SUSTAINABLE DEVELOPMENT REPORT 2020

The Sustainable Development Goals and Covid-19

Includes the SDG Index and Dashboards

| BertelsmannStiftung

SUSTAINABLE DEVELOPMENT
SOLUTIONS NETWORK
A GLOBAL INITIATIVE FOR THE UNITED NATIONS

CAMBRIDGE
UNIVERSITY PRESS

CAMBRIDGE
UNIVERSITY PRESS

University Printing House, Cambridge CB2 8BS, United Kingdom

One Liberty Plaza, 20th Floor, New York, NY 10006, USA

477 Williamstown Road, Port Melbourne, VIC 3207, Australia

314–321, 3rd Floor, Plot 3, Splendor Forum, Jasola District Centre, New Delhi – 110025, India

103 Penang Road, #05-06/07, Visioncrest Commercial, Singapore 238467

Cambridge University Press is part of the University of Cambridge. It furthers the University's mission by disseminating knowledge in the pursuit of education, learning, and research at the highest international levels of excellence.

www.cambridge.org
Information on this title: www.cambridge.org/9781108834209
DOI: 10.1017/9781108992411

First published 2021

The views expressed in this report do not reflect the views of any organizations, agency or programme of the United Nations. This report has been prepared with the extensive advice and consultation of the SDSN Leadership Council members. Members of the Leadership Council serve in their personal capacities, so the opinions expressed in this paper may not reflect the opinions of their host institutions. Members are not necessarily in agreement with every detail of this report.

Printed in the United Kingdom by TJ Books Limited, Padstow Cornwall

A catalogue record for this publication is available from the British Library.

Library of Congress Cataloging-in-Publication Data

ISBN 978-1-108-83420-9 Hardback
ISBN 978-1-108-99465-1 Paperback

Cambridge University Press has no responsibility for the persistence or accuracy of URLs for external or third-party internet websites referred to in this publication and does not guarantee that any content on such websites is, or will remain, accurate or appropriate.

Contents

Figures

Tables

List of Boxes

Acknowledgements

The report was coordinated by Guillaume Lafortune under the direction of Christian Kroll and Guido Schmidt-Traub and the overall supervision of Jeffrey D. Sachs. Lead writers are Jeffrey D. Sachs, Guido Schmidt-Traub, Christian Kroll, Guillaume Lafortune, Grayson Fuller and Finn Woelm. We are grateful to Carmina Baez Sarita for statistical support, as well as to Jessica Espey, Hayden Dahmm, and Maryam Rabiee from the Thematic Research Network on Data and Statistics (TReNDs) for their valuable comments.

The views expressed in this report do not reflect the views of any organizations, agencies or programmes of the United Nations.

The report combines data and analyses produced by international organizations, civil society organizations, and research centers. We thank all for their contributions and collaboration in producing the report. The full list of contributing organizations can be found in the References section of this report.

We also thank the regional and national SDSN networks, experts, and government officials for responding to the 2020 survey on "national implementation and coordination mechanisms for the SDGs at the central/federal level." We also thank respondents to SDSN's 2020 public-opinion surveys on "SDG Progress and Challenges" and on "Covid-19 and the SDGs."

María Cortes-Puch, Elena Crete, Cheyenne Maddox, and Ryan Swaney provided communication support for the launch of the report. Cambridge University Press and Roberto Rossi of Pica Publishing prepared the manuscript for publication. We thank all staff members at SDSN and its member institutions, at Bertelsmann Stiftung and at Cambridge University Press, especially Phil Good, who have supported this report.

Please notify us of any publications that use the SDG Index and Dashboards data or the *Sustainable Development Report*, and share your publication with us at info@sdgindex.org.

An interactive online dashboard and all data used in this report can be accessed at:
http://sustainabledevelopment.report.

Please cite this report as:

Sachs, J., Schmidt-Traub, G., Kroll, C., Lafortune, G., Fuller, G., Woelm, F. 2020.
The Sustainable Development Goals and COVID-19. Sustainable Development Report 2020. Cambridge: Cambridge University Press.

This report has been prepared with the extensive advice and consultation of the SDSN Leadership Council members. Members of the Leadership Council serve in their personal capacities, so the opinions expressed in this paper may not reflect the opinions of their host institutions. Members are not necessarily in agreement with every detail of this report.

Design and Layout by Pica Publishing Ltd – www.pica-publishing.com

Executive Summary

Covid-19 will have severe negative impacts on most SDGs. The world is facing the worst public health and economic crisis in a century. As of June 20th, 2020, around 463,000 people had died from Covid-19 across the world. The health crisis is affecting all countries, including high-income countries in Europe and North America. The necessary measures taken to respond to the immediate threat of Covid-19, including the shut-down of many economic activities for weeks, have led to a global economic crisis with massive job losses and major impacts especially on vulnerable groups. This is a significant setback for the world's ambition to achieve the SDGs, in particular for poor countries and population groups. The only bright spot in this foreboding picture is the reduction in environmental impacts resulting from declines in economic activity: a key objective will be to restore economic activity without simply restoring old patterns of environmental degradation. However, all long-term consequences of the pandemic remain highly uncertain at this point.

All countries need to strengthen the resilience of their health systems and prevention programs. Some countries have outperformed others in containing the pandemic, yet all remain at serious risk. No country has attained so-called herd immunity; all remain highly vulnerable to new outbreaks. In line with SDG 3 (Good Health and Well-Being), all countries need to "Strengthen the capacity for early warning, risk reduction and management of national and global health risks." The Covid-19 pandemic has shed considerable light on the vulnerability of health systems, notably in high-income countries that were thought best prepared to face epidemics. Besides greater investments, this crisis shows that better measures and reporting are needed to track prevention programs, healthcare system preparedness, and resilience to pandemics.

The SDGs and the Six SDG Transformations can inform the recovery from Covid-19. As the international community, regional organizations, and countries plan the post-Covid-19 recovery, it will be important to put the SDGs at the heart of policymaking. Covid-19 does not resolve the climate and biodiversity crises, and it is gravely amplifying income inequalities and other forms of inequality. It has also shown us that countries will only be able to protect themselves from global pandemics if health systems are strengthened in every country. The SDR2020 shows that significant progress has been achieved in many regions and on many goals over the past five years. Here we describe how the SDGs and the six SDG Transformations (Sachs et al., 2019a) can guide the immediate post-crisis recovery and frame long-term strategies towards more resilient and sustainable societies.

Asian countries have made the most progress towards the SDGs since the adoption of the goals in 2015. Asian countries have also responded most effectively to the Covid-19 outbreak. While the world as a whole has made progress on the SDGs, countries in East and South Asia in particular have progressed the most in terms of their SDG Index score. Countries in this region have also managed the Covid-19 outbreak more effectively than in other parts of the world. While the situation is still evolving, the shift of the geopolitical and economic global center of gravity from the North Atlantic region to the Asia-Pacific region is likely to be accelerated by the crisis.

Solidarity and partnerships are critical to address and prevent health, economic, and humanitarian crises. Globalization and the destruction of wildlife habitats facilitate the rapid spread of viruses around the world. Yet rather than losing the vast benefits that globalization offers for economics, poverty reduction, technological advance, and the enjoyment of each other's cultures, it is important instead to make globalization more fair, sustainable, and resilient to shocks. Concerted international action by policymakers, business, civil society, and the scientific community can accelerate the identification of solutions to the immediate crisis and strengthen globalization for the long term. Stronger international and multisectoral partnerships can support mitigation strategies by sharing best practices, and help prevent future disruptive events. The health, economic, and social crises call for increased international collaboration and solidarity to support the most vulnerable countries.

Data gaps and time lags in official statistics require urgent investments in statistical capacity and increased coordination between governments and the private sector. The pandemic has taught us once again the value of real-time information, and the enormous costs of flying blind into a storm. Early detection of Covid-19 outbreaks can make all the difference between suppression of the pandemic and a full-scale outbreak. The same is true across many SDG indicators, where timing matters enormously to save lives, ecosystems, and effective governance. This year's edition of the SDG Index and Dashboards cannot integrate the impact of Covid-19 on the SDGs due to time lags in official statistics and reporting. This illustrates how crucial timely and disaggregated data are across the SDGs. Major efforts should focus on increasing data availability and reducing time lags in official statistics, and on leveraging the wealth of real-time data available from non-traditional sources, including the research community and the private sector.

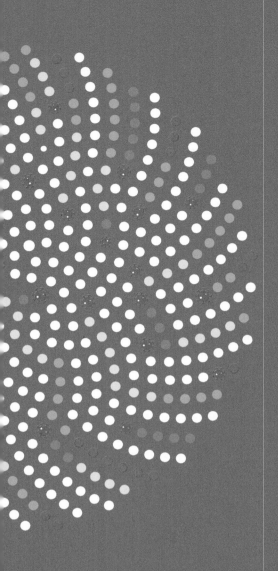

Part 1

Covid-19, the SDGs, and the Recovery

Part 1

Covid-19, the SDGs, and the Recovery

———

The world is still in the early phase of the vast Covid-19 crisis. Deaths and infections continue to mount (JHU, 2020; Worldometer, 2020). Economies are in a deep and growing crisis. Inequalities within and among countries are rising, as the poorest suffer a disproportionate share of the infections and deaths, and struggle more to make ends meet. Poverty and hunger are soaring. And global tensions are rising. United Nations Secretary-General António Guterres has rightly called this crisis the worst since World War II. The economic ramifications could rival those of the Great Depression in the 1930s (IMF, 2020a).

The implications of the pandemic encompass public health, economics, social stability, politics, and geopolitics. The crisis is unprecedented in severity at least since the influenza epidemic at the end of World War I, and still very uncertain in its trajectory. The world will change markedly. However, if we take the right approach to crisis management, we may learn important positive lessons for the future – and if not, we may fall into a downward spiral of crisis.

The *Sustainable Development Report 2020* (SDR2020) presents some early thoughts on the Covid-19 crisis and the future of sustainable development.

This opening section is divided into two parts:

In the first part, we review early responses and identify short-term priorities for action by governments and their partners around the world, including the international community. We also describe how the Sustainable Development Goals (SDGs) can help chart medium-term and longer-term responses to recover from the health, economic, social, and environmental impacts of the pandemic. We believe that success will require deep changes to how countries and the international community operate, which we try to outline.

In the second part, we review how governments have responded to the immediate health crisis and describe emerging lessons for public health authorities, governments at large, and the public. The crisis has shown profound weaknesses in our public health systems, including in many of the richest countries that were deemed to be well prepared for such a pandemic. Meanwhile, some countries, particularly in the Asia-Pacific region, have (so far) been successful in containing Covid-19 and minimizing the damage to their societies. We present a novel approach and a pilot index to measure the effectiveness of the OECD countries' early responses

to Covid-19 which integrates health and economic considerations.

Poor performance on this index does not necessarily mean that countries have not responded appropriately to the Covid-19 outbreak under the circumstances they were confronted with. In countries where personal protective equipment (PPE) (e.g. masks) and test kits were lacking and where capacities in intensive care units were more limited, a strict and prolonged lockdown was most probably required for containing the spread of the virus and reducing death rates. Yet, we also underline how some countries that were better prepared (e.g. South Korea) managed to deal with the disease outbreak more efficiently so far by testing, tracing, and isolating rapidly confirmed Covid-19 cases and through the immediate use of PPE among most of the population, which has greatly help in mitigating the negative economic impacts. Besides government actions, other factors can explain lower mortality rates from Covid-19 such as geography, demography, and other contextual factors including recent experiences with viruses' outbreaks.

1.1 Covid-19 and the future of sustainable development

Clearly, the pandemic will have profound implications on progress towards the SDGs, which this report has been tracking since 2016. The data we present in this 2020 report mostly dates from before the onset of the pandemic, so it does not account for the Covid-19 impact. For this reason, this section outlines likely implications on the SDGs by drawing on emerging data and findings from around the world. We underscore the preliminary and uncertain nature of these findings, but we hope they will help the global discussion on Covid-19 and the SDGs.

This section also seeks to lay out a vision for the future of sustainable development and the SDGs. It is necessarily preliminary since we are only at what some have called the end of the beginning of Covid-19. Previous pandemics suggest that there may well be several new rounds of outbreaks, and the implications on economies, social cohesion, the environment, and international diplomacy are impossible to predict. As the UN Secretary-General (UN 2020) has reminded us, some of the worst can be avoided, but only if countries act decisively and in unison, with strong international solidarity.

The SDGs are the world's shared goals for sustainable development, and Covid-19 makes them more relevant than ever. It is critical that we "build back better," but the question is of course how to do so. In this section we outline some preliminary ideas for how the SDGs can provide the framework for national action and international cooperation in the wake of Covid-19.

We distinguish between short-run and longer-term priorities. In the short run, the absolute priority is to control the spread of the virus in every country, including the poorest ones. Countries and the international community also need to mitigate the impact on achievement of the SDGs, especially in vulnerable countries and population groups. International collaboration and partnerships are needed to speed the fight against the pandemic, support macroeconomic stability, and avoid a disastrous humanitarian crisis. In the longer term, we argue that the SDGs provide the framework to guide the recovery. Countries need to invest in stronger and more resilient health systems and pursue the other SDGs. We outline practical steps for how this might be achieved.

Short-term priorities

Control the disease

The good news is that, in principle, Covid-19 is controllable. The pandemic could be stopped in its tracks if every infected person were kept safely away from susceptible individuals during the period of infectiousness, which is roughly one to two weeks. If that were to happen, the vast majority of those currently infected would recover, while a small proportion, perhaps around 1%, would die from the illness. In a matter of just a few weeks the epidemic would end, since those infected today would not infect others.

Yet the pandemic is not being suppressed in this quick and orderly way. At the time of writing (late May 2020), the number of new cases continues to grow rapidly in many countries and regions, including Brazil, India, Russia, the United States, and several countries in South America and Africa. Infected individuals continue to infect susceptible individuals in large numbers. In many of these countries and regions, new infections are rising at a very fast pace. The virus has reached virtually every country on every continent.

Yet the news on suppressing the pandemic is not all bleak. Several countries, notably in the Asia-Pacific region – including Australia, New Zealand, South Korea, and Vietnam, among others – have shown that it is possible to stop the epidemic, or at least to reduce the number of new infections to small numbers. Success is based heavily on intensive public health services and good hygienic practices among the population. People in these countries who show symptoms are tested and isolated. If their home conditions are too crowded, they are quarantined in public facilities where they will not transmit the virus to family members or neighbors. Their close contacts are rigorously traced, tested, and isolated or quarantined if necessary. People are routinely monitored for symptoms (such as fever) when they move in public places. People wear face masks and regularly wash their hands to avoid spreading the virus, and they keep their physical distance from others when in shops, public places, or their workplaces. Businesses allow employees to work from home whenever possible, monitor their workforce for any symptoms of infection, and quickly isolate any who might be infected. In short, every effort is made to prevent infected individuals from infecting others.

Most countries around the world do not yet have such high-quality public health systems. They lack adequate testing, contact tracing, and quarantine facilities. They do not aggressively monitor public places for people with symptoms such as fever. Individuals do not always honor physical distancing. People take undue risks by meeting together in large groups, such as at beaches, sports events, restaurants, parties, religious services, funerals, and other group occasions. They also often do not, or cannot, adhere to strict hygiene measures, including hand-washing and the wearing of masks. The virus is then easily spread to large numbers of people.

The wealthy countries of Western Europe and North America were in fact among those with the greatest number of infected people and deaths in the first months of the pandemic. The United States alone was reporting 99,807 Covid-19 deaths as of May 26, or 29% of the world's 348,300 total reported Covid-19 deaths at the time, despite accounting for just 4% of the world's population. That comes to a death rate of 302 per million population in the United States, compared with just 3 per million in China, 4 per million in Australia and New Zealand, 5 per million in South Korea, and 7 per million in Japan. Well-financed healthcare systems did not spare the United States and many countries in Western Europe. These countries had hospitals but lacked testing capacities, contact tracers, and other control measures. Standard rankings of preparedness also gave the wrong message: The United States often topped these conventional rankings (box 1), yet the country failed to respond effectively when the virus arrived.

The pandemic especially ravages countries with poor leadership. Countries led by populists or strongmen who dismiss science, weaken public health institutions, or undermine transparency in the management of the disease are performing particularly poorly. The modeling has shown that even a few weeks' delay in response can mean the difference between suppressing the pandemic and suffering a mass outbreak with a vast loss of life. Each failure harms not only the country itself, but the rest of the world as well. It sets back the revival of trade, tourism, investment, higher education, and other global activities.

With widespread transmission of the virus and inadequate public health measures, most countries have resorted to temporary lockdowns of economic and social life. By cutting down sharply on daily contacts throughout society – in shops, restaurants, offices, public transport and public spaces, and at events – transmission of the virus is slowed. Yet lockdowns are very costly and inefficient. Instead of isolating only infected individuals and their contacts, everybody is isolated. The economy grinds to a halt, with very high costs in terms of mass

unemployment, sudden poverty, a rise in hunger, rising domestic abuse, and other impacts of remaining at home.

Yet lifting lockdowns in the absence of adequate public health measures can simply allow the pandemic to return with full force. Every country therefore faces a grim reality. Either build up public-health capacity to contain the pandemic, as have those countries that have succeeded in containing Covid-19, or face the disastrous choice between an uncontained pandemic and economic collapse.

Clearly, the choice between death and economic collapse is really no choice. The only viable option for all societies is to build effective public health systems that can contain the pandemic, which could even allow businesses to operate at a level close to that of before the outbreak (Dorn et al., 2020). In fact, a synergetic relationship between public health and a prosperous economy seems possible even in times of Covid-19. According to illustrative calculations by Dorn et al., a favorable scenario may be one in which the virus's reproduction rate, or R-value, falls to 0.75 (based on data from Germany), which presents the best possible balance between new infections and economic costs due to shutdown measures. We will learn over the coming weeks whether countries that are currently reopening their economies have put in place the necessary public health interventions to monitor, trace, prevent, and treat infections, so as to prevent a second outbreak.

Even though it is possible to contain and even to stop the global pandemic through effective public-health measures, it is more likely that the virus will continue to spread widely and affect vast proportions of the world's population. This is the result of poor public leadership in many rich countries, combined with the lack of the means and financing to contain the epidemic in poorer countries. Poorer countries generally do not have large cadres of public-health officials, though such cadres are an excellent investment not only in pandemic control but also towards meeting other objectives of SDG 3 (Good Health and Well-Being). The poorer countries also do not have adequate testing facilities. It is also very difficult to keep impoverished populations at home even for short periods of time. Some leaders, such as Pakistan's Prime Minister Imran Khan (2020), have simply declared that they do not

Figure 1

Short-term impacts of Covid-19 on the Sustainable Development Goals

 Mainly positive impact

 Mixed or moderately negative impact

 Highly negative impact

 Impact still unclear

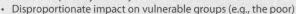

SDG 1
No poverty

Highly negative impact

- Increased poverty due to job losses and economic lockdown
- Disproportionate impact on vulnerable groups (e.g., the poor)

SDG 2
Zero hunger

Highly negative impact

- Food insecurity due to reduction in global food supplies and trade
- Hunger due to fall in incomes and reduced food availability during lockdown
- Higher food loss and waste due to transportation challenges and reduced labor availability
- Poorer nutrition due to interruption of school meals

SDG 3
Good health and well-being

Highly negative impact

- Higher disease incidence and mortality from Covid 19
- Higher mortality from other causes because of overburdening of health systems
- Slight decline in mortality due to reduced economic and social activities (e.g., traffic accidents)
- Potential short-term health gains due to lower environmental pollution
- Negative impact of confinement and lockdown on mental health (e.g., anxiety and depression)

SDG 4
Quality education

Mixed or moderately negative impact

- School and day-care closures
- Loss in the development of human capital
- Poorer nutrition due to interruption of school meals

SDG 5
Gender equality

Mixed or moderately negative impact

- Possible disproportionate economic impacts on women (e.g., job losses, poverty)
- Other social impacts on women from the lockdown (e. g., domestic violence)
- Higher mortality rates from the virus among men (because they suffer from more chronic respiratory diseases due to higher smoking rate)

SDG 6
Clean water and sanitation

Mixed or moderately negative impact

- Limited access to clean water among disadvantaged groups limits possibility of adhering to strict hygiene guidelines

SDG 7
Affordable and clean energy

Mixed or moderately negative impact

- Slowdown in economic growth contributing to a reduction in energy prices (e.g., oil), which might increase access to energy but reduce incentives for renewables

SDG 8
Decent work and economic growth

Highly negative impact

- Economic crisis in virtually all parts of the world
- Trade disruption
- Mass unemployment
- Business closures / bankruptcies
- Sharp decline in tourism activities
- Massive public deficits

SDG 9
Industry, innovation and infrastructure

Mixed or moderately negative impact

- Decline in industrial outputs
- Possible nationalization of some industries, and bankruptcies and closures of others
- Scientific collaboration to find treatments and vaccine
- Accelerated uptake of digital technologies, for e-health, e-education, e-governance, and e-payments

SDG 10
Reduced inequalities

Highly negative impact
- Disproportionate negative health and economic impacts on vulnerable groups (including refugees and migrants), especially in countries with low safety nets
- Loss of jobs of lower-skilled, lower-wage labor

SDG 11
Sustainable cities and communities

Mixed or moderately negative impact
- Rise in urban poverty and vulnerability
- Shut down of public transports
- Lower access to public / green spaces
- Movements of population that vary across countries
- Sharp short-term reduction in pollution levels

SDG 12
Responsible consumption and production

Impact still unclear
- Short-term reduction in natural resource use due to reduced economic activity and consumption
- Pressure to loosen up regulations on circular economy and postpone the adoption of new measures
- Increased plastic pollution (e.g., used to produce personal protective equipment)

SDG 13
Climate action

Impact still unclear
- Short-term reduction in global GHG emissions
- Pressure to reduce environmental safeguards
- Lack of clarity on environmental investments
- Slowdown in economic growth contributing to reduction in energy prices (e.g., oil), which might increase access to energy but reduce incentives for renewables

SDG 14
Life below water

Impact still unclear
- Short-term reduction in threats to marine biodiversity due to reduced global economic activity and consumption
- Pressure to reduce marine biodiversity and ecosystem safeguards

SDG 15
Life on land

Impact still unclear
- Short-term reduction in threats to terrestrial and freshwater biodiversity due to reduced global economic activity and consumption
- Pressure to reduce terrestrial and freshwater biodiversity and ecosystem safeguards, including biodiversity and ecosystem regulations conventions (for instance, on deforestation)

SDG 16
Peace, justice and strong institutions

Mixed or moderately negative impact
- Increased pressure on governments to mitigate the health and economic consequences of the pandemic
- Pressure to increase accessible health care in countries that have not yet achieved universal health coverage
- Increased public deficits and debt
- Disruption of legislative processes and public debates
- Suspension of freedom-of-information laws and transparency policies

SDG 17
Partnerships for the goals

Mixed or moderately negative impact
- Possible reduced responsiveness of international aid community to needs of the poorest countries
- Possible reduction in international remittances and cross-border financing
- Closing of borders
- Slowdown in international trade
- Debt crisis

have the means to contain their county's pandemic. The consequences may well be horrendous for such countries. But they would also be horrendous for other countries, since the virus and the damage it wreaks would continue to spread across borders.

Therefore, the world as a whole is at a decisive moment. With serious public-health efforts in all parts of the world, containing the pandemic is feasible.

Mitigate negative impacts on the SDGs

Many fallouts from the Covid-19 crisis on the SDGs are direct and obvious. Figure 1 summarizes these short-term impacts. Some poor countries will face devastating poverty as they lose a high proportion of their incomes from commodity exports, tourism, and remittance flows. The terms of trade for many commodity exporters will fall sharply, as shown by the collapse in oil prices during the first months of 2020. Domestic lockdowns in the poor countries will deprive the poor of their meagre daily incomes. Poverty and hunger will rise.

Many food-importing developing countries could see plummeting currencies, steeply rising domestic (and real) prices of imported food, and thus growing hunger, both hidden and overt (FAO, 2020; IFPRI, 2020). Much of Africa in particular depends on food imports for staples, and these countries will likely lose a substantial proportion of their foreign-exchange income. The consequences could be dire and could translate into social and political instability, as well as hunger.

Many emerging economies and frontier economies could soon also face devastating challenges in refinancing their debts (Adrian and Natalucci, 2020). As the crisis unfolds, governments face an intense budget squeeze, as revenues decline while social spending rises. Moreover, many developing country currencies will depreciate against the dollar, raising the domestic currency costs of servicing foreign dollar-denominated debts. It would be possible in principle to refinance the debts falling due through new private borrowing, IMF credits, or systematic rollovers of principal and interest. In practice, the international financial system rarely works so systematically. It is more

likely that one or more countries will default, pushing the bond-rating agencies to downgrade sovereign developing-country debts more generally, and leading to a freezing up of the system rather than a refinancing. The result would be a cascade of defaults and balance-of-payments crises that would also touch many countries that have hitherto managed their economies well.

Beyond the most direct impacts on poverty (SDG 1), food security (SDG 2), health (SDG 3), the economy (SDG 8), and multilateralism (SDG 17), Covid-19 has numerous other SDG impacts that are less widely discussed.

Vulnerable countries and population groups (including the elderly, people with pre-conditions, homeless people, low-skilled workers and refugees) are disproportionately affected by the short- and medium-term consequences of the Covid-19 crisis (United Nations, 2020). This can be expected to result in growing inequalities, undermining progress towards the achievement of SDG 10 (Reduced Inequalities). On SDG 5 (Gender Equality), early evidence suggests that women are disproportionally affected in many ways by the Covid-19 health and economic crises, including through their greater exposure to labor market disruptions and the increase in domestic violence stemming from the lockdowns (Inter-Agency Standing Committee, 2020; UNFPA, 2020; Wenham et al., 2020). Meanwhile, the mortality rate of Covid-19 is greater among men, due perhaps to greater pre-existing behavioral risk factors, such as higher smoking rates, other co-morbidities, or biological factors (Reeves and Ford, 2020). The crisis also has negative impacts on access to schools, especially for populations that are poorly equipped with digital technologies.

The crisis also affects the functioning of political and legislative systems and the rule of law (SDG 16). Some governments have introduced exceptional measures that increase their powers, allow them to rule by decree, and limit freedom of speech (Transparency International, 2020). As rightly emphasized by the UN Security Council (Council of Europe, 2020), the consequences of Covid-19 are exacerbated in fragile states, including in countries that face conflicts and civil wars.

At the same time, the crisis has brought about at least some temporary environmental benefits. Emissions of CO_2 around the world have dropped significantly due to reduced industrial activity, lower energy consumption, and reduced transportation of material and people (Le Quéré et al., 2020). CO_2 emissions and emissions of nitrogen dioxide, a major air pollutant, declined sharply in China during the early months of the pandemic (Ghosh, 2020; Myllyvirta, 2020), although they are now rebounding strongly (CREA, 2020). Yet, the virus may also have a negative impact on the enforcement of environmental laws, including on deforestation, as industrial lobbies put pressure on public authorities to loosen up restrictions or even postpone the adoption of new measures (Reuters, 2020). Meanwhile it is unclear what impact Covid-19 will have on investments, policies, and other short-term actions to tackle climate change. Overall, we believe the direction of short-term impacts on environmental and biodiversity goals (SDGs 12–15) is unclear. Most importantly, where Covid-19-related declines in economic activity have reduced environmental degradation, the restoration of economic activity should aim to protect these environmental gains.

While the global health situation remains gloomy, mortality rates due to traffic accidents (covered under SDG 3.6) have sharply declined in many parts of the world (Kopf, 2020). There might also be other short-term health gains due to lower pollution levels. These must be continued as the world recovers from Covid-19.

Medium- and long-term priorities
Guide the recovery with the six SDG Transformations

The SDGs provide an invaluable framework for recovery from Covid-19. The pandemic has laid bare the fragile economic, social, and environmental underpinnings of our world today. Despite the world's vast wealth, scientific and technological prowess, and supposed preparedness for disasters, and despite repeated specific warnings of the risks of pandemics, including many specific warnings of coronavirus pandemics, the world was not ready when the virus struck.

The SDGs were adopted to address unnecessary risks and fragilities across the economic, social, and environmental domains. These include poverty, widening inequalities in income and access to decent lives, continued high disease burdens, and of course massive environmental destruction. These warnings are today more pertinent than ever. If the Covid-19 disaster accomplishes anything good, it should be to shake the world from its complacency, so as seriously commit to the hard work of investing in a sustainable and inclusive future for humanity.

The six SDG Transformations (Sachs et al., 2019a) provide a detailed framework on which to construct integrated strategies to recover from Covid-19 and to build back better. They can be implemented in every country to help address trade-offs and synergies across the SDGs. We presented the SDG Transformations in last year's report and outline here how they will need to be rethought to help guide medium- and longer-term responses to Covid-19.

The core of the six Transformations is the recognition that all 17 SDGs can be achieved through six major societal transformations, focused on: (1) education and skills, (2) health and wellbeing, (3) clean energy and industry, (4) sustainable land use, (5) sustainable cities, and (6) digital technologies. All are guided by the twin principles of "leave no one behind" and "ensure circularity and decoupling" (See Sachs et al., 2019a for details, page 3). The six Transformations provide an action agenda for government ministries, businesses, and civil society. They help governments and the international community, as well as business and civil society, to frame actionable strategies to achieve the SDGs and thereby make our societies more prosperous, inclusive, and sustainable.

To implement these transformations, in the medium-run, relationship between markets and governments must be rebalanced, with governments playing a more central role in the economy through public investments, redistribution of incomes from rich to poor, and regulation of industry to ensure environmental and social sustainability. As a result of the pandemic, government spending will have to increase sharply over the coming one to three years, to mitigate the consequences of the health and economic crises. And at least some of this increase in spending, for example on health coverage and access to public services, should remain permanent.

Already, public workforces including healthcare workers and first responders such as the police force have been heavily mobilized to respond to the health emergency. Large-scale public-private partnerships are underway

Figure 2
Six SDG Transformations

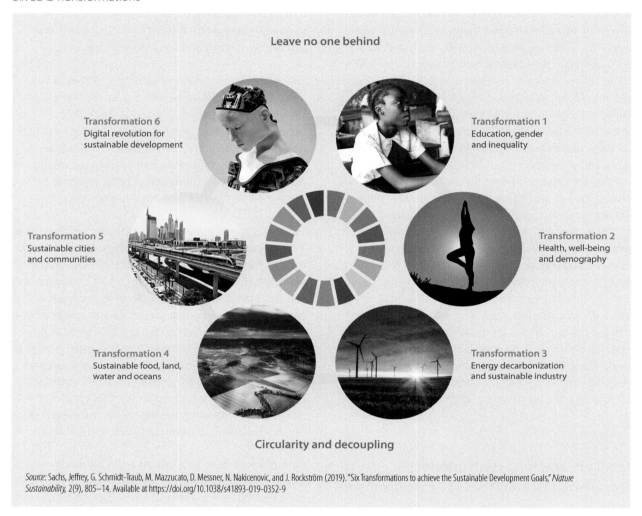

Leave no one behind

Transformation 6
Digital revolution for
sustainable development

Transformation 1
Education, gender
and inequality

Transformation 5
Sustainable cities
and communities

Transformation 2
Health, well-being
and demography

Transformation 4
Sustainable food, land,
water and oceans

Transformation 3
Energy decarbonization
and sustainable industry

Circularity and decoupling

Source: Sachs, Jeffrey, G. Schmidt-Traub, M. Mazzucato, D. Messner, N. Nakicenovic, and J. Rockström (2019). "Six Transformations to achieve the Sustainable Development Goals," *Nature Sustainability,* 2(9), 805–14. Available at https://doi.org/10.1038/s41893-019-0352-9

– in transport for example – and the role of government in the health sector is expanding dramatically. Governments are also stepping in to distribute key medical supplies such as protective equipment and sanitizers, support research for treatments and vaccines, negotiate prices, and avert risks of food shortages (among other interventions). Massive fiscal packages, mainly to support the incomes of workers, combined with falls in GDPs will increase public spending as a share of GDP across the board.

The highest priority of every government must remain the suppression of the pandemic. There can be no economic recovery while the pandemic is raging.

Yet governments need to plan for the post Covid-19 economy. Unemployment will remain very high. Jobs lost in many sectors – retail, office support, construction, tourism, personal services, fossil-fuel energy – will not return, or at least not rapidly and robustly. Budget deficits and financial imbalances will persist. Many enterprises will go out of business. Non-government aggregate demand, including private consumption and investment, will most likely remain depressed.

There are many complex choices ahead, with financing at the core. In many countries, state and local governments provide healthcare, education, social services, and local infrastructure. But state and local governments will be strapped for cash. National governments, backed by their tax authority, their ability to borrow in capital markets, and their access to central bank financing (directly or through open-market operations), will urgently need to share revenues with state and local governments. Many national governments that borrow abroad in foreign currencies and require foreign exchange for vital imports such as food and basic capital equipment will suffer a balance-of-payments crisis. The G20 countries have already granted a debt-service moratorium to low-income countries (in April 2020). This will almost surely have to be extended to many emerging-market middle-income countries as well.

The length and depth of the global economic crisis will depend largely on when the pandemic is brought under control. If a vaccine proves to be successful on a rapid timeline, that is by late 2020 or during the first part of 2021, economic prospects will brighten dramatically – assuming that the vaccine can be manufactured at scale and deployed globally during 2021. Without a vaccine, all will depend on the success or failure of public health measures to suppress virus transmission: testing, isolating, contact-tracing, physical distancing, and safety in public spaces and work places through the use of face masks, sanitizers, and other hygienic measures (e.g., air circulation, UV lights).

As of this writing, in the late spring of 2020, the signs are very worrisome. Major outbreaks continue in large parts of the world, and public health containment and suppression approaches are not yet decisive in many major economies. The epidemic continues to spread rapidly in Brazil, India, Mexico, Russia, the United States, and several other countries in South America and Africa. The outlooks in many highly populous developing countries such as Ethiopia, Indonesia, Nigeria, Pakistan, and South Africa, remain guarded and tenuous.

As the epidemic itself is brought under control or eventually constrained by herd immunity once a large enough proportion of the population has been infected, the time for rebuilding the economy will be at hand. The sooner that moment arrives, the brighter will be the prospects for recovery. As of mid-2020, it seems likely that the Asia-Pacific region will start rebuilding first among the world's major regions.

Yet we will not go back to the pre-Covid-19 economy. Hundreds of millions of jobs will have been lost as a direct consequence of the pandemic. Many of these jobs will never return. E-commerce will boom, but in doing so will further displace the bricks-and-mortar retail sector. Offices will give way to increased teleworking from home. Education and healthcare will move increasingly online. The fossil-fuel industries will not recover, as the world rightly embraces renewable energy as a way out of the crisis. Countries such as Brazil, Indonesia, and Mexico that have recently banked heavily on their hydrocarbon sectors will face a need for deep economic restructuring. So too will traditional oil-exporting countries – including Angola, the Gulf States, Nigeria, and Russia.

In the rebuilding phase, governments should support their economic recovery with a strong focus on infrastructure investments that boost jobs and underpin the transition to a low-carbon economy, in line with the Paris Agreement. Tens of millions of jobs can be created directly by building new clean-energy systems based on solar and wind energy, long-distance power transmission, smart grids, electric vehicles, hydrogen and other synthetic fuels, and energy-efficient buildings. The European Green Deal, a United States "Green New Deal," a sustainable Belt and Road Initiative, and regional "green deals" in the ASEAN, South America, the Middle East, South Asia, and elsewhere, could provide the way forward to massive job creation, renewed economic growth, and environmental sustainability. In short, to the achievement of the SDGs and the objectives of the Paris Agreement.

The *Six Transformations Framework for the SDGs* can be a very useful guide for rebuilding:

Transformation 1 (Education, Gender and Inequality). Countries will need to invest more in their education systems to strengthen their resilience, particularly by drawing on modern communication technologies. The crisis is accelerating the rollout of digital tools in schools and in remote education and training – tools that have been used in many countries to strengthen the resilience of education systems in the midst of the crisis. Further investments in education in science, technology, engineering and mathematics (STEM) subjects and in life-long learning are needed to accompany these transformations and boost skills.

Figure 3

An SDG framework to map out possible short-term and longer-term government responses to Covid-19

Whole-of-government response (transversal)

- Increased role of government in key sectors (economy, health, food, social security)
- Re-think global supply chains and dependence for strategic equipment and materials
- Strengthen development cooperation to support recovery plans in countries most hit and in least developed countries
- Strengthen statistical capacity, and the availability of timely data
- Strengthen government capacities to anticipate and manage unforeseen disruptive events
- Strengthen international platforms, exchanges and transparency among scientists/researchers (open science)

Transformation 1: Education, Gender, and Inequality

- Expand and strengthen public social security systems best suited to address the consequences of disruptive events
- Further investments in STEM education, digital skills, equity, and lifelong learning
- Further streamline basic health prevention measures in school programs (e.g., hand-washing) and provide adequate supplies for good hygiene
- Place women's needs and leadership at the heart of the response to the health and economic crises

Transformation 2: Health, Wellbeing, and Demography

- Strengthen the role of public health and disease prevention and surveillance (for both communicable and chronic diseases).
- Increase the role of public authorities in the research for treatment and vaccines, and in providing access to treatment and vaccines
- Accelerate efforts to achieve universal health care
- Strengthen public health emergency preparedness (including building stocks of essential equipment and increasing flexibility to mobilize staff to respond to emergencies)
- Reduce dependence on other countries for key health supplies and equipment
- Expand digital health solutions (e.g., telehealth) to reduce the burden on hospitals and increase access to care
- Increase the quality and timeliness of health statistics
- Increase the resilience of health systems to respond to shocks/crises (e.g., increase capacity to build hospitals and other infrastructures in record time)

Transformation 3: Energy Decarbonization and Sustainable Industry

- Use the Paris Climate Agreement as the vision for long-term change and to inform investment plans and bailouts
- Build on positive short-term prospects due to plummeting industrial output and further the roll out of digital services and e-commerce to accelerate the transition to climate neutrality
- Reduce international dependence for key industries and sectors in case of major disruptive events (e.g. protective masks, food supply)
- Pursue efforts to enforce environmental treaties and national regulations despite the lockdown and economic turmoil

Transformation 4: Sustainable Food, Land, Water and Oceans

- Strengthen food security and hygiene, including the reduction of risks of zoonotic diseases
- Emphasize the resilience and sustainability of food systems
- Accelerate efforts to provide universal access to water and sanitation, and increase focus on hygiene and handwashing to help curb transmission of oral-fecal diseases
- Pursue efforts to reduce negative impacts on biodiversity and ecosystems to prevent future pandemics

Transformation 5: Sustainable Cities and Communities

- Address immediate threats to vulnerable groups in urban settlements (homeless, refugees), to avoid a deep worsening of their living conditions and to make confinement measures more effective
- Strengthen the territorial distribution of doctors and availability of care, including in rural areas
- Further integrate vulnerable groups in urban settlements, including homeless people, refugees, and migrants
- Adapt public transportation systems to the need for physical distancing and hygiene, and to changing patterns in working and commuting habits
- Develop integrated territorial strategies to address the impact of travel restrictions on business, exports, and tourism activities

Transformation 6: Harnessing the Digital Revolution for Sustainable Development

- Further expand digital health solutions to reduce the burden on hospitals and increase access
- Develop and use online education tools
- Further development of other digital government services and e-commerce
- Further investments in STEMS, digital skills, equity, and lifelong learning
- Accelerate the adoption of measures that support a fair transition for workers affected by the digital and technological revolution

Source: Authors' analysis

The economic shocks from Covid-19 threaten to increase inequalities in all countries: the policy focus on lowering these inequalities will likely rise in importance. Countries will need to strengthen their social-protection systems (SDG 1.3 and SDG 10.4), including their ability to respond quickly to major crises. Gender-sensitive policies are also needed to mitigate risks of disproportionate economic and social impacts on women and girls.

Transformation 2 (Good Health and Well-Being) obviously has the most prominent implications right now. In the short- and medium-term, the role of public health systems in disease prevention and surveillance will need to increase to prevent further waves of Covid-19 and future health crises. Governments will play a key role in developing and distributing Covid-19 treatments and vaccines at global scale. As in the case of education, the crisis will likely accelerate the transformation towards digital healthcare and telemedicine to increase access to and efficiency of healthcare systems.

The Covid-19 crisis has made it very clear that countries equipped with effective social protection systems and universal health coverage are best equipped to respond to such crises. This is also less costly, and it is precisely for this reason that the SDGs call for countries to strengthen their social safety nets and move towards universal health coverage for key medical services. Meanwhile, nearly 40% of the world's population has no health insurance or access to national health services (ILO, 2020). Providing universal social-protection floors is within fiscal reach, although low-income countries might need financial support to close the fiscal gap. Another benefit of effective social safety nets is that they mitigate the consequences of lockdowns and thereby reduce the temptation to open up economies too early, risking a new Covid-19 wave.

Transformation 3 (Energy Decarbonization and Sustainable Industry) provides the long-term direction for a clean, green economy. This should guide government investment plans and support to companies and industries. Ironically, the crisis could lead to a decline in the enforcement of environmental laws and major international conventions in some parts of the world. Throughout, a major challenge during and post Covid-19 will be to direct the attention of senior policymakers to the climate crisis. The scientific community should be

vocal on the need to connect the Covid-19 recovery to investments in clean energy.

Transformation 4 (Sustainable Food, Land, Water and Oceans) draws attention to the shorter-term risks of food shortages, especially in low-income countries, due to disruption in trade and supply chains and the sudden collapse of incomes. Vulnerable households, including in rich countries, will need financial support to mitigate the risks of food insecurity. In the medium and longer run, governments will need to accelerate the further integration of healthy diets, food security, agricultural systems, and natural resource management. This is becoming self-evident not only to respond to the increased percentage of undernourished people and obese people, but also to reduce the risks of future zoonotic diseases. Governments should seize the post Covid-19 recovery as an opportunity to accelerate the transition towards sustainable and resilient food systems.

Transformation 5 (Sustainable Cities and Communities). In the short run, there is an urgent need to meet the needs of vulnerable groups (including homeless people and refugees) in urban settlements. This is critical to avoid rapid deterioration of the living conditions of vulnerable people during the lockdown phase of pandemic control, but also to ensure that confinement measures are effective. This crisis will amplify inequalities in access to water, sanitation, and health services. Effective medium-term and long-term responses will therefore require increased investments to accelerate the provision of universal access to water, sanitation, and clean energy services. There will also be lasting implications of Covid-19 on territorial development, urban planning, and public transportation systems (OECD,2020). Regional and local policy leaders will need to guide the transformation of their territories in order to adapt to new realities including social distancing, changes in workplace practices and commuting patterns, and travel restrictions, which will impact business and tourism activities.

Transformation 6 (Harnessing the Digital Revolution for Sustainable Development) has been greatly accelerated by the Covid-19 epidemic. Countries that can afford it are accelerating the roll-out of digital technologies and services in response to the crisis. The digital technologies are playing an important role in sustaining social services, payments, schooling, and health care during the lockdowns, and in enabling working from home to be effective for many occupations. The importance of digital applications underscores the vital importance of universal access to broadband services as key to social inclusion, economic opportunity, and public health. Governments, businesses, schools, health facilities, and others will be turning increasingly to online service delivery as a vital part of their activities in the years ahead.

The urgent need for international cooperation

The current crisis, including hostilities among major powers, raises the specter of global conflict instead of global cooperation. We are reminded of the great work of economic historian Charles Kindleberger in *The World in Depression, 1929–1939*. It was Kindleberger's thesis that the Great Depression was so severe because there was no global leader (no "hegemon" in the language of international affairs) and no adequate cooperation among the major powers. The result was a breakdown of the global monetary and trading system that opened the way to Hitler in Germany in 1933, and then on to World War II.

The early signs of this crisis are not good. The United States is attacking the WHO as being too pro-Chinese, and is cutting off funding rather than supporting the WHO for its vital work in suppressing the pandemic. In general, the United States is intensifying its attacks on China and trying to divide the world between pro-US and pro-Chinese camps. The risk of a new Cold War is very grave and should be avoided by all nations.

The good news is that most of the world urgently wants multilateralism and cooperation. The bad news is that some countries do not, while others are paralyzed by their own crises, budget deficits, and divisions of local politics. The multilateral situation is therefore fraught and needs bolstering. A possible outcome is a kind of limping multilateralism, rather than strong and decisive cooperation, in which accomplishments on the ground are modest and countless opportunities to avoid hardships and suffering are lost.

International cooperation could speed a favorable and rapid resolution to the pandemic. Indeed, there is no other way to succeed. Global cooperation would include the following measures:

(1) Disseminate best practices rapidly.
The world needs urgently to learn from and to emulate the strategies for fighting Covid-19 adopted in the East Asia and the Pacific region. The WHO should urgently facilitate a rapid dissemination of best practices.

(2) Strengthen financing mechanisms for developing countries. The IMF was created for global crises like this one. It needs ample firepower, including far greater latitude to extend credits, either under existing facilities or through a new issuance of Special Drawing Rights (SDRs). Private creditors will need to refinance or capitalize debts falling due.

(3) Address hunger hotspots. We need global support for the lead United Nations agencies, including the Office for the Coordination of Humanitarian Affairs (OCHA), the Food and Agriculture Organization (FAO), and the World Food Program (WFP), so that they can head off impending hunger crises and food insecurity.

(4) Ensure social protection. As part of any comprehensive response to the pandemic, governments should promote new instruments of social protection, including a new Global Fund for Social Protection that was proposed to address SDG 1 (No Poverty) even before the pandemic, but which is even more urgently needed now in response to it.

(5) Promote new drugs and vaccines. Financing R&D for Covid-19 drugs and vaccines is an urgent global public good. Without global cooperation, R&D will be inadequate and duplicative. And when breakthroughs are achieved, they will in turn require global cooperation for their mass uptake. The Global Fund and Gavi, the Vaccine Alliance are two exemplary institutions that serve as historical precedents for what will be needed for the rapid uptake of new drugs and vaccines, and can lead the effort on the ground.

Box 1. Lessons on preparedness

The risk of a pandemic – and specifically a coronavirus pandemic – has been widely forewarned year after year. Yet many regions, including the United States and Europe, have not taken heed of these warnings in any meaningful way. Countries failed to invest sufficiently in public health systems and now suffer the consequences.

The Covid-19 pandemic has highlighted the lack of preparedness of health systems to respond to such public-health emergencies, including those of many OECD countries that before the crisis were thought better prepared. As of June 20th, the United States had the highest number of reported cases and deaths due to Covid-19. As a share of their populations, apart from a few small city-states, it is the OECD countries Belgium, Spain, the United Kingdom, Italy and France that have reported the highest number of deaths per capita. By contrast, several countries located closer to China, where the disease outbreak started – notably South Korea – have managed the Covid-19 outbreak more effectively.

Before the Covid-19 outbreak, the United States and many Western European countries were rated highest for health preparedness. For example, the United States and the United Kingdom topped the Global Health Security Index released in November 2019, shortly before the first outbreak of Covid-19 (NTI, JHU, and EIU, 2019). President Trump cited this index early in the pandemic, in February 2020, to argue that the United States was rated "Number 1" in terms of preparedness (Hub staff report, 2020). But it quickly became obvious that the level of preparation was not particularly great in the United States and in many other OECD countries.

There does not seem to be anything wrong with the assessment framework for preparedness to health threats adopted by the researchers. Yet the Index seems to have overestimated the capacity of some countries, including the United States, the United Kingdom, and France, to implement widespread testing of suspected cases and to isolate them. For example, the United States scored better (98.2) than Germany (84.6) and South Korea (92.1) on the dimension "detection and reporting capacity," yet the United States took much more time than Germany and South Korea to test a significant proportion of its population (see figure 4, below).

Figure 4

Despite good performance in the 2019 Global Health Security Index on "Detection and Reporting," the United States took longer than Germany and South Korea to test its population during the Covid-19 pandemic.

Cumulative Covid-19 tests per 1,000 population

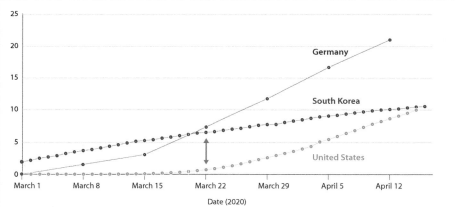

Performance in Global Health Security Index, November 2019
Category 2: Detection and Reporting

COUNTRY	RANK	SCORE
United States	1	98.2
South Korea	5	92.1
Germany	10	84.6

↑↓ US gap in Covid-19 tests performed in March

Date (2020)

Source: Official sources collected by Our World in Data

Another interpretation of the gap between predicted and actual responses to Covid-19 is that some countries *should have* been able to respond well to the Covid-19 health crisis but failed to do so because of a lack of information, poor political leadership, and other factors. These might be "omitted variables" in the Global Health Security assessment framework or variables that go beyond the scope of the GHS exercise (e.g. political leadership). As the world recovers from the Covid-19 crisis, it will be important to learn lessons from countries that were the most effective in dealing with the pandemic outbreak, but also to strengthen existing indicators and monitoring systems to track countries' preparedness and resilience capacities.

Source: Authors analysis. Based on Lafortune, G (2020). "How much do we know about countries' preparedness to respond to pandemics? Insights from two country-level indices." SDSN Blog Post. Paris. https://www.unsdsn.org/how-much-do-we-know-about-countries-preparedness-to-respond-to-pandemics-insights-from-two-country-level-indices

1.2 Comparing early Covid-19 control in the OECD countries

It is important to understand why some of the richest countries have failed to contain mass deaths from Covid-19 even thought they had ample warning. This section presents a simple quantitative model of the emergency response and introduces an index to measure the effectiveness of early responses to Covid-19 in OECD countries.

There is an enormous variation in the early Covid-19 pandemic control measures taken across the OECD countries, covering the period March 4 through May 12. The most marked difference is in the Covid-19 death rate per 1 million population, even given that death rates are difficult to compare across countries owing to widely differing reporting standards. In some OECD countries, such as Australia, Japan, Korea, and New Zealand, reported Covid-19 deaths remain below than 10 per million population. In other OECD countries, including Belgium, France, Germany, Sweden, and the United States, deaths are above 100 per million population, and in some cases many times higher.

A second important difference lies in the overall extent to which the pandemic was suppressed during this early phase, which is measured by epidemiologists according to the effective reproduction rate (ERR). An ERR < 1 signifies effective suppression, while an ERR > 1 signifies ongoing epidemic conditions. Some OECD countries suppressed the transmission of the virus during March and April, for example South Korea and New Zealand. Other countries had epidemic conditions with ERRs averaging far above 1.0. These include France, Germany, the United Kingdom, and the United States, among many others.

A third difference lies in the efficiency with which the pandemic is controlled. One way to cut the ERR below 1 is to lock down the economy. This reduces the viral transmission but at the cost of an enormous disruption to the economy and to daily life. Another way to cut the ERR is through more focused strategies that emphasize the isolation or quarantine of infected individuals, contact tracing, quarantine of people exposed to carriers of the virus, and improved hygienic practices, such as wearing face masks. Through such targeted means, the pandemic

can be suppressed at minimal economic cost. Some countries, such as South Korea, have succeeded in cutting their ERR through more targeted means, while others including Italy, Spain, and the United States have had to resort to the cruder and costlier approach of economic lockdowns. Strict and prolonged lockdowns, although costly, was most probably the right policy response for countries lacking PPE and with lower testing and hospital intensive care capacities. Strict and prolonged lockdowns contributed to saving many thousands of lives (Flaxman et al, 2020).

This section introduces a pilot index of Covid-19 control that summarizes each country's performance over the three dimensions (mortality rate, ERR, and efficiency of control). We study all OECD countries except for the three middle-income countries of Latin America (Chile, Colombia, and Mexico), where the virus came later, and Iceland due to the lack of relevant data on physical mobility, which we use to construct the efficiency index. We are therefore left with 33 OECD countries in our sample.

Mortality rate

The mortality rate per million population for the OECD countries as of May 12 is shown in table 1. We see that the mortality rate varies from a low value of 4 in Australia and New Zealand to a high of 762 in Belgium. It is important to emphasize that Covid-19 mortality rates are imperfectly measured, both within countries and across countries. Some countries count only the deaths of individuals who have tested positive for Covid-19, while others, such as Belgium, include deaths that were likely due to Covid-19, even if those deaths were not confirmed with a positive Covid-19 test. Many countries exclude deaths that occur at home or in nursing homes, which might account for some 40% of their total. Nonetheless, even taking into account the inevitable errors in the measurements, the actual differences in mortality rates are striking.

The high variation in mortality rates across the OECD countries reflects several factors. Perhaps most importantly, mortality per million depends on the infection rate per million. Unfortunately, insufficient testing and reporting in most countries mean that, at this stage, we lack accurate, comparable data on the infection rates of their populations.

The variation in the mortality rate across countries also reflects other structural factors, such as the intensive-care capacity of the hospital system; the population age structure (because of high mortality rates among the elderly); the burden of co-morbidities, such as obesity, respiratory infections, and hypertension in the population; and the protections given to vulnerable groups, especially in settings such as nursing homes, retirement homes, worker hostels, and prisons. Some also suspect that genetic differences might contribute to variations in mortality, but these issues are poorly understood at present.

Effective reproduction rate

The effective reproduction rate is defined as the average number of infections that an infectious individual transmits to susceptible individuals. In the most basic standard model of epidemics, the ERR(t) as of day t is given as follows:

(1) $ERR(t) = N(t) \times P(t) \times D(t) \times S(t)$

In this equation, N(t) is the average number of contacts per day for an individual in the community; P(t) is the probability that a contact between an infectious individual and a susceptible individual actually transmits the virus; D(t) is the average number of days that an infectious individual is circulating in an infectious state in the community; and S(t) is the share of the population susceptible to infection as of day t. We see that N(t) x D(t) therefore is the average number of community contacts by an infectious person during the period of infectiousness. P(t) times the number of community contacts measures the number of times the virus will be transmitted. Since a fraction – S(t) – of those infectious contacts are susceptible to becoming infected, we have equation (1).

At the start of an epidemic – on day 0 – ERR is designated as R0, the basic reproduction rate. In the case of Covid-19, S(0) is assumed to be equal to 1, that is, the entire population is assumed to be susceptible, since there is no known intrinsic or acquired immunity. R0 is generally estimated to

be between 2 and 3, with a typical estimate of around 2.4. D(0) is usually assumed to be around 6 days. Assuming these parameters (and acknowledging the many continuing uncertainties about the virus), we can surmise an average of 0.4 infections transmitted per day (= 2.4/6). If each individual plausibly has around 20 contacts per day, a typical assumption in the epidemiological literature, the probability of the virus being transmitted in any single contact (e.g., in a casual conversation, or interpersonal proximity in a retail shop, or sitting nearby an infected individual in a restaurant, theater, or sports event) can be calculated as 0.4 infections per day/20 contacts per day = 0.02 infections per contact, or a 2% risk of transmission in any single contact.

In the basic model, the daily change in the number of infected individuals I(t) as of day t is given by:

(2) $I(t+1) - I(t) = N(t)*P(t)*I(t)*S(t) - [1/D(t)]*I(t)$

N(t)*P(t)*I(t)*S(t) is the number of new infections in day t, while (1/D)*(t) is the number of currently infected individuals on day t who cease being infected, either because they die on day t or recover on day t. With a bit of simple algebraic rearrangement of equations (1) and (2), we can derive a basic relationship between the daily growth of new infections g(t) = [I(t+1) – I(t)]/I(t) and the ERR(t):

(3) $ERR(t) = 1 + D(t)*g(t)$

The relationship in equation (3) is helpful in two ways. First, we see that the growth of new infections g(t) is positive when ERR(t) > 1 and negative when ERR(t) < 1. Thus, the ERR(t) determines whether the epidemic is expanding or contracting. Second, since we observe (or at least can estimate) the growth of the epidemic day by day, we can also estimate ERR(t) for each day.

Several epidemiologists are now publishing estimates of ERR(t) on a daily basis. We use the estimates of Prof. Simas Kucinskas (2020) of Humboldt University of Berlin. The estimated ERR(t) averaged by day for the interval March 4 to May 12 is shown in table 1. We see that South Korea had the lowest average ERR in this period, at 0.76, while the United States, the United Kingdom, Turkey, Canada, France and Spain had the highest average values of ERR, above 1.5 for the period.

Epidemic control efficiency

According to equation 3, the epidemic is suppressed by reducing ERR(t) to below 1.0. This can occur in four basic ways.

First, the average number of contacts per day N(t) in the population can be reduced sharply. This is the basic motivation of the "temporary lockdown" that was put in place in many parts of the world in mid-March. Second, the probability of transmitting the disease per each contact P(t) can be reduced by changes in personal behavior, such as by wearing face masks, using hand sanitizers, and observing social distancing. Third, the infectious individual himself or herself can stop circulating in the public very early in the course of the illness by self-isolating at home or through quarantine in a public facility. In this case, an infectious individual only circulates for one or two days before isolating. The number of days D(t) for which they are potentially spreading the infection is thereby cut sharply. Fourth, the proportion of the population susceptible to infection S(t) will fall over time, assuming that a bout of illness also confers persistent immunity. If the pandemic therefore infects enough of the population, S(t) will fall by enough to reduce ERR(t) to below 1.0. That is the painful way to stop the epidemic, which comes to a halt only after a substantial proportion of the population has fallen victim to the disease. Assuming an R0 of 2.4, and assuming no other behavioral changes that affect N(t), P(t), and D(t), we see that S(t) would have to decline to below 41.6% (= 1/2.4) in order for ERR to fall below 1.0. In other words, almost 60% of a population would need to incur the infection before "herd immunity" of the community is acquired.

A lockdown is an inefficient way to suppress the pandemic, and herd immunity is a deadly way to do so. In the case of a lockdown, daily contacts are slashed for everybody in the community across the board, whether or not they are infectious – putting aside the question of "essential workers" and partial lockdowns for the sake of the discussion. The economy declines sharply. In the case of herd immunity, more than half of the population incurs the infection, which if the infection mortality rate (IMR) is around 1%, as is generally believed, suggests that around 0.5% of the population would succumb to the disease, a horrendously high toll. In fact, in an uncontrolled

pandemic the attack rate – meaning the proportion ever infected in the population – would be considerably above 1/2.4, with the mortality rate being commensurately higher as well.

It is far more efficient to cut ERR(t) by slashing P(t) through improved personal hygiene or by reducing D(t) through early isolation or quarantine in public facilities. Cutting D(t) efficiently limits the circulation of the few who are infected, rather than the many who are susceptible.

Thanks to Google Community Mobility Reports (2020), we have smartphone-based measurements for dozens of countries of daily mobility within the community, including visits to retail establishments, restaurants, grocery stores, pharmacies, transit stations and workplaces. The Google mobility measurements GM(t) therefore offer a useful proxy measurement of the decline in daily contacts N(t) in a community. The data show the decline in visits relative to a baseline GM(0) during the interval from January 3 to February 6, 2020.

Using the Google data, we show the proportionate decline in mobility, [GM(0) – GM(t)]/GM(0), in the final (sixth) column of table 1. To calculate the decline, we take the simple daily average of four of Google's community mobility measures: visits to retail outlets and recreation, visits to grocery stores and pharmacies, visits to transit stations, and visits to workplaces. In all cases, the variable is equal to the decline in visits relative to the baseline period.

The data show that visits among the community have declined relative to the baseline in all OECD countries, but by widely varying amounts. South Korea, which has not had a lockdown, shows a decline of 0.10, or 10%. On the other extreme, Italy and Spain show a decline in mobility of 62% and 60% respectively – the most extreme lockdowns in the OECD group. A few countries have reduced mobility by 25% or less – Australia, Japan, Latvia, South Korea, and Sweden – while several show reductions greater than 40%.

A useful measure of the *efficiency* of epidemic control is to compare the decline in ERR(t) with the decline in N(t), as proxied by the Google data. If most of the reduction in ERR(t) is brought about by a reduction in N(t), we can say that the epidemic control is inefficient. If most of the decline in ERR(t) is achieved not by a reduction of N(t), but (implicitly) by a reduction in P(t)*D(t), we can say that the epidemic control is efficient.

We therefore propose the following measure of epidemic control efficiency, ECE(t):

(4) $ECE(t) = [R0 - ERR(t)]/R0 - [GM(t) - GM(0)]/GM(0)$

The first term on the right-hand side measures the proportionate reduction in ERR(t), while the second term measures the proportion reduction in average daily contacts. When the proportionate reduction in ERR(t) exceeds the proportionate reduction of mobility, ECE(t) > 0, and we deem the epidemic control to be efficient. When ECE(t) ≤ 0, we deem epidemic control to be inefficient. The ECE Is shown in the fourth column of table 1, while its two right-hand-side components are shown in the fifth and sixth columns. We see that South Korea has demonstrated by far the most efficient epidemic control during the period of observation (March 4 to May 12), while Spain shows the least efficient control.

Index of epidemic control

We now create an overall index of epidemic control among the 33 OECD countries, by combining the data on Covid-19 mortality rates, effective reproduction rates, and epidemic control efficiency. To construct the index, we follow the usual procedure of the SDG Index described in this report. For each variable X_i for country i, we create a normalized variable X_i^N on a scale from 0 to 100, calculated as follows:

(5) $X_i^N = [X_i - X_{MIN}]/[X_{MAX} - X_{MIN}] \times 100$

X_{MIN} is the minimum value of X among the 33 OECD countries. X_{MAX} is the maximum value. Clearly, when $X_i = X_{MIN}$, then $X_i^N = 0$, and when $X_i = X_{MAX}$, then $X_i^N = 1$. For all other X_i, we have $0 < X_i^N < 1$.

To construct the index, we use the mortality rate M (Column 1), the ERR (Column 2), and the ECE (Column 3). The final index score is denoted as the Covid Index of Epidemic Control (CIEC), and is calculated by averaging across the three variables:

(6) $CIEC_i = (1/3) * (M_i^N + ERR_i^N + ECE_i^N)$

According to this index, the top performing country is South Korea. Indeed, South Korea has excelled on all three dimensions of epidemic control. It has kept the death rate low, the ERR far below 1, and its economy has remained open during the entire epidemic. The worst performing economy is Spain, where the mortality rate is among the highest, its ERR averages far above 1, and the economy has been in substantial lockdown nonetheless. Some countries may have been artificially penalized in the data presented in this table due to their more-thorough reporting of Covid-19 deaths (counting probable cases as well as tested cases). Thus, we should also mention the five other very poor performers: Belgium, France, Italy, the United Kingdom and the United States.

Many governments, including Spain, have learned rapidly during the process and adapted policies accordingly. From April 6 onward, Spain has had an estimated R(t) less than 1, thereby dramatically curtailing the epidemic.

In general, South Korea owes its top ranking to its high-quality public health system. Its remarkable early efforts are described in an important report (Government of the Republic of Korea, 2020): not only did South Korea go into high alert upon the first news of the Covid-19 epidemic in China, its biotech companies moved rapidly to develop effective tests. By February 4, just three weeks after Chinese scientists had posted the genome of Covid-19, the company KogeneBiotech had developed an effective diagnostic kit (Lee, 2020). Five other companies followed soon after. ICTs were put to use in many ways: for emergency notifications from the government; in contact-tracing apps to let individuals know of virus "hotspots" visited by Covid-19-infected individuals; to develop distance-learning curricula and protocols; to provide advice for companies; and in many other applications that were developed and deployed within weeks.

It is useful to point out some other patterns among OECD countries in the early control period. First, the Asia-Pacific region in general has been high performing, exemplified in the following rankings on our index of epidemic control: South Korea, 1; Australia, 3; Japan, 6 and New Zealand, 9. With the exception of Japan, OECD countries with a population of greater than 50 million people did quite poorly, however. Germany ranks highest among large OECD countries, at 19, followed by Turkey, 26; the United States, 28; Italy, 29; France, 30; the United Kingdom, 31; and Spain, 33. No doubt these large countries all received many infected travelers early in the pandemic, both visitors from China and residents returning from China. In this sense, the major countries, being the major travel hubs, were heavily "seeded" with Covid-19 early on. Yet they all evinced low levels of control, not only of their borders, but also of transmission within the community.

In general, Northern Europe has outperformed Southern Europe, and Eastern Europe has outperformed Western Europe. The Baltic states have all done well: Latvia, 2; Lithuania, 4; and Estonia, 5. Within the Nordic countries, Sweden is a distinctive outlier, not only in its policies, but also in its ranking, with Norway ranking 10; Denmark, 12; Finland, 14; and Sweden, 22. Sweden alone of these countries tried to avoid a shutdown. Mobility fell by only 19% in Sweden, compared with Denmark, 29%; Norway, 30%; and Finland, 32%. Yet the ERR remains much higher in Sweden, as does the mortality rate. Sweden has received little benefit from its heterodox stand, at least as of early May. Swedish public health officials claim that Sweden will be better able to weather a second wave in the fall, however, because of a higher level of acquired immunity. Time will tell whether this approach will prove to be correct in the long run, but it is more costly in the short run.

The United States has generally underperformed in its Covid-19 response in relation to the average of the OECD countries. In the United States too, there was no move to a nationwide lockdown. Decisions were left mainly to states and their governors. Most states introduced partial lockdowns in mid-March but began to lift these by early May. In any event, observance of the lockdowns was decidedly uneven. Mobility declined by a relatively modest 27%, and its ERR remains among the highest in the OECD. Mortality rates have also been high, although below that of the highest mortality rates of Western Europe.

Concluding thoughts

This section offers just a first attempt by the SDSN to compare responses across countries, and considers only the first months of the global pandemic. Yet even this first glimpse reveals stark differences in policies and outcomes across the OECD countries. Since it is vital for countries to learn from each other in this pandemic, the SDSN will continue to monitor and compare the public-health performance of nations in the coming years as part of our overall effort to measure progress towards the SDGs and to thereby foster best practices and accelerated learning among national and local policy makers.

Table 1

Covid-19 pilot Index and performance indicators for the OECD countries

Rank	Country	Covid Index	Deaths Per Million	Effective Reproduction Rate (ERR)	Epidemic Control Efficiency (ECE)	ERR Decline	Mobility Decline
1	South Korea	0.90	5.00	0.76	0.63	0.36	0.10
2	Latvia	0.78	9.34	0.95	0.29	0.63	0.24
3	Australia	0.76	3.88	1.06	0.27	0.67	0.24
4	Lithuania	0.75	17.85	0.90	0.15	0.61	0.36
5	Estonia	0.75	46.14	0.94	0.21	0.73	0.31
6	Japan	0.73	5.08	1.25	0.29	0.70	0.16
7	Slovenia	0.72	49.18	0.83	0.07	0.78	0.46
8	Slovak Republic	0.72	4.77	0.96	0.07	0.74	0.42
9	New Zealand	0.71	4.34	0.80	-0.03	0.86	0.44
10	Norway	0.71	42.17	1.13	0.18	0.72	0.30
11	Greece	0.71	14.07	0.99	0.07	0.62	0.43
12	Denmark	0.70	92.00	1.11	0.19	0.73	0.29
13	Czech Republic	0.70	26.53	1.11	0.11	0.67	0.33
14	Finland	0.69	49.13	1.18	0.12	0.65	0.32
15	Hungary	0.68	43.48	1.14	0.06	0.63	0.32
16	Austria	0.65	70.13	1.16	0.00	0.58	0.44
17	Israel	0.64	29.04	1.22	-0.06	0.82	0.42
18	Luxembourg	0.64	166.13	0.95	-0.07	0.78	0.50
19	Germany	0.63	90.86	1.38	0.07	0.70	0.31
20	Switzerland	0.63	181.13	1.23	0.06	0.78	0.37
21	Poland	0.63	21.36	1.34	-0.05	0.52	0.38
22	Sweden	0.61	319.99	1.36	0.21	0.60	0.19
23	Netherlands	0.58	316.63	1.30	0.08	0.72	0.32
24	Canada	0.56	134.74	1.51	-0.10	0.63	0.37
25	Portugal	0.55	111.24	1.39	-0.21	0.65	0.49
26	Turkey	0.53	46.66	1.56	-0.25	0.65	0.38
27	Ireland	0.53	301.40	1.31	-0.14	0.73	0.44
28	United States	0.51	246.98	1.73	-0.05	0.63	0.27
29	Italy	0.49	508.74	1.19	-0.15	0.69	0.62
30	France	0.46	397.79	1.50	-0.21	0.68	0.54
31	United Kingdom	0.43	482.47	1.60	-0.15	0.60	0.43
32	Belgium	0.40	761.55	1.39	-0.10	0.67	0.45
33	Spain	0.39	575.26	1.50	-0.28	0.64	0.60

Source: Authors' analysis.
Deaths per million are for May 12, 2020. The effective reproduction rate (ERR), epidemic control efficiency (ECE), and mobility decline are all calculated for the period March 4 to May 12, 2020. ERR decline is calculated as (2.4 − ERR)/2.4, assuming R0 = 2.4.

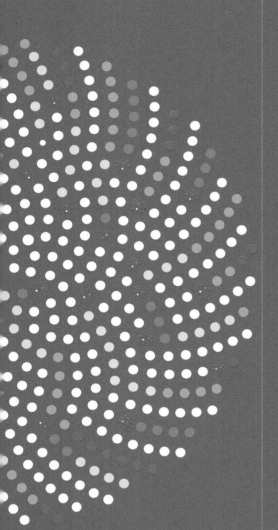

Part 2

The SDG Index and Dashboards

Part 2
The SDG Index and Dashboards

As in previous years, the *Sustainable Development Report 2020* (SDR2020) presents and aggregates data on country performance towards the SDGs. It is not an official SDG monitoring tool, but instead complements efforts of national statistical offices and international organizations to collect data on and standardize SDG indicators. To this end, the SDR2020 presents the most up-to-date data from official sources (the United Nations, the World Bank, and others) as well as from non-official sources (research institutions and non-governmental organizations).

Due to time lags in data generation and reporting, this year's SDG Index and Dashboards do not reflect the impact of Covid-19. The projection of country trajectories based on recent progress (business-as-usual, or BAU, scenarios) may not provide a realistic sense of the likely future, as Covid-19 risks changing trajectories relating to many SDGs (see section 1).

Nevertheless, the "pre-Covid-19" SDG Index and Dashboards remain useful for understanding goal-by-goal progress across countries and regions since the adoption of the SDGs in 2015. This serves three purposes in a world that is being transformed by the effects of Covid-19.

First, the SDG data presented in this report can help countries understand pre-crisis vulnerabilities and challenges, which partly explain why so many countries were ill-prepared to respond to Covid-19 (see Box 1). The SDG Index and Dashboards can support such diagnostics in every country.

Second, as highlighted in section 1, the SDGs provide the framework for the long-term recovery from Covid-19. The six SDG Transformations described in section 1 can help operationalize such a strategy. For example, our report highlights high levels of inequalities that must be addressed as part of the Covid-19 recovery (SDG Transformation 1). Over the longer term, the impacts of climate change might dwarf the dislocations caused by Covid-19, so countries need to understand where they stand in terms of decarbonizing energy systems (SDG Transformation 3); making their use of land and oceans sustainable (SDG Transformation 4); and developing low-carbon, resilient cities (SDG Transformation 5). The SDG dashboards provide a tool for such diagnoses (Box 2).

Third, the SDG dashboards underscore the urgent need for investments in more timely and comprehensive SDG data. As one example, SDSN's Thematic Research Network on Data and Statistics (TReNDs), in collaboration with various partners, has launched the Data4Now initiative, which aims to provide real-time updates on certain key SDG metrics.

Using the same methodology as in previous years, the SDG Index and Dashboards summarize countries' current performance and trends in relation to the 17 SDGs. This year we include data for 166 countries. Owing to slight changes in the indicator selection (see section 4), the 2020 rankings and scores are not comparable with last year's results. For the first time, we are now able to estimate changes in performance on the SDG Index using the SDR2020 indicators, which are described in section 2.2. As every year, we encourage readers to look beyond the aggregate SDG Index score and to consider countries' performances at the goal and indicator level.

Detailed methodological information, sensitivity tests, and the independent statistical audit of the SDG Index conducted by the European Commission in 2019 are available on our website (www.sdgindex.org).

Box 2. National and subnational SDG indices and dashboards

Good data and clear metrics are critical for each country to take stock of where it stands on the SDGs, devise pathways for achieving the goals, and track progress. Since 2016, the SDSN and Bertelsmann Stiftung have published the annual global SDG Index and Dashboards. The methodology has been peer-reviewed (Schmidt-Traub et al., 2017) and was audited in 2019 by the European Commission Joint Research Centre (Papadimitriou, Neves, and Becker, 2019).

To provide a better analysis of country and regional contexts, and to improve policy relevance, the SDSN in collaboration with numerous partners has also developed regional and sub-national SDG indices and dashboards. Regional assessments are available for Africa (2018, 2019 and 2020), the Arab Region (2019), the European Union (2019), the Mediterranean Countries (2019), and Latin America and the Caribbean (2020). These reports differ from the global edition in three ways: (i) they tailor the indicator selection to SDG challenges in each specific region; (ii) they use data and statistics from the region (e.g., the European Commission in Europe, UN/ECLAC in Latin America), which can greatly improve the analysis compared with the global Sustainable Development Report; and (iii) they include policy sections that discuss regional policy challenges and implementation efforts. For these reasons, regional SDG indices and dashboards have been generating a lot of interest from governments and other stakeholders.

Another priority is sub-national assessments of SDG progress, which can highlight disparities across cities, provinces, and regions within a country. The SDSN estimates that almost two-thirds (65%) of the 169 SDG targets underlying the 17 SDGs will not be reached without the engagement of and coordination with local, provincial, and regional governments. Similarly, UN-Habitat estimates that around one-third of all SDG indicators have a local or urban component. SDSN and local partner organizations have therefore supported the development of sub-national SDG indices and dashboards in Bolivia, Italy, Spain, and the United States, as well as the European Union. Many other sub-national reports are in preparation.

Figure 5

SDG index and Dashboards: global, regional and subnational editions (2016–2020)

Global editions

Regional editions

Subnational editions

Source: Authors' analysis. Download the reports and databases at: www.sdgindex.org.

2.1 The 2020 SDG Index

The SDG Index tracks country performance on the 17 SDGs, as agreed by the international community in 2015 with equal weight to all 17 goals. The score signifies a country's position between the worst (0) and the best or target (100) outcomes. For example, Sweden's overall Index score (85) suggest that the country is on average 85% of the way to the best possible outcome across the 17 SDGs. To ensure transparency and encourage further analyses, all underlying data is made available publicly on www.sdgindex.org.

Following minor changes to the indicator selection for this report, and last year's audit by the European Commission Joint Research Centre, the methodology and data for the SDG Index and Dashboards are now mature and stable. This year's SDG Index and Dashboards include 85 global indicators plus an additional 30 indicators for the OECD countries. We separated imported biodiversity threats into terrestrial, freshwater (under SDG 15 – Life on Land), and marine (under SDG 14 – Life Below Water). We have also added an indicator to track profit-shifting (under SDG 17 – Partnerships for the Goals). This year, we are also able for the first time to compile trends on transboundary impacts embodied in trade and consumption. All changes to the indicator selection are described in section 4 of this report.

As in previous editions, three Nordic countries top the 2020 SDG Index: Sweden, Denmark, and Finland. Most countries in the top 20 are OECD countries. Yet even these countries face significant challenges in achieving several SDGs. Every country has a "red" score on at least one SDG in the dashboards (Figure 14). High-income countries perform poorly on spillover indicators (Table 13). Looking at trends, many high-income countries are not making significant progress on sustainable consumption and production or the protection of biodiversity, particularly in relation to Goal 14 (Life Below Water), for which most high-income countries are stagnating. Covid-19 will likely negatively impact progress towards most SDGs in the short and medium-term, including in high-income countries.

Low-income countries tend to have lower SDG Index scores. This is partly due to the nature of the SDGs, which focus to a large extent on ending extreme poverty and on access to basic services and infrastructure (SDGs 1–9). Moreover, poorer countries tend to lack adequate infrastructure and mechanisms to manage key environmental challenges covered under SDGs 12–15. Except for countries that face armed conflicts and civil wars, however, most low-income countries are making progress in ending extreme poverty and in providing access to basic services and infrastructure, particularly under SDG 3 (Good Health and Well-Being) and SDG 8 (Decent Work and Economic Growth), as illustrated by the SDG trends dashboards.

2.2 The SDG Index score over time

Overall, the world has been making progress towards the SDGs. Figure 6 presents the evolution of SDG Index scores since 2010 by region. The chart suggests some convergence overall, with regions that had lower 2010 SDG Index scores progressing faster. Countries in East and South Asia have progressed the most since 2010, and since the adoption of the SDGs in 2015. Africa made significant progress during the MDG period (2000–2015) and has also made some progress since the adoption of the SDGs. Latin America and the Caribbean, Eastern Europe and Central Asia, and the Middle East and North Africa region also made progress between 2010 and 2019 and have increased their SDG Index score by more than one point on average. Finally, OECD countries, which have on average the highest SDG Index score, progressed moderately since 2015. On average, progress since 2015 has been faster in low- and middle-income countries compared with high-income countries (Figure 7).

There are significant disparities in the progress that countries have made on the SDGs, including within regions. The three countries that have progressed the most in terms of the SDG Index score are Côte d'Ivoire, Burkina Faso, and Cambodia. By contrast, the three countries that have declined the most are Venezuela, Zimbabwe, and the Republic of the Congo. In general, conflicts and civil wars lead to reversal in SDG progress.

Table 2

The 2020 SDG Index scores

Rank	Country	Score	Rank	Country	Score
1	Sweden	84.7	43	Greece	74.3
2	Denmark	84.6	44	Luxembourg	74.3
3	Finland	83.8	45	Uruguay	74.3
4	France	81.1	46	Ecuador	74.3
5	Germany	80.8	47	Ukraine	74.2
6	Norway	80.8	48	China	73.9
7	Austria	80.7	49	Vietnam	73.8
8	Czech Republic	80.6	50	Bosnia and Herzegovina	73.5
9	Netherlands	80.4	51	Argentina	73.2
10	Estonia	80.1	52	Kyrgyz Republic	73.0
11	Belgium	80.0	53	Brazil	72.7
12	Slovenia	79.8	54	Azerbaijan	72.6
13	United Kingdom	79.8	55	Cuba	72.6
14	Ireland	79.4	56	Algeria	72.3
15	Switzerland	79.4	57	Russian Federation	71.9
16	New Zealand	79.2	58	Georgia	71.9
17	Japan	79.2	59	Iran, Islamic Rep.	71.8
18	Belarus	78.8	60	Malaysia	71.8
19	Croatia	78.4	61	Peru	71.8
20	Korea, Rep.	78.3	62	North Macedonia	71.4
21	Canada	78.2	63	Tunisia	71.4
22	Spain	78.1	64	Morocco	71.3
23	Poland	78.1	65	Kazakhstan	71.1
24	Latvia	77.7	66	Uzbekistan	71.0
25	Portugal	77.6	67	Colombia	70.9
26	Iceland	77.5	68	Albania	70.8
27	Slovak Republic	77.5	69	Mexico	70.4
28	Chile	77.4	70	Turkey	70.3
29	Hungary	77.3	71	United Arab Emirates	70.3
30	Italy	77.0	72	Montenegro	70.2
31	United States	76.4	73	Dominican Republic	70.2
32	Malta	76.0	74	Fiji	69.9
33	Serbia	75.2	75	Armenia	69.9
34	Cyprus	75.2	76	Oman	69.7
35	Costa Rica	75.1	77	El Salvador	69.6
36	Lithuania	75.0	78	Tajikistan	69.4
37	Australia	74.9	79	Bolivia	69.3
38	Romania	74.8	80	Bhutan	69.3
39	Bulgaria	74.8	81	Panama	69.2
40	Israel	74.6	82	Bahrain	68.8
41	Thailand	74.5	83	Egypt, Arab Rep.	68.8
42	Moldova	74.4	84	Jamaica	68.7

Rank	Country	Score	Rank	Country	Score
85	Nicaragua	68.7	126	Syrian Arab Republic	59.3
86	Suriname	68.4	127	Senegal	58.3
87	Barbados	68.3	128	Côte d'Ivoire	57.9
88	Brunei Darussalam	68.2	129	The Gambia	57.9
89	Jordan	68.1	130	Mauritania	57.7
90	Paraguay	67.7	131	Tanzania	56.6
91	Maldives	67.6	132	Rwanda	56.6
92	Cabo Verde	67.2	133	Cameroon	56.5
93	Singapore	67.0	134	Pakistan	56.2
94	Sri Lanka	66.9	135	Congo, Rep.	55.2
95	Lebanon	66.7	136	Ethiopia	55.2
96	Nepal	65.9	137	Burkina Faso	55.2
97	Saudi Arabia	65.8	138	Djibouti	54.6
98	Trinidad and Tobago	65.8	139	Afghanistan	54.2
99	Philippines	65.5	140	Mozambique	54.1
100	Ghana	65.4	141	Lesotho	54.0
101	Indonesia	65.3	142	Uganda	53.5
102	Belize	65.1	143	Burundi	53.5
103	Qatar	64.7	144	Eswatini	53.4
104	Myanmar	64.6	145	Benin	53.3
105	Honduras	64.4	146	Comoros	53.1
106	Cambodia	64.4	147	Togo	52.7
107	Mongolia	64.0	148	Zambia	52.7
108	Mauritius	63.8	149	Angola	52.6
109	Bangladesh	63.5	150	Guinea	52.5
110	South Africa	63.4	151	Yemen, Rep.	52.3
111	Gabon	63.4	152	Malawi	52.2
112	Kuwait	63.1	153	Sierra Leone	51.9
113	Iraq	63.1	154	Haiti	51.7
114	Turkmenistan	63.0	155	Papua New Guinea	51.7
115	São Tomé and Príncipe	62.6	156	Mali	51.4
116	Lao PDR	62.1	157	Niger	50.1
117	India	61.9	158	Dem. Rep. Congo	49.7
118	Venezuela, RB	61.7	159	Sudan	49.6
119	Namibia	61.6	160	Nigeria	49.3
120	Guatemala	61.5	161	Madagascar	49.1
121	Botswana	61.5	162	Liberia	47.1
122	Vanuatu	60.9	163	Somalia	46.2
123	Kenya	60.2	164	Chad	43.8
124	Guyana	59.7	165	South Sudan	43.7
125	Zimbabwe	59.5	166	Central African Republic	38.5

Annual assessments of progress on the SDG Index score are affected by limited data availability and time lags for certain indicators. Due to gaps in data availability and time lags, these longitudinal trend lines include many imputations based on closest available years. As noted above, Covid-19 will likely have a strongly negative impact on SDG performance in many countries, but this has not been reflected in the data available to date. See the detailed trend database accessible on the SDG Index website: https://www.sdgindex.org/.

Figure 6

Progress on the SDG Index by regions (2010–2019)

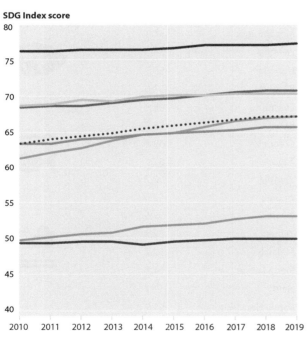

SDG Index score

..... World
— East and South Asia
— Eastern Europe and Central Asia
— Latin America and the Caribbean
— Middle East and North Africa
— Oceania
— OECD countries
— Sub-Saharan Africa

Figure 7

Progress on the SDG Index by income group (2010–2019)

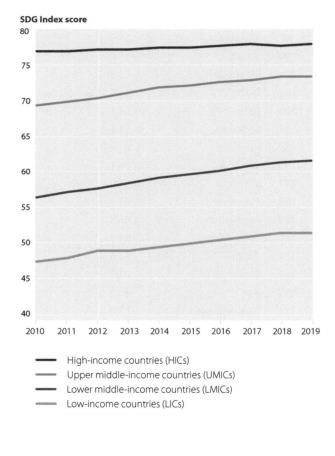

SDG Index score

— High-income countries (HICs)
— Upper middle-income countries (UMICs)
— Lower middle-income countries (LMICs)
— Low-income countries (LICs)

Figure 8

Countries whose SDG Index score has improved or decreased the most since 2015

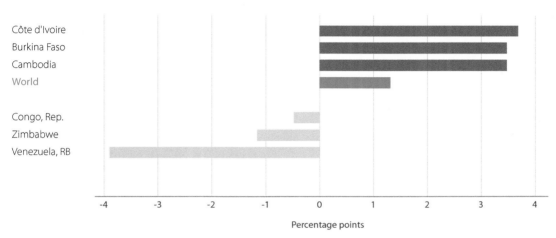

Note: Population-weighted averages.
Source: Authors' analysis

Progress by SDGs

Since 2015, the world has seen the most rapid progress towards SDG 1 (No Poverty), SDG 9 (Industry, Innovation and Infrastructure), and SDG 11 (Sustainable Cities and Communities). Overall, as underlined by the United Nations Statistics Division, the percentage of people living in extreme poverty globally in 2018 had decreased by 1.4 percentage points from the adoption of the SDGs: from 10% in 2015 to 8.6% in 2018 (United Nations, 2019). Following these historic trends, this figure was projected to reach 6% by 2030, however Covid-19 now threatens to increase extreme poverty in many countries. Access to basic transport infrastructure and broadband connection has also been growing rapidly. Ninety percent of the world's population live within range of a 3G or higher-quality mobile network (United Nations, 2019). Global investment in research and development has also been growing. At the same time, SDG 9 (Industry, Innovation and Infrastructure) is the goal that exhibits the largest spread between top and bottom performers. This emphasizes the need to accelerate the spread of technologies and innovation globally and to strengthen capacities and skills. As highlighted in the SDG dashboards, the historic pace of progress may not be sufficient to achieve these SDGs by 2030 – including ending extreme poverty.

By contrast, even before Covid-19, many parts of the world were progressing slowly or experiencing reversals in progress made towards SDG 2 (Zero Hunger) and SDG 15 (Life on Land). The lack of progress towards SDG 2 is driven by increases in the number of people who suffer from undernourishment as well as a growing share of people who are overweight or obese. It is likely that Covid-19 will increase food insecurity and malnutrition, especially for low-income people (FAO, 2020; IFPRI, 2020; World Food Programme, 2020). The accelerated loss of terrestrial and freshwater biodiversity is affecting performance on SDG 15 (Life on Land). Despite an increase in protected areas, reversals on this goal in many countries are driven by biodiversity threats and deforestation, caused at least in part by unsustainable supply chains. This is confirmed by many international reports (IPCC, 2019; IPBES, 2019).

There are indications that historic trends in progress towards SDG 10 (Reduced Inequalities) and SDG 17 (Partnerships for the Goals) have also been declining slightly, however global trend data is sparse, so we do not present longitudinal charts for these goals.

Figure 9

Progress by SDGs and regions

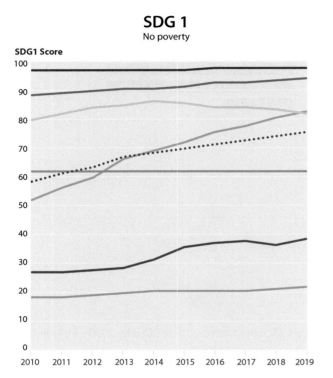

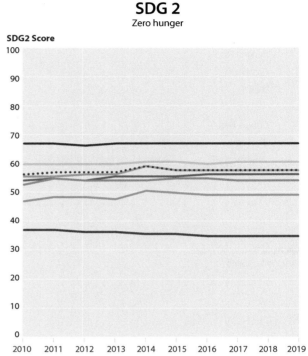

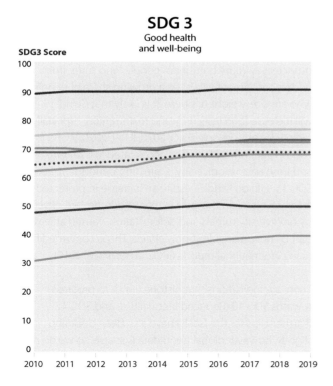

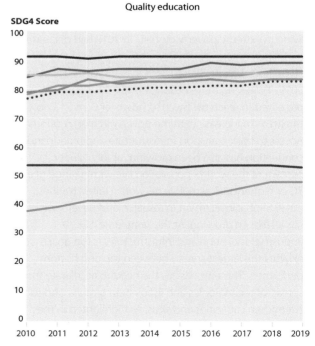

Figure 9

Progress by SDGs and regions (continued)

- ····· World
- —— East and South Asia
- —— Eastern Europe and Central Asia
- —— Latin America and the Caribbean
- —— Middle East and North Africa
- —— Oceania
- —— OECD countries
- —— Sub-Saharan Africa

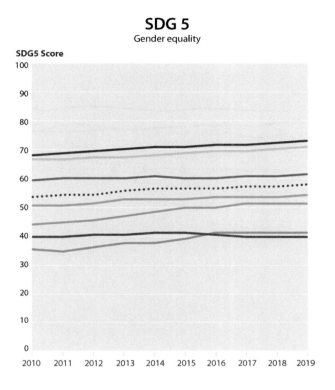

SDG 5
Gender equality

SDG5 Score

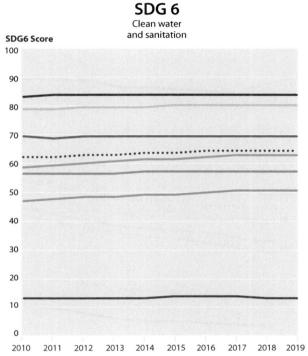

SDG 6
Clean water and sanitation

SDG6 Score

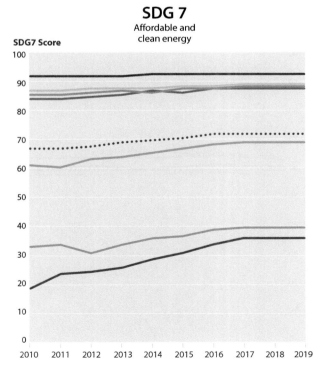

SDG 7
Affordable and clean energy

SDG7 Score

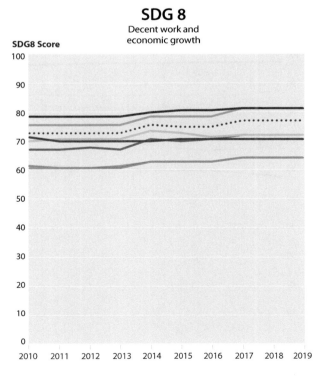

SDG 8
Decent work and economic growth

SDG8 Score

Figure 9

Progress by SDGs and regions (continued)

····· World
— East and South Asia
— Eastern Europe and Central Asia
— Latin America and the Caribbean
— Middle East and North Africa
— Oceania
— OECD countries
— Sub-Saharan Africa

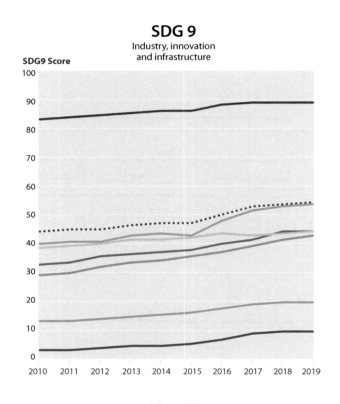

SDG 9
Industry, innovation and infrastructure

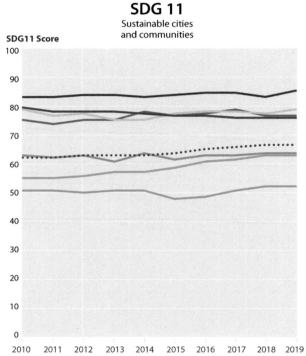

SDG 11
Sustainable cities and communities

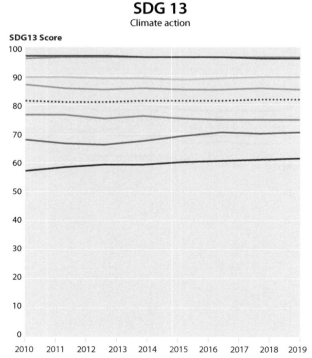

SDG 13
Climate action

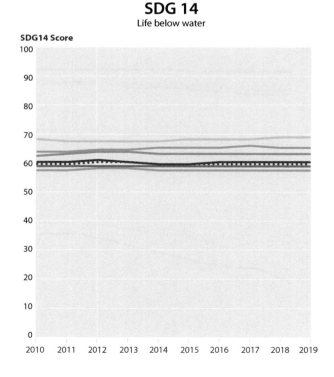

SDG 14
Life below water

Figure 9

Progress by SDGs and regions (continued)

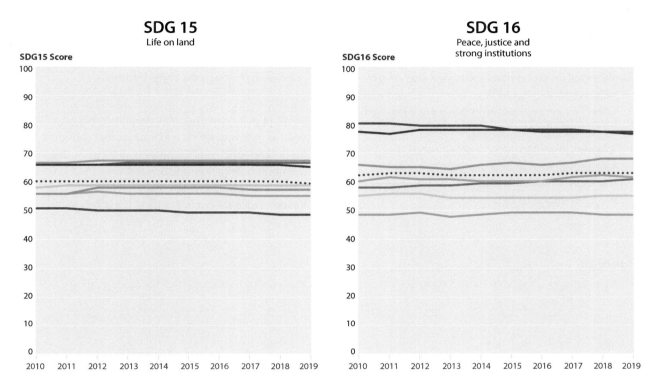

Note: Trend data for SDG 10 (Reduced Inequalities), SDG 12 (Responsible Consumption and Production), and SDG 17 (Partnerships for the Goals) are not presented due to data gaps. For SDG 13 (Climate Action), goal score is based on the headline indicator "CO_2 emissions per capita." Other indicators for SDG 13 are included in the country profiles and dashboards. Due to incomplete trend data, longitudinal results on SDG 14 (Life Below Water) are not presented for Oceania. See country profiles and dashboards for more information on indicator and goal trajectories.

Source: Authors' analysis

2.3 International spillovers

Strategies to achieve the SDGs need to be implemented domestically without generating negative impacts on other countries ("spillovers"). The 2030 Agenda and the SDGs recognize the importance of international spillovers. SDG 12 (Responsible Consumption and Production) requires developed countries to take the lead in tackling spillovers. Greta Thunberg and others have accused rich countries of "creative carbon accounting" by counting only "production-based" emissions, leaving aside consumption-based emissions embodied into trade.[1]

Spillovers must be understood, measured, and carefully managed. Since 2017, the *Sustainable Development Report* has presented the best available data on countries' positive and negative spillovers, and these have been consolidated into a Spillover Index. The index score and rank are available for all countries in the Annex and have been included in the country profiles. We group spillovers into three categories:

- Environmental spillovers cover international spillovers related to the use of natural resources and pollution. Environmental spillovers can be generated in two ways: i) through transboundary effects embodied in trade, and ii) through direct cross-border flows in air and water.

---

1. https://www.economist.com/finance-and-economics/2019/10/17/greta-thunberg-accuses-rich-countries-of-creative-carbon-accounting

Trade-related spillover measures are obtained using the consumption-based accounting (CBA) framework and isolating the "import" component. Using tools such as multiregional input–output (MRIO) databases, combined with databases on environmental, biodiversity and social factors, we can estimate transboundary impacts embodied in consumption and trade. Generating better measures of cross-border flows (through air and water) for each country remains an important research agenda.

• Spillovers related to the economy, finance, and governance cover international development finance (e.g., ODA), unfair tax competition, banking secrecy, and international labor standards.

• Security spillovers include negative externalities – such as the trade in arms, particularly in small arms (Adeniyi, 2017), and organized international crime – which can have a destabilizing impact on poor countries. Among the positive spillovers are investments in conflict-prevention and peacekeeping, including through the United Nations.

Overall, high-income countries generate the largest negative spillovers, which undermine other countries' efforts to achieve the SDGs. Small countries – such as Luxembourg, Singapore and Switzerland – tend to trade more than larger economies, and therefore generate high per-capita spillovers. Yet, there is a large variation

Figure 10

Average spillover score against gross domestic product per capita (GDP per capita, constant 2010 US$, PPP)

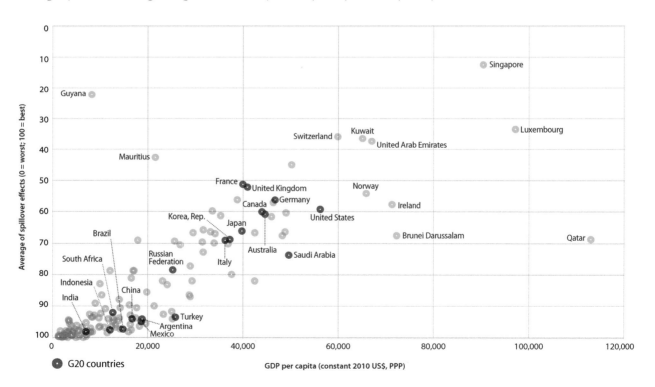

Note: The Spillover Index measures transboundary impacts generated by one country on others, which undermine their ability to achieve the SDGs. The Spillover Index covers financial spillovers (e.g., financial secrecy, profit-shifting), environmental and social impacts embodied into trade and consumption (e.g., imported CO_2 emissions, imported biodiversity threats, accidents at work embodied into trade) and security/development cooperation (ODA, weapons exports). ODA is an example of a positive spillover. Scores should be interpreted in the same way as for the SDG Index, ranging from 0 (worst performance i.e., significant negative spillovers) to 100 (best possible performance, i.e., no significant negative spillovers). To allow for international comparisons, most spillover indicators are expressed on a per capita basis. The Spillover Index scores and ranks are available in Table 13.

Source: Authors' analysis.

in spillovers among countries with similar per-capita incomes. This suggests that countries can reduce their negative spillovers without reducing their per-capita incomes. The spillover index is presented in each individual country profile.

Data on cross-border spillovers tends to be sparse and incomplete, and several spillovers lack clear conceptual frameworks for measurement. The lack of data and measurement concepts derive partly from the complexity of the issues. Another challenge is that national statistical offices are rarely mandated to measure international spillovers. Moreover, a lot of work on international spillovers focuses on individual supply chains (e.g., production of a pair of jeans) or specific products, such as palm oil from South-East Asia. Such case studies have made a tremendous contribution towards our understanding of international spillovers, but they cannot directly be incorporated into national-level assessments. Translating the findings from case studies into national metrics is a priority for future research into international spillover indicators.

Focusing on spillovers embodied into trade, there is a crucial need to better integrate consumption-based accounting within monitoring and policy frameworks, including in tracking and reducing greenhouse gas emissions (Kander et al., 2015). Consumption-based accounting has the advantage of incorporating the impacts generated by international transport. It also incorporates carbon leakages and attributes them to the countries that externalize CO_2 emissions (or other types of impacts). As such, it brings complementary policy implications to production-based accounting. While production-based accounting rightfully emphasizes the principle of "product liability," which states that producers are responsible for the quality and safety of their products, consumption-based accounting emphasizes the responsibility of consumers and international trade policies and agreements.

For the first time, the report this year integrates trends over time for trade-related spillovers. Constructing MRIO databases and satellite datasets is very time consuming, which leads to time lags in data reporting of three to six years (Svenja Wiebe et al., 2018). This is an important limitation of consumption-based and trade-related spillover measures. Efforts to increase the timeliness of global MRIOs are under way (Miao and Fortanier, 2018; Stadler et al., 2018)

In contrast to domestic impacts, we see no clear signs of sustained reductions in spillovers generated by OECD countries. CO_2 emissions in OECD countries declined between 2010 and 2015 but imported CO_2 emissions have increased overall compared to 2000 and have risen further since 2009 (Figure 11). OECD countries are reducing their impact on domestic water scarcity. However, while scarce water use embodied in imports has declined overall since 2000, no progress was seen between 2009 and 2013.

More data-driven conversations are also needed to reform the governance of global supply chains. Many international supply chains, particularly relating to land-use and food systems are unsustainable. The ability of individual companies to correct these failings can be limited, so industry- and supply-chain-wide approaches are needed. Several such industry initiatives exist (for coffee, palm oil, cocoa, and many other products). As part of a larger consortium, SDSN released a study in 2019 on the governance of the soybean supply chain, and in particular on the impact of trade imports from Europe and China on major soybean producers, such as Argentina and Brazil (Czaplicki Cabezas et al., 2019). More work is needed to understand how the governance of international supply chains can be and need to be reformed to curb cross-country spillovers.

Figure 11

Domestic vs transboundary impacts (CO_2 emissions and scarce water use)

━━ OECD countries
── Rest of the World (ROW)

Domestic: Energy-related CO_2 emissions per capita (tCO_2/capita)

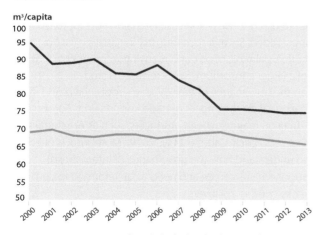

Source: Authors' analysis. Based on Gütschow et al (2016)

Spillover: CO_2 emissions embodied into imports (tCO_2/capita)

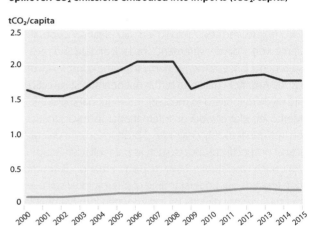

Source: Authors' analysis. Based on Lenzen, M. et al. (2020)

Domestic: Scarce water use for domestic consumption and exports (m³/Capita)

Source: Authors' analysis. Based on Lenzen, M. et al. (2013)

Spillover: Scarce water use embodied into imports (m³/capita)

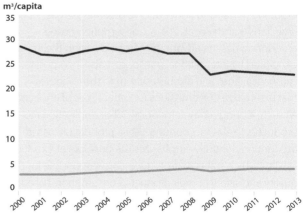

Source: Authors' analysis. Based on Lenzen, M. et al. (2013)

2.4 The SDG dashboards

The SDG dashboards highlight the strengths and weaknesses of each country in relation to each of the 17 SDGs. As described in the methodology section, dashboard ratings are based on data for the two indicators under each goal for which the country performs worst. This means that, for example, good performance on five out of seven indicators does not compensate for poor performance on two indicators. In other words, our methodology assumes low substitutability or compensation across indicators in the construction of our composite index.

This year, the dashboards include population-weighted averages for each region and by income groups (Figure 12). These regional comparisons are based on the same set of indicators as used for the SDG Index. The OECD dashboards (Figure 14) include more indicators than the other dashboards, however, owing to the greater availability of data for these countries. SDSN is also promoting regional editions of the *SDG Index and Dashboards*, including editions on Africa, the Arab Region, Europe, and Latin America (Box 2).

OECD countries

The OECD dashboard reveals that, before the Covid-19 outbreak, OECD countries were not on track to achieve the SDGs. Compared to the rest of the world, OECD countries perform better on goals related to socioeconomic outcomes and basic access to infrastructure, including SDG 1 (No Poverty), SDG 3 (Good Health and Well-Being), SDG 6 (Clean Water and Sanitation), and SDG 7 (Affordable and Clean Energy). Yet the indicator set does not capture well a country's preparedness for health security challenges, due to the absence of a robust international measure (Box 1). Covid-19 has indeed highlighted the vulnerability of health systems, including those of OECD countries (section 1.2), and the need to strengthen resilience and prevention.

Major efforts are needed to accelerate progress towards climate mitigation and biodiversity protection – SDGs 12 to 15. In particular, some OECD countries perform especially poorly on associated spillover indicators. Based on available

data, trends on SDG 13 (Climate Action), SDG 14 (Life Below Water) and, where available, on transboundary impacts embodied in trade and consumption are alarming in most OECD countries. These countries need to undertake greater efforts to decouple economic growth from negative environmental impacts, particularly in the wake of Covid-19.

OECD countries face persistent challenges related to sustainable agriculture and diets – which are also major drivers of greenhouse gas emissions and biodiversity loss. OECD countries perform relatively poorly on the indicators on trophic levels (capturing the energy intensity and long-term sustainability of average diets) and obesity. Meanwhile, the closure of yield-gap remains well below the 80% target in numerous OECD countries and below 50% in some. This underscores the need to increase the efficiency of agricultural and land-use systems and to improve diets and sustainable food consumption.

Inequalities in incomes as well as in access to services and opportunities are growing challenges in most OECD countries. Palma ratios, adjusted GINI coefficients, and elderly poverty rates are all high and are increasing in the majority of the OECD countries. Disparities in health and education outcomes by income and territorial area are also high. Finally, gender pay gaps and the gender gap in minutes spent doing unpaid work need to be substantially reduced to achieve SDG 5 (Gender Equality) in OECD countries.

East and South Asia

Overall, East and South Asia is the region that has progressed most on the SDG Index since the adoption of the goals in 2015. Most countries in the region also managed the Covid-19 outbreak more effectively than many other parts of the world (section 1).

Countries in East and South Asia differ greatly in size and in level of economic development. Correspondingly, SDG challenges also vary greatly across countries in this region. Overall, the best performances are obtained on SDG 1 (No Poverty), SDG 4 (Quality Education), SDG 7 (Affordable and Clean Energy), although for each of these goals, at least one country in the region has a red rating (major SDG challenge). Major challenges persist in most countries on SDG 2 (Zero Hunger), SDG 3 (Good Health and Well-Being), SDG 5 (Gender Equality), SDGs 12–15 on climate change mitigation and biodiversity protection, and SDG 16 (Peace, Justice and Strong Institutions). Trends on SDG 1 (No Poverty) are especially positive, with most countries in the region on track to eradicate extreme poverty. By contrast, negative trends on SDG 13 (Climate Action) and SDG 15 (Life on Land) need to be reversed and will require a significant acceleration of progress to achieve the 2030 targets in most countries. Vigilance is needed to ensure that Covid-19 does not change positive trajectories.

Eastern Europe and Central Asia

Countries in Eastern Europe and Central Asia obtain their best performance on SDG 1 (No Poverty) and SDG 7 (Affordable and Clean Energy). Compared to other regions, SDG 16 (Peace, Justice and Strong Institutions) remains problematic, due to relatively high perceived corruption in some countries, low freedom of speech, or high insecurity. As for other parts of the world, poor performance on SDGs 12 to 15 on climate mitigation and biodiversity protection require urgent policy attention. Access to basic services and infrastructure, covered notably under SDG 6 (Clean Water and Sanitation) and SDG 7 (Affordable and Clean Energy), is improving rapidly. By contrast, trends on SDG 15 (Life on Land) and SDG 17 (Partnerships for the Goals) are stagnating or reversing in most countries in this region.

Latin America and the Caribbean

Latin American and Caribbean countries perform best on SDG 1 (No Poverty) and SDG 7 (Affordable and Clean Energy). They have also been experiencing progress on SDG 6 (Clean Water and Sanitation) and SDG 8 (Decent Work and Economic Growth). Yet, compared to other parts of the world, greater efforts are needed to reduce income and wealth inequalities, which is underlined by the poor performance of all countries in the region on SDG 10 (Reduced Inequalities). Improving access to and quality of key services would help strengthen performance on SDG 3

(Good Health and Well-Being) and SDG 4 (Quality Education). In most countries in the region, a high homicide rate is associated with a low share of people who feel safe walking alone at night. Combined with high and often stagnating (or even increasing) perceptions of corruption, these factors explain poor performance and trends on SDG 16 (Peace, Justice and Strong Institutions). Finally, as for other parts of the world, economic growth has not been decoupled from negative environmental impact, which is evident in large achievement gaps on SDGs 12 through to 15.

Middle East and North Africa

The SDG performance of Middle East and North African countries varies greatly. Conflicts in some countries lead to poor and declining performance on most SDGs, particularly on SDG 2 (Zero Hunger), SDG 3 (Good Health and Well-Being), and SDG 16 (Peace, Justice and Strong Institutions).

Countries less affected by conflicts perform best on SDG 1 (No Poverty) and SDG 17 (Partnerships for the Goals). Still, all countries in the region face major challenges in reaching SDG 2 (Zero Hunger), due to undernourishment, stunting, obesity, or issues related to agriculture and sustainable land-use (such as poor nitrogen management). Access to infrastructure, primarily covered under SDG 6 (Clean Water and Sanitation) and SDG 7 (Affordable and Clean Energy), is generally high or improving at a fast pace. However, further efforts are needed to strengthen domestic labor rights and standards and to tackle negative spillovers under SDG 8 (Decent Work and Economic Growth); to enhance freedom of speech and address high levels of perceived corruption under SDG 16 (Peace, Justice and Strong Institutions); and to make the transition towards more circular and green economies (SDGs 12 to 15). High CO_2 emissions embodied in fossil-fuel exports have a strongly negative impact on the performance of most countries in the region on SDG 13 (Climate Action).

There are persistent data gaps in the Gulf States for tracking poverty at 1.90$/day and 3.20$/day, income inequality (GINI coefficient), and working conditions (e.g., modern slavery). Greater investments are therefore needed in budget surveys, household surveys, and data availability.

Sub-Saharan Africa

The average SDG Index score for countries in Sub-Saharan Africa has improved significantly since 2015. Yet, all sub-Saharan African countries continue to face major challenges in achieving the SDGs, and Covid-19 threatens to undo much of the progress made in recent years. Owing to the poverty in the region, performance on socioeconomic goals and access to basic services and infrastructure (SDGs 1 to 9) are poor compared to other world regions. In some countries, insecurity and conflict have lowered performance on various goals, including SDG 16 (Peace, Justice and Strong Institutions). To improve the low performance on this and SDG 17 (Partnerships for the Goals), countries need to strengthen their institutions and increase domestic resource mobilization. Relatively low levels of consumption lead to somewhat better performances on SDGs 12 to 15 on climate mitigation and biodiversity protection, although trends in pollution in urban areas, covered under SDG 11 (Sustainable Cities and Communities), and forest loss and biodiversity protection, covered under SDG 15 (Life on Land), are flat for the region as a whole and moving in the wrong direction in some countries.

The Covid-19 outbreak and the disruption in international supply chains, including the food supply chain, are likely to have very negative impacts on SDG performance in many sub-Saharan countries. International solidarity and support will be needed to prevent losing the development gains of recent decades.

Oceania

The SDG dashboards for Oceania reveal the relative lack of comparable data across the region. Due to this lack of data, it is impossible to benchmark many small island developing states in Oceania against other countries. On the basis of the data available, small island states in the region perform best on SDG 12 (Responsible Consumption and Production) and SDG 17 (Partnerships for the Goals). By contrast, access to services, and their quality, covered under SDG 3 (Good Health and Well-Being) and SDG 4 (Quality Education), need to improve. Similarly, access to infrastructure, covered under SDG 6 (Clean Water and Sanitation), SDG 7 (Affordable and Clean Energy), and SDG 9 (Industry, Innovation, and Infrastructure), is lower than in most other regions. Small island states perform well compared to the rest of the world on climate mitigation (SDG 13), but they are of course among the countries that are the most vulnerable to climate change.

Figure 12

2020 SDG dashboards (levels and trends) by United Nations sub-regions and income groups

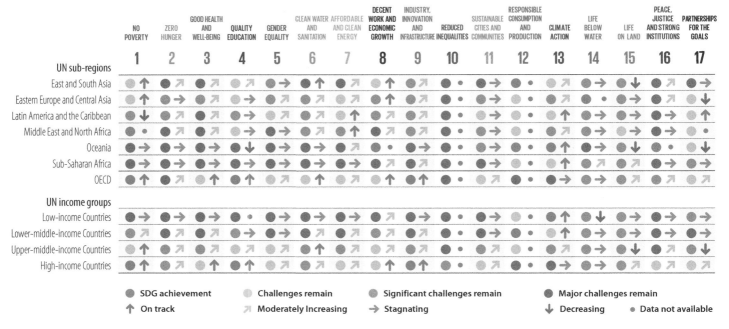

Note: Excluding OECD specific indicators. Population-weighted averages.   *Source:* Authors' analysis

Figure 13

2020 SDG dashboards (levels and trends) for East and South Asia

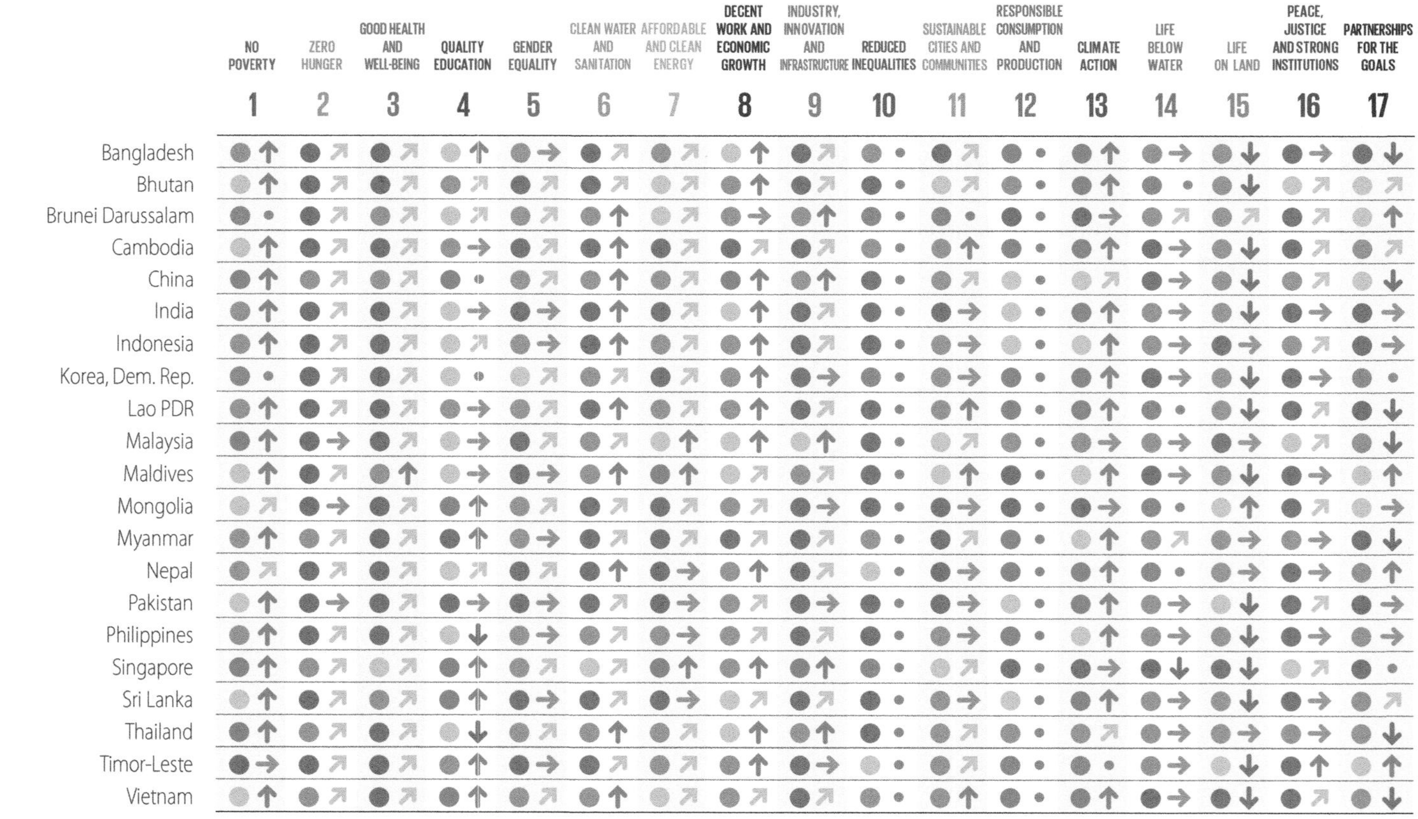

Source: Authors' analysis

Figure 14

2020 SDG dashboards (levels and trends) for OECD countries

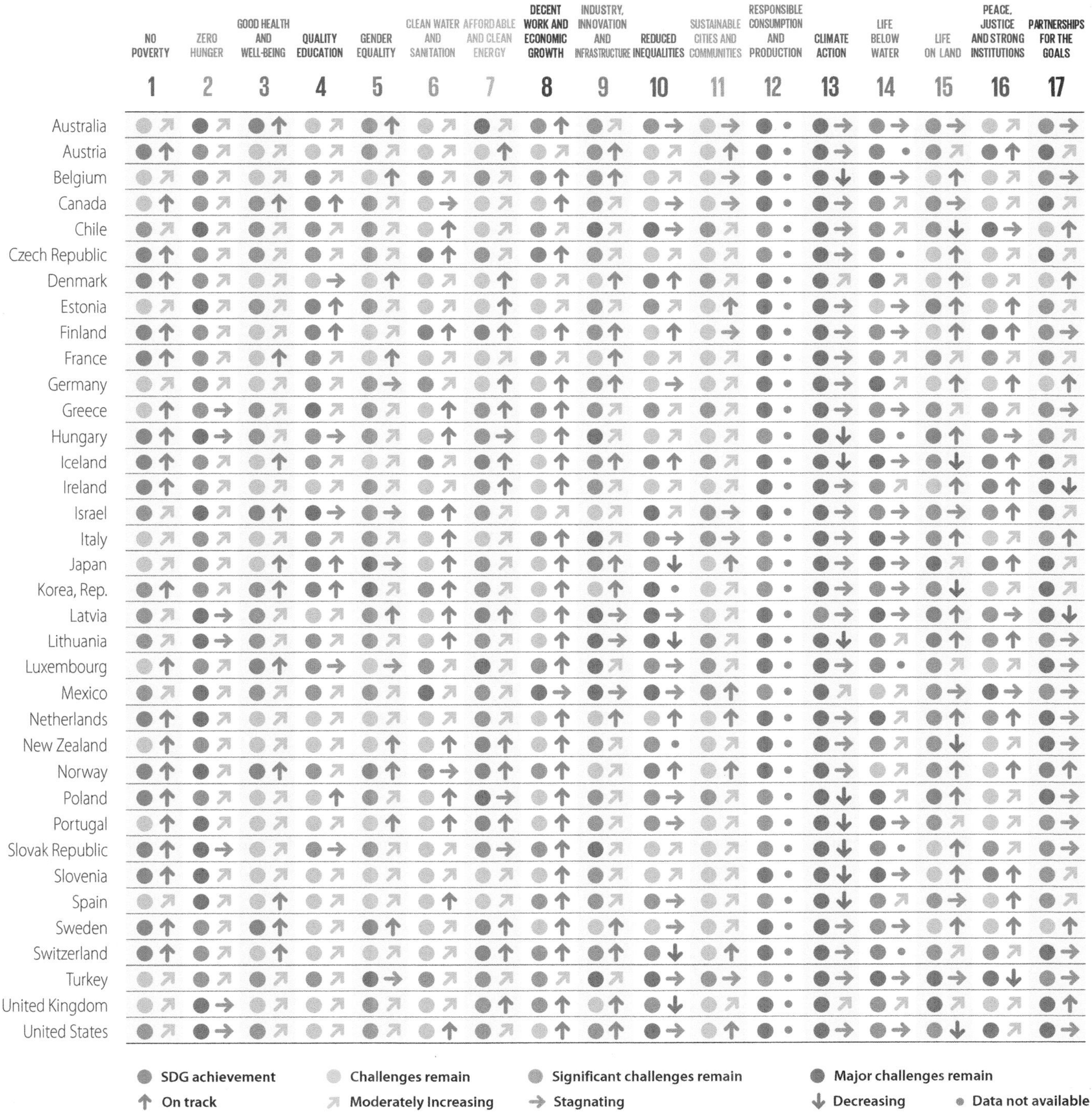

	NO POVERTY	ZERO HUNGER	GOOD HEALTH AND WELL-BEING	QUALITY EDUCATION	GENDER EQUALITY	CLEAN WATER AND SANITATION	AFFORDABLE AND CLEAN ENERGY	DECENT WORK AND ECONOMIC GROWTH	INDUSTRY, INNOVATION AND INFRASTRUCTURE	REDUCED INEQUALITIES	SUSTAINABLE CITIES AND COMMUNITIES	RESPONSIBLE CONSUMPTION AND PRODUCTION	CLIMATE ACTION	LIFE BELOW WATER	LIFE ON LAND	PEACE, JUSTICE AND STRONG INSTITUTIONS	PARTNERSHIPS FOR THE GOALS
	1	2	3	4	5	6	7	8	9	10	11	12	13	14	15	16	17
Australia																	
Austria																	
Belgium																	
Canada																	
Chile																	
Czech Republic																	
Denmark																	
Estonia																	
Finland																	
France																	
Germany																	
Greece																	
Hungary																	
Iceland																	
Ireland																	
Israel																	
Italy																	
Japan																	
Korea, Rep.																	
Latvia																	
Lithuania																	
Luxembourg																	
Mexico																	
Netherlands																	
New Zealand																	
Norway																	
Poland																	
Portugal																	
Slovak Republic																	
Slovenia																	
Spain																	
Sweden																	
Switzerland																	
Turkey																	
United Kingdom																	
United States																	

● SDG achievement   ● Challenges remain   ● Significant challenges remain   ● Major challenges remain

↑ On track   ↗ Moderately Increasing   → Stagnating   ↓ Decreasing   • Data not available

Note: Including OECD specific indicators.   *Source:* Authors' analysis

Figure 15

2020 SDG dashboards (levels and trends) for Eastern Europe and Central Asia

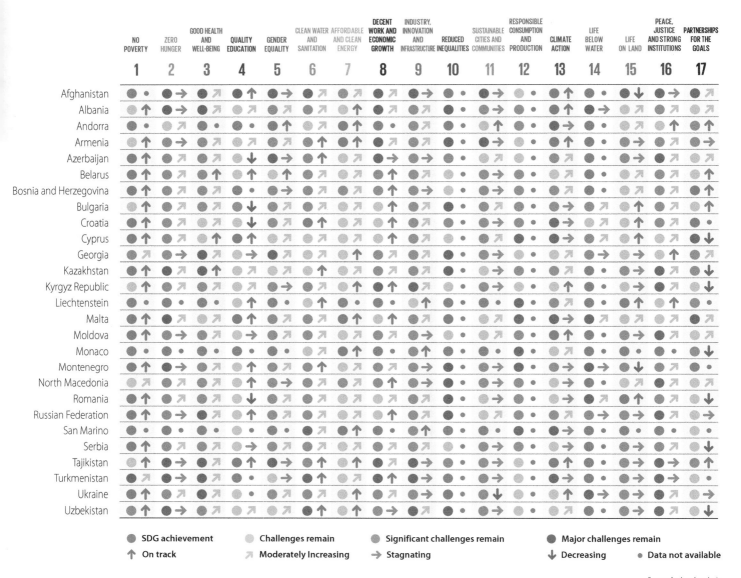

Source: Authors' analysis

Figure 16

2020 SDG dashboards (levels and trends) for Latin America and the Caribbean

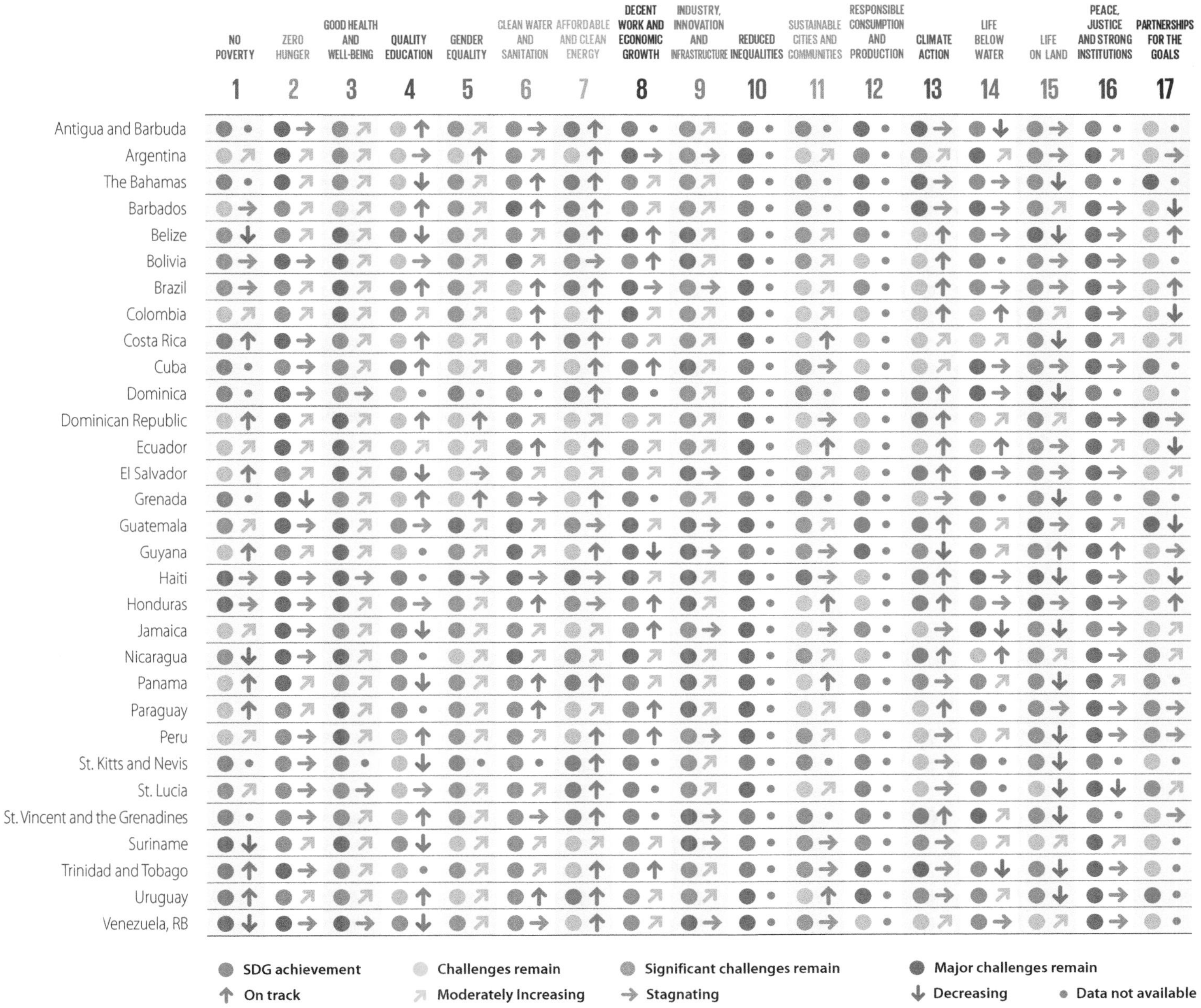

	NO POVERTY	ZERO HUNGER	GOOD HEALTH AND WELL-BEING	QUALITY EDUCATION	GENDER EQUALITY	CLEAN WATER AND SANITATION	AFFORDABLE AND CLEAN ENERGY	DECENT WORK AND ECONOMIC GROWTH	INDUSTRY, INNOVATION AND INFRASTRUCTURE	REDUCED INEQUALITIES	SUSTAINABLE CITIES AND COMMUNITIES	RESPONSIBLE CONSUMPTION AND PRODUCTION	CLIMATE ACTION	LIFE BELOW WATER	LIFE ON LAND	PEACE, JUSTICE AND STRONG INSTITUTIONS	PARTNERSHIPS FOR THE GOALS
	1	2	3	4	5	6	7	8	9	10	11	12	13	14	15	16	17
Antigua and Barbuda																	
Argentina																	
The Bahamas																	
Barbados																	
Belize																	
Bolivia																	
Brazil																	
Colombia																	
Costa Rica																	
Cuba																	
Dominica																	
Dominican Republic																	
Ecuador																	
El Salvador																	
Grenada																	
Guatemala																	
Guyana																	
Haiti																	
Honduras																	
Jamaica																	
Nicaragua																	
Panama																	
Paraguay																	
Peru																	
St. Kitts and Nevis																	
St. Lucia																	
St. Vincent and the Grenadines																	
Suriname																	
Trinidad and Tobago																	
Uruguay																	
Venezuela, RB																	

● SDG achievement ◐ Challenges remain ◑ Significant challenges remain ● Major challenges remain

↑ On track ↗ Moderately Increasing → Stagnating ↓ Decreasing • Data not available

Source: Authors' analysis

Figure 17

2020 SDG dashboards (levels and trends) for the Middle East and North Africa

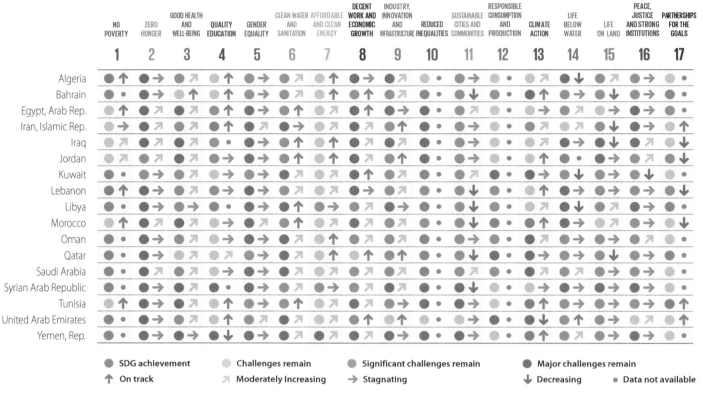

Source: Authors' analysis

Figure 18

2020 SDG dashboards (levels and trends) for Oceania

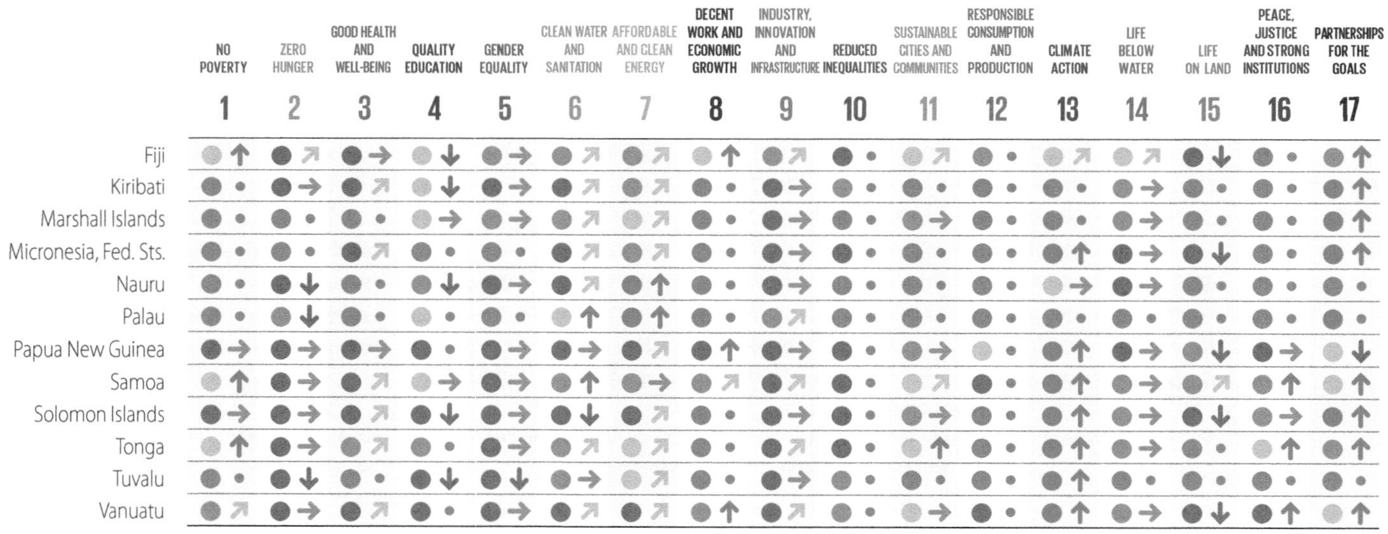

Source: Authors' analysis

Figure 19

2020 SDG dashboards (levels and trends) for Sub-Saharan Africa

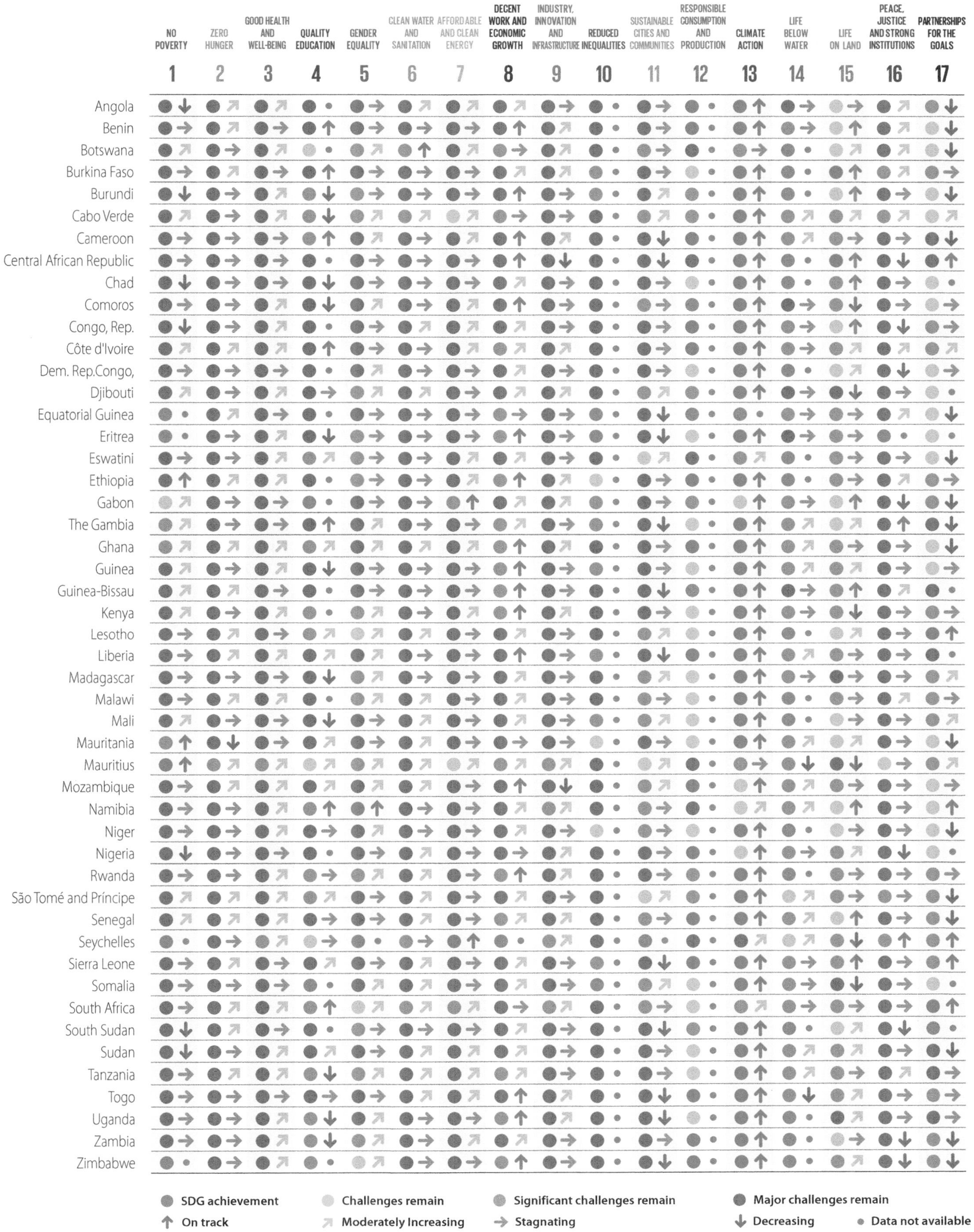
1 NO POVERTY
2 ZERO HUNGER
3 GOOD HEALTH AND WELL-BEING
4 QUALITY EDUCATION
5 GENDER EQUALITY
6 CLEAN WATER AND SANITATION
7 AFFORDABLE AND CLEAN ENERGY
8 DECENT WORK AND ECONOMIC GROWTH
9 INDUSTRY, INNOVATION AND INFRASTRUCTURE
10 REDUCED INEQUALITIES
11 SUSTAINABLE CITIES AND COMMUNITIES
12 RESPONSIBLE CONSUMPTION AND PRODUCTION
13 CLIMATE ACTION
14 LIFE BELOW WATER
15 LIFE ON LAND
16 PEACE, JUSTICE AND STRONG INSTITUTIONS
17 PARTNERSHIPS FOR THE GOALS
Angola
Benin
Botswana
Burkina Faso
Burundi
Cabo Verde
Cameroon
Central African Republic
Chad
Comoros
Congo, Rep.
Côte d'Ivoire
Dem. Rep.Congo,
Djibouti
Equatorial Guinea
Eritrea
Eswatini
Ethiopia
Gabon
The Gambia
Ghana
Guinea
Guinea-Bissau
Kenya
Lesotho
Liberia
Madagascar
Malawi
Mali
Mauritania
Mauritius
Mozambique
Namibia
Niger
Nigeria
Rwanda
São Tomé and Príncipe
Senegal
Seychelles
Sierra Leone
Somalia
South Africa
South Sudan
Sudan
Tanzania
Togo
Uganda
Zambia
Zimbabwe
SDG achievement
Challenges remain
Significant challenges remain
Major challenges remain
On track
Moderately Increasing
Stagnating
Decreasing
Data not available

Source: Authors' analysis

2.5 Absolute SDG performance gaps in G20 countries

G20 countries comprise two-thirds of the world's population and account for 85% of global gross domestic product and over 75% of global trade. They also generate 80% of global energy-related carbon-dioxide emissions. Table 3 illustrates the importance of G20 countries by showing estimated absolute SDG performance gaps (in %) for each Goal to complement the per-capita analyses in the SDG Index and Dashboards.

Absolute SDG performance gaps emphasize the importance of the G20 countries in the post-Covid-19 recovery. Apart from SDG 1 (No Poverty) and SDG 4 (Quality Education), for which sub-Saharan Africa accounts for most of the achievement gap, the G20 countries represent close to or more than 50% of the total performance gap for each Goal. A lack of action and commitments from the G20 countries would make it impossible to achieve the SDGs, depriving large shares of the world's population from achieving sustainable development and improved living conditions.

Due to their large populations, China and India account for the largest shares of global SDG performance gaps. For example: China, the United States, and the European Union together represent close to 50% of the global performance gap on Goal 13 (Climate Action).[2] Focusing on just one of the underlying metrics – energy-related CO_2 emissions – we see that if China was to reduce emissions to 2 tonnes of CO_2 per capita per year (equivalent to a total reduction of 69.2% from current levels), the world would be 31% closer to achieving the SDG target on CO_2 emissions. Similarly, India alone represents 23.8% of the total achievement gap on SDG 2 (Zero Hunger).[3] If India eradicated undernourishment (currently 14.5% of the Indian population) the world would be 27.4% closer to achieving the SDG target on undernourishment. The European Union also generates negative spillovers, in particular through trade and consumption, which undermine other countries' abilities to achieve the SDGs.

As G20 countries design recovery plans, it will be important to maintain the commitments, efforts, and momentum for sustainable development if we are to avoid major setbacks on SDG 7 (Affordable and Clean Energy) and SDGs 12 to 15 on climate and biodiversity. The G20 countries can also play a pivotal role in promoting sustainable supply chains by focusing on deforestation and other environmental damage. This will help to achieve the SDGs and reduce risks of zoonotic diseases and future pandemics.

2. SDG 13 (Climate Action) is measured using three indicators: energy-related CO_2 emissions per capita, imported CO_2 emissions, and CO_2 emissions embodied in fossil-fuel exports.

3. SDG 2 (Zero Hunger) is measured using seven indicators: prevalence of undernourishment, prevalence of stunting, prevalence of wasting, prevalence of obesity, human trophic level, cereal yield, and sustainable nitrogen management. The full title of SDG 2 is "End hunger, achieve food security and improved nutrition and promote sustainable agriculture."

Table 3

Absolute SDG performance gaps in 2020 (%)

Country	SDG1	SDG2	SDG3	SDG4	SDG5	SDG6	SDG7	SDG8	SDG9	SDG10	SDG11	SDG12	SDG13	SDG14	SDG15	SDG16	SDG17	Spillovers
Argentina	0.1	0.5	0.3	0.2	0.3	0.4	0.2	0.8	0.7	0.7	0.2	0.8	0.7	0.7	0.6	0.6	0.4	0.4
Australia	0.0	0.3	0.0	0.0	0.2	0.0	0.1	0.3	0.1	0.2	0.2	1.2	2.5	0.4	0.3	0.1	0.3	1.4
Brazil	1.8	2.2	1.8	2.3	2.0	1.1	0.6	3.3	2.3	4.6	1.7	3.6	1.4	2.0	2.9	3.3	1.5	0.9
Canada	0.0	0.4	0.1	0.0	0.2	0.2	0.1	0.3	0.2	0.2	0.2	1.5	2.1	0.5	0.5	0.2	0.4	2.2
China	1.8	10.5	11.7	5.4	10.7	17.2	20.1	10.3	10.5	16.0	13.5	13.7	17.2	23.2	18.7	18.2	22.8	12.4
Germany	0.0	0.8	0.2	0.1	0.6	0.5	0.3	0.7	0.2	0.4	0.4	3.3	3.7	1.3	0.6	0.5	0.5	5.3
France	0.0	0.6	0.2	0.0	0.3	0.3	0.1	0.8	0.2	0.3	0.3	2.3	2.0	0.7	0.6	0.6	0.6	4.7
United Kingdom	0.0	0.7	0.2	0.1	0.3	0.2	0.2	0.7	0.2	0.5	0.2	2.6	3.2	0.8	0.5	0.4	0.9	4.8
Indonesia	4.1	3.7	4.1	1.8	3.2	3.5	3.3	3.8	4.3	5.1	3.6	2.7	2.2	3.6	4.9	2.6	4.2	1.0
India	21.8	23.8	24.5	17.3	29.2	23.1	19.7	14.0	21.5	17.6	27.2	8.8	5.2	16.6	22.0	18.7	20.8	2.5
Italy	0.1	0.6	0.2	0.1	0.5	0.4	0.2	0.7	0.3	0.6	0.7	1.9	1.5	1.0	0.4	0.5	0.7	2.8
Japan	0.1	1.0	0.3	0.0	1.6	0.7	0.4	0.9	0.3	0.8	1.2	3.3	4.7	2.0	1.4	0.4	1.2	6.3
Korea, Rep.	0.0	0.3	0.2	0.1	0.5	0.5	0.2	0.4	0.0	0.2	0.4	1.2	2.1	0.7	0.8	0.4	0.7	2.4
Mexico	1.0	1.7	1.0	0.0	0.9	1.0	0.8	1.9	1.8	2.9	0.9	2.0	1.6	1.1	2.2	2.1	1.5	1.0
Russian Federation	0.0	2.3	1.4	0.6	1.5	1.6	0.6	1.7	1.3	2.0	1.0	2.7	4.0	2.3	1.6	2.5	1.3	4.7
Saudi Arabia	0.1	0.5	0.3	0.1	0.6	0.7	0.2	0.6	0.3	0.4	0.8	1.0	1.7	0.5	0.6	0.4	0.3	1.3
Turkey	0.0	1.0	0.6	0.1	1.4	0.8	0.4	1.5	0.9	1.5	1.0	1.3	1.1	1.5	1.3	1.0	0.7	0.8
United States	0.2	3.5	1.5	0.1	2.6	2.1	1.0	2.8	0.5	5.0	1.4	12.5	16.3	3.9	4.3	2.9	3.0	20.0
South Africa	1.8	0.7	1.2	0.9	0.3	0.7	0.6	1.3	0.7	1.7	0.5	0.9	1.4	0.7	0.8	1.0	0.4	0.7
European Union	0.3	4.6	1.5	1.1	3.1	2.6	1.4	4.7	2.1	3.1	2.7	14.7	14.6	6.1	2.9	3.1	4.7	23.5
Total G20	33.30	57.80	50.80	30.20	58.70	56.30	49.70	49.20	47.60	62.40	56.80	74.70	81.90	66.30	66.30	57.90	65.10	86.30

>20%	10-20%	2-10%	0-2%

Source: Authors' analysis

2. The SDG Index and Dashboards

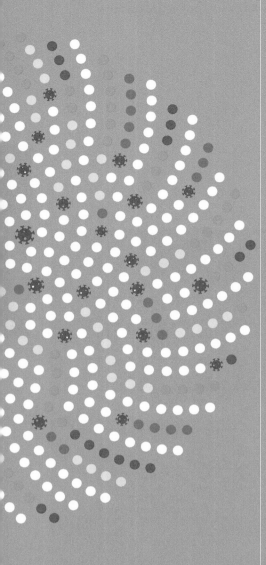

Part 3

Policy and Monitoring Frameworks for the SDGs

Part 3

Policy and Monitoring Frameworks for the SDGs

This section assesses policy efforts to implement the SDGs. It presents new expert and public opinion survey data to gauge political leadership in support of the SDGs at the country level. As in other sections, our data does not account for the impact of Covid-19 in most countries. Results confirm that the SDGs have quickly become a widely used framework for many national statistical institutes and other data providers. Yet further efforts are needed to address persistent data gaps and data time lags in relation to the SDG indicators. The section therefore provides an overview of major data and statistics initiatives introduced globally since the adoption of the SDGs in 2015. We argue that more policy trackers are needed to increase visibility on how governments are pursuing the SDGs, strengthen accountability, and share data on best practices and lessons learnt, which will help other countries accelerate progress towards the SDGs.

3.1 Political leadership and policy environment

Performance and outcome data provide essential information to track the implementation of the SDGs, but they should be complemented by other, more qualitative, assessments of policy efforts and other actions in support of the goals. Performance and outcome data (e.g., poverty rate, life expectancy, CO_2 emissions) have limitations. There is typically a two- to three-year lag (sometimes more) in data reporting, particularly for cross-country comparisons. So tracking SDGs using outcome data alone means adopting a "rear-mirror view." Such a view tracks historic trends, which may be a poor guide to the future. Governments that have introduced major policy reforms might only see these efforts reflected in outcome data after many years. Similarly, the impact of Covid-19 will take a long time to feed into outcome data. We therefore need greater investments in real-time data. In addition, we need "forward-looking" assessments of policies that provide a better sense of where countries are heading and track the efforts of current administrations. As in previous years, this report therefore contributes to measuring the efforts made by governments in support of the SDGs.

Measuring government efforts in support of the SDGs is challenging, due to the broad and complex nature of the goals. In the SDR2019, we introduced three layers for mea-suring government efforts to implement the long-term objectives of the 2030 Agenda and the Paris Agreement:

(1) High-level public statements by governments in support of sustainable development.

(2) Strategic use of public practices and procedures towards achieving the goals (coordination mech-anisms, budgets, procurement, human-resource management, data collection and audits);

(3) The content of government strategies and policy actions.

Monitoring all three layers is important, but layer 3 provides the most actionable and valuable information on governments' efforts to achieve the SDGs. In this section we present primary data collected by the SDSN, combined with third-party data that help track policy efforts and commitments for the SDGs. For the first time, we present findings from two public opinion surveys, conducted by the SDSN in March and April 2020, on "SDG Progress and Challenges" and "Covid-19 and the SDGs."

Public statements and public management practices for the SDGs

The SDSN mobilizes its global network of experts every year to track public statements by governments (layer 1) and the strategic use of some public practices (layer 2) in support of the SDGs. Since 2018, this information has been collected through the *SDSN survey on national coordination and implementation mechanisms at the central/federal level of government*. The 2020 results and an indication of trends over time are presented in table 4. This year's survey covers 30 countries, including most of the G20 and OECD countries, as well as countries with a population greater than 100 million people.

We find a discrepancy between expressed political support for the SDGs and the integration of the SDGs in strategic public policy processes, including national budgets. As in previous years, a large majority of governments (25 out of 30) have made public statements in support of the SDGs and the 2030 Agenda via heads of states, ministers, or other cabinet members. These statements often highlight implementation mechanisms and country initiatives to achieve key SDG transformations. We also find evidence in most surveyed countries that the SDGs are being integrated into a dedicated strategy or action plan, or into sectoral policies (e.g., health, education, industrial strategy, or economic development). Most countries have also identified a coordinating unit or agency responsible for coordinating implementation of the SDGs.

Yet only about a third of the countries surveyed (12/30) mention the SDGs or use related terms in their latest official budget document. Of these 12 countries, only 4 mention the SDGs in their national budget as a dedicated section or budget line. The other 8 mention the SDGs only in the overall narrative. In only half of the countries surveyed do the SDGs or related terms apply both to domestic implementation (e.g., national health, education, social protection, economic development reforms) and international cooperation (e.g., aid allocation, foreign policy). The cross-sectional budget analysis and tools developed by the Ministry of the Economy in Argentina provides a good example of how a country has linked its national budget with the SDGs.[1]

Over time, we find an increase in national monitoring efforts. Most countries covered in the survey (28 out of 30) have either identified a national set of SDG indicators or have launched dedicated platforms to report on the availability of SDG indicators at the national level. On average, countries that have developed national SDG indicator sets use about 112 indicators. These efforts to strengthen monitoring mechanisms for sustainable development are very much aligned with the SDGs. These findings are discussed in greater detail in section 3.2.

By contrast, we find a slight decrease in stakeholder engagement mechanisms for the SDGs. While many countries have launched stakeholder engagement processes for specific objectives and deliverables (e.g., for Voluntary National Reviews, or the development

of national SDG action plans), only some countries have adopted more permanent stakeholder engagement mechanisms to inform policies, indicator selection, or budgets (stakeholder engagement mechanisms at the subnational level – regions, provinces, municipalities – were not covered by the survey.) The Finnish Citizens' Panel for Sustainable Development, established in 2018, is a good example of a national stakeholder engagement mechanism for the SDGs.

Content of government strategies and policy actions

To improve assessments of government efforts, one needs to assess the content of policies – including national targets, long-term pathways, and intermediate objectives – to determine if they are consistent with achieving the SDGs (layer 3). Such assessments would also track policy implementation. Unfortunately, such "policy trackers" are complex and costly to undertake. Moreover, most international organizations do not have the mandate to assess their members' policies in such ways.

The Covid-19 outbreak saw a rapid increase in available policy trackers to track government responses to the health crisis, including but not limited to:

- The IMF Policy Response to Covid-19 (IMF, 2020*b*)

- The OECD Country Policy Tracker (OECD, 2020*a*)

- The Oxford Covid-19 Government Response Tracker (Oxford, 2020)

- The Yale School of Management Covid-19 Financial Response Tracker and Visualization (Yale School of Management, 2020)

- The IGC Covid-19 policy response tracker (IGC, 2020)

The Climate Action Tracker (CAT) provides the best example of an SDG Policy Tracker. Developed by a research consortium specialized in the field of climate mitigation, CAT uses a methodology that evaluates

---

1. https://www.minhacienda.gob.ar/onp/presupuesto_ciudadano/seccion6.html

Table 4

National government efforts to implement the SDGs

	VNR	High-level statements	SDG strategy/ SDGs into sectoral action plans	Budget		National monitoring		Stakeholder engagement
	Date submitted	yes/no	yes/no	yes/no	overarching narrative/section or budget line	*DI/IC	yes/no	no. of indicators	yes/no
Argentina	2017 and 2020	yes	yes	yes	section or budget line	DI and IC	no, but online reporting		yes
Australia	2018	no	no	no			no, but online reporting		no
Austria	2020	yes	yes	yes	section or budget line	DI and IC	yes	200	yes
Bangladesh	2017 and 2020	yes	yes	no			yes	40	yes
Brazil	2017	no	yes	no			no, but online reporting		no
Canada	2018	yes	yes	yes	overarching narrative	IC	yes	60	yes
Chile	2017 and 2019	yes	yes	no			yes	112	yes
China	2016	yes	yes	no			no, but it is planned		no
Denmark	2017	yes	yes	no			no, but online reporting		yes
Ethiopia	2017	yes	yes	yes	overarching narrative	DI	yes	60	no
European Union	not applicable	yes	yes	yes	overarching narrative	DI and IC	yes	100	yes
Finland	2016 and 2020	yes	yes	yes	overarching narrative	DI and IC	no, but online reporting		yes
Germany	2016	yes	yes	yes	overarching narrative	DI and IC	yes	65	yes
Hungary	2018	no	yes	no			yes	83	no
Israel	2019	yes	yes	no			no, but online reporting		no
Japan	2017	yes	yes	yes	section or budget line	DI and IC	no, but online reporting		yes
Mexico	2016 and 2018	yes	yes	no			yes	169	yes
New Zealand	2019	yes	yes	no			yes	100	no
Norway	2016	yes	yes	no			no, but it is planned		yes
Pakistan	2019	yes	yes	yes	section or budget line	DI	yes	46	yes
Poland	2018	yes	yes	no			yes	126	yes
Portugal	2017	yes	yes	yes	overarching narrative	DI	yes	146	yes
Russia	2020	no	no	no			no, but online reporting		no
Saudi Arabia	2018	yes	yes	no			yes	96	no
Slovenia	2017 and 2020	yes	yes	yes	overarching narrative	IC	yes	70	yes
South Africa	2019	yes	yes	no			yes	128	yes
Spain	2018	yes	yes	yes	overarching narrative	DI and IC	yes	125	yes
Sweden	2017	yes	yes	no			yes	294	yes
United Kingdom	2019	yes	yes	no			no, but online reporting		yes
United States	Not planned	no	no	no			no, but online reporting		no
TOTAL "yes"		**25**	**27**	**12**			**28**	**112**	**20**
Trend	...	=	=	=	...	...	+	...	-

Note: Trend calculated based on the results of the 2018 and 2019 SDSN surveys. A positive or negative trend denotes a change of +/− 2 in the totals.

Source: SDSN 2020 Survey on national coordination and implementation mechanisms at the central/federal level of government (April, 2020).

* Di = Domestic Implementation   Ic = International Cooperation

Figure 20

Comparative assessment of government strategies and policy actions for climate mitigation

| CRITICALLY INSUFFICIENT | HIGHLY INSUFFICIENT | INSUFFICIENT | 2°C COMPATIBLE | 1.5°C PARIS AGREEMENT COMPATIBLE | ROLE MODEL |

Source: Climate action tracker (March, 2020)

both the content of Intended Nationally Determined Contributions (INDCs) (*what governments propose to do*) and current policies (*what governments are actually doing*) to meet the objectives of the Paris Agreement. The latest CAT assessment covers 32 countries, including all G20 countries, and the European Union (Climate Action Tracker, 2020).

The conclusions from the latest CAT assessment are very clear: only six countries (Bhutan, Costa Rica, Ethiopia, India, Kenya, and the Philippines) have made sufficient commitments and efforts to hold global warming well below 2°C, and only two countries (Morocco and The Gambia) are on track to hold warming below 1.5°C. Government strategies and policy actions in the Russian Federation, Saudi Arabia, Turkey, Ukraine, the United States, and Vietnam are "critically insufficient" (the worst label possible).

Similar evaluations are needed for other SDG transformations. The SDSN, in collaboration with partners, aims to promote the development of policy trackers for the six SDG transformations (Sachs et al., 2019a). As one example, as part of the Food and Land-Use Coalition, SDSN and partners are launching the Food, Environment, Land, and Development (FELD) Policy Action Tracker to measure progress on SDG Transformation 4 (Sustainable Food, Land, Water, and Oceans).

Covid-19 makes policy trackers even more relevant, given the long-term impacts of recovery strategies. As an example, the Climate Action Tracker has released a roadmap for addressing the climate impact of Covid-19 and emerging recovery strategies (Climate Action Tracker, 2020). Other organizations are proposing sustainability tests to assess recovery plans (Think Sustainable Europe, 2020). These need to be tracked across countries.

Box 3. Public opinion survey on SDG Progress and Challenges

In April 2020, the SDSN surveyed the SDG community on progress made and major challenges and barriers faced in implementing the SDGs. In total, 715 respondents from 104 countries participated. Respondents represented university and research organizations (32%), non-governmental organizations (22%), the private sector (14%), students (14%), governments (8%), international organizations (5%), and other (5%).

Overall, respondents considered that before the outbreak of the Covid-19 pandemic, the world was not on track to achieve the SDGs. Two-thirds of the SDG community believed that their country would only achieve up to half of the goals. Only 16% of respondents believed that their country was on track to achieving all or most of the SDGs. This is broadly consistent with the findings of the SDR2018, SDR2019 and SDR2020.

According to the respondents, governments should strengthen efforts to respond to the climate and biodiversity crises. More than 50% of respondents considered that their governments had made only minor efforts over the past five years to implement Transformation 3 (Energy Decarbonization and Sustainable Industry) and Transformation 4 (Sustainable Food, Land, Water, and Oceans). These findings remain consistent when combined with the next survey question, which asked about the importance and relevance of each transformation in the respondents' countries. This resonates quite well with the findings of major reports (IPCC, 2019; IPBES, 2019). Of the six SDG Transformations, respondents perceived that their governments had made the greatest efforts towards implementing Transformation 6 (Digital Revolution for Sustainable Development).

Finally, respondents identified three major challenges that impede further implementation of the SDG Transformations and progress towards the SDGs. The first and most significant barrier in many countries is a lack of political leadership to implement the 2030 Agenda. A second barrier is a lack of awareness of the SDGs among policymakers and the general public. Lastly, short-termism and a focus on responding to immediate events over the pursuit of longer-term objectives such as the SDGs represents a third barrier. This third barrier is likely to increase in relevance as countries shift their focus to managing the consequences of the Covid-19 pandemic.

Figure 21

Q.1. In your view, is your country on track to achieve the SDGs by 2030?

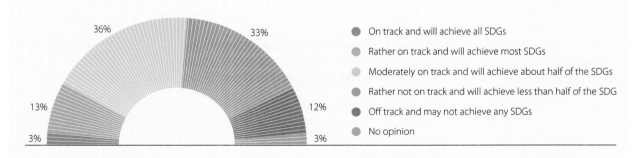

- On track and will achieve all SDGs
- Rather on track and will achieve most SDGs
- Moderately on track and will achieve about half of the SDGs
- Rather not on track and will achieve less than half of the SDG
- Off track and may not achieve any SDGs
- No opinion

Box 3. (continued)

Figure 22

Q.2. Since 2015, how do you perceive government efforts and actions to implement the six transformations in your country?

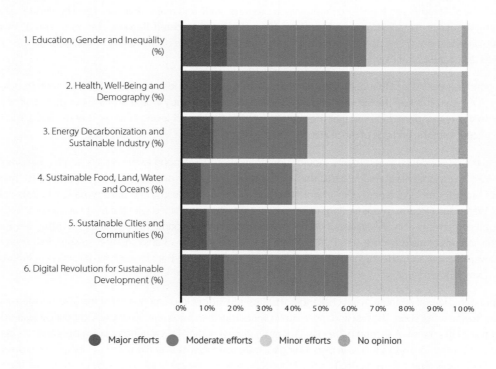

Figure 23

Q.4. In your view, what are the main barriers to achieving the SDGs in your country?

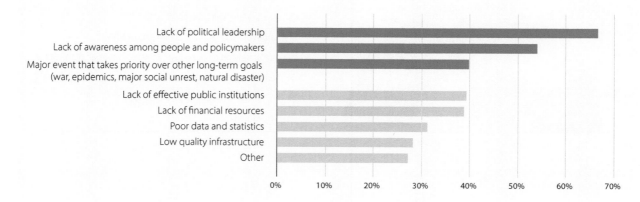

Source: SDSN Public opinion survey on SDG Progress and Challenges (April, 2020). n=715.

Box 4. Public opinion survey on Covid-19 and the SDGs

In April 2020, the SDSN surveyed the SDG community on the impact of the Covid-19 pandemic on the achievement of the SDGs. A total of 1,034 respondents from 110 countries participated in the survey. Respondents represented university and research organizations (28%), the private sector (20%), non-governmental organizations (16%), students (14%), governments (11%), international organizations (6%), and other (5%).

While the short-term impacts of Covid-19 on most SDGs were expected to most likely be negative, a majority of respondents considered that in the long run there might still be certain positive impacts. In total, 53% of respondents considered that the impact of Covid-19 would not be negative *across the board* for the achievement of the SDGs by 2030, and that positive transformations might occur on some SDGs. Respondents also felt that uncertainty prevailed. Close to 10% of respondents mentioned that it was too early to tell what the long-term impact of Covid-19 on the SDGs would be.

Respondents also expected differentiated impacts of Covid-19 on the six SDG Transformations. The greatest negative impacts were expected on Transformation 1 (Education, Gender, and Inequality) and Transformation 2 (Health, Well-Being, and Demography). At the same time, many respondents felt that the Covid-19 crisis may provide an opportunity to strengthen healthcare system preparedness and resilience, as well as improving prevention programs in the longer term. Respondents expected more mixed impacts on Transformation 3 (Energy Decarbonization and Sustainable Industry), Transformation 4 (Sustainable Food, Land, Water, and Oceans), and Transformation 5 (Sustainable Cities and Communities). Respondents considered that the short-term benefits that the lockdown measures had on air pollution and CO_2 emissions might be offset in the long run by unsustainable recovery plans, the low cost of fossil fuels, and the lack of enforcement of environmental and biodiversity conventions. Finally, respondents expected more positive impacts on Transformation 6 (Digital Revolution for Sustainable Development), pointing to the growth of e-commerce, remote working, digital health services, and online education services.

Finally, most respondents considered that the SDGs provide a framework that could help inform the recovery phase and contribute to preventing future global health and other crises. Only 28% of respondents considered the SDGs completely useless in helping to prevent and mitigate major global risks (e.g., pandemics) in the future. Yet even those who believed that the SDGs could be a useful framework mentioned that monitoring and reporting processes must be strengthened. Respondents also felt that the SDG reporting process, including voluntary national reviews (VNRs), should have a stronger focus on the resilience of health and other systems, as well as on crisis prevention. Finally, respondents considered that political leadership will be crucial to retain the SDGs as shared global priorities when countries recover from the Covid-19 outbreak.

Figure 24

Q.1. In your view, in your country, what will be the impact of the Covid-19 pandemic on the achievement of the SDGs by 2030?

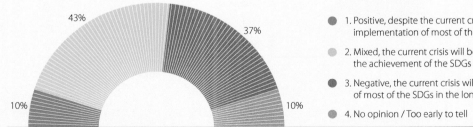

43%

37%

10%

10%

● 1. Positive, despite the current crisis it will accelerate the implementation of most of the SDGs in the long run

● 2. Mixed, the current crisis will both accelerate and slow down the achievement of the SDGs in the same proportion

● 3. Negative, the current crisis will slow down the implementation of most of the SDGs in the long run

● 4. No opinion / Too early to tell

Box 4. (continued)

Figure 25

Q.2. In your view, in your country, what will be the impact of Covid-19 on each of the six SDG Transformations?

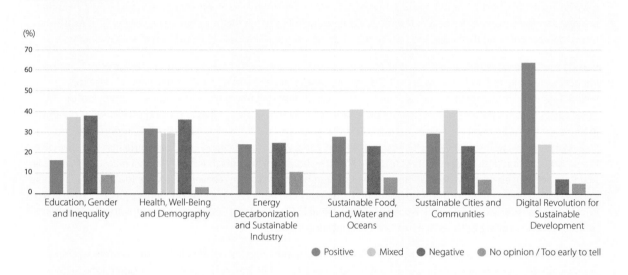

Figure 26

Q.3. In your view, is the current SDG framework and reporting process suited to help prevent and mitigate major global risks (e.g., pandemics)?

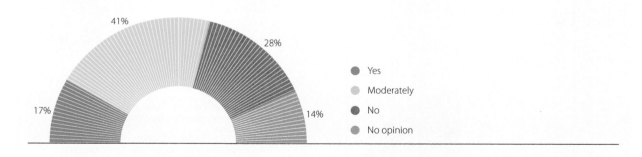

Source: SDSN Public opinion survey on "Covid-19 and the SDGs" (April, 2020). n=1,034.

3.2 Data, statistics and monitoring

Data and monitoring initiatives

The 2030 Agenda emphasizes the importance of reliable data and statistics. The focus on data and statistics is stronger than that of the MDGs (SDSN, 2015). The 2030 Agenda states that "the goals and targets will be followed up and reviewed using a set of global indicators," while a dedicated section provides key principles of tracking progress and contextualizes SDG assessment processes and instruments at all levels. The Agenda mandates that the Inter-agency and Expert Group on SDG Indicators (IAEG-SDGs), the Statistical Commission, and the Economic and Social Council (ECOSOC) are to develop and frequently update an SDG indicator framework. As of March 2020, 231 official SDG indicators, classified in three tiers, are used to monitor the 17 SDGs and 169 targets (IAEG-SDGs, 2019).

National governments, multilateral organizations, civil society, and businesses have also launched numerous initiatives to monitor progress on the SDGs since 2015. We identify seven major types of SDG data initiatives below, but there are probably many others.

1. **International SDG monitoring reports** focus on all 17 SDGs and provide comparative assessments of SDG performance and progress across countries. At the global level, such initiatives include the *SDG Index and Dashboards* (Sachs et al., 2017, 2018, 2019), the *UN Sustainable Development Goals Report* and Progress Cards (United Nations, 2019), and the *OECD Measuring Distance to the SDG Targets reports* (OECD, 2017, 2019). Several regional reports have also become available. In the European Union, for instance, Eurostat publishes *Sustainable development in the European Union*, the official SDG monitoring report (Eurostat, 2017, 2018, 2019). The SDSN, in collaboration with partners, has supported the production of SDG baseline assessments for several regions since 2015 (SDG Center for Africa and SDSN, 2018, 2019; Luomi et al., 2019; SDSN and IEEP, 2019; Sachs et al., 2019b) – see also box 2.

2. **National SDG indicator and monitoring reports** are based on a national set of indicators identified by the government and/or civil society. Voluntary national reviews (VNRs), the main annual and government-led SDG review mechanism, typically assess a country's key challenges to and priorities for achieving the SDGs. VNR indicators are not harmonized internationally and lack comparability (Schmidt-Traub et al., 2017). Some countries publish annual SDG reports, led by government and/or civil society (National Sustainable Development Council of Australia, 2019; NITI Aayog, 2019).

3. **Goal-specific monitoring initiatives** focus on monitoring progress towards individual SDG outcomes. Examples include the Global Hunger Index (GHI) tracking SDG 2, and Goalkeepers, tracking SDGs 1 to 6 (Concern Worldwide and Welthungerhilfe, 2019; Bill & Melinda Gates Foundation, 2019). Equal Measures 2030 focuses on data and metrics to track progress on the "leave no one behind" principle of the 2030 Agenda (Equal Measures 2030, 2019), and the Global Slavery Index monitors progress on SDG 8.7 (Minderoo Foundation Walk Free Initiative, 2018). Other goal-specific SDG monitoring initiatives include *Tracking SDG7: The Energy Progress Report* (World Bank et al., 2019) and the *SDG 11 Synthesis Report 2018 on Cities and Communities* (UNHABITAT, 2018).

4. **Policy trackers** are needed to create forward-looking assessments of countries' trajectories towards the SDGs. As discussed in the previous section, the Climate Action Tracker tracks national commitments and policies relating to SDG Transformation 3 (Energy Decarbonization), in support of SDG 13 and the objectives of the Paris Agreement (Climate Action Tracker, 2018a). SDSN is launching the Food, Environment, Land, and Development (FELD) Action Tracker as part of the Food and Land-Use Coalition. Similar policy trackers are urgently needed for the other SDG Transformations.

5. **Subnational and city-level SDG assessments** track the efforts and performance of cities, provinces, and regions. The SDSN has released monitoring instruments for cities in Italy, Spain, the United States, and across the European Union. The Local Data Action Solutions Initiative (LDA-SI) – a project

run by the SDSN's USA-Sustainable Cities Initiative (USA-SCI) and TReNDS – supports sub-national actors in engaging with the SDGs through local monitoring. The OECD has launched *A Territorial Approach to the Sustainable Development Goals*, which assesses the distance of SDG targets for more than 600 cities and regions (OECD, 2020). Local Governments for Sustainability (ICLEI), C40 Cities, and UN-Habitat have also launched SDG monitoring initiatives in cities. The European Commission, through its Joint Research Centre (JRC) and the Directorate-General for Regional and Urban Policy (DG REGIO), is also working on monitoring the urban dimension of the 2030 Agenda for Sustainable Development.

6. **Corporate benchmarks and sustainability metrics.** The SDGs are increasingly used by large companies as the underlying framework for environmental, social, and governance (ESG) reporting. The World Benchmarking Alliance is developing corporate benchmarks for major industries, while in close collaboration, the "Fixing the Business of Food" coalition initiated by the Barilla Center for Nutrition is developing monitoring frameworks for the food sector (World Benchmarking Alliance, 2019); SDSN and BCFN, 2019). The World Business Council on Sustainable Development (WBCSD) facilitates the exchange of best practices on SDG data (WBCSD, 2018). Many financial institutions and development banks have also developed SDG tools and procedures to track the SDG impact of their investments.

7. **Capacity-building and partnerships to develop alternative data sources.** PARIS21 has been named the custodian agency to support statistical capacity-building in low- and middle-income countries (PARIS21 and Partners for Review, 2019). The Thematic Research Group on Data and Statistics (TReNDS) supports better SDG monitoring, evolving data governance, and new data-sharing policy and practice standards (TReNDS, 2019). The Global Partnership for Sustainable Development Data (GPSDD) was established to help stakeholders across countries and sectors fully harness the data revolution for sustainable development. Together they are implementing DATA4Now to increase the timeliness of SDG metrics (GPSDD et al., 2019).

Data availability and timeliness for the SDGs

Timely data is crucial for accurate monitoring of SDG progress and for evidence-based policymaking. This is even more true after Covid-19. To assess the current state of data and monitoring, we assessed data availability and timeliness of the indicators included in this SDR2020. Our analysis highlights three major findings.

First, the inclusion of non-official statistics, including model-based estimates, helps fill data gaps and can reduce time lags in official statistics. Using only official statistics from United Nations custodian agencies, data availability varies significantly among regions, from 95% in OECD countries to 54% in Oceania (table 5). The average year of reference is 2016 for most regions (Eastern Europe and Central Asia, East and South Asia, Middle East and North Africa, Oceania, and Sub-Saharan Africa) and 2017 for OECD countries. Both data coverage and timeliness improve when adding model-based estimates (e.g., from IHME and the World Data Lab) and population surveys conducted by analytics companies (e.g., Gallup World Poll).

Non-official statistics obtained through modelling, population surveys, or other techniques come with limitations. While they increase data availability and timeliness, they do remain predictions. The accuracy of the underlying models have been questioned, and significant discrepancies have been found between model-based estimates and official statistics obtained several years after (Boerma, Victora, and Abouzahr, 2018; Shiffman and Shawar, 2020). Also, the models and underlying assumptions are not always made transparent. Finally, the availability of such estimates may reduce incentives to strengthen statistical capacity. Large-scale household surveys conducted by analytics companies typically have much lower sample sizes (usually 1,000 people) than national statistical offices require, which in turn will affect the reliability of the data. Data are not always collected face-to-face and the questions and scales used may not represent the most valid and reliable measurement approaches (OECD, 2017; Praia City Group, 2020).

Second, it remains difficult to assess if the adoption of the SDGs has had a positive impact on the availability and timeliness of official statistics. On one hand, we find that there is now more data available to measure sustainable development than there was in 2015. Improvements have been particularly pronounced in Oceania and Sub-Saharan Africa. On the other hand, many of the data points available now have a year of reference that predates the adoption of the SDGs. When comparing data availability of 2010–2015 vs 2015–2020, we find that availability has declined in all regions except in OECD countries (+0.3%). The slight increase in data availability for OECD countries is primarily due to new data on freshwater withdrawals (FAO) and mortality from air pollution (WHO).

There are several ways to interpret these findings. First, it might be too early to evaluate the impact of statistical projects and programs launched since the adoption of the SDGs in 2015. It takes many years to collect and standardize official statistics in collaboration with national statistical offices, especially when there are no agreed definitions or methods. Second, it is possible that datapoints collected and published between 2015 and 2020 have reference years before 2015. We could not trace from international data portals the date when the data was collected. So, a data point obtained in 2016 with a reference year of 2014 is counted under data available for 2010–2015 but not for the SDG period (2015–2020). Hence these findings may just reinforce the point made earlier on significant time lags in official data reporting. Third, we have limited our analysis to data from official sources that is presented in the SDR2020. A similar analysis conducted for all official UN indicators might yield other findings.

Finally, we find that data availability and timeliness vary extensively across the SDGs. Using both official and non-official data sources, we find that data coverage and timeliness tend to be better for socioeconomic goals such as SDG 3 (Good Health and Well-Being) and SDG 5 (Gender Equality). Data availability and timeliness to track SDG 10 (Reduced Inequalities) is more problematic, with many countries reporting outdated information or no information for the GINI coefficient. At the global level, data availability and timeliness are also low for environmental and biodiversity goals, including SDG 12 (Responsible Consumption and Production) and SDG 14 (Life Below Water).

Table 5

Non-official data sources help address data gaps and time lags in official statistics

Data availability and year of reference by sub-regions (official data sources), including and excluding model-based estimates

	Official data sources (excluding model-based estimates and subjective measures)		Official data sources (including model-based estimates and subjective measures)	
	Coverage (%)	Avg. Year	Coverage (%)	Avg. Year
Eastern Europe & Central Asia	76.6	2016	78.3	2017
East and South Asia	82.3	2016	84.7	2017
Latin America and the Caribbean	76.7	2016	77.9	2017
Middle East and North Africa	73.3	2016	76.8	2016
OECD	95.0	2017	96.1	2017
Oceania	54.5	2016	53.1	2016
Sub-Saharan Africa	80.1	2016	82.9	2017

Note: This table focuses on indicators from official sources (e.g., UN custodian agencies) included in the SDR2020. It does not cover all official SDG indicators. Model-based estimates include data from the World Poverty Lab and IHME. Subjective measures include population surveys conducted by the Gallup World Poll.

Source: Authors' analysis

Figure 27

Overall, there are more official data available in 2020 than between 2010–2015 to measure sustainable development globally...

Change in data availability (official data sources[1]), 2010–2015 vs 2010–2020 (%)

Figure 28

...Yet, it might be too soon to see an "SDG effect" on data availability and timeliness

Change in data availability (official data sources[1]), 2010–2015 vs 2015–2020 (%)

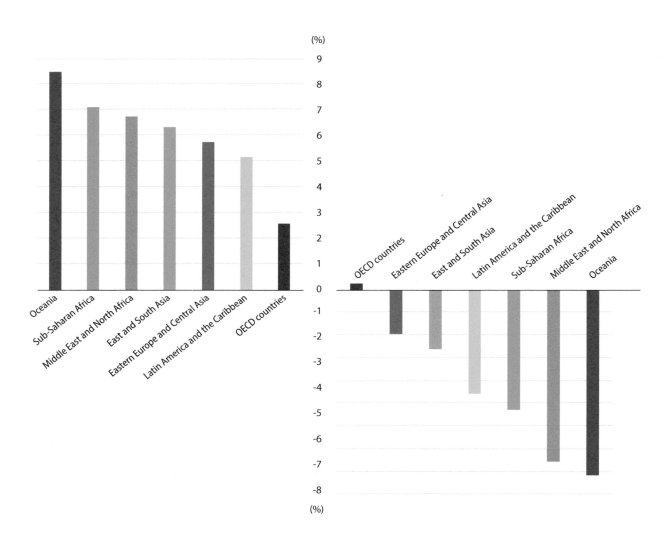

Note: (1) Excluding model-based estimates and other non-official statistics.
Source: Authors' analysis

Figure 29

Data availability and timeliness vary extensively across the SDGs

Global data availability (in %) and average year of reference (in years) by SDGs (official and non-official data sources)

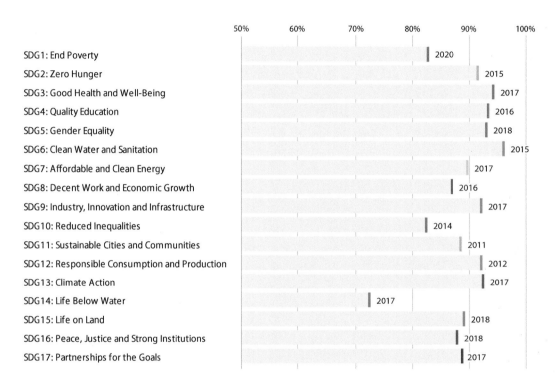

Source: Authors' analysis

The outbreak of Covid-19 underlines the need for more timely and disaggregated data. Beyond data needed on incidence, hospitalization, mortality, and the effective reproduction rate (ERR), countries need timely, accurate, and disaggregated data to design policy interventions that address the needs of their most vulnerable population groups (Dahmm, 2020; Marks, 2020). For comparison, the average time lag for data reported in the SDR2020 is three years.

At the same time, Covid-19 and its aftermath pose serious challenges for statistical systems. These include delays in planned censuses and surveys and reduced funding for

and capacity within national statistical offices. The need for real-time contact tracing also brings to the fore ethical and other concerns about new sources of data and the role private providers play in generating and using the data (Orrell, 2020; Marks, 2020; Espey, 2020). The SDSN TReNDS network and Data4Now support partnerships between governments and other stakeholders (including the private sector) to increase data availability and timeliness for the SDGs (GPSDD et al., 2019), while the Contract for Data Collaborations (C4DC) project supports governments in developing and executing data-sharing agreements for cross-sector data initiatives (GOVLAB, University of Washington, World Economic Forum and TRENDs, 2020).

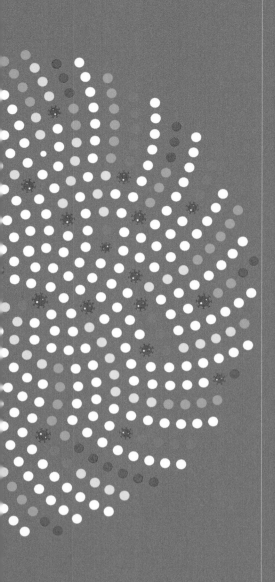

Part 4

Methods Summary
and Data Tables

Part 4

Methods Summary and Data Tables

4.1 Interpreting the Index and Dashboards results

The *Sustainable Development Report 2020* describes each country's progress towards achieving the SDGs and indicates areas requiring faster progress. A country's overall SDG Index score and its scores on individual SDGs can be interpreted as a percentage of optimal performance. The difference between the score and 100 is therefore the distance, in percentage points, that needs to be overcome to reach optimum performance. The same basket of indicators is used for all countries to generate comparable scores and rankings.

Substantial differences in rankings may be due to small differences in the aggregate SDG Index score. Differences of two or three places between countries should not be interpreted as "significant," whereas differences of 10 places or more can show a meaningful difference (JRC, 2019).

The SDG dashboards provide a visual representation of each country's performance on the 17 SDGs. The "traffic light" color scheme (green, yellow, orange, and red) illustrates how far a country is from achieving a particular goal. As in previous years, the dashboards and country profiles for OECD countries include additional metrics that are not available for non-OECD member countries.

The SDG trend dashboards indicate whether a country is on track to achieve a particular goal by 2030, based on its recent performance on given indicators. Indicator trends are aggregated at the goal level to give a trend indication of how the country is progressing towards that SDG.

This section describes how the SDG Index and dashboards are computed. A **detailed methodology paper** is accessible online (Lafortune et al., 2018).

The European Commission Joint Research Centre (JRC) conducted an independent statistical audit of the report's methodology and results in 2019. The audit reviewed the conceptual and statistical coherence of the index structure. The detailed statistical audit report is also available on our website (http://sustainabledevelopment.report).

4.2 Changes made to the 2020 edition, and main limitations

Changes made to the 2020 SDG Index and Dashboards

The 2020 SDG Index covers 166 countries, compared with 162 countries in 2019. The additional countries included this year are Barbados, Brunei Darussalam, Somalia, and South Sudan. The 2020 report also incorporates several new indicators. These are shown in table 6, which also identifies indicators that were replaced or modified due to changes in the methodology, and estimates produced by data providers. The data for this year's edition was extracted between February and April 2020.

For the first time, the 2020 edition of the report features time series data for several spillovers. This includes the following indicators:

- CO_2 emissions embodied in imports (tCO_2/capita)
- Scarce water consumption embodied in imports (m^3/capita),
- Fatal work-related accidents embodied in imports (per 100,000 population)

Limitations and data gaps

Due to changes in the indicators as well as some refinements in the methodology, SDG Index rankings and scores cannot be compared with those of previous editions. In spite of our best efforts to identify data for the SDGs, several indicator and data gaps persist (table 7).

Table 6

New indicators and modifications

SDG	Indicator	Change
3	Universal health coverage (UHC) index of service coverage (worst 0–100 best)	Modification: Changed data source to WHO (2020)
4	Participation rate in pre-primary organized learning (% of children aged 4 to 6)	Modification: Changed data source to UNESCO (2020)
6	Anthropogenic wastewater that receives treatment (%)	Modification: Underlying data source changed for a few countries. See https://epi.envirocenter.yale.edu/ for more information
6	Scarce water consumption embodied in imports (m³/capita)	New, replaces "Imported groundwater depletion"
7	Share of renewable energy in total primary energy supply (%)	Modification: Changed data source to OECD (2020)
12	Production-based SO_2 emissions (kg/capita)	Modification: To increase timeliness and country coverage, data source was changed to Lenzen, M. et al. (2020)
12	SO_2 emissions embodied in imports (kg/capita)	Modification: To increase timeliness and country coverage data source was changed to Lenzen, M. et al. (2020)
12	Non-recycled municipal solid waste (kg/capita/day)	Modification: Indicator now excludes composted waste in addition to recycled waste
13	CO_2 emissions embodied in imports (tCO_2/capita)	Modification: To increase timeliness and country coverage data source was changed to Lenzen, M. et al. (2020). Carbon accounting is no longer technology-adjusted
13	CO_2 emissions embodied in fossil fuel exports (kg/capita)	Modification: To avoid penalizing trade and transit countries, fuel exports are now capped at the country's level of production
14	Marine biodiversity threats embodied in imports (per million population)	New addition
15	Terrestrial and freshwater biodiversity threats embodied in imports (per million population)	New addition
16	Unsentenced detainees (% of prison population)	Modification: Data now calculated as 3-year averages because of volatility
17	Government spending on health and education (% of GDP)	Modification: Changed data source for OECD countries to be consistent with non-OECD countries
17	Corporate Tax Haven Score (best 0–100 worst)	New, replaces "Tax Haven Score (best 0–5 worst)"
17	Shifted profits of multinationals (US$ billion)	New addition

Source: Authors' analysis

Table 7

Major indicator and data gaps for the SDGs

SDG	Issue	Desired metrics
2	Agriculture and nutrition	Resource-use efficiency (nutrients, water, energy)
		Risky pesticides
		Food loss and food waste
		Greenhouse gas emissions from land use
3	Health	Affordability of healthcare
		Health-care system resilience and preparedness to face global health risks
4	Education	Internationally comparable primary and secondary education outcomes
		Early childhood development
5	Women empowerment	Gender pay gap and other empowerment measures
		Violence against women
6	Water	Quality of drinking water and surface waters
8	Decent work	Decent work
		Labor rights protections
10	Inequality	Wealth inequality
		Vertical mobility
12	Sustainable consumption and production	Environmental impact of material flows
		Recycling and re-use (circular economy)
		Chemicals
		Waste shipments
13	Climate change	Leading indicators for decarbonization
		Greenhouse gas emissions from land use
14	Marine ecosystems	Maximum sustainable yields for fisheries
		Impact of high-sea and cross-border fishing
		Protected areas by level of protection
15	Terrestrial ecosystems	Leading indicators for ecosystem health
		Trade in endangered species
		Protected areas by level of protection
16	Peace and justice	Access to justice
		Violence against children
		Protection of the rights of civil society organizations
17	Means of implementation	Non-concessional development finance
		Climate finance
		Unfair tax competition
		Development impact of trade practices

Source: Authors' analysis

4. Methods Summary and Data Tables

As underscored in previous editions of this report, governments and the international community must increase investments in SDG data and monitoring systems to close these gaps.

To ensure maximum data comparability, we only use data from internationally comparable sources. The providers of this data may adjust national data to ensure international comparability. As a result, some data points presented in this report may differ from data available from national statistical offices or other national sources. Moreover, the length of the validation processes followed by international organizations can lead to significant delays in publishing some data. National statistical offices may therefore have more recent data for some indicators than presented in this report.

Looking forward

In future editions we will include additional and improved SDG metrics as they become available, and we will aim for greater comparability over time. In particular, a major priority in future editions will be to present trend data on additional spillover metrics; such as SO_2 emissions, nitrogen emissions, and biodiversity threats embodied in imports.

To better inform regional and national discussions on the implementation of the SDGs, we support the creation of SDG indices and dashboards for regions (e.g., the Africa SDG Index and Dashboards Report) and at sub-national levels (e.g., the US Cities Sustainable Development Report). SDSN is also working with partners to produce more regional and sub-national editions that can promote evidence-based policymaking, mobilize regional and local communities, and identify persisting data gaps for monitoring the SDGs.

4.3 Methodology (summary)

The SDR2020 provides a comprehensive assessment of distance to targets based on the most up to date data available covering all 193 United Nations Member States. This year's report includes a total of 115 indicators with 85 global indicators and 30 indicators added specifically for OECD countries, including several new indicators to fill data gaps.

The following sections provide an overview of the methodology for indicator selection, normalization, aggregation and for generating indications on trends. Additional information including raw data, additional data tables and sensitivity tests are available online.

A. Data selection

Where possible, the SDR2020 uses official SDG indicators endorsed by the UN Statistical Commission. Where insufficient data is available for an official indicator and to close data gaps, we include other metrics from official and unofficial providers. Five criteria for indicator selection were used to determine suitable metrics for inclusion in the report:

1. **Global relevance and applicability to a broad range of country settings:** The indicators are relevant to monitoring achievement of the SDGs and applicable to the entire continent. They are internationally comparable and allow for direct comparison of performance across countries. In particular, they allow for the definition of quantitative performance thresholds that signify SDG achievement.

2. **Statistical adequacy:** The indicators selected represent valid and reliable measures.

3. **Timeliness:** The indicators selected are up to date and published on a reasonably prompt schedule.

4. **Data quality:** The data series used represent the best available measure for a specific issue and derive from official national or international sources (e.g., national statistical offices or international organizations) or other reputable sources, such as peer-reviewed

publications. No imputations of self-reported national estimates are included.

5. **Coverage:** Data must be available for at least 80% of the United Nations Member States with a national population of more than 1 million people.

Data sources

The data included in the SDR2020 come from a mix of official and non-official data sources. Most of the data come from international organizations (World Bank, OECD, WHO, FAO, ILO, UNICEF, and others) which have extensive and rigorous data-validation processes. Other data sources include household surveys (Gallup World Poll), civil society organizations and networks (Oxfam, Tax Justice Network, and others) and peer-reviewed journals. The full list of indicators and data sources is presented in table 9.

B. Missing data and imputations

The purpose of the SDR2020 is to guide countries' discussions of their current SDG priorities based on available and robust data. To minimize biases from missing data, the SDG Index only includes countries that have data for at least 80% of the variables included in the global SDG Index. The list of countries not included in the SDG Index due to insufficient data availability is presented in table 10. We include all United Nations Member States in the SDG dashboards and country profiles, which illustrates gaps in available SDG data for some countries.

Considering that many SDG priorities lack widely accepted statistical models for imputing country-level data, we generally did not impute or model any missing data. We made exceptions for the variables listed in table 8, often because they would otherwise have not been included due to missing data.

To reduce missing-data biases in the computation of the SDG Index, we impute the regional mean goal scores to those goal scores that are missing or are missing data for more than 75% of the indicators under that goal. This applies primarily to Goal 10 (Reduced Inequalities) and

Goal 14 (Life Below Water). Imputed goal scores are used solely for the computation of the index, and they are not reported in the SDG dashboards or country profiles. Similarly, we impute regional scores for each indicator under Goal 4 to those countries missing data for that indicator. This is done exceptionally to reduce missing bias from the many data gaps in the education data. In the case of Goal 14 (Life Below Water), we hope to identify more metrics in the future to gauge the impact of landlocked countries on oceans. Imputed values are clearly marked in the online datasets and in the country profiles.

C. Method for constructing the SDG Index

The procedure for calculating the SDG Index comprised three steps: (i) censor extreme values from the distribution of each indicator; (ii) rescale the data to ensure comparability across indicators; (iii) aggregate the indicators within and across SDGs.

Normalization

To make the data comparable across indicators, each variable was rescaled from 0 to 100, with 0 denoting worst performance and 100 describing the optimum. Rescaling is usually very sensitive to the choice of limits and extreme values (outliers) at both tails of the distribution. The latter may become unintended thresholds and introduce spurious variability in the data. Consequently, the choice of upper and lower bounds can affect the relative ranking of countries in the index.

The upper bound for each indicator was determined using a five-step decision tree:

1. **Use absolute quantitative thresholds in SDGs and targets:** e.g., zero poverty, universal school completion, universal access to water and sanitation, full gender equality. Some SDG targets propose relative changes (such as Target 3.4: "reduce by one third premature mortality from non-communicable diseases … ") that cannot be translated into a global baseline today. Such targets are addressed in step 5 (page 69).

2. **Where no explicit SDG target is available, apply the principle of "leave no one behind" in setting the upper bound to universal access or zero deprivation for the following types of indicators:**

   a. Measures of extreme poverty (e.g., wasting), consistent with the SDG ambition to end extreme poverty in all its forms.

   b. Public service coverage (e.g., access to contraception).

   c. Access to basic infrastructure (e.g., mobile phone coverage, wastewater treatment).

3. **Where science-based targets exist that must be achieved by 2030 or later, use these to set a 100% upper bound** (e.g., 100% sustainable management of fisheries, or greenhouse gas emissions from electricity to reach net-zero by 2070 at the latest to limit warming to below 2°C).

4. **Where several countries already exceed an SDG target, use the average of the top 5 performers** (e.g., child mortality).

5. **For all other indicators, use the average of the top performers.** For global indicators, the upper bound was set by taking the average value of the top 5 global performers. For OECD indicators, the average of the top 3 performers was used.

These principles interpret the SDGs as "stretch targets" and focus attention on the indicators on which a country is lagging behind. Each indicator distribution was censored, so that all values exceeding the upper bound scored 100 and values below the lower bound scored 0.

In some cases, the upper bound exceeded the thresholds to be met by 2030 in order to achieve the SDGs. For example, the SDGs call for reducing child mortality to no more than 25 deaths per 1000 live births, but many countries have already exceeded this threshold (i.e., have mortality rates lower than 25 in 1000). By defining the upper bound as the "best" outcome (e.g., 0 mortality per 1000 live births) – rather than the SDG achievement threshold – the SDG Index rewards improvements across the full distribution. This is particularly important for countries that have already achieved some SDG thresholds, but still lag behind others on this metric.

Some countries already exceed the upper bound of certain indicators today, and more will do so in the coming years as the world progresses towards the SDGs.

To remove the effect of extreme values, which can skew the results of a composite index, the JRC (OECD and JRC, 2008) recommends censoring data at the bottom 2.5[th] percentile as the minimum value for the normalization – as long as that value does not include observations that are still part of the ordinary distribution. However, sometimes the 2.5[th] percentile may contain outliers and values that are part of a normally distributed set of data. When clear outliers were identified, an intermediate value between the weakest outlier and the most extreme "normal" value in the distribution was selected as the lower bound and we censored data at this level.

After establishing the upper and lower bounds, variables were transformed linearly to a scale of 0 to 100 using the following rescaling formula for the range [0; 100]:

$$x' = \frac{x - min(x)}{max(x) - min(x)} * 100 \ (Eq.S1)$$

where x is raw data value; max/min denote the bounds for best and worst performance, respectively; and x' is the normalized value after rescaling.

The rescaling equation ensured that all rescaled variables were expressed as ascending variables (i.e., higher values denoted better performance). In this way, the rescaled data became easy to interpret and compare across all indicators: a country that scores 50 on a variable is half-way towards achieving the optimum value; a country with a score of 75 has covered three-quarters of the distance from worst to best.

Table 8

Imputations

SDG	Indicator	Imputation
1	Poverty headcount ratio at $1.90/day (%)	Data was not reported for those countries where no survey data was available.
1	Poverty headcount ratio at $3.20/day (%)	Data was not reported for those countries where no survey data was available.
2	Prevalence of undernourishment (%)	FAO et al. (2015) report 14.7 million undernourished people in developed regions, which corresponds to an average prevalence of 1.17% in the developed regions. We assumed a 1.2% prevalence rate for each high-income country with missing data.
2	Prevalence of stunting in children under 5 years of age (%)	UNICEF et al. (2016) report an average prevalence of stunting in high-income countries of 2.58%. We assumed this value for high-income countries with missing data.
2	Prevalence of wasting in children under 5 years of age (%)	UNICEF et al. (2016) report an average prevalence of wasting in high-income countries of 0.75%. We assumed this value for high-income countries with missing data.
4	Net primary enrollment rate (%)	For OECD countries, we imputed values from OECD enrollment data. For Japan and Lebanon, the datapoint in the 2019 SDR was reported for this year.
4	Lower secondary completion rate (%)	For OECD countries, we imputed values from OECD enrollment data. For Bulgaria, Japan, Lebanon, and Namibia, the datapoint in the 2019 SDR was reported for this year.
5	Demand for family planning satisfied by modern methods (% of females aged 15 to 49 who are married or in unions)	We impute modeled estimates from UNDESA Population Division for countries missing administrative data.
8	Victims of modern slavery (per 1,000 population)	We assume missing data points for those countries in which the Walk Free Foundation's methodology has less confidence due to survey unavailability.
9	The Times Higher Education Universities Ranking: Average score of top 3 universities (worst 0–100 best)	We impute values from the Global Innovation Index's indicator on university scores in the QS University Rankings for countries with missing data. We assumed a value of 0 for countries with no universities in the rankings.
9	Expenditure on research and development (% of GDP)	We assumed zero R&D expenditure for low-income countries that did not report any data for this variable.
10	Gini coefficient adjusted for top income	We impute the World Bank Gini coefficients for those countries missing data on the adjusted Gini coefficient from Brookings.
13	CO_2 emissions embodied in fossil fuel exports (kg/capita)	We assumed a value of 0 for countries with unreported export data and no production across all three fossil-fuel types (coal, gas, oil).
15	Permanent deforestation (% of forest area, 5-year average)	We did not report data for countries with insignificant forest area as per the Environmental Performance Index (2018). Countries with forest area but no data on drivers of permanent deforestation (shifting agriculture, urbanization, and land use for commodity production) were assigned a value of 0.
16	Homicides (per 100,000 population)	Countries with missing values in the most current extraction from the UNODC were assigned the values that were available for the 2019 Sustainable Development Report.
16	Children involved in child labor (% of population aged 5 to 14)	The best performing upper-middle-income countries have a child labor rate of 1% (UNICEF, 2015). We assumed 0% child labor for high-income OECD members for which no data was reported.

Table 8

(continued)

SDG	Indicator	Imputation
16	Exports of major conventional weapons (TIV constant million USD per 100,000 population)	We assumed a value of 0 for countries with unreported export data and from which there are no major companies that produce weapons.
17	Government spending on health and education (% of GDP)	When data are missing from WHO or UNESCO, values were imputed from the OECD System of National Accounts data. Alternatively, when OECD SNA data wasn't available, values for health spending were imputed from the OECD Health expenditure and financing database while values for education spending were imputed from the Education at a glance: Educational finance indicators database.
17	Other countries: Government revenue excluding grants (% of GDP)	IMF data (taxes, social contributions, and other revenue, excluding grants) is imputed when countries are missing data in the World Bank database. The IMF data used is from the central government (incl. social security funds) sector. If that is not available, we use data for the budgetary central government sector
17	Corporate Tax Haven Score (best 0–100 worst)	A value of 0 was imputed to all countries not included in the index. Missing data was assigned to those countries not included in the index and indicated in the OECD Automatic Exchange of Information Implementation Report 2018 (Nauru, Qatar and Bahrain). According to the report, these countries have no system for direct taxation in place and do not have reciprocal information-exchanges.

Weighting and aggregation

The results of several rounds of expert consultations on earlier drafts of the SDG Index made clear that there is no consensus across different epistemic communities on assigning higher weights to some SDGs over others. As a normative assumption, we therefore opted for a fixed, equal weight to be given to every SDG to reflect policymakers' commitments to treating all SDGs equally and as an "integrated and indivisible" set of goals (United Nations, 2015, para. 5). This implies that to improve their SDG Index score, countries need to place attention on all goals, with a particular focus on goals that they are furthest from achieving and where incremental progress might therefore be expected to be fastest.

To compute the SDG Index, we first estimate scores for each goal using the arithmetic mean of indicators for that goal. These goal scores are then averaged across all 17 SDGs to obtain the SDG Index score. Various sensitivity tests have been available online, including comparisons of arithmetic mean versus geometric mean and Monte-Carlo simulations at the Index and Goal level. Monte-Carlo simulations call for prudence in interpreting small differences in the Index scores and rankings between countries, as those may be sensitive to the weighting scheme.

D. Method for constructing the dashboards

We have introduced additional quantitative **thresholds** for each indicator, to group countries in a "traffic light" table. Aggregating across all indicators for each goal yields an overall score for each SDG and for each country. Table 11 presents these thresholds for each indicator.

Thresholds

To assess a country's progress on a particular indicator, we considered four bands. The green band is bounded by the maximum rating that can be achieved for each variable (i.e., the upper bound) and the threshold for achieving the SDG. Three color bands, moving from yellow to orange and then red, denote increasing distance from SDG achievement. The red band is bound at the bottom by the value of the 2.5th percentile of the distribution. Upper and lower bounds are the same as for the SDG Index.

Additional thresholds were established based on statistical techniques and in consultation with experts. The country assessments were subject to a public consultation as well as direct consultations with members of the Sustainable Development Solutions Network. All thresholds were specified in absolute terms and apply to all countries.

Weighting and aggregation

The purpose of the global SDG dashboards is to highlight those SDGs that require particular attention in each country, and therefore should be prioritized for early action. For the design of the dashboards, the same issues related to weighting and aggregation of indicators apply, as discussed above for the SDG Index.

Averaging across all indicators for an SDG might hide areas of policy concern when a country performs well on most indicators but faces serious shortfalls on one or two metrics within the same SDG. This applies particularly to high-income and upper-middle-income countries that have made significant progress on many SDG dimensions but may face serious shortfalls on individual variables.

As a result, the global SDG dashboards aggregate indicator ratings for each SDG by estimating the average of the two variables on which a country performed worst. To this end, the indicator values were first rescaled from 0 to 3, where 0 corresponds to the lower bound, 1 to the value of the threshold between red and orange ("red threshold"), 2 to the value of the threshold between yellow and green ("green threshold"), and 3 to the upper bound. For all indicators, the yellow–orange threshold was set as the value halfway between the red and green thresholds (1.5). Each interval between 0 and 3 is continuous.

We then took the average of the two rescaled variables on which the country performed worst to identify its rating for that goal. We applied an additional rule that, in order to score green for the goal, both indicators had to be green – otherwise the goal would be rated yellow. Similarly, a red score was applied only if both worst-performing indicators scored red. If a country has only one data point under an SDG, then the color rating for that indicator determines its overall rating for the goal. If a country has data available on fewer than 50% of the indicators under a goal, its dashboard color for that goal will be gray.

E. SDG trends

Using historic data, we estimate how fast a country has been progressing towards an SDG and determine whether – if extrapolated into the future – this pace will be sufficient to achieve the SDG by 2030. For each indicator, SDG achievement is defined by the green threshold set for the SDG dashboards. The difference in percentage points between the green threshold and the normalized country score denotes the gap that must be closed to meet that goal. To estimate trends at the indicator level, we calculated the linear annual growth rates (i.e., annual percentage improvement) needed to achieve the target by 2030 (i.e., 2010–2030), which we compared to the average annual growth rate over the most recent period, for example, from 2015–2018. Progress towards achievement on a particular indicator is described using a four-arrow system (figure 30). Figure 31 illustrates the methodology graphically.

Specifically, each indicator trend was re-normalized on a scale of 0 to 4, similar to the dashboard methodology. Decreasing indicators were assigned a value of 0–1, where 0 is the highest rate of score decrease and 1 corresponds to no change whatsoever in the score over time. Indicator trends that are "stagnating" were assigned a value of 1–2, where 2 corresponds to 50% of the growth rate needed to meet the target by 2030. Indicators that are "moderately improving" were assigned a value of 2–3, where 3 is the exact growth rate needed to achieve the target by 2030. Those indicators that are "on track" were assigned values of 3–4, where 4 corresponds to the greatest improvement over the period. Indicators that are "maintaining SDG achievement" were assigned a score of exactly 3. The individual bands are linear, but the continuous 0-to-4 scale is not linear as a whole.

Overall goal trends were calculated as the arithmetic average of the rescaled values for all trend indicators under each goal. An average of 0–1 corresponds to a "decreasing" goal trend, 1–2 to a "stagnating" trend, 2–3 to "moderate improvement," and 3–4 to "on track or maintaining achievement." The trend for an SDG was calculated as the arithmetic average of all trend indicators for that goal.

Figure 30

The Four-arrow system for denoting SDG trends

Decreasing	**Stagnating**	**Moderately improving**	**On track or Maintaining SDG achievement**
Decreasing score, i.e. country moves in the wrong direction	Score remains stagnant or increases at a rate below 50% of the growth rate needed to achieve the SDG by 2030	Score increases at a rate above 50% of the required growth rate but below the rate needed to achieve the SDG by 2030	Score increases at the rate needed to achieve the SDG by 2030 or performance has already exceeded SDG achievement threshold

Figure 31

Graphic representation of the SDG trends methodology

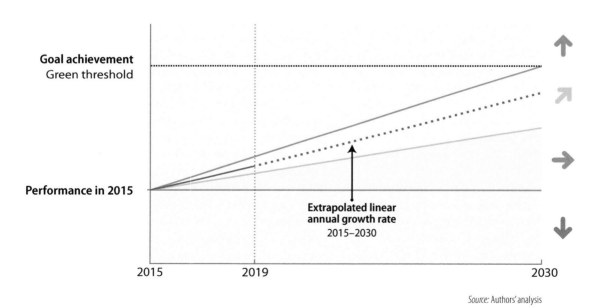

Source: Authors' analysis

Table 12 also provides the complete list of indicators used to compute SDG Trends. Trend indicators were selected from the indicators included in the SDG dashboards based on the availability of trend data. When the value for one year was not available, we used the closest available value with a maximum one-year difference for calculating the trend indications. The table also indicates the period over which the trend was calculated. For several indicators, trends were calculated using data in 2015 as the start year. These indicators demonstrate how the situation in the country has changed since adoption of the SDGs. These indicators are particularly insightful for understanding how policy implementation efforts have corresponded to changing outcomes, and are marked with an asterisk in table 12. Other SDG trends are calculated based on data points that preceded the adoption of SDGs, because data is reported with long lags at the international level due to lengthy validation processes.

Small decreases in countries that are top performers are treated differently from small decreases in countries that are average or low performers. For top performers only, very small decreases are now treated as "stagnating" trends. They are reported as such at the indicator level and treated as such when calculating the overall goal trend. However, countries that used to be above the green threshold and that decrease to a score lower than the green threshold obtain a "decreasing" trend.

Several other calculation methods were considered. For instance, we tested the sensitivity of the results when using technical optimums (100 score) as "goal achievement" and calculated distance to these optimums. This approach yielded harsher results and is not consistent with our conceptual assumption that lower green thresholds correspond to goal achievement. We also considered using compound annual growth rates (CAGR) instead of linear growth rates. The two approaches yield rather similar results however, and we could not identify a strong argument for using the more sophisticated CAGR method. Finally, while the dashboards are based only on the two worst indicators, trends are generated using all indicators under the goal. This is because the dashboards aim to highlight goals where action is urgently required due to poor performance on some of the underlying indicators, whereas the trends aim to reflect the evolution of overall performance on the goal over time, including all indicators.

4. Methods Summary and Data Tables

4.4 Data tables

Table 9

Indicators included in the Sustainable Development Report 2020

Legend

[a]   denotes OECD-only indicators

[b]   denotes indicators not used in OECD dashboard but that are used in the calculation of OECD countries' index scores.

SDG	Notes	Indicator	Reference Year	Source	Description
1		Poverty headcount ratio at $1.90/day (%)	2020	World Data Lab (2020)	Estimated percentage of the population that is living under the poverty threshold of US$1.90 a day. Estimated using historical estimates of the income distribution, projections of population changes by age and educational attainment, and GDP projections.
1		Poverty headcount ratio at $3.20/day (%)	2020	World Data Lab (2020)	Estimated percentage of the population that is living under the poverty threshold of US$3.20 a day. Estimated using historical estimates of the income distribution, projections of population changes by age and educational attainment, and GDP projections.
1	[a]	Poverty rate after taxes and transfers (%)	2017	OECD (2020)	Relative poverty is measured as the share of the population whose incomes fall below half the median disposable income for the entire population. The income threshold for relative poverty changes over time with changes in median disposable income.
2		Prevalence of undernourishment (%)	2017	FAO (2020)	The percentage of the population whose food intake is insufficient to meet dietary energy requirements for a minimum of one year. Dietary energy requirements are defined as the amount of dietary energy required by an individual to maintain body functions, health and normal activity. FAO et al. (2015) report 14.7 million undernourished people in developed regions, which corresponds to an average prevalence of 1.17% in the developed regions. We assumed a 1.2% prevalence rate for each high-income country (World Bank, 2019) with missing data.
2		Prevalence of stunting in children under 5 years of age (%)	2016	UNICEF et al. (2020)	The percentage of children up to the age of 5 years that are stunted, measured as the percentage that fall below minus two standard deviations from the median height for their age, according to the WHO Child Growth Standards. UNICEF et al. (2016) report an average prevalence of wasting in high-income countries of 2.58%. We assumed this value for high-income countries with missing data.
2		Prevalence of wasting in children under 5 years of age (%)	2016	UNICEF et al. (2020)	The percentage of children up to the age of 5 years whose weight falls below minus two standard deviations from the median weight for their age, according to the WHO Child Growth Standards. UNICEF et al. (2016) report an average prevalence of wasting in high-income countries of 0.75%. We assumed this value for high-income countries with missing data.
2		Prevalence of obesity, BMI ≥ 30 (% of adult population)	2016	WHO (2020)	The percentage of the adult population that has a body mass index (BMI) of 30kg/m^2 or higher, based on measured height and weight.
2		Human Trophic Level (best 2-3 worst)	2017	Bonhommeau et al. (2013)	Trophic levels are a measure of the energy intensity of diet composition and reflect the relative amounts of plants as opposed to animals eaten in a given country. A higher trophic level represents a greater level of consumption of energy-intensive animals.
2		Cereal yield (tonnes per hectare of harvested land)	2017	FAO (2020)	Cereal yield, measured as tonnes per hectare of harvested land. Production data on cereals relate to crops harvested for dry grain only and excludes crops harvested for hay or green for food, feed, or silage and those used for grazing.
2		Sustainable Nitrogen Management Index (best 0-1.41 worst)	2015	Zhang and Davidson (2019)	The Sustainable Nitrogen Management Index (SNMI) is a one-dimensional ranking score that combines two efficiency measures in crop production: Nitrogen use efficiency (NUE) and land use efficiency (crop yield).
2	[a]	Yield gap closure (% of potential yield)	2015	Global Yield Gap Atlas (2015)	A country's yield expressed as a percentage of its potential yield in the three annual crops using the most land area, weighted for the relative importance of each crop in terms of surface area.

Table 9

(continued)

SDG	Notes	Indicator	Reference Year	Source	Description
3		Maternal mortality rate (per 100,000 live births)	2017	WHO et al. (2020)	The estimated number of women, between the age of 15-49, who die from pregnancy-related causes while pregnant or within 42 days of termination of pregnancy, per 100,000 live births.
3		Neonatal mortality rate (per 1,000 live births)	2018	UNICEF et al. (2020)	The number of newborn infants (neonates) who die before reaching 28 days of age, per 1,000 live births.
3		Mortality rate, under-5 (per 1,000 live births)	2018	UNICEF et al. (2020)	The probability that a newborn baby will die before reaching age five, if subject to age-specific mortality rates of the specified year, per 1,000 live births.
3		Incidence of tuberculosis (per 100,000 population)	2018	WHO (2020)	The estimated rate of new and relapse cases of tuberculosis in a given year, expressed per 100,000 people. All forms of tuberculosis are included, including cases of people living with HIV.
3		New HIV infections (per 1,000 uninfected population)	2018	UNAIDS (2020)	Number of people newly infected with HIV per 1,000 uninfected population.
3		Age-standardized death rate due to cardiovascular disease, cancer, diabetes, or chronic respiratory disease in adults aged 30–70 years (%)	2016	WHO (2018)	The probability of dying between the ages of 30 and 70 years from cardiovascular diseases, cancer, diabetes or chronic respiratory diseases, defined as the percent of 30-year-old-people who would die before their 70th birthday from these diseases, assuming current mortality rates at every age and that individuals would not die from any other cause of death (e.g. injuries or HIV/AIDS).
3		Age-standardized death rate attributable to household air pollution and ambient air pollution (per 100,000 population)	2016	WHO (2020)	Mortality rate that is attributable to the joint effects of fuels used for cooking indoors and ambient outdoor air pollution.
3		Traffic deaths (per 100,000 population)	2016	WHO (2020)	Estimated number of fatal road traffic injuries per 100,000 people.
3		Life expectancy at birth (years)	2016	WHO (2020)	The average number of years that a newborn could expect to live, if he or she were to pass through life exposed to the sex- and age-specific death rates prevailing at the time of his or her birth, for a specific year, in a given country, territory, or geographic area.
3		Adolescent fertility rate (births per 1,000 adolescent females aged 15 to 19)	2017	UNDESA (2020)	The number of births per 1,000 women between the age of 15 to 19.
3		Births attended by skilled health personnel (%)	2016	UNICEF (2020)	The percentage of births attended by personnel trained to give the necessary supervision, care, and advice to women during pregnancy, labor, and the postpartum period, to conduct deliveries on their own, and to care for newborns.
3		Percentage of surviving infants who received 2 WHO-recommended vaccines (%)	2018	WHO and UNICEF (2020)	Estimated national routine immunization coverage of infants, expressed as the percentage of surviving infants children under the age of 12 months who received two WHO-recommended vaccines (3rd dose of DTP and 1st dose of measles). Calculated as the minimum value between the percentage of infants who have received the 3rd dose of DTP and the percentage who have received the 1st dose of measles.
3		Universal health coverage (UHC) index of service coverage (worst 0–100 best)	2017	WHO (2019)	Coverage of essential health services (defined as the average coverage of essential services based on tracer interventions that include reproductive, maternal, newborn and child health, infectious diseases, non-communicable diseases and service capacity and access, among the general and the most disadvantaged population). The indicator is an index reported on a unitless scale of 0 to 100, which is computed as the geometric mean of 14 tracer indicators of health service coverage.
3		Subjective well-being (average ladder score, worst 0–10 best)	2019	Gallup (2020)	Subjective self-evaluation of life, where respondents are asked to evaluate where they feel they stand on a ladder where 0 represents the worst possible life and 10 the best possible life.
3	[a]	Gap in life expectancy at birth among regions (years)	2016	OECD (2020)	Difference between maximum and minimum regional life expectancy at birth among regions.

4. Methods Summary and Data Tables

Table 9

(continued)

SDG	Notes	Indicator	Reference Year	Source	Description
3	[a]	Gap in self-reported health status by income (percentage points)	2018	OECD (2020)	Gap in percentage of people who perceive their health status as good or very good between the poorest 20% and the richest 20% of the population.
3	[a]	Daily smokers (% of population aged 15 and over)	2018	OECD (2020)	The percentage of the population aged 15 years and older who are reported to smoke daily.
4		Net primary enrollment rate (%)	2018	UNESCO (2020)	The percentage of children of the official school age population who are enrolled in primary education.
4		Lower secondary completion rate (%)	2018	UNESCO (2020)	Lower secondary education completion rate measured as the gross intake ratio to the last grade of lower secondary education (general and pre-vocational). It is calculated as the number of new entrants in the last grade of lower secondary education, regardless of age, divided by the population at the entrance age for the last grade of lower secondary education.
4		Literacy rate (% of population aged 15 to 24)	2018	UNESCO (2020)	The percentage of youth, aged 15 to 24, who can both read and write a short simple statement on everyday life with understanding.
4	[a]	Participation rate in pre-primary organized learning (% of children aged 4 to 6)	2018	UNESCO (2020)	Participation rate in organized learning one year before the official primary entry age.
4	[a]	Tertiary educational attainment (% of population aged 25 to 34)	2018	OECD (2020)	The percentage of the population, aged 25 to 34, who have completed tertiary education.
4	[a]	PISA score (worst 0–600 best)	2018	OECD (2018)	National scores in the Programme for International Student Assessment (PISA), an internationally standardized assessment that is administered to 15-year-olds in schools. It assesses how far students near the end of compulsory education have acquired some of the knowledge and skills that are essential for full participation in society. Country PISA scores for reading, mathematics, and science were averaged to obtain an overall PISA score.
4	[a]	Variation in science performance explained by socio-economic status (%)	2018	OECD (2018)	Percentage of variation in science performance explained by students' socio-economic status.
4	[a]	Underachievers in science (% of 15-year-olds)	2018	OECD (2018)	Percentage of students with a performance in science below level 2 (less than 409.54 score points).
4	[a]	Resilient students in science (% of 15-year-olds)	2018	OECD (2018)	Percentage of students who are in the bottom quarter of the PISA index of economic, social and cultural status (ESCS) in the country/economy of assessment and are in the top quarter of science performers among all countries/economies, after accounting for socio-economic status.
5		Demand for family planning satisfied by modern methods (% of females aged 15 to 49 who are married or in unions)	2018	UNDESA (2020)	The percentage of women of reproductive age, either married or in a union, whose demand for family planning has been met using modern methods of contraception.
5		Ratio of female-to-male mean years of education received (%)	2018	UNESCO (2020)	The mean years of education received by women aged 25 and older divided by the mean years of education received by men aged 25 and older.
5		Ratio of female-to-male labor force participation rate (%)	2019	ILO (2020)	Modeled estimate of the proportion of the female population aged 15 years and older that is economically active, divided by the same proportion for men.
5		Seats held by women in national parliament (%)	2020	IPU (2020)	The number of seats held by women in single or lower chambers of national parliaments, expressed as a percentage of all occupied seats. Seats refer to the number of parliamentary mandates, or the number of members of parliament.
5	[a]	Gender wage gap (% of male median wage)	2018	OECD (2020)	The difference between male and female median wages of full-time employees and those self-employed, divided by the male median wage.
5	[a]	Gender gap in time spent doing unpaid work (minutes/day)	2015	OECD (2020)	The difference in time spent in unpaid work between men and women in minutes per day. Unpaid work includes work, such as childcare, meal preparation, and cleaning.

Table 9

(continued)

SDG	Notes	Indicator	Reference Year	Source	Description
6		Population using at least basic drinking water services (%)	2017	JMP (2020)	The percentage of the population using at least a basic drinking water service, such as drinking water from an improved source, provided that the collection time is not more than 30 minutes for a round trip, including queuing.
6		Population using at least basic sanitation services (%)	2017	JMP (2020)	The percentage of the population using at least a basic sanitation service, such as an improved sanitation facility that is not shared with other households.
6		Freshwater withdrawal (% of available freshwater resources)	2015	FAO (2020)	The level of water stress: freshwater withdrawal as a proportion of available freshwater resources is the ratio between total freshwater withdrawn by all major sectors and total renewable freshwater resources, after taking into account environmental water requirements. Main sectors, as defined by ISIC standards, include agriculture, forestry and fishing, manufacturing, electricity industry, and services. This indicator is also known as water withdrawal intensity.
6		Anthropogenic wastewater that receives treatment (%)	2018	EPI (2018)	The percentage of collected, generated, or produced wastewater that is treated, normalized by the population connected to centralized wastewater treatment facilities. Scores were calculated by multiplying the wastewater treatment summary values, based on decadal averages, with the sewerage connection values to arrive at an overall total percentage of wastewater treated.
6		Scarce water consumption embodied in imports (m^3/capita)	2013	Lenzen et al. (2013)	Water scarcity is measured as water consumption weighted by scarcity indices. In order to incorporate water scarcity into the virtual water flow calculus, a new satellite account was constructed where water use entries are weighted so that they reflect the scarcity of the water being used. The weight used is a measure of water withdrawals as a percentage of the existing local renewable freshwater resources. The Water Scarcity Index was used for converting total water use into scarce water use.
6	[a]	Population using safely managed water services (%)	2017	JMP (2020)	The percentage of the population using a safely managed drinking water service. A safely managed drinking water service is one where people use an "improved" source meeting three criteria: it is accessible on premises, water is available when needed, and the water supplied is free from contamination. Improved sources are those that have the potential to deliver safe water by nature of their design and construction.
6	[a]	Population using safely managed sanitation services (%)	2017	JMP (2020)	The percentage of the population using safely managed sanitation services. Safely managed sanitation services are "improved" sanitation facilities that are not shared with other households, and where the excreta produced should either be treated and disposed of in situ, stored temporarily and then emptied, transported and treated off-site, or transported through a sewer with wastewater and then treated off-site. Improved sanitation facilities are those designed to hygienically separate excreta from human contact.
7		Population with access to electricity (%)	2017	SE4All (2020)	The percentage of the population who has access to electricity.
7		Population with access to clean fuels and technology for cooking (%)	2016	SE4All (2020)	The percentage of the population primarily using clean cooking fuels and technologies for cooking. Under WHO guidelines, kerosene is excluded from clean cooking fuels.
7		CO_2 emissions from fuel combustion for electricity and heating per total electricity output ($MtCO_2$/TWh)	2017	IEA (2019)	A measure of the carbon intensity of energy production, calculated by dividing CO_2 emissions from the combustion of fuel by electricity output.
7	[a]	Share of renewable energy in total primary energy supply (%)	2018	OECD (2020)	The share of renewable energy in the total primary energy supply. Renewables include the primary energy equivalent of hydro (excluding pumped storage), geothermal, solar, wind, tide and wave sources. Energy derived from solid biofuels, biogasoline, biodiesels, other liquid biofuels, biogases and the renewable fraction of municipal waste are also included.
8		Adjusted GDP growth (%)	2018	World Bank (2020)	The growth rate of GDP adjusted to income levels (where rich countries are expected to grow less) and expressed relative to the US growth performance. GDP is the sum of gross value added by all resident producers in the economy, plus any product taxes and minus any subsidies not included in the value of the products.

4. Methods Summary and Data Tables

Table 9

(continued)

SDG	Notes	Indicator	Reference Year	Source	Description
8		Victims of modern slavery (per 1,000 population)	2018	Walk Free Foundation (2018)	Estimation of the number of people in modern slavery. Modern slavery is defined as people in forced labor or forced marriage. It is calculated based on standardized surveys and Multiple Systems Estimation (MSE).
8		Adults with an account at a bank or other financial institution or with a mobile-money-service provider (% of population aged 15 or over)	2017	Demirguc-Kunt et al. (2018)	The percentage of adults, 15 years and older, who report having an account (by themselves or with someone else) at a bank or another type of financial institution, or who have personally used a mobile money service within the past 12 months.
8	[b]	Unemployment rate (% of total labor force)	2019	ILO (2020)	Modeled estimate of the share of the labor force that is without work but is available and actively seeking employment. The indicator reflects the inability of an economy to generate employment for people who want to work but are not doing so.
8		Fatal work-related accidents embodied in imports (per 100,000 population)	2010	Alsamawi et al. (2017)	The number of fatal work-related accidents associated with imported goods. Calculated using extensions to a multiregional input-output table.
8	[a]	Employment-to-population ratio (%)	2019	OECD (2020)	The ratio of the employed to the working age population. Employed people are those aged 15 or older who were in paid employment or self-employed during a specified period. The working age population refers to people aged 15 to 64.
8	[a]	Youth not in employment, education or training (NEET) (% of population aged 15 to 29)	2018	OECD (2020)	The percentage of young people who are not in employment, education or training (NEET). Education includes part-time or full-time education, but exclude those in non-formal education and in educational activities of very short duration. Employment is defined according to the ILO Guidelines and covers all those who have been in paid work for at least one hour in the reference week or were temporarily absent from such work.
9		Population using the internet (%)	2018	ITU (2020)	The percentage of the population who used the Internet from any location in the last three months. Access could be via a fixed or mobile network.
9		Mobile broadband subscriptions (per 100 population)	2018	ITU (2020)	The number of mobile broadband subscriptions per 100 population. Mobile broadband subscriptions refer to subscriptions to mobile cellular networks with access to data communications (e.g. the Internet) at broadband speeds, irrespective of the device used to access the internet.
9		Logistics Performance Index: Quality of trade and transport-related infrastructure (worst 1–5 best)	2018	World Bank (2018)	Survey-based average assessment of the quality of trade and transport related infrastructure, e.g. ports, roads, railroads and information technology, on a scale from 1 (worst) to 5 (best).
9		The Times Higher Education Universities Ranking: Average score of top 3 universities (worst 0–100 best)	2020	Times Higher Education (2020)	The average score of the top three universities in each country that are listed in the global top 1,000 universities in the world. For countries with at least one university on the list, only the score of the ranked university was taken into account. When a university score was missing in the Times Higher Education World University Ranking, an indicator from the Global Innovation Index on the top 3 universities in Quacquarelli Symonds (QS) University Ranking was used as a source when available.
9		Scientific and technical journal articles (per 1,000 population)	2018	National Science Foundation (2020)	The number of scientific and technical journal articles published, that are covered by the Science Citation Index (SCI) or the Social Sciences Citation Index (SSCI). Articles are counted and assigned to a country based on the institutional address(es) listed in the article.
9		Expenditure on research and development (% of GDP)	2017	UNESCO (2020)	Gross domestic expenditure on scientific research and experimental development (R&D) expressed as a percentage of Gross Domestic Product (GDP). We assumed zero R&D expenditure for low-income countries that do not report any data.
9	[a]	Researchers (per 1,000 employed population)	2018	OECD (2020)	The number of researchers per thousand employed people. Researchers are professionals engaged in the conception or creation of new knowledge, products, processes, methods and systems, as well as in the management of the projects concerned

Table 9

(continued)

SDG	Notes	Indicator	Reference Year	Source	Description
9	[a]	Triadic patent families filed (per million population)	2017	OECD (2020)	A triadic patent family is defined as a set of patents registered in various countries (i.e. patent offices) to protect the same invention. Triadic patent families are a set of patents filed at three of these major patent offices: the European Patent Office (EPO), the Japan Patent Office (JPO) and the United States Patent and Trademark Office (USPTO). The number of triadic patent families is "nowcast" for timeliness.
9	[a]	Gap in internet access by income (percentage points)	2019	OECD (2020)	The difference in the percentage of household Internet access between the top and bottom income quartiles.
9	[a]	Women in science and engineering (% of tertiary graduates in science and engineering)	2015	OECD (2020)	Percentage of women tertiary graduates in natural sciences and engineering out of total tertiary graduates in natural sciences and engineering.
10		Gini coefficient adjusted for top income	2017	Chandy and Seidel (2017)	The Gini coefficient adjusted for top revenues unaccounted for in household surveys. This indicator takes the average of the unadjusted Gini and the adjusted Gini.
10	[a]	Palma ratio	2017	OECD (2020)	The share of all income received by the 10% people with highest disposable income divided by the share of all income received by the 40% people with the lowest disposable income.
10	[a]	Elderly poverty rate (% of population aged 66 or over)	2017	OECD (2020)	The percentage of people of 66 years of age or more whose income falls below half the median household income of the total population.
11		Annual mean concentration of particulate matter of less than 2.5 microns in diameter (PM2.5) ($\mu g/m^3$)	2017	IHME (2017)	Air pollution measured as the population-weighted mean annual concentration of PM2.5 for the urban population in a country. PM2.5 is suspended particles measuring less than 2.5 microns in aerodynamic diameter, which are capable of penetrating deep into the respiratory tract and can cause severe health damage.
11		Access to improved water source, piped (% of urban population)	2017	WHO and UNICEF (2020)	The percentage of the urban population with access to improved drinking water piped on premises. An "improved" drinking-water source is one that, by the nature of its construction and when properly used, adequately protects the source from outside contamination, particularly fecal matter.
11		Satisfaction with public transport (%)	2019	Gallup (2020)	The percentage of the surveyed population that responded "satisfied" to the question "In the city or area where you live, are you satisfied or dissatisfied with the public transportation systems?".
11	[a]	Population with rent overburden (%)	2017	OECD (2011)	Percentage of the population living in households where the total housing costs represent more than 40 % of disposable income.
12	[b]	Municipal solid waste (kg/capita/day)	2016	World Bank (2018)	The amount of waste collected by or on behalf of municipal authorities and disposed of through the waste management system. Waste from agriculture and from industries are not included.
12		Electronic waste (kg/capita)	2016	UNU-IAS (2017)	Waste from electrical and electronic equipment, estimated based on figures for domestic production, imports and exports of electronic products, as well as product lifespan data.
12		Production-based SO_2 emissions (kg/capita)	2012	Lenzen et al. (2020)	SO_2 emissions associated with the production of goods and services, which are then either exported or consumed domestically.
12		SO_2 emissions embodied in imports (kg/capita)	2012	Lenzen et al. (2020)	Emissions of SO_2 embodied in imported goods and services. SO_2 emissions have severe health impacts and are a significant cause of premature mortality worldwide.
12		Production-based nitrogen emissions (kg/capita)	2010	Oita et al. (2016)	Reactive nitrogen emitted during the production of commodities, which are then either exported or consumed domestically. Reactive nitrogen corresponds to emissions of ammonia, nitrogen oxides and nitrous oxide to the atmosphere, and of reactive nitrogen potentially exportable to water bodies, all of which can be harmful to human health and the environment.
12		Nitrogen emissions embodied in imports (kg/capita)	2010	Oita et al. (2016)	Emissions of reactive nitrogen embodied in imported goods and services. Reactive nitrogen corresponds here to emissions of ammonia, nitrogen oxides and nitrous oxide to the atmosphere, and of reactive nitrogen potentially exportable to water bodies, all of which can be harmful to human health and the environment.
12	[a]	Non-recycled municipal solid waste (kg/capita/day)	2018	OECD (2020)	The amount of municipal solid waste (MSW), including household waste, that is neither recycled nor composted.

Table 9

(continued)

SDG	Notes	Indicator	Reference Year	Source	Description
13		Energy-related CO_2 emissions (tCO_2/capita)	2017	Gütschow et al. (2019)	Emissions of CO_2 that arise from the consumption of energy. This includes emissions due to the consumption of petroleum, natural gas, coal, and also from natural gas flaring.
13		CO_2 emissions embodied in imports (tCO_2/capita)	2015	Lenzen et al. (2020)	CO_2 emissions embodied in imported goods and services.
13		CO_2 emissions embodied in fossil fuel exports (kg/capita)	2019	UN Comtrade (2020); EIA (2020)	CO_2 emissions embodied in the exports of coal, gas, and oil. Calculated using a 5-year average of fossil fuel exports and converting exports into their equivalent CO_2 emissions. Exports for each fossil fuel are capped at the country's level of production.
13	[a]	Effective carbon rate (EUR/tCO_2)	2016	OECD (2016)	The price of carbon emissions resulting from taxes and emissions trading systems, excluding CO_2 emissions from biomass.
14		Mean area that is protected in marine sites important to biodiversity (%)	2018	Birdlife International et al. (2020)	The mean percentage area of marine Key Biodiversity Areas (sites that are important for the global persistence of marine biodiversity) that are protected.
14		Ocean Health Index: Clean Waters score (worst 0–100 best)	2019	Ocean Health Index (2019)	The clean waters subgoal of the Ocean Health Index measures to what degree marine waters under national jurisdictions have been contaminated by chemicals, excessive nutrients (eutrophication), human pathogens, and trash.
14		Fish caught from overexploited or collapsed stocks (% of total catch)	2014	Sea around Us (2018); EPI (2018)	The percentage of a country's total catch, within its exclusive economic zone (EEZ), that is comprised of species that are overexploited or collapsed, weighted by the quality of fish catch data.
14		Fish caught by trawling (%)	2014	Sea Around Us (2018)	The percentage of fish caught by trawling, a method of fishing in which industrial fishing vessels drag large nets (trawls) along the seabed.
14		Marine biodiversity threats embodied in imports (per million population)	2018	Lenzen et al. (2020)	Threats to marine species embodied in imports of goods and services.
15		Mean area that is protected in terrestrial sites important to biodiversity (%)	2018	Birdlife International et al. (2020)	The mean percentage area of terrestrial Key Biodiversity Areas (sites that are important for the global persistence of biodiversity) that are protected.
15		Mean area that is protected in freshwater sites important to biodiversity (%)	2018	Birdlife International et al. (2020)	The mean percentage area of freshwater Key Biodiversity Areas (sites that are important for the global persistence of biodiversity) that are protected.
15		Red List Index of species survival (worst 0–1 best)	2019	IUCN and Birdlife International (2020)	The change in aggregate extinction risk across groups of species. The index is based on genuine changes in the number of species in each category of extinction risk on The IUCN Red List of Threatened Species.
15		Permanent deforestation (% of forest area, 5-year average)	2018	Curtis et al. (2018)	The mean annual percentage of permanent deforestation over the period 2014 to 2018. Permanent deforestation refers to tree cover removal for urbanization, commodity production and certain types of small-scale agriculture. It does not include temporary forest loss due to the forestry sector or wildfires.
15		Terrestrial and freshwater biodiversity threats embodied in imports (per million population)	2018	Lenzen et al. (2020)	Threats to terrestrial and freshwater species embodied in imports of goods and services.
16		Homicides (per 100,000 population)	2017	UNODC (2020)	The number of intentional homicides per 100,000 people. Intentional homicides are estimates of unlawful homicides purposely inflicted as a result of domestic disputes, interpersonal violence, violent conflicts over land resources, intergang violence over turf or control, and predatory violence and killing by armed groups. Intentional homicide does not include all intentional killing, such as killing in armed conflict.
16		Unsentenced detainees (% of prison population)	2018	UNODC (2020)	Unsentenced prisoners as a percentage of overall prison population. Persons held unsentenced or pre-trial refers to persons held in prisons, penal institutions or correctional institutions who are untried, pre-trial or awaiting a first instance decision on their case from a competent authority regarding their conviction or acquittal.

Table 9

(continued)

SDG	Notes	Indicator	Reference Year	Source	Description
16		Percentage of population who feel safe walking alone at night in the city or area where they live (%)	2019	Gallup (2020)	The percentage of the surveyed population that responded "Yes" to the question "Do you feel safe walking alone at night in the city or area where you live?"
16		Property Rights (worst 1–7 best)	2019	World Economic Forum (2019)	Survey-based assessment of protection of property rights, on a scale from 1 (worst) to 7 (best). The indicator reports respondents' qualitative assessment based on answers to several questions on the protection of property rights and intellectual property rights protection.
16		Birth registrations with civil authority (% of children under age 5)	2018	UNICEF (2020)	The percentage of children under the age of five whose births are reported as being registered with the relevant national civil authorities.
16		Corruption Perception Index (worst 0–100 best)	2019	Transparency International (2020)	The perceived levels of public sector corruption, on a scale from 0 (highest level of perceived corruption) to 100 (lowest level of perceived corruption). The CPI aggregates data from a number of different sources that provide perceptions of business people and country experts.
16		Children involved in child labor (% of population aged 5 to 14)	2016	UNICEF (2017)	The percentage of children, between the age of 5-14 years old, involved in child labor at the time of the survey. A child is considered to be involved in child labor under the following conditions: (a) children 5-11 years old who, during the reference week, did at least one hour of economic activity or at least 28 hours of household chores, or (b) children 12-14 years old who, during the reference week, did at least 14 hours of economic activity or at least 28 hours of household chores. We assumed 0% child labor for high-income countries for which no data was reported.
16		Exports of major conventional weapons (TIV constant million USD per 100,000 population)	2019	Stockholm Peace Research Institute (2020)	Volume of major conventional weapons exported, expressed in constant 1990 US$ millions per 100,000 population. It is calculated based on the trend-indicator value, which is based on the known unit production cost of a core set of weapons, and does not reflect the financial value of the exports. Small arms, light weapons, ammunition and other support material are not included.
16		Press Freedom Index (best 0–100 worst)	2019	Reporters sans frontières (2019)	Degree of freedom available to journalists in 180 countries and regions, determined by pooling the responses of experts to a questionnaire devised by RSF.
16	[a]	Persons held in prison (per 100,000 population)	2017	UNODC (2020)	The prison population is composed of persons held in prisons, penal institutions, or correctional institutions.
17		Government spending on health and education (% of GDP)	2016	UNESCO (2020); WHO (2020)	The sum of public expenditure on health from domestic sources and general government expenditure on education (current, capital, and transfers) expressed as a percentage of GDP.
17		For high-income and all OECD DAC countries: International concessional public finance, including official development assistance (% of GNI)	2017	OECD (2020)	The amount of official development assistance (ODA) as a share of gross national income (GNI). It includes grants, "soft" loans (where the grant element is at least 25% of the total) and the provision of technical assistance, and excludes grants and loans for military purposes.
17		Other countries: Government revenue excluding grants (% of GDP)	2018	IMF (2020)	Government revenue measured as cash receipts from taxes, social contributions, and other revenues such as fines, fees, rent, and income from property or sales. Grants are also considered as revenue but are excluded here.
17		Corporate Tax Haven Score (best 0–100 worst)	2019	Tax Justice Network (2019)	The Corporate Tax Haven Score measures a jurisdiction's potential to poach the tax base of others, as enshrined in its laws, regulations and documented administrative practices. For countries with multiple jurisdictions, the value of the worst-performing jurisdiction was retained.
17	[a]	Financial Secrecy Score (best 0–100 worst)	2020	Tax Justice Network (2020)	The Index measures the contribution of each jurisdiction to financial secrecy, on a scale from 0 (best) to 100 (worst). It is calculated using qualitative data to prepare a secrecy score for each jurisdiction and quantitative data to create a global scale weighting for each jurisdiction according to its share of offshore financial services activity in the global total. For countries with multiple jurisdictions, the average score of the jurisdictions was used.
17	[a]	Shifted profits of multinationals (US$ billion)	2016	Zucman et al. (2019)	Estimation of how much profit is shifted into tax havens and how much non-haven countries lose in profits from such shifting. Based on macroeconomic data known as foreign affiliates statistics. Negative values indicate profit shifting.

Table 10

Countries not included in the 2020 SDG Index due to insufficient data availability

Country	Missing Values	Percentage of Missing Values
Andorra	37	46%
Antigua and Barbuda	24	29%
The Bahamas	20	24%
Dominica	39	46%
Eritrea	17	20%
Micronesia, Fed. Sts.	39	46%
Guinea-Bissau	17	20%
Equatorial Guinea	27	32%
Grenada	34	41%
Kiribati	37	44%
St. Kitts and Nevis	44	52%
Libya	18	21%
St. Lucia	25	30%
Liechtenstein	47	59%
Monaco	45	54%
Marshall Islands	45	54%
Nauru	49	58%
Palau	48	57%
Korea, Dem. Rep.	20	24%
Solomon Islands	24	29%
San Marino	45	54%
Seychelles	23	27%
Timor-Leste	21	25%
Tonga	28	33%
Tuvalu	47	56%
St. Vincent and the Grenadines	30	36%
Samoa	18	21%

Table 11

Indicator thresholds and justifications for the optimum values

SDG	Indicator	Optimum (value = 100)	Green	Yellow	Orange	Red	Lower Bound	Justification for Optimum
1	Poverty headcount ratio at $1.90/day (%)	0	≤2	2 < x ≤ 7.5	7.5 < x ≤ 13	>13	72.6	SDG Target
1	Poverty headcount ratio at $3.20/day (%)	0	≤2	2 < x ≤ 7.5	7.5 < x ≤ 13	>13	51.5	SDG Target
1	Poverty rate after taxes and transfers (%)	6.1	≤10	10 < x ≤ 12.5	12.5 < x ≤ 15	>15	17.7	Average of 3 best OECD performers
2	Prevalence of undernourishment (%)	0	≤7.5	7.5 < x ≤ 11.25	11.25 < x ≤ 15	>15	42.3	SDG Target
2	Prevalence of stunting in children under 5 years of age (%)	0	≤7.5	7.5 < x ≤ 11.25	11.25 < x ≤ 15	>15	50.2	SDG Target
2	Prevalence of wasting in children under 5 years of age (%)	0	≤5	5 < x ≤ 7.5	7.5 < x ≤ 10	>10	16.3	SDG Target
2	Prevalence of obesity, BMI ≥ 30 (% of adult population)	2.8	≤10	10 < x ≤ 17.5	17.5 < x ≤ 25	>25	35.1	Average of 5 best performers
2	Human Trophic Level (best 2–3 worst)	2.04	≤2.2	2.2 < x ≤ 2.3	2.3 < x ≤ 2.4	>2.4	2.47	Average of 5 best performers
2	Cereal yield (tonnes per hectare of harvested land)	7	≥2.5	2.5 > x ≥ 2	2 > x ≥ 1.5	>1.5	0.2	Average of 5 best performers minus outliers (1 & 1/2SD)
2	Sustainable Nitrogen Management Index (best 0–1.41 worst)	0	≤0.3	0.3 < x ≤ 0.5	0.5 < x ≤ 0.7	>0.7	1.2	Technical Optimum
2	Yield gap closure (% of potential yield)	77	≥75	75 > x ≥ 62.5	62.5 > x ≥ 50	>50	28	Average of 5 best performers
3	Maternal mortality rate (per 100,000 live births)	3.4	≤70	70 < x ≤ 105	105 < x ≤ 140	>140	814	Average of 5 best performers
3	Neonatal mortality rate (per 1,000 live births)	1.1	≤12	12 < x ≤ 15	15 < x ≤ 18	>18	39.7	Average of 5 best performers
3	Mortality rate, under-5 (per 1,000 live births)	2.6	≤25	25 < x ≤ 37.5	37.5 < x ≤ 50	>50	130.1	Average of 5 best performers
3	Incidence of tuberculosis (per 100,000 population)	0	≤10	10 < x ≤ 42.5	42.5 < x ≤ 75	>75	561	SDG Target
3	New HIV infections (per 1,000 uninfected population)	0	≤0.2	0.2 < x ≤ 0.6	0.6 < x ≤ 1	>1	5.5	SDG Target
3	Age-standardized death rate due to cardiovascular disease, cancer, diabetes, or chronic respiratory disease in adults aged 30–70 years (%)	9.3	≤15	15 < x ≤ 20	20 < x ≤ 25	>25	31	Average of 5 best performers
3	Age-standardized death rate attributable to household air pollution and ambient air pollution (per 100,000 population)	0	≤18	18 < x ≤ 84	84 < x ≤ 150	>150	368.8	SDG Target
3	Traffic deaths (per 100,000 population)	3.2	≤8.4	8.4 < x ≤ 12.6	12.6 < x ≤ 16.8	>16.8	33.7	Average of 5 best performers
3	Life expectancy at birth (years)	83	≥80	80 > x ≥ 75	75 > x ≥ 70	>70	54	Average of 5 best performers
3	Adolescent fertility rate (births per 1,000 adolescent females aged 15 to 19)	2.5	≤25	25 < x ≤ 37.5	37.5 < x ≤ 50	>50	139.6	Average of 5 best performers
3	Births attended by skilled health personnel (%)	100	≥98	98 > x ≥ 94	94 > x ≥ 90	>90	23.1	Leave no one behind
3	Percentage of surviving infants who received 2 WHO-recommended vaccines (%)	100	≥90	90 > x ≥ 85	85 > x ≥ 80	>80	41	Leave no one behind
3	Universal health coverage (UHC) index of service coverage (worst 0–100 best)	100	≥80	80 > x ≥ 70	70 > x ≥ 60	>60	38.2	Leave no one behind
3	Subjective well-being (average ladder score, worst 0–10 best)	7.6	≥6	6 > x ≥ 5.5	5.5 > x ≥ 5	>5	3.3	Average of 5 best performers
3	Gap in life expectancy at birth among regions (years)	0	≤3	3 < x ≤ 5	5 < x ≤ 7	>7	11	Leave no one behind

4. Methods Summary and Data Tables

Table 11

(continued)

SDG	Indicator	Optimum (value = 100)	Green	Yellow	Orange	Red	Lower Bound	Justification for Optimum
3	Gap in self-reported health status by income (percentage points)	0	≤20	20 < x ≤ 30	30 < x ≤ 40	>40	45	Leave no one behind
3	Daily smokers (% of population aged 15 and over)	10.1	≤18	18 < x ≤ 25	25 < x ≤ 32	>32	35	Average of 3 best OECD performers
4	Net primary enrollment rate (%)	100	≥97	97 > x ≥ 88.5	88.5 > x ≥ 80	>80	53.8	SDG Target
4	Lower secondary completion rate (%)	100	≥90	90 > x ≥ 82.5	82.5 > x ≥ 75	>75	18	SDG Target
4	Literacy rate (% of population aged 15 to 24)	100	≥95	95 > x ≥ 90	90 > x ≥ 85	>85	45.2	Leave no one behind
4	Participation rate in pre-primary organized learning (% of children aged 4 to 6)	100	≥90	90 > x ≥ 80	80 > x ≥ 70	>70	35	SDG Target
4	Tertiary educational attainment (% of population aged 25 to 34)	52.2	≥40	40 > x ≥ 25	25 > x ≥ 10	>10	0	Average of 3 best OECD performers
4	PISA score (worst 0–600 best)	525.6	≥493	493 > x ≥ 446.5	446.5 > x ≥ 400	>400	350	Average of 3 best OECD performers
4	Variation in science performance explained by socio-economic status (%)	8.3	≤10.5	10.5 < x ≤ 15.25	15.25 < x ≤ 20	>20	21.4	Average of 3 best OECD performers
4	Underachievers in science (% of 15-year-olds)	10	≤15	15 < x ≤ 22.5	22.5 < x ≤ 30	>30	48	Average of 3 best OECD performers
4	Resilient students in science (% of 15-year-olds)	46.6	≥38	38 > x ≥ 29	29 > x ≥ 20	>20	12.8	Average of 3 best OECD performers
5	Demand for family planning satisfied by modern methods (% of females aged 15 to 49 who are married or in unions)	100	≥80	80 > x ≥ 70	70 > x ≥ 60	>60	17.5	Leave no one behind
5	Ratio of female-to-male mean years of education received (%)	100	≥98	98 > x ≥ 86.5	86.5 > x ≥ 75	>75	41.8	SDG Target
5	Ratio of female-to-male labor force participation rate (%)	100	≥70	70 > x ≥ 60	60 > x ≥ 50	>50	21.5	SDG Target
5	Seats held by women in national parliament (%)	50	≥40	40 > x ≥ 30	30 > x ≥ 20	>20	1.2	SDG Target
5	Gender wage gap (% of male median wage)	0	≤8	8 < x ≤ 14	14 < x ≤ 20	>20	36.7	Technical Optimum
5	Gender gap in time spent doing unpaid work (minutes/day)	0	≤90	90 < x ≤ 135	135 < x ≤ 180	>180	245	Technical Optimum
6	Population using at least basic drinking water services (%)	100	≥98	98 > x ≥ 89	89 > x ≥ 80	>80	40	Leave no one behind
6	Population using at least basic sanitation services (%)	100	≥95	95 > x ≥ 85	85 > x ≥ 75	>75	9.7	Leave no one behind
6	Freshwater withdrawal (% of available freshwater resources)	12.5	≤25	25 < x ≤ 50	50 < x ≤ 75	>75	100	Technical Optimum
6	Anthropogenic wastewater that receives treatment (%)	100	≥50	50 > x ≥ 32.5	32.5 > x ≥ 15	>15	0	Technical Optimum
6	Scarce water consumption embodied in imports (m³/capita)	0	≤25	25 < x ≤ 37.5	37.5 < x ≤ 50	>50	100	Average of 5 best performers
6	Population using safely managed water services (%)	100	≥95	95 > x ≥ 87.5	87.5 > x ≥ 80	>80	10.5	Leave no one behind
6	Population using safely managed sanitation services (%)	100	≥90	90 > x ≥ 77.5	77.5 > x ≥ 65	>65	14.1	Leave no one behind
7	Population with access to electricity (%)	100	≥98	98 > x ≥ 89	89 > x ≥ 80	>80	9.1	Leave no one behind
7	Population with access to clean fuels and technology for cooking (%)	100	≥85	85 > x ≥ 67.5	67.5 > x ≥ 50	>50	2	Average of 3 best OECD performers
7	CO_2 emissions from fuel combustion for electricity and heating per total electricity output ($MtCO_2$/TWh)	0	≤1	1 < x ≤ 1.25	1.25 < x ≤ 1.5	>1.5	5.9	Technical Optimum
7	Share of renewable energy in total primary energy supply (%)	51	≥20	20 > x ≥ 15	15 > x ≥ 10	>10	3	Average of 3 best OECD performers

Table 11

(continued)

SDG	Indicator	Optimum (value = 100)	Green	Yellow	Orange	Red	Lower Bound	Justification for Optimum
8	Adjusted GDP growth (%)	5	≥0	0 > x ≥ -1.5	-1.5 > x ≥ -3	>-3	-14.7	Average of 5 best performers
8	Victims of modern slavery (per 1,000 population)	0	≤4	4 < x ≤ 7	7 < x ≤ 10	>10	22	Leave no one behind
8	Adults with an account at a bank or other financial institution or with a mobile-money-service provider (% of population aged 15 or over)	100	≥80	80 > x ≥ 65	65 > x ≥ 50	>50	8	Technical Optimum
8	Unemployment rate (% of total labor force)	0.5	≤5	5 < x ≤ 7.5	7.5 < x ≤ 10	>10	25.9	Average of 5 best performers
8	Fatal work-related accidents embodied in imports (per 100,000 population)	0	≤1	1 < x ≤ 1.75	1.75 < x ≤ 2.5	>2.5	6	Technical Optimum
8	Employment-to-population ratio (%)	77.8	≥60	60 > x ≥ 55	55 > x ≥ 50	>50	50	Average of 3 best OECD performers
8	Youth not in employment, education or training (NEET) (% of population aged 15 to 29)	8.1	≤10	10 < x ≤ 12.5	12.5 < x ≤ 15	>15	28.2	Average of 3 best OECD performers
9	Population using the internet (%)	100	≥80	80 > x ≥ 65	65 > x ≥ 50	>50	2.2	Leave no one behind
9	Mobile broadband subscriptions (per 100 population)	100	≥75	75 > x ≥ 57.5	57.5 > x ≥ 40	>40	1.4	Leave no one behind
9	Logistics Performance Index: Quality of trade and transport-related infrastructure (worst 1–5 best)	3.8	≥3	3 > x ≥ 2.5	2.5 > x ≥ 2	>2	1.6	Average of 5 best performers
9	The Times Higher Education Universities Ranking: Average score of top 3 universities (worst 0–100 best)	50	≥30	30 > x ≥ 15	15 > x ≥ 0	>0	0	Average of 5 best performers
9	Scientific and technical journal articles (per 1,000 population)	1.2	≥0.7	0.7 > x ≥ 0.375	0.375 > x ≥ 0.05	>0.05	0	Average of 5 best performers
9	Expenditure on research and development (% of GDP)	3.7	≥1.5	1.5 > x ≥ 1.25	1.25 > x ≥ 1	>1	0	Average of 5 best performers
9	Researchers (per 1,000 employed population)	15.6	≥8	8 > x ≥ 7.5	7.5 > x ≥ 7	>7	0.8	Average of 3 best OECD performers
9	Triadic patent families filed (per million population)	115.7	≥20	20 > x ≥ 15	15 > x ≥ 10	>10	0.1	Average of 3 best OECD performers
9	Gap in internet access by income (percentage points)	0	≤7	7 < x ≤ 26	26 < x ≤ 45	>45	63.6	Leave no one behind
9	Women in science and engineering (% of tertiary graduates in science and engineering)	38.1	≥33	33 > x ≥ 29	29 > x ≥ 25	>25	16.2	Average of 3 best OECD performers
10	Gini coefficient adjusted for top income	27.5	≤30	30 < x ≤ 35	35 < x ≤ 40	>40	63	Average of 5 best performers
10	Palma ratio	0.9	≤1	1 < x ≤ 1.15	1.15 < x ≤ 1.3	>1.3	2.5	Average of 3 best OECD performers
10	Elderly poverty rate (% of population aged 66 or over)	3.2	≤5	5 < x ≤ 15	15 < x ≤ 25	>25	45.7	Average of 3 best OECD performers
11	Annual mean concentration of particulate matter of less than 2.5 microns in diameter (PM2.5) (µg/m³)	6.3	≤10	10 < x ≤ 17.5	17.5 < x ≤ 25	>25	87	Average of 5 best performers
11	Access to improved water source, piped (% of urban population)	100	≥98	98 > x ≥ 86.5	86.5 > x ≥ 75	>75	6.1	Leave no one behind
11	Satisfaction with public transport (%)	82.6	≥72	72 > x ≥ 57.5	57.5 > x ≥ 43	>43	21	Average of 5 best performers
11	Population with rent overburden (%)	4.6	≤7	7 < x ≤ 12	12 < x ≤ 17	>17	25.6	Average of 3 best OECD performers
12	Municipal solid waste (kg/capita/day)	0.1	≤1	1 < x ≤ 1.5	1.5 < x ≤ 2	>2	3.7	Average of 5 best performers

4. Methods Summary and Data Tables

Table 11

(continued)

SDG	Indicator	Optimum (value = 100)	Green	Yellow	Orange	Red	Lower Bound	Justification for Optimum
12	Electronic waste (kg/capita)	0.2	≤5	5 < x ≤ 7.5	7.5 < x ≤ 10	>10	23.5	Average of 5 best performers
12	Production-based SO_2 emissions (kg/capita)	0	≤30	30 < x ≤ 65	65 < x ≤ 100	>100	525	Average of 5 best performers
12	SO_2 emissions embodied in imports (kg/capita)	0	≤5	5 < x ≤ 7.5	7.5 < x ≤ 10	>10	30	Technical Optimum
12	Production-based nitrogen emissions (kg/capita)	2	≤20	20 < x ≤ 35	35 < x ≤ 50	>50	100	Average of 5 best performers
12	Nitrogen emissions embodied in imports (kg/capita)	0	≤5	5 < x ≤ 10	10 < x ≤ 15	>15	45	Technical Optimum
12	Non-recycled municipal solid waste (kg/capita/day)	0.6	≤0.8	0.8 < x ≤ 0.9	0.9 < x ≤ 1	>1	1.5	Average of 3 best OECD performers
13	Energy-related CO_2 emissions (tCO_2/capita)	0	≤2	2 < x ≤ 3	3 < x ≤ 4	>4	23.7	Technical Optimum
13	CO_2 emissions embodied in imports (tCO_2/capita)	0	≤0.5	0.5 < x ≤ 0.75	0.75 < x ≤ 1	>1	3.2	Technical Optimum
13	CO_2 emissions embodied in fossil fuel exports (kg/capita)	0	≤100	100 < x ≤ 4050	4,050 < x ≤ 8,000	>8,000	44,000	Technical Optimum
13	Effective carbon rate (EUR/tCO_2)	100	≥70	70 > x ≥ 50	50 > x ≥ 30	>30	-0.1	Technical Optimum
14	Mean area that is protected in marine sites important to biodiversity (%)	100	≥50	50 > x ≥ 30	30 > x ≥ 10	>10	0	Technical Optimum
14	Ocean Health Index: Clean Waters score (worst 0–100 best)	100	≥70	70 > x ≥ 65	65 > x ≥ 60	>60	28.6	Technical Optimum
14	Fish caught from overexploited or collapsed stocks (% of total catch)	0	≤25	25 < x ≤ 37.5	37.5 < x ≤ 50	>50	90.7	Technical Optimum
14	Fish caught by trawling (%)	1	≤7	7 < x ≤ 33.5	33.5 < x ≤ 60	>60	90	Average of 5 best performers
14	Marine biodiversity threats embodied in imports (per million population)	0	≤0.2	0.2 < x ≤ 0.6	0.6 < x ≤ 1	>1	2	Technical Optimum
15	Mean area that is protected in terrestrial sites important to biodiversity (%)	100	≥50	50 > x ≥ 30	30 > x ≥ 10	>10	4.6	Technical Optimum
15	Mean area that is protected in freshwater sites important to biodiversity (%)	100	≥50	50 > x ≥ 30	30 > x ≥ 10	>10	0	Technical Optimum
15	Red List Index of species survival (worst 0–1 best)	1	≥0.9	0.9 > x ≥ 0.85	0.85 > x ≥ 0.8	>0.8	0.6	Technical Optimum
15	Permanent deforestation (% of forest area, 5-year average)	0	≤0.05	0.05 < x ≤ 0.275	0.275 < x ≤ 0.5	>0.5	1.5	SDG Target
15	Terrestrial and freshwater biodiversity threats embodied in imports (per million population)	0	≤1	1 < x ≤ 2	2 < x ≤ 3	>3	10	Technical Optimum
16	Homicides (per 100,000 population)	0.3	≤1.5	1.5 < x ≤ 2.75	2.75 < x ≤ 4	>4	38	Average of 5 best performers
16	Unsentenced detainees (% of prison population)	7	≤30	30 < x ≤ 40	40 < x ≤ 50	>50	75	Average of 5 best performers
16	Percentage of population who feel safe walking alone at night in the city or area where they live (%)	90	≥70	70 > x ≥ 60	60 > x ≥ 50	>50	33	Average of 5 best performers
16	Property Rights (worst 1–7 best)	6.3	≥4.5	4.5 > x ≥ 3.75	3.75 > x ≥ 3	>3	2.5	Average of 5 best performers
16	Birth registrations with civil authority (% of children under age 5)	100	≥98	98 > x ≥ 86.5	86.5 > x ≥ 75	>75	11	Leave no one behind
16	Corruption Perception Index (worst 0–100 best)	88.6	≥60	60 > x ≥ 50	50 > x ≥ 40	>40	13	Average of 5 best performers
16	Children involved in child labor (% of population aged 5 to 14)	0	≤2	2 < x ≤ 6	6 < x ≤ 10	>10	39.3	Leave no one behind
16	Exports of major conventional weapons (TIV constant million USD per 100,000 population)	0	≤1	1 < x ≤ 1.75	1.75 < x ≤ 2.5	>2.5	3.4	Technical Optimum
16	Press Freedom Index (best 0–100 worst)	10	≤30	30 < x ≤ 40	40 < x ≤ 50	>50	80	Average of 5 best performers

Table 11

(continued)

SDG	Indicator	Optimum (value = 100)	Green	Yellow	Orange	Red	Lower Bound	Justification for Optimum
16	Persons held in prison (per 100,000 population)	25	≤100	100 < x ≤ 175	175 < x ≤ 250	>250	475	Average of 5 best performers
17	Government spending on health and education (% of GDP)	15	≥10	10 > x ≥ 7.5	7.5 > x ≥ 5	>5	0	Average of 5 best performers
17	For high-income and all OECD DAC countries: International concessional public finance, including official development assistance (% of GNI)	1	≥0.7	0.7 > x ≥ 0.525	0.525 > x ≥ 0.35	>0.35	0.1	Average of 5 best performers
17	Other countries: Government revenue excluding grants (% of GDP)	40	≥30	30 > x ≥ 23	23 > x ≥ 16	>16	10	Average of 5 best performers
17	Corporate Tax Haven Score (best 0–100 worst)	40	≤60	60 < x ≤ 65	65 < x ≤ 70	>70	100	Average of best performers (EU Report)
17	Financial Secrecy Score (best 0–100 worst)	42.7	≤45	45 < x ≤ 50	50 < x ≤ 55	>55	76.5	Average of 5 best performers
17	Shifted profits of multinationals (US$ billion)	0	≥0	0 > x ≥ -15	-15 > x ≥ -30	>-30	-70	Technical Optimum

Table 12

Indicators used for SDG Trends and period for trend estimation

(* The trend estimations since the adoption of the SDGs are marked below)

SDG	Indicator	Period Covered
1	Poverty headcount ratio at $1.90/day (%)	2015–2019*
1	Poverty headcount ratio at $3.20/day (%)	2015–2019*
1	Poverty rate after taxes and transfers (%)	2013–2016
2	Prevalence of undernourishment (%)	2014–2017
2	Prevalence of stunting in children under 5 years of age (%)	2014–2017
2	Prevalence of wasting in children under 5 years of age (%)	2014–2017
2	Prevalence of obesity, BMI ≥ 30 (% of adult population)	2013–2016
2	Human Trophic Level (best 2–3 worst)	2014–2017
2	Cereal yield (tonnes per hectare of harvested land)	2014–2017
2	Sustainable Nitrogen Management Index (best 0–1.41 worst)	2012–2015
3	Maternal mortality rate (per 100,000 live births)	2014–2017
3	Neonatal mortality rate (per 1,000 live births)	2015–2018*
3	Mortality rate, under-5 (per 1,000 live births)	2015–2018*
3	Incidence of tuberculosis (per 100,000 population)	2015–2018*
3	New HIV infections (per 1,000 uninfected population)	2015–2018*
3	Age-standardized death rate due to cardiovascular disease, cancer, diabetes, or chronic respiratory disease in adults aged 30–70 years (%)	2010–2016
3	Traffic deaths (per 100,000 population)	2013–2016
3	Life expectancy at birth (years)	2013–2016
3	Adolescent fertility rate (births per 1,000 adolescent females aged 15 to 19)	2014–2017
3	Births attended by skilled health personnel (%)	2012–2016
3	Percentage of surviving infants who received 2 WHO-recommended vaccines (%)	2015–2018*
3	Universal health coverage (UHC) index of service coverage (worst 0–100 best)	2010–2017
3	Subjective well-being (average ladder score, worst 0–10 best)	2015–2019*
3	Gap in self-reported health status by income (percentage points)	2014–2017
3	Daily smokers (% of population aged 15 and over)	2014–2017
4	Net primary enrollment rate (%)	2014–2017
4	Lower secondary completion rate (%)	2015–2018*
4	Participation rate in pre-primary organized learning (% of children aged 4 to 6)	2014–2017
4	Tertiary educational attainment (% of population aged 25 to 34)	2015–2018*
4	PISA score (worst 0–600 best)	2015–2018*
4	Variation in science performance explained by socio-economic status (%)	2015–2018*
4	Underachievers in science (% of 15-year-olds)	2015–2018*
4	Resilient students in science (% of 15-year-olds)	2015–2018*
5	Ratio of female-to-male mean years of education received (%)	2015–2018*
5	Ratio of female-to-male labor force participation rate (%)	2015–2019*
5	Seats held by women in national parliament (%)	2015–2019*
5	Gender wage gap (% of male median wage)	2014–2017
6	Population using at least basic drinking water services (%)	2014–2017
6	Population using at least basic sanitation services (%)	2014–2017
6	Scarce water consumption embodied in imports (m³/capita)	2010–2013
6	Population using safely managed water services (%)	2014–2017
6	Population using safely managed sanitation services (%)	2014–2017

Table 12

(continued)

SDG	Indicator	Period Covered
7	Population with access to electricity (%)	2014–2017
7	Population with access to clean fuels and technology for cooking (%)	2013–2016
7	CO_2 emissions from fuel combustion for electricity and heating per total electricity output ($MtCO_2$/TWh)	2014–2017
7	Share of renewable energy in total primary energy supply (%)	2014–2017
8	Adults with an account at a bank or other financial institution or with a mobile-money-service provider (% of population aged 15 or over)	2014–2017
8	Unemployment rate (% of total labor force)	2015–2019*
8	Fatal work-related accidents embodied in imports (per 100,000 population)	2007–2010
8	Employment-to-population ratio (%)	2015–2019*
8	Youth not in employment, education or training (NEET) (% of population aged 15 to 29)	2015–2018*
9	Population using the internet (%)	2014–2017
9	Mobile broadband subscriptions (per 100 population)	2015–2018*
9	Logistics Performance Index: Quality of trade and transport-related infrastructure (worst 1–5 best)	2014–2018
9	Scientific and technical journal articles (per 1,000 population)	2015–2018*
9	Expenditure on research and development (% of GDP)	2014–2017
9	Researchers (per 1,000 employed population)	2014–2017
9	Triadic patent families filed (per million population)	2014–2017
9	Gap in internet access by income (percentage points)	2015–2018*
10	Gini coefficient adjusted for top income	2012–2015
10	Palma ratio	2013–2016
10	Elderly poverty rate (% of population aged 66 or over)	2013–2016
11	Annual mean concentration of particulate matter of less than 2.5 microns in diameter (PM2.5) ($\mu g/m^3$)	2014–2017
11	Access to improved water source, piped (% of urban population)	2014–2017
11	Satisfaction with public transport (%)	2015–2019*
11	Population with rent overburden (%)	2014–2017
13	Energy-related CO_2 emissions (tCO_2/capita)	2014–2017
13	CO_2 emissions embodied in imports (tCO_2/capita)	2012–2015
14	Mean area that is protected in marine sites important to biodiversity (%)	2015–2018*
14	Ocean Health Index: Clean Waters score (worst 0–100 best)	2015–2019*
14	Fish caught from overexploited or collapsed stocks (% of total catch)	2010–2014
14	Fish caught by trawling (%)	2010–2014
15	Mean area that is protected in terrestrial sites important to biodiversity (%)	2015–2018*
15	Mean area that is protected in freshwater sites important to biodiversity (%)	2015–2018*
15	Red List Index of species survival (worst 0–1 best)	2015–2019*
16	Homicides (per 100,000 population)	2014–2017
16	Unsentenced detainees (% of prison population)	2015–2018*
16	Percentage of population who feel safe walking alone at night in the city or area where they live (%)	2015–2019*
16	Corruption Perception Index (worst 0–100 best)	2015–2019*
16	Press Freedom Index (best 0–100 worst)	2015–2019*
16	Persons held in prison (per 100,000 population)	2014–2017
17	Government spending on health and education (% of GDP)	2013–2016
17	For high-income and all OECD DAC countries: International concessional public finance, including official development assistance (% of GNI)	2014–2017
17	Other countries: Government revenue excluding grants (% of GDP)	2014–2017

Table 13

Spillover Index Score and Rank (compared with SDG Index Rank)

The Spillover Index measures transboundary impacts generated by one country on others, which may in turn undermine the other countries' capacities to achieve the SDGs. The Spillover Index covers financial spillovers (e.g., financial secrecy, profit shifting), environmental and social impacts embodied into trade and consumption (e.g., imported CO_2 emissions, imported biodiversity threats, accidents at work embodied into trade), and security/development cooperation (ODA, weapons exports). ODA is an example of a positive spillover. Scores should be interpreted in the same way as the SDG Index score: from 0 (poor performance, i.e., significant negative spillovers) to 100 (good performance, i.e., no significant negative spillovers). To allow for international comparisons, most spillover indicators are expressed in per-capita terms.

Country	Spillover Index Score	Spillover Index Rank	SDG Index Rank
Afghanistan	99.3	24	139
Albania	94.3	82	68
Algeria	97.4	58	56
Angola	96.7	65	149
Argentina	94.0	86	51
Armenia	96.7	66	75
Australia	61.6	145	37
Austria	56.3	154	7
Azerbaijan	97.6	55	54
Bahrain	82.0	115	82
Bangladesh	99.4	23	109
Barbados	78.6	121	87
Belarus	96.3	69	18
Belgium	59.9	149	11
Belize	93.4	92	102
Benin	99.5	20	145
Bhutan	93.7	90	80
Bolivia	97.9	51	79
Bosnia and Herzegovina	95.8	73	50
Botswana	78.5	122	121
Brazil	97.3	60	53
Brunei Darussalam	67.6	136	88
Bulgaria	85.4	112	39
Burkina Faso	99.3	25	137
Burundi	99.8	7	143
Cabo Verde	95.3	76	92
Cambodia	98.8	34	106
Cameroon	99.5	19	133
Canada	60.6	147	21
Central African Republic	99.6	12	166
Chad	99.8	6	164
Chile	92.6	97	28
China	94.2	84	48
Colombia	94.7	79	67

Table 13

(continued)

Country	Spillover Index Score	Spillover Index Rank	SDG Index Rank
Comoros	100.0	1	146
Congo, Rep.	97.7	54	135
Costa Rica	89.6	106	35
Côte d'Ivoire	99.5	18	128
Croatia	83.1	113	19
Cuba	97.1	61	55
Cyprus	59.9	150	34
Czech Republic	69.7	129	8
Dem. Rep. Congo	99.4	22	158
Denmark	66.4	141	2
Djibouti	98.2	43	138
Dominican Republic	95.9	72	73
Ecuador	96.8	63	46
Egypt, Arab Rep.	98.5	37	83
El Salvador	92.6	98	77
Estonia	69.4	130	10
Eswatini	82.9	114	144
Ethiopia	99.7	9	136
Fiji	92.4	99	74
Finland	66.6	140	3
France	51.1	158	4
Gabon	93.0	95	111
The Gambia	97.9	52	129
Georgia	90.8	102	58
Germany	57.0	153	5
Ghana	97.4	59	100
Greece	69.4	131	43
Guatemala	97.0	62	120
Guinea	99.5	17	150
Guyana	22.2	165	124
Haiti	99.6	13	154
Honduras	96.0	71	105
Hungary	77.1	124	29
Iceland	60.3	148	26
India	98.8	36	117
Indonesia	97.6	56	101
Iran, Islamic Rep.	95.5	74	59
Iraq	98.3	40	113
Ireland	57.8	152	14
Israel	66.7	138	40
Italy	69.0	132	30
Jamaica	92.9	96	84

Table 13

(continued)

Country	Spillover Index Score	Spillover Index Rank	SDG Index Rank
Japan	66.1	143	17
Jordan	89.2	107	89
Kazakhstan	94.0	87	65
Kenya	94.5	81	123
Korea, Rep.	68.6	135	20
Kuwait	36.6	162	112
Kyrgyz Republic	96.1	70	52
Lao PDR	99.2	27	116
Latvia	70.4	127	24
Lebanon	78.8	120	95
Lesotho	94.5	80	141
Liberia	98.0	49	162
Lithuania	65.6	144	36
Luxembourg	33.5	164	44
Madagascar	99.5	21	161
Malawi	98.9	32	152
Malaysia	86.3	111	60
Maldives	87.8	108	91
Mali	99.5	16	156
Malta	56.3	155	32
Mauritania	98.0	50	130
Mauritius	42.6	160	108
Mexico	94.9	78	69
Moldova	99.8	8	42
Mongolia	95.0	77	107
Montenegro	68.9	133	72
Morocco	98.1	47	64
Mozambique	99.5	15	140
Myanmar	100.0	2	104
Namibia	86.3	110	119
Nepal	99.1	29	96
Netherlands	44.9	159	9
New Zealand	70.1	128	16
Nicaragua	97.9	53	85
Niger	99.6	11	157
Nigeria	99.2	28	160
North Macedonia	93.8	88	62
Norway	54.1	156	6
Oman	79.8	119	76
Pakistan	99.6	10	134
Panama	81.9	116	81
Papua New Guinea	98.2	44	155
Paraguay	93.7	91	90
Peru	96.7	64	61
Philippines	98.1	45	99

Table 13

(continued)

Country	Spillover Index Score	Spillover Index Rank	SDG Index Rank
Poland	81.8	117	23
Portugal	66.7	139	25
Qatar	68.7	134	103
Romania	91.6	101	38
Russian Federation	78.3	123	57
Rwanda	98.8	35	132
São Tomé and Príncipe	95.4	75	115
Saudi Arabia	73.8	125	97
Senegal	99.0	31	127
Serbia	80.9	118	33
Sierra Leone	99.6	14	153
Singapore	12.4	166	93
Slovak Republic	72.7	126	27
Slovenia	66.4	142	12
Somalia	100.0	4	163
South Africa	92.0	100	110
South Sudan	99.9	5	165
Spain	61.3	146	22
Sri Lanka	96.5	67	94
Sudan	100.0	3	159
Suriname	90.6	103	86
Sweden	67.4	137	1
Switzerland	35.8	163	15
Syrian Arab Republic	98.4	38	126
Tajikistan	97.5	57	78
Tanzania	98.3	41	131
Thailand	93.8	89	41
Togo	99.3	26	147
Trinidad and Tobago	86.8	109	98
Tunisia	94.2	85	63
Turkey	93.3	94	70
Turkmenistan	90.4	104	114
Uganda	99.1	30	142
Ukraine	93.3	93	47
United Arab Emirates	37.4	161	71
United Kingdom	52.1	157	13
United States	59.2	151	31
Uruguay	90.0	105	45
Uzbekistan	98.1	48	66
Vanuatu	94.3	83	122
Venezuela, RB	96.4	68	118
Vietnam	98.3	39	49
Yemen, Rep.	98.9	33	151
Zambia	98.1	46	148
Zimbabwe	98.2	42	125

Source: Authors' analysis

References

Cited in the text

Adeniyi, A. (2017). "The human cost of uncontrolled arms in Africa." Oxfam, Oxford, UK.

Adrian and Natalucci, 2020. Adrian, Tobias, and Natalucci Fabio. 'COVID-19 Worsens Pre-Existing Financial Vulnerabilities'. IMF Blog (blog), 2020. https://blogs.imf.org/2020/05/22/covid-19-worsens-pre-existing-financial-vulnerabilities/.

AEG-SDGs, 2019. https://unstats.un.org/sdgs/iaeg-sdgs/

Arroyo Marioli, F., F. Bullano, S. Kucinskas, and C. Rondón-Moreno (2020). "Tracking R of COVID-19: a new real-time estimation using the Kalman filter," *SSRN Scholarly Paper* No. ID 3581633, Social Science Research Network, Rochester, NY.

Beltram, S. (2020). "How to minimize the impact of Coronavirus on food security." *Insight*, World Food Programme (WFP).

Bill & Melinda Gates Foundation (2019). *The Goalkeepers Report 2019*. The Bill & Melinda Gates Foundation.

Boerma, T., C. Victora, and C. Abouzahr (2018). "Monitoring country progress and achievements by making global predictions: is the tail wagging the dog?" *The Lancet*, 392(10147), 607–609.

Climate Action Tracker (2018). *Some Progress since Paris, but Not Enough, as Governments Amble towards 3°c of Warming*. Warming projections global update. New Climate Institute and Climate Analytics, December 2018.

Climate Action Tracker (2020). A Government Roadmap for Addressing the Climate and Post Covid-19 Economic Crises. New Climate Institute and Climate Analytics.

Concern Worldwide and Welthungerhilfe (2019). *Global Hunger Index*. Concern Worldwide, Welthungerhilfe, and the International Food and Policy Research Institute.

Council of Europe (2020). "COVID-19: Refugees are in a vicious circle that make them particularly vulnerable." Council of Europe, Parliamentary Assembly. http://assembly.coe.int/nw/xml/News/News-View-EN.asp?newsid=7852&lang=2

CREA (2020). China's Air Pollution Overshoots Pre-Crisis Levels for the First Time. Centre for Research on Energy and Clean Air.

Cullen, M. (2020). *Coronavirus: Food Supply Chain under Strain. What to Do?* Food and Agriculture Organization (FAO), 24 March.

Czaplicki Cabezas, S., H. Bellfield, G. Lafortune, C. Streck, and B. Hermann (2019). Towards More Sustainability in the Soy Supply Chain: How Can EU Actors Support Zero Deforestation and SDG Efforts? Climate Focus, Global Canopy, SDSN and GIZ.

Dahmm, H. (2020). "In low-income countries fundamental data issues remain for COVID-19 response." *Insights*, UNSDSN TReNDs – Thematic Research Network on Data and Statistics.

Davies, E., S. Harman, J. True, and C. Wenham (2020). "Why gender matters in the impact and recovery from Covid-19." *The Interpreter*, the Lowy Institute, 2020. https://www.lowyinstitute.org/the-interpreter/why-gender-matters-impact-and-recovery-covid-19

Dorn, F., C. Fuest, M. Göttert, C. Krolage, S. Lautenbacher, S. Link, A. Peichl, M. Reif, S. Sauer, M. Stöckli, K. Wohlrabe, and T. Wollmershäuser (2020). "Die volkswirtschaftlichen Kosten des Corona-Shutdown für Deutschland: Eine Szenarienrechnung'". *ifo Schnelldienst* 73, no. 04 (2020): 29–35.

Equal Measures 2030 (2019). Harnessing the Power of Data for Gender Equality: 2019 Global Report. Equal Measures 2030.

Espey, J. (2020). "Big data in a time of crisis: maximizing its value – and avoiding its risks – in the fight against COVID-19." *Insights,* UNSDSN TReNDs – Thematic Research Network on Data and Statistics.

Eurostat (2017). Sustainable Development in the European Union — Monitoring Report on Progress towards the SDGs in an EU context, 2017 Edition. Publications Office of the European Union, Luxembourg.

Eurostat (2018). *Sustainable Development in the European Union — Monitoring Report on Progress towards the SDGs in an EU context, 2018 Edition*. Publications Office of the European Union, Luxembourg.

Eurostat (2019). Sustainable Development in the European Union — Monitoring Report on Progress towards the SDGs in an EU context, 2019 Edition. Publications Office of the European Union, Luxembourg.

Flaxman, Seth, Swapnil Mishra, Axel Gandy, H. Juliette T. Unwin, Thomas A. Mellan, Helen Coupland, Charles Whittaker, et al. (2020). 'Estimating the Effects of Non-Pharmaceutical Interventions on COVID-19 in Europe'. Nature, 8 June 2020, 1–8. https://doi.org/10.1038/s41586-020-2405-7.

Ghosh, I (2020). "These satellite photos show how COVID-19 lockdowns have impacted global emissions." World Economic Forum, 2020. https://www.weforum.org/agenda/2020/03/emissions-impact-coronavirus-lockdowns-satellites/.

Google (2020). *Community Mobility Reports*. Google. https://www.google.com/covid19/mobility/

Government of the Republic of Korea (2020). "Flattening the curve on COVID-19: how Korea responded to a pandemic using ICT." UNDP Seoul Policy Centre for Knowledge Exchange through SDG Partnerships, UNDP. http://www.undp.org/content/seoul_policy_center/en/home/presscenter/articles/2019/flattening-the-curve-on-covid-19.html, accessed May 26, 2020.

GPSDD, World Bank Group, United Nations, and SDSN (2019). *Data4Now: Accelerating SDG progress through timely information (Concept Note)*. Global Partnership for Sustainable Development Data (GPSDD).

Gütschow, J.; L. Jeffery, R. Gieseke, R. Gebel, D. Stevens, M. Krapp, and M. Rocha (2016) "The PRIMAP-hist national historical emissions time series." *Earth System Science Data*, Volume 8, Issue 2, Page 571-603. Munich: European Geopyhsical Union.

Hub staff report, 2020. Hub staff report. 'Here's the Johns Hopkins Study President Trump Referenced in His Coronavirus News Conference'. The Hub, 27 February 2020.

https://hub.jhu.edu/2020/02/27/trump-johns-hopkins-study-pandemic-coronaviruscovid-19-649-em0-art1-dtd-health/.

IFPRI (2020). *Preventing global food security crisis under COVID-19 emergency*. International Food Policy Research Institute (IFPRI).

IGC (2020). COVID-19 policy response tracker. https://www.theigc.org/covid-19/tracker/, accessed May 26, 2020.

IMF (2020a). *World Economic Outlook, April 2020: The Great Lockdown*, International Monetary Fund. Washington. D.C.

IMF (2020b). *Policy Responses to COVID19*. International Monetary Fund (IMF).

IPBES (2019). Global Assessment Report on Biodiversity and Ecosystem Services,Summary for Policymakers. Intergovernmental Science-Policy Platform on Biodiversity and Ecosystem Services (IPBES). Advance unedited version.

IPCC (2019). *Climate Change and Land*. IPCC Special Report, Summary for Policymakers. Intergovernmental Panel on Climate Change (IPCC).

JHU (2020). COVID-19 Dashboard and Map. Center for Systems Science and Engineering (CSSE) at Johns Hopkins University (JHU). https://coronavirus.jhu.edu/map.html, accessed May 22, 2020.

Kander, A., M. Jiborn, D. D. Moran, and T. O. Wiedmann (2015). "National greenhouse-gas accounting for effective climate policy on international trade." *Nature Climate Change*, 5(5), 431–435.

Kopf, D. (2020). "Traffic collisions are plummeting in several US cities." *Quartz*, 24 March 2020. https://qz.com/1822492/traffic-accidents-are-plummeting-because-of-the-pandemic/.

Lafortune, G., G. Fuller, J. Moreno, G. Schmidt-Traub, and C. Kroll (2018). "SDG Index and Dashboards: detailed methodological pape." Bertelsmann Stiftung and Sustainable Development Solutions Network, Paris.

Lederer, E. (2020). "UN chief says COVID-19 is worst crisis since World War II." Associated Press News, March 31, 2020.

Lee, G. (2020). "South Korea approves first four COVID-19 test kits under urgent-use license." Bioworld. https://www.bioworld.com/articles/433783-south-korea-approves-first-four-covid-19-test-kits-under-urgent-use-license, accessed May 26, 2020.

Le Quéré et al., 2020. Le Quéré, Corinne, Robert B. Jackson, Matthew W. Jones, Adam J. P. Smith, Sam Abernethy, Robbie M. Andrew, Anthony J. De-Gol, et al. 'Temporary Reduction in Daily Global CO 2 Emissions during the COVID-19 Forced Confinement'. Nature Climate Change, 19 May 2020, 1–7. https://doi.org/10.1038/s41558-020-0797-x.

Luomi, M., G. Fuller, L. Dahan, K. Lisboa Båsund, E. Karoubi, and G. Lafortune (2019). *Arab Region SDG Index and Dashboards Report 2019*, Abu Dhabi and New York: SDG Centre of Excellence for the Arab Region/Emirates Diplomatic Academy and Sustainable Development Solutions Network.

Marks, A. (2020). "In the fight against Covid-19: What do we know and to whom can we turn for answers?" *Insights*, UNSDSN TReNDs – Thematic Research Network on Data and Statistics.

Miao, G., and F. Fortanier (2018). *Nowcast TiVA Estimates: Methodology*. OECD and WTO, Paris.

Minderoo Foundation. (2020). Protecting People in a Pandemic. Walk Free, Mindaroo Foundation https://cdn.minderoo.org/content/uploads/2020/04/30211819/Walk-Free-Foundation-COVID-19-Report.pdf

Myllyvirta, Lauri (2020). "Analysis: Coronavirus temporarily reduced China's CO_2 emissions by a quarter." *Carbon Brief*, 19 February 2020. https://www.carbonbrief.org/analysis-coronavirus-has-temporarily-reduced-chinas-co2-emissions-by-a-quarter.

National Sustainable Development Council of Australia (2019). *SDG Progress Report: Australia*. Monash University, Melbourne, Australia.

NITI Aayog (2019). *SDG India: Index & Dashboard 2019–20*. NITI Aayog, New Delhi, India.

NTI et al., 2019. NTI, JHU, and EIU. 'Global Health Security Index'. Nuclear Threat Initiative, Johns Hopkins Center for Health Security and Economist Intelligence Unit, November 2019. https://www.ghsindex.org/about/.

OECD (2017). *OECD Guidelines on Measuring Trust*. OECD Publishing, Paris.

OECD (2020a). "Tackling the coronavirus (COVID-19) crisis together: OECD policy contributions for co-ordinated action." OECD, Paris. https://www.oecd.org/coronavirus/en/, accessed May 26, 2020.

OECD (2020b). A Territorial Approach to the Sustainable Development Goals: Synthesis Report. OECD Urban Policy Reviews, OECD Publishing, Paris.

OECD and JRC (2008). Handbook on Constructing Composite Indicators: Methodology and User Guide. OECD, Joint Research Committee, Paris.

Orrell, T. (2020). "Checking our instincts: We need to remain evidence-based and standards-driven in times of crisis." *Insights*, UNSDSN TReNDs – Thematic Research Network on Data and Statistics.

Oxford University (2020). Oxford COVID-19 Government Response Tracker. Blavatnik School of Government, University of Oxford, Oxford UK. https://covidtracker.bsg.ox.ac.uk/, accessed May 26, 2020.

Papadimitriou, E., A. Neves, and W. Becker. 'JRC Statistical Audit of the Sustainable Development Goals Index and Dashboards'. European Commission, Joint Research Centre, July 2019. doi:10.2760/723763, JRC116857.

PARIS21 and Partners for Review (2019). *National SDG Review: Data Challenges and Opportunities*. Partnership in Statistics for Development in the 21st Century (PARIS21).

Polglase, K., G. Mezzofiore, and M. Foster (2020). "Here's why the coronavirus may be killing more men than women. The US should take note." *CNN Health.* https://edition.cnn.com/2020/03/24/health/coronavirus-gender-mortality-intl/index.html

Praia City Group (2020). *Handbook on Governance Statistics.* Praia Group on Governance Statistics.

Reeves, R. V. and T. Ford (2020). "Covid-19 much more fatal for men, especially taking age into account." Brookings (blog), 15 May 2020. https://www.brookings.edu/blog/up-front/2020/05/15/covid-19-much-more-fatal-for-men-especially-taking-age-into-account/.

Reuters (2020). "Brazil scales back environmental enforcement amid coronavirus outbreak." *The Guardian,* 27 March, 2020. https://www.theguardian.com/world/2020/mar/27/brazil-scales-back-environmental-enforcement-coronavirus-outbreak-deforestation

Sachs, J., G. Schmidt-Traub, M. Mazzucato, D. Messner, N. Nakicenovic, and J. Rockström (2019a). "Six Transformations to achieve the Sustainable Development Goals." *Nature Sustainability,* 2(9), 805–814. https://doi.org/10.1038/s41893-019-0352-9

Sachs, J., G. Schmidt-Traub, R. Pulselli, S. Cresti, and A. Riccaboni (2019b). *Sustainable Development Report 2019 – Mediterranean Countries Edition.* Sustainable Development Solutions Network for the Mediterranean Area (SDSN-Mediterranean), Siena, Italy.

Schmidt-Traub, G., C. Kroll, K. Teksoz, D. Durand-Delacre, and J.D. Sachs (2017). "National baselines for the Sustainable Development Goals assessed in the SDG Index and Dashboards." *Nature Geoscience,* 10(8), 547–555.

SDG Center for Africa and SDSN (2018). *Africa SDG Index and Dashboards Report 2018.* SDG Center for Africa and the Sustainable Development Solutions Network, Kigali and New York.

SDG Center for Africa and SDSN (2019). *Africa SDG Index and Dashboards Report 2019.* SDG Center for Africa and the Sustainable Development Solutions Network, Kigali and New York.

SDSN (2015). *Indicators and a monitoring framework for Sustainable Development Goals: Launching a Data Revolution for the SDGs.* Sustainable Development Solutions Network, Paris and New York.

SDSN and BCFN (2019). *Fixing the Business of Food.* Sustainable Development Solutions Network and Barilla Center for Food and Nutrition, New York and Milan.

SDSN and IEEP (2019). *2019 Europe Sustainable Development Report.* Sustainable Development Solutions Network and the Institute for European Environmental Policy, Paris and Brussels.

Shiffman, J., and Y.R. Shawar (2020). "Strengthening accountability of the global health metrics enterprise." *The Lancet,* 395(10234), 1452–1456.

Stadler K, R. Wood, T. Bulavskaya, C.J. Sodersten, M. Simas, S. Schmidt, A. Usubiaga, J. Acosta-Fernandez, J. Kuenen, M. Bruckner, S. Giljum, S. Lutter, S. Merciai, J.H. Schmidt, M.C. Theurl, C. Plutzar, T. Kastner, M. Eisenmenger, K. Erb, A. de Koning, A. Tukker (2018). "EXIOBASE 3: Developing a time series of detailed environmentally extended multi-regional input-output tables." *Journal of Industrial Ecology* 22(3)502–5. doi: 10.1111/jiec.12715

Svenja Wiebe, K., E. Lekve Bielle, J. Többen, and R. Wood (2018). "Implementing exogenous scenarios in a global MRIO model for the estimation of future environmental footprints." *Journal of Economic Structures,* 7, Article number: 20 (2018).

Think Sustainable Europe (2020). "Europe's recovery plans must pass five sustainability tests." Euractiv. https://www.euractiv.com/section/energy-environment/opinion/europes-recovery-plans-must-pass-five-sustainability-tests/

TReNDs (2019). *Counting on the World to Act: A Roadmap for Governments to Achieve Modern Data Systems for Sustainable Development.* UNSDSN and TReNDs – Thematic Research Network on Data and Statistics. https://countingontheworld.sdsntrends.org/static/files/19COTW.pdf

UN-HABITAT (2018). *SDG 11 Synthesis Report 2018 on Sustainable Cities and Communities.* United Nations Human Settlements Programme (UN-HABITAT), Nairobi.

United Nations (2019). *The Sustainable Development Goals Report 2019,* United Nations. New York.

United Nations (2020). "Shared responsibility, global solidarity: responding to the socio-economic impacts of COVID-19." United Nations, March 2020.

Walk Free Foundation (2018). *Global Slavery Index* 2018. Walk Free Foundation, Broadway Nedlands, Australia.

WBCSD (2018). SDG Sector Roadmaps: How to leverage the power of sectoral collaboration to maximize business impact on the Sustainable Development Goals. World Business Council on Sustainable Development.

World Bank, IEA, IRENA, UNSD, and WHO (2019). *Tracking SDG7: The Energy Progress Report 2019.* The World Bank, Washington DC.

World Benchmarking Alliance (2019). *Systems Transformations.* World Benchmarking Alliance. https://www.worldbenchmarkingalliance.org/system-transformations/, accessed February 7, 2019.

Worldometer (2020). COVID-19 Coronavirus Pandemic. Live updates. https://www.worldometers.info/coronavirus/, accessed May 22, 2020.

Yale School of Management (2020). *COVID-19 Financial Response Tracker Visualization (CFRTV).* https://som.yale.edu/faculty-research-centers/centers-initiatives/program-on-financial-stability/covid-19-tracker, accessed May 26, 2020.

Databases

Alsamawi, A., J. Murray, M. Lenzen, and R. C. Reyes (2017). "Trade in occupational safety and health: tracing the embodied human and economic harm in labour along the global supply chain." *Journal of Cleaner Production*, 147, 187–196.

Baldé, C.P., V. Forti, V. Gray, R. Kuehr, P. Stegmann (2017). *The Global E-waste Monitor 2017*. United Nations University (UNU), International Telecommunication Union (ITU) and the International Solid Waste Association (ISWA), Bonn/Geneva/Vienna

BirdLife International, IUCN, and UNEP-WCMC (2020). *Resources and Data*. BirdLife International, International Union for Conservation of Nature and the United Nations Environment Programme – World Conservation Monitoring Center. https://unstats.un.org/sdgs/indicators/database/

Bonhommeau, S., L. Dubroca, O. Le Pape, J. Barde, D. M. Kaplan, E. Chassot, and A. E. Nieblas (2013). "Eating up the world's food web and the human trophic level." *Proceedings of the National Academy of Sciences*, 110(51), 20617–20. https://doi.org/10.1073/pnas.1305827110

Cashion, T., D. Al-Abdulrazzak, D. Belhabib, B. Derrick, E. Divovich, D. Moutopoulos, S.-L. Noël, M. L.D. Palomares, L. Teh, D. Zeller, and D. Pauly (2018). "A global fishing gear dataset for integration into the Sea Around Us global fisheries databases (in review)." Sea Around Us, Vancouver, Canada.

Chandy, L., Seidel B. (2017). The Brookings Institution. https://www.brookings.edu/opinions/how-much-do-we-really-know-about-inequality-within-countries-around-the-world/

Cuaresma, J. C., W. Fengler, H. Kharas, K. Bekhtiar, M. Brottrager, and M. Hofer (2019). "Will the Sustainable Development Goals be fulfilled? Assessing present and future global poverty." *Palgrave Communications*, 4(1), 29.

Curtis et al. (2018). "Classifying drivers of global forest loss." *Science*, Vol. 361 - 6407, pp. 1108–11. Data updated in 2020.

Demirguc-Kunt et al. (2018). Global Financial Inclusion Database. World Bank, Washington, D.C. https://data.worldbank.org/indicator/FX.OWN.TOTL.ZS

FAO (2020). Cereal Yield (kg per hectare). Food and Agriculture Organization, Rome. http://data.worldbank.org/indicator/AG.YLD.CREL.KG

FAO (2020). Level of water stress: freshwater withdrawal as a proportion of available freshwater resources (%). AQUASTAT, Food and Agriculture Organization, Rome. http://www.fao.org/nr/water/aquastat/data/query/index.html?lang=en

FAO (2020). Prevalence of undernourishment (% of population). Food and Agriculture Organization, Rome. http://data.worldbank.org/indicator/SN.ITK.DEFC.ZS

FAO, IFAD, and WFP (2015). *The State of Food Insecurity in the World 2015. Meeting the 2015 international hunger targets: taking stock of uneven progress*. FAO, Rome.

Gallup (2020). Gallup World Poll.

Global Yield Gap Atlas (2015). A joint initiative of Wageningen University and Research and University of Nebraska-Lincoln. http://www.yieldgap.org

Gütschow, J., Jeffery, L., Gieseke, R. (2019): The PRIMAP-hist national historical emissions time series (1850–2016). v2.0. GFZ Data Services. https://doi.org/10.5880/pik.2019.001

IEA (2019). CO_2 Emissions From Fuel Combustion 2019. International Energy Agency, Paris. https://www.iea.org/reports/co2-emissions-from-fuel-combustion-2019

IHME (2017). Global Burden of Disease Study 2017 (GBD 2017). Health-related Sustainable Development Goals (SDG)

ILO (2020). Ratio of female-to-male labour force participation rate (%) (modeled ILO estimate). International Labour Organization, Geneva. https://data.worldbank.org/indicator/SL.TLF.CACT.FM.ZS

ILO (2020). Unemployment, total (% of total labor force) (modeled ILO estimate). International Labour Organization, Geneva. http://data.worldbank.org/indicator/SL.UEM.TOTL.ZS

International Monetary Fund (2020). Government Finance Statistics Yearbook. https://data.worldbank.org/indicator/GC.REV.XGRT.GD.ZS?view=chart

IPU (2020). Proportion of seats held by women in national parliaments (%). Inter-Parliamentary Union, Geneva. http://data.worldbank.org/indicator/SG.GEN.PARL.ZS

ITU (2020). World Telecommunication/ICT Indicators database. International Telecommunication Union, Geneva. http://www.itu.int/en/ITU-D/Statistics/Pages/publications/wtid.aspx

IUCN, BirdLife International (2020). IUCN Red List. International Union for Conservation of Nature and Birdlife International. http://unstats.un.org/sdgs/indicators/database/?indicator=15.5.1

Kaza, Silpa; Yao, Lisa C.; Bhada-Tata, Perinaz; Van Woerden, Frank. 2018. What a Waste 2.0 : A Global Snapshot of Solid Waste Management to 2050. Urban Development;. Washington, DC: World Bank.

Lenzen, M., D. Moran, A. Bhaduri, K. Kanemoto, M. Bekchanov, A. Geschke, and B. Foran. (2013). "International trade of scarce water." *Ecological Economics*, Vol. 94, pp. 78–85.

Lenzen, M., D. Moran, K. Kanemoto, B. Foran, L. Lobefaro, and A. Geschke. (2012). "International trade drives biodiversity threats in developing nations." *Nature*, 486, 109–112. (Dataset updated to 2015 by Isaac Russell Peterson, Matthew Selinkske, and colleagues), doi: 10.1038/nature11145

Lenzen, M., Malik, A., Li, M., Fry, J., Weisz, H., Pichler, P-P., Chaves, L.S.M., Capon, A. Pencheon, D. 2020 (under review), The global environmental footprint of healthcare, The Lancet Planetary Health.

National Science Foundation (2020). Scientific and Technical Journal Articles. National Science Foundation, Arlington, VA. http://data.worldbank.org/indicator/IP.JRN.ARTC.SC

Ocean Health Index (2019). Ocean Health Index 2019 global assessment. National Center for Ecological Analysis and Synthesis, University of California, Santa Barbara. http://data.oceanhealthindex.org/data-and-downloads

OECD (2011). How's Life? Measuring well-being. Table 4.2 Housing cost overburden rate by tenure status. Dataset updated to 2018 by Marissa Plouin, Pauline Fron, and colleagues (Affordable Housing Database). https://doi.org/10.1787/9789264121164-en

OECD (2016). Effective Carbon Rates: Pricing CO_2 through Taxes and Emissions Trading Systems, OECD Publishing, Paris. https://doi.org/10.1787/9789264260115-en.

OECD (2018). PISA Database. Organisation for Economic Cooperation and Development, Paris. http://pisadataexplorer.oecd.org/ide/idepisa/dataset.aspx.

OECD (2020). OECD Statistics. Organisation for Economic Cooperation and Development, Paris. http://stats.oecd.org/

Oita, A., et al. (2016). Substantial nitrogen pollution embedded in international trade. Nature Geoscience, 9, pp. 111–115, doi: 10.1038/ngeo2635

Pauly D., and D. Zeller (2018). *Sea Around Us. Concepts, Design and Data.* Sea Around Us, Vancouver, Canada. www.seaaroundus.org.

Reporters Without Borders (2019). World Press Freedom Index 2019. Reporters Without Borders (RSF). https://rsf.org/en/ranking/2019

Schwab, K. (2019). *The Global Competitiveness Report 2019.* World Economic Forum, Geneva. https://reports.weforum.org/global-competitiveness-report-2019

SE4All (2020). Access to clean fuels and technologies for cooking (% of population). Sustainable Energy for All. https://data.worldbank.org/indicator/EG.CFT.ACCS.ZS

SE4All (2020). Access to electricity (% of population). Sustainable Energy for All. http://data.worldbank.org/indicator/EG.ELC.ACCS.ZS

SIPRI (2020). SIPRI Arms Transfers Database. Stockholm International Peace Research Institute, Stockholm. https://www.sipri.org/ databases/armstransfers.

Tax Justice Network (2019). Corporate Tax Haven Index 2019. Tax Justice Network, London. https://corporatetaxhavenindex.org/introduction/cthi-2019-results

Tax Justice Network (2020). Financial Secrecy Index 2020. Tax Justice Network, London. https://www.financialsecrecyindex.com/introduction/fsi-2018-results

Times Higher Education (2020). World University Rankings 2020. *Times Higher Education* and the World Universities Insights, London. https://www.timeshighereducation.com/world-university-rankings

Transparency International (2020*). Corruption Perceptions Index 2019.* Transparency International, Berlin. https://www.transparency.org/cpi2019?/news/feature/cpi-2019

UN IGME (2020). Mortality rate, neonatal (per 1,000 live births). United Nations Inter-agency Group for Child Mortality Estimation (UNICEF, WHO, the World Bank Group, and the United Nations Population Division). http://data.worldbank.org/indicator/SH.DYN.NMRT

UN IGME (2020). Mortality rate, under-5 (per 1,000 live births). United Nations Inter-agency Group for Child Mortality Estimation (UNICEF, WHO, the World Bank Group, and the United Nations Population Division). http://data.worldbank.org/indicator/SH.DYN.MORT

UNAIDS (2020). HIV incidence per 1000 population (15–49). Aidsinfo, Joint United Nations Programme on HIV and AIDS, Geneva. http://aidsinfo.unaids.rg?did=55da49cd64e925b9 4e70b0ce&r=world&t=2018&tb=d&bt=dnli&ts=0, 0&tr=world&aid=5970eccef7341ed11f26de5d&sav= Population: All ages&tl=2

UNDESA (2020). Adolescent fertility rate (births per 1,000 women ages 15-19). *World Population Prospects*, United Nations Population Division, United Nations Department of Economic and Social Affairs, New York. http://data.worldbank.org/indicator/SP.ADO.TFRT

UNDESA (2020). Family Planning – Model. United Nations Department of Economic and Social Affairs, New York. http://www.un.org/en/development/desa/population/theme/family- planning/cp_model.shtml

UNDESA (2020). Proportion of women of reproductive age (aged 15-49 years) who have their need for family planning satisfied with modern methods (% of women aged 15-49 years). World Contraceptive Use 2018 (POP/DB/CP/Rev2018). United Nations Department of Economic and Social Affairs, New York. https://www.un.org/en/development/desa/population/publications/dataset/contraception/wcu2018.asp

UNESCO (2020). UIS.stat. Government expenditure on education. UNESCO Institute for Statistics (UIS), Montréal, Canada. http://data.uis.unesco.org/

UNESCO (2020). UIS.stat. Lower secondary completion rate, total (% of relevant age group). UNESCO Institute for Statistics (UIS), Montréal, Canada. http://data.uis.unesco.org/

UNESCO (2020). UIS.stat. Net enrolment rate, primary, both sexes (%). UNESCO Institute for Statistics (UIS), Montréal, Canada. http://data.uis.unesco.org/

UNESCO (2020). UIS.stat. UNESCO Institute for Statistics (UIS), Montréal, Canada. http://data.uis.unesco.org/

UNESCO (2020). UIS.stat. Youth literacy rate, population 15-24 years, both sexes (%). UNESCO Institute for Statistics (UIS), Montréal, Canada. http://data.uis.unesco.org/

UNICEF (2017). Child labour. http://data.unicef.org/topic/child-protection/child-labour/

UNICEF (2017). Birth registration. United Nations Children's Fund, New York. http://data.unicef.org/topic/child-protection/birth-registration/

UNICEF (2020). Births attended by skilled health staff (% of total). United Nations Children's Fund, New York. http://data.worldbank.org/indicator/SH.STA.BRTC.ZS

UNICEF, WHO, and the World Bank Group (2020). Prevalence of stunting, height for age (% of children under 5). United Nations Children's Fund (UNICEF), the World Health Organization, and the International Bank for Reconstruction and Development/The World Bank. https://data.worldbank.org/indicator/SH.STA.STNT.ZS

UNICEF, WHO, and the World Bank Group (2020). Prevalence of wasting, weight for height (% of children under 5). United Nations Children's Fund (UNICEF), the World Health Organization, and the International Bank for Reconstruction and Development/The World Bank. http://data.worldbank.org/indicator/SH.STA.WAST.ZS

United Nations (2020). UN Comtrade Database. United Nations, NY. https://comtrade.un.org/data/

UNODC (2020). Global Study on Homicides. United Nations Office on Drugs and Crime, Vienna. https://dataunodc.un.org/GSH_app

UNODC (2020). Total Persons Held Unsentenced. United Nations Office on Drugs and Crime, Vienna. https://dataunodc.un.org/data/prison/total%20persons%20held%20unsentenced

UNODC (2020). Total Prison Population. United Nations Office on Drugs and Crime, Vienna. https://dataunodc.un.org/crime/total-prison-population

Walk Free Foundation (2018). Global Slavery Index 2018. Walk Free Foundation, Broadway Nedlands, Australia. https://www.globalslaveryindex.org/

Wendling, Z. A., Emerson, J. W., Esty, D. C., Levy, M. A., de Sherbinin, A., et al. (2018). 2018 Environmental Performance Index. New Haven, CT: Yale Center for Environmental Law and Policy. http://epi.yale.edu.

WHO (2018). Age-standardized death rate due to cardiovascular disease, cancer, diabetes, and chronic respiratory disease in populations age 30–70 years, per 100 000 population. World Health Organization, Geneva. https://apps.who.int/gho/data/view.main.GSWCAH21v

WHO (2019). Tracking universal health coverage: 2019 Global Monitoring Report. World Health Organization, Geneva. http://www.who.int/healthinfo/universal_health_coverage/report/2019/en/

WHO (2020). Age-standardized death rate attributable to household air pollution and ambient air pollution, per 100 000 population. World Health Organization, Geneva. https://apps.who.int/gho/data/view.main.GSWCAH37v

WHO (2020). GHO Life expectancy and healthy life expectancy. World Health Organization, Geneva. http://apps.who.int/gho/data/node.main.688

WHO (2020). GHO Obesity (age- standardized estimate). World Health Organization, Geneva. http://apps.who.int/gho/data/view.main.CTRY2450A?lang=en

WHO (2020). GHO Road traffic deaths. World Health Organization, Geneva. http://apps.who.int/gho/data/node.main.A997

WHO (2020). Incidence of tuberculosis (per 100,000 people). World Health Organization, Geneva. http://data.worldbank.org/indicator/SH.TBS.INCD

WHO (2020). World Health Expenditure Database. World Health Organization, Geneva. http://apps.who.int/nha/database

WHO, et al. (2020). Maternal mortality ratio (modeled estimate, per 100,000 live births). World Health Organization, Geneva. http://data.worldbank.org/indicator/SH.STA.MMRT

WHO, UNICEF (2020). Immunization Coverage. World Health Organization and United Nations Children's Fund, Geneva and New York. http://data.unicef.org/topic/child-health/immunization/

WHO, UNICEF (2020). WHO / UNICEF Joint Monitoring Programme: Data and estimates. People using at least basic drinking water services (% of population). World Health Organization and United Nations Children's Fund, Geneva and New York. https://washdata.org/data

WHO, UNICEF (2020). WHO / UNICEF Joint Monitoring Programme: Data and estimates. People using at least basic sanitation services (% of population). World Health Organization and United Nations Children's Fund, Geneva and New York. https://washdata.org/data

WHO, UNICEF (2020). WHO / UNICEF Joint Monitoring Programme: Data and estimates. World Health Organization and United Nations Children's Fund, Geneva and New York. https://washdata.org/data

World Bank (2018). 2018 Logistics Performance Index (LPI). World Bank, Washington, D.C. http://lpi.worldbank.org/international/global

World Bank (2020). GDP per capita, PPP (current international $). World Bank, Washington, D.C. https://data.worldbank.org/indicator/NY.GDP.PCAP.PP.CD

World Data Lab (2020). World Poverty Clock. World Data Lab, Vienna. http://worldpoverty.io/

Zhang, X., and E. Davidson (2019). Sustainable Nitrogen Management Index. Earth and Space Science Open Archive. https://doi.org/10.1002/essoar.10501111.1

Zucman, G., T. Tørsløv, and L. Weir (2019). The Missing Profits of Nations: 2016 Figures. https://missingprofits.world

Part 5

Country Profiles

▼ OVERALL PERFORMANCE

Index score

54.2

Regional average score

70.9

SDG Global rank **139** (OF 166)

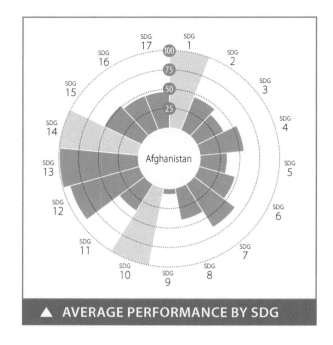

▲ AVERAGE PERFORMANCE BY SDG

▼ SPILLOVER INDEX

100 (best) to 0 (worst)

▼ CURRENT ASSESSMENT – SDG DASHBOARD

■ Major challenges ■ Significant challenges ■ Challenges remain ■ SDG achieved ■ Information unavailable

▼ SDG TRENDS

↓ Decreasing   → Stagnating   ↗ Moderately improving   ↑ On track or maintaining SDG achievement   ● Information unavailable

Notes: The full title of Goal 2 "Zero Hunger" is "End hunger, achieve food security and improved nutrition and promote sustainable agriculture".
The full title of each SDG is available here: https://sustainabledevelopment.un.org/topics/sustainabledevelopmentgoals

SDG1 – No Poverty

Indicator	Value	Year	Rating	Trend
Poverty headcount ratio at $1.90/day (%)	* NA	NA	●	●
Poverty headcount ratio at $3.20/day (%)	* NA	NA	●	●

SDG2 – Zero Hunger

Indicator	Value	Year	Rating	Trend
Prevalence of undernourishment (%)	29.8	2017	●	↓
Prevalence of stunting in children under 5 years of age (%)	40.9	2013	●	→
Prevalence of wasting in children under 5 years of age (%)	9.5	2013	●	↑
Prevalence of obesity, BMI ≥ 30 (% of adult population)	5.5	2016	●	↑
Human Trophic Level (best 2–3 worst)	2.2	2017	●	↑
Cereal yield (tonnes per hectare of harvested land)	2.0	2017	●	→
Sustainable Nitrogen Management Index (best 0–1.41 worst)	0.7	2015	●	↓

SDG3 – Good Health and Well-Being

Indicator	Value	Year	Rating	Trend
Maternal mortality rate (per 100,000 live births)	638	2017	●	↑
Neonatal mortality rate (per 1,000 live births)	37.1	2018	●	↗
Mortality rate, under-5 (per 1,000 live births)	62.3	2018	●	↗
Incidence of tuberculosis (per 100,000 population)	189.0	2018	●	→
New HIV infections (per 1,000 uninfected population)	0.0	2018	●	↑
Age-standardized death rate due to cardiovascular disease, cancer, diabetes, or chronic respiratory disease in adults aged 30–70 years (%)	29.8	2016	●	→
Age-standardized death rate attributable to household air pollution and ambient air pollution (per 100,000 population)	211	2016	●	●
Traffic deaths (per 100,000 population)	15.1	2016	●	→
Life expectancy at birth (years)	62.7	2016	●	→
Adolescent fertility rate (births per 1,000 adolescent females aged 15 to 19)	69.0	2017	●	↑
Births attended by skilled health personnel (%)	50.5	2015	●	↑
Percentage of surviving infants who received 2 WHO-recommended vaccines (%)	64	2018	●	→
Universal health coverage (UHC) index of service coverage (worst 0–100 best)	37.0	2017	●	→
Subjective well-being (average ladder score, worst 0–10 best)	2.7	2018	●	↓

SDG4 – Quality Education

Indicator	Value	Year	Rating	Trend
Net primary enrollment rate (%)	NA	NA	●	●
Lower secondary completion rate (%)	53.2	2017	●	↑
Literacy rate (% of population aged 15 to 24)	65.4	2018	●	●

SDG5 – Gender Equality

Indicator	Value	Year	Rating	Trend
Demand for family planning satisfied by modern methods (% of females aged 15 to 49 who are married or in unions)	42.2	2016	●	↗
Ratio of female-to-male mean years of education received (%)	31.7	2018	●	→
Ratio of female-to-male labor force participation rate (%)	59.5	2019	●	↗
Seats held by women in national parliament (%)	27.0	2020	●	↓

SDG6 – Clean Water and Sanitation

Indicator	Value	Year	Rating	Trend
Population using at least basic drinking water services (%)	67.1	2017	●	↑
Population using at least basic sanitation services (%)	43.4	2017	●	→
Freshwater withdrawal (% of available freshwater resources)	54.8	2000	●	●
Anthropogenic wastewater that receives treatment (%)	0.0	2018	●	●
Scarce water consumption embodied in imports (m³/capita)	2.5	2013	●	↑

SDG7 – Affordable and Clean Energy

Indicator	Value	Year	Rating	Trend
Population with access to electricity (%)	97.7	2017	●	↑
Population with access to clean fuels and technology for cooking (%)	32.4	2016	●	↗
CO_2 emissions from fuel combustion for electricity and heating per total electricity output (MtCO₂/TWh)	NA	NA	●	●

SDG8 – Decent Work and Economic Growth

Indicator	Value	Year	Rating	Trend
Adjusted GDP growth (%)	-7.3	2018	●	●
Victims of modern slavery (per 1,000 population)	22.2	2018	●	●
Adults with an account at a bank or other financial institution or with a mobile-money-service provider (% of population aged 15 or over)	14.9	2017	●	→
Unemployment rate (% of total labor force)	11.1	2019	●	→
Fatal work-related accidents embodied in imports (per 100,000 population)	0.0	2010	●	↑

SDG9 – Industry, Innovation and Infrastructure

Indicator	Value	Year	Rating	Trend
Population using the internet (%)	13.5	2017	●	→
Mobile broadband subscriptions (per 100 population)	18.8	2018	●	↗
Logistics Performance Index: Quality of trade and transport-related infrastructure (worst 1–5 best)	1.8	2018	●	↓
The Times Higher Education Universities Ranking: Average score of top 3 universities (worst 0–100 best)	* 0.0	2020	●	●
Scientific and technical journal articles (per 1,000 population)	0.0	2018	●	→
Expenditure on research and development (% of GDP)	* 0.0	2017	●	●

SDG10 – Reduced Inequalities

Indicator	Value	Year	Rating	Trend
Gini coefficient adjusted for top income	NA	NA	●	●

SDG11 – Sustainable Cities and Communities

Indicator	Value	Year	Rating	Trend
Annual mean concentration of particulate matter of less than 2.5 microns in diameter (PM2.5) (μg/m³)	56.9	2017	●	→
Access to improved water source, piped (% of urban population)	45.1	2017	●	→
Satisfaction with public transport (%)	45.3	2018	●	↓

SDG12 – Responsible Consumption and Production

Indicator	Value	Year	Rating	Trend
Municipal solid waste (kg/capita/day)	1.7	2016	●	●
Electronic waste (kg/capita)	0.6	2016	●	●
Production-based SO_2 emissions (kg/capita)	5.1	2012	●	●
SO_2 emissions embodied in imports (kg/capita)	0.4	2012	●	●
Production-based nitrogen emissions (kg/capita)	9.1	2010	●	●
Nitrogen emissions embodied in imports (kg/capita)	0.2	2010	●	●

SDG13 – Climate Action

Indicator	Value	Year	Rating	Trend
Energy-related CO_2 emissions (tCO₂/capita)	0.4	2017	●	↑
CO_2 emissions embodied in imports (tCO₂/capita)	0.0	2015	●	↑
CO_2 emissions embodied in fossil fuel exports (kg/capita)	22.4	2015	●	●

SDG14 – Life Below Water

Indicator	Value	Year	Rating	Trend
Mean area that is protected in marine sites important to biodiversity (%)	NA	NA	●	●
Ocean Health Index: Clean Waters score (worst 0–100 best)	NA	NA	●	●
Fish caught from overexploited or collapsed stocks (% of total catch)	NA	NA	●	●
Fish caught by trawling (%)	NA	NA	●	●
Marine biodiversity threats embodied in imports (per million population)	0.0	2018	●	●

SDG15 – Life on Land

Indicator	Value	Year	Rating	Trend
Mean area that is protected in terrestrial sites important to biodiversity (%)	6.1	2018	●	→
Mean area that is protected in freshwater sites important to biodiversity (%)	0.1	2018	●	→
Red List Index of species survival (worst 0–1 best)	0.8	2019	●	↓
Permanent deforestation (% of forest area, 5-year average)	0.0	2018	●	●
Terrestrial and freshwater biodiversity threats embodied in imports (per million population)	0.0	2018	●	●

SDG16 – Peace, Justice and Strong Institutions

Indicator	Value	Year	Rating	Trend
Homicides (per 100,000 population)	7.1	2017	●	↑
Unsentenced detainees (% of prison population)	31.3	2015	●	●
Percentage of population who feel safe walking alone at night in the city or area where they live (%)	12.5	2018	●	↓
Property Rights (worst 1–7 best)	NA	NA	●	●
Birth registrations with civil authority (% of children under age 5)	42.3	2018	●	●
Corruption Perception Index (worst 0–100 best)	16	2019	●	→
Children involved in child labor (% of population aged 5 to 14)	29.4	2016	●	●
Exports of major conventional weapons (TIV constant million USD per 100,000 population)	* 0.0	2019	●	●
Press Freedom Index (best 0–100 worst)	36.6	2019	●	↗

SDG17 – Partnerships for the Goals

Indicator	Value	Year	Rating	Trend
Government spending on health and education (% of GDP)	4.8	2016	●	↗
For high-income and all OECD DAC countries: International concessional public finance, including official development assistance (% of GNI)	NA	NA	●	●
Other countries: Government revenue excluding grants (% of GDP)	12.2	2017	●	↗
Corporate Tax Haven Score (best 0–100 worst)	* 0.0	2019	●	●

* Imputed data point

5. Country Profiles

ALBANIA

Eastern Europe and Central Asia

▼ OVERALL PERFORMANCE

Index score

70.8

Regional average score

70.9

SDG Global rank 68 (OF 166)

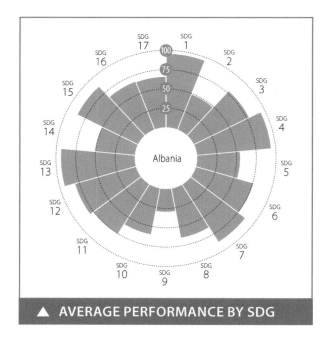

▲ AVERAGE PERFORMANCE BY SDG

▼ SPILLOVER INDEX

100 (best) to 0 (worst)

▼ CURRENT ASSESSMENT – SDG DASHBOARD

■ Major challenges ■ Significant challenges ■ Challenges remain ■ SDG achieved ■ Information unavailable

▼ SDG TRENDS

⬇ Decreasing ➡ Stagnating ↗ Moderately improving ⬆ On track or maintaining SDG achievement ● Information unavailable

Notes: The full title of Goal 2 "Zero Hunger" is "End hunger, achieve food security and improved nutrition and promote sustainable agriculture".
The full title of each SDG is available here: https://sustainabledevelopment.un.org/topics/sustainabledevelopmentgoals

104 | Sustainable Development Report 2020 ◯ The Sustainable Development Goals and Covid-19

SDG1 – No Poverty

	Value	Year	Rating	Trend
Poverty headcount ratio at $1.90/day (%)	0.4	2020	●	↑
Poverty headcount ratio at $3.20/day (%)	4.4	2020	○	↑

SDG2 – Zero Hunger

	Value	Year	Rating	Trend
Prevalence of undernourishment (%)	6.2	2017	●	↑
Prevalence of stunting in children under 5 years of age (%)	23.1	2009	●	→
Prevalence of wasting in children under 5 years of age (%)	9.4	2009	●	↗
Prevalence of obesity, BMI ≥ 30 (% of adult population)	21.7	2016	●	↓
Human Trophic Level (best 2–3 worst)	2.4	2017	●	↓
Cereal yield (tonnes per hectare of harvested land)	4.8	2017	●	↑
Sustainable Nitrogen Management Index (best 0–1.41 worst)	0.8	2015	●	→

SDG3 – Good Health and Well-Being

	Value	Year	Rating	Trend
Maternal mortality rate (per 100,000 live births)	15	2017	●	↑
Neonatal mortality rate (per 1,000 live births)	6.5	2018	●	↑
Mortality rate, under-5 (per 1,000 live births)	8.8	2018	●	↑
Incidence of tuberculosis (per 100,000 population)	18.0	2018	○	→
New HIV infections (per 1,000 uninfected population)	NA	NA	●	●
Age-standardized death rate due to cardiovascular disease, cancer, diabetes, or chronic respiratory disease in adults aged 30–70 years (%)	17.0	2016	○	↑
Age-standardized death rate attributable to household air pollution and ambient air pollution (per 100,000 population)	68	2016	○	●
Traffic deaths (per 100,000 population)	13.6	2016	●	↑
Life expectancy at birth (years)	76.4	2016	●	↗
Adolescent fertility rate (births per 1,000 adolescent females aged 15 to 19)	19.6	2017	●	↑
Births attended by skilled health personnel (%)	99.8	2018	●	↑
Percentage of surviving infants who received 2 WHO-recommended vaccines (%)	94	2018	●	↑
Universal health coverage (UHC) index of service coverage (worst 0–100 best)	59.0	2017	●	→
Subjective well-being (average ladder score, worst 0–10 best)	5.0	2019	●	↑

SDG4 – Quality Education

	Value	Year	Rating	Trend
Net primary enrollment rate (%)	94.5	2018	○	↗
Lower secondary completion rate (%)	96.3	2018	●	↑
Literacy rate (% of population aged 15 to 24)	99.3	2018	●	●

SDG5 – Gender Equality

	Value	Year	Rating	Trend
Demand for family planning satisfied by modern methods (% of females aged 15 to 49 who are married or in unions)	4.9	2018	●	↗
Ratio of female-to-male mean years of education received (%)	97.1	2018	○	↑
Ratio of female-to-male labor force participation rate (%)	72.7	2019	●	↑
Seats held by women in national parliament (%)	29.5	2020	●	↑

SDG6 – Clean Water and Sanitation

	Value	Year	Rating	Trend
Population using at least basic drinking water services (%)	91.0	2017	○	→
Population using at least basic sanitation services (%)	97.7	2017	●	↑
Freshwater withdrawal (% of available freshwater resources)	7.9	2005	●	●
Anthropogenic wastewater that receives treatment (%)	2.7	2018	●	●
Scarce water consumption embodied in imports (m3/capita)	5.7	2013	●	↑

SDG7 – Affordable and Clean Energy

	Value	Year	Rating	Trend
Population with access to electricity (%)	100.0	2017	●	↑
Population with access to clean fuels and technology for cooking (%)	77.4	2016	●	↑
CO2 emissions from fuel combustion for electricity and heating per total electricity output (MtCO2/TWh)	1.0	2017	●	↑

SDG8 – Decent Work and Economic Growth

	Value	Year	Rating	Trend
Adjusted GDP growth (%)	-1.1	2018	○	●
Victims of modern slavery (per 1,000 population)	6.9	2018	○	●
Adults with an account at a bank or other financial institution or with a mobile-money-service provider (% of population aged 15 or over)	40.0	2017	●	→
Unemployment rate (% of total labor force)	12.3	2019	●	↑
Fatal work-related accidents embodied in imports (per 100,000 population)	0.2	2010	●	↑

SDG9 – Industry, Innovation and Infrastructure

	Value	Year	Rating	Trend
Population using the internet (%)	71.8	2017	○	↑
Mobile broadband subscriptions (per 100 population)	62.8	2018	○	↑
Logistics Performance Index: Quality of trade and transport-related infrastructure (worst 1–5 best)	2.3	2018	●	●
The Times Higher Education Universities Ranking: Average score of top 3 universities (worst 0–100 best) *	0.0	2020	●	●
Scientific and technical journal articles (per 1,000 population)	0.1	2018	●	→
Expenditure on research and development (% of GDP)	0.2	2008	●	●

SDG10 – Reduced Inequalities

	Value	Year	Rating	Trend
Gini coefficient adjusted for top income	41.7	2012	●	●

SDG11 – Sustainable Cities and Communities

	Value	Year	Rating	Trend
Annual mean concentration of particulate matter of less than 2.5 microns in diameter (PM2.5) (µg/m3)	18.2	2017	●	→
Access to improved water source, piped (% of urban population)	92.4	2017	○	→
Satisfaction with public transport (%)	50.5	2019	●	→

SDG12 – Responsible Consumption and Production

	Value	Year	Rating	Trend
Municipal solid waste (kg/capita/day)	1.8	2015	●	●
Electronic waste (kg/capita)	7.1	2016	●	●
Production-based SO2 emissions (kg/capita)	49.3	2012	●	●
SO2 emissions embodied in imports (kg/capita)	4.7	2012	●	●
Production-based nitrogen emissions (kg/capita)	17.0	2010	●	●
Nitrogen emissions embodied in imports (kg/capita)	2.0	2010	●	●

SDG13 – Climate Action

	Value	Year	Rating	Trend
Energy-related CO2 emissions (tCO2/capita)	1.5	2017	●	↑
CO2 emissions embodied in imports (tCO2/capita)	0.4	2015	●	↑
CO2 emissions embodied in fossil fuel exports (kg/capita)	0.0	2016	●	●

SDG14 – Life Below Water

	Value	Year	Rating	Trend
Mean area that is protected in marine sites important to biodiversity (%)	60.1	2018	●	↑
Ocean Health Index: Clean Waters score (worst 0–100 best)	56.7	2019	●	→
Fish caught from overexploited or collapsed stocks (% of total catch)	NA	NA	●	●
Fish caught by trawling (%)	86.3	2014	●	→
Marine biodiversity threats embodied in imports (per million population)	0.0	2018	●	●

SDG15 – Life on Land

	Value	Year	Rating	Trend
Mean area that is protected in terrestrial sites important to biodiversity (%)	76.1	2018	●	↑
Mean area that is protected in freshwater sites important to biodiversity (%)	99.0	2018	●	↑
Red List Index of species survival (worst 0–1 best)	0.8	2019	●	↓
Permanent deforestation (% of forest area, 5-year average)	0.0	2018	●	●
Terrestrial and freshwater biodiversity threats embodied in imports (per million population)	0.6	2018	●	●

SDG16 – Peace, Justice and Strong Institutions

	Value	Year	Rating	Trend
Homicides (per 100,000 population)	2.3	2017	○	↑
Unsentenced detainees (% of prison population)	44.3	2018	●	↗
Percentage of population who feel safe walking alone at night in the city or area where they live (%)	63.0	2019	○	↗
Property Rights (worst 1–7 best)	3.3	2019	●	●
Birth registrations with civil authority (% of children under age 5)	98.4	2018	●	●
Corruption Perception Index (worst 0–100 best)	35	2019	●	↓
Children involved in child labor (% of population aged 5 to 14)	5.1	2016	●	●
Exports of major conventional weapons (TIV constant million USD per 100,000 population) *	0.0	2019	●	●
Press Freedom Index (best 0–100 worst)	29.8	2019	●	↑

SDG17 – Partnerships for the Goals

	Value	Year	Rating	Trend
Government spending on health and education (% of GDP)	6.7	2016	●	↗
For high-income and all OECD DAC countries: International concessional public finance, including official development assistance (% of GNI)	NA	NA	●	●
Other countries: Government revenue excluding grants (% of GDP)	25.6	2018	○	↗
Corporate Tax Haven Score (best 0–100 worst) *	0.0	2019	●	●

* Imputed data point

5. Country Profiles

▼ OVERALL PERFORMANCE

Index score

72.3

Regional average score

66.3

SDG Global rank 56 (OF 166)

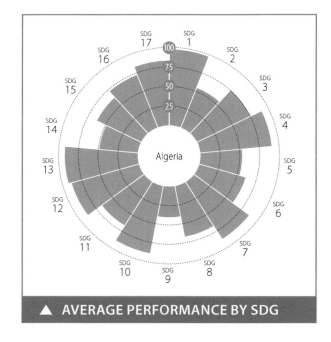

▲ AVERAGE PERFORMANCE BY SDG

▼ SPILLOVER INDEX

100 (best) to 0 (worst)

▼ CURRENT ASSESSMENT – SDG DASHBOARD

▼ SDG TRENDS

↓ Decreasing → Stagnating ↗ Moderately improving ↑ On track or maintaining SDG achievement ● Information unavailable

Notes: The full title of Goal 2 "Zero Hunger" is "End hunger, achieve food security and improved nutrition and promote sustainable agriculture".
The full title of each SDG is available here: https://sustainabledevelopment.un.org/topics/sustainabledevelopmentgoals

SDG1 – No Poverty

	Value	Year	Rating	Trend
Poverty headcount ratio at $1.90/day (%)	0.3	2020	●	↑
Poverty headcount ratio at $3.20/day (%)	2.0	2020	●	↑

SDG2 – Zero Hunger

	Value	Year	Rating	Trend
Prevalence of undernourishment (%)	3.9	2017	●	↑
Prevalence of stunting in children under 5 years of age (%)	11.7	2012	●	→
Prevalence of wasting in children under 5 years of age (%)	4.1	2012	●	↑
Prevalence of obesity, BMI ≥ 30 (% of adult population)	27.4	2016	●	↓
Human Trophic Level (best 2–3 worst)	2.2	2017	●	↑
Cereal yield (tonnes per hectare of harvested land)	1.0	2017	●	↓
Sustainable Nitrogen Management Index (best 0–1.41 worst)	0.7	2015	●	→

SDG3 – Good Health and Well-Being

	Value	Year	Rating	Trend
Maternal mortality rate (per 100,000 live births)	112	2017	●	→
Neonatal mortality rate (per 1,000 live births)	14.6	2018	●	↑
Mortality rate, under-5 (per 1,000 live births)	23.5	2018	●	↑
Incidence of tuberculosis (per 100,000 population)	69.0	2018	●	→
New HIV infections (per 1,000 uninfected population)	0.0	2018	●	↑
Age-standardized death rate due to cardiovascular disease, cancer, diabetes, or chronic respiratory disease in adults aged 30–70 years (%)	14.2	2016	●	↑
Age-standardized death rate attributable to household air pollution and ambient air pollution (per 100,000 population)	50	2016	●	●
Traffic deaths (per 100,000 population)	23.8	2013	●	●
Life expectancy at birth (years)	76.4	2016	●	↗
Adolescent fertility rate (births per 1,000 adolescent females aged 15 to 19)	10.1	2017	●	↑
Births attended by skilled health personnel (%)	96.6	2013	●	●
Percentage of surviving infants who received 2 WHO-recommended vaccines (%)	80	2018	●	↓
Universal health coverage (UHC) index of service coverage (worst 0–100 best)	78.0	2017	●	↑
Subjective well-being (average ladder score, worst 0–10 best)	5.0	2018	●	↓

SDG4 – Quality Education

	Value	Year	Rating	Trend
Net primary enrollment rate (%)	97.6	2018	●	↑
Lower secondary completion rate (%)	84.6	2018	●	↑
Literacy rate (% of population aged 15 to 24)	97.4	2018	●	●

SDG5 – Gender Equality

	Value	Year	Rating	Trend
Demand for family planning satisfied by modern methods (% of females aged 15 to 49 who are married or in unions)	77.2	2013	●	↑
Ratio of female-to-male mean years of education received (%)	92.8	2018	●	↑
Ratio of female-to-male labor force participation rate (%)	22.2	2019	●	↓
Seats held by women in national parliament (%)	25.8	2020	●	↓

SDG6 – Clean Water and Sanitation

	Value	Year	Rating	Trend
Population using at least basic drinking water services (%)	93.6	2017	●	→
Population using at least basic sanitation services (%)	87.6	2017	●	→
Freshwater withdrawal (% of available freshwater resources)	127.7	2015	●	●
Anthropogenic wastewater that receives treatment (%)	33.1	2018	●	●
Scarce water consumption embodied in imports (m³/capita)	3.5	2013	●	↑

SDG7 – Affordable and Clean Energy

	Value	Year	Rating	Trend
Population with access to electricity (%)	100.0	2017	●	↑
Population with access to clean fuels and technology for cooking (%)	92.6	2016	●	↑
CO_2 emissions from fuel combustion for electricity and heating per total electricity output (MtCO$_2$/TWh)	1.8	2017	●	↑

SDG8 – Decent Work and Economic Growth

	Value	Year	Rating	Trend
Adjusted GDP growth (%)	-3.7	2018	●	●
Victims of modern slavery (per 1,000 population)	2.7	2018	●	●
Adults with an account at a bank or other financial institution or with a mobile-money-service provider (% of population aged 15 or over)	42.8	2017	●	↓
Unemployment rate (% of total labor force)	11.7	2019	●	↓
Fatal work-related accidents embodied in imports (per 100,000 population)	0.1	2010	●	↑

SDG9 – Industry, Innovation and Infrastructure

	Value	Year	Rating	Trend
Population using the internet (%)	49.0	2018	●	↑
Mobile broadband subscriptions (per 100 population)	81.7	2018	●	↑
Logistics Performance Index: Quality of trade and transport-related infrastructure (worst 1–5 best)	2.4	2018	●	↓
The Times Higher Education Universities Ranking: Average score of top 3 universities (worst 0–100 best)	24.5	2020	●	●
Scientific and technical journal articles (per 1,000 population)	0.1	2018	●	→
Expenditure on research and development (% of GDP)	0.5	2017	●	●

SDG10 – Reduced Inequalities

	Value	Year	Rating	Trend
Gini coefficient adjusted for top income	31.5	2011	●	●

SDG11 – Sustainable Cities and Communities

	Value	Year	Rating	Trend
Annual mean concentration of particulate matter of less than 2.5 microns in diameter (PM2.5) (µg/m³)	38.9	2017	●	↓
Access to improved water source, piped (% of urban population)	81.9	2017	●	↓
Satisfaction with public transport (%)	57.7	2018	●	↑

SDG12 – Responsible Consumption and Production

	Value	Year	Rating	Trend
Municipal solid waste (kg/capita/day)	1.1	2016	●	●
Electronic waste (kg/capita)	6.2	2016	●	●
Production-based SO_2 emissions (kg/capita)	5.3	2012	●	●
SO_2 emissions embodied in imports (kg/capita)	1.4	2012	●	●
Production-based nitrogen emissions (kg/capita)	9.9	2010	●	●
Nitrogen emissions embodied in imports (kg/capita)	1.0	2010	●	●

SDG13 – Climate Action

	Value	Year	Rating	Trend
Energy-related CO_2 emissions (tCO$_2$/capita)	3.4	2017	●	→
CO_2 emissions embodied in imports (tCO$_2$/capita)	0.2	2015	●	↑
CO_2 emissions embodied in fossil fuel exports (kg/capita)	918.8	2017	●	●

SDG14 – Life Below Water

	Value	Year	Rating	Trend
Mean area that is protected in marine sites important to biodiversity (%)	30.0	2018	●	→
Ocean Health Index: Clean Waters score (worst 0–100 best)	41.4	2019	●	→
Fish caught from overexploited or collapsed stocks (% of total catch)	64.9	2014	●	↓
Fish caught by trawling (%)	29.6	2014	●	↓
Marine biodiversity threats embodied in imports (per million population)	0.0	2018	●	●

SDG15 – Life on Land

	Value	Year	Rating	Trend
Mean area that is protected in terrestrial sites important to biodiversity (%)	40.2	2018	●	→
Mean area that is protected in freshwater sites important to biodiversity (%)	52.5	2018	●	↑
Red List Index of species survival (worst 0–1 best)	0.9	2019	●	↑
Permanent deforestation (% of forest area, 5-year average)	0.8	2018	●	●
Terrestrial and freshwater biodiversity threats embodied in imports (per million population)	0.3	2018	●	●

SDG16 – Peace, Justice and Strong Institutions

	Value	Year	Rating	Trend
Homicides (per 100,000 population)	1.4	2015	●	●
Unsentenced detainees (% of prison population)	12.0	2018	●	↑
Percentage of population who feel safe walking alone at night in the city or area where they live (%)	64.3	2018	●	●
Property Rights (worst 1–7 best)	4.1	2019	●	●
Birth registrations with civil authority (% of children under age 5)	99.6	2018	●	●
Corruption Perception Index (worst 0–100 best)	35	2019	●	↓
Children involved in child labor (% of population aged 5 to 14)	5.0	2016	●	●
Exports of major conventional weapons (TIV constant million USD per 100,000 population)	0.0	2019	●	●
Press Freedom Index (best 0–100 worst)	45.8	2019	●	↓

SDG17 – Partnerships for the Goals

	Value	Year	Rating	Trend
Government spending on health and education (% of GDP)	7.4	2008	●	●
For high-income and all OECD DAC countries: International concessional public finance, including official development assistance (% of GNI)	NA	NA	●	●
Other countries: Government revenue excluding grants (% of GDP)	* 40.4	2011	●	●
Corporate Tax Haven Score (best 0–100 worst)	* 0.0	2019	●	●

* Imputed data point

5. Country Profiles

ANDORRA

▼ OVERALL PERFORMANCE

Index score

na

Regional average score

70.9

SDG Global rank   NA (OF 166)

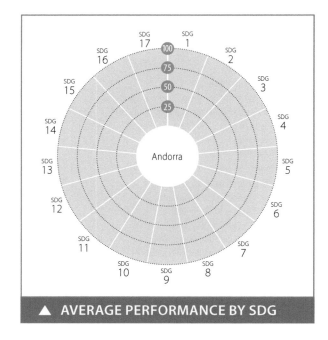

▲ AVERAGE PERFORMANCE BY SDG

▼ SPILLOVER INDEX

100 (best) to 0 (worst)

▼ CURRENT ASSESSMENT – SDG DASHBOARD

■ Major challenges   ■ Significant challenges   ■ Challenges remain   ■ SDG achieved   ■ Information unavailable

▼ SDG TRENDS

↓ Decreasing   → Stagnating   ↗ Moderately improving   ↑ On track or maintaining SDG achievement   ● Information unavailable

Notes: The full title of Goal 2 "Zero Hunger" is "End hunger, achieve food security and improved nutrition and promote sustainable agriculture".
The full title of each SDG is available here: https://sustainabledevelopment.un.org/topics/sustainabledevelopmentgoals

SDG1 – No Poverty

	Value	Year	Rating	Trend
Poverty headcount ratio at $1.90/day (%)	NA	NA	●	●
Poverty headcount ratio at $3.20/day (%)	NA	NA	●	●

SDG2 – Zero Hunger

		Value	Year	Rating	Trend
Prevalence of undernourishment (%)	*	1.2	2017	●	●
Prevalence of stunting in children under 5 years of age (%)	*	2.6	2016	●	↑
Prevalence of wasting in children under 5 years of age (%)	*	0.7	2016	●	↑
Prevalence of obesity, BMI ≥ 30 (% of adult population)		25.6	2016	●	↓
Human Trophic Level (best 2–3 worst)		NA	NA	●	●
Cereal yield (tonnes per hectare of harvested land)		NA	NA	●	●
Sustainable Nitrogen Management Index (best 0–1.41 worst)		NA	NA	●	●

SDG3 – Good Health and Well-Being

	Value	Year	Rating	Trend
Maternal mortality rate (per 100,000 live births)	NA	NA	●	●
Neonatal mortality rate (per 1,000 live births)	1.4	2018	●	↑
Mortality rate, under-5 (per 1,000 live births)	2.9	2018	●	↑
Incidence of tuberculosis (per 100,000 population)	3.0	2018	●	↑
New HIV infections (per 1,000 uninfected population)	NA	NA	●	●
Age-standardized death rate due to cardiovascular disease, cancer, diabetes, or chronic respiratory disease in adults aged 30–70 years (%)	NA	NA	●	●
Age-standardized death rate attributable to household air pollution and ambient air pollution (per 100,000 population)	NA	NA	●	●
Traffic deaths (per 100,000 population)	7.6	2013	●	●
Life expectancy at birth (years)	NA	NA	●	●
Adolescent fertility rate (births per 1,000 adolescent females aged 15 to 19)	NA	NA	●	●
Births attended by skilled health personnel (%)	NA	NA	●	●
Percentage of surviving infants who received 2 WHO-recommended vaccines (%)	99	2018	●	↑
Universal health coverage (UHC) index of service coverage (worst 0–100 best)	NA	NA	●	●
Subjective well-being (average ladder score, worst 0–10 best)	NA	NA	●	●

SDG4 – Quality Education

	Value	Year	Rating	Trend
Net primary enrollment rate (%)	NA	NA	●	●
Lower secondary completion rate (%)	NA	NA	●	●
Literacy rate (% of population aged 15 to 24)	NA	NA	●	●

SDG5 – Gender Equality

	Value	Year	Rating	Trend
Demand for family planning satisfied by modern methods (% of females aged 15 to 49 who are married or in unions)	NA	NA	●	●
Ratio of female-to-male mean years of education received (%)	99.0	2018	●	↑
Ratio of female-to-male labor force participation rate (%)	NA	NA	●	●
Seats held by women in national parliament (%)	46.4	2020	●	↑

SDG6 – Clean Water and Sanitation

	Value	Year	Rating	Trend
Population using at least basic drinking water services (%)	100.0	2017	●	↑
Population using at least basic sanitation services (%)	100.0	2017	●	↑
Freshwater withdrawal (% of available freshwater resources)	NA	NA	●	●
Anthropogenic wastewater that receives treatment (%)	100.0	2018	●	●
Scarce water consumption embodied in imports (m³/capita)	33.8	2013	●	→

SDG7 – Affordable and Clean Energy

	Value	Year	Rating	Trend
Population with access to electricity (%)	100.0	2017	●	↑
Population with access to clean fuels and technology for cooking (%)	100.0	2016	●	↑
CO_2 emissions from fuel combustion for electricity and heating per total electricity output (MtCO$_2$/TWh)	NA	NA	●	●

SDG8 – Decent Work and Economic Growth

		Value	Year	Rating	Trend
Adjusted GDP growth (%)		NA	NA	●	●
Victims of modern slavery (per 1,000 population)		NA	NA	●	●
Adults with an account at a bank or other financial institution or with a mobile-money-service provider (% of population aged 15 or over)		NA	NA	●	●
Unemployment rate (% of total labor force)		NA	NA	●	●
Fatal work-related accidents embodied in imports (per 100,000 population)		1.5	2010	●	↑

SDG9 – Industry, Innovation and Infrastructure

		Value	Year	Rating	Trend
Population using the internet (%)		91.6	2017	●	↑
Mobile broadband subscriptions (per 100 population)		60.4	2018	●	↑
Logistics Performance Index: Quality of trade and transport-related infrastructure (worst 1–5 best)		NA	NA	●	●
The Times Higher Education Universities Ranking: Average score of top 3 universities (worst 0–100 best)	*	0.0	2020	●	●
Scientific and technical journal articles (per 1,000 population)		0.0	2018	●	↓
Expenditure on research and development (% of GDP)		NA	NA	●	●

SDG10 – Reduced Inequalities

	Value	Year	Rating	Trend
Gini coefficient adjusted for top income	NA	NA	●	●

SDG11 – Sustainable Cities and Communities

	Value	Year	Rating	Trend
Annual mean concentration of particulate matter of less than 2.5 microns in diameter (PM2.5) (μg/m³)	10.3	2017	●	↑
Access to improved water source, piped (% of urban population)	99.0	2017	●	↑
Satisfaction with public transport (%)	NA	NA	●	●

SDG12 – Responsible Consumption and Production

	Value	Year	Rating	Trend
Municipal solid waste (kg/capita/day)	1.7	2012	●	●
Electronic waste (kg/capita)	NA	NA	●	●
Production-based SO_2 emissions (kg/capita)	40.1	2012	●	●
SO_2 emissions embodied in imports (kg/capita)	21.3	2012	●	●
Production-based nitrogen emissions (kg/capita)	22.5	2010	●	●
Nitrogen emissions embodied in imports (kg/capita)	14.1	2010	●	●

SDG13 – Climate Action

	Value	Year	Rating	Trend
Energy-related CO_2 emissions (tCO$_2$/capita)	6.2	2017	●	→
CO_2 emissions embodied in imports (tCO$_2$/capita)	2.7	2015	●	→
CO_2 emissions embodied in fossil fuel exports (kg/capita)	0.7	2017	●	●

SDG14 – Life Below Water

	Value	Year	Rating	Trend
Mean area that is protected in marine sites important to biodiversity (%)	NA	NA	●	●
Ocean Health Index: Clean Waters score (worst 0–100 best)	NA	NA	●	●
Fish caught from overexploited or collapsed stocks (% of total catch)	NA	NA	●	●
Fish caught by trawling (%)	NA	NA	●	●
Marine biodiversity threats embodied in imports (per million population)	0.0	2018	●	●

SDG15 – Life on Land

	Value	Year	Rating	Trend
Mean area that is protected in terrestrial sites important to biodiversity (%)	26.1	2018	●	→
Mean area that is protected in freshwater sites important to biodiversity (%)	NA	NA	●	●
Red List Index of species survival (worst 0–1 best)	0.9	2019	●	↑
Permanent deforestation (% of forest area, 5-year average)	NA	NA	●	●
Terrestrial and freshwater biodiversity threats embodied in imports (per million population)	0.6	2018	●	●

SDG16 – Peace, Justice and Strong Institutions

		Value	Year	Rating	Trend
Homicides (per 100,000 population)		1.2	2011	●	●
Unsentenced detainees (% of prison population)		50.6	2018	●	↑
Percentage of population who feel safe walking alone at night in the city or area where they live (%)		NA	NA	●	●
Property Rights (worst 1–7 best)		NA	NA	●	●
Birth registrations with civil authority (% of children under age 5)		100.0	2018	●	●
Corruption Perception Index (worst 0–100 best)		NA	NA	●	●
Children involved in child labor (% of population aged 5 to 14)		NA	NA	●	●
Exports of major conventional weapons (TIV constant million USD per 100,000 population)	*	0.0	2019	●	●
Press Freedom Index (best 0–100 worst)		24.6	2019	●	↑

SDG17 – Partnerships for the Goals

	Value	Year	Rating	Trend
Government spending on health and education (% of GDP)	8.4	2016	●	↑
For high-income and all OECD DAC countries: International concessional public finance, including official development assistance (% of GNI)	NA	NA	●	●
Other countries: Government revenue excluding grants (% of GDP)	NA	NA	●	●
Corporate Tax Haven Score (best 0–100 worst)	69.0	2019	●	●

* Imputed data point

5. Country Profiles

ANGOLA

Sub-Saharan Africa

OVERALL PERFORMANCE

Index score

52.6

Regional average score

53.1

SDG Global rank 149 (OF 166)

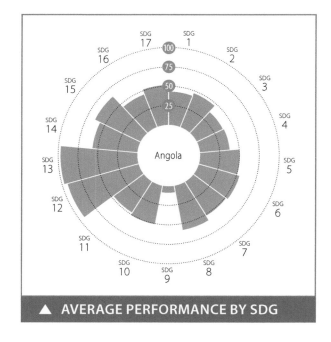

AVERAGE PERFORMANCE BY SDG

SPILLOVER INDEX

100 (best) to 0 (worst)

CURRENT ASSESSMENT – SDG DASHBOARD

■ Major challenges   ■ Significant challenges   ■ Challenges remain   ■ SDG achieved   ■ Information unavailable

SDG TRENDS

↓ Decreasing   → Stagnating   ↗ Moderately improving   ↑ On track or maintaining SDG achievement   ● Information unavailable

Notes: The full title of Goal 2 "Zero Hunger" is "End hunger, achieve food security and improved nutrition and promote sustainable agriculture". The full title of each SDG is available here: https://sustainabledevelopment.un.org/topics/sustainabledevelopmentgoals

ANGOLA

SDG1 – No Poverty

Indicator	Value	Year	Rating	Trend
Poverty headcount ratio at $1.90/day (%)	21.0	2020	●	↓
Poverty headcount ratio at $3.20/day (%)	42.9	2020	●	↓

SDG2 – Zero Hunger

Indicator	Value	Year	Rating	Trend
Prevalence of undernourishment (%)	25.0	2017	●	↗
Prevalence of stunting in children under 5 years of age (%)	37.6	2016	●	→
Prevalence of wasting in children under 5 years of age (%)	4.9	2016	●	↑
Prevalence of obesity, BMI ≥ 30 (% of adult population)	8.2	2016	●	↑
Human Trophic Level (best 2–3 worst)	2.1	2017	●	↑
Cereal yield (tonnes per hectare of harvested land)	0.9	2017	●	→
Sustainable Nitrogen Management Index (best 0–1.41 worst)	0.9	2015	●	↓

SDG3 – Good Health and Well-Being

Indicator	Value	Year	Rating	Trend
Maternal mortality rate (per 100,000 live births)	241	2017	●	→
Neonatal mortality rate (per 1,000 live births)	28.5	2018	●	↗
Mortality rate, under-5 (per 1,000 live births)	77.2	2018	●	↗
Incidence of tuberculosis (per 100,000 population)	355.0	2018	●	→
New HIV infections (per 1,000 uninfected population)	1.0	2018	●	→
Age-standardized death rate due to cardiovascular disease, cancer, diabetes, or chronic respiratory disease in adults aged 30–70 years (%)	16.5	2016	●	↑
Age-standardized death rate attributable to household air pollution and ambient air pollution (per 100,000 population)	119	2016	●	●
Traffic deaths (per 100,000 population)	23.6	2016	●	↑
Life expectancy at birth (years)	62.6	2016	●	→
Adolescent fertility rate (births per 1,000 adolescent females aged 15 to 19)	150.5	2017	●	→
Births attended by skilled health personnel (%)	49.6	2016	●	●
Percentage of surviving infants who received 2 WHO-recommended vaccines (%)	50	2018	●	↓
Universal health coverage (UHC) index of service coverage (worst 0–100 best)	40.0	2017	●	→
Subjective well-being (average ladder score, worst 0–10 best)	3.8	2014	●	●

SDG4 – Quality Education

Indicator	Value	Year	Rating	Trend
Net primary enrollment rate (%)	78.0	2011	●	●
Lower secondary completion rate (%)	20.7	2011	●	●
Literacy rate (% of population aged 15 to 24)	77.4	2014	●	●

SDG5 – Gender Equality

Indicator	Value	Year	Rating	Trend
Demand for family planning satisfied by modern methods (% of females aged 15 to 49 who are married or in unions)	29.8	2016	●	→
Ratio of female-to-male mean years of education received (%)	62.5	2018	●	↓
Ratio of female-to-male labor force participation rate (%)	94.2	2019	●	↑
Seats held by women in national parliament (%)	30.0	2020	●	↓

SDG6 – Clean Water and Sanitation

Indicator	Value	Year	Rating	Trend
Population using at least basic drinking water services (%)	55.8	2017	●	→
Population using at least basic sanitation services (%)	49.9	2017	●	→
Freshwater withdrawal (% of available freshwater resources)	1.9	2005	●	●
Anthropogenic wastewater that receives treatment (%)	0.0	2018	●	●
Scarce water consumption embodied in imports (m³/capita)	1.1	2013	●	↑

SDG7 – Affordable and Clean Energy

Indicator	Value	Year	Rating	Trend
Population with access to electricity (%)	41.9	2017	●	↗
Population with access to clean fuels and technology for cooking (%)	48.1	2016	●	→
CO_2 emissions from fuel combustion for electricity and heating per total electricity output (MtCO$_2$/TWh)	1.7	2017	●	↑

SDG8 – Decent Work and Economic Growth

Indicator	Value	Year	Rating	Trend
Adjusted GDP growth (%)	-9.6	2018	●	●
Victims of modern slavery (per 1,000 population)	7.2	2018	●	●
Adults with an account at a bank or other financial institution or with a mobile-money-service provider (% of population aged 15 or over)	29.3	2014	●	●
Unemployment rate (% of total labor force)	6.9	2019	●	↗
Fatal work-related accidents embodied in imports (per 100,000 population)	0.1	2010	●	↑

SDG9 – Industry, Innovation and Infrastructure

Indicator	Value	Year	Rating	Trend
Population using the internet (%)	14.3	2017	●	↓
Mobile broadband subscriptions (per 100 population)	18.9	2018	●	→
Logistics Performance Index: Quality of trade and transport-related infrastructure (worst 1–5 best)	1.9	2018	●	↓
The Times Higher Education Universities Ranking: Average score of top 3 universities (worst 0–100 best) *	0.0	2020	●	●
Scientific and technical journal articles (per 1,000 population)	0.0	2018	●	→
Expenditure on research and development (% of GDP)	NA	NA	●	●

SDG10 – Reduced Inequalities

Indicator	Value	Year	Rating	Trend
Gini coefficient adjusted for top income	45.1	2008	●	●

SDG11 – Sustainable Cities and Communities

Indicator	Value	Year	Rating	Trend
Annual mean concentration of particulate matter of less than 2.5 microns in diameter (PM2.5) (µg/m³)	32.4	2017	●	→
Access to improved water source, piped (% of urban population)	58.0	2017	●	↗
Satisfaction with public transport (%)	32.2	2014	●	●

SDG12 – Responsible Consumption and Production

Indicator	Value	Year	Rating	Trend
Municipal solid waste (kg/capita/day)	0.6	2012	●	●
Electronic waste (kg/capita)	3.3	2016	●	●
Production-based SO$_2$ emissions (kg/capita)	6.9	2012	●	●
SO$_2$ emissions embodied in imports (kg/capita)	1.6	2012	●	●
Production-based nitrogen emissions (kg/capita)	10.0	2010	●	●
Nitrogen emissions embodied in imports (kg/capita)	0.9	2010	●	●

SDG13 – Climate Action

Indicator	Value	Year	Rating	Trend
Energy-related CO_2 emissions (tCO$_2$/capita)	1.3	2017	●	↑
CO_2 emissions embodied in imports (tCO$_2$/capita)	0.1	2015	●	↑
CO_2 emissions embodied in fossil fuel exports (kg/capita)	88.3	2018	●	●

SDG14 – Life Below Water

Indicator	Value	Year	Rating	Trend
Mean area that is protected in marine sites important to biodiversity (%)	0.9	2018	●	→
Ocean Health Index: Clean Waters score (worst 0–100 best)	55.0	2019	●	↓
Fish caught from overexploited or collapsed stocks (% of total catch)	12.1	2014	●	↑
Fish caught by trawling (%)	28.9	2014	●	↗
Marine biodiversity threats embodied in imports (per million population)	0.2	2018	●	●

SDG15 – Life on Land

Indicator	Value	Year	Rating	Trend
Mean area that is protected in terrestrial sites important to biodiversity (%)	28.4	2018	●	→
Mean area that is protected in freshwater sites important to biodiversity (%)	33.3	2018	●	→
Red List Index of species survival (worst 0–1 best)	0.9	2019	●	↑
Permanent deforestation (% of forest area, 5-year average)	0.2	2018	●	●
Terrestrial and freshwater biodiversity threats embodied in imports (per million population)	0.6	2018	●	●

SDG16 – Peace, Justice and Strong Institutions

Indicator	Value	Year	Rating	Trend
Homicides (per 100,000 population)	4.8	2012	●	●
Unsentenced detainees (% of prison population)	48.0	2018	●	↗
Percentage of population who feel safe walking alone at night in the city or area where they live (%)	46.2	2014	●	●
Property Rights (worst 1–7 best)	3.2	2019	●	●
Birth registrations with civil authority (% of children under age 5)	25.0	2018	●	●
Corruption Perception Index (worst 0–100 best)	26	2019	●	↗
Children involved in child labor (% of population aged 5 to 14)	23.4	2016	●	●
Exports of major conventional weapons (TIV constant million USD per 100,000 population) *	0.0	2019	●	●
Press Freedom Index (best 0–100 worst)	35.0	2019	●	↑

SDG17 – Partnerships for the Goals

Indicator	Value	Year	Rating	Trend
Government spending on health and education (% of GDP)	5.1	2010	●	●
For high-income and all OECD DAC countries: International concessional public finance, including official development assistance (% of GNI)	NA	NA	●	●
Other countries: Government revenue excluding grants (% of GDP)	16.4	2017	●	↓
Corporate Tax Haven Score (best 0–100 worst) *	0.0	2019	●	●

* Imputed data point

5. Country Profiles

▼ OVERALL PERFORMANCE

Index score
na

Regional average score
70.4

SDG Global rank **NA** (OF 166)

▼ SPILLOVER INDEX

100 (best) to 0 (worst)

100
80
60
40
20
0

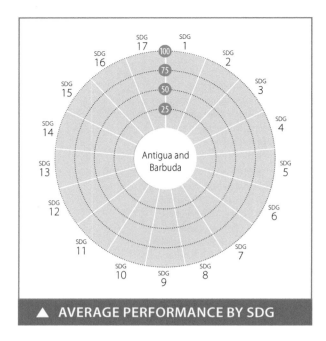

▲ AVERAGE PERFORMANCE BY SDG

Antigua and Barbuda

SDG 1
SDG 2
SDG 3
SDG 4
SDG 5
SDG 6
SDG 7
SDG 8
SDG 9
SDG 10
SDG 11
SDG 12
SDG 13
SDG 14
SDG 15
SDG 16
SDG 17

100
75
50
25

▼ CURRENT ASSESSMENT – SDG DASHBOARD

- ■ Major challenges
- ■ Significant challenges
- ☐ Challenges remain
- ■ SDG achieved
- ■ Information unavailable

▼ SDG TRENDS

- ↓ Decreasing
- → Stagnating
- ↗ Moderately improving
- ↑ On track or maintaining SDG achievement
- ● Information unavailable

Notes: The full title of Goal 2 "Zero Hunger" is "End hunger, achieve food security and improved nutrition and promote sustainable agriculture".
The full title of each SDG is available here: https://sustainabledevelopment.un.org/topics/sustainabledevelopmentgoals

SDG1 – No Poverty

Indicator	Value	Year	Rating	Trend
Poverty headcount ratio at $1.90/day (%)	NA	NA	●	●
Poverty headcount ratio at $3.20/day (%)	NA	NA	●	●

SDG2 – Zero Hunger

Indicator	Value	Year	Rating	Trend
Prevalence of undernourishment (%)	* 1.2	2017	●	●
Prevalence of stunting in children under 5 years of age (%)	* 2.6	2016	●	↑
Prevalence of wasting in children under 5 years of age (%)	* 0.7	2016	●	↑
Prevalence of obesity, BMI ≥ 30 (% of adult population)	18.9	2016	●	↓
Human Trophic Level (best 2–3 worst)	2.4	2017	●	→
Cereal yield (tonnes per hectare of harvested land)	1.6	2017	●	↓
Sustainable Nitrogen Management Index (best 0–1.41 worst)	1.3	2015	●	→

SDG3 – Good Health and Well-Being

Indicator	Value	Year	Rating	Trend
Maternal mortality rate (per 100,000 live births)	42	2017	●	↑
Neonatal mortality rate (per 1,000 live births)	3.4	2018	●	↑
Mortality rate, under-5 (per 1,000 live births)	6.4	2018	●	↑
Incidence of tuberculosis (per 100,000 population)	6.0	2018	●	↑
New HIV infections (per 1,000 uninfected population)	0.6	2018	●	→
Age-standardized death rate due to cardiovascular disease, cancer, diabetes, or chronic respiratory disease in adults aged 30–70 years (%)	22.6	2016	●	↓
Age-standardized death rate attributable to household air pollution and ambient air pollution (per 100,000 population)	30	2016	●	●
Traffic deaths (per 100,000 population)	7.9	2016	●	↑
Life expectancy at birth (years)	75.0	2016	●	→
Adolescent fertility rate (births per 1,000 adolescent females aged 15 to 19)	42.8	2017	●	↗
Births attended by skilled health personnel (%)	100.0	2014	●	●
Percentage of surviving infants who received 2 WHO-recommended vaccines (%)	95	2018	●	↑
Universal health coverage (UHC) index of service coverage (worst 0–100 best)	73.0	2017	●	↑
Subjective well-being (average ladder score, worst 0–10 best)	NA	NA	●	●

SDG4 – Quality Education

Indicator	Value	Year	Rating	Trend
Net primary enrollment rate (%)	95.7	2018	●	↑
Lower secondary completion rate (%)	98.6	2018	●	↑
Literacy rate (% of population aged 15 to 24)	NA	NA	●	●

SDG5 – Gender Equality

Indicator	Value	Year	Rating	Trend
Demand for family planning satisfied by modern methods (% of females aged 15 to 49 who are married or in unions)	* 79.4	2017	●	↑
Ratio of female-to-male mean years of education received (%)	NA	NA	●	●
Ratio of female-to-male labor force participation rate (%)	NA	NA	●	●
Seats held by women in national parliament (%)	11.1	2020	●	→

SDG6 – Clean Water and Sanitation

Indicator	Value	Year	Rating	Trend
Population using at least basic drinking water services (%)	96.7	2017	●	→
Population using at least basic sanitation services (%)	87.5	2017	●	→
Freshwater withdrawal (% of available freshwater resources)	8.5	2010	●	●
Anthropogenic wastewater that receives treatment (%)	1.3	2018	●	●
Scarce water consumption embodied in imports (m³/capita)	15.2	2013	●	↑

SDG7 – Affordable and Clean Energy

Indicator	Value	Year	Rating	Trend
Population with access to electricity (%)	100.0	2017	●	↑
Population with access to clean fuels and technology for cooking (%)	98.8	2016	●	↑
CO₂ emissions from fuel combustion for electricity and heating per total electricity output (MtCO₂/TWh)	NA	NA	●	●

SDG8 – Decent Work and Economic Growth

Indicator	Value	Year	Rating	Trend
Adjusted GDP growth (%)	1.4	2018	●	●
Victims of modern slavery (per 1,000 population)	NA	NA	●	●
Adults with an account at a bank or other financial institution or with a mobile-money-service provider (% of population aged 15 or over)	NA	NA	●	●
Unemployment rate (% of total labor force)	NA	NA	●	●
Fatal work-related accidents embodied in imports (per 100,000 population)	0.9	2010	●	↑

SDG9 – Industry, Innovation and Infrastructure

Indicator	Value	Year	Rating	Trend
Population using the internet (%)	76.0	2017	●	↑
Mobile broadband subscriptions (per 100 population)	50.3	2017	●	↑
Logistics Performance Index: Quality of trade and transport-related infrastructure (worst 1–5 best)	NA	NA	●	●
The Times Higher Education Universities Ranking: Average score of top 3 universities (worst 0–100 best)	* 0.0	2020	●	●
Scientific and technical journal articles (per 1,000 population)	0.1	2018	●	→
Expenditure on research and development (% of GDP)	NA	NA	●	●

SDG10 – Reduced Inequalities

Indicator	Value	Year	Rating	Trend
Gini coefficient adjusted for top income	NA	NA	●	●

SDG11 – Sustainable Cities and Communities

Indicator	Value	Year	Rating	Trend
Annual mean concentration of particulate matter of less than 2.5 microns in diameter (PM2.5) (μg/m³)	18.6	2017	●	↗
Access to improved water source, piped (% of urban population)	NA	NA	●	●
Satisfaction with public transport (%)	NA	NA	●	●

SDG12 – Responsible Consumption and Production

Indicator	Value	Year	Rating	Trend
Municipal solid waste (kg/capita/day)	3.3	2012	●	●
Electronic waste (kg/capita)	12.0	2016	●	●
Production-based SO₂ emissions (kg/capita)	1201.9	2012	●	●
SO₂ emissions embodied in imports (kg/capita)	17.6	2012	●	●
Production-based nitrogen emissions (kg/capita)	37.4	2010	●	●
Nitrogen emissions embodied in imports (kg/capita)	12.7	2010	●	●

SDG13 – Climate Action

Indicator	Value	Year	Rating	Trend
Energy-related CO₂ emissions (tCO₂/capita)	5.9	2017	●	→
CO₂ emissions embodied in imports (tCO₂/capita)	2.0	2015	●	→
CO₂ emissions embodied in fossil fuel exports (kg/capita)	* 0.0	2018	●	●

SDG14 – Life Below Water

Indicator	Value	Year	Rating	Trend
Mean area that is protected in marine sites important to biodiversity (%)	35.5	2018	●	→
Ocean Health Index: Clean Waters score (worst 0–100 best)	61.6	2019	●	↓
Fish caught from overexploited or collapsed stocks (% of total catch)	68.9	2014	●	↓
Fish caught by trawling (%)	NA	NA	●	●
Marine biodiversity threats embodied in imports (per million population)	0.9	2018	●	●

SDG15 – Life on Land

Indicator	Value	Year	Rating	Trend
Mean area that is protected in terrestrial sites important to biodiversity (%)	14.9	2018	●	→
Mean area that is protected in freshwater sites important to biodiversity (%)	NA	NA	●	●
Red List Index of species survival (worst 0–1 best)	0.9	2019	●	→
Permanent deforestation (% of forest area, 5-year average)	0.3	2018	●	●
Terrestrial and freshwater biodiversity threats embodied in imports (per million population)	0.3	2018	●	●

SDG16 – Peace, Justice and Strong Institutions

Indicator	Value	Year	Rating	Trend
Homicides (per 100,000 population)	10.3	2012	●	●
Unsentenced detainees (% of prison population)	38.5	2018	●	↑
Percentage of population who feel safe walking alone at night in the city or area where they live	NA	NA	●	●
Property Rights (worst 1–7 best)	NA	NA	●	●
Birth registrations with civil authority (% of children under age 5)	NA	NA	●	●
Corruption Perception Index (worst 0–100 best)	NA	NA	●	●
Children involved in child labor (% of population aged 5 to 14)	NA	NA	●	●
Exports of major conventional weapons (TIV constant million USD per 100,000 population)	* 0.0	2019	●	●
Press Freedom Index (best 0–100 worst)	NA	NA	●	●

SDG17 – Partnerships for the Goals

Indicator	Value	Year	Rating	Trend
Government spending on health and education (% of GDP)	5.8	2009	●	●
For high-income and all OECD DAC countries: International concessional public finance, including official development assistance (% of GNI)	NA	NA	●	●
Other countries: Government revenue excluding grants (% of GDP)	* NA	NA	●	●
Corporate Tax Haven Score (best 0–100 worst)	* 0.0	2019	●	●

* Imputed data point

5. Country Profiles

▼ OVERALL PERFORMANCE

Index score

73.2

Regional average score

70.4

SDG Global rank 51 (OF 166)

▼ SPILLOVER INDEX

100 (best) to 0 (worst)

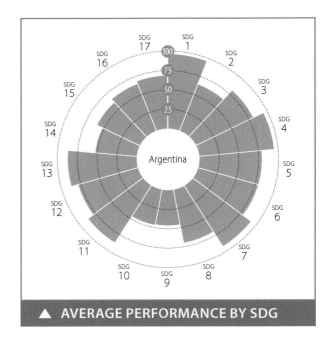

▲ AVERAGE PERFORMANCE BY SDG

▼ CURRENT ASSESSMENT – SDG DASHBOARD

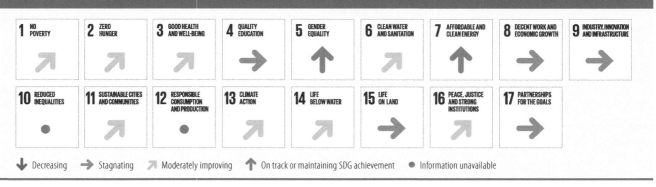

■ Major challenges   ■ Significant challenges   ■ Challenges remain   ■ SDG achieved   ■ Information unavailable

▼ SDG TRENDS

1 NO POVERTY	2 ZERO HUNGER	3 GOOD HEALTH AND WELL-BEING	4 QUALITY EDUCATION	5 GENDER EQUALITY	6 CLEAN WATER AND SANITATION	7 AFFORDABLE AND CLEAN ENERGY	8 DECENT WORK AND ECONOMIC GROWTH	9 INDUSTRY, INNOVATION AND INFRASTRUCTURE
↗	↗	↗	→	↑	↗	↑	→	→

10 REDUCED INEQUALITIES	11 SUSTAINABLE CITIES AND COMMUNITIES	12 RESPONSIBLE CONSUMPTION AND PRODUCTION	13 CLIMATE ACTION	14 LIFE BELOW WATER	15 LIFE ON LAND	16 PEACE, JUSTICE AND STRONG INSTITUTIONS	17 PARTNERSHIPS FOR THE GOALS
●	↗	●	↗	↗	→	↗	→

↓ Decreasing   → Stagnating   ↗ Moderately improving   ↑ On track or maintaining SDG achievement   ● Information unavailable

Notes: The full title of Goal 2 "Zero Hunger" is "End hunger, achieve food security and improved nutrition and promote sustainable agriculture".
The full title of each SDG is available here: https://sustainabledevelopment.un.org/topics/sustainabledevelopmentgoals

SDG1 – No Poverty

Indicator	Value	Year	Rating	Trend
Poverty headcount ratio at $1.90/day (%)	0.7	2020	●	↑
Poverty headcount ratio at $3.20/day (%)	2.9	2020	●	→

SDG2 – Zero Hunger

Indicator	Value	Year	Rating	Trend
Prevalence of undernourishment (%)	4.6	2017	●	↑
Prevalence of stunting in children under 5 years of age (%)	8.2	2005	●	↑
Prevalence of wasting in children under 5 years of age (%)	1.2	2005	●	↑
Prevalence of obesity, BMI ≥ 30 (% of adult population)	28.3	2016	●	↓
Human Trophic Level (best 2–3 worst)	2.4	2017	●	→
Cereal yield (tonnes per hectare of harvested land)	5.4	2017	●	↑
Sustainable Nitrogen Management Index (best 0–1.41 worst)	0.3	2015	●	↑

SDG3 – Good Health and Well-Being

Indicator	Value	Year	Rating	Trend
Maternal mortality rate (per 100,000 live births)	39	2017	●	↑
Neonatal mortality rate (per 1,000 live births)	6.4	2018	●	↑
Mortality rate, under-5 (per 1,000 live births)	9.9	2018	●	↑
Incidence of tuberculosis (per 100,000 population)	27.0	2018	●	→
New HIV infections (per 1,000 uninfected population)	0.2	2018	●	↑
Age-standardized death rate due to cardiovascular disease, cancer, diabetes, or chronic respiratory disease in adults aged 30–70 years (%)	15.8	2016	●	↑
Age-standardized death rate attributable to household air pollution and ambient air pollution (per 100,000 population)	27	2016	●	●
Traffic deaths (per 100,000 population)	14.0	2016	●	↓
Life expectancy at birth (years)	76.9	2016	●	↗
Adolescent fertility rate (births per 1,000 adolescent females aged 15 to 19)	62.8	2017	●	→
Births attended by skilled health personnel (%)	99.6	2015	●	↑
Percentage of surviving infants who received 2 WHO-recommended vaccines (%)	86	2018	●	↓
Universal health coverage (UHC) index of service coverage (worst 0–100 best)	76.0	2017	●	↑
Subjective well-being (average ladder score, worst 0–10 best)	6.1	2019	●	↑

SDG4 – Quality Education

Indicator	Value	Year	Rating	Trend
Net primary enrollment rate (%)	99.2	2017	●	↑
Lower secondary completion rate (%)	89.8	2017	●	↓
Literacy rate (% of population aged 15 to 24)	99.5	2018	●	●

SDG5 – Gender Equality

Indicator	Value	Year	Rating	Trend
Demand for family planning satisfied by modern methods (% of females aged 15 to 49 who are married or in unions) *	81.4	2017	●	↑
Ratio of female-to-male mean years of education received (%)	101.9	2018	●	↑
Ratio of female-to-male labor force participation rate (%)	67.2	2019	●	↑
Seats held by women in national parliament (%)	40.9	2020	●	↑

SDG6 – Clean Water and Sanitation

Indicator	Value	Year	Rating	Trend
Population using at least basic drinking water services (%)	99.1	2016	●	↑
Population using at least basic sanitation services (%)	94.3	2016	●	↗
Freshwater withdrawal (% of available freshwater resources)	10.5	2010	●	●
Anthropogenic wastewater that receives treatment (%)	5.9	2018	●	●
Scarce water consumption embodied in imports (m³/capita)	2.7	2013	●	↑

SDG7 – Affordable and Clean Energy

Indicator	Value	Year	Rating	Trend
Population with access to electricity (%)	100.0	2017	●	↑
Population with access to clean fuels and technology for cooking (%)	98.4	2016	●	↑
CO_2 emissions from fuel combustion for electricity and heating per total electricity output (MtCO₂/TWh)	1.3	2017	●	↑

SDG8 – Decent Work and Economic Growth

Indicator	Value	Year	Rating	Trend
Adjusted GDP growth (%)	-4.8	2018	●	●
Victims of modern slavery (per 1,000 population)	1.3	2018	●	●
Adults with an account at a bank or other financial institution or with a mobile-money-service provider (% of population aged 15 or over)	48.7	2017	●	↓
Unemployment rate (% of total labor force)	9.8	2019	●	↓
Fatal work-related accidents embodied in imports (per 100,000 population)	0.3	2010	●	↑

SDG9 – Industry, Innovation and Infrastructure

Indicator	Value	Year	Rating	Trend
Population using the internet (%)	74.3	2017	●	↑
Mobile broadband subscriptions (per 100 population)	80.7	2017	●	↑
Logistics Performance Index: Quality of trade and transport-related infrastructure (worst 1–5 best)	2.8	2018	●	↓
The Times Higher Education Universities Ranking: Average score of top 3 universities (worst 0–100 best)	16.4	2020	●	●
Scientific and technical journal articles (per 1,000 population)	0.2	2018	●	→
Expenditure on research and development (% of GDP)	0.5	2016	●	↓

SDG10 – Reduced Inequalities

Indicator	Value	Year	Rating	Trend
Gini coefficient adjusted for top income	46.7	2016	●	●

SDG11 – Sustainable Cities and Communities

Indicator	Value	Year	Rating	Trend
Annual mean concentration of particulate matter of less than 2.5 microns in diameter (PM2.5) (µg/m³)	13.3	2017	●	↑
Access to improved water source, piped (% of urban population)	98.0	2017	●	↑
Satisfaction with public transport (%)	63.5	2019	●	↓

SDG12 – Responsible Consumption and Production

Indicator	Value	Year	Rating	Trend
Municipal solid waste (kg/capita/day)	1.2	2014	●	●
Electronic waste (kg/capita)	8.4	2016	●	●
Production-based SO_2 emissions (kg/capita)	22.2	2012	●	●
SO_2 emissions embodied in imports (kg/capita)	3.8	2012	●	●
Production-based nitrogen emissions (kg/capita)	46.6	2010	●	●
Nitrogen emissions embodied in imports (kg/capita)	2.4	2010	●	●

SDG13 – Climate Action

Indicator	Value	Year	Rating	Trend
Energy-related CO_2 emissions (tCO₂/capita)	4.6	2017	●	→
CO_2 emissions embodied in imports (tCO₂/capita)	0.7	2015	●	↑
CO_2 emissions embodied in fossil fuel exports (kg/capita)	3.9	2018	●	●

SDG14 – Life Below Water

Indicator	Value	Year	Rating	Trend
Mean area that is protected in marine sites important to biodiversity (%)	35.3	2018	●	↑
Ocean Health Index: Clean Waters score (worst 0–100 best)	81.9	2019	●	↑
Fish caught from overexploited or collapsed stocks (% of total catch)	74.0	2014	●	↓
Fish caught by trawling (%)	60.5	2014	●	→
Marine biodiversity threats embodied in imports (per million population)	0.0	2018	●	●

SDG15 – Life on Land

Indicator	Value	Year	Rating	Trend
Mean area that is protected in terrestrial sites important to biodiversity (%)	32.4	2018	●	→
Mean area that is protected in freshwater sites important to biodiversity (%)	39.6	2018	●	→
Red List Index of species survival (worst 0–1 best)	0.9	2019	●	→
Permanent deforestation (% of forest area, 5-year average)	0.4	2018	●	●
Terrestrial and freshwater biodiversity threats embodied in imports (per million population)	0.5	2018	●	●

SDG16 – Peace, Justice and Strong Institutions

Indicator	Value	Year	Rating	Trend
Homicides (per 100,000 population)	5.2	2017	●	↑
Unsentenced detainees (% of prison population)	46.3	2018	●	↑
Percentage of population who feel safe walking alone at night in the city or area where they live (%)	44.2	2019	●	→
Property Rights (worst 1–7 best)	3.8	2019	●	●
Birth registrations with civil authority (% of children under age 5)	99.5	2018	●	●
Corruption Perception Index (worst 0–100 best)	45	2019	●	↑
Children involved in child labor (% of population aged 5 to 14)	4.4	2016	●	●
Exports of major conventional weapons (TIV constant million USD per 100,000 population) *	0.0	2019	●	●
Press Freedom Index (best 0–100 worst)	28.3	2019	●	↑

SDG17 – Partnerships for the Goals

Indicator	Value	Year	Rating	Trend
Government spending on health and education (% of GDP)	11.2	2016	●	↑
For high-income and all OECD DAC countries: International concessional public finance, including official development assistance (% of GNI)	NA	NA	●	●
Other countries: Government revenue excluding grants (% of GDP)	19.4	2017	●	↓
Corporate Tax Haven Score (best 0–100 worst) *	0.0	2019	●	●

* Imputed data point

5. Country Profiles

ARMENIA

Eastern Europe and Central Asia

▼ OVERALL PERFORMANCE

Index score
69.9

Regional average score
70.9

SDG Global rank **75** (OF 166)

▼ SPILLOVER INDEX

100 (best) to 0 (worst)

100
80
60
40
20
0

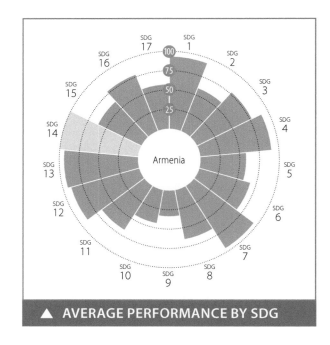

▲ AVERAGE PERFORMANCE BY SDG

▼ CURRENT ASSESSMENT – SDG DASHBOARD

■ Major challenges ■ Significant challenges ■ Challenges remain ■ SDG achieved ■ Information unavailable

▼ SDG TRENDS

↓ Decreasing → Stagnating ↗ Moderately improving ↑ On track or maintaining SDG achievement ● Information unavailable

Notes: The full title of Goal 2 "Zero Hunger" is "End hunger, achieve food security and improved nutrition and promote sustainable agriculture".
The full title of each SDG is available here: https://sustainabledevelopment.un.org/topics/sustainabledevelopmentgoals

ARMENIA

SDG1 – No Poverty

Indicator	Value	Year	Rating	Trend
Poverty headcount ratio at $1.90/day (%)	0.7	2020	●	↑
Poverty headcount ratio at $3.20/day (%)	6.5	2020	○	↑

SDG2 – Zero Hunger

Indicator	Value	Year	Rating	Trend
Prevalence of undernourishment (%)	4.3	2017	●	↑
Prevalence of stunting in children under 5 years of age (%)	9.4	2016	○	↑
Prevalence of wasting in children under 5 years of age (%)	4.2	2016	●	↑
Prevalence of obesity, BMI ≥ 30 (% of adult population)	20.2	2016	●	↓
Human Trophic Level (best 2–3 worst)	2.3	2017	●	→
Cereal yield (tonnes per hectare of harvested land)	2.0	2017	●	↓
Sustainable Nitrogen Management Index (best 0–1.41 worst)	0.6	2015	●	↓

SDG3 – Good Health and Well-Being

Indicator	Value	Year	Rating	Trend
Maternal mortality rate (per 100,000 live births)	26	2017	●	↑
Neonatal mortality rate (per 1,000 live births)	6.5	2018	●	↑
Mortality rate, under-5 (per 1,000 live births)	12.4	2018	●	↑
Incidence of tuberculosis (per 100,000 population)	31.0	2018	○	↑
New HIV infections (per 1,000 uninfected population)	0.1	2018	●	↑
Age-standardized death rate due to cardiovascular disease, cancer, diabetes, or chronic respiratory disease in adults aged 30–70 years (%)	22.3	2016	●	↑
Age-standardized death rate attributable to household air pollution and ambient air pollution (per 100,000 population)	55	2016	●	●
Traffic deaths (per 100,000 population)	17.1	2016	●	↗
Life expectancy at birth (years)	74.8	2016	●	→
Adolescent fertility rate (births per 1,000 adolescent females aged 15 to 19)	21.5	2017	●	↑
Births attended by skilled health personnel (%)	99.8	2016	●	↑
Percentage of surviving infants who received 2 WHO-recommended vaccines (%)	92	2018	●	↑
Universal health coverage (UHC) index of service coverage (worst 0–100 best)	69.0	2017	●	↑
Subjective well-being (average ladder score, worst 0–10 best)	5.1	2018	●	↑

SDG4 – Quality Education

Indicator	Value	Year	Rating	Trend
Net primary enrollment rate (%)	90.7	2018	○	↓
Lower secondary completion rate (%)	93.3	2018	●	↑
Literacy rate (% of population aged 15 to 24)	99.8	2017	●	●

SDG5 – Gender Equality

Indicator	Value	Year	Rating	Trend
Demand for family planning satisfied by modern methods (% of females aged 15 to 49 who are married or in unions)	36.9	2016	●	→
Ratio of female-to-male mean years of education received (%)	100.0	2018	●	↑
Ratio of female-to-male labor force participation rate (%)	71.0	2019	●	↑
Seats held by women in national parliament (%)	23.5	2020	●	↑

SDG6 – Clean Water and Sanitation

Indicator	Value	Year	Rating	Trend
Population using at least basic drinking water services (%)	99.9	2017	●	↑
Population using at least basic sanitation services (%)	93.6	2017	○	↑
Freshwater withdrawal (% of available freshwater resources)	64.2	2015	●	●
Anthropogenic wastewater that receives treatment (%)	8.8	2018	●	●
Scarce water consumption embodied in imports (m³/capita)	5.1	2013	●	↑

SDG7 – Affordable and Clean Energy

Indicator	Value	Year	Rating	Trend
Population with access to electricity (%)	100.0	2017	●	↑
Population with access to clean fuels and technology for cooking (%)	96.9	2016	●	↑
CO_2 emissions from fuel combustion for electricity and heating per total electricity output (MtCO_2/TWh)	0.7	2017	●	↑

SDG8 – Decent Work and Economic Growth

Indicator	Value	Year	Rating	Trend
Adjusted GDP growth (%)	-0.4	2018	○	●
Victims of modern slavery (per 1,000 population)	5.3	2018	○	●
Adults with an account at a bank or other financial institution or with a mobile-money-service provider (% of population aged 15 or over)	47.8	2017	●	↑
Unemployment rate (% of total labor force)	17.0	2019	●	→
Fatal work-related accidents embodied in imports (per 100,000 population)	0.1	2010	●	↑

SDG9 – Industry, Innovation and Infrastructure

Indicator	Value	Year	Rating	Trend
Population using the internet (%)	64.7	2017	●	↑
Mobile broadband subscriptions (per 100 population)	75.9	2018	●	↑
Logistics Performance Index: Quality of trade and transport-related infrastructure (worst 1–5 best)	2.5	2018	●	↗
The Times Higher Education Universities Ranking: Average score of top 3 universities (worst 0–100 best) *	0.0	2020	●	●
Scientific and technical journal articles (per 1,000 population)	0.2	2018	●	↓
Expenditure on research and development (% of GDP)	0.2	2017	●	↓

SDG10 – Reduced Inequalities

Indicator	Value	Year	Rating	Trend
Gini coefficient adjusted for top income	47.5	2017	●	●

SDG11 – Sustainable Cities and Communities

Indicator	Value	Year	Rating	Trend
Annual mean concentration of particulate matter of less than 2.5 microns in diameter (PM2.5) (µg/m³)	32.5	2017	●	→
Access to improved water source, piped (% of urban population)	99.0	2017	●	↑
Satisfaction with public transport (%)	42.7	2018	●	↓

SDG12 – Responsible Consumption and Production

Indicator	Value	Year	Rating	Trend
Municipal solid waste (kg/capita/day)	0.7	2014	●	●
Electronic waste (kg/capita)	4.7	2016	●	●
Production-based SO_2 emissions (kg/capita)	41.3	2012	○	●
SO_2 emissions embodied in imports (kg/capita)	2.6	2012	●	●
Production-based nitrogen emissions (kg/capita)	9.1	2010	●	●
Nitrogen emissions embodied in imports (kg/capita)	1.2	2010	●	●

SDG13 – Climate Action

Indicator	Value	Year	Rating	Trend
Energy-related CO_2 emissions (tCO_2/capita)	2.0	2017	●	↑
CO_2 emissions embodied in imports (tCO_2/capita)	0.3	2015	●	↑
CO_2 emissions embodied in fossil fuel exports (kg/capita)	0.0	2019	●	●

SDG14 – Life Below Water

Indicator	Value	Year	Rating	Trend
Mean area that is protected in marine sites important to biodiversity (%)	NA	NA	●	●
Ocean Health Index: Clean Waters score (worst 0–100 best)	NA	NA	●	●
Fish caught from overexploited or collapsed stocks (% of total catch)	NA	NA	●	●
Fish caught by trawling (%)	NA	NA	●	●
Marine biodiversity threats embodied in imports (per million population)	0.0	2018	●	●

SDG15 – Life on Land

Indicator	Value	Year	Rating	Trend
Mean area that is protected in terrestrial sites important to biodiversity (%)	21.5	2018	●	→
Mean area that is protected in freshwater sites important to biodiversity (%)	26.8	2018	●	→
Red List Index of species survival (worst 0–1 best)	0.8	2019	●	→
Permanent deforestation (% of forest area, 5-year average) *	0.0	2018	●	●
Terrestrial and freshwater biodiversity threats embodied in imports (per million population)	0.1	2018	●	●

SDG16 – Peace, Justice and Strong Institutions

Indicator	Value	Year	Rating	Trend
Homicides (per 100,000 population)	2.4	2017	○	↗
Unsentenced detainees (% of prison population)	36.3	2018	○	↓
Percentage of population who feel safe walking alone at night in the city or area where they live	89.1	2018	●	↑
Property Rights (worst 1–7 best)	4.8	2019	●	●
Birth registrations with civil authority (% of children under age 5)	98.7	2018	●	●
Corruption Perception Index (worst 0–100 best)	42	2019	●	↑
Children involved in child labor (% of population aged 5 to 14)	8.7	2016	●	●
Exports of major conventional weapons (TIV constant million USD per 100,000 population) *	0.0	2019	●	●
Press Freedom Index (best 0–100 worst)	29.0	2019	●	↑

SDG17 – Partnerships for the Goals

Indicator	Value	Year	Rating	Trend
Government spending on health and education (% of GDP)	4.4	2016	●	→
For high-income and all OECD DAC countries: International concessional public finance, including official development assistance (% of GNI)	NA	NA	●	●
Other countries: Government revenue excluding grants (% of GDP)	22.5	2018	●	↓
Corporate Tax Haven Score (best 0–100 worst) *	0.0	2019	●	●

* Imputed data point

5. Country Profiles

▼ OVERALL PERFORMANCE

Index score

74.9

Regional average score

77.3

SDG Global rank **37** (OF 166)

▼ SPILLOVER INDEX

100 (best) to 0 (worst)

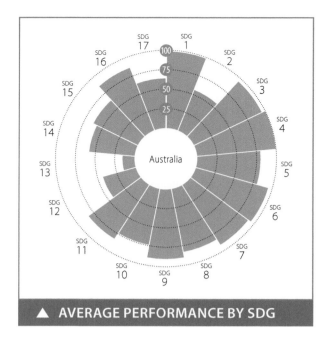

Australia

▲ AVERAGE PERFORMANCE BY SDG

▼ CURRENT ASSESSMENT – SDG DASHBOARD

■ Major challenges　■ Significant challenges　■ Challenges remain　■ SDG achieved　■ Information unavailable

▼ SDG TRENDS

↓ Decreasing　→ Stagnating　↗ Moderately improving　↑ On track or maintaining SDG achievement　● Information unavailable

Notes: The full title of Goal 2 "Zero Hunger" is "End hunger, achieve food security and improved nutrition and promote sustainable agriculture".
The full title of each SDG is available here: https://sustainabledevelopment.un.org/topics/sustainabledevelopmentgoals

SDG1 – No Poverty

Indicator	Value	Year	Rating	Trend
Poverty headcount ratio at $1.90/day (%)	0.5	2020	●	↑
Poverty headcount ratio at $3.20/day (%)	0.6	2020	●	↑
Poverty rate after taxes and transfers (%)	12.4	2018	◐	↗

SDG2 – Zero Hunger

Indicator	Value	Year	Rating	Trend
Prevalence of undernourishment (%)	2.5	2017	●	↑
Prevalence of stunting in children under 5 years of age (%)	2.0	2007	●	↑
Prevalence of wasting in children under 5 years of age (%)	0.0	2007	●	↑
Prevalence of obesity, BMI ≥ 30 (% of adult population)	29.0	2016	●	↓
Human Trophic Level (best 2–3 worst)	2.5	2017	●	→
Cereal yield (tonnes per hectare of harvested land)	2.7	2017	●	↑
Sustainable Nitrogen Management Index (best 0–1.41 worst)	0.6	2015	●	→
Yield gap closure (% of potential yield)	47.7	2015	●	●

SDG3 – Good Health and Well-Being

Indicator	Value	Year	Rating	Trend
Maternal mortality rate (per 100,000 live births)	6	2017	●	↑
Neonatal mortality rate (per 1,000 live births)	2.3	2018	●	↑
Mortality rate, under-5 (per 1,000 live births)	3.7	2018	●	↑
Incidence of tuberculosis (per 100,000 population)	6.6	2018	●	↑
New HIV infections (per 1,000 uninfected population)	0.0	2018	●	↑
Age-standardized death rate due to cardiovascular disease, cancer, diabetes, or chronic respiratory disease in adults aged 30–70 years (%)	9.1	2016	●	↑
Age-standardized death rate attributable to household air pollution and ambient air pollution (per 100,000 population)	8	2016	●	●
Traffic deaths (per 100,000 population)	5.6	2016	●	↑
Life expectancy at birth (years)	82.9	2016	●	↑
Adolescent fertility rate (births per 1,000 adolescent females aged 15 to 19)	11.7	2017	●	↑
Births attended by skilled health personnel (%)	99.7	2015	●	↑
Percentage of surviving infants who received 2 WHO-recommended vaccines (%)	95.0	2018	●	↑
Universal health coverage (UHC) index of service coverage (worst 0–100 best)	87.0	2017	●	↑
Subjective well-being (average ladder score, worst 0–10 best)	7.2	2019	●	↑
Gap in life expectancy at birth among regions (years)	2.4	2015	●	●
Gap in self-reported health status by income (percentage points)	8.9	2017	●	↑
Daily smokers (% of population aged 15 and over)	12.4	2016	●	↑

SDG4 – Quality Education

Indicator	Value	Year	Rating	Trend
Net primary enrollment rate (%)	* 100.0	2017	●	↑
Lower secondary completion rate (%)	* 100.0	2017	●	↑
Literacy rate (% of population aged 15 to 24)	NA	NA	●	●
Participation rate in pre-primary organized learning (% of children aged 4 to 6)	86.4	2017	◐	↑
Tertiary educational attainment (% of population aged 25 to 34)	51.4	2018	●	↑
PISA score (worst 0–600 best)	499.0	2018	●	↑
Variation in science performance explained by socio-economic status (%)	10.0	2018	●	↑
Underachievers in science (% of 15-year-olds)	18.9	2018	◐	↓
Resilient students in science (% of 15-year-olds)	35.3	2018	◐	↑

SDG5 – Gender Equality

Indicator	Value	Year	Rating	Trend
Demand for family planning satisfied by modern methods (% of females aged 15 to 49 who are married or in unions)	* 83.1	2017	●	↑
Ratio of female-to-male mean years of education received (%)	100.8	2018	●	↑
Ratio of female-to-male labor force participation rate (%)	84.7	2019	●	↑
Seats held by women in national parliament (%)	30.5	2020	◐	↗
Gender wage gap (% of male median wage)	11.7	2018	●	↑
Gender gap in time spent doing unpaid work (minutes/day)	139.4	2006	●	●

SDG6 – Clean Water and Sanitation

Indicator	Value	Year	Rating	Trend
Population using at least basic drinking water services (%)	100.0	2017	●	●
Population using at least basic sanitation services (%)	100.0	2017	●	●
Freshwater withdrawal (% of available freshwater resources)	6.2	2015	●	●
Anthropogenic wastewater that receives treatment (%)	92.7	2018	●	●
Scarce water consumption embodied in imports (m³/capita)	17.9	2013	●	↑
Population using safely managed water services (%)	* 100.0	2017	●	●
Population using safely managed sanitation services (%)	75.6	2017	●	↗

SDG7 – Affordable and Clean Energy

Indicator	Value	Year	Rating	Trend
Population with access to electricity (%)	100.0	2017	●	↑
Population with access to clean fuels and technology for cooking (%)	100.0	2016	●	↑
CO2 emissions from fuel combustion for electricity and heating per total electricity output (MtCO2/TWh)	1.6	2017	●	→
Share of renewable energy in total primary energy supply (%)	6.9	2018	●	→

SDG8 – Decent Work and Economic Growth

Indicator	Value	Year	Rating	Trend
Adjusted GDP growth (%)	0.0	2018	●	●
Victims of modern slavery (per 1,000 population)	0.6	2018	●	●
Adults with an account at a bank or other financial institution or with a mobile-money-service provider (% of population aged 15 or over)	99.5	2017	●	↑
Fatal work-related accidents embodied in imports (per 100,000 population)	2.4	2010	●	↑
Employment-to-population ratio (%)	74.3	2019	●	↑
Youth not in employment, education or training (NEET) (% of population aged 15 to 29)	10.8	2018	◐	↑

SDG9 – Industry, Innovation and Infrastructure

Indicator	Value	Year	Rating	Trend
Population using the internet (%)	86.5	2017	●	↑
Mobile broadband subscriptions (per 100 population)	129.6	2018	●	↑
Logistics Performance Index: Quality of trade and transport-related infrastructure (worst 1–5 best)	4.0	2018	●	↑
The Times Higher Education Universities Ranking: Average score of top 3 universities (worst 0–100 best)	73.1	2020	●	●
Scientific and technical journal articles (per 1,000 population)	2.2	2018	●	↑
Expenditure on research and development (% of GDP)	1.9	2015	●	●
Researchers (per 1,000 employed population)	9.0	2010	●	●
Triadic patent families filed (per million population)	13.5	2017	●	↓
Gap in internet access by income (percentage points)	57.0	2008	●	●
Women in science and engineering (% of tertiary graduates in science and engineering)	27.6	2015	●	●

SDG10 – Reduced Inequalities

Indicator	Value	Year	Rating	Trend
Gini coefficient adjusted for top income	36.9	2014	●	●
Palma ratio	1.3	2018	●	→
Elderly poverty rate (% of population aged 66 or over)	23.7	2018	●	→

SDG11 – Sustainable Cities and Communities

Indicator	Value	Year	Rating	Trend
Annual mean concentration of particulate matter of less than 2.5 microns in diameter (PM2.5) (µg/m³)	8.6	2017	●	↑
Access to improved water source, piped (% of urban population)	92.4	2017	◐	→
Satisfaction with public transport (%)	56.6	2019	●	→
Population with rent overburden (%)	9.9	2017	◐	↓

SDG12 – Responsible Consumption and Production

Indicator	Value	Year	Rating	Trend
Electronic waste (kg/capita)	23.6	2016	●	●
Production-based SO2 emissions (kg/capita)	144.6	2012	●	●
SO2 emissions embodied in imports (kg/capita)	15.2	2012	●	●
Production-based nitrogen emissions (kg/capita)	105.4	2010	●	●
Nitrogen emissions embodied in imports (kg/capita)	9.0	2010	●	●
Non-recycled municipal solid waste (kg/capita/day)	0.8	2017	●	●

SDG13 – Climate Action

Indicator	Value	Year	Rating	Trend
Energy-related CO2 emissions (tCO2/capita)	14.8	2017	●	→
CO2 emissions embodied in imports (tCO2/capita)	3.0	2015	●	→
CO2 emissions embodied in fossil fuel exports (kg/capita)	45100.5	2018	●	●
Effective carbon rate (EUR/tCO2)	2.6	2016	●	●

SDG14 – Life Below Water

Indicator	Value	Year	Rating	Trend
Mean area that is protected in marine sites important to biodiversity (%)	66.0	2018	●	↑
Ocean Health Index: Clean Waters score (worst 0–100 best)	80.3	2019	●	↑
Fish caught from overexploited or collapsed stocks (% of total catch)	73.7	2014	●	↓
Fish caught by trawling (%)	28.3	2014	◐	↓
Marine biodiversity threats embodied in imports (per million population)	0.8	2018	●	●

SDG15 – Life on Land

Indicator	Value	Year	Rating	Trend
Mean area that is protected in terrestrial sites important to biodiversity (%)	52.7	2018	●	↑
Mean area that is protected in freshwater sites important to biodiversity (%)	36.6	2018	●	→
Red List Index of species survival (worst 0–1 best)	0.8	2019	●	↓
Permanent deforestation (% of forest area, 5-year average)	0.0	2018	●	●
Terrestrial and freshwater biodiversity threats embodied in imports (per million population)	2.7	2018	●	●

SDG16 – Peace, Justice and Strong Institutions

Indicator	Value	Year	Rating	Trend
Homicides (per 100,000 population)	0.8	2017	●	↑
Unsentenced detainees (% of prison population)	31.6	2018	◐	↓
Percentage of population who feel safe walking alone at night in the city or area where they live	64.3	2019	◐	↗
Property Rights (worst 1–7 best)	6.1	2019	●	●
Birth registrations with civil authority (% of children under age 5)	100.0	2018	●	●
Corruption Perception Index (worst 0–100 best)	77.0	2019	●	↑
Children involved in child labor (% of population aged 5 to 14)	* 0.0	2016	●	●
Exports of major conventional weapons (TIV constant million USD per 100,000 population)	0.4	2019	●	●
Press Freedom Index (best 0–100 worst)	16.6	2019	●	↑
Persons held in prison (per 100,000 population)	168.5	2017	◐	↓

SDG17 – Partnerships for the Goals

Indicator	Value	Year	Rating	Trend
Government spending on health and education (% of GDP)	11.6	2016	●	↑
For high-income and all OECD DAC countries: International concessional public finance, including official development assistance (% of GNI)	0.2	2017	●	↓
Other countries: Government revenue excluding grants (% of GDP)	NA	NA	●	●
Corporate Tax Haven Score (best 0–100 worst)	* 0.0	2019	●	●
Financial Secrecy Score (best 0–100 worst)	50.1	2020	●	●
Shifted profits of multinationals (US$ billion)	15.2	2016	●	●

* Imputed data point

5. Country Profiles

▼ OVERALL PERFORMANCE

Index score

80.7

Regional average score

77.3

SDG Global rank **7** (OF 166)

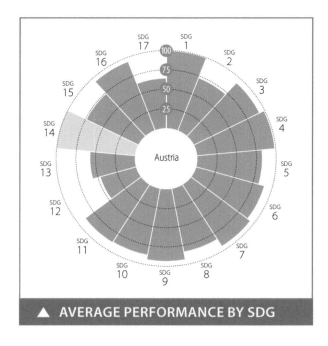

▲ AVERAGE PERFORMANCE BY SDG

▼ SPILLOVER INDEX

100 (best) to 0 (worst)

▼ CURRENT ASSESSMENT – SDG DASHBOARD

■ Major challenges ■ Significant challenges ■ Challenges remain ■ SDG achieved ■ Information unavailable

▼ SDG TRENDS

↓ Decreasing → Stagnating ↗ Moderately improving ↑ On track or maintaining SDG achievement ● Information unavailable

Notes: The full title of Goal 2 "Zero Hunger" is "End hunger, achieve food security and improved nutrition and promote sustainable agriculture".
The full title of each SDG is available here: https://sustainabledevelopment.un.org/topics/sustainabledevelopmentgoals

AUSTRIA

SDG1 – No Poverty

	Value	Year	Rating	Trend
Poverty headcount ratio at $1.90/day (%)	0.4	2020		
Poverty headcount ratio at $3.20/day (%)	0.5	2020		
Poverty rate after taxes and transfers (%)	9.4	2017		

SDG2 – Zero Hunger

	Value	Year	Rating	Trend
Prevalence of undernourishment (%)	2.5	2017		
Prevalence of stunting in children under 5 years of age (%)	* 2.6	2016		
Prevalence of wasting in children under 5 years of age (%)	* 0.7	2016		
Prevalence of obesity, BMI ≥ 30 (% of adult population)	20.1	2016		
Human Trophic Level (best 2–3 worst)	2.4	2017		
Cereal yield (tonnes per hectare of harvested land)	6.3	2017		
Sustainable Nitrogen Management Index (best 0–1.41 worst)	0.4	2015		
Yield gap closure (% of potential yield)	69.7	2015		

SDG3 – Good Health and Well-Being

	Value	Year	Rating	Trend
Maternal mortality rate (per 100,000 live births)	5	2017		
Neonatal mortality rate (per 1,000 live births)	2.1	2018		
Mortality rate, under-5 (per 1,000 live births)	3.5	2018		
Incidence of tuberculosis (per 100,000 population)	7.1	2018		
New HIV infections (per 1,000 uninfected population)	NA	NA		
Age-standardized death rate due to cardiovascular disease, cancer, diabetes, or chronic respiratory disease in adults aged 30–70 years (%)	11.4	2016		
Age-standardized death rate attributable to household air pollution and ambient air pollution (per 100,000 population)	15	2016		
Traffic deaths (per 100,000 population)	5.2	2016		
Life expectancy at birth (years)	81.9	2016		
Adolescent fertility rate (births per 1,000 adolescent females aged 15 to 19)	7.3	2017		
Births attended by skilled health personnel (%)	98.4	2016		
Percentage of surviving infants who received 2 WHO-recommended vaccines (%)	85.0	2018		
Universal health coverage (UHC) index of service coverage (worst 0–100 best)	79.0	2017		
Subjective well-being (average ladder score, worst 0–10 best)	7.2	2019		
Gap in life expectancy at birth among regions (years)	1.9	2016		
Gap in self-reported health status by income (percentage points)	20.6	2018		
Daily smokers (% of population aged 15 and over)	24.3	2014		

SDG4 – Quality Education

	Value	Year	Rating	Trend
Net primary enrollment rate (%)	* 98.6	2017		
Lower secondary completion rate (%)	* 98.6	2017		
Literacy rate (% of population aged 15 to 24)	NA	NA		
Participation rate in pre-primary organized learning (% of children aged 4 to 6)	100.0	2017		
Tertiary educational attainment (% of population aged 25 to 34)	40.5	2018		
PISA score (worst 0–600 best)	491.0	2018		
Variation in science performance explained by socio-economic status (%)	14.8	2018		
Underachievers in science (% of 15-year-olds)	21.9	2018		
Resilient students in science (% of 15-year-olds)	28.3	2018		

SDG5 – Gender Equality

	Value	Year	Rating	Trend
Demand for family planning satisfied by modern methods (% of females aged 15 to 49 who are married or in unions)	* 83.6	2017		
Ratio of female-to-male mean years of education received (%)	94.6	2018		
Ratio of female-to-male labor force participation rate (%)	83.4	2019		
Seats held by women in national parliament (%)	39.3	2020		
Gender wage gap (% of male median wage)	15.4	2017		
Gender gap in time spent doing unpaid work (minutes/day)	133.9	2009		

SDG6 – Clean Water and Sanitation

	Value	Year	Rating	Trend
Population using at least basic drinking water services (%)	100.0	2017		
Population using at least basic sanitation services (%)	100.0	2017		
Freshwater withdrawal (% of available freshwater resources)	9.5	2010		
Anthropogenic wastewater that receives treatment (%)	94.0	2018		
Scarce water consumption embodied in imports (m³/capita)	46.0	2013		
Population using safely managed water services (%)	98.9	2017		
Population using safely managed sanitation services (%)	96.7	2017		

SDG7 – Affordable and Clean Energy

	Value	Year	Rating	Trend
Population with access to electricity (%)	100.0	2017		
Population with access to clean fuels and technology for cooking (%)	100.0	2016		
CO_2 emissions from fuel combustion for electricity and heating per total electricity output (MtCO₂/TWh)	1.0	2017		
Share of renewable energy in total primary energy supply (%)	29.4	2018		

SDG8 – Decent Work and Economic Growth

	Value	Year	Rating	Trend
Adjusted GDP growth (%)	0.0	2018		
Victims of modern slavery (per 1,000 population)	1.7	2018		
Adults with an account at a bank or other financial institution or with a mobile-money-service provider (% of population aged 15 or over)	98.2	2017		
Fatal work-related accidents embodied in imports (per 100,000 population)	1.9	2010		
Employment-to-population ratio (%)	73.5	2019		
Youth not in employment, education or training (NEET) (% of population aged 15 to 29)	11.1	2018		

SDG9 – Industry, Innovation and Infrastructure

	Value	Year	Rating	Trend
Population using the internet (%)	87.5	2018		
Mobile broadband subscriptions (per 100 population)	88.0	2018		
Logistics Performance Index: Quality of trade and transport-related infrastructure (worst 1–5 best)	4.2	2018		
The Times Higher Education Universities Ranking: Average score of top 3 universities (worst 0–100 best)	54.1	2020		
Scientific and technical journal articles (per 1,000 population)	1.4	2018		
Expenditure on research and development (% of GDP)	3.2	2017		
Researchers (per 1,000 employed population)	11.4	2018		
Triadic patent families filed (per million population)	42.7	2017		
Gap in internet access by income (percentage points)	13.6	2019		
Women in science and engineering (% of tertiary graduates in science and engineering)	23.4	2015		

SDG10 – Reduced Inequalities

	Value	Year	Rating	Trend
Gini coefficient adjusted for top income	32.0	2015		
Palma ratio	1.0	2017		
Elderly poverty rate (% of population aged 66 or over)	9.7	2017		

SDG11 – Sustainable Cities and Communities

	Value	Year	Rating	Trend
Annual mean concentration of particulate matter of less than 2.5 microns in diameter (PM2.5) (μg/m³)	12.5	2017		
Access to improved water source, piped (% of urban population)	NA	NA		
Satisfaction with public transport (%)	73.0	2019		
Population with rent overburden (%)	5.0	2017		

SDG12 – Responsible Consumption and Production

	Value	Year	Rating	Trend
Electronic waste (kg/capita)	20.9	2016		
Production-based SO_2 emissions (kg/capita)	58.5	2012		
SO_2 emissions embodied in imports (kg/capita)	20.6	2012		
Production-based nitrogen emissions (kg/capita)	41.4	2010		
Nitrogen emissions embodied in imports (kg/capita)	18.7	2010		
Non-recycled municipal solid waste (kg/capita/day)	0.7	2018		

SDG13 – Climate Action

	Value	Year	Rating	Trend
Energy-related CO_2 emissions (tCO₂/capita)	7.1	2017		
CO_2 emissions embodied in imports (tCO₂/capita)	3.6	2015		
CO_2 emissions embodied in fossil fuel exports (kg/capita)	295.2	2018		
Effective carbon rate (EUR/tCO₂)	29.3	2016		

SDG14 – Life Below Water

	Value	Year	Rating	Trend
Mean area that is protected in marine sites important to biodiversity (%)	NA	NA		
Ocean Health Index: Clean Waters score (worst 0–100 best)	NA	NA		
Fish caught from overexploited or collapsed stocks (% of total catch)	NA	NA		
Fish caught by trawling (%)	NA	NA		
Marine biodiversity threats embodied in imports (per million population)	0.1	2018		

SDG15 – Life on Land

	Value	Year	Rating	Trend
Mean area that is protected in terrestrial sites important to biodiversity (%)	66.6	2018		
Mean area that is protected in freshwater sites important to biodiversity (%)	71.2	2018		
Red List Index of species survival (worst 0–1 best)	0.9	2019		
Permanent deforestation (% of forest area, 5-year average)	0.0	2018		
Terrestrial and freshwater biodiversity threats embodied in imports (per million population)	4.5	2018		

SDG16 – Peace, Justice and Strong Institutions

	Value	Year	Rating	Trend
Homicides (per 100,000 population)	0.7	2016		
Unsentenced detainees (% of prison population)	21.0	2018		
Percentage of population who feel safe walking alone at night in the city or area where they live (%)	87.3	2019		
Property Rights (worst 1–7 best)	6.2	2019		
Birth registrations with civil authority (% of children under age 5)	100.0	2018		
Corruption Perception Index (worst 0–100 best)	77.0	2019		
Children involved in child labor (% of population aged 5 to 14)	* 0.0	2016		
Exports of major conventional weapons (TIV constant million USD per 100,000 population)	0.1	2019		
Press Freedom Index (best 0–100 worst)	15.3	2019		
Persons held in prison (per 100,000 population)	99.5	2017		

SDG17 – Partnerships for the Goals

	Value	Year	Rating	Trend
Government spending on health and education (% of GDP)	13.1	2016		
For high-income and all OECD DAC countries: International concessional public finance, including official development assistance (% of GNI)	0.3	2017		
Other countries: Government revenue excluding grants (% of GDP)	NA	NA		
Corporate Tax Haven Score (best 0–100 worst)	51.6	2019		
Financial Secrecy Score (best 0–100 worst)	56.5	2020		
Shifted profits of multinationals (US$ billion)	4.3	2016		

* Imputed data point

5. Country Profiles

AZERBAIJAN

Eastern Europe and Central Asia

▼ OVERALL PERFORMANCE

Index score

72.6

Regional average score

70.9

SDG Global rank 54 (OF 166)

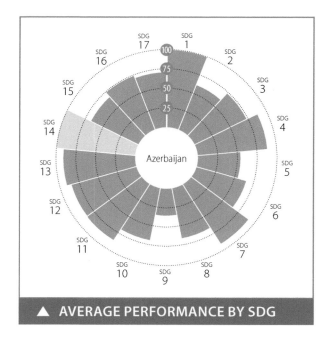

▲ AVERAGE PERFORMANCE BY SDG

▼ SPILLOVER INDEX

100 (best) to 0 (worst)

▼ CURRENT ASSESSMENT – SDG DASHBOARD

■ Major challenges ■ Significant challenges ▨ Challenges remain ■ SDG achieved ■ Information unavailable

▼ SDG TRENDS

↓ Decreasing   → Stagnating   ↗ Moderately improving   ↑ On track or maintaining SDG achievement   ● Information unavailable

Notes: The full title of Goal 2 "Zero Hunger" is "End hunger, achieve food security and improved nutrition and promote sustainable agriculture".
The full title of each SDG is available here: https://sustainabledevelopment.un.org/topics/sustainabledevelopmentgoals

SDG1 – No Poverty

Indicator	Value	Year	Rating	Trend
Poverty headcount ratio at $1.90/day (%)	0.0	2020	●	↑
Poverty headcount ratio at $3.20/day (%)	0.0	2020	●	↑

SDG2 – Zero Hunger

Indicator	Value	Year	Rating	Trend
Prevalence of undernourishment (%)	2.5	2017	●	↑
Prevalence of stunting in children under 5 years of age (%)	18.0	2013	●	↗
Prevalence of wasting in children under 5 years of age (%)	3.1	2013	●	↑
Prevalence of obesity, BMI ≥ 30 (% of adult population)	19.9	2016	●	↓
Human Trophic Level (best 2–3 worst)	2.2	2017	●	→
Cereal yield (tonnes per hectare of harvested land)	2.9	2017	●	↑
Sustainable Nitrogen Management Index (best 0–1.41 worst)	0.6	2015	●	→

SDG3 – Good Health and Well-Being

Indicator	Value	Year	Rating	Trend
Maternal mortality rate (per 100,000 live births)	26	2017	●	↑
Neonatal mortality rate (per 1,000 live births)	11.2	2018	●	↑
Mortality rate, under-5 (per 1,000 live births)	21.5	2018	●	↑
Incidence of tuberculosis (per 100,000 population)	63.0	2018	●	↗
New HIV infections (per 1,000 uninfected population)	NA	NA	●	●
Age-standardized death rate due to cardiovascular disease, cancer, diabetes, or chronic respiratory disease in adults aged 30–70 years (%)	22.2	2016	●	↗
Age-standardized death rate attributable to household air pollution and ambient air pollution (per 100,000 population)	64	2016	●	●
Traffic deaths (per 100,000 population)	8.7	2016	●	↑
Life expectancy at birth (years)	73.1	2016	●	↗
Adolescent fertility rate (births per 1,000 adolescent females aged 15 to 19)	55.8	2017	●	↓
Births attended by skilled health personnel (%)	99.8	2016	●	↑
Percentage of surviving infants who received 2 WHO-recommended vaccines (%)	95	2018	●	↑
Universal health coverage (UHC) index of service coverage (worst 0–100 best)	65.0	2017	●	↑
Subjective well-being (average ladder score, worst 0–10 best)	5.2	2019	●	→

SDG4 – Quality Education

Indicator	Value	Year	Rating	Trend
Net primary enrollment rate (%)	92.4	2018	●	↓
Lower secondary completion rate (%)	84.7	2018	●	↓
Literacy rate (% of population aged 15 to 24)	99.9	2017	●	●

SDG5 – Gender Equality

Indicator	Value	Year	Rating	Trend
Demand for family planning satisfied by modern methods (% of females aged 15 to 49 who are married or in unions)	21.5	2006	●	→
Ratio of female-to-male mean years of education received (%)	94.4	2018	●	→
Ratio of female-to-male labor force participation rate (%)	90.7	2019	●	↑
Seats held by women in national parliament (%)	17.4	2020	●	→

SDG6 – Clean Water and Sanitation

Indicator	Value	Year	Rating	Trend
Population using at least basic drinking water services (%)	91.4	2017	●	↑
Population using at least basic sanitation services (%)	92.5	2017	●	↑
Freshwater withdrawal (% of available freshwater resources)	56.4	2015	●	●
Anthropogenic wastewater that receives treatment (%)	3.8	2018	●	●
Scarce water consumption embodied in imports (m3/capita)	3.2	2013	●	↑

SDG7 – Affordable and Clean Energy

Indicator	Value	Year	Rating	Trend
Population with access to electricity (%)	100.0	2017	●	↑
Population with access to clean fuels and technology for cooking (%)	95.5	2016	●	↑
CO_2 emissions from fuel combustion for electricity and heating per total electricity output (MtCO2/TWh)	1.3	2017	●	→

SDG8 – Decent Work and Economic Growth

Indicator	Value	Year	Rating	Trend
Adjusted GDP growth (%)	-5.0	2018	●	●
Victims of modern slavery (per 1,000 population)	4.5	2018	●	●
Adults with an account at a bank or other financial institution or with a mobile-money-service provider (% of population aged 15 or over)	28.6	2017	●	↓
Unemployment rate (% of total labor force)	5.5	2019	●	↓
Fatal work-related accidents embodied in imports (per 100,000 population)	0.1	2010	●	↑

SDG9 – Industry, Innovation and Infrastructure

Indicator	Value	Year	Rating	Trend
Population using the internet (%)	79.8	2018	●	↑
Mobile broadband subscriptions (per 100 population)	59.6	2018	●	↓
Logistics Performance Index: Quality of trade and transport-related infrastructure (worst 1–5 best)	2.7	2014	●	●
The Times Higher Education Universities Ranking: Average score of top 3 * universities (worst 0–100 best)	3.7	2019	●	●
Scientific and technical journal articles (per 1,000 population)	0.1	2018	●	→
Expenditure on research and development (% of GDP)	0.2	2017	●	↓

SDG10 – Reduced Inequalities

Indicator	Value	Year	Rating	Trend
Gini coefficient adjusted for top income	38.6	2008	●	●

SDG11 – Sustainable Cities and Communities

Indicator	Value	Year	Rating	Trend
Annual mean concentration of particulate matter of less than 2.5 microns in diameter (PM2.5) (μg/m3)	19.9	2017	●	→
Access to improved water source, piped (% of urban population)	98.5	2017	●	↑
Satisfaction with public transport (%)	67.1	2019	●	↑

SDG12 – Responsible Consumption and Production

Indicator	Value	Year	Rating	Trend
Municipal solid waste (kg/capita/day)	1.5	2015	●	●
Electronic waste (kg/capita)	6.7	2016	●	●
Production-based SO_2 emissions (kg/capita)	25.2	2012	●	●
SO_2 emissions embodied in imports (kg/capita)	1.8	2012	●	●
Production-based nitrogen emissions (kg/capita)	15.1	2010	●	●
Nitrogen emissions embodied in imports (kg/capita)	0.7	2010	●	●

SDG13 – Climate Action

Indicator	Value	Year	Rating	Trend
Energy-related CO_2 emissions (tCO2/capita)	3.9	2017	●	→
CO_2 emissions embodied in imports (tCO2/capita)	0.3	2015	●	↑
CO_2 emissions embodied in fossil fuel exports (kg/capita)	1795.8	2019	●	●

SDG14 – Life Below Water

Indicator	Value	Year	Rating	Trend
Mean area that is protected in marine sites important to biodiversity (%)	NA	NA	●	●
Ocean Health Index: Clean Waters score (worst 0–100 best)	NA	NA	●	●
Fish caught from overexploited or collapsed stocks (% of total catch)	NA	NA	●	●
Fish caught by trawling (%)	NA	NA	●	●
Marine biodiversity threats embodied in imports (per million population)	0.0	2018	●	●

SDG15 – Life on Land

Indicator	Value	Year	Rating	Trend
Mean area that is protected in terrestrial sites important to biodiversity (%)	38.2	2018	●	→
Mean area that is protected in freshwater sites important to biodiversity (%)	21.0	2018	●	→
Red List Index of species survival (worst 0–1 best)	0.9	2019	●	↑
Permanent deforestation (% of forest area, 5-year average)	0.0	2018	●	●
Terrestrial and freshwater biodiversity threats embodied in imports (per million population)	0.1	2018	●	●

SDG16 – Peace, Justice and Strong Institutions

Indicator	Value	Year	Rating	Trend
Homicides (per 100,000 population)	2.0	2017	●	↑
Unsentenced detainees (% of prison population)	15.5	2018	●	↑
Percentage of population who feel safe walking alone at night in the city or area where they live (%)	82.4	2019	●	↑
Property Rights (worst 1–7 best)	5.1	2019	●	●
Birth registrations with civil authority (% of children under age 5)	93.6	2018	●	●
Corruption Perception Index (worst 0–100 best)	30	2019	●	→
Children involved in child labor (% of population aged 5 to 14)	6.5	2016	●	●
Exports of major conventional weapons (TIV constant million USD per 100,000 population) *	0.0	2019	●	●
Press Freedom Index (best 0–100 worst)	59.1	2019	●	↓

SDG17 – Partnerships for the Goals

Indicator	Value	Year	Rating	Trend
Government spending on health and education (% of GDP)	4.3	2016	●	↗
For high-income and all OECD DAC countries: International concessional public finance, including official development assistance (% of GNI)	NA	NA	●	●
Other countries: Government revenue excluding grants (% of GDP)	35.1	2017	●	↑
Corporate Tax Haven Score (best 0–100 worst) *	0.0	2019	●	●

* Imputed data point

5. Country Profiles

▼ OVERALL PERFORMANCE

Index score
na

Regional average score
70.4

SDG Global rank NA (OF 166)

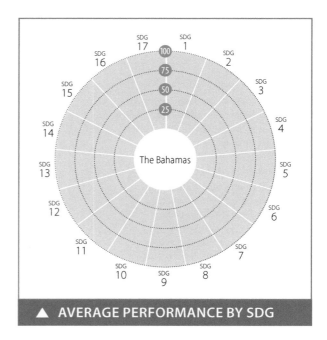

▲ AVERAGE PERFORMANCE BY SDG

▼ SPILLOVER INDEX

100 (best) to 0 (worst)

▼ CURRENT ASSESSMENT – SDG DASHBOARD

■ Major challenges ■ Significant challenges ▨ Challenges remain ■ SDG achieved ▨ Information unavailable

▼ SDG TRENDS

↓ Decreasing   → Stagnating   ↗ Moderately improving   ↑ On track or maintaining SDG achievement   ● Information unavailable

Notes: The full title of Goal 2 "Zero Hunger" is "End hunger, achieve food security and improved nutrition and promote sustainable agriculture".
The full title of each SDG is available here: https://sustainabledevelopment.un.org/topics/sustainabledevelopmentgoals

SDG1 – No Poverty

Indicator	Value	Year	Rating	Trend
Poverty headcount ratio at $1.90/day (%)	* NA	NA	●	●
Poverty headcount ratio at $3.20/day (%)	* NA	NA	●	●

SDG2 – Zero Hunger

Indicator	Value	Year	Rating	Trend
Prevalence of undernourishment (%)	* 1.2	2017	●	●
Prevalence of stunting in children under 5 years of age (%)	* 2.6	2016	●	↑
Prevalence of wasting in children under 5 years of age (%)	* 0.7	2016	●	↑
Prevalence of obesity, BMI ≥ 30 (% of adult population)	31.6	2016	●	↓
Human Trophic Level (best 2–3 worst)	2.3	2017	●	↗
Cereal yield (tonnes per hectare of harvested land)	8.8	2017	●	↑
Sustainable Nitrogen Management Index (best 0–1.41 worst)	1.1	2015	●	↓

SDG3 – Good Health and Well-Being

Indicator	Value	Year	Rating	Trend
Maternal mortality rate (per 100,000 live births)	70	2017	●	↑
Neonatal mortality rate (per 1,000 live births)	5.4	2018	●	↑
Mortality rate, under-5 (per 1,000 live births)	10.2	2018	●	↑
Incidence of tuberculosis (per 100,000 population)	14.0	2018	●	↑
New HIV infections (per 1,000 uninfected population)	0.6	2018	●	↑
Age-standardized death rate due to cardiovascular disease, cancer, diabetes, or chronic respiratory disease in adults aged 30–70 years (%)	15.5	2016	●	↑
Age-standardized death rate attributable to household air pollution and ambient air pollution (per 100,000 population)	20	2016	●	●
Traffic deaths (per 100,000 population)	13.8	2013	●	●
Life expectancy at birth (years)	75.7	2016	●	↗
Adolescent fertility rate (births per 1,000 adolescent females aged 15 to 19)	30.0	2017	●	↑
Births attended by skilled health personnel (%)	99.6	2014	●	●
Percentage of surviving infants who received 2 WHO-recommended vaccines (%)	89	2018	●	↓
Universal health coverage (UHC) index of service coverage (worst 0–100 best)	75.0	2017	●	↑
Subjective well-being (average ladder score, worst 0–10 best)	NA	NA	●	●

SDG4 – Quality Education

Indicator	Value	Year	Rating	Trend
Net primary enrollment rate (%)	74.2	2018	●	↓
Lower secondary completion rate (%)	92.2	2010	●	●
Literacy rate (% of population aged 15 to 24)	NA	NA	●	●

SDG5 – Gender Equality

Indicator	Value	Year	Rating	Trend
Demand for family planning satisfied by modern methods (% of females aged 15 to 49 who are married or in unions)	* 82.8	2017	●	↑
Ratio of female-to-male mean years of education received (%)	102.6	2018	●	↑
Ratio of female-to-male labor force participation rate (%)	82.4	2019	●	↑
Seats held by women in national parliament (%)	12.8	2020	●	↓

SDG6 – Clean Water and Sanitation

Indicator	Value	Year	Rating	Trend
Population using at least basic drinking water services (%)	98.9	2017	●	↑
Population using at least basic sanitation services (%)	94.9	2017	●	↑
Freshwater withdrawal (% of available freshwater resources)	NA	NA	●	●
Anthropogenic wastewater that receives treatment (%)	1.4	2018	●	●
Scarce water consumption embodied in imports (m³/capita)	15.5	2013	●	↑

SDG7 – Affordable and Clean Energy

Indicator	Value	Year	Rating	Trend
Population with access to electricity (%)	100.0	2017	●	↑
Population with access to clean fuels and technology for cooking (%)	100.0	2016	●	↑
CO_2 emissions from fuel combustion for electricity and heating per total electricity output (MtCO₂/TWh)	NA	NA	●	●

SDG8 – Decent Work and Economic Growth

Indicator	Value	Year	Rating	Trend
Adjusted GDP growth (%)	-2.8	2018	●	●
Victims of modern slavery (per 1,000 population)	NA	NA	●	●
Adults with an account at a bank or other financial institution or with a mobile-money-service provider (% of population aged 15 or over)	NA	NA	●	●
Unemployment rate (% of total labor force)	10.4	2019	●	↗
Fatal work-related accidents embodied in imports (per 100,000 population)	0.5	2010	●	↑

SDG9 – Industry, Innovation and Infrastructure

Indicator	Value	Year	Rating	Trend
Population using the internet (%)	85.0	2017	●	↑
Mobile broadband subscriptions (per 100 population)	60.8	2018	●	↑
Logistics Performance Index: Quality of trade and transport-related infrastructure (worst 1–5 best)	2.4	2018	●	↓
The Times Higher Education Universities Ranking: Average score of top 3 universities (worst 0–100 best)	* 0.0	2020	●	●
Scientific and technical journal articles (per 1,000 population)	0.1	2018	●	→
Expenditure on research and development (% of GDP)	NA	NA	●	●

SDG10 – Reduced Inequalities

Indicator	Value	Year	Rating	Trend
Gini coefficient adjusted for top income	NA	NA	●	●

SDG11 – Sustainable Cities and Communities

Indicator	Value	Year	Rating	Trend
Annual mean concentration of particulate matter of less than 2.5 microns in diameter (PM2.5) (µg/m³)	17.4	2017	●	↗
Access to improved water source, piped (% of urban population)	NA	NA	●	●
Satisfaction with public transport (%)	NA	NA	●	●

SDG12 – Responsible Consumption and Production

Indicator	Value	Year	Rating	Trend
Municipal solid waste (kg/capita/day)	2.2	2015	●	●
Electronic waste (kg/capita)	13.2	2016	●	●
Production-based SO_2 emissions (kg/capita)	413.9	2012	●	●
SO_2 emissions embodied in imports (kg/capita)	10.3	2012	●	●
Production-based nitrogen emissions (kg/capita)	44.1	2010	●	●
Nitrogen emissions embodied in imports (kg/capita)	15.4	2010	●	●

SDG13 – Climate Action

Indicator	Value	Year	Rating	Trend
Energy-related CO_2 emissions (tCO₂/capita)	6.6	2017	●	→
CO_2 emissions embodied in imports (tCO₂/capita)	2.6	2015	●	→
CO_2 emissions embodied in fossil fuel exports (kg/capita)	0.0	2015	●	●

SDG14 – Life Below Water

Indicator	Value	Year	Rating	Trend
Mean area that is protected in marine sites important to biodiversity (%)	29.4	2018	●	→
Ocean Health Index: Clean Waters score (worst 0–100 best)	61.8	2019	●	↗
Fish caught from overexploited or collapsed stocks (% of total catch)	28.1	2014	●	↓
Fish caught by trawling (%)	NA	NA	●	●
Marine biodiversity threats embodied in imports (per million population)	1.7	2018	●	●

SDG15 – Life on Land

Indicator	Value	Year	Rating	Trend
Mean area that is protected in terrestrial sites important to biodiversity (%)	24.1	2018	●	→
Mean area that is protected in freshwater sites important to biodiversity (%)	NA	NA	●	●
Red List Index of species survival (worst 0–1 best)	0.7	2019	●	↓
Permanent deforestation (% of forest area, 5-year average)	0.4	2018	●	●
Terrestrial and freshwater biodiversity threats embodied in imports (per million population)	0.4	2018	●	●

SDG16 – Peace, Justice and Strong Institutions

Indicator	Value	Year	Rating	Trend
Homicides (per 100,000 population)	30.9	2017	●	→
Unsentenced detainees (% of prison population)	43.0	2015	●	●
Percentage of population who feel safe walking alone at night in the city or area where they live (%)	NA	NA	●	●
Property Rights (worst 1–7 best)	NA	NA	●	●
Birth registrations with civil authority (% of children under age 5)	NA	NA	●	●
Corruption Perception Index (worst 0–100 best)	64	2019	●	↑
Children involved in child labor (% of population aged 5 to 14)	NA	NA	●	●
Exports of major conventional weapons (TIV constant million USD per 100,000 population)	0.0	2019	●	●
Press Freedom Index (best 0–100 worst)	NA	NA	●	●

SDG17 – Partnerships for the Goals

Indicator	Value	Year	Rating	Trend
Government spending on health and education (% of GDP)	4.1	2000	●	●
For high-income and all OECD DAC countries: International concessional public finance, including official development assistance (% of GNI)	NA	NA	●	●
Other countries: Government revenue excluding grants (% of GDP)	NA	NA	●	●
Corporate Tax Haven Score (best 0–100 worst)	100.0	2019	●	●

* Imputed data point

▼ OVERALL PERFORMANCE

Index score

68.8

Regional average score

66.3

SDG Global rank 82 (OF 166)

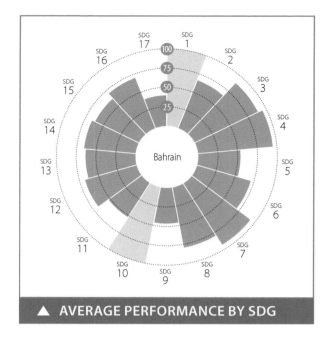

▲ AVERAGE PERFORMANCE BY SDG

▼ SPILLOVER INDEX

100 (best) to 0 (worst)

▼ CURRENT ASSESSMENT – SDG DASHBOARD

■ Major challenges ■ Significant challenges ■ Challenges remain ■ SDG achieved ■ Information unavailable

▼ SDG TRENDS

↓ Decreasing → Stagnating ↗ Moderately improving ↑ On track or maintaining SDG achievement ● Information unavailable

Notes: The full title of Goal 2 "Zero Hunger" is "End hunger, achieve food security and improved nutrition and promote sustainable agriculture".
The full title of each SDG is available here: https://sustainabledevelopment.un.org/topics/sustainabledevelopmentgoals

SDG1 – No Poverty

Indicator		Value	Year	Rating	Trend
Poverty headcount ratio at $1.90/day (%)	*	NA	NA	●	●
Poverty headcount ratio at $3.20/day (%)	*	NA	NA	●	●

SDG2 – Zero Hunger

Indicator		Value	Year	Rating	Trend
Prevalence of undernourishment (%)	*	1.2	2017	●	●
Prevalence of stunting in children under 5 years of age (%)	*	2.6	2016	●	↑
Prevalence of wasting in children under 5 years of age (%)	*	0.7	2016	●	↑
Prevalence of obesity, BMI ≥ 30 (% of adult population)		29.8	2016	●	↓
Human Trophic Level (best 2–3 worst)		NA	NA	●	●
Cereal yield (tonnes per hectare of harvested land)		NA	NA	●	●
Sustainable Nitrogen Management Index (best 0–1.41 worst)		0.9	2015	●	↓

SDG3 – Good Health and Well-Being

Indicator	Value	Year	Rating	Trend
Maternal mortality rate (per 100,000 live births)	14	2017	●	↑
Neonatal mortality rate (per 1,000 live births)	3.0	2018	●	↑
Mortality rate, under-5 (per 1,000 live births)	7.1	2018	●	↑
Incidence of tuberculosis (per 100,000 population)	11.0	2018	●	●
New HIV infections (per 1,000 uninfected population)	NA	NA	●	●
Age-standardized death rate due to cardiovascular disease, cancer, diabetes, or chronic respiratory disease in adults aged 30–70 years (%)	11.3	2016	●	↑
Age-standardized death rate attributable to household air pollution and ambient air pollution (per 100,000 population)	40	2016	●	●
Traffic deaths (per 100,000 population)	8.0	2013	●	●
Life expectancy at birth (years)	79.1	2016	●	↑
Adolescent fertility rate (births per 1,000 adolescent females aged 15 to 19)	13.4	2017	●	↑
Births attended by skilled health personnel (%)	99.7	2015	●	↑
Percentage of surviving infants who received 2 WHO-recommended vaccines (%)	99	2018	●	↑
Universal health coverage (UHC) index of service coverage (worst 0–100 best)	77.0	2017	●	↑
Subjective well-being (average ladder score, worst 0–10 best)	6.2	2017	●	●

SDG4 – Quality Education

Indicator	Value	Year	Rating	Trend
Net primary enrollment rate (%)	96.7	2018	●	↑
Lower secondary completion rate (%)	94.3	2018	●	↑
Literacy rate (% of population aged 15 to 24)	99.7	2018	●	●

SDG5 – Gender Equality

Indicator		Value	Year	Rating	Trend
Demand for family planning satisfied by modern methods (% of females aged 15 to 49 who are married or in unions)	*	61.6	2017	●	→
Ratio of female-to-male mean years of education received (%)		97.9	2018	●	↓
Ratio of female-to-male labor force participation rate (%)		51.0	2019	●	→
Seats held by women in national parliament (%)		15.0	2020	●	↗

SDG6 – Clean Water and Sanitation

Indicator	Value	Year	Rating	Trend
Population using at least basic drinking water services (%)	100.0	2017	●	↑
Population using at least basic sanitation services (%)	100.0	2017	●	↑
Freshwater withdrawal (% of available freshwater resources)	132.2	2015	●	●
Anthropogenic wastewater that receives treatment (%)	86.9	2018	●	●
Scarce water consumption embodied in imports (m³/capita)	30.1	2013	●	→

SDG7 – Affordable and Clean Energy

Indicator	Value	Year	Rating	Trend
Population with access to electricity (%)	100.0	2017	●	↑
Population with access to clean fuels and technology for cooking (%)	100.0	2016	●	↑
CO₂ emissions from fuel combustion for electricity and heating per total electricity output (MtCO₂/TWh)	1.1	2017	●	↑

SDG8 – Decent Work and Economic Growth

Indicator		Value	Year	Rating	Trend
Adjusted GDP growth (%)		-3.4	2018	●	●
Victims of modern slavery (per 1,000 population)	*	NA	NA	●	●
Adults with an account at a bank or other financial institution or with a mobile-money-service provider (% of population aged 15 or over)		82.6	2017	●	↑
Unemployment rate (% of total labor force)		0.7	2019	●	↑
Fatal work-related accidents embodied in imports (per 100,000 population)		1.2	2010	●	↑

SDG9 – Industry, Innovation and Infrastructure

Indicator		Value	Year	Rating	Trend
Population using the internet (%)		98.6	2018	●	↑
Mobile broadband subscriptions (per 100 population)		126.0	2018	●	↑
Logistics Performance Index: Quality of trade and transport-related infrastructure (worst 1–5 best)		2.7	2018	●	↓
The Times Higher Education Universities Ranking: Average score of top 3 universities (worst 0–100 best)	*	4.5	2019	●	●
Scientific and technical journal articles (per 1,000 population)		0.2	2018	●	↗
Expenditure on research and development (% of GDP)		0.1	2014	●	●

SDG10 – Reduced Inequalities

Indicator	Value	Year	Rating	Trend
Gini coefficient adjusted for top income	NA	NA	●	●

SDG11 – Sustainable Cities and Communities

Indicator	Value	Year	Rating	Trend
Annual mean concentration of particulate matter of less than 2.5 microns in diameter (PM2.5) (µg/m³)	70.8	2017	●	↓
Access to improved water source, piped (% of urban population)	NA	NA	●	●
Satisfaction with public transport (%)	72.7	2017	●	●

SDG12 – Responsible Consumption and Production

Indicator	Value	Year	Rating	Trend
Municipal solid waste (kg/capita/day)	1.9	2016	●	●
Electronic waste (kg/capita)	15.5	2016	●	●
Production-based SO₂ emissions (kg/capita)	87.5	2012	●	●
SO₂ emissions embodied in imports (kg/capita)	9.3	2012	●	●
Production-based nitrogen emissions (kg/capita)	17.3	2010	●	●
Nitrogen emissions embodied in imports (kg/capita)	7.5	2010	●	●

SDG13 – Climate Action

Indicator	Value	Year	Rating	Trend
Energy-related CO₂ emissions (tCO₂/capita)	15.5	2017	●	↑
CO₂ emissions embodied in imports (tCO₂/capita)	1.5	2015	●	↗
CO₂ emissions embodied in fossil fuel exports (kg/capita)	0.0	2018	●	●

SDG14 – Life Below Water

Indicator	Value	Year	Rating	Trend
Mean area that is protected in marine sites important to biodiversity (%)	36.6	2018	●	→
Ocean Health Index: Clean Waters score (worst 0–100 best)	54.6	2019	●	↗
Fish caught from overexploited or collapsed stocks (% of total catch)	NA	NA	●	●
Fish caught by trawling (%)	11.7	2014	●	↗
Marine biodiversity threats embodied in imports (per million population)	0.0	2018	●	●

SDG15 – Life on Land

Indicator	Value	Year	Rating	Trend
Mean area that is protected in terrestrial sites important to biodiversity (%)	27.5	2018	●	→
Mean area that is protected in freshwater sites important to biodiversity (%)	NA	NA	●	●
Red List Index of species survival (worst 0–1 best)	0.8	2019	●	↓
Permanent deforestation (% of forest area, 5-year average)	NA	NA	●	●
Terrestrial and freshwater biodiversity threats embodied in imports (per million population)	0.1	2018	●	●

SDG16 – Peace, Justice and Strong Institutions

Indicator		Value	Year	Rating	Trend
Homicides (per 100,000 population)		0.5	2014	●	●
Unsentenced detainees (% of prison population)		25.7	2018	●	↑
Percentage of population who feel safe walking alone at night in the city or area where they live		59.9	2011	●	●
Property Rights (worst 1–7 best)		5.7	2019	●	●
Birth registrations with civil authority (% of children under age 5)		NA	NA	●	●
Corruption Perception Index (worst 0–100 best)		42	2019	●	↓
Children involved in child labor (% of population aged 5 to 14)		4.6	2016	●	●
Exports of major conventional weapons (TIV constant million USD per 100,000 population)	*	0.0	2019	●	●
Press Freedom Index (best 0–100 worst)		61.3	2019	●	↓

SDG17 – Partnerships for the Goals

Indicator		Value	Year	Rating	Trend
Government spending on health and education (% of GDP)		5.9	2015	●	↑
For high-income and all OECD DAC countries: International concessional public finance, including official development assistance (% of GNI)		NA	NA	●	●
Other countries: Government revenue excluding grants (% of GDP)		NA	NA	●	●
Corporate Tax Haven Score (best 0–100 worst)	*	NA	NA	●	●

* Imputed data point

▼ OVERALL PERFORMANCE

Index score	Regional average score
63.5	67.2

SDG Global rank 109 (OF 166)

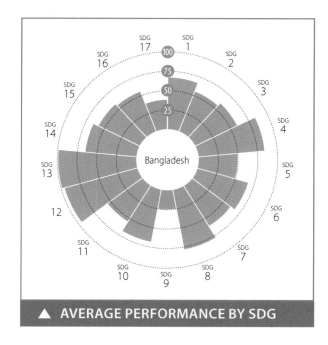

▲ AVERAGE PERFORMANCE BY SDG

▼ SPILLOVER INDEX

100 (best) to 0 (worst)

▼ CURRENT ASSESSMENT – SDG DASHBOARD

■ Major challenges   ■ Significant challenges   ▨ Challenges remain   ■ SDG achieved   ■ Information unavailable

▼ SDG TRENDS

↓ Decreasing   → Stagnating   ↗ Moderately improving   ↑ On track or maintaining SDG achievement   ● Information unavailable

Notes: The full title of Goal 2 "Zero Hunger" is "End hunger, achieve food security and improved nutrition and promote sustainable agriculture".
The full title of each SDG is available here: https://sustainabledevelopment.un.org/topics/sustainabledevelopmentgoals

SDG1 – No Poverty

	Value	Year	Rating	Trend
Poverty headcount ratio at $1.90/day (%)	4.3	2020	○	↑
Poverty headcount ratio at $3.20/day (%)	31.0	2020	●	↑

SDG2 – Zero Hunger

	Value	Year	Rating	Trend
Prevalence of undernourishment (%)	14.7	2017	●	↗
Prevalence of stunting in children under 5 years of age (%)	36.1	2014	●	→
Prevalence of wasting in children under 5 years of age (%)	14.3	2014	●	→
Prevalence of obesity, BMI ≥ 30 (% of adult population)	3.6	2016	●	↑
Human Trophic Level (best 2–3 worst)	2.1	2017	●	↑
Cereal yield (tonnes per hectare of harvested land)	4.4	2017	●	↑
Sustainable Nitrogen Management Index (best 0–1.41 worst)	0.7	2015	●	→

SDG3 – Good Health and Well-Being

	Value	Year	Rating	Trend
Maternal mortality rate (per 100,000 live births)	173	2017	●	↑
Neonatal mortality rate (per 1,000 live births)	17.1	2018	●	↑
Mortality rate, under-5 (per 1,000 live births)	30.2	2018	○	↑
Incidence of tuberculosis (per 100,000 population)	221.0	2018	●	→
New HIV infections (per 1,000 uninfected population)	0.0	2018	●	↑
Age-standardized death rate due to cardiovascular disease, cancer, diabetes, or chronic respiratory disease in adults aged 30–70 years (%)	21.6	2016	●	→
Age-standardized death rate attributable to household air pollution and ambient air pollution (per 100,000 population)	149	2016	●	●
Traffic deaths (per 100,000 population)	15.3	2016	●	↓
Life expectancy at birth (years)	72.7	2016	●	↗
Adolescent fertility rate (births per 1,000 adolescent females aged 15 to 19)	83.0	2017	●	→
Births attended by skilled health personnel (%)	49.8	2016	●	↗
Percentage of surviving infants who received 2 WHO-recommended vaccines (%)	97	2018	●	↑
Universal health coverage (UHC) index of service coverage (worst 0–100 best)	48.0	2017	●	↗
Subjective well-being (average ladder score, worst 0–10 best)	5.1	2019	●	↑

SDG4 – Quality Education

	Value	Year	Rating	Trend
Net primary enrollment rate (%)	90.5	2010	○	●
Lower secondary completion rate (%)	88.0	2018	○	↑
Literacy rate (% of population aged 15 to 24)	93.3	2018	○	●

SDG5 – Gender Equality

	Value	Year	Rating	Trend
Demand for family planning satisfied by modern methods (% of females aged 15 to 49 who are married or in unions)	72.6	2014	●	↗
Ratio of female-to-male mean years of education received (%)	77.9	2018	●	↓
Ratio of female-to-male labor force participation rate (%)	44.5	2019	●	↗
Seats held by women in national parliament (%)	20.9	2020	●	→

SDG6 – Clean Water and Sanitation

	Value	Year	Rating	Trend
Population using at least basic drinking water services (%)	97.0	2017	○	↑
Population using at least basic sanitation services (%)	48.2	2017	●	→
Freshwater withdrawal (% of available freshwater resources)	5.7	2010	●	●
Anthropogenic wastewater that receives treatment (%)	0.0	2018	●	●
Scarce water consumption embodied in imports (m3/capita)	1.0	2013	●	↑

SDG7 – Affordable and Clean Energy

	Value	Year	Rating	Trend
Population with access to electricity (%)	88.0	2017	●	↑
Population with access to clean fuels and technology for cooking (%)	17.7	2016	●	→
CO2 emissions from fuel combustion for electricity and heating per total electricity output (MtCO2/TWh)	1.1	2017	○	↑

SDG8 – Decent Work and Economic Growth

	Value	Year	Rating	Trend
Adjusted GDP growth (%)	0.6	2018	●	●
Victims of modern slavery (per 1,000 population)	3.7	2018	●	●
Adults with an account at a bank or other financial institution or with a mobile-money-service provider (% of population aged 15 or over)	50.0	2017	●	↑
Unemployment rate (% of total labor force)	4.2	2019	●	↑
Fatal work-related accidents embodied in imports (per 100,000 population)	0.0	2010	●	↑

SDG9 – Industry, Innovation and Infrastructure

	Value	Year	Rating	Trend
Population using the internet (%)	15.0	2017	●	→
Mobile broadband subscriptions (per 100 population)	41.2	2018	●	↑
Logistics Performance Index: Quality of trade and transport-related infrastructure (worst 1–5 best)	2.4	2018	●	↑
The Times Higher Education Universities Ranking: Average score of top 3 universities (worst 0–100 best)	16.4	2020	○	●
Scientific and technical journal articles (per 1,000 population)	0.0	2018	●	→
Expenditure on research and development (% of GDP)	NA	NA	●	●

SDG10 – Reduced Inequalities

	Value	Year	Rating	Trend
Gini coefficient adjusted for top income	38.7	2016	●	●

SDG11 – Sustainable Cities and Communities

	Value	Year	Rating	Trend
Annual mean concentration of particulate matter of less than 2.5 microns in diameter (PM2.5) (µg/m3)	60.8	2017	●	↗
Access to improved water source, piped (% of urban population)	37.1	2017	●	→
Satisfaction with public transport (%)	81.8	2019	●	↑

SDG12 – Responsible Consumption and Production

	Value	Year	Rating	Trend
Municipal solid waste (kg/capita/day)	0.7	2012	●	●
Electronic waste (kg/capita)	0.9	2016	●	●
Production-based SO2 emissions (kg/capita)	1.7	2012	●	●
SO2 emissions embodied in imports (kg/capita)	0.4	2012	●	●
Production-based nitrogen emissions (kg/capita)	8.5	2010	●	●
Nitrogen emissions embodied in imports (kg/capita)	0.2	2010	●	●

SDG13 – Climate Action

	Value	Year	Rating	Trend
Energy-related CO2 emissions (tCO2/capita)	0.5	2017	●	↑
CO2 emissions embodied in imports (tCO2/capita)	0.1	2015	●	↑
CO2 emissions embodied in fossil fuel exports (kg/capita)	0.0	2015	●	●

SDG14 – Life Below Water

	Value	Year	Rating	Trend
Mean area that is protected in marine sites important to biodiversity (%)	34.5	2018	○	→
Ocean Health Index: Clean Waters score (worst 0–100 best)	33.5	2019	●	→
Fish caught from overexploited or collapsed stocks (% of total catch)	1.7	2014	●	↑
Fish caught by trawling (%)	15.6	2014	○	↓
Marine biodiversity threats embodied in imports (per million population)	0.0	2018	●	●

SDG15 – Life on Land

	Value	Year	Rating	Trend
Mean area that is protected in terrestrial sites important to biodiversity (%)	48.0	2018	○	→
Mean area that is protected in freshwater sites important to biodiversity (%)	20.8	2018	●	→
Red List Index of species survival (worst 0–1 best)	0.8	2019	●	↓
Permanent deforestation (% of forest area, 5-year average)	0.2	2018	●	●
Terrestrial and freshwater biodiversity threats embodied in imports (per million population)	0.0	2018	●	●

SDG16 – Peace, Justice and Strong Institutions

	Value	Year	Rating	Trend
Homicides (per 100,000 population)	2.2	2017	○	↑
Unsentenced detainees (% of prison population)	78.2	2018	●	↓
Percentage of population who feel safe walking alone at night in the city or area where they live (%)	68.4	2019	○	↓
Property Rights (worst 1–7 best)	4.0	2019	●	●
Birth registrations with civil authority (% of children under age 5)	56.2	2018	●	●
Corruption Perception Index (worst 0–100 best)	26	2019	●	→
Children involved in child labor (% of population aged 5 to 14)	4.3	2016	●	●
Exports of major conventional weapons (TIV constant million USD per 100,000 population) *	0.0	2019	●	●
Press Freedom Index (best 0–100 worst)	50.7	2019	●	↓

SDG17 – Partnerships for the Goals

	Value	Year	Rating	Trend
Government spending on health and education (% of GDP)	2.0	2016	●	↓
For high-income and all OECD DAC countries: International concessional public finance, including official development assistance (% of GNI)	NA	NA	●	●
Other countries: Government revenue excluding grants (% of GDP)	10.2	2016	●	↓
Corporate Tax Haven Score (best 0–100 worst) *	0.0	2019	●	●

* Imputed data point

5. Country Profiles

▼ OVERALL PERFORMANCE

Index score	Regional average score
68.3	**70.4**

SDG Global rank **87** (OF 166)

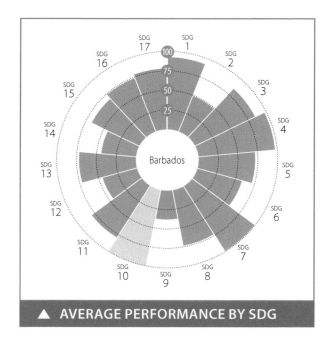

▲ AVERAGE PERFORMANCE BY SDG

▼ SPILLOVER INDEX

100 (best) to 0 (worst)

▼ CURRENT ASSESSMENT – SDG DASHBOARD

■ Major challenges   ■ Significant challenges   ▨ Challenges remain   ■ SDG achieved   ■ Information unavailable

▼ SDG TRENDS

⬇ Decreasing   ➡ Stagnating   ↗ Moderately improving   ⬆ On track or maintaining SDG achievement   ● Information unavailable

Notes: The full title of Goal 2 "Zero Hunger" is "End hunger, achieve food security and improved nutrition and promote sustainable agriculture".
The full title of each SDG is available here: https://sustainabledevelopment.un.org/topics/sustainabledevelopmentgoals

SDG1 – No Poverty

	Value	Year	Rating	Trend
Poverty headcount ratio at $1.90/day (%)	2.4	2020	○	→
Poverty headcount ratio at $3.20/day (%)	6.2	2020	○	→

SDG2 – Zero Hunger

	Value	Year	Rating	Trend
Prevalence of undernourishment (%)	3.9	2017	●	↑
Prevalence of stunting in children under 5 years of age (%)	7.7	2012	○	↑
Prevalence of wasting in children under 5 years of age (%)	6.8	2012	○	↑
Prevalence of obesity, BMI ≥ 30 (% of adult population)	23.1	2016	●	↓
Human Trophic Level (best 2–3 worst)	2.3	2017	●	→
Cereal yield (tonnes per hectare of harvested land)	2.9	2017	●	↑
Sustainable Nitrogen Management Index (best 0–1.41 worst)	1.2	2015	●	→

SDG3 – Good Health and Well-Being

	Value	Year	Rating	Trend
Maternal mortality rate (per 100,000 live births)	27	2017	●	↑
Neonatal mortality rate (per 1,000 live births)	7.9	2018	●	↑
Mortality rate, under-5 (per 1,000 live births)	12.2	2018	●	↑
Incidence of tuberculosis (per 100,000 population)	0.4	2018	●	↑
New HIV infections (per 1,000 uninfected population)	0.6	2018	○	→
Age-standardized death rate due to cardiovascular disease, cancer, diabetes, or chronic respiratory disease in adults aged 30–70 years (%)	16.2	2016	○	↑
Age-standardized death rate attributable to household air pollution and ambient air pollution (per 100,000 population)	31	2016	○	●
Traffic deaths (per 100,000 population)	5.6	2016	●	↑
Life expectancy at birth (years)	75.6	2016	○	→
Adolescent fertility rate (births per 1,000 adolescent females aged 15 to 19)	33.6	2017	○	↑
Births attended by skilled health personnel (%)	99.0	2015	●	↑
Percentage of surviving infants who received 2 WHO-recommended vaccines (%)	85	2018	○	↓
Universal health coverage (UHC) index of service coverage (worst 0–100 best)	77.0	2017	○	↑
Subjective well-being (average ladder score, worst 0–10 best)	NA	NA	●	●

SDG4 – Quality Education

	Value	Year	Rating	Trend
Net primary enrollment rate (%)	96.7	2018	○	↑
Lower secondary completion rate (%)	100.7	2009	●	●
Literacy rate (% of population aged 15 to 24)	99.9	2014	●	●

SDG5 – Gender Equality

	Value	Year	Rating	Trend
Demand for family planning satisfied by modern methods (% of females aged 15 to 49 who are married or in unions)	70.0	2012	○	↗
Ratio of female-to-male mean years of education received (%)	105.8	2018	●	↑
Ratio of female-to-male labor force participation rate (%)	89.0	2019	●	↑
Seats held by women in national parliament (%)	20.0	2020	●	→

SDG6 – Clean Water and Sanitation

	Value	Year	Rating	Trend
Population using at least basic drinking water services (%)	98.5	2017	●	↑
Population using at least basic sanitation services (%)	97.3	2017	●	↑
Freshwater withdrawal (% of available freshwater resources)	87.5	2005	●	●
Anthropogenic wastewater that receives treatment (%)	1.2	2018	●	●
Scarce water consumption embodied in imports (m³/capita)	13.5	2013	●	↑

SDG7 – Affordable and Clean Energy

	Value	Year	Rating	Trend
Population with access to electricity (%)	100.0	2017	●	↑
Population with access to clean fuels and technology for cooking (%)	99.4	2016	●	↑
CO_2 emissions from fuel combustion for electricity and heating per total electricity output (MtCO$_2$/TWh)	NA	NA	●	●

SDG8 – Decent Work and Economic Growth

	Value	Year	Rating	Trend
Adjusted GDP growth (%)	-3.0	2018	●	●
Victims of modern slavery (per 1,000 population)	2.7	2018	●	●
Adults with an account at a bank or other financial institution or with a mobile-money-service provider (% of population aged 15 or over)	NA	NA	●	●
Unemployment rate (% of total labor force)	10.3	2019	●	↗
Fatal work-related accidents embodied in imports (per 100,000 population)	0.8	2010	●	↑

SDG9 – Industry, Innovation and Infrastructure

	Value	Year	Rating	Trend
Population using the internet (%)	81.8	2017	●	↑
Mobile broadband subscriptions (per 100 population)	59.9	2018	○	↑
Logistics Performance Index: Quality of trade and transport-related infrastructure (worst 1–5 best)	NA	NA	●	●
The Times Higher Education Universities Ranking: Average score of top 3 universities (worst 0–100 best) *	0.0	2020	●	●
Scientific and technical journal articles (per 1,000 population)	0.1	2018	●	↓
Expenditure on research and development (% of GDP)	NA	NA	●	●

SDG10 – Reduced Inequalities

	Value	Year	Rating	Trend
Gini coefficient adjusted for top income	NA	NA	●	●

SDG11 – Sustainable Cities and Communities

	Value	Year	Rating	Trend
Annual mean concentration of particulate matter of less than 2.5 microns in diameter (PM2.5) (µg/m³)	23.1	2017	●	↗
Access to improved water source, piped (% of urban population)	NA	NA	●	●
Satisfaction with public transport (%)	NA	NA	●	●

SDG12 – Responsible Consumption and Production

	Value	Year	Rating	Trend
Municipal solid waste (kg/capita/day)	5.4	2011	●	●
Electronic waste (kg/capita)	13.7	2016	●	●
Production-based SO$_2$ emissions (kg/capita)	433.6	2012	●	●
SO$_2$ emissions embodied in imports (kg/capita)	12.6	2012	●	●
Production-based nitrogen emissions (kg/capita)	25.9	2010	○	●
Nitrogen emissions embodied in imports (kg/capita)	11.3	2010	●	●

SDG13 – Climate Action

	Value	Year	Rating	Trend
Energy-related CO_2 emissions (tCO$_2$/capita)	4.4	2017	●	→
CO_2 emissions embodied in imports (tCO$_2$/capita)	2.2	2015	●	→
CO_2 emissions embodied in fossil fuel exports (kg/capita)	0.0	2018	●	●

SDG14 – Life Below Water

	Value	Year	Rating	Trend
Mean area that is protected in marine sites important to biodiversity (%)	7.6	2018	●	→
Ocean Health Index: Clean Waters score (worst 0–100 best)	64.1	2019	●	↗
Fish caught from overexploited or collapsed stocks (% of total catch)	52.2	2014	●	→
Fish caught by trawling (%)	NA	NA	●	●
Marine biodiversity threats embodied in imports (per million population)	0.5	2018	○	●

SDG15 – Life on Land

	Value	Year	Rating	Trend
Mean area that is protected in terrestrial sites important to biodiversity (%)	2.5	2018	●	→
Mean area that is protected in freshwater sites important to biodiversity (%)	NA	NA	●	●
Red List Index of species survival (worst 0–1 best)	0.9	2019	●	↑
Permanent deforestation (% of forest area, 5-year average)	0.1	2018	○	●
Terrestrial and freshwater biodiversity threats embodied in imports (per million population)	0.6	2018	●	●

SDG16 – Peace, Justice and Strong Institutions

	Value	Year	Rating	Trend
Homicides (per 100,000 population)	10.5	2017	●	↓
Unsentenced detainees (% of prison population)	56.1	2018	●	↓
Percentage of population who feel safe walking alone at night in the city or area where they live (%)	NA	NA	●	●
Property Rights (worst 1–7 best)	4.5	2019	●	●
Birth registrations with civil authority (% of children under age 5)	98.7	2018	●	●
Corruption Perception Index (worst 0–100 best)	62	2019	●	↑
Children involved in child labor (% of population aged 5 to 14)	1.9	2016	●	●
Exports of major conventional weapons (TIV constant million USD per 100,000 population) *	0.0	2019	●	●
Press Freedom Index (best 0–100 worst)	NA	NA	●	●

SDG17 – Partnerships for the Goals

	Value	Year	Rating	Trend
Government spending on health and education (% of GDP)	8.3	2016	○	↓
For high-income and all OECD DAC countries: International concessional public finance, including official development assistance (% of GNI)	NA	NA	●	●
Other countries: Government revenue excluding grants (% of GDP)	NA	NA	●	●
Corporate Tax Haven Score (best 0–100 worst) *	0.0	2019	●	●

* Imputed data point

5. Country Profiles

BELARUS

▼ OVERALL PERFORMANCE

Index score

78.8

Regional average score
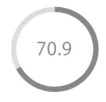
70.9

SDG Global rank 18 (OF 166)

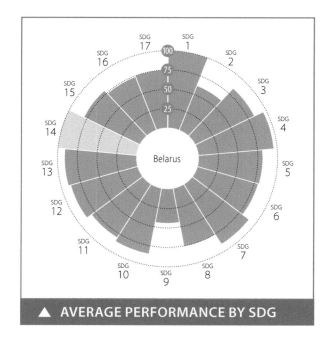

▲ AVERAGE PERFORMANCE BY SDG

Belarus

▼ SPILLOVER INDEX

100 (best) to 0 (worst)

```
100
 80
 60
 40
 20
  0
```

▼ CURRENT ASSESSMENT – SDG DASHBOARD

■ Major challenges ■ Significant challenges ■ Challenges remain ■ SDG achieved ■ Information unavailable

▼ SDG TRENDS

↓ Decreasing → Stagnating ↗ Moderately improving ↑ On track or maintaining SDG achievement ● Information unavailable

Notes: The full title of Goal 2 "Zero Hunger" is "End hunger, achieve food security and improved nutrition and promote sustainable agriculture".
The full title of each SDG is available here: https://sustainabledevelopment.un.org/topics/sustainabledevelopmentgoals

SDG1 – No Poverty

	Value	Year	Rating	Trend
Poverty headcount ratio at $1.90/day (%)	0.0	2020	●	↑
Poverty headcount ratio at $3.20/day (%)	0.1	2020	●	↑

SDG2 – Zero Hunger

	Value	Year	Rating	Trend
Prevalence of undernourishment (%)	2.5	2017	●	↑
Prevalence of stunting in children under 5 years of age (%)	4.5	2005	●	↑
Prevalence of wasting in children under 5 years of age (%)	2.2	2005	●	↑
Prevalence of obesity, BMI ≥ 30 (% of adult population)	24.5	2016	●	↓
Human Trophic Level (best 2–3 worst)	2.3	2017	●	↗
Cereal yield (tonnes per hectare of harvested land)	3.4	2017	●	↑
Sustainable Nitrogen Management Index (best 0–1.41 worst)	0.8	2015	●	→

SDG3 – Good Health and Well-Being

	Value	Year	Rating	Trend
Maternal mortality rate (per 100,000 live births)	2	2017	●	↑
Neonatal mortality rate (per 1,000 live births)	1.3	2018	●	↑
Mortality rate, under-5 (per 1,000 live births)	3.4	2018	●	↑
Incidence of tuberculosis (per 100,000 population)	31.0	2018	●	↑
New HIV infections (per 1,000 uninfected population)	0.2	2018	●	↑
Age-standardized death rate due to cardiovascular disease, cancer, diabetes, or chronic respiratory disease in adults aged 30–70 years (%)	23.7	2016	●	↑
Age-standardized death rate attributable to household air pollution and ambient air pollution (per 100,000 population)	61	2016	●	●
Traffic deaths (per 100,000 population)	8.9	2016	●	↑
Life expectancy at birth (years)	74.2	2016	●	↑
Adolescent fertility rate (births per 1,000 adolescent females aged 15 to 19)	14.5	2017	●	↑
Births attended by skilled health personnel (%)	99.8	2014	●	●
Percentage of surviving infants who received 2 WHO-recommended vaccines (%)	97	2018	●	↑
Universal health coverage (UHC) index of service coverage (worst 0–100 best)	76.0	2017	●	↑
Subjective well-being (average ladder score, worst 0–10 best)	5.8	2019	●	↑

SDG4 – Quality Education

	Value	Year	Rating	Trend
Net primary enrollment rate (%)	94.9	2018	●	↑
Lower secondary completion rate (%)	97.8	2018	●	↑
Literacy rate (% of population aged 15 to 24)	99.9	2018	●	●

SDG5 – Gender Equality

	Value	Year	Rating	Trend
Demand for family planning satisfied by modern methods (% of females aged 15 to 49 who are married or in unions)	74.2	2012	●	↑
Ratio of female-to-male mean years of education received (%)	98.4	2018	●	↑
Ratio of female-to-male labor force participation rate (%)	82.7	2019	●	↑
Seats held by women in national parliament (%)	40.0	2020	●	↑

SDG6 – Clean Water and Sanitation

	Value	Year	Rating	Trend
Population using at least basic drinking water services (%)	96.5	2017	●	→
Population using at least basic sanitation services (%)	97.8	2017	●	↑
Freshwater withdrawal (% of available freshwater resources)	4.8	2015	●	●
Anthropogenic wastewater that receives treatment (%)	7.2	2018	●	●
Scarce water consumption embodied in imports (m³/capita)	0.3	2013	●	↑

SDG7 – Affordable and Clean Energy

	Value	Year	Rating	Trend
Population with access to electricity (%)	100.0	2017	●	↑
Population with access to clean fuels and technology for cooking (%)	98.2	2016	●	↑
CO_2 emissions from fuel combustion for electricity and heating per total electricity output (MtCO$_2$/TWh)	1.7	2017	●	↗

SDG8 – Decent Work and Economic Growth

	Value	Year	Rating	Trend
Adjusted GDP growth (%)	-2.3	2018	●	●
Victims of modern slavery (per 1,000 population)	10.9	2018	●	●
Adults with an account at a bank or other financial institution or with a mobile-money-service provider (% of population aged 15 or over)	81.2	2017	●	↑
Unemployment rate (% of total labor force)	4.6	2019	●	↑
Fatal work-related accidents embodied in imports (per 100,000 population)	0.0	2010	●	↑

SDG9 – Industry, Innovation and Infrastructure

	Value	Year	Rating	Trend
Population using the internet (%)	79.1	2018	●	↑
Mobile broadband subscriptions (per 100 population)	86.3	2018	●	↑
Logistics Performance Index: Quality of trade and transport-related infrastructure (worst 1–5 best)	2.4	2018	●	↓
The Times Higher Education Universities Ranking: Average score of top 3 universities (worst 0–100 best)	16.4	2020	●	●
Scientific and technical journal articles (per 1,000 population)	0.1	2018	●	→
Expenditure on research and development (% of GDP)	0.6	2017	●	→

SDG10 – Reduced Inequalities

	Value	Year	Rating	Trend
Gini coefficient adjusted for top income	32.7	2017	●	●

SDG11 – Sustainable Cities and Communities

	Value	Year	Rating	Trend
Annual mean concentration of particulate matter of less than 2.5 microns in diameter (PM2.5) (µg/m³)	18.8	2017	●	↗
Access to improved water source, piped (% of urban population)	97.8	2017	●	↑
Satisfaction with public transport (%)	57.3	2019	●	↓

SDG12 – Responsible Consumption and Production

	Value	Year	Rating	Trend
Municipal solid waste (kg/capita/day)	1.6	2015	●	●
Electronic waste (kg/capita)	7.6	2016	●	●
Production-based SO_2 emissions (kg/capita)	0.7	2012	●	●
SO_2 emissions embodied in imports (kg/capita)	0.3	2012	●	●
Production-based nitrogen emissions (kg/capita)	0.5	2010	●	●
Nitrogen emissions embodied in imports (kg/capita)	0.0	2010	●	●

SDG13 – Climate Action

	Value	Year	Rating	Trend
Energy-related CO_2 emissions (tCO$_2$/capita)	6.5	2017	●	→
CO_2 emissions embodied in imports (tCO$_2$/capita)	0.0	2015	●	↑
CO_2 emissions embodied in fossil fuel exports (kg/capita)	0.0	2018	●	●

SDG14 – Life Below Water

	Value	Year	Rating	Trend
Mean area that is protected in marine sites important to biodiversity (%)	NA	NA	●	●
Ocean Health Index: Clean Waters score (worst 0–100 best)	NA	NA	●	●
Fish caught from overexploited or collapsed stocks (% of total catch)	NA	NA	●	●
Fish caught by trawling (%)	NA	NA	●	●
Marine biodiversity threats embodied in imports (per million population)	0.0	2018	●	●

SDG15 – Life on Land

	Value	Year	Rating	Trend
Mean area that is protected in terrestrial sites important to biodiversity (%)	48.6	2018	●	→
Mean area that is protected in freshwater sites important to biodiversity (%)	54.9	2018	●	↑
Red List Index of species survival (worst 0–1 best)	1.0	2019	●	↑
Permanent deforestation (% of forest area, 5-year average)	0.0	2018	●	●
Terrestrial and freshwater biodiversity threats embodied in imports (per million population)	0.0	2018	●	●

SDG16 – Peace, Justice and Strong Institutions

	Value	Year	Rating	Trend
Homicides (per 100,000 population)	3.6	2014	●	●
Unsentenced detainees (% of prison population)	9.4	2018	●	↑
Percentage of population who feel safe walking alone at night in the city or area where they live (%)	61.5	2019	●	↑
Property Rights (worst 1–7 best)	NA	NA	●	●
Birth registrations with civil authority (% of children under age 5)	100.0	2018	●	●
Corruption Perception Index (worst 0–100 best)	45	2019	●	↑
Children involved in child labor (% of population aged 5 to 14)	1.4	2016	●	●
Exports of major conventional weapons (TIV constant million USD per 100,000 population)	1.1	2019	●	●
Press Freedom Index (best 0–100 worst)	51.7	2019	●	→

SDG17 – Partnerships for the Goals

	Value	Year	Rating	Trend
Government spending on health and education (% of GDP)	8.8	2016	●	↗
For high-income and all OECD DAC countries: International concessional public finance, including official development assistance (% of GNI)	NA	NA	●	●
Other countries: Government revenue excluding grants (% of GDP)	29.5	2017	●	↑
Corporate Tax Haven Score (best 0–100 worst) *	0.0	2019	●	●

* Imputed data point

▼ OVERALL PERFORMANCE

Index score

80.0

Regional average score

77.3

SDG Global rank 11 (OF 166)

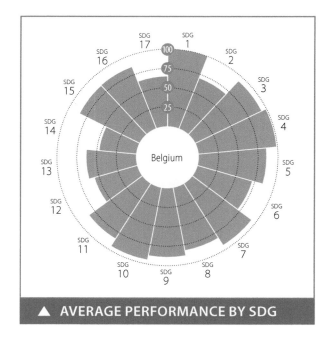

▲ AVERAGE PERFORMANCE BY SDG

▼ SPILLOVER INDEX

100 (best) to 0 (worst)

▼ CURRENT ASSESSMENT – SDG DASHBOARD

■ Major challenges   ■ Significant challenges   ■ Challenges remain   ■ SDG achieved   ■ Information unavailable

▼ SDG TRENDS

↓ Decreasing   → Stagnating   ↗ Moderately improving   ↑ On track or maintaining SDG achievement   ● Information unavailable

Notes: The full title of Goal 2 "Zero Hunger" is "End hunger, achieve food security and improved nutrition and promote sustainable agriculture".
The full title of each SDG is available here: https://sustainabledevelopment.un.org/topics/sustainabledevelopmentgoals

SDG1 – No Poverty

Indicator	Value	Year	Rating	Trend
Poverty headcount ratio at $1.90/day (%)	0.2	2020	●	↑
Poverty headcount ratio at $3.20/day (%)	0.3	2020	●	↑
Poverty rate after taxes and transfers (%)	10.2	2017	○	↓

SDG2 – Zero Hunger

Indicator	Value	Year	Rating	Trend
Prevalence of undernourishment (%)	2.5	2017	●	↑
Prevalence of stunting in children under 5 years of age (%)	* 2.6	2016	●	↑
Prevalence of wasting in children under 5 years of age (%)	* 0.7	2016	●	↑
Prevalence of obesity, BMI ≥ 30 (% of adult population)	22.1	2016	●	↓
Human Trophic Level (best 2–3 worst)	2.4	2017	●	↗
Cereal yield (tonnes per hectare of harvested land)	9.1	2017	●	↑
Sustainable Nitrogen Management Index (best 0–1.41 worst)	0.7	2015	●	→
Yield gap closure (% of potential yield)	77.2	2015	●	●

SDG3 – Good Health and Well-Being

Indicator	Value	Year	Rating	Trend
Maternal mortality rate (per 100,000 live births)	5	2017	●	↑
Neonatal mortality rate (per 1,000 live births)	2.0	2018	●	↑
Mortality rate, under-5 (per 1,000 live births)	3.7	2018	●	↑
Incidence of tuberculosis (per 100,000 population)	9.0	2018	●	↑
New HIV infections (per 1,000 uninfected population)	NA	NA	●	●
Age-standardized death rate due to cardiovascular disease, cancer, diabetes, or chronic respiratory disease in adults aged 30–70 years (%)	11.4	2016	●	↑
Age-standardized death rate attributable to household air pollution and ambient air pollution (per 100,000 population)	16	2016	●	●
Traffic deaths (per 100,000 population)	5.8	2016	●	↑
Life expectancy at birth (years)	81.2	2016	●	↑
Adolescent fertility rate (births per 1,000 adolescent females aged 15 to 19)	4.7	2017	●	↑
Births attended by skilled health personnel (%)	NA	NA	●	●
Percentage of surviving infants who received 2 WHO-recommended vaccines (%)	96.0	2018	●	↑
Universal health coverage (UHC) index of service coverage (worst 0–100 best)	84.0	2017	●	↑
Subjective well-being (average ladder score, worst 0–10 best)	6.8	2019	●	↑
Gap in life expectancy at birth among regions (years)	2.8	2016	●	●
Gap in self-reported health status by income (percentage points)	27.6	2017	○	→
Daily smokers (% of population aged 15 and over)	18.9	2013	○	●

SDG4 – Quality Education

Indicator	Value	Year	Rating	Trend
Net primary enrollment rate (%)	* 98.8	2017	●	↑
Lower secondary completion rate (%)	* 98.8	2017	●	↑
Literacy rate (% of population aged 15 to 24)	NA	NA	●	●
Participation rate in pre-primary organized learning (% of children aged 4 to 6)	98.4	2017	●	↑
Tertiary educational attainment (% of population aged 25 to 34)	47.4	2018	●	↑
PISA score (worst 0–600 best)	500.0	2018	●	↑
Variation in science performance explained by socio-economic status (%)	20.0	2018	●	↓
Underachievers in science (% of 15-year-olds)	20.0	2018	○	↓
Resilient students in science (% of 15-year-olds)	30.7	2018	○	↑

SDG5 – Gender Equality

Indicator	Value	Year	Rating	Trend
Demand for family planning satisfied by modern methods (% of females aged 15 to 49 who are married or in unions)	* 89.9	2017	●	↑
Ratio of female-to-male mean years of education received (%)	97.5	2018	●	↑
Ratio of female-to-male labor force participation rate (%)	81.6	2019	●	↑
Seats held by women in national parliament (%)	40.7	2020	●	↑
Gender wage gap (% of male median wage)	3.7	2016	●	↑
Gender gap in time spent doing unpaid work (minutes/day)	93.2	2013	○	●

SDG6 – Clean Water and Sanitation

Indicator	Value	Year	Rating	Trend
Population using at least basic drinking water services (%)	100.0	2017	●	●
Population using at least basic sanitation services (%)	99.5	2017	●	●
Freshwater withdrawal (% of available freshwater resources)	73.8	2010	●	●
Anthropogenic wastewater that receives treatment (%)	67.9	2018	●	●
Scarce water consumption embodied in imports (m³/capita)	38.6	2013	●	↗
Population using safely managed water services (%)	99.5	2017	●	↑
Population using safely managed sanitation services (%)	97.1	2017	●	↑

SDG7 – Affordable and Clean Energy

Indicator	Value	Year	Rating	Trend
Population with access to electricity (%)	100.0	2017	●	↑
Population with access to clean fuels and technology for cooking (%)	100.0	2016	●	↑
CO2 emissions from fuel combustion for electricity and heating per total electricity output (MtCO2/TWh)	1.1	2017	○	↑
Share of renewable energy in total primary energy supply (%)	7.9	2018	●	→

SDG8 – Decent Work and Economic Growth

Indicator	Value	Year	Rating	Trend
Adjusted GDP growth (%)	-0.1	2018	○	●
Victims of modern slavery (per 1,000 population)	2.0	2018	●	●
Adults with an account at a bank or other financial institution or with a mobile-money-service provider (% of population aged 15 or over)	98.6	2017	●	↑
Fatal work-related accidents embodied in imports (per 100,000 population)	1.9	2010	●	↑
Employment-to-population ratio (%)	65.3	2019	●	↑
Youth not in employment, education or training (NEET) (% of population aged 15 to 29)	12.8	2018	●	↑

SDG9 – Industry, Innovation and Infrastructure

Indicator	Value	Year	Rating	Trend
Population using the internet (%)	88.7	2018	●	↑
Mobile broadband subscriptions (per 100 population)	75.7	2018	●	↑
Logistics Performance Index: Quality of trade and transport-related infrastructure (worst 1–5 best)	4.0	2018	●	↑
The Times Higher Education Universities Ranking: Average score of top 3 universities (worst 0–100 best)	63.4	2020	●	●
Scientific and technical journal articles (per 1,000 population)	1.4	2018	●	↑
Expenditure on research and development (% of GDP)	2.6	2017	●	↑
Researchers (per 1,000 employed population)	12.0	2018	●	↑
Triadic patent families filed (per million population)	35.7	2017	●	↑
Gap in internet access by income (percentage points)	28.0	2019	●	↑
Women in science and engineering (% of tertiary graduates in science and engineering)	26.0	2015	●	●

SDG10 – Reduced Inequalities

Indicator	Value	Year	Rating	Trend
Gini coefficient adjusted for top income	29.4	2015	●	↑
Palma ratio	0.9	2017	●	↑
Elderly poverty rate (% of population aged 66 or over)	8.8	2017	○	→

SDG11 – Sustainable Cities and Communities

Indicator	Value	Year	Rating	Trend
Annual mean concentration of particulate matter of less than 2.5 microns in diameter (PM2.5) (µg/m³)	12.9	2017	○	↗
Access to improved water source, piped (% of urban population)	99.0	2017	●	↑
Satisfaction with public transport (%)	58.5	2019	●	↓
Population with rent overburden (%)	8.9	2017	○	→

SDG12 – Responsible Consumption and Production

Indicator	Value	Year	Rating	Trend
Electronic waste (kg/capita)	21.2	2016	●	●
Production-based SO2 emissions (kg/capita)	54.5	2012	○	●
SO2 emissions embodied in imports (kg/capita)	13.7	2012	●	●
Production-based nitrogen emissions (kg/capita)	51.7	2010	●	●
Nitrogen emissions embodied in imports (kg/capita)	17.8	2010	●	●
Non-recycled municipal solid waste (kg/capita/day)	0.5	2018	●	●

SDG13 – Climate Action

Indicator	Value	Year	Rating	Trend
Energy-related CO2 emissions (tCO2/capita)	8.8	2017	●	↓
CO2 emissions embodied in imports (tCO2/capita)	2.4	2015	●	→
CO2 emissions embodied in fossil fuel exports (kg/capita)	0.0	2019	●	●
Effective carbon rate (EUR/tCO2)	7.6	2016	●	●

SDG14 – Life Below Water

Indicator	Value	Year	Rating	Trend
Mean area that is protected in marine sites important to biodiversity (%)	93.4	2018	●	↑
Ocean Health Index: Clean Waters score (worst 0–100 best)	31.9	2019	●	↓
Fish caught from overexploited or collapsed stocks (% of total catch)	NA	NA	●	●
Fish caught by trawling (%)	97.1	2014	●	→
Marine biodiversity threats embodied in imports (per million population)	0.2	2018	○	●

SDG15 – Life on Land

Indicator	Value	Year	Rating	Trend
Mean area that is protected in terrestrial sites important to biodiversity (%)	81.0	2018	●	↑
Mean area that is protected in freshwater sites important to biodiversity (%)	92.8	2018	●	↑
Red List Index of species survival (worst 0–1 best)	1.0	2019	●	↑
Permanent deforestation (% of forest area, 5-year average)	0.0	2018	●	●
Terrestrial and freshwater biodiversity threats embodied in imports (per million population)	4.7	2018	●	●

SDG16 – Peace, Justice and Strong Institutions

Indicator	Value	Year	Rating	Trend
Homicides (per 100,000 population)	1.7	2017	○	↑
Unsentenced detainees (% of prison population)	35.6	2018	○	↓
Percentage of population who feel safe walking alone at night in the city or area where they live (%)	61.7	2019	○	↓
Property Rights (worst 1–7 best)	5.7	2019	●	●
Birth registrations with civil authority (% of children under age 5)	100.0	2018	●	●
Corruption Perception Index (worst 0–100 best)	75.0	2019	●	↑
Children involved in child labor (% of population aged 5 to 14)	* 0.0	2016	●	●
Exports of major conventional weapons (TIV constant million USD per 100,000 population)	0.2	2019	●	●
Press Freedom Index (best 0–100 worst)	12.1	2019	●	↑
Persons held in prison (per 100,000 population)	88.1	2017	●	↑

SDG17 – Partnerships for the Goals

Indicator	Value	Year	Rating	Trend
Government spending on health and education (% of GDP)	15.0	2016	●	↑
For high-income and all OECD DAC countries: International concessional public finance, including official development assistance (% of GNI)	0.5	2017	●	↓
Other countries: Government revenue excluding grants (% of GDP)	NA	NA	●	●
Corporate Tax Haven Score (best 0–100 worst)	67.8	2019	●	●
Financial Secrecy Score (best 0–100 worst)	45.1	2020	○	●
Shifted profits of multinationals (US$ billion)	-15.2	2016	●	●

* Imputed data point

5. Country Profiles

▼ OVERALL PERFORMANCE

Index score	Regional average score
65.1	70.4

SDG Global rank 102 (OF 166)

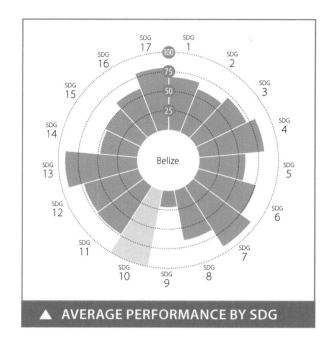

▲ AVERAGE PERFORMANCE BY SDG

▼ SPILLOVER INDEX

100 (best) to 0 (worst)

▼ CURRENT ASSESSMENT – SDG DASHBOARD

■ Major challenges ■ Significant challenges ■ Challenges remain ■ SDG achieved ■ Information unavailable

▼ SDG TRENDS

↓ Decreasing → Stagnating ↗ Moderately improving ↑ On track or maintaining SDG achievement ● Information unavailable

Notes: The full title of Goal 2 "Zero Hunger" is "End hunger, achieve food security and improved nutrition and promote sustainable agriculture".
The full title of each SDG is available here: https://sustainabledevelopment.un.org/topics/sustainabledevelopmentgoals

SDG1 – No Poverty

Indicator	Value	Year	Rating	Trend
Poverty headcount ratio at $1.90/day (%)	11.5	2020	●	↓
Poverty headcount ratio at $3.20/day (%)	24.1	2020	●	↓

SDG2 – Zero Hunger

Indicator	Value	Year	Rating	Trend
Prevalence of undernourishment (%)	7.5	2017	●	↑
Prevalence of stunting in children under 5 years of age (%)	15.0	2015	●	↗
Prevalence of wasting in children under 5 years of age (%)	1.8	2015	●	↑
Prevalence of obesity, BMI ≥ 30 (% of adult population)	24.1	2016	●	↓
Human Trophic Level (best 2–3 worst)	2.2	2017	●	↓
Cereal yield (tonnes per hectare of harvested land)	4.2	2017	●	↑
Sustainable Nitrogen Management Index (best 0–1.41 worst)	0.9	2015	●	↓

SDG3 – Good Health and Well-Being

Indicator	Value	Year	Rating	Trend
Maternal mortality rate (per 100,000 live births)	36	2017	●	↑
Neonatal mortality rate (per 1,000 live births)	8.6	2018	●	↑
Mortality rate, under-5 (per 1,000 live births)	13.0	2018	●	↑
Incidence of tuberculosis (per 100,000 population)	30.0	2018	●	→
New HIV infections (per 1,000 uninfected population)	0.8	2018	●	→
Age-standardized death rate due to cardiovascular disease, cancer, diabetes, or chronic respiratory disease in adults aged 30–70 years (%)	22.1	2016	●	→
Age-standardized death rate attributable to household air pollution and ambient air pollution (per 100,000 population)	69	2016	●	●
Traffic deaths (per 100,000 population)	28.3	2016	●	↓
Life expectancy at birth (years)	70.5	2016	●	→
Adolescent fertility rate (births per 1,000 adolescent females aged 15 to 19)	68.5	2017	●	→
Births attended by skilled health personnel (%)	96.8	2016	●	↑
Percentage of surviving infants who received 2 WHO-recommended vaccines (%)	96	2018	●	↑
Universal health coverage (UHC) index of service coverage (worst 0–100 best)	64.0	2017	●	→
Subjective well-being (average ladder score, worst 0–10 best)	6.0	2014	●	●

SDG4 – Quality Education

Indicator	Value	Year	Rating	Trend
Net primary enrollment rate (%)	95.9	2018	●	→
Lower secondary completion rate (%)	67.2	2018	●	↓
Literacy rate (% of population aged 15 to 24)	NA	NA	●	●

SDG5 – Gender Equality

Indicator	Value	Year	Rating	Trend
Demand for family planning satisfied by modern methods (% of females aged 15 to 49 who are married or in unions)	65.9	2016	●	→
Ratio of female-to-male mean years of education received (%)	102.1	2018	●	↑
Ratio of female-to-male labor force participation rate (%)	65.8	2019	●	↗
Seats held by women in national parliament (%)	9.4	2020	●	↗

SDG6 – Clean Water and Sanitation

Indicator	Value	Year	Rating	Trend
Population using at least basic drinking water services (%)	98.0	2017	●	↑
Population using at least basic sanitation services (%)	87.9	2017	●	↗
Freshwater withdrawal (% of available freshwater resources)	1.3	2000	●	●
Anthropogenic wastewater that receives treatment (%)	0.6	2018	●	●
Scarce water consumption embodied in imports (m³/capita)	4.4	2013	●	↑

SDG7 – Affordable and Clean Energy

Indicator	Value	Year	Rating	Trend
Population with access to electricity (%)	98.3	2017	●	↑
Population with access to clean fuels and technology for cooking (%)	85.4	2016	●	↑
CO_2 emissions from fuel combustion for electricity and heating per total electricity output (MtCO$_2$/TWh)	NA	NA	●	●

SDG8 – Decent Work and Economic Growth

Indicator	Value	Year	Rating	Trend
Adjusted GDP growth (%)	-5.2	2018	●	●
Victims of modern slavery (per 1,000 population)	NA	NA	●	●
Adults with an account at a bank or other financial institution or with a mobile-money-service provider (% of population aged 15 or over)	48.2	2014	●	●
Unemployment rate (% of total labor force)	6.4	2019	●	↑
Fatal work-related accidents embodied in imports (per 100,000 population)	0.3	2010	●	↑

SDG9 – Industry, Innovation and Infrastructure

Indicator	Value	Year	Rating	Trend
Population using the internet (%)	47.1	2017	●	↑
Mobile broadband subscriptions (per 100 population)	38.0	2017	●	↑
Logistics Performance Index: Quality of trade and transport-related infrastructure (worst 1–5 best)	NA	NA	●	●
The Times Higher Education Universities Ranking: Average score of top 3 universities (worst 0–100 best) *	0.0	2020	●	●
Scientific and technical journal articles (per 1,000 population)	0.0	2018	●	→
Expenditure on research and development (% of GDP)	NA	NA	●	●

SDG10 – Reduced Inequalities

Indicator	Value	Year	Rating	Trend
Gini coefficient adjusted for top income	NA	NA	●	●

SDG11 – Sustainable Cities and Communities

Indicator	Value	Year	Rating	Trend
Annual mean concentration of particulate matter of less than 2.5 microns in diameter (PM2.5) (µg/m³)	23.0	2017	●	↗
Access to improved water source, piped (% of urban population)	95.4	2017	●	↑
Satisfaction with public transport (%)	49.1	2014	●	●

SDG12 – Responsible Consumption and Production

Indicator	Value	Year	Rating	Trend
Municipal solid waste (kg/capita/day)	1.6	2015	●	●
Electronic waste (kg/capita)	6.0	2016	●	●
Production-based SO_2 emissions (kg/capita)	303.7	2012	●	●
SO_2 emissions embodied in imports (kg/capita)	5.1	2012	●	●
Production-based nitrogen emissions (kg/capita)	19.8	2010	●	●
Nitrogen emissions embodied in imports (kg/capita)	3.6	2010	●	●

SDG13 – Climate Action

Indicator	Value	Year	Rating	Trend
Energy-related CO_2 emissions (tCO$_2$/capita)	1.7	2017	●	↑
CO_2 emissions embodied in imports (tCO$_2$/capita)	0.6	2015	●	↑
CO_2 emissions embodied in fossil fuel exports (kg/capita)	0.0	2019	●	●

SDG14 – Life Below Water

Indicator	Value	Year	Rating	Trend
Mean area that is protected in marine sites important to biodiversity (%)	27.7	2018	●	→
Ocean Health Index: Clean Waters score (worst 0–100 best)	66.3	2019	●	↑
Fish caught from overexploited or collapsed stocks (% of total catch)	NA	NA	●	●
Fish caught by trawling (%)	78.2	2014	●	↓
Marine biodiversity threats embodied in imports (per million population)	0.1	2018	●	●

SDG15 – Life on Land

Indicator	Value	Year	Rating	Trend
Mean area that is protected in terrestrial sites important to biodiversity (%)	46.0	2018	●	→
Mean area that is protected in freshwater sites important to biodiversity (%)	18.3	2018	●	→
Red List Index of species survival (worst 0–1 best)	0.7	2019	●	↓
Permanent deforestation (% of forest area, 5-year average)	0.7	2018	●	●
Terrestrial and freshwater biodiversity threats embodied in imports (per million population)	0.2	2018	●	●

SDG16 – Peace, Justice and Strong Institutions

Indicator	Value	Year	Rating	Trend
Homicides (per 100,000 population)	37.9	2017	●	↓
Unsentenced detainees (% of prison population)	56.9	2018	●	↓
Percentage of population who feel safe walking alone at night in the city or area where they live (%)	50.2	2014	●	●
Property Rights (worst 1–7 best)	NA	NA	●	●
Birth registrations with civil authority (% of children under age 5)	95.7	2018	●	●
Corruption Perception Index (worst 0–100 best)	NA	NA	●	●
Children involved in child labor (% of population aged 5 to 14)	3.2	2016	●	●
Exports of major conventional weapons (TIV constant million USD per 100,000 population) *	0.0	2019	●	●
Press Freedom Index (best 0–100 worst)	27.5	2019	●	↑

SDG17 – Partnerships for the Goals

Indicator	Value	Year	Rating	Trend
Government spending on health and education (% of GDP)	11.2	2016	●	↑
For high-income and all OECD DAC countries: International concessional public finance, including official development assistance (% of GNI)	NA	NA	●	●
Other countries: Government revenue excluding grants (% of GDP)	29.4	2017	●	↑
Corporate Tax Haven Score (best 0–100 worst) *	0.0	2019	●	●

* Imputed data point

5. Country Profiles

▼ OVERALL PERFORMANCE

Index score

53.3

Regional average score

53.1

SDG Global rank 145 (OF 166)

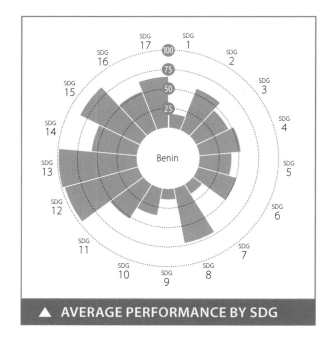

▲ AVERAGE PERFORMANCE BY SDG

▼ SPILLOVER INDEX

100 (best) to 0 (worst)

▼ CURRENT ASSESSMENT – SDG DASHBOARD

■ Major challenges　■ Significant challenges　■ Challenges remain　■ SDG achieved　■ Information unavailable

▼ SDG TRENDS

　Decreasing　→ Stagnating　↗ Moderately improving　↑ On track or maintaining SDG achievement　● Information unavailable

Notes: The full title of Goal 2 "Zero Hunger" is "End hunger, achieve food security and improved nutrition and promote sustainable agriculture".
　　　 The full title of each SDG is available here: https://sustainabledevelopment.un.org/topics/sustainabledevelopmentgoals

BENIN

SDG1 – No Poverty	Value	Year	Rating	Trend
Poverty headcount ratio at $1.90/day (%)	45.8	2020	●	→
Poverty headcount ratio at $3.20/day (%)	69.8	2020	●	→

SDG2 – Zero Hunger	Value	Year	Rating	Trend
Prevalence of undernourishment (%)	10.1	2017	◐	→
Prevalence of stunting in children under 5 years of age (%)	34.0	2014	●	↗
Prevalence of wasting in children under 5 years of age (%)	4.5	2014	●	↑
Prevalence of obesity, BMI ≥ 30 (% of adult population)	9.6	2016	●	↑
Human Trophic Level (best 2–3 worst)	2.1	2017	●	↑
Cereal yield (tonnes per hectare of harvested land)	1.5	2017	●	→
Sustainable Nitrogen Management Index (best 0–1.41 worst)	0.8	2015	●	→

SDG3 – Good Health and Well-Being	Value	Year	Rating	Trend
Maternal mortality rate (per 100,000 live births)	397	2017	●	↗
Neonatal mortality rate (per 1,000 live births)	31.3	2018	●	→
Mortality rate, under-5 (per 1,000 live births)	93.0	2018	●	→
Incidence of tuberculosis (per 100,000 population)	56.0	2018	●	→
New HIV infections (per 1,000 uninfected population)	0.3	2018	◐	↑
Age-standardized death rate due to cardiovascular disease, cancer, diabetes, or chronic respiratory disease in adults aged 30–70 years (%)	19.6	2016	◐	→
Age-standardized death rate attributable to household air pollution and ambient air pollution (per 100,000 population)	205	2016	●	●
Traffic deaths (per 100,000 population)	27.5	2016	●	→
Life expectancy at birth (years)	61.1	2016	●	→
Adolescent fertility rate (births per 1,000 adolescent females aged 15 to 19)	86.1	2017	●	→
Births attended by skilled health personnel (%)	78.1	2018	●	↓
Percentage of surviving infants who received 2 WHO-recommended vaccines (%)	71	2018	●	↗
Universal health coverage (UHC) index of service coverage (worst 0–100 best)	40.0	2017	●	→
Subjective well-being (average ladder score, worst 0–10 best)	5.0	2019	●	↑

SDG4 – Quality Education	Value	Year	Rating	Trend
Net primary enrollment rate (%)	97.2	2018	●	↑
Lower secondary completion rate (%)	45.8	2016	●	●
Literacy rate (% of population aged 15 to 24)	60.9	2018	●	●

SDG5 – Gender Equality	Value	Year	Rating	Trend
Demand for family planning satisfied by modern methods (% of females aged 15 to 49 who are married or in unions)	25.9	2018	●	→
Ratio of female-to-male mean years of education received (%)	68.2	2018	●	→
Ratio of female-to-male labor force participation rate (%)	94.6	2019	●	↑
Seats held by women in national parliament (%)	7.2	2020	●	→

SDG6 – Clean Water and Sanitation	Value	Year	Rating	Trend
Population using at least basic drinking water services (%)	66.4	2017	●	→
Population using at least basic sanitation services (%)	16.5	2017	●	→
Freshwater withdrawal (% of available freshwater resources)	1.0	2000	●	●
Anthropogenic wastewater that receives treatment (%)	0.0	2018	●	●
Scarce water consumption embodied in imports (m³/capita)	0.4	2013	●	↑

SDG7 – Affordable and Clean Energy	Value	Year	Rating	Trend
Population with access to electricity (%)	43.1	2017	●	↗
Population with access to clean fuels and technology for cooking (%)	6.4	2016	●	→
CO$_2$ emissions from fuel combustion for electricity and heating per total electricity output (MtCO$_2$/TWh)	21.7	2017	●	↓

SDG8 – Decent Work and Economic Growth	Value	Year	Rating	Trend
Adjusted GDP growth (%)	-3.8	2018	●	●
Victims of modern slavery (per 1,000 population)	5.5	2018	◐	●
Adults with an account at a bank or other financial institution or with a mobile-money-service provider (% of population aged 15 or over)	38.5	2017	●	↑
Unemployment rate (% of total labor force)	2.2	2019	●	↑
Fatal work-related accidents embodied in imports (per 100,000 population)	0.0	2010	●	↑

SDG9 – Industry, Innovation and Infrastructure	Value	Year	Rating	Trend
Population using the internet (%)	20.0	2017	●	↑
Mobile broadband subscriptions (per 100 population)	19.8	2018	●	↑
Logistics Performance Index: Quality of trade and transport-related infrastructure (worst 1–5 best)	2.5	2018	●	↗
The Times Higher Education Universities Ranking: Average score of top 3 universities (worst 0–100 best) *	0.0	2020	●	●
Scientific and technical journal articles (per 1,000 population)	0.0	2018	●	→
Expenditure on research and development (% of GDP) *	0.0	2017	●	●

SDG10 – Reduced Inequalities	Value	Year	Rating	Trend
Gini coefficient adjusted for top income	50.5	2015	●	●

SDG11 – Sustainable Cities and Communities	Value	Year	Rating	Trend
Annual mean concentration of particulate matter of less than 2.5 microns in diameter (PM2.5) (µg/m³)	39.0	2017	●	↓
Access to improved water source, piped (% of urban population)	54.2	2017	●	↓
Satisfaction with public transport (%)	49.3	2019	●	↑

SDG12 – Responsible Consumption and Production	Value	Year	Rating	Trend
Municipal solid waste (kg/capita/day)	NA	NA	●	●
Electronic waste (kg/capita)	0.7	2016	●	●
Production-based SO$_2$ emissions (kg/capita)	15.1	2012	●	●
SO$_2$ emissions embodied in imports (kg/capita)	0.4	2012	●	●
Production-based nitrogen emissions (kg/capita)	13.9	2010	●	●
Nitrogen emissions embodied in imports (kg/capita)	0.3	2010	●	●

SDG13 – Climate Action	Value	Year	Rating	Trend
Energy-related CO$_2$ emissions (tCO$_2$/capita)	0.6	2017	●	↑
CO$_2$ emissions embodied in imports (tCO$_2$/capita)	0.0	2015	●	↑
CO$_2$ emissions embodied in fossil fuel exports (kg/capita)	0.0	2015	●	●

SDG14 – Life Below Water	Value	Year	Rating	Trend
Mean area that is protected in marine sites important to biodiversity (%)	30.6	2018	◐	→
Ocean Health Index: Clean Waters score (worst 0–100 best)	23.8	2019	●	→
Fish caught from overexploited or collapsed stocks (% of total catch)	NA	NA	●	●
Fish caught by trawling (%)	1.5	2014	●	↑
Marine biodiversity threats embodied in imports (per million population)	0.0	2018	●	●

SDG15 – Life on Land	Value	Year	Rating	Trend
Mean area that is protected in terrestrial sites important to biodiversity (%)	77.4	2018	●	↑
Mean area that is protected in freshwater sites important to biodiversity (%)	NA	NA	●	●
Red List Index of species survival (worst 0–1 best)	0.9	2019	●	↑
Permanent deforestation (% of forest area, 5-year average)	0.2	2018	●	●
Terrestrial and freshwater biodiversity threats embodied in imports (per million population)	0.0	2018	●	●

SDG16 – Peace, Justice and Strong Institutions	Value	Year	Rating	Trend
Homicides (per 100,000 population) *	1.1	2017	●	↑
Unsentenced detainees (% of prison population)	62.3	2018	●	●
Percentage of population who feel safe walking alone at night in the city or area where they live (%)	54.1	2019	●	↑
Property Rights (worst 1–7 best)	3.9	2019	●	●
Birth registrations with civil authority (% of children under age 5)	85.6	2018	●	●
Corruption Perception Index (worst 0–100 best)	41	2019	●	↗
Children involved in child labor (% of population aged 5 to 14)	52.5	2016	●	●
Exports of major conventional weapons (TIV constant million USD per 100,000 population) *	0.0	2019	●	●
Press Freedom Index (best 0–100 worst)	31.7	2019	◐	↓

SDG17 – Partnerships for the Goals	Value	Year	Rating	Trend
Government spending on health and education (% of GDP)	4.8	2016	●	↓
For high-income and all OECD DAC countries: International concessional public finance, including official development assistance (% of GNI)	NA	NA	●	●
Other countries: Government revenue excluding grants (% of GDP)	NA	NA	●	●
Corporate Tax Haven Score (best 0–100 worst) *	0.0	2019	●	●

* Imputed data point

5. Country Profiles

BHUTAN

East and South Asia

▼ OVERALL PERFORMANCE

Index score

69.3

Regional average score

67.2

SDG Global rank **80** (OF 166)

▼ SPILLOVER INDEX

100 (best) to 0 (worst)

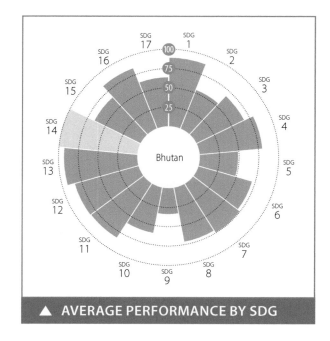

▲ AVERAGE PERFORMANCE BY SDG

▼ CURRENT ASSESSMENT – SDG DASHBOARD

■ Major challenges ■ Significant challenges ■ Challenges remain ■ SDG achieved ■ Information unavailable

▼ SDG TRENDS

↓ Decreasing → Stagnating ↗ Moderately improving ↑ On track or maintaining SDG achievement ● Information unavailable

Notes: The full title of Goal 2 "Zero Hunger" is "End hunger, achieve food security and improved nutrition and promote sustainable agriculture".
The full title of each SDG is available here: https://sustainabledevelopment.un.org/topics/sustainabledevelopmentgoals

SDG1 – No Poverty

Indicator	Value	Year	Rating	Trend
Poverty headcount ratio at $1.90/day (%)	0.0	2020	●	↑
Poverty headcount ratio at $3.20/day (%)	10.5	2020	●	↑

SDG2 – Zero Hunger

Indicator	Value	Year	Rating	Trend
Prevalence of undernourishment (%)	NA	NA	●	●
Prevalence of stunting in children under 5 years of age (%)	33.6	2010	●	→
Prevalence of wasting in children under 5 years of age (%)	5.9	2010	◐	↑
Prevalence of obesity, BMI ≥ 30 (% of adult population)	6.4	2016	●	↑
Human Trophic Level (best 2–3 worst)	NA	NA	●	●
Cereal yield (tonnes per hectare of harvested land)	3.4	2017	●	↑
Sustainable Nitrogen Management Index (best 0–1.41 worst)	0.7	2015	●	→

SDG3 – Good Health and Well-Being

Indicator	Value	Year	Rating	Trend
Maternal mortality rate (per 100,000 live births)	183	2017	●	↑
Neonatal mortality rate (per 1,000 live births)	16.4	2018	●	↑
Mortality rate, under-5 (per 1,000 live births)	29.7	2018	◐	↑
Incidence of tuberculosis (per 100,000 population)	149.0	2018	●	↗
New HIV infections (per 1,000 uninfected population)	0.1	2018	●	↑
Age-standardized death rate due to cardiovascular disease, cancer, diabetes, or chronic respiratory disease in adults aged 30–70 years (%)	23.3	2016	●	↗
Age-standardized death rate attributable to household air pollution and ambient air pollution (per 100,000 population)	124	2016	●	●
Traffic deaths (per 100,000 population)	17.4	2016	●	↓
Life expectancy at birth (years)	70.6	2016	●	↗
Adolescent fertility rate (births per 1,000 adolescent females aged 15 to 19)	20.2	2017	●	↑
Births attended by skilled health personnel (%)	89.0	2016	●	↑
Percentage of surviving infants who received 2 WHO-recommended vaccines (%)	97	2018	●	↑
Universal health coverage (UHC) index of service coverage (worst 0–100 best)	62.0	2017	●	↑
Subjective well-being (average ladder score, worst 0–10 best)	5.1	2015	●	●

SDG4 – Quality Education

Indicator	Value	Year	Rating	Trend
Net primary enrollment rate (%)	88.0	2018	●	↓
Lower secondary completion rate (%)	82.5	2018	●	↑
Literacy rate (% of population aged 15 to 24)	93.1	2017	◐	●

SDG5 – Gender Equality

Indicator	Value	Year	Rating	Trend
Demand for family planning satisfied by modern methods (% of females aged 15 to 49 who are married or in unions)	84.6	2010	●	↑
Ratio of female-to-male mean years of education received (%)	50.0	2018	●	↓
Ratio of female-to-male labor force participation rate (%)	78.3	2019	●	↑
Seats held by women in national parliament (%)	14.9	2020	●	↗

SDG6 – Clean Water and Sanitation

Indicator	Value	Year	Rating	Trend
Population using at least basic drinking water services (%)	97.2	2017	◐	↑
Population using at least basic sanitation services (%)	69.3	2017	●	↗
Freshwater withdrawal (% of available freshwater resources)	1.4	2010	●	●
Anthropogenic wastewater that receives treatment (%)	0.0	2018	●	●
Scarce water consumption embodied in imports (m³/capita)	6.3	2013	●	↑

SDG7 – Affordable and Clean Energy

Indicator	Value	Year	Rating	Trend
Population with access to electricity (%)	97.7	2017	◐	↑
Population with access to clean fuels and technology for cooking (%)	52.5	2016	●	→
CO$_2$ emissions from fuel combustion for electricity and heating per total electricity output (MtCO$_2$/TWh)	NA	NA	●	●

SDG8 – Decent Work and Economic Growth

Indicator	Value	Year	Rating	Trend
Adjusted GDP growth (%)	-0.6	2018	◐	●
Victims of modern slavery (per 1,000 population)	NA	NA	●	●
Adults with an account at a bank or other financial institution or with a mobile-money-service provider (% of population aged 15 or over)	33.7	2014	●	●
Unemployment rate (% of total labor force)	2.3	2019	●	↑
Fatal work-related accidents embodied in imports (per 100,000 population)	0.5	2010	●	↑

SDG9 – Industry, Innovation and Infrastructure

Indicator	Value	Year	Rating	Trend
Population using the internet (%)	48.1	2017	●	↑
Mobile broadband subscriptions (per 100 population)	101.6	2018	●	↑
Logistics Performance Index: Quality of trade and transport-related infrastructure (worst 1–5 best)	1.9	2018	●	↓
The Times Higher Education Universities Ranking: Average score of top 3 universities (worst 0–100 best) *	0.0	2020	●	●
Scientific and technical journal articles (per 1,000 population)	0.1	2018	●	→
Expenditure on research and development (% of GDP)	NA	NA	●	●

SDG10 – Reduced Inequalities

Indicator	Value	Year	Rating	Trend
Gini coefficient adjusted for top income	41.8	2017	●	●

SDG11 – Sustainable Cities and Communities

Indicator	Value	Year	Rating	Trend
Annual mean concentration of particulate matter of less than 2.5 microns in diameter (PM2.5) (μg/m³)	37.9	2017	●	↗
Access to improved water source, piped (% of urban population)	99.0	2017	●	↑
Satisfaction with public transport (%)	75.2	2015	●	●

SDG12 – Responsible Consumption and Production

Indicator	Value	Year	Rating	Trend
Municipal solid waste (kg/capita/day)	0.9	2007	●	●
Electronic waste (kg/capita)	2.5	2016	●	●
Production-based SO$_2$ emissions (kg/capita)	149.5	2012	●	●
SO$_2$ emissions embodied in imports (kg/capita)	5.9	2012	◐	●
Production-based nitrogen emissions (kg/capita)	14.3	2010	●	●
Nitrogen emissions embodied in imports (kg/capita)	2.7	2010	●	●

SDG13 – Climate Action

Indicator	Value	Year	Rating	Trend
Energy-related CO$_2$ emissions (tCO$_2$/capita)	0.8	2017	●	↑
CO$_2$ emissions embodied in imports (tCO$_2$/capita)	0.4	2015	●	↑
CO$_2$ emissions embodied in fossil fuel exports (kg/capita)	NA	NA	●	●

SDG14 – Life Below Water

Indicator	Value	Year	Rating	Trend
Mean area that is protected in marine sites important to biodiversity (%)	NA	NA	●	●
Ocean Health Index: Clean Waters score (worst 0–100 best)	NA	NA	●	●
Fish caught from overexploited or collapsed stocks (% of total catch)	NA	NA	●	●
Fish caught by trawling (%)	NA	NA	●	●
Marine biodiversity threats embodied in imports (per million population)	0.1	2018	●	●

SDG15 – Life on Land

Indicator	Value	Year	Rating	Trend
Mean area that is protected in terrestrial sites important to biodiversity (%)	47.3	2018	◐	→
Mean area that is protected in freshwater sites important to biodiversity (%)	34.3	2018	◐	→
Red List Index of species survival (worst 0–1 best)	0.8	2019	●	↓
Permanent deforestation (% of forest area, 5-year average)	0.0	2018	●	●
Terrestrial and freshwater biodiversity threats embodied in imports (per million population)	0.2	2018	●	●

SDG16 – Peace, Justice and Strong Institutions

Indicator	Value	Year	Rating	Trend
Homicides (per 100,000 population)	1.6	2017	◐	↓
Unsentenced detainees (% of prison population)	NA	NA	●	●
Percentage of population who feel safe walking alone at night in the city or area where they live (%)	63.1	2015	◐	●
Property Rights (worst 1–7 best)	NA	NA	●	●
Birth registrations with civil authority (% of children under age 5)	99.9	2018	●	●
Corruption Perception Index (worst 0–100 best)	68	2019	●	↑
Children involved in child labor (% of population aged 5 to 14)	2.9	2016	◐	●
Exports of major conventional weapons (TIV constant million USD per 100,000 population) *	0.0	2019	●	●
Press Freedom Index (best 0–100 worst)	29.8	2019	●	↑

SDG17 – Partnerships for the Goals

Indicator	Value	Year	Rating	Trend
Government spending on health and education (% of GDP)	9.4	2016	◐	↑
For high-income and all OECD DAC countries: International concessional public finance, including official development assistance (% of GNI)	NA	NA	●	●
Other countries: Government revenue excluding grants (% of GDP)	18.5	2017	●	↓
Corporate Tax Haven Score (best 0–100 worst) *	0.0	2019	●	●

* Imputed data point

5. Country Profiles

BOLIVIA

Latin America and the Caribbean

▼ OVERALL PERFORMANCE

Index score

69.3

Regional average score

70.4

SDG Global rank 79 (OF 166)

▼ SPILLOVER INDEX

100 (best) to 0 (worst)

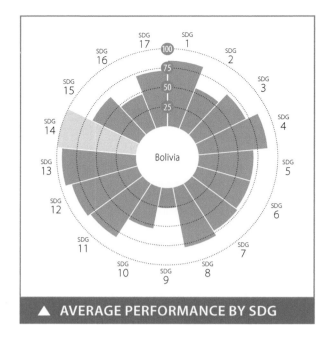

▲ AVERAGE PERFORMANCE BY SDG

▼ CURRENT ASSESSMENT – SDG DASHBOARD

■ Major challenges ■ Significant challenges ▨ Challenges remain ■ SDG achieved ■ Information unavailable

▼ SDG TRENDS

↓ Decreasing → Stagnating ↗ Moderately improving ↑ On track or maintaining SDG achievement ● Information unavailable

Notes: The full title of Goal 2 "Zero Hunger" is "End hunger, achieve food security and improved nutrition and promote sustainable agriculture".
The full title of each SDG is available here: https://sustainabledevelopment.un.org/topics/sustainabledevelopmentgoals

SDG1 – No Poverty

Indicator	Value	Year	Rating	Trend
Poverty headcount ratio at $1.90/day (%)	4.7	2020	●	↗
Poverty headcount ratio at $3.20/day (%)	11.3	2020	●	→

SDG2 – Zero Hunger

Indicator	Value	Year	Rating	Trend
Prevalence of undernourishment (%)	17.1	2017	●	↑
Prevalence of stunting in children under 5 years of age (%)	16.1	2016	●	↑
Prevalence of wasting in children under 5 years of age (%)	2.0	2016	●	↑
Prevalence of obesity, BMI ≥ 30 (% of adult population)	20.2	2016	●	↓
Human Trophic Level (best 2–3 worst)	2.3	2017	●	→
Cereal yield (tonnes per hectare of harvested land)	1.9	2017	●	↓
Sustainable Nitrogen Management Index (best 0–1.41 worst)	0.5	2015	●	↗

SDG3 – Good Health and Well-Being

Indicator	Value	Year	Rating	Trend
Maternal mortality rate (per 100,000 live births)	155	2017	●	↑
Neonatal mortality rate (per 1,000 live births)	14.3	2018	●	↑
Mortality rate, under-5 (per 1,000 live births)	26.8	2018	●	↑
Incidence of tuberculosis (per 100,000 population)	108.0	2018	●	→
New HIV infections (per 1,000 uninfected population)	0.1	2018	●	↑
Age-standardized death rate due to cardiovascular disease, cancer, diabetes, or chronic respiratory disease in adults aged 30–70 years (%)	17.2	2016	●	↑
Age-standardized death rate attributable to household air pollution and ambient air pollution (per 100,000 population)	64	2016	●	●
Traffic deaths (per 100,000 population)	15.5	2016	●	↑
Life expectancy at birth (years)	71.5	2016	●	↗
Adolescent fertility rate (births per 1,000 adolescent females aged 15 to 19)	64.9	2017	●	↗
Births attended by skilled health personnel (%)	89.8	2016	●	↑
Percentage of surviving infants who received 2 WHO-recommended vaccines (%)	83	2018	●	↓
Universal health coverage (UHC) index of service coverage (worst 0–100 best)	68.0	2017	●	↑
Subjective well-being (average ladder score, worst 0–10 best)	5.9	2018	●	↑

SDG4 – Quality Education

Indicator	Value	Year	Rating	Trend
Net primary enrollment rate (%)	92.9	2018	●	↑
Lower secondary completion rate (%)	82.5	2017	●	↓
Literacy rate (% of population aged 15 to 24)	99.4	2015	●	●

SDG5 – Gender Equality

Indicator	Value	Year	Rating	Trend
Demand for family planning satisfied by modern methods (% of females aged 15 to 49 who are married or in unions)	50.3	2016	●	↗
Ratio of female-to-male mean years of education received (%)	84.7	2018	●	↓
Ratio of female-to-male labor force participation rate (%)	71.3	2019	●	↑
Seats held by women in national parliament (%)	53.1	2020	●	↑

SDG6 – Clean Water and Sanitation

Indicator	Value	Year	Rating	Trend
Population using at least basic drinking water services (%)	92.8	2017	●	↑
Population using at least basic sanitation services (%)	60.7	2017	●	↗
Freshwater withdrawal (% of available freshwater resources)	1.2	2010	●	●
Anthropogenic wastewater that receives treatment (%)	3.5	2018	●	●
Scarce water consumption embodied in imports (m³/capita)	1.1	2013	●	↑

SDG7 – Affordable and Clean Energy

Indicator	Value	Year	Rating	Trend
Population with access to electricity (%)	91.8	2017	●	↑
Population with access to clean fuels and technology for cooking (%)	64.0	2016	●	↓
CO_2 emissions from fuel combustion for electricity and heating per total electricity output (MtCO$_2$/TWh)	2.3	2017	●	→

SDG8 – Decent Work and Economic Growth

Indicator	Value	Year	Rating	Trend
Adjusted GDP growth (%)	-2.0	2018	●	●
Victims of modern slavery (per 1,000 population)	2.1	2018	●	●
Adults with an account at a bank or other financial institution or with a mobile-money-service provider (% of population aged 15 or over)	54.4	2017	●	↑
Unemployment rate (% of total labor force)	3.5	2019	●	↑
Fatal work-related accidents embodied in imports (per 100,000 population)	0.1	2010	●	↑

SDG9 – Industry, Innovation and Infrastructure

Indicator	Value	Year	Rating	Trend
Population using the internet (%)	44.3	2018	●	↗
Mobile broadband subscriptions (per 100 population)	79.9	2018	●	↑
Logistics Performance Index: Quality of trade and transport-related infrastructure (worst 1–5 best)	2.2	2018	●	↓
The Times Higher Education Universities Ranking: Average score of top 3 universities (worst 0–100 best) *	0.0	2020	●	●
Scientific and technical journal articles (per 1,000 population)	0.0	2018	●	→
Expenditure on research and development (% of GDP)	0.2	2009	●	●

SDG10 – Reduced Inequalities

Indicator	Value	Year	Rating	Trend
Gini coefficient adjusted for top income	44.0	2017	●	●

SDG11 – Sustainable Cities and Communities

Indicator	Value	Year	Rating	Trend
Annual mean concentration of particulate matter of less than 2.5 microns in diameter (PM2.5) (µg/m³)	21.6	2017	●	↑
Access to improved water source, piped (% of urban population)	87.9	2017	●	↓
Satisfaction with public transport (%)	68.2	2018	●	↑

SDG12 – Responsible Consumption and Production

Indicator	Value	Year	Rating	Trend
Municipal solid waste (kg/capita/day)	0.8	2015	●	●
Electronic waste (kg/capita)	3.3	2016	●	●
Production-based SO$_2$ emissions (kg/capita)	17.0	2012	●	●
SO$_2$ emissions embodied in imports (kg/capita)	1.5	2012	●	●
Production-based nitrogen emissions (kg/capita)	43.8	2010	●	●
Nitrogen emissions embodied in imports (kg/capita)	1.3	2010	●	●

SDG13 – Climate Action

Indicator	Value	Year	Rating	Trend
Energy-related CO_2 emissions (tCO$_2$/capita)	1.6	2017	●	↑
CO_2 emissions embodied in imports (tCO$_2$/capita)	0.2	2015	●	↑
CO_2 emissions embodied in fossil fuel exports (kg/capita)	2797.2	2018	●	●

SDG14 – Life Below Water

Indicator	Value	Year	Rating	Trend
Mean area that is protected in marine sites important to biodiversity (%)	NA	NA	●	●
Ocean Health Index: Clean Waters score (worst 0–100 best)	NA	NA	●	●
Fish caught from overexploited or collapsed stocks (% of total catch)	NA	NA	●	●
Fish caught by trawling (%)	NA	NA	●	●
Marine biodiversity threats embodied in imports (per million population)	0.0	2018	●	●

SDG15 – Life on Land

Indicator	Value	Year	Rating	Trend
Mean area that is protected in terrestrial sites important to biodiversity (%)	50.2	2018	●	↑
Mean area that is protected in freshwater sites important to biodiversity (%)	49.4	2018	●	→
Red List Index of species survival (worst 0–1 best)	0.9	2019	●	→
Permanent deforestation (% of forest area, 5-year average)	0.5	2018	●	●
Terrestrial and freshwater biodiversity threats embodied in imports (per million population)	0.2	2018	●	●

SDG16 – Peace, Justice and Strong Institutions

Indicator	Value	Year	Rating	Trend
Homicides (per 100,000 population)	6.3	2016	●	↑
Unsentenced detainees (% of prison population)	69.9	2018	●	↑
Percentage of population who feel safe walking alone at night in the city or area where they live (%)	46.1	2018	●	→
Property Rights (worst 1–7 best)	2.7	2019	●	●
Birth registrations with civil authority (% of children under age 5)	91.9	2018	●	●
Corruption Perception Index (worst 0–100 best)	31	2019	●	↓
Children involved in child labor (% of population aged 5 to 14)	26.4	2016	●	●
Exports of major conventional weapons (TIV constant million USD per 100,000 population) *	0.0	2019	●	●
Press Freedom Index (best 0–100 worst)	35.4	2019	●	↓

SDG17 – Partnerships for the Goals

Indicator	Value	Year	Rating	Trend
Government spending on health and education (% of GDP)	NA	NA	●	●
For high-income and all OECD DAC countries: International concessional public finance, including official development assistance (% of GNI)	NA	NA	●	●
Other countries: Government revenue excluding grants (% of GDP)	23.3	2007	●	●
Corporate Tax Haven Score (best 0–100 worst) *	0.0	2019	●	●

* Imputed data point

5. Country Profiles

▼ OVERALL PERFORMANCE

Index score

73.5

Regional average score
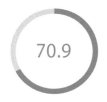
70.9

SDG Global rank 50 (OF 166)

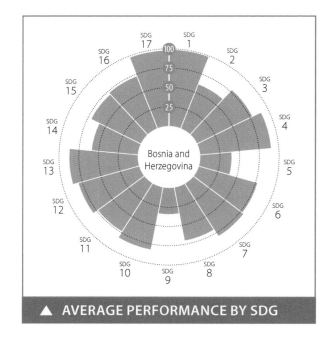

▲ AVERAGE PERFORMANCE BY SDG

▼ SPILLOVER INDEX

100 (best) to 0 (worst)

100
80
60
40
20
0

▼ CURRENT ASSESSMENT – SDG DASHBOARD

■ Major challenges ■ Significant challenges ■ Challenges remain ■ SDG achieved ■ Information unavailable

▼ SDG TRENDS

↓ Decreasing → Stagnating ↗ Moderately improving ↑ On track or maintaining SDG achievement ● Information unavailable

Notes: The full title of Goal 2 "Zero Hunger" is "End hunger, achieve food security and improved nutrition and promote sustainable agriculture".
The full title of each SDG is available here: https://sustainabledevelopment.un.org/topics/sustainabledevelopmentgoals

SDG1 – No Poverty

Indicator	Value	Year	Rating	Trend
Poverty headcount ratio at $1.90/day (%)	0.1	2020	●	↑
Poverty headcount ratio at $3.20/day (%)	0.2	2020	●	↑

SDG2 – Zero Hunger

Indicator	Value	Year	Rating	Trend
Prevalence of undernourishment (%)	2.5	2017	●	↑
Prevalence of stunting in children under 5 years of age (%)	8.9	2012	●	↑
Prevalence of wasting in children under 5 years of age (%)	2.3	2012	●	↑
Prevalence of obesity, BMI ≥ 30 (% of adult population)	17.9	2016	●	↓
Human Trophic Level (best 2–3 worst)	2.3	2017	●	↗
Cereal yield (tonnes per hectare of harvested land)	3.7	2017	●	↑
Sustainable Nitrogen Management Index (best 0–1.41 worst)	1.0	2015	●	↓

SDG3 – Good Health and Well-Being

Indicator	Value	Year	Rating	Trend
Maternal mortality rate (per 100,000 live births)	10	2017	●	↑
Neonatal mortality rate (per 1,000 live births)	4.1	2018	●	↑
Mortality rate, under-5 (per 1,000 live births)	5.8	2018	●	↑
Incidence of tuberculosis (per 100,000 population)	25.0	2018	●	↑
New HIV infections (per 1,000 uninfected population)	0.0	2018	●	↑
Age-standardized death rate due to cardiovascular disease, cancer, diabetes, or chronic respiratory disease in adults aged 30–70 years (%)	17.8	2016	●	↑
Age-standardized death rate attributable to household air pollution and ambient air pollution (per 100,000 population)	80	2016	●	●
Traffic deaths (per 100,000 population)	15.7	2016	●	↑
Life expectancy at birth (years)	77.3	2016	●	↑
Adolescent fertility rate (births per 1,000 adolescent females aged 15 to 19)	9.6	2017	●	↑
Births attended by skilled health personnel (%)	99.9	2015	●	↑
Percentage of surviving infants who received 2 WHO-recommended vaccines (%)	68	2018	●	↓
Universal health coverage (UHC) index of service coverage (worst 0–100 best)	61.0	2017	●	↗
Subjective well-being (average ladder score, worst 0–10 best)	5.9	2018	●	↑

SDG4 – Quality Education

Indicator	Value	Year	Rating	Trend
Net primary enrollment rate (%)	NA	NA	●	●
Lower secondary completion rate (%)	NA	NA	●	●
Literacy rate (% of population aged 15 to 24)	99.7	2013	●	●

SDG5 – Gender Equality

Indicator	Value	Year	Rating	Trend
Demand for family planning satisfied by modern methods (% of females aged 15 to 49 who are married or in unions)	21.9	2012	●	→
Ratio of female-to-male mean years of education received (%)	78.9	2018	●	→
Ratio of female-to-male labor force participation rate (%)	60.8	2019	●	↓
Seats held by women in national parliament (%)	21.4	2020	●	→

SDG6 – Clean Water and Sanitation

Indicator	Value	Year	Rating	Trend
Population using at least basic drinking water services (%)	96.1	2017	●	→
Population using at least basic sanitation services (%)	95.4	2017	●	↑
Freshwater withdrawal (% of available freshwater resources)	2.7	2015	●	●
Anthropogenic wastewater that receives treatment (%)	1.1	2018	●	●
Scarce water consumption embodied in imports (m³/capita)	2.9	2013	●	↑

SDG7 – Affordable and Clean Energy

Indicator	Value	Year	Rating	Trend
Population with access to electricity (%)	100.0	2017	●	↑
Population with access to clean fuels and technology for cooking (%)	63.4	2016	●	↗
CO_2 emissions from fuel combustion for electricity and heating per total electricity output (MtCO₂/TWh)	1.4	2017	●	→

SDG8 – Decent Work and Economic Growth

Indicator	Value	Year	Rating	Trend
Adjusted GDP growth (%)	1.0	2018	●	●
Victims of modern slavery (per 1,000 population)	3.4	2018	●	●
Adults with an account at a bank or other financial institution or with a mobile-money-service provider (% of population aged 15 or over)	58.8	2017	●	↑
Unemployment rate (% of total labor force)	18.4	2019	●	↑
Fatal work-related accidents embodied in imports (per 100,000 population)	0.1	2010	●	↑

SDG9 – Industry, Innovation and Infrastructure

Indicator	Value	Year	Rating	Trend
Population using the internet (%)	70.1	2018	●	↑
Mobile broadband subscriptions (per 100 population)	55.4	2018	●	↑
Logistics Performance Index: Quality of trade and transport-related infrastructure (worst 1–5 best)	2.4	2018	●	↓
The Times Higher Education Universities Ranking: Average score of top 3 universities (worst 0–100 best) *	7.0	2019	●	●
Scientific and technical journal articles (per 1,000 population)	0.2	2018	●	→
Expenditure on research and development (% of GDP)	0.2	2017	●	↓

SDG10 – Reduced Inequalities

Indicator	Value	Year	Rating	Trend
Gini coefficient adjusted for top income	34.1	2015	●	●

SDG11 – Sustainable Cities and Communities

Indicator	Value	Year	Rating	Trend
Annual mean concentration of particulate matter of less than 2.5 microns in diameter (PM2.5) (µg/m³)	27.7	2017	●	→
Access to improved water source, piped (% of urban population)	97.6	2017	●	→
Satisfaction with public transport (%)	49.4	2018	●	↗

SDG12 – Responsible Consumption and Production

Indicator	Value	Year	Rating	Trend
Municipal solid waste (kg/capita/day)	2.0	2015	●	●
Electronic waste (kg/capita)	6.5	2016	●	●
Production-based SO_2 emissions (kg/capita)	73.8	2012	●	●
SO_2 emissions embodied in imports (kg/capita)	3.3	2012	●	●
Production-based nitrogen emissions (kg/capita)	17.0	2010	●	●
Nitrogen emissions embodied in imports (kg/capita)	1.5	2010	●	●

SDG13 – Climate Action

Indicator	Value	Year	Rating	Trend
Energy-related CO_2 emissions (tCO₂/capita)	6.7	2017	●	→
CO_2 emissions embodied in imports (tCO₂/capita)	0.4	2015	●	↑
CO_2 emissions embodied in fossil fuel exports (kg/capita)	90.1	2019	●	●

SDG14 – Life Below Water

Indicator	Value	Year	Rating	Trend
Mean area that is protected in marine sites important to biodiversity (%)	NA	NA	●	●
Ocean Health Index: Clean Waters score (worst 0–100 best)	40.6	2019	●	→
Fish caught from overexploited or collapsed stocks (% of total catch)	NA	NA	●	●
Fish caught by trawling (%)	NA	NA	●	●
Marine biodiversity threats embodied in imports (per million population)	0.0	2018	●	●

SDG15 – Life on Land

Indicator	Value	Year	Rating	Trend
Mean area that is protected in terrestrial sites important to biodiversity (%)	18.2	2018	●	→
Mean area that is protected in freshwater sites important to biodiversity (%)	66.7	2018	●	↑
Red List Index of species survival (worst 0–1 best)	0.9	2019	●	↑
Permanent deforestation (% of forest area, 5-year average)	0.0	2018	●	●
Terrestrial and freshwater biodiversity threats embodied in imports (per million population)	0.5	2018	●	●

SDG16 – Peace, Justice and Strong Institutions

Indicator	Value	Year	Rating	Trend
Homicides (per 100,000 population)	1.2	2017	●	↑
Unsentenced detainees (% of prison population)	15.4	2018	●	↑
Percentage of population who feel safe walking alone at night in the city or area where they live (%)	67.1	2018	●	↓
Property Rights (worst 1–7 best)	3.3	2019	●	●
Birth registrations with civil authority (% of children under age 5)	99.5	2018	●	●
Corruption Perception Index (worst 0–100 best)	36	2019	●	↓
Children involved in child labor (% of population aged 5 to 14)	5.3	2016	●	●
Exports of major conventional weapons (TIV constant million USD per 100,000 population) *	0.0	2019	●	●
Press Freedom Index (best 0–100 worst)	29.0	2019	●	↑

SDG17 – Partnerships for the Goals

Indicator	Value	Year	Rating	Trend
Government spending on health and education (% of GDP)	NA	NA	●	●
For high-income and all OECD DAC countries: International concessional public finance, including official development assistance (% of GNI)	NA	NA	●	●
Other countries: Government revenue excluding grants (% of GDP)	38.9	2018	●	↑
Corporate Tax Haven Score (best 0–100 worst) *	0.0	2019	●	●

* Imputed data point

5. Country Profiles

OVERALL PERFORMANCE

Index score
61.5

Regional average score
53.1

SDG Global rank 121 (OF 166)

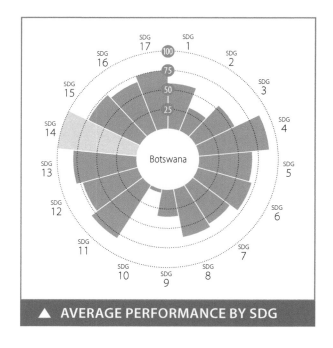

AVERAGE PERFORMANCE BY SDG

SPILLOVER INDEX

100 (best) to 0 (worst)

CURRENT ASSESSMENT – SDG DASHBOARD

■ Major challenges ■ Significant challenges □ Challenges remain ■ SDG achieved ■ Information unavailable

SDG TRENDS

↓ Decreasing → Stagnating ↗ Moderately improving ↑ On track or maintaining SDG achievement ● Information unavailable

Notes: The full title of Goal 2 "Zero Hunger" is "End hunger, achieve food security and improved nutrition and promote sustainable agriculture".
The full title of each SDG is available here: https://sustainabledevelopment.un.org/topics/sustainabledevelopmentgoals

BOTSWANA

SDG1 – No Poverty

Indicator	Value	Year
Poverty headcount ratio at $1.90/day (%)	16.1	2020
Poverty headcount ratio at $3.20/day (%)	31.3	2020

SDG2 – Zero Hunger

Indicator	Value	Year
Prevalence of undernourishment (%)	26.4	2017
Prevalence of stunting in children under 5 years of age (%)	31.4	2007
Prevalence of wasting in children under 5 years of age (%)	7.2	2007
Prevalence of obesity, BMI ≥ 30 (% of adult population)	18.9	2016
Human Trophic Level (best 2–3 worst)	2.3	2017
Cereal yield (tonnes per hectare of harvested land)	0.4	2017
Sustainable Nitrogen Management Index (best 0–1.41 worst)	1.3	2015

SDG3 – Good Health and Well-Being

Indicator	Value	Year
Maternal mortality rate (per 100,000 live births)	144	2017
Neonatal mortality rate (per 1,000 live births)	24.5	2018
Mortality rate, under-5 (per 1,000 live births)	36.5	2018
Incidence of tuberculosis (per 100,000 population)	275.0	2018
New HIV infections (per 1,000 uninfected population)	4.4	2018
Age-standardized death rate due to cardiovascular disease, cancer, diabetes, or chronic respiratory disease in adults aged 30–70 years (%)	20.3	2016
Age-standardized death rate attributable to household air pollution and ambient air pollution (per 100,000 population)	101	2016
Traffic deaths (per 100,000 population)	23.8	2016
Life expectancy at birth (years)	66.1	2016
Adolescent fertility rate (births per 1,000 adolescent females aged 15 to 19)	46.1	2017
Births attended by skilled health personnel (%)	99.7	2015
Percentage of surviving infants who received 2 WHO-recommended vaccines (%)	95	2018
Universal health coverage (UHC) index of service coverage (worst 0–100 best)	61.0	2017
Subjective well-being (average ladder score, worst 0–10 best)	3.5	2018

SDG4 – Quality Education

Indicator	Value	Year
Net primary enrollment rate (%)	87.7	2014
Lower secondary completion rate (%)	98.0	2014
Literacy rate (% of population aged 15 to 24)	97.5	2013

SDG5 – Gender Equality

Indicator	Value	Year
Demand for family planning satisfied by modern methods (% of females aged 15 to 49 who are married or in unions) *	78.2	2017
Ratio of female-to-male mean years of education received (%)	96.8	2018
Ratio of female-to-male labor force participation rate (%)	84.4	2019
Seats held by women in national parliament (%)	10.8	2020

SDG6 – Clean Water and Sanitation

Indicator	Value	Year
Population using at least basic drinking water services (%)	90.3	2017
Population using at least basic sanitation services (%)	77.3	2017
Freshwater withdrawal (% of available freshwater resources)	2.1	2015
Anthropogenic wastewater that receives treatment (%)	1.0	2018
Scarce water consumption embodied in imports (m³/capita)	6.8	2013

SDG7 – Affordable and Clean Energy

Indicator	Value	Year
Population with access to electricity (%)	62.8	2017
Population with access to clean fuels and technology for cooking (%)	64.1	2016
CO_2 emissions from fuel combustion for electricity and heating per total electricity output ($MtCO_2$/TWh)	2.7	2017

SDG8 – Decent Work and Economic Growth

Indicator	Value	Year
Adjusted GDP growth (%)	-1.6	2018
Victims of modern slavery (per 1,000 population)	3.4	2018
Adults with an account at a bank or other financial institution or with a mobile-money-service provider (% of population aged 15 or over)	51.0	2017
Unemployment rate (% of total labor force)	18.2	2019
Fatal work-related accidents embodied in imports (per 100,000 population)	0.8	2010

SDG9 – Industry, Innovation and Infrastructure

Indicator	Value	Year
Population using the internet (%)	47.0	2017
Mobile broadband subscriptions (per 100 population)	77.6	2018
Logistics Performance Index: Quality of trade and transport-related infrastructure (worst 1–5 best)	3.0	2016
The Times Higher Education Universities Ranking: Average score of top 3 universities (worst 0–100 best) *	0.0	2020
Scientific and technical journal articles (per 1,000 population)	0.1	2018
Expenditure on research and development (% of GDP)	0.5	2013

SDG10 – Reduced Inequalities

Indicator	Value	Year
Gini coefficient adjusted for top income	61.3	2015

SDG11 – Sustainable Cities and Communities

Indicator	Value	Year
Annual mean concentration of particulate matter of less than 2.5 microns in diameter (PM2.5) (µg/m³)	23.1	2017
Access to improved water source, piped (% of urban population)	96.8	2017
Satisfaction with public transport (%)	62.2	2018

SDG12 – Responsible Consumption and Production

Indicator	Value	Year
Municipal solid waste (kg/capita/day)	0.4	2010
Electronic waste (kg/capita)	7.6	2016
Production-based SO_2 emissions (kg/capita)	108.0	2012
SO_2 emissions embodied in imports (kg/capita)	12.4	2012
Production-based nitrogen emissions (kg/capita)	55.6	2010
Nitrogen emissions embodied in imports (kg/capita)	5.3	2010

SDG13 – Climate Action

Indicator	Value	Year
Energy-related CO_2 emissions (tCO_2/capita)	3.5	2017
CO_2 emissions embodied in imports (tCO_2/capita)	1.5	2015
CO_2 emissions embodied in fossil fuel exports (kg/capita)	45.1	2018

SDG14 – Life Below Water

Indicator	Value	Year
Mean area that is protected in marine sites important to biodiversity (%)	NA	NA
Ocean Health Index: Clean Waters score (worst 0–100 best)	NA	NA
Fish caught from overexploited or collapsed stocks (% of total catch)	NA	NA
Fish caught by trawling (%)	NA	NA
Marine biodiversity threats embodied in imports (per million population)	0.5	2018

SDG15 – Life on Land

Indicator	Value	Year
Mean area that is protected in terrestrial sites important to biodiversity (%)	51.1	2018
Mean area that is protected in freshwater sites important to biodiversity (%)	46.0	2018
Red List Index of species survival (worst 0–1 best)	1.0	2019
Permanent deforestation (% of forest area, 5-year average)	0.0	2018
Terrestrial and freshwater biodiversity threats embodied in imports (per million population)	2.5	2018

SDG16 – Peace, Justice and Strong Institutions

Indicator	Value	Year
Homicides (per 100,000 population)	15.0	2010
Unsentenced detainees (% of prison population)	25.4	2015
Percentage of population who feel safe walking alone at night in the city or area where they live (%)	34.4	2018
Property Rights (worst 1–7 best)	4.9	2019
Birth registrations with civil authority (% of children under age 5)	87.5	2018
Corruption Perception Index (worst 0–100 best)	61	2019
Children involved in child labor (% of population aged 5 to 14)	9.0	2016
Exports of major conventional weapons (TIV constant million USD per 100,000 population) *	0.0	2019
Press Freedom Index (best 0–100 worst)	25.1	2019

SDG17 – Partnerships for the Goals

Indicator	Value	Year
Government spending on health and education (% of GDP)	14.1	2009
For high-income and all OECD DAC countries: International concessional public finance, including official development assistance (% of GNI)	NA	NA
Other countries: Government revenue excluding grants (% of GDP)	26.8	2018
Corporate Tax Haven Score (best 0–100 worst)	55.3	2019

* Imputed data point

5. Country Profiles

▼ OVERALL PERFORMANCE

Index score

72.7

Regional average score

70.4

SDG Global rank **53** (OF 166)

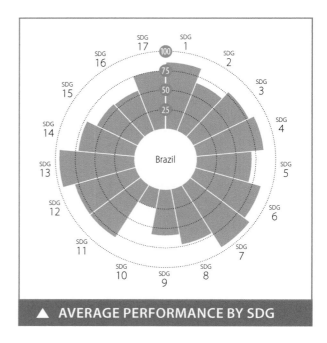

▲ AVERAGE PERFORMANCE BY SDG

▼ SPILLOVER INDEX

100 (best) to 0 (worst)

▼ CURRENT ASSESSMENT – SDG DASHBOARD

■ Major challenges ■ Significant challenges ■ Challenges remain ■ SDG achieved ■ Information unavailable

▼ SDG TRENDS

↓ Decreasing   → Stagnating   ↗ Moderately improving   ↑ On track or maintaining SDG achievement   ● Information unavailable

Notes: The full title of Goal 2 "Zero Hunger" is "End hunger, achieve food security and improved nutrition and promote sustainable agriculture".
The full title of each SDG is available here: https://sustainabledevelopment.un.org/topics/sustainabledevelopmentgoals

SDG1 – No Poverty	Value	Year	Rating	Trend
Poverty headcount ratio at $1.90/day (%)	4.2	2020	○	→
Poverty headcount ratio at $3.20/day (%)	11.1	2020	○	→

SDG2 – Zero Hunger	Value	Year	Rating	Trend
Prevalence of undernourishment (%)	2.5	2017	●	↑
Prevalence of stunting in children under 5 years of age (%)	7.1	2007	●	↑
Prevalence of wasting in children under 5 years of age (%)	1.6	2007	●	↑
Prevalence of obesity, BMI ≥ 30 (% of adult population)	22.1	2016	●	↓
Human Trophic Level (best 2–3 worst)	2.4	2017	●	→
Cereal yield (tonnes per hectare of harvested land)	5.2	2017	●	↑
Sustainable Nitrogen Management Index (best 0–1.41 worst)	0.5	2015	●	↓

SDG3 – Good Health and Well-Being	Value	Year	Rating	Trend
Maternal mortality rate (per 100,000 live births)	60	2017	●	↑
Neonatal mortality rate (per 1,000 live births)	8.1	2018	●	↑
Mortality rate, under-5 (per 1,000 live births)	14.4	2018	●	↑
Incidence of tuberculosis (per 100,000 population)	45.0	2018	●	→
New HIV infections (per 1,000 uninfected population)	0.3	2018	○	→
Age-standardized death rate due to cardiovascular disease, cancer, diabetes, or chronic respiratory disease in adults aged 30–70 years (%)	16.6	2016	●	↑
Age-standardized death rate attributable to household air pollution and ambient air pollution (per 100,000 population)	30	2016	○	●
Traffic deaths (per 100,000 population)	19.7	2016	●	↑
Life expectancy at birth (years)	75.1	2016	●	↗
Adolescent fertility rate (births per 1,000 adolescent females aged 15 to 19)	59.1	2017	●	→
Births attended by skilled health personnel (%)	99.2	2015	●	↑
Percentage of surviving infants who received 2 WHO-recommended vaccines (%)	83	2018	●	↓
Universal health coverage (UHC) index of service coverage (worst 0–100 best)	79.0	2017	●	↑
Subjective well-being (average ladder score, worst 0–10 best)	6.5	2019	●	↑

SDG4 – Quality Education	Value	Year	Rating	Trend
Net primary enrollment rate (%)	96.3	2017	○	↑
Lower secondary completion rate (%)	71.8	2011	●	●
Literacy rate (% of population aged 15 to 24)	99.2	2018	●	●

SDG5 – Gender Equality	Value	Year	Rating	Trend
Demand for family planning satisfied by modern methods (% of females aged 15 to 49 who are married or in unions)	89.0	2007	●	↑
Ratio of female-to-male mean years of education received (%)	106.6	2018	●	↑
Ratio of female-to-male labor force participation rate (%)	72.6	2019	●	↑
Seats held by women in national parliament (%)	14.6	2020	●	→

SDG6 – Clean Water and Sanitation	Value	Year	Rating	Trend
Population using at least basic drinking water services (%)	98.2	2017	●	↑
Population using at least basic sanitation services (%)	88.3	2017	○	↑
Freshwater withdrawal (% of available freshwater resources)	3.0	2015	●	●
Anthropogenic wastewater that receives treatment (%)	49.3	2018	○	●
Scarce water consumption embodied in imports (m³/capita)	2.1	2013	●	↑

SDG7 – Affordable and Clean Energy	Value	Year	Rating	Trend
Population with access to electricity (%)	100.0	2017	●	↑
Population with access to clean fuels and technology for cooking (%)	95.6	2016	●	↑
CO$_2$ emissions from fuel combustion for electricity and heating per total electricity output (MtCO$_2$/TWh)	0.7	2017	●	↑

SDG8 – Decent Work and Economic Growth	Value	Year	Rating	Trend
Adjusted GDP growth (%)	-4.7	2018	●	●
Victims of modern slavery (per 1,000 population)	1.8	2018	●	●
Adults with an account at a bank or other financial institution or with a mobile-money-service provider (% of population aged 15 or over)	70.0	2017	○	↗
Unemployment rate (% of total labor force)	12.1	2019	●	↓
Fatal work-related accidents embodied in imports (per 100,000 population)	0.1	2010	●	↑

SDG9 – Industry, Innovation and Infrastructure	Value	Year	Rating	Trend
Population using the internet (%)	70.4	2018	○	↑
Mobile broadband subscriptions (per 100 population)	88.1	2018	●	↑
Logistics Performance Index: Quality of trade and transport-related infrastructure (worst 1–5 best)	2.9	2018	○	→
The Times Higher Education Universities Ranking: Average score of top 3 universities (worst 0–100 best)	39.1	2020	●	●
Scientific and technical journal articles (per 1,000 population)	0.3	2018	○	→
Expenditure on research and development (% of GDP)	1.3	2016	○	↓

SDG10 – Reduced Inequalities	Value	Year	Rating	Trend
Gini coefficient adjusted for top income	54.2	2017	●	●

SDG11 – Sustainable Cities and Communities	Value	Year	Rating	Trend
Annual mean concentration of particulate matter of less than 2.5 microns in diameter (PM2.5) (µg/m³)	12.7	2017	○	↑
Access to improved water source, piped (% of urban population)	99.0	2017	●	↑
Satisfaction with public transport (%)	50.3	2019	●	→

SDG12 – Responsible Consumption and Production	Value	Year	Rating	Trend
Municipal solid waste (kg/capita/day)	1.2	2015	○	●
Electronic waste (kg/capita)	7.4	2016	○	●
Production-based SO$_2$ emissions (kg/capita)	11.4	2012	●	●
SO$_2$ emissions embodied in imports (kg/capita)	1.4	2012	●	●
Production-based nitrogen emissions (kg/capita)	53.5	2010	●	●
Nitrogen emissions embodied in imports (kg/capita)	1.2	2010	●	●

SDG13 – Climate Action	Value	Year	Rating	Trend
Energy-related CO$_2$ emissions (tCO$_2$/capita)	2.1	2017	○	↑
CO$_2$ emissions embodied in imports (tCO$_2$/capita)	0.2	2015	●	↑
CO$_2$ emissions embodied in fossil fuel exports (kg/capita)	2.3	2018	●	●

SDG14 – Life Below Water	Value	Year	Rating	Trend
Mean area that is protected in marine sites important to biodiversity (%)	65.2	2018	●	↑
Ocean Health Index: Clean Waters score (worst 0–100 best)	60.2	2019	●	→
Fish caught from overexploited or collapsed stocks (% of total catch)	31.6	2014	○	↓
Fish caught by trawling (%)	17.5	2014	○	↓
Marine biodiversity threats embodied in imports (per million population)	0.0	2018	●	●

SDG15 – Life on Land	Value	Year	Rating	Trend
Mean area that is protected in terrestrial sites important to biodiversity (%)	42.2	2018	○	→
Mean area that is protected in freshwater sites important to biodiversity (%)	12.5	2018	●	→
Red List Index of species survival (worst 0–1 best)	0.9	2019	●	↑
Permanent deforestation (% of forest area, 5-year average)	0.6	2018	●	●
Terrestrial and freshwater biodiversity threats embodied in imports (per million population)	0.3	2018	●	●

SDG16 – Peace, Justice and Strong Institutions	Value	Year	Rating	Trend
Homicides (per 100,000 population)	30.5	2017	●	↓
Unsentenced detainees (% of prison population)	37.2	2018	○	↑
Percentage of population who feel safe walking alone at night in the city or area where they live (%)	40.2	2019	●	→
Property Rights (worst 1–7 best)	3.9	2019	●	●
Birth registrations with civil authority (% of children under age 5)	96.4	2018	○	●
Corruption Perception Index (worst 0–100 best)	35	2019	●	↓
Children involved in child labor (% of population aged 5 to 14)	6.6	2016	●	●
Exports of major conventional weapons (TIV constant million USD per 100,000 population)	0.0	2019	●	●
Press Freedom Index (best 0–100 worst)	32.8	2019	○	→

SDG17 – Partnerships for the Goals	Value	Year	Rating	Trend
Government spending on health and education (% of GDP)	10.0	2015	●	↑
For high-income and all OECD DAC countries: International concessional public finance, including official development assistance (% of GNI)	NA	NA	●	●
Other countries: Government revenue excluding grants (% of GDP)	27.2	2017	○	↑
Corporate Tax Haven Score (best 0–100 worst) *	0.0	2019	●	●

* Imputed data point

5. Country Profiles

▼ OVERALL PERFORMANCE

Index score	Regional average score
68.2	67.2

SDG Global rank 88 (OF 166)

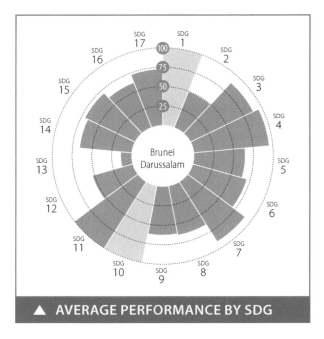

▲ AVERAGE PERFORMANCE BY SDG

▼ SPILLOVER INDEX

100 (best) to 0 (worst)

▼ CURRENT ASSESSMENT – SDG DASHBOARD

■ Major challenges　■ Significant challenges　■ Challenges remain　■ SDG achieved　■ Information unavailable

▼ SDG TRENDS

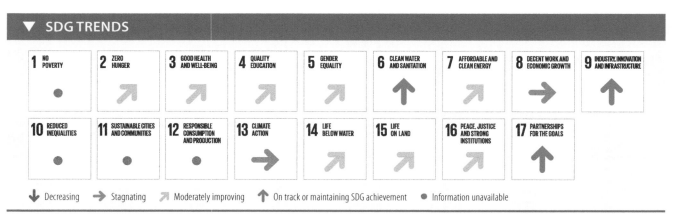

↓ Decreasing　→ Stagnating　↗ Moderately improving　↑ On track or maintaining SDG achievement　● Information unavailable

Notes: The full title of Goal 2 "Zero Hunger" is "End hunger, achieve food security and improved nutrition and promote sustainable agriculture".
The full title of each SDG is available here: https://sustainabledevelopment.un.org/topics/sustainabledevelopmentgoals

SDG1 – No Poverty

Indicator		Value	Year	Rating	Trend
Poverty headcount ratio at $1.90/day (%)	*	NA	NA	●	●
Poverty headcount ratio at $3.20/day (%)	*	NA	NA	●	●

SDG2 – Zero Hunger

Indicator	Value	Year	Rating	Trend
Prevalence of undernourishment (%)	3.2	2017	●	↑
Prevalence of stunting in children under 5 years of age (%)	19.7	2009	●	↗
Prevalence of wasting in children under 5 years of age (%)	2.9	2009	●	↑
Prevalence of obesity, BMI ≥ 30 (% of adult population)	14.1	2016	◐	↓
Human Trophic Level (best 2–3 worst)	2.4	2013	●	●
Cereal yield (tonnes per hectare of harvested land)	2.6	2017	●	↑
Sustainable Nitrogen Management Index (best 0–1.41 worst)	1.4	2015	●	→

SDG3 – Good Health and Well-Being

Indicator	Value	Year	Rating	Trend
Maternal mortality rate (per 100,000 live births)	31	2017	●	↑
Neonatal mortality rate (per 1,000 live births)	5.5	2018	●	↑
Mortality rate, under-5 (per 1,000 live births)	11.6	2018	●	↑
Incidence of tuberculosis (per 100,000 population)	68.0	2018	●	→
New HIV infections (per 1,000 uninfected population)	NA	NA	●	●
Age-standardized death rate due to cardiovascular disease, cancer, diabetes, or chronic respiratory disease in adults aged 30–70 years (%)	16.6	2016	◐	↑
Age-standardized death rate attributable to household air pollution and ambient air pollution (per 100,000 population)	13	2016	●	●
Traffic deaths (per 100,000 population)	8.0	2013	●	●
Life expectancy at birth (years)	76.4	2016	◐	→
Adolescent fertility rate (births per 1,000 adolescent females aged 15 to 19)	10.3	2017	●	↑
Births attended by skilled health personnel (%)	100.0	2016	●	↑
Percentage of surviving infants who received 2 WHO-recommended vaccines (%)	99	2018	●	↑
Universal health coverage (UHC) index of service coverage (worst 0–100 best)	81.0	2017	●	↑
Subjective well-being (average ladder score, worst 0–10 best)	NA	NA	●	●

SDG4 – Quality Education

Indicator	Value	Year	Rating	Trend
Net primary enrollment rate (%)	93.1	2018	◐	↗
Lower secondary completion rate (%)	105.8	2018	●	↑
Literacy rate (% of population aged 15 to 24)	99.7	2018	●	●

SDG5 – Gender Equality

Indicator	Value	Year	Rating	Trend
Demand for family planning satisfied by modern methods (% of females aged 15 to 49 who are married or in unions)	NA	NA	●	●
Ratio of female-to-male mean years of education received (%)	100.0	2018	●	↑
Ratio of female-to-male labor force participation rate (%)	81.4	2019	●	↑
Seats held by women in national parliament (%)	9.1	2020	●	→

SDG6 – Clean Water and Sanitation

Indicator	Value	Year	Rating	Trend
Population using at least basic drinking water services (%)	99.9	2017	●	↑
Population using at least basic sanitation services (%)	96.3	2015	●	●
Freshwater withdrawal (% of available freshwater resources)	NA	NA	●	●
Anthropogenic wastewater that receives treatment (%)	6.1	2018	●	●
Scarce water consumption embodied in imports (m³/capita)	19.6	2013	●	↑

SDG7 – Affordable and Clean Energy

Indicator	Value	Year	Rating	Trend
Population with access to electricity (%)	100.0	2017	●	↑
Population with access to clean fuels and technology for cooking (%)	100.0	2016	●	↑
CO_2 emissions from fuel combustion for electricity and heating per total electricity output (MtCO$_2$/TWh)	1.7	2017	●	→

SDG8 – Decent Work and Economic Growth

Indicator	Value	Year	Rating	Trend
Adjusted GDP growth (%)	-2.6	2018	●	●
Victims of modern slavery (per 1,000 population)	10.9	2018	●	●
Adults with an account at a bank or other financial institution or with a mobile-money-service provider (% of population aged 15 or over)	NA	NA	●	●
Unemployment rate (% of total labor force)	9.1	2019	●	↓
Fatal work-related accidents embodied in imports (per 100,000 population)	1.3	2010	◐	↑

SDG9 – Industry, Innovation and Infrastructure

Indicator	Value	Year	Rating	Trend
Population using the internet (%)	94.9	2017	●	↑
Mobile broadband subscriptions (per 100 population)	130.0	2018	●	↑
Logistics Performance Index: Quality of trade and transport-related infrastructure (worst 1–5 best)	2.5	2018	●	●
The Times Higher Education Universities Ranking: Average score of top 3 universities (worst 0–100 best)	40.6	2020	●	●
Scientific and technical journal articles (per 1,000 population)	0.7	2018	◐	↑
Expenditure on research and development (% of GDP)	0.0	2004	●	●

SDG10 – Reduced Inequalities

Indicator	Value	Year	Rating	Trend
Gini coefficient adjusted for top income	NA	NA	●	●

SDG11 – Sustainable Cities and Communities

Indicator	Value	Year	Rating	Trend
Annual mean concentration of particulate matter of less than 2.5 microns in diameter (PM2.5) (μg/m³)	5.9	2017	●	↑
Access to improved water source, piped (% of urban population)	NA	NA	●	●
Satisfaction with public transport (%)	NA	NA	●	●

SDG12 – Responsible Consumption and Production

Indicator	Value	Year	Rating	Trend
Municipal solid waste (kg/capita/day)	1.8	2016	●	●
Electronic waste (kg/capita)	18.3	2016	●	●
Production-based SO_2 emissions (kg/capita)	242.5	2012	●	●
SO_2 emissions embodied in imports (kg/capita)	23.0	2012	●	●
Production-based nitrogen emissions (kg/capita)	23.2	2010	◐	●
Nitrogen emissions embodied in imports (kg/capita)	8.4	2010	◐	●

SDG13 – Climate Action

Indicator	Value	Year	Rating	Trend
Energy-related CO_2 emissions (tCO$_2$/capita)	25.0	2017	●	↓
CO_2 emissions embodied in imports (tCO$_2$/capita)	2.2	2015	●	↗
CO_2 emissions embodied in fossil fuel exports (kg/capita)	40507.6	2018	●	●

SDG14 – Life Below Water

Indicator	Value	Year	Rating	Trend
Mean area that is protected in marine sites important to biodiversity (%)	60.9	2018	●	↑
Ocean Health Index: Clean Waters score (worst 0–100 best)	57.2	2019	●	→
Fish caught from overexploited or collapsed stocks (% of total catch)	NA	NA	●	●
Fish caught by trawling (%)	33.3	2014	◐	↗
Marine biodiversity threats embodied in imports (per million population)	0.0	2018	●	●

SDG15 – Life on Land

Indicator	Value	Year	Rating	Trend
Mean area that is protected in terrestrial sites important to biodiversity (%)	63.1	2018	●	↑
Mean area that is protected in freshwater sites important to biodiversity (%)	50.0	2018	●	↑
Red List Index of species survival (worst 0–1 best)	0.8	2019	●	↓
Permanent deforestation (% of forest area, 5-year average)	0.2	2018	●	●
Terrestrial and freshwater biodiversity threats embodied in imports (per million population)	0.4	2018	●	●

SDG16 – Peace, Justice and Strong Institutions

Indicator		Value	Year	Rating	Trend
Homicides (per 100,000 population)		0.5	2013	●	●
Unsentenced detainees (% of prison population)		7.1	2015	●	●
Percentage of population who feel safe walking alone at night in the city or area where they live (%)		NA	NA	●	●
Property Rights (worst 1–7 best)		4.3	2019	◐	●
Birth registrations with civil authority (% of children under age 5)		NA	NA	●	●
Corruption Perception Index (worst 0–100 best)		60	2019	●	↑
Children involved in child labor (% of population aged 5 to 14)		NA	NA	●	●
Exports of major conventional weapons (TIV constant million USD per 100,000 population)		2.8	2019	●	●
Press Freedom Index (best 0–100 worst)		51.5	2019	●	→

SDG17 – Partnerships for the Goals

Indicator		Value	Year	Rating	Trend
Government spending on health and education (% of GDP)		6.6	2016	●	↑
For high-income and all OECD DAC countries: International concessional public finance, including official development assistance (% of GNI)		NA	NA	●	●
Other countries: Government revenue excluding grants (% of GDP)		NA	NA	●	●
Corporate Tax Haven Score (best 0–100 worst)	*	0.0	2019	●	●

* Imputed data point

5. Country Profiles

▼ OVERALL PERFORMANCE

Index score
74.8

Regional average score
70.9

SDG Global rank   39 (OF 166)

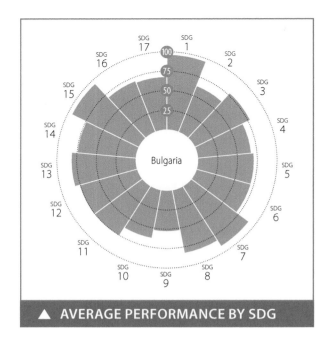

▲ AVERAGE PERFORMANCE BY SDG

▼ SPILLOVER INDEX

100 (best) to 0 (worst)

▼ CURRENT ASSESSMENT – SDG DASHBOARD

■ Major challenges   ■ Significant challenges   ■ Challenges remain   ■ SDG achieved   ■ Information unavailable

▼ SDG TRENDS

↓ Decreasing   → Stagnating   ↗ Moderately improving   ↑ On track or maintaining SDG achievement   ● Information unavailable

Notes: The full title of Goal 2 "Zero Hunger" is "End hunger, achieve food security and improved nutrition and promote sustainable agriculture".
The full title of each SDG is available here: https://sustainabledevelopment.un.org/topics/sustainabledevelopmentgoals

SDG1 – No Poverty

	Value	Year	Rating	Trend
Poverty headcount ratio at $1.90/day (%)	1.3	2020	○	↑
Poverty headcount ratio at $3.20/day (%)	2.0	2020	○	↑

SDG2 – Zero Hunger

	Value	Year	Rating	Trend
Prevalence of undernourishment (%)	3.6	2017	●	↑
Prevalence of stunting in children under 5 years of age (%)	8.8	2004	●	↗
Prevalence of wasting in children under 5 years of age (%)	3.2	2004	●	↑
Prevalence of obesity, BMI ≥ 30 (% of adult population)	25.0	2016	●	↓
Human Trophic Level (best 2–3 worst)	2.4	2017	●	→
Cereal yield (tonnes per hectare of harvested land)	5.5	2017	●	↑
Sustainable Nitrogen Management Index (best 0–1.41 worst)	0.5	2015	●	↗

SDG3 – Good Health and Well-Being

	Value	Year	Rating	Trend
Maternal mortality rate (per 100,000 live births)	10	2017	●	↑
Neonatal mortality rate (per 1,000 live births)	3.6	2018	●	↑
Mortality rate, under-5 (per 1,000 live births)	7.1	2018	●	↑
Incidence of tuberculosis (per 100,000 population)	22.0	2018	●	↑
New HIV infections (per 1,000 uninfected population)	0.1	2018	●	↑
Age-standardized death rate due to cardiovascular disease, cancer, diabetes, or chronic respiratory disease in adults aged 30–70 years (%)	23.6	2016	●	→
Age-standardized death rate attributable to household air pollution and ambient air pollution (per 100,000 population)	62	2016	●	●
Traffic deaths (per 100,000 population)	10.2	2016	●	↓
Life expectancy at birth (years)	74.8	2016	●	→
Adolescent fertility rate (births per 1,000 adolescent females aged 15 to 19)	39.9	2017	●	↗
Births attended by skilled health personnel (%)	99.8	2015	●	↑
Percentage of surviving infants who received 2 WHO-recommended vaccines (%)	92	2018	●	↑
Universal health coverage (UHC) index of service coverage (worst 0–100 best)	66.0	2017	●	↗
Subjective well-being (average ladder score, worst 0–10 best)	5.1	2018	●	↑

SDG4 – Quality Education

	Value	Year	Rating	Trend
Net primary enrollment rate (%)	86.4	2017	●	↓
Lower secondary completion rate (%)	47.6	2016	●	↓
Literacy rate (% of population aged 15 to 24)	97.9	2011	●	●

SDG5 – Gender Equality

	Value	Year	Rating	Trend
Demand for family planning satisfied by modern methods (% of females aged 15 to 49 who are married or in unions) *	63.4	2017	●	↗
Ratio of female-to-male mean years of education received (%)	100.8	2018	●	↑
Ratio of female-to-male labor force participation rate (%)	80.4	2019	●	↑
Seats held by women in national parliament (%)	26.7	2020	●	↗

SDG6 – Clean Water and Sanitation

	Value	Year	Rating	Trend
Population using at least basic drinking water services (%)	99.1	2017	●	↑
Population using at least basic sanitation services (%)	86.0	2017	●	→
Freshwater withdrawal (% of available freshwater resources)	41.6	2015	●	●
Anthropogenic wastewater that receives treatment (%)	13.9	2018	●	●
Scarce water consumption embodied in imports (m³/capita)	9.3	2013	●	↑

SDG7 – Affordable and Clean Energy

	Value	Year	Rating	Trend
Population with access to electricity (%)	100.0	2017	●	↑
Population with access to clean fuels and technology for cooking (%)	88.7	2016	●	↑
CO_2 emissions from fuel combustion for electricity and heating per total electricity output (MtCO₂/TWh)	1.0	2017	●	↓

SDG8 – Decent Work and Economic Growth

	Value	Year	Rating	Trend
Adjusted GDP growth (%)	1.4	2018	●	●
Victims of modern slavery (per 1,000 population)	4.5	2018	●	●
Adults with an account at a bank or other financial institution or with a mobile-money-service provider (% of population aged 15 or over)	72.2	2017	●	↑
Unemployment rate (% of total labor force)	4.3	2019	●	↑
Fatal work-related accidents embodied in imports (per 100,000 population)	0.4	2010	●	↑

SDG9 – Industry, Innovation and Infrastructure

	Value	Year	Rating	Trend
Population using the internet (%)	64.8	2018	●	↑
Mobile broadband subscriptions (per 100 population)	101.0	2018	●	↑
Logistics Performance Index: Quality of trade and transport-related infrastructure (worst 1–5 best)	2.8	2018	●	↓
The Times Higher Education Universities Ranking: Average score of top 3 universities (worst 0–100 best)	16.4	2020	○	●
Scientific and technical journal articles (per 1,000 population)	0.5	2018	○	↑
Expenditure on research and development (% of GDP)	0.8	2017	●	↓

SDG10 – Reduced Inequalities

	Value	Year	Rating	Trend
Gini coefficient adjusted for top income	40.9	2014	●	●

SDG11 – Sustainable Cities and Communities

	Value	Year	Rating	Trend
Annual mean concentration of particulate matter of less than 2.5 microns in diameter (PM2.5) (µg/m³)	19.1	2017	●	↗
Access to improved water source, piped (% of urban population)	99.0	2017	●	↑
Satisfaction with public transport (%)	45.8	2018	●	↓

SDG12 – Responsible Consumption and Production

	Value	Year	Rating	Trend
Municipal solid waste (kg/capita/day)	1.6	2015	●	●
Electronic waste (kg/capita)	11.1	2016	●	●
Production-based SO_2 emissions (kg/capita)	62.0	2012	○	●
SO_2 emissions embodied in imports (kg/capita)	5.9	2012	●	●
Production-based nitrogen emissions (kg/capita)	24.9	2010	○	●
Nitrogen emissions embodied in imports (kg/capita)	3.5	2010	●	●

SDG13 – Climate Action

	Value	Year	Rating	Trend
Energy-related CO_2 emissions (tCO₂/capita)	6.2	2017	●	→
CO_2 emissions embodied in imports (tCO₂/capita)	1.0	2015	●	→
CO_2 emissions embodied in fossil fuel exports (kg/capita)	15.3	2018	●	●

SDG14 – Life Below Water

	Value	Year	Rating	Trend
Mean area that is protected in marine sites important to biodiversity (%)	99.3	2018	●	↑
Ocean Health Index: Clean Waters score (worst 0–100 best)	42.3	2019	●	→
Fish caught from overexploited or collapsed stocks (% of total catch)	NA	NA	●	●
Fish caught by trawling (%)	20.6	2014	○	↑
Marine biodiversity threats embodied in imports (per million population)	0.0	2018	●	●

SDG15 – Life on Land

	Value	Year	Rating	Trend
Mean area that is protected in terrestrial sites important to biodiversity (%)	98.9	2018	●	↑
Mean area that is protected in freshwater sites important to biodiversity (%)	98.6	2018	●	↑
Red List Index of species survival (worst 0–1 best)	0.9	2019	●	↑
Permanent deforestation (% of forest area, 5-year average)	0.0	2018	●	●
Terrestrial and freshwater biodiversity threats embodied in imports (per million population)	1.1	2018	○	●

SDG16 – Peace, Justice and Strong Institutions

	Value	Year	Rating	Trend
Homicides (per 100,000 population)	1.5	2017	●	↑
Unsentenced detainees (% of prison population)	8.8	2018	●	↑
Percentage of population who feel safe walking alone at night in the city or area where they live (%)	58.4	2018	●	→
Property Rights (worst 1–7 best)	3.9	2019	●	●
Birth registrations with civil authority (% of children under age 5)	100.0	2018	●	●
Corruption Perception Index (worst 0–100 best)	43	2019	●	→
Children involved in child labor (% of population aged 5 to 14)	NA	NA	●	●
Exports of major conventional weapons (TIV constant million USD per 100,000 population)	0.6	2019	●	●
Press Freedom Index (best 0–100 worst)	35.1	2019	○	→

SDG17 – Partnerships for the Goals

	Value	Year	Rating	Trend
Government spending on health and education (% of GDP)	8.1	2013	●	●
For high-income and all OECD DAC countries: International concessional public finance, including official development assistance (% of GNI)	NA	NA	●	●
Other countries: Government revenue excluding grants (% of GDP)	32.8	2017	●	↑
Corporate Tax Haven Score (best 0–100 worst)	55.6	2019	●	●

* Imputed data point

5. Country Profiles

▼ OVERALL PERFORMANCE

Index score	Regional average score
55.2	53.1

SDG Global rank 137 (OF 166)

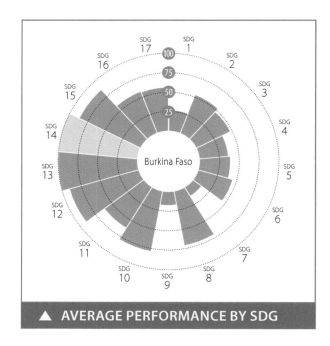

▲ AVERAGE PERFORMANCE BY SDG

▼ SPILLOVER INDEX

100 (best) to 0 (worst)

▼ CURRENT ASSESSMENT – SDG DASHBOARD

■ Major challenges   ■ Significant challenges   ■ Challenges remain   ■ SDG achieved   ■ Information unavailable

▼ SDG TRENDS

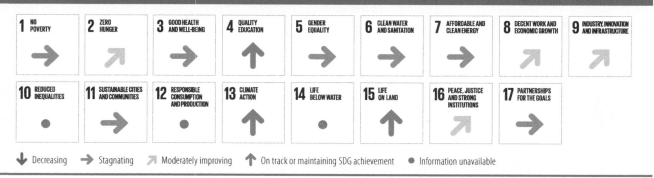

⬇ Decreasing   ➡ Stagnating   ↗ Moderately improving   ⬆ On track or maintaining SDG achievement   • Information unavailable

Notes: The full title of Goal 2 "Zero Hunger" is "End hunger, achieve food security and improved nutrition and promote sustainable agriculture".
The full title of each SDG is available here: https://sustainabledevelopment.un.org/topics/sustainabledevelopmentgoals

SDG1 – No Poverty

	Value	Year	Rating	Trend
Poverty headcount ratio at $1.90/day (%)	33.2	2020	●	↗
Poverty headcount ratio at $3.20/day (%)	67.7	2020	●	→

SDG2 – Zero Hunger

	Value	Year	Rating	Trend
Prevalence of undernourishment (%)	20.0	2017	●	→
Prevalence of stunting in children under 5 years of age (%)	27.3	2016	●	↗
Prevalence of wasting in children under 5 years of age (%)	7.6	2016	●	↑
Prevalence of obesity, BMI ≥ 30 (% of adult population)	5.6	2016	●	↑
Human Trophic Level (best 2–3 worst)	2.1	2017	●	↑
Cereal yield (tonnes per hectare of harvested land)	1.0	2017	●	↓
Sustainable Nitrogen Management Index (best 0–1.41 worst)	0.8	2015	●	→

SDG3 – Good Health and Well-Being

	Value	Year	Rating	Trend
Maternal mortality rate (per 100,000 live births)	320	2017	●	↗
Neonatal mortality rate (per 1,000 live births)	24.7	2018	●	↗
Mortality rate, under-5 (per 1,000 live births)	76.4	2018	●	↗
Incidence of tuberculosis (per 100,000 population)	48.0	2018	●	→
New HIV infections (per 1,000 uninfected population)	0.1	2018	●	↑
Age-standardized death rate due to cardiovascular disease, cancer, diabetes, or chronic respiratory disease in adults aged 30–70 years (%)	21.7	2016	●	→
Age-standardized death rate attributable to household air pollution and ambient air pollution (per 100,000 population)	206	2016	●	●
Traffic deaths (per 100,000 population)	30.5	2016	●	↓
Life expectancy at birth (years)	60.3	2016	●	→
Adolescent fertility rate (births per 1,000 adolescent females aged 15 to 19)	104.3	2017	●	→
Births attended by skilled health personnel (%)	79.8	2015	●	●
Percentage of surviving infants who received 2 WHO-recommended vaccines (%)	88	2018	●	→
Universal health coverage (UHC) index of service coverage (worst 0–100 best)	40.0	2017	●	→
Subjective well-being (average ladder score, worst 0–10 best)	4.7	2019	●	↗

SDG4 – Quality Education

	Value	Year	Rating	Trend
Net primary enrollment rate (%)	78.6	2018	●	↑
Lower secondary completion rate (%)	43.0	2018	●	↑
Literacy rate (% of population aged 15 to 24)	58.3	2018	●	●

SDG5 – Gender Equality

	Value	Year	Rating	Trend
Demand for family planning satisfied by modern methods (% of females aged 15 to 49 who are married or in unions)	56.4	2018	●	↗
Ratio of female-to-male mean years of education received (%)	47.6	2018	●	↓
Ratio of female-to-male labor force participation rate (%)	77.8	2019	●	↑
Seats held by women in national parliament (%)	13.4	2020	●	→

SDG6 – Clean Water and Sanitation

	Value	Year	Rating	Trend
Population using at least basic drinking water services (%)	47.9	2017	●	↓
Population using at least basic sanitation services (%)	19.4	2017	●	→
Freshwater withdrawal (% of available freshwater resources)	7.8	2005	●	●
Anthropogenic wastewater that receives treatment (%)	0.0	2018	●	●
Scarce water consumption embodied in imports (m³/capita)	0.6	2013	●	↑

SDG7 – Affordable and Clean Energy

	Value	Year	Rating	Trend
Population with access to electricity (%)	25.5	2017	●	→
Population with access to clean fuels and technology for cooking (%)	8.9	2016	●	→
CO_2 emissions from fuel combustion for electricity and heating per total electricity output (MtCO_2/TWh)	NA	NA	●	●

SDG8 – Decent Work and Economic Growth

	Value	Year	Rating	Trend
Adjusted GDP growth (%)	-3.5	2018	●	●
Victims of modern slavery (per 1,000 population)	4.5	2018	●	●
Adults with an account at a bank or other financial institution or with a mobile-money-service provider (% of population aged 15 or over)	43.2	2017	●	↑
Unemployment rate (% of total labor force)	6.3	2019	●	→
Fatal work-related accidents embodied in imports (per 100,000 population)	0.0	2010	●	↑

SDG9 – Industry, Innovation and Infrastructure

	Value	Year	Rating	Trend
Population using the internet (%)	16.0	2017	●	→
Mobile broadband subscriptions (per 100 population)	29.9	2018	●	↑
Logistics Performance Index: Quality of trade and transport-related infrastructure (worst 1–5 best)	2.4	2018	●	↗
The Times Higher Education Universities Ranking: Average score of top 3 universities (worst 0–100 best) *	0.0	2020	●	●
Scientific and technical journal articles (per 1,000 population)	0.0	2018	●	→
Expenditure on research and development (% of GDP)	0.7	2017	●	↑

SDG10 – Reduced Inequalities

	Value	Year	Rating	Trend
Gini coefficient adjusted for top income	35.3	2014	●	●

SDG11 – Sustainable Cities and Communities

	Value	Year	Rating	Trend
Annual mean concentration of particulate matter of less than 2.5 microns in diameter (PM2.5) (µg/m³)	42.9	2017	●	↓
Access to improved water source, piped (% of urban population)	74.3	2017	●	↓
Satisfaction with public transport (%)	55.4	2019	●	↑

SDG12 – Responsible Consumption and Production

	Value	Year	Rating	Trend
Municipal solid waste (kg/capita/day)	1.2	2015	●	●
Electronic waste (kg/capita)	0.6	2016	●	●
Production-based SO_2 emissions (kg/capita)	8.9	2012	●	●
SO_2 emissions embodied in imports (kg/capita)	0.6	2012	●	●
Production-based nitrogen emissions (kg/capita)	24.9	2010	●	●
Nitrogen emissions embodied in imports (kg/capita)	0.5	2010	●	●

SDG13 – Climate Action

	Value	Year	Rating	Trend
Energy-related CO_2 emissions (tCO_2/capita)	0.2	2017	●	↑
CO_2 emissions embodied in imports (tCO_2/capita)	0.0	2015	●	↑
CO_2 emissions embodied in fossil fuel exports (kg/capita) *	0.0	2018	●	●

SDG14 – Life Below Water

	Value	Year	Rating	Trend
Mean area that is protected in marine sites important to biodiversity (%)	NA	NA	●	●
Ocean Health Index: Clean Waters score (worst 0–100 best)	NA	NA	●	●
Fish caught from overexploited or collapsed stocks (% of total catch)	NA	NA	●	●
Fish caught by trawling (%)	NA	NA	●	●
Marine biodiversity threats embodied in imports (per million population)	0.0	2018	●	●

SDG15 – Life on Land

	Value	Year	Rating	Trend
Mean area that is protected in terrestrial sites important to biodiversity (%)	71.8	2018	●	↑
Mean area that is protected in freshwater sites important to biodiversity (%)	63.0	2018	●	↑
Red List Index of species survival (worst 0–1 best)	1.0	2019	●	↑
Permanent deforestation (% of forest area, 5-year average)	0.0	2018	●	●
Terrestrial and freshwater biodiversity threats embodied in imports (per million population)	0.0	2018	●	●

SDG16 – Peace, Justice and Strong Institutions

	Value	Year	Rating	Trend
Homicides (per 100,000 population)	1.3	2017	●	↑
Unsentenced detainees (% of prison population)	42.0	2018	●	↗
Percentage of population who feel safe walking alone at night in the city or area where they live (%)	57.7	2019	●	→
Property Rights (worst 1–7 best)	4.0	2019	●	●
Birth registrations with civil authority (% of children under age 5)	76.9	2018	●	●
Corruption Perception Index (worst 0–100 best)	40	2019	●	→
Children involved in child labor (% of population aged 5 to 14)	39.2	2016	●	●
Exports of major conventional weapons (TIV constant million USD per 100,000 population) *	0.0	2019	●	●
Press Freedom Index (best 0–100 worst)	24.5	2019	●	↑

SDG17 – Partnerships for the Goals

	Value	Year	Rating	Trend
Government spending on health and education (% of GDP)	5.8	2015	●	↓
For high-income and all OECD DAC countries: International concessional public finance, including official development assistance (% of GNI)	NA	NA	●	●
Other countries: Government revenue excluding grants (% of GDP)	18.9	2018	●	→
Corporate Tax Haven Score (best 0–100 worst) *	0.0	2019	●	●

* Imputed data point

5. Country Profiles

BURUNDI

▼ OVERALL PERFORMANCE

Index score
53.5

Regional average score
53.1

SDG Global rank 143 (OF 166)

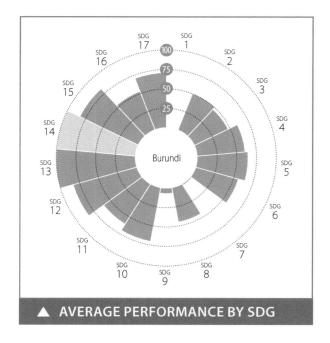

Burundi

▲ AVERAGE PERFORMANCE BY SDG

▼ SPILLOVER INDEX

100 (best) to 0 (worst)

▼ CURRENT ASSESSMENT – SDG DASHBOARD

■ Major challenges ■ Significant challenges ▨ Challenges remain ■ SDG achieved ▨ Information unavailable

▼ SDG TRENDS

↓ Decreasing → Stagnating ↗ Moderately improving ↑ On track or maintaining SDG achievement ● Information unavailable

Notes: The full title of Goal 2 "Zero Hunger" is "End hunger, achieve food security and improved nutrition and promote sustainable agriculture".
The full title of each SDG is available here: https://sustainabledevelopment.un.org/topics/sustainabledevelopmentgoals

BURUNDI

SDG1 – No Poverty	Value	Year	Rating	Trend
Poverty headcount ratio at $1.90/day (%)	75.9	2020	●	↓
Poverty headcount ratio at $3.20/day (%)	92.8	2020	●	↓

SDG2 – Zero Hunger	Value	Year	Rating	Trend
Prevalence of undernourishment (%)	NA	NA	●	●
Prevalence of stunting in children under 5 years of age (%)	55.9	2016	●	→
Prevalence of wasting in children under 5 years of age (%)	5.1	2016	◐	→
Prevalence of obesity, BMI ≥ 30 (% of adult population)	5.4	2016	●	↑
Human Trophic Level (best 2–3 worst)	2.0	2007	●	●
Cereal yield (tonnes per hectare of harvested land)	1.4	2017	●	→
Sustainable Nitrogen Management Index (best 0–1.41 worst)	0.9	2015	●	↓

SDG3 – Good Health and Well-Being	Value	Year	Rating	Trend
Maternal mortality rate (per 100,000 live births)	548	2017	●	→
Neonatal mortality rate (per 1,000 live births)	21.7	2018	●	↗
Mortality rate, under-5 (per 1,000 live births)	58.5	2018	●	↑
Incidence of tuberculosis (per 100,000 population)	111.0	2018	●	→
New HIV infections (per 1,000 uninfected population)	0.2	2018	●	↑
Age-standardized death rate due to cardiovascular disease, cancer, diabetes, or chronic respiratory disease in adults aged 30–70 years (%)	22.9	2016	●	↓
Age-standardized death rate attributable to household air pollution and ambient air pollution (per 100,000 population)	180	2016	●	●
Traffic deaths (per 100,000 population)	34.7	2016	●	↓
Life expectancy at birth (years)	60.1	2016	●	→
Adolescent fertility rate (births per 1,000 adolescent females aged 15 to 19)	55.6	2017	●	→
Births attended by skilled health personnel (%)	85.1	2017	●	↑
Percentage of surviving infants who received 2 WHO-recommended vaccines (%)	88	2018	●	↓
Universal health coverage (UHC) index of service coverage (worst 0–100 best)	42.0	2017	●	→
Subjective well-being (average ladder score, worst 0–10 best)	3.8	2018	●	↑

SDG4 – Quality Education	Value	Year	Rating	Trend
Net primary enrollment rate (%)	92.8	2018	◐	●
Lower secondary completion rate (%)	32.6	2018	●	↓
Literacy rate (% of population aged 15 to 24)	88.2	2017	●	●

SDG5 – Gender Equality	Value	Year	Rating	Trend
Demand for family planning satisfied by modern methods (% of females aged 15 to 49 who are married or in unions)	38.0	2017	●	→
Ratio of female-to-male mean years of education received (%)	75.0	2018	●	↗
Ratio of female-to-male labor force participation rate (%)	103.6	2019	●	↑
Seats held by women in national parliament (%)	36.4	2020	◐	→

SDG6 – Clean Water and Sanitation	Value	Year	Rating	Trend
Population using at least basic drinking water services (%)	60.8	2017	●	→
Population using at least basic sanitation services (%)	45.8	2017	●	↓
Freshwater withdrawal (% of available freshwater resources)	10.5	2000	●	●
Anthropogenic wastewater that receives treatment (%)	0.0	2018	●	●
Scarce water consumption embodied in imports (m³/capita)	0.2	2013	●	↑

SDG7 – Affordable and Clean Energy	Value	Year	Rating	Trend
Population with access to electricity (%)	9.3	2017	●	→
Population with access to clean fuels and technology for cooking (%)	0.9	2016	●	→
CO₂ emissions from fuel combustion for electricity and heating per total electricity output (MtCO₂/TWh)	NA	NA	●	●

SDG8 – Decent Work and Economic Growth	Value	Year	Rating	Trend
Adjusted GDP growth (%)	-10.7	2018	●	●
Victims of modern slavery (per 1,000 population)	40.0	2018	●	●
Adults with an account at a bank or other financial institution or with a mobile-money-service provider (% of population aged 15 or over)	7.1	2014	●	●
Unemployment rate (% of total labor force)	1.4	2019	●	↑
Fatal work-related accidents embodied in imports (per 100,000 population)	0.0	2010	●	↑

SDG9 – Industry, Innovation and Infrastructure	Value	Year	Rating	Trend
Population using the internet (%)	2.7	2017	●	→
Mobile broadband subscriptions (per 100 population)	11.4	2018	●	→
Logistics Performance Index: Quality of trade and transport-related infrastructure (worst 1–5 best)	2.0	2018	●	↓
The Times Higher Education Universities Ranking: Average score of top 3 universities (worst 0–100 best) *	0.0	2020	●	●
Scientific and technical journal articles (per 1,000 population)	0.0	2018	●	→
Expenditure on research and development (% of GDP)	0.1	2011	●	●

SDG10 – Reduced Inequalities	Value	Year	Rating	Trend
Gini coefficient adjusted for top income	38.6	2013	●	●

SDG11 – Sustainable Cities and Communities	Value	Year	Rating	Trend
Annual mean concentration of particulate matter of less than 2.5 microns in diameter (PM2.5) (μg/m³)	38.9	2017	●	→
Access to improved water source, piped (% of urban population)	89.4	2017	◐	↑
Satisfaction with public transport (%)	39.4	2018	●	↗

SDG12 – Responsible Consumption and Production	Value	Year	Rating	Trend
Municipal solid waste (kg/capita/day)	3.5	2002	●	●
Electronic waste (kg/capita)	0.5	2016	●	●
Production-based SO₂ emissions (kg/capita)	13.8	2012	●	●
SO₂ emissions embodied in imports (kg/capita)	0.2	2012	●	●
Production-based nitrogen emissions (kg/capita)	5.8	2010	●	●
Nitrogen emissions embodied in imports (kg/capita)	0.1	2010	●	●

SDG13 – Climate Action	Value	Year	Rating	Trend
Energy-related CO₂ emissions (tCO₂/capita)	0.0	2017	●	↑
CO₂ emissions embodied in imports (tCO₂/capita)	0.0	2015	●	↑
CO₂ emissions embodied in fossil fuel exports (kg/capita) *	0.0	2018	●	●

SDG14 – Life Below Water	Value	Year	Rating	Trend
Mean area that is protected in marine sites important to biodiversity (%)	NA	NA	●	●
Ocean Health Index: Clean Waters score (worst 0–100 best)	NA	NA	●	●
Fish caught from overexploited or collapsed stocks (% of total catch)	NA	NA	●	●
Fish caught by trawling (%)	NA	NA	●	●
Marine biodiversity threats embodied in imports (per million population)	0.0	2018	●	●

SDG15 – Life on Land	Value	Year	Rating	Trend
Mean area that is protected in terrestrial sites important to biodiversity (%)	67.3	2018	●	↑
Mean area that is protected in freshwater sites important to biodiversity (%)	81.4	2018	●	↑
Red List Index of species survival (worst 0–1 best)	0.9	2019	●	↑
Permanent deforestation (% of forest area, 5-year average)	0.2	2018	◐	●
Terrestrial and freshwater biodiversity threats embodied in imports (per million population)	0.0	2018	●	●

SDG16 – Peace, Justice and Strong Institutions	Value	Year	Rating	Trend
Homicides (per 100,000 population)	6.0	2016	●	→
Unsentenced detainees (% of prison population)	52.7	2018	●	→
Percentage of population who feel safe walking alone at night in the city or area where they live (%)	65.7	2018	◐	↑
Property Rights (worst 1–7 best)	4.3	2019	◐	●
Birth registrations with civil authority (% of children under age 5)	83.5	2018	●	●
Corruption Perception Index (worst 0–100 best)	19	2019	●	↓
Children involved in child labor (% of population aged 5 to 14)	26.3	2016	●	●
Exports of major conventional weapons (TIV constant million USD per 100,000 population) *	0.0	2019	●	●
Press Freedom Index (best 0–100 worst)	52.9	2019	●	→

SDG17 – Partnerships for the Goals	Value	Year	Rating	Trend
Government spending on health and education (% of GDP)	6.5	2016	●	↓
For high-income and all OECD DAC countries: International concessional public finance, including official development assistance (% of GNI)	NA	NA	●	●
Other countries: Government revenue excluding grants (% of GDP)	NA	NA	●	●
Corporate Tax Haven Score (best 0–100 worst) *	0.0	2019	●	●

* Imputed data point

▼ OVERALL PERFORMANCE

Index score

67.2

Regional average score

53.1

SDG Global rank 92 (OF 166)

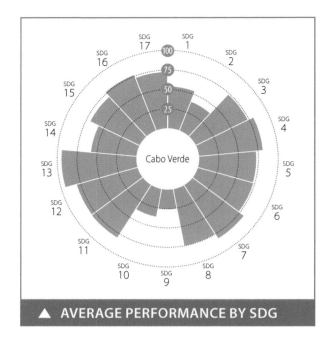

▲ AVERAGE PERFORMANCE BY SDG

▼ SPILLOVER INDEX

100 (best) to 0 (worst)

▼ CURRENT ASSESSMENT – SDG DASHBOARD

■ Major challenges   ■ Significant challenges   ■ Challenges remain   ■ SDG achieved   ■ Information unavailable

▼ SDG TRENDS

1 NO POVERTY	2 ZERO HUNGER	3 GOOD HEALTH AND WELL-BEING	4 QUALITY EDUCATION	5 GENDER EQUALITY	6 CLEAN WATER AND SANITATION	7 AFFORDABLE AND CLEAN ENERGY	8 DECENT WORK AND ECONOMIC GROWTH	9 INDUSTRY, INNOVATION AND INFRASTRUCTURE
↗	→	↗	↓	↗	↗	↗	→	→

10 REDUCED INEQUALITIES	11 SUSTAINABLE CITIES AND COMMUNITIES	12 RESPONSIBLE CONSUMPTION AND PRODUCTION	13 CLIMATE ACTION	14 LIFE BELOW WATER	15 LIFE ON LAND	16 PEACE, JUSTICE AND STRONG INSTITUTIONS	17 PARTNERSHIPS FOR THE GOALS
●	↗	●	↑	↗	↗	↗	↗

↓ Decreasing   → Stagnating   ↗ Moderately improving   ↑ On track or maintaining SDG achievement   ● Information unavailable

Notes: The full title of Goal 2 "Zero Hunger" is "End hunger, achieve food security and improved nutrition and promote sustainable agriculture".
The full title of each SDG is available here: https://sustainabledevelopment.un.org/topics/sustainabledevelopmentgoals

SDG1 – No Poverty

Indicator	Value	Year	Rating	Trend
Poverty headcount ratio at $1.90/day (%)	15.8	2020	●	↗
Poverty headcount ratio at $3.20/day (%)	35.5	2020	●	↗

SDG2 – Zero Hunger

Indicator	Value	Year	Rating	Trend
Prevalence of undernourishment (%)	12.6	2017	●	↗
Prevalence of stunting in children under 5 years of age (%)	NA	NA	●	●
Prevalence of wasting in children under 5 years of age (%)	NA	NA	●	●
Prevalence of obesity, BMI ≥ 30 (% of adult population)	11.8	2016	●	↓
Human Trophic Level (best 2–3 worst)	2.2	2017	●	→
Cereal yield (tonnes per hectare of harvested land)	0.2	2017	●	→
Sustainable Nitrogen Management Index (best 0–1.41 worst)	1.2	2015	●	→

SDG3 – Good Health and Well-Being

Indicator	Value	Year	Rating	Trend
Maternal mortality rate (per 100,000 live births)	58	2017	●	↑
Neonatal mortality rate (per 1,000 live births)	11.6	2018	●	↑
Mortality rate, under-5 (per 1,000 live births)	19.5	2018	●	↑
Incidence of tuberculosis (per 100,000 population)	46.0	2018	●	↑
New HIV infections (per 1,000 uninfected population)	0.2	2018	●	↑
Age-standardized death rate due to cardiovascular disease, cancer, diabetes, or chronic respiratory disease in adults aged 30–70 years (%)	17.2	2016	●	↑
Age-standardized death rate attributable to household air pollution and ambient air pollution (per 100,000 population)	99	2016	●	●
Traffic deaths (per 100,000 population)	25.0	2016	●	→
Life expectancy at birth (years)	73.2	2016	●	↗
Adolescent fertility rate (births per 1,000 adolescent females aged 15 to 19)	73.8	2017	●	→
Births attended by skilled health personnel (%)	91.4	2015	●	→
Percentage of surviving infants who received 2 WHO-recommended vaccines (%)	98	2018	●	↑
Universal health coverage (UHC) index of service coverage (worst 0–100 best)	69.0	2017	●	↑
Subjective well-being (average ladder score, worst 0–10 best)	NA	NA	●	●

SDG4 – Quality Education

Indicator	Value	Year	Rating	Trend
Net primary enrollment rate (%)	93.4	2018	●	→
Lower secondary completion rate (%)	68.2	2018	●	↓
Literacy rate (% of population aged 15 to 24)	98.1	2015	●	●

SDG5 – Gender Equality

Indicator	Value	Year	Rating	Trend
Demand for family planning satisfied by modern methods (% of females aged 15 to 49 who are married or in unions)	73.2	2005	●	↑
Ratio of female-to-male mean years of education received (%)	92.3	2018	●	→
Ratio of female-to-male labor force participation rate (%)	89.5	2019	●	↑
Seats held by women in national parliament (%)	25.0	2020	●	↗

SDG6 – Clean Water and Sanitation

Indicator	Value	Year	Rating	Trend
Population using at least basic drinking water services (%)	87.1	2017	●	↗
Population using at least basic sanitation services (%)	73.9	2017	●	↑
Freshwater withdrawal (% of available freshwater resources)	9.0	2000	●	●
Anthropogenic wastewater that receives treatment (%)	20.9	2018	●	●
Scarce water consumption embodied in imports (m³/capita)	4.9	2013	●	↑

SDG7 – Affordable and Clean Energy

Indicator	Value	Year	Rating	Trend
Population with access to electricity (%)	92.9	2017	●	↑
Population with access to clean fuels and technology for cooking (%)	71.1	2016	●	↗
CO_2 emissions from fuel combustion for electricity and heating per total electricity output (MtCO$_2$/TWh)	NA	NA	●	●

SDG8 – Decent Work and Economic Growth

Indicator	Value	Year	Rating	Trend
Adjusted GDP growth (%)	-1.5	2018	●	●
Victims of modern slavery (per 1,000 population)	4.1	2018	●	●
Adults with an account at a bank or other financial institution or with a mobile-money-service provider (% of population aged 15 or over)	NA	NA	●	●
Unemployment rate (% of total labor force)	12.2	2019	●	↓
Fatal work-related accidents embodied in imports (per 100,000 population)	0.3	2010	●	↑

SDG9 – Industry, Innovation and Infrastructure

Indicator	Value	Year	Rating	Trend
Population using the internet (%)	57.2	2017	●	↑
Mobile broadband subscriptions (per 100 population)	66.8	2018	●	↓
Logistics Performance Index: Quality of trade and transport-related infrastructure (worst 1–5 best)	NA	NA	●	●
The Times Higher Education Universities Ranking: Average score of top 3 universities (worst 0–100 best) *	0.0	2020	●	●
Scientific and technical journal articles (per 1,000 population)	0.0	2018	●	↓
Expenditure on research and development (% of GDP)	0.1	2011	●	●

SDG10 – Reduced Inequalities

Indicator	Value	Year	Rating	Trend
Gini coefficient adjusted for top income	50.2	2007	●	●

SDG11 – Sustainable Cities and Communities

Indicator	Value	Year	Rating	Trend
Annual mean concentration of particulate matter of less than 2.5 microns in diameter (PM2.5) (µg/m³)	34.8	2017	●	↓
Access to improved water source, piped (% of urban population)	95.8	2017	●	↑
Satisfaction with public transport (%)	NA	NA	●	●

SDG12 – Responsible Consumption and Production

Indicator	Value	Year	Rating	Trend
Municipal solid waste (kg/capita/day)	1.0	2012	●	●
Electronic waste (kg/capita)	4.6	2016	●	●
Production-based SO_2 emissions (kg/capita)	231.9	2012	●	●
SO_2 emissions embodied in imports (kg/capita)	4.4	2012	●	●
Production-based nitrogen emissions (kg/capita)	16.7	2010	●	●
Nitrogen emissions embodied in imports (kg/capita)	2.3	2010	●	●

SDG13 – Climate Action

Indicator	Value	Year	Rating	Trend
Energy-related CO_2 emissions (tCO$_2$/capita)	1.5	2017	●	↑
CO_2 emissions embodied in imports (tCO$_2$/capita)	0.4	2015	●	↑
CO_2 emissions embodied in fossil fuel exports (kg/capita) *	0.0	2018	●	●

SDG14 – Life Below Water

Indicator	Value	Year	Rating	Trend
Mean area that is protected in marine sites important to biodiversity (%)	3.1	2018	●	→
Ocean Health Index: Clean Waters score (worst 0–100 best)	62.2	2019	●	↑
Fish caught from overexploited or collapsed stocks (% of total catch)	24.4	2014	●	↑
Fish caught by trawling (%)	33.7	2014	●	●
Marine biodiversity threats embodied in imports (per million population)	0.0	2018	●	●

SDG15 – Life on Land

Indicator	Value	Year	Rating	Trend
Mean area that is protected in terrestrial sites important to biodiversity (%)	13.0	2018	●	→
Mean area that is protected in freshwater sites important to biodiversity (%)	NA	NA	●	●
Red List Index of species survival (worst 0–1 best)	0.9	2019	●	↑
Permanent deforestation (% of forest area, 5-year average)	0.0	2018	●	●
Terrestrial and freshwater biodiversity threats embodied in imports (per million population)	0.2	2018	●	●

SDG16 – Peace, Justice and Strong Institutions

Indicator	Value	Year	Rating	Trend
Homicides (per 100,000 population)	11.5	2016	●	↗
Unsentenced detainees (% of prison population)	19.3	2018	●	●
Percentage of population who feel safe walking alone at night in the city or area where they live (%)	NA	NA	●	●
Property Rights (worst 1–7 best)	4.2	2019	●	●
Birth registrations with civil authority (% of children under age 5)	91.0	2018	●	●
Corruption Perception Index (worst 0–100 best)	58	2019	●	↑
Children involved in child labor (% of population aged 5 to 14)	6.4	2016	●	●
Exports of major conventional weapons (TIV constant million USD per 100,000 population) *	0.0	2019	●	●
Press Freedom Index (best 0–100 worst)	19.8	2019	●	↑

SDG17 – Partnerships for the Goals

Indicator	Value	Year	Rating	Trend
Government spending on health and education (% of GDP)	8.3	2016	●	↗
For high-income and all OECD DAC countries: International concessional public finance, including official development assistance (% of GNI)	NA	NA	●	●
Other countries: Government revenue excluding grants (% of GDP)	28.8	2017	●	↑
Corporate Tax Haven Score (best 0–100 worst) *	0.0	2019	●	●

* Imputed data point

5. Country Profiles

▼ OVERALL PERFORMANCE

Index score

64.4

Regional average score

67.2

SDG Global rank **106** (OF 166)

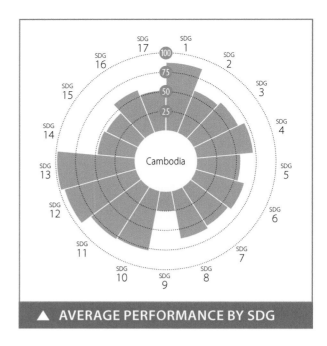

▲ AVERAGE PERFORMANCE BY SDG

▼ SPILLOVER INDEX

100 (best) to 0 (worst)

▼ CURRENT ASSESSMENT – SDG DASHBOARD

■ Major challenges ■ Significant challenges ■ Challenges remain ■ SDG achieved ■ Information unavailable

▼ SDG TRENDS

↓ Decreasing → Stagnating ↗ Moderately improving ↑ On track or maintaining SDG achievement • Information unavailable

Notes: The full title of Goal 2 "Zero Hunger" is "End hunger, achieve food security and improved nutrition and promote sustainable agriculture".
The full title of each SDG is available here: https://sustainabledevelopment.un.org/topics/sustainabledevelopmentgoals

SDG1 – No Poverty

Indicator	Value	Year	Rating	Trend
Poverty headcount ratio at $1.90/day (%)	0.2	2020	●	↑
Poverty headcount ratio at $3.20/day (%)	12.3	2020	●	↑

SDG2 – Zero Hunger

Indicator	Value	Year	Rating	Trend
Prevalence of undernourishment (%)	16.4	2017	●	↗
Prevalence of stunting in children under 5 years of age (%)	32.4	2014	●	→
Prevalence of wasting in children under 5 years of age (%)	9.6	2014	●	↗
Prevalence of obesity, BMI ≥ 30 (% of adult population)	3.9	2016	●	↑
Human Trophic Level (best 2–3 worst)	2.2	2017	●	↑
Cereal yield (tonnes per hectare of harvested land)	3.6	2017	●	↑
Sustainable Nitrogen Management Index (best 0–1.41 worst)	0.6	2015	●	→

SDG3 – Good Health and Well-Being

Indicator	Value	Year	Rating	Trend
Maternal mortality rate (per 100,000 live births)	160	2017	●	↑
Neonatal mortality rate (per 1,000 live births)	14.4	2018	●	↑
Mortality rate, under-5 (per 1,000 live births)	28.0	2018	●	↑
Incidence of tuberculosis (per 100,000 population)	302.0	2018	●	↗
New HIV infections (per 1,000 uninfected population)	0.1	2018	●	↑
Age-standardized death rate due to cardiovascular disease, cancer, diabetes, or chronic respiratory disease in adults aged 30–70 years (%)	21.1	2016	●	↗
Age-standardized death rate attributable to household air pollution and ambient air pollution (per 100,000 population)	150	2016	●	●
Traffic deaths (per 100,000 population)	17.8	2016	●	↓
Life expectancy at birth (years)	69.4	2016	●	↗
Adolescent fertility rate (births per 1,000 adolescent females aged 15 to 19)	50.2	2017	●	↓
Births attended by skilled health personnel (%)	89.0	2014	●	●
Percentage of surviving infants who received 2 WHO-recommended vaccines (%)	84	2018	●	→
Universal health coverage (UHC) index of service coverage (worst 0–100 best)	60.0	2017	●	↗
Subjective well-being (average ladder score, worst 0–10 best)	5.0	2019	●	↑

SDG4 – Quality Education

Indicator	Value	Year	Rating	Trend
Net primary enrollment rate (%)	90.3	2018	●	↓
Lower secondary completion rate (%)	58.4	2018	●	↑
Literacy rate (% of population aged 15 to 24)	92.2	2015	●	●

SDG5 – Gender Equality

Indicator	Value	Year	Rating	Trend
Demand for family planning satisfied by modern methods (% of females aged 15 to 49 who are married or in unions)	56.5	2014	●	↗
Ratio of female-to-male mean years of education received (%)	71.9	2018	●	→
Ratio of female-to-male labor force participation rate (%)	85.6	2019	●	↑
Seats held by women in national parliament (%)	20.0	2020	●	↓

SDG6 – Clean Water and Sanitation

Indicator	Value	Year	Rating	Trend
Population using at least basic drinking water services (%)	78.5	2017	●	↑
Population using at least basic sanitation services (%)	59.2	2017	●	↑
Freshwater withdrawal (% of available freshwater resources)	1.0	2005	●	●
Anthropogenic wastewater that receives treatment (%)	0.0	2018	●	●
Scarce water consumption embodied in imports (m³/capita)	0.9	2013	●	↑

SDG7 – Affordable and Clean Energy

Indicator	Value	Year	Rating	Trend
Population with access to electricity (%)	89.1	2017	●	↑
Population with access to clean fuels and technology for cooking (%)	17.7	2016	●	→
CO_2 emissions from fuel combustion for electricity and heating per total electricity output (MtCO₂/TWh)	1.6	2017	●	↑

SDG8 – Decent Work and Economic Growth

Indicator	Value	Year	Rating	Trend
Adjusted GDP growth (%)	-0.1	2018	●	●
Victims of modern slavery (per 1,000 population)	16.8	2018	●	●
Adults with an account at a bank or other financial institution or with a mobile-money-service provider (% of population aged 15 or over)	21.7	2017	●	↓
Unemployment rate (% of total labor force)	0.7	2019	●	↑
Fatal work-related accidents embodied in imports (per 100,000 population)	0.1	2010	●	↑

SDG9 – Industry, Innovation and Infrastructure

Indicator	Value	Year	Rating	Trend
Population using the internet (%)	40.0	2018	●	↑
Mobile broadband subscriptions (per 100 population)	82.8	2018	●	↑
Logistics Performance Index: Quality of trade and transport-related infrastructure (worst 1–5 best)	2.1	2018	●	↓
The Times Higher Education Universities Ranking: Average score of top 3 universities (worst 0–100 best) *	0.0	2020	●	●
Scientific and technical journal articles (per 1,000 population)	0.0	2018	●	→
Expenditure on research and development (% of GDP)	0.1	2015	●	●

SDG10 – Reduced Inequalities

Indicator	Value	Year	Rating	Trend
Gini coefficient adjusted for top income	35.4	2004	●	●

SDG11 – Sustainable Cities and Communities

Indicator	Value	Year	Rating	Trend
Annual mean concentration of particulate matter of less than 2.5 microns in diameter (PM2.5) (µg/m³)	25.6	2017	●	↗
Access to improved water source, piped (% of urban population)	77.3	2017	●	↑
Satisfaction with public transport (%)	73.8	2019	●	↑

SDG12 – Responsible Consumption and Production

Indicator	Value	Year	Rating	Trend
Municipal solid waste (kg/capita/day)	0.8	2014	●	●
Electronic waste (kg/capita)	0.9	2016	●	●
Production-based SO_2 emissions (kg/capita)	11.0	2012	●	●
SO_2 emissions embodied in imports (kg/capita)	1.0	2012	●	●
Production-based nitrogen emissions (kg/capita)	11.9	2010	●	●
Nitrogen emissions embodied in imports (kg/capita)	0.5	2010	●	●

SDG13 – Climate Action

Indicator	Value	Year	Rating	Trend
Energy-related CO_2 emissions (tCO₂/capita)	0.5	2017	●	↑
CO_2 emissions embodied in imports (tCO₂/capita)	0.1	2015	●	↑
CO_2 emissions embodied in fossil fuel exports (kg/capita)	0.0	2018	●	●

SDG14 – Life Below Water

Indicator	Value	Year	Rating	Trend
Mean area that is protected in marine sites important to biodiversity (%)	19.2	2018	●	→
Ocean Health Index: Clean Waters score (worst 0–100 best)	53.1	2019	●	↗
Fish caught from overexploited or collapsed stocks (% of total catch)	44.9	2014	●	↓
Fish caught by trawling (%)	61.4	2014	●	↓
Marine biodiversity threats embodied in imports (per million population)	0.0	2018	●	●

SDG15 – Life on Land

Indicator	Value	Year	Rating	Trend
Mean area that is protected in terrestrial sites important to biodiversity (%)	39.5	2018	●	→
Mean area that is protected in freshwater sites important to biodiversity (%)	33.0	2018	●	→
Red List Index of species survival (worst 0–1 best)	0.8	2019	●	↓
Permanent deforestation (% of forest area, 5-year average)	1.8	2018	●	●
Terrestrial and freshwater biodiversity threats embodied in imports (per million population)	0.0	2018	●	●

SDG16 – Peace, Justice and Strong Institutions

Indicator	Value	Year	Rating	Trend
Homicides (per 100,000 population)	1.8	2011	●	●
Unsentenced detainees (% of prison population)	28.7	2018	●	↑
Percentage of population who feel safe walking alone at night in the city or area where they live (%)	55.5	2019	●	↑
Property Rights (worst 1–7 best)	4.2	2019	●	●
Birth registrations with civil authority (% of children under age 5)	73.3	2018	●	●
Corruption Perception Index (worst 0–100 best)	20	2019	●	↓
Children involved in child labor (% of population aged 5 to 14)	19.3	2016	●	●
Exports of major conventional weapons (TIV constant million USD per 100,000 population) *	0.0	2019	●	●
Press Freedom Index (best 0–100 worst)	45.9	2019	●	↓

SDG17 – Partnerships for the Goals

Indicator	Value	Year	Rating	Trend
Government spending on health and education (% of GDP)	3.1	2014	●	●
For high-income and all OECD DAC countries: International concessional public finance, including official development assistance (% of GNI)	NA	NA	●	●
Other countries: Government revenue excluding grants (% of GDP)	19.9	2018	●	↗
Corporate Tax Haven Score (best 0–100 worst) *	0.0	2019	●	●

* Imputed data point

5. Country Profiles

CAMEROON

Sub-Saharan Africa

▼ OVERALL PERFORMANCE

Index score

56.5

Regional average score

53.1

SDG Global rank 133 (OF 166)

▼ SPILLOVER INDEX

100 (best) to 0 (worst)

▲ AVERAGE PERFORMANCE BY SDG

Cameroon

▼ CURRENT ASSESSMENT – SDG DASHBOARD

■ Major challenges ■ Significant challenges ■ Challenges remain ■ SDG achieved ■ Information unavailable

▼ SDG TRENDS

↓ Decreasing   → Stagnating   ↗ Moderately improving   ↑ On track or maintaining SDG achievement   • Information unavailable

Notes: The full title of Goal 2 "Zero Hunger" is "End hunger, achieve food security and improved nutrition and promote sustainable agriculture".
The full title of each SDG is available here: https://sustainabledevelopment.un.org/topics/sustainabledevelopmentgoals

CAMEROON

SDG1 – No Poverty	Value	Year	Rating	Trend
Poverty headcount ratio at $1.90/day (%)	19.5	2020	●	↗
Poverty headcount ratio at $3.20/day (%)	36.9	2020	●	→

SDG2 – Zero Hunger	Value	Year	Rating	Trend
Prevalence of undernourishment (%)	9.9	2017	●	↓
Prevalence of stunting in children under 5 years of age (%)	31.7	2014	●	→
Prevalence of wasting in children under 5 years of age (%)	5.2	2014	●	↑
Prevalence of obesity, BMI ≥ 30 (% of adult population)	11.4	2016	●	↓
Human Trophic Level (best 2–3 worst)	2.1	2017	●	↑
Cereal yield (tonnes per hectare of harvested land)	1.7	2017	●	→
Sustainable Nitrogen Management Index (best 0–1.41 worst)	0.8	2015	●	→

SDG3 – Good Health and Well-Being	Value	Year	Rating	Trend
Maternal mortality rate (per 100,000 live births)	529	2017	●	→
Neonatal mortality rate (per 1,000 live births)	26.6	2018	●	→
Mortality rate, under-5 (per 1,000 live births)	76.1	2018	●	↗
Incidence of tuberculosis (per 100,000 population)	186.0	2018	●	↗
New HIV infections (per 1,000 uninfected population)	1.0	2018	●	↑
Age-standardized death rate due to cardiovascular disease, cancer, diabetes, or chronic respiratory disease in adults aged 30–70 years (%)	21.6	2016	●	→
Age-standardized death rate attributable to household air pollution and ambient air pollution (per 100,000 population)	208	2016	●	●
Traffic deaths (per 100,000 population)	30.1	2016	●	↓
Life expectancy at birth (years)	58.1	2016	●	→
Adolescent fertility rate (births per 1,000 adolescent females aged 15 to 19)	105.8	2017	●	↗
Births attended by skilled health personnel (%)	64.7	2014	●	●
Percentage of surviving infants who received 2 WHO-recommended vaccines (%)	71	2018	●	↓
Universal health coverage (UHC) index of service coverage (worst 0–100 best)	46.0	2017	●	↗
Subjective well-being (average ladder score, worst 0–10 best)	4.9	2019	●	↓

SDG4 – Quality Education	Value	Year	Rating	Trend
Net primary enrollment rate (%)	92.9	2017	●	↑
Lower secondary completion rate (%)	47.2	2016	●	●
Literacy rate (% of population aged 15 to 24)	85.1	2018	●	●

SDG5 – Gender Equality	Value	Year	Rating	Trend
Demand for family planning satisfied by modern methods (% of females aged 15 to 49 who are married or in unions)	47.0	2014	●	↗
Ratio of female-to-male mean years of education received (%)	61.5	2018	●	↓
Ratio of female-to-male labor force participation rate (%)	87.4	2019	●	↑
Seats held by women in national parliament (%)	33.9	2020	●	↗

SDG6 – Clean Water and Sanitation	Value	Year	Rating	Trend
Population using at least basic drinking water services (%)	60.4	2017	●	→
Population using at least basic sanitation services (%)	39.1	2017	●	→
Freshwater withdrawal (% of available freshwater resources)	1.4	2000	●	●
Anthropogenic wastewater that receives treatment (%)	0.0	2018	●	●
Scarce water consumption embodied in imports (m³/capita)	0.5	2013	●	↑

SDG7 – Affordable and Clean Energy	Value	Year	Rating	Trend
Population with access to electricity (%)	61.4	2017	●	↗
Population with access to clean fuels and technology for cooking (%)	23.0	2016	●	→
CO_2 emissions from fuel combustion for electricity and heating per total electricity output (MtCO₂/TWh)	0.7	2017	●	↑

SDG8 – Decent Work and Economic Growth	Value	Year	Rating	Trend
Adjusted GDP growth (%)	-4.4	2018	●	●
Victims of modern slavery (per 1,000 population)	6.9	2018	●	●
Adults with an account at a bank or other financial institution or with a mobile-money-service provider (% of population aged 15 or over)	34.6	2017	●	↑
Unemployment rate (% of total labor force)	3.4	2019	●	↑
Fatal work-related accidents embodied in imports (per 100,000 population)	0.0	2010	●	↑

SDG9 – Industry, Innovation and Infrastructure	Value	Year	Rating	Trend
Population using the internet (%)	23.2	2017	●	↗
Mobile broadband subscriptions (per 100 population)	14.0	2018	●	↗
Logistics Performance Index: Quality of trade and transport-related infrastructure (worst 1–5 best)	2.6	2018	●	↑
The Times Higher Education Universities Ranking: Average score of top 3 * universities (worst 0–100 best)	0.0	2020	●	●
Scientific and technical journal articles (per 1,000 population)	0.0	2018	●	→
Expenditure on research and development (% of GDP)	NA	NA	●	●

SDG10 – Reduced Inequalities	Value	Year	Rating	Trend
Gini coefficient adjusted for top income	47.7	2014	●	●

SDG11 – Sustainable Cities and Communities	Value	Year	Rating	Trend
Annual mean concentration of particulate matter of less than 2.5 microns in diameter (PM2.5) (μg/m³)	72.8	2017	●	↓
Access to improved water source, piped (% of urban population)	60.8	2017	●	↓
Satisfaction with public transport (%)	45.9	2019	●	→

SDG12 – Responsible Consumption and Production	Value	Year	Rating	Trend
Municipal solid waste (kg/capita/day)	0.6	2013	●	●
Electronic waste (kg/capita)	0.8	2016	●	●
Production-based SO_2 emissions (kg/capita)	7.2	2012	●	●
SO_2 emissions embodied in imports (kg/capita)	0.3	2012	●	●
Production-based nitrogen emissions (kg/capita)	10.9	2010	●	●
Nitrogen emissions embodied in imports (kg/capita)	0.3	2010	●	●

SDG13 – Climate Action	Value	Year	Rating	Trend
Energy-related CO_2 emissions (tCO₂/capita)	0.5	2017	●	↑
CO_2 emissions embodied in imports (tCO₂/capita)	0.0	2015	●	↑
CO_2 emissions embodied in fossil fuel exports (kg/capita)	0.0	2017	●	●

SDG14 – Life Below Water	Value	Year	Rating	Trend
Mean area that is protected in marine sites important to biodiversity (%)	NA	NA	●	●
Ocean Health Index: Clean Waters score (worst 0–100 best)	36.1	2019	●	→
Fish caught from overexploited or collapsed stocks (% of total catch)	NA	NA	●	●
Fish caught by trawling (%)	7.9	2014	●	↑
Marine biodiversity threats embodied in imports (per million population)	0.0	2018	●	●

SDG15 – Life on Land	Value	Year	Rating	Trend
Mean area that is protected in terrestrial sites important to biodiversity (%)	35.3	2018	●	→
Mean area that is protected in freshwater sites important to biodiversity (%)	54.5	2018	●	↑
Red List Index of species survival (worst 0–1 best)	0.8	2019	●	↓
Permanent deforestation (% of forest area, 5-year average)	0.2	2018	●	●
Terrestrial and freshwater biodiversity threats embodied in imports (per million population)	0.0	2018	●	●

SDG16 – Peace, Justice and Strong Institutions	Value	Year	Rating	Trend
Homicides (per 100,000 population)	1.4	2017	●	↑
Unsentenced detainees (% of prison population)	54.7	2018	●	↗
Percentage of population who feel safe walking alone at night in the city or area where they live (%)	43.6	2019	●	↓
Property Rights (worst 1–7 best)	3.9	2019	●	●
Birth registrations with civil authority (% of children under age 5)	66.1	2018	●	●
Corruption Perception Index (worst 0–100 best)	25	2019	●	↓
Children involved in child labor (% of population aged 5 to 14)	47.0	2016	●	●
Exports of major conventional weapons (TIV constant million USD per 100,000 population)	* 0.0	2019	●	●
Press Freedom Index (best 0–100 worst)	43.3	2019	●	↓

SDG17 – Partnerships for the Goals	Value	Year	Rating	Trend
Government spending on health and education (% of GDP)	3.3	2016	●	↓
For high-income and all OECD DAC countries: International concessional public finance, including official development assistance (% of GNI)	NA	NA	●	●
Other countries: Government revenue excluding grants (% of GDP)	15.1	2017	●	↓
Corporate Tax Haven Score (best 0–100 worst)	* 0.0	2019	●	●

* Imputed data point

5. Country Profiles

CANADA

▼ OVERALL PERFORMANCE

Index score
78.2

Regional average score
77.3

SDG Global rank 21 (OF 166)

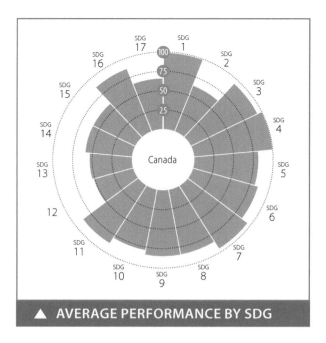

▲ AVERAGE PERFORMANCE BY SDG

▼ SPILLOVER INDEX

100 (best) to 0 (worst)

▼ CURRENT ASSESSMENT – SDG DASHBOARD

■ Major challenges ■ Significant challenges ▨ Challenges remain ■ SDG achieved ■ Information unavailable

▼ SDG TRENDS

1 NO POVERTY	2 ZERO HUNGER	3 GOOD HEALTH AND WELL-BEING	4 QUALITY EDUCATION	5 GENDER EQUALITY	6 CLEAN WATER AND SANITATION	7 AFFORDABLE AND CLEAN ENERGY	8 DECENT WORK AND ECONOMIC GROWTH	9 INDUSTRY, INNOVATION AND INFRASTRUCTURE
↑	↗	↑	↑	↗	→	↗	↑	↗

10 REDUCED INEQUALITIES	11 SUSTAINABLE CITIES AND COMMUNITIES	12 RESPONSIBLE CONSUMPTION AND PRODUCTION	13 CLIMATE ACTION	14 LIFE BELOW WATER	15 LIFE ON LAND	16 PEACE, JUSTICE AND STRONG INSTITUTIONS	17 PARTNERSHIPS FOR THE GOALS
→	→	●	→	↗	→	↗	↗

↓ Decreasing → Stagnating ↗ Moderately improving ↑ On track or maintaining SDG achievement ● Information unavailable

Notes: The full title of Goal 2 "Zero Hunger" is "End hunger, achieve food security and improved nutrition and promote sustainable agriculture".
The full title of each SDG is available here: https://sustainabledevelopment.un.org/topics/sustainabledevelopmentgoals

SDG1 – No Poverty

Indicator	Value	Year	Rating	Trend
Poverty headcount ratio at $1.90/day (%)	0.4	2020	●	↑
Poverty headcount ratio at $3.20/day (%)	0.5	2020	●	↑
Poverty rate after taxes and transfers (%)	12.1	2017	○	↑

SDG2 – Zero Hunger

Indicator	Value	Year	Rating	Trend
Prevalence of undernourishment (%)	2.5	2017	●	↑
Prevalence of stunting in children under 5 years of age (%)	* 2.6	2016	●	↑
Prevalence of wasting in children under 5 years of age (%)	* 0.7	2016	●	↑
Prevalence of obesity, BMI ≥ 30 (% of adult population)	29.4	2016	●	↓
Human Trophic Level (best 2–3 worst)	2.4	2017	●	↗
Cereal yield (tonnes per hectare of harvested land)	4.0	2017	●	↑
Sustainable Nitrogen Management Index (best 0–1.41 worst)	0.5	2015	○	↓
Yield gap closure (% of potential yield)	NA	NA	●	●

SDG3 – Good Health and Well-Being

Indicator	Value	Year	Rating	Trend
Maternal mortality rate (per 100,000 live births)	10	2017	●	↑
Neonatal mortality rate (per 1,000 live births)	3.4	2018	●	↑
Mortality rate, under-5 (per 1,000 live births)	5.0	2018	●	↑
Incidence of tuberculosis (per 100,000 population)	5.6	2018	●	↑
New HIV infections (per 1,000 uninfected population)	NA	NA	●	●
Age-standardized death rate due to cardiovascular disease, cancer, diabetes, or chronic respiratory disease in adults aged 30–70 years (%)	9.8	2016	●	↑
Age-standardized death rate attributable to household air pollution and ambient air pollution (per 100,000 population)	7	2016	●	●
Traffic deaths (per 100,000 population)	5.8	2016	●	↑
Life expectancy at birth (years)	82.8	2016	●	↑
Adolescent fertility rate (births per 1,000 adolescent females aged 15 to 19)	8.4	2017	●	↑
Births attended by skilled health personnel (%)	97.9	2014	○	●
Percentage of surviving infants who received 2 WHO-recommended vaccines (%)	90.0	2018	●	↑
Universal health coverage (UHC) index of service coverage (worst 0–100 best)	89.0	2017	●	↑
Subjective well-being (average ladder score, worst 0–10 best)	7.1	2019	●	↑
Gap in life expectancy at birth among regions (years)	11.5	2014	●	●
Gap in self-reported health status by income (percentage points)	13.2	2017	●	↑
Daily smokers (% of population aged 15 and over)	12.0	2017	●	↑

SDG4 – Quality Education

Indicator	Value	Year	Rating	Trend
Net primary enrollment rate (%)	* 100.0	2017	●	↑
Lower secondary completion rate (%)	* 100.0	2017	●	↑
Literacy rate (% of population aged 15 to 24)	NA	NA	●	●
Participation rate in pre-primary organized learning (% of children aged 4 to 6)	* 92.5	2016	●	●
Tertiary educational attainment (% of population aged 25 to 34)	61.8	2018	●	↑
PISA score (worst 0–600 best)	516.7	2018	●	↑
Variation in science performance explained by socio-economic status (%)	6.4	2018	●	↑
Underachievers in science (% of 15-year-olds)	13.4	2018	●	↑
Resilient students in science (% of 15-year-olds)	40.7	2018	●	↑

SDG5 – Gender Equality

Indicator	Value	Year	Rating	Trend
Demand for family planning satisfied by modern methods (% of females aged 15 to 49 who are married or in unions)	* 87.8	2017	●	↑
Ratio of female-to-male mean years of education received (%)	103.1	2018	●	↑
Ratio of female-to-male labor force participation rate (%)	87.4	2019	●	↑
Seats held by women in national parliament (%)	29.0	2020	●	↗
Gender wage gap (% of male median wage)	18.5	2018	●	→
Gender gap in time spent doing unpaid work (minutes/day)	75.5	2015	●	●

SDG6 – Clean Water and Sanitation

Indicator	Value	Year	Rating	Trend
Population using at least basic drinking water services (%)	99.4	2017	●	●
Population using at least basic sanitation services (%)	99.3	2017	●	●
Freshwater withdrawal (% of available freshwater resources)	3.6	2015	●	●
Anthropogenic wastewater that receives treatment (%)	67.4	2018	●	●
Scarce water consumption embodied in imports (m³/capita)	36.2	2013	●	→
Population using safely managed water services (%)	98.9	2017	●	↑
Population using safely managed sanitation services (%)	82.3	2017	○	↓

SDG7 – Affordable and Clean Energy

Indicator	Value	Year	Rating	Trend
Population with access to electricity (%)	100.0	2017	●	↑
Population with access to clean fuels and technology for cooking (%)	100.0	2016	●	↑
CO$_2$ emissions from fuel combustion for electricity and heating per total electricity output (MtCO$_2$/TWh)	0.9	2017	●	↑
Share of renewable energy in total primary energy supply (%)	16.4	2018	○	↓

SDG8 – Decent Work and Economic Growth

Indicator	Value	Year	Rating	Trend
Adjusted GDP growth (%)	-1.2	2018	○	●
Victims of modern slavery (per 1,000 population)	0.5	2018	●	●
Adults with an account at a bank or other financial institution or with a mobile-money-service provider (% of population aged 15 or over)	99.7	2017	●	↑
Fatal work-related accidents embodied in imports (per 100,000 population)	1.5	2010	○	↑
Employment-to-population ratio (%)	74.4	2019	●	↑
Youth not in employment, education or training (NEET) (% of population aged 15 to 29)	11.9	2018	○	↑

SDG9 – Industry, Innovation and Infrastructure

Indicator	Value	Year	Rating	Trend
Population using the internet (%)	91.0	2017	●	↑
Mobile broadband subscriptions (per 100 population)	76.4	2018	●	↑
Logistics Performance Index: Quality of trade and transport-related infrastructure (worst 1–5 best)	3.8	2018	●	↑
The Times Higher Education Universities Ranking: Average score of top 3 universities (worst 0–100 best)	78.7	2020	●	●
Scientific and technical journal articles (per 1,000 population)	1.6	2018	●	↑
Expenditure on research and development (% of GDP)	1.6	2017	●	↑
Researchers (per 1,000 employed population)	8.4	2016	●	↑
Triadic patent families filed (per million population)	15.3	2017	○	↓
Gap in internet access by income (percentage points)	52.4	2007	●	●
Women in science and engineering (% of tertiary graduates in science and engineering)	27.7	2015	●	●

SDG10 – Reduced Inequalities

Indicator	Value	Year	Rating	Trend
Gini coefficient adjusted for top income	35.0	2013	●	●
Palma ratio	1.1	2017	○	↑
Elderly poverty rate (% of population aged 66 or over)	12.2	2017	○	↓

SDG11 – Sustainable Cities and Communities

Indicator	Value	Year	Rating	Trend
Annual mean concentration of particulate matter of less than 2.5 microns in diameter (PM2.5) (µg/m³)	6.4	2017	●	↑
Access to improved water source, piped (% of urban population)	99.0	2017	●	↓
Satisfaction with public transport (%)	59.7	2019	●	↓
Population with rent overburden (%)	8.6	2016	●	↓

SDG12 – Responsible Consumption and Production

Indicator	Value	Year	Rating	Trend
Electronic waste (kg/capita)	20.0	2016	●	●
Production-based SO$_2$ emissions (kg/capita)	58.1	2012	●	●
SO$_2$ emissions embodied in imports (kg/capita)	12.4	2012	●	●
Production-based nitrogen emissions (kg/capita)	57.3	2010	●	●
Nitrogen emissions embodied in imports (kg/capita)	17.2	2010	●	●
Non-recycled municipal solid waste (kg/capita/day)	NA	NA	●	●

SDG13 – Climate Action

Indicator	Value	Year	Rating	Trend
Energy-related CO$_2$ emissions (tCO$_2$/capita)	14.4	2017	●	→
CO$_2$ emissions embodied in imports (tCO$_2$/capita)	2.3	2015	●	→
CO$_2$ emissions embodied in fossil fuel exports (kg/capita)	3453.1	2019	○	●
Effective carbon rate (EUR/tCO$_2$)	3.8	2016	●	●

SDG14 – Life Below Water

Indicator	Value	Year	Rating	Trend
Mean area that is protected in marine sites important to biodiversity (%)	33.1	2018	○	↗
Ocean Health Index: Clean Waters score (worst 0–100 best)	94.0	2019	●	↑
Fish caught from overexploited or collapsed stocks (% of total catch)	45.5	2014	●	→
Fish caught by trawling (%)	30.9	2014	○	↗
Marine biodiversity threats embodied in imports (per million population)	0.9	2018	●	●

SDG15 – Life on Land

Indicator	Value	Year	Rating	Trend
Mean area that is protected in terrestrial sites important to biodiversity (%)	26.5	2018	●	→
Mean area that is protected in freshwater sites important to biodiversity (%)	20.8	2018	●	→
Red List Index of species survival (worst 0–1 best)	1.0	2019	●	↑
Permanent deforestation (% of forest area, 5-year average)	0.0	2018	●	●
Terrestrial and freshwater biodiversity threats embodied in imports (per million population)	4.1	2018	●	●

SDG16 – Peace, Justice and Strong Institutions

Indicator	Value	Year	Rating	Trend
Homicides (per 100,000 population)	1.8	2017	○	↓
Unsentenced detainees (% of prison population)	38.9	2018	○	↓
Percentage of population who feel safe walking alone at night in the city or area where they live (%)	81.4	2019	●	↑
Property Rights (worst 1–7 best)	5.6	2019	●	●
Birth registrations with civil authority (% of children under age 5)	100.0	2018	●	●
Corruption Perception Index (worst 0–100 best)	77.0	2019	●	↑
Children involved in child labor (% of population aged 5 to 14)	* 0.0	2016	●	●
Exports of major conventional weapons (TIV constant million USD per 100,000 population)	0.4	2019	●	●
Press Freedom Index (best 0–100 worst)	15.7	2019	●	↑
Persons held in prison (per 100,000 population)	113.4	2016	○	→

SDG17 – Partnerships for the Goals

Indicator	Value	Year	Rating	Trend
Government spending on health and education (% of GDP)	* 11.9	2015	●	↑
For high-income and all OECD DAC countries: International concessional public finance, including official development assistance (% of GNI)	0.3	2017	●	→
Other countries: Government revenue excluding grants (% of GDP)	NA	NA	●	●
Corporate Tax Haven Score (best 0–100 worst)	* 0.0	2019	●	●
Financial Secrecy Score (best 0–100 worst)	55.8	2020	●	●
Shifted profits of multinationals (US$ billion)	15.2	2016	●	●

* Imputed data point

CENTRAL AFRICAN REPUBLIC   Sub-Saharan Africa

▼ OVERALL PERFORMANCE

Index score
38.5

Regional average score
53.1

SDG Global rank   **166** (OF 166)

▲ AVERAGE PERFORMANCE BY SDG

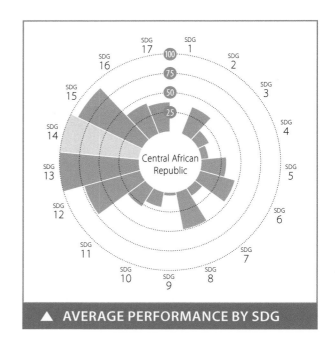

Central African Republic

▼ SPILLOVER INDEX

100 (best) to 0 (worst)

▼ CURRENT ASSESSMENT – SDG DASHBOARD

■ Major challenges   ■ Significant challenges   ■ Challenges remain   ■ SDG achieved   ■ Information unavailable

▼ SDG TRENDS

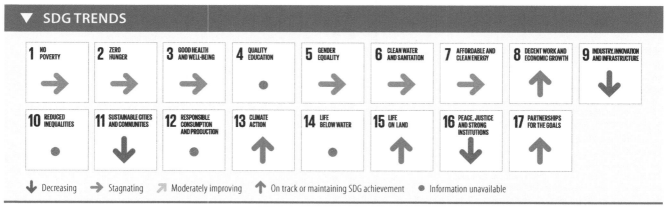

↓ Decreasing   → Stagnating   ↗ Moderately improving   ↑ On track or maintaining SDG achievement   ● Information unavailable

Notes: The full title of Goal 2 "Zero Hunger" is "End hunger, achieve food security and improved nutrition and promote sustainable agriculture".
The full title of each SDG is available here: https://sustainabledevelopment.un.org/topics/sustainabledevelopmentgoals

SDG1 – No Poverty

	Value	Year	Rating	Trend
Poverty headcount ratio at $1.90/day (%)	80.0	2020	●	→
Poverty headcount ratio at $3.20/day (%)	91.5	2020	●	→

SDG2 – Zero Hunger

	Value	Year	Rating	Trend
Prevalence of undernourishment (%)	59.6	2017	●	↓
Prevalence of stunting in children under 5 years of age (%)	40.7	2010	●	→
Prevalence of wasting in children under 5 years of age (%)	7.4	2010	●	↗
Prevalence of obesity, BMI ≥ 30 (% of adult population)	7.5	2016	●	↑
Human Trophic Level (best 2–3 worst)	2.1	2017	●	↑
Cereal yield (tonnes per hectare of harvested land)	0.9	2017	●	→
Sustainable Nitrogen Management Index (best 0–1.41 worst)	1.0	2015	●	↓

SDG3 – Good Health and Well-Being

	Value	Year	Rating	Trend
Maternal mortality rate (per 100,000 live births)	829	2017	●	↗
Neonatal mortality rate (per 1,000 live births)	41.2	2018	●	→
Mortality rate, under-5 (per 1,000 live births)	116.5	2018	●	↗
Incidence of tuberculosis (per 100,000 population)	540.0	2018	●	→
New HIV infections (per 1,000 uninfected population)	1.2	2018	●	↑
Age-standardized death rate due to cardiovascular disease, cancer, diabetes, or chronic respiratory disease in adults aged 30–70 years (%)	23.1	2016	●	↗
Age-standardized death rate attributable to household air pollution and ambient air pollution (per 100,000 population)	212	2016	●	●
Traffic deaths (per 100,000 population)	33.6	2016	●	↓
Life expectancy at birth (years)	53.0	2016	●	↗
Adolescent fertility rate (births per 1,000 adolescent females aged 15 to 19)	129.1	2017	●	→
Births attended by skilled health personnel (%)	40.0	2010	●	●
Percentage of surviving infants who received 2 WHO-recommended vaccines (%)	47	2018	●	→
Universal health coverage (UHC) index of service coverage (worst 0–100 best)	33.0	2017	●	→
Subjective well-being (average ladder score, worst 0–10 best)	3.5	2017	●	●

SDG4 – Quality Education

	Value	Year	Rating	Trend
Net primary enrollment rate (%)	66.3	2012	●	●
Lower secondary completion rate (%)	9.8	2016	●	●
Literacy rate (% of population aged 15 to 24)	38.3	2018	●	●

SDG5 – Gender Equality

	Value	Year	Rating	Trend
Demand for family planning satisfied by modern methods (% of females aged 15 to 49 who are married or in unions)	28.7	2011	●	→
Ratio of female-to-male mean years of education received (%)	53.6	2018	●	→
Ratio of female-to-male labor force participation rate (%)	81.0	2019	●	↑
Seats held by women in national parliament (%)	8.6	2020	●	→

SDG6 – Clean Water and Sanitation

	Value	Year	Rating	Trend
Population using at least basic drinking water services (%)	46.3	2016	●	→
Population using at least basic sanitation services (%)	25.3	2016	●	→
Freshwater withdrawal (% of available freshwater resources)	0.3	2005	●	●
Anthropogenic wastewater that receives treatment (%)	0.0	2018	●	●
Scarce water consumption embodied in imports (m³/capita)	0.3	2013	●	↑

SDG7 – Affordable and Clean Energy

	Value	Year	Rating	Trend
Population with access to electricity (%)	30.0	2017	●	↗
Population with access to clean fuels and technology for cooking (%)	1.0	2016	●	→
CO2 emissions from fuel combustion for electricity and heating per total electricity output (MtCO2/TWh)	NA	NA	●	●

SDG8 – Decent Work and Economic Growth

	Value	Year	Rating	Trend
Adjusted GDP growth (%)	-5.0	2018	●	●
Victims of modern slavery (per 1,000 population)	22.3	2018	●	●
Adults with an account at a bank or other financial institution or with a mobile-money-service provider (% of population aged 15 or over)	13.7	2017	●	●
Unemployment rate (% of total labor force)	3.7	2019	●	↑
Fatal work-related accidents embodied in imports (per 100,000 population)	0.0	2010	●	↑

SDG9 – Industry, Innovation and Infrastructure

	Value	Year	Rating	Trend
Population using the internet (%)	4.3	2017	●	→
Mobile broadband subscriptions (per 100 population)	5.3	2018	●	→
Logistics Performance Index: Quality of trade and transport-related infrastructure (worst 1–5 best)	1.9	2018	●	↓
The Times Higher Education Universities Ranking: Average score of top 3 universities (worst 0–100 best) *	0.0	2020	●	●
Scientific and technical journal articles (per 1,000 population)	0.0	2018	●	→
Expenditure on research and development (% of GDP) *	0.0	2017	●	●

SDG10 – Reduced Inequalities

	Value	Year	Rating	Trend
Gini coefficient adjusted for top income	56.2	2008	●	●

SDG11 – Sustainable Cities and Communities

	Value	Year	Rating	Trend
Annual mean concentration of particulate matter of less than 2.5 microns in diameter (PM2.5) (µg/m³)	56.8	2017	●	↓
Access to improved water source, piped (% of urban population)	42.9	2016	●	→
Satisfaction with public transport (%)	25.1	2017	●	●

SDG12 – Responsible Consumption and Production

	Value	Year	Rating	Trend
Municipal solid waste (kg/capita/day)	1.5	2014	●	●
Electronic waste (kg/capita)	0.5	2016	●	●
Production-based SO2 emissions (kg/capita)	108.3	2012	●	●
SO2 emissions embodied in imports (kg/capita)	0.3	2012	●	●
Production-based nitrogen emissions (kg/capita)	197.8	2010	●	●
Nitrogen emissions embodied in imports (kg/capita)	0.2	2010	●	●

SDG13 – Climate Action

	Value	Year	Rating	Trend
Energy-related CO2 emissions (tCO2/capita)	0.1	2017	●	↑
CO2 emissions embodied in imports (tCO2/capita)	0.0	2015	●	↑
CO2 emissions embodied in fossil fuel exports (kg/capita) *	0.0	2018	●	●

SDG14 – Life Below Water

	Value	Year	Rating	Trend
Mean area that is protected in marine sites important to biodiversity (%)	NA	NA	●	●
Ocean Health Index: Clean Waters score (worst 0–100 best)	NA	NA	●	●
Fish caught from overexploited or collapsed stocks (% of total catch)	NA	NA	●	●
Fish caught by trawling (%)	NA	NA	●	●
Marine biodiversity threats embodied in imports (per million population)	0.0	2018	●	●

SDG15 – Life on Land

	Value	Year	Rating	Trend
Mean area that is protected in terrestrial sites important to biodiversity (%)	74.4	2018	●	↑
Mean area that is protected in freshwater sites important to biodiversity (%)	95.9	2018	●	↑
Red List Index of species survival (worst 0–1 best)	0.9	2019	●	↑
Permanent deforestation (% of forest area, 5-year average)	0.0	2018	●	●
Terrestrial and freshwater biodiversity threats embodied in imports (per million population)	0.0	2018	●	●

SDG16 – Peace, Justice and Strong Institutions

	Value	Year	Rating	Trend
Homicides (per 100,000 population)	19.8	2016	●	●
Unsentenced detainees (% of prison population)	70.1	2012	●	●
Percentage of population who feel safe walking alone at night in the city or area where they live (%)	52.1	2017	●	●
Property Rights (worst 1–7 best)	NA	NA	●	●
Birth registrations with civil authority (% of children under age 5)	61.0	2018	●	●
Corruption Perception Index (worst 0–100 best)	25	2019	●	→
Children involved in child labor (% of population aged 5 to 14)	28.5	2016	●	●
Exports of major conventional weapons (TIV constant million USD per 100,000 population) *	0.0	2019	●	●
Press Freedom Index (best 0–100 worst)	47.3	2019	●	↓

SDG17 – Partnerships for the Goals

	Value	Year	Rating	Trend
Government spending on health and education (% of GDP)	2.0	2011	●	●
For high-income and all OECD DAC countries: International concessional public finance, including official development assistance (% of GNI)	NA	NA	●	●
Other countries: Government revenue excluding grants (% of GDP)	7.5	2016	●	↑
Corporate Tax Haven Score (best 0–100 worst) *	0.0	2019	●	●

* Imputed data point

5. Country Profiles

▼ OVERALL PERFORMANCE

Index score

43.8

Regional average score

53.1

SDG Global rank **164** (OF 166)

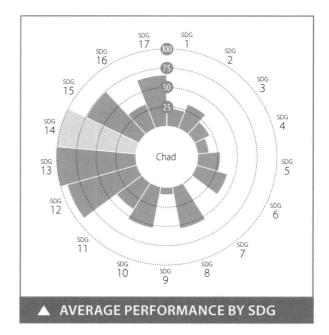

▲ AVERAGE PERFORMANCE BY SDG

▼ SPILLOVER INDEX

100 (best) to 0 (worst)

▼ CURRENT ASSESSMENT – SDG DASHBOARD

■ Major challenges   ■ Significant challenges   ■ Challenges remain   ■ SDG achieved   ■ Information unavailable

▼ SDG TRENDS

↓ Decreasing   → Stagnating   ↗ Moderately improving   ↑ On track or maintaining SDG achievement   ● Information unavailable

Notes: The full title of Goal 2 "Zero Hunger" is "End hunger, achieve food security and improved nutrition and promote sustainable agriculture".
The full title of each SDG is available here: https://sustainabledevelopment.un.org/topics/sustainabledevelopmentgoals

CHAD

SDG1 – No Poverty	Value	Year	Rating	Trend
Poverty headcount ratio at $1.90/day (%)	39.0	2020	●	↓
Poverty headcount ratio at $3.20/day (%)	64.1	2020	●	↓

SDG2 – Zero Hunger	Value	Year	Rating	Trend
Prevalence of undernourishment (%)	37.5	2017	●	↓
Prevalence of stunting in children under 5 years of age (%)	39.9	2015	●	→
Prevalence of wasting in children under 5 years of age (%)	13.0	2015	●	→
Prevalence of obesity, BMI ≥ 30 (% of adult population)	6.1	2016	●	↑
Human Trophic Level (best 2–3 worst)	2.3	2017	●	↓
Cereal yield (tonnes per hectare of harvested land)	0.8	2017	●	↓
Sustainable Nitrogen Management Index (best 0–1.41 worst)	0.8	2015	●	→

SDG3 – Good Health and Well-Being	Value	Year	Rating	Trend
Maternal mortality rate (per 100,000 live births)	1140	2017	●	→
Neonatal mortality rate (per 1,000 live births)	34.2	2018	●	→
Mortality rate, under-5 (per 1,000 live births)	119.0	2018	●	↗
Incidence of tuberculosis (per 100,000 population)	142.0	2018	●	→
New HIV infections (per 1,000 uninfected population)	0.4	2018	●	↗
Age-standardized death rate due to cardiovascular disease, cancer, diabetes, or chronic respiratory disease in adults aged 30–70 years (%)	23.9	2016	●	→
Age-standardized death rate attributable to household air pollution and ambient air pollution (per 100,000 population)	280	2016	●	●
Traffic deaths (per 100,000 population)	27.6	2016	●	↓
Life expectancy at birth (years)	54.3	2016	●	→
Adolescent fertility rate (births per 1,000 adolescent females aged 15 to 19)	161.1	2017	●	→
Births attended by skilled health personnel (%)	20.2	2015	●	●
Percentage of surviving infants who received 2 WHO-recommended vaccines (%)	37	2018	●	↓
Universal health coverage (UHC) index of service coverage (worst 0–100 best)	28.0	2017	●	→
Subjective well-being (average ladder score, worst 0–10 best)	4.5	2018	●	→

SDG4 – Quality Education	Value	Year	Rating	Trend
Net primary enrollment rate (%)	73.2	2016	●	↓
Lower secondary completion rate (%)	15.0	2016	●	●
Literacy rate (% of population aged 15 to 24)	30.8	2016	●	●

SDG5 – Gender Equality	Value	Year	Rating	Trend
Demand for family planning satisfied by modern methods (% of females aged 15 to 49 who are married or in unions)	20.2	2015	●	→
Ratio of female-to-male mean years of education received (%)	36.1	2018	●	→
Ratio of female-to-male labor force participation rate (%)	83.3	2019	●	↑
Seats held by women in national parliament (%)	15.4	2020	●	→

SDG6 – Clean Water and Sanitation	Value	Year	Rating	Trend
Population using at least basic drinking water services (%)	38.7	2017	●	↓
Population using at least basic sanitation services (%)	8.3	2017	●	↓
Freshwater withdrawal (% of available freshwater resources)	4.3	2005	●	●
Anthropogenic wastewater that receives treatment (%)	0.0	2018	●	●
Scarce water consumption embodied in imports (m³/capita)	0.2	2013	●	↑

SDG7 – Affordable and Clean Energy	Value	Year	Rating	Trend
Population with access to electricity (%)	10.9	2017	●	→
Population with access to clean fuels and technology for cooking (%)	3.1	2016	●	↓
CO$_2$ emissions from fuel combustion for electricity and heating per total electricity output (MtCO$_2$/TWh)	NA	NA	●	●

SDG8 – Decent Work and Economic Growth	Value	Year	Rating	Trend
Adjusted GDP growth (%)	-11.8	2018	●	●
Victims of modern slavery (per 1,000 population)	12.0	2018	●	●
Adults with an account at a bank or other financial institution or with a mobile-money-service provider (% of population aged 15 or over)	21.8	2017	●	↗
Unemployment rate (% of total labor force)	1.9	2019	●	↑
Fatal work-related accidents embodied in imports (per 100,000 population)	0.0	2010	●	↑

SDG9 – Industry, Innovation and Infrastructure	Value	Year	Rating	Trend
Population using the internet (%)	6.5	2017	●	→
Mobile broadband subscriptions (per 100 population)	4.0	2018	●	→
Logistics Performance Index: Quality of trade and transport-related infrastructure (worst 1–5 best)	2.4	2018	●	→
The Times Higher Education Universities Ranking: Average score of top 3 universities (worst 0–100 best) *	0.0	2020	●	●
Scientific and technical journal articles (per 1,000 population)	0.0	2018	●	→
Expenditure on research and development (% of GDP)	0.3	2016	●	●

SDG10 – Reduced Inequalities	Value	Year	Rating	Trend
Gini coefficient adjusted for top income	44.0	2011	●	●

SDG11 – Sustainable Cities and Communities	Value	Year	Rating	Trend
Annual mean concentration of particulate matter of less than 2.5 microns in diameter (PM2.5) (µg/m³)	66.0	2017	●	↓
Access to improved water source, piped (% of urban population)	52.7	2017	●	↓
Satisfaction with public transport (%)	47.1	2018	●	↑

SDG12 – Responsible Consumption and Production	Value	Year	Rating	Trend
Municipal solid waste (kg/capita/day)	1.1	2010	●	●
Electronic waste (kg/capita)	0.7	2016	●	●
Production-based SO$_2$ emissions (kg/capita)	11.9	2012	●	●
SO$_2$ emissions embodied in imports (kg/capita)	0.2	2012	●	●
Production-based nitrogen emissions (kg/capita)	24.0	2010	●	●
Nitrogen emissions embodied in imports (kg/capita)	0.1	2010	●	●

SDG13 – Climate Action	Value	Year	Rating	Trend
Energy-related CO$_2$ emissions (tCO$_2$/capita)	0.1	2017	●	↑
CO$_2$ emissions embodied in imports (tCO$_2$/capita)	0.0	2015	●	↑
CO$_2$ emissions embodied in fossil fuel exports (kg/capita)	NA	NA	●	●

SDG14 – Life Below Water	Value	Year	Rating	Trend
Mean area that is protected in marine sites important to biodiversity (%)	NA	NA	●	●
Ocean Health Index: Clean Waters score (worst 0–100 best)	NA	NA	●	●
Fish caught from overexploited or collapsed stocks (% of total catch)	NA	NA	●	●
Fish caught by trawling (%)	NA	NA	●	●
Marine biodiversity threats embodied in imports (per million population)	0.0	2018	●	●

SDG15 – Life on Land	Value	Year	Rating	Trend
Mean area that is protected in terrestrial sites important to biodiversity (%)	70.6	2018	●	↑
Mean area that is protected in freshwater sites important to biodiversity (%)	70.2	2018	●	↑
Red List Index of species survival (worst 0–1 best)	0.9	2019	●	↑
Permanent deforestation (% of forest area, 5-year average)	0.7	2018	●	●
Terrestrial and freshwater biodiversity threats embodied in imports (per million population)	0.0	2018	●	●

SDG16 – Peace, Justice and Strong Institutions	Value	Year	Rating	Trend
Homicides (per 100,000 population) *	9.0	2015	●	●
Unsentenced detainees (% of prison population)	63.4	2012	●	●
Percentage of population who feel safe walking alone at night in the city or area where they live (%)	42.9	2018	●	↓
Property Rights (worst 1–7 best)	3.1	2019	●	●
Birth registrations with civil authority (% of children under age 5)	12.0	2018	●	●
Corruption Perception Index (worst 0–100 best)	20	2019	●	↓
Children involved in child labor (% of population aged 5 to 14)	51.5	2016	●	●
Exports of major conventional weapons (TIV constant million USD per 100,000 population) *	0.0	2019	●	●
Press Freedom Index (best 0–100 worst)	36.7	2019	●	↑

SDG17 – Partnerships for the Goals	Value	Year	Rating	Trend
Government spending on health and education (% of GDP)	4.7	2013	●	●
For high-income and all OECD DAC countries: International concessional public finance, including official development assistance (% of GNI)	NA	NA	●	●
Other countries: Government revenue excluding grants (% of GDP)	NA	NA	●	●
Corporate Tax Haven Score (best 0–100 worst) *	0.0	2019	●	●

5. Country Profiles

* Imputed data point

▼ OVERALL PERFORMANCE

Index score

77.4

Regional average score

77.3

SDG Global rank 28 (OF 166)

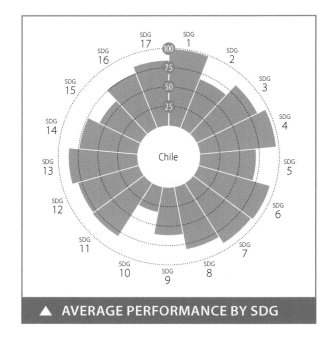

▲ AVERAGE PERFORMANCE BY SDG

▼ SPILLOVER INDEX

100 (best) to 0 (worst)

▼ CURRENT ASSESSMENT – SDG DASHBOARD

■ Major challenges   ■ Significant challenges   ▧ Challenges remain   ■ SDG achieved   ■ Information unavailable

▼ SDG TRENDS

1 NO POVERTY	2 ZERO HUNGER	3 GOOD HEALTH AND WELL-BEING	4 QUALITY EDUCATION	5 GENDER EQUALITY	6 CLEAN WATER AND SANITATION	7 AFFORDABLE AND CLEAN ENERGY	8 DECENT WORK AND ECONOMIC GROWTH	9 INDUSTRY, INNOVATION AND INFRASTRUCTURE
↗	↗	↗	↗	↗	↑	↗	↗	↗

10 REDUCED INEQUALITIES	11 SUSTAINABLE CITIES AND COMMUNITIES	12 RESPONSIBLE CONSUMPTION AND PRODUCTION	13 CLIMATE ACTION	14 LIFE BELOW WATER	15 LIFE ON LAND	16 PEACE, JUSTICE AND STRONG INSTITUTIONS	17 PARTNERSHIPS FOR THE GOALS
→	↗	●	→	↗	↓	→	↑

↓ Decreasing   → Stagnating   ↗ Moderately improving   ↑ On track or maintaining SDG achievement   ● Information unavailable

Notes: The full title of Goal 2 "Zero Hunger" is "End hunger, achieve food security and improved nutrition and promote sustainable agriculture".
The full title of each SDG is available here: https://sustainabledevelopment.un.org/topics/sustainabledevelopmentgoals

SDG1 – No Poverty

Indicator	Value	Year	Rating	Trend
Poverty headcount ratio at $1.90/day (%)	0.2	2020	●	↑
Poverty headcount ratio at $3.20/day (%)	0.9	2020	●	↑
Poverty rate after taxes and transfers (%)	16.5	2017	●	→

SDG2 – Zero Hunger

Indicator	Value	Year	Rating	Trend
Prevalence of undernourishment (%)	2.7	2017	●	↑
Prevalence of stunting in children under 5 years of age (%)	1.8	2014	●	↑
Prevalence of wasting in children under 5 years of age (%)	0.3	2014	●	↑
Prevalence of obesity, BMI ≥ 30 (% of adult population)	28.0	2016	●	↓
Human Trophic Level (best 2–3 worst)	2.3	2017	●	↓
Cereal yield (tonnes per hectare of harvested land)	6.8	2017	●	↑
Sustainable Nitrogen Management Index (best 0–1.41 worst)	0.8	2015	●	→
Yield gap closure (% of potential yield)	NA	NA	●	●

SDG3 – Good Health and Well-Being

Indicator	Value	Year	Rating	Trend
Maternal mortality rate (per 100,000 live births)	13	2017	●	↑
Neonatal mortality rate (per 1,000 live births)	4.9	2018	●	↑
Mortality rate, under-5 (per 1,000 live births)	7.2	2018	●	↑
Incidence of tuberculosis (per 100,000 population)	18.0	2018	●	→
New HIV infections (per 1,000 uninfected population)	0.3	2018	●	→
Age-standardized death rate due to cardiovascular disease, cancer, diabetes, or chronic respiratory disease in adults aged 30–70 years (%)	12.4	2016	●	↑
Age-standardized death rate attributable to household air pollution and ambient air pollution (per 100,000 population)	25	2016	●	●
Traffic deaths (per 100,000 population)	12.5	2016	●	↓
Life expectancy at birth (years)	79.5	2016	●	↑
Adolescent fertility rate (births per 1,000 adolescent females aged 15 to 19)	41.1	2017	●	↑
Births attended by skilled health personnel (%)	99.7	2015	●	↑
Percentage of surviving infants who received 2 WHO-recommended vaccines (%)	93.0	2018	●	↑
Universal health coverage (UHC) index of service coverage (worst 0–100 best)	70.0	2017	●	↑
Subjective well-being (average ladder score, worst 0–10 best)	6.4	2018	●	↑
Gap in life expectancy at birth among regions (years)	2.0	2016	●	↑
Gap in self-reported health status by income (percentage points)	19.7	2017	●	↑
Daily smokers (% of population aged 15 and over)	24.5	2016	●	●

SDG4 – Quality Education

Indicator	Value	Year	Rating	Trend
Net primary enrollment rate (%)	* 97.4	2017	●	↑
Lower secondary completion rate (%)	* 97.4	2017	●	↑
Literacy rate (% of population aged 15 to 24)	99.0	2017	●	●
Participation rate in pre-primary organized learning (% of children aged 4 to 6)	93.6	2017	●	↑
Tertiary educational attainment (% of population aged 25 to 34)	33.7	2017	●	↑
PISA score (worst 0–600 best)	437.7	2018	●	↓
Variation in science performance explained by socio-economic status (%)	14.1	2018	●	↑
Underachievers in science (% of 15-year-olds)	35.3	2018	●	↓
Resilient students in science (% of 15-year-olds)	22.1	2018	●	↑

SDG5 – Gender Equality

Indicator	Value	Year	Rating	Trend
Demand for family planning satisfied by modern methods (% of females aged 15 to 49 who are married or in unions)	* 86.3	2017	●	↑
Ratio of female-to-male mean years of education received (%)	97.2	2018	●	→
Ratio of female-to-male labor force participation rate (%)	68.9	2019	●	↑
Seats held by women in national parliament (%)	22.6	2020	●	↗
Gender wage gap (% of male median wage)	12.5	2017	●	↑
Gender gap in time spent doing unpaid work (minutes/day)	NA	NA	●	●

SDG6 – Clean Water and Sanitation

Indicator	Value	Year	Rating	Trend
Population using at least basic drinking water services (%)	99.8	2017	●	●
Population using at least basic sanitation services (%)	100.0	2017	●	●
Freshwater withdrawal (% of available freshwater resources)	9.0	2005	●	●
Anthropogenic wastewater that receives treatment (%)	71.9	2018	●	●
Scarce water consumption embodied in imports (m³/capita)	5.0	2013	●	↑
Population using safely managed water services (%)	98.6	2017	●	↑
Population using safely managed sanitation services (%)	77.5	2017	●	↑

SDG7 – Affordable and Clean Energy

Indicator	Value	Year	Rating	Trend
Population with access to electricity (%)	100.0	2017	●	●
Population with access to clean fuels and technology for cooking (%)	92.3	2016	●	↑
CO$_2$ emissions from fuel combustion for electricity and heating per total electricity output (MtCO$_2$/TWh)	1.1	2017	●	→
Share of renewable energy in total primary energy supply (%)	27.6	2018	●	↑

SDG8 – Decent Work and Economic Growth

Indicator	Value	Year	Rating	Trend
Adjusted GDP growth (%)	-1.2	2018	●	●
Victims of modern slavery (per 1,000 population)	0.8	2018	●	●
Adults with an account at a bank or other financial institution or with a mobile-money-service provider (% of population aged 15 or over)	74.3	2017	●	↑
Fatal work-related accidents embodied in imports (per 100,000 population)	0.3	2010	●	↑
Employment-to-population ratio (%)	62.6	2018	●	↑
Youth not in employment, education or training (NEET) (% of population aged 15 to 29)	18.4	2017	●	↓

SDG9 – Industry, Innovation and Infrastructure

Indicator	Value	Year	Rating	Trend
Population using the internet (%)	82.3	2017	●	↑
Mobile broadband subscriptions (per 100 population)	91.6	2018	●	↑
Logistics Performance Index: Quality of trade and transport-related infrastructure (worst 1–5 best)	3.2	2018	●	↑
The Times Higher Education Universities Ranking: Average score of top 3 universities (worst 0–100 best)	39.4	2020	●	●
Scientific and technical journal articles (per 1,000 population)	0.4	2018	●	↗
Expenditure on research and development (% of GDP)	0.4	2016	●	↓
Researchers (per 1,000 employed population)	1.1	2017	●	→
Triadic patent families filed (per million population)	0.5	2017	●	→
Gap in internet access by income (percentage points)	7.5	2017	●	↑
Women in science and engineering (% of tertiary graduates in science and engineering)	16.2	2015	●	●

SDG10 – Reduced Inequalities

Indicator	Value	Year	Rating	Trend
Gini coefficient adjusted for top income	51.5	2017	●	→
Palma ratio	2.6	2017	●	→
Elderly poverty rate (% of population aged 66 or over)	17.6	2017	●	↓

SDG11 – Sustainable Cities and Communities

Indicator	Value	Year	Rating	Trend
Annual mean concentration of particulate matter of less than 2.5 microns in diameter (PM2.5) (µg/m³)	21.0	2017	●	↗
Access to improved water source, piped (% of urban population)	99.0	2017	●	↑
Satisfaction with public transport (%)	58.1	2018	●	↑
Population with rent overburden (%)	13.9	2017	●	↓

SDG12 – Responsible Consumption and Production

Indicator	Value	Year	Rating	Trend
Electronic waste (kg/capita)	8.7	2016	●	●
Production-based SO$_2$ emissions (kg/capita)	66.4	2012	●	●
SO$_2$ emissions embodied in imports (kg/capita)	4.1	2012	●	●
Production-based nitrogen emissions (kg/capita)	27.5	2010	●	●
Nitrogen emissions embodied in imports (kg/capita)	3.8	2010	●	●
Non-recycled municipal solid waste (kg/capita/day)	1.2	2017	●	●

SDG13 – Climate Action

Indicator	Value	Year	Rating	Trend
Energy-related CO$_2$ emissions (tCO$_2$/capita)	4.6	2017	●	↓
CO$_2$ emissions embodied in imports (tCO$_2$/capita)	0.7	2015	●	↑
CO$_2$ emissions embodied in fossil fuel exports (kg/capita)	112.2	2017	●	●
Effective carbon rate (EUR/tCO$_2$)	-0.1	2016	●	●

SDG14 – Life Below Water

Indicator	Value	Year	Rating	Trend
Mean area that is protected in marine sites important to biodiversity (%)	24.8	2018	●	→
Ocean Health Index: Clean Waters score (worst 0–100 best)	93.8	2019	●	↑
Fish caught from overexploited or collapsed stocks (% of total catch)	41.5	2014	●	↗
Fish caught by trawling (%)	2.3	2014	●	↑
Marine biodiversity threats embodied in imports (per million population)	0.0	2018	●	●

SDG15 – Life on Land

Indicator	Value	Year	Rating	Trend
Mean area that is protected in terrestrial sites important to biodiversity (%)	34.8	2018	●	→
Mean area that is protected in freshwater sites important to biodiversity (%)	33.2	2018	●	→
Red List Index of species survival (worst 0–1 best)	0.8	2019	●	↓
Permanent deforestation (% of forest area, 5-year average)	0.0	2018	●	●
Terrestrial and freshwater biodiversity threats embodied in imports (per million population)	1.1	2018	●	●

SDG16 – Peace, Justice and Strong Institutions

Indicator	Value	Year	Rating	Trend
Homicides (per 100,000 population)	* 4.3	2017	●	↓
Unsentenced detainees (% of prison population)	31.3	2018	●	↓
Percentage of population who feel safe walking alone at night in the city or area where they live (%)	47.4	2018	●	↓
Property Rights (worst 1–7 best)	5.3	2019	●	●
Birth registrations with civil authority (% of children under age 5)	99.4	2018	●	●
Corruption Perception Index (worst 0–100 best)	67.0	2019	●	↑
Children involved in child labor (% of population aged 5 to 14)	6.6	2016	●	●
Exports of major conventional weapons (TIV constant million USD per 100,000 population)	0.0	2019	●	●
Press Freedom Index (best 0–100 worst)	25.7	2019	●	↑
Persons held in prison (per 100,000 population)	231.3	2017	●	↑

SDG17 – Partnerships for the Goals

Indicator	Value	Year	Rating	Trend
Government spending on health and education (% of GDP)	10.3	2016	●	↑
For high-income and all OECD DAC countries: International concessional public finance, including official development assistance (% of GNI)	NA	NA	●	●
Other countries: Government revenue excluding grants (% of GDP)	NA	NA	●	●
Corporate Tax Haven Score (best 0–100 worst)	* 0.0	2019	●	●
Financial Secrecy Score (best 0–100 worst)	55.8	2020	●	●
Shifted profits of multinationals (US$ billion)	5.3	2016	●	●

* Imputed data point

CHINA

East and South Asia

▼ OVERALL PERFORMANCE

Index score

73.9

Regional average score

67.2

SDG Global rank **48** (OF 166)

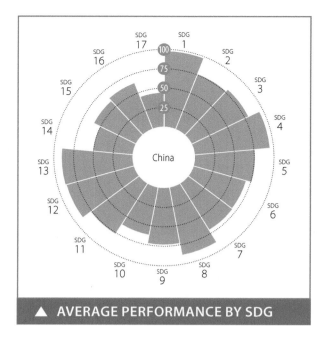

▲ AVERAGE PERFORMANCE BY SDG

▼ SPILLOVER INDEX

100 (best) to 0 (worst)

▼ CURRENT ASSESSMENT – SDG DASHBOARD

■ Major challenges ■ Significant challenges ■ Challenges remain ■ SDG achieved ■ Information unavailable

▼ SDG TRENDS

↓ Decreasing → Stagnating ↗ Moderately improving ↑ On track or maintaining SDG achievement ● Information unavailable

Notes: The full title of Goal 2 "Zero Hunger" is "End hunger, achieve food security and improved nutrition and promote sustainable agriculture".
The full title of each SDG is available here: https://sustainabledevelopment.un.org/topics/sustainabledevelopmentgoals

172 | Sustainable Development Report 2020 ○ The Sustainable Development Goals and Covid-19

SDG1 – No Poverty

	Value	Year	Rating	Trend
Poverty headcount ratio at $1.90/day (%)	0.2	2020	●	↑
Poverty headcount ratio at $3.20/day (%)	2.0	2020	●	↑

SDG2 – Zero Hunger

	Value	Year	Rating	Trend
Prevalence of undernourishment (%)	8.6	2017	●	↑
Prevalence of stunting in children under 5 years of age (%)	8.1	2013	●	↗
Prevalence of wasting in children under 5 years of age (%)	1.9	2013	●	↑
Prevalence of obesity, BMI ≥ 30 (% of adult population)	6.2	2016	●	↑
Human Trophic Level (best 2–3 worst)	2.2	2017	●	↑
Cereal yield (tonnes per hectare of harvested land)	6.0	2017	●	↑
Sustainable Nitrogen Management Index (best 0–1.41 worst)	0.7	2015	●	→

SDG3 – Good Health and Well-Being

	Value	Year	Rating	Trend
Maternal mortality rate (per 100,000 live births)	29	2017	●	↑
Neonatal mortality rate (per 1,000 live births)	4.3	2018	●	↑
Mortality rate, under-5 (per 1,000 live births)	8.6	2018	●	↑
Incidence of tuberculosis (per 100,000 population)	61.0	2018	●	→
New HIV infections (per 1,000 uninfected population)	NA	NA	●	●
Age-standardized death rate due to cardiovascular disease, cancer, diabetes, or chronic respiratory disease in adults aged 30–70 years (%)	17.0	2016	●	↑
Age-standardized death rate attributable to household air pollution and ambient air pollution (per 100,000 population)	113	2016	●	●
Traffic deaths (per 100,000 population)	18.2	2016	●	→
Life expectancy at birth (years)	76.4	2016	●	↗
Adolescent fertility rate (births per 1,000 adolescent females aged 15 to 19)	7.6	2017	●	↑
Births attended by skilled health personnel (%)	99.9	2015	●	↑
Percentage of surviving infants who received 2 WHO-recommended vaccines (%)	99	2018	●	↑
Universal health coverage (UHC) index of service coverage (worst 0–100 best)	79.0	2017	●	↑
Subjective well-being (average ladder score, worst 0–10 best)	5.1	2018	●	↓

SDG4 – Quality Education

	Value	Year	Rating	Trend
Net primary enrollment rate (%)	NA	NA	●	●
Lower secondary completion rate (%)	99.5	2011	●	●
Literacy rate (% of population aged 15 to 24)	99.8	2018	●	●

SDG5 – Gender Equality

	Value	Year	Rating	Trend
Demand for family planning satisfied by modern methods (% of females aged 15 to 49 who are married or in unions)	96.6	2001	●	↑
Ratio of female-to-male mean years of education received (%)	90.4	2018	●	↗
Ratio of female-to-male labor force participation rate (%)	80.4	2019	●	↑
Seats held by women in national parliament (%)	24.9	2020	●	→

SDG6 – Clean Water and Sanitation

	Value	Year	Rating	Trend
Population using at least basic drinking water services (%)	92.8	2017	●	↑
Population using at least basic sanitation services (%)	84.8	2017	●	↑
Freshwater withdrawal (% of available freshwater resources)	43.4	2015	●	
Anthropogenic wastewater that receives treatment (%)	9.4	2018	●	●
Scarce water consumption embodied in imports (m³/capita)	2.3	2013	●	↑

SDG7 – Affordable and Clean Energy

	Value	Year	Rating	Trend
Population with access to electricity (%)	100.0	2017	●	↑
Population with access to clean fuels and technology for cooking (%)	59.3	2016	●	→
CO₂ emissions from fuel combustion for electricity and heating per total electricity output (MtCO₂/TWh)	3.0	2017	●	↗

SDG8 – Decent Work and Economic Growth

	Value	Year	Rating	Trend
Adjusted GDP growth (%)	2.6	2018	●	●
Victims of modern slavery (per 1,000 population)	2.8	2018	●	●
Adults with an account at a bank or other financial institution or with a mobile-money-service provider (% of population aged 15 or over)	80.2	2017	●	↑
Unemployment rate (% of total labor force)	4.3	2019	●	↑
Fatal work-related accidents embodied in imports (per 100,000 population)	0.1	2010	●	↑

SDG9 – Industry, Innovation and Infrastructure

	Value	Year	Rating	Trend
Population using the internet (%)	54.3	2017	●	↑
Mobile broadband subscriptions (per 100 population)	93.5	2018	●	↑
Logistics Performance Index: Quality of trade and transport-related infrastructure (worst 1–5 best)	3.8	2018	●	↑
The Times Higher Education Universities Ranking: Average score of top 3 universities (worst 0–100 best)	76.3	2020	●	●
Scientific and technical journal articles (per 1,000 population)	0.4	2018	●	↗
Expenditure on research and development (% of GDP)	2.1	2017	●	↑

SDG10 – Reduced Inequalities

	Value	Year	Rating	Trend
Gini coefficient adjusted for top income	41.2	2014	●	●

SDG11 – Sustainable Cities and Communities

	Value	Year	Rating	Trend
Annual mean concentration of particulate matter of less than 2.5 microns in diameter (PM2.5) (μg/m³)	52.7	2017	●	↗
Access to improved water source, piped (% of urban population)	92.2	2017	●	↗
Satisfaction with public transport (%)	78.6	2018	●	●

SDG12 – Responsible Consumption and Production

	Value	Year	Rating	Trend
Municipal solid waste (kg/capita/day)	0.7	2015	●	●
Electronic waste (kg/capita)	5.2	2016	●	●
Production-based SO₂ emissions (kg/capita)	30.0	2012	●	●
SO₂ emissions embodied in imports (kg/capita)	0.7	2012	●	●
Production-based nitrogen emissions (kg/capita)	23.1	2010	●	●
Nitrogen emissions embodied in imports (kg/capita)	0.7	2010	●	●

SDG13 – Climate Action

	Value	Year	Rating	Trend
Energy-related CO₂ emissions (tCO₂/capita)	6.5	2017	●	→
CO₂ emissions embodied in imports (tCO₂/capita)	0.1	2015	●	↑
CO₂ emissions embodied in fossil fuel exports (kg/capita)	16.4	2018	●	●

SDG14 – Life Below Water

	Value	Year	Rating	Trend
Mean area that is protected in marine sites important to biodiversity (%)	21.7	2018	●	→
Ocean Health Index: Clean Waters score (worst 0–100 best)	35.0	2019	●	→
Fish caught from overexploited or collapsed stocks (% of total catch)	8.8	2014	●	↑
Fish caught by trawling (%)	60.0	2014	●	↓
Marine biodiversity threats embodied in imports (per million population)	0.0	2018	●	●

SDG15 – Life on Land

	Value	Year	Rating	Trend
Mean area that is protected in terrestrial sites important to biodiversity (%)	37.8	2018	●	→
Mean area that is protected in freshwater sites important to biodiversity (%)	34.4	2018	●	→
Red List Index of species survival (worst 0–1 best)	0.7	2019	●	↓
Permanent deforestation (% of forest area, 5-year average)	0.0	2018	●	●
Terrestrial and freshwater biodiversity threats embodied in imports (per million population)	0.6	2018	●	●

SDG16 – Peace, Justice and Strong Institutions

	Value	Year	Rating	Trend
Homicides (per 100,000 population)	0.6	2017	●	↑
Unsentenced detainees (% of prison population)	NA	NA	●	●
Percentage of population who feel safe walking alone at night in the city or area where they live (%)	86.4	2018	●	●
Property Rights (worst 1–7 best)	4.6	2019	●	●
Birth registrations with civil authority (% of children under age 5)	NA	NA	●	●
Corruption Perception Index (worst 0–100 best)	41	2019	●	↗
Children involved in child labor (% of population aged 5 to 14)	NA	NA	●	●
Exports of major conventional weapons (TIV constant million USD per 100,000 population)	0.1	2019	●	●
Press Freedom Index (best 0–100 worst)	78.9	2019	●	→

SDG17 – Partnerships for the Goals

	Value	Year	Rating	Trend
Government spending on health and education (% of GDP)	NA	NA	●	●
For high-income and all OECD DAC countries: International concessional public finance, including official development assistance (% of GNI)	NA	NA	●	●
Other countries: Government revenue excluding grants (% of GDP)	15.8	2016	●	↓
Corporate Tax Haven Score (best 0–100 worst)	58.3	2019	●	●

* Imputed data point

5. Country Profiles

▼ OVERALL PERFORMANCE

Index score

70.9

Regional average score

70.4

SDG Global rank **67** (OF 166)

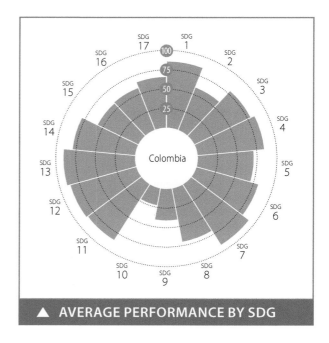

▲ AVERAGE PERFORMANCE BY SDG

▼ SPILLOVER INDEX

100 (best) to 0 (worst)

▼ CURRENT ASSESSMENT – SDG DASHBOARD

■ Major challenges ■ Significant challenges ■ Challenges remain ■ SDG achieved ■ Information unavailable

▼ SDG TRENDS

1 NO POVERTY ↗	2 ZERO HUNGER ↗	3 GOOD HEALTH AND WELL-BEING ↗	4 QUALITY EDUCATION ↗	5 GENDER EQUALITY ↗	6 CLEAN WATER AND SANITATION ↑	7 AFFORDABLE AND CLEAN ENERGY ↑	8 DECENT WORK AND ECONOMIC GROWTH ↗	9 INDUSTRY, INNOVATION AND INFRASTRUCTURE ↗
10 REDUCED INEQUALITIES ●	11 SUSTAINABLE CITIES AND COMMUNITIES ↗	12 RESPONSIBLE CONSUMPTION AND PRODUCTION ●	13 CLIMATE ACTION ↑	14 LIFE BELOW WATER ↑	15 LIFE ON LAND ↗	16 PEACE, JUSTICE AND STRONG INSTITUTIONS →	17 PARTNERSHIPS FOR THE GOALS ↓	

 ↓ Decreasing → Stagnating ↗ Moderately improving ↑ On track or maintaining SDG achievement ● Information unavailable

Notes: The full title of Goal 2 "Zero Hunger" is "End hunger, achieve food security and improved nutrition and promote sustainable agriculture".
The full title of each SDG is available here: https://sustainabledevelopment.un.org/topics/sustainabledevelopmentgoals

COLOMBIA

SDG1 – No Poverty

	Value	Year	Rating	Trend
Poverty headcount ratio at $1.90/day (%)	3.5	2020	●	↑
Poverty headcount ratio at $3.20/day (%)	11.3	2020	●	↗

SDG2 – Zero Hunger

	Value	Year	Rating	Trend
Prevalence of undernourishment (%)	4.8	2017	●	↑
Prevalence of stunting in children under 5 years of age (%)	12.7	2010	●	↗
Prevalence of wasting in children under 5 years of age (%)	0.9	2010	●	↑
Prevalence of obesity, BMI ≥ 30 (% of adult population)	22.3	2016	●	↓
Human Trophic Level (best 2–3 worst)	2.3	2017	●	↑
Cereal yield (tonnes per hectare of harvested land)	4.3	2017	●	↑
Sustainable Nitrogen Management Index (best 0–1.41 worst)	1.1	2015	●	↓

SDG3 – Good Health and Well-Being

	Value	Year	Rating	Trend
Maternal mortality rate (per 100,000 live births)	83	2017	●	↗
Neonatal mortality rate (per 1,000 live births)	7.8	2018	●	↑
Mortality rate, under-5 (per 1,000 live births)	14.2	2018	●	↑
Incidence of tuberculosis (per 100,000 population)	33.0	2018	●	→
New HIV infections (per 1,000 uninfected population)	0.1	2018	●	↑
Age-standardized death rate due to cardiovascular disease, cancer, diabetes, or chronic respiratory disease in adults aged 30–70 years (%)	15.8	2016	●	↑
Age-standardized death rate attributable to household air pollution and ambient air pollution (per 100,000 population)	37	2016	●	●
Traffic deaths (per 100,000 population)	18.5	2016	●	↓
Life expectancy at birth (years)	75.1	2016	●	↗
Adolescent fertility rate (births per 1,000 adolescent females aged 15 to 19)	66.7	2017	●	→
Births attended by skilled health personnel (%)	99.2	2016	●	↑
Percentage of surviving infants who received 2 WHO-recommended vaccines (%)	92	2018	●	↑
Universal health coverage (UHC) index of service coverage (worst 0–100 best)	76.0	2017	●	↑
Subjective well-being (average ladder score, worst 0–10 best)	6.4	2019	●	↑

SDG4 – Quality Education

	Value	Year	Rating	Trend
Net primary enrollment rate (%)	92.9	2018	●	↑
Lower secondary completion rate (%)	75.7	2018	●	→
Literacy rate (% of population aged 15 to 24)	98.9	2018	●	●

SDG5 – Gender Equality

	Value	Year	Rating	Trend
Demand for family planning satisfied by modern methods (% of females aged 15 to 49 who are married or in unions)	86.6	2016	●	↑
Ratio of female-to-male mean years of education received (%)	103.7	2018	●	↑
Ratio of female-to-male labor force participation rate (%)	71.5	2019	●	↑
Seats held by women in national parliament (%)	18.3	2020	●	↓

SDG6 – Clean Water and Sanitation

	Value	Year	Rating	Trend
Population using at least basic drinking water services (%)	97.3	2017	●	↑
Population using at least basic sanitation services (%)	89.6	2017	●	↑
Freshwater withdrawal (% of available freshwater resources)	1.8	2010	●	●
Anthropogenic wastewater that receives treatment (%)	25.6	2018	●	●
Scarce water consumption embodied in imports (m³/capita)	3.8	2013	●	↑

SDG7 – Affordable and Clean Energy

	Value	Year	Rating	Trend
Population with access to electricity (%)	99.6	2017	●	↑
Population with access to clean fuels and technology for cooking (%)	91.8	2016	●	↑
CO$_2$ emissions from fuel combustion for electricity and heating per total electricity output (MtCO$_2$/TWh)	1.0	2017	●	↑

SDG8 – Decent Work and Economic Growth

	Value	Year	Rating	Trend
Adjusted GDP growth (%)	-3.2	2018	●	●
Victims of modern slavery (per 1,000 population)	2.7	2018	●	●
Adults with an account at a bank or other financial institution or with a mobile-money-service provider (% of population aged 15 or over)	45.8	2017	●	↗
Unemployment rate (% of total labor force)	9.7	2019	●	↓
Fatal work-related accidents embodied in imports (per 100,000 population)	0.2	2010	●	↑

SDG9 – Industry, Innovation and Infrastructure

	Value	Year	Rating	Trend
Population using the internet (%)	64.1	2018	●	↑
Mobile broadband subscriptions (per 100 population)	52.3	2018	●	↑
Logistics Performance Index: Quality of trade and transport-related infrastructure (worst 1–5 best)	2.7	2018	●	↑
The Times Higher Education Universities Ranking: Average score of top 3 universities (worst 0–100 best)	29.6	2020	●	●
Scientific and technical journal articles (per 1,000 population)	0.1	2018	●	→
Expenditure on research and development (% of GDP)	0.2	2017	●	↓

SDG10 – Reduced Inequalities

	Value	Year	Rating	Trend
Gini coefficient adjusted for top income	55.2	2017	●	●

SDG11 – Sustainable Cities and Communities

	Value	Year	Rating	Trend
Annual mean concentration of particulate matter of less than 2.5 microns in diameter (PM2.5) (μg/m³)	16.5	2017	●	↑
Access to improved water source, piped (% of urban population)	95.2	2017	●	→
Satisfaction with public transport (%)	64.3	2019	●	↑

SDG12 – Responsible Consumption and Production

	Value	Year	Rating	Trend
Municipal solid waste (kg/capita/day)	0.8	2011	●	●
Electronic waste (kg/capita)	5.6	2016	●	●
Production-based SO$_2$ emissions (kg/capita)	11.8	2012	●	●
SO$_2$ emissions embodied in imports (kg/capita)	2.6	2012	●	●
Production-based nitrogen emissions (kg/capita)	24.6	2010	●	●
Nitrogen emissions embodied in imports (kg/capita)	2.5	2010	●	●

SDG13 – Climate Action

	Value	Year	Rating	Trend
Energy-related CO$_2$ emissions (tCO$_2$/capita)	1.7	2017	●	↑
CO$_2$ emissions embodied in imports (tCO$_2$/capita)	0.4	2015	●	↑
CO$_2$ emissions embodied in fossil fuel exports (kg/capita)	4223.2	2018	●	●

SDG14 – Life Below Water

	Value	Year	Rating	Trend
Mean area that is protected in marine sites important to biodiversity (%)	65.2	2018	●	↑
Ocean Health Index: Clean Waters score (worst 0–100 best)	63.5	2019	●	↑
Fish caught from overexploited or collapsed stocks (% of total catch)	11.8	2014	●	↑
Fish caught by trawling (%)	4.0	2014	●	↑
Marine biodiversity threats embodied in imports (per million population)	0.1	2018	●	●

SDG15 – Life on Land

	Value	Year	Rating	Trend
Mean area that is protected in terrestrial sites important to biodiversity (%)	41.4	2018	●	↑
Mean area that is protected in freshwater sites important to biodiversity (%)	39.3	2018	●	↑
Red List Index of species survival (worst 0–1 best)	0.7	2019	●	↓
Permanent deforestation (% of forest area, 5-year average)	0.2	2018	●	●
Terrestrial and freshwater biodiversity threats embodied in imports (per million population)	1.0	2018	●	●

SDG16 – Peace, Justice and Strong Institutions

	Value	Year	Rating	Trend
Homicides (per 100,000 population)	24.9	2017	●	↗
Unsentenced detainees (% of prison population)	32.0	2018	●	↑
Percentage of population who feel safe walking alone at night in the city or area where they live (%)	47.5	2019	●	→
Property Rights (worst 1–7 best)	4.1	2019	●	●
Birth registrations with civil authority (% of children under age 5)	96.8	2018	●	●
Corruption Perception Index (worst 0–100 best)	37	2019	●	→
Children involved in child labor (% of population aged 5 to 14)	7.8	2016	●	●
Exports of major conventional weapons (TIV constant million USD per 100,000 population)	0.0	2019	●	●
Press Freedom Index (best 0–100 worst)	42.8	2019	●	→

SDG17 – Partnerships for the Goals

	Value	Year	Rating	Trend
Government spending on health and education (% of GDP)	8.2	2016	●	↓
For high-income and all OECD DAC countries: International concessional public finance, including official development assistance (% of GNI)	NA	NA	●	●
Other countries: Government revenue excluding grants (% of GDP)	22.9	2017	●	↓
Corporate Tax Haven Score (best 0–100 worst) *	0.0	2019	●	●

* Imputed data point

5. Country Profiles

COMOROS

Sub-Saharan Africa

OVERALL PERFORMANCE

Index score

53.1

Regional average score

53.1

SDG Global rank **146** (OF 166)

SPILLOVER INDEX
100 (best) to 0 (worst)

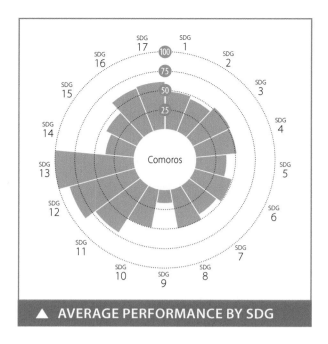

AVERAGE PERFORMANCE BY SDG

CURRENT ASSESSMENT – SDG DASHBOARD

■ Major challenges　■ Significant challenges　■ Challenges remain　■ SDG achieved　■ Information unavailable

SDG TRENDS

↓ Decreasing　→ Stagnating　↗ Moderately improving　↑ On track or maintaining SDG achievement　● Information unavailable

Notes: The full title of Goal 2 "Zero Hunger" is "End hunger, achieve food security and improved nutrition and promote sustainable agriculture".
The full title of each SDG is available here: https://sustainabledevelopment.un.org/topics/sustainabledevelopmentgoals

176 | Sustainable Development Report 2020　The Sustainable Development Goals and Covid-19

SDG1 – No Poverty

Indicator	Value	Year	Rating	Trend
Poverty headcount ratio at $1.90/day (%)	20.0	2020	●	→
Poverty headcount ratio at $3.20/day (%)	37.6	2020	●	→

SDG2 – Zero Hunger

Indicator	Value	Year	Rating	Trend
Prevalence of undernourishment (%)	NA	NA	●	●
Prevalence of stunting in children under 5 years of age (%)	32.1	2012	●	→
Prevalence of wasting in children under 5 years of age (%)	11.1	2012	●	↗
Prevalence of obesity, BMI ≥ 30 (% of adult population)	7.8	2016	●	↑
Human Trophic Level (best 2–3 worst)	2.1	2007	●	●
Cereal yield (tonnes per hectare of harvested land)	1.4	2017	●	↓
Sustainable Nitrogen Management Index (best 0–1.41 worst)	0.9	2015	●	→

SDG3 – Good Health and Well-Being

Indicator	Value	Year	Rating	Trend
Maternal mortality rate (per 100,000 live births)	273	2017	●	→
Neonatal mortality rate (per 1,000 live births)	31.6	2018	●	→
Mortality rate, under-5 (per 1,000 live births)	67.5	2018	●	↗
Incidence of tuberculosis (per 100,000 population)	35.0	2018	●	→
New HIV infections (per 1,000 uninfected population)	0.0	2018	●	↑
Age-standardized death rate due to cardiovascular disease, cancer, diabetes, or chronic respiratory disease in adults aged 30–70 years (%)	22.9	2016	●	→
Age-standardized death rate attributable to household air pollution and ambient air pollution (per 100,000 population)	172	2016	●	●
Traffic deaths (per 100,000 population)	26.5	2016	●	→
Life expectancy at birth (years)	63.9	2016	●	→
Adolescent fertility rate (births per 1,000 adolescent females aged 15 to 19)	65.4	2017	●	↗
Births attended by skilled health personnel (%)	82.2	2012	●	●
Percentage of surviving infants who received 2 WHO-recommended vaccines (%)	90	2018	●	↑
Universal health coverage (UHC) index of service coverage (worst 0–100 best)	52.0	2017	●	↗
Subjective well-being (average ladder score, worst 0–10 best)	4.6	2019	●	●

SDG4 – Quality Education

Indicator	Value	Year	Rating	Trend
Net primary enrollment rate (%)	80.8	2018	●	↓
Lower secondary completion rate (%)	48.3	2014	●	●
Literacy rate (% of population aged 15 to 24)	78.3	2018	●	●

SDG5 – Gender Equality

Indicator	Value	Year	Rating	Trend
Demand for family planning satisfied by modern methods (% of females aged 15 to 49 who are married or in unions)	28.8	2012	●	→
Ratio of female-to-male mean years of education received (%)	66.1	2018	●	→
Ratio of female-to-male labor force participation rate (%)	74.1	2019	●	↑
Seats held by women in national parliament (%)	16.7	2020	●	↑

SDG6 – Clean Water and Sanitation

Indicator	Value	Year	Rating	Trend
Population using at least basic drinking water services (%)	80.2	2017	●	↓
Population using at least basic sanitation services (%)	35.9	2017	●	→
Freshwater withdrawal (% of available freshwater resources)	1.2	2000	●	●
Anthropogenic wastewater that receives treatment (%)	0.1	2018	●	●
Scarce water consumption embodied in imports (m3/capita)	NA	NA	●	●

SDG7 – Affordable and Clean Energy

Indicator	Value	Year	Rating	Trend
Population with access to electricity (%)	79.9	2017	●	↑
Population with access to clean fuels and technology for cooking (%)	9.3	2016	●	→
CO2 emissions from fuel combustion for electricity and heating per total electricity output (MtCO2/TWh)	NA	NA	●	●

SDG8 – Decent Work and Economic Growth

Indicator	Value	Year	Rating	Trend
Adjusted GDP growth (%)	-5.0	2018	●	●
Victims of modern slavery (per 1,000 population)	NA	NA	●	●
Adults with an account at a bank or other financial institution or with a mobile-money-service provider (% of population aged 15 or over)	21.7	2011	●	●
Unemployment rate (% of total labor force)	4.3	2019	●	↑
Fatal work-related accidents embodied in imports (per 100,000 population)	NA	NA	●	●

SDG9 – Industry, Innovation and Infrastructure

Indicator	Value	Year	Rating	Trend
Population using the internet (%)	8.5	2017	●	→
Mobile broadband subscriptions (per 100 population)	60.0	2018	●	↑
Logistics Performance Index: Quality of trade and transport-related infrastructure (worst 1–5 best)	2.3	2018	●	↓
The Times Higher Education Universities Ranking: Average score of top 3 universities (worst 0–100 best) *	0.0	2020	●	●
Scientific and technical journal articles (per 1,000 population)	0.0	2018	●	→
Expenditure on research and development (% of GDP) *	0.0	2017	●	●

SDG10 – Reduced Inequalities

Indicator	Value	Year	Rating	Trend
Gini coefficient adjusted for top income	45.6	2013	●	●

SDG11 – Sustainable Cities and Communities

Indicator	Value	Year	Rating	Trend
Annual mean concentration of particulate matter of less than 2.5 microns in diameter (PM2.5) (µg/m3)	20.5	2017	●	→
Access to improved water source, piped (% of urban population)	76.1	2017	●	→
Satisfaction with public transport (%)	54.0	2019	●	●

SDG12 – Responsible Consumption and Production

Indicator	Value	Year	Rating	Trend
Municipal solid waste (kg/capita/day)	1.0	2015	●	●
Electronic waste (kg/capita)	0.8	2016	●	●
Production-based SO2 emissions (kg/capita)	NA	NA	●	●
SO2 emissions embodied in imports (kg/capita)	NA	NA	●	●
Production-based nitrogen emissions (kg/capita)	NA	NA	●	●
Nitrogen emissions embodied in imports (kg/capita)	NA	NA	●	●

SDG13 – Climate Action

Indicator	Value	Year	Rating	Trend
Energy-related CO2 emissions (tCO2/capita)	0.2	2017	●	↑
CO2 emissions embodied in imports (tCO2/capita)	NA	NA	●	●
CO2 emissions embodied in fossil fuel exports (kg/capita)	0.0	2018	●	●

SDG14 – Life Below Water

Indicator	Value	Year	Rating	Trend
Mean area that is protected in marine sites important to biodiversity (%)	0.0	2018	●	→
Ocean Health Index: Clean Waters score (worst 0–100 best)	38.6	2019	●	↓
Fish caught from overexploited or collapsed stocks (% of total catch)	5.6	2014	●	↑
Fish caught by trawling (%)	NA	NA	●	●
Marine biodiversity threats embodied in imports (per million population)	NA	NA	●	●

SDG15 – Life on Land

Indicator	Value	Year	Rating	Trend
Mean area that is protected in terrestrial sites important to biodiversity (%)	13.0	2018	●	→
Mean area that is protected in freshwater sites important to biodiversity (%)	NA	NA	●	●
Red List Index of species survival (worst 0–1 best)	0.8	2019	●	↓
Permanent deforestation (% of forest area, 5-year average)	0.3	2018	●	●
Terrestrial and freshwater biodiversity threats embodied in imports (per million population)	NA	NA	●	●

SDG16 – Peace, Justice and Strong Institutions

Indicator	Value	Year	Rating	Trend
Homicides (per 100,000 population) *	7.7	2015	●	●
Unsentenced detainees (% of prison population)	60.4	2015	●	●
Percentage of population who feel safe walking alone at night in the city or area where they live (%)	67.0	2019	●	●
Property Rights (worst 1–7 best)	NA	NA	●	●
Birth registrations with civil authority (% of children under age 5)	87.3	2018	●	●
Corruption Perception Index (worst 0–100 best)	25	2019	●	↓
Children involved in child labor (% of population aged 5 to 14)	22.0	2016	●	●
Exports of major conventional weapons (TIV constant million USD per 100,000 population) *	0.0	2019	●	●
Press Freedom Index (best 0–100 worst)	27.9	2019	●	↑

SDG17 – Partnerships for the Goals

Indicator	Value	Year	Rating	Trend
Government spending on health and education (% of GDP)	3.5	2015	●	→
For high-income and all OECD DAC countries: International concessional public finance, including official development assistance (% of GNI)	NA	NA	●	●
Other countries: Government revenue excluding grants (% of GDP)	NA	NA	●	●
Corporate Tax Haven Score (best 0–100 worst) *	0.0	2019	●	●

* Imputed data point

5. Country Profiles

CONGO, REPUBLIC OF

▼ OVERALL PERFORMANCE

Index score

55.2

Regional average score

53.1

SDG Global rank **135** (OF 166)

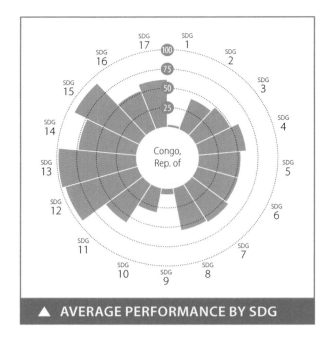

▲ AVERAGE PERFORMANCE BY SDG

▼ SPILLOVER INDEX

100 (best) to 0 (worst)

100
80
60
40
20
0

▼ CURRENT ASSESSMENT – SDG DASHBOARD

■ Major challenges ■ Significant challenges ▨ Challenges remain ■ SDG achieved ■ Information unavailable

▼ SDG TRENDS

↓ Decreasing → Stagnating ↗ Moderately improving ↑ On track or maintaining SDG achievement ● Information unavailable

Notes: The full title of Goal 2 "Zero Hunger" is "End hunger, achieve food security and improved nutrition and promote sustainable agriculture".
The full title of each SDG is available here: https://sustainabledevelopment.un.org/topics/sustainabledevelopmentgoals

SDG1 – No Poverty

	Value	Year	Rating	Trend
Poverty headcount ratio at $1.90/day (%)	67.0	2020	●	↓
Poverty headcount ratio at $3.20/day (%)	85.8	2020	●	↓

SDG2 – Zero Hunger

	Value	Year	Rating	Trend
Prevalence of undernourishment (%)	40.3	2017	●	↓
Prevalence of stunting in children under 5 years of age (%)	21.2	2015	●	↗
Prevalence of wasting in children under 5 years of age (%)	8.2	2015	●	↓
Prevalence of obesity, BMI ≥ 30 (% of adult population)	9.6	2016	●	↑
Human Trophic Level (best 2–3 worst)	2.2	2017	●	↑
Cereal yield (tonnes per hectare of harvested land)	0.8	2017	●	→
Sustainable Nitrogen Management Index (best 0–1.41 worst)	0.9	2015	●	↓

SDG3 – Good Health and Well-Being

	Value	Year	Rating	Trend
Maternal mortality rate (per 100,000 live births)	378	2017	●	↗
Neonatal mortality rate (per 1,000 live births)	20.3	2018	●	↗
Mortality rate, under-5 (per 1,000 live births)	50.1	2018	●	↗
Incidence of tuberculosis (per 100,000 population)	375.0	2018	●	→
New HIV infections (per 1,000 uninfected population)	1.0	2018	●	↗
Age-standardized death rate due to cardiovascular disease, cancer, diabetes, or chronic respiratory disease in adults aged 30–70 years (%)	16.7	2016	●	↑
Age-standardized death rate attributable to household air pollution and ambient air pollution (per 100,000 population)	131	2016	●	●
Traffic deaths (per 100,000 population)	27.4	2016	●	↓
Life expectancy at birth (years)	64.3	2016	●	→
Adolescent fertility rate (births per 1,000 adolescent females aged 15 to 19)	112.2	2017	●	→
Births attended by skilled health personnel (%)	94.4	2015	●	↑
Percentage of surviving infants who received 2 WHO-recommended vaccines (%)	75	2018	●	↓
Universal health coverage (UHC) index of service coverage (worst 0–100 best)	39.0	2017	●	↗
Subjective well-being (average ladder score, worst 0–10 best)	5.2	2019	●	↑

SDG4 – Quality Education

	Value	Year	Rating	Trend
Net primary enrollment rate (%)	87.9	2012	●	●
Lower secondary completion rate (%)	50.1	2012	●	●
Literacy rate (% of population aged 15 to 24)	82.1	2018	●	●

SDG5 – Gender Equality

	Value	Year	Rating	Trend
Demand for family planning satisfied by modern methods (% of females aged 15 to 49 who are married or in unions)	43.2	2015	●	↗
Ratio of female-to-male mean years of education received (%)	81.3	2018	●	↓
Ratio of female-to-male labor force participation rate (%)	93.5	2019	●	↑
Seats held by women in national parliament (%)	11.3	2020	●	→

SDG6 – Clean Water and Sanitation

	Value	Year	Rating	Trend
Population using at least basic drinking water services (%)	73.2	2017	●	↗
Population using at least basic sanitation services (%)	20.2	2017	●	→
Freshwater withdrawal (% of available freshwater resources)	0.0	2000	●	●
Anthropogenic wastewater that receives treatment (%)	0.3	2018	●	●
Scarce water consumption embodied in imports (m3/capita)	1.6	2013	●	↑

SDG7 – Affordable and Clean Energy

	Value	Year	Rating	Trend
Population with access to electricity (%)	66.2	2017	●	↑
Population with access to clean fuels and technology for cooking (%)	24.1	2016	●	→
CO_2 emissions from fuel combustion for electricity and heating per total electricity output (MtCO2/TWh)	0.9	2017	●	↑

SDG8 – Decent Work and Economic Growth

	Value	Year	Rating	Trend
Adjusted GDP growth (%)	-9.1	2018	●	●
Victims of modern slavery (per 1,000 population)	8.0	2018	●	●
Adults with an account at a bank or other financial institution or with a mobile-money-service provider (% of population aged 15 or over)	26.1	2017	●	↗
Unemployment rate (% of total labor force)	9.5	2019	●	→
Fatal work-related accidents embodied in imports (per 100,000 population)	0.2	2010	●	↑

SDG9 – Industry, Innovation and Infrastructure

	Value	Year	Rating	Trend
Population using the internet (%)	8.7	2017	●	→
Mobile broadband subscriptions (per 100 population)	6.0	2017	●	●
Logistics Performance Index: Quality of trade and transport-related infrastructure (worst 1–5 best)	2.1	2018	●	↗
The Times Higher Education Universities Ranking: Average score of top 3 universities (worst 0–100 best) *	0.0	2020	●	●
Scientific and technical journal articles (per 1,000 population)	0.0	2018	●	↓
Expenditure on research and development (% of GDP)	NA	NA	●	●

SDG10 – Reduced Inequalities

	Value	Year	Rating	Trend
Gini coefficient adjusted for top income	52.0	2011	●	●

SDG11 – Sustainable Cities and Communities

	Value	Year	Rating	Trend
Annual mean concentration of particulate matter of less than 2.5 microns in diameter (PM2.5) (μg/m3)	46.6	2017	●	↓
Access to improved water source, piped (% of urban population)	72.8	2017	●	↓
Satisfaction with public transport (%)	53.2	2019	●	↗

SDG12 – Responsible Consumption and Production

	Value	Year	Rating	Trend
Municipal solid waste (kg/capita/day)	NA	NA	●	●
Electronic waste (kg/capita)	3.0	2016	●	●
Production-based SO_2 emissions (kg/capita)	23.7	2012	●	●
SO_2 emissions embodied in imports (kg/capita)	1.4	2012	●	●
Production-based nitrogen emissions (kg/capita)	7.8	2010	●	●
Nitrogen emissions embodied in imports (kg/capita)	1.1	2010	●	●

SDG13 – Climate Action

	Value	Year	Rating	Trend
Energy-related CO_2 emissions (tCO2/capita)	0.5	2017	●	↑
CO_2 emissions embodied in imports (tCO2/capita)	0.1	2015	●	↑
CO_2 emissions embodied in fossil fuel exports (kg/capita)	0.0	2017	●	↑

SDG14 – Life Below Water

	Value	Year	Rating	Trend
Mean area that is protected in marine sites important to biodiversity (%)	NA	NA	●	●
Ocean Health Index: Clean Waters score (worst 0–100 best)	49.1	2019	●	↗
Fish caught from overexploited or collapsed stocks (% of total catch)	NA	NA	●	●
Fish caught by trawling (%)	8.0	2014	●	→
Marine biodiversity threats embodied in imports (per million population)	0.0	2018	●	●

SDG15 – Life on Land

	Value	Year	Rating	Trend
Mean area that is protected in terrestrial sites important to biodiversity (%)	74.3	2018	●	↑
Mean area that is protected in freshwater sites important to biodiversity (%)	100.0	2018	●	↑
Red List Index of species survival (worst 0–1 best)	1.0	2019	●	↑
Permanent deforestation (% of forest area, 5-year average)	0.1	2018	●	●
Terrestrial and freshwater biodiversity threats embodied in imports (per million population)	0.3	2018	●	●

SDG16 – Peace, Justice and Strong Institutions

	Value	Year	Rating	Trend
Homicides (per 100,000 population) *	9.3	2015	●	●
Unsentenced detainees (% of prison population)	60.0	2015	●	●
Percentage of population who feel safe walking alone at night in the city or area where they live (%)	44.8	2019	●	↓
Property Rights (worst 1–7 best)	NA	NA	●	●
Birth registrations with civil authority (% of children under age 5)	95.9	2018	●	●
Corruption Perception Index (worst 0–100 best)	19	2019	●	↓
Children involved in child labor (% of population aged 5 to 14)	23.3	2016	●	●
Exports of major conventional weapons (TIV constant million USD per 100,000 population) *	0.0	2019	●	●
Press Freedom Index (best 0–100 worst)	36.0	2019	●	↓

SDG17 – Partnerships for the Goals

	Value	Year	Rating	Trend
Government spending on health and education (% of GDP)	6.1	2015	●	↑
For high-income and all OECD DAC countries: International concessional public finance, including official development assistance (% of GNI)	NA	NA	●	●
Other countries: Government revenue excluding grants (% of GDP)	23.3	2016	●	↓
Corporate Tax Haven Score (best 0–100 worst) *	0.0	2019	●	●

* Imputed data point

5. Country Profiles

▼ OVERALL PERFORMANCE

Index score

75.1

Regional average score

70.4

SDG Global rank 35 (OF 166)

▲ AVERAGE PERFORMANCE BY SDG

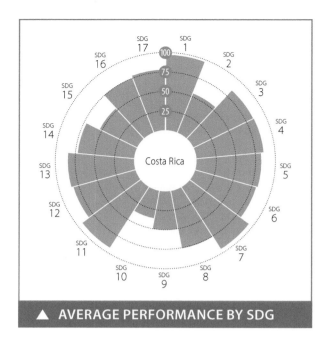

Costa Rica

▼ SPILLOVER INDEX

100 (best) to 0 (worst)

▼ CURRENT ASSESSMENT – SDG DASHBOARD

■ Major challenges ■ Significant challenges ■ Challenges remain ■ SDG achieved ■ Information unavailable

▼ SDG TRENDS

1 NO POVERTY	2 ZERO HUNGER	3 GOOD HEALTH AND WELL-BEING	4 QUALITY EDUCATION	5 GENDER EQUALITY	6 CLEAN WATER AND SANITATION	7 AFFORDABLE AND CLEAN ENERGY	8 DECENT WORK AND ECONOMIC GROWTH	9 INDUSTRY, INNOVATION AND INFRASTRUCTURE
↑	→	↗	↑	↗	↑	↑	↗	↗

10 REDUCED INEQUALITIES	11 SUSTAINABLE CITIES AND COMMUNITIES	12 RESPONSIBLE CONSUMPTION AND PRODUCTION	13 CLIMATE ACTION	14 LIFE BELOW WATER	15 LIFE ON LAND	16 PEACE, JUSTICE AND STRONG INSTITUTIONS	17 PARTNERSHIPS FOR THE GOALS
●	↑	●	↗	↗	↓	↗	↗

↓ Decreasing → Stagnating ↗ Moderately improving ↑ On track or maintaining SDG achievement ● Information unavailable

Notes: The full title of Goal 2 "Zero Hunger" is "End hunger, achieve food security and improved nutrition and promote sustainable agriculture".
The full title of each SDG is available here: https://sustainabledevelopment.un.org/topics/sustainabledevelopmentgoals

SDG1 – No Poverty

	Value	Year	Rating	Trend
Poverty headcount ratio at $1.90/day (%)	0.8	2020	●	↑
Poverty headcount ratio at $3.20/day (%)	1.9	2020	●	↑

SDG2 – Zero Hunger

	Value	Year	Rating	Trend
Prevalence of undernourishment (%)	4.8	2017	●	↑
Prevalence of stunting in children under 5 years of age (%)	5.6	2008	●	↑
Prevalence of wasting in children under 5 years of age (%)	1.0	2008	●	↑
Prevalence of obesity, BMI ≥ 30 (% of adult population)	25.7	2016	●	↓
Human Trophic Level (best 2–3 worst)	2.4	2017	●	→
Cereal yield (tonnes per hectare of harvested land)	4.2	2017	●	↑
Sustainable Nitrogen Management Index (best 0–1.41 worst)	1.1	2015	●	↓

SDG3 – Good Health and Well-Being

	Value	Year	Rating	Trend
Maternal mortality rate (per 100,000 live births)	27	2017	●	↑
Neonatal mortality rate (per 1,000 live births)	5.9	2018	●	↑
Mortality rate, under-5 (per 1,000 live births)	8.8	2018	●	↑
Incidence of tuberculosis (per 100,000 population)	10.0	2018	●	↑
New HIV infections (per 1,000 uninfected population)	0.2	2018	●	↓
Age-standardized death rate due to cardiovascular disease, cancer, diabetes, or chronic respiratory disease in adults aged 30–70 years (%)	11.5	2016	●	↑
Age-standardized death rate attributable to household air pollution and ambient air pollution (per 100,000 population)	23	2016	●	●
Traffic deaths (per 100,000 population)	16.7	2016	●	↓
Life expectancy at birth (years)	79.6	2016	●	↑
Adolescent fertility rate (births per 1,000 adolescent females aged 15 to 19)	53.5	2017	●	↗
Births attended by skilled health personnel (%)	90.0	2015	●	↓
Percentage of surviving infants who received 2 WHO-recommended vaccines (%)	94	2018	●	↑
Universal health coverage (UHC) index of service coverage (worst 0–100 best)	77.0	2017	●	↑
Subjective well-being (average ladder score, worst 0–10 best)	7.0	2019	●	↑

SDG4 – Quality Education

	Value	Year	Rating	Trend
Net primary enrollment rate (%)	97.3	2018	●	↑
Lower secondary completion rate (%)	70.3	2018	●	↑
Literacy rate (% of population aged 15 to 24)	99.4	2018	●	●

SDG5 – Gender Equality

	Value	Year	Rating	Trend
Demand for family planning satisfied by modern methods (% of females aged 15 to 49 who are married or in unions)	89.1	2011	●	↑
Ratio of female-to-male mean years of education received (%)	103.5	2018	●	↑
Ratio of female-to-male labor force participation rate (%)	61.6	2019	●	↓
Seats held by women in national parliament (%)	45.6	2020	●	↑

SDG6 – Clean Water and Sanitation

	Value	Year	Rating	Trend
Population using at least basic drinking water services (%)	99.7	2017	●	↑
Population using at least basic sanitation services (%)	97.8	2017	●	↑
Freshwater withdrawal (% of available freshwater resources)	4.7	2015	●	●
Anthropogenic wastewater that receives treatment (%)	9.7	2018	●	●
Scarce water consumption embodied in imports (m³/capita)	4.8	2013	●	↑

SDG7 – Affordable and Clean Energy

	Value	Year	Rating	Trend
Population with access to electricity (%)	99.6	2017	●	↑
Population with access to clean fuels and technology for cooking (%)	93.5	2016	●	↑
CO_2 emissions from fuel combustion for electricity and heating per total electricity output (MtCO₂/TWh)	0.7	2017	●	↑

SDG8 – Decent Work and Economic Growth

	Value	Year	Rating	Trend
Adjusted GDP growth (%)	-1.1	2018	●	●
Victims of modern slavery (per 1,000 population)	1.3	2018	●	●
Adults with an account at a bank or other financial institution or with a mobile-money-service provider (% of population aged 15 or over)	67.8	2017	●	↑
Unemployment rate (% of total labor force)	11.9	2019	●	↓
Fatal work-related accidents embodied in imports (per 100,000 population)	0.5	2010	●	↑

SDG9 – Industry, Innovation and Infrastructure

	Value	Year	Rating	Trend
Population using the internet (%)	74.1	2018	●	↑
Mobile broadband subscriptions (per 100 population)	97.2	2018	●	↑
Logistics Performance Index: Quality of trade and transport-related infrastructure (worst 1–5 best)	2.5	2018	●	→
The Times Higher Education Universities Ranking: Average score of top 3 universities (worst 0–100 best)	31.8	2020	●	●
Scientific and technical journal articles (per 1,000 population)	0.1	2018	●	→
Expenditure on research and development (% of GDP)	0.5	2016	●	↓

SDG10 – Reduced Inequalities

	Value	Year	Rating	Trend
Gini coefficient adjusted for top income	50.4	2017	●	●

SDG11 – Sustainable Cities and Communities

	Value	Year	Rating	Trend
Annual mean concentration of particulate matter of less than 2.5 microns in diameter (PM2.5) (µg/m³)	15.7	2017	●	↑
Access to improved water source, piped (% of urban population)	99.0	2017	●	↑
Satisfaction with public transport (%)	76.2	2019	●	↑

SDG12 – Responsible Consumption and Production

	Value	Year	Rating	Trend
Municipal solid waste (kg/capita/day)	1.0	2014	●	●
Electronic waste (kg/capita)	9.7	2016	●	●
Production-based SO_2 emissions (kg/capita)	31.7	2012	●	●
SO_2 emissions embodied in imports (kg/capita)	4.9	2012	●	●
Production-based nitrogen emissions (kg/capita)	14.7	2010	●	●
Nitrogen emissions embodied in imports (kg/capita)	4.8	2010	●	●

SDG13 – Climate Action

	Value	Year	Rating	Trend
Energy-related CO_2 emissions (tCO₂/capita)	1.8	2017	●	↑
CO_2 emissions embodied in imports (tCO₂/capita)	0.8	2015	●	→
CO_2 emissions embodied in fossil fuel exports (kg/capita)	NA	NA	●	●

SDG14 – Life Below Water

	Value	Year	Rating	Trend
Mean area that is protected in marine sites important to biodiversity (%)	54.9	2018	●	↑
Ocean Health Index: Clean Waters score (worst 0–100 best)	72.6	2019	●	↑
Fish caught from overexploited or collapsed stocks (% of total catch)	25.1	2014	●	↓
Fish caught by trawling (%)	16.3	2014	●	↗
Marine biodiversity threats embodied in imports (per million population)	0.2	2018	●	●

SDG15 – Life on Land

	Value	Year	Rating	Trend
Mean area that is protected in terrestrial sites important to biodiversity (%)	41.7	2018	●	→
Mean area that is protected in freshwater sites important to biodiversity (%)	0.0	2018	●	→
Red List Index of species survival (worst 0–1 best)	0.8	2019	●	↓
Permanent deforestation (% of forest area, 5-year average)	0.2	2018	●	●
Terrestrial and freshwater biodiversity threats embodied in imports (per million population)	1.6	2018	●	●

SDG16 – Peace, Justice and Strong Institutions

	Value	Year	Rating	Trend
Homicides (per 100,000 population)	12.3	2017	●	↓
Unsentenced detainees (% of prison population)	20.6	2018	●	↑
Percentage of population who feel safe walking alone at night in the city or area where they live (%)	47.8	2019	●	↓
Property Rights (worst 1–7 best)	5.0	2019	●	●
Birth registrations with civil authority (% of children under age 5)	99.6	2018	●	●
Corruption Perception Index (worst 0–100 best)	56	2019	●	↗
Children involved in child labor (% of population aged 5 to 14)	4.1	2016	●	●
Exports of major conventional weapons (TIV constant million USD per 100,000 population)	* 0.0	2019	●	●
Press Freedom Index (best 0–100 worst)	12.2	2019	●	↑

SDG17 – Partnerships for the Goals

	Value	Year	Rating	Trend
Government spending on health and education (% of GDP)	12.7	2016	●	↑
For high-income and all OECD DAC countries: International concessional public finance, including official development assistance (% of GNI)	NA	NA	●	●
Other countries: Government revenue excluding grants (% of GDP)	25.2	2018	●	↗
Corporate Tax Haven Score (best 0–100 worst)	* 0.0	2019	●	●

* Imputed data point

5. Country Profiles

▼ OVERALL PERFORMANCE

Index score

57.9

Regional average score

53.1

SDG Global rank 128 (OF 166)

Côte d'Ivoire

▲ AVERAGE PERFORMANCE BY SDG

▼ SPILLOVER INDEX

100 (best) to 0 (worst)

▼ CURRENT ASSESSMENT – SDG DASHBOARD

■ Major challenges   ■ Significant challenges   ■ Challenges remain   ■ SDG achieved   ■ Information unavailable

▼ SDG TRENDS

↓ Decreasing   → Stagnating   ↗ Moderately improving   ↑ On track or maintaining SDG achievement   ● Information unavailable

Notes: The full title of Goal 2 "Zero Hunger" is "End hunger, achieve food security and improved nutrition and promote sustainable agriculture".
The full title of each SDG is available here: https://sustainabledevelopment.un.org/topics/sustainabledevelopmentgoals

SDG1 – No Poverty

	Value	Year	Rating	Trend
Poverty headcount ratio at $1.90/day (%)	18.3	2020	●	↑
Poverty headcount ratio at $3.20/day (%)	40.8	2020	●	↗

SDG2 – Zero Hunger

	Value	Year	Rating	Trend
Prevalence of undernourishment (%)	19.0	2017	●	↗
Prevalence of stunting in children under 5 years of age (%)	21.6	2016	●	↗
Prevalence of wasting in children under 5 years of age (%)	6.0	2016	●	↑
Prevalence of obesity, BMI ≥ 30 (% of adult population)	10.3	2016	●	↓
Human Trophic Level (best 2–3 worst)	2.1	2017	●	↑
Cereal yield (tonnes per hectare of harvested land)	2.1	2017	●	→
Sustainable Nitrogen Management Index (best 0–1.41 worst)	0.9	2015	●	→

SDG3 – Good Health and Well-Being

	Value	Year	Rating	Trend
Maternal mortality rate (per 100,000 live births)	617	2017	●	↗
Neonatal mortality rate (per 1,000 live births)	33.5	2018	●	→
Mortality rate, under-5 (per 1,000 live births)	80.9	2018	●	↗
Incidence of tuberculosis (per 100,000 population)	142.0	2018	●	↗
New HIV infections (per 1,000 uninfected population)	0.7	2018	●	↑
Age-standardized death rate due to cardiovascular disease, cancer, diabetes, or chronic respiratory disease in adults aged 30–70 years (%)	29.1	2016	●	↓
Age-standardized death rate attributable to household air pollution and ambient air pollution (per 100,000 population)	269	2016	●	●
Traffic deaths (per 100,000 population)	23.6	2016	●	→
Life expectancy at birth (years)	54.6	2016	●	→
Adolescent fertility rate (births per 1,000 adolescent females aged 15 to 19)	117.6	2017	●	→
Births attended by skilled health personnel (%)	73.6	2016	●	↑
Percentage of surviving infants who received 2 WHO-recommended vaccines (%)	71	2018	●	↑
Universal health coverage (UHC) index of service coverage (worst 0–100 best)	47.0	2017	●	↗
Subjective well-being (average ladder score, worst 0–10 best)	5.4	2019	●	↑

SDG4 – Quality Education

	Value	Year	Rating	Trend
Net primary enrollment rate (%)	90.3	2018	●	↑
Lower secondary completion rate (%)	49.4	2018	●	↑
Literacy rate (% of population aged 15 to 24)	58.4	2018	●	●

SDG5 – Gender Equality

	Value	Year	Rating	Trend
Demand for family planning satisfied by modern methods (% of females aged 15 to 49 who are married or in unions)	39.4	2018	●	→
Ratio of female-to-male mean years of education received (%)	65.1	2018	●	→
Ratio of female-to-male labor force participation rate (%)	73.4	2019	●	↑
Seats held by women in national parliament (%)	11.4	2020	●	→

SDG6 – Clean Water and Sanitation

	Value	Year	Rating	Trend
Population using at least basic drinking water services (%)	72.9	2017	●	→
Population using at least basic sanitation services (%)	32.1	2017	●	→
Freshwater withdrawal (% of available freshwater resources)	5.1	2015	●	●
Anthropogenic wastewater that receives treatment (%)	0.6	2018	●	●
Scarce water consumption embodied in imports (m³/capita)	0.4	2013	●	↑

SDG7 – Affordable and Clean Energy

	Value	Year	Rating	Trend
Population with access to electricity (%)	65.6	2017	●	↗
Population with access to clean fuels and technology for cooking (%)	18.2	2016	●	↓
CO_2 emissions from fuel combustion for electricity and heating per total electricity output (MtCO$_2$/TWh)	1.1	2017	●	↑

SDG8 – Decent Work and Economic Growth

	Value	Year	Rating	Trend
Adjusted GDP growth (%)	-0.7	2018	●	●
Victims of modern slavery (per 1,000 population)	5.9	2018	●	●
Adults with an account at a bank or other financial institution or with a mobile-money-service provider (% of population aged 15 or over)	41.3	2017	●	↗
Unemployment rate (% of total labor force)	3.3	2019	●	↑
Fatal work-related accidents embodied in imports (per 100,000 population)	0.0	2010	●	↑

SDG9 – Industry, Innovation and Infrastructure

	Value	Year	Rating	Trend
Population using the internet (%)	46.8	2018	●	↑
Mobile broadband subscriptions (per 100 population)	53.6	2018	●	↑
Logistics Performance Index: Quality of trade and transport-related infrastructure (worst 1–5 best)	2.9	2018	●	↑
The Times Higher Education Universities Ranking: Average score of top 3 universities (worst 0–100 best) *	0.0	2020	●	●
Scientific and technical journal articles (per 1,000 population)	0.0	2018	●	→
Expenditure on research and development (% of GDP)	0.1	2016	●	●

SDG10 – Reduced Inequalities

	Value	Year	Rating	Trend
Gini coefficient adjusted for top income	47.0	2015	●	●

SDG11 – Sustainable Cities and Communities

	Value	Year	Rating	Trend
Annual mean concentration of particulate matter of less than 2.5 microns in diameter (PM2.5) (µg/m³)	25.9	2017	●	↓
Access to improved water source, piped (% of urban population)	62.4	2017	●	↓
Satisfaction with public transport (%)	47.6	2019	●	↑

SDG12 – Responsible Consumption and Production

	Value	Year	Rating	Trend
Municipal solid waste (kg/capita/day)	1.0	2010	●	●
Electronic waste (kg/capita)	0.9	2016	●	●
Production-based SO_2 emissions (kg/capita)	5.7	2012	●	●
SO_2 emissions embodied in imports (kg/capita)	0.3	2012	●	●
Production-based nitrogen emissions (kg/capita)	4.2	2010	●	●
Nitrogen emissions embodied in imports (kg/capita)	0.3	2010	●	●

SDG13 – Climate Action

	Value	Year	Rating	Trend
Energy-related CO_2 emissions (tCO$_2$/capita)	0.5	2017	●	↑
CO_2 emissions embodied in imports (tCO$_2$/capita)	0.0	2015	●	↑
CO_2 emissions embodied in fossil fuel exports (kg/capita)	0.0	2018	●	●

SDG14 – Life Below Water

	Value	Year	Rating	Trend
Mean area that is protected in marine sites important to biodiversity (%)	NA	NA	●	●
Ocean Health Index: Clean Waters score (worst 0–100 best)	40.7	2019	●	↓
Fish caught from overexploited or collapsed stocks (% of total catch)	25.8	2014	●	↓
Fish caught by trawling (%)	4.3	2014	●	↑
Marine biodiversity threats embodied in imports (per million population)	0.0	2018	●	●

SDG15 – Life on Land

	Value	Year	Rating	Trend
Mean area that is protected in terrestrial sites important to biodiversity (%)	71.2	2018	●	↑
Mean area that is protected in freshwater sites important to biodiversity (%)	75.6	2018	●	↑
Red List Index of species survival (worst 0–1 best)	0.9	2019	●	→
Permanent deforestation (% of forest area, 5-year average)	1.1	2018	●	●
Terrestrial and freshwater biodiversity threats embodied in imports (per million population)	0.0	2018	●	●

SDG16 – Peace, Justice and Strong Institutions

		Value	Year	Rating	Trend
Homicides (per 100,000 population)	*	11.6	2015	●	●
Unsentenced detainees (% of prison population)		34.7	2018	●	↑
Percentage of population who feel safe walking alone at night in the city or area where they live		45.5	2019	●	↓
Property Rights (worst 1–7 best)		3.9	2019	●	●
Birth registrations with civil authority (% of children under age 5)		71.7	2018	●	●
Corruption Perception Index (worst 0–100 best)		35	2019	●	→
Children involved in child labor (% of population aged 5 to 14)		26.4	2016	●	●
Exports of major conventional weapons (TIV constant million USD per 100,000 population)		0.0	2019	●	●
Press Freedom Index (best 0–100 worst)		29.5	2019	●	↑

SDG17 – Partnerships for the Goals

		Value	Year	Rating	Trend
Government spending on health and education (% of GDP)		6.5	2016	●	↗
For high-income and all OECD DAC countries: International concessional public finance, including official development assistance (% of GNI)		NA	NA	●	●
Other countries: Government revenue excluding grants (% of GDP)		16.5	2017	●	↗
Corporate Tax Haven Score (best 0–100 worst)	*	0.0	2019	●	●

* Imputed data point

5. Country Profiles

CROATIA

▼ OVERALL PERFORMANCE

Index score
78.4

Regional average score
70.9

SDG Global rank **19** (OF 166)

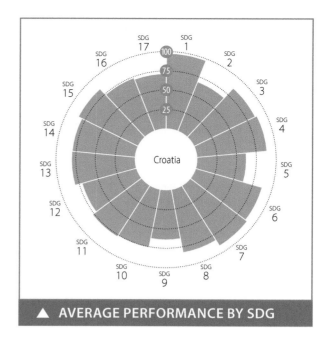

▲ AVERAGE PERFORMANCE BY SDG

▼ SPILLOVER INDEX

100 (best) to 0 (worst)

▼ CURRENT ASSESSMENT – SDG DASHBOARD

■ Major challenges   ■ Significant challenges   ■ Challenges remain   ■ SDG achieved   ■ Information unavailable

▼ SDG TRENDS

1 NO POVERTY	2 ZERO HUNGER	3 GOOD HEALTH AND WELL-BEING	4 QUALITY EDUCATION	5 GENDER EQUALITY	6 CLEAN WATER AND SANITATION	7 AFFORDABLE AND CLEAN ENERGY	8 DECENT WORK AND ECONOMIC GROWTH	9 INDUSTRY, INNOVATION AND INFRASTRUCTURE
↑	↗	↗	↓	↗	↑	↗	↑	↗

10 REDUCED INEQUALITIES	11 SUSTAINABLE CITIES AND COMMUNITIES	12 RESPONSIBLE CONSUMPTION AND PRODUCTION	13 CLIMATE ACTION	14 LIFE BELOW WATER	15 LIFE ON LAND	16 PEACE, JUSTICE AND STRONG INSTITUTIONS	17 PARTNERSHIPS FOR THE GOALS
●	→	●	→	↗	↑	↗	●

↓ Decreasing   → Stagnating   ↗ Moderately improving   ↑ On track or maintaining SDG achievement   ● Information unavailable

Notes: The full title of Goal 2 "Zero Hunger" is "End hunger, achieve food security and improved nutrition and promote sustainable agriculture".
The full title of each SDG is available here: https://sustainabledevelopment.un.org/topics/sustainabledevelopmentgoals

CROATIA

SDG1 – No Poverty

	Value	Year	Rating	Trend
Poverty headcount ratio at $1.90/day (%)	0.6	2020	●	↑
Poverty headcount ratio at $3.20/day (%)	1.1	2020	●	↑

SDG2 – Zero Hunger

	Value	Year	Rating	Trend
Prevalence of undernourishment (%)	2.5	2017	●	↑
Prevalence of stunting in children under 5 years of age (%) *	2.6	2016	●	↑
Prevalence of wasting in children under 5 years of age (%) *	0.7	2016	●	↑
Prevalence of obesity, BMI ≥ 30 (% of adult population)	24.4	2016	●	↓
Human Trophic Level (best 2–3 worst)	2.4	2017	●	↑
Cereal yield (tonnes per hectare of harvested land)	5.7	2017	●	↑
Sustainable Nitrogen Management Index (best 0–1.41 worst)	0.5	2015	●	↑

SDG3 – Good Health and Well-Being

	Value	Year	Rating	Trend
Maternal mortality rate (per 100,000 live births)	8	2017	●	↑
Neonatal mortality rate (per 1,000 live births)	2.6	2018	●	↑
Mortality rate, under-5 (per 1,000 live births)	4.7	2018	●	↑
Incidence of tuberculosis (per 100,000 population)	8.4	2018	●	↑
New HIV infections (per 1,000 uninfected population)	0.0	2018	●	↑
Age-standardized death rate due to cardiovascular disease, cancer, diabetes, or chronic respiratory disease in adults aged 30–70 years (%)	16.7	2016	●	↑
Age-standardized death rate attributable to household air pollution and ambient air pollution (per 100,000 population)	35	2016	●	●
Traffic deaths (per 100,000 population)	8.1	2016	●	↑
Life expectancy at birth (years)	78.3	2016	●	↑
Adolescent fertility rate (births per 1,000 adolescent females aged 15 to 19)	8.7	2017	●	↑
Births attended by skilled health personnel (%)	99.9	2015	●	↑
Percentage of surviving infants who received 2 WHO-recommended vaccines (%)	93	2018	●	↑
Universal health coverage (UHC) index of service coverage (worst 0–100 best)	71.0	2017	●	→
Subjective well-being (average ladder score, worst 0–10 best)	5.5	2018	●	↑

SDG4 – Quality Education

	Value	Year	Rating	Trend
Net primary enrollment rate (%)	88.0	2017	●	↓
Lower secondary completion rate (%)	93.1	2016	●	●
Literacy rate (% of population aged 15 to 24)	99.7	2011	●	●

SDG5 – Gender Equality

	Value	Year	Rating	Trend
Demand for family planning satisfied by modern methods (% of females aged 15 to 49 who are married or in unions) *	61.5	2017	●	↗
Ratio of female-to-male mean years of education received (%)	90.8	2018	●	→
Ratio of female-to-male labor force participation rate (%)	78.8	2019	●	↑
Seats held by women in national parliament (%)	19.2	2020	●	→

SDG6 – Clean Water and Sanitation

	Value	Year	Rating	Trend
Population using at least basic drinking water services (%)	99.6	2017	●	↑
Population using at least basic sanitation services (%)	96.5	2017	●	↑
Freshwater withdrawal (% of available freshwater resources)	1.5	2015	●	●
Anthropogenic wastewater that receives treatment (%)	51.7	2018	●	●
Scarce water consumption embodied in imports (m3/capita)	13.2	2013	●	↑

SDG7 – Affordable and Clean Energy

	Value	Year	Rating	Trend
Population with access to electricity (%)	100.0	2017	●	↑
Population with access to clean fuels and technology for cooking (%)	92.7	2016	●	↑
CO_2 emissions from fuel combustion for electricity and heating per total electricity output (MtCO2/TWh)	1.4	2017	●	→

SDG8 – Decent Work and Economic Growth

	Value	Year	Rating	Trend
Adjusted GDP growth (%)	1.5	2018	●	●
Victims of modern slavery (per 1,000 population)	6.0	2018	●	●
Adults with an account at a bank or other financial institution or with a mobile-money-service provider (% of population aged 15 or over)	86.1	2017	●	↑
Unemployment rate (% of total labor force)	6.9	2019	●	↑
Fatal work-related accidents embodied in imports (per 100,000 population)	0.6	2010	●	↑

SDG9 – Industry, Innovation and Infrastructure

	Value	Year	Rating	Trend
Population using the internet (%)	75.3	2018	●	↑
Mobile broadband subscriptions (per 100 population)	79.5	2018	●	↑
Logistics Performance Index: Quality of trade and transport-related infrastructure (worst 1–5 best)	3.0	2018	●	↑
The Times Higher Education Universities Ranking: Average score of top 3 universities (worst 0–100 best)	24.1	2020	●	●
Scientific and technical journal articles (per 1,000 population)	1.0	2018	●	↑
Expenditure on research and development (% of GDP)	0.9	2017	●	↗

SDG10 – Reduced Inequalities

	Value	Year	Rating	Trend
Gini coefficient adjusted for top income	36.6	2015	●	●

SDG11 – Sustainable Cities and Communities

	Value	Year	Rating	Trend
Annual mean concentration of particulate matter of less than 2.5 microns in diameter (PM2.5) ($\mu g/m^3$)	17.9	2017	●	→
Access to improved water source, piped (% of urban population)	99.0	2017	●	↑
Satisfaction with public transport (%)	47.8	2018	●	↓

SDG12 – Responsible Consumption and Production

	Value	Year	Rating	Trend
Municipal solid waste (kg/capita/day)	1.9	2015	●	●
Electronic waste (kg/capita)	12.6	2016	●	●
Production-based SO_2 emissions (kg/capita)	57.6	2012	●	●
SO_2 emissions embodied in imports (kg/capita)	9.5	2012	●	●
Production-based nitrogen emissions (kg/capita)	20.5	2010	●	●
Nitrogen emissions embodied in imports (kg/capita)	5.7	2010	●	●

SDG13 – Climate Action

	Value	Year	Rating	Trend
Energy-related CO_2 emissions (tCO2/capita)	4.2	2017	●	→
CO_2 emissions embodied in imports (tCO2/capita)	1.4	2015	●	→
CO_2 emissions embodied in fossil fuel exports (kg/capita)	115.8	2018	●	●

SDG14 – Life Below Water

	Value	Year	Rating	Trend
Mean area that is protected in marine sites important to biodiversity (%)	75.2	2018	●	↑
Ocean Health Index: Clean Waters score (worst 0–100 best)	64.6	2019	●	↗
Fish caught from overexploited or collapsed stocks (% of total catch)	7.0	2014	●	↑
Fish caught by trawling (%)	17.9	2014	●	↑
Marine biodiversity threats embodied in imports (per million population)	0.0	2018	●	●

SDG15 – Life on Land

	Value	Year	Rating	Trend
Mean area that is protected in terrestrial sites important to biodiversity (%)	74.1	2018	●	↑
Mean area that is protected in freshwater sites important to biodiversity (%)	86.8	2018	●	↑
Red List Index of species survival (worst 0–1 best)	0.9	2019	●	↑
Permanent deforestation (% of forest area, 5-year average)	0.0	2018	●	●
Terrestrial and freshwater biodiversity threats embodied in imports (per million population)	1.4	2018	●	●

SDG16 – Peace, Justice and Strong Institutions

	Value	Year	Rating	Trend
Homicides (per 100,000 population)	1.1	2017	●	↑
Unsentenced detainees (% of prison population)	27.6	2018	●	↑
Percentage of population who feel safe walking alone at night in the city or area where they live (%)	75.1	2018	●	↑
Property Rights (worst 1–7 best)	3.8	2019	●	●
Birth registrations with civil authority (% of children under age 5)	100.0	2018	●	●
Corruption Perception Index (worst 0–100 best)	47	2019	●	↓
Children involved in child labor (% of population aged 5 to 14)	NA	NA	●	●
Exports of major conventional weapons (TIV constant million USD per 100,000 population)	0.1	2019	●	●
Press Freedom Index (best 0–100 worst)	29.0	2019	●	↑

SDG17 – Partnerships for the Goals

	Value	Year	Rating	Trend
Government spending on health and education (% of GDP)	10.1	2013	●	●
For high-income and all OECD DAC countries: International concessional public finance, including official development assistance (% of GNI)	NA	NA	●	●
Other countries: Government revenue excluding grants (% of GDP)	NA	NA	●	●
Corporate Tax Haven Score (best 0–100 worst)	54.5	2019	●	●

* Imputed data point

CUBA

▼ OVERALL PERFORMANCE

Index score

72.6

Regional average score

70.4

SDG Global rank **55** (OF 166)

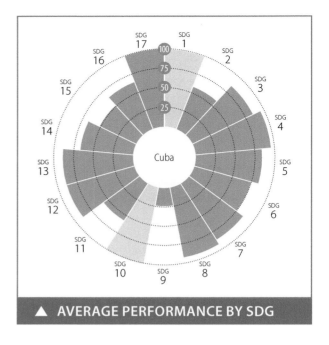

Cuba

▲ AVERAGE PERFORMANCE BY SDG

▼ SPILLOVER INDEX

100 (best) to 0 (worst)

▼ CURRENT ASSESSMENT – SDG DASHBOARD

■ Major challenges   ■ Significant challenges   ■ Challenges remain   ■ SDG achieved   ■ Information unavailable

▼ SDG TRENDS

↓ Decreasing   → Stagnating   ↗ Moderately improving   ↑ On track or maintaining SDG achievement   ● Information unavailable

Notes: The full title of Goal 2 "Zero Hunger" is "End hunger, achieve food security and improved nutrition and promote sustainable agriculture".
The full title of each SDG is available here: https://sustainabledevelopment.un.org/topics/sustainabledevelopmentgoals

CUBA

SDG1 – No Poverty		Value	Year	Rating	Trend
Poverty headcount ratio at $1.90/day (%)	*	NA	NA	●	●
Poverty headcount ratio at $3.20/day (%)	*	NA	NA	●	●

SDG2 – Zero Hunger	Value	Year	Rating	Trend
Prevalence of undernourishment (%)	2.5	2017	●	↑
Prevalence of stunting in children under 5 years of age (%)	7.0	2000	●	↑
Prevalence of wasting in children under 5 years of age (%)	2.4	2000	●	↑
Prevalence of obesity, BMI ≥ 30 (% of adult population)	24.6	2016	●	↓
Human Trophic Level (best 2–3 worst)	2.2	2017	●	→
Cereal yield (tonnes per hectare of harvested land)	2.9	2017	●	↑
Sustainable Nitrogen Management Index (best 0–1.41 worst)	1.1	2015	●	↓

SDG3 – Good Health and Well-Being	Value	Year	Rating	Trend
Maternal mortality rate (per 100,000 live births)	36	2017	●	↑
Neonatal mortality rate (per 1,000 live births)	2.1	2018	●	↑
Mortality rate, under-5 (per 1,000 live births)	5.0	2018	●	↑
Incidence of tuberculosis (per 100,000 population)	7.2	2018	●	↑
New HIV infections (per 1,000 uninfected population)	0.2	2018	●	↑
Age-standardized death rate due to cardiovascular disease, cancer, diabetes, or chronic respiratory disease in adults aged 30–70 years (%)	16.4	2016	◔	↑
Age-standardized death rate attributable to household air pollution and ambient air pollution (per 100,000 population)	50	2016	◔	●
Traffic deaths (per 100,000 population)	8.5	2016	◔	↓
Life expectancy at birth (years)	79.0	2016	◔	↗
Adolescent fertility rate (births per 1,000 adolescent females aged 15 to 19)	51.6	2017	●	→
Births attended by skilled health personnel (%)	99.9	2016	●	↑
Percentage of surviving infants who received 2 WHO-recommended vaccines (%)	99	2018	●	↑
Universal health coverage (UHC) index of service coverage (worst 0–100 best)	83.0	2017	●	↑
Subjective well-being (average ladder score, worst 0–10 best)	5.4	2006	●	●

SDG4 – Quality Education	Value	Year	Rating	Trend
Net primary enrollment rate (%)	97.7	2018	●	↑
Lower secondary completion rate (%)	93.0	2018	●	↑
Literacy rate (% of population aged 15 to 24)	99.9	2012	●	●

SDG5 – Gender Equality	Value	Year	Rating	Trend
Demand for family planning satisfied by modern methods (% of females aged 15 to 49 who are married or in unions)	88.8	2014	●	↑
Ratio of female-to-male mean years of education received (%)	100.9	2018	●	↑
Ratio of female-to-male labor force participation rate (%)	59.3	2019	●	↓
Seats held by women in national parliament (%)	53.2	2020	●	↑

SDG6 – Clean Water and Sanitation	Value	Year	Rating	Trend
Population using at least basic drinking water services (%)	95.3	2017	◔	→
Population using at least basic sanitation services (%)	92.8	2017	◔	↑
Freshwater withdrawal (% of available freshwater resources)	23.9	2015	●	●
Anthropogenic wastewater that receives treatment (%)	3.6	2018	●	●
Scarce water consumption embodied in imports (m³/capita)	2.3	2013	●	↑

SDG7 – Affordable and Clean Energy	Value	Year	Rating	Trend
Population with access to electricity (%)	100.0	2017	●	↑
Population with access to clean fuels and technology for cooking (%)	79.4	2016	◔	↑
CO$_2$ emissions from fuel combustion for electricity and heating per total electricity output (MtCO$_2$/TWh)	1.4	2017	●	↑

SDG8 – Decent Work and Economic Growth	Value	Year	Rating	Trend
Adjusted GDP growth (%)	NA	NA	●	●
Victims of modern slavery (per 1,000 population)	3.8	2018	●	●
Adults with an account at a bank or other financial institution or with a mobile-money-service provider (% of population aged 15 or over)	NA	NA	●	●
Unemployment rate (% of total labor force)	1.6	2019	●	↑
Fatal work-related accidents embodied in imports (per 100,000 population)	0.2	2010	●	↑

SDG9 – Industry, Innovation and Infrastructure	Value	Year	Rating	Trend
Population using the internet (%)	57.1	2017	●	↑
Mobile broadband subscriptions (per 100 population)	14.3	2018	●	↗
Logistics Performance Index: Quality of trade and transport-related infrastructure (worst 1–5 best)	2.0	2018	●	↗
The Times Higher Education Universities Ranking: Average score of top 3 universities (worst 0–100 best)	16.4	2020	◌	●
Scientific and technical journal articles (per 1,000 population)	0.1	2018	●	↓
Expenditure on research and development (% of GDP)	0.3	2016	●	↓

SDG10 – Reduced Inequalities	Value	Year	Rating	Trend
Gini coefficient adjusted for top income	NA	NA	●	●

SDG11 – Sustainable Cities and Communities	Value	Year	Rating	Trend
Annual mean concentration of particulate matter of less than 2.5 microns in diameter (PM2.5) (µg/m³)	19.7	2017	●	↗
Access to improved water source, piped (% of urban population)	86.1	2017	●	→
Satisfaction with public transport (%)	7.9	2006	●	●

SDG12 – Responsible Consumption and Production	Value	Year	Rating	Trend
Municipal solid waste (kg/capita/day)	0.8	2007	●	●
Electronic waste (kg/capita)	NA	NA	●	●
Production-based SO$_2$ emissions (kg/capita)	55.8	2012	◌	●
SO$_2$ emissions embodied in imports (kg/capita)	1.9	2012	●	●
Production-based nitrogen emissions (kg/capita)	20.6	2010	◌	●
Nitrogen emissions embodied in imports (kg/capita)	1.2	2010	●	●

SDG13 – Climate Action	Value	Year	Rating	Trend
Energy-related CO$_2$ emissions (tCO$_2$/capita)	3.3	2017	●	→
CO$_2$ emissions embodied in imports (tCO$_2$/capita)	0.3	2015	●	↑
CO$_2$ emissions embodied in fossil fuel exports (kg/capita)	NA	NA	●	●

SDG14 – Life Below Water	Value	Year	Rating	Trend
Mean area that is protected in marine sites important to biodiversity (%)	60.0	2018	●	↑
Ocean Health Index: Clean Waters score (worst 0–100 best)	58.1	2019	●	↓
Fish caught from overexploited or collapsed stocks (% of total catch)	58.0	2014	●	→
Fish caught by trawling (%)	2.9	2014	●	↑
Marine biodiversity threats embodied in imports (per million population)	0.0	2018	●	●

SDG15 – Life on Land	Value	Year	Rating	Trend
Mean area that is protected in terrestrial sites important to biodiversity (%)	55.9	2018	●	↑
Mean area that is protected in freshwater sites important to biodiversity (%)	15.9	2018	●	→
Red List Index of species survival (worst 0–1 best)	0.7	2019	●	↓
Permanent deforestation (% of forest area, 5-year average)	0.3	2018	●	●
Terrestrial and freshwater biodiversity threats embodied in imports (per million population)	0.2	2018	●	●

SDG16 – Peace, Justice and Strong Institutions		Value	Year	Rating	Trend
Homicides (per 100,000 population)		5.0	2016	●	→
Unsentenced detainees (% of prison population)		NA	NA	●	●
Percentage of population who feel safe walking alone at night in the city or area where they live (%)		50.8	2006	●	●
Property Rights (worst 1–7 best)		NA	NA	●	●
Birth registrations with civil authority (% of children under age 5)		100.0	2018	●	●
Corruption Perception Index (worst 0–100 best)		48	2019	●	→
Children involved in child labor (% of population aged 5 to 14)		NA	NA	◌	●
Exports of major conventional weapons (TIV constant million USD per 100,000 population)	*	0.0	2019	●	●
Press Freedom Index (best 0–100 worst)		63.8	2019	●	↗

SDG17 – Partnerships for the Goals		Value	Year	Rating	Trend
Government spending on health and education (% of GDP)		22.5	2010	●	●
For high-income and all OECD DAC countries: International concessional public finance, including official development assistance (% of GNI)		NA	NA	●	●
Other countries: Government revenue excluding grants (% of GDP)		NA	NA	●	●
Corporate Tax Haven Score (best 0–100 worst)	*	0.0	2019	●	●

* Imputed data point

5. Country Profiles

▼ OVERALL PERFORMANCE

Index score

75.2

Regional average score

70.9

SDG Global rank 34 (OF 166)

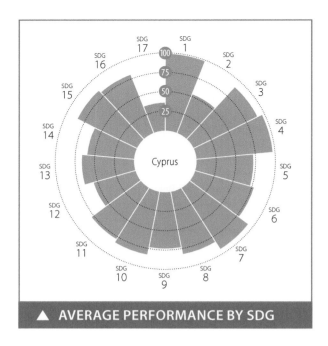

▲ AVERAGE PERFORMANCE BY SDG

▼ SPILLOVER INDEX

100 (best) to 0 (worst)

▼ CURRENT ASSESSMENT – SDG DASHBOARD

■ Major challenges ■ Significant challenges ■ Challenges remain ■ SDG achieved ■ Information unavailable

▼ SDG TRENDS

↓ Decreasing → Stagnating ↗ Moderately improving ↑ On track or maintaining SDG achievement ● Information unavailable

Notes: The full title of Goal 2 "Zero Hunger" is "End hunger, achieve food security and improved nutrition and promote sustainable agriculture".
The full title of each SDG is available here: https://sustainabledevelopment.un.org/topics/sustainabledevelopmentgoals

SDG1 – No Poverty

	Value	Year	Rating	Trend
Poverty headcount ratio at $1.90/day (%)	0.1	2020	●	↑
Poverty headcount ratio at $3.20/day (%)	0.1	2020	●	↑

SDG2 – Zero Hunger

		Value	Year	Rating	Trend
Prevalence of undernourishment (%)		5.6	2017	●	↑
Prevalence of stunting in children under 5 years of age (%)	*	2.6	2016	●	↑
Prevalence of wasting in children under 5 years of age (%)	*	0.7	2016	●	↑
Prevalence of obesity, BMI ≥ 30 (% of adult population)		21.8	2016	●	↓
Human Trophic Level (best 2–3 worst)		2.4	2017	●	→
Cereal yield (tonnes per hectare of harvested land)		2.0	2017	○	↑
Sustainable Nitrogen Management Index (best 0–1.41 worst)		1.1	2015	●	→

SDG3 – Good Health and Well-Being

	Value	Year	Rating	Trend
Maternal mortality rate (per 100,000 live births)	6	2017	●	↑
Neonatal mortality rate (per 1,000 live births)	1.4	2018	●	↑
Mortality rate, under-5 (per 1,000 live births)	2.4	2018	●	↑
Incidence of tuberculosis (per 100,000 population)	5.4	2018	●	↑
New HIV infections (per 1,000 uninfected population)	NA	NA	●	●
Age-standardized death rate due to cardiovascular disease, cancer, diabetes, or chronic respiratory disease in adults aged 30–70 years (%)	11.3	2016	●	↑
Age-standardized death rate attributable to household air pollution and ambient air pollution (per 100,000 population)	20	2016	○	●
Traffic deaths (per 100,000 population)	5.1	2016	●	↑
Life expectancy at birth (years)	80.7	2016	●	↑
Adolescent fertility rate (births per 1,000 adolescent females aged 15 to 19)	4.6	2017	●	↑
Births attended by skilled health personnel (%)	97.4	2014	○	●
Percentage of surviving infants who received 2 WHO-recommended vaccines (%)	90	2018	●	↑
Universal health coverage (UHC) index of service coverage (worst 0–100 best)	78.0	2017	○	↑
Subjective well-being (average ladder score, worst 0–10 best)	6.3	2018	●	↑

SDG4 – Quality Education

	Value	Year	Rating	Trend
Net primary enrollment rate (%)	97.5	2017	●	↑
Lower secondary completion rate (%)	97.6	2015	●	●
Literacy rate (% of population aged 15 to 24)	99.8	2011	●	●

SDG5 – Gender Equality

	Value	Year	Rating	Trend
Demand for family planning satisfied by modern methods (% of females aged 15 to 49 who are married or in unions)	NA	NA	●	●
Ratio of female-to-male mean years of education received (%)	98.4	2018	●	↑
Ratio of female-to-male labor force participation rate (%)	85.5	2019	●	↑
Seats held by women in national parliament (%)	19.6	2020	●	↗

SDG6 – Clean Water and Sanitation

	Value	Year	Rating	Trend
Population using at least basic drinking water services (%)	99.6	2017	●	↑
Population using at least basic sanitation services (%)	99.2	2017	●	↑
Freshwater withdrawal (% of available freshwater resources)	29.8	2015	○	●
Anthropogenic wastewater that receives treatment (%)	50.0	2018	●	●
Scarce water consumption embodied in imports (m³/capita)	42.1	2013	●	→

SDG7 – Affordable and Clean Energy

	Value	Year	Rating	Trend
Population with access to electricity (%)	100.0	2017	●	↑
Population with access to clean fuels and technology for cooking (%)	100.0	2016	●	↑
CO₂ emissions from fuel combustion for electricity and heating per total electricity output (MtCO₂/TWh)	1.3	2017	●	↗

SDG8 – Decent Work and Economic Growth

	Value	Year	Rating	Trend
Adjusted GDP growth (%)	2.2	2018	●	●
Victims of modern slavery (per 1,000 population)	4.2	2018	○	●
Adults with an account at a bank or other financial institution or with a mobile-money-service provider (% of population aged 15 or over)	88.7	2017	●	↑
Unemployment rate (% of total labor force)	7.3	2019	○	↑
Fatal work-related accidents embodied in imports (per 100,000 population)	1.3	2010	○	↑

SDG9 – Industry, Innovation and Infrastructure

	Value	Year	Rating	Trend
Population using the internet (%)	84.4	2018	●	↑
Mobile broadband subscriptions (per 100 population)	111.2	2018	●	↑
Logistics Performance Index: Quality of trade and transport-related infrastructure (worst 1–5 best)	2.9	2018	○	↗
The Times Higher Education Universities Ranking: Average score of top 3 universities (worst 0–100 best)	43.1	2020	●	●
Scientific and technical journal articles (per 1,000 population)	1.0	2018	●	↑
Expenditure on research and development (% of GDP)	0.6	2017	●	→

SDG10 – Reduced Inequalities

	Value	Year	Rating	Trend
Gini coefficient adjusted for top income	34.0	2015	○	●

SDG11 – Sustainable Cities and Communities

	Value	Year	Rating	Trend
Annual mean concentration of particulate matter of less than 2.5 microns in diameter (PM2.5) (μg/m³)	17.3	2017	○	↗
Access to improved water source, piped (% of urban population)	99.0	2017	●	↑
Satisfaction with public transport (%)	49.8	2018	●	↓

SDG12 – Responsible Consumption and Production

	Value	Year	Rating	Trend
Municipal solid waste (kg/capita/day)	1.9	2015	●	●
Electronic waste (kg/capita)	19.1	2016	●	●
Production-based SO₂ emissions (kg/capita)	193.1	2012	●	●
SO₂ emissions embodied in imports (kg/capita)	16.6	2012	●	●
Production-based nitrogen emissions (kg/capita)	27.3	2010	●	●
Nitrogen emissions embodied in imports (kg/capita)	10.9	2010	●	●

SDG13 – Climate Action

	Value	Year	Rating	Trend
Energy-related CO₂ emissions (tCO₂/capita)	5.5	2017	●	→
CO₂ emissions embodied in imports (tCO₂/capita)	2.5	2015	●	→
CO₂ emissions embodied in fossil fuel exports (kg/capita)	0.0	2017	●	●

SDG14 – Life Below Water

	Value	Year	Rating	Trend
Mean area that is protected in marine sites important to biodiversity (%)	39.2	2018	○	→
Ocean Health Index: Clean Waters score (worst 0–100 best)	58.6	2019	●	↗
Fish caught from overexploited or collapsed stocks (% of total catch)	25.1	2014	○	↑
Fish caught by trawling (%)	NA	NA	●	●
Marine biodiversity threats embodied in imports (per million population)	0.3	2018	○	●

SDG15 – Life on Land

	Value	Year	Rating	Trend
Mean area that is protected in terrestrial sites important to biodiversity (%)	66.1	2018	●	↑
Mean area that is protected in freshwater sites important to biodiversity (%)	NA	NA	●	●
Red List Index of species survival (worst 0–1 best)	1.0	2019	●	↑
Permanent deforestation (% of forest area, 5-year average)	0.1	2019	●	●
Terrestrial and freshwater biodiversity threats embodied in imports (per million population)	1.3	2018	○	●

SDG16 – Peace, Justice and Strong Institutions

		Value	Year	Rating	Trend
Homicides (per 100,000 population)		0.6	2017	●	↑
Unsentenced detainees (% of prison population)		26.3	2018	●	↑
Percentage of population who feel safe walking alone at night in the city or area where they live (%)		73.6	2018	●	↑
Property Rights (worst 1–7 best)		5.0	2019	●	●
Birth registrations with civil authority (% of children under age 5)		100.0	2018	●	●
Corruption Perception Index (worst 0–100 best)		58	2019	○	↓
Children involved in child labor (% of population aged 5 to 14)		NA	NA	●	●
Exports of major conventional weapons (TIV constant million USD per 100,000 population)	*	0.0	2019	●	●
Press Freedom Index (best 0–100 worst)		21.7	2019	●	↑

SDG17 – Partnerships for the Goals

	Value	Year	Rating	Trend
Government spending on health and education (% of GDP)	9.2	2016	○	↓
For high-income and all OECD DAC countries: International concessional public finance, including official development assistance (% of GNI)	0.1	2015	●	●
Other countries: Government revenue excluding grants (% of GDP)	NA	NA	●	●
Corporate Tax Haven Score (best 0–100 worst)	71.1	2019	●	●

* Imputed data point

▼ OVERALL PERFORMANCE

Index score	Regional average score
80.6	77.3

SDG Global rank 8 (OF 166)

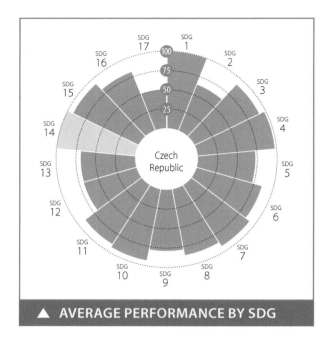

▲ AVERAGE PERFORMANCE BY SDG

▼ SPILLOVER INDEX

100 (best) to 0 (worst)

▼ CURRENT ASSESSMENT – SDG DASHBOARD

■ Major challenges   ■ Significant challenges   ■ Challenges remain   ■ SDG achieved   ■ Information unavailable

▼ SDG TRENDS

↓ Decreasing   → Stagnating   ↗ Moderately improving   ↑ On track or maintaining SDG achievement   ● Information unavailable

Notes: The full title of Goal 2 "Zero Hunger" is "End hunger, achieve food security and improved nutrition and promote sustainable agriculture".
    The full title of each SDG is available here: https://sustainabledevelopment.un.org/topics/sustainabledevelopmentgoals

SDG1 – No Poverty

Indicator	Value	Year	Rating	Trend
Poverty headcount ratio at $1.90/day (%)	0.3	2020	●	↑
Poverty headcount ratio at $3.20/day (%)	0.4	2020	●	↑
Poverty rate after taxes and transfers (%)	5.6	2017	●	↑

SDG2 – Zero Hunger

Indicator	Value	Year	Rating	Trend
Prevalence of undernourishment (%)	2.5	2017	●	↑
Prevalence of stunting in children under 5 years of age (%)	2.6	2001	●	↑
Prevalence of wasting in children under 5 years of age (%)	4.6	2001	●	↑
Prevalence of obesity, BMI ≥ 30 (% of adult population)	26.0	2016	●	↓
Human Trophic Level (best 2–3 worst)	2.4	2017	●	↓
Cereal yield (tonnes per hectare of harvested land)	5.5	2017	●	↑
Sustainable Nitrogen Management Index (best 0–1.41 worst)	0.5	2015	●	↓
Yield gap closure (% of potential yield)	57.8	2015	●	●

SDG3 – Good Health and Well-Being

Indicator	Value	Year	Rating	Trend
Maternal mortality rate (per 100,000 live births)	3	2017	●	↑
Neonatal mortality rate (per 1,000 live births)	1.8	2018	●	↑
Mortality rate, under-5 (per 1,000 live births)	3.4	2018	●	↑
Incidence of tuberculosis (per 100,000 population)	5.4	2018	●	↑
New HIV infections (per 1,000 uninfected population)	0.1	2018	●	↑
Age-standardized death rate due to cardiovascular disease, cancer, diabetes, or chronic respiratory disease in adults aged 30–70 years (%)	15.0	2016	●	↑
Age-standardized death rate attributable to household air pollution and ambient air pollution (per 100,000 population)	30	2016	●	●
Traffic deaths (per 100,000 population)	5.9	2016	●	↑
Life expectancy at birth (years)	79.2	2016	●	↑
Adolescent fertility rate (births per 1,000 adolescent females aged 15 to 19)	12.0	2017	●	↑
Births attended by skilled health personnel (%)	99.8	2013	●	●
Percentage of surviving infants who received 2 WHO-recommended vaccines (%)	96.0	2018	●	↑
Universal health coverage (UHC) index of service coverage (worst 0–100 best)	76.0	2017	●	↑
Subjective well-being (average ladder score, worst 0–10 best)	7.0	2018	●	↑
Gap in life expectancy at birth among regions (years)	3.4	2016	●	●
Gap in self-reported health status by income (percentage points)	41.8	2018	●	↓
Daily smokers (% of population aged 15 and over)	18.4	2017	●	↑

SDG4 – Quality Education

Indicator	Value	Year	Rating	Trend
Net primary enrollment rate (%)	* 98.1	2017	●	↑
Lower secondary completion rate (%)	* 98.1	2017	●	↑
Literacy rate (% of population aged 15 to 24)	NA	NA	●	●
Participation rate in pre-primary organized learning (% of children aged 4 to 6)	89.4	2017	●	↓
Tertiary educational attainment (% of population aged 25 to 34)	33.3	2018	●	↑
PISA score (worst 0–600 best)	495.3	2018	●	↑
Variation in science performance explained by socio-economic status (%)	16.9	2018	●	↑
Underachievers in science (% of 15-year-olds)	18.8	2018	●	↑
Resilient students in science (% of 15-year-olds)	30.5	2018	●	↑

SDG5 – Gender Equality

Indicator	Value	Year	Rating	Trend
Demand for family planning satisfied by modern methods (% of females aged 15 to 49 who are married or in unions)	85.7	2008	●	↑
Ratio of female-to-male mean years of education received (%)	96.2	2018	●	↓
Ratio of female-to-male labor force participation rate (%)	76.9	2019	●	↑
Seats held by women in national parliament (%)	22.5	2020	●	→
Gender wage gap (% of male median wage)	15.1	2018	●	↗
Gender gap in time spent doing unpaid work (minutes/day)	NA	NA	●	●

SDG6 – Clean Water and Sanitation

Indicator	Value	Year	Rating	Trend
Population using at least basic drinking water services (%)	99.9	2017	●	●
Population using at least basic sanitation services (%)	99.1	2017	●	●
Freshwater withdrawal (% of available freshwater resources)	24.9	2015	●	●
Anthropogenic wastewater that receives treatment (%)	60.8	2018	●	●
Scarce water consumption embodied in imports (m³/capita)	17.7	2013	●	↑
Population using safely managed water services (%)	97.9	2017	●	↑
Population using safely managed sanitation services (%)	94.5	2017	●	↑

SDG7 – Affordable and Clean Energy

Indicator	Value	Year	Rating	Trend
Population with access to electricity (%)	100.0	2017	●	↑
Population with access to clean fuels and technology for cooking (%)	97.1	2016	●	↑
CO_2 emissions from fuel combustion for electricity and heating per total electricity output (MtCO₂/TWh)	1.3	2017	●	→
Share of renewable energy in total primary energy supply (%)	10.3	2018	●	→

SDG8 – Decent Work and Economic Growth

Indicator	Value	Year	Rating	Trend
Adjusted GDP growth (%)	1.5	2018	●	●
Victims of modern slavery (per 1,000 population)	2.9	2018	●	●
Adults with an account at a bank or other financial institution or with a mobile-money-service provider (% of population aged 15 or over)	81.0	2017	●	↑
Fatal work-related accidents embodied in imports (per 100,000 population)	0.8	2010	●	↑
Employment-to-population ratio (%)	75.1	2019	●	↑
Youth not in employment, education or training (NEET) (% of population aged 15 to 29)	10.0	2018	●	↑

SDG9 – Industry, Innovation and Infrastructure

Indicator	Value	Year	Rating	Trend
Population using the internet (%)	80.7	2018	●	↑
Mobile broadband subscriptions (per 100 population)	88.0	2018	●	↑
Logistics Performance Index: Quality of trade and transport-related infrastructure (worst 1–5 best)	3.5	2018	●	↑
The Times Higher Education Universities Ranking: Average score of top 3 universities (worst 0–100 best)	34.7	2020	●	●
Scientific and technical journal articles (per 1,000 population)	1.5	2018	●	↑
Expenditure on research and development (% of GDP)	1.8	2017	●	↑
Researchers (per 1,000 employed population)	7.6	2018	●	↑
Triadic patent families filed (per million population)	4.2	2017	●	→
Gap in internet access by income (percentage points)	35.5	2019	●	↑
Women in science and engineering (% of tertiary graduates in science and engineering)	32.2	2015	●	●

SDG10 – Reduced Inequalities

Indicator	Value	Year	Rating	Trend
Gini coefficient adjusted for top income	30.0	2015	●	↑
Palma ratio	0.9	2017	●	↑
Elderly poverty rate (% of population aged 66 or over)	7.4	2017	●	↓

SDG11 – Sustainable Cities and Communities

Indicator	Value	Year	Rating	Trend
Annual mean concentration of particulate matter of less than 2.5 microns in diameter (PM2.5) (µg/m³)	16.1	2017	●	↗
Access to improved water source, piped (% of urban population)	99.0	2017	●	↑
Satisfaction with public transport (%)	70.5	2018	●	→
Population with rent overburden (%)	2.5	2017	●	●

SDG12 – Responsible Consumption and Production

Indicator	Value	Year	Rating	Trend
Electronic waste (kg/capita)	15.9	2016	●	●
Production-based SO_2 emissions (kg/capita)	51.8	2012	●	●
SO_2 emissions embodied in imports (kg/capita)	9.1	2012	●	●
Production-based nitrogen emissions (kg/capita)	31.7	2010	●	●
Nitrogen emissions embodied in imports (kg/capita)	7.5	2010	●	●
Non-recycled municipal solid waste (kg/capita/day)	0.6	2018	●	●

SDG13 – Climate Action

Indicator	Value	Year	Rating	Trend
Energy-related CO_2 emissions (tCO₂/capita)	9.1	2017	●	↓
CO_2 emissions embodied in imports (tCO₂/capita)	1.7	2015	●	→
CO_2 emissions embodied in fossil fuel exports (kg/capita)	671.4	2019	●	●
Effective carbon rate (EUR/tCO₂)	7.6	2016	●	●

SDG14 – Life Below Water

Indicator	Value	Year	Rating	Trend
Mean area that is protected in marine sites important to biodiversity (%)	NA	NA	●	●
Ocean Health Index: Clean Waters score (worst 0–100 best)	NA	NA	●	●
Fish caught from overexploited or collapsed stocks (% of total catch)	NA	NA	●	●
Fish caught by trawling (%)	NA	NA	●	●
Marine biodiversity threats embodied in imports (per million population)	0.1	2018	●	●

SDG15 – Life on Land

Indicator	Value	Year	Rating	Trend
Mean area that is protected in terrestrial sites important to biodiversity (%)	92.3	2018	●	↑
Mean area that is protected in freshwater sites important to biodiversity (%)	92.1	2018	●	↑
Red List Index of species survival (worst 0–1 best)	1.0	2019	●	↑
Permanent deforestation (% of forest area, 5-year average)	0.0	2018	●	●
Terrestrial and freshwater biodiversity threats embodied in imports (per million population)	1.6	2018	●	●

SDG16 – Peace, Justice and Strong Institutions

Indicator	Value	Year	Rating	Trend
Homicides (per 100,000 population)	0.6	2017	●	↑
Unsentenced detainees (% of prison population)	8.4	2018	●	↑
Percentage of population who feel safe walking alone at night in the city or area where they live (%)	72.4	2018	●	↑
Property Rights (worst 1–7 best)	4.7	2019	●	●
Birth registrations with civil authority (% of children under age 5)	100.0	2018	●	●
Corruption Perception Index (worst 0–100 best)	56.0	2019	●	→
Children involved in child labor (% of population aged 5 to 14)	* 0.0	2016	●	●
Exports of major conventional weapons (TIV constant million USD per 100,000 population)	0.9	2019	●	●
Press Freedom Index (best 0–100 worst)	24.9	2019	●	↑
Persons held in prison (per 100,000 population)	208.7	2017	●	↓

SDG17 – Partnerships for the Goals

Indicator	Value	Year	Rating	Trend
Government spending on health and education (% of GDP)	11.4	2016	●	↑
For high-income and all OECD DAC countries: International concessional public finance, including official development assistance (% of GNI)	0.2	2017	●	→
Other countries: Government revenue excluding grants (% of GDP)	NA	NA	●	●
Corporate Tax Haven Score (best 0–100 worst)	58.9	2019	●	●
Financial Secrecy Score (best 0–100 worst)	55.4	2020	●	●
Shifted profits of multinationals (US$ billion)	2.2	2016	●	●

* Imputed data point

5. Country Profiles

DEMOCRATIC REPUBLIC OF THE CONGO Sub-Saharan Africa

▼ OVERALL PERFORMANCE

Index score	Regional average score
49.7	53.1

SDG Global rank 158 (OF 166)

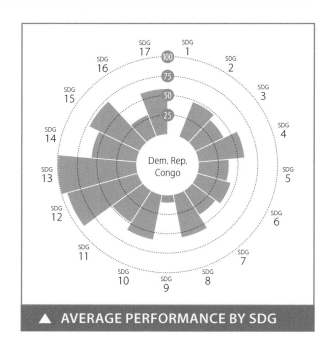

▲ AVERAGE PERFORMANCE BY SDG

▼ SPILLOVER INDEX

100 (best) to 0 (worst)

▼ CURRENT ASSESSMENT – SDG DASHBOARD

■ Major challenges   ■ Significant challenges   ■ Challenges remain   ■ SDG achieved   ■ Information unavailable

▼ SDG TRENDS

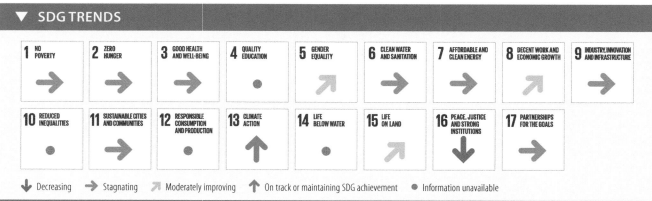

↓ Decreasing   → Stagnating   ↗ Moderately improving   ↑ On track or maintaining SDG achievement   ● Information unavailable

Notes: The full title of Goal 2 "Zero Hunger" is "End hunger, achieve food security and improved nutrition and promote sustainable agriculture".
The full title of each SDG is available here: https://sustainabledevelopment.un.org/topics/sustainabledevelopmentgoals

SDG1 – No Poverty

	Value	Year	Rating	Trend
Poverty headcount ratio at $1.90/day (%)	74.2	2020	●	→
Poverty headcount ratio at $3.20/day (%)	91.3	2020	●	→

SDG2 – Zero Hunger

	Value	Year	Rating	Trend
Prevalence of undernourishment (%)	NA	NA	●	●
Prevalence of stunting in children under 5 years of age (%)	42.6	2013	●	→
Prevalence of wasting in children under 5 years of age (%)	8.1	2013	●	↑
Prevalence of obesity, BMI ≥ 30 (% of adult population)	6.7	2016	●	↑
Human Trophic Level (best 2–3 worst)	2.0	2007	●	●
Cereal yield (tonnes per hectare of harvested land)	0.8	2017	●	↓
Sustainable Nitrogen Management Index (best 0–1.41 worst)	0.9	2015	●	↓

SDG3 – Good Health and Well-Being

	Value	Year	Rating	Trend
Maternal mortality rate (per 100,000 live births)	473	2017	●	→
Neonatal mortality rate (per 1,000 live births)	28.3	2018	●	→
Mortality rate, under-5 (per 1,000 live births)	88.1	2018	●	↗
Incidence of tuberculosis (per 100,000 population)	321.0	2018	●	→
New HIV infections (per 1,000 uninfected population)	0.2	2018	◐	↑
Age-standardized death rate due to cardiovascular disease, cancer, diabetes, or chronic respiratory disease in adults aged 30–70 years (%)	19.4	2016	◐	→
Age-standardized death rate attributable to household air pollution and ambient air pollution (per 100,000 population)	164	2016	●	●
Traffic deaths (per 100,000 population)	33.7	2016	●	↓
Life expectancy at birth (years)	60.5	2016	●	→
Adolescent fertility rate (births per 1,000 adolescent females aged 15 to 19)	124.2	2017	●	→
Births attended by skilled health personnel (%)	80.1	2014	●	●
Percentage of surviving infants who received 2 WHO-recommended vaccines (%)	80	2018	●	→
Universal health coverage (UHC) index of service coverage (worst 0–100 best)	41.0	2017	●	↗
Subjective well-being (average ladder score, worst 0–10 best)	4.3	2017	●	●

SDG4 – Quality Education

	Value	Year	Rating	Trend
Net primary enrollment rate (%)	NA	NA	●	●
Lower secondary completion rate (%)	50.4	2014	●	●
Literacy rate (% of population aged 15 to 24)	85.0	2016	●	●

SDG5 – Gender Equality

	Value	Year	Rating	Trend
Demand for family planning satisfied by modern methods (% of females aged 15 to 49 who are married or in unions)	18.9	2014	●	→
Ratio of female-to-male mean years of education received (%)	63.1	2018	●	↗
Ratio of female-to-male labor force participation rate (%)	91.4	2019	●	↑
Seats held by women in national parliament (%)	12.8	2020	●	→

SDG6 – Clean Water and Sanitation

	Value	Year	Rating	Trend
Population using at least basic drinking water services (%)	43.2	2017	●	→
Population using at least basic sanitation services (%)	20.5	2017	●	→
Freshwater withdrawal (% of available freshwater resources)	0.2	2005	●	●
Anthropogenic wastewater that receives treatment (%)	0.0	2018	●	●
Scarce water consumption embodied in imports (m³/capita)	0.2	2013	●	↑

SDG7 – Affordable and Clean Energy

	Value	Year	Rating	Trend
Population with access to electricity (%)	19.1	2017	●	→
Population with access to clean fuels and technology for cooking (%)	4.0	2016	●	→
CO$_2$ emissions from fuel combustion for electricity and heating per total electricity output (MtCO$_2$/TWh)	0.2	2017	●	↑

SDG8 – Decent Work and Economic Growth

	Value	Year	Rating	Trend
Adjusted GDP growth (%)	-7.2	2018	●	●
Victims of modern slavery (per 1,000 population)	13.7	2018	●	●
Adults with an account at a bank or other financial institution or with a mobile-money-service provider (% of population aged 15 or over)	25.8	2017	●	↗
Unemployment rate (% of total labor force)	4.2	2019	●	↑
Fatal work-related accidents embodied in imports (per 100,000 population)	0.1	2010	●	↑

SDG9 – Industry, Innovation and Infrastructure

	Value	Year	Rating	Trend
Population using the internet (%)	8.6	2017	●	→
Mobile broadband subscriptions (per 100 population)	15.9	2018	●	↗
Logistics Performance Index: Quality of trade and transport-related infrastructure (worst 1–5 best)	2.1	2018	●	↗
The Times Higher Education Universities Ranking: Average score of top 3 universities (worst 0–100 best) *	0.0	2020	●	●
Scientific and technical journal articles (per 1,000 population)	0.0	2018	●	→
Expenditure on research and development (% of GDP)	0.4	2015	●	●

SDG10 – Reduced Inequalities

	Value	Year	Rating	Trend
Gini coefficient adjusted for top income	42.1	2012	●	●

SDG11 – Sustainable Cities and Communities

	Value	Year	Rating	Trend
Annual mean concentration of particulate matter of less than 2.5 microns in diameter (PM2.5) (μg/m³)	44.9	2017	●	↓
Access to improved water source, piped (% of urban population)	62.9	2017	●	→
Satisfaction with public transport (%)	40.8	2017	●	●

SDG12 – Responsible Consumption and Production

	Value	Year	Rating	Trend
Municipal solid waste (kg/capita/day)	1.1	2016	◐	●
Electronic waste (kg/capita)	NA	NA	●	●
Production-based SO$_2$ emissions (kg/capita)	4.0	2012	●	●
SO$_2$ emissions embodied in imports (kg/capita)	0.3	2012	●	●
Production-based nitrogen emissions (kg/capita)	9.9	2010	●	●
Nitrogen emissions embodied in imports (kg/capita)	0.2	2010	●	●

SDG13 – Climate Action

	Value	Year	Rating	Trend
Energy-related CO$_2$ emissions (tCO$_2$/capita)	0.0	2017	●	↑
CO$_2$ emissions embodied in imports (tCO$_2$/capita)	0.0	2015	●	↑
CO$_2$ emissions embodied in fossil fuel exports (kg/capita)	NA	NA	●	●

SDG14 – Life Below Water

	Value	Year	Rating	Trend
Mean area that is protected in marine sites important to biodiversity (%)	NA	NA	●	●
Ocean Health Index: Clean Waters score (worst 0–100 best)	39.5	2019	●	↓
Fish caught from overexploited or collapsed stocks (% of total catch)	NA	NA	●	●
Fish caught by trawling (%)	NA	NA	●	●
Marine biodiversity threats embodied in imports (per million population)	0.0	2018	●	●

SDG15 – Life on Land

	Value	Year	Rating	Trend
Mean area that is protected in terrestrial sites important to biodiversity (%)	52.7	2018	●	↑
Mean area that is protected in freshwater sites important to biodiversity (%)	58.3	2018	●	↑
Red List Index of species survival (worst 0–1 best)	0.9	2019	◐	→
Permanent deforestation (% of forest area, 5-year average)	0.3	2018	●	●
Terrestrial and freshwater biodiversity threats embodied in imports (per million population)	0.2	2018	●	●

SDG16 – Peace, Justice and Strong Institutions

		Value	Year	Rating	Trend
Homicides (per 100,000 population)	*	13.5	2015	●	●
Unsentenced detainees (% of prison population)		73.0	2015	●	●
Percentage of population who feel safe walking alone at night in the city or area where they live (%)		45.2	2017	●	●
Property Rights (worst 1–7 best)		3.1	2019	●	●
Birth registrations with civil authority (% of children under age 5)		24.6	2018	●	●
Corruption Perception Index (worst 0–100 best)		18	2019	●	↓
Children involved in child labor (% of population aged 5 to 14)		38.4	2016	●	●
Exports of major conventional weapons (TIV constant million USD per 100,000 population)	*	0.0	2019	●	●
Press Freedom Index (best 0–100 worst)		51.7	2019	●	↓

SDG17 – Partnerships for the Goals

		Value	Year	Rating	Trend
Government spending on health and education (% of GDP)		2.6	2016	●	→
For high-income and all OECD DAC countries: International concessional public finance, including official development assistance (% of GNI)		NA	NA	●	●
Other countries: Government revenue excluding grants (% of GDP)		NA	NA	●	●
Corporate Tax Haven Score (best 0–100 worst)	*	0.0	2019	●	●

* Imputed data point

DENMARK

Index score

84.6

Regional average score

77.3

SDG Global rank 2 (OF 166)

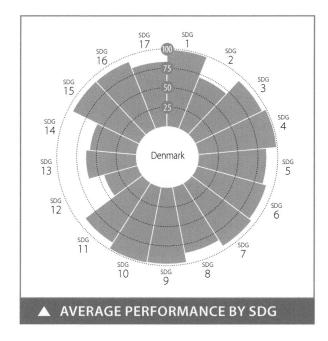

AVERAGE PERFORMANCE BY SDG

SPILLOVER INDEX

100 (best) to 0 (worst)

CURRENT ASSESSMENT – SDG DASHBOARD

■ Major challenges ■ Significant challenges ■ Challenges remain ■ SDG achieved ■ Information unavailable

SDG TRENDS

↓ Decreasing → Stagnating ↗ Moderately improving ↑ On track or maintaining SDG achievement ● Information unavailable

Notes: The full title of Goal 2 "Zero Hunger" is "End hunger, achieve food security and improved nutrition and promote sustainable agriculture".
The full title of each SDG is available here: https://sustainabledevelopment.un.org/topics/sustainabledevelopmentgoals

194 | Sustainable Development Report 2020 ● The Sustainable Development Goals and Covid-19

DENMARK

SDG1 – No Poverty

	Value	Year	Rating	Trend
Poverty headcount ratio at $1.90/day (%)	0.2	2020	●	↑
Poverty headcount ratio at $3.20/day (%)	0.3	2020	●	↑
Poverty rate after taxes and transfers (%)	5.8	2016	●	↑

SDG2 – Zero Hunger

	Value	Year	Rating	Trend
Prevalence of undernourishment (%)	2.5	2017	●	↑
Prevalence of stunting in children under 5 years of age (%)	* 2.6	2016	●	↑
Prevalence of wasting in children under 5 years of age (%)	* 0.7	2016	●	↑
Prevalence of obesity, BMI ≥ 30 (% of adult population)	19.7	2016	●	↓
Human Trophic Level (best 2–3 worst)	2.5	2017	●	↓
Cereal yield (tonnes per hectare of harvested land)	6.9	2017	●	↑
Sustainable Nitrogen Management Index (best 0–1.41 worst)	0.4	2015	◐	→
Yield gap closure (% of potential yield)	76.7	2015	●	●

SDG3 – Good Health and Well-Being

	Value	Year	Rating	Trend
Maternal mortality rate (per 100,000 live births)	4	2017	●	↑
Neonatal mortality rate (per 1,000 live births)	3.1	2018	●	↑
Mortality rate, under-5 (per 1,000 live births)	4.2	2018	●	↑
Incidence of tuberculosis (per 100,000 population)	5.4	2018	●	↑
New HIV infections (per 1,000 uninfected population)	0.0	2018	●	↑
Age-standardized death rate due to cardiovascular disease, cancer, diabetes, or chronic respiratory disease in adults aged 30–70 years (%)	11.3	2016	●	↑
Age-standardized death rate attributable to household air pollution and ambient air pollution (per 100,000 population)	13	2016	●	●
Traffic deaths (per 100,000 population)	4.0	2016	●	↑
Life expectancy at birth (years)	81.2	2016	●	↑
Adolescent fertility rate (births per 1,000 adolescent females aged 15 to 19)	4.1	2017	●	↑
Births attended by skilled health personnel (%)	94.4	2016	◐	↓
Percentage of surviving infants who received 2 WHO-recommended vaccines (%)	95.0	2018	●	↑
Universal health coverage (UHC) index of service coverage (worst 0–100 best)	81.0	2017	●	↑
Subjective well-being (average ladder score, worst 0–10 best)	7.7	2019	●	↑
Gap in life expectancy at birth among regions (years)	1.3	2016	●	●
Gap in self-reported health status by income (percentage points)	17.0	2018	●	↑
Daily smokers (% of population aged 15 and over)	16.9	2017	●	↑

SDG4 – Quality Education

	Value	Year	Rating	Trend
Net primary enrollment rate (%)	* 99.4	2017	●	↑
Lower secondary completion rate (%)	* 99.4	2017	●	↑
Literacy rate (% of population aged 15 to 24)	NA	NA	●	●
Participation rate in pre-primary organized learning (% of children aged 4 to 6)	93.7	2017	●	↑
Tertiary educational attainment (% of population aged 25 to 34)	44.8	2018	●	↑
PISA score (worst 0–600 best)	501.0	2018	●	↑
Variation in science performance explained by socio-economic status (%)	11.6	2018	◐	↓
Underachievers in science (% of 15-year-olds)	18.7	2018	●	↓
Resilient students in science (% of 15-year-olds)	24.8	2018	●	↓

SDG5 – Gender Equality

	Value	Year	Rating	Trend
Demand for family planning satisfied by modern methods (% of females aged 15 to 49 who are married or in unions)	* 83.7	2017	●	↑
Ratio of female-to-male mean years of education received (%)	102.4	2018	●	↑
Ratio of female-to-male labor force participation rate (%)	88.1	2019	●	↑
Seats held by women in national parliament (%)	39.7	2020	●	↑
Gender wage gap (% of male median wage)	5.3	2017	●	↑
Gender gap in time spent doing unpaid work (minutes/day)	56.7	2001	●	●

SDG6 – Clean Water and Sanitation

	Value	Year	Rating	Trend
Population using at least basic drinking water services (%)	100.0	2017	●	●
Population using at least basic sanitation services (%)	99.6	2017	●	●
Freshwater withdrawal (% of available freshwater resources)	17.2	2010	●	●
Anthropogenic wastewater that receives treatment (%)	100.0	2018	●	●
Scarce water consumption embodied in imports (m³/capita)	39.6	2013	●	→
Population using safely managed water services (%)	96.7	2017	●	↑
Population using safely managed sanitation services (%)	94.8	2017	●	↑

SDG7 – Affordable and Clean Energy

	Value	Year	Rating	Trend
Population with access to electricity (%)	100.0	2017	●	●
Population with access to clean fuels and technology for cooking (%)	100.0	2016	●	↑
CO₂ emissions from fuel combustion for electricity and heating per total electricity output (MtCO₂/TWh)	1.0	2017	◐	↑
Share of renewable energy in total primary energy supply (%)	33.4	2018	●	↑

SDG8 – Decent Work and Economic Growth

	Value	Year	Rating	Trend
Adjusted GDP growth (%)	0.7	2018	●	●
Victims of modern slavery (per 1,000 population)	1.6	2018	●	●
Adults with an account at a bank or other financial institution or with a mobile-money-service provider (% of population aged 15 or over)	99.9	2017	●	↑
Fatal work-related accidents embodied in imports (per 100,000 population)	1.6	2010	◐	↑
Employment-to-population ratio (%)	75.0	2019	●	↑
Youth not in employment, education or training (NEET) (% of population aged 15 to 29)	10.8	2018	◐	→

SDG9 – Industry, Innovation and Infrastructure

	Value	Year	Rating	Trend
Population using the internet (%)	97.3	2018	●	↑
Mobile broadband subscriptions (per 100 population)	136.7	2018	●	↑
Logistics Performance Index: Quality of trade and transport-related infrastructure (worst 1–5 best)	4.0	2018	●	↑
The Times Higher Education Universities Ranking: Average score of top 3 universities (worst 0–100 best)	59.1	2020	●	●
Scientific and technical journal articles (per 1,000 population)	2.4	2018	●	↑
Expenditure on research and development (% of GDP)	3.1	2017	●	↑
Researchers (per 1,000 employed population)	15.7	2018	●	↑
Triadic patent families filed (per million population)	55.0	2017	●	↑
Gap in internet access by income (percentage points)	9.8	2019	◐	↑
Women in science and engineering (% of tertiary graduates in science and engineering)	27.8	2015	●	●

SDG10 – Reduced Inequalities

	Value	Year	Rating	Trend
Gini coefficient adjusted for top income	28.4	2015	●	↑
Palma ratio	0.9	2016	●	↑
Elderly poverty rate (% of population aged 66 or over)	3.0	2016	●	↑

SDG11 – Sustainable Cities and Communities

	Value	Year	Rating	Trend
Annual mean concentration of particulate matter of less than 2.5 microns in diameter (PM2.5) (µg/m³)	10.0	2017	◐	↑
Access to improved water source, piped (% of urban population)	99.0	2017	●	↑
Satisfaction with public transport (%)	66.4	2019	◐	↑
Population with rent overburden (%)	15.7	2017	●	↓

SDG12 – Responsible Consumption and Production

	Value	Year	Rating	Trend
Electronic waste (kg/capita)	24.8	2016	●	●
Production-based SO₂ emissions (kg/capita)	124.3	2012	●	●
SO₂ emissions embodied in imports (kg/capita)	19.1	2012	●	●
Production-based nitrogen emissions (kg/capita)	57.3	2010	●	●
Nitrogen emissions embodied in imports (kg/capita)	16.1	2010	●	●
Non-recycled municipal solid waste (kg/capita/day)	1.1	2018	●	●

SDG13 – Climate Action

	Value	Year	Rating	Trend
Energy-related CO₂ emissions (tCO₂/capita)	5.3	2017	●	↗
CO₂ emissions embodied in imports (tCO₂/capita)	2.9	2015	●	→
CO₂ emissions embodied in fossil fuel exports (kg/capita)	0.0	2019	●	●
Effective carbon rate (EUR/tCO₂)	67.0	2016	◐	●

SDG14 – Life Below Water

	Value	Year	Rating	Trend
Mean area that is protected in marine sites important to biodiversity (%)	89.4	2018	●	↑
Ocean Health Index: Clean Waters score (worst 0–100 best)	52.5	2019	●	↓
Fish caught from overexploited or collapsed stocks (% of total catch)	45.1	2014	●	↑
Fish caught by trawling (%)	71.2	2014	●	→
Marine biodiversity threats embodied in imports (per million population)	0.1	2018	●	●

SDG15 – Life on Land

	Value	Year	Rating	Trend
Mean area that is protected in terrestrial sites important to biodiversity (%)	89.7	2018	●	↑
Mean area that is protected in freshwater sites important to biodiversity (%)	100.0	2018	●	↑
Red List Index of species survival (worst 0–1 best)	1.0	2019	●	↑
Permanent deforestation (% of forest area, 5-year average)	0.0	2018	●	●
Terrestrial and freshwater biodiversity threats embodied in imports (per million population)	1.7	2018	◐	●

SDG16 – Peace, Justice and Strong Institutions

	Value	Year	Rating	Trend
Homicides (per 100,000 population)	1.2	2017	●	↑
Unsentenced detainees (% of prison population)	32.8	2018	◐	↓
Percentage of population who feel safe walking alone at night in the city or area where they live (%)	87.5	2019	●	↑
Property Rights (worst 1–7 best)	6.0	2019	●	●
Birth registrations with civil authority (% of children under age 5)	100.0	2018	●	●
Corruption Perception Index (worst 0–100 best)	87.0	2019	●	↑
Children involved in child labor (% of population aged 5 to 14)	* 0.0	2016	●	●
Exports of major conventional weapons (TIV constant million USD per 100,000 population)	0.4	2019	●	●
Press Freedom Index (best 0–100 worst)	9.9	2019	●	↑
Persons held in prison (per 100,000 population)	63.4	2017	●	↑

SDG17 – Partnerships for the Goals

	Value	Year	Rating	Trend
Government spending on health and education (% of GDP)	16.2	2014	●	●
For high-income and all OECD DAC countries: International concessional public finance, including official development assistance (% of GNI)	0.7	2017	●	↑
Other countries: Government revenue excluding grants (% of GDP)	NA	NA	●	●
Corporate Tax Haven Score (best 0–100 worst)	51.7	2019	●	●
Financial Secrecy Score (best 0–100 worst)	45.3	2020	◐	●
Shifted profits of multinationals (US$ billion)	4.5	2016	●	●

* Imputed data point

▼ OVERALL PERFORMANCE

Index score

54.6

Regional average score

53.1

SDG Global rank 138 (OF 166)

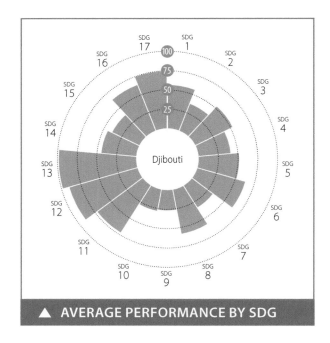

▲ AVERAGE PERFORMANCE BY SDG

▼ SPILLOVER INDEX

100 (best) to 0 (worst)

▼ CURRENT ASSESSMENT – SDG DASHBOARD

■ Major challenges ■ Significant challenges ■ Challenges remain ■ SDG achieved ■ Information unavailable

▼ SDG TRENDS

1 NO POVERTY	2 ZERO HUNGER	3 GOOD HEALTH AND WELL-BEING	4 QUALITY EDUCATION	5 GENDER EQUALITY	6 CLEAN WATER AND SANITATION	7 AFFORDABLE AND CLEAN ENERGY	8 DECENT WORK AND ECONOMIC GROWTH	9 INDUSTRY, INNOVATION AND INFRASTRUCTURE
↗	→	↗	→	↗	↗	→	↗	↗

10 REDUCED INEQUALITIES	11 SUSTAINABLE CITIES AND COMMUNITIES	12 RESPONSIBLE CONSUMPTION AND PRODUCTION	13 CLIMATE ACTION	14 LIFE BELOW WATER	15 LIFE ON LAND	16 PEACE, JUSTICE AND STRONG INSTITUTIONS	17 PARTNERSHIPS FOR THE GOALS
●	↗	●	↑	→	↓	→	●

↓ Decreasing → Stagnating ↗ Moderately improving ↑ On track or maintaining SDG achievement ● Information unavailable

Notes: The full title of Goal 2 "Zero Hunger" is "End hunger, achieve food security and improved nutrition and promote sustainable agriculture".
The full title of each SDG is available here: https://sustainabledevelopment.un.org/topics/sustainabledevelopmentgoals

SDG1 – No Poverty

Indicator	Value	Year	Rating	Trend
Poverty headcount ratio at $1.90/day (%)	13.9	2020	●	↑
Poverty headcount ratio at $3.20/day (%)	34.4	2020	●	↗

SDG2 – Zero Hunger

Indicator	Value	Year	Rating	Trend
Prevalence of undernourishment (%)	18.9	2017	●	→
Prevalence of stunting in children under 5 years of age (%)	33.5	2012	●	→
Prevalence of wasting in children under 5 years of age (%)	21.5	2012	●	→
Prevalence of obesity, BMI ≥ 30 (% of adult population)	13.5	2016	○	↓
Human Trophic Level (best 2–3 worst)	2.1	2017	●	↑
Cereal yield (tonnes per hectare of harvested land)	1.9	2017	●	→
Sustainable Nitrogen Management Index (best 0–1.41 worst)	1.2	2015	●	→

SDG3 – Good Health and Well-Being

Indicator	Value	Year	Rating	Trend
Maternal mortality rate (per 100,000 live births)	248	2017	●	→
Neonatal mortality rate (per 1,000 live births)	31.7	2018	●	↗
Mortality rate, under-5 (per 1,000 live births)	59.3	2018	●	↗
Incidence of tuberculosis (per 100,000 population)	260.0	2018	●	↑
New HIV infections (per 1,000 uninfected population)	0.6	2018	○	→
Age-standardized death rate due to cardiovascular disease, cancer, diabetes, or chronic respiratory disease in adults aged 30–70 years (%)	19.6	2016	○	↓
Age-standardized death rate attributable to household air pollution and ambient air pollution (per 100,000 population)	159	2016	●	●
Traffic deaths (per 100,000 population)	24.7	2013	●	●
Life expectancy at birth (years)	63.8	2016	●	→
Adolescent fertility rate (births per 1,000 adolescent females aged 15 to 19)	18.8	2017	●	↑
Births attended by skilled health personnel (%)	87.4	2012	●	●
Percentage of surviving infants who received 2 WHO-recommended vaccines (%)	84	2018	●	↑
Universal health coverage (UHC) index of service coverage (worst 0–100 best)	47.0	2017	●	↗
Subjective well-being (average ladder score, worst 0–10 best)	4.4	2011	●	●

SDG4 – Quality Education

Indicator	Value	Year	Rating	Trend
Net primary enrollment rate (%)	66.5	2019	●	→
Lower secondary completion rate (%)	49.9	2019	●	→
Literacy rate (% of population aged 15 to 24)	NA	NA	◐	●

SDG5 – Gender Equality

Indicator	Value	Year	Rating	Trend
Demand for family planning satisfied by modern methods (% of females aged 15 to 49 who are married or in unions) *	44.9	2017	●	↗
Ratio of female-to-male mean years of education received (%)	NA	NA	●	●
Ratio of female-to-male labor force participation rate (%)	77.2	2019	●	↑
Seats held by women in national parliament (%)	26.2	2020	○	↑

SDG6 – Clean Water and Sanitation

Indicator	Value	Year	Rating	Trend
Population using at least basic drinking water services (%)	75.6	2017	●	→
Population using at least basic sanitation services (%)	63.6	2017	●	↗
Freshwater withdrawal (% of available freshwater resources)	6.3	2000	●	●
Anthropogenic wastewater that receives treatment (%)	0.0	2018	●	●
Scarce water consumption embodied in imports (m3/capita)	2.0	2013	●	↑

SDG7 – Affordable and Clean Energy

Indicator	Value	Year	Rating	Trend
Population with access to electricity (%)	60.2	2017	●	→
Population with access to clean fuels and technology for cooking (%)	11.5	2016	●	→
CO_2 emissions from fuel combustion for electricity and heating per total electricity output (MtCO2/TWh)	NA	NA	●	●

SDG8 – Decent Work and Economic Growth

Indicator	Value	Year	Rating	Trend
Adjusted GDP growth (%)	NA	NA	●	●
Victims of modern slavery (per 1,000 population)	7.1	2018	●	●
Adults with an account at a bank or other financial institution or with a mobile-money-service provider (% of population aged 15 or over)	12.3	2011	●	●
Unemployment rate (% of total labor force)	10.3	2019	●	→
Fatal work-related accidents embodied in imports (per 100,000 population)	0.2	2010	●	↑

SDG9 – Industry, Innovation and Infrastructure

Indicator	Value	Year	Rating	Trend
Population using the internet (%)	55.7	2017	●	↑
Mobile broadband subscriptions (per 100 population)	20.6	2018	●	↑
Logistics Performance Index: Quality of trade and transport-related infrastructure (worst 1–5 best)	2.8	2018	○	↑
The Times Higher Education Universities Ranking: Average score of top 3 universities (worst 0–100 best) *	0.0	2020	●	●
Scientific and technical journal articles (per 1,000 population)	0.0	2018	●	→
Expenditure on research and development (% of GDP)	NA	NA	●	●

SDG10 – Reduced Inequalities

Indicator	Value	Year	Rating	Trend
Gini coefficient adjusted for top income	53.2	2017	●	●

SDG11 – Sustainable Cities and Communities

Indicator	Value	Year	Rating	Trend
Annual mean concentration of particulate matter of less than 2.5 microns in diameter (PM2.5) ($\mu g/m^3$)	45.6	2017	●	↓
Access to improved water source, piped (% of urban population)	97.9	2017	○	↑
Satisfaction with public transport (%)	60.8	2011	○	●

SDG12 – Responsible Consumption and Production

Indicator	Value	Year	Rating	Trend
Municipal solid waste (kg/capita/day)	0.4	2002	●	●
Electronic waste (kg/capita)	0.9	2016	●	●
Production-based SO_2 emissions (kg/capita)	147.2	2012	●	●
SO_2 emissions embodied in imports (kg/capita)	1.6	2012	●	●
Production-based nitrogen emissions (kg/capita)	19.6	2010	●	●
Nitrogen emissions embodied in imports (kg/capita)	0.8	2010	●	●

SDG13 – Climate Action

Indicator	Value	Year	Rating	Trend
Energy-related CO_2 emissions (tCO2/capita)	0.6	2017	●	↑
CO_2 emissions embodied in imports (tCO2/capita)	0.1	2015	●	↑
CO_2 emissions embodied in fossil fuel exports (kg/capita) *	0.0	2018	●	●

SDG14 – Life Below Water

Indicator	Value	Year	Rating	Trend
Mean area that is protected in marine sites important to biodiversity (%)	0.0	2018	●	→
Ocean Health Index: Clean Waters score (worst 0–100 best)	51.6	2019	●	→
Fish caught from overexploited or collapsed stocks (% of total catch)	NA	NA	●	●
Fish caught by trawling (%)	NA	NA	●	●
Marine biodiversity threats embodied in imports (per million population)	0.0	2018	●	●

SDG15 – Life on Land

Indicator	Value	Year	Rating	Trend
Mean area that is protected in terrestrial sites important to biodiversity (%)	0.9	2018	●	→
Mean area that is protected in freshwater sites important to biodiversity (%)	0.0	2018	●	→
Red List Index of species survival (worst 0–1 best)	0.8	2018	●	↓
Permanent deforestation (% of forest area, 5-year average)	NA	NA	●	●
Terrestrial and freshwater biodiversity threats embodied in imports (per million population)	0.0	2018	●	●

SDG16 – Peace, Justice and Strong Institutions

Indicator	Value	Year	Rating	Trend
Homicides (per 100,000 population) *	6.5	2015	●	●
Unsentenced detainees (% of prison population)	38.0	2018	○	↑
Percentage of population who feel safe walking alone at night in the city or area where they live (%)	71.6	2011	●	●
Property Rights (worst 1–7 best)	NA	NA	●	●
Birth registrations with civil authority (% of children under age 5)	91.7	2018	○	●
Corruption Perception Index (worst 0–100 best)	30	2019	●	↓
Children involved in child labor (% of population aged 5 to 14)	7.7	2016	●	●
Exports of major conventional weapons (TIV constant million USD per 100,000 population) *	0.0	2019	●	●
Press Freedom Index (best 0–100 worst)	71.4	2019	●	↓

SDG17 – Partnerships for the Goals

Indicator	Value	Year	Rating	Trend
Government spending on health and education (% of GDP)	7.4	2016	●	●
For high-income and all OECD DAC countries: International concessional public finance, including official development assistance (% of GNI)	NA	NA	●	●
Other countries: Government revenue excluding grants (% of GDP)	NA	NA	●	●
Corporate Tax Haven Score (best 0–100 worst) *	0.0	2019	●	●

* Imputed data point

5. Country Profiles

▼ OVERALL PERFORMANCE

Index score

na

Regional average score

70.4

SDG Global rank   NA (OF 166)

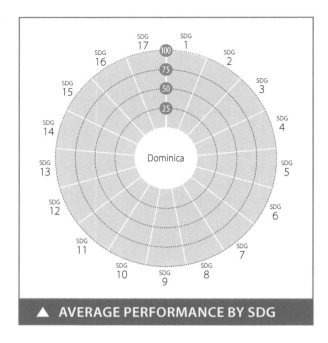

▲ AVERAGE PERFORMANCE BY SDG

▼ SPILLOVER INDEX

100 (best) to 0 (worst)

▼ CURRENT ASSESSMENT – SDG DASHBOARD

■ Major challenges   ■ Significant challenges   ■ Challenges remain   ■ SDG achieved   ■ Information unavailable

▼ SDG TRENDS

↓ Decreasing   → Stagnating   ↗ Moderately improving   ↑ On track or maintaining SDG achievement   ● Information unavailable

Notes: The full title of Goal 2 "Zero Hunger" is "End hunger, achieve food security and improved nutrition and promote sustainable agriculture".
The full title of each SDG is available here: https://sustainabledevelopment.un.org/topics/sustainabledevelopmentgoals

DOMINICA

SDG1 – No Poverty	Value	Year	Rating	Trend
Poverty headcount ratio at $1.90/day (%)	NA	NA	●	●
Poverty headcount ratio at $3.20/day (%)	NA	NA	●	●

SDG2 – Zero Hunger	Value	Year	Rating	Trend
Prevalence of undernourishment (%)	6.2	2017	●	↑
Prevalence of stunting in children under 5 years of age (%)	NA	NA	●	●
Prevalence of wasting in children under 5 years of age (%)	NA	NA	●	●
Prevalence of obesity, BMI ≥ 30 (% of adult population)	27.9	2016	●	↓
Human Trophic Level (best 2–3 worst)	2.2	2017	●	→
Cereal yield (tonnes per hectare of harvested land)	1.7	2017	●	↗
Sustainable Nitrogen Management Index (best 0–1.41 worst)	1.1	2015	●	→

SDG3 – Good Health and Well-Being	Value	Year	Rating	Trend
Maternal mortality rate (per 100,000 live births)	NA	NA	●	●
Neonatal mortality rate (per 1,000 live births)	28.3	2018	●	↓
Mortality rate, under-5 (per 1,000 live births)	35.7	2018	●	↓
Incidence of tuberculosis (per 100,000 population)	6.4	2018	●	↑
New HIV infections (per 1,000 uninfected population)	0.3	2018	●	→
Age-standardized death rate due to cardiovascular disease, cancer, diabetes, or chronic respiratory disease in adults aged 30–70 years (%)	NA	NA	●	●
Age-standardized death rate attributable to household air pollution and ambient air pollution (per 100,000 population)	NA	NA	●	●
Traffic deaths (per 100,000 population)	10.9	2016	●	↑
Life expectancy at birth (years)	NA	NA	●	●
Adolescent fertility rate (births per 1,000 adolescent females aged 15 to 19)	NA	NA	●	●
Births attended by skilled health personnel (%)	96.0	2016	●	↓
Percentage of surviving infants who received 2 WHO-recommended vaccines (%)	84	2018	●	↓
Universal health coverage (UHC) index of service coverage (worst 0–100 best)	NA	NA	●	●
Subjective well-being (average ladder score, worst 0–10 best)	NA	NA	●	●

SDG4 – Quality Education	Value	Year	Rating	Trend
Net primary enrollment rate (%)	95.4	2016	●	●
Lower secondary completion rate (%)	90.7	2015	●	●
Literacy rate (% of population aged 15 to 24)	NA	NA	●	●

SDG5 – Gender Equality	Value	Year	Rating	Trend
Demand for family planning satisfied by modern methods (% of females aged 15 to 49 who are married or in unions)	NA	NA	●	●
Ratio of female-to-male mean years of education received (%)	NA	NA	●	●
Ratio of female-to-male labor force participation rate (%)	NA	NA	●	●
Seats held by women in national parliament (%)	34.4	2020	●	↑

SDG6 – Clean Water and Sanitation	Value	Year	Rating	Trend
Population using at least basic drinking water services (%)	96.5	2015	●	●
Population using at least basic sanitation services (%)	77.9	2015	●	●
Freshwater withdrawal (% of available freshwater resources)	10.0	2010	●	●
Anthropogenic wastewater that receives treatment (%)	1.0	2018	●	●
Scarce water consumption embodied in imports (m³/capita)	NA	NA	●	●

SDG7 – Affordable and Clean Energy	Value	Year	Rating	Trend
Population with access to electricity (%)	100.0	2017	●	↑
Population with access to clean fuels and technology for cooking (%)	90.6	2016	●	↑
CO_2 emissions from fuel combustion for electricity and heating per total electricity output (MtCO₂/TWh)	NA	NA	●	●

SDG8 – Decent Work and Economic Growth	Value	Year	Rating	Trend
Adjusted GDP growth (%)	-5.1	2018	●	●
Victims of modern slavery (per 1,000 population)	NA	NA	●	●
Adults with an account at a bank or other financial institution or with a mobile-money-service provider (% of population aged 15 or over)	NA	NA	●	●
Unemployment rate (% of total labor force)	NA	NA	●	●
Fatal work-related accidents embodied in imports (per 100,000 population)	NA	NA	●	●

SDG9 – Industry, Innovation and Infrastructure	Value	Year	Rating	Trend
Population using the internet (%)	69.6	2017	●	↑
Mobile broadband subscriptions (per 100 population)	93.9	2018	●	↑
Logistics Performance Index: Quality of trade and transport-related infrastructure (worst 1–5 best)	NA	NA	●	●
The Times Higher Education Universities Ranking: Average score of top 3 universities (worst 0–100 best) *	0.0	2020	●	●
Scientific and technical journal articles (per 1,000 population)	0.2	2018	●	→
Expenditure on research and development (% of GDP)	NA	NA	●	●

SDG10 – Reduced Inequalities	Value	Year	Rating	Trend
Gini coefficient adjusted for top income	NA	NA	●	●

SDG11 – Sustainable Cities and Communities	Value	Year	Rating	Trend
Annual mean concentration of particulate matter of less than 2.5 microns in diameter (PM2.5) (µg/m³)	19.5	2017	●	↗
Access to improved water source, piped (% of urban population)	NA	NA	●	●
Satisfaction with public transport (%)	NA	NA	●	●

SDG12 – Responsible Consumption and Production	Value	Year	Rating	Trend
Municipal solid waste (kg/capita/day)	0.7	2013	●	●
Electronic waste (kg/capita)	7.7	2016	●	●
Production-based SO_2 emissions (kg/capita)	NA	NA	●	●
SO_2 emissions embodied in imports (kg/capita)	NA	NA	●	●
Production-based nitrogen emissions (kg/capita)	NA	NA	●	●
Nitrogen emissions embodied in imports (kg/capita)	NA	NA	●	●

SDG13 – Climate Action	Value	Year	Rating	Trend
Energy-related CO_2 emissions (tCO₂/capita)	2.0	2017	●	↑
CO_2 emissions embodied in imports (tCO₂/capita)	NA	NA	●	●
CO_2 emissions embodied in fossil fuel exports (kg/capita) *	0.0	2018	●	●

SDG14 – Life Below Water	Value	Year	Rating	Trend
Mean area that is protected in marine sites important to biodiversity (%)	0.0	2018	●	→
Ocean Health Index: Clean Waters score (worst 0–100 best)	58.9	2019	●	↗
Fish caught from overexploited or collapsed stocks (% of total catch)	NA	NA	●	●
Fish caught by trawling (%)	92.1	2014	●	→
Marine biodiversity threats embodied in imports (per million population)	NA	NA	●	●

SDG15 – Life on Land	Value	Year	Rating	Trend
Mean area that is protected in terrestrial sites important to biodiversity (%)	29.5	2018	●	→
Mean area that is protected in freshwater sites important to biodiversity (%)	0.1	2018	●	→
Red List Index of species survival (worst 0–1 best)	0.7	2019	●	↓
Permanent deforestation (% of forest area, 5-year average)	4.3	2018	●	●
Terrestrial and freshwater biodiversity threats embodied in imports (per million population)	NA	NA	●	●

SDG16 – Peace, Justice and Strong Institutions	Value	Year	Rating	Trend
Homicides (per 100,000 population)	25.7	2017	●	↓
Unsentenced detainees (% of prison population)	30.4	2018	●	↓
Percentage of population who feel safe walking alone at night in the city or area where they live (%)	NA	NA	●	●
Property Rights (worst 1–7 best)	NA	NA	●	●
Birth registrations with civil authority (% of children under age 5)	NA	NA	●	●
Corruption Perception Index (worst 0–100 best)	55	2019	●	↓
Children involved in child labor (% of population aged 5 to 14)	NA	NA	●	●
Exports of major conventional weapons (TIV constant million USD per 100,000 population) *	0.0	2019	●	●
Press Freedom Index (best 0–100 worst)	NA	NA	●	●

SDG17 – Partnerships for the Goals	Value	Year	Rating	Trend
Government spending on health and education (% of GDP)	7.0	2015	●	●
For high-income and all OECD DAC countries: International concessional public finance, including official development assistance (% of GNI)	NA	NA	●	●
Other countries: Government revenue excluding grants (% of GDP) *	26.3	2014	●	●
Corporate Tax Haven Score (best 0–100 worst) *	0.0	2019	●	●

* Imputed data point

5. Country Profiles

Latin America and the Caribbean

▼ OVERALL PERFORMANCE

Index score

70.2

Regional average score

70.4

SDG Global rank   73 (OF 166)

▼ SPILLOVER INDEX

100 (best) to 0 (worst)

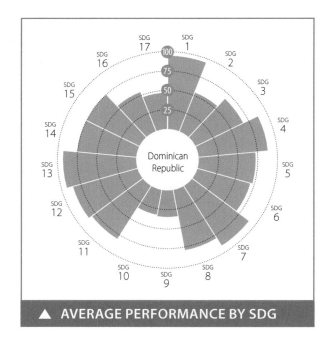

▲ AVERAGE PERFORMANCE BY SDG

▼ CURRENT ASSESSMENT – SDG DASHBOARD

■ Major challenges ■ Significant challenges ■ Challenges remain ■ SDG achieved ■ Information unavailable

▼ SDG TRENDS

↓ Decreasing → Stagnating ↗ Moderately improving ↑ On track or maintaining SDG achievement ● Information unavailable

Notes: The full title of Goal 2 "Zero Hunger" is "End hunger, achieve food security and improved nutrition and promote sustainable agriculture".
The full title of each SDG is available here: https://sustainabledevelopment.un.org/topics/sustainabledevelopmentgoals

SDG1 – No Poverty

	Value	Year	Rating	Trend
Poverty headcount ratio at $1.90/day (%)	0.0	2020	●	↑
Poverty headcount ratio at $3.20/day (%)	4.8	2020	◐	↑

SDG2 – Zero Hunger

	Value	Year	Rating	Trend
Prevalence of undernourishment (%)	9.5	2017	◐	↑
Prevalence of stunting in children under 5 years of age (%)	7.1	2013	●	↑
Prevalence of wasting in children under 5 years of age (%)	2.4	2013	●	↑
Prevalence of obesity, BMI ≥ 30 (% of adult population)	27.6	2016	●	↓
Human Trophic Level (best 2–3 worst)	2.2	2017	●	→
Cereal yield (tonnes per hectare of harvested land)	3.2	2017	●	↑
Sustainable Nitrogen Management Index (best 0–1.41 worst)	1.0	2015	●	→

SDG3 – Good Health and Well-Being

	Value	Year	Rating	Trend
Maternal mortality rate (per 100,000 live births)	95	2017	◐	→
Neonatal mortality rate (per 1,000 live births)	19.4	2018	●	↗
Mortality rate, under-5 (per 1,000 live births)	28.8	2018	◐	↑
Incidence of tuberculosis (per 100,000 population)	45.0	2018	◐	↑
New HIV infections (per 1,000 uninfected population)	0.3	2018	◐	↑
Age-standardized death rate due to cardiovascular disease, cancer, diabetes, or chronic respiratory disease in adults aged 30–70 years (%)	19.0	2016	◐	→
Age-standardized death rate attributable to household air pollution and ambient air pollution (per 100,000 population)	43	2016	◐	●
Traffic deaths (per 100,000 population)	34.6	2016	●	↓
Life expectancy at birth (years)	73.5	2016	●	↗
Adolescent fertility rate (births per 1,000 adolescent females aged 15 to 19)	94.3	2017	●	→
Births attended by skilled health personnel (%)	99.6	2015	●	↑
Percentage of surviving infants who received 2 WHO-recommended vaccines (%)	94	2018	●	↑
Universal health coverage (UHC) index of service coverage (worst 0–100 best)	74.0	2017	●	↑
Subjective well-being (average ladder score, worst 0–10 best)	5.4	2018	◐	↑

SDG4 – Quality Education

	Value	Year	Rating	Trend
Net primary enrollment rate (%)	92.7	2018	◐	↑
Lower secondary completion rate (%)	85.4	2017	●	↑
Literacy rate (% of population aged 15 to 24)	98.8	2016	●	●

SDG5 – Gender Equality

	Value	Year	Rating	Trend
Demand for family planning satisfied by modern methods (% of females aged 15 to 49 who are married or in unions)	81.7	2014	●	↑
Ratio of female-to-male mean years of education received (%)	109.2	2018	●	↑
Ratio of female-to-male labor force participation rate (%)	65.7	2019	●	↑
Seats held by women in national parliament (%)	27.9	2020	●	↑

SDG6 – Clean Water and Sanitation

	Value	Year	Rating	Trend
Population using at least basic drinking water services (%)	96.7	2017	◐	↑
Population using at least basic sanitation services (%)	83.9	2017	●	→
Freshwater withdrawal (% of available freshwater resources)	39.7	2010	◐	●
Anthropogenic wastewater that receives treatment (%)	5.8	2018	●	●
Scarce water consumption embodied in imports (m³/capita)	2.8	2013	●	↑

SDG7 – Affordable and Clean Energy

	Value	Year	Rating	Trend
Population with access to electricity (%)	100.0	2017	●	↑
Population with access to clean fuels and technology for cooking (%)	90.4	2016	●	↑
CO₂ emissions from fuel combustion for electricity and heating per total electricity output (MtCO₂/TWh)	1.2	2017	◐	→

SDG8 – Decent Work and Economic Growth

	Value	Year	Rating	Trend
Adjusted GDP growth (%)	1.4	2018	●	●
Victims of modern slavery (per 1,000 population)	4.0	2018	◐	●
Adults with an account at a bank or other financial institution or with a mobile-money-service provider (% of population aged 15 or over)	56.2	2017	●	→
Unemployment rate (% of total labor force)	5.8	2019	◐	↑
Fatal work-related accidents embodied in imports (per 100,000 population)	0.1	2010	●	↑

SDG9 – Industry, Innovation and Infrastructure

	Value	Year	Rating	Trend
Population using the internet (%)	74.8	2018	◐	↑
Mobile broadband subscriptions (per 100 population)	60.8	2018	◐	↑
Logistics Performance Index: Quality of trade and transport-related infrastructure (worst 1–5 best)	2.4	2018	●	↓
The Times Higher Education Universities Ranking: Average score of top 3 universities (worst 0–100 best) *	0.0	2020	●	●
Scientific and technical journal articles (per 1,000 population)	0.0	2018	●	→
Expenditure on research and development (% of GDP)	NA	NA	●	●

SDG10 – Reduced Inequalities

	Value	Year	Rating	Trend
Gini coefficient adjusted for top income	51.5	2016	●	●

SDG11 – Sustainable Cities and Communities

	Value	Year	Rating	Trend
Annual mean concentration of particulate matter of less than 2.5 microns in diameter (PM2.5) (µg/m³)	13.7	2017*	◐	↗
Access to improved water source, piped (% of urban population)	84.2	2017	●	↓
Satisfaction with public transport (%)	62.1	2018	◐	↓

SDG12 – Responsible Consumption and Production

	Value	Year	Rating	Trend
Municipal solid waste (kg/capita/day)	1.3	2015	◐	●
Electronic waste (kg/capita)	5.8	2016	◐	●
Production-based SO₂ emissions (kg/capita)	31.2	2012	●	●
SO₂ emissions embodied in imports (kg/capita)	2.3	2012	●	●
Production-based nitrogen emissions (kg/capita)	18.6	2010	●	●
Nitrogen emissions embodied in imports (kg/capita)	1.6	2010	●	●

SDG13 – Climate Action

	Value	Year	Rating	Trend
Energy-related CO₂ emissions (tCO₂/capita)	1.9	2017	●	↑
CO₂ emissions embodied in imports (tCO₂/capita)	0.4	2015	●	↑
CO₂ emissions embodied in fossil fuel exports (kg/capita)	0.0	2017	●	●

SDG14 – Life Below Water

	Value	Year	Rating	Trend
Mean area that is protected in marine sites important to biodiversity (%)	79.2	2018	●	↑
Ocean Health Index: Clean Waters score (worst 0–100 best)	50.4	2019	●	→
Fish caught from overexploited or collapsed stocks (% of total catch)	3.8	2014	●	↑
Fish caught by trawling (%)	NA	NA	●	●
Marine biodiversity threats embodied in imports (per million population)	0.1	2018	●	●

SDG15 – Life on Land

	Value	Year	Rating	Trend
Mean area that is protected in terrestrial sites important to biodiversity (%)	73.6	2018	●	↑
Mean area that is protected in freshwater sites important to biodiversity (%)	98.9	2018	●	↑
Red List Index of species survival (worst 0–1 best)	0.7	2019	●	↓
Permanent deforestation (% of forest area, 5-year average)	0.4	2018	●	●
Terrestrial and freshwater biodiversity threats embodied in imports (per million population)	0.2	2018	●	●

SDG16 – Peace, Justice and Strong Institutions

	Value	Year	Rating	Trend
Homicides (per 100,000 population)	11.3	2017	●	↑
Unsentenced detainees (% of prison population)	60.3	2018	●	↓
Percentage of population who feel safe walking alone at night in the city or area where they live (%)	36.8	2018	●	→
Property Rights (worst 1–7 best)	4.3	2019	◐	●
Birth registrations with civil authority (% of children under age 5)	88.0	2018	◐	●
Corruption Perception Index (worst 0–100 best)	28	2019	●	↓
Children involved in child labor (% of population aged 5 to 14)	12.8	2016	●	●
Exports of major conventional weapons (TIV constant million USD per 100,000 population)	0.0	2019	●	●
Press Freedom Index (best 0–100 worst)	27.9	2019	●	↑

SDG17 – Partnerships for the Goals

	Value	Year	Rating	Trend
Government spending on health and education (% of GDP)	3.7	2007	●	●
For high-income and all OECD DAC countries: International concessional public finance, including official development assistance (% of GNI)	NA	NA	●	●
Other countries: Government revenue excluding grants (% of GDP)	15.2	2018	●	→
Corporate Tax Haven Score (best 0–100 worst) *	0.0	2019	●	●

* Imputed data point

▼ OVERALL PERFORMANCE

Index score
74.3

Regional average score
70.4

SDG Global rank 46 (OF 166)

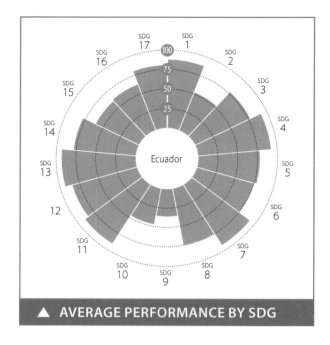

▲ AVERAGE PERFORMANCE BY SDG

▼ SPILLOVER INDEX

100 (best) to 0 (worst)

▼ CURRENT ASSESSMENT – SDG DASHBOARD

■ Major challenges   ■ Significant challenges   ■ Challenges remain   ■ SDG achieved   ■ Information unavailable

▼ SDG TRENDS

↓ Decreasing   → Stagnating   ↗ Moderately improving   ↑ On track or maintaining SDG achievement   ● Information unavailable

Notes: The full title of Goal 2 "Zero Hunger" is "End hunger, achieve food security and improved nutrition and promote sustainable agriculture".
   The full title of each SDG is available here: https://sustainabledevelopment.un.org/topics/sustainabledevelopmentgoals

SDG1 – No Poverty

	Value	Year	Rating	Trend
Poverty headcount ratio at $1.90/day (%)	2.7	2020	●	↑
Poverty headcount ratio at $3.20/day (%)	10.1	2020	●	→

SDG2 – Zero Hunger

	Value	Year	Rating	Trend
Prevalence of undernourishment (%)	7.9	2017	●	↑
Prevalence of stunting in children under 5 years of age (%)	23.9	2014	●	↗
Prevalence of wasting in children under 5 years of age (%)	1.6	2014	●	↑
Prevalence of obesity, BMI ≥ 30 (% of adult population)	19.9	2016	●	↓
Human Trophic Level (best 2–3 worst)	2.3	2017	●	↗
Cereal yield (tonnes per hectare of harvested land)	3.4	2017	●	↑
Sustainable Nitrogen Management Index (best 0–1.41 worst)	1.0	2015	●	→

SDG3 – Good Health and Well-Being

	Value	Year	Rating	Trend
Maternal mortality rate (per 100,000 live births)	59	2017	●	↑
Neonatal mortality rate (per 1,000 live births)	7.2	2018	●	↑
Mortality rate, under-5 (per 1,000 live births)	14.2	2018	●	↑
Incidence of tuberculosis (per 100,000 population)	44.0	2018	●	→
New HIV infections (per 1,000 uninfected population)	0.1	2018	●	↑
Age-standardized death rate due to cardiovascular disease, cancer, diabetes, or chronic respiratory disease in adults aged 30–70 years (%)	13.0	2016	●	↑
Age-standardized death rate attributable to household air pollution and ambient air pollution (per 100,000 population)	25	2016	●	●
Traffic deaths (per 100,000 population)	21.3	2016	●	↓
Life expectancy at birth (years)	76.5	2016	●	↗
Adolescent fertility rate (births per 1,000 adolescent females aged 15 to 19)	79.3	2017	●	→
Births attended by skilled health personnel (%)	96.7	2016	●	↑
Percentage of surviving infants who received 2 WHO-recommended vaccines (%)	83	2018	●	↑
Universal health coverage (UHC) index of service coverage (worst 0–100 best)	77.0	2017	●	↑
Subjective well-being (average ladder score, worst 0–10 best)	5.8	2019	●	↓

SDG4 – Quality Education

	Value	Year	Rating	Trend
Net primary enrollment rate (%)	90.9	2018	●	→
Lower secondary completion rate (%)	97.8	2017	●	↑
Literacy rate (% of population aged 15 to 24)	99.3	2017	●	●

SDG5 – Gender Equality

	Value	Year	Rating	Trend
Demand for family planning satisfied by modern methods (% of females aged 15 to 49 who are married or in unions)	79.4	2012	●	↑
Ratio of female-to-male mean years of education received (%)	97.8	2018	●	↑
Ratio of female-to-male labor force participation rate (%)	69.3	2019	●	↑
Seats held by women in national parliament (%)	39.4	2020	●	↓

SDG6 – Clean Water and Sanitation

	Value	Year	Rating	Trend
Population using at least basic drinking water services (%)	94.0	2017	●	↑
Population using at least basic sanitation services (%)	88.0	2017	●	↑
Freshwater withdrawal (% of available freshwater resources)	6.8	2005	●	●
Anthropogenic wastewater that receives treatment (%)	0.0	2018	●	●
Scarce water consumption embodied in imports (m³/capita)	1.6	2013	●	↑

SDG7 – Affordable and Clean Energy

	Value	Year	Rating	Trend
Population with access to electricity (%)	100.0	2017	●	↑
Population with access to clean fuels and technology for cooking (%)	95.6	2016	●	↑
CO_2 emissions from fuel combustion for electricity and heating per total electricity output (MtCO₂/TWh)	1.2	2017	●	↑

SDG8 – Decent Work and Economic Growth

	Value	Year	Rating	Trend
Adjusted GDP growth (%)	-4.9	2018	●	●
Victims of modern slavery (per 1,000 population)	2.4	2018	●	●
Adults with an account at a bank or other financial institution or with a mobile-money-service provider (% of population aged 15 or over)	51.2	2017	●	↗
Unemployment rate (% of total labor force)	4.0	2019	●	↑
Fatal work-related accidents embodied in imports (per 100,000 population)	0.1	2010	●	↑

SDG9 – Industry, Innovation and Infrastructure

	Value	Year	Rating	Trend
Population using the internet (%)	57.3	2017	●	↑
Mobile broadband subscriptions (per 100 population)	54.7	2018	●	↑
Logistics Performance Index: Quality of trade and transport-related infrastructure (worst 1–5 best)	2.7	2018	●	↑
The Times Higher Education Universities Ranking: Average score of top 3 universities (worst 0–100 best) *	13.6	2019	●	●
Scientific and technical journal articles (per 1,000 population)	0.1	2018	●	↗
Expenditure on research and development (% of GDP)	0.4	2014	●	●

SDG10 – Reduced Inequalities

	Value	Year	Rating	Trend
Gini coefficient adjusted for top income	46.4	2017	●	●

SDG11 – Sustainable Cities and Communities

	Value	Year	Rating	Trend
Annual mean concentration of particulate matter of less than 2.5 microns in diameter (PM2.5) (µg/m³)	14.9	2017	●	↑
Access to improved water source, piped (% of urban population)	97.9	2017	●	↑
Satisfaction with public transport (%)	71.9	2019	●	↑

SDG12 – Responsible Consumption and Production

	Value	Year	Rating	Trend
Municipal solid waste (kg/capita/day)	1.3	2015	●	●
Electronic waste (kg/capita)	5.5	2016	●	●
Production-based SO_2 emissions (kg/capita)	24.2	2012	●	●
SO_2 emissions embodied in imports (kg/capita)	1.9	2012	●	●
Production-based nitrogen emissions (kg/capita)	22.6	2010	●	●
Nitrogen emissions embodied in imports (kg/capita)	1.4	2010	●	●

SDG13 – Climate Action

	Value	Year	Rating	Trend
Energy-related CO_2 emissions (tCO₂/capita)	2.2	2017	●	↑
CO_2 emissions embodied in imports (tCO₂/capita)	0.3	2015	●	↑
CO_2 emissions embodied in fossil fuel exports (kg/capita)	0.0	2018	●	●

SDG14 – Life Below Water

	Value	Year	Rating	Trend
Mean area that is protected in marine sites important to biodiversity (%)	76.9	2018	●	↑
Ocean Health Index: Clean Waters score (worst 0–100 best)	68.5	2019	●	↑
Fish caught from overexploited or collapsed stocks (% of total catch)	29.2	2014	●	↑
Fish caught by trawling (%)	5.9	2014	●	↑
Marine biodiversity threats embodied in imports (per million population)	0.0	2018	●	●

SDG15 – Life on Land

	Value	Year	Rating	Trend
Mean area that is protected in terrestrial sites important to biodiversity (%)	29.7	2018	●	↗
Mean area that is protected in freshwater sites important to biodiversity (%)	70.9	2018	●	↑
Red List Index of species survival (worst 0–1 best)	0.7	2019	●	↓
Permanent deforestation (% of forest area, 5-year average)	0.1	2018	●	●
Terrestrial and freshwater biodiversity threats embodied in imports (per million population)	0.3	2018	●	●

SDG16 – Peace, Justice and Strong Institutions

	Value	Year	Rating	Trend
Homicides (per 100,000 population)	5.8	2017	●	↑
Unsentenced detainees (% of prison population)	33.8	2018	●	↑
Percentage of population who feel safe walking alone at night in the city or area where they live	45.3	2019	●	↓
Property Rights (worst 1–7 best)	3.7	2019	●	●
Birth registrations with civil authority (% of children under age 5)	82.1	2018	●	●
Corruption Perception Index (worst 0–100 best)	38	2019	●	↗
Children involved in child labor (% of population aged 5 to 14)	4.9	2016	●	●
Exports of major conventional weapons (TIV constant million USD per 100,000 population)	0.0	2019	●	●
Press Freedom Index (best 0–100 worst)	31.9	2019	●	↑

SDG17 – Partnerships for the Goals

	Value	Year	Rating	Trend
Government spending on health and education (% of GDP)	9.2	2015	●	↓
For high-income and all OECD DAC countries: International concessional public finance, including official development assistance (% of GNI)	NA	NA	●	●
Other countries: Government revenue excluding grants (% of GDP)	NA	NA	●	●
Corporate Tax Haven Score (best 0–100 worst) *	0.0	2019	●	●

* Imputed data point

5. Country Profiles

EGYPT, ARAB REPUBLIC OF Middle East and North Africa

▼ OVERALL PERFORMANCE

Index score
68.8

Regional average score
66.3

SDG Global rank **83** (OF 166)

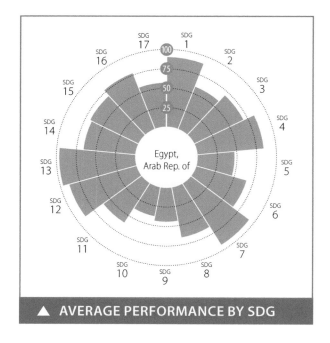

▲ AVERAGE PERFORMANCE BY SDG

▼ SPILLOVER INDEX

100 (best) to 0 (worst)

▼ CURRENT ASSESSMENT – SDG DASHBOARD

■ Major challenges ■ Significant challenges ■ Challenges remain ■ SDG achieved ■ Information unavailable

▼ SDG TRENDS

⬇ Decreasing ➡ Stagnating ↗ Moderately improving ⬆ On track or maintaining SDG achievement ● Information unavailable

Notes: The full title of Goal 2 "Zero Hunger" is "End hunger, achieve food security and improved nutrition and promote sustainable agriculture".
The full title of each SDG is available here: https://sustainabledevelopment.un.org/topics/sustainabledevelopmentgoals

SDG1 – No Poverty	Value	Year	Rating	Trend
Poverty headcount ratio at $1.90/day (%)	0.5	2020	●	↑
Poverty headcount ratio at $3.20/day (%)	9.5	2020	●	↑

SDG2 – Zero Hunger	Value	Year	Rating	Trend
Prevalence of undernourishment (%)	4.5	2017	●	↑
Prevalence of stunting in children under 5 years of age (%)	22.3	2014	●	↑
Prevalence of wasting in children under 5 years of age (%)	9.5	2014	●	↑
Prevalence of obesity, BMI ≥ 30 (% of adult population)	32.0	2016	●	↓
Human Trophic Level (best 2–3 worst)	2.2	2017	●	↑
Cereal yield (tonnes per hectare of harvested land)	7.3	2017	●	↑
Sustainable Nitrogen Management Index (best 0–1.41 worst)	0.6	2015	●	↓

SDG3 – Good Health and Well-Being	Value	Year	Rating	Trend
Maternal mortality rate (per 100,000 live births)	37	2017	●	↑
Neonatal mortality rate (per 1,000 live births)	11.2	2018	●	↑
Mortality rate, under-5 (per 1,000 live births)	21.2	2018	●	↑
Incidence of tuberculosis (per 100,000 population)	12.0	2018	●	↑
New HIV infections (per 1,000 uninfected population)	0.0	2018	●	↑
Age-standardized death rate due to cardiovascular disease, cancer, diabetes, or chronic respiratory disease in adults aged 30–70 years (%)	27.7	2016	●	→
Age-standardized death rate attributable to household air pollution and ambient air pollution (per 100,000 population)	109	2016	●	●
Traffic deaths (per 100,000 population)	9.7	2016	●	↑
Life expectancy at birth (years)	70.5	2016	●	↓
Adolescent fertility rate (births per 1,000 adolescent females aged 15 to 19)	53.8	2017	●	→
Births attended by skilled health personnel (%)	91.5	2014	●	●
Percentage of surviving infants who received 2 WHO-recommended vaccines (%)	94	2018	●	↑
Universal health coverage (UHC) index of service coverage (worst 0–100 best)	68.0	2017	●	↗
Subjective well-being (average ladder score, worst 0–10 best)	4.0	2018	●	↓

SDG4 – Quality Education	Value	Year	Rating	Trend
Net primary enrollment rate (%)	97.0	2018	●	↑
Lower secondary completion rate (%)	84.6	2018	●	↑
Literacy rate (% of population aged 15 to 24)	88.2	2017	●	●

SDG5 – Gender Equality	Value	Year	Rating	Trend
Demand for family planning satisfied by modern methods (% of females aged 15 to 49 who are married or in unions)	80.0	2014	●	↑
Ratio of female-to-male mean years of education received (%)	83.8	2018	●	↗
Ratio of female-to-male labor force participation rate (%)	31.3	2019	●	→
Seats held by women in national parliament (%)	15.1	2020	●	→

SDG6 – Clean Water and Sanitation	Value	Year	Rating	Trend
Population using at least basic drinking water services (%)	99.1	2017	●	↑
Population using at least basic sanitation services (%)	94.2	2017	●	↑
Freshwater withdrawal (% of available freshwater resources)	118.9	2015	●	●
Anthropogenic wastewater that receives treatment (%)	42.0	2018	●	●
Scarce water consumption embodied in imports (m³/capita)	1.6	2013	●	↑

SDG7 – Affordable and Clean Energy	Value	Year	Rating	Trend
Population with access to electricity (%)	100.0	2017	●	↑
Population with access to clean fuels and technology for cooking (%)	97.6	2016	●	↑
CO_2 emissions from fuel combustion for electricity and heating per total electricity output (MtCO₂/TWh)	1.1	2017	●	↗

SDG8 – Decent Work and Economic Growth	Value	Year	Rating	Trend
Adjusted GDP growth (%)	-1.6	2018	●	●
Victims of modern slavery (per 1,000 population)	5.5	2018	●	●
Adults with an account at a bank or other financial institution or with a mobile-money-service provider (% of population aged 15 or over)	32.8	2017	●	↑
Unemployment rate (% of total labor force)	10.8	2019	●	↑
Fatal work-related accidents embodied in imports (per 100,000 population)	0.1	2010	●	↑

SDG9 – Industry, Innovation and Infrastructure	Value	Year	Rating	Trend
Population using the internet (%)	46.9	2018	●	↑
Mobile broadband subscriptions (per 100 population)	53.9	2018	●	↑
Logistics Performance Index: Quality of trade and transport-related infrastructure (worst 1–5 best)	2.8	2018	●	↓
The Times Higher Education Universities Ranking: Average score of top 3 universities (worst 0–100 best)	39.4	2020	●	●
Scientific and technical journal articles (per 1,000 population)	0.1	2018	●	→
Expenditure on research and development (% of GDP)	0.6	2017	●	↓

SDG10 – Reduced Inequalities	Value	Year	Rating	Trend
Gini coefficient adjusted for top income	49.6	2015	●	●

SDG11 – Sustainable Cities and Communities	Value	Year	Rating	Trend
Annual mean concentration of particulate matter of less than 2.5 microns in diameter (PM2.5) (µg/m³)	87.0	2017	●	↓
Access to improved water source, piped (% of urban population)	98.6	2017	●	↑
Satisfaction with public transport (%)	71.0	2018	●	↑

SDG12 – Responsible Consumption and Production	Value	Year	Rating	Trend
Municipal solid waste (kg/capita/day)	1.4	2012	●	●
Electronic waste (kg/capita)	5.5	2016	●	●
Production-based SO_2 emissions (kg/capita)	8.8	2012	●	●
SO_2 emissions embodied in imports (kg/capita)	0.7	2012	●	●
Production-based nitrogen emissions (kg/capita)	10.9	2010	●	●
Nitrogen emissions embodied in imports (kg/capita)	0.6	2010	●	●

SDG13 – Climate Action	Value	Year	Rating	Trend
Energy-related CO_2 emissions (tCO₂/capita)	2.0	2017	●	↓
CO_2 emissions embodied in imports (tCO₂/capita)	0.1	2015	●	↑
CO_2 emissions embodied in fossil fuel exports (kg/capita)	13.2	2018	●	●

SDG14 – Life Below Water	Value	Year	Rating	Trend
Mean area that is protected in marine sites important to biodiversity (%)	66.2	2018	●	↑
Ocean Health Index: Clean Waters score (worst 0–100 best)	50.4	2019	●	↓
Fish caught from overexploited or collapsed stocks (% of total catch)	27.7	2014	●	↑
Fish caught by trawling (%)	34.5	2014	●	↑
Marine biodiversity threats embodied in imports (per million population)	0.0	2018	●	●

SDG15 – Life on Land	Value	Year	Rating	Trend
Mean area that is protected in terrestrial sites important to biodiversity (%)	40.3	2018	●	→
Mean area that is protected in freshwater sites important to biodiversity (%)	28.5	2018	●	→
Red List Index of species survival (worst 0–1 best)	0.9	2019	●	↑
Permanent deforestation (% of forest area, 5-year average)	0.0	2018	●	●
Terrestrial and freshwater biodiversity threats embodied in imports (per million population)	0.1	2018	●	●

SDG16 – Peace, Justice and Strong Institutions	Value	Year	Rating	Trend
Homicides (per 100,000 population)	2.5	2012	●	●
Unsentenced detainees (% of prison population)	9.9	2018	●	●
Percentage of population who feel safe walking alone at night in the city or area where they live (%)	87.0	2018	●	↑
Property Rights (worst 1–7 best)	5.1	2019	●	●
Birth registrations with civil authority (% of children under age 5)	99.4	2018	●	●
Corruption Perception Index (worst 0–100 best)	35	2019	●	↓
Children involved in child labor (% of population aged 5 to 14)	7.0	2016	●	●
Exports of major conventional weapons (TIV constant million USD per 100,000 population)	0.0	2019	●	●
Press Freedom Index (best 0–100 worst)	56.5	2019	●	↓

SDG17 – Partnerships for the Goals	Value	Year	Rating	Trend
Government spending on health and education (% of GDP)	5.3	2008	●	●
For high-income and all OECD DAC countries: International concessional public finance, including official development assistance (% of GNI)	NA	NA	●	●
Other countries: Government revenue excluding grants (% of GDP)	21.0	2015	●	●
Corporate Tax Haven Score (best 0–100 worst) *	0.0	2019	●	●

* Imputed data point

5. Country Profiles

▼ OVERALL PERFORMANCE

Index score
69.6

Regional average score
70.4

SDG Global rank 77 (OF 166)

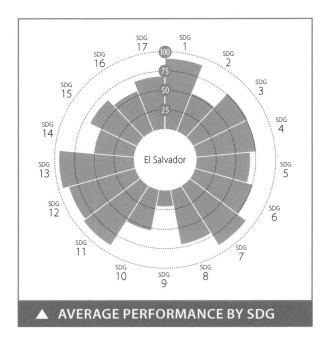

▲ AVERAGE PERFORMANCE BY SDG

▼ SPILLOVER INDEX

100 (best) to 0 (worst)

▼ CURRENT ASSESSMENT – SDG DASHBOARD

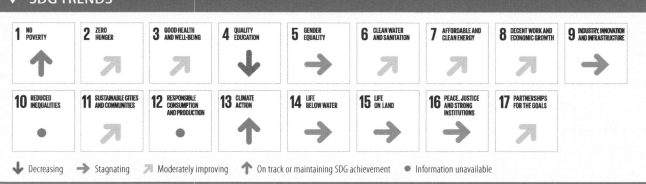

■ Major challenges ■ Significant challenges ■ Challenges remain ■ SDG achieved ■ Information unavailable

▼ SDG TRENDS

1 NO POVERTY	2 ZERO HUNGER	3 GOOD HEALTH AND WELL-BEING	4 QUALITY EDUCATION	5 GENDER EQUALITY	6 CLEAN WATER AND SANITATION	7 AFFORDABLE AND CLEAN ENERGY	8 DECENT WORK AND ECONOMIC GROWTH	9 INDUSTRY, INNOVATION AND INFRASTRUCTURE
↑	↗	↗	↓	→	↗	↗	↗	→

10 REDUCED INEQUALITIES	11 SUSTAINABLE CITIES AND COMMUNITIES	12 RESPONSIBLE CONSUMPTION AND PRODUCTION	13 CLIMATE ACTION	14 LIFE BELOW WATER	15 LIFE ON LAND	16 PEACE, JUSTICE AND STRONG INSTITUTIONS	17 PARTNERSHIPS FOR THE GOALS
●	↗	●	↑	→	→	→	↗

↓ Decreasing → Stagnating ↗ Moderately improving ↑ On track or maintaining SDG achievement ● Information unavailable

Notes: The full title of Goal 2 "Zero Hunger" is "End hunger, achieve food security and improved nutrition and promote sustainable agriculture".
The full title of each SDG is available here: https://sustainabledevelopment.un.org/topics/sustainabledevelopmentgoals

SDG1 – No Poverty

Indicator	Value	Year	Rating	Trend
Poverty headcount ratio at $1.90/day (%)	1.1	2020	●	↑
Poverty headcount ratio at $3.20/day (%)	7.4	2020	○	↑

SDG2 – Zero Hunger

Indicator	Value	Year	Rating	Trend
Prevalence of undernourishment (%)	9.0	2017	○	↑
Prevalence of stunting in children under 5 years of age (%)	13.6	2014	●	↑
Prevalence of wasting in children under 5 years of age (%)	2.1	2014	●	↑
Prevalence of obesity, BMI ≥ 30 (% of adult population)	24.6	2016	●	↓
Human Trophic Level (best 2–3 worst)	2.3	2017	○	↑
Cereal yield (tonnes per hectare of harvested land)	2.8	2017	●	↑
Sustainable Nitrogen Management Index (best 0–1.41 worst)	1.0	2015	●	→

SDG3 – Good Health and Well-Being

Indicator	Value	Year	Rating	Trend
Maternal mortality rate (per 100,000 live births)	46	2017	●	↑
Neonatal mortality rate (per 1,000 live births)	6.7	2018	●	↑
Mortality rate, under-5 (per 1,000 live births)	13.7	2018	●	↑
Incidence of tuberculosis (per 100,000 population)	70.0	2018	●	↓
New HIV infections (per 1,000 uninfected population)	0.1	2018	●	↑
Age-standardized death rate due to cardiovascular disease, cancer, diabetes, or chronic respiratory disease in adults aged 30–70 years (%)	14.0	2016	●	↑
Age-standardized death rate attributable to household air pollution and ambient air pollution (per 100,000 population)	42	2016	○	●
Traffic deaths (per 100,000 population)	22.2	2016	●	↓
Life expectancy at birth (years)	73.7	2016	●	↗
Adolescent fertility rate (births per 1,000 adolescent females aged 15 to 19)	69.5	2017	●	→
Births attended by skilled health personnel (%)	99.9	2016	●	↑
Percentage of surviving infants who received 2 WHO-recommended vaccines (%)	81	2018	●	↓
Universal health coverage (UHC) index of service coverage (worst 0–100 best)	76.0	2017	○	↑
Subjective well-being (average ladder score, worst 0–10 best)	6.3	2018	●	↑

SDG4 – Quality Education

Indicator	Value	Year	Rating	Trend
Net primary enrollment rate (%)	81.0	2018	●	↓
Lower secondary completion rate (%)	77.8	2017	●	↓
Literacy rate (% of population aged 15 to 24)	98.0	2018	●	●

SDG5 – Gender Equality

Indicator	Value	Year	Rating	Trend
Demand for family planning satisfied by modern methods (% of females aged 15 to 49 who are married or in unions)	80.0	2014	●	↑
Ratio of female-to-male mean years of education received (%)	90.4	2018	○	→
Ratio of female-to-male labor force participation rate (%)	58.6	2019	●	↓
Seats held by women in national parliament (%)	33.3	2020	○	→

SDG6 – Clean Water and Sanitation

Indicator	Value	Year	Rating	Trend
Population using at least basic drinking water services (%)	97.4	2017	○	↑
Population using at least basic sanitation services (%)	87.4	2017	○	→
Freshwater withdrawal (% of available freshwater resources)	13.2	2005	●	●
Anthropogenic wastewater that receives treatment (%)	0.1	2018	●	●
Scarce water consumption embodied in imports (m³/capita)	2.0	2013	●	↑

SDG7 – Affordable and Clean Energy

Indicator	Value	Year	Rating	Trend
Population with access to electricity (%)	99.5	2017	●	↑
Population with access to clean fuels and technology for cooking (%)	86.0	2016	●	↑
CO_2 emissions from fuel combustion for electricity and heating per total electricity output (MtCO₂/TWh)	1.1	2017	○	↓

SDG8 – Decent Work and Economic Growth

Indicator	Value	Year	Rating	Trend
Adjusted GDP growth (%)	-2.7	2018	●	●
Victims of modern slavery (per 1,000 population)	2.5	2018	●	●
Adults with an account at a bank or other financial institution or with a mobile-money-service provider (% of population aged 15 or over)	30.4	2017	●	↓
Unemployment rate (% of total labor force)	4.1	2019	●	↑
Fatal work-related accidents embodied in imports (per 100,000 population)	0.4	2010	●	↑

SDG9 – Industry, Innovation and Infrastructure

Indicator	Value	Year	Rating	Trend
Population using the internet (%)	33.8	2017	●	↗
Mobile broadband subscriptions (per 100 population)	54.5	2018	●	↑
Logistics Performance Index: Quality of trade and transport-related infrastructure (worst 1–5 best)	2.2	2018	●	↓
The Times Higher Education Universities Ranking: Average score of top 3 universities (worst 0–100 best) *	0.0	2020	●	●
Scientific and technical journal articles (per 1,000 population)	0.0	2018	●	→
Expenditure on research and development (% of GDP)	0.1	2016	●	→

SDG10 – Reduced Inequalities

Indicator	Value	Year	Rating	Trend
Gini coefficient adjusted for top income	44.4	2017	●	●

SDG11 – Sustainable Cities and Communities

Indicator	Value	Year	Rating	Trend
Annual mean concentration of particulate matter of less than 2.5 microns in diameter (PM2.5) (μg/m³)	24.5	2017	●	↗
Access to improved water source, piped (% of urban population)	94.6	2017	○	↗
Satisfaction with public transport (%)	80.3	2018	●	↑

SDG12 – Responsible Consumption and Production

Indicator	Value	Year	Rating	Trend
Municipal solid waste (kg/capita/day)	1.0	2010	●	●
Electronic waste (kg/capita)	5.8	2016	●	●
Production-based SO_2 emissions (kg/capita)	30.1	2012	●	●
SO_2 emissions embodied in imports (kg/capita)	3.3	2012	●	●
Production-based nitrogen emissions (kg/capita)	13.9	2010	●	●
Nitrogen emissions embodied in imports (kg/capita)	2.7	2010	●	●

SDG13 – Climate Action

Indicator	Value	Year	Rating	Trend
Energy-related CO_2 emissions (tCO₂/capita)	1.2	2017	●	↑
CO_2 emissions embodied in imports (tCO₂/capita)	0.4	2015	●	↑
CO_2 emissions embodied in fossil fuel exports (kg/capita)	0.0	2019	●	●

SDG14 – Life Below Water

Indicator	Value	Year	Rating	Trend
Mean area that is protected in marine sites important to biodiversity (%)	46.6	2018	○	→
Ocean Health Index: Clean Waters score (worst 0–100 best)	44.2	2019	●	↓
Fish caught from overexploited or collapsed stocks (% of total catch)	100.0	2014	●	↓
Fish caught by trawling (%)	11.5	2014	○	↑
Marine biodiversity threats embodied in imports (per million population)	0.2	2018	●	●

SDG15 – Life on Land

Indicator	Value	Year	Rating	Trend
Mean area that is protected in terrestrial sites important to biodiversity (%)	26.6	2018	●	→
Mean area that is protected in freshwater sites important to biodiversity (%)	81.6	2018	●	↑
Red List Index of species survival (worst 0–1 best)	0.8	2019	●	↓
Permanent deforestation (% of forest area, 5-year average)	0.2	2018	●	●
Terrestrial and freshwater biodiversity threats embodied in imports (per million population)	1.8	2018	○	●

SDG16 – Peace, Justice and Strong Institutions

Indicator	Value	Year	Rating	Trend
Homicides (per 100,000 population)	61.8	2017	●	→
Unsentenced detainees (% of prison population)	30.4	2018	○	↓
Percentage of population who feel safe walking alone at night in the city or area where they live (%)	52.8	2018	●	↑
Property Rights (worst 1–7 best)	3.6	2019	●	●
Birth registrations with civil authority (% of children under age 5)	98.5	2018	●	●
Corruption Perception Index (worst 0–100 best)	34	2019	●	↓
Children involved in child labor (% of population aged 5 to 14)	8.9	2016	●	●
Exports of major conventional weapons (TIV constant million USD per 100,000 population) *	0.0	2019	●	●
Press Freedom Index (best 0–100 worst)	29.8	2019	●	↑

SDG17 – Partnerships for the Goals

Indicator	Value	Year	Rating	Trend
Government spending on health and education (% of GDP)	8.3	2016	○	→
For high-income and all OECD DAC countries: International concessional public finance, including official development assistance (% of GNI)	NA	NA	●	●
Other countries: Government revenue excluding grants (% of GDP)	25.1	2017	○	↑
Corporate Tax Haven Score (best 0–100 worst) *	0.0	2019	●	●

* Imputed data point

5. Country Profiles

EQUATORIAL GUINEA

▼ OVERALL PERFORMANCE

Index score

na

Regional average score

53.1

SDG Global rank   NA (OF 166)

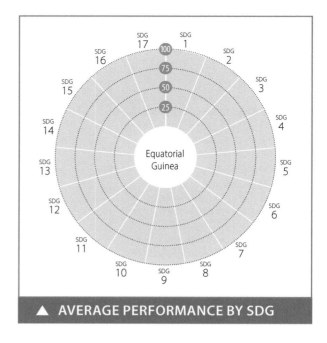

▲ AVERAGE PERFORMANCE BY SDG

▼ SPILLOVER INDEX

100 (best) to 0 (worst)

▼ CURRENT ASSESSMENT – SDG DASHBOARD

■ Major challenges   ■ Significant challenges   ▨ Challenges remain   ■ SDG achieved   ■ Information unavailable

▼ SDG TRENDS

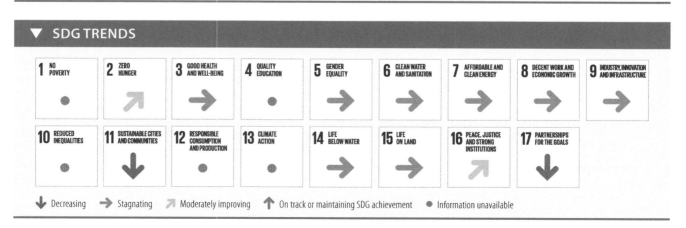

↓ Decreasing   → Stagnating   ↗ Moderately improving   ↑ On track or maintaining SDG achievement   ● Information unavailable

Notes: The full title of Goal 2 "Zero Hunger" is "End hunger, achieve food security and improved nutrition and promote sustainable agriculture".
The full title of each SDG is available here: https://sustainabledevelopment.un.org/topics/sustainabledevelopmentgoals

SDG1 – No Poverty

Indicator	Value	Year	Rating	Trend
Poverty headcount ratio at $1.90/day (%)	* NA	NA	●	●
Poverty headcount ratio at $3.20/day (%)	* NA	NA	●	●

SDG2 – Zero Hunger

Indicator	Value	Year	Rating	Trend
Prevalence of undernourishment (%)	NA	NA	●	●
Prevalence of stunting in children under 5 years of age (%)	26.2	2011	●	↗
Prevalence of wasting in children under 5 years of age (%)	3.1	2011	●	↑
Prevalence of obesity, BMI ≥ 30 (% of adult population)	8.0	2016	●	↑
Human Trophic Level (best 2–3 worst)	NA	NA	●	●
Cereal yield (tonnes per hectare of harvested land)	NA	NA	●	●
Sustainable Nitrogen Management Index (best 0–1.41 worst)	1.0	2015	●	→

SDG3 – Good Health and Well-Being

Indicator	Value	Year	Rating	Trend
Maternal mortality rate (per 100,000 live births)	301	2017	●	→
Neonatal mortality rate (per 1,000 live births)	29.9	2018	●	→
Mortality rate, under-5 (per 1,000 live births)	85.3	2018	●	↗
Incidence of tuberculosis (per 100,000 population)	201.0	2018	●	↓
New HIV infections (per 1,000 uninfected population)	4.2	2018	●	→
Age-standardized death rate due to cardiovascular disease, cancer, diabetes, or chronic respiratory disease in adults aged 30–70 years (%)	22.0	2016	●	→
Age-standardized death rate attributable to household air pollution and ambient air pollution (per 100,000 population)	178	2016	●	●
Traffic deaths (per 100,000 population)	24.6	2016	●	↓
Life expectancy at birth (years)	59.5	2016	●	→
Adolescent fertility rate (births per 1,000 adolescent females aged 15 to 19)	155.6	2017	●	→
Births attended by skilled health personnel (%)	68.3	2011	●	●
Percentage of surviving infants who received 2 WHO-recommended vaccines (%)	25	2018	●	↗
Universal health coverage (UHC) index of service coverage (worst 0–100 best)	45.0	2017	●	↗
Subjective well-being (average ladder score, worst 0–10 best)	NA	NA	●	●

SDG4 – Quality Education

Indicator	Value	Year	Rating	Trend
Net primary enrollment rate (%)	43.5	2015	●	●
Lower secondary completion rate (%)	24.2	2015	●	●
Literacy rate (% of population aged 15 to 24)	98.0	2010	●	●

SDG5 – Gender Equality

Indicator	Value	Year	Rating	Trend
Demand for family planning satisfied by modern methods (% of females aged 15 to 49 who are married or in unions)	20.7	2011	●	→
Ratio of female-to-male mean years of education received (%)	54.2	2018	●	↓
Ratio of female-to-male labor force participation rate (%)	82.1	2019	●	↑
Seats held by women in national parliament (%)	21.0	2020	●	↓

SDG6 – Clean Water and Sanitation

Indicator	Value	Year	Rating	Trend
Population using at least basic drinking water services (%)	64.7	2017	●	→
Population using at least basic sanitation services (%)	66.3	2017	●	→
Freshwater withdrawal (% of available freshwater resources)	0.2	2000	●	●
Anthropogenic wastewater that receives treatment (%)	1.3	2018	●	●
Scarce water consumption embodied in imports (m3/capita)	NA	NA	●	●

SDG7 – Affordable and Clean Energy

Indicator	Value	Year	Rating	Trend
Population with access to electricity (%)	67.2	2017	●	→
Population with access to clean fuels and technology for cooking (%)	34.4	2016	●	→
CO_2 emissions from fuel combustion for electricity and heating per total electricity output ($MtCO_2$/TWh)	NA	NA	●	●

SDG8 – Decent Work and Economic Growth

Indicator	Value	Year	Rating	Trend
Adjusted GDP growth (%)	-12.8	2018	●	●
Victims of modern slavery (per 1,000 population)	6.4	2018	●	●
Adults with an account at a bank or other financial institution or with a mobile-money-service provider (% of population aged 15 or over)	NA	NA	●	●
Unemployment rate (% of total labor force)	6.4	2019	●	→
Fatal work-related accidents embodied in imports (per 100,000 population)	NA	NA	●	●

SDG9 – Industry, Innovation and Infrastructure

Indicator	Value	Year	Rating	Trend
Population using the internet (%)	26.2	2017	●	↗
Mobile broadband subscriptions (per 100 population)	0.1	2018	●	→
Logistics Performance Index: Quality of trade and transport-related infrastructure (worst 1–5 best)	1.9	2018	●	↓
The Times Higher Education Universities Ranking: Average score of top 3 universities (worst 0–100 best)	* 0.0	2020	●	●
Scientific and technical journal articles (per 1,000 population)	0.0	2018	●	↓
Expenditure on research and development (% of GDP)	NA	NA	●	●

SDG10 – Reduced Inequalities

Indicator	Value	Year	Rating	Trend
Gini coefficient adjusted for top income	NA	NA	●	●

SDG11 – Sustainable Cities and Communities

Indicator	Value	Year	Rating	Trend
Annual mean concentration of particulate matter of less than 2.5 microns in diameter (PM2.5) ($\mu g/m^3$)	53.2	2017	●	↓
Access to improved water source, piped (% of urban population)	48.1	2017	●	→
Satisfaction with public transport (%)	NA	NA	●	●

SDG12 – Responsible Consumption and Production

Indicator	Value	Year	Rating	Trend
Municipal solid waste (kg/capita/day)	0.6	2016	●	●
Electronic waste (kg/capita)	NA	NA	●	●
Production-based SO_2 emissions (kg/capita)	NA	NA	●	●
SO_2 emissions embodied in imports (kg/capita)	NA	NA	●	●
Production-based nitrogen emissions (kg/capita)	NA	NA	●	●
Nitrogen emissions embodied in imports (kg/capita)	NA	NA	●	●

SDG13 – Climate Action

Indicator	Value	Year	Rating	Trend
Energy-related CO_2 emissions (tCO_2/capita)	4.8	2017	●	→
CO_2 emissions embodied in imports (tCO_2/capita)	NA	NA	●	●
CO_2 emissions embodied in fossil fuel exports (kg/capita)	NA	NA	●	●

SDG14 – Life Below Water

Indicator	Value	Year	Rating	Trend
Mean area that is protected in marine sites important to biodiversity (%)	100.0	2018	●	↑
Ocean Health Index: Clean Waters score (worst 0–100 best)	57.5	2019	●	↓
Fish caught from overexploited or collapsed stocks (% of total catch)	13.8	2014	●	↑
Fish caught by trawling (%)	23.2	2014	●	↓
Marine biodiversity threats embodied in imports (per million population)	NA	NA	●	●

SDG15 – Life on Land

Indicator	Value	Year	Rating	Trend
Mean area that is protected in terrestrial sites important to biodiversity (%)	100.0	2018	●	↑
Mean area that is protected in freshwater sites important to biodiversity (%)	NA	NA	●	●
Red List Index of species survival (worst 0–1 best)	0.8	2019	●	↓
Permanent deforestation (% of forest area, 5-year average)	0.2	2018	●	●
Terrestrial and freshwater biodiversity threats embodied in imports (per million population)	NA	NA	●	●

SDG16 – Peace, Justice and Strong Institutions

Indicator	Value	Year	Rating	Trend
Homicides (per 100,000 population)	* 2.3	2015	●	●
Unsentenced detainees (% of prison population)	NA	NA	●	●
Percentage of population who feel safe walking alone at night in the city or area where they live (%)	NA	NA	●	●
Property Rights (worst 1–7 best)	NA	NA	●	●
Birth registrations with civil authority (% of children under age 5)	53.5	2018	●	●
Corruption Perception Index (worst 0–100 best)	16	2019	●	●
Children involved in child labor (% of population aged 5 to 14)	27.8	2016	●	●
Exports of major conventional weapons (TIV constant million USD per 100,000 population)	* 0.0	2019	●	●
Press Freedom Index (best 0–100 worst)	58.4	2019	●	↗

SDG17 – Partnerships for the Goals

Indicator	Value	Year	Rating	Trend
Government spending on health and education (% of GDP)	NA	NA	●	●
For high-income and all OECD DAC countries: International concessional public finance, including official development assistance (% of GNI)	NA	NA	●	●
Other countries: Government revenue excluding grants (% of GDP)	17.2	2017	●	↓
Corporate Tax Haven Score (best 0–100 worst)	* 0.0	2019	●	●

* Imputed data point

5. Country Profiles

▼ OVERALL PERFORMANCE

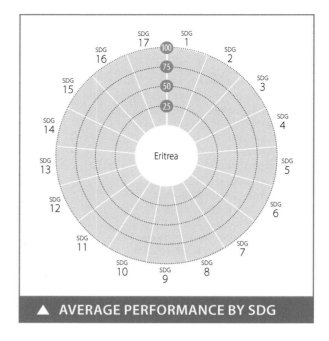

Index score

na

Regional average score

53.1

SDG Global rank NA (OF 166)

▲ AVERAGE PERFORMANCE BY SDG

▼ SPILLOVER INDEX

100 (best) to 0 (worst)

100	
80	
60	
40	
20	
0	

▼ CURRENT ASSESSMENT – SDG DASHBOARD

■ Major challenges   ■ Significant challenges   ■ Challenges remain   ■ SDG achieved   ■ Information unavailable

▼ SDG TRENDS

↓ Decreasing   → Stagnating   ↗ Moderately improving   ↑ On track or maintaining SDG achievement   ● Information unavailable

Notes: The full title of Goal 2 "Zero Hunger" is "End hunger, achieve food security and improved nutrition and promote sustainable agriculture".
   The full title of each SDG is available here: https://sustainabledevelopment.un.org/topics/sustainabledevelopmentgoals

SDG1 – No Poverty

Indicator		Value	Year	Rating	Trend
Poverty headcount ratio at $1.90/day (%)	*	NA	NA	●	●
Poverty headcount ratio at $3.20/day (%)	*	NA	NA	●	●

SDG2 – Zero Hunger

Indicator	Value	Year	Rating	Trend
Prevalence of undernourishment (%)	NA	NA	●	●
Prevalence of stunting in children under 5 years of age (%)	50.3	2010	●	→
Prevalence of wasting in children under 5 years of age (%)	15.3	2010	●	→
Prevalence of obesity, BMI ≥ 30 (% of adult population)	5.0	2016	●	↑
Human Trophic Level (best 2–3 worst)	2.1	2007	●	●
Cereal yield (tonnes per hectare of harvested land)	0.6	2017	●	↓
Sustainable Nitrogen Management Index (best 0–1.41 worst)	1.0	2015	●	→

SDG3 – Good Health and Well-Being

Indicator	Value	Year	Rating	Trend
Maternal mortality rate (per 100,000 live births)	480	2017	●	↗
Neonatal mortality rate (per 1,000 live births)	18.4	2018	●	↗
Mortality rate, under-5 (per 1,000 live births)	41.9	2018	●	↑
Incidence of tuberculosis (per 100,000 population)	89.0	2018	●	↗
New HIV infections (per 1,000 uninfected population)	0.2	2018	●	↑
Age-standardized death rate due to cardiovascular disease, cancer, diabetes, or chronic respiratory disease in adults aged 30–70 years (%)	23.9	2016	●	→
Age-standardized death rate attributable to household air pollution and ambient air pollution (per 100,000 population)	174	2016	●	●
Traffic deaths (per 100,000 population)	25.3	2016	●	↓
Life expectancy at birth (years)	65.0	2016	●	→
Adolescent fertility rate (births per 1,000 adolescent females aged 15 to 19)	52.6	2017	●	↗
Births attended by skilled health personnel (%)	34.1	2010	●	●
Percentage of surviving infants who received 2 WHO-recommended vaccines (%)	95	2018	●	↑
Universal health coverage (UHC) index of service coverage (worst 0–100 best)	38.0	2017	●	→
Subjective well-being (average ladder score, worst 0–10 best)	NA	NA	●	●

SDG4 – Quality Education

Indicator	Value	Year	Rating	Trend
Net primary enrollment rate (%)	51.5	2018	●	↓
Lower secondary completion rate (%)	47.2	2017	●	↓
Literacy rate (% of population aged 15 to 24)	93.3	2018	○	●

SDG5 – Gender Equality

Indicator	Value	Year	Rating	Trend
Demand for family planning satisfied by modern methods (% of females aged 15 to 49 who are married or in unions)	21.0	2010	●	→
Ratio of female-to-male mean years of education received (%)	NA	NA	●	●
Ratio of female-to-male labor force participation rate (%)	85.2	2019	●	↑
Seats held by women in national parliament (%)	22.0	2019	●	→

SDG6 – Clean Water and Sanitation

Indicator	Value	Year	Rating	Trend
Population using at least basic drinking water services (%)	51.9	2016	●	→
Population using at least basic sanitation services (%)	11.9	2016	●	→
Freshwater withdrawal (% of available freshwater resources)	11.2	2005	●	●
Anthropogenic wastewater that receives treatment (%)	0.0	2018	●	●
Scarce water consumption embodied in imports (m3/capita)	0.3	2013	●	↑

SDG7 – Affordable and Clean Energy

Indicator	Value	Year	Rating	Trend
Population with access to electricity (%)	48.4	2017	●	→
Population with access to clean fuels and technology for cooking (%)	16.3	2016	●	→
CO_2 emissions from fuel combustion for electricity and heating per total electricity output (MtCO2/TWh)	1.6	2017	●	→

SDG8 – Decent Work and Economic Growth

Indicator	Value	Year	Rating	Trend
Adjusted GDP growth (%)	NA	NA	●	●
Victims of modern slavery (per 1,000 population)	93.0	2018	●	●
Adults with an account at a bank or other financial institution or with a mobile-money-service provider (% of population aged 15 or over)	NA	NA	●	●
Unemployment rate (% of total labor force)	5.1	2019	○	↑
Fatal work-related accidents embodied in imports (per 100,000 population)	0.0	2010	●	↑

SDG9 – Industry, Innovation and Infrastructure

Indicator		Value	Year	Rating	Trend
Population using the internet (%)		1.3	2017	●	→
Mobile broadband subscriptions (per 100 population)		0.0	2017	●	→
Logistics Performance Index: Quality of trade and transport-related infrastructure (worst 1–5 best)		1.9	2018	●	↗
The Times Higher Education Universities Ranking: Average score of top 3 universities (worst 0–100 best)	*	0.0	2020	●	●
Scientific and technical journal articles (per 1,000 population)		0.0	2018	●	→
Expenditure on research and development (% of GDP)	*	0.0	2017	●	●

SDG10 – Reduced Inequalities

Indicator	Value	Year	Rating	Trend
Gini coefficient adjusted for top income	NA	NA	●	●

SDG11 – Sustainable Cities and Communities

Indicator	Value	Year	Rating	Trend
Annual mean concentration of particulate matter of less than 2.5 microns in diameter (PM2.5) ($\mu g/m^3$)	48.0	2017	●	↓
Access to improved water source, piped (% of urban population)	69.0	2016	●	→
Satisfaction with public transport (%)	NA	NA	●	●

SDG12 – Responsible Consumption and Production

Indicator	Value	Year	Rating	Trend
Municipal solid waste (kg/capita/day)	1.0	2011	●	●
Electronic waste (kg/capita)	0.6	2016	●	●
Production-based SO_2 emissions (kg/capita)	38.0	2012	○	●
SO_2 emissions embodied in imports (kg/capita)	0.3	2012	●	●
Production-based nitrogen emissions (kg/capita)	28.0	2010	○	●
Nitrogen emissions embodied in imports (kg/capita)	0.2	2010	●	●

SDG13 – Climate Action

Indicator		Value	Year	Rating	Trend
Energy-related CO_2 emissions (tCO2/capita)		0.2	2017	●	↑
CO_2 emissions embodied in imports (tCO2/capita)		0.0	2015	●	↑
CO_2 emissions embodied in fossil fuel exports (kg/capita)	*	0.0	2018	●	●

SDG14 – Life Below Water

Indicator	Value	Year	Rating	Trend
Mean area that is protected in marine sites important to biodiversity (%)	0.0	2018	●	→
Ocean Health Index: Clean Waters score (worst 0–100 best)	54.0	2019	●	↓
Fish caught from overexploited or collapsed stocks (% of total catch)	10.7	2014	●	↑
Fish caught by trawling (%)	NA	NA	●	●
Marine biodiversity threats embodied in imports (per million population)	0.0	2018	●	●

SDG15 – Life on Land

Indicator	Value	Year	Rating	Trend
Mean area that is protected in terrestrial sites important to biodiversity (%)	13.3	2018	●	→
Mean area that is protected in freshwater sites important to biodiversity (%)	0.0	2018	●	→
Red List Index of species survival (worst 0–1 best)	0.9	2019	●	↑
Permanent deforestation (% of forest area, 5-year average)	NA	NA	●	●
Terrestrial and freshwater biodiversity threats embodied in imports (per million population)	0.0	2018	●	●

SDG16 – Peace, Justice and Strong Institutions

Indicator		Value	Year	Rating	Trend
Homicides (per 100,000 population)	*	8.0	2015	●	●
Unsentenced detainees (% of prison population)		NA	NA	●	●
Percentage of population who feel safe walking alone at night in the city or area where they live (%)		NA	NA	●	●
Property Rights (worst 1–7 best)		NA	NA	●	●
Birth registrations with civil authority (% of children under age 5)		NA	NA	●	●
Corruption Perception Index (worst 0–100 best)		23	2019	●	→
Children involved in child labor (% of population aged 5 to 14)		NA	NA	●	●
Exports of major conventional weapons (TIV constant million USD per 100,000 population)	*	0.0	2019	●	●
Press Freedom Index (best 0–100 worst)		80.3	2019	●	→

SDG17 – Partnerships for the Goals

Indicator		Value	Year	Rating	Trend
Government spending on health and education (% of GDP)		2.8	2006	●	●
For high-income and all OECD DAC countries: International concessional public finance, including official development assistance (% of GNI)		NA	NA	●	●
Other countries: Government revenue excluding grants (% of GDP)		NA	NA	●	●
Corporate Tax Haven Score (best 0–100 worst)	*	0.0	2019	●	●

* Imputed data point

▼ OVERALL PERFORMANCE

Index score

80.1

Regional average score

77.3

SDG Global rank **10** (OF 166)

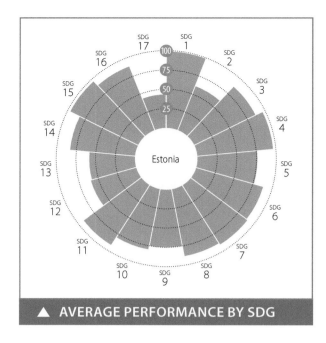

▲ AVERAGE PERFORMANCE BY SDG

▼ SPILLOVER INDEX

100 (best) to 0 (worst)

▼ CURRENT ASSESSMENT – SDG DASHBOARD

■ Major challenges ■ Significant challenges ■ Challenges remain ■ SDG achieved ▒ Information unavailable

▼ SDG TRENDS

↓ Decreasing → Stagnating ↗ Moderately improving ↑ On track or maintaining SDG achievement ● Information unavailable

Notes: The full title of Goal 2 "Zero Hunger" is "End hunger, achieve food security and improved nutrition and promote sustainable agriculture".
The full title of each SDG is available here: https://sustainabledevelopment.un.org/topics/sustainabledevelopmentgoals

SDG1 – No Poverty

	Value	Year	Rating	Trend
Poverty headcount ratio at $1.90/day (%)	0.1	2020	●	↑
Poverty headcount ratio at $3.20/day (%)	0.2	2020	●	↑
Poverty rate after taxes and transfers (%)	15.8	2017	●	→

SDG2 – Zero Hunger

		Value	Year	Rating	Trend
Prevalence of undernourishment (%)		2.9	2017	●	↑
Prevalence of stunting in children under 5 years of age (%)	*	2.6	2016	●	↑
Prevalence of wasting in children under 5 years of age (%)	*	0.7	2016	●	↑
Prevalence of obesity, BMI ≥ 30 (% of adult population)		21.2	2016	●	↓
Human Trophic Level (best 2–3 worst)		2.5	2017	●	↓
Cereal yield (tonnes per hectare of harvested land)		4.0	2017	●	↑
Sustainable Nitrogen Management Index (best 0–1.41 worst)		0.6	2015	●	→
Yield gap closure (% of potential yield)		40.7	2015	●	●

SDG3 – Good Health and Well-Being

	Value	Year	Rating	Trend
Maternal mortality rate (per 100,000 live births)	9	2017	●	↑
Neonatal mortality rate (per 1,000 live births)	1.2	2018	●	↑
Mortality rate, under-5 (per 1,000 live births)	2.6	2018	●	↑
Incidence of tuberculosis (per 100,000 population)	13.0	2018	●	↑
New HIV infections (per 1,000 uninfected population)	0.2	2018	●	↑
Age-standardized death rate due to cardiovascular disease, cancer, diabetes, or chronic respiratory disease in adults aged 30–70 years (%)	17.0	2016	●	↑
Age-standardized death rate attributable to household air pollution and ambient air pollution (per 100,000 population)	25	2016	●	●
Traffic deaths (per 100,000 population)	6.1	2016	●	↑
Life expectancy at birth (years)	77.8	2016	●	↑
Adolescent fertility rate (births per 1,000 adolescent females aged 15 to 19)	7.7	2017	●	↑
Births attended by skilled health personnel (%)	99.4	2016	●	↑
Percentage of surviving infants who received 2 WHO-recommended vaccines (%)	87.0	2018	●	↓
Universal health coverage (UHC) index of service coverage (worst 0–100 best)	75.0	2017	●	↑
Subjective well-being (average ladder score, worst 0–10 best)	6.0	2019	●	↑
Gap in life expectancy at birth among regions (years)	3.7	2015	●	●
Gap in self-reported health status by income (percentage points)	44.7	2017	●	↓
Daily smokers (% of population aged 15 and over)	17.2	2018	●	↑

SDG4 – Quality Education

		Value	Year	Rating	Trend
Net primary enrollment rate (%)	*	97.1	2017	●	↑
Lower secondary completion rate (%)	*	97.1	2017	●	↑
Literacy rate (% of population aged 15 to 24)		99.9	2011	●	●
Participation rate in pre-primary organized learning (% of children aged 4 to 6)		93.2	2017	●	↑
Tertiary educational attainment (% of population aged 25 to 34)		43.6	2018	●	↑
PISA score (worst 0–600 best)		525.3	2018	●	↑
Variation in science performance explained by socio-economic status (%)		7.2	2018	●	↑
Underachievers in science (% of 15-year-olds)		8.8	2018	●	↑
Resilient students in science (% of 15-year-olds)		54.0	2018	●	↑

SDG5 – Gender Equality

		Value	Year	Rating	Trend
Demand for family planning satisfied by modern methods (% of females aged 15 to 49 who are married or in unions)	*	78.4	2017	●	↑
Ratio of female-to-male mean years of education received (%)		106.3	2018	●	↑
Ratio of female-to-male labor force participation rate (%)		80.5	2019	●	↑
Seats held by women in national parliament (%)		28.7	2020	●	↗
Gender wage gap (% of male median wage)		28.3	2014	●	●
Gender gap in time spent doing unpaid work (minutes/day)		89.0	2010	●	●

SDG6 – Clean Water and Sanitation

	Value	Year	Rating	Trend
Population using at least basic drinking water services (%)	99.7	2017	●	●
Population using at least basic sanitation services (%)	99.1	2017	●	●
Freshwater withdrawal (% of available freshwater resources)	18.6	2015	●	●
Anthropogenic wastewater that receives treatment (%)	69.6	2018	●	●
Scarce water consumption embodied in imports (m³/capita)	18.7	2013	●	↑
Population using safely managed water services (%)	93.3	2017	●	↓
Population using safely managed sanitation services (%)	97.4	2017	●	↑

SDG7 – Affordable and Clean Energy

	Value	Year	Rating	Trend
Population with access to electricity (%)	100.0	2017	●	●
Population with access to clean fuels and technology for cooking (%)	92.9	2016	●	↑
CO₂ emissions from fuel combustion for electricity and heating per total electricity output (MtCO₂/TWh)	1.3	2017	●	●
Share of renewable energy in total primary energy supply (%)	19.2	2018	●	↑

SDG8 – Decent Work and Economic Growth

		Value	Year	Rating	Trend
Adjusted GDP growth (%)		2.6	2018	●	●
Victims of modern slavery (per 1,000 population)		3.6	2018	●	●
Adults with an account at a bank or other financial institution or with a mobile-money-service provider (% of population aged 15 or over)		98.0	2017	●	↑
Fatal work-related accidents embodied in imports (per 100,000 population)		0.7	2010	●	↑
Employment-to-population ratio (%)		75.3	2019	●	↑
Youth not in employment, education or training (NEET) (% of population aged 15 to 29)		12.7	2018	●	→

SDG9 – Industry, Innovation and Infrastructure

	Value	Year	Rating	Trend
Population using the internet (%)	89.4	2018	●	↑
Mobile broadband subscriptions (per 100 population)	146.7	2018	●	↑
Logistics Performance Index: Quality of trade and transport-related infrastructure (worst 1–5 best)	3.1	2018	●	↑
The Times Higher Education Universities Ranking: Average score of top 3 universities (worst 0–100 best)	32.0	2020	●	●
Scientific and technical journal articles (per 1,000 population)	1.1	2018	●	↑
Expenditure on research and development (% of GDP)	1.3	2017	●	↓
Researchers (per 1,000 employed population)	7.7	2018	●	↑
Triadic patent families filed (per million population)	3.0	2017	●	↓
Gap in internet access by income (percentage points)	25.3	2019	●	↗
Women in science and engineering (% of tertiary graduates in science and engineering)	35.0	2015	●	●

SDG10 – Reduced Inequalities

	Value	Year	Rating	Trend
Gini coefficient adjusted for top income	34.9	2015	●	↑
Palma ratio	1.1	2017	●	↑
Elderly poverty rate (% of population aged 66 or over)	37.2	2017	●	↓

SDG11 – Sustainable Cities and Communities

	Value	Year	Rating	Trend
Annual mean concentration of particulate matter of less than 2.5 microns in diameter (PM2.5) (µg/m³)	6.7	2017	●	↑
Access to improved water source, piped (% of urban population)	99.0	2017	●	↑
Satisfaction with public transport (%)	67.4	2019	●	↑
Population with rent overburden (%)	4.7	2017	●	↑

SDG12 – Responsible Consumption and Production

	Value	Year	Rating	Trend
Electronic waste (kg/capita)	14.4	2016	●	●
Production-based SO₂ emissions (kg/capita)	186.6	2012	●	●
SO₂ emissions embodied in imports (kg/capita)	16.0	2012	●	●
Production-based nitrogen emissions (kg/capita)	40.5	2010	●	●
Nitrogen emissions embodied in imports (kg/capita)	7.9	2010	●	●
Non-recycled municipal solid waste (kg/capita/day)	0.8	2018	●	●

SDG13 – Climate Action

	Value	Year	Rating	Trend
Energy-related CO₂ emissions (tCO₂/capita)	15.5	2017	●	↓
CO₂ emissions embodied in imports (tCO₂/capita)	2.0	2015	●	→
CO₂ emissions embodied in fossil fuel exports (kg/capita)	0.0	2019	●	●
Effective carbon rate (EUR/tCO₂)	12.1	2016	●	●

SDG14 – Life Below Water

	Value	Year	Rating	Trend
Mean area that is protected in marine sites important to biodiversity (%)	97.8	2018	●	↑
Ocean Health Index: Clean Waters score (worst 0–100 best)	66.0	2019	●	↓
Fish caught from overexploited or collapsed stocks (% of total catch)	1.4	2014	●	↑
Fish caught by trawling (%)	29.6	2014	●	↓
Marine biodiversity threats embodied in imports (per million population)	0.1	2018	●	●

SDG15 – Life on Land

	Value	Year	Rating	Trend
Mean area that is protected in terrestrial sites important to biodiversity (%)	94.8	2018	●	↑
Mean area that is protected in freshwater sites important to biodiversity (%)	93.5	2018	●	↑
Red List Index of species survival (worst 0–1 best)	1.0	2019	●	↑
Permanent deforestation (% of forest area, 5-year average)	0.0	2018	●	●
Terrestrial and freshwater biodiversity threats embodied in imports (per million population)	0.3	2018	●	●

SDG16 – Peace, Justice and Strong Institutions

		Value	Year	Rating	Trend
Homicides (per 100,000 population)		2.2	2017	●	↑
Unsentenced detainees (% of prison population)		20.7	2018	●	↑
Percentage of population who feel safe walking alone at night in the city or area where they live (%)		72.1	2019	●	↑
Property Rights (worst 1–7 best)		5.4	2019	●	●
Birth registrations with civil authority (% of children under age 5)		100.0	2018	●	●
Corruption Perception Index (worst 0–100 best)		74.0	2019	●	↑
Children involved in child labor (% of population aged 5 to 14)	*	0.0	2016	●	●
Exports of major conventional weapons (TIV constant million USD per 100,000 population)		0.0	2019	●	●
Press Freedom Index (best 0–100 worst)		12.3	2019	●	↑
Persons held in prison (per 100,000 population)		196.6	2017	●	↑

SDG17 – Partnerships for the Goals

	Value	Year	Rating	Trend
Government spending on health and education (% of GDP)	10.2	2016	●	↑
For high-income and all OECD DAC countries: International concessional public finance, including official development assistance (% of GNI)	0.2	2017	●	→
Other countries: Government revenue excluding grants (% of GDP)	NA	NA	●	●
Corporate Tax Haven Score (best 0–100 worst)	66.5	2019	●	●
Financial Secrecy Score (best 0–100 worst)	43.1	2020	●	●
Shifted profits of multinationals (US$ billion)	0.3	2016	●	●

* Imputed data point

5. Country Profiles

ESWATINI

▼ OVERALL PERFORMANCE

Index score
53.4

Regional average score
53.1

SDG Global rank **144** (OF 166)

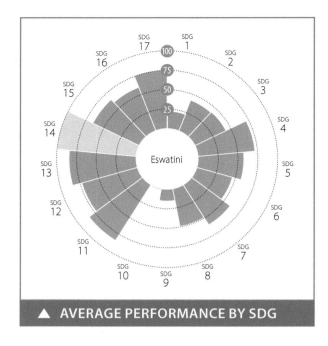

▲ AVERAGE PERFORMANCE BY SDG

▼ SPILLOVER INDEX

100 (best) to 0 (worst)

▼ CURRENT ASSESSMENT – SDG DASHBOARD

■ Major challenges   ■ Significant challenges   ▊ Challenges remain   ■ SDG achieved   ■ Information unavailable

▼ SDG TRENDS

↓ Decreasing   → Stagnating   ↗ Moderately improving   ↑ On track or maintaining SDG achievement   ● Information unavailable

Notes: The full title of Goal 2 "Zero Hunger" is "End hunger, achieve food security and improved nutrition and promote sustainable agriculture".
The full title of each SDG is available here: https://sustainabledevelopment.un.org/topics/sustainabledevelopmentgoals

ESWATINI

SDG1 – No Poverty	Value	Year	Rating	Trend
Poverty headcount ratio at $1.90/day (%)	39.3	2020	●	→
Poverty headcount ratio at $3.20/day (%)	59.5	2020	●	→

SDG2 – Zero Hunger	Value	Year	Rating	Trend
Prevalence of undernourishment (%)	20.6	2017	●	↗
Prevalence of stunting in children under 5 years of age (%)	25.5	2014	●	↑
Prevalence of wasting in children under 5 years of age (%)	2.0	2014	●	↑
Prevalence of obesity, BMI ≥ 30 (% of adult population)	16.5	2016	●	↓
Human Trophic Level (best 2–3 worst)	4.0	2017	●	↓
Cereal yield (tonnes per hectare of harvested land)	1.1	2017	●	→
Sustainable Nitrogen Management Index (best 0–1.41 worst)	0.8	2015	●	→

SDG3 – Good Health and Well-Being	Value	Year	Rating	Trend
Maternal mortality rate (per 100,000 live births)	437	2017	●	↓
Neonatal mortality rate (per 1,000 live births)	17.2	2018	●	↗
Mortality rate, under-5 (per 1,000 live births)	54.4	2018	●	↑
Incidence of tuberculosis (per 100,000 population)	329.0	2018	●	↑
New HIV infections (per 1,000 uninfected population)	8.6	2018	●	↑
Age-standardized death rate due to cardiovascular disease, cancer, diabetes, or chronic respiratory disease in adults aged 30–70 years (%)	26.7	2016	●	↓
Age-standardized death rate attributable to household air pollution and ambient air pollution (per 100,000 population)	137	2016	●	●
Traffic deaths (per 100,000 population)	26.9	2016	●	↓
Life expectancy at birth (years)	57.7	2016	●	→
Adolescent fertility rate (births per 1,000 adolescent females aged 15 to 19)	76.7	2017	●	→
Births attended by skilled health personnel (%)	88.3	2014	●	●
Percentage of surviving infants who received 2 WHO-recommended vaccines (%)	89	2018	●	→
Universal health coverage (UHC) index of service coverage (worst 0–100 best)	63.0	2017	●	↗
Subjective well-being (average ladder score, worst 0–10 best)	4.4	2019	●	●

SDG4 – Quality Education	Value	Year	Rating	Trend
Net primary enrollment rate (%)	82.5	2017	●	↓
Lower secondary completion rate (%)	67.4	2017	●	↑
Literacy rate (% of population aged 15 to 24)	95.5	2018	●	●

SDG5 – Gender Equality	Value	Year	Rating	Trend
Demand for family planning satisfied by modern methods (% of females aged 15 to 49 who are married or in unions)	82.9	2014	●	↑
Ratio of female-to-male mean years of education received (%)	87.5	2018	●	↓
Ratio of female-to-male labor force participation rate (%)	62.9	2019	●	→
Seats held by women in national parliament (%)	9.6	2020	●	→

SDG6 – Clean Water and Sanitation	Value	Year	Rating	Trend
Population using at least basic drinking water services (%)	69.0	2017	●	→
Population using at least basic sanitation services (%)	58.4	2017	●	→
Freshwater withdrawal (% of available freshwater resources)	75.7	2000	●	●
Anthropogenic wastewater that receives treatment (%)	5.3	2018	●	●
Scarce water consumption embodied in imports (m³/capita)	6.3	2013	●	↑

SDG7 – Affordable and Clean Energy	Value	Year	Rating	Trend
Population with access to electricity (%)	73.5	2017	●	↑
Population with access to clean fuels and technology for cooking (%)	49.7	2016	●	↗
CO_2 emissions from fuel combustion for electricity and heating per total electricity output (MtCO₂/TWh)	NA	NA	●	●

SDG8 – Decent Work and Economic Growth	Value	Year	Rating	Trend
Adjusted GDP growth (%)	-3.3	2018	●	●
Victims of modern slavery (per 1,000 population)	8.8	2018	●	●
Adults with an account at a bank or other financial institution or with a mobile-money-service provider (% of population aged 15 or over)	28.6	2011	●	●
Unemployment rate (% of total labor force)	22.1	2019	●	→
Fatal work-related accidents embodied in imports (per 100,000 population)	0.7	2010	●	↑

SDG9 – Industry, Innovation and Infrastructure	Value	Year	Rating	Trend
Population using the internet (%)	47.0	2017	●	↑
Mobile broadband subscriptions (per 100 population)	15.9	2017	●	→
Logistics Performance Index: Quality of trade and transport-related infrastructure (worst 1–5 best)	NA	NA	●	●
The Times Higher Education Universities Ranking: Average score of top 3 universities (worst 0–100 best) *	0.0	2020	●	●
Scientific and technical journal articles (per 1,000 population)	0.0	2018	●	→
Expenditure on research and development (% of GDP)	0.3	2015	●	●

SDG10 – Reduced Inequalities	Value	Year	Rating	Trend
Gini coefficient adjusted for top income	65.9	2009	●	●

SDG11 – Sustainable Cities and Communities	Value	Year	Rating	Trend
Annual mean concentration of particulate matter of less than 2.5 microns in diameter (PM2.5) (μg/m³)	17.2	2017	●	↗
Access to improved water source, piped (% of urban population)	94.8	2017	●	↑
Satisfaction with public transport (%)	63.6	2019	●	●

SDG12 – Responsible Consumption and Production	Value	Year	Rating	Trend
Municipal solid waste (kg/capita/day)	1.8	2016	●	●
Electronic waste (kg/capita)	5.1	2016	●	●
Production-based SO_2 emissions (kg/capita)	114.8	2012	●	●
SO_2 emissions embodied in imports (kg/capita)	12.1	2012	●	●
Production-based nitrogen emissions (kg/capita)	27.2	2010	●	●
Nitrogen emissions embodied in imports (kg/capita)	5.3	2010	●	●

SDG13 – Climate Action	Value	Year	Rating	Trend
Energy-related CO_2 emissions (tCO₂/capita)	1.2	2017	●	↑
CO_2 emissions embodied in imports (tCO₂/capita)	1.4	2015	●	→
CO_2 emissions embodied in fossil fuel exports (kg/capita)	162.7	2019	●	●

SDG14 – Life Below Water	Value	Year	Rating	Trend
Mean area that is protected in marine sites important to biodiversity (%)	NA	NA	●	●
Ocean Health Index: Clean Waters score (worst 0–100 best)	NA	NA	●	●
Fish caught from overexploited or collapsed stocks (% of total catch)	NA	NA	●	●
Fish caught by trawling (%)	NA	NA	●	●
Marine biodiversity threats embodied in imports (per million population)	0.5	2018	●	●

SDG15 – Life on Land	Value	Year	Rating	Trend
Mean area that is protected in terrestrial sites important to biodiversity (%)	30.6	2018	●	→
Mean area that is protected in freshwater sites important to biodiversity (%)	NA	NA	●	●
Red List Index of species survival (worst 0–1 best)	0.8	2019	●	→
Permanent deforestation (% of forest area, 5-year average)	0.1	2018	●	●
Terrestrial and freshwater biodiversity threats embodied in imports (per million population)	1.7	2018	●	●

SDG16 – Peace, Justice and Strong Institutions	Value	Year	Rating	Trend
Homicides (per 100,000 population)	9.5	2017	●	→
Unsentenced detainees (% of prison population)	18.1	2012	●	●
Percentage of population who feel safe walking alone at night in the city or area where they live (%)	45.3	2019	●	●
Property Rights (worst 1–7 best)	4.6	2019	●	●
Birth registrations with civil authority (% of children under age 5)	53.5	2018	●	●
Corruption Perception Index (worst 0–100 best)	34	2019	●	↓
Children involved in child labor (% of population aged 5 to 14)	7.3	2016	●	●
Exports of major conventional weapons (TIV constant million USD per 100,000 population) *	0.0	2019	●	●
Press Freedom Index (best 0–100 worst)	49.1	2019	●	↗

SDG17 – Partnerships for the Goals	Value	Year	Rating	Trend
Government spending on health and education (% of GDP)	11.6	2014	●	●
For high-income and all OECD DAC countries: International concessional public finance, including official development assistance (% of GNI)	NA	NA	●	●
Other countries: Government revenue excluding grants (% of GDP) *	24.5	2018	●	↓
Corporate Tax Haven Score (best 0–100 worst) *	0.0	2019	●	●

* Imputed data point

5. Country Profiles

ETHIOPIA

▼ OVERALL PERFORMANCE

Index score

55.2

Regional average score

53.1

SDG Global rank 136 (OF 166)

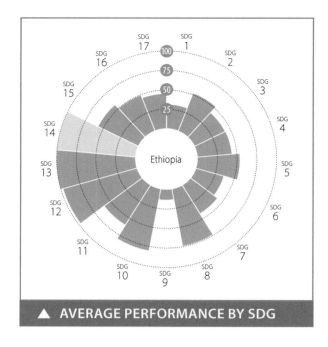

▲ AVERAGE PERFORMANCE BY SDG

▼ SPILLOVER INDEX

100 (best) to 0 (worst)

▼ CURRENT ASSESSMENT – SDG DASHBOARD

■ Major challenges   ■ Significant challenges   ■ Challenges remain   ■ SDG achieved   ■ Information unavailable

▼ SDG TRENDS

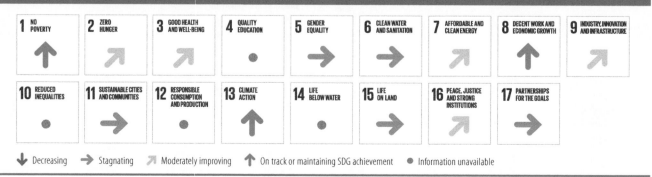

↓ Decreasing   → Stagnating   ↗ Moderately improving   ↑ On track or maintaining SDG achievement   ● Information unavailable

Notes: The full title of Goal 2 "Zero Hunger" is "End hunger, achieve food security and improved nutrition and promote sustainable agriculture".
The full title of each SDG is available here: https://sustainabledevelopment.un.org/topics/sustainabledevelopmentgoals

216 | Sustainable Development Report 2020 ◉ The Sustainable Development Goals and Covid-19

ETHIOPIA

SDG1 – No Poverty

Indicator	Value	Year	Rating	Trend
Poverty headcount ratio at $1.90/day (%)	25.3	2020	●	↑
Poverty headcount ratio at $3.20/day (%)	59.3	2020	●	↗

SDG2 – Zero Hunger

Indicator	Value	Year	Rating	Trend
Prevalence of undernourishment (%)	20.6	2017	●	↑
Prevalence of stunting in children under 5 years of age (%)	38.4	2016	●	→
Prevalence of wasting in children under 5 years of age (%)	9.9	2016	●	→
Prevalence of obesity, BMI ≥ 30 (% of adult population)	4.5	2016	●	↑
Human Trophic Level (best 2–3 worst)	2.1	2017	●	↑
Cereal yield (tonnes per hectare of harvested land)	2.5	2017	●	↑
Sustainable Nitrogen Management Index (best 0–1.41 worst)	0.7	2015	●	→

SDG3 – Good Health and Well-Being

Indicator	Value	Year	Rating	Trend
Maternal mortality rate (per 100,000 live births)	401	2017	●	↗
Neonatal mortality rate (per 1,000 live births)	28.1	2018	●	↗
Mortality rate, under-5 (per 1,000 live births)	55.2	2018	●	↑
Incidence of tuberculosis (per 100,000 population)	151.0	2018	●	↑
New HIV infections (per 1,000 uninfected population)	0.2	2018	●	↑
Age-standardized death rate due to cardiovascular disease, cancer, diabetes, or chronic respiratory disease in adults aged 30–70 years (%)	18.3	2016	●	↗
Age-standardized death rate attributable to household air pollution and ambient air pollution (per 100,000 population)	144	2016	●	●
Traffic deaths (per 100,000 population)	26.7	2016	●	↓
Life expectancy at birth (years)	65.5	2016	●	↗
Adolescent fertility rate (births per 1,000 adolescent females aged 15 to 19)	66.7	2017	●	↗
Births attended by skilled health personnel (%)	27.7	2016	●	→
Percentage of surviving infants who received 2 WHO-recommended vaccines (%)	61	2018	●	↓
Universal health coverage (UHC) index of service coverage (worst 0–100 best)	39.0	2017	●	↗
Subjective well-being (average ladder score, worst 0–10 best)	4.1	2019	●	↓

SDG4 – Quality Education

Indicator	Value	Year	Rating	Trend
Net primary enrollment rate (%)	84.6	2015	●	●
Lower secondary completion rate (%)	29.5	2015	●	●
Literacy rate (% of population aged 15 to 24)	72.8	2017	●	●

SDG5 – Gender Equality

Indicator	Value	Year	Rating	Trend
Demand for family planning satisfied by modern methods (% of females aged 15 to 49 who are married or in unions)	62.3	2018	●	→
Ratio of female-to-male mean years of education received (%)	41.0	2018	●	↓
Ratio of female-to-male labor force participation rate (%)	86.0	2019	●	↑
Seats held by women in national parliament (%)	38.8	2020	●	→

SDG6 – Clean Water and Sanitation

Indicator	Value	Year	Rating	Trend
Population using at least basic drinking water services (%)	41.1	2017	●	→
Population using at least basic sanitation services (%)	7.3	2017	●	→
Freshwater withdrawal (% of available freshwater resources)	32.3	2015	●	●
Anthropogenic wastewater that receives treatment (%)	0.0	2018	●	●
Scarce water consumption embodied in imports (m³/capita)	0.4	2013	●	↑

SDG7 – Affordable and Clean Energy

Indicator	Value	Year	Rating	Trend
Population with access to electricity (%)	44.3	2017	●	↑
Population with access to clean fuels and technology for cooking (%)	3.5	2016	●	→
CO_2 emissions from fuel combustion for electricity and heating per total electricity output (MtCO$_2$/TWh)	1.0	2017	●	↑

SDG8 – Decent Work and Economic Growth

Indicator	Value	Year	Rating	Trend
Adjusted GDP growth (%)	-1.1	2018	●	●
Victims of modern slavery (per 1,000 population)	6.2	2018	●	●
Adults with an account at a bank or other financial institution or with a mobile-money-service provider (% of population aged 15 or over)	34.8	2017	●	↑
Unemployment rate (% of total labor force)	2.1	2019	●	↑
Fatal work-related accidents embodied in imports (per 100,000 population)	0.0	2010	●	↑

SDG9 – Industry, Innovation and Infrastructure

Indicator	Value	Year	Rating	Trend
Population using the internet (%)	18.6	2017	●	↗
Mobile broadband subscriptions (per 100 population)	13.9	2017	●	↑
Logistics Performance Index: Quality of trade and transport-related infrastructure (worst 1–5 best)	2.1	2016	●	●
The Times Higher Education Universities Ranking: Average score of top 3 universities (worst 0–100 best) *	0.0	2020	●	●
Scientific and technical journal articles (per 1,000 population)	0.0	2018	●	→
Expenditure on research and development (% of GDP)	0.6	2013	●	●

SDG10 – Reduced Inequalities

Indicator	Value	Year	Rating	Trend
Gini coefficient adjusted for top income	35.0	2015	●	●

SDG11 – Sustainable Cities and Communities

Indicator	Value	Year	Rating	Trend
Annual mean concentration of particulate matter of less than 2.5 microns in diameter (PM2.5) (µg/m³)	39.0	2017	●	↓
Access to improved water source, piped (% of urban population)	87.2	2017	●	→
Satisfaction with public transport (%)	39.9	2019	●	→

SDG12 – Responsible Consumption and Production

Indicator	Value	Year	Rating	Trend
Municipal solid waste (kg/capita/day)	0.8	2015	●	●
Electronic waste (kg/capita)	0.5	2016	●	●
Production-based SO_2 emissions (kg/capita)	0.5	2012	●	●
SO_2 emissions embodied in imports (kg/capita)	0.2	2012	●	●
Production-based nitrogen emissions (kg/capita)	2.9	2010	●	●
Nitrogen emissions embodied in imports (kg/capita)	0.1	2010	●	●

SDG13 – Climate Action

Indicator	Value	Year	Rating	Trend
Energy-related CO_2 emissions (tCO$_2$/capita)	0.1	2017	●	↑
CO_2 emissions embodied in imports (tCO$_2$/capita)	0.0	2015	●	↑
CO_2 emissions embodied in fossil fuel exports (kg/capita)	0.0	2017	●	●

SDG14 – Life Below Water

Indicator	Value	Year	Rating	Trend
Mean area that is protected in marine sites important to biodiversity (%)	NA	NA	●	●
Ocean Health Index: Clean Waters score (worst 0–100 best)	NA	NA	●	●
Fish caught from overexploited or collapsed stocks (% of total catch)	NA	NA	●	●
Fish caught by trawling (%)	NA	NA	●	●
Marine biodiversity threats embodied in imports (per million population)	0.0	2018	●	●

SDG15 – Life on Land

Indicator	Value	Year	Rating	Trend
Mean area that is protected in terrestrial sites important to biodiversity (%)	18.6	2018	●	→
Mean area that is protected in freshwater sites important to biodiversity (%)	16.2	2018	●	→
Red List Index of species survival (worst 0–1 best)	0.8	2019	●	→
Permanent deforestation (% of forest area, 5-year average)	0.1	2018	●	●
Terrestrial and freshwater biodiversity threats embodied in imports (per million population)	0.0	2018	●	●

SDG16 – Peace, Justice and Strong Institutions

Indicator	Value	Year	Rating	Trend
Homicides (per 100,000 population) *	7.6	2015	●	●
Unsentenced detainees (% of prison population)	14.6	2015	●	●
Percentage of population who feel safe walking alone at night in the city or area where they live (%)	53.7	2019	●	↓
Property Rights (worst 1–7 best)	3.3	2019	●	●
Birth registrations with civil authority (% of children under age 5)	2.7	2018	●	●
Corruption Perception Index (worst 0–100 best)	37	2019	●	↗
Children involved in child labor (% of population aged 5 to 14)	27.4	2016	●	●
Exports of major conventional weapons (TIV constant million USD per 100,000 population) *	0.0	2019	●	●
Press Freedom Index (best 0–100 worst)	35.1	2019	●	↑

SDG17 – Partnerships for the Goals

Indicator	Value	Year	Rating	Trend
Government spending on health and education (% of GDP)	5.8	2015	●	→
For high-income and all OECD DAC countries: International concessional public finance, including official development assistance (% of GNI)	NA	NA	●	●
Other countries: Government revenue excluding grants (% of GDP)	9.0	2018	●	↓
Corporate Tax Haven Score (best 0–100 worst) *	0.0	2019	●	●

* Imputed data point

5. Country Profiles

▼ OVERALL PERFORMANCE

Index score

69.9

Regional average score

49.6

SDG Global rank 74 (OF 166)

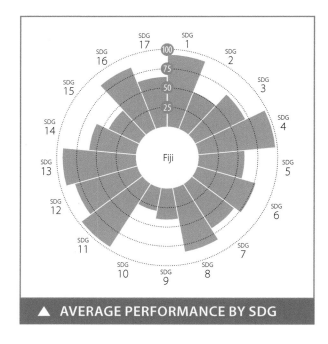

▲ AVERAGE PERFORMANCE BY SDG

▼ SPILLOVER INDEX

100 (best) to 0 (worst)

▼ CURRENT ASSESSMENT – SDG DASHBOARD

■ Major challenges ■ Significant challenges ■ Challenges remain ■ SDG achieved ■ Information unavailable

▼ SDG TRENDS

↓ Decreasing   → Stagnating   ↗ Moderately improving   ↑ On track or maintaining SDG achievement   ● Information unavailable

Notes: The full title of Goal 2 "Zero Hunger" is "End hunger, achieve food security and improved nutrition and promote sustainable agriculture".
The full title of each SDG is available here: https://sustainabledevelopment.un.org/topics/sustainabledevelopmentgoals

SDG1 – No Poverty

Indicator	Value	Year	Rating	Trend
Poverty headcount ratio at $1.90/day (%)	0.2	2020	●	↑
Poverty headcount ratio at $3.20/day (%)	6.7	2020	◐	↑

SDG2 – Zero Hunger

Indicator	Value	Year	Rating	Trend
Prevalence of undernourishment (%)	3.7	2017	●	↑
Prevalence of stunting in children under 5 years of age (%)	7.5	2004	●	↑
Prevalence of wasting in children under 5 years of age (%)	6.3	2004	◐	→
Prevalence of obesity, BMI ≥ 30 (% of adult population)	30.2	2016	●	↓
Human Trophic Level (best 2–3 worst)	2.2	2017	●	↑
Cereal yield (tonnes per hectare of harvested land)	3.0	2017	●	↑
Sustainable Nitrogen Management Index (best 0–1.41 worst)	1.2	2015	●	↓

SDG3 – Good Health and Well-Being

Indicator	Value	Year	Rating	Trend
Maternal mortality rate (per 100,000 live births)	34	2017	●	↑
Neonatal mortality rate (per 1,000 live births)	10.9	2018	●	↑
Mortality rate, under-5 (per 1,000 live births)	25.6	2018	◐	↓
Incidence of tuberculosis (per 100,000 population)	54.0	2018	●	→
New HIV infections (per 1,000 uninfected population)	NA	NA	●	
Age-standardized death rate due to cardiovascular disease, cancer, diabetes, or chronic respiratory disease in adults aged 30–70 years (%)	30.6	2016	●	→
Age-standardized death rate attributable to household air pollution and ambient air pollution (per 100,000 population)	99	2016	●	
Traffic deaths (per 100,000 population)	9.6	2016	◐	↓
Life expectancy at birth (years)	69.9	2016	●	→
Adolescent fertility rate (births per 1,000 adolescent females aged 15 to 19)	49.4	2017	●	↓
Births attended by skilled health personnel (%)	99.9	2015	●	↑
Percentage of surviving infants who received 2 WHO-recommended vaccines (%)	94	2018	●	↑
Universal health coverage (UHC) index of service coverage (worst 0–100 best)	64.0	2017	●	↑
Subjective well-being (average ladder score, worst 0–10 best)	NA	NA	●	

SDG4 – Quality Education

Indicator	Value	Year	Rating	Trend
Net primary enrollment rate (%)	96.8	2016	◐	↓
Lower secondary completion rate (%)	102.6	2016	●	
Literacy rate (% of population aged 15 to 24)	99.7	2017	●	

SDG5 – Gender Equality

Indicator	Value	Year	Rating	Trend
Demand for family planning satisfied by modern methods (% of females aged 15 to 49 who are married or in unions) *	65.8	2017	●	→
Ratio of female-to-male mean years of education received (%)	102.8	2018	●	↑
Ratio of female-to-male labor force participation rate (%)	50.4	2019	●	↓
Seats held by women in national parliament (%)	19.6	2020	●	→

SDG6 – Clean Water and Sanitation

Indicator	Value	Year	Rating	Trend
Population using at least basic drinking water services (%)	93.8	2017	◐	→
Population using at least basic sanitation services (%)	95.1	2017	●	↑
Freshwater withdrawal (% of available freshwater resources)	0.5	2005	●	
Anthropogenic wastewater that receives treatment (%)	3.9	2018	●	
Scarce water consumption embodied in imports (m³/capita)	4.4	2013	●	↑

SDG7 – Affordable and Clean Energy

Indicator	Value	Year	Rating	Trend
Population with access to electricity (%)	96.0	2017	◐	↑
Population with access to clean fuels and technology for cooking (%)	39.6	2016	●	→
CO$_2$ emissions from fuel combustion for electricity and heating per total electricity output (MtCO$_2$/TWh)	NA	NA	●	●

SDG8 – Decent Work and Economic Growth

Indicator	Value	Year	Rating	Trend
Adjusted GDP growth (%)	-1.0	2018	◐	●
Victims of modern slavery (per 1,000 population)	NA	NA	●	●
Adults with an account at a bank or other financial institution or with a mobile-money-service provider (% of population aged 15 or over)	NA	NA	●	●
Unemployment rate (% of total labor force)	4.1	2019	●	↑
Fatal work-related accidents embodied in imports (per 100,000 population)	0.3	2010	●	↑

SDG9 – Industry, Innovation and Infrastructure

Indicator	Value	Year	Rating	Trend
Population using the internet (%)	50.0	2017	●	↑
Mobile broadband subscriptions (per 100 population)	147.5	2018	●	↑
Logistics Performance Index: Quality of trade and transport-related infrastructure (worst 1–5 best)	2.4	2018	●	↓
The Times Higher Education Universities Ranking: Average score of top 3 universities (worst 0–100 best) *	0.0	2020	●	●
Scientific and technical journal articles (per 1,000 population)	0.2	2018	●	→
Expenditure on research and development (% of GDP)	NA	NA	●	●

SDG10 – Reduced Inequalities

Indicator	Value	Year	Rating	Trend
Gini coefficient adjusted for top income	52.4	2013	●	●

SDG11 – Sustainable Cities and Communities

Indicator	Value	Year	Rating	Trend
Annual mean concentration of particulate matter of less than 2.5 microns in diameter (PM2.5) (µg/m³)	10.8	2017	◐	↑
Access to improved water source, piped (% of urban population)	97.0	2017	◐	→
Satisfaction with public transport (%)	NA	NA	●	●

SDG12 – Responsible Consumption and Production

Indicator	Value	Year	Rating	Trend
Municipal solid waste (kg/capita/day)	1.0	2011	●	●
Electronic waste (kg/capita)	5.1	2016	●	●
Production-based SO$_2$ emissions (kg/capita)	127.4	2012	●	●
SO$_2$ emissions embodied in imports (kg/capita)	6.4	2012	◐	●
Production-based nitrogen emissions (kg/capita)	16.5	2010	●	●
Nitrogen emissions embodied in imports (kg/capita)	2.8	2010	●	●

SDG13 – Climate Action

Indicator	Value	Year	Rating	Trend
Energy-related CO$_2$ emissions (tCO$_2$/capita)	1.7	2017	●	↑
CO$_2$ emissions embodied in imports (tCO$_2$/capita)	0.5	2015	◐	↗
CO$_2$ emissions embodied in fossil fuel exports (kg/capita)	0.0	2018	●	●

SDG14 – Life Below Water

Indicator	Value	Year	Rating	Trend
Mean area that is protected in marine sites important to biodiversity (%)	15.9	2018	●	→
Ocean Health Index: Clean Waters score (worst 0–100 best)	73.1	2019	●	↑
Fish caught from overexploited or collapsed stocks (% of total catch)	24.4	2014	●	↑
Fish caught by trawling (%)	NA	NA	●	●
Marine biodiversity threats embodied in imports (per million population)	0.3	2018	◐	●

SDG15 – Life on Land

Indicator	Value	Year	Rating	Trend
Mean area that is protected in terrestrial sites important to biodiversity (%)	9.4	2018	●	→
Mean area that is protected in freshwater sites important to biodiversity (%)	0.1	2018	●	→
Red List Index of species survival (worst 0–1 best)	0.7	2019	●	↓
Permanent deforestation (% of forest area, 5-year average)	0.1	2018	●	●
Terrestrial and freshwater biodiversity threats embodied in imports (per million population)	0.0	2018	●	●

SDG16 – Peace, Justice and Strong Institutions

Indicator	Value	Year	Rating	Trend
Homicides (per 100,000 population)	2.3	2014	◐	●
Unsentenced detainees (% of prison population)	25.9	2018	●	↑
Percentage of population who feel safe walking alone at night in the city or area where they live (%)	NA	NA	●	●
Property Rights (worst 1–7 best)	NA	NA	●	●
Birth registrations with civil authority (% of children under age 5)	NA	NA	●	●
Corruption Perception Index (worst 0–100 best)	NA	NA	●	●
Children involved in child labor (% of population aged 5 to 14)	NA	NA	●	●
Exports of major conventional weapons (TIV constant million USD per 100,000 population) *	0.0	2019	●	●
Press Freedom Index (best 0–100 worst)	27.2	2019	●	↑

SDG17 – Partnerships for the Goals

Indicator	Value	Year	Rating	Trend
Government spending on health and education (% of GDP)	5.9	2013	●	●
For high-income and all OECD DAC countries: International concessional public finance, including official development assistance (% of GNI)	NA	NA	●	●
Other countries: Government revenue excluding grants (% of GDP)	26.4	2018	◐	↑
Corporate Tax Haven Score (best 0–100 worst) *	0.0	2019	●	●

* Imputed data point

5. Country Profiles

▼ OVERALL PERFORMANCE

Index score

83.8

Regional average score

77.3

SDG Global rank **3** (OF 166)

▼ AVERAGE PERFORMANCE BY SDG

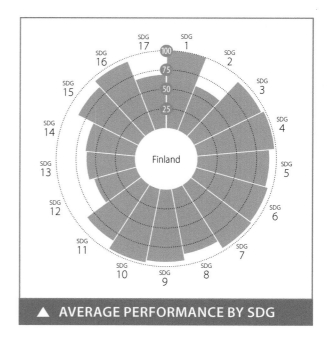

Finland

▼ SPILLOVER INDEX

100 (best) to 0 (worst)

▼ CURRENT ASSESSMENT – SDG DASHBOARD

■ Major challenges   ■ Significant challenges   ▨ Challenges remain   ■ SDG achieved   ■ Information unavailable

▼ SDG TRENDS

1 NO POVERTY	2 ZERO HUNGER	3 GOOD HEALTH AND WELL-BEING	4 QUALITY EDUCATION	5 GENDER EQUALITY	6 CLEAN WATER AND SANITATION	7 AFFORDABLE AND CLEAN ENERGY	8 DECENT WORK AND ECONOMIC GROWTH	9 INDUSTRY, INNOVATION AND INFRASTRUCTURE
↑	↗	↗	↑	↗	↑	↑	↑	↑

10 REDUCED INEQUALITIES	11 SUSTAINABLE CITIES AND COMMUNITIES	12 RESPONSIBLE CONSUMPTION AND PRODUCTION	13 CLIMATE ACTION	14 LIFE BELOW WATER	15 LIFE ON LAND	16 PEACE, JUSTICE AND STRONG INSTITUTIONS	17 PARTNERSHIPS FOR THE GOALS
↑	→	●	→	→	↑	↑	→

 Decreasing   Stagnating   Moderately improving   ↑ On track or maintaining SDG achievement   ● Information unavailable

Notes: The full title of Goal 2 "Zero Hunger" is "End hunger, achieve food security and improved nutrition and promote sustainable agriculture".
The full title of each SDG is available here: https://sustainabledevelopment.un.org/topics/sustainabledevelopmentgoals

SDG1 – No Poverty

Indicator	Value	Year	Rating	Trend
Poverty headcount ratio at $1.90/day (%)	0.1	2020	●	↑
Poverty headcount ratio at $3.20/day (%)	0.1	2020	●	↑
Poverty rate after taxes and transfers (%)	6.3	2017	●	↑

SDG2 – Zero Hunger

Indicator	Value	Year	Rating	Trend
Prevalence of undernourishment (%)	2.5	2017	●	↑
Prevalence of stunting in children under 5 years of age (%)	* 2.6	2016	●	↑
Prevalence of wasting in children under 5 years of age (%)	* 0.7	2016	●	↑
Prevalence of obesity, BMI ≥ 30 (% of adult population)	22.2	2016	●	↓
Human Trophic Level (best 2–3 worst)	2.6	2017	●	↓
Cereal yield (tonnes per hectare of harvested land)	4.0	2017	●	↑
Sustainable Nitrogen Management Index (best 0–1.41 worst)	0.6	2015	●	↓
Yield gap closure (% of potential yield)	51.6	2015	●	●

SDG3 – Good Health and Well-Being

Indicator	Value	Year	Rating	Trend
Maternal mortality rate (per 100,000 live births)	3	2017	●	↑
Neonatal mortality rate (per 1,000 live births)	1.0	2018	●	↑
Mortality rate, under-5 (per 1,000 live births)	1.7	2018	●	↑
Incidence of tuberculosis (per 100,000 population)	4.7	2018	●	↑
New HIV infections (per 1,000 uninfected population)	0.0	2018	●	↑
Age-standardized death rate due to cardiovascular disease, cancer, diabetes, or chronic respiratory disease in adults aged 30–70 years (%)	10.2	2016	●	↑
Age-standardized death rate attributable to household air pollution and ambient air pollution (per 100,000 population)	7	2016	●	●
Traffic deaths (per 100,000 population)	4.7	2016	●	↑
Life expectancy at birth (years)	81.4	2016	●	↑
Adolescent fertility rate (births per 1,000 adolescent females aged 15 to 19)	5.8	2017	●	↑
Births attended by skilled health personnel (%)	99.9	2015	●	↑
Percentage of surviving infants who received 2 WHO-recommended vaccines (%)	91.0	2018	●	↑
Universal health coverage (UHC) index of service coverage (worst 0–100 best)	78.0	2017	●	→
Subjective well-being (average ladder score, worst 0–10 best)	7.8	2019	●	↑
Gap in life expectancy at birth among regions (years)	1.1	2016	●	●
Gap in self-reported health status by income (percentage points)	26.3	2018	●	↓
Daily smokers (% of population aged 15 and over)	14.0	2018	●	↑

SDG4 – Quality Education

Indicator	Value	Year	Rating	Trend
Net primary enrollment rate (%)	* 98.5	2017	●	↑
Lower secondary completion rate (%)	* 98.5	2017	●	↑
Literacy rate (% of population aged 15 to 24)	NA	NA	●	●
Participation rate in pre-primary organized learning (% of children aged 4 to 6)	99.1	2017	●	↑
Tertiary educational attainment (% of population aged 25 to 34)	41.3	2018	●	↑
PISA score (worst 0–600 best)	516.3	2018	●	↑
Variation in science performance explained by socio-economic status (%)	10.5	2018	●	↑
Underachievers in science (% of 15-year-olds)	12.9	2018	●	↑
Resilient students in science (% of 15-year-olds)	41.5	2018	●	↑

SDG5 – Gender Equality

Indicator	Value	Year	Rating	Trend
Demand for family planning satisfied by modern methods (% of females aged 15 to 49 who are married or in unions)	* 89.9	2017	●	↑
Ratio of female-to-male mean years of education received (%)	102.4	2018	●	↑
Ratio of female-to-male labor force participation rate (%)	88.5	2019	●	↑
Seats held by women in national parliament (%)	46.0	2020	●	↑
Gender wage gap (% of male median wage)	17.7	2017	●	↗
Gender gap in time spent doing unpaid work (minutes/day)	78.3	2010	●	●

SDG6 – Clean Water and Sanitation

Indicator	Value	Year	Rating	Trend
Population using at least basic drinking water services (%)	100.0	2017	●	●
Population using at least basic sanitation services (%)	99.4	2017	●	●
Freshwater withdrawal (% of available freshwater resources)	15.6	2005	●	●
Anthropogenic wastewater that receives treatment (%)	100.0	2018	●	●
Scarce water consumption embodied in imports (m³/capita)	23.6	2013	●	↑
Population using safely managed water services (%)	99.6	2017	●	↑
Population using safely managed sanitation services (%)	99.2	2017	●	↑

SDG7 – Affordable and Clean Energy

Indicator	Value	Year	Rating	Trend
Population with access to electricity (%)	100.0	2017	●	●
Population with access to clean fuels and technology for cooking (%)	100.0	2016	●	↑
CO2 emissions from fuel combustion for electricity and heating per total electricity output (MtCO2/TWh)	0.7	2017	●	↑
Share of renewable energy in total primary energy supply (%)	33.8	2018	●	↑

SDG8 – Decent Work and Economic Growth

Indicator	Value	Year	Rating	Trend
Adjusted GDP growth (%)	0.6	2018	●	●
Victims of modern slavery (per 1,000 population)	1.7	2018	●	●
Adults with an account at a bank or other financial institution or with a mobile-money-service provider (% of population aged 15 or over)	99.8	2017	●	↑
Fatal work-related accidents embodied in imports (per 100,000 population)	1.0	2010	●	↑
Employment-to-population ratio (%)	72.1	2018	●	↑
Youth not in employment, education or training (NEET) (% of population aged 15 to 29)	11.9	2018	●	↑

SDG9 – Industry, Innovation and Infrastructure

Indicator	Value	Year	Rating	Trend
Population using the internet (%)	88.9	2018	●	↑
Mobile broadband subscriptions (per 100 population)	154.5	2018	●	↑
Logistics Performance Index: Quality of trade and transport-related infrastructure (worst 1–5 best)	4.0	2018	●	↑
The Times Higher Education Universities Ranking: Average score of top 3 universities (worst 0–100 best)	55.2	2020	●	●
Scientific and technical journal articles (per 1,000 population)	1.9	2018	●	↑
Expenditure on research and development (% of GDP)	2.8	2017	●	↑
Researchers (per 1,000 employed population)	14.5	2018	●	↑
Triadic patent families filed (per million population)	47.0	2017	●	↑
Gap in internet access by income (percentage points)	14.9	2019	●	↑
Women in science and engineering (% of tertiary graduates in science and engineering)	23.0	2015	●	●

SDG10 – Reduced Inequalities

Indicator	Value	Year	Rating	Trend
Gini coefficient adjusted for top income	28.7	2015	●	↑
Palma ratio	0.9	2017	●	↑
Elderly poverty rate (% of population aged 66 or over)	6.3	2017	●	↑

SDG11 – Sustainable Cities and Communities

Indicator	Value	Year	Rating	Trend
Annual mean concentration of particulate matter of less than 2.5 microns in diameter (PM2.5) (μg/m³)	5.9	2017	●	↑
Access to improved water source, piped (% of urban population)	99.0	2017	●	↑
Satisfaction with public transport (%)	56.2	2019	●	↓
Population with rent overburden (%)	8.4	2017	●	↓

SDG12 – Responsible Consumption and Production

Indicator	Value	Year	Rating	Trend
Electronic waste (kg/capita)	21.1	2016	●	●
Production-based SO2 emissions (kg/capita)	96.1	2012	●	●
SO2 emissions embodied in imports (kg/capita)	16.3	2012	●	●
Production-based nitrogen emissions (kg/capita)	43.0	2010	●	●
Nitrogen emissions embodied in imports (kg/capita)	11.9	2010	●	●
Non-recycled municipal solid waste (kg/capita/day)	0.9	2018	●	●

SDG13 – Climate Action

Indicator	Value	Year	Rating	Trend
Energy-related CO2 emissions (tCO2/capita)	8.1	2017	●	→
CO2 emissions embodied in imports (tCO2/capita)	2.6	2015	●	→
CO2 emissions embodied in fossil fuel exports (kg/capita)	0.0	2018	●	●
Effective carbon rate (EUR/tCO2)	38.8	2016	●	●

SDG14 – Life Below Water

Indicator	Value	Year	Rating	Trend
Mean area that is protected in marine sites important to biodiversity (%)	54.3	2018	●	↑
Ocean Health Index: Clean Waters score (worst 0–100 best)	70.0	2019	●	↓
Fish caught from overexploited or collapsed stocks (% of total catch)	6.2	2014	●	↑
Fish caught by trawling (%)	79.3	2014	●	↓
Marine biodiversity threats embodied in imports (per million population)	0.1	2018	●	●

SDG15 – Life on Land

Indicator	Value	Year	Rating	Trend
Mean area that is protected in terrestrial sites important to biodiversity (%)	74.8	2018	●	↑
Mean area that is protected in freshwater sites important to biodiversity (%)	74.0	2018	●	↑
Red List Index of species survival (worst 0–1 best)	1.0	2019	●	●
Permanent deforestation (% of forest area, 5-year average)	0.0	2018	●	●
Terrestrial and freshwater biodiversity threats embodied in imports (per million population)	2.0	2018	●	●

SDG16 – Peace, Justice and Strong Institutions

Indicator	Value	Year	Rating	Trend
Homicides (per 100,000 population)	1.2	2017	●	↑
Unsentenced detainees (% of prison population)	19.0	2018	●	↑
Percentage of population who feel safe walking alone at night in the city or area where they live (%)	84.3	2019	●	↑
Property Rights (worst 1–7 best)	6.6	2019	●	●
Birth registrations with civil authority (% of children under age 5)	100.0	2018	●	●
Corruption Perception Index (worst 0–100 best)	86.0	2019	●	↑
Children involved in child labor (% of population aged 5 to 14)	* 0.0	2016	●	●
Exports of major conventional weapons (TIV constant million USD per 100,000 population)	0.6	2019	●	●
Press Freedom Index (best 0–100 worst)	7.9	2019	●	↑
Persons held in prison (per 100,000 population)	55.8	2017	●	↑

SDG17 – Partnerships for the Goals

Indicator	Value	Year	Rating	Trend
Government spending on health and education (% of GDP)	14.2	2016	●	↑
For high-income and all OECD DAC countries: International concessional public finance, including official development assistance (% of GNI)	0.4	2017	●	↓
Other countries: Government revenue excluding grants (% of GDP)	NA	NA	●	●
Corporate Tax Haven Score (best 0–100 worst)	55.0	2019	●	●
Financial Secrecy Score (best 0–100 worst)	52.1	2020	●	●
Shifted profits of multinationals (US$ billion)	3.2	2016	●	●

* Imputed data point

5. Country Profiles

▼ OVERALL PERFORMANCE

Index score

81.1

Regional average score

77.3

SDG Global rank **4** (OF 166)

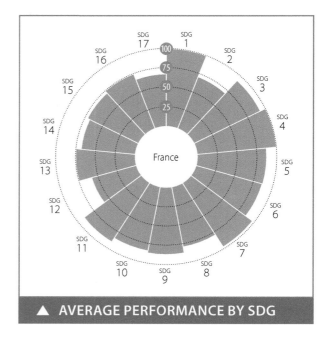

▲ AVERAGE PERFORMANCE BY SDG

▼ SPILLOVER INDEX

100 (best) to 0 (worst)

▼ CURRENT ASSESSMENT – SDG DASHBOARD

■ Major challenges　■ Significant challenges　■ Challenges remain　■ SDG achieved　■ Information unavailable

▼ SDG TRENDS

1 NO POVERTY	2 ZERO HUNGER	3 GOOD HEALTH AND WELL-BEING	4 QUALITY EDUCATION	5 GENDER EQUALITY	6 CLEAN WATER AND SANITATION	7 AFFORDABLE AND CLEAN ENERGY	8 DECENT WORK AND ECONOMIC GROWTH	9 INDUSTRY, INNOVATION AND INFRASTRUCTURE
↑	↗	↑	↗	↑	↗	↗	↗	↑

10 REDUCED INEQUALITIES	11 SUSTAINABLE CITIES AND COMMUNITIES	12 RESPONSIBLE CONSUMPTION AND PRODUCTION	13 CLIMATE ACTION	14 LIFE BELOW WATER	15 LIFE ON LAND	16 PEACE, JUSTICE AND STRONG INSTITUTIONS	17 PARTNERSHIPS FOR THE GOALS
↗	↗	●	→	↗	↗	↗	↗

↓ Decreasing　→ Stagnating　↗ Moderately improving　↑ On track or maintaining SDG achievement　● Information unavailable

Notes: The full title of Goal 2 "Zero Hunger" is "End hunger, achieve food security and improved nutrition and promote sustainable agriculture".
The full title of each SDG is available here: https://sustainabledevelopment.un.org/topics/sustainabledevelopmentgoals

SDG1 – No Poverty

Indicator	Value	Year	Rating	Trend
Poverty headcount ratio at $1.90/day (%)	0.2	2020	●	↑
Poverty headcount ratio at $3.20/day (%)	0.3	2020	●	↑
Poverty rate after taxes and transfers (%)	8.1	2017	●	↑

SDG2 – Zero Hunger

Indicator	Value	Year	Rating	Trend
Prevalence of undernourishment (%)	2.5	2017	●	↑
Prevalence of stunting in children under 5 years of age (%)	* 2.6	2016	●	↑
Prevalence of wasting in children under 5 years of age (%)	* 0.7	2016	●	↑
Prevalence of obesity, BMI ≥ 30 (% of adult population)	21.6	2016	●	↓
Human Trophic Level (best 2–3 worst)	2.5	2017	●	→
Cereal yield (tonnes per hectare of harvested land)	6.9	2017	●	↑
Sustainable Nitrogen Management Index (best 0–1.41 worst)	0.4	2015	●	↓
Yield gap closure (% of potential yield)	77.3	2015	●	●

SDG3 – Good Health and Well-Being

Indicator	Value	Year	Rating	Trend
Maternal mortality rate (per 100,000 live births)	8	2017	●	↑
Neonatal mortality rate (per 1,000 live births)	2.5	2018	●	↑
Mortality rate, under-5 (per 1,000 live births)	4.0	2018	●	↑
Incidence of tuberculosis (per 100,000 population)	8.9	2018	●	↑
New HIV infections (per 1,000 uninfected population)	0.1	2018	●	↑
Age-standardized death rate due to cardiovascular disease, cancer, diabetes, or chronic respiratory disease in adults aged 30–70 years (%)	10.6	2016	●	↑
Age-standardized death rate attributable to household air pollution and ambient air pollution (per 100,000 population)	10	2016	●	↑
Traffic deaths (per 100,000 population)	5.5	2016	●	↑
Life expectancy at birth (years)	82.9	2016	●	↑
Adolescent fertility rate (births per 1,000 adolescent females aged 15 to 19)	4.7	2017	●	↑
Births attended by skilled health personnel (%)	97.4	2016	●	↑
Percentage of surviving infants who received 2 WHO-recommended vaccines (%)	90.0	2018	●	↑
Universal health coverage (UHC) index of service coverage (worst 0–100 best)	78.0	2017	●	↑
Subjective well-being (average ladder score, worst 0–10 best)	6.7	2019	●	↑
Gap in life expectancy at birth among regions (years)	3.7	2016	●	●
Gap in self-reported health status by income (percentage points)	9.6	2017	●	●
Daily smokers (% of population aged 15 and over)	22.4	2014	●	●

SDG4 – Quality Education

Indicator	Value	Year	Rating	Trend
Net primary enrollment rate (%)	* 99.7	2017	●	↑
Lower secondary completion rate (%)	* 99.7	2017	●	↑
Literacy rate (% of population aged 15 to 24)	NA	NA	●	●
Participation rate in pre-primary organized learning (% of children aged 4 to 6)	99.8	2017	●	↑
Tertiary educational attainment (% of population aged 25 to 34)	46.9	2018	●	↑
PISA score (worst 0–600 best)	493.7	2018	●	↑
Variation in science performance explained by socio-economic status (%)	20.1	2018	●	→
Underachievers in science (% of 15-year-olds)	20.5	2018	●	↑
Resilient students in science (% of 15-year-olds)	28.9	2018	●	↑

SDG5 – Gender Equality

Indicator	Value	Year	Rating	Trend
Demand for family planning satisfied by modern methods (% of females aged 15 to 49 who are married or in unions)	95.5	2005	●	↑
Ratio of female-to-male mean years of education received (%)	96.6	2018	●	↑
Ratio of female-to-male labor force participation rate (%)	84.1	2019	●	↑
Seats held by women in national parliament (%)	39.5	2020	●	↑
Gender wage gap (% of male median wage)	13.0	2015	●	●
Gender gap in time spent doing unpaid work (minutes/day)	89.1	2010	●	●

SDG6 – Clean Water and Sanitation

Indicator	Value	Year	Rating	Trend
Population using at least basic drinking water services (%)	100.0	2017	●	●
Population using at least basic sanitation services (%)	98.7	2017	●	●
Freshwater withdrawal (% of available freshwater resources)	26.1	2010	●	●
Anthropogenic wastewater that receives treatment (%)	88.0	2018	●	●
Scarce water consumption embodied in imports (m³/capita)	41.0	2013	●	↗
Population using safely managed water services (%)	97.9	2017	●	↑
Population using safely managed sanitation services (%)	88.4	2017	●	→

SDG7 – Affordable and Clean Energy

Indicator	Value	Year	Rating	Trend
Population with access to electricity (%)	100.0	2017	●	↑
Population with access to clean fuels and technology for cooking (%)	100.0	2016	●	↑
CO₂ emissions from fuel combustion for electricity and heating per total electricity output (MtCO₂/TWh)	0.6	2017	●	↑
Share of renewable energy in total primary energy supply (%)	10.5	2018	●	↗

SDG8 – Decent Work and Economic Growth

Indicator	Value	Year	Rating	Trend
Adjusted GDP growth (%)	-0.3	2018	●	●
Victims of modern slavery (per 1,000 population)	2.0	2018	●	●
Adults with an account at a bank or other financial institution or with a mobile-money-service provider (% of population aged 15 or over)	94.0	2017	●	↑
Fatal work-related accidents embodied in imports (per 100,000 population)	2.0	2010	●	↑
Employment-to-population ratio (%)	65.6	2019	●	↑
Youth not in employment, education or training (NEET) (% of population aged 15 to 29)	16.1	2018	●	↗

SDG9 – Industry, Innovation and Infrastructure

Indicator	Value	Year	Rating	Trend
Population using the internet (%)	82.0	2018	●	↑
Mobile broadband subscriptions (per 100 population)	91.6	2018	●	↑
Logistics Performance Index: Quality of trade and transport-related infrastructure (worst 1–5 best)	4.0	2018	●	↑
The Times Higher Education Universities Ranking: Average score of top 3 universities (worst 0–100 best)	66.6	2020	●	●
Scientific and technical journal articles (per 1,000 population)	1.0	2018	●	↑
Expenditure on research and development (% of GDP)	2.2	2017	●	↑
Researchers (per 1,000 employed population)	10.9	2018	●	↑
Triadic patent families filed (per million population)	33.4	2017	●	↑
Gap in internet access by income (percentage points)	20.7	2019	●	↑
Women in science and engineering (% of tertiary graduates in science and engineering)	29.2	2015	●	●

SDG10 – Reduced Inequalities

Indicator	Value	Year	Rating	Trend
Gini coefficient adjusted for top income	33.3	2015	●	↗
Palma ratio	1.1	2017	●	→
Elderly poverty rate (% of population aged 66 or over)	3.6	2017	●	↑

SDG11 – Sustainable Cities and Communities

Indicator	Value	Year	Rating	Trend
Annual mean concentration of particulate matter of less than 2.5 microns in diameter (PM2.5) (µg/m³)	11.8	2017	●	↑
Access to improved water source, piped (% of urban population)	99.0	2017	●	↑
Satisfaction with public transport (%)	67.9	2019	●	↓
Population with rent overburden (%)	5.2	2017	●	↑

SDG12 – Responsible Consumption and Production

Indicator	Value	Year	Rating	Trend
Electronic waste (kg/capita)	21.3	2016	●	●
Production-based SO₂ emissions (kg/capita)	26.5	2012	●	●
SO₂ emissions embodied in imports (kg/capita)	11.2	2012	●	●
Production-based nitrogen emissions (kg/capita)	42.1	2010	●	●
Nitrogen emissions embodied in imports (kg/capita)	16.3	2010	●	●
Non-recycled municipal solid waste (kg/capita/day)	0.8	2018	●	●

SDG13 – Climate Action

Indicator	Value	Year	Rating	Trend
Energy-related CO₂ emissions (tCO₂/capita)	4.8	2017	●	→
CO₂ emissions embodied in imports (tCO₂/capita)	1.9	2015	●	→
CO₂ emissions embodied in fossil fuel exports (kg/capita)	0.8	2018	●	●
Effective carbon rate (EUR/tCO₂)	11.8	2016	●	●

SDG14 – Life Below Water

Indicator	Value	Year	Rating	Trend
Mean area that is protected in marine sites important to biodiversity (%)	79.4	2018	●	↑
Ocean Health Index: Clean Waters score (worst 0–100 best)	49.1	2019	●	↓
Fish caught from overexploited or collapsed stocks (% of total catch)	16.0	2014	●	↑
Fish caught by trawling (%)	27.8	2014	●	↗
Marine biodiversity threats embodied in imports (per million population)	0.4	2018	●	●

SDG15 – Life on Land

Indicator	Value	Year	Rating	Trend
Mean area that is protected in terrestrial sites important to biodiversity (%)	80.9	2018	●	↑
Mean area that is protected in freshwater sites important to biodiversity (%)	78.0	2018	●	↑
Red List Index of species survival (worst 0–1 best)	0.9	2019	●	↓
Permanent deforestation (% of forest area, 5-year average)	0.0	2018	●	●
Terrestrial and freshwater biodiversity threats embodied in imports (per million population)	7.1	2018	●	●

SDG16 – Peace, Justice and Strong Institutions

Indicator	Value	Year	Rating	Trend
Homicides (per 100,000 population)	1.3	2017	●	↑
Unsentenced detainees (% of prison population)	28.6	2018	●	↑
Percentage of population who feel safe walking alone at night in the city or area where they live (%)	74.1	2019	●	↑
Property Rights (worst 1–7 best)	5.2	2019	●	●
Birth registrations with civil authority (% of children under age 5)	100.0	2018	●	●
Corruption Perception Index (worst 0–100 best)	69.0	2019	●	↑
Children involved in child labor (% of population aged 5 to 14)	* 0.0	2016	●	●
Exports of major conventional weapons (TIV constant million USD per 100,000 population)	3.5	2019	●	●
Press Freedom Index (best 0–100 worst)	22.2	2019	●	↑
Persons held in prison (per 100,000 population)	106.1	2017	●	→

SDG17 – Partnerships for the Goals

Indicator	Value	Year	Rating	Trend
Government spending on health and education (% of GDP)	* 13.2	2018	●	↑
For high-income and all OECD DAC countries: International concessional public finance, including official development assistance (% of GNI)	0.4	2017	●	↗
Other countries: Government revenue excluding grants (% of GDP)	NA	NA	●	●
Corporate Tax Haven Score (best 0–100 worst)	55.7	2019	●	●
Financial Secrecy Score (best 0–100 worst)	49.9	2020	●	●
Shifted profits of multinationals (US$ billion)	36.0	2016	●	●

* Imputed data point

5. Country Profiles

GABON

Sub-Saharan Africa

▼ OVERALL PERFORMANCE

Index score

63.4

Regional average score

53.1

SDG Global rank **111** (OF 166)

▼ SPILLOVER INDEX

100 (best) to 0 (worst)

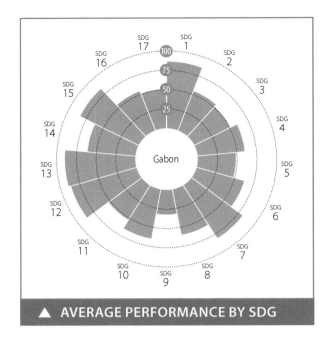

▲ AVERAGE PERFORMANCE BY SDG

▼ CURRENT ASSESSMENT – SDG DASHBOARD

■ Major challenges ■ Significant challenges ■ Challenges remain ■ SDG achieved ■ Information unavailable

▼ SDG TRENDS

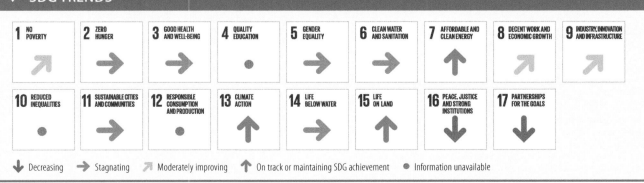

↓ Decreasing   → Stagnating   ↗ Moderately improving   ↑ On track or maintaining SDG achievement   ● Information unavailable

Notes: The full title of Goal 2 "Zero Hunger" is "End hunger, achieve food security and improved nutrition and promote sustainable agriculture".
The full title of each SDG is available here: https://sustainabledevelopment.un.org/topics/sustainabledevelopmentgoals

SDG1 – No Poverty

	Value	Year	Rating	Trend
Poverty headcount ratio at $1.90/day (%)	2.5	2020	○	↑
Poverty headcount ratio at $3.20/day (%)	12.4	2020	●	↗

SDG2 – Zero Hunger

	Value	Year	Rating	Trend
Prevalence of undernourishment (%)	10.5	2017	○	↓
Prevalence of stunting in children under 5 years of age (%)	17.5	2012	●	↗
Prevalence of wasting in children under 5 years of age (%)	3.4	2012	●	↑
Prevalence of obesity, BMI ≥ 30 (% of adult population)	15.0	2016	●	↓
Human Trophic Level (best 2–3 worst)	2.2	2017	●	↑
Cereal yield (tonnes per hectare of harvested land)	1.6	2017	●	→
Sustainable Nitrogen Management Index (best 0–1.41 worst)	1.0	2015	●	↓

SDG3 – Good Health and Well-Being

	Value	Year	Rating	Trend
Maternal mortality rate (per 100,000 live births)	252	2017	●	→
Neonatal mortality rate (per 1,000 live births)	21.0	2018	●	↗
Mortality rate, under-5 (per 1,000 live births)	44.8	2018	●	↑
Incidence of tuberculosis (per 100,000 population)	525.0	2018	●	→
New HIV infections (per 1,000 uninfected population)	1.0	2018	●	↑
Age-standardized death rate due to cardiovascular disease, cancer, diabetes, or chronic respiratory disease in adults aged 30–70 years (%)	14.4	2016	●	↑
Age-standardized death rate attributable to household air pollution and ambient air pollution (per 100,000 population)	76	2016	○	●
Traffic deaths (per 100,000 population)	23.2	2016	●	↓
Life expectancy at birth (years)	66.4	2016	●	↗
Adolescent fertility rate (births per 1,000 adolescent females aged 15 to 19)	96.2	2017	●	→
Births attended by skilled health personnel (%)	89.3	2012	●	●
Percentage of surviving infants who received 2 WHO-recommended vaccines (%)	59	2018	●	↓
Universal health coverage (UHC) index of service coverage (worst 0–100 best)	49.0	2017	●	↓
Subjective well-being (average ladder score, worst 0–10 best)	4.9	2019	●	↗

SDG4 – Quality Education

	Value	Year	Rating	Trend
Net primary enrollment rate (%)	NA	NA	●	●
Lower secondary completion rate (%)	NA	NA	●	●
Literacy rate (% of population aged 15 to 24)	89.8	2018	●	●

SDG5 – Gender Equality

	Value	Year	Rating	Trend
Demand for family planning satisfied by modern methods (% of females aged 15 to 49 who are married or in unions)	44.0	2012	●	→
Ratio of female-to-male mean years of education received (%)	81.5	2018	●	→
Ratio of female-to-male labor force participation rate (%)	72.5	2019	●	↑
Seats held by women in national parliament (%)	14.8	2020	●	→

SDG6 – Clean Water and Sanitation

	Value	Year	Rating	Trend
Population using at least basic drinking water services (%)	85.8	2017	●	→
Population using at least basic sanitation services (%)	47.4	2017	●	→
Freshwater withdrawal (% of available freshwater resources)	0.5	2005	●	●
Anthropogenic wastewater that receives treatment (%)	0.0	2018	●	●
Scarce water consumption embodied in imports (m3/capita)	4.0	2013	●	↑

SDG7 – Affordable and Clean Energy

	Value	Year	Rating	Trend
Population with access to electricity (%)	92.2	2017	○	↑
Population with access to clean fuels and technology for cooking (%)	79.1	2016	○	↑
CO2 emissions from fuel combustion for electricity and heating per total electricity output (MtCO2/TWh)	1.5	2017	●	↑

SDG8 – Decent Work and Economic Growth

	Value	Year	Rating	Trend
Adjusted GDP growth (%)	-5.0	2018	●	●
Victims of modern slavery (per 1,000 population)	4.8	2018	○	●
Adults with an account at a bank or other financial institution or with a mobile-money-service provider (% of population aged 15 or over)	58.6	2017	●	↑
Unemployment rate (% of total labor force)	20.0	2019	●	→
Fatal work-related accidents embodied in imports (per 100,000 population)	0.2	2010	●	↑

SDG9 – Industry, Innovation and Infrastructure

	Value	Year	Rating	Trend
Population using the internet (%)	62.0	2017	●	↑
Mobile broadband subscriptions (per 100 population)	91.8	2018	●	↑
Logistics Performance Index: Quality of trade and transport-related infrastructure (worst 1–5 best)	2.1	2018	●	→
The Times Higher Education Universities Ranking: Average score of top 3 universities (worst 0–100 best) *	0.0	2020	●	●
Scientific and technical journal articles (per 1,000 population)	0.0	2018	●	↓
Expenditure on research and development (% of GDP)	0.6	2009	●	●

SDG10 – Reduced Inequalities

	Value	Year	Rating	Trend
Gini coefficient adjusted for top income	39.8	2017	●	●

SDG11 – Sustainable Cities and Communities

	Value	Year	Rating	Trend
Annual mean concentration of particulate matter of less than 2.5 microns in diameter (PM2.5) (μg/m3)	44.4	2017	●	↓
Access to improved water source, piped (% of urban population)	94.5	2017	○	→
Satisfaction with public transport (%)	27.7	2019	●	→

SDG12 – Responsible Consumption and Production

	Value	Year	Rating	Trend
Municipal solid waste (kg/capita/day)	NA	NA	●	●
Electronic waste (kg/capita)	7.6	2016	●	●
Production-based SO2 emissions (kg/capita)	74.2	2012	●	●
SO2 emissions embodied in imports (kg/capita)	3.0	2012	●	●
Production-based nitrogen emissions (kg/capita)	7.2	2010	●	●
Nitrogen emissions embodied in imports (kg/capita)	2.8	2010	●	●

SDG13 – Climate Action

	Value	Year	Rating	Trend
Energy-related CO2 emissions (tCO2/capita)	2.2	2017	○	↑
CO2 emissions embodied in imports (tCO2/capita)	0.4	2015	●	↑
CO2 emissions embodied in fossil fuel exports (kg/capita)	NA	NA	●	●

SDG14 – Life Below Water

	Value	Year	Rating	Trend
Mean area that is protected in marine sites important to biodiversity (%)	51.3	2018	●	↑
Ocean Health Index: Clean Waters score (worst 0–100 best)	63.6	2019	●	↑
Fish caught from overexploited or collapsed stocks (% of total catch)	43.2	2014	●	↓
Fish caught by trawling (%)	39.6	2014	●	↓
Marine biodiversity threats embodied in imports (per million population)	0.1	2018	●	●

SDG15 – Life on Land

	Value	Year	Rating	Trend
Mean area that is protected in terrestrial sites important to biodiversity (%)	61.7	2018	●	↑
Mean area that is protected in freshwater sites important to biodiversity (%)	93.6	2018	●	↑
Red List Index of species survival (worst 0–1 best)	1.0	2018	●	↑
Permanent deforestation (% of forest area, 5-year average)	0.1	2018	○	●
Terrestrial and freshwater biodiversity threats embodied in imports (per million population)	2.5	2018	●	●

SDG16 – Peace, Justice and Strong Institutions

		Value	Year	Rating	Trend
Homicides (per 100,000 population)	*	8.0	2015	●	●
Unsentenced detainees (% of prison population)		50.0	2015	●	●
Percentage of population who feel safe walking alone at night in the city or area where they live (%)		28.4	2019	●	↓
Property Rights (worst 1–7 best)		3.5	2019	●	●
Birth registrations with civil authority (% of children under age 5)		89.6	2018	○	●
Corruption Perception Index (worst 0–100 best)		31	2019	●	↓
Children involved in child labor (% of population aged 5 to 14)		13.4	2016	●	●
Exports of major conventional weapons (TIV constant million USD per 100,000 population)	*	0.0	2019	●	●
Press Freedom Index (best 0–100 worst)		35.6	2019	○	↓

SDG17 – Partnerships for the Goals

		Value	Year	Rating	Trend
Government spending on health and education (% of GDP)		4.2	2014	●	●
For high-income and all OECD DAC countries: International concessional public finance, including official development assistance (% of GNI)		NA	NA	●	●
Other countries: Government revenue excluding grants (% of GDP)		16.8	2018	●	↓
Corporate Tax Haven Score (best 0–100 worst)	*	0.0	2019	●	●

* Imputed data point

5. Country Profiles

THE GAMBIA

 Sub-Saharan Africa

▼ OVERALL PERFORMANCE

Index score
57.9

Regional average score
53.1

SDG Global rank 129 (OF 166)

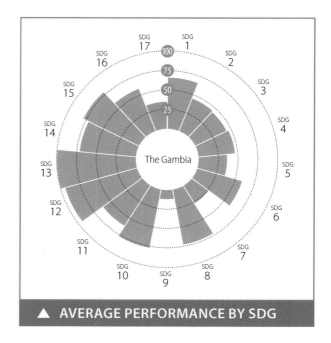

▲ AVERAGE PERFORMANCE BY SDG

▼ SPILLOVER INDEX

100 (best) to 0 (worst)

▼ CURRENT ASSESSMENT – SDG DASHBOARD

■ Major challenges ■ Significant challenges ■ Challenges remain ■ SDG achieved ■ Information unavailable

▼ SDG TRENDS

↓ Decreasing → Stagnating ↗ Moderately improving ↑ On track or maintaining SDG achievement ● Information unavailable

Notes: The full title of Goal 2 "Zero Hunger" is "End hunger, achieve food security and improved nutrition and promote sustainable agriculture".
The full title of each SDG is available here: https://sustainabledevelopment.un.org/topics/sustainabledevelopmentgoals

226 Sustainable Development Report 2020   The Sustainable Development Goals and Covid-19

THE GAMBIA

SDG1 – No Poverty	Value	Year	Rating	Trend
Poverty headcount ratio at $1.90/day (%)	6.6	2020	○	↑
Poverty headcount ratio at $3.20/day (%)	29.1	2020	●	↗

SDG2 – Zero Hunger	Value	Year	Rating	Trend
Prevalence of undernourishment (%)	10.2	2017	○	→
Prevalence of stunting in children under 5 years of age (%)	25.0	2013	●	→
Prevalence of wasting in children under 5 years of age (%)	11.1	2013	●	↓
Prevalence of obesity, BMI ≥ 30 (% of adult population)	10.3	2016	○	↓
Human Trophic Level (best 2–3 worst)	2.3	2017	●	→
Cereal yield (tonnes per hectare of harvested land)	0.8	2017	●	→
Sustainable Nitrogen Management Index (best 0–1.41 worst)	0.9	2015	●	↓

SDG3 – Good Health and Well-Being	Value	Year	Rating	Trend
Maternal mortality rate (per 100,000 live births)	597	2017	●	→
Neonatal mortality rate (per 1,000 live births)	26.3	2018	●	↗
Mortality rate, under-5 (per 1,000 live births)	58.4	2018	●	↗
Incidence of tuberculosis (per 100,000 population)	174.0	2018	●	→
New HIV infections (per 1,000 uninfected population)	1.1	2018	●	→
Age-standardized death rate due to cardiovascular disease, cancer, diabetes, or chronic respiratory disease in adults aged 30–70 years (%)	20.4	2016	●	→
Age-standardized death rate attributable to household air pollution and ambient air pollution (per 100,000 population)	237	2016	●	●
Traffic deaths (per 100,000 population)	29.7	2016	●	↓
Life expectancy at birth (years)	61.9	2016	●	→
Adolescent fertility rate (births per 1,000 adolescent females aged 15 to 19)	78.2	2017	●	↗
Births attended by skilled health personnel (%)	57.2	2013	●	●
Percentage of surviving infants who received 2 WHO-recommended vaccines (%)	91	2018	●	↑
Universal health coverage (UHC) index of service coverage (worst 0–100 best)	44.0	2017	●	→
Subjective well-being (average ladder score, worst 0–10 best)	5.2	2019	●	●

SDG4 – Quality Education	Value	Year	Rating	Trend
Net primary enrollment rate (%)	76.8	2018	●	↑
Lower secondary completion rate (%)	59.2	2014	●	↑
Literacy rate (% of population aged 15 to 24)	67.2	2015	●	●

SDG5 – Gender Equality	Value	Year	Rating	Trend
Demand for family planning satisfied by modern methods (% of females aged 15 to 49 who are married or in unions)	26.7	2013	●	→
Ratio of female-to-male mean years of education received (%)	69.8	2018	●	↑
Ratio of female-to-male labor force participation rate (%)	76.6	2019	●	↑
Seats held by women in national parliament (%)	8.6	2020	●	↓

SDG6 – Clean Water and Sanitation	Value	Year	Rating	Trend
Population using at least basic drinking water services (%)	78.0	2017	●	→
Population using at least basic sanitation services (%)	39.2	2017	●	↓
Freshwater withdrawal (% of available freshwater resources)	2.0	2000	●	●
Anthropogenic wastewater that receives treatment (%)	0.0	2018	●	●
Scarce water consumption embodied in imports (m³/capita)	0.6	2013	●	↑

SDG7 – Affordable and Clean Energy	Value	Year	Rating	Trend
Population with access to electricity (%)	56.2	2017	●	→
Population with access to clean fuels and technology for cooking (%)	3.3	2016	●	→
CO₂ emissions from fuel combustion for electricity and heating per total electricity output (MtCO₂/TWh)	NA	NA	●	●

SDG8 – Decent Work and Economic Growth	Value	Year	Rating	Trend
Adjusted GDP growth (%)	-5.0	2018	●	●
Victims of modern slavery (per 1,000 population)	5.8	2018	○	●
Adults with an account at a bank or other financial institution or with a mobile-money-service provider (% of population aged 15 or over)	NA	NA	●	●
Unemployment rate (% of total labor force)	9.1	2019	●	→
Fatal work-related accidents embodied in imports (per 100,000 population)	0.1	2010	●	↑

SDG9 – Industry, Innovation and Infrastructure	Value	Year	Rating	Trend
Population using the internet (%)	19.8	2017	●	→
Mobile broadband subscriptions (per 100 population)	36.8	2018	●	↑
Logistics Performance Index: Quality of trade and transport-related infrastructure (worst 1–5 best)	1.8	2018	●	↓
The Times Higher Education Universities Ranking: Average score of top 3 * universities (worst 0–100 best)	0.0	2020	●	●
Scientific and technical journal articles (per 1,000 population)	0.0	2018	●	↓
Expenditure on research and development (% of GDP)	0.1	2011	●	●

SDG10 – Reduced Inequalities	Value	Year	Rating	Trend
Gini coefficient adjusted for top income	35.9	2015	●	●

SDG11 – Sustainable Cities and Communities	Value	Year	Rating	Trend
Annual mean concentration of particulate matter of less than 2.5 microns in diameter (PM2.5) (µg/m³)	34.0	2017	●	↓
Access to improved water source, piped (% of urban population)	83.9	2017	●	↓
Satisfaction with public transport (%)	42.7	2019	●	●

SDG12 – Responsible Consumption and Production	Value	Year	Rating	Trend
Municipal solid waste (kg/capita/day)	0.4	2002	●	●
Electronic waste (kg/capita)	1.1	2016	●	●
Production-based SO₂ emissions (kg/capita)	62.5	2012	○	●
SO₂ emissions embodied in imports (kg/capita)	0.5	2012	●	●
Production-based nitrogen emissions (kg/capita)	13.5	2010	●	●
Nitrogen emissions embodied in imports (kg/capita)	0.3	2010	●	●

SDG13 – Climate Action	Value	Year	Rating	Trend
Energy-related CO₂ emissions (tCO₂/capita)	0.3	2017	●	↑
CO₂ emissions embodied in imports (tCO₂/capita)	0.0	2015	●	↑
CO₂ emissions embodied in fossil fuel exports (kg/capita)	0.0	2017	●	●

SDG14 – Life Below Water	Value	Year	Rating	Trend
Mean area that is protected in marine sites important to biodiversity (%)	54.4	2018	●	↑
Ocean Health Index: Clean Waters score (worst 0–100 best)	50.1	2019	●	→
Fish caught from overexploited or collapsed stocks (% of total catch)	NA	NA	●	●
Fish caught by trawling (%)	1.4	2014	●	↑
Marine biodiversity threats embodied in imports (per million population)	0.0	2018	●	●

SDG15 – Life on Land	Value	Year	Rating	Trend
Mean area that is protected in terrestrial sites important to biodiversity (%)	34.6	2018	○	→
Mean area that is protected in freshwater sites important to biodiversity (%)	NA	NA	●	●
Red List Index of species survival (worst 0–1 best)	1.0	2019	●	↑
Permanent deforestation (% of forest area, 5-year average)	0.2	2018	○	●
Terrestrial and freshwater biodiversity threats embodied in imports (per million population)	0.0	2018	●	●

SDG16 – Peace, Justice and Strong Institutions	Value	Year	Rating	Trend
Homicides (per 100,000 population) *	9.1	2015	●	●
Unsentenced detainees (% of prison population)	24.1	2015	●	●
Percentage of population who feel safe walking alone at night in the city or area where they live (%)	44.5	2019	●	●
Property Rights (worst 1–7 best)	4.5	2019	○	●
Birth registrations with civil authority (% of children under age 5)	57.9	2018	●	●
Corruption Perception Index (worst 0–100 best)	37	2019	●	↑
Children involved in child labor (% of population aged 5 to 14)	19.2	2016	●	●
Exports of major conventional weapons (TIV constant million USD per 100,000 population) *	0.0	2019	●	●
Press Freedom Index (best 0–100 worst)	31.4	2019	○	↑

SDG17 – Partnerships for the Goals	Value	Year	Rating	Trend
Government spending on health and education (% of GDP)	2.9	2016	●	↓
For high-income and all OECD DAC countries: International concessional public finance, including official development assistance (% of GNI)	NA	NA	●	●
Other countries: Government revenue excluding grants (% of GDP)	10.1	2009	●	●
Corporate Tax Haven Score (best 0–100 worst)	48.0	2019	●	●

* Imputed data point

5. Country Profiles

▼ OVERALL PERFORMANCE

Index score

71.9

Regional average score

70.9

SDG Global rank 58 (OF 166)

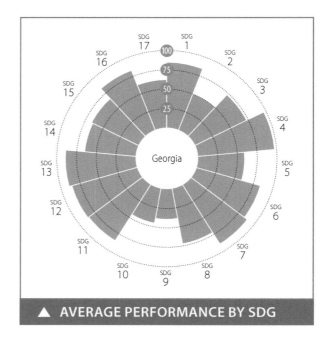

Georgia

▲ AVERAGE PERFORMANCE BY SDG

▼ SPILLOVER INDEX

100 (best) to 0 (worst)

▼ CURRENT ASSESSMENT – SDG DASHBOARD

 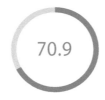

■ Major challenges ■ Significant challenges ☐ Challenges remain ■ SDG achieved ▨ Information unavailable

▼ SDG TRENDS

↓ Decreasing → Stagnating ↗ Moderately improving ↑ On track or maintaining SDG achievement ● Information unavailable

Notes: The full title of Goal 2 "Zero Hunger" is "End hunger, achieve food security and improved nutrition and promote sustainable agriculture".
The full title of each SDG is available here: https://sustainabledevelopment.un.org/topics/sustainabledevelopmentgoals

SDG1 – No Poverty

Indicator	Value	Year	Rating	Trend
Poverty headcount ratio at $1.90/day (%)	2.8	2020	○	↑
Poverty headcount ratio at $3.20/day (%)	12.7	2020	●	↗

SDG2 – Zero Hunger

Indicator	Value	Year	Rating	Trend
Prevalence of undernourishment (%)	7.9	2017	●	↓
Prevalence of stunting in children under 5 years of age (%)	11.3	2009	●	↗
Prevalence of wasting in children under 5 years of age (%)	1.6	2009	●	↑
Prevalence of obesity, BMI ≥ 30 (% of adult population)	21.7	2016	●	↓
Human Trophic Level (best 2–3 worst)	2.3	2017	●	→
Cereal yield (tonnes per hectare of harvested land)	2.0	2017	●	↓
Sustainable Nitrogen Management Index (best 0–1.41 worst)	1.1	2015	●	↓

SDG3 – Good Health and Well-Being

Indicator	Value	Year	Rating	Trend
Maternal mortality rate (per 100,000 live births)	25	2017	●	↑
Neonatal mortality rate (per 1,000 live births)	5.9	2018	●	↑
Mortality rate, under-5 (per 1,000 live births)	9.8	2018	●	↑
Incidence of tuberculosis (per 100,000 population)	80.0	2018	●	↑
New HIV infections (per 1,000 uninfected population)	0.2	2018	●	↑
Age-standardized death rate due to cardiovascular disease, cancer, diabetes, or chronic respiratory disease in adults aged 30–70 years (%)	24.9	2016	●	→
Age-standardized death rate attributable to household air pollution and ambient air pollution (per 100,000 population)	102	2016	●	●
Traffic deaths (per 100,000 population)	15.3	2016	●	↓
Life expectancy at birth (years)	72.6	2016	●	↓
Adolescent fertility rate (births per 1,000 adolescent females aged 15 to 19)	46.4	2017	●	↗
Births attended by skilled health personnel (%)	99.9	2015	●	↑
Percentage of surviving infants who received 2 WHO-recommended vaccines (%)	93	2018	●	↑
Universal health coverage (UHC) index of service coverage (worst 0–100 best)	66.0	2017	●	↗
Subjective well-being (average ladder score, worst 0–10 best)	4.9	2019	●	↑

SDG4 – Quality Education

Indicator	Value	Year	Rating	Trend
Net primary enrollment rate (%)	96.4	2018	○	↓
Lower secondary completion rate (%)	101.8	2018	●	↑
Literacy rate (% of population aged 15 to 24)	99.6	2017	●	●

SDG5 – Gender Equality

Indicator	Value	Year	Rating	Trend
Demand for family planning satisfied by modern methods (% of females aged 15 to 49 who are married or in unions)	52.8	2010	●	→
Ratio of female-to-male mean years of education received (%)	100.0	2018	●	↑
Ratio of female-to-male labor force participation rate (%)	73.5	2019	●	↑
Seats held by women in national parliament (%)	14.1	2020	●	→

SDG6 – Clean Water and Sanitation

Indicator	Value	Year	Rating	Trend
Population using at least basic drinking water services (%)	98.4	2017	●	↑
Population using at least basic sanitation services (%)	90.0	2017	○	→
Freshwater withdrawal (% of available freshwater resources)	5.9	2010	●	●
Anthropogenic wastewater that receives treatment (%)	46.6	2018	○	●
Scarce water consumption embodied in imports (m³/capita)	15.4	2013	●	↑

SDG7 – Affordable and Clean Energy

Indicator	Value	Year	Rating	Trend
Population with access to electricity (%)	100.0	2017	●	↑
Population with access to clean fuels and technology for cooking (%)	77.8	2016	○	↑
CO_2 emissions from fuel combustion for electricity and heating per total electricity output (MtCO₂/TWh)	0.8	2017	●	↑

SDG8 – Decent Work and Economic Growth

Indicator	Value	Year	Rating	Trend
Adjusted GDP growth (%)	0.0	2018	●	●
Victims of modern slavery (per 1,000 population)	4.3	2018	●	●
Adults with an account at a bank or other financial institution or with a mobile-money-service provider (% of population aged 15 or over)	61.2	2017	●	↑
Unemployment rate (% of total labor force)	14.4	2019	●	↗
Fatal work-related accidents embodied in imports (per 100,000 population)	0.3	2010	●	↑

SDG9 – Industry, Innovation and Infrastructure

Indicator	Value	Year	Rating	Trend
Population using the internet (%)	62.7	2018	●	↑
Mobile broadband subscriptions (per 100 population)	73.7	2018	●	↑
Logistics Performance Index: Quality of trade and transport-related infrastructure (worst 1–5 best)	2.4	2018	●	↓
The Times Higher Education Universities Ranking: Average score of top 3 universities (worst 0–100 best)	16.4	2020	○	●
Scientific and technical journal articles (per 1,000 population)	0.1	2018	●	→
Expenditure on research and development (% of GDP)	0.3	2017	●	→

SDG10 – Reduced Inequalities

Indicator	Value	Year	Rating	Trend
Gini coefficient adjusted for top income	47.6	2017	●	●

SDG11 – Sustainable Cities and Communities

Indicator	Value	Year	Rating	Trend
Annual mean concentration of particulate matter of less than 2.5 microns in diameter (PM2.5) (μg/m³)	22.2	2017	●	→
Access to improved water source, piped (% of urban population)	95.9	2017	○	↑
Satisfaction with public transport (%)	66.5	2019	○	↓

SDG12 – Responsible Consumption and Production

Indicator	Value	Year	Rating	Trend
Municipal solid waste (kg/capita/day)	1.0	2015	●	●
Electronic waste (kg/capita)	5.7	2016	●	●
Production-based SO_2 emissions (kg/capita)	54.7	2012	●	●
SO_2 emissions embodied in imports (kg/capita)	5.2	2012	●	●
Production-based nitrogen emissions (kg/capita)	13.0	2010	●	●
Nitrogen emissions embodied in imports (kg/capita)	2.6	2010	●	●

SDG13 – Climate Action

Indicator	Value	Year	Rating	Trend
Energy-related CO_2 emissions (tCO₂/capita)	1.7	2017	●	↑
CO_2 emissions embodied in imports (tCO₂/capita)	0.9	2015	●	↗
CO_2 emissions embodied in fossil fuel exports (kg/capita)	4.8	2019	●	●

SDG14 – Life Below Water

Indicator	Value	Year	Rating	Trend
Mean area that is protected in marine sites important to biodiversity (%)	26.5	2018	●	→
Ocean Health Index: Clean Waters score (worst 0–100 best)	55.0	2019	●	↓
Fish caught from overexploited or collapsed stocks (% of total catch)	NA	NA	●	●
Fish caught by trawling (%)	6.4	2014	●	↑
Marine biodiversity threats embodied in imports (per million population)	0.0	2018	●	●

SDG15 – Life on Land

Indicator	Value	Year	Rating	Trend
Mean area that is protected in terrestrial sites important to biodiversity (%)	37.8	2018	○	→
Mean area that is protected in freshwater sites important to biodiversity (%)	36.1	2018	●	→
Red List Index of species survival (worst 0–1 best)	0.9	2019	●	→
Permanent deforestation (% of forest area, 5-year average)	0.0	2018	●	●
Terrestrial and freshwater biodiversity threats embodied in imports (per million population)	0.7	2018	●	●

SDG16 – Peace, Justice and Strong Institutions

Indicator	Value	Year	Rating	Trend
Homicides (per 100,000 population)	1.0	2016	●	↑
Unsentenced detainees (% of prison population)	11.8	2018	●	↑
Percentage of population who feel safe walking alone at night in the city or area where they live (%)	82.4	2019	●	↑
Property Rights (worst 1–7 best)	4.8	2019	●	●
Birth registrations with civil authority (% of children under age 5)	99.6	2018	●	●
Corruption Perception Index (worst 0–100 best)	56	2019	●	↑
Children involved in child labor (% of population aged 5 to 14)	4.2	2016	●	●
Exports of major conventional weapons (TIV constant million USD per 100,000 population)	0.2	2019	●	●
Press Freedom Index (best 0–100 worst)	29.0	2019	●	↑

SDG17 – Partnerships for the Goals

Indicator	Value	Year	Rating	Trend
Government spending on health and education (% of GDP)	6.9	2016	●	↑
For high-income and all OECD DAC countries: International concessional public finance, including official development assistance (% of GNI)	NA	NA	●	●
Other countries: Government revenue excluding grants (% of GDP)	23.0	2018	●	→
Corporate Tax Haven Score (best 0–100 worst) *	0.0	2019	●	●

* Imputed data point

▼ OVERALL PERFORMANCE

Index score

80.8

Regional average score

77.3

SDG Global rank 5 (OF 166)

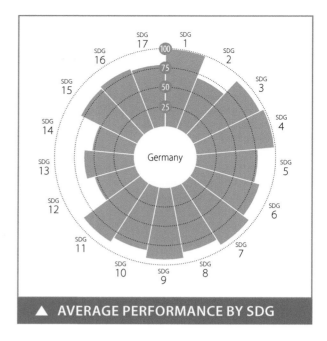

▲ AVERAGE PERFORMANCE BY SDG

▼ SPILLOVER INDEX

100 (best) to 0 (worst)

▼ CURRENT ASSESSMENT – SDG DASHBOARD

■ Major challenges   ■ Significant challenges   ■ Challenges remain   ■ SDG achieved   ■ Information unavailable

▼ SDG TRENDS

↓ Decreasing   → Stagnating   ↗ Moderately improving   ↑ On track or maintaining SDG achievement   ● Information unavailable

Notes: The full title of Goal 2 "Zero Hunger" is "End hunger, achieve food security and improved nutrition and promote sustainable agriculture".
The full title of each SDG is available here: https://sustainabledevelopment.un.org/topics/sustainabledevelopmentgoals

SDG1 – No Poverty

Indicator	Value	Year	Rating	Trend
Poverty headcount ratio at $1.90/day (%)	0.2	2020	●	↑
Poverty headcount ratio at $3.20/day (%)	0.2	2020	●	↑
Poverty rate after taxes and transfers (%)	10.4	2017	○	↓

SDG2 – Zero Hunger

Indicator	Value	Year	Rating	Trend
Prevalence of undernourishment (%)	2.5	2017	●	↑
Prevalence of stunting in children under 5 years of age (%)	1.3	2005	●	↑
Prevalence of wasting in children under 5 years of age (%)	1.0	2005	●	↑
Prevalence of obesity, BMI ≥ 30 (% of adult population)	22.3	2016	●	↓
Human Trophic Level (best 2–3 worst)	2.4	2017	●	↓
Cereal yield (tonnes per hectare of harvested land)	7.3	2017	●	↑
Sustainable Nitrogen Management Index (best 0–1.41 worst)	0.5	2015	●	↓
Yield gap closure (% of potential yield)	77.3	2015	●	●

SDG3 – Good Health and Well-Being

Indicator	Value	Year	Rating	Trend
Maternal mortality rate (per 100,000 live births)	7	2017	●	↑
Neonatal mortality rate (per 1,000 live births)	2.2	2018	●	↑
Mortality rate, under-5 (per 1,000 live births)	3.7	2018	●	↑
Incidence of tuberculosis (per 100,000 population)	7.3	2018	●	↑
New HIV infections (per 1,000 uninfected population)	0.0	2018	●	↑
Age-standardized death rate due to cardiovascular disease, cancer, diabetes, or chronic respiratory disease in adults aged 30–70 years (%)	12.1	2016	●	↑
Age-standardized death rate attributable to household air pollution and ambient air pollution (per 100,000 population)	16	2016	●	●
Traffic deaths (per 100,000 population)	4.1	2016	●	↑
Life expectancy at birth (years)	81.0	2016	●	↑
Adolescent fertility rate (births per 1,000 adolescent females aged 15 to 19)	8.1	2017	●	↑
Births attended by skilled health personnel (%)	98.7	2015	●	↑
Percentage of surviving infants who received 2 WHO-recommended vaccines (%)	93.0	2018	●	↑
Universal health coverage (UHC) index of service coverage (worst 0–100 best)	83.0	2017	●	↑
Subjective well-being (average ladder score, worst 0–10 best)	7.0	2019	●	↑
Gap in life expectancy at birth among regions (years)	2.2	2016	●	↑
Gap in self-reported health status by income (percentage points)	29.8	2017	○	↓
Daily smokers (% of population aged 15 and over)	18.8	2017	○	↑

SDG4 – Quality Education

Indicator	Value	Year	Rating	Trend
Net primary enrollment rate (%)	* 98.7	2017	●	↑
Lower secondary completion rate (%)	* 98.7	2017	●	↑
Literacy rate (% of population aged 15 to 24)	NA	NA	●	●
Participation rate in pre-primary organized learning (% of children aged 4 to 6)	98.8	2017	●	↑
Tertiary educational attainment (% of population aged 25 to 34)	32.3	2018	●	↑
PISA score (worst 0–600 best)	500.3	2018	●	↑
Variation in science performance explained by socio-economic status (%)	18.6	2018	●	↓
Underachievers in science (% of 15-year-olds)	19.6	2018	●	↓
Resilient students in science (% of 15-year-olds)	37.5	2018	○	↑

SDG5 – Gender Equality

Indicator	Value	Year	Rating	Trend
Demand for family planning satisfied by modern methods (% of females aged 15 to 49 who are married or in unions)	* 83.0	2017	●	↑
Ratio of female-to-male mean years of education received (%)	93.8	2018	○	→
Ratio of female-to-male labor force participation rate (%)	83.6	2019	●	↑
Seats held by women in national parliament (%)	31.2	2020	●	↓
Gender wage gap (% of male median wage)	16.2	2017	●	↗
Gender gap in time spent doing unpaid work (minutes/day)	91.8	2013	●	●

SDG6 – Clean Water and Sanitation

Indicator	Value	Year	Rating	Trend
Population using at least basic drinking water services (%)	100.0	2017	●	●
Population using at least basic sanitation services (%)	99.2	2017	●	●
Freshwater withdrawal (% of available freshwater resources)	34.4	2010	○	●
Anthropogenic wastewater that receives treatment (%)	97.0	2018	●	●
Scarce water consumption embodied in imports (m³/capita)	48.6	2013	●	→
Population using safely managed water services (%)	99.8	2017	●	↑
Population using safely managed sanitation services (%)	97.2	2017	●	↑

SDG7 – Affordable and Clean Energy

Indicator	Value	Year	Rating	Trend
Population with access to electricity (%)	100.0	2017	●	↑
Population with access to clean fuels and technology for cooking (%)	100.0	2016	●	↑
CO₂ emissions from fuel combustion for electricity and heating per total electricity output (MtCO₂/TWh)	1.2	2017	●	↑
Share of renewable energy in total primary energy supply (%)	14.1	2018	●	↑

SDG8 – Decent Work and Economic Growth

Indicator	Value	Year	Rating	Trend
Adjusted GDP growth (%)	0.0	2018	○	●
Victims of modern slavery (per 1,000 population)	2.0	2018	●	●
Adults with an account at a bank or other financial institution or with a mobile-money-service provider (% of population aged 15 or over)	99.1	2017	●	↑
Fatal work-related accidents embodied in imports (per 100,000 population)	1.8	2010	●	↑
Employment-to-population ratio (%)	76.7	2019	●	↑
Youth not in employment, education or training (NEET) (% of population aged 15 to 29)	9.2	2018	●	↑

SDG9 – Industry, Innovation and Infrastructure

Indicator	Value	Year	Rating	Trend
Population using the internet (%)	89.7	2018	●	↑
Mobile broadband subscriptions (per 100 population)	82.6	2018	●	↑
Logistics Performance Index: Quality of trade and transport-related infrastructure (worst 1–5 best)	4.4	2018	●	↑
The Times Higher Education Universities Ranking: Average score of top 3 universities (worst 0–100 best)	75.1	2020	●	●
Scientific and technical journal articles (per 1,000 population)	1.3	2018	●	↑
Expenditure on research and development (% of GDP)	3.0	2017	●	↑
Researchers (per 1,000 employed population)	9.7	2018	●	↑
Triadic patent families filed (per million population)	56.4	2017	●	↑
Gap in internet access by income (percentage points)	14.5	2019	●	↑
Women in science and engineering (% of tertiary graduates in science and engineering)	24.7	2015	●	●

SDG10 – Reduced Inequalities

Indicator	Value	Year	Rating	Trend
Gini coefficient adjusted for top income	33.7	2015	○	↓
Palma ratio	1.1	2017	○	↗
Elderly poverty rate (% of population aged 66 or over)	10.2	2017	○	↓

SDG11 – Sustainable Cities and Communities

Indicator	Value	Year	Rating	Trend
Annual mean concentration of particulate matter of less than 2.5 microns in diameter (PM2.5) (µg/m³)	12.0	2017	○	↑
Access to improved water source, piped (% of urban population)	99.0	2017	●	↑
Satisfaction with public transport	67.3	2019	○	↓
Population with rent overburden (%)	4.8	2017	●	↑

SDG12 – Responsible Consumption and Production

Indicator	Value	Year	Rating	Trend
Electronic waste (kg/capita)	22.8	2016	●	●
Production-based SO₂ emissions (kg/capita)	34.5	2012	●	●
SO₂ emissions embodied in imports (kg/capita)	15.0	2012	●	●
Production-based nitrogen emissions (kg/capita)	37.1	2010	●	●
Nitrogen emissions embodied in imports (kg/capita)	17.0	2010	●	●
Non-recycled municipal solid waste (kg/capita/day)	0.5	2018	●	●

SDG13 – Climate Action

Indicator	Value	Year	Rating	Trend
Energy-related CO₂ emissions (tCO₂/capita)	8.7	2017	●	↓
CO₂ emissions embodied in imports (tCO₂/capita)	2.4	2015	●	→
CO₂ emissions embodied in fossil fuel exports (kg/capita)	231.9	2018	○	●
Effective carbon rate (EUR/tCO₂)	25.4	2016	●	●

SDG14 – Life Below Water

Indicator	Value	Year	Rating	Trend
Mean area that is protected in marine sites important to biodiversity (%)	85.6	2018	●	↑
Ocean Health Index: Clean Waters score (worst 0–100 best)	51.0	2019	●	→
Fish caught from overexploited or collapsed stocks (% of total catch)	46.6	2014	●	↑
Fish caught by trawling (%)	80.6	2014	●	→
Marine biodiversity threats embodied in imports (per million population)	0.3	2018	●	●

SDG15 – Life on Land

Indicator	Value	Year	Rating	Trend
Mean area that is protected in terrestrial sites important to biodiversity (%)	78.3	2018	●	↑
Mean area that is protected in freshwater sites important to biodiversity (%)	81.1	2018	●	↑
Red List Index of species survival (worst 0–1 best)	1.0	2019	●	↑
Permanent deforestation (% of forest area, 5-year average)	0.0	2018	●	●
Terrestrial and freshwater biodiversity threats embodied in imports (per million population)	5.7	2018	●	●

SDG16 – Peace, Justice and Strong Institutions

Indicator	Value	Year	Rating	Trend
Homicides (per 100,000 population)	1.0	2017	●	↑
Unsentenced detainees (% of prison population)	23.6	2018	●	↑
Percentage of population who feel safe walking alone at night in the city or area where they live (%)	71.3	2019	●	↑
Property Rights (worst 1–7 best)	5.3	2019	●	●
Birth registrations with civil authority (% of children under age 5)	100.0	2018	●	●
Corruption Perception Index (worst 0–100 best)	80.0	2019	●	↑
Children involved in child labor (% of population aged 5 to 14)	* 0.0	2016	●	●
Exports of major conventional weapons (TIV constant million USD per 100,000 population)	2.0	2019	●	●
Press Freedom Index (best 0–100 worst)	14.6	2019	●	↑
Persons held in prison (per 100,000 population)	76.6	2017	●	↑

SDG17 – Partnerships for the Goals

Indicator	Value	Year	Rating	Trend
Government spending on health and education (% of GDP)	14.2	2016	●	↑
For high-income and all OECD DAC countries: International concessional public finance, including official development assistance (% of GNI)	0.7	2017	○	↑
Other countries: Government revenue excluding grants (% of GDP)	NA	NA	●	●
Corporate Tax Haven Score (best 0–100 worst)	52.3	2019	●	●
Financial Secrecy Score (best 0–100 worst)	51.7	2020	●	●
Shifted profits of multinationals (US$ billion)	65.4	2016	●	●

* Imputed data point

▼ OVERALL PERFORMANCE

Index score

65.4

Regional average score

53.1

SDG Global rank 100 (OF 166)

▼ SPILLOVER INDEX

100 (best) to 0 (worst)

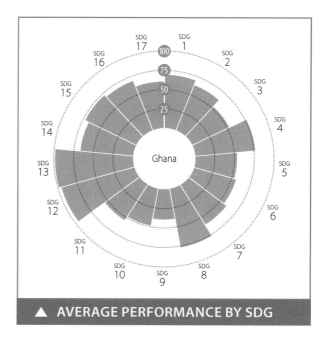

▲ AVERAGE PERFORMANCE BY SDG

▼ CURRENT ASSESSMENT – SDG DASHBOARD

■ Major challenges ■ Significant challenges ▨ Challenges remain ■ SDG achieved ▨ Information unavailable

▼ SDG TRENDS

↓ Decreasing → Stagnating ↗ Moderately improving ↑ On track or maintaining SDG achievement ● Information unavailable

Notes: The full title of Goal 2 "Zero Hunger" is "End hunger, achieve food security and improved nutrition and promote sustainable agriculture".
The full title of each SDG is available here: https://sustainabledevelopment.un.org/topics/sustainabledevelopmentgoals

SDG1 – No Poverty

Indicator	Value	Year	Rating	Trend
Poverty headcount ratio at $1.90/day (%)	9.9	2020	●	↑
Poverty headcount ratio at $3.20/day (%)	23.6	2020	●	↗

SDG2 – Zero Hunger

Indicator	Value	Year	Rating	Trend
Prevalence of undernourishment (%)	5.5	2017	●	↑
Prevalence of stunting in children under 5 years of age (%)	18.8	2014	●	↑
Prevalence of wasting in children under 5 years of age (%)	4.7	2014	●	↑
Prevalence of obesity, BMI ≥ 30 (% of adult population)	10.9	2016	●	↓
Human Trophic Level (best 2–3 worst)	2.1	2017	●	↑
Cereal yield (tonnes per hectare of harvested land)	1.9	2017	●	↑
Sustainable Nitrogen Management Index (best 0–1.41 worst)	0.8	2015	●	→

SDG3 – Good Health and Well-Being

Indicator	Value	Year	Rating	Trend
Maternal mortality rate (per 100,000 live births)	308	2017	●	→
Neonatal mortality rate (per 1,000 live births)	23.9	2018	●	↗
Mortality rate, under-5 (per 1,000 live births)	47.9	2018	●	↑
Incidence of tuberculosis (per 100,000 population)	148.0	2018	●	→
New HIV infections (per 1,000 uninfected population)	0.7	2018	●	↗
Age-standardized death rate due to cardiovascular disease, cancer, diabetes, or chronic respiratory disease in adults aged 30–70 years (%)	20.8	2016	●	↓
Age-standardized death rate attributable to household air pollution and ambient air pollution (per 100,000 population)	204	2016	●	●
Traffic deaths (per 100,000 population)	24.9	2016	●	→
Life expectancy at birth (years)	63.4	2016	●	→
Adolescent fertility rate (births per 1,000 adolescent females aged 15 to 19)	66.6	2017	●	→
Births attended by skilled health personnel (%)	70.8	2014	●	●
Percentage of surviving infants who received 2 WHO-recommended vaccines (%)	92	2018	●	↑
Universal health coverage (UHC) index of service coverage (worst 0–100 best)	47.0	2017	●	↗
Subjective well-being (average ladder score, worst 0–10 best)	5.0	2018	●	↑

SDG4 – Quality Education

Indicator	Value	Year	Rating	Trend
Net primary enrollment rate (%)	86.2	2019	●	↓
Lower secondary completion rate (%)	78.0	2018	●	↑
Literacy rate (% of population aged 15 to 24)	92.5	2018	●	●

SDG5 – Gender Equality

Indicator	Value	Year	Rating	Trend
Demand for family planning satisfied by modern methods (% of females aged 15 to 49 who are married or in unions)	46.2	2017	●	↗
Ratio of female-to-male mean years of education received (%)	81.0	2018	●	↑
Ratio of female-to-male labor force participation rate (%)	88.9	2019	●	↑
Seats held by women in national parliament (%)	13.1	2020	●	→

SDG6 – Clean Water and Sanitation

Indicator	Value	Year	Rating	Trend
Population using at least basic drinking water services (%)	81.5	2017	●	↗
Population using at least basic sanitation services (%)	18.5	2017	●	→
Freshwater withdrawal (% of available freshwater resources)	6.1	2015	●	●
Anthropogenic wastewater that receives treatment (%)	0.0	2018	●	●
Scarce water consumption embodied in imports (m³/capita)	0.7	2013	●	↑

SDG7 – Affordable and Clean Energy

Indicator	Value	Year	Rating	Trend
Population with access to electricity (%)	79.0	2017	●	→
Population with access to clean fuels and technology for cooking (%)	21.7	2016	●	→
CO_2 emissions from fuel combustion for electricity and heating per total electricity output (MtCO$_2$/TWh)	1.0	2017	●	↑

SDG8 – Decent Work and Economic Growth

Indicator	Value	Year	Rating	Trend
Adjusted GDP growth (%)	-1.9	2018	●	●
Victims of modern slavery (per 1,000 population)	4.8	2018	●	●
Adults with an account at a bank or other financial institution or with a mobile-money-service provider (% of population aged 15 or over)	57.7	2017	●	↑
Unemployment rate (% of total labor force)	4.3	2019	●	↑
Fatal work-related accidents embodied in imports (per 100,000 population)	0.0	2010	●	↑

SDG9 – Industry, Innovation and Infrastructure

Indicator	Value	Year	Rating	Trend
Population using the internet (%)	39.0	2017	●	↑
Mobile broadband subscriptions (per 100 population)	91.8	2018	●	↑
Logistics Performance Index: Quality of trade and transport-related infrastructure (worst 1–5 best)	2.4	2018	●	↓
The Times Higher Education Universities Ranking: Average score of top 3 universities (worst 0–100 best)	25.2	2020	●	●
Scientific and technical journal articles (per 1,000 population)	0.0	2018	●	→
Expenditure on research and development (% of GDP)	0.4	2010	●	●

SDG10 – Reduced Inequalities

Indicator	Value	Year	Rating	Trend
Gini coefficient adjusted for top income	46.0	2016	●	●

SDG11 – Sustainable Cities and Communities

Indicator	Value	Year	Rating	Trend
Annual mean concentration of particulate matter of less than 2.5 microns in diameter (PM2.5) (µg/m³)	34.7	2017	●	↓
Access to improved water source, piped (% of urban population)	39.9	2017	●	↓
Satisfaction with public transport (%)	58.4	2018	●	↑

SDG12 – Responsible Consumption and Production

Indicator	Value	Year	Rating	Trend
Municipal solid waste (kg/capita/day)	0.6	2005	●	●
Electronic waste (kg/capita)	1.4	2016	●	●
Production-based SO$_2$ emissions (kg/capita)	8.6	2012	●	●
SO$_2$ emissions embodied in imports (kg/capita)	0.6	2012	●	●
Production-based nitrogen emissions (kg/capita)	6.5	2010	●	●
Nitrogen emissions embodied in imports (kg/capita)	0.3	2010	●	●

SDG13 – Climate Action

Indicator	Value	Year	Rating	Trend
Energy-related CO_2 emissions (tCO$_2$/capita)	0.5	2017	●	↑
CO_2 emissions embodied in imports (tCO$_2$/capita)	0.1	2015	●	↑
CO_2 emissions embodied in fossil fuel exports (kg/capita)	0.0	2018	●	●

SDG14 – Life Below Water

Indicator	Value	Year	Rating	Trend
Mean area that is protected in marine sites important to biodiversity (%)	72.4	2018	●	↑
Ocean Health Index: Clean Waters score (worst 0–100 best)	36.2	2019	●	→
Fish caught from overexploited or collapsed stocks (% of total catch)	37.0	2014	●	↑
Fish caught by trawling (%)	7.8	2014	●	↑
Marine biodiversity threats embodied in imports (per million population)	0.0	2018	●	●

SDG15 – Life on Land

Indicator	Value	Year	Rating	Trend
Mean area that is protected in terrestrial sites important to biodiversity (%)	85.6	2018	●	↑
Mean area that is protected in freshwater sites important to biodiversity (%)	NA	NA	●	●
Red List Index of species survival (worst 0–1 best)	0.8	2019	●	↓
Permanent deforestation (% of forest area, 5-year average)	0.8	2018	●	●
Terrestrial and freshwater biodiversity threats embodied in imports (per million population)	0.0	2018	●	●

SDG16 – Peace, Justice and Strong Institutions

Indicator	Value	Year	Rating	Trend
Homicides (per 100,000 population)	2.1	2017	●	→
Unsentenced detainees (% of prison population)	12.5	2018	●	↑
Percentage of population who feel safe walking alone at night in the city or area where they live (%)	66.7	2018	●	↓
Property Rights (worst 1–7 best)	4.1	2019	●	●
Birth registrations with civil authority (% of children under age 5)	70.5	2018	●	●
Corruption Perception Index (worst 0–100 best)	41	2019	●	↓
Children involved in child labor (% of population aged 5 to 14)	21.8	2016	●	●
Exports of major conventional weapons (TIV constant million USD per 100,000 population)	0.0 *	2019	●	●
Press Freedom Index (best 0–100 worst)	20.8	2019	●	↑

SDG17 – Partnerships for the Goals

Indicator	Value	Year	Rating	Trend
Government spending on health and education (% of GDP)	6.2	2016	●	↓
For high-income and all OECD DAC countries: International concessional public finance, including official development assistance (% of GNI)	NA	NA	●	●
Other countries: Government revenue excluding grants (% of GDP)	27.2	2015	●	●
Corporate Tax Haven Score (best 0–100 worst)	49.5	2019	●	●

* Imputed data point

5. Country Profiles

▼ OVERALL PERFORMANCE

Index score

74.3

Regional average score

77.3

SDG Global rank 43 (OF 166)

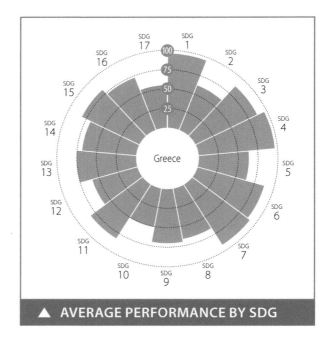

▲ AVERAGE PERFORMANCE BY SDG

▼ SPILLOVER INDEX

100 (best) to 0 (worst)

▼ CURRENT ASSESSMENT – SDG DASHBOARD

■ Major challenges   ■ Significant challenges   ■ Challenges remain   ■ SDG achieved   ■ Information unavailable

▼ SDG TRENDS

↓ Decreasing   → Stagnating   ↗ Moderately improving   ↑ On track or maintaining SDG achievement   ● Information unavailable

Notes: The full title of Goal 2 "Zero Hunger" is "End hunger, achieve food security and improved nutrition and promote sustainable agriculture".
The full title of each SDG is available here: https://sustainabledevelopment.un.org/topics/sustainabledevelopmentgoals

SDG1 – No Poverty

	Value	Year	Rating	Trend
Poverty headcount ratio at $1.90/day (%)	1.4	2020	●	↑
Poverty headcount ratio at $3.20/day (%)	2.4	2020	◐	↗
Poverty rate after taxes and transfers (%)	12.6	2017	●	↑

SDG2 – Zero Hunger

		Value	Year	Rating	Trend
Prevalence of undernourishment (%)		2.5	2017	●	↑
Prevalence of stunting in children under 5 years of age (%)	*	2.6	2016	●	↑
Prevalence of wasting in children under 5 years of age (%)	*	0.7	2016	●	↑
Prevalence of obesity, BMI ≥ 30 (% of adult population)		24.9	2016	●	↓
Human Trophic Level (best 2–3 worst)		2.4	2017	●	→
Cereal yield (tonnes per hectare of harvested land)		3.8	2017	●	↑
Sustainable Nitrogen Management Index (best 0–1.41 worst)		0.6	2015	●	↓
Yield gap closure (% of potential yield)		51.7	2015	●	●

SDG3 – Good Health and Well-Being

	Value	Year	Rating	Trend
Maternal mortality rate (per 100,000 live births)	3	2017	●	↑
Neonatal mortality rate (per 1,000 live births)	2.6	2018	●	↑
Mortality rate, under-5 (per 1,000 live births)	4.5	2018	●	↑
Incidence of tuberculosis (per 100,000 population)	4.5	2018	●	↑
New HIV infections (per 1,000 uninfected population)	NA	NA	●	●
Age-standardized death rate due to cardiovascular disease, cancer, diabetes, or chronic respiratory disease in adults aged 30–70 years (%)	12.4	2016	●	↑
Age-standardized death rate attributable to household air pollution and ambient air pollution (per 100,000 population)	28	2016	◐	●
Traffic deaths (per 100,000 population)	9.2	2016	◐	→
Life expectancy at birth (years)	81.2	2016	●	↑
Adolescent fertility rate (births per 1,000 adolescent females aged 15 to 19)	7.2	2017	●	↑
Births attended by skilled health personnel (%)	NA	NA	●	●
Percentage of surviving infants who received 2 WHO-recommended vaccines (%)	97.0	2018	●	↑
Universal health coverage (UHC) index of service coverage (worst 0–100 best)	75.0	2017	●	↑
Subjective well-being (average ladder score, worst 0–10 best)	5.4	2018	●	↓
Gap in life expectancy at birth among regions (years)	2.4	2016	●	●
Gap in self-reported health status by income (percentage points)	6.5	2017	●	↑
Daily smokers (% of population aged 15 and over)	27.3	2014	●	●

SDG4 – Quality Education

		Value	Year	Rating	Trend
Net primary enrollment rate (%)	*	97.5	2017	●	↑
Lower secondary completion rate (%)	*	97.5	2017	●	↑
Literacy rate (% of population aged 15 to 24)		99.2	2018	●	●
Participation rate in pre-primary organized learning (% of children aged 4 to 6)		92.7	2017	●	↑
Tertiary educational attainment (% of population aged 25 to 34)		42.8	2018	●	↑
PISA score (worst 0–600 best)		453.3	2018	●	↓
Variation in science performance explained by socio-economic status (%)		10.9	2018	●	↑
Underachievers in science (% of 15-year-olds)		31.7	2018	●	→
Resilient students in science (% of 15-year-olds)		19.5	2018	●	→

SDG5 – Gender Equality

		Value	Year	Rating	Trend
Demand for family planning satisfied by modern methods (% of females aged 15 to 49 who are married or in unions)	*	62.0	2017	◐	↗
Ratio of female-to-male mean years of education received (%)		95.4	2018	◐	↑
Ratio of female-to-male labor force participation rate (%)		74.8	2019	●	↑
Seats held by women in national parliament (%)		20.7	2020	●	→
Gender wage gap (% of male median wage)		4.5	2017	●	↑
Gender gap in time spent doing unpaid work (minutes/day)		164.4	2013	●	●

SDG6 – Clean Water and Sanitation

	Value	Year	Rating	Trend
Population using at least basic drinking water services (%)	100.0	2017	●	●
Population using at least basic sanitation services (%)	99.0	2017	●	●
Freshwater withdrawal (% of available freshwater resources)	19.3	2005	●	●
Anthropogenic wastewater that receives treatment (%)	81.7	2018	●	●
Scarce water consumption embodied in imports (m3/capita)	34.8	2013	●	↑
Population using safely managed water services (%)	100.0	2017	●	↑
Population using safely managed sanitation services (%)	90.4	2017	●	↑

SDG7 – Affordable and Clean Energy

	Value	Year	Rating	Trend
Population with access to electricity (%)	100.0	2017	●	↑
Population with access to clean fuels and technology for cooking (%)	94.3	2016	●	↑
CO2 emissions from fuel combustion for electricity and heating per total electricity output (MtCO2/TWh)	1.2	2017	●	↑
Share of renewable energy in total primary energy supply (%)	13.0	2018	●	↑

SDG8 – Decent Work and Economic Growth

	Value	Year	Rating	Trend
Adjusted GDP growth (%)	-1.3	2018	◐	●
Victims of modern slavery (per 1,000 population)	7.9	2018	●	●
Adults with an account at a bank or other financial institution or with a mobile-money-service provider (% of population aged 15 or over)	85.5	2017	●	↑
Fatal work-related accidents embodied in imports (per 100,000 population)	1.3	2010	●	↑
Employment-to-population ratio (%)	56.5	2019	●	↑
Youth not in employment, education or training (NEET) (% of population aged 15 to 29)	21.5	2018	●	↑

SDG9 – Industry, Innovation and Infrastructure

		Value	Year	Rating	Trend
Population using the internet (%)		73.0	2018	◐	↑
Mobile broadband subscriptions (per 100 population)		81.4	2018	●	↑
Logistics Performance Index: Quality of trade and transport-related infrastructure (worst 1–5 best)		3.2	2018	●	↑
The Times Higher Education Universities Ranking: Average score of top 3 universities (worst 0–100 best)		37.4	2020	●	●
Scientific and technical journal articles (per 1,000 population)		1.0	2018	●	↑
Expenditure on research and development (% of GDP)		1.1	2017	●	↑
Researchers (per 1,000 employed population)		8.6	2018	●	↑
Triadic patent families filed (per million population)		1.3	2017	●	↓
Gap in internet access by income (percentage points)		36.9	2019	●	↗
Women in science and engineering (% of tertiary graduates in science and engineering)		NA	NA	●	●

SDG10 – Reduced Inequalities

	Value	Year	Rating	Trend
Gini coefficient adjusted for top income	45.1	2015	●	→
Palma ratio	1.2	2017	●	↑
Elderly poverty rate (% of population aged 66 or over)	7.2	2017	◐	↑

SDG11 – Sustainable Cities and Communities

	Value	Year	Rating	Trend
Annual mean concentration of particulate matter of less than 2.5 microns in diameter (PM2.5) (μg/m3)	16.2	2017	◐	↗
Access to improved water source, piped (% of urban population)	99.0	2017	●	↑
Satisfaction with public transport (%)	57.0	2018	●	↗
Population with rent overburden (%)	19.7	2017	●	↗

SDG12 – Responsible Consumption and Production

	Value	Year	Rating	Trend
Electronic waste (kg/capita)	17.5	2016	●	●
Production-based SO2 emissions (kg/capita)	102.5	2012	●	●
SO2 emissions embodied in imports (kg/capita)	9.5	2012	●	●
Production-based nitrogen emissions (kg/capita)	50.6	2010	●	●
Nitrogen emissions embodied in imports (kg/capita)	12.9	2010	●	●
Non-recycled municipal solid waste (kg/capita/day)	1.1	2017	●	●

SDG13 – Climate Action

	Value	Year	Rating	Trend
Energy-related CO2 emissions (tCO2/capita)	6.1	2017	●	↓
CO2 emissions embodied in imports (tCO2/capita)	1.6	2015	●	→
CO2 emissions embodied in fossil fuel exports (kg/capita)	5.1	2019	●	●
Effective carbon rate (EUR/tCO2)	22.6	2016	●	●

SDG14 – Life Below Water

	Value	Year	Rating	Trend
Mean area that is protected in marine sites important to biodiversity (%)	86.4	2018	●	↑
Ocean Health Index: Clean Waters score (worst 0–100 best)	58.5	2019	●	↓
Fish caught from overexploited or collapsed stocks (% of total catch)	48.5	2014	●	↓
Fish caught by trawling (%)	21.8	2014	◐	↗
Marine biodiversity threats embodied in imports (per million population)	0.2	2018	●	●

SDG15 – Life on Land

	Value	Year	Rating	Trend
Mean area that is protected in terrestrial sites important to biodiversity (%)	85.8	2018	●	↑
Mean area that is protected in freshwater sites important to biodiversity (%)	87.2	2018	●	↑
Red List Index of species survival (worst 0–1 best)	0.8	2019	●	→
Permanent deforestation (% of forest area, 5-year average)	0.0	2018	●	●
Terrestrial and freshwater biodiversity threats embodied in imports (per million population)	2.9	2018	●	●

SDG16 – Peace, Justice and Strong Institutions

		Value	Year	Rating	Trend
Homicides (per 100,000 population)		0.7	2017	●	↑
Unsentenced detainees (% of prison population)		31.1	2018	◐	↓
Percentage of population who feel safe walking alone at night in the city or area where they live		57.5	2018	●	↓
Property Rights (worst 1–7 best)		4.0	2019	●	●
Birth registrations with civil authority (% of children under age 5)		100.0	2018	●	●
Corruption Perception Index (worst 0–100 best)		48.0	2019	●	↗
Children involved in child labor (% of population aged 5 to 14)	*	0.0	2016	●	●
Exports of major conventional weapons (TIV constant million USD per 100,000 population)		0.3	2019	●	●
Press Freedom Index (best 0–100 worst)		29.1	2019	●	↑
Persons held in prison (per 100,000 population)		89.7	2017	●	↑

SDG17 – Partnerships for the Goals

		Value	Year	Rating	Trend
Government spending on health and education (% of GDP)	*	8.9	2018	◐	↓
For high-income and all OECD DAC countries: International concessional public finance, including official development assistance (% of GNI)		0.2	2017	●	→
Other countries: Government revenue excluding grants (% of GDP)		NA	NA	●	●
Corporate Tax Haven Score (best 0–100 worst)		39.1	2019	●	●
Financial Secrecy Score (best 0–100 worst)		51.5	2020	●	●
Shifted profits of multinationals (US$ billion)		1.7	2016	●	●

* Imputed data point

▼ OVERALL PERFORMANCE

Index score

na

Regional average score

70.4

SDG Global rank NA (OF 166)

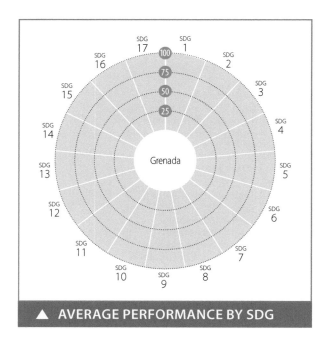

▲ AVERAGE PERFORMANCE BY SDG

▼ SPILLOVER INDEX

100 (best) to 0 (worst)

▼ CURRENT ASSESSMENT – SDG DASHBOARD

■ Major challenges ■ Significant challenges ■ Challenges remain ■ SDG achieved ■ Information unavailable

▼ SDG TRENDS

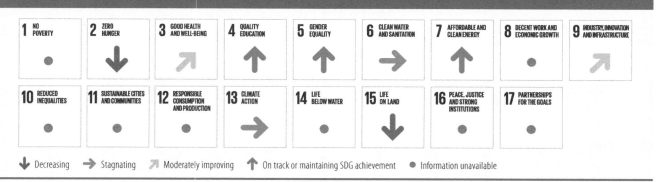

↓ Decreasing   → Stagnating   ↗ Moderately improving   ↑ On track or maintaining SDG achievement   ● Information unavailable

Notes: The full title of Goal 2 "Zero Hunger" is "End hunger, achieve food security and improved nutrition and promote sustainable agriculture".
The full title of each SDG is available here: https://sustainabledevelopment.un.org/topics/sustainabledevelopmentgoals

SDG1 – No Poverty

	Value	Year	Rating	Trend
Poverty headcount ratio at $1.90/day (%)	NA	NA	●	●
Poverty headcount ratio at $3.20/day (%)	NA	NA	●	●

SDG2 – Zero Hunger

	Value	Year	Rating	Trend
Prevalence of undernourishment (%)	NA	NA	●	●
Prevalence of stunting in children under 5 years of age (%)	NA	NA	●	●
Prevalence of wasting in children under 5 years of age (%)	NA	NA	●	●
Prevalence of obesity, BMI ≥ 30 (% of adult population)	21.3	2016	●	↓
Human Trophic Level (best 2–3 worst)	2.3	2017	●	→
Cereal yield (tonnes per hectare of harvested land)	1.0	2017	●	→
Sustainable Nitrogen Management Index (best 0–1.41 worst)	1.0	2015	●	→

SDG3 – Good Health and Well-Being

	Value	Year	Rating	Trend
Maternal mortality rate (per 100,000 live births)	25	2017	●	↑
Neonatal mortality rate (per 1,000 live births)	9.9	2018	●	↑
Mortality rate, under-5 (per 1,000 live births)	15.2	2018	●	↑
Incidence of tuberculosis (per 100,000 population)	2.1	2018	●	↑
New HIV infections (per 1,000 uninfected population)	0.3	2018	●	↑
Age-standardized death rate due to cardiovascular disease, cancer, diabetes, or chronic respiratory disease in adults aged 30–70 years (%)	21.4	2016	●	↗
Age-standardized death rate attributable to household air pollution and ambient air pollution (per 100,000 population)	45	2016	●	●
Traffic deaths (per 100,000 population)	9.3	2016	●	↓
Life expectancy at birth (years)	73.4	2016	●	→
Adolescent fertility rate (births per 1,000 adolescent females aged 15 to 19)	29.2	2017	●	↑
Births attended by skilled health personnel (%)	99.3	2016	●	↑
Percentage of surviving infants who received 2 WHO-recommended vaccines (%)	84	2018	●	↓
Universal health coverage (UHC) index of service coverage (worst 0–100 best)	72.0	2017	●	↑
Subjective well-being (average ladder score, worst 0–10 best)	NA	NA	●	●

SDG4 – Quality Education

	Value	Year	Rating	Trend
Net primary enrollment rate (%)	95.9	2018	●	●
Lower secondary completion rate (%)	104.8	2017	●	↑
Literacy rate (% of population aged 15 to 24)	99.2	2014	●	●

SDG5 – Gender Equality

	Value	Year	Rating	Trend
Demand for family planning satisfied by modern methods (% of females aged 15 to 49 who are married or in unions) *	79.7	2017	●	↑
Ratio of female-to-male mean years of education received (%)	NA	NA	●	●
Ratio of female-to-male labor force participation rate (%)	NA	NA	●	●
Seats held by women in national parliament (%)	46.7	2020	●	↑

SDG6 – Clean Water and Sanitation

	Value	Year	Rating	Trend
Population using at least basic drinking water services (%)	95.6	2017	●	→
Population using at least basic sanitation services (%)	91.5	2017	●	→
Freshwater withdrawal (% of available freshwater resources)	7.1	2015	●	●
Anthropogenic wastewater that receives treatment (%)	0.9	2018	●	●
Scarce water consumption embodied in imports (m³/capita)	NA	NA	●	●

SDG7 – Affordable and Clean Energy

	Value	Year	Rating	Trend
Population with access to electricity (%)	94.7	2017	●	↑
Population with access to clean fuels and technology for cooking (%)	96.6	2016	●	↑
CO₂ emissions from fuel combustion for electricity and heating per total electricity output (MtCO₂/TWh)	NA	NA	●	●

SDG8 – Decent Work and Economic Growth

	Value	Year	Rating	Trend
Adjusted GDP growth (%)	-0.2	2018	●	●
Victims of modern slavery (per 1,000 population)	NA	NA	●	●
Adults with an account at a bank or other financial institution or with a mobile-money-service provider (% of population aged 15 or over)	NA	NA	●	●
Unemployment rate (% of total labor force)	NA	NA	●	●
Fatal work-related accidents embodied in imports (per 100,000 population)	NA	NA	●	●

SDG9 – Industry, Innovation and Infrastructure

	Value	Year	Rating	Trend
Population using the internet (%)	59.1	2017	●	↑
Mobile broadband subscriptions (per 100 population)	32.9	2017	●	↗
Logistics Performance Index: Quality of trade and transport-related infrastructure (worst 1–5 best)	NA	NA	●	●
The Times Higher Education Universities Ranking: Average score of top 3 universities (worst 0–100 best) *	0.0	2020	●	●
Scientific and technical journal articles (per 1,000 population)	0.4	2018	●	↑
Expenditure on research and development (% of GDP)	NA	NA	●	●

SDG10 – Reduced Inequalities

	Value	Year	Rating	Trend
Gini coefficient adjusted for top income	NA	NA	●	●

SDG11 – Sustainable Cities and Communities

	Value	Year	Rating	Trend
Annual mean concentration of particulate matter of less than 2.5 microns in diameter (PM2.5) (μg/m³)	22.7	2017	●	↗
Access to improved water source, piped (% of urban population)	NA	NA	●	●
Satisfaction with public transport (%)	NA	NA	●	●

SDG12 – Responsible Consumption and Production

	Value	Year	Rating	Trend
Municipal solid waste (kg/capita/day)	2.1	2012	●	●
Electronic waste (kg/capita)	7.8	2016	●	●
Production-based SO₂ emissions (kg/capita)	NA	NA	●	●
SO₂ emissions embodied in imports (kg/capita)	NA	NA	●	●
Production-based nitrogen emissions (kg/capita)	NA	NA	●	●
Nitrogen emissions embodied in imports (kg/capita)	NA	NA	●	●

SDG13 – Climate Action

	Value	Year	Rating	Trend
Energy-related CO₂ emissions (tCO₂/capita)	2.3	2017	●	→
CO₂ emissions embodied in imports (tCO₂/capita)	NA	NA	●	●
CO₂ emissions embodied in fossil fuel exports (kg/capita) *	0.0	2018	●	●

SDG14 – Life Below Water

	Value	Year	Rating	Trend
Mean area that is protected in marine sites important to biodiversity (%)	52.2	2018	●	↑
Ocean Health Index: Clean Waters score (worst 0–100 best)	59.9	2019	●	↗
Fish caught from overexploited or collapsed stocks (% of total catch)	NA	NA	●	●
Fish caught by trawling (%)	NA	NA	●	●
Marine biodiversity threats embodied in imports (per million population)	NA	NA	●	●

SDG15 – Life on Land

	Value	Year	Rating	Trend
Mean area that is protected in terrestrial sites important to biodiversity (%)	34.5	2018	●	→
Mean area that is protected in freshwater sites important to biodiversity (%)	NA	NA	●	●
Red List Index of species survival (worst 0–1 best)	0.8	2019	●	↓
Permanent deforestation (% of forest area, 5-year average)	0.2	2018	●	●
Terrestrial and freshwater biodiversity threats embodied in imports (per million population)	NA	NA	●	●

SDG16 – Peace, Justice and Strong Institutions

	Value	Year	Rating	Trend
Homicides (per 100,000 population)	11.1	2017	●	↓
Unsentenced detainees (% of prison population)	19.9	2018	●	↑
Percentage of population who feel safe walking alone at night in the city or area where they live (%)	NA	NA	●	●
Property Rights (worst 1–7 best)	NA	NA	●	●
Birth registrations with civil authority (% of children under age 5)	NA	NA	●	●
Corruption Perception Index (worst 0–100 best)	53	2019	●	↓
Children involved in child labor (% of population aged 5 to 14)	NA	NA	●	●
Exports of major conventional weapons (TIV constant million USD per 100,000 population) *	0.0	2019	●	●
Press Freedom Index (best 0–100 worst)	NA	NA	●	●

SDG17 – Partnerships for the Goals

	Value	Year	Rating	Trend
Government spending on health and education (% of GDP)	6.2	2003	●	●
For high-income and all OECD DAC countries: International concessional public finance, including official development assistance (% of GNI)	NA	NA	●	●
Other countries: Government revenue excluding grants (% of GDP) *	20.4	2014	●	●
Corporate Tax Haven Score (best 0–100 worst) *	0.0	2019	●	●

* Imputed data point

5. Country Profiles

▼ OVERALL PERFORMANCE

Index score

61.5

Regional average score

70.4

SDG Global rank **120** (OF 166)

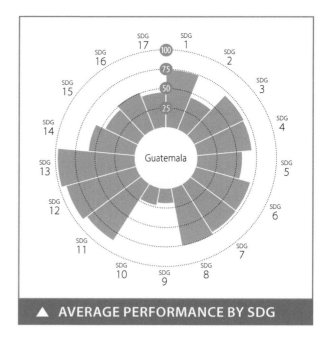

▲ AVERAGE PERFORMANCE BY SDG

▼ SPILLOVER INDEX

100 (best) to 0 (worst)

▼ CURRENT ASSESSMENT – SDG DASHBOARD

■ Major challenges   ■ Significant challenges   ■ Challenges remain   ■ SDG achieved   ■ Information unavailable

▼ SDG TRENDS

↓ Decreasing   → Stagnating   ↗ Moderately improving   ↑ On track or maintaining SDG achievement   ● Information unavailable

Notes: The full title of Goal 2 "Zero Hunger" is "End hunger, achieve food security and improved nutrition and promote sustainable agriculture".
The full title of each SDG is available here: https://sustainabledevelopment.un.org/topics/sustainabledevelopmentgoals

SDG1 – No Poverty

Indicator	Value	Year	Rating	Trend
Poverty headcount ratio at $1.90/day (%)	6.9	2020	○	↗
Poverty headcount ratio at $3.20/day (%)	20.4	2020	●	→

SDG2 – Zero Hunger

Indicator	Value	Year	Rating	Trend
Prevalence of undernourishment (%)	15.2	2017	●	↗
Prevalence of stunting in children under 5 years of age (%)	46.5	2015	●	→
Prevalence of wasting in children under 5 years of age (%)	0.7	2015	●	↑
Prevalence of obesity, BMI ≥ 30 (% of adult population)	21.2	2016	●	↓
Human Trophic Level (best 2–3 worst)	2.2	2017	●	→
Cereal yield (tonnes per hectare of harvested land)	2.2	2017	●	↑
Sustainable Nitrogen Management Index (best 0–1.41 worst)	1.0	2015	●	↓

SDG3 – Good Health and Well-Being

Indicator	Value	Year	Rating	Trend
Maternal mortality rate (per 100,000 live births)	95	2017	●	↑
Neonatal mortality rate (per 1,000 live births)	12.3	2018	●	↑
Mortality rate, under-5 (per 1,000 live births)	26.2	2018	●	↑
Incidence of tuberculosis (per 100,000 population)	26.0	2018	●	→
New HIV infections (per 1,000 uninfected population)	0.1	2018	●	↑
Age-standardized death rate due to cardiovascular disease, cancer, diabetes, or chronic respiratory disease in adults aged 30–70 years (%)	14.9	2016	●	↑
Age-standardized death rate attributable to household air pollution and ambient air pollution (per 100,000 population)	74	2016	●	●
Traffic deaths (per 100,000 population)	16.6	2016	●	↑
Life expectancy at birth (years)	73.2	2016	●	↗
Adolescent fertility rate (births per 1,000 adolescent females aged 15 to 19)	70.9	2017	●	→
Births attended by skilled health personnel (%)	65.5	2015	●	↗
Percentage of surviving infants who received 2 WHO-recommended vaccines (%)	86	2018	●	↑
Universal health coverage (UHC) index of service coverage (worst 0–100 best)	55.0	2017	●	↓
Subjective well-being (average ladder score, worst 0–10 best)	6.3	2019	●	↑

SDG4 – Quality Education

Indicator	Value	Year	Rating	Trend
Net primary enrollment rate (%)	86.9	2018	●	→
Lower secondary completion rate (%)	56.4	2018	●	↓
Literacy rate (% of population aged 15 to 24)	94.4	2014	●	●

SDG5 – Gender Equality

Indicator	Value	Year	Rating	Trend
Demand for family planning satisfied by modern methods (% of females aged 15 to 49 who are married or in unions)	66.1	2015	●	↗
Ratio of female-to-male mean years of education received (%)	98.5	2018	●	↑
Ratio of female-to-male labor force participation rate (%)	48.3	2019	●	→
Seats held by women in national parliament (%)	19.4	2020	●	↗

SDG6 – Clean Water and Sanitation

Indicator	Value	Year	Rating	Trend
Population using at least basic drinking water services (%)	94.2	2017	●	↑
Population using at least basic sanitation services (%)	65.1	2017	●	→
Freshwater withdrawal (% of available freshwater resources)	5.7	2005	●	●
Anthropogenic wastewater that receives treatment (%)	6.8	2018	●	●
Scarce water consumption embodied in imports (m³/capita)	1.4	2013	●	↑

SDG7 – Affordable and Clean Energy

Indicator	Value	Year	Rating	Trend
Population with access to electricity (%)	93.3	2017	●	↑
Population with access to clean fuels and technology for cooking (%)	45.2	2016	●	→
CO_2 emissions from fuel combustion for electricity and heating per total electricity output (MtCO$_2$/TWh)	1.3	2017	●	→

SDG8 – Decent Work and Economic Growth

Indicator	Value	Year	Rating	Trend
Adjusted GDP growth (%)	-3.6	2018	●	●
Victims of modern slavery (per 1,000 population)	2.9	2018	●	●
Adults with an account at a bank or other financial institution or with a mobile-money-service provider (% of population aged 15 or over)	44.1	2017	●	→
Unemployment rate (% of total labor force)	2.5	2019	●	↑
Fatal work-related accidents embodied in imports (per 100,000 population)	0.1	2010	●	↑

SDG9 – Industry, Innovation and Infrastructure

Indicator	Value	Year	Rating	Trend
Population using the internet (%)	65.0	2017	●	↑
Mobile broadband subscriptions (per 100 population)	16.5	2017	●	↗
Logistics Performance Index: Quality of trade and transport-related infrastructure (worst 1–5 best)	2.2	2018	●	↓
The Times Higher Education Universities Ranking: Average score of top 3 universities (worst 0–100 best) *	0.0	2020	●	●
Scientific and technical journal articles (per 1,000 population)	0.0	2018	●	→
Expenditure on research and development (% of GDP)	0.0	2015	●	●

SDG10 – Reduced Inequalities

Indicator	Value	Year	Rating	Trend
Gini coefficient adjusted for top income	55.3	2014	●	●

SDG11 – Sustainable Cities and Communities

Indicator	Value	Year	Rating	Trend
Annual mean concentration of particulate matter of less than 2.5 microns in diameter (PM2.5) (µg/m³)	24.1	2017	●	↗
Access to improved water source, piped (% of urban population)	92.1	2017	●	→
Satisfaction with public transport (%)	72.5	2019	●	↑

SDG12 – Responsible Consumption and Production

Indicator	Value	Year	Rating	Trend
Municipal solid waste (kg/capita/day)	0.9	2015	●	●
Electronic waste (kg/capita)	4.0	2016	●	●
Production-based SO_2 emissions (kg/capita)	14.2	2012	●	●
SO_2 emissions embodied in imports (kg/capita)	1.6	2012	●	●
Production-based nitrogen emissions (kg/capita)	10.9	2010	●	●
Nitrogen emissions embodied in imports (kg/capita)	1.4	2010	●	●

SDG13 – Climate Action

Indicator	Value	Year	Rating	Trend
Energy-related CO_2 emissions (tCO$_2$/capita)	0.9	2017	●	↑
CO_2 emissions embodied in imports (tCO$_2$/capita)	0.2	2015	●	↑
CO_2 emissions embodied in fossil fuel exports (kg/capita)	0.0	2019	●	●

SDG14 – Life Below Water

Indicator	Value	Year	Rating	Trend
Mean area that is protected in marine sites important to biodiversity (%)	39.3	2018	●	↑
Ocean Health Index: Clean Waters score (worst 0–100 best)	31.9	2019	●	→
Fish caught from overexploited or collapsed stocks (% of total catch)	15.0	2014	●	↑
Fish caught by trawling (%)	30.9	2014	●	↑
Marine biodiversity threats embodied in imports (per million population)	0.1	2018	●	●

SDG15 – Life on Land

Indicator	Value	Year	Rating	Trend
Mean area that is protected in terrestrial sites important to biodiversity (%)	29.6	2018	●	→
Mean area that is protected in freshwater sites important to biodiversity (%)	24.8	2018	●	→
Red List Index of species survival (worst 0–1 best)	0.7	2019	●	↓
Permanent deforestation (% of forest area, 5-year average)	0.7	2018	●	●
Terrestrial and freshwater biodiversity threats embodied in imports (per million population)	0.5	2018	●	●

SDG16 – Peace, Justice and Strong Institutions

Indicator	Value	Year	Rating	Trend
Homicides (per 100,000 population)	26.1	2017	●	↗
Unsentenced detainees (% of prison population)	51.8	2018	●	↓
Percentage of population who feel safe walking alone at night in the city or area where they live (%)	56.3	2019	●	↑
Property Rights (worst 1–7 best)	4.2	2019	●	●
Birth registrations with civil authority (% of children under age 5)	96.4	2018	●	●
Corruption Perception Index (worst 0–100 best)	26	2019	●	↓
Children involved in child labor (% of population aged 5 to 14)	25.8	2016	●	●
Exports of major conventional weapons (TIV constant million USD per 100,000 population) *	0.0	2019	●	●
Press Freedom Index (best 0–100 worst)	35.9	2019	●	↗

SDG17 – Partnerships for the Goals

Indicator	Value	Year	Rating	Trend
Government spending on health and education (% of GDP)	5.0	2016	●	↓
For high-income and all OECD DAC countries: International concessional public finance, including official development assistance (% of GNI)	NA	NA	●	●
Other countries: Government revenue excluding grants (% of GDP)	11.0	2016	●	↓
Corporate Tax Haven Score (best 0–100 worst) *	0.0	2019	●	●

* Imputed data point

5. Country Profiles

▼ OVERALL PERFORMANCE

Index score

52.5

Regional average score

53.1

SDG Global rank 150 (OF 166)

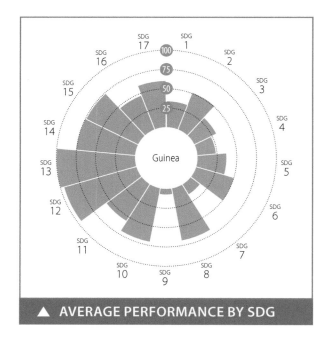

▼ SPILLOVER INDEX

100 (best) to 0 (worst)

▲ AVERAGE PERFORMANCE BY SDG

▼ CURRENT ASSESSMENT – SDG DASHBOARD

■ Major challenges   ■ Significant challenges   ■ Challenges remain   ■ SDG achieved   ■ Information unavailable

▼ SDG TRENDS

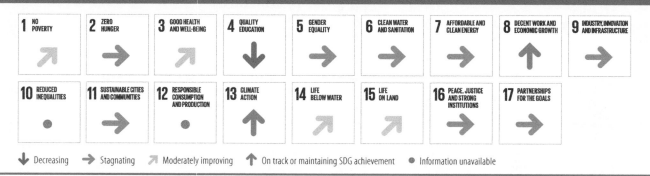

↓ Decreasing   → Stagnating   ↗ Moderately improving   ↑ On track or maintaining SDG achievement   • Information unavailable

Notes: The full title of Goal 2 "Zero Hunger" is "End hunger, achieve food security and improved nutrition and promote sustainable agriculture".
The full title of each SDG is available here: https://sustainabledevelopment.un.org/topics/sustainabledevelopmentgoals

SDG1 – No Poverty

	Value	Year	Rating	Trend
Poverty headcount ratio at $1.90/day (%)	22.2	2020	●	↑
Poverty headcount ratio at $3.20/day (%)	54.4	2020	●	↗

SDG2 – Zero Hunger

	Value	Year	Rating	Trend
Prevalence of undernourishment (%)	16.5	2017	●	↓
Prevalence of stunting in children under 5 years of age (%)	32.4	2016	●	↗
Prevalence of wasting in children under 5 years of age (%)	8.1	2016	●	→
Prevalence of obesity, BMI ≥ 30 (% of adult population)	7.7	2016	●	↑
Human Trophic Level (best 2–3 worst)	2.1	2017	●	↑
Cereal yield (tonnes per hectare of harvested land)	1.2	2017	●	→
Sustainable Nitrogen Management Index (best 0–1.41 worst)	0.9	2015	●	↓

SDG3 – Good Health and Well-Being

	Value	Year	Rating	Trend
Maternal mortality rate (per 100,000 live births)	576	2017	●	↑
Neonatal mortality rate (per 1,000 live births)	31.1	2018	●	→
Mortality rate, under-5 (per 1,000 live births)	100.8	2018	●	→
Incidence of tuberculosis (per 100,000 population)	176.0	2018	●	→
New HIV infections (per 1,000 uninfected population)	0.5	2018	○	↑
Age-standardized death rate due to cardiovascular disease, cancer, diabetes, or chronic respiratory disease in adults aged 30–70 years (%)	22.4	2016	●	→
Age-standardized death rate attributable to household air pollution and ambient air pollution (per 100,000 population)	243	2016	●	●
Traffic deaths (per 100,000 population)	28.2	2016	●	↓
Life expectancy at birth (years)	59.8	2016	●	→
Adolescent fertility rate (births per 1,000 adolescent females aged 15 to 19)	135.3	2017	●	→
Births attended by skilled health personnel (%)	62.7	2016	●	↑
Percentage of surviving infants who received 2 WHO-recommended vaccines (%)	45	2018	●	→
Universal health coverage (UHC) index of service coverage (worst 0–100 best)	37.0	2017	●	→
Subjective well-being (average ladder score, worst 0–10 best)	4.8	2019	●	↑

SDG4 – Quality Education

	Value	Year	Rating	Trend
Net primary enrollment rate (%)	76.0	2016	●	↓
Lower secondary completion rate (%)	35.4	2014	●	●
Literacy rate (% of population aged 15 to 24)	46.3	2014	●	●

SDG5 – Gender Equality

	Value	Year	Rating	Trend
Demand for family planning satisfied by modern methods (% of females aged 15 to 49 who are married or in unions)	21.5	2016	●	→
Ratio of female-to-male mean years of education received (%)	38.5	2018	●	→
Ratio of female-to-male labor force participation rate (%)	98.5	2019	●	↑
Seats held by women in national parliament (%)	22.8	2019	●	→

SDG6 – Clean Water and Sanitation

	Value	Year	Rating	Trend
Population using at least basic drinking water services (%)	61.9	2017	●	↓
Population using at least basic sanitation services (%)	22.7	2017	●	→
Freshwater withdrawal (% of available freshwater resources)	0.9	2000	●	●
Anthropogenic wastewater that receives treatment (%)	0.0	2018	●	●
Scarce water consumption embodied in imports (m³/capita)	0.5	2013	●	↑

SDG7 – Affordable and Clean Energy

	Value	Year	Rating	Trend
Population with access to electricity (%)	35.4	2017	●	→
Population with access to clean fuels and technology for cooking (%)	1.2	2016	●	→
CO_2 emissions from fuel combustion for electricity and heating per total electricity output (MtCO₂/TWh)	NA	NA	●	●

SDG8 – Decent Work and Economic Growth

	Value	Year	Rating	Trend
Adjusted GDP growth (%)	-0.4	2018	○	●
Victims of modern slavery (per 1,000 population)	7.8	2018	●	●
Adults with an account at a bank or other financial institution or with a mobile-money-service provider (% of population aged 15 or over)	23.5	2017	●	↑
Unemployment rate (% of total labor force)	4.3	2019	●	↑
Fatal work-related accidents embodied in imports (per 100,000 population)	0.0	2010	●	↑

SDG9 – Industry, Innovation and Infrastructure

	Value	Year	Rating	Trend
Population using the internet (%)	18.0	2017	●	↗
Mobile broadband subscriptions (per 100 population)	23.8	2018	●	↗
Logistics Performance Index: Quality of trade and transport-related infrastructure (worst 1–5 best)	1.6	2018	●	↓
The Times Higher Education Universities Ranking: Average score of top 3 universities (worst 0–100 best) *	0.0	2020	○	●
Scientific and technical journal articles (per 1,000 population)	0.0	2018	●	↓
Expenditure on research and development (% of GDP) *	0.0	2017	●	●

SDG10 – Reduced Inequalities

	Value	Year	Rating	Trend
Gini coefficient adjusted for top income	38.3	2012	●	●

SDG11 – Sustainable Cities and Communities

	Value	Year	Rating	Trend
Annual mean concentration of particulate matter of less than 2.5 microns in diameter (PM2.5) (µg/m³)	26.1	2017	●	↓
Access to improved water source, piped (% of urban population)	65.0	2017	●	↓
Satisfaction with public transport (%)	37.6	2019	●	↑

SDG12 – Responsible Consumption and Production

	Value	Year	Rating	Trend
Municipal solid waste (kg/capita/day)	NA	NA	●	●
Electronic waste (kg/capita)	0.6	2016	●	●
Production-based SO_2 emissions (kg/capita)	16.6	2012	●	●
SO_2 emissions embodied in imports (kg/capita)	0.4	2012	●	●
Production-based nitrogen emissions (kg/capita)	21.9	2010	○	●
Nitrogen emissions embodied in imports (kg/capita)	0.2	2010	●	●

SDG13 – Climate Action

	Value	Year	Rating	Trend
Energy-related CO_2 emissions (tCO₂/capita)	0.3	2017	●	↑
CO_2 emissions embodied in imports (tCO₂/capita)	0.0	2015	●	↑
CO_2 emissions embodied in fossil fuel exports (kg/capita) *	0.0	2018	●	●

SDG14 – Life Below Water

	Value	Year	Rating	Trend
Mean area that is protected in marine sites important to biodiversity (%)	74.3	2018	●	↑
Ocean Health Index: Clean Waters score (worst 0–100 best)	44.0	2019	●	→
Fish caught from overexploited or collapsed stocks (% of total catch)	3.5	2014	●	↑
Fish caught by trawling (%)	17.4	2014	○	↑
Marine biodiversity threats embodied in imports (per million population)	0.0	2018	●	●

SDG15 – Life on Land

	Value	Year	Rating	Trend
Mean area that is protected in terrestrial sites important to biodiversity (%)	78.9	2018	●	↑
Mean area that is protected in freshwater sites important to biodiversity (%)	98.5	2018	●	↑
Red List Index of species survival (worst 0–1 best)	0.9	2019	○	→
Permanent deforestation (% of forest area, 5-year average)	1.2	2018	●	●
Terrestrial and freshwater biodiversity threats embodied in imports (per million population)	0.0	2018	●	●

SDG16 – Peace, Justice and Strong Institutions

	Value	Year	Rating	Trend
Homicides (per 100,000 population) *	8.8	2015	●	●
Unsentenced detainees (% of prison population)	68.1	2009	●	●
Percentage of population who feel safe walking alone at night in the city or area where they live (%)	54.3	2019	●	↗
Property Rights (worst 1–7 best)	3.6	2019	●	●
Birth registrations with civil authority (% of children under age 5)	62.0	2018	●	●
Corruption Perception Index (worst 0–100 best)	29	2019	●	→
Children involved in child labor (% of population aged 5 to 14)	28.3	2016	●	●
Exports of major conventional weapons (TIV constant million USD per 100,000 population) *	0.0	2019	●	●
Press Freedom Index (best 0–100 worst)	33.5	2019	○	→

SDG17 – Partnerships for the Goals

	Value	Year	Rating	Trend
Government spending on health and education (% of GDP)	3.2	2016	●	→
For high-income and all OECD DAC countries: International concessional public finance, including official development assistance (% of GNI)	NA	NA	●	●
Other countries: Government revenue excluding grants (% of GDP)	NA	NA	●	●
Corporate Tax Haven Score (best 0–100 worst) *	0.0	2019	●	●

* Imputed data point

5. Country Profiles

▼ OVERALL PERFORMANCE

Index score

na

Regional average score

53.1

SDG Global rank NA (OF 166)

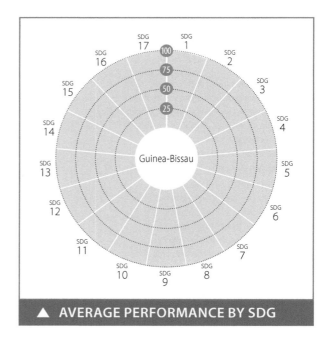

▲ AVERAGE PERFORMANCE BY SDG

▼ SPILLOVER INDEX

100 (best) to 0 (worst)

▼ CURRENT ASSESSMENT – SDG DASHBOARD

■ Major challenges ■ Significant challenges ■ Challenges remain ■ SDG achieved ■ Information unavailable

▼ SDG TRENDS

↓ Decreasing → Stagnating ↗ Moderately improving ↑ On track or maintaining SDG achievement ● Information unavailable

Notes: The full title of Goal 2 "Zero Hunger" is "End hunger, achieve food security and improved nutrition and promote sustainable agriculture".
The full title of each SDG is available here: https://sustainabledevelopment.un.org/topics/sustainabledevelopmentgoals

SDG1 – No Poverty

	Value	Year	Rating	Trend
Poverty headcount ratio at $1.90/day (%)	52.2	2020	●	↗
Poverty headcount ratio at $3.20/day (%)	75.6	2020	●	→

SDG2 – Zero Hunger

	Value	Year	Rating	Trend
Prevalence of undernourishment (%)	28.0	2017	●	↓
Prevalence of stunting in children under 5 years of age (%)	27.6	2014	●	↗
Prevalence of wasting in children under 5 years of age (%)	6.0	2014	●	↑
Prevalence of obesity, BMI ≥ 30 (% of adult population)	9.5	2016	●	↑
Human Trophic Level (best 2–3 worst)	2.1	2017	●	↑
Cereal yield (tonnes per hectare of harvested land)	1.6	2017	●	↗
Sustainable Nitrogen Management Index (best 0–1.41 worst)	1.0	2015	●	↓

SDG3 – Good Health and Well-Being

	Value	Year	Rating	Trend
Maternal mortality rate (per 100,000 live births)	667	2017	●	→
Neonatal mortality rate (per 1,000 live births)	36.6	2018	●	→
Mortality rate, under-5 (per 1,000 live births)	81.5	2018	●	↗
Incidence of tuberculosis (per 100,000 population)	361.0	2018	●	→
New HIV infections (per 1,000 uninfected population)	1.4	2018	●	↗
Age-standardized death rate due to cardiovascular disease, cancer, diabetes, or chronic respiratory disease in adults aged 30–70 years (%)	20.0	2016	●	↗
Age-standardized death rate attributable to household air pollution and ambient air pollution (per 100,000 population)	215	2016	●	●
Traffic deaths (per 100,000 population)	31.1	2016	●	↓
Life expectancy at birth (years)	59.8	2016	●	→
Adolescent fertility rate (births per 1,000 adolescent females aged 15 to 19)	104.8	2017	●	→
Births attended by skilled health personnel (%)	45.0	2014	●	●
Percentage of surviving infants who received 2 WHO-recommended vaccines (%)	86	2018	●	↗
Universal health coverage (UHC) index of service coverage (worst 0–100 best)	40.0	2017	●	→
Subjective well-being (average ladder score, worst 0–10 best)	NA	NA	●	●

SDG4 – Quality Education

	Value	Year	Rating	Trend
Net primary enrollment rate (%)	71.3	2010	●	●
Lower secondary completion rate (%)	36.8	2010	●	●
Literacy rate (% of population aged 15 to 24)	60.4	2014	●	●

SDG5 – Gender Equality

	Value	Year	Rating	Trend
Demand for family planning satisfied by modern methods (% of females aged 15 to 49 who are married or in unions)	55.7	2014	●	→
Ratio of female-to-male mean years of education received (%)	NA	NA	●	●
Ratio of female-to-male labor force participation rate (%)	85.5	2019	●	↑
Seats held by women in national parliament (%)	13.7	2020	●	→

SDG6 – Clean Water and Sanitation

	Value	Year	Rating	Trend
Population using at least basic drinking water services (%)	66.6	2017	●	→
Population using at least basic sanitation services (%)	20.5	2017	●	→
Freshwater withdrawal (% of available freshwater resources)	1.5	2000	●	●
Anthropogenic wastewater that receives treatment (%)	0.0	2018	●	●
Scarce water consumption embodied in imports (m³/capita)	NA	NA	●	●

SDG7 – Affordable and Clean Energy

	Value	Year	Rating	Trend
Population with access to electricity (%)	26.0	2017	●	↗
Population with access to clean fuels and technology for cooking (%)	1.5	2016	●	→
CO_2 emissions from fuel combustion for electricity and heating per total electricity output (MtCO$_2$/TWh)	NA	NA	●	●

SDG8 – Decent Work and Economic Growth

	Value	Year	Rating	Trend
Adjusted GDP growth (%)	-4.2	2018	●	●
Victims of modern slavery (per 1,000 population)	7.5	2018	●	●
Adults with an account at a bank or other financial institution or with a mobile-money-service provider (% of population aged 15 or over)	NA	NA	●	●
Unemployment rate (% of total labor force)	2.5	2019	●	↑
Fatal work-related accidents embodied in imports (per 100,000 population)	NA	NA	●	●

SDG9 – Industry, Innovation and Infrastructure

		Value	Year	Rating	Trend
Population using the internet (%)		3.9	2017	●	→
Mobile broadband subscriptions (per 100 population)		17.7	2018	●	↑
Logistics Performance Index: Quality of trade and transport-related infrastructure (worst 1–5 best)		1.8	2018	●	↓
The Times Higher Education Universities Ranking: Average score of top 3 universities (worst 0–100 best)	*	0.0	2020	●	●
Scientific and technical journal articles (per 1,000 population)		0.0	2018	●	→
Expenditure on research and development (% of GDP)	*	0.0	2017	●	●

SDG10 – Reduced Inequalities

	Value	Year	Rating	Trend
Gini coefficient adjusted for top income	55.1	2010	●	●

SDG11 – Sustainable Cities and Communities

	Value	Year	Rating	Trend
Annual mean concentration of particulate matter of less than 2.5 microns in diameter (PM2.5) (µg/m³)	29.8	2017	●	↓
Access to improved water source, piped (% of urban population)	35.6	2016	●	→
Satisfaction with public transport (%)	NA	NA	●	●

SDG12 – Responsible Consumption and Production

	Value	Year	Rating	Trend
Municipal solid waste (kg/capita/day)	1.0	2015	●	●
Electronic waste (kg/capita)	0.5	2016	●	●
Production-based SO_2 emissions (kg/capita)	NA	NA	●	●
SO_2 emissions embodied in imports (kg/capita)	NA	NA	●	●
Production-based nitrogen emissions (kg/capita)	NA	NA	●	●
Nitrogen emissions embodied in imports (kg/capita)	NA	NA	●	●

SDG13 – Climate Action

		Value	Year	Rating	Trend
Energy-related CO_2 emissions (tCO$_2$/capita)		0.2	2017	●	↑
CO_2 emissions embodied in imports (tCO$_2$/capita)		NA	NA	●	●
CO_2 emissions embodied in fossil fuel exports (kg/capita)	*	0.0	2018	●	●

SDG14 – Life Below Water

	Value	Year	Rating	Trend
Mean area that is protected in marine sites important to biodiversity (%)	53.8	2018	●	↑
Ocean Health Index: Clean Waters score (worst 0–100 best)	56.1	2019	●	→
Fish caught from overexploited or collapsed stocks (% of total catch)	54.1	2014	●	↓
Fish caught by trawling (%)	1.2	2003	●	●
Marine biodiversity threats embodied in imports (per million population)	NA	NA	●	●

SDG15 – Life on Land

	Value	Year	Rating	Trend
Mean area that is protected in terrestrial sites important to biodiversity (%)	52.6	2018	●	↑
Mean area that is protected in freshwater sites important to biodiversity (%)	NA	NA	●	●
Red List Index of species survival (worst 0–1 best)	1.0	2019	●	↑
Permanent deforestation (% of forest area, 5-year average)	0.6	2018	●	●
Terrestrial and freshwater biodiversity threats embodied in imports (per million population)	NA	NA	●	●

SDG16 – Peace, Justice and Strong Institutions

		Value	Year	Rating	Trend
Homicides (per 100,000 population)	*	1.1	2017	●	↑
Unsentenced detainees (% of prison population)		55.5	2018	●	↑
Percentage of population who feel safe walking alone at night in the city or area where they live (%)		NA	NA	●	●
Property Rights (worst 1–7 best)		NA	NA	●	●
Birth registrations with civil authority (% of children under age 5)		23.7	2018	●	●
Corruption Perception Index (worst 0–100 best)		18	2019	●	→
Children involved in child labor (% of population aged 5 to 14)		51.1	2016	●	●
Exports of major conventional weapons (TIV constant million USD per 100,000 population)	*	0.0	2019	●	●
Press Freedom Index (best 0–100 worst)		31.0	2019	●	↓

SDG17 – Partnerships for the Goals

		Value	Year	Rating	Trend
Government spending on health and education (% of GDP)		4.0	2013	●	●
For high-income and all OECD DAC countries: International concessional public finance, including official development assistance (% of GNI)		NA	NA	●	●
Other countries: Government revenue excluding grants (% of GDP)		12.7	2017	●	●
Corporate Tax Haven Score (best 0–100 worst)	*	0.0	2019	●	●

* Imputed data point

GUYANA

Latin America and the Caribbean

▼ OVERALL PERFORMANCE

Index score
59.7

Regional average score
70.4

SDG Global rank 124 (OF 166)

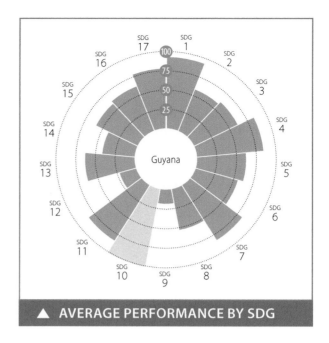

▼ SPILLOVER INDEX

100 (best) to 0 (worst)

▲ AVERAGE PERFORMANCE BY SDG

▼ CURRENT ASSESSMENT – SDG DASHBOARD

■ Major challenges ■ Significant challenges ■ Challenges remain ■ SDG achieved ■ Information unavailable

▼ SDG TRENDS

↓ Decreasing → Stagnating ↗ Moderately improving ↑ On track or maintaining SDG achievement ● Information unavailable

Notes: The full title of Goal 2 "Zero Hunger" is "End hunger, achieve food security and improved nutrition and promote sustainable agriculture".
The full title of each SDG is available here: https://sustainabledevelopment.un.org/topics/sustainabledevelopmentgoals

GUYANA

SDG1 – No Poverty

	Value	Year	Rating	Trend
Poverty headcount ratio at $1.90/day (%)	2.5	2020	○	↑
Poverty headcount ratio at $3.20/day (%)	4.5	2020	○	↑

SDG2 – Zero Hunger

	Value	Year	Rating	Trend
Prevalence of undernourishment (%)	8.1	2017	●	↑
Prevalence of stunting in children under 5 years of age (%)	12.0	2014	●	↑
Prevalence of wasting in children under 5 years of age (%)	6.4	2014	●	↗
Prevalence of obesity, BMI ≥ 30 (% of adult population)	20.2	2016	●	↓
Human Trophic Level (best 2–3 worst)	2.2	2017	●	↑
Cereal yield (tonnes per hectare of harvested land)	3.6	2017	●	↑
Sustainable Nitrogen Management Index (best 0–1.41 worst)	0.7	2015	●	↓

SDG3 – Good Health and Well-Being

	Value	Year	Rating	Trend
Maternal mortality rate (per 100,000 live births)	169	2017	●	→
Neonatal mortality rate (per 1,000 live births)	18.2	2018	●	↑
Mortality rate, under-5 (per 1,000 live births)	30.1	2018	●	↑
Incidence of tuberculosis (per 100,000 population)	83.0	2018	●	↗
New HIV infections (per 1,000 uninfected population)	0.5	2018	●	↗
Age-standardized death rate due to cardiovascular disease, cancer, diabetes, or chronic respiratory disease in adults aged 30–70 years (%)	30.5	2016	●	→
Age-standardized death rate attributable to household air pollution and ambient air pollution (per 100,000 population)	108	2016	●	●
Traffic deaths (per 100,000 population)	24.6	2016	●	↓
Life expectancy at birth (years)	66.2	2016	●	→
Adolescent fertility rate (births per 1,000 adolescent females aged 15 to 19)	74.4	2017	●	↗
Births attended by skilled health personnel (%)	85.7	2014	●	●
Percentage of surviving infants who received 2 WHO-recommended vaccines (%)	95	2018	●	↑
Universal health coverage (UHC) index of service coverage (worst 0–100 best)	72.0	2017	●	↑
Subjective well-being (average ladder score, worst 0–10 best)	6.0	2007	○	●

SDG4 – Quality Education

	Value	Year	Rating	Trend
Net primary enrollment rate (%)	93.1	2012	○	●
Lower secondary completion rate (%)	79.1	2010	●	●
Literacy rate (% of population aged 15 to 24)	96.7	2014	●	●

SDG5 – Gender Equality

	Value	Year	Rating	Trend
Demand for family planning satisfied by modern methods (% of females aged 15 to 49 who are married or in unions)	51.5	2014	●	↗
Ratio of female-to-male mean years of education received (%)	111.3	2018	●	↑
Ratio of female-to-male labor force participation rate (%)	56.2	2019	●	→
Seats held by women in national parliament (%)	31.9	2019	○	↗

SDG6 – Clean Water and Sanitation

	Value	Year	Rating	Trend
Population using at least basic drinking water services (%)	95.5	2017	●	↑
Population using at least basic sanitation services (%)	85.8	2017	●	→
Freshwater withdrawal (% of available freshwater resources)	3.3	2010	●	●
Anthropogenic wastewater that receives treatment (%)	0.0	2018	●	●
Scarce water consumption embodied in imports (m³/capita)	101.6	2013	●	↑

SDG7 – Affordable and Clean Energy

	Value	Year	Rating	Trend
Population with access to electricity (%)	90.9	2017	○	↑
Population with access to clean fuels and technology for cooking (%)	74.5	2016	○	↑
CO$_2$ emissions from fuel combustion for electricity and heating per total electricity output (MtCO$_2$/TWh)	NA	NA	●	●

SDG8 – Decent Work and Economic Growth

	Value	Year	Rating	Trend
Adjusted GDP growth (%)	-1.9	2018	●	●
Victims of modern slavery (per 1,000 population)	2.6	2018	●	●
Adults with an account at a bank or other financial institution or with a mobile-money-service provider (% of population aged 15 or over)	NA	NA	●	●
Unemployment rate (% of total labor force)	11.9	2019	●	→
Fatal work-related accidents embodied in imports (per 100,000 population)	20.1	2010	●	↓

SDG9 – Industry, Innovation and Infrastructure

	Value	Year	Rating	Trend
Population using the internet (%)	37.3	2017	●	↗
Mobile broadband subscriptions (per 100 population)	26.4	2017	●	↑
Logistics Performance Index: Quality of trade and transport-related infrastructure (worst 1–5 best)	2.1	2018	●	↓
The Times Higher Education Universities Ranking: Average score of top 3 universities (worst 0–100 best) *	0.0	2020	●	●
Scientific and technical journal articles (per 1,000 population)	0.0	2018	●	→
Expenditure on research and development (% of GDP)	NA	NA	●	●

SDG10 – Reduced Inequalities

	Value	Year	Rating	Trend
Gini coefficient adjusted for top income	NA	NA	●	●

SDG11 – Sustainable Cities and Communities

	Value	Year	Rating	Trend
Annual mean concentration of particulate matter of less than 2.5 microns in diameter (PM2.5) (µg/m³)	22.4	2017	●	→
Access to improved water source, piped (% of urban population)	86.8	2017	○	→
Satisfaction with public transport (%)	71.8	2007	○	●

SDG12 – Responsible Consumption and Production

	Value	Year	Rating	Trend
Municipal solid waste (kg/capita/day)	2.4	2010	●	●
Electronic waste (kg/capita)	6.1	2016	○	●
Production-based SO$_2$ emissions (kg/capita)	438.2	2012	●	●
SO$_2$ emissions embodied in imports (kg/capita)	134.3	2012	●	●
Production-based nitrogen emissions (kg/capita)	234.2	2010	●	●
Nitrogen emissions embodied in imports (kg/capita)	166.9	2010	●	●

SDG13 – Climate Action

	Value	Year	Rating	Trend
Energy-related CO$_2$ emissions (tCO$_2$/capita)	2.7	2017	○	→
CO$_2$ emissions embodied in imports (tCO$_2$/capita)	36.7	2015	●	↓
CO$_2$ emissions embodied in fossil fuel exports (kg/capita)	0.0	2018	●	●

SDG14 – Life Below Water

	Value	Year	Rating	Trend
Mean area that is protected in marine sites important to biodiversity (%)	NA	NA	●	●
Ocean Health Index: Clean Waters score (worst 0–100 best)	74.8	2019	●	↑
Fish caught from overexploited or collapsed stocks (% of total catch)	35.4	2014	○	↑
Fish caught by trawling (%)	54.8	2014	●	↓
Marine biodiversity threats embodied in imports (per million population)	5.4	2018	●	●

SDG15 – Life on Land

	Value	Year	Rating	Trend
Mean area that is protected in terrestrial sites important to biodiversity (%)	NA	NA	●	●
Mean area that is protected in freshwater sites important to biodiversity (%)	NA	NA	●	●
Red List Index of species survival (worst 0–1 best)	0.9	2019	●	↑
Permanent deforestation (% of forest area, 5-year average)	0.0	2018	●	●
Terrestrial and freshwater biodiversity threats embodied in imports (per million population)	47.2	2018	●	●

SDG16 – Peace, Justice and Strong Institutions

	Value	Year	Rating	Trend
Homicides (per 100,000 population)	14.8	2017	●	↑
Unsentenced detainees (% of prison population)	32.1	2018	○	↑
Percentage of population who feel safe walking alone at night in the city or area where they live	46.7	2007	●	●
Property Rights (worst 1–7 best)	NA	NA	●	●
Birth registrations with civil authority (% of children under age 5)	88.7	2018	○	●
Corruption Perception Index (worst 0–100 best)	40	2019	●	↑
Children involved in child labor (% of population aged 5 to 14)	18.3	2016	●	●
Exports of major conventional weapons (TIV constant million USD per 100,000 population) *	0.0	2019	●	●
Press Freedom Index (best 0–100 worst)	26.6	2019	●	↑

SDG17 – Partnerships for the Goals

	Value	Year	Rating	Trend
Government spending on health and education (% of GDP)	8.6	2016	○	→
For high-income and all OECD DAC countries: International concessional public finance, including official development assistance (% of GNI)	NA	NA	●	●
Other countries: Government revenue excluding grants (% of GDP)	NA	NA	●	●
Corporate Tax Haven Score (best 0–100 worst) *	0.0	2019	●	●

* Imputed data point

▼ OVERALL PERFORMANCE

Index score

51.7

Regional average score

70.4

SDG Global rank   154 (OF 166)

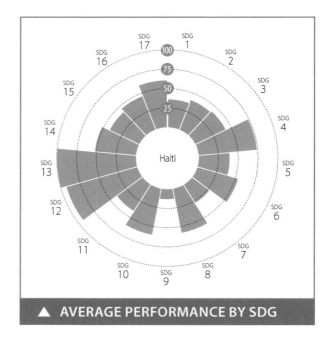

▲ AVERAGE PERFORMANCE BY SDG

▼ SPILLOVER INDEX

100 (best) to 0 (worst)

▼ CURRENT ASSESSMENT – SDG DASHBOARD

■ Major challenges   ■ Significant challenges   ■ Challenges remain   ■ SDG achieved   ■ Information unavailable

▼ SDG TRENDS

↓ Decreasing   → Stagnating   ↗ Moderately improving   ↑ On track or maintaining SDG achievement   ● Information unavailable

Notes: The full title of Goal 2 "Zero Hunger" is "End hunger, achieve food security and improved nutrition and promote sustainable agriculture".
The full title of each SDG is available here: https://sustainabledevelopment.un.org/topics/sustainabledevelopmentgoals

SDG1 – No Poverty	Value	Year	Rating	Trend
Poverty headcount ratio at $1.90/day (%)	23.5	2020	●	→
Poverty headcount ratio at $3.20/day (%)	48.3	2020	●	→

SDG2 – Zero Hunger				
Prevalence of undernourishment (%)	49.3	2017	●	→
Prevalence of stunting in children under 5 years of age (%)	21.9	2012	●	→
Prevalence of wasting in children under 5 years of age (%)	5.2	2012	●	↑
Prevalence of obesity, BMI ≥ 30 (% of adult population)	22.7	2016	●	↓
Human Trophic Level (best 2–3 worst)	2.1	2017	●	↑
Cereal yield (tonnes per hectare of harvested land)	1.1	2017	●	→
Sustainable Nitrogen Management Index (best 0–1.41 worst)	0.9	2015	●	→

SDG3 – Good Health and Well-Being				
Maternal mortality rate (per 100,000 live births)	480	2017	●	→
Neonatal mortality rate (per 1,000 live births)	26.0	2018	●	→
Mortality rate, under-5 (per 1,000 live births)	64.8	2018	●	↗
Incidence of tuberculosis (per 100,000 population)	176.0	2018	●	→
New HIV infections (per 1,000 uninfected population)	0.7	2018	●	↗
Age-standardized death rate due to cardiovascular disease, cancer, diabetes, or chronic respiratory disease in adults aged 30–70 years (%)	26.5	2016	●	↓
Age-standardized death rate attributable to household air pollution and ambient air pollution (per 100,000 population)	184	2016	●	●
Traffic deaths (per 100,000 population)	15.1	2013	●	●
Life expectancy at birth (years)	63.5	2016	●	→
Adolescent fertility rate (births per 1,000 adolescent females aged 15 to 19)	51.7	2017	●	↗
Births attended by skilled health personnel (%)	41.6	2017	●	→
Percentage of surviving infants who received 2 WHO-recommended vaccines (%)	64	2018	●	→
Universal health coverage (UHC) index of service coverage (worst 0–100 best)	49.0	2017	●	↗
Subjective well-being (average ladder score, worst 0–10 best)	3.6	2018	●	→

SDG4 – Quality Education				
Net primary enrollment rate (%)	NA	NA	●	●
Lower secondary completion rate (%)	NA	NA	●	●
Literacy rate (% of population aged 15 to 24)	83.0	2016	●	●

SDG5 – Gender Equality				
Demand for family planning satisfied by modern methods (% of females aged 15 to 49 who are married or in unions)	43.1	2017	●	→
Ratio of female-to-male mean years of education received (%)	65.2	2018	●	↗
Ratio of female-to-male labor force participation rate (%)	87.1	2019	●	↑
Seats held by women in national parliament (%)	2.5	2019	●	↓

SDG6 – Clean Water and Sanitation				
Population using at least basic drinking water services (%)	65.5	2017	●	→
Population using at least basic sanitation services (%)	34.7	2017	●	→
Freshwater withdrawal (% of available freshwater resources)	13.4	2010	●	●
Anthropogenic wastewater that receives treatment (%)	0.0	2018	●	●
Scarce water consumption embodied in imports (m³/capita)	0.3	2013	●	↑

SDG7 – Affordable and Clean Energy				
Population with access to electricity (%)	43.8	2017	●	→
Population with access to clean fuels and technology for cooking (%)	4.3	2016	●	→
CO_2 emissions from fuel combustion for electricity and heating per total electricity output (MtCO₂/TWh)	3.4	2017	●	→

SDG8 – Decent Work and Economic Growth				
Adjusted GDP growth (%)	-6.7	2018	●	●
Victims of modern slavery (per 1,000 population)	5.6	2018	●	●
Adults with an account at a bank or other financial institution or with a mobile-money-service provider (% of population aged 15 or over)	32.6	2017	●	↑
Unemployment rate (% of total labor force)	13.8	2019	●	→
Fatal work-related accidents embodied in imports (per 100,000 population)	0.0	2010	●	↑

SDG9 – Industry, Innovation and Infrastructure	Value	Year	Rating	Trend
Population using the internet (%)	32.5	2018	●	↑
Mobile broadband subscriptions (per 100 population)	30.0	2018	●	↑
Logistics Performance Index: Quality of trade and transport-related infrastructure (worst 1–5 best)	1.9	2018	●	↓
The Times Higher Education Universities Ranking: Average score of top 3 universities (worst 0–100 best)	* 0.0	2020	●	●
Scientific and technical journal articles (per 1,000 population)	0.0	2018	●	→
Expenditure on research and development (% of GDP)	* 0.0	2017	●	●

SDG10 – Reduced Inequalities				
Gini coefficient adjusted for top income	41.5	2012	●	●

SDG11 – Sustainable Cities and Communities				
Annual mean concentration of particulate matter of less than 2.5 microns in diameter (PM2.5) (µg/m³)	15.0	2017	●	↑
Access to improved water source, piped (% of urban population)	20.7	2017	●	↓
Satisfaction with public transport (%)	30.0	2018	●	→

SDG12 – Responsible Consumption and Production				
Municipal solid waste (kg/capita/day)	1.0	2015	●	●
Electronic waste (kg/capita)	NA	NA	●	●
Production-based SO₂ emissions (kg/capita)	13.1	2012	●	●
SO₂ emissions embodied in imports (kg/capita)	0.3	2012	●	●
Production-based nitrogen emissions (kg/capita)	9.8	2010	●	●
Nitrogen emissions embodied in imports (kg/capita)	0.2	2010	●	●

SDG13 – Climate Action				
Energy-related CO_2 emissions (tCO₂/capita)	0.3	2017	●	↑
CO_2 emissions embodied in imports (tCO₂/capita)	0.0	2015	●	↑
CO_2 emissions embodied in fossil fuel exports (kg/capita)	* 0.0	2018	●	●

SDG14 – Life Below Water				
Mean area that is protected in marine sites important to biodiversity (%)	0.0	2018	●	→
Ocean Health Index: Clean Waters score (worst 0–100 best)	41.6	2019	●	→
Fish caught from overexploited or collapsed stocks (% of total catch)	9.7	2014	●	↑
Fish caught by trawling (%)	NA	NA	●	●
Marine biodiversity threats embodied in imports (per million population)	0.0	2018	●	●

SDG15 – Life on Land				
Mean area that is protected in terrestrial sites important to biodiversity (%)	10.5	2018	●	→
Mean area that is protected in freshwater sites important to biodiversity (%)	0.0	2018	●	→
Red List Index of species survival (worst 0–1 best)	0.7	2019	●	↓
Permanent deforestation (% of forest area, 5-year average)	0.4	2018	●	●
Terrestrial and freshwater biodiversity threats embodied in imports (per million population)	0.0	2018	●	●

SDG16 – Peace, Justice and Strong Institutions				
Homicides (per 100,000 population)	9.5	2016	●	→
Unsentenced detainees (% of prison population)	66.8	2018	●	→
Percentage of population who feel safe walking alone at night in the city or area where they live (%)	49.5	2018	●	→
Property Rights (worst 1–7 best)	2.4	2019	●	●
Birth registrations with civil authority (% of children under age 5)	84.8	2018	●	●
Corruption Perception Index (worst 0–100 best)	18	2019	●	→
Children involved in child labor (% of population aged 5 to 14)	24.4	2016	●	●
Exports of major conventional weapons (TIV constant million USD per 100,000 population)	* 0.0	2019	●	●
Press Freedom Index (best 0–100 worst)	29.0	2019	●	↑

SDG17 – Partnerships for the Goals				
Government spending on health and education (% of GDP)	3.3	2016	●	↓
For high-income and all OECD DAC countries: International concessional public finance, including official development assistance (% of GNI)	NA	NA	●	●
Other countries: Government revenue excluding grants (% of GDP)	NA	NA	●	●
Corporate Tax Haven Score (best 0–100 worst)	* 0.0	2019	●	●

* Imputed data point

5. Country Profiles

▼ OVERALL PERFORMANCE

Index score
64.4

Regional average score
70.4

SDG Global rank 105 (OF 166)

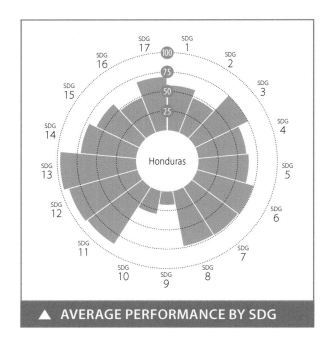

▲ AVERAGE PERFORMANCE BY SDG

▼ SPILLOVER INDEX

100 (best) to 0 (worst)

▼ CURRENT ASSESSMENT – SDG DASHBOARD

■ Major challenges ■ Significant challenges ■ Challenges remain ■ SDG achieved ■ Information unavailable

▼ SDG TRENDS

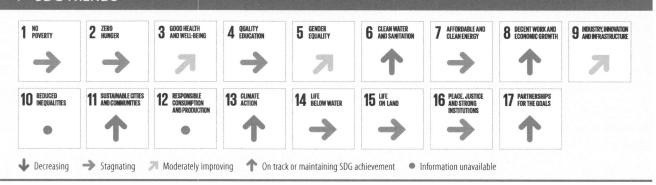

↓ Decreasing → Stagnating ↗ Moderately improving ↑ On track or maintaining SDG achievement ● Information unavailable

Notes: The full title of Goal 2 "Zero Hunger" is "End hunger, achieve food security and improved nutrition and promote sustainable agriculture".
The full title of each SDG is available here: https://sustainabledevelopment.un.org/topics/sustainabledevelopmentgoals

SDG1 – No Poverty

Indicator	Value	Year	Rating	Trend
Poverty headcount ratio at $1.90/day (%)	17.1	2020	●	→
Poverty headcount ratio at $3.20/day (%)	30.3	2020	●	→

SDG2 – Zero Hunger

Indicator	Value	Year	Rating	Trend
Prevalence of undernourishment (%)	12.9	2017	●	↑
Prevalence of stunting in children under 5 years of age (%)	22.7	2012	●	→
Prevalence of wasting in children under 5 years of age (%)	1.4	2012	●	↑
Prevalence of obesity, BMI ≥ 30 (% of adult population)	21.4	2016	●	↓
Human Trophic Level (best 2–3 worst)	2.3	2017	●	↗
Cereal yield (tonnes per hectare of harvested land)	1.8	2017	●	→
Sustainable Nitrogen Management Index (best 0–1.41 worst)	1.0	2015	●	↓

SDG3 – Good Health and Well-Being

Indicator	Value	Year	Rating	Trend
Maternal mortality rate (per 100,000 live births)	65	2017	●	↑
Neonatal mortality rate (per 1,000 live births)	9.6	2018	●	↑
Mortality rate, under-5 (per 1,000 live births)	17.6	2018	●	↑
Incidence of tuberculosis (per 100,000 population)	37.0	2018	●	↗
New HIV infections (per 1,000 uninfected population)	0.1	2018	●	↑
Age-standardized death rate due to cardiovascular disease, cancer, diabetes, or chronic respiratory disease in adults aged 30–70 years (%)	14.0	2016	●	↑
Age-standardized death rate attributable to household air pollution and ambient air pollution (per 100,000 population)	61	2016	●	
Traffic deaths (per 100,000 population)	16.7	2016	●	→
Life expectancy at birth (years)	75.2	2016	●	↗
Adolescent fertility rate (births per 1,000 adolescent females aged 15 to 19)	72.9	2017	●	→
Births attended by skilled health personnel (%)	82.8	2012	●	●
Percentage of surviving infants who received 2 WHO-recommended vaccines (%)	89	2018	●	↓
Universal health coverage (UHC) index of service coverage (worst 0–100 best)	65.0	2017	●	→
Subjective well-being (average ladder score, worst 0–10 best)	5.9	2019	●	↑

SDG4 – Quality Education

Indicator	Value	Year	Rating	Trend
Net primary enrollment rate (%)	80.1	2017	●	●
Lower secondary completion rate (%)	45.8	2016	●	●
Literacy rate (% of population aged 15 to 24)	96.5	2018	●	●

SDG5 – Gender Equality

Indicator	Value	Year	Rating	Trend
Demand for family planning satisfied by modern methods (% of females aged 15 to 49 who are married or in unions)	76.0	2012	●	↑
Ratio of female-to-male mean years of education received (%)	100.0	2018	●	●
Ratio of female-to-male labor force participation rate (%)	56.6	2019	●	→
Seats held by women in national parliament (%)	21.1	2020	●	↓

SDG6 – Clean Water and Sanitation

Indicator	Value	Year	Rating	Trend
Population using at least basic drinking water services (%)	94.8	2017	●	↑
Population using at least basic sanitation services (%)	81.3	2017	●	↗
Freshwater withdrawal (% of available freshwater resources)	4.6	2005	●	●
Anthropogenic wastewater that receives treatment (%)	3.2	2018	●	●
Scarce water consumption embodied in imports (m³/capita)	1.3	2013	●	↑

SDG7 – Affordable and Clean Energy

Indicator	Value	Year	Rating	Trend
Population with access to electricity (%)	86.5	2017	●	↓
Population with access to clean fuels and technology for cooking (%)	53.1	2016	●	↗
CO$_2$ emissions from fuel combustion for electricity and heating per total electricity output (MtCO$_2$/TWh)	1.1	2017	●	→

SDG8 – Decent Work and Economic Growth

Indicator	Value	Year	Rating	Trend
Adjusted GDP growth (%)	-2.9	2018	●	●
Victims of modern slavery (per 1,000 population)	3.4	2018	●	●
Adults with an account at a bank or other financial institution or with a mobile-money-service provider (% of population aged 15 or over)	45.3	2017	●	↑
Unemployment rate (% of total labor force)	5.4	2019	●	↑
Fatal work-related accidents embodied in imports (per 100,000 population)	0.2	2010	●	↑

SDG9 – Industry, Innovation and Infrastructure

Indicator	Value	Year	Rating	Trend
Population using the internet (%)	31.7	2017	●	↑
Mobile broadband subscriptions (per 100 population)	32.1	2018	●	↑
Logistics Performance Index: Quality of trade and transport-related infrastructure (worst 1–5 best)	2.5	2018	●	↑
The Times Higher Education Universities Ranking: Average score of top 3 universities (worst 0–100 best) *	0.0	2020	●	●
Scientific and technical journal articles (per 1,000 population)	0.0	2018	●	→
Expenditure on research and development (% of GDP)	0.0	2015	●	●

SDG10 – Reduced Inequalities

Indicator	Value	Year	Rating	Trend
Gini coefficient adjusted for top income	52.3	2017	●	●

SDG11 – Sustainable Cities and Communities

Indicator	Value	Year	Rating	Trend
Annual mean concentration of particulate matter of less than 2.5 microns in diameter (PM2.5) (μg/m³)	20.6	2017	●	↑
Access to improved water source, piped (% of urban population)	96.1	2017	●	↑
Satisfaction with public transport (%)	71.9	2019	●	↑

SDG12 – Responsible Consumption and Production

Indicator	Value	Year	Rating	Trend
Municipal solid waste (kg/capita/day)	1.1	2016	●	●
Electronic waste (kg/capita)	2.3	2016	●	●
Production-based SO$_2$ emissions (kg/capita)	23.6	2012	●	●
SO$_2$ emissions embodied in imports (kg/capita)	1.9	2012	●	●
Production-based nitrogen emissions (kg/capita)	13.2	2010	●	●
Nitrogen emissions embodied in imports (kg/capita)	1.7	2010	●	●

SDG13 – Climate Action

Indicator	Value	Year	Rating	Trend
Energy-related CO$_2$ emissions (tCO$_2$/capita)	1.0	2017	●	↑
CO$_2$ emissions embodied in imports (tCO$_2$/capita)	0.3	2015	●	↑
CO$_2$ emissions embodied in fossil fuel exports (kg/capita)	0.0	2015	●	●

SDG14 – Life Below Water

Indicator	Value	Year	Rating	Trend
Mean area that is protected in marine sites important to biodiversity (%)	48.9	2018	●	→
Ocean Health Index: Clean Waters score (worst 0–100 best)	59.2	2019	●	↓
Fish caught from overexploited or collapsed stocks (% of total catch)	12.6	2014	●	↑
Fish caught by trawling (%)	18.3	2014	●	↓
Marine biodiversity threats embodied in imports (per million population)	0.1	2018	●	●

SDG15 – Life on Land

Indicator	Value	Year	Rating	Trend
Mean area that is protected in terrestrial sites important to biodiversity (%)	65.4	2018	●	↑
Mean area that is protected in freshwater sites important to biodiversity (%)	NA	NA	●	●
Red List Index of species survival (worst 0–1 best)	0.7	2019	●	↓
Permanent deforestation (% of forest area, 5-year average)	0.8	2018	●	●
Terrestrial and freshwater biodiversity threats embodied in imports (per million population)	0.6	2018	●	●

SDG16 – Peace, Justice and Strong Institutions

Indicator	Value	Year	Rating	Trend
Homicides (per 100,000 population)	41.7	2017	●	↑
Unsentenced detainees (% of prison population)	55.4	2018	●	↓
Percentage of population who feel safe walking alone at night in the city or area where they live (%)	59.4	2019	●	↑
Property Rights (worst 1–7 best)	4.1	2019	●	●
Birth registrations with civil authority (% of children under age 5)	93.6	2018	●	●
Corruption Perception Index (worst 0–100 best)	26	2019	●	↓
Children involved in child labor (% of population aged 5 to 14)	14.1	2016	●	●
Exports of major conventional weapons (TIV constant million USD per 100,000 population) *	0.0	2019	●	●
Press Freedom Index (best 0–100 worst)	48.5	2019	●	↓

SDG17 – Partnerships for the Goals

Indicator	Value	Year	Rating	Trend
Government spending on health and education (% of GDP)	9.4	2015	●	↑
For high-income and all OECD DAC countries: International concessional public finance, including official development assistance (% of GNI)	NA	NA	●	●
Other countries: Government revenue excluding grants (% of GDP)	23.4	2015	●	●
Corporate Tax Haven Score (best 0–100 worst) *	0.0	2019	●	●

* Imputed data point

5. Country Profiles

▼ OVERALL PERFORMANCE

Index score

77.3

Regional average score

77.3

SDG Global rank 29 (OF 166)

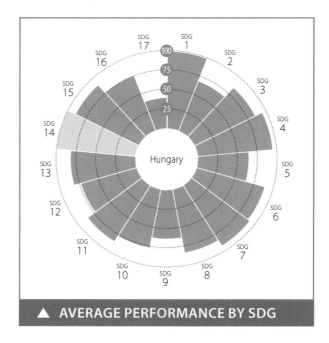

▲ AVERAGE PERFORMANCE BY SDG

▼ SPILLOVER INDEX

100 (best) to 0 (worst)

▼ CURRENT ASSESSMENT – SDG DASHBOARD

■ Major challenges ■ Significant challenges ■ Challenges remain ■ SDG achieved ■ Information unavailable

▼ SDG TRENDS

↓ Decreasing → Stagnating ↗ Moderately improving ↑ On track or maintaining SDG achievement ● Information unavailable

Notes: The full title of Goal 2 "Zero Hunger" is "End hunger, achieve food security and improved nutrition and promote sustainable agriculture".
The full title of each SDG is available here: https://sustainabledevelopment.un.org/topics/sustainabledevelopmentgoals

SDG1 – No Poverty

Indicator	Value	Year	Rating	Trend
Poverty headcount ratio at $1.90/day (%)	0.5	2020	●	↑
Poverty headcount ratio at $3.20/day (%)	0.7	2020	●	↑
Poverty rate after taxes and transfers (%)	8.0	2017	●	↑

SDG2 – Zero Hunger

Indicator		Value	Year	Rating	Trend
Prevalence of undernourishment (%)		2.5	2017	●	↑
Prevalence of stunting in children under 5 years of age (%)	*	2.6	2016	●	↑
Prevalence of wasting in children under 5 years of age (%)	*	0.7	2016	●	↑
Prevalence of obesity, BMI ≥ 30 (% of adult population)		26.4	2016	●	↓
Human Trophic Level (best 2–3 worst)		2.4	2017	●	↓
Cereal yield (tonnes per hectare of harvested land)		5.8	2017	●	↑
Sustainable Nitrogen Management Index (best 0–1.41 worst)		0.4	2015	●	→
Yield gap closure (% of potential yield)		64.4	2015	●	●

SDG3 – Good Health and Well-Being

Indicator	Value	Year	Rating	Trend
Maternal mortality rate (per 100,000 live births)	12	2017	●	↑
Neonatal mortality rate (per 1,000 live births)	2.3	2018	●	↑
Mortality rate, under-5 (per 1,000 live births)	4.3	2018	●	↑
Incidence of tuberculosis (per 100,000 population)	6.4	2018	●	↑
New HIV infections (per 1,000 uninfected population)	0.0	2018	●	↑
Age-standardized death rate due to cardiovascular disease, cancer, diabetes, or chronic respiratory disease in adults aged 30–70 years (%)	23.0	2016	●	→
Age-standardized death rate attributable to household air pollution and ambient air pollution (per 100,000 population)	39	2016	●	●
Traffic deaths (per 100,000 population)	7.8	2016	●	↑
Life expectancy at birth (years)	76.0	2016	●	↗
Adolescent fertility rate (births per 1,000 adolescent females aged 15 to 19)	24.0	2017	●	↑
Births attended by skilled health personnel (%)	99.2	2014	●	●
Percentage of surviving infants who received 2 WHO-recommended vaccines (%)	99.0	2018	●	↑
Universal health coverage (UHC) index of service coverage (worst 0–100 best)	74.0	2017	●	↑
Subjective well-being (average ladder score, worst 0–10 best)	6.0	2019	●	↑
Gap in life expectancy at birth among regions (years)	3.0	2016	●	●
Gap in self-reported health status by income (percentage points)	21.6	2018	●	↓
Daily smokers (% of population aged 15 and over)	25.8	2014	●	●

SDG4 – Quality Education

Indicator		Value	Year	Rating	Trend
Net primary enrollment rate (%)	*	95.5	2017	●	↓
Lower secondary completion rate (%)	*	95.5	2017	●	↑
Literacy rate (% of population aged 15 to 24)		98.8	2014	●	●
Participation rate in pre-primary organized learning (% of children aged 4 to 6)		87.1	2017	●	↓
Tertiary educational attainment (% of population aged 25 to 34)		30.6	2018	●	↓
PISA score (worst 0–600 best)		479.3	2018	●	↑
Variation in science performance explained by socio-economic status (%)		21.2	2018	●	→
Underachievers in science (% of 15-year-olds)		24.1	2018	●	↗
Resilient students in science (% of 15-year-olds)		22.7	2018	●	↗

SDG5 – Gender Equality

Indicator		Value	Year	Rating	Trend
Demand for family planning satisfied by modern methods (% of females aged 15 to 49 who are married or in unions)	*	75.6	2017	●	↑
Ratio of female-to-male mean years of education received (%)		96.7	2018	●	↑
Ratio of female-to-male labor force participation rate (%)		74.5	2019	●	↑
Seats held by women in national parliament (%)		12.1	2020	●	→
Gender wage gap (% of male median wage)		9.4	2016	●	↓
Gender gap in time spent doing unpaid work (minutes/day)		131.4	2010	●	●

SDG6 – Clean Water and Sanitation

Indicator	Value	Year	Rating	Trend
Population using at least basic drinking water services (%)	100.0	2017	●	●
Population using at least basic sanitation services (%)	98.0	2017	●	●
Freshwater withdrawal (% of available freshwater resources)	7.2	2015	●	●
Anthropogenic wastewater that receives treatment (%)	53.8	2018	●	●
Scarce water consumption embodied in imports (m³/capita)	8.0	2013	●	↑
Population using safely managed water services (%)	89.6	2017	●	↑
Population using safely managed sanitation services (%)	95.7	2017	●	↑

SDG7 – Affordable and Clean Energy

Indicator	Value	Year	Rating	Trend
Population with access to electricity (%)	100.0	2017	●	●
Population with access to clean fuels and technology for cooking (%)	100.0	2016	●	↑
CO$_2$ emissions from fuel combustion for electricity and heating per total electricity output (MtCO$_2$/TWh)	1.5	2017	●	→
Share of renewable energy in total primary energy supply (%)	10.6	2018	●	↓

SDG8 – Decent Work and Economic Growth

Indicator		Value	Year	Rating	Trend
Adjusted GDP growth (%)		0.7	2018	●	●
Victims of modern slavery (per 1,000 population)		3.7	2018	●	●
Adults with an account at a bank or other financial institution or with a mobile-money-service provider (% of population aged 15 or over)		74.9	2017	●	↑
Fatal work-related accidents embodied in imports (per 100,000 population)		0.4	2010	●	↑
Employment-to-population ratio (%)		70.1	2019	●	↑
Youth not in employment, education or training (NEET) (% of population aged 15 to 29)		13.5	2018	●	↑

SDG9 – Industry, Innovation and Infrastructure

Indicator	Value	Year	Rating	Trend
Population using the internet (%)	76.1	2018	●	→
Mobile broadband subscriptions (per 100 population)	67.8	2018	●	↑
Logistics Performance Index: Quality of trade and transport-related infrastructure (worst 1–5 best)	3.3	2018	●	↑
The Times Higher Education Universities Ranking: Average score of top 3 universities (worst 0–100 best)	32.5	2020	●	●
Scientific and technical journal articles (per 1,000 population)	0.7	2018	●	↑
Expenditure on research and development (% of GDP)	1.4	2017	●	→
Researchers (per 1,000 employed population)	6.8	2018	●	↑
Triadic patent families filed (per million population)	3.4	2017	●	↓
Gap in internet access by income (percentage points)	50.5	2019	●	→
Women in science and engineering (% of tertiary graduates in science and engineering)	29.2	2015	●	●

SDG10 – Reduced Inequalities

Indicator	Value	Year	Rating	Trend
Gini coefficient adjusted for top income	35.8	2015	●	↑
Palma ratio	1.0	2017	●	→
Elderly poverty rate (% of population aged 66 or over)	4.9	2017	●	↑

SDG11 – Sustainable Cities and Communities

Indicator	Value	Year	Rating	Trend
Annual mean concentration of particulate matter of less than 2.5 microns in diameter (PM2.5) (µg/m³)	15.9	2017	●	→
Access to improved water source, piped (% of urban population)	99.0	2017	●	↑
Satisfaction with public transport (%)	63.1	2019	●	↑
Population with rent overburden (%)	8.9	2017	●	↑

SDG12 – Responsible Consumption and Production

Indicator	Value	Year	Rating	Trend
Electronic waste (kg/capita)	13.8	2016	●	●
Production-based SO$_2$ emissions (kg/capita)	38.2	2012	●	●
SO$_2$ emissions embodied in imports (kg/capita)	5.9	2012	●	●
Production-based nitrogen emissions (kg/capita)	32.8	2010	●	●
Nitrogen emissions embodied in imports (kg/capita)	3.4	2010	●	●
Non-recycled municipal solid waste (kg/capita/day)	0.7	2018	●	●

SDG13 – Climate Action

Indicator	Value	Year	Rating	Trend
Energy-related CO$_2$ emissions (tCO$_2$/capita)	4.8	2017	●	↓
CO$_2$ emissions embodied in imports (tCO$_2$/capita)	1.1	2015	●	→
CO$_2$ emissions embodied in fossil fuel exports (kg/capita)	266.3	2019	●	●
Effective carbon rate (EUR/tCO$_2$)	5.9	2016	●	●

SDG14 – Life Below Water

Indicator	Value	Year	Rating	Trend
Mean area that is protected in marine sites important to biodiversity (%)	NA	NA	●	●
Ocean Health Index: Clean Waters score (worst 0–100 best)	NA	NA	●	●
Fish caught from overexploited or collapsed stocks (% of total catch)	NA	NA	●	●
Fish caught by trawling (%)	NA	NA	●	●
Marine biodiversity threats embodied in imports (per million population)	0.0	2018	●	●

SDG15 – Life on Land

Indicator	Value	Year	Rating	Trend
Mean area that is protected in terrestrial sites important to biodiversity (%)	83.1	2018	●	↑
Mean area that is protected in freshwater sites important to biodiversity (%)	84.9	2018	●	↑
Red List Index of species survival (worst 0–1 best)	0.9	2019	●	↑
Permanent deforestation (% of forest area, 5-year average)	0.0	2018	●	●
Terrestrial and freshwater biodiversity threats embodied in imports (per million population)	0.4	2018	●	●

SDG16 – Peace, Justice and Strong Institutions

Indicator		Value	Year	Rating	Trend
Homicides (per 100,000 population)		2.5	2017	●	↓
Unsentenced detainees (% of prison population)		20.1	2018	●	↑
Percentage of population who feel safe walking alone at night in the city or area where they live (%)		63.2	2019	●	↑
Property Rights (worst 1–7 best)		4.0	2019	●	●
Birth registrations with civil authority (% of children under age 5)		100.0	2018	●	●
Corruption Perception Index (worst 0–100 best)		44.0	2019	●	↓
Children involved in child labor (% of population aged 5 to 14)	*	0.0	2016	●	●
Exports of major conventional weapons (TIV constant million USD per 100,000 population)	*	0.0	2019	●	●
Press Freedom Index (best 0–100 worst)		30.4	2019	●	↓
Persons held in prison (per 100,000 population)		178.4	2017	●	→

SDG17 – Partnerships for the Goals

Indicator	Value	Year	Rating	Trend
Government spending on health and education (% of GDP)	9.6	2016	●	↑
For high-income and all OECD DAC countries: International concessional public finance, including official development assistance (% of GNI)	0.1	2017	●	→
Other countries: Government revenue excluding grants (% of GDP)	NA	NA	●	●
Corporate Tax Haven Score (best 0–100 worst)	69.1	2019	●	●
Financial Secrecy Score (best 0–100 worst)	53.8	2020	●	●
Shifted profits of multinationals (US$ billion)	3.7	2016	●	●

* Imputed data point

▼ OVERALL PERFORMANCE

Index score

77.5

Regional average score

77.3

SDG Global rank 26 (OF 166)

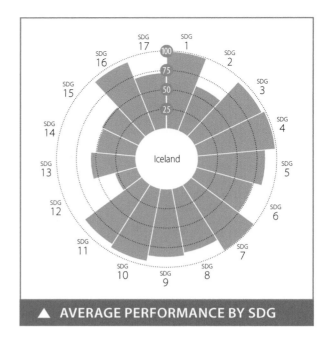

▲ AVERAGE PERFORMANCE BY SDG

▼ SPILLOVER INDEX

100 (best) to 0 (worst)

▼ CURRENT ASSESSMENT – SDG DASHBOARD

■ Major challenges   ■ Significant challenges   ■ Challenges remain   ■ SDG achieved   ■ Information unavailable

▼ SDG TRENDS

↓ Decreasing   → Stagnating   ↗ Moderately improving   ↑ On track or maintaining SDG achievement   ● Information unavailable

Notes: The full title of Goal 2 "Zero Hunger" is "End hunger, achieve food security and improved nutrition and promote sustainable agriculture".
The full title of each SDG is available here: https://sustainabledevelopment.un.org/topics/sustainabledevelopmentgoals

SDG1 – No Poverty

	Value	Year	Rating	Trend
Poverty headcount ratio at $1.90/day (%)	0.2	2020	●	↑
Poverty headcount ratio at $3.20/day (%)	0.2	2020	●	↑
Poverty rate after taxes and transfers (%)	5.4	2015	●	↑

SDG2 – Zero Hunger

	Value	Year	Rating	Trend
Prevalence of undernourishment (%)	2.5	2017	●	↑
Prevalence of stunting in children under 5 years of age (%)	* 2.6	2016	●	↑
Prevalence of wasting in children under 5 years of age (%)	* 0.7	2016	●	↑
Prevalence of obesity, BMI ≥ 30 (% of adult population)	21.9	2016	●	↓
Human Trophic Level (best 2–3 worst)	2.6	2017	●	→
Cereal yield (tonnes per hectare of harvested land)	NA	NA	●	●
Sustainable Nitrogen Management Index (best 0–1.41 worst)	0.6	2015	●	→
Yield gap closure (% of potential yield)	NA	NA	●	●

SDG3 – Good Health and Well-Being

	Value	Year	Rating	Trend
Maternal mortality rate (per 100,000 live births)	4	2017	●	↑
Neonatal mortality rate (per 1,000 live births)	1.0	2018	●	↑
Mortality rate, under-5 (per 1,000 live births)	2.0	2018	●	↑
Incidence of tuberculosis (per 100,000 population)	2.7	2018	●	↑
New HIV infections (per 1,000 uninfected population)	0.1	2018	●	↑
Age-standardized death rate due to cardiovascular disease, cancer, diabetes, or chronic respiratory disease in adults aged 30–70 years (%)	9.1	2016	●	↑
Age-standardized death rate attributable to household air pollution and ambient air pollution (per 100,000 population)	9	2016	●	●
Traffic deaths (per 100,000 population)	6.6	2016	●	↑
Life expectancy at birth (years)	82.4	2016	●	↑
Adolescent fertility rate (births per 1,000 adolescent females aged 15 to 19)	6.3	2017	●	↑
Births attended by skilled health personnel (%)	97.9	2016	○	↑
Percentage of surviving infants who received 2 WHO-recommended vaccines (%)	91.0	2018	●	↑
Universal health coverage (UHC) index of service coverage (worst 0–100 best)	84.0	2017	●	↑
Subjective well-being (average ladder score, worst 0–10 best)	7.5	2017	●	↑
Gap in life expectancy at birth among regions (years)	NA	NA	●	●
Gap in self-reported health status by income (percentage points)	14.5	2016	●	↑
Daily smokers (% of population aged 15 and over)	8.6	2018	●	↑

SDG4 – Quality Education

	Value	Year	Rating	Trend
Net primary enrollment rate (%)	* 99.0	2017	●	↑
Lower secondary completion rate (%)	* 99.0	2017	●	↑
Literacy rate (% of population aged 15 to 24)	NA	NA	●	●
Participation rate in pre-primary organized learning (% of children aged 4 to 6)	94.2	2017	●	↑
Tertiary educational attainment (% of population aged 25 to 34)	47.0	2018	●	↑
PISA score (worst 0–600 best)	481.3	2018	○	→
Variation in science performance explained by socio-economic status (%)	8.9	2018	●	↑
Underachievers in science (% of 15-year-olds)	25.0	2018	●	→
Resilient students in science (% of 15-year-olds)	18.6	2018	●	→

SDG5 – Gender Equality

	Value	Year	Rating	Trend
Demand for family planning satisfied by modern methods (% of females aged 15 to 49 who are married or in unions)	NA	NA	●	●
Ratio of female-to-male mean years of education received (%)	96.9	2018	○	→
Ratio of female-to-male labor force participation rate (%)	89.5	2019	●	↑
Seats held by women in national parliament (%)	38.1	2020	●	↓
Gender wage gap (% of male median wage)	11.5	2016	●	↑
Gender gap in time spent doing unpaid work (minutes/day)	NA	NA	●	●

SDG6 – Clean Water and Sanitation

	Value	Year	Rating	Trend
Population using at least basic drinking water services (%)	100.0	2017	●	●
Population using at least basic sanitation services (%)	98.8	2017	●	●
Freshwater withdrawal (% of available freshwater resources)	0.4	2015	●	●
Anthropogenic wastewater that receives treatment (%)	15.5	2018	●	●
Scarce water consumption embodied in imports (m³/capita)	40.9	2013	●	↓
Population using safely managed water services (%)	100.0	2017	●	↑
Population using safely managed sanitation services (%)	81.8	2017	○	↑

SDG7 – Affordable and Clean Energy

	Value	Year	Rating	Trend
Population with access to electricity (%)	100.0	2017	●	↑
Population with access to clean fuels and technology for cooking (%)	100.0	2016	●	↑
CO₂ emissions from fuel combustion for electricity and heating per total electricity output (MtCO₂/TWh)	0.1	2017	●	↑
Share of renewable energy in total primary energy supply (%)	88.7	2018	●	↑

SDG8 – Decent Work and Economic Growth

	Value	Year	Rating	Trend
Adjusted GDP growth (%)	1.9	2018	●	●
Victims of modern slavery (per 1,000 population)	2.1	2018	●	●
Adults with an account at a bank or other financial institution or with a mobile-money-service provider (% of population aged 15 or over)	NA	NA	●	●
Fatal work-related accidents embodied in imports (per 100,000 population)	2.0	2010	●	↑
Employment-to-population ratio (%)	85.1	2018	●	↑
Youth not in employment, education or training (NEET) (% of population aged 15 to 29)	6.1	2018	●	↑

SDG9 – Industry, Innovation and Infrastructure

	Value	Year	Rating	Trend
Population using the internet (%)	99.0	2018	●	↑
Mobile broadband subscriptions (per 100 population)	125.1	2018	●	↑
Logistics Performance Index: Quality of trade and transport-related infrastructure (worst 1–5 best)	3.2	2018	●	↑
The Times Higher Education Universities Ranking: Average score of top 3 universities (worst 0–100 best)	44.5	2020	●	●
Scientific and technical journal articles (per 1,000 population)	2.0	2018	●	↑
Expenditure on research and development (% of GDP)	2.2	2017	●	↑
Researchers (per 1,000 employed population)	10.3	2017	●	↑
Triadic patent families filed (per million population)	7.0	2017	●	↑
Gap in internet access by income (percentage points)	4.9	2017	●	↑
Women in science and engineering (% of tertiary graduates in science and engineering)	NA	NA	●	●

SDG10 – Reduced Inequalities

	Value	Year	Rating	Trend
Gini coefficient adjusted for top income	29.7	2014	●	↑
Palma ratio	0.9	2015	●	↑
Elderly poverty rate (% of population aged 66 or over)	3.0	2015	●	↑

SDG11 – Sustainable Cities and Communities

	Value	Year	Rating	Trend
Annual mean concentration of particulate matter of less than 2.5 microns in diameter (PM2.5) (µg/m³)	6.5	2017	●	↑
Access to improved water source, piped (% of urban population)	99.0	2017	●	↑
Satisfaction with public transport (%)	64.1	2017	○	●
Population with rent overburden (%)	18.0	2016	●	→

SDG12 – Responsible Consumption and Production

	Value	Year	Rating	Trend
Electronic waste (kg/capita)	22.6	2016	●	●
Production-based SO₂ emissions (kg/capita)	344.9	2012	●	●
SO₂ emissions embodied in imports (kg/capita)	29.7	2012	●	●
Production-based nitrogen emissions (kg/capita)	34.6	2010	○	●
Nitrogen emissions embodied in imports (kg/capita)	18.0	2010	●	●
Non-recycled municipal solid waste (kg/capita/day)	1.4	2017	●	●

SDG13 – Climate Action

	Value	Year	Rating	Trend
Energy-related CO₂ emissions (tCO₂/capita)	7.8	2017	●	↓
CO₂ emissions embodied in imports (tCO₂/capita)	4.5	2015	●	→
CO₂ emissions embodied in fossil fuel exports (kg/capita)	0.0	2017	●	●
Effective carbon rate (EUR/tCO₂)	18.1	2016	●	●

SDG14 – Life Below Water

	Value	Year	Rating	Trend
Mean area that is protected in marine sites important to biodiversity (%)	14.6	2018	●	→
Ocean Health Index: Clean Waters score (worst 0–100 best)	79.3	2019	●	↑
Fish caught from overexploited or collapsed stocks (% of total catch)	58.3	2014	●	↓
Fish caught by trawling (%)	70.3	2014	●	↓
Marine biodiversity threats embodied in imports (per million population)	0.0	2018	●	●

SDG15 – Life on Land

	Value	Year	Rating	Trend
Mean area that is protected in terrestrial sites important to biodiversity (%)	15.0	2018	●	→
Mean area that is protected in freshwater sites important to biodiversity (%)	33.9	2018	○	→
Red List Index of species survival (worst 0–1 best)	0.9	2019	○	↓
Permanent deforestation (% of forest area, 5-year average)	NA	NA	●	●
Terrestrial and freshwater biodiversity threats embodied in imports (per million population)	0.4	2018	●	●

SDG16 – Peace, Justice and Strong Institutions

	Value	Year	Rating	Trend
Homicides (per 100,000 population)	0.9	2017	●	↑
Unsentenced detainees (% of prison population)	10.6	2018	●	↑
Percentage of population who feel safe walking alone at night in the city or area where they live (%)	84.0	2017	●	●
Property Rights (worst 1–7 best)	5.9	2019	●	●
Birth registrations with civil authority (% of children under age 5)	100.0	2018	●	●
Corruption Perception Index (worst 0–100 best)	78.0	2019	●	↑
Children involved in child labor (% of population aged 5 to 14)	* 0.0	2016	●	●
Exports of major conventional weapons (TIV constant million USD per 100,000 population)	* 0.0	2019	●	●
Press Freedom Index (best 0–100 worst)	14.7	2019	●	↑
Persons held in prison (per 100,000 population)	39.1	2017	●	↑

SDG17 – Partnerships for the Goals

	Value	Year	Rating	Trend
Government spending on health and education (% of GDP)	14.2	2016	●	↑
For high-income and all OECD DAC countries: International concessional public finance, including official development assistance (% of GNI)	0.3	2017	●	↗
Other countries: Government revenue excluding grants (% of GDP)	NA	NA	●	●
Corporate Tax Haven Score (best 0–100 worst)	* 0.0	2019	●	●
Financial Secrecy Score (best 0–100 worst)	57.4	2020	●	●
Shifted profits of multinationals (US$ billion)	0.5	2016	●	●

* Imputed data point

5. Country Profiles

▼ OVERALL PERFORMANCE

Index score

61.9

Regional average score

67.2

SDG Global rank 117 (OF 166)

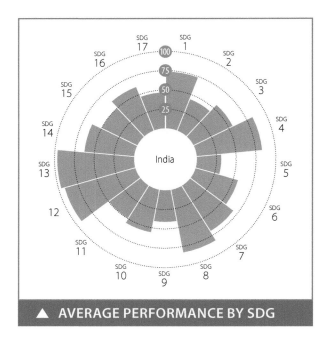

India

SDG 17, SDG 16, SDG 15, SDG 14, SDG 13, 12, 11, 10, SDG 9, SDG 8, SDG 7, SDG 6, SDG 5, SDG 4, SDG 3, SDG 2, SDG 1

100, 75, 50, 25

▲ AVERAGE PERFORMANCE BY SDG

▼ SPILLOVER INDEX

100 (best) to 0 (worst)

100
80
60
40
20
0

▼ CURRENT ASSESSMENT – SDG DASHBOARD

■ Major challenges ■ Significant challenges ▨ Challenges remain ■ SDG achieved ■ Information unavailable

▼ SDG TRENDS

↓ Decreasing → Stagnating ↗ Moderately improving ↑ On track or maintaining SDG achievement • Information unavailable

Notes: The full title of Goal 2 "Zero Hunger" is "End hunger, achieve food security and improved nutrition and promote sustainable agriculture".
The full title of each SDG is available here: https://sustainabledevelopment.un.org/topics/sustainabledevelopmentgoals

SDG1 – No Poverty

Indicator	Value	Year	Rating	Trend
Poverty headcount ratio at $1.90/day (%)	2.3	2020	●	↑
Poverty headcount ratio at $3.20/day (%)	24.6	2020	●	↑

SDG2 – Zero Hunger

Indicator	Value	Year	Rating	Trend
Prevalence of undernourishment (%)	14.5	2017	●	↑
Prevalence of stunting in children under 5 years of age (%)	38.4	2015	●	↗
Prevalence of wasting in children under 5 years of age (%)	21.0	2015	●	→
Prevalence of obesity, BMI ≥ 30 (% of adult population)	3.9	2016	●	↑
Human Trophic Level (best 2–3 worst)	2.2	2017	●	→
Cereal yield (tonnes per hectare of harvested land)	3.2	2017	●	↑
Sustainable Nitrogen Management Index (best 0–1.41 worst)	0.9	2015	●	→

SDG3 – Good Health and Well-Being

Indicator	Value	Year	Rating	Trend
Maternal mortality rate (per 100,000 live births)	145	2017	●	↑
Neonatal mortality rate (per 1,000 live births)	22.7	2018	●	↑
Mortality rate, under-5 (per 1,000 live births)	36.6	2018	●	↑
Incidence of tuberculosis (per 100,000 population)	199.0	2018	●	→
New HIV infections (per 1,000 uninfected population)	NA	NA	●	●
Age-standardized death rate due to cardiovascular disease, cancer, diabetes, or chronic respiratory disease in adults aged 30–70 years (%)	23.3	2016	●	→
Age-standardized death rate attributable to household air pollution and ambient air pollution (per 100,000 population)	184	2016	●	●
Traffic deaths (per 100,000 population)	22.6	2016	●	↓
Life expectancy at birth (years)	68.8	2016	●	→
Adolescent fertility rate (births per 1,000 adolescent females aged 15 to 19)	13.2	2017	●	↑
Births attended by skilled health personnel (%)	81.4	2016	●	●
Percentage of surviving infants who received 2 WHO-recommended vaccines (%)	89	2018	●	↑
Universal health coverage (UHC) index of service coverage (worst 0–100 best)	55.0	2017	●	↗
Subjective well-being (average ladder score, worst 0–10 best)	3.8	2018	●	↓

SDG4 – Quality Education

Indicator	Value	Year	Rating	Trend
Net primary enrollment rate (%)	92.3	2013	●	●
Lower secondary completion rate (%)	85.0	2017	●	→
Literacy rate (% of population aged 15 to 24)	91.7	2018	●	●

SDG5 – Gender Equality

Indicator	Value	Year	Rating	Trend
Demand for family planning satisfied by modern methods (% of females aged 15 to 49 who are married or in unions)	67.2	2016	●	↗
Ratio of female-to-male mean years of education received (%)	57.3	2018	●	↓
Ratio of female-to-male labor force participation rate (%)	29.8	2019	●	→
Seats held by women in national parliament (%)	14.4	2020	●	→

SDG6 – Clean Water and Sanitation

Indicator	Value	Year	Rating	Trend
Population using at least basic drinking water services (%)	92.7	2017	●	↑
Population using at least basic sanitation services (%)	59.5	2017	●	↗
Freshwater withdrawal (% of available freshwater resources)	66.5	2010	●	●
Anthropogenic wastewater that receives treatment (%)	2.2	2018	●	●
Scarce water consumption embodied in imports (m³/capita)	2.9	2013	●	↑

SDG7 – Affordable and Clean Energy

Indicator	Value	Year	Rating	Trend
Population with access to electricity (%)	92.6	2017	●	↑
Population with access to clean fuels and technology for cooking (%)	41.0	2016	●	→
CO_2 emissions from fuel combustion for electricity and heating per total electricity output (MtCO$_2$/TWh)	1.5	2017	●	↑

SDG8 – Decent Work and Economic Growth

Indicator	Value	Year	Rating	Trend
Adjusted GDP growth (%)	1.4	2018	●	●
Victims of modern slavery (per 1,000 population)	6.1	2018	●	●
Adults with an account at a bank or other financial institution or with a mobile-money-service provider (% of population aged 15 or over)	79.9	2017	●	↑
Unemployment rate (% of total labor force)	5.4	2019	●	↑
Fatal work-related accidents embodied in imports (per 100,000 population)	0.1	2010	●	↑

SDG9 – Industry, Innovation and Infrastructure

Indicator	Value	Year	Rating	Trend
Population using the internet (%)	34.5	2017	●	↑
Mobile broadband subscriptions (per 100 population)	37.5	2018	●	↑
Logistics Performance Index: Quality of trade and transport-related infrastructure (worst 1–5 best)	2.9	2018	●	↗
The Times Higher Education Universities Ranking: Average score of top 3 universities (worst 0–100 best)	44.9	2020	●	●
Scientific and technical journal articles (per 1,000 population)	0.1	2018	●	→
Expenditure on research and development (% of GDP)	0.6	2015	●	●

SDG10 – Reduced Inequalities

Indicator	Value	Year	Rating	Trend
Gini coefficient adjusted for top income	43.2	2011	●	●

SDG11 – Sustainable Cities and Communities

Indicator	Value	Year	Rating	Trend
Annual mean concentration of particulate matter of less than 2.5 microns in diameter (PM2.5) (µg/m³)	90.9	2017	●	↓
Access to improved water source, piped (% of urban population)	67.9	2017	●	↓
Satisfaction with public transport (%)	71.9	2018	●	↑

SDG12 – Responsible Consumption and Production

Indicator	Value	Year	Rating	Trend
Municipal solid waste (kg/capita/day)	1.0	2001	●	●
Electronic waste (kg/capita)	1.5	2016	●	●
Production-based SO_2 emissions (kg/capita)	7.0	2012	●	●
SO_2 emissions embodied in imports (kg/capita)	0.4	2012	●	●
Production-based nitrogen emissions (kg/capita)	13.2	2010	●	●
Nitrogen emissions embodied in imports (kg/capita)	0.6	2010	●	●

SDG13 – Climate Action

Indicator	Value	Year	Rating	Trend
Energy-related CO_2 emissions (tCO$_2$/capita)	1.8	2017	●	↑
CO_2 emissions embodied in imports (tCO$_2$/capita)	0.1	2015	●	↑
CO_2 emissions embodied in fossil fuel exports (kg/capita)	1.6	2018	●	●

SDG14 – Life Below Water

Indicator	Value	Year	Rating	Trend
Mean area that is protected in marine sites important to biodiversity (%)	37.7	2018	●	→
Ocean Health Index: Clean Waters score (worst 0–100 best)	29.5	2019	●	↑
Fish caught from overexploited or collapsed stocks (% of total catch)	12.0	2014	●	↑
Fish caught by trawling (%)	10.2	2014	●	→
Marine biodiversity threats embodied in imports (per million population)	0.0	2018	●	●

SDG15 – Life on Land

Indicator	Value	Year	Rating	Trend
Mean area that is protected in terrestrial sites important to biodiversity (%)	25.7	2018	●	→
Mean area that is protected in freshwater sites important to biodiversity (%)	15.1	2018	●	→
Red List Index of species survival (worst 0–1 best)	0.7	2019	●	↓
Permanent deforestation (% of forest area, 5-year average)	0.0	2018	●	●
Terrestrial and freshwater biodiversity threats embodied in imports (per million population)	0.1	2018	●	●

SDG16 – Peace, Justice and Strong Institutions

Indicator	Value	Year	Rating	Trend
Homicides (per 100,000 population)	3.2	2016	●	↑
Unsentenced detainees (% of prison population)	67.7	2018	●	↓
Percentage of population who feel safe walking alone at night in the city or area where they live (%)	69.3	2018	●	↑
Property Rights (worst 1–7 best)	4.4	2019	●	●
Birth registrations with civil authority (% of children under age 5)	79.7	2018	●	●
Corruption Perception Index (worst 0–100 best)	41	2019	●	↗
Children involved in child labor (% of population aged 5 to 14)	11.8	2016	●	●
Exports of major conventional weapons (TIV constant million USD per 100,000 population)	0.0	2019	●	●
Press Freedom Index (best 0–100 worst)	45.7	2019	●	↓

SDG17 – Partnerships for the Goals

Indicator	Value	Year	Rating	Trend
Government spending on health and education (% of GDP)	4.7	2013	●	●
For high-income and all OECD DAC countries: International concessional public finance, including official development assistance (% of GNI)	NA	NA	●	●
Other countries: Government revenue excluding grants (% of GDP)	12.9	2017	●	→
Corporate Tax Haven Score (best 0–100 worst) *	0.0	2019	●	●

5. Country Profiles

* Imputed data point

▼ OVERALL PERFORMANCE

Index score

65.3

Regional average score

67.2

SDG Global rank 101 (OF 166)

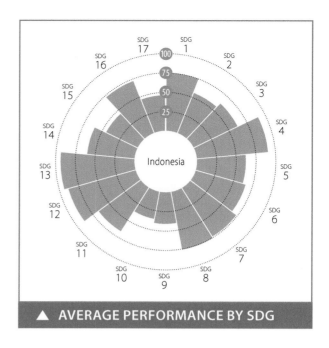

▲ AVERAGE PERFORMANCE BY SDG

▼ SPILLOVER INDEX

100 (best) to 0 (worst)

▼ CURRENT ASSESSMENT – SDG DASHBOARD

■ Major challenges   ■ Significant challenges   ■ Challenges remain   ■ SDG achieved   ■ Information unavailable

▼ SDG TRENDS

↓ Decreasing   → Stagnating   ↗ Moderately improving   ↑ On track or maintaining SDG achievement   ● Information unavailable

Notes: The full title of Goal 2 "Zero Hunger" is "End hunger, achieve food security and improved nutrition and promote sustainable agriculture".
The full title of each SDG is available here: https://sustainabledevelopment.un.org/topics/sustainabledevelopmentgoals

SDG1 – No Poverty

	Value	Year	Rating	Trend
Poverty headcount ratio at $1.90/day (%)	3.7	2020	○	↑
Poverty headcount ratio at $3.20/day (%)	22.2	2020	●	↑

SDG2 – Zero Hunger

	Value	Year	Rating	Trend
Prevalence of undernourishment (%)	8.3	2017	○	↑
Prevalence of stunting in children under 5 years of age (%)	36.4	2013	●	→
Prevalence of wasting in children under 5 years of age (%)	13.5	2013	●	↗
Prevalence of obesity, BMI ≥ 30 (% of adult population)	6.9	2016	●	↑
Human Trophic Level (best 2–3 worst)	2.2	2017	●	↑
Cereal yield (tonnes per hectare of harvested land)	5.2	2017	●	↑
Sustainable Nitrogen Management Index (best 0–1.41 worst)	0.7	2015	●	→

SDG3 – Good Health and Well-Being

	Value	Year	Rating	Trend
Maternal mortality rate (per 100,000 live births)	177	2017	●	↗
Neonatal mortality rate (per 1,000 live births)	12.7	2018	○	↑
Mortality rate, under-5 (per 1,000 live births)	25.0	2018	●	↑
Incidence of tuberculosis (per 100,000 population)	316.0	2018	●	→
New HIV infections (per 1,000 uninfected population)	0.2	2018	●	↑
Age-standardized death rate due to cardiovascular disease, cancer, diabetes, or chronic respiratory disease in adults aged 30–70 years (%)	26.4	2016	●	→
Age-standardized death rate attributable to household air pollution and ambient air pollution (per 100,000 population)	112	2016	●	●
Traffic deaths (per 100,000 population)	12.2	2016	○	↑
Life expectancy at birth (years)	69.3	2016	●	→
Adolescent fertility rate (births per 1,000 adolescent females aged 15 to 19)	47.4	2017	●	→
Births attended by skilled health personnel (%)	92.6	2016	●	↑
Percentage of surviving infants who received 2 WHO-recommended vaccines (%)	75	2018	●	→
Universal health coverage (UHC) index of service coverage (worst 0–100 best)	57.0	2017	●	↑
Subjective well-being (average ladder score, worst 0–10 best)	5.3	2019	●	↑

SDG4 – Quality Education

	Value	Year	Rating	Trend
Net primary enrollment rate (%)	93.5	2018	○	↑
Lower secondary completion rate (%)	90.0	2017	○	↓
Literacy rate (% of population aged 15 to 24)	99.7	2018	●	●

SDG5 – Gender Equality

	Value	Year	Rating	Trend
Demand for family planning satisfied by modern methods (% of females aged 15 to 49 who are married or in unions)	77.6	2017	○	↓
Ratio of female-to-male mean years of education received (%)	90.5	2018	○	↗
Ratio of female-to-male labor force participation rate (%)	63.9	2019	●	↑
Seats held by women in national parliament (%)	20.4	2020	○	→

SDG6 – Clean Water and Sanitation

	Value	Year	Rating	Trend
Population using at least basic drinking water services (%)	89.3	2017	○	↑
Population using at least basic sanitation services (%)	73.1	2017	●	↑
Freshwater withdrawal (% of available freshwater resources)	28.0	2015	○	●
Anthropogenic wastewater that receives treatment (%)	0.0	2018	●	●
Scarce water consumption embodied in imports (m³/capita)	2.7	2013	●	↑

SDG7 – Affordable and Clean Energy

	Value	Year	Rating	Trend
Population with access to electricity (%)	98.1	2017	●	↑
Population with access to clean fuels and technology for cooking (%)	58.4	2016	●	↑
CO_2 emissions from fuel combustion for electricity and heating per total electricity output (MtCO₂/TWh)	2.1	2017	●	→

SDG8 – Decent Work and Economic Growth

	Value	Year	Rating	Trend
Adjusted GDP growth (%)	-0.1	2018	○	●
Victims of modern slavery (per 1,000 population)	4.7	2018	○	●
Adults with an account at a bank or other financial institution or with a mobile-money-service provider (% of population aged 15 or over)	48.9	2017	●	↑
Unemployment rate (% of total labor force)	4.7	2019	●	↑
Fatal work-related accidents embodied in imports (per 100,000 population)	0.1	2010	●	↑

SDG9 – Industry, Innovation and Infrastructure

	Value	Year	Rating	Trend
Population using the internet (%)	39.9	2018	●	↑
Mobile broadband subscriptions (per 100 population)	87.1	2018	●	↑
Logistics Performance Index: Quality of trade and transport-related infrastructure (worst 1–5 best)	2.9	2018	○	→
The Times Higher Education Universities Ranking: Average score of top 3 universities (worst 0–100 best)	21.5	2020	○	●
Scientific and technical journal articles (per 1,000 population)	0.1	2018	●	↗
Expenditure on research and development (% of GDP)	0.2	2017	●	→

SDG10 – Reduced Inequalities

	Value	Year	Rating	Trend
Gini coefficient adjusted for top income	50.5	2016	●	●

SDG11 – Sustainable Cities and Communities

	Value	Year	Rating	Trend
Annual mean concentration of particulate matter of less than 2.5 microns in diameter (PM2.5) (µg/m³)	16.5	2017	○	→
Access to improved water source, piped (% of urban population)	22.7	2017	●	↓
Satisfaction with public transport (%)	78.4	2019	●	↑

SDG12 – Responsible Consumption and Production

	Value	Year	Rating	Trend
Municipal solid waste (kg/capita/day)	1.2	2016	○	●
Electronic waste (kg/capita)	4.9	2016	●	●
Production-based SO_2 emissions (kg/capita)	10.8	2012	●	●
SO_2 emissions embodied in imports (kg/capita)	1.2	2012	●	●
Production-based nitrogen emissions (kg/capita)	14.1	2010	●	●
Nitrogen emissions embodied in imports (kg/capita)	1.1	2010	●	●

SDG13 – Climate Action

	Value	Year	Rating	Trend
Energy-related CO_2 emissions (tCO₂/capita)	1.7	2017	●	↑
CO_2 emissions embodied in imports (tCO₂/capita)	0.2	2015	●	↑
CO_2 emissions embodied in fossil fuel exports (kg/capita)	3001.8	2018	○	●

SDG14 – Life Below Water

	Value	Year	Rating	Trend
Mean area that is protected in marine sites important to biodiversity (%)	23.4	2018	●	→
Ocean Health Index: Clean Waters score (worst 0–100 best)	58.0	2019	●	→
Fish caught from overexploited or collapsed stocks (% of total catch)	21.2	2014	●	↑
Fish caught by trawling (%)	36.9	2014	●	↓
Marine biodiversity threats embodied in imports (per million population)	0.0	2018	●	●

SDG15 – Life on Land

	Value	Year	Rating	Trend
Mean area that is protected in terrestrial sites important to biodiversity (%)	24.4	2018	●	→
Mean area that is protected in freshwater sites important to biodiversity (%)	35.5	2018	○	→
Red List Index of species survival (worst 0–1 best)	0.8	2019	●	↓
Permanent deforestation (% of forest area, 5-year average)	1.1	2018	●	●
Terrestrial and freshwater biodiversity threats embodied in imports (per million population)	0.2	2018	●	●

SDG16 – Peace, Justice and Strong Institutions

	Value	Year	Rating	Trend
Homicides (per 100,000 population)	0.4	2017	●	↑
Unsentenced detainees (% of prison population)	32.7	2018	○	↗
Percentage of population who feel safe walking alone at night in the city or area where they live (%)	80.8	2019	●	↑
Property Rights (worst 1–7 best)	4.7	2019	●	●
Birth registrations with civil authority (% of children under age 5)	71.9	2018	●	●
Corruption Perception Index (worst 0–100 best)	40	2019	●	↗
Children involved in child labor (% of population aged 5 to 14)	6.9	2016	●	●
Exports of major conventional weapons (TIV constant million USD per 100,000 population)	0.0	2019	●	●
Press Freedom Index (best 0–100 worst)	36.8	2019	○	↑

SDG17 – Partnerships for the Goals

	Value	Year	Rating	Trend
Government spending on health and education (% of GDP)	4.8	2015	●	↗
For high-income and all OECD DAC countries: International concessional public finance, including official development assistance (% of GNI)	NA	NA	●	●
Other countries: Government revenue excluding grants (% of GDP)	12.2	2017	●	↓
Corporate Tax Haven Score (best 0–100 worst) *	0.0	2019	●	●

* Imputed data point

5. Country Profiles

▼ OVERALL PERFORMANCE

Index score
71.8

Regional average score
66.3

SDG Global rank **59** (OF 166)

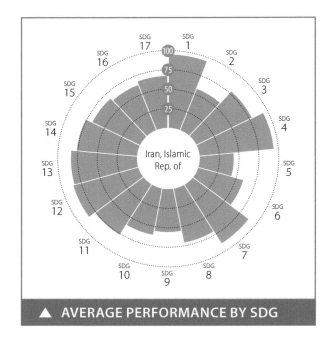

▲ AVERAGE PERFORMANCE BY SDG

▼ SPILLOVER INDEX

100 (best) to 0 (worst)

▼ CURRENT ASSESSMENT – SDG DASHBOARD

1 NO POVERTY	2 ZERO HUNGER	3 GOOD HEALTH AND WELL-BEING	4 QUALITY EDUCATION	5 GENDER EQUALITY	6 CLEAN WATER AND SANITATION	7 AFFORDABLE AND CLEAN ENERGY	8 DECENT WORK AND ECONOMIC GROWTH	9 INDUSTRY, INNOVATION AND INFRASTRUCTURE
10 REDUCED INEQUALITIES	11 SUSTAINABLE CITIES AND COMMUNITIES	12 RESPONSIBLE CONSUMPTION AND PRODUCTION	13 CLIMATE ACTION	14 LIFE BELOW WATER	15 LIFE ON LAND	16 PEACE, JUSTICE AND STRONG INSTITUTIONS	17 PARTNERSHIPS FOR THE GOALS	SUSTAINABLE DEVELOPMENT GOALS

■ Major challenges ■ Significant challenges ■ Challenges remain ■ SDG achieved ■ Information unavailable

▼ SDG TRENDS

1 NO POVERTY →	2 ZERO HUNGER ↗	3 GOOD HEALTH AND WELL-BEING ↗	4 QUALITY EDUCATION ↑	5 GENDER EQUALITY ↗	6 CLEAN WATER AND SANITATION →	7 AFFORDABLE AND CLEAN ENERGY ↗	8 DECENT WORK AND ECONOMIC GROWTH ↗	9 INDUSTRY, INNOVATION AND INFRASTRUCTURE ↑
10 REDUCED INEQUALITIES ●	11 SUSTAINABLE CITIES AND COMMUNITIES →	12 RESPONSIBLE CONSUMPTION AND PRODUCTION ●	13 CLIMATE ACTION ↗	14 LIFE BELOW WATER ↗	15 LIFE ON LAND ↓	16 PEACE, JUSTICE AND STRONG INSTITUTIONS →	17 PARTNERSHIPS FOR THE GOALS ↑	

↓ Decreasing → Stagnating ↗ Moderately improving ↑ On track or maintaining SDG achievement ● Information unavailable

Notes: The full title of Goal 2 "Zero Hunger" is "End hunger, achieve food security and improved nutrition and promote sustainable agriculture".
The full title of each SDG is available here: https://sustainabledevelopment.un.org/topics/sustainabledevelopmentgoals

SDG1 – No Poverty

Indicator	Value	Year
Poverty headcount ratio at $1.90/day (%)	0.2	2020
Poverty headcount ratio at $3.20/day (%)	4.2	2020

SDG2 – Zero Hunger

Indicator	Value	Year
Prevalence of undernourishment (%)	4.9	2017
Prevalence of stunting in children under 5 years of age (%)	6.8	2011
Prevalence of wasting in children under 5 years of age (%)	4.0	2011
Prevalence of obesity, BMI ≥ 30 (% of adult population)	25.8	2016
Human Trophic Level (best 2–3 worst)	2.2	2017
Cereal yield (tonnes per hectare of harvested land)	2.3	2017
Sustainable Nitrogen Management Index (best 0–1.41 worst)	0.8	2015

SDG3 – Good Health and Well-Being

Indicator	Value	Year
Maternal mortality rate (per 100,000 live births)	16	2017
Neonatal mortality rate (per 1,000 live births)	8.9	2018
Mortality rate, under-5 (per 1,000 live births)	14.4	2018
Incidence of tuberculosis (per 100,000 population)	14.0	2018
New HIV infections (per 1,000 uninfected population)	0.1	2018
Age-standardized death rate due to cardiovascular disease, cancer, diabetes, or chronic respiratory disease in adults aged 30–70 years (%)	14.8	2016
Age-standardized death rate attributable to household air pollution and ambient air pollution (per 100,000 population)	51	2016
Traffic deaths (per 100,000 population)	20.5	2016
Life expectancy at birth (years)	75.7	2016
Adolescent fertility rate (births per 1,000 adolescent females aged 15 to 19)	40.6	2017
Births attended by skilled health personnel (%)	99.0	2014
Percentage of surviving infants who received 2 WHO-recommended vaccines (%)	99	2018
Universal health coverage (UHC) index of service coverage (worst 0–100 best)	72.0	2017
Subjective well-being (average ladder score, worst 0–10 best)	5.0	2019

SDG4 – Quality Education

Indicator	Value	Year
Net primary enrollment rate (%)	99.7	2017
Lower secondary completion rate (%)	90.2	2017
Literacy rate (% of population aged 15 to 24)	98.1	2016

SDG5 – Gender Equality

Indicator	Value	Year
Demand for family planning satisfied by modern methods (% of females aged 15 to 49 who are married or in unions)	68.6	2011
Ratio of female-to-male mean years of education received (%)	98.0	2018
Ratio of female-to-male labor force participation rate (%)	23.3	2019
Seats held by women in national parliament (%)	8.2	2020

SDG6 – Clean Water and Sanitation

Indicator	Value	Year
Population using at least basic drinking water services (%)	95.2	2017
Population using at least basic sanitation services (%)	88.4	2017
Freshwater withdrawal (% of available freshwater resources)	81.4	2005
Anthropogenic wastewater that receives treatment (%)	3.7	2018
Scarce water consumption embodied in imports (m³/capita)	6.5	2013

SDG7 – Affordable and Clean Energy

Indicator	Value	Year
Population with access to electricity (%)	100.0	2017
Population with access to clean fuels and technology for cooking (%)	98.5	2016
CO_2 emissions from fuel combustion for electricity and heating per total electricity output (MtCO$_2$/TWh)	2.0	2017

SDG8 – Decent Work and Economic Growth

Indicator	Value	Year
Adjusted GDP growth (%)	0.5	2018
Victims of modern slavery (per 1,000 population)	16.2	2018
Adults with an account at a bank or other financial institution or with a mobile-money-service provider (% of population aged 15 or over)	94.0	2017
Unemployment rate (% of total labor force)	11.4	2019
Fatal work-related accidents embodied in imports (per 100,000 population)	0.2	2010

SDG9 – Industry, Innovation and Infrastructure

Indicator	Value	Year
Population using the internet (%)	70.0	2018
Mobile broadband subscriptions (per 100 population)	68.2	2018
Logistics Performance Index: Quality of trade and transport-related infrastructure (worst 1–5 best)	2.8	2018
The Times Higher Education Universities Ranking: Average score of top 3 universities (worst 0–100 best)	40.3	2020
Scientific and technical journal articles (per 1,000 population)	0.6	2018
Expenditure on research and development (% of GDP)	0.3	2013

SDG10 – Reduced Inequalities

Indicator	Value	Year
Gini coefficient adjusted for top income	41.7	2016

SDG11 – Sustainable Cities and Communities

Indicator	Value	Year
Annual mean concentration of particulate matter of less than 2.5 microns in diameter (PM2.5) (μg/m³)	39.0	2017
Access to improved water source, piped (% of urban population)	95.8	2017
Satisfaction with public transport (%)	64.6	2019

SDG12 – Responsible Consumption and Production

Indicator	Value	Year
Municipal solid waste (kg/capita/day)	0.8	2017
Electronic waste (kg/capita)	7.8	2016
Production-based SO_2 emissions (kg/capita)	22.0	2012
SO_2 emissions embodied in imports (kg/capita)	2.3	2012
Production-based nitrogen emissions (kg/capita)	26.8	2010
Nitrogen emissions embodied in imports (kg/capita)	1.4	2010

SDG13 – Climate Action

Indicator	Value	Year
Energy-related CO_2 emissions (tCO$_2$/capita)	8.1	2017
CO_2 emissions embodied in imports (tCO$_2$/capita)	0.5	2015
CO_2 emissions embodied in fossil fuel exports (kg/capita)	387.8	2017

SDG14 – Life Below Water

Indicator	Value	Year
Mean area that is protected in marine sites important to biodiversity (%)	60.3	2018
Ocean Health Index: Clean Waters score (worst 0–100 best)	66.1	2019
Fish caught from overexploited or collapsed stocks (% of total catch)	25.4	2014
Fish caught by trawling (%)	5.1	2014
Marine biodiversity threats embodied in imports (per million population)	0.0	2018

SDG15 – Life on Land

Indicator	Value	Year
Mean area that is protected in terrestrial sites important to biodiversity (%)	45.0	2018
Mean area that is protected in freshwater sites important to biodiversity (%)	36.2	2018
Red List Index of species survival (worst 0–1 best)	0.8	2019
Permanent deforestation (% of forest area, 5-year average)	0.0	2018
Terrestrial and freshwater biodiversity threats embodied in imports (per million population)	0.2	2018

SDG16 – Peace, Justice and Strong Institutions

Indicator	Value	Year
Homicides (per 100,000 population)	2.5	2014
Unsentenced detainees (% of prison population)	25.1	2015
Percentage of population who feel safe walking alone at night in the city or area where they live (%)	70.9	2019
Property Rights (worst 1–7 best)	3.5	2019
Birth registrations with civil authority (% of children under age 5)	98.6	2018
Corruption Perception Index (worst 0–100 best)	26	2019
Children involved in child labor (% of population aged 5 to 14)	11.4	2016
Exports of major conventional weapons (TIV constant million USD per 100,000 population)	0.0	2019
Press Freedom Index (best 0–100 worst)	64.4	2019

SDG17 – Partnerships for the Goals

Indicator	Value	Year
Government spending on health and education (% of GDP)	7.8	2016
For high-income and all OECD DAC countries: International concessional public finance, including official development assistance (% of GNI)	NA	NA
Other countries: Government revenue excluding grants (% of GDP)	25.4	2009
Corporate Tax Haven Score (best 0–100 worst) *	0.0	2019

* Imputed data point

5. Country Profiles

IRAQ

▼ OVERALL PERFORMANCE

Index score
63.1

Regional average score
66.3

SDG Global rank **113** (OF 166)

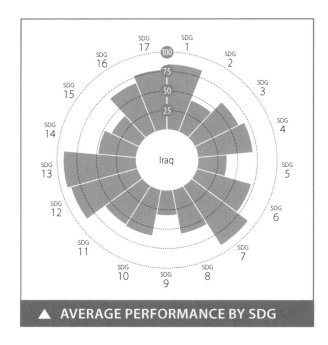

▲ AVERAGE PERFORMANCE BY SDG

▼ SPILLOVER INDEX

100 (best) to 0 (worst)

▼ CURRENT ASSESSMENT – SDG DASHBOARD

■ Major challenges ■ Significant challenges ■ Challenges remain ■ SDG achieved ■ Information unavailable

▼ SDG TRENDS

↓ Decreasing → Stagnating ↗ Moderately improving ↑ On track or maintaining SDG achievement ● Information unavailable

Notes: The full title of Goal 2 "Zero Hunger" is "End hunger, achieve food security and improved nutrition and promote sustainable agriculture".
The full title of each SDG is available here: https://sustainabledevelopment.un.org/topics/sustainabledevelopmentgoals

SDG1 – No Poverty

Indicator	Value	Year	Rating	Trend
Poverty headcount ratio at $1.90/day (%)	1.1	2020	●	↑
Poverty headcount ratio at $3.20/day (%)	14.5	2020	●	↗

SDG2 – Zero Hunger

Indicator	Value	Year	Rating	Trend
Prevalence of undernourishment (%)	29.0	2017	●	↓
Prevalence of stunting in children under 5 years of age (%)	22.6	2011	●	↗
Prevalence of wasting in children under 5 years of age (%)	7.4	2011	●	↗
Prevalence of obesity, BMI ≥ 30 (% of adult population)	30.4	2016	●	↓
Human Trophic Level (best 2–3 worst)	2.1	2017	●	↑
Cereal yield (tonnes per hectare of harvested land)	2.8	2017	●	↑
Sustainable Nitrogen Management Index (best 0–1.41 worst)	0.8	2015	●	↗

SDG3 – Good Health and Well-Being

Indicator	Value	Year	Rating	Trend
Maternal mortality rate (per 100,000 live births)	79	2017	●	↑
Neonatal mortality rate (per 1,000 live births)	15.3	2018	●	↑
Mortality rate, under-5 (per 1,000 live births)	26.7	2018	●	↑
Incidence of tuberculosis (per 100,000 population)	42.0	2018	●	→
New HIV infections (per 1,000 uninfected population)	NA	NA	●	●
Age-standardized death rate due to cardiovascular disease, cancer, diabetes, or chronic respiratory disease in adults aged 30–70 years (%)	21.3	2016	●	↗
Age-standardized death rate attributable to household air pollution and ambient air pollution (per 100,000 population)	75	2016	●	●
Traffic deaths (per 100,000 population)	20.7	2016	●	↓
Life expectancy at birth (years)	69.8	2016	●	↓
Adolescent fertility rate (births per 1,000 adolescent females aged 15 to 19)	71.7	2017	●	→
Births attended by skilled health personnel (%)	70.4	2012	●	●
Percentage of surviving infants who received 2 WHO-recommended vaccines (%)	83	2018	●	↑
Universal health coverage (UHC) index of service coverage (worst 0–100 best)	61.0	2017	●	↗
Subjective well-being (average ladder score, worst 0–10 best)	5.1	2018	●	↑

SDG4 – Quality Education

Indicator	Value	Year	Rating	Trend
Net primary enrollment rate (%)	92.8	2007	●	●
Lower secondary completion rate (%)	48.4	2007	●	●
Literacy rate (% of population aged 15 to 24)	93.5	2017	●	●

SDG5 – Gender Equality

Indicator	Value	Year	Rating	Trend
Demand for family planning satisfied by modern methods (% of females aged 15 to 49 who are married or in unions)	54.6	2018	●	↗
Ratio of female-to-male mean years of education received (%)	69.8	2018	●	→
Ratio of female-to-male labor force participation rate (%)	17.1	2019	●	→
Seats held by women in national parliament (%)	26.4	2020	●	↓

SDG6 – Clean Water and Sanitation

Indicator	Value	Year	Rating	Trend
Population using at least basic drinking water services (%)	96.5	2017	●	↑
Population using at least basic sanitation services (%)	94.1	2017	●	↑
Freshwater withdrawal (% of available freshwater resources)	54.1	2015	●	●
Anthropogenic wastewater that receives treatment (%)	19.5	2018	●	●
Scarce water consumption embodied in imports (m³/capita)	1.9	2013	●	↑

SDG7 – Affordable and Clean Energy

Indicator	Value	Year	Rating	Trend
Population with access to electricity (%)	100.0	2017	●	↑
Population with access to clean fuels and technology for cooking (%)	97.6	2016	●	↑
CO_2 emissions from fuel combustion for electricity and heating per total electricity output (MtCO$_2$/TWh)	1.7	2017	●	↑

SDG8 – Decent Work and Economic Growth

Indicator	Value	Year	Rating	Trend
Adjusted GDP growth (%)	-2.4	2018	●	●
Victims of modern slavery (per 1,000 population) *	NA	NA	●	●
Adults with an account at a bank or other financial institution or with a mobile-money-service provider (% of population aged 15 or over)	22.7	2017	●	↗
Unemployment rate (% of total labor force)	12.8	2019	●	↓
Fatal work-related accidents embodied in imports (per 100,000 population)	0.1	2010	●	↑

SDG9 – Industry, Innovation and Infrastructure

Indicator	Value	Year	Rating	Trend
Population using the internet (%)	75.0	2018	●	↑
Mobile broadband subscriptions (per 100 population)	39.8	2018	●	↑
Logistics Performance Index: Quality of trade and transport-related infrastructure (worst 1–5 best)	2.0	2018	●	↓
The Times Higher Education Universities Ranking: Average score of top 3 universities (worst 0–100 best)	20.8	2020	●	●
Scientific and technical journal articles (per 1,000 population)	0.2	2018	●	↗
Expenditure on research and development (% of GDP)	0.0	2017	●	→

SDG10 – Reduced Inequalities

Indicator	Value	Year	Rating	Trend
Gini coefficient adjusted for top income	41.8	2012	●	●

SDG11 – Sustainable Cities and Communities

Indicator	Value	Year	Rating	Trend
Annual mean concentration of particulate matter of less than 2.5 microns in diameter (PM2.5) (µg/m³)	61.6	2017	●	↓
Access to improved water source, piped (% of urban population)	84.5	2017	●	↓
Satisfaction with public transport (%)	57.9	2018	●	↗

SDG12 – Responsible Consumption and Production

Indicator	Value	Year	Rating	Trend
Municipal solid waste (kg/capita/day)	1.3	2015	●	●
Electronic waste (kg/capita)	6.1	2016	●	●
Production-based SO$_2$ emissions (kg/capita)	30.0	2012	●	●
SO$_2$ emissions embodied in imports (kg/capita)	1.1	2012	●	●
Production-based nitrogen emissions (kg/capita)	13.2	2010	●	●
Nitrogen emissions embodied in imports (kg/capita)	0.6	2010	●	●

SDG13 – Climate Action

Indicator	Value	Year	Rating	Trend
Energy-related CO_2 emissions (tCO$_2$/capita)	5.0	2017	●	→
CO_2 emissions embodied in imports (tCO$_2$/capita)	0.2	2015	●	↑
CO_2 emissions embodied in fossil fuel exports (kg/capita)	0.0	2016	●	●

SDG14 – Life Below Water

Indicator	Value	Year	Rating	Trend
Mean area that is protected in marine sites important to biodiversity (%)	0.0	2018	●	→
Ocean Health Index: Clean Waters score (worst 0–100 best)	44.9	2019	●	↓
Fish caught from overexploited or collapsed stocks (% of total catch)	NA	NA	●	●
Fish caught by trawling (%)	30.0	2014	●	→
Marine biodiversity threats embodied in imports (per million population)	0.0	2018	●	●

SDG15 – Life on Land

Indicator	Value	Year	Rating	Trend
Mean area that is protected in terrestrial sites important to biodiversity (%)	3.8	2018	●	→
Mean area that is protected in freshwater sites important to biodiversity (%)	5.1	2018	●	→
Red List Index of species survival (worst 0–1 best)	0.8	2019	●	↓
Permanent deforestation (% of forest area, 5-year average)	NA	NA	●	●
Terrestrial and freshwater biodiversity threats embodied in imports (per million population)	0.0	2018	●	●

SDG16 – Peace, Justice and Strong Institutions

Indicator	Value	Year	Rating	Trend
Homicides (per 100,000 population)	9.9	2013	●	●
Unsentenced detainees (% of prison population)	26.5	2015	●	●
Percentage of population who feel safe walking alone at night in the city or area where they live (%)	67.0	2018	●	↑
Property Rights (worst 1–7 best)	NA	NA	●	●
Birth registrations with civil authority (% of children under age 5)	98.8	2018	●	●
Corruption Perception Index (worst 0–100 best)	20	2019	●	→
Children involved in child labor (% of population aged 5 to 14)	4.7	2016	●	●
Exports of major conventional weapons (TIV constant million USD per 100,000 population) *	0.0	2019	●	●
Press Freedom Index (best 0–100 worst)	52.6	2019	●	→

SDG17 – Partnerships for the Goals

Indicator	Value	Year	Rating	Trend
Government spending on health and education (% of GDP)	NA	NA	●	●
For high-income and all OECD DAC countries: International concessional public finance, including official development assistance (% of GNI)	NA	NA	●	●
Other countries: Government revenue excluding grants (% of GDP)	26.3	2016	●	↓
Corporate Tax Haven Score (best 0–100 worst) *	0.0	2019	●	●

* Imputed data point

5. Country Profiles

▼ OVERALL PERFORMANCE

Index score

79.4

Regional average score

77.3

SDG Global rank 14 (OF 166)

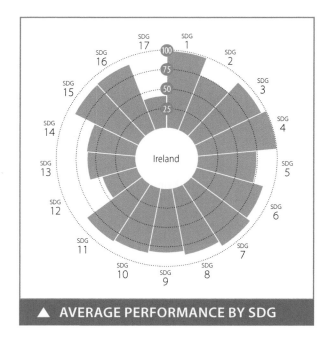

▲ AVERAGE PERFORMANCE BY SDG

▼ SPILLOVER INDEX

100 (best) to 0 (worst)

▼ CURRENT ASSESSMENT – SDG DASHBOARD

■ Major challenges ■ Significant challenges ■ Challenges remain ■ SDG achieved ■ Information unavailable

▼ SDG TRENDS

↓ Decreasing   → Stagnating   ↗ Moderately improving   ↑ On track or maintaining SDG achievement   ● Information unavailable

Notes: The full title of Goal 2 "Zero Hunger" is "End hunger, achieve food security and improved nutrition and promote sustainable agriculture".
The full title of each SDG is available here: https://sustainabledevelopment.un.org/topics/sustainabledevelopmentgoals

SDG1 – No Poverty

	Value	Year	Rating	Trend
Poverty headcount ratio at $1.90/day (%)	0.2	2020	●	↑
Poverty headcount ratio at $3.20/day (%)	0.2	2020	●	↑
Poverty rate after taxes and transfers (%)	9.0	2017	●	↑

SDG2 – Zero Hunger

	Value	Year	Rating	Trend
Prevalence of undernourishment (%)	2.5	2017	◐	↑
Prevalence of stunting in children under 5 years of age (%)	* 2.6	2016	●	↑
Prevalence of wasting in children under 5 years of age (%)	* 0.7	2016	●	↑
Prevalence of obesity, BMI ≥ 30 (% of adult population)	25.3	2016	●	↓
Human Trophic Level (best 2–3 worst)	2.4	2017	●	↗
Cereal yield (tonnes per hectare of harvested land)	8.8	2017	●	↑
Sustainable Nitrogen Management Index (best 0–1.41 worst)	0.0	2015	●	↑
Yield gap closure (% of potential yield)	74.5	2015	◔	

SDG3 – Good Health and Well-Being

	Value	Year	Rating	Trend
Maternal mortality rate (per 100,000 live births)	5	2017	●	↑
Neonatal mortality rate (per 1,000 live births)	2.3	2018	●	↑
Mortality rate, under-5 (per 1,000 live births)	3.7	2018	●	↑
Incidence of tuberculosis (per 100,000 population)	7.0	2018	●	↑
New HIV infections (per 1,000 uninfected population)	0.1	2018	●	↑
Age-standardized death rate due to cardiovascular disease, cancer, diabetes, or chronic respiratory disease in adults aged 30–70 years (%)	10.3	2016	●	↑
Age-standardized death rate attributable to household air pollution and ambient air pollution (per 100,000 population)	12	2016	●	●
Traffic deaths (per 100,000 population)	4.1	2016	●	↑
Life expectancy at birth (years)	81.5	2016	●	↑
Adolescent fertility rate (births per 1,000 adolescent females aged 15 to 19)	7.5	2017	●	↑
Births attended by skilled health personnel (%)	99.7	2015	●	↑
Percentage of surviving infants who received 2 WHO-recommended vaccines (%)	92.0	2018	●	↑
Universal health coverage (UHC) index of service coverage (worst 0–100 best)	76.0	2017	●	↗
Subjective well-being (average ladder score, worst 0–10 best)	7.3	2019	●	↑
Gap in life expectancy at birth among regions (years)	0.1	2016	●	↑
Gap in self-reported health status by income (percentage points)	20.0	2017	●	↑
Daily smokers (% of population aged 15 and over)	17.0	2018	●	↑

SDG4 – Quality Education

	Value	Year	Rating	Trend
Net primary enrollment rate (%)	* 100.0	2017	●	↑
Lower secondary completion rate (%)	* 100.0	2017	●	↑
Literacy rate (% of population aged 15 to 24)	NA	NA	●	●
Participation rate in pre-primary organized learning (% of children aged 4 to 6)	99.9	2017	●	↑
Tertiary educational attainment (% of population aged 25 to 34)	56.2	2018	●	↑
PISA score (worst 0–600 best)	504.7	2018	●	↑
Variation in science performance explained by socio-economic status (%)	11.1	2018	◔	↑
Underachievers in science (% of 15-year-olds)	17.0	2018	●	↓
Resilient students in science (% of 15-year-olds)	34.0	2018	◔	↑

SDG5 – Gender Equality

	Value	Year	Rating	Trend
Demand for family planning satisfied by modern methods (% of females aged 15 to 49 who are married or in unions)	* 80.2	2017	●	↑
Ratio of female-to-male mean years of education received (%)	103.3	2018	●	↑
Ratio of female-to-male labor force participation rate (%)	81.2	2019	●	↑
Seats held by women in national parliament (%)	22.5	2020	●	↗
Gender wage gap (% of male median wage)	10.6	2014	●	●
Gender gap in time spent doing unpaid work (minutes/day)	165.5	2005	●	●

SDG6 – Clean Water and Sanitation

	Value	Year	Rating	Trend
Population using at least basic drinking water services (%)	97.4	2017	◔	●
Population using at least basic sanitation services (%)	91.2	2017	◔	●
Freshwater withdrawal (% of available freshwater resources)	3.6	2010	●	●
Anthropogenic wastewater that receives treatment (%)	89.7	2018	●	●
Scarce water consumption embodied in imports (m³/capita)	39.3	2013	●	↗
Population using safely managed water services (%)	97.3	2017	●	↑
Population using safely managed sanitation services (%)	82.4	2017	◔	↑

SDG7 – Affordable and Clean Energy

	Value	Year	Rating	Trend
Population with access to electricity (%)	100.0	2017	●	↑
Population with access to clean fuels and technology for cooking (%)	100.0	2016	●	↑
CO₂ emissions from fuel combustion for electricity and heating per total electricity output (MtCO₂/TWh)	1.2	2017	●	↑
Share of renewable energy in total primary energy supply (%)	10.3	2018	●	↗

SDG8 – Decent Work and Economic Growth

	Value	Year	Rating	Trend
Adjusted GDP growth (%)	3.3	2018	●	●
Victims of modern slavery (per 1,000 population)	1.7	2018	●	●
Adults with an account at a bank or other financial institution or with a mobile-money-service provider (% of population aged 15 or over)	95.3	2017	●	↑
Fatal work-related accidents embodied in imports (per 100,000 population)	1.7	2010	◔	↑
Employment-to-population ratio (%)	69.6	2019	●	↑
Youth not in employment, education or training (NEET) (% of population aged 15 to 29)	11.7	2018	◔	↑

SDG9 – Industry, Innovation and Infrastructure

	Value	Year	Rating	Trend
Population using the internet (%)	84.5	2018	●	↑
Mobile broadband subscriptions (per 100 population)	103.8	2018	●	↑
Logistics Performance Index: Quality of trade and transport-related infrastructure (worst 1–5 best)	3.3	2018	●	↑
The Times Higher Education Universities Ranking: Average score of top 3 universities (worst 0–100 best)	53.4	2020	●	●
Scientific and technical journal articles (per 1,000 population)	1.5	2018	●	↑
Expenditure on research and development (% of GDP)	1.0	2017	●	↓
Researchers (per 1,000 employed population)	11.6	2018	●	↑
Triadic patent families filed (per million population)	21.8	2017	●	↑
Gap in internet access by income (percentage points)	25.4	2018	●	●
Women in science and engineering (% of tertiary graduates in science and engineering)	23.4	2015	●	●

SDG10 – Reduced Inequalities

	Value	Year	Rating	Trend
Gini coefficient adjusted for top income	33.1	2015	◔	↑
Palma ratio	1.1	2017	◔	↑
Elderly poverty rate (% of population aged 66 or over)	11.4	2017	◔	↓

SDG11 – Sustainable Cities and Communities

	Value	Year	Rating	Trend
Annual mean concentration of particulate matter of less than 2.5 microns in diameter (PM2.5) (µg/m³)	8.2	2017	●	↑
Access to improved water source, piped (% of urban population)	97.0	2017	◔	→
Satisfaction with public transport (%)	60.6	2019	◔	→
Population with rent overburden (%)	6.9	2017	●	↑

SDG12 – Responsible Consumption and Production

	Value	Year	Rating	Trend
Electronic waste (kg/capita)	19.9	2016	●	●
Production-based SO₂ emissions (kg/capita)	103.0	2012	●	●
SO₂ emissions embodied in imports (kg/capita)	19.5	2012	●	●
Production-based nitrogen emissions (kg/capita)	57.0	2010	●	●
Nitrogen emissions embodied in imports (kg/capita)	19.8	2010	●	●
Non-recycled municipal solid waste (kg/capita/day)	0.9	2017	●	●

SDG13 – Climate Action

	Value	Year	Rating	Trend
Energy-related CO₂ emissions (tCO₂/capita)	7.6	2017	●	↓
CO₂ emissions embodied in imports (tCO₂/capita)	2.8	2015	●	→
CO₂ emissions embodied in fossil fuel exports (kg/capita)	10.1	2018	●	●
Effective carbon rate (EUR/tCO₂)	21.8	2016	●	●

SDG14 – Life Below Water

	Value	Year	Rating	Trend
Mean area that is protected in marine sites important to biodiversity (%)	84.5	2018	●	↑
Ocean Health Index: Clean Waters score (worst 0–100 best)	61.3	2019	●	→
Fish caught from overexploited or collapsed stocks (% of total catch)	21.4	2014	●	↑
Fish caught by trawling (%)	85.9	2014	●	→
Marine biodiversity threats embodied in imports (per million population)	0.1	2018	●	●

SDG15 – Life on Land

	Value	Year	Rating	Trend
Mean area that is protected in terrestrial sites important to biodiversity (%)	87.7	2018	●	↑
Mean area that is protected in freshwater sites important to biodiversity (%)	97.7	2018	●	↑
Red List Index of species survival (worst 0–1 best)	0.9	2019	●	↑
Permanent deforestation (% of forest area, 5-year average)	0.0	2018	●	●
Terrestrial and freshwater biodiversity threats embodied in imports (per million population)	1.7	2018	●	●

SDG16 – Peace, Justice and Strong Institutions

	Value	Year	Rating	Trend
Homicides (per 100,000 population)	0.9	2017	●	↑
Unsentenced detainees (% of prison population)	18.7	2018	●	↑
Percentage of population who feel safe walking alone at night in the city or area where they live (%)	75.9	2019	●	↑
Property Rights (worst 1–7 best)	5.7	2019	●	●
Birth registrations with civil authority (% of children under age 5)	100.0	2018	●	●
Corruption Perception Index (worst 0–100 best)	74.0	2019	●	↑
Children involved in child labor (% of population aged 5 to 14)	* 0.0	2016	●	●
Exports of major conventional weapons (TIV constant million USD per 100,000 population)	* 0.0	2019	●	●
Press Freedom Index (best 0–100 worst)	15.0	2019	●	↑
Persons held in prison (per 100,000 population)	78.5	2017	●	↑

SDG17 – Partnerships for the Goals

	Value	Year	Rating	Trend
Government spending on health and education (% of GDP)	9.0	2016	◔	↓
For high-income and all OECD DAC countries: International concessional public finance, including official development assistance (% of GNI)	0.3	2017	●	↓
Other countries: Government revenue excluding grants (% of GDP)	NA	NA	●	●
Corporate Tax Haven Score (best 0–100 worst)	75.7	2019	●	●
Financial Secrecy Score (best 0–100 worst)	48.2	2020	●	●
Shifted profits of multinationals (US$ billion)	-117.1	2016	●	●

* Imputed data point

5. Country Profiles

▼ OVERALL PERFORMANCE

Index score

74.6

Regional average score

77.3

SDG Global rank 40 (OF 166)

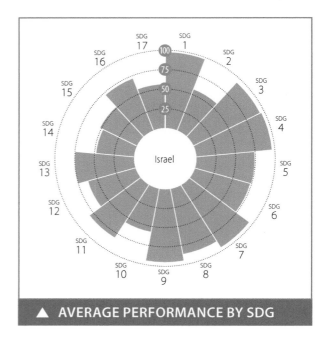

▲ AVERAGE PERFORMANCE BY SDG

▼ SPILLOVER INDEX

100 (best) to 0 (worst)

▼ CURRENT ASSESSMENT – SDG DASHBOARD

■ Major challenges ■ Significant challenges ■ Challenges remain ■ SDG achieved ■ Information unavailable

▼ SDG TRENDS

⬇ Decreasing ➡ Stagnating ↗ Moderately improving ⬆ On track or maintaining SDG achievement ● Information unavailable

Notes: The full title of Goal 2 "Zero Hunger" is "End hunger, achieve food security and improved nutrition and promote sustainable agriculture".
The full title of each SDG is available here: https://sustainabledevelopment.un.org/topics/sustainabledevelopmentgoals

SDG1 – No Poverty

	Value	Year	Rating	Trend
Poverty headcount ratio at $1.90/day (%)	0.2	2020	●	↑
Poverty headcount ratio at $3.20/day (%)	0.6	2020	●	↑
Poverty rate after taxes and transfers (%)	16.9	2018	●	↗

SDG2 – Zero Hunger

	Value	Year	Rating	Trend
Prevalence of undernourishment (%)	2.5	2017	●	↑
Prevalence of stunting in children under 5 years of age (%)	* 2.6	2016	●	↑
Prevalence of wasting in children under 5 years of age (%)	* 0.7	2016	●	↑
Prevalence of obesity, BMI ≥ 30 (% of adult population)	26.1	2016	●	↓
Human Trophic Level (best 2–3 worst)	2.4	2017	●	↓
Cereal yield (tonnes per hectare of harvested land)	3.6	2017	●	↑
Sustainable Nitrogen Management Index (best 0–1.41 worst)	0.9	2015	●	→
Yield gap closure (% of potential yield)	NA	NA	●	●

SDG3 – Good Health and Well-Being

	Value	Year	Rating	Trend
Maternal mortality rate (per 100,000 live births)	3	2017	●	↑
Neonatal mortality rate (per 1,000 live births)	1.9	2018	●	↑
Mortality rate, under-5 (per 1,000 live births)	3.7	2018	●	↑
Incidence of tuberculosis (per 100,000 population)	4.0	2018	●	↑
New HIV infections (per 1,000 uninfected population)	0.1	2018	●	↑
Age-standardized death rate due to cardiovascular disease, cancer, diabetes, or chronic respiratory disease in adults aged 30–70 years (%)	9.6	2016	●	↑
Age-standardized death rate attributable to household air pollution and ambient air pollution (per 100,000 population)	15	2016	●	●
Traffic deaths (per 100,000 population)	4.2	2016	●	↑
Life expectancy at birth (years)	82.3	2016	●	↑
Adolescent fertility rate (births per 1,000 adolescent females aged 15 to 19)	9.6	2017	●	↑
Births attended by skilled health personnel (%)	NA	NA	●	●
Percentage of surviving infants who received 2 WHO-recommended vaccines (%)	98.0	2018	●	↑
Universal health coverage (UHC) index of service coverage (worst 0–100 best)	82.0	2017	●	↑
Subjective well-being (average ladder score, worst 0–10 best)	6.9	2018	●	↑
Gap in life expectancy at birth among regions (years)	2.7	2016	●	●
Gap in self-reported health status by income (percentage points)	8.7	2017	●	↑
Daily smokers (% of population aged 15 and over)	16.9	2017	●	↑

SDG4 – Quality Education

	Value	Year	Rating	Trend
Net primary enrollment rate (%)	* 97.0	2017	●	↓
Lower secondary completion rate (%)	* 97.0	2017	●	↑
Literacy rate (% of population aged 15 to 24)	NA	NA	●	●
Participation rate in pre-primary organized learning (% of children aged 4 to 6)	99.1	2017	●	↑
Tertiary educational attainment (% of population aged 25 to 34)	48.0	2017	●	↑
PISA score (worst 0–600 best)	465.0	2018	●	↓
Variation in science performance explained by socio-economic status (%)	13.6	2018	●	↓
Underachievers in science (% of 15-year-olds)	33.1	2018	●	↓
Resilient students in science (% of 15-year-olds)	16.0	2018	●	→

SDG5 – Gender Equality

	Value	Year	Rating	Trend
Demand for family planning satisfied by modern methods (% of females aged 15 to 49 who are married or in unions)	* 71.1	2017	●	→
Ratio of female-to-male mean years of education received (%)	100.0	2018	●	↑
Ratio of female-to-male labor force participation rate (%)	85.8	2019	●	↑
Seats held by women in national parliament (%)	25.0	2020	●	↓
Gender wage gap (% of male median wage)	21.8	2017	●	↓
Gender gap in time spent doing unpaid work (minutes/day)	NA	NA	●	●

SDG6 – Clean Water and Sanitation

	Value	Year	Rating	Trend
Population using at least basic drinking water services (%)	100.0	2017	●	●
Population using at least basic sanitation services (%)	100.0	2017	●	●
Freshwater withdrawal (% of available freshwater resources)	122.4	2005	●	●
Anthropogenic wastewater that receives treatment (%)	81.7	2018	●	●
Scarce water consumption embodied in imports (m³/capita)	17.8	2013	●	↑
Population using safely managed water services (%)	99.4	2017	●	↑
Population using safely managed sanitation services (%)	93.7	2017	●	↑

SDG7 – Affordable and Clean Energy

	Value	Year	Rating	Trend
Population with access to electricity (%)	100.0	2017	●	↑
Population with access to clean fuels and technology for cooking (%)	100.0	2016	●	↑
CO_2 emissions from fuel combustion for electricity and heating per total electricity output (MtCO₂/TWh)	1.0	2017	●	↑
Share of renewable energy in total primary energy supply (%)	2.6	2018	●	→

SDG8 – Decent Work and Economic Growth

	Value	Year	Rating	Trend
Adjusted GDP growth (%)	-0.1	2018	●	●
Victims of modern slavery (per 1,000 population)	3.9	2018	●	●
Adults with an account at a bank or other financial institution or with a mobile-money-service provider (% of population aged 15 or over)	92.8	2017	●	↑
Fatal work-related accidents embodied in imports (per 100,000 population)	0.7	2010	●	↑
Employment-to-population ratio (%)	68.9	2019	●	↑
Youth not in employment, education or training (NEET) (% of population aged 15 to 29)	13.3	2018	●	↗

SDG9 – Industry, Innovation and Infrastructure

	Value	Year	Rating	Trend
Population using the internet (%)	83.7	2018	●	↑
Mobile broadband subscriptions (per 100 population)	113.3	2018	●	↑
Logistics Performance Index: Quality of trade and transport-related infrastructure (worst 1–5 best)	3.3	2018	●	↑
The Times Higher Education Universities Ranking: Average score of top 3 universities (worst 0–100 best)	48.9	2020	●	●
Scientific and technical journal articles (per 1,000 population)	1.5	2018	●	↑
Expenditure on research and development (% of GDP)	4.6	2017	●	↑
Researchers (per 1,000 employed population)	NA	NA	●	●
Triadic patent families filed (per million population)	59.4	2017	●	↑
Gap in internet access by income (percentage points)	39.5	2017	●	↗
Women in science and engineering (% of tertiary graduates in science and engineering)	NA	NA	●	●

SDG10 – Reduced Inequalities

	Value	Year	Rating	Trend
Gini coefficient adjusted for top income	43.2	2016	●	↗
Palma ratio	1.4	2018	●	↗
Elderly poverty rate (% of population aged 66 or over)	20.6	2018	●	↗

SDG11 – Sustainable Cities and Communities

	Value	Year	Rating	Trend
Annual mean concentration of particulate matter of less than 2.5 microns in diameter (PM2.5) (µg/m³)	21.4	2017	●	→
Access to improved water source, piped (% of urban population)	99.0	2017	●	↑
Satisfaction with public transport (%)	57.4	2018	●	↓
Population with rent overburden (%)	NA	NA	●	●

SDG12 – Responsible Consumption and Production

	Value	Year	Rating	Trend
Electronic waste (kg/capita)	14.1	2016	●	●
Production-based SO_2 emissions (kg/capita)	113.8	2012	●	●
SO_2 emissions embodied in imports (kg/capita)	8.0	2012	●	●
Production-based nitrogen emissions (kg/capita)	60.5	2010	●	●
Nitrogen emissions embodied in imports (kg/capita)	6.2	2010	●	●
Non-recycled municipal solid waste (kg/capita/day)	1.4	2018	●	●

SDG13 – Climate Action

	Value	Year	Rating	Trend
Energy-related CO_2 emissions (tCO₂/capita)	8.2	2017	●	→
CO_2 emissions embodied in imports (tCO₂/capita)	1.4	2015	●	→
CO_2 emissions embodied in fossil fuel exports (kg/capita)	17.5	2018	●	→
Effective carbon rate (EUR/tCO₂)	28.8	2016	●	●

SDG14 – Life Below Water

	Value	Year	Rating	Trend
Mean area that is protected in marine sites important to biodiversity (%)	NA	NA	●	●
Ocean Health Index: Clean Waters score (worst 0–100 best)	30.2	2019	●	→
Fish caught from overexploited or collapsed stocks (% of total catch)	NA	NA	●	●
Fish caught by trawling (%)	52.3	2014	●	↗
Marine biodiversity threats embodied in imports (per million population)	0.0	2018	●	●

SDG15 – Life on Land

	Value	Year	Rating	Trend
Mean area that is protected in terrestrial sites important to biodiversity (%)	20.9	2018	●	→
Mean area that is protected in freshwater sites important to biodiversity (%)	26.1	2018	●	→
Red List Index of species survival (worst 0–1 best)	0.8	2019	●	→
Permanent deforestation (% of forest area, 5-year average)	0.0	2018	●	●
Terrestrial and freshwater biodiversity threats embodied in imports (per million population)	2.1	2018	●	●

SDG16 – Peace, Justice and Strong Institutions

	Value	Year	Rating	Trend
Homicides (per 100,000 population)	1.4	2015	●	●
Unsentenced detainees (% of prison population)	27.0	2015	●	●
Percentage of population who feel safe walking alone at night in the city or area where they live (%)	75.1	2018	●	↑
Property Rights (worst 1–7 best)	5.4	2019	●	●
Birth registrations with civil authority (% of children under age 5)	100.0	2018	●	●
Corruption Perception Index (worst 0–100 best)	60.0	2019	●	↑
Children involved in child labor (% of population aged 5 to 14)	* 0.0	2016	●	●
Exports of major conventional weapons (TIV constant million USD per 100,000 population)	10.2	2019	●	●
Press Freedom Index (best 0–100 worst)	30.8	2019	●	↑
Persons held in prison (per 100,000 population)	232.2	2017	●	↗

SDG17 – Partnerships for the Goals

	Value	Year	Rating	Trend
Government spending on health and education (% of GDP)	10.4	2016	●	↑
For high-income and all OECD DAC countries: International concessional public finance, including official development assistance (% of GNI)	0.1	2017	●	→
Other countries: Government revenue excluding grants (% of GDP)	NA	NA	●	●
Corporate Tax Haven Score (best 0–100 worst)	* 0.0	2019	●	●
Financial Secrecy Score (best 0–100 worst)	58.7	2020	●	●
Shifted profits of multinationals (US$ billion)	2.4	2016	●	●

* Imputed data point

5. Country Profiles

▼ OVERALL PERFORMANCE

Index score

77.0

Regional average score

77.3

SDG Global rank **30** (OF 166)

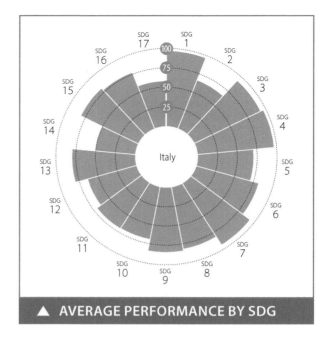

▲ AVERAGE PERFORMANCE BY SDG

▼ SPILLOVER INDEX

100 (best) to 0 (worst)

▼ CURRENT ASSESSMENT – SDG DASHBOARD

■ Major challenges   ■ Significant challenges   ■ Challenges remain   ■ SDG achieved   ■ Information unavailable

▼ SDG TRENDS

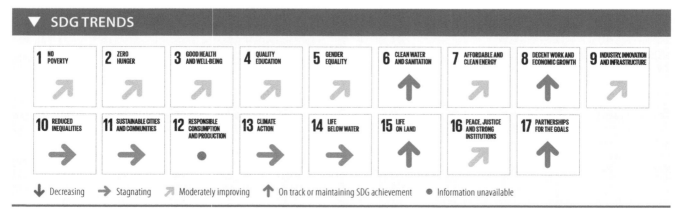

↓ Decreasing   → Stagnating   ↗ Moderately improving   ↑ On track or maintaining SDG achievement   ● Information unavailable

Notes: The full title of Goal 2 "Zero Hunger" is "End hunger, achieve food security and improved nutrition and promote sustainable agriculture".
The full title of each SDG is available here: https://sustainabledevelopment.un.org/topics/sustainabledevelopmentgoals

SDG1 – No Poverty

Indicator	Value	Year	Rating	Trend
Poverty headcount ratio at $1.90/day (%)	1.4	2020	●	↑
Poverty headcount ratio at $3.20/day (%)	1.8	2020	●	↑
Poverty rate after taxes and transfers (%)	13.9	2017	●	↓

SDG2 – Zero Hunger

Indicator	Value	Year	Rating	Trend
Prevalence of undernourishment (%)	2.5	2017	●	↑
Prevalence of stunting in children under 5 years of age (%)	* 2.6	2016	●	↑
Prevalence of wasting in children under 5 years of age (%)	* 0.7	2016	●	↑
Prevalence of obesity, BMI ≥ 30 (% of adult population)	19.9	2016	●	↓
Human Trophic Level (best 2–3 worst)	2.4	2017	●	→
Cereal yield (tonnes per hectare of harvested land)	5.2	2017	●	↑
Sustainable Nitrogen Management Index (best 0–1.41 worst)	0.6	2015	●	→
Yield gap closure (% of potential yield)	58.9	2015	●	●

SDG3 – Good Health and Well-Being

Indicator	Value	Year	Rating	Trend
Maternal mortality rate (per 100,000 live births)	2	2017	●	↑
Neonatal mortality rate (per 1,000 live births)	2.0	2018	●	↑
Mortality rate, under-5 (per 1,000 live births)	3.0	2018	●	↑
Incidence of tuberculosis (per 100,000 population)	7.0	2018	●	↑
New HIV infections (per 1,000 uninfected population)	0.1	2018	●	↑
Age-standardized death rate due to cardiovascular disease, cancer, diabetes, or chronic respiratory disease in adults aged 30–70 years (%)	9.5	2016	●	↑
Age-standardized death rate attributable to household air pollution and ambient air pollution (per 100,000 population)	15	2016	●	●
Traffic deaths (per 100,000 population)	5.6	2016	●	↑
Life expectancy at birth (years)	82.8	2016	●	↑
Adolescent fertility rate (births per 1,000 adolescent females aged 15 to 19)	5.2	2017	●	↑
Births attended by skilled health personnel (%)	99.9	2014	●	●
Percentage of surviving infants who received 2 WHO-recommended vaccines (%)	93.0	2018	●	↑
Universal health coverage (UHC) index of service coverage (worst 0–100 best)	82.0	2017	●	↑
Subjective well-being (average ladder score, worst 0–10 best)	6.4	2019	●	↑
Gap in life expectancy at birth among regions (years)	2.6	2016	●	↑
Gap in self-reported health status by income (percentage points)	7.6	2017	●	↑
Daily smokers (% of population aged 15 and over)	19.9	2017	●	→

SDG4 – Quality Education

Indicator	Value	Year	Rating	Trend
Net primary enrollment rate (%)	* 97.6	2017	●	↑
Lower secondary completion rate (%)	* 97.6	2017	●	↑
Literacy rate (% of population aged 15 to 24)	99.9	2018	●	●
Participation rate in pre-primary organized learning (% of children aged 4 to 6)	93.9	2017	●	↑
Tertiary educational attainment (% of population aged 25 to 34)	27.7	2018	●	↗
PISA score (worst 0–600 best)	477.0	2018	●	↓
Variation in science performance explained by socio-economic status (%)	8.5	2018	●	↑
Underachievers in science (% of 15-year-olds)	25.9	2018	●	↓
Resilient students in science (% of 15-year-olds)	27.4	2018	●	→

SDG5 – Gender Equality

Indicator	Value	Year	Rating	Trend
Demand for family planning satisfied by modern methods (% of females aged 15 to 49 who are married or in unions)	* 68.2	2017	●	↗
Ratio of female-to-male mean years of education received (%)	95.2	2018	●	↓
Ratio of female-to-male labor force participation rate (%)	68.7	2019	●	↑
Seats held by women in national parliament (%)	35.7	2020	●	↑
Gender wage gap (% of male median wage)	5.6	2016	●	↑
Gender gap in time spent doing unpaid work (minutes/day)	175.6	2014	●	●

SDG6 – Clean Water and Sanitation

Indicator	Value	Year	Rating	Trend
Population using at least basic drinking water services (%)	99.4	2017	●	●
Population using at least basic sanitation services (%)	98.8	2017	●	●
Freshwater withdrawal (% of available freshwater resources)	30.1	2015	●	●
Anthropogenic wastewater that receives treatment (%)	58.8	2018	●	●
Scarce water consumption embodied in imports (m³/capita)	25.8	2013	●	↑
Population using safely managed water services (%)	95.0	2017	●	↑
Population using safely managed sanitation services (%)	96.2	2017	●	↑

SDG7 – Affordable and Clean Energy

Indicator	Value	Year	Rating	Trend
Population with access to electricity (%)	100.0	2017	●	↑
Population with access to clean fuels and technology for cooking (%)	100.0	2016	●	↑
CO_2 emissions from fuel combustion for electricity and heating per total electricity output (MtCO2/TWh)	1.1	2017	●	↑
Share of renewable energy in total primary energy supply (%)	17.9	2018	●	↓

SDG8 – Decent Work and Economic Growth

Indicator	Value	Year	Rating	Trend
Adjusted GDP growth (%)	0.2	2018	●	●
Victims of modern slavery (per 1,000 population)	2.4	2018	●	●
Adults with an account at a bank or other financial institution or with a mobile-money-service provider (% of population aged 15 or over)	93.8	2017	●	↑
Fatal work-related accidents embodied in imports (per 100,000 population)	1.0	2010	●	↑
Employment-to-population ratio (%)	59.1	2019	●	↑
Youth not in employment, education or training (NEET) (% of population aged 15 to 29)	23.9	2018	●	↑

SDG9 – Industry, Innovation and Infrastructure

Indicator	Value	Year	Rating	Trend
Population using the internet (%)	74.4	2018	●	↑
Mobile broadband subscriptions (per 100 population)	89.9	2018	●	↑
Logistics Performance Index: Quality of trade and transport-related infrastructure (worst 1–5 best)	3.9	2018	●	↑
The Times Higher Education Universities Ranking: Average score of top 3 universities (worst 0–100 best)	56.8	2020	●	●
Scientific and technical journal articles (per 1,000 population)	1.2	2018	●	↑
Expenditure on research and development (% of GDP)	1.4	2017	●	↗
Researchers (per 1,000 employed population)	5.5	2018	●	↗
Triadic patent families filed (per million population)	12.8	2017	●	↓
Gap in internet access by income (percentage points)	47.4	2013	●	●
Women in science and engineering (% of tertiary graduates in science and engineering)	NA	NA	●	●

SDG10 – Reduced Inequalities

Indicator	Value	Year	Rating	Trend
Gini coefficient adjusted for top income	38.8	2015	●	→
Palma ratio	1.3	2017	●	↓
Elderly poverty rate (% of population aged 66 or over)	9.7	2017	●	↓

SDG11 – Sustainable Cities and Communities

Indicator	Value	Year	Rating	Trend
Annual mean concentration of particulate matter of less than 2.5 microns in diameter (PM2.5) (µg/m³)	16.8	2017	●	↗
Access to improved water source, piped (% of urban population)	97.5	2016	●	→
Satisfaction with public transport (%)	34.4	2019	●	↓
Population with rent overburden (%)	9.1	2017	●	↗

SDG12 – Responsible Consumption and Production

Indicator	Value	Year	Rating	Trend
Electronic waste (kg/capita)	18.9	2016	●	●
Production-based SO_2 emissions (kg/capita)	38.7	2012	●	●
SO_2 emissions embodied in imports (kg/capita)	8.2	2012	●	●
Production-based nitrogen emissions (kg/capita)	37.3	2010	●	●
Nitrogen emissions embodied in imports (kg/capita)	10.1	2010	●	●
Non-recycled municipal solid waste (kg/capita/day)	0.6	2018	●	●

SDG13 – Climate Action

Indicator	Value	Year	Rating	Trend
Energy-related CO_2 emissions (tCO2/capita)	5.4	2017	●	↓
CO_2 emissions embodied in imports (tCO2/capita)	1.3	2015	●	→
CO_2 emissions embodied in fossil fuel exports (kg/capita)	8.2	2018	●	●
Effective carbon rate (EUR/tCO2)	20.5	2016	●	●

SDG14 – Life Below Water

Indicator	Value	Year	Rating	Trend
Mean area that is protected in marine sites important to biodiversity (%)	73.8	2018	●	↑
Ocean Health Index: Clean Waters score (worst 0–100 best)	50.0	2019	●	↓
Fish caught from overexploited or collapsed stocks (% of total catch)	75.1	2014	●	↓
Fish caught by trawling (%)	51.8	2014	●	↗
Marine biodiversity threats embodied in imports (per million population)	0.3	2018	●	●

SDG15 – Life on Land

Indicator	Value	Year	Rating	Trend
Mean area that is protected in terrestrial sites important to biodiversity (%)	77.9	2018	●	↑
Mean area that is protected in freshwater sites important to biodiversity (%)	84.7	2018	●	↑
Red List Index of species survival (worst 0–1 best)	0.9	2019	●	↑
Permanent deforestation (% of forest area, 5-year average)	0.0	2018	●	●
Terrestrial and freshwater biodiversity threats embodied in imports (per million population)	3.5	2018	●	●

SDG16 – Peace, Justice and Strong Institutions

Indicator	Value	Year	Rating	Trend
Homicides (per 100,000 population)	0.7	2016	●	↑
Unsentenced detainees (% of prison population)	18.1	2018	●	↑
Percentage of population who feel safe walking alone at night in the city or area where they live (%)	68.3	2019	●	↑
Property Rights (worst 1–7 best)	4.4	2019	●	●
Birth registrations with civil authority (% of children under age 5)	100.0	2018	●	●
Corruption Perception Index (worst 0–100 best)	53.0	2019	●	↑
Children involved in child labor (% of population aged 5 to 14)	* 0.0	2016	●	●
Exports of major conventional weapons (TIV constant million USD per 100,000 population)	1.0	2019	●	●
Press Freedom Index (best 0–100 worst)	25.0	2019	●	↑
Persons held in prison (per 100,000 population)	100.5	2017	●	↓

SDG17 – Partnerships for the Goals

Indicator	Value	Year	Rating	Trend
Government spending on health and education (% of GDP)	10.5	2016	●	↑
For high-income and all OECD DAC countries: International concessional public finance, including official development assistance (% of GNI)	0.3	2017	●	↑
Other countries: Government revenue excluding grants (% of GDP)	NA	NA	●	●
Corporate Tax Haven Score (best 0–100 worst)	50.5	2019	●	●
Financial Secrecy Score (best 0–100 worst)	50.4	2020	●	●
Shifted profits of multinationals (US$ billion)	24.0	2016	●	●

* Imputed data point

5. Country Profiles

▼ OVERALL PERFORMANCE

Index score

68.7

Regional average score

70.4

SDG Global rank 84 (OF 166)

▼ SPILLOVER INDEX

100 (best) to 0 (worst)

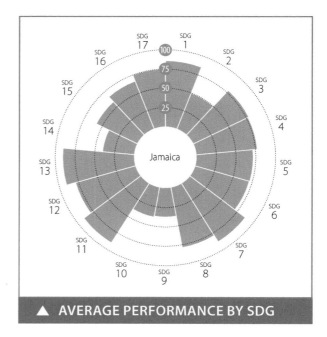

▲ AVERAGE PERFORMANCE BY SDG

▼ CURRENT ASSESSMENT – SDG DASHBOARD

■ Major challenges ■ Significant challenges ■ Challenges remain ■ SDG achieved ■ Information unavailable

▼ SDG TRENDS

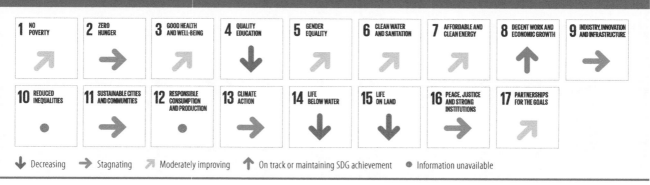

↓ Decreasing → Stagnating ↗ Moderately improving ↑ On track or maintaining SDG achievement ● Information unavailable

Notes: The full title of Goal 2 "Zero Hunger" is "End hunger, achieve food security and improved nutrition and promote sustainable agriculture".
The full title of each SDG is available here: https://sustainabledevelopment.un.org/topics/sustainabledevelopmentgoals

SDG1 – No Poverty

	Value	Year	Rating	Trend
Poverty headcount ratio at $1.90/day (%)	1.0	2020	●	↑
Poverty headcount ratio at $3.20/day (%)	13.7	2020	●	→

SDG2 – Zero Hunger

	Value	Year	Rating	Trend
Prevalence of undernourishment (%)	8.0	2017	◐	↑
Prevalence of stunting in children under 5 years of age (%)	6.2	2014	●	↑
Prevalence of wasting in children under 5 years of age (%)	3.6	2014	●	↑
Prevalence of obesity, BMI ≥ 30 (% of adult population)	24.7	2016	●	↓
Human Trophic Level (best 2–3 worst)	2.3	2017	●	→
Cereal yield (tonnes per hectare of harvested land)	1.2	2017	●	→
Sustainable Nitrogen Management Index (best 0–1.41 worst)	1.1	2015	●	→

SDG3 – Good Health and Well-Being

	Value	Year	Rating	Trend
Maternal mortality rate (per 100,000 live births)	80	2017	◐	→
Neonatal mortality rate (per 1,000 live births)	10.2	2018	●	↑
Mortality rate, under-5 (per 1,000 live births)	14.4	2018	●	↑
Incidence of tuberculosis (per 100,000 population)	2.9	2018	●	↑
New HIV infections (per 1,000 uninfected population)	NA	NA	●	●
Age-standardized death rate due to cardiovascular disease, cancer, diabetes, or chronic respiratory disease in adults aged 30–70 years (%)	14.7	2016	●	↑
Age-standardized death rate attributable to household air pollution and ambient air pollution (per 100,000 population)	25	2016	●	●
Traffic deaths (per 100,000 population)	13.6	2016	●	↓
Life expectancy at birth (years)	76.0	2016	●	↗
Adolescent fertility rate (births per 1,000 adolescent females aged 15 to 19)	52.8	2017	●	↗
Births attended by skilled health personnel (%)	99.1	2011	●	●
Percentage of surviving infants who received 2 WHO-recommended vaccines (%)	89	2018	●	↓
Universal health coverage (UHC) index of service coverage (worst 0–100 best)	65.0	2017	●	↗
Subjective well-being (average ladder score, worst 0–10 best)	5.9	2017	●	●

SDG4 – Quality Education

	Value	Year	Rating	Trend
Net primary enrollment rate (%)	81.0	2018	●	↓
Lower secondary completion rate (%)	82.4	2018	●	↓
Literacy rate (% of population aged 15 to 24)	96.3	2014	●	●

SDG5 – Gender Equality

	Value	Year	Rating	Trend
Demand for family planning satisfied by modern methods (% of females aged 15 to 49 who are married or in unions)	79.2	2009	◐	↑
Ratio of female-to-male mean years of education received (%)	105.3	2018	●	↑
Ratio of female-to-male labor force participation rate (%)	82.0	2019	●	↑
Seats held by women in national parliament (%)	17.5	2020	●	↗

SDG6 – Clean Water and Sanitation

	Value	Year	Rating	Trend
Population using at least basic drinking water services (%)	90.6	2017	◐	→
Population using at least basic sanitation services (%)	87.3	2017	◐	→
Freshwater withdrawal (% of available freshwater resources)	26.9	2015	◐	●
Anthropogenic wastewater that receives treatment (%)	3.0	2018	●	●
Scarce water consumption embodied in imports (m³/capita)	3.7	2013	●	↑

SDG7 – Affordable and Clean Energy

	Value	Year	Rating	Trend
Population with access to electricity (%)	99.5	2017	●	↑
Population with access to clean fuels and technology for cooking (%)	90.5	2016	●	↑
CO_2 emissions from fuel combustion for electricity and heating per total electricity output (MtCO₂/TWh)	1.7	2017	●	↗

SDG8 – Decent Work and Economic Growth

	Value	Year	Rating	Trend
Adjusted GDP growth (%)	-3.5	2018	●	●
Victims of modern slavery (per 1,000 population)	2.6	2018	●	●
Adults with an account at a bank or other financial institution or with a mobile-money-service provider (% of population aged 15 or over)	78.5	2014	◐	
Unemployment rate (% of total labor force)	8.0	2019	●	↑
Fatal work-related accidents embodied in imports (per 100,000 population)	0.2	2010	●	↑

SDG9 – Industry, Innovation and Infrastructure

	Value	Year	Rating	Trend
Population using the internet (%)	55.1	2017	●	↑
Mobile broadband subscriptions (per 100 population)	51.2	2018	●	↓
Logistics Performance Index: Quality of trade and transport-related infrastructure (worst 1–5 best)	2.3	2018	●	↓
The Times Higher Education Universities Ranking: Average score of top 3 universities (worst 0–100 best)	37.0	2020	●	●
Scientific and technical journal articles (per 1,000 population)	0.1	2018	◐	→
Expenditure on research and development (% of GDP)	0.1	2002	●	●

SDG10 – Reduced Inequalities

	Value	Year	Rating	Trend
Gini coefficient adjusted for top income	49.6	2004	●	●

SDG11 – Sustainable Cities and Communities

	Value	Year	Rating	Trend
Annual mean concentration of particulate matter of less than 2.5 microns in diameter (PM2.5) (μg/m³)	13.4	2017	◐	↗
Access to improved water source, piped (% of urban population)	93.4	2017	◐	→
Satisfaction with public transport (%)	72.2	2017	●	●

SDG12 – Responsible Consumption and Production

	Value	Year	Rating	Trend
Municipal solid waste (kg/capita/day)	1.8	2016	●	●
Electronic waste (kg/capita)	5.9	2016	●	●
Production-based SO_2 emissions (kg/capita)	138.4	2012	●	●
SO_2 emissions embodied in imports (kg/capita)	3.4	2012	●	●
Production-based nitrogen emissions (kg/capita)	16.5	2010	●	●
Nitrogen emissions embodied in imports (kg/capita)	3.2	2010	●	●

SDG13 – Climate Action

	Value	Year	Rating	Trend
Energy-related CO_2 emissions (tCO₂/capita)	2.5	2017	◐	→
CO_2 emissions embodied in imports (tCO₂/capita)	0.6	2015	◐	→
CO_2 emissions embodied in fossil fuel exports (kg/capita)	0.0	2017	●	●

SDG14 – Life Below Water

	Value	Year	Rating	Trend
Mean area that is protected in marine sites important to biodiversity (%)	30.6	2018	◐	→
Ocean Health Index: Clean Waters score (worst 0–100 best)	44.7	2019	●	→
Fish caught from overexploited or collapsed stocks (% of total catch)	74.1	2014	●	↓
Fish caught by trawling (%)	NA	NA	●	●
Marine biodiversity threats embodied in imports (per million population)	0.2	2018	◐	●

SDG15 – Life on Land

	Value	Year	Rating	Trend
Mean area that is protected in terrestrial sites important to biodiversity (%)	20.4	2018	●	→
Mean area that is protected in freshwater sites important to biodiversity (%)	NA	NA	●	●
Red List Index of species survival (worst 0–1 best)	0.7	2019	●	↓
Permanent deforestation (% of forest area, 5-year average)	0.2	2018	◐	●
Terrestrial and freshwater biodiversity threats embodied in imports (per million population)	0.6	2018	●	●

SDG16 – Peace, Justice and Strong Institutions

	Value	Year	Rating	Trend
Homicides (per 100,000 population)	57.0	2017	●	↓
Unsentenced detainees (% of prison population)	29.3	2018	●	↑
Percentage of population who feel safe walking alone at night in the city or area where they live (%)	62.1	2017	◐	●
Property Rights (worst 1–7 best)	4.4	2019	●	●
Birth registrations with civil authority (% of children under age 5)	98.0	2018	●	●
Corruption Perception Index (worst 0–100 best)	43	2019	●	→
Children involved in child labor (% of population aged 5 to 14)	3.3	2016	●	●
Exports of major conventional weapons (TIV constant million USD per 100,000 population)	* 0.0	2019	●	●
Press Freedom Index (best 0–100 worst)	11.1	2019	●	↑

SDG17 – Partnerships for the Goals

	Value	Year	Rating	Trend
Government spending on health and education (% of GDP)	9.0	2016	◐	↓
For high-income and all OECD DAC countries: International concessional public finance, including official development assistance (% of GNI)	NA	NA	●	●
Other countries: Government revenue excluding grants (% of GDP)	29.3	2017	◐	↑
Corporate Tax Haven Score (best 0–100 worst)	* 0.0	2019	●	●

* Imputed data point

5. Country Profiles

▼ OVERALL PERFORMANCE

Index score	Regional average score
79.2	77.3

SDG Global rank   17 (OF 166)

▼ SPILLOVER INDEX

100 (best) to 0 (worst)

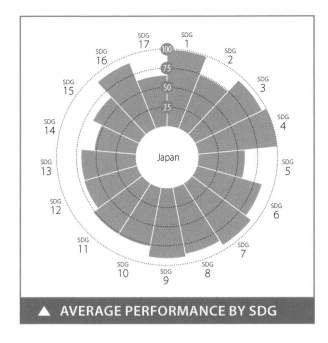

▲ AVERAGE PERFORMANCE BY SDG

▼ CURRENT ASSESSMENT – SDG DASHBOARD

■ Major challenges ■ Significant challenges ■ Challenges remain ■ SDG achieved ■ Information unavailable

▼ SDG TRENDS

↓ Decreasing → Stagnating ↗ Moderately improving ↑ On track or maintaining SDG achievement ● Information unavailable

Notes: The full title of Goal 2 "Zero Hunger" is "End hunger, achieve food security and improved nutrition and promote sustainable agriculture".
The full title of each SDG is available here: https://sustainabledevelopment.un.org/topics/sustainabledevelopmentgoals

JAPAN

SDG1 – No Poverty

Indicator	Value	Year	Rating	Trend
Poverty headcount ratio at $1.90/day (%)	0.5	2020	●	↑
Poverty headcount ratio at $3.20/day (%)	0.7	2020	●	↑
Poverty rate after taxes and transfers (%)	15.7	2015	●	→

SDG2 – Zero Hunger

Indicator	Value	Year	Rating	Trend
Prevalence of undernourishment (%)	2.5	2017	●	↑
Prevalence of stunting in children under 5 years of age (%)	7.1	2010	●	↑
Prevalence of wasting in children under 5 years of age (%)	2.3	2010	●	↑
Prevalence of obesity, BMI ≥ 30 (% of adult population)	4.3	2016	●	↑
Human Trophic Level (best 2–3 worst)	2.4	2017	●	→
Cereal yield (tonnes per hectare of harvested land)	6.0	2017	●	↑
Sustainable Nitrogen Management Index (best 0–1.41 worst)	0.6	2015	●	↓
Yield gap closure (% of potential yield)	NA	NA	●	●

SDG3 – Good Health and Well-Being

Indicator	Value	Year	Rating	Trend
Maternal mortality rate (per 100,000 live births)	5	2017	●	↑
Neonatal mortality rate (per 1,000 live births)	0.9	2018	●	↑
Mortality rate, under-5 (per 1,000 live births)	2.5	2018	●	↑
Incidence of tuberculosis (per 100,000 population)	14.0	2018	◐	↑
New HIV infections (per 1,000 uninfected population)	0.0	2018	●	↑
Age-standardized death rate due to cardiovascular disease, cancer, diabetes, or chronic respiratory disease in adults aged 30–70 years (%)	8.4	2016	●	↑
Age-standardized death rate attributable to household air pollution and ambient air pollution (per 100,000 population)	12	2016	●	●
Traffic deaths (per 100,000 population)	4.1	2016	●	↑
Life expectancy at birth (years)	84.2	2016	●	↑
Adolescent fertility rate (births per 1,000 adolescent females aged 15 to 19)	3.8	2017	●	↑
Births attended by skilled health personnel (%)	99.9	2015	●	↑
Percentage of surviving infants who received 2 WHO-recommended vaccines (%)	97.0	2018	●	↑
Universal health coverage (UHC) index of service coverage (worst 0–100 best)	83.0	2017	●	↑
Subjective well-being (average ladder score, worst 0–10 best)	5.9	2019	◐	↗
Gap in life expectancy at birth among regions (years)	0.9	2016	●	●
Gap in self-reported health status by income (percentage points)	11.4	2016	●	↑
Daily smokers (% of population aged 15 and over)	17.7	2017	●	↑

SDG4 – Quality Education

Indicator	Value	Year	Rating	Trend
Net primary enrollment rate (%)	* 100.0	2017	●	↑
Lower secondary completion rate (%)	* 100.0	2017	●	↑
Literacy rate (% of population aged 15 to 24)	NA	NA	●	●
Participation rate in pre-primary organized learning (% of children aged 4 to 6)	* 91.0	2016	●	●
Tertiary educational attainment (% of population aged 25 to 34)	60.7	2018	●	↑
PISA score (worst 0–600 best)	520.0	2018	●	↑
Variation in science performance explained by socio-economic status (%)	7.7	2018	●	↑
Underachievers in science (% of 15-year-olds)	10.8	2018	●	↑
Resilient students in science (% of 15-year-olds)	50.2	2018	●	↑

SDG5 – Gender Equality

Indicator	Value	Year	Rating	Trend
Demand for family planning satisfied by modern methods (% of females aged 15 to 49 who are married or in unions)	* 60.1	2017	●	↓
Ratio of female-to-male mean years of education received (%)	103.2	2018	●	↑
Ratio of female-to-male labor force participation rate (%)	73.0	2019	●	↑
Seats held by women in national parliament (%)	9.9	2020	●	→
Gender wage gap (% of male median wage)	24.5	2017	●	→
Gender gap in time spent doing unpaid work (minutes/day)	183.5	2016	●	●

SDG6 – Clean Water and Sanitation

Indicator	Value	Year	Rating	Trend
Population using at least basic drinking water services (%)	99.0	2017	●	●
Population using at least basic sanitation services (%)	99.9	2017	●	●
Freshwater withdrawal (% of available freshwater resources)	37.3	2010	◐	●
Anthropogenic wastewater that receives treatment (%)	75.3	2018	●	●
Scarce water consumption embodied in imports (m³/capita)	20.9	2013	●	↑
Population using safely managed water services (%)	98.5	2017	●	↑
Population using safely managed sanitation services (%)	98.8	2017	●	↑

SDG7 – Affordable and Clean Energy

Indicator	Value	Year	Rating	Trend
Population with access to electricity (%)	100.0	2017	●	↑
Population with access to clean fuels and technology for cooking (%)	100.0	2016	●	↑
CO2 emissions from fuel combustion for electricity and heating per total electricity output (MtCO2/TWh)	1.1	2017	◐	↗
Share of renewable energy in total primary energy supply (%)	5.9	2018	●	→

SDG8 – Decent Work and Economic Growth

Indicator	Value	Year	Rating	Trend
Adjusted GDP growth (%)	-2.0	2018	●	●
Victims of modern slavery (per 1,000 population)	0.3	2018	●	●
Adults with an account at a bank or other financial institution or with a mobile-money-service provider (% of population aged 15 or over)	98.2	2017	●	↑
Fatal work-related accidents embodied in imports (per 100,000 population)	1.2	2010	◐	↑
Employment-to-population ratio (%)	77.7	2019	●	↑
Youth not in employment, education or training (NEET) (% of population aged 15 to 29)	9.8	2014	●	●

SDG9 – Industry, Innovation and Infrastructure

Indicator	Value	Year	Rating	Trend
Population using the internet (%)	91.3	2018	●	↑
Mobile broadband subscriptions (per 100 population)	193.3	2018	●	↑
Logistics Performance Index: Quality of trade and transport-related infrastructure (worst 1–5 best)	4.2	2018	●	↑
The Times Higher Education Universities Ranking: Average score of top 3 universities (worst 0–100 best)	64.0	2020	●	●
Scientific and technical journal articles (per 1,000 population)	0.8	2018	●	↑
Expenditure on research and development (% of GDP)	3.2	2017	●	↑
Researchers (per 1,000 employed population)	9.8	2018	●	↑
Triadic patent families filed (per million population)	142.9	2017	●	↑
Gap in internet access by income (percentage points)	NA	NA	●	●
Women in science and engineering (% of tertiary graduates in science and engineering)	NA	NA	●	●

SDG10 – Reduced Inequalities

Indicator	Value	Year	Rating	Trend
Gini coefficient adjusted for top income	35.7	2008	●	●
Palma ratio	1.3	2015	●	↓
Elderly poverty rate (% of population aged 66 or over)	19.6	2015	●	↓

SDG11 – Sustainable Cities and Communities

Indicator	Value	Year	Rating	Trend
Annual mean concentration of particulate matter of less than 2.5 microns in diameter (PM2.5) (µg/m³)	11.7	2017	◐	↑
Access to improved water source, piped (% of urban population)	NA	NA	◐	●
Satisfaction with public transport (%)	58.0	2019	◐	↗
Population with rent overburden (%)	8.1	2016	◐	●

SDG12 – Responsible Consumption and Production

Indicator	Value	Year	Rating	Trend
Electronic waste (kg/capita)	16.9	2016	●	●
Production-based SO2 emissions (kg/capita)	42.0	2012	●	●
SO2 emissions embodied in imports (kg/capita)	9.5	2012	●	●
Production-based nitrogen emissions (kg/capita)	28.3	2010	●	●
Nitrogen emissions embodied in imports (kg/capita)	9.5	2010	●	●
Non-recycled municipal solid waste (kg/capita/day)	0.7	2017	●	●

SDG13 – Climate Action

Indicator	Value	Year	Rating	Trend
Energy-related CO2 emissions (tCO2/capita)	8.8	2017	●	→
CO2 emissions embodied in imports (tCO2/capita)	1.8	2015	●	→
CO2 emissions embodied in fossil fuel exports (kg/capita)	0.0	2019	●	●
Effective carbon rate (EUR/tCO2)	7.8	2016	●	●

SDG14 – Life Below Water

Indicator	Value	Year	Rating	Trend
Mean area that is protected in marine sites important to biodiversity (%)	73.5	2018	●	↑
Ocean Health Index: Clean Waters score (worst 0–100 best)	59.4	2019	●	↓
Fish caught from overexploited or collapsed stocks (% of total catch)	70.8	2014	●	↓
Fish caught by trawling (%)	24.2	2014	◐	↓
Marine biodiversity threats embodied in imports (per million population)	1.0	2018	●	●

SDG15 – Life on Land

Indicator	Value	Year	Rating	Trend
Mean area that is protected in terrestrial sites important to biodiversity (%)	65.8	2018	●	↑
Mean area that is protected in freshwater sites important to biodiversity (%)	67.0	2018	●	↑
Red List Index of species survival (worst 0–1 best)	0.8	2019	●	↓
Permanent deforestation (% of forest area, 5-year average)	0.0	2018	●	●
Terrestrial and freshwater biodiversity threats embodied in imports (per million population)	5.1	2018	●	●

SDG16 – Peace, Justice and Strong Institutions

Indicator	Value	Year	Rating	Trend
Homicides (per 100,000 population)	0.2	2017	●	↑
Unsentenced detainees (% of prison population)	11.3	2018	●	↑
Percentage of population who feel safe walking alone at night in the city or area where they live	73.3	2019	●	↑
Property Rights (worst 1–7 best)	6.2	2019	●	●
Birth registrations with civil authority (% of children under age 5)	100.0	2018	●	●
Corruption Perception Index (worst 0–100 best)	73.0	2019	●	↑
Children involved in child labor (% of population aged 5 to 14)	* 0.0	2016	●	●
Exports of major conventional weapons (TIV constant million USD per 100,000 population)	0.0	2019	●	●
Press Freedom Index (best 0–100 worst)	29.4	2019	●	↑
Persons held in prison (per 100,000 population)	40.6	2017	●	↑

SDG17 – Partnerships for the Goals

Indicator	Value	Year	Rating	Trend
Government spending on health and education (% of GDP)	12.3	2016	●	↑
For high-income and all OECD DAC countries: International concessional public finance, including official development assistance (% of GNI)	0.2	2017	●	→
Other countries: Government revenue excluding grants (% of GDP)	NA	NA	●	●
Corporate Tax Haven Score (best 0–100 worst)	* 0.0	2019	●	●
Financial Secrecy Score (best 0–100 worst)	62.9	2020	●	●
Shifted profits of multinationals (US$ billion)	11.8	2016	●	●

* Imputed data point

5. Country Profiles

JORDAN

Middle East and North Africa

▼ OVERALL PERFORMANCE

Index score
68.1

Regional average score
66.3

SDG Global rank 89 (OF 166)

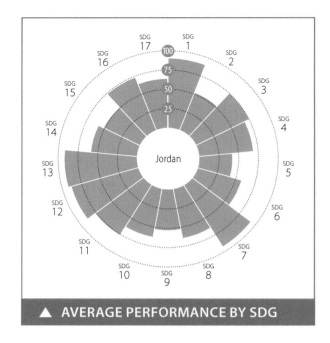

▲ AVERAGE PERFORMANCE BY SDG

▼ SPILLOVER INDEX

100 (best) to 0 (worst)

▼ CURRENT ASSESSMENT – SDG DASHBOARD

■ Major challenges ■ Significant challenges ■ Challenges remain ■ SDG achieved ▦ Information unavailable

▼ SDG TRENDS

↓ Decreasing → Stagnating ↗ Moderately improving ↑ On track or maintaining SDG achievement ● Information unavailable

Notes: The full title of Goal 2 "Zero Hunger" is "End hunger, achieve food security and improved nutrition and promote sustainable agriculture".
The full title of each SDG is available here: https://sustainabledevelopment.un.org/topics/sustainabledevelopmentgoals

JORDAN

SDG1 – No Poverty	Value	Year	Rating	Trend
Poverty headcount ratio at $1.90/day (%)	0.4	2020	●	↑
Poverty headcount ratio at $3.20/day (%)	9.2	2020	●	→

SDG2 – Zero Hunger	Value	Year	Rating	Trend
Prevalence of undernourishment (%)	12.2	2017	●	↓
Prevalence of stunting in children under 5 years of age (%)	7.8	2012	●	↑
Prevalence of wasting in children under 5 years of age (%)	2.4	2012	●	↑
Prevalence of obesity, BMI ≥ 30 (% of adult population)	35.5	2016	●	↓
Human Trophic Level (best 2–3 worst)	2.2	2017	●	↑
Cereal yield (tonnes per hectare of harvested land)	1.6	2017	●	↗
Sustainable Nitrogen Management Index (best 0–1.41 worst)	0.6	2015	●	↑

SDG3 – Good Health and Well-Being	Value	Year	Rating	Trend
Maternal mortality rate (per 100,000 live births)	46	2017	●	↑
Neonatal mortality rate (per 1,000 live births)	9.5	2018	●	↑
Mortality rate, under-5 (per 1,000 live births)	16.2	2018	●	↑
Incidence of tuberculosis (per 100,000 population)	5.0	2018	●	↑
New HIV infections (per 1,000 uninfected population)	0.0	2018	●	↑
Age-standardized death rate due to cardiovascular disease, cancer, diabetes, or chronic respiratory disease in adults aged 30–70 years (%)	19.2	2016	●	↗
Age-standardized death rate attributable to household air pollution and ambient air pollution (per 100,000 population)	51	2016	●	●
Traffic deaths (per 100,000 population)	24.4	2016	●	↗
Life expectancy at birth (years)	74.3	2016	●	→
Adolescent fertility rate (births per 1,000 adolescent females aged 15 to 19)	25.9	2017	●	↑
Births attended by skilled health personnel (%)	99.7	2018	●	↑
Percentage of surviving infants who received 2 WHO-recommended vaccines (%)	92	2018	●	↑
Universal health coverage (UHC) index of service coverage (worst 0–100 best)	76.0	2017	●	↗
Subjective well-being (average ladder score, worst 0–10 best)	4.5	2019	●	↓

SDG4 – Quality Education	Value	Year	Rating	Trend
Net primary enrollment rate (%)	80.9	2018	●	↗
Lower secondary completion rate (%)	59.0	2018	●	↓
Literacy rate (% of population aged 15 to 24)	99.3	2018	●	●

SDG5 – Gender Equality	Value	Year	Rating	Trend
Demand for family planning satisfied by modern methods (% of females aged 15 to 49 who are married or in unions)	56.7	2018	●	→
Ratio of female-to-male mean years of education received (%)	95.3	2018	●	↑
Ratio of female-to-male labor force participation rate (%)	22.2	2019	●	→
Seats held by women in national parliament (%)	15.4	2020	●	→

SDG6 – Clean Water and Sanitation	Value	Year	Rating	Trend
Population using at least basic drinking water services (%)	98.9	2017	●	↑
Population using at least basic sanitation services (%)	97.3	2017	●	↑
Freshwater withdrawal (% of available freshwater resources)	100.1	2015	●	●
Anthropogenic wastewater that receives treatment (%)	18.6	2018	●	●
Scarce water consumption embodied in imports (m³/capita)	26.3	2013	●	↑

SDG7 – Affordable and Clean Energy	Value	Year	Rating	Trend
Population with access to electricity (%)	100.0	2017	●	↑
Population with access to clean fuels and technology for cooking (%)	99.1	2016	●	↑
CO₂ emissions from fuel combustion for electricity and heating per total electricity output (MtCO₂/TWh)	1.3	2017	●	↑

SDG8 – Decent Work and Economic Growth	Value	Year	Rating	Trend
Adjusted GDP growth (%)	-4.7	2018	●	●
Victims of modern slavery (per 1,000 population)	1.8	2018	●	●
Adults with an account at a bank or other financial institution or with a mobile-money-service provider (% of population aged 15 or over)	42.5	2017	●	↑
Unemployment rate (% of total labor force)	14.7	2019	●	↓
Fatal work-related accidents embodied in imports (per 100,000 population)	0.4	2010	●	↑

SDG9 – Industry, Innovation and Infrastructure	Value	Year	Rating	Trend
Population using the internet (%)	66.8	2017	●	↑
Mobile broadband subscriptions (per 100 population)	87.6	2018	●	↑
Logistics Performance Index: Quality of trade and transport-related infrastructure (worst 1–5 best)	2.7	2018	●	↑
The Times Higher Education Universities Ranking: Average score of top 3 universities (worst 0–100 best)	31.3	2020	●	●
Scientific and technical journal articles (per 1,000 population)	0.3	2018	●	↗
Expenditure on research and development (% of GDP)	0.7	2016	●	●

SDG10 – Reduced Inequalities	Value	Year	Rating	Trend
Gini coefficient adjusted for top income	41.1	2010	●	●

SDG11 – Sustainable Cities and Communities	Value	Year	Rating	Trend
Annual mean concentration of particulate matter of less than 2.5 microns in diameter (PM2.5) (μg/m³)	33.0	2017	●	→
Access to improved water source, piped (% of urban population)	88.8	2017	●	↓
Satisfaction with public transport (%)	63.9	2019	●	↑

SDG12 – Responsible Consumption and Production	Value	Year	Rating	Trend
Municipal solid waste (kg/capita/day)	0.8	2013	●	●
Electronic waste (kg/capita)	5.6	2016	●	●
Production-based SO₂ emissions (kg/capita)	29.1	2012	●	●
SO₂ emissions embodied in imports (kg/capita)	4.0	2012	●	●
Production-based nitrogen emissions (kg/capita)	10.0	2010	●	●
Nitrogen emissions embodied in imports (kg/capita)	3.4	2010	●	●

SDG13 – Climate Action	Value	Year	Rating	Trend
Energy-related CO₂ emissions (tCO₂/capita)	1.8	2017	●	↑
CO₂ emissions embodied in imports (tCO₂/capita)	0.6	2015	●	↑
CO₂ emissions embodied in fossil fuel exports (kg/capita)	0.0	2017	●	●

SDG14 – Life Below Water	Value	Year	Rating	Trend
Mean area that is protected in marine sites important to biodiversity (%)	NA	NA	●	●
Ocean Health Index: Clean Waters score (worst 0–100 best)	47.2	2019	●	↓
Fish caught from overexploited or collapsed stocks (% of total catch)	NA	NA	●	●
Fish caught by trawling (%)	NA	NA	●	●
Marine biodiversity threats embodied in imports (per million population)	0.2	2018	●	●

SDG15 – Life on Land	Value	Year	Rating	Trend
Mean area that is protected in terrestrial sites important to biodiversity (%)	8.7	2018	●	→
Mean area that is protected in freshwater sites important to biodiversity (%)	9.8	2018	●	→
Red List Index of species survival (worst 0–1 best)	1.0	2019	●	↑
Permanent deforestation (% of forest area, 5-year average)	NA	NA	●	●
Terrestrial and freshwater biodiversity threats embodied in imports (per million population)	0.2	2018	●	●

SDG16 – Peace, Justice and Strong Institutions	Value	Year	Rating	Trend
Homicides (per 100,000 population)	1.4	2017	●	↑
Unsentenced detainees (% of prison population)	41.7	2015	●	●
Percentage of population who feel safe walking alone at night in the city or area where they live (%)	73.4	2019	●	↑
Property Rights (worst 1–7 best)	5.0	2019	●	●
Birth registrations with civil authority (% of children under age 5)	98.0	2018	●	●
Corruption Perception Index (worst 0–100 best)	48	2019	●	↓
Children involved in child labor (% of population aged 5 to 14)	1.7	2016	●	●
Exports of major conventional weapons (TIV constant million USD per 100,000 population)	0.4	2019	●	●
Press Freedom Index (best 0–100 worst)	43.1	2019	●	→

SDG17 – Partnerships for the Goals	Value	Year	Rating	Trend
Government spending on health and education (% of GDP)	7.3	2016	●	●
For high-income and all OECD DAC countries: International concessional public finance, including official development assistance (% of GNI)	NA	NA	●	●
Other countries: Government revenue excluding grants (% of GDP)	23.2	2017	●	↓
Corporate Tax Haven Score (best 0–100 worst) *	0.0	2019	●	●

* Imputed data point

5. Country Profiles

▼ OVERALL PERFORMANCE

Index score

71.1

Regional average score

70.9

SDG Global rank 65 (OF 166)

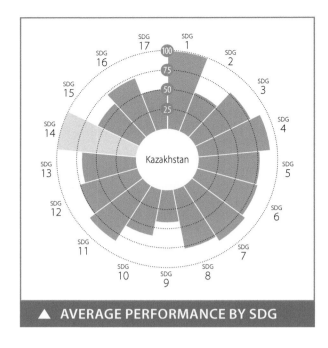

▲ AVERAGE PERFORMANCE BY SDG

▼ SPILLOVER INDEX

100 (best) to 0 (worst)

▼ CURRENT ASSESSMENT – SDG DASHBOARD

■ Major challenges   ■ Significant challenges   ■ Challenges remain   ■ SDG achieved   ■ Information unavailable

▼ SDG TRENDS

1 NO POVERTY	2 ZERO HUNGER	3 GOOD HEALTH AND WELL-BEING	4 QUALITY EDUCATION	5 GENDER EQUALITY	6 CLEAN WATER AND SANITATION	7 AFFORDABLE AND CLEAN ENERGY	8 DECENT WORK AND ECONOMIC GROWTH	9 INDUSTRY, INNOVATION AND INFRASTRUCTURE
↑	↗	↑	↗	↗	↑	↗	↗	↗

10 REDUCED INEQUALITIES	11 SUSTAINABLE CITIES AND COMMUNITIES	12 RESPONSIBLE CONSUMPTION AND PRODUCTION	13 CLIMATE ACTION	14 LIFE BELOW WATER	15 LIFE ON LAND	16 PEACE, JUSTICE AND STRONG INSTITUTIONS	17 PARTNERSHIPS FOR THE GOALS
●	→	●	↗	●	→	↗	↓

↓ Decreasing   → Stagnating   ↗ Moderately improving   ↑ On track or maintaining SDG achievement   ● Information unavailable

Notes: The full title of Goal 2 "Zero Hunger" is "End hunger, achieve food security and improved nutrition and promote sustainable agriculture".
The full title of each SDG is available here: https://sustainabledevelopment.un.org/topics/sustainabledevelopmentgoals

SDG1 – No Poverty

Indicator	Value	Year	Rating	Trend
Poverty headcount ratio at $1.90/day (%)	0.0	2020	●	↑
Poverty headcount ratio at $3.20/day (%)	0.1	2020	●	↑

SDG2 – Zero Hunger

Indicator	Value	Year	Rating	Trend
Prevalence of undernourishment (%)	2.5	2017	●	↑
Prevalence of stunting in children under 5 years of age (%)	8.0	2015	●	↑
Prevalence of wasting in children under 5 years of age (%)	3.1	2015	●	↑
Prevalence of obesity, BMI ≥ 30 (% of adult population)	21.0	2016	●	↓
Human Trophic Level (best 2–3 worst)	2.4	2017	●	↓
Cereal yield (tonnes per hectare of harvested land)	1.4	2017	●	↗
Sustainable Nitrogen Management Index (best 0–1.41 worst)	0.8	2015	●	→

SDG3 – Good Health and Well-Being

Indicator	Value	Year	Rating	Trend
Maternal mortality rate (per 100,000 live births)	10	2017	●	↑
Neonatal mortality rate (per 1,000 live births)	5.6	2018	●	↑
Mortality rate, under-5 (per 1,000 live births)	9.9	2018	●	↑
Incidence of tuberculosis (per 100,000 population)	68.0	2018	●	↗
New HIV infections (per 1,000 uninfected population)	0.1	2018	●	↑
Age-standardized death rate due to cardiovascular disease, cancer, diabetes, or chronic respiratory disease in adults aged 30–70 years (%)	26.8	2016	●	↑
Age-standardized death rate attributable to household air pollution and ambient air pollution (per 100,000 population)	63	2016	●	●
Traffic deaths (per 100,000 population)	17.6	2016	●	↑
Life expectancy at birth (years)	71.1	2016	●	↗
Adolescent fertility rate (births per 1,000 adolescent females aged 15 to 19)	29.8	2017	●	↗
Births attended by skilled health personnel (%)	99.4	2015	●	↑
Percentage of surviving infants who received 2 WHO-recommended vaccines (%)	98	2018	●	↑
Universal health coverage (UHC) index of service coverage (worst 0–100 best)	76.0	2017	●	↑
Subjective well-being (average ladder score, worst 0–10 best)	6.3	2019	●	↑

SDG4 – Quality Education

Indicator	Value	Year	Rating	Trend
Net primary enrollment rate (%)	86.9	2019	●	→
Lower secondary completion rate (%)	113.6	2018	●	↑
Literacy rate (% of population aged 15 to 24)	99.9	2018	●	●

SDG5 – Gender Equality

Indicator	Value	Year	Rating	Trend
Demand for family planning satisfied by modern methods (% of females aged 15 to 49 who are married or in unions)	79.4	2018	●	↗
Ratio of female-to-male mean years of education received (%)	101.7	2018	●	↑
Ratio of female-to-male labor force participation rate (%)	84.3	2019	●	↑
Seats held by women in national parliament (%)	27.1	2020	●	→

SDG6 – Clean Water and Sanitation

Indicator	Value	Year	Rating	Trend
Population using at least basic drinking water services (%)	95.6	2017	●	↑
Population using at least basic sanitation services (%)	97.9	2017	●	↑
Freshwater withdrawal (% of available freshwater resources)	27.7	2010	●	●
Anthropogenic wastewater that receives treatment (%)	28.6	2018	●	●
Scarce water consumption embodied in imports (m³/capita)	7.5	2013	●	↑

SDG7 – Affordable and Clean Energy

Indicator	Value	Year	Rating	Trend
Population with access to electricity (%)	100.0	2017	●	↑
Population with access to clean fuels and technology for cooking (%)	95.3	2016	●	↑
CO_2 emissions from fuel combustion for electricity and heating per total electricity output (MtCO$_2$/TWh)	2.6	2017	●	→

SDG8 – Decent Work and Economic Growth

Indicator	Value	Year	Rating	Trend
Adjusted GDP growth (%)	-1.1	2018	●	●
Victims of modern slavery (per 1,000 population)	4.2	2018	●	●
Adults with an account at a bank or other financial institution or with a mobile-money-service provider (% of population aged 15 or over)	58.7	2017	●	↗
Unemployment rate (% of total labor force)	4.6	2019	●	↑
Fatal work-related accidents embodied in imports (per 100,000 population)	0.3	2010	●	↑

SDG9 – Industry, Innovation and Infrastructure

Indicator	Value	Year	Rating	Trend
Population using the internet (%)	78.9	2018	●	↑
Mobile broadband subscriptions (per 100 population)	77.6	2018	●	↑
Logistics Performance Index: Quality of trade and transport-related infrastructure (worst 1–5 best)	2.5	2018	●	↑
The Times Higher Education Universities Ranking: Average score of top 3 universities (worst 0–100 best)	16.4	2020	●	●
Scientific and technical journal articles (per 1,000 population)	0.1	2018	●	→
Expenditure on research and development (% of GDP)	0.1	2017	●	↓

SDG10 – Reduced Inequalities

Indicator	Value	Year	Rating	Trend
Gini coefficient adjusted for top income	41.7	2017	●	●

SDG11 – Sustainable Cities and Communities

Indicator	Value	Year	Rating	Trend
Annual mean concentration of particulate matter of less than 2.5 microns in diameter (PM2.5) (µg/m³)	13.8	2017	●	→
Access to improved water source, piped (% of urban population)	94.0	2017	●	↗
Satisfaction with public transport (%)	62.1	2019	●	↗

SDG12 – Responsible Consumption and Production

Indicator	Value	Year	Rating	Trend
Municipal solid waste (kg/capita/day)	1.2	2012	●	●
Electronic waste (kg/capita)	8.2	2016	●	●
Production-based SO$_2$ emissions (kg/capita)	100.3	2012	●	●
SO$_2$ emissions embodied in imports (kg/capita)	3.6	2012	●	●
Production-based nitrogen emissions (kg/capita)	46.4	2010	●	●
Nitrogen emissions embodied in imports (kg/capita)	2.4	2010	●	●

SDG13 – Climate Action

Indicator	Value	Year	Rating	Trend
Energy-related CO_2 emissions (tCO$_2$/capita)	14.9	2017	●	→
CO_2 emissions embodied in imports (tCO$_2$/capita)	0.7	2015	●	↑
CO_2 emissions embodied in fossil fuel exports (kg/capita)	4963.3	2019	●	●

SDG14 – Life Below Water

Indicator	Value	Year	Rating	Trend
Mean area that is protected in marine sites important to biodiversity (%)	NA	NA	●	●
Ocean Health Index: Clean Waters score (worst 0–100 best)	NA	NA	●	●
Fish caught from overexploited or collapsed stocks (% of total catch)	NA	NA	●	●
Fish caught by trawling (%)	NA	NA	●	●
Marine biodiversity threats embodied in imports (per million population)	0.0	2018	●	●

SDG15 – Life on Land

Indicator	Value	Year	Rating	Trend
Mean area that is protected in terrestrial sites important to biodiversity (%)	15.7	2018	●	→
Mean area that is protected in freshwater sites important to biodiversity (%)	17.0	2018	●	→
Red List Index of species survival (worst 0–1 best)	0.9	2019	●	→
Permanent deforestation (% of forest area, 5-year average)	0.0	2018	●	●
Terrestrial and freshwater biodiversity threats embodied in imports (per million population)	0.3	2018	●	●

SDG16 – Peace, Justice and Strong Institutions

Indicator	Value	Year	Rating	Trend
Homicides (per 100,000 population)	5.0	2017	●	→
Unsentenced detainees (% of prison population)	11.3	2018	●	↑
Percentage of population who feel safe walking alone at night in the city or area where they live (%)	70.2	2019	●	↑
Property Rights (worst 1–7 best)	4.4	2019	●	●
Birth registrations with civil authority (% of children under age 5)	99.7	2018	●	●
Corruption Perception Index (worst 0–100 best)	34	2019	●	↗
Children involved in child labor (% of population aged 5 to 14)	2.2	2016	●	●
Exports of major conventional weapons (TIV constant million USD per 100,000 population)	* 0.0	2019	●	●
Press Freedom Index (best 0–100 worst)	52.8	2019	●	→

SDG17 – Partnerships for the Goals

Indicator	Value	Year	Rating	Trend
Government spending on health and education (% of GDP)	5.1	2016	●	●
For high-income and all OECD DAC countries: International concessional public finance, including official development assistance (% of GNI)	NA	NA	●	●
Other countries: Government revenue excluding grants (% of GDP)	16.0	2018	●	↓
Corporate Tax Haven Score (best 0–100 worst)	* 0.0	2019	●	●

* Imputed data point

5. Country Profiles

KENYA

▼ OVERALL PERFORMANCE

Index score
60.2

Regional average score
53.1

SDG Global rank **123** (OF 166)

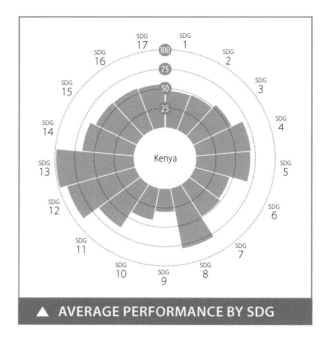

▲ AVERAGE PERFORMANCE BY SDG

▼ SPILLOVER INDEX

100 (best) to 0 (worst)

▼ CURRENT ASSESSMENT – SDG DASHBOARD

■ Major challenges ■ Significant challenges ■ Challenges remain ■ SDG achieved ■ Information unavailable

▼ SDG TRENDS

↓ Decreasing   → Stagnating   ↗ Moderately improving   ↑ On track or maintaining SDG achievement   ● Information unavailable

Notes: The full title of Goal 2 "Zero Hunger" is "End hunger, achieve food security and improved nutrition and promote sustainable agriculture".
The full title of each SDG is available here: https://sustainabledevelopment.un.org/topics/sustainabledevelopmentgoals

SDG1 – No Poverty

Indicator	Value	Year	Rating	Trend
Poverty headcount ratio at $1.90/day (%)	15.9	2020	●	↗
Poverty headcount ratio at $3.20/day (%)	41.8	2020	●	→

SDG2 – Zero Hunger

Indicator	Value	Year	Rating	Trend
Prevalence of undernourishment (%)	29.4	2017	●	↓
Prevalence of stunting in children under 5 years of age (%)	26.0	2014	●	→
Prevalence of wasting in children under 5 years of age (%)	4.0	2014	●	↑
Prevalence of obesity, BMI ≥ 30 (% of adult population)	7.1	2016	●	↑
Human Trophic Level (best 2–3 worst)	2.2	2017	●	→
Cereal yield (tonnes per hectare of harvested land)	1.5	2017	●	↓
Sustainable Nitrogen Management Index (best 0–1.41 worst)	0.9	2015	●	→

SDG3 – Good Health and Well-Being

Indicator	Value	Year	Rating	Trend
Maternal mortality rate (per 100,000 live births)	342	2017	●	→
Neonatal mortality rate (per 1,000 live births)	19.6	2018	●	↗
Mortality rate, under-5 (per 1,000 live births)	41.1	2018	●	↑
Incidence of tuberculosis (per 100,000 population)	292.0	2018	●	↑
New HIV infections (per 1,000 uninfected population)	1.0	2018	●	↑
Age-standardized death rate due to cardiovascular disease, cancer, diabetes, or chronic respiratory disease in adults aged 30–70 years (%)	13.4	2016	●	↑
Age-standardized death rate attributable to household air pollution and ambient air pollution (per 100,000 population)	78	2016	●	●
Traffic deaths (per 100,000 population)	27.8	2016	●	→
Life expectancy at birth (years)	66.7	2016	●	↗
Adolescent fertility rate (births per 1,000 adolescent females aged 15 to 19)	75.1	2017	●	↗
Births attended by skilled health personnel (%)	61.8	2014	●	●
Percentage of surviving infants who received 2 WHO-recommended vaccines (%)	89	2018	●	→
Universal health coverage (UHC) index of service coverage (worst 0–100 best)	55.0	2017	●	→
Subjective well-being (average ladder score, worst 0–10 best)	4.6	2019	●	↗

SDG4 – Quality Education

Indicator	Value	Year	Rating	Trend
Net primary enrollment rate (%)	80.0	2012	●	●
Lower secondary completion rate (%)	79.2	2016	●	●
Literacy rate (% of population aged 15 to 24)	87.8	2018	●	●

SDG5 – Gender Equality

Indicator	Value	Year	Rating	Trend
Demand for family planning satisfied by modern methods (% of females aged 15 to 49 who are married or in unions)	76.0	2017	●	↑
Ratio of female-to-male mean years of education received (%)	83.3	2018	●	↗
Ratio of female-to-male labor force participation rate (%)	92.0	2019	●	↑
Seats held by women in national parliament (%)	21.8	2020	●	→

SDG6 – Clean Water and Sanitation

Indicator	Value	Year	Rating	Trend
Population using at least basic drinking water services (%)	58.9	2017	●	→
Population using at least basic sanitation services (%)	29.1	2017	●	↓
Freshwater withdrawal (% of available freshwater resources)	33.2	2015	●	●
Anthropogenic wastewater that receives treatment (%)	0.5	2018	●	●
Scarce water consumption embodied in imports (m³/capita)	2.2	2013	●	↑

SDG7 – Affordable and Clean Energy

Indicator	Value	Year	Rating	Trend
Population with access to electricity (%)	63.8	2017	●	↑
Population with access to clean fuels and technology for cooking (%)	13.4	2016	●	→
CO_2 emissions from fuel combustion for electricity and heating per total electricity output (MtCO$_2$/TWh)	1.6	2017	●	→

SDG8 – Decent Work and Economic Growth

Indicator	Value	Year	Rating	Trend
Adjusted GDP growth (%)	-2.7	2018	●	●
Victims of modern slavery (per 1,000 population)	6.9	2018	●	●
Adults with an account at a bank or other financial institution or with a mobile-money-service provider (% of population aged 15 or over)	81.6	2017	●	↑
Unemployment rate (% of total labor force)	2.6	2019	●	↑
Fatal work-related accidents embodied in imports (per 100,000 population)	0.5	2010	●	↑

SDG9 – Industry, Innovation and Infrastructure

Indicator	Value	Year	Rating	Trend
Population using the internet (%)	17.8	2017	●	→
Mobile broadband subscriptions (per 100 population)	41.9	2018	●	↑
Logistics Performance Index: Quality of trade and transport-related infrastructure (worst 1–5 best)	2.6	2018	●	↑
The Times Higher Education Universities Ranking: Average score of top 3 universities (worst 0–100 best)	25.2	2020	●	●
Scientific and technical journal articles (per 1,000 population)	0.0	2018	●	→
Expenditure on research and development (% of GDP)	0.8	2010	●	●

SDG10 – Reduced Inequalities

Indicator	Value	Year	Rating	Trend
Gini coefficient adjusted for top income	48.5	2015	●	●

SDG11 – Sustainable Cities and Communities

Indicator	Value	Year	Rating	Trend
Annual mean concentration of particulate matter of less than 2.5 microns in diameter (PM2.5) (μg/m³)	28.6	2017	●	→
Access to improved water source, piped (% of urban population)	61.7	2017	●	↓
Satisfaction with public transport (%)	60.6	2019	●	↑

SDG12 – Responsible Consumption and Production

Indicator	Value	Year	Rating	Trend
Municipal solid waste (kg/capita/day)	1.1	2010	●	●
Electronic waste (kg/capita)	0.8	2016	●	●
Production-based SO_2 emissions (kg/capita)	7.4	2012	●	●
SO_2 emissions embodied in imports (kg/capita)	0.9	2012	●	●
Production-based nitrogen emissions (kg/capita)	26.8	2010	●	●
Nitrogen emissions embodied in imports (kg/capita)	2.3	2010	●	●

SDG13 – Climate Action

Indicator	Value	Year	Rating	Trend
Energy-related CO_2 emissions (tCO$_2$/capita)	0.3	2017	●	↑
CO_2 emissions embodied in imports (tCO$_2$/capita)	0.1	2015	●	↑
CO_2 emissions embodied in fossil fuel exports (kg/capita)	0.0	2018	●	●

SDG14 – Life Below Water

Indicator	Value	Year	Rating	Trend
Mean area that is protected in marine sites important to biodiversity (%)	60.2	2018	●	↑
Ocean Health Index: Clean Waters score (worst 0–100 best)	46.9	2019	●	↓
Fish caught from overexploited or collapsed stocks (% of total catch)	44.9	2014	●	↓
Fish caught by trawling (%)	8.0	2014	●	→
Marine biodiversity threats embodied in imports (per million population)	0.0	2018	●	●

SDG15 – Life on Land

Indicator	Value	Year	Rating	Trend
Mean area that is protected in terrestrial sites important to biodiversity (%)	35.1	2018	●	→
Mean area that is protected in freshwater sites important to biodiversity (%)	34.4	2018	●	→
Red List Index of species survival (worst 0–1 best)	0.8	2019	●	↓
Permanent deforestation (% of forest area, 5-year average)	0.2	2018	●	●
Terrestrial and freshwater biodiversity threats embodied in imports (per million population)	0.7	2018	●	●

SDG16 – Peace, Justice and Strong Institutions

Indicator	Value	Year	Rating	Trend
Homicides (per 100,000 population)	5.0	2017	●	→
Unsentenced detainees (% of prison population)	38.8	2018	●	↗
Percentage of population who feel safe walking alone at night in the city or area where they live	57.5	2019	●	↗
Property Rights (worst 1–7 best)	4.4	2019	●	●
Birth registrations with civil authority (% of children under age 5)	66.9	2018	●	●
Corruption Perception Index (worst 0–100 best)	28	2019	●	→
Children involved in child labor (% of population aged 5 to 14)	25.9	2016	●	●
Exports of major conventional weapons (TIV constant million USD per 100,000 population)	* 0.0	2019	●	●
Press Freedom Index (best 0–100 worst)	32.4	2019	●	↓

SDG17 – Partnerships for the Goals

Indicator	Value	Year	Rating	Trend
Government spending on health and education (% of GDP)	7.0	2016	●	↓
For high-income and all OECD DAC countries: International concessional public finance, including official development assistance (% of GNI)	NA	NA	●	●
Other countries: Government revenue excluding grants (% of GDP)	22.0	2017	●	→
Corporate Tax Haven Score (best 0–100 worst)	50.8	2019	●	●

* Imputed data point

5. Country Profiles

▼ OVERALL PERFORMANCE

Index score

na

Regional average score

49.6

SDG Global rank NA (OF 166)

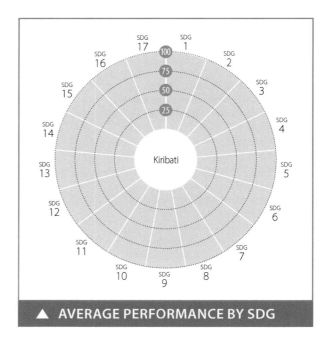

▲ AVERAGE PERFORMANCE BY SDG

▼ SPILLOVER INDEX

100 (best) to 0 (worst)

▼ CURRENT ASSESSMENT – SDG DASHBOARD

■ Major challenges ■ Significant challenges ■ Challenges remain ■ SDG achieved ■ Information unavailable

▼ SDG TRENDS

↓ Decreasing → Stagnating ↗ Moderately improving ↑ On track or maintaining SDG achievement ● Information unavailable

Notes: The full title of Goal 2 "Zero Hunger" is "End hunger, achieve food security and improved nutrition and promote sustainable agriculture".
The full title of each SDG is available here: https://sustainabledevelopment.un.org/topics/sustainabledevelopmentgoals

SDG1 – No Poverty

Indicator	Value	Year	Rating	Trend
Poverty headcount ratio at $1.90/day (%)	NA	NA	●	●
Poverty headcount ratio at $3.20/day (%)	NA	NA	●	●

SDG2 – Zero Hunger

Indicator	Value	Year	Rating	Trend
Prevalence of undernourishment (%)	2.7	2017	●	↑
Prevalence of stunting in children under 5 years of age (%)	NA	NA	●	●
Prevalence of wasting in children under 5 years of age (%)	NA	NA	●	●
Prevalence of obesity, BMI ≥ 30 (% of adult population)	46.0	2016	●	↓
Human Trophic Level (best 2–3 worst)	2.3	2017	●	→
Cereal yield (tonnes per hectare of harvested land)	NA	NA	●	●
Sustainable Nitrogen Management Index (best 0–1.41 worst)	1.0	2015	●	↓

SDG3 – Good Health and Well-Being

Indicator	Value	Year	Rating	Trend
Maternal mortality rate (per 100,000 live births)	92	2017	●	↑
Neonatal mortality rate (per 1,000 live births)	22.8	2018	●	↗
Mortality rate, under-5 (per 1,000 live births)	52.5	2018	●	↗
Incidence of tuberculosis (per 100,000 population)	349.0	2018	●	↑
New HIV infections (per 1,000 uninfected population)	NA	NA	●	●
Age-standardized death rate due to cardiovascular disease, cancer, diabetes, or chronic respiratory disease in adults aged 30–70 years (%)	28.4	2016	●	→
Age-standardized death rate attributable to household air pollution and ambient air pollution (per 100,000 population)	140	2016	●	●
Traffic deaths (per 100,000 population)	4.4	2016	●	↑
Life expectancy at birth (years)	66.1	2016	●	→
Adolescent fertility rate (births per 1,000 adolescent females aged 15 to 19)	16.2	2017	●	↑
Births attended by skilled health personnel (%)	98.3	2010	●	●
Percentage of surviving infants who received 2 WHO-recommended vaccines (%)	84	2018	●	↑
Universal health coverage (UHC) index of service coverage (worst 0–100 best)	41.0	2017	●	→
Subjective well-being (average ladder score, worst 0–10 best)	NA	NA	●	●

SDG4 – Quality Education

Indicator	Value	Year	Rating	Trend
Net primary enrollment rate (%)	94.7	2017	●	↓
Lower secondary completion rate (%)	94.6	2016	●	●
Literacy rate (% of population aged 15 to 24)	NA	NA	●	●

SDG5 – Gender Equality

Indicator	Value	Year	Rating	Trend
Demand for family planning satisfied by modern methods (% of females aged 15 to 49 who are married or in unions)	35.8	2009	●	→
Ratio of female-to-male mean years of education received (%)	NA	NA	●	●
Ratio of female-to-male labor force participation rate (%)	NA	NA	●	●
Seats held by women in national parliament (%)	8.9	2020	●	→

SDG6 – Clean Water and Sanitation

Indicator	Value	Year	Rating	Trend
Population using at least basic drinking water services (%)	71.6	2017	●	↗
Population using at least basic sanitation services (%)	47.8	2017	●	→
Freshwater withdrawal (% of available freshwater resources)	NA	NA	●	●
Anthropogenic wastewater that receives treatment (%)	0.0	2018	●	●
Scarce water consumption embodied in imports (m³/capita)	NA	NA	●	●

SDG7 – Affordable and Clean Energy

Indicator	Value	Year	Rating	Trend
Population with access to electricity (%)	98.6	2017	●	↑
Population with access to clean fuels and technology for cooking (%)	5.5	2016	●	→
CO₂ emissions from fuel combustion for electricity and heating per total electricity output (MtCO₂/TWh)	NA	NA	●	●

SDG8 – Decent Work and Economic Growth

Indicator	Value	Year	Rating	Trend
Adjusted GDP growth (%)	-5.5	2018	●	●
Victims of modern slavery (per 1,000 population)	NA	NA	●	●
Adults with an account at a bank or other financial institution or with a mobile-money-service provider (% of population aged 15 or over)	NA	NA	●	●
Unemployment rate (% of total labor force)	NA	NA	●	●
Fatal work-related accidents embodied in imports (per 100,000 population)	NA	NA	●	●

SDG9 – Industry, Innovation and Infrastructure

Indicator	Value	Year	Rating	Trend
Population using the internet (%)	14.6	2017	●	→
Mobile broadband subscriptions (per 100 population)	1.5	2017	●	→
Logistics Performance Index: Quality of trade and transport-related infrastructure (worst 1–5 best)	NA	NA	●	●
The Times Higher Education Universities Ranking: Average score of top 3 universities (worst 0–100 best) *	0.0	2020	●	●
Scientific and technical journal articles (per 1,000 population)	0.0	2018	●	↓
Expenditure on research and development (% of GDP)	NA	NA	●	●

SDG10 – Reduced Inequalities

Indicator	Value	Year	Rating	Trend
Gini coefficient adjusted for top income	37.0	2006	●	●

SDG11 – Sustainable Cities and Communities

Indicator	Value	Year	Rating	Trend
Annual mean concentration of particulate matter of less than 2.5 microns in diameter (PM2.5) (µg/m³)	10.6	2017	●	↑
Access to improved water source, piped (% of urban population)	NA	NA	●	●
Satisfaction with public transport (%)	NA	NA	●	●

SDG12 – Responsible Consumption and Production

Indicator	Value	Year	Rating	Trend
Municipal solid waste (kg/capita/day)	1.5	2016	●	●
Electronic waste (kg/capita)	0.8	2016	●	●
Production-based SO₂ emissions (kg/capita)	NA	NA	●	●
SO₂ emissions embodied in imports (kg/capita)	NA	NA	●	●
Production-based nitrogen emissions (kg/capita)	NA	NA	●	●
Nitrogen emissions embodied in imports (kg/capita)	NA	NA	●	●

SDG13 – Climate Action

Indicator	Value	Year	Rating	Trend
Energy-related CO₂ emissions (tCO₂/capita)	0.7	2017	●	↑
CO₂ emissions embodied in imports (tCO₂/capita)	NA	NA	●	●
CO₂ emissions embodied in fossil fuel exports (kg/capita)	NA	NA	●	●

SDG14 – Life Below Water

Indicator	Value	Year	Rating	Trend
Mean area that is protected in marine sites important to biodiversity (%)	40.2	2018	●	→
Ocean Health Index: Clean Waters score (worst 0–100 best)	28.2	2019	●	→
Fish caught from overexploited or collapsed stocks (% of total catch)	3.6	2014	●	↑
Fish caught by trawling (%)	NA	NA	●	●
Marine biodiversity threats embodied in imports (per million population)	NA	NA	●	●

SDG15 – Life on Land

Indicator	Value	Year	Rating	Trend
Mean area that is protected in terrestrial sites important to biodiversity (%)	32.0	2018	●	→
Mean area that is protected in freshwater sites important to biodiversity (%)	NA	NA	●	●
Red List Index of species survival (worst 0–1 best)	0.8	2019	●	↓
Permanent deforestation (% of forest area, 5-year average)	NA	NA	●	●
Terrestrial and freshwater biodiversity threats embodied in imports (per million population)	NA	NA	●	●

SDG16 – Peace, Justice and Strong Institutions

Indicator	Value	Year	Rating	Trend
Homicides (per 100,000 population)	7.5	2012	●	●
Unsentenced detainees (% of prison population)	5.4	2018	●	●
Percentage of population who feel safe walking alone at night in the city or area where they live (%)	NA	NA	●	●
Property Rights (worst 1–7 best)	NA	NA	●	●
Birth registrations with civil authority (% of children under age 5)	93.5	2018	●	●
Corruption Perception Index (worst 0–100 best)	NA	NA	●	●
Children involved in child labor (% of population aged 5 to 14)	NA	NA	●	●
Exports of major conventional weapons (TIV constant million USD per 100,000 population) *	0.0	2019	●	●
Press Freedom Index (best 0–100 worst)	NA	NA	●	●

SDG17 – Partnerships for the Goals

Indicator	Value	Year	Rating	Trend
Government spending on health and education (% of GDP)	23.9	2001	●	●
For high-income and all OECD DAC countries: International concessional public finance, including official development assistance (% of GNI)	NA	NA	●	●
Other countries: Government revenue excluding grants (% of GDP)	100.5	2017	●	↑
Corporate Tax Haven Score (best 0–100 worst) *	0.0	2019	●	●

* Imputed data point

KOREA, DEMOCRATIC REPUBLIC OF East and South Asia

▼ OVERALL PERFORMANCE

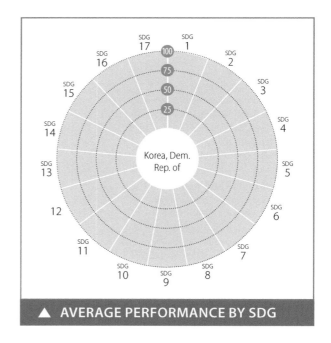

Index score

na

Regional average score

67.2

SDG Global rank   NA (OF 166)

▲ AVERAGE PERFORMANCE BY SDG

▼ SPILLOVER INDEX

100 (best) to 0 (worst)

▼ CURRENT ASSESSMENT – SDG DASHBOARD

■ Major challenges   ■ Significant challenges   ■ Challenges remain   ■ SDG achieved   ■ Information unavailable

▼ SDG TRENDS

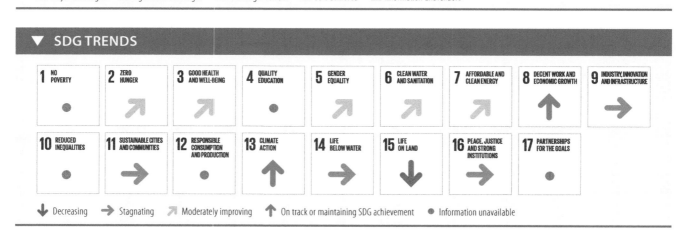

↓ Decreasing   → Stagnating   ↗ Moderately improving   ↑ On track or maintaining SDG achievement   ● Information unavailable

Notes: The full title of Goal 2 "Zero Hunger" is "End hunger, achieve food security and improved nutrition and promote sustainable agriculture".
The full title of each SDG is available here: https://sustainabledevelopment.un.org/topics/sustainabledevelopmentgoals

SDG1 – No Poverty

		Value	Year	Rating	Trend
Poverty headcount ratio at $1.90/day (%)	*	NA	NA	●	●
Poverty headcount ratio at $3.20/day (%)	*	NA	NA	●	●

SDG2 – Zero Hunger

	Value	Year	Rating	Trend
Prevalence of undernourishment (%)	47.8	2017	●	↓
Prevalence of stunting in children under 5 years of age (%)	27.9	2012	●	↗
Prevalence of wasting in children under 5 years of age (%)	4.0	2012	●	↑
Prevalence of obesity, BMI ≥ 30 (% of adult population)	6.8	2016	●	↑
Human Trophic Level (best 2–3 worst)	2.1	2017	●	↑
Cereal yield (tonnes per hectare of harvested land)	4.0	2017	●	↑
Sustainable Nitrogen Management Index (best 0–1.41 worst)	0.5	2015	●	→

SDG3 – Good Health and Well-Being

	Value	Year	Rating	Trend
Maternal mortality rate (per 100,000 live births)	89	2017	●	↗
Neonatal mortality rate (per 1,000 live births)	9.7	2018	●	↑
Mortality rate, under-5 (per 1,000 live births)	18.2	2018	●	↑
Incidence of tuberculosis (per 100,000 population)	513.0	2018	●	→
New HIV infections (per 1,000 uninfected population)	NA	NA	●	●
Age-standardized death rate due to cardiovascular disease, cancer, diabetes, or chronic respiratory disease in adults aged 30–70 years (%)	25.6	2016	●	→
Age-standardized death rate attributable to household air pollution and ambient air pollution (per 100,000 population)	207	2016	●	●
Traffic deaths (per 100,000 population)	20.8	2013	●	●
Life expectancy at birth (years)	71.9	2016	●	→
Adolescent fertility rate (births per 1,000 adolescent females aged 15 to 19)	0.3	2017	●	↑
Births attended by skilled health personnel (%)	100.0	2009	●	↑
Percentage of surviving infants who received 2 WHO-recommended vaccines (%)	97	2018	●	↑
Universal health coverage (UHC) index of service coverage (worst 0–100 best)	71.0	2017	●	↑
Subjective well-being (average ladder score, worst 0–10 best)	NA	NA	●	●

SDG4 – Quality Education

	Value	Year	Rating	Trend
Net primary enrollment rate (%)	94.0	2009	●	●
Lower secondary completion rate (%)	NA	NA	●	●
Literacy rate (% of population aged 15 to 24)	100.0	2008	●	●

SDG5 – Gender Equality

	Value	Year	Rating	Trend
Demand for family planning satisfied by modern methods (% of females aged 15 to 49 who are married or in unions)	89.8	2014	●	↑
Ratio of female-to-male mean years of education received (%)	NA	NA	●	●
Ratio of female-to-male labor force participation rate (%)	85.1	2019	●	↑
Seats held by women in national parliament (%)	17.6	2020	●	→

SDG6 – Clean Water and Sanitation

	Value	Year	Rating	Trend
Population using at least basic drinking water services (%)	94.5	2017	●	→
Population using at least basic sanitation services (%)	83.2	2017	●	↗
Freshwater withdrawal (% of available freshwater resources)	27.7	2005	●	●
Anthropogenic wastewater that receives treatment (%)	0.0	2018	●	●
Scarce water consumption embodied in imports (m³/capita)	0.2	2013	●	↑

SDG7 – Affordable and Clean Energy

	Value	Year	Rating	Trend
Population with access to electricity (%)	43.9	2017	●	↗
Population with access to clean fuels and technology for cooking (%)	10.8	2016	●	→
CO₂ emissions from fuel combustion for electricity and heating per total electricity output (MtCO₂/TWh)	1.2	2017	●	↑

SDG8 – Decent Work and Economic Growth

		Value	Year	Rating	Trend
Adjusted GDP growth (%)		NA	NA	●	●
Victims of modern slavery (per 1,000 population)		104.6	2018	●	●
Adults with an account at a bank or other financial institution or with a mobile-money-service provider (% of population aged 15 or over)		NA	NA	●	●
Unemployment rate (% of total labor force)		2.7	2019	●	↑
Fatal work-related accidents embodied in imports (per 100,000 population)		0.0	2010	●	↑

SDG9 – Industry, Innovation and Infrastructure

		Value	Year	Rating	Trend
Population using the internet (%)		0.0	2012	●	●
Mobile broadband subscriptions (per 100 population)		15.0	2017	●	→
Logistics Performance Index: Quality of trade and transport-related infrastructure (worst 1–5 best)		NA	NA	●	●
The Times Higher Education Universities Ranking: Average score of top 3 universities (worst 0–100 best)	*	0.0	2020	●	●
Scientific and technical journal articles (per 1,000 population)		0.0	2018	●	→
Expenditure on research and development (% of GDP)	*	0.0	2017	●	●

SDG10 – Reduced Inequalities

	Value	Year	Rating	Trend
Gini coefficient adjusted for top income	NA	NA	●	●

SDG11 – Sustainable Cities and Communities

	Value	Year	Rating	Trend
Annual mean concentration of particulate matter of less than 2.5 microns in diameter (PM2.5) (μg/m³)	32.0	2017	●	↗
Access to improved water source, piped (% of urban population)	76.0	2017	●	↓
Satisfaction with public transport (%)	NA	NA	●	●

SDG12 – Responsible Consumption and Production

	Value	Year	Rating	Trend
Municipal solid waste (kg/capita/day)	NA	NA	●	●
Electronic waste (kg/capita)	NA	NA	●	●
Production-based SO₂ emissions (kg/capita)	24.5	2012	●	●
SO₂ emissions embodied in imports (kg/capita)	0.1	2012	●	●
Production-based nitrogen emissions (kg/capita)	5.5	2010	●	●
Nitrogen emissions embodied in imports (kg/capita)	0.1	2010	●	●

SDG13 – Climate Action

	Value	Year	Rating	Trend
Energy-related CO₂ emissions (tCO₂/capita)	1.8	2017	●	↑
CO₂ emissions embodied in imports (tCO₂/capita)	0.0	2015	●	↑
CO₂ emissions embodied in fossil fuel exports (kg/capita)	NA	NA	●	●

SDG14 – Life Below Water

	Value	Year	Rating	Trend
Mean area that is protected in marine sites important to biodiversity (%)	0.0	2018	●	→
Ocean Health Index: Clean Waters score (worst 0–100 best)	53.6	2019	●	→
Fish caught from overexploited or collapsed stocks (% of total catch)	21.8	2014	●	↑
Fish caught by trawling (%)	30.0	2014	●	↓
Marine biodiversity threats embodied in imports (per million population)	0.0	2018	●	●

SDG15 – Life on Land

	Value	Year	Rating	Trend
Mean area that is protected in terrestrial sites important to biodiversity (%)	11.6	2018	●	→
Mean area that is protected in freshwater sites important to biodiversity (%)	0.0	2018	●	→
Red List Index of species survival (worst 0–1 best)	0.9	2019	●	↓
Permanent deforestation (% of forest area, 5-year average)	0.1	2018	●	●
Terrestrial and freshwater biodiversity threats embodied in imports (per million population)	0.0	2018	●	●

SDG16 – Peace, Justice and Strong Institutions

		Value	Year	Rating	Trend
Homicides (per 100,000 population)	*	4.4	2015	●	●
Unsentenced detainees (% of prison population)		NA	NA	●	●
Percentage of population who feel safe walking alone at night in the city or area where they live (%)		NA	NA	●	●
Property Rights (worst 1–7 best)		NA	NA	●	●
Birth registrations with civil authority (% of children under age 5)		100.0	2018	●	●
Corruption Perception Index (worst 0–100 best)		17	2019	●	↗
Children involved in child labor (% of population aged 5 to 14)		NA	NA	●	●
Exports of major conventional weapons (TIV constant million USD per 100,000 population)	*	0.0	2019	●	●
Press Freedom Index (best 0–100 worst)		83.4	2019	●	→

SDG17 – Partnerships for the Goals

		Value	Year	Rating	Trend
Government spending on health and education (% of GDP)		NA	NA	●	●
For high-income and all OECD DAC countries: International concessional public finance, including official development assistance (% of GNI)		NA	NA	●	●
Other countries: Government revenue excluding grants (% of GDP)		NA	NA	●	●
Corporate Tax Haven Score (best 0–100 worst)	*	0.0	2019	●	●

* Imputed data point

▼ OVERALL PERFORMANCE

Index score

78.3

Regional average score

77.3

SDG Global rank 20 (OF 166)

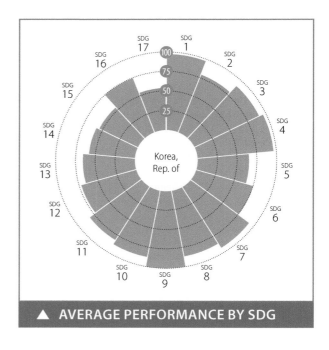

▲ AVERAGE PERFORMANCE BY SDG

▼ SPILLOVER INDEX

100 (best) to 0 (worst)

▼ CURRENT ASSESSMENT – SDG DASHBOARD

■ Major challenges　■ Significant challenges　■ Challenges remain　■ SDG achieved　■ Information unavailable

▼ SDG TRENDS

 ↓ Decreasing　→ Stagnating　↗ Moderately improving　↑ On track or maintaining SDG achievement　● Information unavailable

Notes: The full title of Goal 2 "Zero Hunger" is "End hunger, achieve food security and improved nutrition and promote sustainable agriculture".
The full title of each SDG is available here: https://sustainabledevelopment.un.org/topics/sustainabledevelopmentgoals

SDG1 – No Poverty

Indicator	Value	Year	Rating	Trend
Poverty headcount ratio at $1.90/day (%)	0.5	2020	●	↑
Poverty headcount ratio at $3.20/day (%)	0.7	2020	●	↑
Poverty rate after taxes and transfers (%)	17.4	2017	●	●

SDG2 – Zero Hunger

Indicator	Value	Year	Rating	Trend
Prevalence of undernourishment (%)	2.5	2017	●	↑
Prevalence of stunting in children under 5 years of age (%)	2.5	2010	●	↑
Prevalence of wasting in children under 5 years of age (%)	1.2	2010	●	↑
Prevalence of obesity, BMI ≥ 30 (% of adult population)	4.7	2016	●	↑
Human Trophic Level (best 2–3 worst)	2.3	2017	●	↓
Cereal yield (tonnes per hectare of harvested land)	6.7	2017	●	↑
Sustainable Nitrogen Management Index (best 0–1.41 worst)	0.6	2015	●	↓
Yield gap closure (% of potential yield)	NA	NA	●	●

SDG3 – Good Health and Well-Being

Indicator	Value	Year	Rating	Trend
Maternal mortality rate (per 100,000 live births)	11	2017	●	↑
Neonatal mortality rate (per 1,000 live births)	1.5	2018	●	↑
Mortality rate, under-5 (per 1,000 live births)	3.2	2018	●	↑
Incidence of tuberculosis (per 100,000 population)	66.0	2018	●	↗
New HIV infections (per 1,000 uninfected population)	NA	NA	●	●
Age-standardized death rate due to cardiovascular disease, cancer, diabetes, or chronic respiratory disease in adults aged 30–70 years (%)	7.8	2016	●	↑
Age-standardized death rate attributable to household air pollution and ambient air pollution (per 100,000 population)	20	2016	●	●
Traffic deaths (per 100,000 population)	9.8	2016	●	↑
Life expectancy at birth (years)	82.7	2016	●	↑
Adolescent fertility rate (births per 1,000 adolescent females aged 15 to 19)	1.4	2017	●	↑
Births attended by skilled health personnel (%)	100.0	2015	●	↑
Percentage of surviving infants who received 2 WHO-recommended vaccines (%)	98.0	2018	●	↑
Universal health coverage (UHC) index of service coverage (worst 0–100 best)	86.0	2017	●	↑
Subjective well-being (average ladder score, worst 0–10 best)	5.9	2019	●	↑
Gap in life expectancy at birth among regions (years)	2.5	2014	●	●
Gap in self-reported health status by income (percentage points)	14.4	2017	●	↑
Daily smokers (% of population aged 15 and over)	17.5	2017	●	↑

SDG4 – Quality Education

Indicator	Value	Year	Rating	Trend
Net primary enrollment rate (%)	* 97.4	2017	●	↑
Lower secondary completion rate (%)	* 97.4	2017	●	↑
Literacy rate (% of population aged 15 to 24)	NA	NA	●	●
Participation rate in pre-primary organized learning (% of children aged 4 to 6)	95.9	2017	●	↑
Tertiary educational attainment (% of population aged 25 to 34)	69.6	2018	●	↑
PISA score (worst 0–600 best)	519.7	2018	●	↑
Variation in science performance explained by socio-economic status (%)	8.0	2018	●	↑
Underachievers in science (% of 15-year-olds)	14.2	2018	●	↑
Resilient students in science (% of 15-year-olds)	45.0	2018	●	↑

SDG5 – Gender Equality

Indicator	Value	Year	Rating	Trend
Demand for family planning satisfied by modern methods (% of females aged 15 to 49 who are married or in unions)	* 83.4	2017	●	↑
Ratio of female-to-male mean years of education received (%)	89.1	2018	●	→
Ratio of female-to-male labor force participation rate (%)	71.9	2019	●	↑
Seats held by women in national parliament (%)	19.0	2020	●	→
Gender wage gap (% of male median wage)	34.1	2018	●	→
Gender gap in time spent doing unpaid work (minutes/day)	166.0	2014	●	●

SDG6 – Clean Water and Sanitation

Indicator	Value	Year	Rating	Trend
Population using at least basic drinking water services (%)	99.8	2017	●	●
Population using at least basic sanitation services (%)	100.0	2017	●	●
Freshwater withdrawal (% of available freshwater resources)	84.8	2005	●	●
Anthropogenic wastewater that receives treatment (%)	76.8	2018	●	●
Scarce water consumption embodied in imports (m³/capita)	17.7	2013	●	↑
Population using safely managed water services (%)	98.2	2017	●	↑
Population using safely managed sanitation services (%)	99.9	2017	●	↑

SDG7 – Affordable and Clean Energy

Indicator	Value	Year	Rating	Trend
Population with access to electricity (%)	100.0	2017	●	●
Population with access to clean fuels and technology for cooking (%)	96.7	2016	●	↑
CO$_2$ emissions from fuel combustion for electricity and heating per total electricity output (MtCO$_2$/TWh)	1.1	2017	●	→
Share of renewable energy in total primary energy supply (%)	1.9	2018	●	→

SDG8 – Decent Work and Economic Growth

Indicator	Value	Year	Rating	Trend
Adjusted GDP growth (%)	-0.2	2018	●	●
Victims of modern slavery (per 1,000 population)	1.9	2018	●	●
Adults with an account at a bank or other financial institution or with a mobile-money-service provider (% of population aged 15 or over)	94.9	2017	●	↑
Fatal work-related accidents embodied in imports (per 100,000 population)	1.0	2010	●	↑
Employment-to-population ratio (%)	66.8	2019	●	↑
Youth not in employment, education or training (NEET) (% of population aged 15 to 29)	NA	NA	●	●

SDG9 – Industry, Innovation and Infrastructure

Indicator	Value	Year	Rating	Trend
Population using the internet (%)	96.0	2018	●	↑
Mobile broadband subscriptions (per 100 population)	113.6	2018	●	↑
Logistics Performance Index: Quality of trade and transport-related infrastructure (worst 1–5 best)	3.7	2018	●	↑
The Times Higher Education Universities Ranking: Average score of top 3 universities (worst 0–100 best)	64.1	2020	●	●
Scientific and technical journal articles (per 1,000 population)	1.3	2018	●	↑
Expenditure on research and development (% of GDP)	4.6	2017	●	↑
Researchers (per 1,000 employed population)	15.3	2018	●	↑
Triadic patent families filed (per million population)	42.8	2017	●	↑
Gap in internet access by income (percentage points)	1.9	2018	●	↑
Women in science and engineering (% of tertiary graduates in science and engineering)	24.0	2015	●	●

SDG10 – Reduced Inequalities

Indicator	Value	Year	Rating	Trend
Gini coefficient adjusted for top income	32.3	2012	○	●
Palma ratio	1.4	2017	●	●
Elderly poverty rate (% of population aged 66 or over)	43.8	2017	●	●

SDG11 – Sustainable Cities and Communities

Indicator	Value	Year	Rating	Trend
Annual mean concentration of particulate matter of less than 2.5 microns in diameter (PM2.5) (µg/m³)	25.0	2017	●	↗
Access to improved water source, piped (% of urban population)	NA	NA	●	●
Satisfaction with public transport (%)	73.2	2019	●	↑
Population with rent overburden (%)	3.1	2012	●	●

SDG12 – Responsible Consumption and Production

Indicator	Value	Year	Rating	Trend
Electronic waste (kg/capita)	13.1	2016	●	●
Production-based SO$_2$ emissions (kg/capita)	39.7	2012	●	●
SO$_2$ emissions embodied in imports (kg/capita)	9.9	2012	●	●
Production-based nitrogen emissions (kg/capita)	30.2	2010	●	●
Nitrogen emissions embodied in imports (kg/capita)	6.9	2010	●	●
Non-recycled municipal solid waste (kg/capita/day)	0.4	2016	●	●

SDG13 – Climate Action

Indicator	Value	Year	Rating	Trend
Energy-related CO$_2$ emissions (tCO$_2$/capita)	11.8	2017	●	↓
CO$_2$ emissions embodied in imports (tCO$_2$/capita)	1.7	2015	●	→
CO$_2$ emissions embodied in fossil fuel exports (kg/capita)	1.3	2018	●	●
Effective carbon rate (EUR/tCO$_2$)	9.9	2016	●	●

SDG14 – Life Below Water

Indicator	Value	Year	Rating	Trend
Mean area that is protected in marine sites important to biodiversity (%)	24.2	2018	●	→
Ocean Health Index: Clean Waters score (worst 0–100 best)	59.8	2019	●	↓
Fish caught from overexploited or collapsed stocks (% of total catch)	6.1	2014	●	↑
Fish caught by trawling (%)	45.1	2014	●	→
Marine biodiversity threats embodied in imports (per million population)	0.4	2018	●	●

SDG15 – Life on Land

Indicator	Value	Year	Rating	Trend
Mean area that is protected in terrestrial sites important to biodiversity (%)	32.5	2018	○	→
Mean area that is protected in freshwater sites important to biodiversity (%)	36.8	2018	○	→
Red List Index of species survival (worst 0–1 best)	0.7	2019	●	↓
Permanent deforestation (% of forest area, 5-year average)	0.0	2018	●	●
Terrestrial and freshwater biodiversity threats embodied in imports (per million population)	2.5	2018	●	●

SDG16 – Peace, Justice and Strong Institutions

Indicator	Value	Year	Rating	Trend
Homicides (per 100,000 population)	0.6	2017	●	↑
Unsentenced detainees (% of prison population)	35.4	2018	○	↓
Percentage of population who feel safe walking alone at night in the city or area where they live (%)	74.8	2019	●	↑
Property Rights (worst 1–7 best)	5.0	2019	●	●
Birth registrations with civil authority (% of children under age 5)	NA	NA	●	●
Corruption Perception Index (worst 0–100 best)	59.0	2019	●	↑
Children involved in child labor (% of population aged 5 to 14)	* 0.0	2016	●	●
Exports of major conventional weapons (TIV constant million USD per 100,000 population)	1.2	2019	●	●
Press Freedom Index (best 0–100 worst)	24.9	2019	●	↑
Persons held in prison (per 100,000 population)	108.3	2017	○	→

SDG17 – Partnerships for the Goals

Indicator	Value	Year	Rating	Trend
Government spending on health and education (% of GDP)	* 8.9	2017	○	↑
For high-income and all OECD DAC countries: International concessional public finance, including official development assistance (% of GNI)	0.1	2017	●	→
Other countries: Government revenue excluding grants (% of GDP)	NA	NA	●	●
Corporate Tax Haven Score (best 0–100 worst)	* 0.0	2019	●	●
Financial Secrecy Score (best 0–100 worst)	61.6	2020	●	●
Shifted profits of multinationals (US$ billion)	4.7	2016	●	●

* Imputed data point

5. Country Profiles

KUWAIT

Middle East and North Africa

▼ OVERALL PERFORMANCE

Index score

63.1

Regional average score

66.3

SDG Global rank **112** (OF 166)

▼ SPILLOVER INDEX

100 (best) to 0 (worst)

▲ AVERAGE PERFORMANCE BY SDG

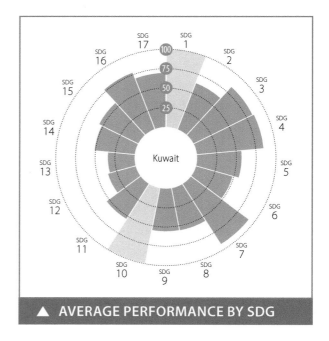

Kuwait

▼ CURRENT ASSESSMENT – SDG DASHBOARD

■ Major challenges ■ Significant challenges ■ Challenges remain ■ SDG achieved ■ Information unavailable

▼ SDG TRENDS

1 NO POVERTY	2 ZERO HUNGER	3 GOOD HEALTH AND WELL-BEING	4 QUALITY EDUCATION	5 GENDER EQUALITY	6 CLEAN WATER AND SANITATION	7 AFFORDABLE AND CLEAN ENERGY	8 DECENT WORK AND ECONOMIC GROWTH	9 INDUSTRY, INNOVATION AND INFRASTRUCTURE
●	→	↗	→	→	↗	↗	↑	↗

10 REDUCED INEQUALITIES	11 SUSTAINABLE CITIES AND COMMUNITIES	12 RESPONSIBLE CONSUMPTION AND PRODUCTION	13 CLIMATE ACTION	14 LIFE BELOW WATER	15 LIFE ON LAND	16 PEACE, JUSTICE AND STRONG INSTITUTIONS	17 PARTNERSHIPS FOR THE GOALS
●	↗	●	→	↓	→	↓	●

↓ Decreasing → Stagnating ↗ Moderately improving ↑ On track or maintaining SDG achievement ● Information unavailable

Notes: The full title of Goal 2 "Zero Hunger" is "End hunger, achieve food security and improved nutrition and promote sustainable agriculture".
The full title of each SDG is available here: https://sustainabledevelopment.un.org/topics/sustainabledevelopmentgoals

284 | Sustainable Development Report 2020 ○ The Sustainable Development Goals and Covid-19

KUWAIT

SDG1 – No Poverty

Indicator		Value	Year	Rating	Trend
Poverty headcount ratio at $1.90/day (%)	*	NA	NA	●	●
Poverty headcount ratio at $3.20/day (%)	*	NA	NA	●	●

SDG2 – Zero Hunger

Indicator	Value	Year	Rating	Trend
Prevalence of undernourishment (%)	2.8	2017	●	↑
Prevalence of stunting in children under 5 years of age (%)	4.9	2015	●	↑
Prevalence of wasting in children under 5 years of age (%)	3.1	2015	●	↑
Prevalence of obesity, BMI ≥ 30 (% of adult population)	37.9	2016	●	↓
Human Trophic Level (best 2–3 worst)	2.2	2017	●	↓
Cereal yield (tonnes per hectare of harvested land)	5.7	2017	●	↑
Sustainable Nitrogen Management Index (best 0–1.41 worst)	0.7	2015	●	↓

SDG3 – Good Health and Well-Being

Indicator	Value	Year	Rating	Trend
Maternal mortality rate (per 100,000 live births)	12	2017	●	↑
Neonatal mortality rate (per 1,000 live births)	4.5	2018	●	↑
Mortality rate, under-5 (per 1,000 live births)	7.9	2018	●	↑
Incidence of tuberculosis (per 100,000 population)	23.0	2018	●	→
New HIV infections (per 1,000 uninfected population)	0.0	2018	●	↑
Age-standardized death rate due to cardiovascular disease, cancer, diabetes, or chronic respiratory disease in adults aged 30–70 years (%)	17.4	2016	●	↑
Age-standardized death rate attributable to household air pollution and ambient air pollution (per 100,000 population)	104	2016	●	●
Traffic deaths (per 100,000 population)	17.6	2016	●	↗
Life expectancy at birth (years)	74.8	2016	●	→
Adolescent fertility rate (births per 1,000 adolescent females aged 15 to 19)	8.2	2017	●	↑
Births attended by skilled health personnel (%)	99.9	2015	●	↑
Percentage of surviving infants who received 2 WHO-recommended vaccines (%)	99	2018	●	↑
Universal health coverage (UHC) index of service coverage (worst 0–100 best)	76.0	2017	●	↑
Subjective well-being (average ladder score, worst 0–10 best)	6.2	2018	●	↑

SDG4 – Quality Education

Indicator	Value	Year	Rating	Trend
Net primary enrollment rate (%)	82.6	2018	●	↓
Lower secondary completion rate (%)	94.3	2018	●	↑
Literacy rate (% of population aged 15 to 24)	99.1	2018	●	●

SDG5 – Gender Equality

Indicator		Value	Year	Rating	Trend
Demand for family planning satisfied by modern methods (% of females aged 15 to 49 who are married or in unions)	*	64.6	2017	●	→
Ratio of female-to-male mean years of education received (%)		115.9	2018	●	↑
Ratio of female-to-male labor force participation rate (%)		67.2	2019	●	→
Seats held by women in national parliament (%)		6.4	2020	●	→

SDG6 – Clean Water and Sanitation

Indicator	Value	Year	Rating	Trend
Population using at least basic drinking water services (%)	100.0	2017	●	↑
Population using at least basic sanitation services (%)	100.0	2017	●	↑
Freshwater withdrawal (% of available freshwater resources)	2075.0	2000	●	●
Anthropogenic wastewater that receives treatment (%)	43.1	2018	●	●
Scarce water consumption embodied in imports (m³/capita)	287.9	2013	●	↗

SDG7 – Affordable and Clean Energy

Indicator	Value	Year	Rating	Trend
Population with access to electricity (%)	100.0	2017	●	↑
Population with access to clean fuels and technology for cooking (%)	100.0	2016	●	↑
CO_2 emissions from fuel combustion for electricity and heating per total electricity output ($MtCO_2$/TWh)	1.3	2017	●	↗

SDG8 – Decent Work and Economic Growth

Indicator		Value	Year	Rating	Trend
Adjusted GDP growth (%)		-3.9	2018	●	●
Victims of modern slavery (per 1,000 population)	*	NA	NA	●	●
Adults with an account at a bank or other financial institution or with a mobile-money-service provider (% of population aged 15 or over)		79.8	2017	●	↑
Unemployment rate (% of total labor force)		2.2	2019	●	↑
Fatal work-related accidents embodied in imports (per 100,000 population)		7.3	2010	●	↑

SDG9 – Industry, Innovation and Infrastructure

Indicator	Value	Year	Rating	Trend
Population using the internet (%)	99.6	2018	●	↑
Mobile broadband subscriptions (per 100 population)	131.1	2018	●	↑
Logistics Performance Index: Quality of trade and transport-related infrastructure (worst 1–5 best)	3.0	2018	●	↑
The Times Higher Education Universities Ranking: Average score of top 3 universities (worst 0–100 best)	25.2	2020	●	●
Scientific and technical journal articles (per 1,000 population)	0.2	2018	●	→
Expenditure on research and development (% of GDP)	0.1	2017	●	↓

SDG10 – Reduced Inequalities

Indicator	Value	Year	Rating	Trend
Gini coefficient adjusted for top income	NA	NA	●	●

SDG11 – Sustainable Cities and Communities

Indicator	Value	Year	Rating	Trend
Annual mean concentration of particulate matter of less than 2.5 microns in diameter (PM2.5) (µg/m³)	60.7	2017	●	↓
Access to improved water source, piped (% of urban population)	NA	NA	●	●
Satisfaction with public transport (%)	67.9	2018	●	↑

SDG12 – Responsible Consumption and Production

Indicator	Value	Year	Rating	Trend
Municipal solid waste (kg/capita/day)	1.1	2010	●	●
Electronic waste (kg/capita)	15.8	2016	●	●
Production-based SO_2 emissions (kg/capita)	284.2	2012	●	●
SO_2 emissions embodied in imports (kg/capita)	35.5	2012	●	●
Production-based nitrogen emissions (kg/capita)	32.0	2010	●	●
Nitrogen emissions embodied in imports (kg/capita)	57.8	2010	●	●

SDG13 – Climate Action

Indicator	Value	Year	Rating	Trend
Energy-related CO_2 emissions (tCO_2/capita)	23.3	2017	●	→
CO_2 emissions embodied in imports (tCO_2/capita)	4.7	2015	●	↗
CO_2 emissions embodied in fossil fuel exports (kg/capita)	0.3	2018	●	●

SDG14 – Life Below Water

Indicator	Value	Year	Rating	Trend
Mean area that is protected in marine sites important to biodiversity (%)	32.1	2018	●	→
Ocean Health Index: Clean Waters score (worst 0–100 best)	59.6	2019	●	↓
Fish caught from overexploited or collapsed stocks (% of total catch)	NA	NA	●	●
Fish caught by trawling (%)	48.4	2014	●	↓
Marine biodiversity threats embodied in imports (per million population)	0.4	2018	●	●

SDG15 – Life on Land

Indicator	Value	Year	Rating	Trend
Mean area that is protected in terrestrial sites important to biodiversity (%)	59.0	2018	●	↑
Mean area that is protected in freshwater sites important to biodiversity (%)	NA	NA	●	●
Red List Index of species survival (worst 0–1 best)	0.8	2019	●	↓
Permanent deforestation (% of forest area, 5-year average)	NA	NA	●	●
Terrestrial and freshwater biodiversity threats embodied in imports (per million population)	5.2	2018	●	●

SDG16 – Peace, Justice and Strong Institutions

Indicator		Value	Year	Rating	Trend
Homicides (per 100,000 population)		1.8	2012	●	●
Unsentenced detainees (% of prison population)		9.1	2015	●	●
Percentage of population who feel safe walking alone at night in the city or area where they live (%)		85.8	2006	●	●
Property Rights (worst 1–7 best)		4.4	2019	●	●
Birth registrations with civil authority (% of children under age 5)		NA	NA	●	●
Corruption Perception Index (worst 0–100 best)		40	2019	●	↓
Children involved in child labor (% of population aged 5 to 14)		NA	NA	●	●
Exports of major conventional weapons (TIV constant million USD per 100,000 population)	*	0.0	2019	●	●
Press Freedom Index (best 0–100 worst)		33.9	2019	●	↓

SDG17 – Partnerships for the Goals

Indicator		Value	Year	Rating	Trend
Government spending on health and education (% of GDP)		5.6	2006	●	●
For high-income and all OECD DAC countries: International concessional public finance, including official development assistance (% of GNI)		NA	NA	●	●
Other countries: Government revenue excluding grants (% of GDP)		NA	NA	●	●
Corporate Tax Haven Score (best 0–100 worst)	*	0.0	2019	●	●

* Imputed data point

5. Country Profiles

KYRGYZ REPUBLIC

▼ OVERALL PERFORMANCE

Index score

73.0

Regional average score

70.9

SDG Global rank 52 (OF 166)

▼ AVERAGE PERFORMANCE BY SDG

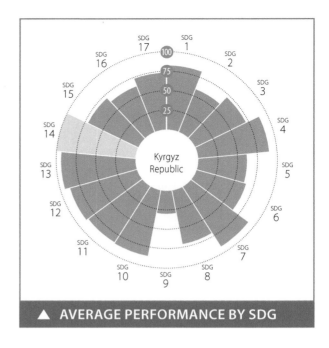

Kyrgyz Republic

▼ SPILLOVER INDEX

100 (best) to 0 (worst)

▼ CURRENT ASSESSMENT – SDG DASHBOARD

■ Major challenges ■ Significant challenges ■ Challenges remain ■ SDG achieved ■ Information unavailable

▼ SDG TRENDS

| 1 NO POVERTY ↑ | 2 ZERO HUNGER ↗ | 3 GOOD HEALTH AND WELL-BEING ↗ | 4 QUALITY EDUCATION ↗ | 5 GENDER EQUALITY → | 6 CLEAN WATER AND SANITATION ↗ | 7 AFFORDABLE AND CLEAN ENERGY ↑ | 8 DECENT WORK AND ECONOMIC GROWTH ↑ | 9 INDUSTRY, INNOVATION AND INFRASTRUCTURE ↗ |
| 10 REDUCED INEQUALITIES ● | 11 SUSTAINABLE CITIES AND COMMUNITIES → | 12 RESPONSIBLE CONSUMPTION AND PRODUCTION ● | 13 CLIMATE ACTION ↑ | 14 LIFE BELOW WATER ● | 15 LIFE ON LAND → | 16 PEACE, JUSTICE AND STRONG INSTITUTIONS ↗ | 17 PARTNERSHIPS FOR THE GOALS ↓ | |

↓ Decreasing   → Stagnating   ↗ Moderately improving   ↑ On track or maintaining SDG achievement   ● Information unavailable

Notes: The full title of Goal 2 "Zero Hunger" is "End hunger, achieve food security and improved nutrition and promote sustainable agriculture".
The full title of each SDG is available here: https://sustainabledevelopment.un.org/topics/sustainabledevelopmentgoals

SDG1 – No Poverty

Indicator	Value	Year	Rating	Trend
Poverty headcount ratio at $1.90/day (%)	0.8	2020	●	↑
Poverty headcount ratio at $3.20/day (%)	15.6	2020	●	↑

SDG2 – Zero Hunger

Indicator	Value	Year	Rating	Trend
Prevalence of undernourishment (%)	7.1	2017	●	↑
Prevalence of stunting in children under 5 years of age (%)	12.9	2014	●	↗
Prevalence of wasting in children under 5 years of age (%)	2.8	2014	●	↑
Prevalence of obesity, BMI ≥ 30 (% of adult population)	16.6	2016	●	↓
Human Trophic Level (best 2–3 worst)	2.3	2017	●	↗
Cereal yield (tonnes per hectare of harvested land)	3.1	2017	●	↑
Sustainable Nitrogen Management Index (best 0–1.41 worst)	0.6	2015	●	↓

SDG3 – Good Health and Well-Being

Indicator	Value	Year	Rating	Trend
Maternal mortality rate (per 100,000 live births)	60	2017	●	↑
Neonatal mortality rate (per 1,000 live births)	13.2	2018	●	↑
Mortality rate, under-5 (per 1,000 live births)	18.9	2018	●	↑
Incidence of tuberculosis (per 100,000 population)	116.0	2018	●	↗
New HIV infections (per 1,000 uninfected population)	0.1	2018	●	↑
Age-standardized death rate due to cardiovascular disease, cancer, diabetes, or chronic respiratory disease in adults aged 30–70 years (%)	24.9	2016	●	↗
Age-standardized death rate attributable to household air pollution and ambient air pollution (per 100,000 population)	111	2016	●	●
Traffic deaths (per 100,000 population)	15.4	2016	●	↑
Life expectancy at birth (years)	71.4	2016	●	↗
Adolescent fertility rate (births per 1,000 adolescent females aged 15 to 19)	32.8	2017	●	↑
Births attended by skilled health personnel (%)	98.4	2014	●	●
Percentage of surviving infants who received 2 WHO-recommended vaccines (%)	94	2018	●	↑
Universal health coverage (UHC) index of service coverage (worst 0–100 best)	70.0	2017	●	↑
Subjective well-being (average ladder score, worst 0–10 best)	5.7	2019	●	↑

SDG4 – Quality Education

Indicator	Value	Year	Rating	Trend
Net primary enrollment rate (%)	89.9	2018	●	→
Lower secondary completion rate (%)	95.1	2018	●	↑
Literacy rate (% of population aged 15 to 24)	99.8	2018	●	●

SDG5 – Gender Equality

Indicator	Value	Year	Rating	Trend
Demand for family planning satisfied by modern methods (% of females aged 15 to 49 who are married or in unions)	66.2	2014	●	→
Ratio of female-to-male mean years of education received (%)	101.9	2018	●	↑
Ratio of female-to-male labor force participation rate (%)	63.0	2019	●	↓
Seats held by women in national parliament (%)	19.2	2020	●	↓

SDG6 – Clean Water and Sanitation

Indicator	Value	Year	Rating	Trend
Population using at least basic drinking water services (%)	87.5	2017	●	→
Population using at least basic sanitation services (%)	96.5	2017	●	↑
Freshwater withdrawal (% of available freshwater resources)	50.0	2005	●	●
Anthropogenic wastewater that receives treatment (%)	0.2	2018	●	●
Scarce water consumption embodied in imports (m³/capita)	6.8	2013	●	↑

SDG7 – Affordable and Clean Energy

Indicator	Value	Year	Rating	Trend
Population with access to electricity (%)	100.0	2017	●	↑
Population with access to clean fuels and technology for cooking (%)	81.3	2016	●	↑
CO_2 emissions from fuel combustion for electricity and heating per total electricity output (MtCO₂/TWh)	0.6	2017	●	↑

SDG8 – Decent Work and Economic Growth

Indicator	Value	Year	Rating	Trend
Adjusted GDP growth (%)	-3.6	2018	●	●
Victims of modern slavery (per 1,000 population)	4.1	2018	●	●
Adults with an account at a bank or other financial institution or with a mobile-money-service provider (% of population aged 15 or over)	39.9	2017	●	↑
Unemployment rate (% of total labor force)	6.3	2019	●	↑
Fatal work-related accidents embodied in imports (per 100,000 population)	0.1	2010	●	↑

SDG9 – Industry, Innovation and Infrastructure

Indicator	Value	Year	Rating	Trend
Population using the internet (%)	38.0	2017	●	↑
Mobile broadband subscriptions (per 100 population)	94.0	2018	●	↑
Logistics Performance Index: Quality of trade and transport-related infrastructure (worst 1–5 best)	2.4	2018	●	↑
The Times Higher Education Universities Ranking: Average score of top 3 * universities (worst 0–100 best)	0.0	2020	●	●
Scientific and technical journal articles (per 1,000 population)	0.0	2018	●	→
Expenditure on research and development (% of GDP)	0.1	2017	●	↓

SDG10 – Reduced Inequalities

Indicator	Value	Year	Rating	Trend
Gini coefficient adjusted for top income	32.8	2017	●	●

SDG11 – Sustainable Cities and Communities

Indicator	Value	Year	Rating	Trend
Annual mean concentration of particulate matter of less than 2.5 microns in diameter (PM2.5) (μg/m³)	22.7	2017	●	→
Access to improved water source, piped (% of urban population)	97.8	2017	●	↓
Satisfaction with public transport (%)	66.7	2019	●	→

SDG12 – Responsible Consumption and Production

Indicator	Value	Year	Rating	Trend
Municipal solid waste (kg/capita/day)	1.4	2015	●	●
Electronic waste (kg/capita)	1.2	2016	●	●
Production-based SO_2 emissions (kg/capita)	67.3	2012	●	●
SO_2 emissions embodied in imports (kg/capita)	2.4	2012	●	●
Production-based nitrogen emissions (kg/capita)	18.9	2010	●	●
Nitrogen emissions embodied in imports (kg/capita)	0.8	2010	●	●

SDG13 – Climate Action

Indicator	Value	Year	Rating	Trend
Energy-related CO_2 emissions (tCO₂/capita)	1.4	2017	●	↑
CO_2 emissions embodied in imports (tCO₂/capita)	0.5	2015	●	↑
CO_2 emissions embodied in fossil fuel exports (kg/capita)	114.5	2018	●	●

SDG14 – Life Below Water

Indicator	Value	Year	Rating	Trend
Mean area that is protected in marine sites important to biodiversity (%)	NA	NA	●	●
Ocean Health Index: Clean Waters score (worst 0–100 best)	NA	NA	●	●
Fish caught from overexploited or collapsed stocks (% of total catch)	NA	NA	●	●
Fish caught by trawling (%)	NA	NA	●	●
Marine biodiversity threats embodied in imports (per million population)	0.0	2018	●	●

SDG15 – Life on Land

Indicator	Value	Year	Rating	Trend
Mean area that is protected in terrestrial sites important to biodiversity (%)	26.7	2018	●	→
Mean area that is protected in freshwater sites important to biodiversity (%)	36.7	2018	●	→
Red List Index of species survival (worst 0–1 best)	1.0	2019	●	↑
Permanent deforestation (% of forest area, 5-year average)	0.0	2018	●	●
Terrestrial and freshwater biodiversity threats embodied in imports (per million population)	0.0	2018	●	●

SDG16 – Peace, Justice and Strong Institutions

Indicator	Value	Year	Rating	Trend
Homicides (per 100,000 population)	4.2	2017	●	↑
Unsentenced detainees (% of prison population)	16.5	2018	●	↑
Percentage of population who feel safe walking alone at night in the city or area where they live (%)	62.3	2019	●	↑
Property Rights (worst 1–7 best)	3.5	2019	●	●
Birth registrations with civil authority (% of children under age 5)	98.9	2018	●	●
Corruption Perception Index (worst 0–100 best)	30	2019	●	→
Children involved in child labor (% of population aged 5 to 14)	25.8	2016	●	●
Exports of major conventional weapons (TIV constant million USD per 100,000 population)	0.1	2019	●	●
Press Freedom Index (best 0–100 worst)	29.9	2019	●	↑

SDG17 – Partnerships for the Goals

Indicator	Value	Year	Rating	Trend
Government spending on health and education (% of GDP)	9.2	2016	●	↓
For high-income and all OECD DAC countries: International concessional public finance, including official development assistance (% of GNI)	NA	NA	●	●
Other countries: Government revenue excluding grants (% of GDP)	28.6	2018	●	↓
Corporate Tax Haven Score (best 0–100 worst) *	0.0	2019	●	●

* Imputed data point

LAO PEOPLE'S DEMOCRATIC REPUBLIC East and South Asia

▼ OVERALL PERFORMANCE

Index score

62.1

Regional average score

67.2

SDG Global rank **116** (OF 166)

▲ AVERAGE PERFORMANCE BY SDG

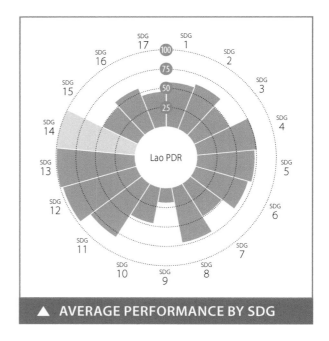

Lao PDR

▼ SPILLOVER INDEX

100 (best) to 0 (worst)

▼ CURRENT ASSESSMENT – SDG DASHBOARD

■ Major challenges ■ Significant challenges ■ Challenges remain ■ SDG achieved ■ Information unavailable

▼ SDG TRENDS

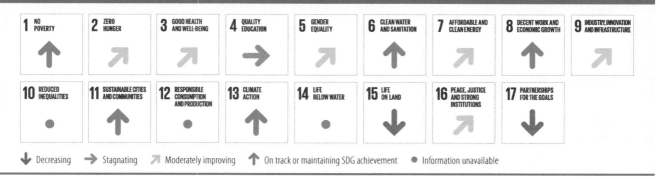

↓ Decreasing → Stagnating ↗ Moderately improving ↑ On track or maintaining SDG achievement ● Information unavailable

Notes: The full title of Goal 2 "Zero Hunger" is "End hunger, achieve food security and improved nutrition and promote sustainable agriculture".
The full title of each SDG is available here: https://sustainabledevelopment.un.org/topics/sustainabledevelopmentgoals

SDG1 – No Poverty

	Value	Year	Rating	Trend
Poverty headcount ratio at $1.90/day (%)	8.9	2020	●	↑
Poverty headcount ratio at $3.20/day (%)	36.2	2020	●	↗

SDG2 – Zero Hunger

	Value	Year	Rating	Trend
Prevalence of undernourishment (%)	16.5	2017	●	→
Prevalence of stunting in children under 5 years of age (%)	43.8	2011	●	→
Prevalence of wasting in children under 5 years of age (%)	6.4	2011	●	→
Prevalence of obesity, BMI ≥ 30 (% of adult population)	5.3	2016	●	↑
Human Trophic Level (best 2–3 worst)	2.1	2017	●	↑
Cereal yield (tonnes per hectare of harvested land)	4.5	2017	●	↑
Sustainable Nitrogen Management Index (best 0–1.41 worst)	0.4	2015	●	→

SDG3 – Good Health and Well-Being

	Value	Year	Rating	Trend
Maternal mortality rate (per 100,000 live births)	185	2017	●	↑
Neonatal mortality rate (per 1,000 live births)	22.7	2018	●	↗
Mortality rate, under-5 (per 1,000 live births)	47.3	2018	●	↑
Incidence of tuberculosis (per 100,000 population)	162.0	2018	●	↗
New HIV infections (per 1,000 uninfected population)	0.1	2018	●	↑
Age-standardized death rate due to cardiovascular disease, cancer, diabetes, or chronic respiratory disease in adults aged 30–70 years (%)	27.0	2016	●	→
Age-standardized death rate attributable to household air pollution and ambient air pollution (per 100,000 population)	188	2016	●	●
Traffic deaths (per 100,000 population)	16.6	2016	●	↓
Life expectancy at birth (years)	65.8	2016	●	→
Adolescent fertility rate (births per 1,000 adolescent females aged 15 to 19)	65.4	2017	●	→
Births attended by skilled health personnel (%)	40.1	2012	●	●
Percentage of surviving infants who received 2 WHO-recommended vaccines (%)	68	2018	●	↓
Universal health coverage (UHC) index of service coverage (worst 0–100 best)	51.0	2017	●	↗
Subjective well-being (average ladder score, worst 0–10 best)	4.9	2018	●	●

SDG4 – Quality Education

	Value	Year	Rating	Trend
Net primary enrollment rate (%)	91.5	2018	●	↓
Lower secondary completion rate (%)	67.1	2018	●	↗
Literacy rate (% of population aged 15 to 24)	92.5	2015	●	●

SDG5 – Gender Equality

	Value	Year	Rating	Trend
Demand for family planning satisfied by modern methods (% of females aged 15 to 49 who are married or in unions)	71.6	2017	●	↗
Ratio of female-to-male mean years of education received (%)	85.7	2018	●	↑
Ratio of female-to-male labor force participation rate (%)	96.3	2019	●	↑
Seats held by women in national parliament (%)	27.5	2020	●	↗

SDG6 – Clean Water and Sanitation

	Value	Year	Rating	Trend
Population using at least basic drinking water services (%)	82.1	2017	●	↑
Population using at least basic sanitation services (%)	74.5	2017	●	↑
Freshwater withdrawal (% of available freshwater resources)	2.3	2005	●	●
Anthropogenic wastewater that receives treatment (%)	0.0	2018	●	●
Scarce water consumption embodied in imports (m³/capita)	0.7	2013	●	↑

SDG7 – Affordable and Clean Energy

	Value	Year	Rating	Trend
Population with access to electricity (%)	93.6	2017	●	↑
Population with access to clean fuels and technology for cooking (%)	5.6	2016	●	→
CO₂ emissions from fuel combustion for electricity and heating per total electricity output (MtCO₂/TWh)	NA	NA	●	●

SDG8 – Decent Work and Economic Growth

	Value	Year	Rating	Trend
Adjusted GDP growth (%)	0.2	2018	●	●
Victims of modern slavery (per 1,000 population)	9.4	2018	●	●
Adults with an account at a bank or other financial institution or with a mobile-money-service provider (% of population aged 15 or over)	29.1	2017	●	●
Unemployment rate (% of total labor force)	0.6	2019	●	↑
Fatal work-related accidents embodied in imports (per 100,000 population)	0.0	2010	●	↑

SDG9 – Industry, Innovation and Infrastructure

	Value	Year	Rating	Trend
Population using the internet (%)	25.5	2017	●	↗
Mobile broadband subscriptions (per 100 population)	42.0	2018	●	↑
Logistics Performance Index: Quality of trade and transport-related infrastructure (worst 1–5 best)	2.4	2018	●	↑
The Times Higher Education Universities Ranking: Average score of top 3 universities (worst 0–100 best) *	0.0	2020	●	●
Scientific and technical journal articles (per 1,000 population)	0.0	2018	●	→
Expenditure on research and development (% of GDP)	0.0	2002	●	●

SDG10 – Reduced Inequalities

	Value	Year	Rating	Trend
Gini coefficient adjusted for top income	46.8	2012	●	●

SDG11 – Sustainable Cities and Communities

	Value	Year	Rating	Trend
Annual mean concentration of particulate matter of less than 2.5 microns in diameter (PM2.5) (μg/m³)	25.1	2017	●	↗
Access to improved water source, piped (% of urban population)	82.3	2017	●	↑
Satisfaction with public transport (%)	71.6	2018	●	●

SDG12 – Responsible Consumption and Production

	Value	Year	Rating	Trend
Municipal solid waste (kg/capita/day)	0.4	2015	●	●
Electronic waste (kg/capita)	1.0	2016	●	●
Production-based SO₂ emissions (kg/capita)	18.7	2012	●	●
SO₂ emissions embodied in imports (kg/capita)	0.6	2012	●	●
Production-based nitrogen emissions (kg/capita)	7.6	2010	●	●
Nitrogen emissions embodied in imports (kg/capita)	0.3	2010	●	●

SDG13 – Climate Action

	Value	Year	Rating	Trend
Energy-related CO₂ emissions (tCO₂/capita)	0.1	2017	●	↑
CO₂ emissions embodied in imports (tCO₂/capita)	0.1	2015	●	↑
CO₂ emissions embodied in fossil fuel exports (kg/capita)	12.7	2018	●	●

SDG14 – Life Below Water

	Value	Year	Rating	Trend
Mean area that is protected in marine sites important to biodiversity (%)	NA	NA	●	●
Ocean Health Index: Clean Waters score (worst 0–100 best)	NA	NA	●	●
Fish caught from overexploited or collapsed stocks (% of total catch)	NA	NA	●	●
Fish caught by trawling (%)	NA	NA	●	●
Marine biodiversity threats embodied in imports (per million population)	0.0	2018	●	●

SDG15 – Life on Land

	Value	Year	Rating	Trend
Mean area that is protected in terrestrial sites important to biodiversity (%)	46.5	2018	●	→
Mean area that is protected in freshwater sites important to biodiversity (%)	19.9	2018	●	→
Red List Index of species survival (worst 0–1 best)	0.8	2019	●	↓
Permanent deforestation (% of forest area, 5-year average)	1.0	2018	●	●
Terrestrial and freshwater biodiversity threats embodied in imports (per million population)	0.0	2018	●	●

SDG16 – Peace, Justice and Strong Institutions

		Value	Year	Rating	Trend
Homicides (per 100,000 population)	*	7.0	2015	●	●
Unsentenced detainees (% of prison population)		NA	NA	●	●
Percentage of population who feel safe walking alone at night in the city or area where they live (%)		60.7	2018	●	●
Property Rights (worst 1–7 best)		3.9	2019	●	●
Birth registrations with civil authority (% of children under age 5)		73.0	2018	●	●
Corruption Perception Index (worst 0–100 best)		29	2019	●	→
Children involved in child labor (% of population aged 5 to 14)		10.1	2016	●	●
Exports of major conventional weapons (TIV constant million USD per 100,000 population)	*	0.0	2019	●	●
Press Freedom Index (best 0–100 worst)		64.5	2019	●	↗

SDG17 – Partnerships for the Goals

		Value	Year	Rating	Trend
Government spending on health and education (% of GDP)		3.6	2014	●	●
For high-income and all OECD DAC countries: International concessional public finance, including official development assistance (% of GNI)		NA	NA	●	●
Other countries: Government revenue excluding grants (% of GDP)	*	14.3	2018	●	↓
Corporate Tax Haven Score (best 0–100 worst)	*	0.0	2019	●	●

* Imputed data point

▼ OVERALL PERFORMANCE

Index score

77.7

Regional average score

77.3

SDG Global rank 24 (OF 166)

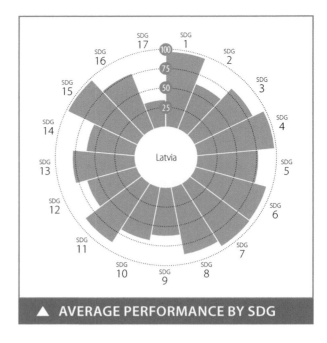

▲ AVERAGE PERFORMANCE BY SDG

▼ SPILLOVER INDEX

100 (best) to 0 (worst)

▼ CURRENT ASSESSMENT – SDG DASHBOARD

■ Major challenges   ■ Significant challenges   ■ Challenges remain   ■ SDG achieved   ■ Information unavailable

▼ SDG TRENDS

↓ Decreasing   → Stagnating   ↗ Moderately improving   ↑ On track or maintaining SDG achievement   ● Information unavailable

Notes: The full title of Goal 2 "Zero Hunger" is "End hunger, achieve food security and improved nutrition and promote sustainable agriculture".
The full title of each SDG is available here: https://sustainabledevelopment.un.org/topics/sustainabledevelopmentgoals

SDG1 – No Poverty

Indicator	Value	Year
Poverty headcount ratio at $1.90/day (%)	0.5	2020
Poverty headcount ratio at $3.20/day (%)	0.9	2020
Poverty rate after taxes and transfers (%)	16.6	2017

SDG2 – Zero Hunger

Indicator	Value	Year
Prevalence of undernourishment (%)	2.5	2017
Prevalence of stunting in children under 5 years of age (%)	* 2.6	2016
Prevalence of wasting in children under 5 years of age (%)	* 0.7	2016
Prevalence of obesity, BMI ≥ 30 (% of adult population)	23.6	2016
Human Trophic Level (best 2–3 worst)	2.4	2017
Cereal yield (tonnes per hectare of harvested land)	4.3	2017
Sustainable Nitrogen Management Index (best 0–1.41 worst)	0.6	2015
Yield gap closure (% of potential yield)	44.6	2015

SDG3 – Good Health and Well-Being

Indicator	Value	Year
Maternal mortality rate (per 100,000 live births)	19	2017
Neonatal mortality rate (per 1,000 live births)	2.0	2018
Mortality rate, under-5 (per 1,000 live births)	3.9	2018
Incidence of tuberculosis (per 100,000 population)	29.0	2018
New HIV infections (per 1,000 uninfected population)	0.2	2018
Age-standardized death rate due to cardiovascular disease, cancer, diabetes, or chronic respiratory disease in adults aged 30–70 years (%)	21.9	2016
Age-standardized death rate attributable to household air pollution and ambient air pollution (per 100,000 population)	41	2016
Traffic deaths (per 100,000 population)	9.3	2016
Life expectancy at birth (years)	75.0	2016
Adolescent fertility rate (births per 1,000 adolescent females aged 15 to 19)	16.2	2017
Births attended by skilled health personnel (%)	99.9	2016
Percentage of surviving infants who received 2 WHO-recommended vaccines (%)	96.0	2018
Universal health coverage (UHC) index of service coverage (worst 0–100 best)	71.0	2017
Subjective well-being (average ladder score, worst 0–10 best)	5.9	2018
Gap in life expectancy at birth among regions (years)	3.4	2015
Gap in self-reported health status by income (percentage points)	45.7	2018
Daily smokers (% of population aged 15 and over)	24.1	2014

SDG4 – Quality Education

Indicator	Value	Year
Net primary enrollment rate (%)	* 98.4	2017
Lower secondary completion rate (%)	* 98.4	2017
Literacy rate (% of population aged 15 to 24)	99.8	2018
Participation rate in pre-primary organized learning (% of children aged 4 to 6)	98.1	2017
Tertiary educational attainment (% of population aged 25 to 34)	41.6	2018
PISA score (worst 0–600 best)	487.3	2018
Variation in science performance explained by socio-economic status (%)	8.4	2018
Underachievers in science (% of 15-year-olds)	18.5	2018
Resilient students in science (% of 15-year-olds)	33.0	2018

SDG5 – Gender Equality

Indicator	Value	Year
Demand for family planning satisfied by modern methods (% of females aged 15 to 49 who are married or in unions)	* 77.9	2017
Ratio of female-to-male mean years of education received (%)	104.8	2018
Ratio of female-to-male labor force participation rate (%)	81.7	2019
Seats held by women in national parliament (%)	30.0	2020
Gender wage gap (% of male median wage)	21.1	2014
Gender gap in time spent doing unpaid work (minutes/day)	123.5	2003

SDG6 – Clean Water and Sanitation

Indicator	Value	Year
Population using at least basic drinking water services (%)	98.6	2017
Population using at least basic sanitation services (%)	92.1	2017
Freshwater withdrawal (% of available freshwater resources)	1.3	2015
Anthropogenic wastewater that receives treatment (%)	90.7	2018
Scarce water consumption embodied in imports (m³/capita)	17.4	2013
Population using safely managed water services (%)	95.2	2017
Population using safely managed sanitation services (%)	85.8	2017

SDG7 – Affordable and Clean Energy

Indicator	Value	Year
Population with access to electricity (%)	100.0	2017
Population with access to clean fuels and technology for cooking (%)	95.3	2016
CO₂ emissions from fuel combustion for electricity and heating per total electricity output (MtCO₂/TWh)	0.9	2017
Share of renewable energy in total primary energy supply (%)	40.0	2018

SDG8 – Decent Work and Economic Growth

Indicator	Value	Year
Adjusted GDP growth (%)	2.2	2018
Victims of modern slavery (per 1,000 population)	3.9	2018
Adults with an account at a bank or other financial institution or with a mobile-money-service provider (% of population aged 15 or over)	93.2	2017
Fatal work-related accidents embodied in imports (per 100,000 population)	0.5	2010
Employment-to-population ratio (%)	72.3	2019
Youth not in employment, education or training (NEET) (% of population aged 15 to 29)	11.2	2018

SDG9 – Industry, Innovation and Infrastructure

Indicator	Value	Year
Population using the internet (%)	83.6	2018
Mobile broadband subscriptions (per 100 population)	130.2	2018
Logistics Performance Index: Quality of trade and transport-related infrastructure (worst 1–5 best)	3.0	2018
The Times Higher Education Universities Ranking: Average score of top 3 universities (worst 0–100 best)	19.3	2020
Scientific and technical journal articles (per 1,000 population)	0.7	2018
Expenditure on research and development (% of GDP)	0.5	2017
Researchers (per 1,000 employed population)	4.1	2018
Triadic patent families filed (per million population)	1.8	2017
Gap in internet access by income (percentage points)	39.6	2019
Women in science and engineering (% of tertiary graduates in science and engineering)	27.0	2015

SDG10 – Reduced Inequalities

Indicator	Value	Year
Gini coefficient adjusted for top income	39.1	2015
Palma ratio	1.4	2017
Elderly poverty rate (% of population aged 66 or over)	35.3	2017

SDG11 – Sustainable Cities and Communities

Indicator	Value	Year
Annual mean concentration of particulate matter of less than 2.5 microns in diameter (PM2.5) (µg/m³)	13.4	2017
Access to improved water source, piped (% of urban population)	97.2	2017
Satisfaction with public transport (%)	66.5	2018
Population with rent overburden (%)	2.9	2017

SDG12 – Responsible Consumption and Production

Indicator	Value	Year
Electronic waste (kg/capita)	11.0	2016
Production-based SO₂ emissions (kg/capita)	114.6	2012
SO₂ emissions embodied in imports (kg/capita)	16.0	2012
Production-based nitrogen emissions (kg/capita)	36.3	2010
Nitrogen emissions embodied in imports (kg/capita)	7.0	2010
Non-recycled municipal solid waste (kg/capita/day)	0.8	2018

SDG13 – Climate Action

Indicator	Value	Year
Energy-related CO₂ emissions (tCO₂/capita)	3.4	2017
CO₂ emissions embodied in imports (tCO₂/capita)	1.7	2015
CO₂ emissions embodied in fossil fuel exports (kg/capita)	0.0	2018
Effective carbon rate (EUR/tCO₂)	NA	NA

SDG14 – Life Below Water

Indicator	Value	Year
Mean area that is protected in marine sites important to biodiversity (%)	95.8	2018
Ocean Health Index: Clean Waters score (worst 0–100 best)	53.6	2019
Fish caught from overexploited or collapsed stocks (% of total catch)	54.0	2014
Fish caught by trawling (%)	61.2	2014
Marine biodiversity threats embodied in imports (per million population)	0.0	2018

SDG15 – Life on Land

Indicator	Value	Year
Mean area that is protected in terrestrial sites important to biodiversity (%)	97.3	2018
Mean area that is protected in freshwater sites important to biodiversity (%)	97.5	2018
Red List Index of species survival (worst 0–1 best)	1.0	2019
Permanent deforestation (% of forest area, 5-year average)	0.0	2018
Terrestrial and freshwater biodiversity threats embodied in imports (per million population)	0.2	2018

SDG16 – Peace, Justice and Strong Institutions

Indicator	Value	Year
Homicides (per 100,000 population)	4.2	2017
Unsentenced detainees (% of prison population)	28.6	2018
Percentage of population who feel safe walking alone at night in the city or area where they live	58.2	2018
Property Rights (worst 1–7 best)	4.7	2019
Birth registrations with civil authority (% of children under age 5)	100.0	2018
Corruption Perception Index (worst 0–100 best)	56.0	2019
Children involved in child labor (% of population aged 5 to 14)	* 0.0	2016
Exports of major conventional weapons (TIV constant million USD per 100,000 population)	* 0.0	2019
Press Freedom Index (best 0–100 worst)	19.5	2019
Persons held in prison (per 100,000 population)	193.1	2017

SDG17 – Partnerships for the Goals

Indicator	Value	Year
Government spending on health and education (% of GDP)	8.1	2016
For high-income and all OECD DAC countries: International concessional public finance, including official development assistance (% of GNI)	0.1	2017
Other countries: Government revenue excluding grants (% of GDP)	NA	NA
Corporate Tax Haven Score (best 0–100 worst)	68.1	2019
Financial Secrecy Score (best 0–100 worst)	59.1	2020
Shifted profits of multinationals (US$ billion)	0.3	2016

* Imputed data point

5. Country Profiles

LEBANON

▼ OVERALL PERFORMANCE

Index score
66.7

Regional average score
66.3

SDG Global rank 95 (OF 166)

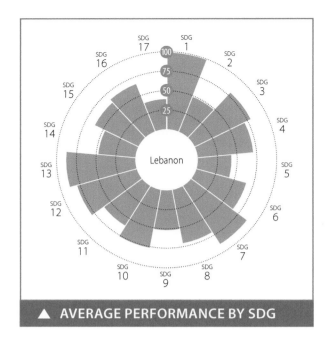

▲ AVERAGE PERFORMANCE BY SDG

▼ SPILLOVER INDEX

100 (best) to 0 (worst)

▼ CURRENT ASSESSMENT – SDG DASHBOARD

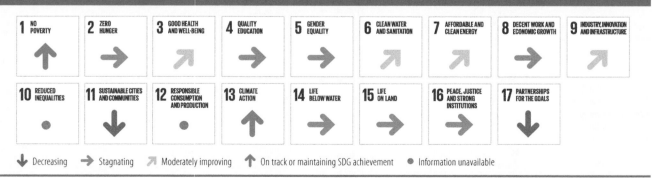

■ Major challenges ■ Significant challenges ■ Challenges remain ■ SDG achieved ■ Information unavailable

▼ SDG TRENDS

1 NO POVERTY	2 ZERO HUNGER	3 GOOD HEALTH AND WELL-BEING	4 QUALITY EDUCATION	5 GENDER EQUALITY	6 CLEAN WATER AND SANITATION	7 AFFORDABLE AND CLEAN ENERGY	8 DECENT WORK AND ECONOMIC GROWTH	9 INDUSTRY, INNOVATION AND INFRASTRUCTURE
↑	→	↗	→	→	↗	↗	→	↗

10 REDUCED INEQUALITIES	11 SUSTAINABLE CITIES AND COMMUNITIES	12 RESPONSIBLE CONSUMPTION AND PRODUCTION	13 CLIMATE ACTION	14 LIFE BELOW WATER	15 LIFE ON LAND	16 PEACE, JUSTICE AND STRONG INSTITUTIONS	17 PARTNERSHIPS FOR THE GOALS
●	↓	●	↑	→	→	→	↓

↓ Decreasing → Stagnating ↗ Moderately improving ↑ On track or maintaining SDG achievement ● Information unavailable

Notes: The full title of Goal 2 "Zero Hunger" is "End hunger, achieve food security and improved nutrition and promote sustainable agriculture".
The full title of each SDG is available here: https://sustainabledevelopment.un.org/topics/sustainabledevelopmentgoals

SDG1 – No Poverty

	Value	Year	Rating	Trend
Poverty headcount ratio at $1.90/day (%)	0.0	2020	○	↑
Poverty headcount ratio at $3.20/day (%)	0.1	2020	○	↑

SDG2 – Zero Hunger

	Value	Year	Rating	Trend
Prevalence of undernourishment (%)	11.0	2017	○	→
Prevalence of stunting in children under 5 years of age (%)	16.5	2004	●	↗
Prevalence of wasting in children under 5 years of age (%)	6.6	2004	●	↑
Prevalence of obesity, BMI ≥ 30 (% of adult population)	32.0	2016	●	↓
Human Trophic Level (best 2–3 worst)	2.2	2017	●	↑
Cereal yield (tonnes per hectare of harvested land)	3.1	2017	●	↑
Sustainable Nitrogen Management Index (best 0–1.41 worst)	0.9	2015	●	↓

SDG3 – Good Health and Well-Being

	Value	Year	Rating	Trend
Maternal mortality rate (per 100,000 live births)	29	2017	●	↑
Neonatal mortality rate (per 1,000 live births)	4.3	2018	●	↑
Mortality rate, under-5 (per 1,000 live births)	7.4	2018	●	↑
Incidence of tuberculosis (per 100,000 population)	11.0	2018	○	↑
New HIV infections (per 1,000 uninfected population)	0.0	2018	●	↑
Age-standardized death rate due to cardiovascular disease, cancer, diabetes, or chronic respiratory disease in adults aged 30–70 years (%)	17.9	2016	●	→
Age-standardized death rate attributable to household air pollution and ambient air pollution (per 100,000 population)	51	2016	●	●
Traffic deaths (per 100,000 population)	18.1	2016	●	↑
Life expectancy at birth (years)	76.3	2016	●	→
Adolescent fertility rate (births per 1,000 adolescent females aged 15 to 19)	14.5	2017	●	↑
Births attended by skilled health personnel (%)	98.2	2004	●	●
Percentage of surviving infants who received 2 WHO-recommended vaccines (%)	82	2018	●	→
Universal health coverage (UHC) index of service coverage (worst 0–100 best)	73.0	2017	○	↑
Subjective well-being (average ladder score, worst 0–10 best)	5.2	2018	●	↓

SDG4 – Quality Education

	Value	Year	Rating	Trend
Net primary enrollment rate (%)	* 86.3	2017	●	↑
Lower secondary completion rate (%)	52.4	2017	●	↓
Literacy rate (% of population aged 15 to 24)	99.8	2018	●	●

SDG5 – Gender Equality

	Value	Year	Rating	Trend
Demand for family planning satisfied by modern methods (% of females aged 15 to 49 who are married or in unions)	* 63.8	2017	●	→
Ratio of female-to-male mean years of education received (%)	95.5	2018	○	→
Ratio of female-to-male labor force participation rate (%)	33.2	2019	●	→
Seats held by women in national parliament (%)	4.7	2020	●	→

SDG6 – Clean Water and Sanitation

	Value	Year	Rating	Trend
Population using at least basic drinking water services (%)	92.6	2017	○	↗
Population using at least basic sanitation services (%)	98.5	2017	●	↑
Freshwater withdrawal (% of available freshwater resources)	57.3	2015	●	●
Anthropogenic wastewater that receives treatment (%)	38.2	2018	○	●
Scarce water consumption embodied in imports (m³/capita)	45.8	2013	●	→

SDG7 – Affordable and Clean Energy

	Value	Year	Rating	Trend
Population with access to electricity (%)	100.0	2017	●	↑
Population with access to clean fuels and technology for cooking (%)	NA	NA	●	●
CO₂ emissions from fuel combustion for electricity and heating per total electricity output (MtCO₂/TWh)	1.4	2017	●	→

SDG8 – Decent Work and Economic Growth

	Value	Year	Rating	Trend
Adjusted GDP growth (%)	-4.6	2018	●	●
Victims of modern slavery (per 1,000 population)	1.7	2018	●	●
Adults with an account at a bank or other financial institution or with a mobile-money-service provider (% of population aged 15 or over)	44.8	2017	●	↓
Unemployment rate (% of total labor force)	6.2	2019	○	→
Fatal work-related accidents embodied in imports (per 100,000 population)	0.7	2010	●	↑

SDG9 – Industry, Innovation and Infrastructure

	Value	Year	Rating	Trend
Population using the internet (%)	78.2	2017	○	↑
Mobile broadband subscriptions (per 100 population)	45.2	2018	●	→
Logistics Performance Index: Quality of trade and transport-related infrastructure (worst 1–5 best)	2.6	2018	○	↗
The Times Higher Education Universities Ranking: Average score of top 3 universities (worst 0–100 best)	31.3	2020	●	●
Scientific and technical journal articles (per 1,000 population)	0.3	2018	●	↗
Expenditure on research and development (% of GDP)	NA	NA	●	●

SDG10 – Reduced Inequalities

	Value	Year	Rating	Trend
Gini coefficient adjusted for top income	36.2	2011	●	●

SDG11 – Sustainable Cities and Communities

	Value	Year	Rating	Trend
Annual mean concentration of particulate matter of less than 2.5 microns in diameter (PM2.5) (μg/m³)	30.6	2017	●	↓
Access to improved water source, piped (% of urban population)	NA	NA	●	●
Satisfaction with public transport (%)	51.8	2018	●	↓

SDG12 – Responsible Consumption and Production

	Value	Year	Rating	Trend
Municipal solid waste (kg/capita/day)	1.0	2014	○	●
Electronic waste (kg/capita)	11.1	2016	●	●
Production-based SO₂ emissions (kg/capita)	55.5	2012	○	●
SO₂ emissions embodied in imports (kg/capita)	5.9	2012	○	●
Production-based nitrogen emissions (kg/capita)	15.1	2010	●	●
Nitrogen emissions embodied in imports (kg/capita)	5.9	2010	○	●

SDG13 – Climate Action

	Value	Year	Rating	Trend
Energy-related CO₂ emissions (tCO₂/capita)	2.1	2017	○	↑
CO₂ emissions embodied in imports (tCO₂/capita)	0.9	2015	●	↑
CO₂ emissions embodied in fossil fuel exports (kg/capita)	0.0	2018	●	●

SDG14 – Life Below Water

	Value	Year	Rating	Trend
Mean area that is protected in marine sites important to biodiversity (%)	5.1	2018	●	→
Ocean Health Index: Clean Waters score (worst 0–100 best)	33.0	2019	●	→
Fish caught from overexploited or collapsed stocks (% of total catch)	NA	NA	●	●
Fish caught by trawling (%)	10.0	2008	○	●
Marine biodiversity threats embodied in imports (per million population)	0.2	2018	●	●

SDG15 – Life on Land

	Value	Year	Rating	Trend
Mean area that is protected in terrestrial sites important to biodiversity (%)	13.3	2018	●	→
Mean area that is protected in freshwater sites important to biodiversity (%)	21.1	2018	●	→
Red List Index of species survival (worst 0–1 best)	1.0	2019	●	↑
Permanent deforestation (% of forest area, 5-year average)	0.1	2018	●	●
Terrestrial and freshwater biodiversity threats embodied in imports (per million population)	0.6	2018	●	●

SDG16 – Peace, Justice and Strong Institutions

	Value	Year	Rating	Trend
Homicides (per 100,000 population)	4.0	2016	●	↗
Unsentenced detainees (% of prison population)	42.3	2018	●	→
Percentage of population who feel safe walking alone at night in the city or area where they live (%)	55.3	2018	●	↓
Property Rights (worst 1–7 best)	4.0	2019	○	●
Birth registrations with civil authority (% of children under age 5)	99.5	2018	●	●
Corruption Perception Index (worst 0–100 best)	28	2019	●	→
Children involved in child labor (% of population aged 5 to 14)	1.9	2016	●	●
Exports of major conventional weapons (TIV constant million USD per 100,000 population)	* 0.0	2019	●	●
Press Freedom Index (best 0–100 worst)	32.4	2019	○	→

SDG17 – Partnerships for the Goals

	Value	Year	Rating	Trend
Government spending on health and education (% of GDP)	6.3	2013	●	●
For high-income and all OECD DAC countries: International concessional public finance, including official development assistance (% of GNI)	NA	NA	●	●
Other countries: Government revenue excluding grants (% of GDP)	19.8	2017	●	↓
Corporate Tax Haven Score (best 0–100 worst)	72.8	2019	●	●

* Imputed data point

5. Country Profiles

▼ OVERALL PERFORMANCE

Index score
54.0

Regional average score
53.1

SDG Global rank 141 (OF 166)

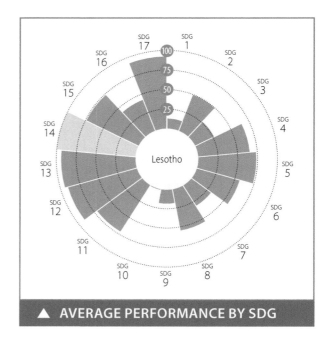

▲ AVERAGE PERFORMANCE BY SDG

▼ SPILLOVER INDEX

100 (best) to 0 (worst)

▼ CURRENT ASSESSMENT – SDG DASHBOARD

■ Major challenges ■ Significant challenges ■ Challenges remain ■ SDG achieved ■ Information unavailable

▼ SDG TRENDS

↓ Decreasing → Stagnating ↗ Moderately improving ↑ On track or maintaining SDG achievement ● Information unavailable

Notes: The full title of Goal 2 "Zero Hunger" is "End hunger, achieve food security and improved nutrition and promote sustainable agriculture".
The full title of each SDG is available here: https://sustainabledevelopment.un.org/topics/sustainabledevelopmentgoals

SDG1 – No Poverty

	Value	Year	Rating	Trend
Poverty headcount ratio at $1.90/day (%)	52.3	2020	●	→
Poverty headcount ratio at $3.20/day (%)	71.6	2020	●	→

SDG2 – Zero Hunger

	Value	Year	Rating	Trend
Prevalence of undernourishment (%)	13.1	2017	●	→
Prevalence of stunting in children under 5 years of age (%)	33.2	2014	●	→
Prevalence of wasting in children under 5 years of age (%)	2.8	2014	●	↑
Prevalence of obesity, BMI ≥ 30 (% of adult population)	16.6	2016	●	↓
Human Trophic Level (best 2–3 worst)	2.1	2017	●	↑
Cereal yield (tonnes per hectare of harvested land)	1.0	2017	●	↑
Sustainable Nitrogen Management Index (best 0–1.41 worst)	1.0	2015	●	→

SDG3 – Good Health and Well-Being

	Value	Year	Rating	Trend
Maternal mortality rate (per 100,000 live births)	544	2017	●	→
Neonatal mortality rate (per 1,000 live births)	34.9	2018	●	→
Mortality rate, under-5 (per 1,000 live births)	81.1	2018	●	↗
Incidence of tuberculosis (per 100,000 population)	611.0	2018	●	↑
New HIV infections (per 1,000 uninfected population)	7.8	2018	●	↑
Age-standardized death rate due to cardiovascular disease, cancer, diabetes, or chronic respiratory disease in adults aged 30–70 years (%)	26.6	2016	●	→
Age-standardized death rate attributable to household air pollution and ambient air pollution (per 100,000 population)	178	2016	●	●
Traffic deaths (per 100,000 population)	28.9	2016	●	↓
Life expectancy at birth (years)	52.9	2016	●	→
Adolescent fertility rate (births per 1,000 adolescent females aged 15 to 19)	92.7	2017	●	↓
Births attended by skilled health personnel (%)	77.9	2014	●	●
Percentage of surviving infants who received 2 WHO-recommended vaccines (%)	90	2018	●	↑
Universal health coverage (UHC) index of service coverage (worst 0–100 best)	48.0	2017	●	→
Subjective well-being (average ladder score, worst 0–10 best)	3.5	2019	●	↓

SDG4 – Quality Education

	Value	Year	Rating	Trend
Net primary enrollment rate (%)	93.3	2017	◐	↑
Lower secondary completion rate (%)	47.4	2017	●	→
Literacy rate (% of population aged 15 to 24)	86.6	2014	●	●

SDG5 – Gender Equality

	Value	Year	Rating	Trend
Demand for family planning satisfied by modern methods (% of females aged 15 to 49 who are married or in unions)	78.9	2014	◐	↑
Ratio of female-to-male mean years of education received (%)	127.3	2018	●	↑
Ratio of female-to-male labor force participation rate (%)	79.7	2019	●	↑
Seats held by women in national parliament (%)	23.3	2020	●	↓

SDG6 – Clean Water and Sanitation

	Value	Year	Rating	Trend
Population using at least basic drinking water services (%)	68.7	2017	●	↗
Population using at least basic sanitation services (%)	42.8	2017	●	↗
Freshwater withdrawal (% of available freshwater resources)	2.2	2015	●	●
Anthropogenic wastewater that receives treatment (%)	0.3	2018	●	●
Scarce water consumption embodied in imports (m³/capita)	3.2	2013	●	↑

SDG7 – Affordable and Clean Energy

	Value	Year	Rating	Trend
Population with access to electricity (%)	33.7	2017	●	→
Population with access to clean fuels and technology for cooking (%)	35.6	2016	●	→
CO$_2$ emissions from fuel combustion for electricity and heating per total electricity output (MtCO$_2$/TWh)	NA	NA	●	●

SDG8 – Decent Work and Economic Growth

	Value	Year	Rating	Trend
Adjusted GDP growth (%)	-6.1	2018	●	●
Victims of modern slavery (per 1,000 population)	4.2	2018	◐	●
Adults with an account at a bank or other financial institution or with a mobile-money-service provider (% of population aged 15 or over)	45.6	2017	●	●
Unemployment rate (% of total labor force)	23.4	2019	●	→
Fatal work-related accidents embodied in imports (per 100,000 population)	0.4	2010	●	↑

SDG9 – Industry, Innovation and Infrastructure

	Value	Year	Rating	Trend
Population using the internet (%)	29.0	2017	●	↗
Mobile broadband subscriptions (per 100 population)	59.0	2018	◐	↑
Logistics Performance Index: Quality of trade and transport-related infrastructure (worst 1–5 best)	2.0	2018	●	↓
The Times Higher Education Universities Ranking: Average score of top 3 universities (worst 0–100 best) *	0.0	2020	●	●
Scientific and technical journal articles (per 1,000 population)	0.0	2018	●	→
Expenditure on research and development (% of GDP)	0.0	2015	●	●

SDG10 – Reduced Inequalities

	Value	Year	Rating	Trend
Gini coefficient adjusted for top income	63.0	2010	●	●

SDG11 – Sustainable Cities and Communities

	Value	Year	Rating	Trend
Annual mean concentration of particulate matter of less than 2.5 microns in diameter (PM2.5) (µg/m³)	28.0	2017	●	↑
Access to improved water source, piped (% of urban population)	88.5	2017	◐	→
Satisfaction with public transport (%)	51.8	2019	●	↗

SDG12 – Responsible Consumption and Production

	Value	Year	Rating	Trend
Municipal solid waste (kg/capita/day)	0.3	2006	●	●
Electronic waste (kg/capita)	0.9	2016	●	●
Production-based SO$_2$ emissions (kg/capita)	63.5	2012	◐	●
SO$_2$ emissions embodied in imports (kg/capita)	4.5	2012	●	●
Production-based nitrogen emissions (kg/capita)	21.5	2010	◐	●
Nitrogen emissions embodied in imports (kg/capita)	2.1	2010	●	●

SDG13 – Climate Action

	Value	Year	Rating	Trend
Energy-related CO$_2$ emissions (tCO$_2$/capita)	1.3	2017	●	↑
CO$_2$ emissions embodied in imports (tCO$_2$/capita)	0.4	2015	●	↑
CO$_2$ emissions embodied in fossil fuel exports (kg/capita)	0.0	2017	●	●

SDG14 – Life Below Water

	Value	Year	Rating	Trend
Mean area that is protected in marine sites important to biodiversity (%)	NA	NA	●	●
Ocean Health Index: Clean Waters score (worst 0–100 best)	NA	NA	●	●
Fish caught from overexploited or collapsed stocks (% of total catch)	NA	NA	●	●
Fish caught by trawling (%)	NA	NA	●	●
Marine biodiversity threats embodied in imports (per million population)	0.0	2018	●	●

SDG15 – Life on Land

	Value	Year	Rating	Trend
Mean area that is protected in terrestrial sites important to biodiversity (%)	16.7	2018	●	→
Mean area that is protected in freshwater sites important to biodiversity (%)	NA	NA	●	●
Red List Index of species survival (worst 0–1 best)	1.0	2019	●	↑
Permanent deforestation (% of forest area, 5-year average)	0.0	2018	●	●
Terrestrial and freshwater biodiversity threats embodied in imports (per million population)	0.5	2018	●	●

SDG16 – Peace, Justice and Strong Institutions

	Value	Year	Rating	Trend
Homicides (per 100,000 population)	41.2	2015	●	●
Unsentenced detainees (% of prison population)	19.5	2015	●	●
Percentage of population who feel safe walking alone at night in the city or area where they live (%)	34.0	2019	●	↓
Property Rights (worst 1–7 best)	3.4	2019	●	●
Birth registrations with civil authority (% of children under age 5)	43.3	2018	●	↓
Corruption Perception Index (worst 0–100 best)	40	2019	●	↓
Children involved in child labor (% of population aged 5 to 14)	22.9	2016	●	●
Exports of major conventional weapons (TIV constant million USD per 100,000 population) *	0.0	2019	●	●
Press Freedom Index (best 0–100 worst)	29.7	2019	●	↑

SDG17 – Partnerships for the Goals

	Value	Year	Rating	Trend
Government spending on health and education (% of GDP)	16.2	2008	●	●
For high-income and all OECD DAC countries: International concessional public finance, including official development assistance (% of GNI)	NA	NA	●	●
Other countries: Government revenue excluding grants (% of GDP)	33.8	2017	●	↑
Corporate Tax Haven Score (best 0–100 worst) *	0.0	2019	●	●

* Imputed data point

5. Country Profiles

▼ OVERALL PERFORMANCE

Index score

47.1

Regional average score

53.1

SDG Global rank 162 (OF 166)

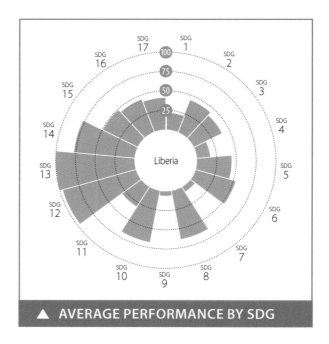

▲ AVERAGE PERFORMANCE BY SDG

▼ SPILLOVER INDEX

100 (best) to 0 (worst)

▼ CURRENT ASSESSMENT – SDG DASHBOARD

■ Major challenges ■ Significant challenges ■ Challenges remain ■ SDG achieved ■ Information unavailable

▼ SDG TRENDS

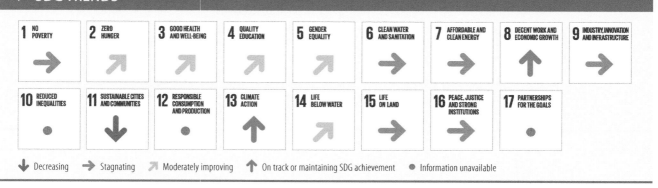

↓ Decreasing → Stagnating ↗ Moderately improving ↑ On track or maintaining SDG achievement ● Information unavailable

Notes: The full title of Goal 2 "Zero Hunger" is "End hunger, achieve food security and improved nutrition and promote sustainable agriculture".
The full title of each SDG is available here: https://sustainabledevelopment.un.org/topics/sustainabledevelopmentgoals

SDG1 – No Poverty

Indicator	Value	Year
Poverty headcount ratio at $1.90/day (%)	39.2	2020
Poverty headcount ratio at $3.20/day (%)	70.4	2020

SDG2 – Zero Hunger

Indicator	Value	Year
Prevalence of undernourishment (%)	37.2	2017
Prevalence of stunting in children under 5 years of age (%)	32.1	2013
Prevalence of wasting in children under 5 years of age (%)	5.6	2013
Prevalence of obesity, BMI ≥ 30 (% of adult population)	9.9	2016
Human Trophic Level (best 2–3 worst)	2.1	2017
Cereal yield (tonnes per hectare of harvested land)	1.3	2017
Sustainable Nitrogen Management Index (best 0–1.41 worst)	1.0	2015

SDG3 – Good Health and Well-Being

Indicator	Value	Year
Maternal mortality rate (per 100,000 live births)	661	2017
Neonatal mortality rate (per 1,000 live births)	24.5	2018
Mortality rate, under-5 (per 1,000 live births)	70.9	2018
Incidence of tuberculosis (per 100,000 population)	308.0	2018
New HIV infections (per 1,000 uninfected population)	0.4	2018
Age-standardized death rate due to cardiovascular disease, cancer, diabetes, or chronic respiratory disease in adults aged 30–70 years (%)	17.6	2016
Age-standardized death rate attributable to household air pollution and ambient air pollution (per 100,000 population)	170	2016
Traffic deaths (per 100,000 population)	35.9	2016
Life expectancy at birth (years)	62.9	2016
Adolescent fertility rate (births per 1,000 adolescent females aged 15 to 19)	136.0	2017
Births attended by skilled health personnel (%)	61.1	2013
Percentage of surviving infants who received 2 WHO-recommended vaccines (%)	84	2018
Universal health coverage (UHC) index of service coverage (worst 0–100 best)	39.0	2017
Subjective well-being (average ladder score, worst 0–10 best)	5.1	2019

SDG4 – Quality Education

Indicator	Value	Year
Net primary enrollment rate (%)	44.3	2017
Lower secondary completion rate (%)	44.2	2017
Literacy rate (% of population aged 15 to 24)	55.4	2017

SDG5 – Gender Equality

Indicator	Value	Year
Demand for family planning satisfied by modern methods (% of females aged 15 to 49 who are married or in unions)	41.4	2013
Ratio of female-to-male mean years of education received (%)	59.3	2018
Ratio of female-to-male labor force participation rate (%)	95.2	2019
Seats held by women in national parliament (%)	12.3	2020

SDG6 – Clean Water and Sanitation

Indicator	Value	Year
Population using at least basic drinking water services (%)	72.9	2017
Population using at least basic sanitation services (%)	17.0	2017
Freshwater withdrawal (% of available freshwater resources)	0.2	2000
Anthropogenic wastewater that receives treatment (%)	0.0	2018
Scarce water consumption embodied in imports (m³/capita)	0.3	2013

SDG7 – Affordable and Clean Energy

Indicator	Value	Year
Population with access to electricity (%)	21.5	2017
Population with access to clean fuels and technology for cooking (%)	0.7	2016
CO$_2$ emissions from fuel combustion for electricity and heating per total electricity output (MtCO$_2$/TWh)	NA	NA

SDG8 – Decent Work and Economic Growth

Indicator	Value	Year
Adjusted GDP growth (%)	-9.1	2018
Victims of modern slavery (per 1,000 population)	7.4	2018
Adults with an account at a bank or other financial institution or with a mobile-money-service provider (% of population aged 15 or over)	35.7	2017
Unemployment rate (% of total labor force)	2.8	2019
Fatal work-related accidents embodied in imports (per 100,000 population)	0.0	2010

SDG9 – Industry, Innovation and Infrastructure

Indicator	Value	Year
Population using the internet (%)	8.0	2017
Mobile broadband subscriptions (per 100 population)	11.7	2017
Logistics Performance Index: Quality of trade and transport-related infrastructure (worst 1–5 best)	1.9	2018
The Times Higher Education Universities Ranking: Average score of top 3 universities (worst 0–100 best) *	0.0	2020
Scientific and technical journal articles (per 1,000 population)	0.0	2018
Expenditure on research and development (% of GDP) *	0.0	2017

SDG10 – Reduced Inequalities

Indicator	Value	Year
Gini coefficient adjusted for top income	39.1	2016

SDG11 – Sustainable Cities and Communities

Indicator	Value	Year
Annual mean concentration of particulate matter of less than 2.5 microns in diameter (PM2.5) (µg/m³)	18.0	2017
Access to improved water source, piped (% of urban population)	9.3	2017
Satisfaction with public transport (%)	16.0	2019

SDG12 – Responsible Consumption and Production

Indicator	Value	Year
Municipal solid waste (kg/capita/day)	0.6	2007
Electronic waste (kg/capita)	NA	NA
Production-based SO$_2$ emissions (kg/capita)	23.1	2012
SO$_2$ emissions embodied in imports (kg/capita)	0.3	2012
Production-based nitrogen emissions (kg/capita)	1.4	2010
Nitrogen emissions embodied in imports (kg/capita)	0.1	2010

SDG13 – Climate Action

Indicator	Value	Year
Energy-related CO$_2$ emissions (tCO$_2$/capita)	0.2	2017
CO$_2$ emissions embodied in imports (tCO$_2$/capita)	0.0	2015
CO$_2$ emissions embodied in fossil fuel exports (kg/capita) *	0.0	2018

SDG14 – Life Below Water

Indicator	Value	Year
Mean area that is protected in marine sites important to biodiversity (%)	NA	NA
Ocean Health Index: Clean Waters score (worst 0–100 best)	49.6	2019
Fish caught from overexploited or collapsed stocks (% of total catch)	13.4	2014
Fish caught by trawling (%)	6.1	2005
Marine biodiversity threats embodied in imports (per million population)	0.0	2018

SDG15 – Life on Land

Indicator	Value	Year
Mean area that is protected in terrestrial sites important to biodiversity (%)	15.9	2018
Mean area that is protected in freshwater sites important to biodiversity (%)	32.4	2018
Red List Index of species survival (worst 0–1 best)	0.9	2019
Permanent deforestation (% of forest area, 5-year average)	1.0	2018
Terrestrial and freshwater biodiversity threats embodied in imports (per million population)	0.0	2018

SDG16 – Peace, Justice and Strong Institutions

Indicator	Value	Year
Homicides (per 100,000 population)	3.2	2012
Unsentenced detainees (% of prison population)	63.0	2018
Percentage of population who feel safe walking alone at night in the city or area where they live (%)	33.0	2019
Property Rights (worst 1–7 best)	NA	NA
Birth registrations with civil authority (% of children under age 5)	24.6	2018
Corruption Perception Index (worst 0–100 best)	28	2019
Children involved in child labor (% of population aged 5 to 14)	20.8	2016
Exports of major conventional weapons (TIV constant million USD per 100,000 population) *	0.0	2019
Press Freedom Index (best 0–100 worst)	31.5	2019

SDG17 – Partnerships for the Goals

Indicator	Value	Year
Government spending on health and education (% of GDP)	3.1	2014
For high-income and all OECD DAC countries: International concessional public finance, including official development assistance (% of GNI)	NA	NA
Other countries: Government revenue excluding grants (% of GDP)	15.7	2013
Corporate Tax Haven Score (best 0–100 worst)	49.0	2019

* Imputed data point

5. Country Profiles

▼ OVERALL PERFORMANCE

Index score

na

Regional average score

66.3

SDG Global rank NA (OF 166)

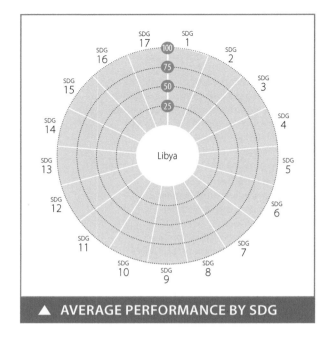

▲ AVERAGE PERFORMANCE BY SDG

▼ SPILLOVER INDEX

100 (best) to 0 (worst)

100
80
60
40
20
0

▼ CURRENT ASSESSMENT – SDG DASHBOARD

■ Major challenges   ■ Significant challenges   ■ Challenges remain   ■ SDG achieved   ■ Information unavailable

▼ SDG TRENDS

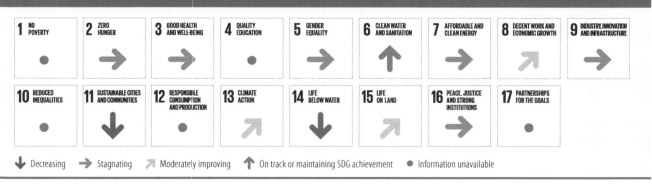

⬇ Decreasing   ➡ Stagnating   ↗ Moderately improving   ⬆ On track or maintaining SDG achievement   ● Information unavailable

Notes: The full title of Goal 2 "Zero Hunger" is "End hunger, achieve food security and improved nutrition and promote sustainable agriculture".
   The full title of each SDG is available here: https://sustainabledevelopment.un.org/topics/sustainabledevelopmentgoals

SDG1 – No Poverty

Indicator		Value	Year	Rating	Trend
Poverty headcount ratio at $1.90/day (%)	*	NA	NA	●	●
Poverty headcount ratio at $3.20/day (%)	*	NA	NA	●	●

SDG2 – Zero Hunger

Indicator	Value	Year	Rating	Trend
Prevalence of undernourishment (%)	NA	NA	●	●
Prevalence of stunting in children under 5 years of age (%)	21.0	2007	●	→
Prevalence of wasting in children under 5 years of age (%)	6.5	2007	●	→
Prevalence of obesity, BMI ≥ 30 (% of adult population)	32.5	2016	●	↓
Human Trophic Level (best 2–3 worst)	2.2	2007	●	→
Cereal yield (tonnes per hectare of harvested land)	0.8	2017	●	→
Sustainable Nitrogen Management Index (best 0–1.41 worst)	0.9	2015	●	→

SDG3 – Good Health and Well-Being

Indicator	Value	Year	Rating	Trend
Maternal mortality rate (per 100,000 live births)	72	2017	●	↓
Neonatal mortality rate (per 1,000 live births)	6.4	2018	●	↑
Mortality rate, under-5 (per 1,000 live births)	12.0	2018	●	↑
Incidence of tuberculosis (per 100,000 population)	40.0	2018	●	→
New HIV infections (per 1,000 uninfected population)	0.1	2018	●	↑
Age-standardized death rate due to cardiovascular disease, cancer, diabetes, or chronic respiratory disease in adults aged 30–70 years (%)	20.1	2016	●	→
Age-standardized death rate attributable to household air pollution and ambient air pollution (per 100,000 population)	72	2016	●	●
Traffic deaths (per 100,000 population)	26.1	2016	●	↓
Life expectancy at birth (years)	71.9	2016	●	↓
Adolescent fertility rate (births per 1,000 adolescent females aged 15 to 19)	5.8	2017	●	↑
Births attended by skilled health personnel (%)	99.9	2013	●	●
Percentage of surviving infants who received 2 WHO-recommended vaccines (%)	97	2018	●	↑
Universal health coverage (UHC) index of service coverage (worst 0–100 best)	64.0	2017	●	→
Subjective well-being (average ladder score, worst 0–10 best)	5.5	2018	●	↓

SDG4 – Quality Education

Indicator	Value	Year	Rating	Trend
Net primary enrollment rate (%)	NA	NA	●	●
Lower secondary completion rate (%)	NA	NA	●	●
Literacy rate (% of population aged 15 to 24)	99.6	2004	●	●

SDG5 – Gender Equality

Indicator	Value	Year	Rating	Trend
Demand for family planning satisfied by modern methods (% of females aged 15 to 49 who are married or in unions)	24.0	2014	●	↗
Ratio of female-to-male mean years of education received (%)	111.1	2018	●	↑
Ratio of female-to-male labor force participation rate (%)	32.6	2019	●	↓
Seats held by women in national parliament (%)	16.0	2020	●	↓

SDG6 – Clean Water and Sanitation

Indicator	Value	Year	Rating	Trend
Population using at least basic drinking water services (%)	98.5	2017	●	↑
Population using at least basic sanitation services (%)	100.0	2017	●	↑
Freshwater withdrawal (% of available freshwater resources)	822.9	2010	●	●
Anthropogenic wastewater that receives treatment (%)	9.6	2018	●	●
Scarce water consumption embodied in imports (m³/capita)	5.0	2013	●	↑

SDG7 – Affordable and Clean Energy

Indicator	Value	Year	Rating	Trend
Population with access to electricity (%)	70.1	2017	●	↓
Population with access to clean fuels and technology for cooking (%)	NA	NA	●	●
CO$_2$ emissions from fuel combustion for electricity and heating per total electricity output (MtCO$_2$/TWh)	1.2	2017	●	↑

SDG8 – Decent Work and Economic Growth

Indicator		Value	Year	Rating	Trend
Adjusted GDP growth (%)		5.1	2018	●	●
Victims of modern slavery (per 1,000 population)	*	NA	NA	●	●
Adults with an account at a bank or other financial institution or with a mobile-money-service provider (% of population aged 15 or over)		65.7	2017	●	●
Unemployment rate (% of total labor force)		18.6	2019	●	→
Fatal work-related accidents embodied in imports (per 100,000 population)		0.1	2010	●	↑

SDG9 – Industry, Innovation and Infrastructure

Indicator		Value	Year	Rating	Trend
Population using the internet (%)		21.8	2017	●	→
Mobile broadband subscriptions (per 100 population)		35.8	2017	●	↗
Logistics Performance Index: Quality of trade and transport-related infrastructure (worst 1–5 best)		2.2	2018	●	↓
The Times Higher Education Universities Ranking: Average score of top 3 universities (worst 0–100 best)	*	0.0	2020	●	●
Scientific and technical journal articles (per 1,000 population)		0.0	2018	●	↓
Expenditure on research and development (% of GDP)		NA	NA	●	●

SDG10 – Reduced Inequalities

Indicator	Value	Year	Rating	Trend
Gini coefficient adjusted for top income	NA	NA	●	●

SDG11 – Sustainable Cities and Communities

Indicator	Value	Year	Rating	Trend
Annual mean concentration of particulate matter of less than 2.5 microns in diameter (PM2.5) (μg/m³)	54.3	2017	●	↓
Access to improved water source, piped (% of urban population)	NA	NA	●	●
Satisfaction with public transport (%)	45.7	2018	●	↓

SDG12 – Responsible Consumption and Production

Indicator	Value	Year	Rating	Trend
Municipal solid waste (kg/capita/day)	1.1	2011	●	●
Electronic waste (kg/capita)	11.0	2016	●	●
Production-based SO$_2$ emissions (kg/capita)	42.4	2012	●	●
SO$_2$ emissions embodied in imports (kg/capita)	3.1	2012	●	●
Production-based nitrogen emissions (kg/capita)	19.7	2010	●	●
Nitrogen emissions embodied in imports (kg/capita)	1.9	2010	●	●

SDG13 – Climate Action

Indicator	Value	Year	Rating	Trend
Energy-related CO$_2$ emissions (tCO$_2$/capita)	7.9	2017	●	↗
CO$_2$ emissions embodied in imports (tCO$_2$/capita)	0.4	2015	●	↑
CO$_2$ emissions embodied in fossil fuel exports (kg/capita)	NA	NA	●	●

SDG14 – Life Below Water

Indicator	Value	Year	Rating	Trend
Mean area that is protected in marine sites important to biodiversity (%)	0.3	2018	●	→
Ocean Health Index: Clean Waters score (worst 0–100 best)	56.4	2019	●	↓
Fish caught from overexploited or collapsed stocks (% of total catch)	67.5	2014	●	↓
Fish caught by trawling (%)	19.9	2014	●	↓
Marine biodiversity threats embodied in imports (per million population)	0.0	2018	●	●

SDG15 – Life on Land

Indicator	Value	Year	Rating	Trend
Mean area that is protected in terrestrial sites important to biodiversity (%)	4.6	2018	●	→
Mean area that is protected in freshwater sites important to biodiversity (%)	NA	NA	●	●
Red List Index of species survival (worst 0–1 best)	1.0	2019	●	↑
Permanent deforestation (% of forest area, 5-year average)	NA	NA	●	●
Terrestrial and freshwater biodiversity threats embodied in imports (per million population)	0.1	2018	●	●

SDG16 – Peace, Justice and Strong Institutions

Indicator		Value	Year	Rating	Trend
Homicides (per 100,000 population)	*	2.5	2015	●	●
Unsentenced detainees (% of prison population)		86.7	2015	●	●
Percentage of population who feel safe walking alone at night in the city or area where they live (%)		54.1	2018	●	●
Property Rights (worst 1–7 best)		NA	NA	●	●
Birth registrations with civil authority (% of children under age 5)		NA	NA	●	●
Corruption Perception Index (worst 0–100 best)		18	2019	●	→
Children involved in child labor (% of population aged 5 to 14)		NA	NA	●	●
Exports of major conventional weapons (TIV constant million USD per 100,000 population)	*	0.0	2019	●	●
Press Freedom Index (best 0–100 worst)		55.8	2019	●	→

SDG17 – Partnerships for the Goals

Indicator		Value	Year	Rating	Trend
Government spending on health and education (% of GDP)		NA	NA	●	●
For high-income and all OECD DAC countries: International concessional public finance, including official development assistance (% of GNI)		NA	NA	●	●
Other countries: Government revenue excluding grants (% of GDP)		NA	NA	●	●
Corporate Tax Haven Score (best 0–100 worst)	*	0.0	2019	●	●

* Imputed data point

5. Country Profiles

LIECHTENSTEIN

▼ OVERALL PERFORMANCE

Index score

na

Regional average score

70.9

SDG Global rank NA (OF 166)

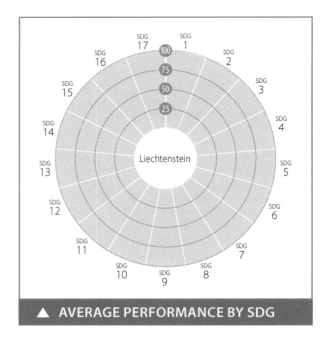

▲ AVERAGE PERFORMANCE BY SDG

▼ SPILLOVER INDEX

100 (best) to 0 (worst)

▼ CURRENT ASSESSMENT – SDG DASHBOARD

■ Major challenges ■ Significant challenges ■ Challenges remain ■ SDG achieved ■ Information unavailable

▼ SDG TRENDS

↓ Decreasing   → Stagnating   ↗ Moderately improving   ↑ On track or maintaining SDG achievement   ● Information unavailable

Notes: The full title of Goal 2 "Zero Hunger" is "End hunger, achieve food security and improved nutrition and promote sustainable agriculture".
The full title of each SDG is available here: https://sustainabledevelopment.un.org/topics/sustainabledevelopmentgoals

LIECHTENSTEIN

SDG1 – No Poverty

	Value	Year	Rating	Trend
Poverty headcount ratio at $1.90/day (%)	NA	NA	●	●
Poverty headcount ratio at $3.20/day (%)	NA	NA	●	●

SDG2 – Zero Hunger

		Value	Year	Rating	Trend
Prevalence of undernourishment (%)	*	1.2	2017	●	●
Prevalence of stunting in children under 5 years of age (%)	*	2.6	2016	●	●
Prevalence of wasting in children under 5 years of age (%)	*	0.7	2016	●	●
Prevalence of obesity, BMI ≥ 30 (% of adult population)		NA	NA	●	●
Human Trophic Level (best 2–3 worst)		NA	NA	●	●
Cereal yield (tonnes per hectare of harvested land)		NA	NA	●	●
Sustainable Nitrogen Management Index (best 0–1.41 worst)		NA	NA	●	●

SDG3 – Good Health and Well-Being

	Value	Year	Rating	Trend
Maternal mortality rate (per 100,000 live births)	NA	NA	●	●
Neonatal mortality rate (per 1,000 live births)	NA	NA	●	●
Mortality rate, under-5 (per 1,000 live births)	NA	NA	●	●
Incidence of tuberculosis (per 100,000 population)	NA	NA	●	●
New HIV infections (per 1,000 uninfected population)	NA	NA	●	●
Age-standardized death rate due to cardiovascular disease, cancer, diabetes, or chronic respiratory disease in adults aged 30–70 years (%)	NA	NA	●	●
Age-standardized death rate attributable to household air pollution and ambient air pollution (per 100,000 population)	NA	NA	●	●
Traffic deaths (per 100,000 population)	NA	NA	●	●
Life expectancy at birth (years)	NA	NA	●	●
Adolescent fertility rate (births per 1,000 adolescent females aged 15 to 19)	NA	NA	●	●
Births attended by skilled health personnel (%)	NA	NA	●	●
Percentage of surviving infants who received 2 WHO-recommended vaccines (%)	NA	NA	●	●
Universal health coverage (UHC) index of service coverage (worst 0–100 best)	NA	NA	●	●
Subjective well-being (average ladder score, worst 0–10 best)	NA	NA	●	●

SDG4 – Quality Education

	Value	Year	Rating	Trend
Net primary enrollment rate (%)	92.1	2016	●	↑
Lower secondary completion rate (%)	86.0	2016	●	●
Literacy rate (% of population aged 15 to 24)	NA	NA	●	●

SDG5 – Gender Equality

	Value	Year	Rating	Trend
Demand for family planning satisfied by modern methods (% of females aged 15 to 49 who are married or in unions)	NA	NA	●	●
Ratio of female-to-male mean years of education received (%)	NA	NA	●	●
Ratio of female-to-male labor force participation rate (%)	NA	NA	●	●
Seats held by women in national parliament (%)	12.0	2019	●	↓

SDG6 – Clean Water and Sanitation

	Value	Year	Rating	Trend
Population using at least basic drinking water services (%)	100.0	2017	●	↑
Population using at least basic sanitation services (%)	100.0	2017	●	↑
Freshwater withdrawal (% of available freshwater resources)	NA	NA	●	●
Anthropogenic wastewater that receives treatment (%)	NA	NA	●	●
Scarce water consumption embodied in imports (m³/capita)	25.5	2013	●	↑

SDG7 – Affordable and Clean Energy

	Value	Year	Rating	Trend
Population with access to electricity (%)	100.0	2017	●	↑
Population with access to clean fuels and technology for cooking (%)	NA	NA	●	●
CO$_2$ emissions from fuel combustion for electricity and heating per total electricity output (MtCO$_2$/TWh)	NA	NA	●	●

SDG8 – Decent Work and Economic Growth

	Value	Year	Rating	Trend
Adjusted GDP growth (%)	NA	NA	●	●
Victims of modern slavery (per 1,000 population)	NA	NA	●	●
Adults with an account at a bank or other financial institution or with a mobile-money-service provider (% of population aged 15 or over)	NA	NA	●	●
Unemployment rate (% of total labor force)	NA	NA	●	●
Fatal work-related accidents embodied in imports (per 100,000 population)	1.8	2010	●	↑

SDG9 – Industry, Innovation and Infrastructure

		Value	Year	Rating	Trend
Population using the internet (%)		98.1	2017	●	↑
Mobile broadband subscriptions (per 100 population)		130.0	2018	●	↑
Logistics Performance Index: Quality of trade and transport-related infrastructure (worst 1–5 best)		NA	NA	●	●
The Times Higher Education Universities Ranking: Average score of top 3 universities (worst 0–100 best)	*	0.0	2020	●	●
Scientific and technical journal articles (per 1,000 population)		0.8	2018	●	↑
Expenditure on research and development (% of GDP)		NA	NA	●	●

SDG10 – Reduced Inequalities

	Value	Year	Rating	Trend
Gini coefficient adjusted for top income	NA	NA	●	●

SDG11 – Sustainable Cities and Communities

	Value	Year	Rating	Trend
Annual mean concentration of particulate matter of less than 2.5 microns in diameter (PM2.5) (µg/m³)	NA	NA	●	●
Access to improved water source, piped (% of urban population)	NA	NA	●	●
Satisfaction with public transport (%)	NA	NA	●	●

SDG12 – Responsible Consumption and Production

	Value	Year	Rating	Trend
Municipal solid waste (kg/capita/day)	16.2	2015	●	●
Electronic waste (kg/capita)	NA	NA	●	●
Production-based SO$_2$ emissions (kg/capita)	85.7	2012	●	●
SO$_2$ emissions embodied in imports (kg/capita)	27.9	2012	●	●
Production-based nitrogen emissions (kg/capita)	42.2	2010	●	●
Nitrogen emissions embodied in imports (kg/capita)	12.0	2010	●	●

SDG13 – Climate Action

	Value	Year	Rating	Trend
Energy-related CO$_2$ emissions (tCO$_2$/capita)	3.7	2017	●	↗
CO$_2$ emissions embodied in imports (tCO$_2$/capita)	1.0	2015	●	↗
CO$_2$ emissions embodied in fossil fuel exports (kg/capita)	NA	NA	●	●

SDG14 – Life Below Water

	Value	Year	Rating	Trend
Mean area that is protected in marine sites important to biodiversity (%)	NA	NA	●	●
Ocean Health Index: Clean Waters score (worst 0–100 best)	NA	NA	●	●
Fish caught from overexploited or collapsed stocks (% of total catch)	NA	NA	●	●
Fish caught by trawling (%)	NA	NA	●	●
Marine biodiversity threats embodied in imports (per million population)	0.0	2018	●	●

SDG15 – Life on Land

	Value	Year	Rating	Trend
Mean area that is protected in terrestrial sites important to biodiversity (%)	75.8	2018	●	↑
Mean area that is protected in freshwater sites important to biodiversity (%)	NA	NA	●	●
Red List Index of species survival (worst 0–1 best)	1.0	2019	●	↑
Permanent deforestation (% of forest area, 5-year average)	NA	NA	●	●
Terrestrial and freshwater biodiversity threats embodied in imports (per million population)	0.4	2018	●	●

SDG16 – Peace, Justice and Strong Institutions

		Value	Year	Rating	Trend
Homicides (per 100,000 population)		2.7	2014	●	●
Unsentenced detainees (% of prison population)		24.7	2018	●	↑
Percentage of population who feel safe walking alone at night in the city or area where they live (%)		NA	NA	●	●
Property Rights (worst 1–7 best)		NA	NA	●	●
Birth registrations with civil authority (% of children under age 5)		100.0	2018	●	●
Corruption Perception Index (worst 0–100 best)		NA	NA	●	●
Children involved in child labor (% of population aged 5 to 14)		NA	NA	●	●
Exports of major conventional weapons (TIV constant million USD per 100,000 population)	*	0.0	2019	●	●
Press Freedom Index (best 0–100 worst)		20.5	2019	●	↑

SDG17 – Partnerships for the Goals

	Value	Year	Rating	Trend
Government spending on health and education (% of GDP)	NA	NA	●	●
For high-income and all OECD DAC countries: International concessional public finance, including official development assistance (% of GNI)	0.5	2014	●	●
Other countries: Government revenue excluding grants (% of GDP)	NA	NA	●	●
Corporate Tax Haven Score (best 0–100 worst)	69.5	2019	●	●

* Imputed data point

▼ OVERALL PERFORMANCE

Index score

75.0

Regional average score

77.3

SDG Global rank 36 (OF 166)

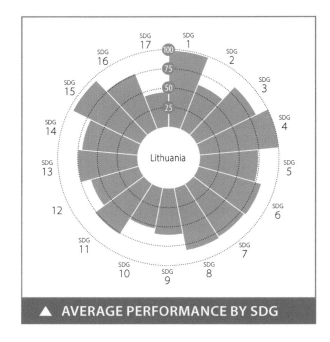

▲ AVERAGE PERFORMANCE BY SDG

▼ SPILLOVER INDEX

100 (best) to 0 (worst)

▼ CURRENT ASSESSMENT – SDG DASHBOARD

1 NO POVERTY	2 ZERO HUNGER

■ Major challenges   ■ Significant challenges   ■ Challenges remain   ■ SDG achieved   ■ Information unavailable

▼ SDG TRENDS

↓ Decreasing   → Stagnating   ↗ Moderately improving   ↑ On track or maintaining SDG achievement   ● Information unavailable

Notes: The full title of Goal 2 "Zero Hunger" is "End hunger, achieve food security and improved nutrition and promote sustainable agriculture".
The full title of each SDG is available here: https://sustainabledevelopment.un.org/topics/sustainabledevelopmentgoals

SDG1 – No Poverty

	Value	Year	Rating	Trend
Poverty headcount ratio at $1.90/day (%)	0.6	2020	●	↑
Poverty headcount ratio at $3.20/day (%)	1.1	2020	●	↑
Poverty rate after taxes and transfers (%)	17.3	2017	●	↓

SDG2 – Zero Hunger

	Value	Year	Rating	Trend
Prevalence of undernourishment (%)	2.5	2017	●	↑
Prevalence of stunting in children under 5 years of age (%)	* 2.6	2016	●	↑
Prevalence of wasting in children under 5 years of age (%)	* 0.7	2016	●	↑
Prevalence of obesity, BMI ≥ 30 (% of adult population)	26.3	2016	●	↓
Human Trophic Level (best 2–3 worst)	2.5	2017	●	↑
Cereal yield (tonnes per hectare of harvested land)	4.2	2017	●	↑
Sustainable Nitrogen Management Index (best 0–1.41 worst)	0.5	2015	○	↑
Yield gap closure (% of potential yield)	45.6	2015	●	●

SDG3 – Good Health and Well-Being

	Value	Year	Rating	Trend
Maternal mortality rate (per 100,000 live births)	8	2017	●	↑
Neonatal mortality rate (per 1,000 live births)	2.1	2018	●	↑
Mortality rate, under-5 (per 1,000 live births)	4.0	2018	●	↑
Incidence of tuberculosis (per 100,000 population)	44.0	2018	●	↑
New HIV infections (per 1,000 uninfected population)	NA	NA	●	●
Age-standardized death rate due to cardiovascular disease, cancer, diabetes, or chronic respiratory disease in adults aged 30–70 years (%)	20.7	2016	●	↑
Age-standardized death rate attributable to household air pollution and ambient air pollution (per 100,000 population)	34	2016	○	●
Traffic deaths (per 100,000 population)	8.0	2016	●	↑
Life expectancy at birth (years)	75.0	2016	○	↑
Adolescent fertility rate (births per 1,000 adolescent females aged 15 to 19)	10.9	2017	●	↑
Births attended by skilled health personnel (%)	100.0	2014	●	●
Percentage of surviving infants who received 2 WHO-recommended vaccines (%)	92.0	2018	●	↑
Universal health coverage (UHC) index of service coverage (worst 0–100 best)	73.0	2017	●	↑
Subjective well-being (average ladder score, worst 0–10 best)	6.3	2018	●	↑
Gap in life expectancy at birth among regions (years)	2.3	2015	●	↑
Gap in self-reported health status by income (percentage points)	40.0	2017	●	↓
Daily smokers (% of population aged 15 and over)	20.3	2014	●	●

SDG4 – Quality Education

	Value	Year	Rating	Trend
Net primary enrollment rate (%)	* 100.0	2017	●	↑
Lower secondary completion rate (%)	* 100.0	2017	●	↑
Literacy rate (% of population aged 15 to 24)	99.9	2011	●	●
Participation rate in pre-primary organized learning (% of children aged 4 to 6)	99.9	2017	●	↑
Tertiary educational attainment (% of population aged 25 to 34)	55.6	2018	●	↑
PISA score (worst 0–600 best)	479.7	2018	○	↑
Variation in science performance explained by socio-economic status (%)	12.5	2018	●	↓
Underachievers in science (% of 15-year-olds)	22.2	2018	●	↑
Resilient students in science (% of 15-year-olds)	26.4	2018	●	↑

SDG5 – Gender Equality

	Value	Year	Rating	Trend
Demand for family planning satisfied by modern methods (% of females aged 15 to 49 who are married or in unions)	* 72.6	2017	○	↗
Ratio of female-to-male mean years of education received (%)	100.0	2018	●	↑
Ratio of female-to-male labor force participation rate (%)	84.6	2019	●	↑
Seats held by women in national parliament (%)	24.1	2020	●	→
Gender wage gap (% of male median wage)	12.5	2014	●	●
Gender gap in time spent doing unpaid work (minutes/day)	140.3	2003	●	●

SDG6 – Clean Water and Sanitation

	Value	Year	Rating	Trend
Population using at least basic drinking water services (%)	97.5	2017	○	●
Population using at least basic sanitation services (%)	93.4	2017	○	●
Freshwater withdrawal (% of available freshwater resources)	19.9	2015	●	●
Anthropogenic wastewater that receives treatment (%)	51.4	2018	●	●
Scarce water consumption embodied in imports (m³/capita)	21.5	2013	●	↑
Population using safely managed water services (%)	92.0	2017	●	↑
Population using safely managed sanitation services (%)	91.3	2017	●	↑

SDG7 – Affordable and Clean Energy

	Value	Year	Rating	Trend
Population with access to electricity (%)	100.0	2017	●	↑
Population with access to clean fuels and technology for cooking (%)	100.0	2016	●	↑
CO₂ emissions from fuel combustion for electricity and heating per total electricity output (MtCO₂/TWh)	3.5	2017	●	→
Share of renewable energy in total primary energy supply (%)	19.3	2018	○	↑

SDG8 – Decent Work and Economic Growth

	Value	Year	Rating	Trend
Adjusted GDP growth (%)	2.7	2018	●	●
Victims of modern slavery (per 1,000 population)	5.8	2018	○	●
Adults with an account at a bank or other financial institution or with a mobile-money-service provider (% of population aged 15 or over)	82.9	2017	●	↑
Fatal work-related accidents embodied in imports (per 100,000 population)	0.6	2010	●	↑
Employment-to-population ratio (%)	73.0	2019	●	↑
Youth not in employment, education or training (NEET) (% of population aged 15 to 29)	10.5	2018	○	↑

SDG9 – Industry, Innovation and Infrastructure

	Value	Year	Rating	Trend
Population using the internet (%)	79.7	2018	○	↑
Mobile broadband subscriptions (per 100 population)	98.6	2018	●	↑
Logistics Performance Index: Quality of trade and transport-related infrastructure (worst 1–5 best)	2.7	2018	○	↓
The Times Higher Education Universities Ranking: Average score of top 3 universities (worst 0–100 best)	19.3	2020	●	●
Scientific and technical journal articles (per 1,000 population)	0.8	2018	●	↑
Expenditure on research and development (% of GDP)	0.9	2017	●	↓
Researchers (per 1,000 employed population)	6.4	2018	●	↓
Triadic patent families filed (per million population)	1.0	2017	●	↓
Gap in internet access by income (percentage points)	41.3	2019	●	↑
Women in science and engineering (% of tertiary graduates in science and engineering)	29.7	2015	○	●

SDG10 – Reduced Inequalities

	Value	Year	Rating	Trend
Gini coefficient adjusted for top income	44.2	2015	●	↓
Palma ratio	1.6	2017	●	↓
Elderly poverty rate (% of population aged 66 or over)	28.2	2017	●	↓

SDG11 – Sustainable Cities and Communities

	Value	Year	Rating	Trend
Annual mean concentration of particulate matter of less than 2.5 microns in diameter (PM2.5) (μg/m³)	11.9	2017	○	↑
Access to improved water source, piped (% of urban population)	99.0	2017	●	↑
Satisfaction with public transport (%)	44.1	2018	●	↓
Population with rent overburden (%)	4.5	2017	●	↑

SDG12 – Responsible Consumption and Production

	Value	Year	Rating	Trend
Electronic waste (kg/capita)	13.4	2016	●	●
Production-based SO₂ emissions (kg/capita)	94.1	2012	●	●
SO₂ emissions embodied in imports (kg/capita)	11.9	2012	●	●
Production-based nitrogen emissions (kg/capita)	48.6	2010	●	●
Nitrogen emissions embodied in imports (kg/capita)	8.0	2010	●	●
Non-recycled municipal solid waste (kg/capita/day)	0.5	2018	●	●

SDG13 – Climate Action

	Value	Year	Rating	Trend
Energy-related CO₂ emissions (tCO₂/capita)	4.9	2017	●	↓
CO₂ emissions embodied in imports (tCO₂/capita)	1.8	2015	●	→
CO₂ emissions embodied in fossil fuel exports (kg/capita)	0.0	2018	●	●
Effective carbon rate (EUR/tCO₂)	NA	NA	●	●

SDG14 – Life Below Water

	Value	Year	Rating	Trend
Mean area that is protected in marine sites important to biodiversity (%)	67.3	2018	●	↑
Ocean Health Index: Clean Waters score (worst 0–100 best)	45.1	2019	●	→
Fish caught from overexploited or collapsed stocks (% of total catch)	NA	NA	●	●
Fish caught by trawling (%)	4.2	2014	●	↑
Marine biodiversity threats embodied in imports (per million population)	0.1	2018	●	●

SDG15 – Life on Land

	Value	Year	Rating	Trend
Mean area that is protected in terrestrial sites important to biodiversity (%)	90.5	2018	●	↑
Mean area that is protected in freshwater sites important to biodiversity (%)	95.2	2018	●	↑
Red List Index of species survival (worst 0–1 best)	1.0	2019	●	↑
Permanent deforestation (% of forest area, 5-year average)	* 0.0	2018	●	●
Terrestrial and freshwater biodiversity threats embodied in imports (per million population)	0.8	2018	●	●

SDG16 – Peace, Justice and Strong Institutions

	Value	Year	Rating	Trend
Homicides (per 100,000 population)	4.5	2017	●	↑
Unsentenced detainees (% of prison population)	9.1	2018	●	↑
Percentage of population who feel safe walking alone at night in the city or area where they live (%)	69.0	2018	○	↑
Property Rights (worst 1–7 best)	4.7	2019	●	●
Birth registrations with civil authority (% of children under age 5)	100.0	2018	●	●
Corruption Perception Index (worst 0–100 best)	60.0	2019	●	↑
Children involved in child labor (% of population aged 5 to 14)	* 0.0	2016	●	●
Exports of major conventional weapons (TIV constant million USD per 100,000 population)	2.2	2019	●	●
Press Freedom Index (best 0–100 worst)	22.1	2019	●	↑
Persons held in prison (per 100,000 population)	228.3	2017	○	↑

SDG17 – Partnerships for the Goals

	Value	Year	Rating	Trend
Government spending on health and education (% of GDP)	8.4	2016	○	↓
For high-income and all OECD DAC countries: International concessional public finance, including official development assistance (% of GNI)	0.1	2017	●	→
Other countries: Government revenue excluding grants (% of GDP)	NA	NA	●	●
Corporate Tax Haven Score (best 0–100 worst)	54.8	2019	●	●
Financial Secrecy Score (best 0–100 worst)	50.3	2020	●	●
Shifted profits of multinationals (US$ billion)	NA	NA	●	●

* Imputed data point

5. Country Profiles

▼ OVERALL PERFORMANCE

Index score

74.3

Regional average score

77.3

SDG Global rank **44** (OF 166)

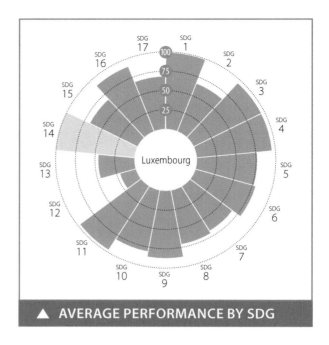

▼ SPILLOVER INDEX

100 (best) to 0 (worst)

```
100
80
60
40
20
0
```

▲ AVERAGE PERFORMANCE BY SDG

▼ CURRENT ASSESSMENT – SDG DASHBOARD

■ Major challenges ■ Significant challenges ■ Challenges remain ■ SDG achieved ■ Information unavailable

▼ SDG TRENDS

↓ Decreasing → Stagnating ↗ Moderately improving ↑ On track or maintaining SDG achievement ● Information unavailable

Notes: The full title of Goal 2 "Zero Hunger" is "End hunger, achieve food security and improved nutrition and promote sustainable agriculture".
The full title of each SDG is available here: https://sustainabledevelopment.un.org/topics/sustainabledevelopmentgoals

SDG1 – No Poverty

Indicator	Value	Year	Rating	Trend
Poverty headcount ratio at $1.90/day (%)	0.1	2020	●	↑
Poverty headcount ratio at $3.20/day (%)	0.1	2020	●	↑
Poverty rate after taxes and transfers (%)	12.2	2017	○	●

SDG2 – Zero Hunger

Indicator	Value	Year	Rating	Trend
Prevalence of undernourishment (%)	2.5	2017	●	↑
Prevalence of stunting in children under 5 years of age (%)	* 2.6	2016	●	↑
Prevalence of wasting in children under 5 years of age (%)	* 0.7	2016	●	↑
Prevalence of obesity, BMI ≥ 30 (% of adult population)	22.6	2016	●	↓
Human Trophic Level (best 2–3 worst)	2.3	2017	●	→
Cereal yield (tonnes per hectare of harvested land)	5.3	2017	●	↑
Sustainable Nitrogen Management Index (best 0–1.41 worst)	0.7	2015	●	↓
Yield gap closure (% of potential yield)	65.0	2015	○	●

SDG3 – Good Health and Well-Being

Indicator	Value	Year	Rating	Trend
Maternal mortality rate (per 100,000 live births)	5	2017	●	↑
Neonatal mortality rate (per 1,000 live births)	1.4	2018	●	↑
Mortality rate, under-5 (per 1,000 live births)	2.4	2018	●	↑
Incidence of tuberculosis (per 100,000 population)	8.0	2018	●	↑
New HIV infections (per 1,000 uninfected population)	0.1	2018	●	↑
Age-standardized death rate due to cardiovascular disease, cancer, diabetes, or chronic respiratory disease in adults aged 30–70 years (%)	10.0	2016	●	↑
Age-standardized death rate attributable to household air pollution and ambient air pollution (per 100,000 population)	12	2016	●	●
Traffic deaths (per 100,000 population)	6.3	2016	●	↑
Life expectancy at birth (years)	82.4	2016	●	↑
Adolescent fertility rate (births per 1,000 adolescent females aged 15 to 19)	4.7	2017	●	↑
Births attended by skilled health personnel (%)	99.9	2009	●	●
Percentage of surviving infants who received 2 WHO-recommended vaccines (%)	99.0	2018	●	↑
Universal health coverage (UHC) index of service coverage (worst 0–100 best)	83.0	2017	●	↑
Subjective well-being (average ladder score, worst 0–10 best)	7.4	2019	●	↑
Gap in life expectancy at birth among regions (years)	NA	NA	●	●
Gap in self-reported health status by income (percentage points)	10.6	2017	●	↑
Daily smokers (% of population aged 15 and over)	14.5	2018	●	↑

SDG4 – Quality Education

Indicator	Value	Year	Rating	Trend
Net primary enrollment rate (%)	* 96.4	2017	○	↓
Lower secondary completion rate (%)	* 96.4	2017	●	↑
Literacy rate (% of population aged 15 to 24)	NA	NA	●	●
Participation rate in pre-primary organized learning (% of children aged 4 to 6)	98.2	2017	●	↑
Tertiary educational attainment (% of population aged 25 to 34)	54.8	2018	●	↑
PISA score (worst 0–600 best)	476.7	2018	●	↓
Variation in science performance explained by socio-economic status (%)	20.9	2018	●	↓
Underachievers in science (% of 15-year-olds)	26.8	2018	●	↓
Resilient students in science (% of 15-year-olds)	24.5	2018	●	↑

SDG5 – Gender Equality

Indicator	Value	Year	Rating	Trend
Demand for family planning satisfied by modern methods (% of females aged 15 to 49 who are married or in unions)	NA	NA	●	●
Ratio of female-to-male mean years of education received (%)	93.7	2018	○	→
Ratio of female-to-male labor force participation rate (%)	85.5	2019	●	↑
Seats held by women in national parliament (%)	30.0	2020	●	→
Gender wage gap (% of male median wage)	3.4	2014	●	●
Gender gap in time spent doing unpaid work (minutes/day)	118.5	2013	○	●

SDG6 – Clean Water and Sanitation

Indicator	Value	Year	Rating	Trend
Population using at least basic drinking water services (%)	99.9	2017	●	●
Population using at least basic sanitation services (%)	97.6	2017	●	●
Freshwater withdrawal (% of available freshwater resources)	3.6	2015	●	●
Anthropogenic wastewater that receives treatment (%)	98.5	2018	●	●
Scarce water consumption embodied in imports (m³/capita)	156.0	2013	●	→
Population using safely managed water services (%)	99.7	2017	●	↑
Population using safely managed sanitation services (%)	96.6	2017	●	↑

SDG7 – Affordable and Clean Energy

Indicator	Value	Year	Rating	Trend
Population with access to electricity (%)	100.0	2017	●	↑
Population with access to clean fuels and technology for cooking (%)	100.0	2016	●	↑
CO₂ emissions from fuel combustion for electricity and heating per total electricity output (MtCO₂/TWh)	22.5	2017	●	↓
Share of renewable energy in total primary energy supply (%)	7.5	2018	●	↗

SDG8 – Decent Work and Economic Growth

Indicator	Value	Year	Rating	Trend
Adjusted GDP growth (%)	0.5	2018	●	●
Victims of modern slavery (per 1,000 population)	1.5	2018	●	●
Adults with an account at a bank or other financial institution or with a mobile-money-service provider (% of population aged 15 or over)	98.8	2017	●	↑
Fatal work-related accidents embodied in imports (per 100,000 population)	6.4	2010	●	↑
Employment-to-population ratio (%)	67.9	2019	●	↑
Youth not in employment, education or training (NEET) (% of population aged 15 to 29)	8.4	2018	●	↑

SDG9 – Industry, Innovation and Infrastructure

Indicator	Value	Year	Rating	Trend
Population using the internet (%)	97.1	2018	●	↑
Mobile broadband subscriptions (per 100 population)	94.0	2018	●	↑
Logistics Performance Index: Quality of trade and transport-related infrastructure (worst 1–5 best)	3.6	2018	●	↑
The Times Higher Education Universities Ranking: Average score of top 3 universities (worst 0–100 best)	51.9	2020	●	●
Scientific and technical journal articles (per 1,000 population)	1.4	2018	●	↑
Expenditure on research and development (% of GDP)	1.3	2017	○	↓
Researchers (per 1,000 employed population)	6.7	2018	●	→
Triadic patent families filed (per million population)	48.2	2017	●	↑
Gap in internet access by income (percentage points)	7.7	2019	○	→
Women in science and engineering (% of tertiary graduates in science and engineering)	18.3	2015	●	●

SDG10 – Reduced Inequalities

Indicator	Value	Year	Rating	Trend
Gini coefficient adjusted for top income	34.8	2015	○	→
Palma ratio	1.2	2017	●	●
Elderly poverty rate (% of population aged 66 or over)	10.9	2017	○	●

SDG11 – Sustainable Cities and Communities

Indicator	Value	Year	Rating	Trend
Annual mean concentration of particulate matter of less than 2.5 microns in diameter (PM2.5) (µg/m³)	10.4	2017	○	↑
Access to improved water source, piped (% of urban population)	99.0	2017	●	↑
Satisfaction with public transport (%)	78.8	2019	●	↑
Population with rent overburden (%)	16.9	2017	●	↓

SDG12 – Responsible Consumption and Production

Indicator	Value	Year	Rating	Trend
Electronic waste (kg/capita)	20.9	2016	●	●
Production-based SO₂ emissions (kg/capita)	225.9	2012	●	●
SO₂ emissions embodied in imports (kg/capita)	81.2	2012	●	●
Production-based nitrogen emissions (kg/capita)	99.5	2010	●	●
Nitrogen emissions embodied in imports (kg/capita)	67.6	2010	●	●
Non-recycled municipal solid waste (kg/capita/day)	0.8	2018	○	●

SDG13 – Climate Action

Indicator	Value	Year	Rating	Trend
Energy-related CO₂ emissions (tCO₂/capita)	15.1	2017	●	↗
CO₂ emissions embodied in imports (tCO₂/capita)	15.7	2015	●	→
CO₂ emissions embodied in fossil fuel exports (kg/capita)	0.0	2018	●	●
Effective carbon rate (EUR/tCO₂)	6.3	2016	●	●

SDG14 – Life Below Water

Indicator	Value	Year	Rating	Trend
Mean area that is protected in marine sites important to biodiversity (%)	NA	NA	●	●
Ocean Health Index: Clean Waters score (worst 0–100 best)	NA	NA	●	●
Fish caught from overexploited or collapsed stocks (% of total catch)	NA	NA	●	●
Fish caught by trawling (%)	NA	NA	●	●
Marine biodiversity threats embodied in imports (per million population)	0.7	2018	●	●

SDG15 – Life on Land

Indicator	Value	Year	Rating	Trend
Mean area that is protected in terrestrial sites important to biodiversity (%)	83.3	2018	●	↑
Mean area that is protected in freshwater sites important to biodiversity (%)	37.1	2018	○	→
Red List Index of species survival (worst 0–1 best)	1.0	2019	●	↑
Permanent deforestation (% of forest area, 5-year average)	0.0	2018	●	●
Terrestrial and freshwater biodiversity threats embodied in imports (per million population)	7.9	2018	●	●

SDG16 – Peace, Justice and Strong Institutions

Indicator	Value	Year	Rating	Trend
Homicides (per 100,000 population)	0.3	2017	●	↑
Unsentenced detainees (% of prison population)	45.9	2018	●	↓
Percentage of population who feel safe walking alone at night in the city or area where they live (%)	86.6	2019	●	↑
Property Rights (worst 1–7 best)	6.1	2019	●	●
Birth registrations with civil authority (% of children under age 5)	100.0	2018	●	●
Corruption Perception Index (worst 0–100 best)	80.0	2019	●	↑
Children involved in child labor (% of population aged 5 to 14)	* 0.0	2016	●	●
Exports of major conventional weapons (TIV constant million USD per 100,000 population)	* 0.0	2019	●	●
Press Freedom Index (best 0–100 worst)	15.7	2019	●	↑
Persons held in prison (per 100,000 population)	111.5	2017	○	→

SDG17 – Partnerships for the Goals

Indicator	Value	Year	Rating	Trend
Government spending on health and education (% of GDP)	9.0	2015	○	↓
For high-income and all OECD DAC countries: International concessional public finance, including official development assistance (% of GNI)	1.0	2017	●	↑
Other countries: Government revenue excluding grants (% of GDP)	NA	NA	●	●
Corporate Tax Haven Score (best 0–100 worst)	72.4	2019	●	●
Financial Secrecy Score (best 0–100 worst)	55.5	2020	●	●
Shifted profits of multinationals (US$ billion)	-50.1	2016	●	●

* Imputed data point

5. Country Profiles

MADAGASCAR

▼ OVERALL PERFORMANCE

Index score

49.1

Regional average score

53.1

SDG Global rank 161 (OF 166)

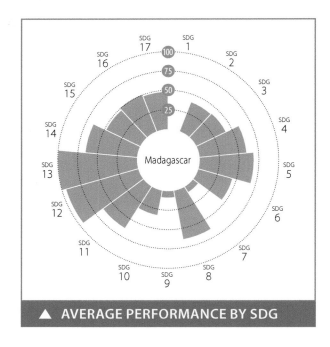

▲ AVERAGE PERFORMANCE BY SDG

▼ SPILLOVER INDEX

100 (best) to 0 (worst)

▼ CURRENT ASSESSMENT – SDG DASHBOARD

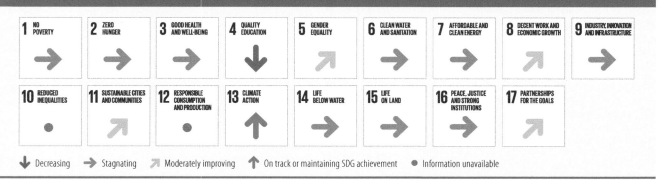

■ Major challenges ■ Significant challenges ■ Challenges remain ■ SDG achieved ■ Information unavailable

▼ SDG TRENDS

1 NO POVERTY	2 ZERO HUNGER	3 GOOD HEALTH AND WELL-BEING	4 QUALITY EDUCATION	5 GENDER EQUALITY	6 CLEAN WATER AND SANITATION	7 AFFORDABLE AND CLEAN ENERGY	8 DECENT WORK AND ECONOMIC GROWTH	9 INDUSTRY, INNOVATION AND INFRASTRUCTURE
→	→	→	↓	↗	→	→	↗	→

10 REDUCED INEQUALITIES	11 SUSTAINABLE CITIES AND COMMUNITIES	12 RESPONSIBLE CONSUMPTION AND PRODUCTION	13 CLIMATE ACTION	14 LIFE BELOW WATER	15 LIFE ON LAND	16 PEACE, JUSTICE AND STRONG INSTITUTIONS	17 PARTNERSHIPS FOR THE GOALS
●	↗	●	↑	→	→	→	↗

↓ Decreasing → Stagnating ↗ Moderately improving ↑ On track or maintaining SDG achievement ● Information unavailable

Notes: The full title of Goal 2 "Zero Hunger" is "End hunger, achieve food security and improved nutrition and promote sustainable agriculture".
The full title of each SDG is available here: https://sustainabledevelopment.un.org/topics/sustainabledevelopmentgoals

SDG1 – No Poverty

Indicator	Value	Year	Rating	Trend
Poverty headcount ratio at $1.90/day (%)	75.7	2020	●	→
Poverty headcount ratio at $3.20/day (%)	92.0	2020	●	→

SDG2 – Zero Hunger

Indicator	Value	Year	Rating	Trend
Prevalence of undernourishment (%)	44.4	2017	●	↓
Prevalence of stunting in children under 5 years of age (%)	49.2	2009	●	→
Prevalence of wasting in children under 5 years of age (%)	15.2	2004	●	→
Prevalence of obesity, BMI ≥ 30 (% of adult population)	5.3	2016	●	↑
Human Trophic Level (best 2–3 worst)	2.1	2017	●	↑
Cereal yield (tonnes per hectare of harvested land)	3.8	2017	●	↑
Sustainable Nitrogen Management Index (best 0–1.41 worst)	0.7	2015	●	→

SDG3 – Good Health and Well-Being

Indicator	Value	Year	Rating	Trend
Maternal mortality rate (per 100,000 live births)	335	2017	●	↗
Neonatal mortality rate (per 1,000 live births)	20.6	2018	●	↗
Mortality rate, under-5 (per 1,000 live births)	53.6	2018	●	↗
Incidence of tuberculosis (per 100,000 population)	233.0	2018	●	→
New HIV infections (per 1,000 uninfected population)	0.2	2018	●	↓
Age-standardized death rate due to cardiovascular disease, cancer, diabetes, or chronic respiratory disease in adults aged 30–70 years (%)	22.9	2016	●	↗
Age-standardized death rate attributable to household air pollution and ambient air pollution (per 100,000 population)	160	2016	●	●
Traffic deaths (per 100,000 population)	28.6	2016	●	↓
Life expectancy at birth (years)	66.1	2016	●	→
Adolescent fertility rate (births per 1,000 adolescent females aged 15 to 19)	109.6	2017	●	→
Births attended by skilled health personnel (%)	44.3	2013	●	●
Percentage of surviving infants who received 2 WHO-recommended vaccines (%)	62	2018	●	↗
Universal health coverage (UHC) index of service coverage (worst 0–100 best)	28.0	2017	●	→
Subjective well-being (average ladder score, worst 0–10 best)	4.3	2019	●	↑

SDG4 – Quality Education

Indicator	Value	Year	Rating	Trend
Net primary enrollment rate (%)	95.6	2018	●	●
Lower secondary completion rate (%)	37.0	2018	●	↓
Literacy rate (% of population aged 15 to 24)	81.2	2018	●	●

SDG5 – Gender Equality

Indicator	Value	Year	Rating	Trend
Demand for family planning satisfied by modern methods (% of females aged 15 to 49 who are married or in unions)	60.5	2017	●	↗
Ratio of female-to-male mean years of education received (%)	110.3	2018	●	↑
Ratio of female-to-male labor force participation rate (%)	93.7	2019	●	↑
Seats held by women in national parliament (%)	15.9	2020	●	↓

SDG6 – Clean Water and Sanitation

Indicator	Value	Year	Rating	Trend
Population using at least basic drinking water services (%)	54.4	2017	●	→
Population using at least basic sanitation services (%)	10.5	2017	●	→
Freshwater withdrawal (% of available freshwater resources)	11.3	2005	●	●
Anthropogenic wastewater that receives treatment (%)	0.0	2018	●	●
Scarce water consumption embodied in imports (m3/capita)	0.6	2013	●	↑

SDG7 – Affordable and Clean Energy

Indicator	Value	Year	Rating	Trend
Population with access to electricity (%)	24.1	2017	●	→
Population with access to clean fuels and technology for cooking (%)	0.9	2016	●	↓
CO_2 emissions from fuel combustion for electricity and heating per total electricity output (MtCO2/TWh)	NA	NA	●	●

SDG8 – Decent Work and Economic Growth

Indicator	Value	Year	Rating	Trend
Adjusted GDP growth (%)	-5.4	2018	●	●
Victims of modern slavery (per 1,000 population)	7.5	2018	●	●
Adults with an account at a bank or other financial institution or with a mobile-money-service provider (% of population aged 15 or over)	17.9	2017	●	↗
Unemployment rate (% of total labor force)	1.8	2019	●	↑
Fatal work-related accidents embodied in imports (per 100,000 population)	0.0	2010	●	↑

SDG9 – Industry, Innovation and Infrastructure

Indicator	Value	Year	Rating	Trend
Population using the internet (%)	9.8	2017	●	→
Mobile broadband subscriptions (per 100 population)	15.6	2018	●	→
Logistics Performance Index: Quality of trade and transport-related infrastructure (worst 1–5 best)	2.2	2018	●	→
The Times Higher Education Universities Ranking: Average score of top 3 universities (worst 0–100 best) *	0.0	2020	●	●
Scientific and technical journal articles (per 1,000 population)	0.0	2018	●	→
Expenditure on research and development (% of GDP)	0.0	2017	●	↓

SDG10 – Reduced Inequalities

Indicator	Value	Year	Rating	Trend
Gini coefficient adjusted for top income	51.7	2012	●	●

SDG11 – Sustainable Cities and Communities

Indicator	Value	Year	Rating	Trend
Annual mean concentration of particulate matter of less than 2.5 microns in diameter (PM2.5) (µg/m3)	22.5	2017	●	→
Access to improved water source, piped (% of urban population)	69.6	2017	●	→
Satisfaction with public transport (%)	46.6	2019	●	↑

SDG12 – Responsible Consumption and Production

Indicator	Value	Year	Rating	Trend
Municipal solid waste (kg/capita/day)	1.1	2016	●	●
Electronic waste (kg/capita)	0.5	2016	●	●
Production-based SO_2 emissions (kg/capita)	5.9	2012	●	●
SO_2 emissions embodied in imports (kg/capita)	0.4	2012	●	●
Production-based nitrogen emissions (kg/capita)	6.6	2010	●	●
Nitrogen emissions embodied in imports (kg/capita)	0.2	2010	●	●

SDG13 – Climate Action

Indicator	Value	Year	Rating	Trend
Energy-related CO_2 emissions (tCO2/capita)	0.1	2017	●	↑
CO_2 emissions embodied in imports (tCO2/capita)	0.0	2015	●	↑
CO_2 emissions embodied in fossil fuel exports (kg/capita)	0.0	2018	●	↑

SDG14 – Life Below Water

Indicator	Value	Year	Rating	Trend
Mean area that is protected in marine sites important to biodiversity (%)	18.3	2018	●	↗
Ocean Health Index: Clean Waters score (worst 0–100 best)	57.7	2019	●	↓
Fish caught from overexploited or collapsed stocks (% of total catch)	17.4	2014	●	↑
Fish caught by trawling (%)	13.6	2014	●	→
Marine biodiversity threats embodied in imports (per million population)	0.0	2018	●	●

SDG15 – Life on Land

Indicator	Value	Year	Rating	Trend
Mean area that is protected in terrestrial sites important to biodiversity (%)	24.6	2018	●	→
Mean area that is protected in freshwater sites important to biodiversity (%)	57.4	2018	●	↑
Red List Index of species survival (worst 0–1 best)	0.8	2019	●	↓
Permanent deforestation (% of forest area, 5-year average)	1.3	2018	●	●
Terrestrial and freshwater biodiversity threats embodied in imports (per million population)	0.0	2018	●	●

SDG16 – Peace, Justice and Strong Institutions

Indicator	Value	Year	Rating	Trend
Homicides (per 100,000 population) *	7.7	2015	●	●
Unsentenced detainees (% of prison population)	56.1	2018	●	↓
Percentage of population who feel safe walking alone at night in the city or area where they live (%)	43.4	2019	●	↓
Property Rights (worst 1–7 best)	3.2	2019	●	●
Birth registrations with civil authority (% of children under age 5)	83.0	2018	●	●
Corruption Perception Index (worst 0–100 best)	24	2019	●	↓
Children involved in child labor (% of population aged 5 to 14)	22.9	2016	●	●
Exports of major conventional weapons (TIV constant million USD per 100,000 population) *	0.0	2019	●	●
Press Freedom Index (best 0–100 worst)	27.8	2019	●	↑

SDG17 – Partnerships for the Goals

Indicator	Value	Year	Rating	Trend
Government spending on health and education (% of GDP)	6.1	2016	●	↑
For high-income and all OECD DAC countries: International concessional public finance, including official development assistance (% of GNI)	NA	NA	●	●
Other countries: Government revenue excluding grants (% of GDP)	11.4	2018	●	→
Corporate Tax Haven Score (best 0–100 worst) *	0.0	2019	●	●

5. Country Profiles

* Imputed data point

MALAWI

▼ OVERALL PERFORMANCE

Index score

52.2

Regional average score

53.1

SDG Global rank **152** (OF 166)

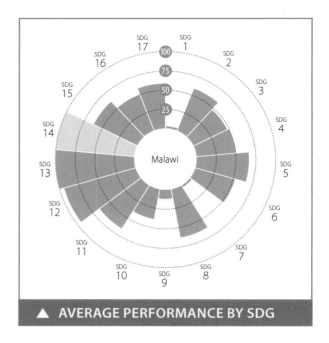

▲ AVERAGE PERFORMANCE BY SDG

▼ SPILLOVER INDEX

100 (best) to 0 (worst)

▼ CURRENT ASSESSMENT – SDG DASHBOARD

■ Major challenges   ■ Significant challenges   ■ Challenges remain   ■ SDG achieved   ■ Information unavailable

▼ SDG TRENDS

↓ Decreasing   → Stagnating   ↗ Moderately improving   ↑ On track or maintaining SDG achievement   ● Information unavailable

Notes: The full title of Goal 2 "Zero Hunger" is "End hunger, achieve food security and improved nutrition and promote sustainable agriculture".
The full title of each SDG is available here: https://sustainabledevelopment.un.org/topics/sustainabledevelopmentgoals

308 | Sustainable Development Report 2020 ⬤ The Sustainable Development Goals and Covid-19

SDG1 – No Poverty

	Value	Year	Rating	Trend
Poverty headcount ratio at $1.90/day (%)	66.5	2020	●	→
Poverty headcount ratio at $3.20/day (%)	87.4	2020	●	→

SDG2 – Zero Hunger

	Value	Year	Rating	Trend
Prevalence of undernourishment (%)	17.5	2017	●	→
Prevalence of stunting in children under 5 years of age (%)	37.1	2015	●	→
Prevalence of wasting in children under 5 years of age (%)	2.7	2015	●	↑
Prevalence of obesity, BMI ≥ 30 (% of adult population)	5.8	2016	●	↑
Human Trophic Level (best 2–3 worst)	2.1	2017	●	↑
Cereal yield (tonnes per hectare of harvested land)	1.9	2017	●	↓
Sustainable Nitrogen Management Index (best 0–1.41 worst)	0.7	2015	●	→

SDG3 – Good Health and Well-Being

	Value	Year	Rating	Trend
Maternal mortality rate (per 100,000 live births)	349	2017	●	↗
Neonatal mortality rate (per 1,000 live births)	22.4	2018	●	↗
Mortality rate, under-5 (per 1,000 live births)	49.7	2018	●	↑
Incidence of tuberculosis (per 100,000 population)	181.0	2018	●	↗
New HIV infections (per 1,000 uninfected population)	2.3	2018	●	↑
Age-standardized death rate due to cardiovascular disease, cancer, diabetes, or chronic respiratory disease in adults aged 30–70 years (%)	16.4	2016	○	↑
Age-standardized death rate attributable to household air pollution and ambient air pollution (per 100,000 population)	115	2016	●	●
Traffic deaths (per 100,000 population)	31.0	2016	●	↗
Life expectancy at birth (years)	64.2	2016	●	↗
Adolescent fertility rate (births per 1,000 adolescent females aged 15 to 19)	132.7	2017	●	→
Births attended by skilled health personnel (%)	89.8	2016	●	●
Percentage of surviving infants who received 2 WHO-recommended vaccines (%)	87	2018	○	→
Universal health coverage (UHC) index of service coverage (worst 0–100 best)	46.0	2017	●	→
Subjective well-being (average ladder score, worst 0–10 best)	3.9	2019	●	→

SDG4 – Quality Education

	Value	Year	Rating	Trend
Net primary enrollment rate (%)	97.6	2009	●	●
Lower secondary completion rate (%)	21.6	2013	●	●
Literacy rate (% of population aged 15 to 24)	72.9	2015	●	●

SDG5 – Gender Equality

	Value	Year	Rating	Trend
Demand for family planning satisfied by modern methods (% of females aged 15 to 49 who are married or in unions)	73.9	2016	○	↑
Ratio of female-to-male mean years of education received (%)	80.4	2018	●	↗
Ratio of female-to-male labor force participation rate (%)	88.6	2019	●	↑
Seats held by women in national parliament (%)	22.9	2020	○	↗

SDG6 – Clean Water and Sanitation

	Value	Year	Rating	Trend
Population using at least basic drinking water services (%)	68.8	2017	●	→
Population using at least basic sanitation services (%)	26.2	2017	●	→
Freshwater withdrawal (% of available freshwater resources)	17.5	2005	●	●
Anthropogenic wastewater that receives treatment (%)	0.0	2018	●	●
Scarce water consumption embodied in imports (m³/capita)	0.4	2013	●	↑

SDG7 – Affordable and Clean Energy

	Value	Year	Rating	Trend
Population with access to electricity (%)	12.7	2017	●	→
Population with access to clean fuels and technology for cooking (%)	2.5	2016	●	→
CO₂ emissions from fuel combustion for electricity and heating per total electricity output (MtCO₂/TWh)	NA	NA	●	●

SDG8 – Decent Work and Economic Growth

	Value	Year	Rating	Trend
Adjusted GDP growth (%)	-6.7	2018	●	●
Victims of modern slavery (per 1,000 population)	7.5	2018	●	●
Adults with an account at a bank or other financial institution or with a mobile-money-service provider (% of population aged 15 or over)	33.7	2017	●	↑
Unemployment rate (% of total labor force)	5.7	2019	○	↗
Fatal work-related accidents embodied in imports (per 100,000 population)	0.1	2010	●	↑

SDG9 – Industry, Innovation and Infrastructure

	Value	Year	Rating	Trend
Population using the internet (%)	13.8	2017	●	↗
Mobile broadband subscriptions (per 100 population)	27.2	2018	●	↗
Logistics Performance Index: Quality of trade and transport-related infrastructure (worst 1–5 best)	2.2	2018	●	↓
The Times Higher Education Universities Ranking: Average score of top 3 universities (worst 0–100 best) *	0.0	2020	●	●
Scientific and technical journal articles (per 1,000 population)	0.0	2018	●	→
Expenditure on research and development (% of GDP) *	0.0	2017	●	●

SDG10 – Reduced Inequalities

	Value	Year	Rating	Trend
Gini coefficient adjusted for top income	49.4	2016	●	●

SDG11 – Sustainable Cities and Communities

	Value	Year	Rating	Trend
Annual mean concentration of particulate matter of less than 2.5 microns in diameter (PM2.5) (μg/m³)	23.6	2017	●	↗
Access to improved water source, piped (% of urban population)	81.5	2017	●	→
Satisfaction with public transport (%)	43.1	2019	●	↗

SDG12 – Responsible Consumption and Production

	Value	Year	Rating	Trend
Municipal solid waste (kg/capita/day)	1.1	2013	○	●
Electronic waste (kg/capita)	0.5	2016	●	●
Production-based SO₂ emissions (kg/capita)	8.2	2012	●	●
SO₂ emissions embodied in imports (kg/capita)	0.4	2012	●	●
Production-based nitrogen emissions (kg/capita)	5.3	2010	●	●
Nitrogen emissions embodied in imports (kg/capita)	0.4	2010	●	●

SDG13 – Climate Action

	Value	Year	Rating	Trend
Energy-related CO₂ emissions (tCO₂/capita)	0.1	2017	●	↑
CO₂ emissions embodied in imports (tCO₂/capita)	0.0	2015	●	↑
CO₂ emissions embodied in fossil fuel exports (kg/capita)	0.8	2017	●	●

SDG14 – Life Below Water

	Value	Year	Rating	Trend
Mean area that is protected in marine sites important to biodiversity (%)	NA	NA	●	●
Ocean Health Index: Clean Waters score (worst 0–100 best)	NA	NA	●	●
Fish caught from overexploited or collapsed stocks (% of total catch)	NA	NA	●	●
Fish caught by trawling (%)	NA	NA	●	●
Marine biodiversity threats embodied in imports (per million population)	0.0	2018	●	●

SDG15 – Life on Land

	Value	Year	Rating	Trend
Mean area that is protected in terrestrial sites important to biodiversity (%)	83.4	2018	●	↑
Mean area that is protected in freshwater sites important to biodiversity (%)	44.7	2018	○	→
Red List Index of species survival (worst 0–1 best)	0.8	2019	●	→
Permanent deforestation (% of forest area, 5-year average)	1.0	2018	●	●
Terrestrial and freshwater biodiversity threats embodied in imports (per million population)	0.3	2018	●	●

SDG16 – Peace, Justice and Strong Institutions

	Value	Year	Rating	Trend
Homicides (per 100,000 population)	1.7	2012	○	●
Unsentenced detainees (% of prison population)	14.4	2018	●	↑
Percentage of population who feel safe walking alone at night in the city or area where they live	47.3	2019	●	↗
Property Rights (worst 1–7 best)	4.2	2019	○	●
Birth registrations with civil authority (% of children under age 5)	5.6	2018	●	●
Corruption Perception Index (worst 0–100 best)	31	2019	●	→
Children involved in child labor (% of population aged 5 to 14)	39.3	2016	●	●
Exports of major conventional weapons (TIV constant million USD per 100,000 population) *	0.0	2019	●	●
Press Freedom Index (best 0–100 worst)	29.4	2019	●	↑

SDG17 – Partnerships for the Goals

	Value	Year	Rating	Trend
Government spending on health and education (% of GDP)	7.5	2016	○	→
For high-income and all OECD DAC countries: International concessional public finance, including official development assistance (% of GNI)	NA	NA	●	●
Other countries: Government revenue excluding grants (% of GDP)	18.1	2018	●	→
Corporate Tax Haven Score (best 0–100 worst) *	0.0	2019	●	●

* Imputed data point

5. Country Profiles

▼ OVERALL PERFORMANCE

Index score

71.8

Regional average score

67.2

SDG Global rank 60 (OF 166)

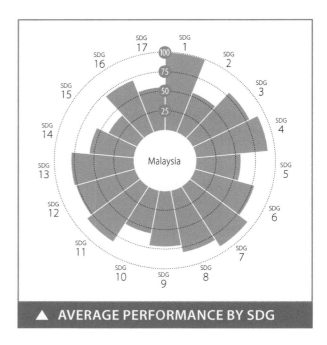

▲ AVERAGE PERFORMANCE BY SDG

▼ SPILLOVER INDEX

100 (best) to 0 (worst)

▼ CURRENT ASSESSMENT – SDG DASHBOARD

■ Major challenges ■ Significant challenges ■ Challenges remain ■ SDG achieved ■ Information unavailable

▼ SDG TRENDS

1 NO POVERTY	2 ZERO HUNGER	3 GOOD HEALTH AND WELL-BEING	4 QUALITY EDUCATION	5 GENDER EQUALITY	6 CLEAN WATER AND SANITATION	7 AFFORDABLE AND CLEAN ENERGY	8 DECENT WORK AND ECONOMIC GROWTH	9 INDUSTRY, INNOVATION AND INFRASTRUCTURE
↑	→	↗	→	↗	↗	↑	↑	↑

10 REDUCED INEQUALITIES	11 SUSTAINABLE CITIES AND COMMUNITIES	12 RESPONSIBLE CONSUMPTION AND PRODUCTION	13 CLIMATE ACTION	14 LIFE BELOW WATER	15 LIFE ON LAND	16 PEACE, JUSTICE AND STRONG INSTITUTIONS	17 PARTNERSHIPS FOR THE GOALS
●	↗	●	→	→	→	↗	↓

↓ Decreasing → Stagnating ↗ Moderately improving ↑ On track or maintaining SDG achievement ● Information unavailable

Notes: The full title of Goal 2 "Zero Hunger" is "End hunger, achieve food security and improved nutrition and promote sustainable agriculture".
The full title of each SDG is available here: https://sustainabledevelopment.un.org/topics/sustainabledevelopmentgoals

SDG1 – No Poverty

Indicator	Value	Year	Rating	Trend
Poverty headcount ratio at $1.90/day (%)	0.0	2020	●	↑
Poverty headcount ratio at $3.20/day (%)	0.0	2020	●	↑

SDG2 – Zero Hunger

Indicator	Value	Year	Rating	Trend
Prevalence of undernourishment (%)	2.5	2017	●	↑
Prevalence of stunting in children under 5 years of age (%)	20.7	2016	●	→
Prevalence of wasting in children under 5 years of age (%)	11.5	2016	●	↓
Prevalence of obesity, BMI ≥ 30 (% of adult population)	15.6	2016	◐	↓
Human Trophic Level (best 2–3 worst)	2.4	2017	●	→
Cereal yield (tonnes per hectare of harvested land)	4.3	2017	●	↑
Sustainable Nitrogen Management Index (best 0–1.41 worst)	0.5	2015	●	↑

SDG3 – Good Health and Well-Being

Indicator	Value	Year	Rating	Trend
Maternal mortality rate (per 100,000 live births)	29	2017	●	↑
Neonatal mortality rate (per 1,000 live births)	4.3	2018	●	↑
Mortality rate, under-5 (per 1,000 live births)	7.8	2018	●	↑
Incidence of tuberculosis (per 100,000 population)	92.0	2018	●	→
New HIV infections (per 1,000 uninfected population)	0.2	2018	●	↑
Age-standardized death rate due to cardiovascular disease, cancer, diabetes, or chronic respiratory disease in adults aged 30–70 years (%)	17.2	2016	◐	↑
Age-standardized death rate attributable to household air pollution and ambient air pollution (per 100,000 population)	47	2016	◐	●
Traffic deaths (per 100,000 population)	23.6	2016	●	→
Life expectancy at birth (years)	75.3	2016	●	↗
Adolescent fertility rate (births per 1,000 adolescent females aged 15 to 19)	13.4	2017	●	↑
Births attended by skilled health personnel (%)	99.4	2015	●	↑
Percentage of surviving infants who received 2 WHO-recommended vaccines (%)	96	2018	●	↑
Universal health coverage (UHC) index of service coverage (worst 0–100 best)	73.0	2017	◐	↑
Subjective well-being (average ladder score, worst 0–10 best)	5.4	2019	●	↓

SDG4 – Quality Education

Indicator	Value	Year	Rating	Trend
Net primary enrollment rate (%)	99.6	2017	●	↑
Lower secondary completion rate (%)	81.8	2018	●	↓
Literacy rate (% of population aged 15 to 24)	96.9	2018	●	●

SDG5 – Gender Equality

Indicator	Value	Year	Rating	Trend
Demand for family planning satisfied by modern methods (% of females aged 15 to 49 who are married or in unions) *	54.5	2017	●	↗
Ratio of female-to-male mean years of education received (%)	97.1	2018	◐	↑
Ratio of female-to-male labor force participation rate (%)	65.9	2019	●	↗
Seats held by women in national parliament (%)	14.4	2020	●	→

SDG6 – Clean Water and Sanitation

Indicator	Value	Year	Rating	Trend
Population using at least basic drinking water services (%)	96.7	2017	◐	↑
Population using at least basic sanitation services (%)	99.6	2017	●	↑
Freshwater withdrawal (% of available freshwater resources)	5.7	2005	●	●
Anthropogenic wastewater that receives treatment (%)	12.4	2018	●	●
Scarce water consumption embodied in imports (m³/capita)	18.7	2013	●	↑

SDG7 – Affordable and Clean Energy

Indicator	Value	Year	Rating	Trend
Population with access to electricity (%)	100.0	2017	●	↑
Population with access to clean fuels and technology for cooking (%)	96.3	2016	●	↑
CO_2 emissions from fuel combustion for electricity and heating per total electricity output (MtCO₂/TWh)	1.4	2017	●	↑

SDG8 – Decent Work and Economic Growth

Indicator	Value	Year	Rating	Trend
Adjusted GDP growth (%)	0.9	2018	●	●
Victims of modern slavery (per 1,000 population)	6.9	2018	◐	●
Adults with an account at a bank or other financial institution or with a mobile-money-service provider (% of population aged 15 or over)	85.3	2017	●	↑
Unemployment rate (% of total labor force)	3.3	2019	●	↑
Fatal work-related accidents embodied in imports (per 100,000 population)	1.0	2010	●	↑

SDG9 – Industry, Innovation and Infrastructure

Indicator	Value	Year	Rating	Trend
Population using the internet (%)	81.2	2018	●	↑
Mobile broadband subscriptions (per 100 population)	116.7	2018	●	↑
Logistics Performance Index: Quality of trade and transport-related infrastructure (worst 1–5 best)	3.1	2018	●	↑
The Times Higher Education Universities Ranking: Average score of top 3 universities (worst 0–100 best)	38.1	2020	●	●
Scientific and technical journal articles (per 1,000 population)	0.8	2018	●	↑
Expenditure on research and development (% of GDP)	1.4	2016	◐	↑

SDG10 – Reduced Inequalities

Indicator	Value	Year	Rating	Trend
Gini coefficient adjusted for top income	43.0	2015	●	●

SDG11 – Sustainable Cities and Communities

Indicator	Value	Year	Rating	Trend
Annual mean concentration of particulate matter of less than 2.5 microns in diameter (PM2.5) (µg/m³)	16.0	2017	◐	↗
Access to improved water source, piped (% of urban population)	98.9	2017	●	↑
Satisfaction with public transport (%)	61.0	2019	◐	↓

SDG12 – Responsible Consumption and Production

Indicator	Value	Year	Rating	Trend
Municipal solid waste (kg/capita/day)	1.5	2014	◐	●
Electronic waste (kg/capita)	8.8	2016	●	●
Production-based SO_2 emissions (kg/capita)	37.5	2012	◐	●
SO_2 emissions embodied in imports (kg/capita)	5.1	2012	◐	●
Production-based nitrogen emissions (kg/capita)	28.1	2010	◐	●
Nitrogen emissions embodied in imports (kg/capita)	5.9	2010	●	●

SDG13 – Climate Action

Indicator	Value	Year	Rating	Trend
Energy-related CO_2 emissions (tCO₂/capita)	7.7	2017	●	→
CO_2 emissions embodied in imports (tCO₂/capita)	0.8	2015	●	↗
CO_2 emissions embodied in fossil fuel exports (kg/capita)	2200.7	2018	◐	●

SDG14 – Life Below Water

Indicator	Value	Year	Rating	Trend
Mean area that is protected in marine sites important to biodiversity (%)	28.5	2018	●	→
Ocean Health Index: Clean Waters score (worst 0–100 best)	57.4	2019	●	↓
Fish caught from overexploited or collapsed stocks (% of total catch)	23.2	2014	●	↑
Fish caught by trawling (%)	47.4	2014	●	→
Marine biodiversity threats embodied in imports (per million population)	0.2	2018	●	●

SDG15 – Life on Land

Indicator	Value	Year	Rating	Trend
Mean area that is protected in terrestrial sites important to biodiversity (%)	39.5	2018	◐	→
Mean area that is protected in freshwater sites important to biodiversity (%)	68.0	2018	●	↑
Red List Index of species survival (worst 0–1 best)	0.7	2019	●	↓
Permanent deforestation (% of forest area, 5-year average)	1.8	2018	●	●
Terrestrial and freshwater biodiversity threats embodied in imports (per million population)	2.1	2018	●	●

SDG16 – Peace, Justice and Strong Institutions

Indicator	Value	Year	Rating	Trend
Homicides (per 100,000 population)	2.1	2013	◐	●
Unsentenced detainees (% of prison population)	31.9	2018	◐	↓
Percentage of population who feel safe walking alone at night in the city or area where they live (%)	61.0	2019	◐	↑
Property Rights (worst 1–7 best)	5.5	2019	●	●
Birth registrations with civil authority (% of children under age 5)	NA	NA	●	●
Corruption Perception Index (worst 0–100 best)	53	2019	◐	↑
Children involved in child labor (% of population aged 5 to 14)	NA	NA	●	●
Exports of major conventional weapons (TIV constant million USD per 100,000 population) *	0.0	2019	●	●
Press Freedom Index (best 0–100 worst)	36.7	2019	◐	↑

SDG17 – Partnerships for the Goals

Indicator	Value	Year	Rating	Trend
Government spending on health and education (% of GDP)	6.7	2016	●	↓
For high-income and all OECD DAC countries: International concessional public finance, including official development assistance (% of GNI)	NA	NA	●	●
Other countries: Government revenue excluding grants (% of GDP)	16.1	2018	●	↓
Corporate Tax Haven Score (best 0–100 worst) *	0.0	2019	●	●

* Imputed data point

5. Country Profiles

▼ OVERALL PERFORMANCE

Index score

67.6

Regional average score

67.2

SDG Global rank **91** (OF 166)

▲ AVERAGE PERFORMANCE BY SDG

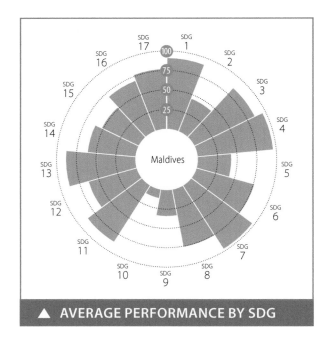

▼ SPILLOVER INDEX

100 (best) to 0 (worst)

▼ CURRENT ASSESSMENT – SDG DASHBOARD

■ Major challenges ■ Significant challenges ■ Challenges remain ■ SDG achieved ■ Information unavailable

▼ SDG TRENDS

↓ Decreasing → Stagnating ↗ Moderately improving ↑ On track or maintaining SDG achievement • Information unavailable

Notes: The full title of Goal 2 "Zero Hunger" is "End hunger, achieve food security and improved nutrition and promote sustainable agriculture".
The full title of each SDG is available here: https://sustainabledevelopment.un.org/topics/sustainabledevelopmentgoals

SDG1 – No Poverty

	Value	Year	Rating	Trend
Poverty headcount ratio at $1.90/day (%)	1.3	2020	●	↑
Poverty headcount ratio at $3.20/day (%)	7.6	2020	●	↑

SDG2 – Zero Hunger

	Value	Year	Rating	Trend
Prevalence of undernourishment (%)	10.3	2017	●	↑
Prevalence of stunting in children under 5 years of age (%)	20.3	2009	●	↗
Prevalence of wasting in children under 5 years of age (%)	10.2	2009	●	↗
Prevalence of obesity, BMI ≥ 30 (% of adult population)	8.6	2016	●	↑
Human Trophic Level (best 2–3 worst)	2.4	2017	●	↑
Cereal yield (tonnes per hectare of harvested land)	2.6	2017	●	↑
Sustainable Nitrogen Management Index (best 0–1.41 worst)	1.1	2015	●	↓

SDG3 – Good Health and Well-Being

	Value	Year	Rating	Trend
Maternal mortality rate (per 100,000 live births)	53	2017	●	↑
Neonatal mortality rate (per 1,000 live births)	4.8	2018	●	↑
Mortality rate, under-5 (per 1,000 live births)	8.6	2018	●	↑
Incidence of tuberculosis (per 100,000 population)	33.0	2018	●	↑
New HIV infections (per 1,000 uninfected population)	NA	NA	●	●
Age-standardized death rate due to cardiovascular disease, cancer, diabetes, or chronic respiratory disease in adults aged 30–70 years (%)	13.4	2016	●	↑
Age-standardized death rate attributable to household air pollution and ambient air pollution (per 100,000 population)	26	2016	●	●
Traffic deaths (per 100,000 population)	0.9	2016	●	↑
Life expectancy at birth (years)	78.4	2016	●	↑
Adolescent fertility rate (births per 1,000 adolescent females aged 15 to 19)	7.8	2017	●	↑
Births attended by skilled health personnel (%)	99.5	2017	●	↑
Percentage of surviving infants who received 2 WHO-recommended vaccines (%)	99	2018	●	↑
Universal health coverage (UHC) index of service coverage (worst 0–100 best)	62.0	2017	●	↗
Subjective well-being (average ladder score, worst 0–10 best)	5.2	2017	●	●

SDG4 – Quality Education

	Value	Year	Rating	Trend
Net primary enrollment rate (%)	95.4	2017	●	↓
Lower secondary completion rate (%)	108.2	2017	●	↑
Literacy rate (% of population aged 15 to 24)	98.8	2016	●	●

SDG5 – Gender Equality

	Value	Year	Rating	Trend
Demand for family planning satisfied by modern methods (% of females aged 15 to 49 who are married or in unions)	42.5	2009	●	↗
Ratio of female-to-male mean years of education received (%)	97.1	2018	●	↑
Ratio of female-to-male labor force participation rate (%)	51.1	2019	●	↓
Seats held by women in national parliament (%)	4.6	2020	●	↓

SDG6 – Clean Water and Sanitation

	Value	Year	Rating	Trend
Population using at least basic drinking water services (%)	99.3	2017	●	↑
Population using at least basic sanitation services (%)	99.4	2017	●	↑
Freshwater withdrawal (% of available freshwater resources)	15.7	2010	●	●
Anthropogenic wastewater that receives treatment (%)	4.6	2018	●	●
Scarce water consumption embodied in imports (m³/capita)	18.9	2013	●	↑

SDG7 – Affordable and Clean Energy

	Value	Year	Rating	Trend
Population with access to electricity (%)	99.8	2017	●	↑
Population with access to clean fuels and technology for cooking (%)	93.8	2016	●	↑
CO$_2$ emissions from fuel combustion for electricity and heating per total electricity output (MtCO$_2$/TWh)	NA	NA	●	●

SDG8 – Decent Work and Economic Growth

	Value	Year	Rating	Trend
Adjusted GDP growth (%)	-1.4	2018	●	●
Victims of modern slavery (per 1,000 population)	NA	NA	●	●
Adults with an account at a bank or other financial institution or with a mobile-money-service provider (% of population aged 15 or over)	NA	NA	●	●
Unemployment rate (% of total labor force)	6.1	2019	●	→
Fatal work-related accidents embodied in imports (per 100,000 population)	1.1	2010	●	↑

SDG9 – Industry, Innovation and Infrastructure

	Value	Year	Rating	Trend
Population using the internet (%)	63.2	2017	●	↑
Mobile broadband subscriptions (per 100 population)	54.5	2018	●	↗
Logistics Performance Index: Quality of trade and transport-related infrastructure (worst 1–5 best)	2.7	2018	●	↑
The Times Higher Education Universities Ranking: Average score of top 3 universities (worst 0–100 best) *	0.0	2020	●	●
Scientific and technical journal articles (per 1,000 population)	0.0	2018	●	↓
Expenditure on research and development (% of GDP)	NA	NA	●	●

SDG10 – Reduced Inequalities

	Value	Year	Rating	Trend
Gini coefficient adjusted for top income	59.1	2009	●	●

SDG11 – Sustainable Cities and Communities

	Value	Year	Rating	Trend
Annual mean concentration of particulate matter of less than 2.5 microns in diameter (PM2.5) (µg/m³)	7.8	2017	●	↑
Access to improved water source, piped (% of urban population)	98.3	2017	●	↑
Satisfaction with public transport (%)	59.0	2017	●	●

SDG12 – Responsible Consumption and Production

	Value	Year	Rating	Trend
Municipal solid waste (kg/capita/day)	3.3	2015	●	●
Electronic waste (kg/capita)	6.9	2016	●	●
Production-based SO$_2$ emissions (kg/capita)	285.8	2012	●	●
SO$_2$ emissions embodied in imports (kg/capita)	8.7	2012	●	●
Production-based nitrogen emissions (kg/capita)	11.7	2010	●	●
Nitrogen emissions embodied in imports (kg/capita)	5.0	2010	●	●

SDG13 – Climate Action

	Value	Year	Rating	Trend
Energy-related CO$_2$ emissions (tCO$_2$/capita)	2.8	2017	●	↑
CO$_2$ emissions embodied in imports (tCO$_2$/capita)	0.8	2015	●	↑
CO$_2$ emissions embodied in fossil fuel exports (kg/capita) *	0.0	2018	●	●

SDG14 – Life Below Water

	Value	Year	Rating	Trend
Mean area that is protected in marine sites important to biodiversity (%)	0.0	2018	●	→
Ocean Health Index: Clean Waters score (worst 0–100 best)	58.4	2019	●	↑
Fish caught from overexploited or collapsed stocks (% of total catch)	30.8	2014	●	↓
Fish caught by trawling (%)	0.0	2010	●	●
Marine biodiversity threats embodied in imports (per million population)	0.1	2018	●	●

SDG15 – Life on Land

	Value	Year	Rating	Trend
Mean area that is protected in terrestrial sites important to biodiversity (%)	0.0	2018	●	→
Mean area that is protected in freshwater sites important to biodiversity (%)	NA	NA	●	●
Red List Index of species survival (worst 0–1 best)	0.8	2019	●	↓
Permanent deforestation (% of forest area, 5-year average)	NA	NA	●	●
Terrestrial and freshwater biodiversity threats embodied in imports (per million population)	0.3	2018	●	●

SDG16 – Peace, Justice and Strong Institutions

	Value	Year	Rating	Trend
Homicides (per 100,000 population)	0.8	2013	●	●
Unsentenced detainees (% of prison population)	NA	NA	●	●
Percentage of population who feel safe walking alone at night in the city or area where they live (%)	49.5	2017	●	●
Property Rights (worst 1–7 best)	NA	NA	●	●
Birth registrations with civil authority (% of children under age 5)	98.8	2018	●	●
Corruption Perception Index (worst 0–100 best)	29	2019	●	↓
Children involved in child labor (% of population aged 5 to 14)	NA	NA	●	●
Exports of major conventional weapons (TIV constant million USD per 100,000 population) *	0.0	2019	●	●
Press Freedom Index (best 0–100 worst)	32.2	2019	●	↑

SDG17 – Partnerships for the Goals

	Value	Year	Rating	Trend
Government spending on health and education (% of GDP)	11.8	2016	●	↑
For high-income and all OECD DAC countries: International concessional public finance, including official development assistance (% of GNI)	NA	NA	●	●
Other countries: Government revenue excluding grants (% of GDP)	25.7	2014	●	●
Corporate Tax Haven Score (best 0–100 worst) *	0.0	2019	●	●

* Imputed data point

5. Country Profiles

▼ OVERALL PERFORMANCE

Index score

51.4

Regional average score

53.1

SDG Global rank 156 (OF 166)

▲ AVERAGE PERFORMANCE BY SDG

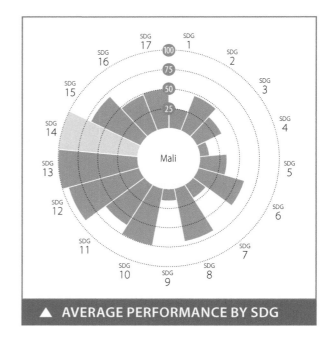

Mali

SDG 1, SDG 2, SDG 3, SDG 4, SDG 5, SDG 6, SDG 7, SDG 8, SDG 9, SDG 10, SDG 11, SDG 12, SDG 13, SDG 14, SDG 15, SDG 16, SDG 17

▼ SPILLOVER INDEX

100 (best) to 0 (worst)

```
100
 80
 60
 40
 20
  0
```

▼ CURRENT ASSESSMENT – SDG DASHBOARD

■ Major challenges ■ Significant challenges ■ Challenges remain ■ SDG achieved ■ Information unavailable

▼ SDG TRENDS

↓ Decreasing → Stagnating ↗ Moderately improving ↑ On track or maintaining SDG achievement ● Information unavailable

Notes: The full title of Goal 2 "Zero Hunger" is "End hunger, achieve food security and improved nutrition and promote sustainable agriculture".
The full title of each SDG is available here: https://sustainabledevelopment.un.org/topics/sustainabledevelopmentgoals

SDG1 – No Poverty

	Value	Year	Rating	Trend
Poverty headcount ratio at $1.90/day (%)	34.3	2020	●	↗
Poverty headcount ratio at $3.20/day (%)	66.7	2020	●	→

SDG2 – Zero Hunger

	Value	Year	Rating	Trend
Prevalence of undernourishment (%)	6.3	2017	●	↑
Prevalence of stunting in children under 5 years of age (%)	30.4	2015	●	→
Prevalence of wasting in children under 5 years of age (%)	13.5	2015	●	↓
Prevalence of obesity, BMI ≥ 30 (% of adult population)	8.6	2016	●	↑
Human Trophic Level (best 2–3 worst)	2.2	2017	●	↑
Cereal yield (tonnes per hectare of harvested land)	1.5	2017	●	↓
Sustainable Nitrogen Management Index (best 0–1.41 worst)	0.8	2015	●	→

SDG3 – Good Health and Well-Being

	Value	Year	Rating	Trend
Maternal mortality rate (per 100,000 live births)	562	2017	●	↗
Neonatal mortality rate (per 1,000 live births)	32.7	2018	●	→
Mortality rate, under-5 (per 1,000 live births)	97.8	2018	●	↗
Incidence of tuberculosis (per 100,000 population)	53.0	2018	●	→
New HIV infections (per 1,000 uninfected population)	0.8	2018	●	→
Age-standardized death rate due to cardiovascular disease, cancer, diabetes, or chronic respiratory disease in adults aged 30–70 years (%)	24.6	2016	●	→
Age-standardized death rate attributable to household air pollution and ambient air pollution (per 100,000 population)	209	2016	●	●
Traffic deaths (per 100,000 population)	23.1	2016	●	↗
Life expectancy at birth (years)	58.0	2016	●	→
Adolescent fertility rate (births per 1,000 adolescent females aged 15 to 19)	169.1	2017	●	→
Births attended by skilled health personnel (%)	43.7	2015	●	↓
Percentage of surviving infants who received 2 WHO-recommended vaccines (%)	70	2018	●	↑
Universal health coverage (UHC) index of service coverage (worst 0–100 best)	38.0	2017	●	→
Subjective well-being (average ladder score, worst 0–10 best)	5.0	2019	●	↑

SDG4 – Quality Education

	Value	Year	Rating	Trend
Net primary enrollment rate (%)	58.9	2018	●	↓
Lower secondary completion rate (%)	29.7	2017	●	↓
Literacy rate (% of population aged 15 to 24)	50.1	2018	●	●

SDG5 – Gender Equality

	Value	Year	Rating	Trend
Demand for family planning satisfied by modern methods (% of females aged 15 to 49 who are married or in unions)	35.0	2015	●	→
Ratio of female-to-male mean years of education received (%)	56.7	2018	●	→
Ratio of female-to-male labor force participation rate (%)	75.8	2019	●	↑
Seats held by women in national parliament (%)	9.5	2019	●	→

SDG6 – Clean Water and Sanitation

	Value	Year	Rating	Trend
Population using at least basic drinking water services (%)	78.3	2017	●	↑
Population using at least basic sanitation services (%)	39.3	2017	●	→
Freshwater withdrawal (% of available freshwater resources)	8.0	2005	●	●
Anthropogenic wastewater that receives treatment (%)	0.0	2018	●	●
Scarce water consumption embodied in imports (m³/capita)	0.3	2013	●	↑

SDG7 – Affordable and Clean Energy

	Value	Year	Rating	Trend
Population with access to electricity (%)	43.1	2017	●	↗
Population with access to clean fuels and technology for cooking (%)	1.0	2016	●	↓
CO_2 emissions from fuel combustion for electricity and heating per total electricity output (MtCO₂/TWh)	NA	NA	●	●

SDG8 – Decent Work and Economic Growth

	Value	Year	Rating	Trend
Adjusted GDP growth (%)	-4.3	2018	●	●
Victims of modern slavery (per 1,000 population)	3.6	2018	●	●
Adults with an account at a bank or other financial institution or with a mobile-money-service provider (% of population aged 15 or over)	35.4	2017	●	↑
Unemployment rate (% of total labor force)	7.2	2019	●	↗
Fatal work-related accidents embodied in imports (per 100,000 population)	0.0	2010	●	↑

SDG9 – Industry, Innovation and Infrastructure

	Value	Year	Rating	Trend
Population using the internet (%)	13.0	2017	●	→
Mobile broadband subscriptions (per 100 population)	30.3	2018	●	↑
Logistics Performance Index: Quality of trade and transport-related infrastructure (worst 1–5 best)	2.3	2018	●	↗
The Times Higher Education Universities Ranking: Average score of top 3 universities (worst 0–100 best) *	0.0	2020	●	●
Scientific and technical journal articles (per 1,000 population)	0.0	2018	●	→
Expenditure on research and development (% of GDP)	0.3	2017	●	↓

SDG10 – Reduced Inequalities

	Value	Year	Rating	Trend
Gini coefficient adjusted for top income	37.0	2009	●	●

SDG11 – Sustainable Cities and Communities

	Value	Year	Rating	Trend
Annual mean concentration of particulate matter of less than 2.5 microns in diameter (PM2.5) (μg/m³)	38.5	2017	●	↓
Access to improved water source, piped (% of urban population)	81.6	2017	●	↑
Satisfaction with public transport (%)	46.0	2019	●	↑

SDG12 – Responsible Consumption and Production

	Value	Year	Rating	Trend
Municipal solid waste (kg/capita/day)	0.7	2012	●	●
Electronic waste (kg/capita)	0.7	2016	●	●
Production-based SO_2 emissions (kg/capita)	9.5	2012	●	●
SO_2 emissions embodied in imports (kg/capita)	0.3	2012	●	●
Production-based nitrogen emissions (kg/capita)	30.5	2010	●	●
Nitrogen emissions embodied in imports (kg/capita)	0.2	2010	●	●

SDG13 – Climate Action

	Value	Year	Rating	Trend
Energy-related CO_2 emissions (tCO₂/capita)	0.1	2017	●	↑
CO_2 emissions embodied in imports (tCO₂/capita)	0.0	2015	●	↑
CO_2 emissions embodied in fossil fuel exports (kg/capita)	0.0	2017	●	●

SDG14 – Life Below Water

	Value	Year	Rating	Trend
Mean area that is protected in marine sites important to biodiversity (%)	NA	NA	●	●
Ocean Health Index: Clean Waters score (worst 0–100 best)	NA	NA	●	●
Fish caught from overexploited or collapsed stocks (% of total catch)	NA	NA	●	●
Fish caught by trawling (%)	NA	NA	●	●
Marine biodiversity threats embodied in imports (per million population)	0.0	2018	●	●

SDG15 – Life on Land

	Value	Year	Rating	Trend
Mean area that is protected in terrestrial sites important to biodiversity (%)	33.8	2018	●	→
Mean area that is protected in freshwater sites important to biodiversity (%)	43.7	2018	●	→
Red List Index of species survival (worst 0–1 best)	1.0	2019	●	↑
Permanent deforestation (% of forest area, 5-year average)	0.3	2018	●	●
Terrestrial and freshwater biodiversity threats embodied in imports (per million population)	0.0	2018	●	●

SDG16 – Peace, Justice and Strong Institutions

	Value	Year	Rating	Trend
Homicides (per 100,000 population) *	10.9	2015	●	●
Unsentenced detainees (% of prison population)	51.5	2015	●	●
Percentage of population who feel safe walking alone at night in the city or area where they live (%)	55.0	2019	●	↓
Property Rights (worst 1–7 best)	3.6	2019	●	●
Birth registrations with civil authority (% of children under age 5)	86.7	2018	●	●
Corruption Perception Index (worst 0–100 best)	29	2019	●	↓
Children involved in child labor (% of population aged 5 to 14)	55.8	2016	●	●
Exports of major conventional weapons (TIV constant million USD per 100,000 population) *	0.0	2019	●	●
Press Freedom Index (best 0–100 worst)	35.2	2019	●	↑

SDG17 – Partnerships for the Goals

	Value	Year	Rating	Trend
Government spending on health and education (% of GDP)	4.3	2016	●	→
For high-income and all OECD DAC countries: International concessional public finance, including official development assistance (% of GNI)	NA	NA	●	●
Other countries: Government revenue excluding grants (% of GDP)	17.4	2017	●	↑
Corporate Tax Haven Score (best 0–100 worst) *	0.0	2019	●	●

* Imputed data point

▼ OVERALL PERFORMANCE

Index score

76.0

Regional average score

70.9

SDG Global rank 32 (OF 166)

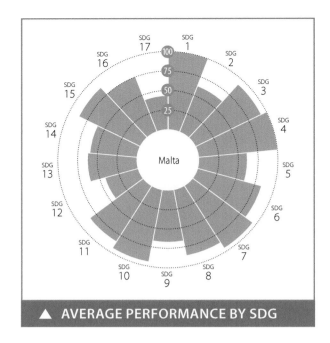

▲ AVERAGE PERFORMANCE BY SDG

▼ SPILLOVER INDEX

100 (best) to 0 (worst)

▼ CURRENT ASSESSMENT – SDG DASHBOARD

■ Major challenges ■ Significant challenges □ Challenges remain ■ SDG achieved ▨ Information unavailable

▼ SDG TRENDS

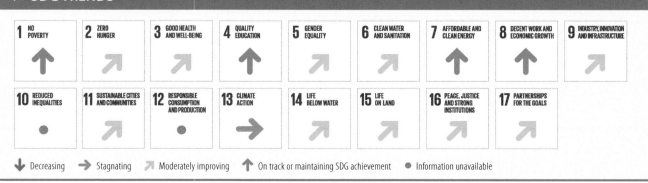

↓ Decreasing → Stagnating ↗ Moderately improving ↑ On track or maintaining SDG achievement ● Information unavailable

Notes: The full title of Goal 2 "Zero Hunger" is "End hunger, achieve food security and improved nutrition and promote sustainable agriculture".
The full title of each SDG is available here: https://sustainabledevelopment.un.org/topics/sustainabledevelopmentgoals

SDG1 – No Poverty

	Value	Year	Rating	Trend
Poverty headcount ratio at $1.90/day (%)	0.1	2020	●	↑
Poverty headcount ratio at $3.20/day (%)	0.2	2020	●	↑

SDG2 – Zero Hunger

		Value	Year	Rating	Trend
Prevalence of undernourishment (%)		2.5	2017	●	↑
Prevalence of stunting in children under 5 years of age (%)	*	2.6	2016	●	↑
Prevalence of wasting in children under 5 years of age (%)	*	0.7	2016	●	↑
Prevalence of obesity, BMI ≥ 30 (% of adult population)		28.9	2016	●	↓
Human Trophic Level (best 2–3 worst)		2.3	2017	●	→
Cereal yield (tonnes per hectare of harvested land)		4.8	2017	●	↑
Sustainable Nitrogen Management Index (best 0–1.41 worst)		0.9	2015	●	↓

SDG3 – Good Health and Well-Being

	Value	Year	Rating	Trend
Maternal mortality rate (per 100,000 live births)	6	2017	●	↑
Neonatal mortality rate (per 1,000 live births)	4.7	2018	●	↑
Mortality rate, under-5 (per 1,000 live births)	7.0	2018	●	↑
Incidence of tuberculosis (per 100,000 population)	14.0	2018	●	↓
New HIV infections (per 1,000 uninfected population)	NA	NA	●	●
Age-standardized death rate due to cardiovascular disease, cancer, diabetes, or chronic respiratory disease in adults aged 30–70 years (%)	10.8	2016	●	↑
Age-standardized death rate attributable to household air pollution and ambient air pollution (per 100,000 population)	20	2016	●	●
Traffic deaths (per 100,000 population)	6.1	2016	●	↑
Life expectancy at birth (years)	81.5	2016	●	↑
Adolescent fertility rate (births per 1,000 adolescent females aged 15 to 19)	12.9	2017	●	↑
Births attended by skilled health personnel (%)	99.8	2016	●	↑
Percentage of surviving infants who received 2 WHO-recommended vaccines (%)	96	2018	●	↑
Universal health coverage (UHC) index of service coverage (worst 0–100 best)	82.0	2017	●	↑
Subjective well-being (average ladder score, worst 0–10 best)	6.7	2019	●	↑

SDG4 – Quality Education

	Value	Year	Rating	Trend
Net primary enrollment rate (%)	99.5	2017	●	↑
Lower secondary completion rate (%)	100.4	2016	●	●
Literacy rate (% of population aged 15 to 24)	99.3	2018	●	●

SDG5 – Gender Equality

		Value	Year	Rating	Trend
Demand for family planning satisfied by modern methods (% of females aged 15 to 49 who are married or in unions)	*	74.8	2017	●	↑
Ratio of female-to-male mean years of education received (%)		94.8	2018	●	→
Ratio of female-to-male labor force participation rate (%)		65.5	2019	●	↑
Seats held by women in national parliament (%)		13.4	2020	●	→

SDG6 – Clean Water and Sanitation

		Value	Year	Rating	Trend
Population using at least basic drinking water services (%)		100.0	2017	●	↑
Population using at least basic sanitation services (%)		100.0	2017	●	↑
Freshwater withdrawal (% of available freshwater resources)		52.3	2015	●	●
Anthropogenic wastewater that receives treatment (%)	*	100.0	2018	●	●
Scarce water consumption embodied in imports (m³/capita)		39.2	2013	●	→

SDG7 – Affordable and Clean Energy

	Value	Year	Rating	Trend
Population with access to electricity (%)	100.0	2017	●	↑
Population with access to clean fuels and technology for cooking (%)	100.0	2016	●	↑
CO₂ emissions from fuel combustion for electricity and heating per total electricity output (MtCO₂/TWh)	1.0	2017	●	↑

SDG8 – Decent Work and Economic Growth

	Value	Year	Rating	Trend
Adjusted GDP growth (%)	1.5	2018	●	●
Victims of modern slavery (per 1,000 population)	NA	NA	●	●
Adults with an account at a bank or other financial institution or with a mobile-money-service provider (% of population aged 15 or over)	97.4	2017	●	●
Unemployment rate (% of total labor force)	3.5	2019	●	↑
Fatal work-related accidents embodied in imports (per 100,000 population)	1.4	2010	●	↑

SDG9 – Industry, Innovation and Infrastructure

	Value	Year	Rating	Trend
Population using the internet (%)	81.7	2018	●	↑
Mobile broadband subscriptions (per 100 population)	104.3	2018	●	↑
Logistics Performance Index: Quality of trade and transport-related infrastructure (worst 1–5 best)	2.9	2018	●	↓
The Times Higher Education Universities Ranking: Average score of top 3 universities (worst 0–100 best)	31.8	2020	●	●
Scientific and technical journal articles (per 1,000 population)	1.0	2018	●	↑
Expenditure on research and development (% of GDP)	0.5	2017	●	↓

SDG10 – Reduced Inequalities

	Value	Year	Rating	Trend
Gini coefficient adjusted for top income	29.6	2015	●	●

SDG11 – Sustainable Cities and Communities

	Value	Year	Rating	Trend
Annual mean concentration of particulate matter of less than 2.5 microns in diameter (PM2.5) (µg/m³)	13.9	2017	●	↗
Access to improved water source, piped (% of urban population)	99.0	2017	●	↑
Satisfaction with public transport (%)	60.3	2019	●	↑

SDG12 – Responsible Consumption and Production

	Value	Year	Rating	Trend
Municipal solid waste (kg/capita/day)	1.8	2015	●	●
Electronic waste (kg/capita)	15.5	2016	●	●
Production-based SO₂ emissions (kg/capita)	555.8	2012	●	●
SO₂ emissions embodied in imports (kg/capita)	17.0	2012	●	●
Production-based nitrogen emissions (kg/capita)	34.3	2010	●	●
Nitrogen emissions embodied in imports (kg/capita)	17.4	2010	●	●

SDG13 – Climate Action

	Value	Year	Rating	Trend
Energy-related CO₂ emissions (tCO₂/capita)**	6.3	2017	●	→
CO₂ emissions embodied in imports (tCO₂/capita)	2.8	2015	●	→
CO₂ emissions embodied in fossil fuel exports (kg/capita)	0.0	2019	●	→

SDG14 – Life Below Water

	Value	Year	Rating	Trend
Mean area that is protected in marine sites important to biodiversity (%)	98.9	2018	●	↑
Ocean Health Index: Clean Waters score (worst 0–100 best)	41.1	2019	●	↓
Fish caught from overexploited or collapsed stocks (% of total catch)	12.5	2014	●	↑
Fish caught by trawling (%)	93.6	2014	●	→
Marine biodiversity threats embodied in imports (per million population)	0.1	2018	●	●

SDG15 – Life on Land

	Value	Year	Rating	Trend
Mean area that is protected in terrestrial sites important to biodiversity (%)	99.3	2018	●	↑
Mean area that is protected in freshwater sites important to biodiversity (%)	NA	NA	●	●
Red List Index of species survival (worst 0–1 best)	0.9	2019	●	→
Permanent deforestation (% of forest area, 5-year average)	NA	NA	●	●
Terrestrial and freshwater biodiversity threats embodied in imports (per million population)	1.1	2018	●	●

SDG16 – Peace, Justice and Strong Institutions

	Value	Year	Rating	Trend
Homicides (per 100,000 population)	0.9	2015	●	●
Unsentenced detainees (% of prison population)	27.9	2018	●	↑
Percentage of population who feel safe walking alone at night in the city or area where they live (%)	74.5	2019	●	↑
Property Rights (worst 1–7 best)	5.1	2019	●	●
Birth registrations with civil authority (% of children under age 5)	100.0	2018	●	●
Corruption Perception Index (worst 0–100 best)	54	2019	●	↓
Children involved in child labor (% of population aged 5 to 14)	NA	NA	●	●
Exports of major conventional weapons (TIV constant million USD per 100,000 population)	1.1	2019	●	●
Press Freedom Index (best 0–100 worst)	29.7	2019	●	↑

SDG17 – Partnerships for the Goals

	Value	Year	Rating	Trend
Government spending on health and education (% of GDP)	10.9	2015	●	↑
For high-income and all OECD DAC countries: International concessional public finance, including official development assistance (% of GNI)	0.2	2017	●	→
Other countries: Government revenue excluding grants (% of GDP)	NA	NA	●	●
Corporate Tax Haven Score (best 0–100 worst)	73.5	2019	●	●

* Imputed data point

**In Malta, the "Country-Reported" data of CO2 emissions from energy is significantly lower than the "Third-Party" estimate used in this report and has improved since 2014 (Gütschow et al, 2019). The "Country-Reported" data reflects the shift made by Malta in 2014 to a gas-fired power plant from a Heavy Fuel Oil (HFO) plant in addition to the 2015 linkage to mainland Europe's interconnector.

5. Country Profiles

MARSHALL ISLANDS

Oceania

▼ OVERALL PERFORMANCE

Index score

na

Regional average score

49.6

SDG Global rank NA (OF 166)

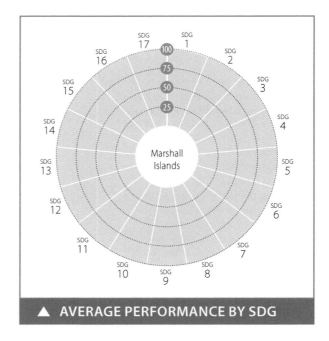

▲ AVERAGE PERFORMANCE BY SDG

▼ SPILLOVER INDEX

100 (best) to 0 (worst)

▼ CURRENT ASSESSMENT – SDG DASHBOARD

■ Major challenges   ■ Significant challenges   ▨ Challenges remain   ■ SDG achieved   ■ Information unavailable

▼ SDG TRENDS

↓ Decreasing   → Stagnating   ↗ Moderately improving   ↑ On track or maintaining SDG achievement   ● Information unavailable

Notes: The full title of Goal 2 "Zero Hunger" is "End hunger, achieve food security and improved nutrition and promote sustainable agriculture".
The full title of each SDG is available here: https://sustainabledevelopment.un.org/topics/sustainabledevelopmentgoals

SDG1 – No Poverty

	Value	Year	Rating	Trend
Poverty headcount ratio at $1.90/day (%)	NA	NA	●	●
Poverty headcount ratio at $3.20/day (%)	NA	NA	●	●

SDG2 – Zero Hunger

	Value	Year	Rating	Trend
Prevalence of undernourishment (%)	NA	NA	●	●
Prevalence of stunting in children under 5 years of age (%)	NA	NA	●	●
Prevalence of wasting in children under 5 years of age (%)	NA	NA	●	●
Prevalence of obesity, BMI ≥ 30 (% of adult population)	52.9	2016	●	↓
Human Trophic Level (best 2–3 worst)	NA	NA	●	●
Cereal yield (tonnes per hectare of harvested land)	NA	NA	●	●
Sustainable Nitrogen Management Index (best 0–1.41 worst)	1.3	2015	●	↓

SDG3 – Good Health and Well-Being

	Value	Year	Rating	Trend
Maternal mortality rate (per 100,000 live births)	NA	NA	●	●
Neonatal mortality rate (per 1,000 live births)	15.5	2018	●	↑
Mortality rate, under-5 (per 1,000 live births)	33.1	2018	●	↑
Incidence of tuberculosis (per 100,000 population)	434.0	2018	●	↓
New HIV infections (per 1,000 uninfected population)	NA	NA	●	●
Age-standardized death rate due to cardiovascular disease, cancer, diabetes, or chronic respiratory disease in adults aged 30–70 years (%)	NA	NA	●	●
Age-standardized death rate attributable to household air pollution and ambient air pollution (per 100,000 population)	NA	NA	●	●
Traffic deaths (per 100,000 population)	5.7	2013	●	●
Life expectancy at birth (years)	NA	NA	●	●
Adolescent fertility rate (births per 1,000 adolescent females aged 15 to 19)	NA	NA	●	●
Births attended by skilled health personnel (%)	90.1	2011	●	●
Percentage of surviving infants who received 2 WHO-recommended vaccines (%)	81	2018	●	↑
Universal health coverage (UHC) index of service coverage (worst 0–100 best)	NA	NA	●	●
Subjective well-being (average ladder score, worst 0–10 best)	NA	NA	●	●

SDG4 – Quality Education

	Value	Year	Rating	Trend
Net primary enrollment rate (%)	73.2	2016	●	→
Lower secondary completion rate (%)	109.5	2011	●	●
Literacy rate (% of population aged 15 to 24)	98.5	2011	●	●

SDG5 – Gender Equality

	Value	Year	Rating	Trend
Demand for family planning satisfied by modern methods (% of females aged 15 to 49 who are married or in unions)	80.5	2007	●	●
Ratio of female-to-male mean years of education received (%)	97.3	2018	●	↑
Ratio of female-to-male labor force participation rate (%)	NA	NA	●	●
Seats held by women in national parliament (%)	6.1	2020	●	↓

SDG6 – Clean Water and Sanitation

	Value	Year	Rating	Trend
Population using at least basic drinking water services (%)	88.5	2017	●	↑
Population using at least basic sanitation services (%)	83.5	2017	●	→
Freshwater withdrawal (% of available freshwater resources)	NA	NA	●	●
Anthropogenic wastewater that receives treatment (%)	0.0	2018	●	●
Scarce water consumption embodied in imports (m³/capita)	NA	NA	●	●

SDG7 – Affordable and Clean Energy

	Value	Year	Rating	Trend
Population with access to electricity (%)	94.8	2017	●	↑
Population with access to clean fuels and technology for cooking (%)	65.4	2016	●	↗
CO$_2$ emissions from fuel combustion for electricity and heating per total electricity output (MtCO$_2$/TWh)	NA	NA	●	●

SDG8 – Decent Work and Economic Growth

	Value	Year	Rating	Trend
Adjusted GDP growth (%)	-3.3	2018	●	●
Victims of modern slavery (per 1,000 population)	NA	NA	●	●
Adults with an account at a bank or other financial institution or with a mobile-money-service provider (% of population aged 15 or over)	NA	NA	●	●
Unemployment rate (% of total labor force)	NA	NA	●	●
Fatal work-related accidents embodied in imports (per 100,000 population)	NA	NA	●	●

SDG9 – Industry, Innovation and Infrastructure

	Value	Year	Rating	Trend
Population using the internet (%)	38.7	2017	●	↑
Mobile broadband subscriptions (per 100 population)	0.0	2017	●	→
Logistics Performance Index: Quality of trade and transport-related infrastructure (worst 1–5 best)	NA	NA	●	●
The Times Higher Education Universities Ranking: Average score of top 3 universities (worst 0–100 best) *	0.0	2020	●	●
Scientific and technical journal articles (per 1,000 population)	0.0	2018	●	↓
Expenditure on research and development (% of GDP)	NA	NA	●	●

SDG10 – Reduced Inequalities

	Value	Year	Rating	Trend
Gini coefficient adjusted for top income	NA	NA	●	●

SDG11 – Sustainable Cities and Communities

	Value	Year	Rating	Trend
Annual mean concentration of particulate matter of less than 2.5 microns in diameter (PM2.5) (µg/m³)	10.2	2017	●	↑
Access to improved water source, piped (% of urban population)	13.0	2017	●	↓
Satisfaction with public transport (%)	NA	NA	●	●

SDG12 – Responsible Consumption and Production

	Value	Year	Rating	Trend
Municipal solid waste (kg/capita/day)	0.6	2013	●	●
Electronic waste (kg/capita)	NA	NA	●	●
Production-based SO$_2$ emissions (kg/capita)	NA	NA	●	●
SO$_2$ emissions embodied in imports (kg/capita)	NA	NA	●	●
Production-based nitrogen emissions (kg/capita)	NA	NA	●	●
Nitrogen emissions embodied in imports (kg/capita)	NA	NA	●	●

SDG13 – Climate Action

	Value	Year	Rating	Trend
Energy-related CO$_2$ emissions (tCO$_2$/capita)	2.4	2017	●	→
CO$_2$ emissions embodied in imports (tCO$_2$/capita)	NA	NA	●	●
CO$_2$ emissions embodied in fossil fuel exports (kg/capita)	NA	NA	●	●

SDG14 – Life Below Water

	Value	Year	Rating	Trend
Mean area that is protected in marine sites important to biodiversity (%)	12.3	2018	●	→
Ocean Health Index: Clean Waters score (worst 0–100 best)	36.3	2019	●	→
Fish caught from overexploited or collapsed stocks (% of total catch)	1.5	2014	●	↑
Fish caught by trawling (%)	NA	NA	●	●
Marine biodiversity threats embodied in imports (per million population)	NA	NA	●	●

SDG15 – Life on Land

	Value	Year	Rating	Trend
Mean area that is protected in terrestrial sites important to biodiversity (%)	15.0	2018	●	→
Mean area that is protected in freshwater sites important to biodiversity (%)	NA	NA	●	●
Red List Index of species survival (worst 0–1 best)	0.8	2019	●	↓
Permanent deforestation (% of forest area, 5-year average)	NA	NA	●	●
Terrestrial and freshwater biodiversity threats embodied in imports (per million population)	NA	NA	●	●

SDG16 – Peace, Justice and Strong Institutions

	Value	Year	Rating	Trend
Homicides (per 100,000 population)	NA	NA	●	●
Unsentenced detainees (% of prison population)	8.5	2015	●	●
Percentage of population who feel safe walking alone at night in the city or area where they live (%)	NA	NA	●	●
Property Rights (worst 1–7 best)	NA	NA	●	●
Birth registrations with civil authority (% of children under age 5)	83.8	2018	●	●
Corruption Perception Index (worst 0–100 best)	NA	NA	●	●
Children involved in child labor (% of population aged 5 to 14)	NA	NA	●	●
Exports of major conventional weapons (TIV constant million USD per 100,000 population) *	0.0	2019	●	●
Press Freedom Index (best 0–100 worst)	NA	NA	●	●

SDG17 – Partnerships for the Goals

	Value	Year	Rating	Trend
Government spending on health and education (% of GDP)	22.5	2003	●	●
For high-income and all OECD DAC countries: International concessional public finance, including official development assistance (% of GNI)	NA	NA	●	●
Other countries: Government revenue excluding grants (% of GDP)	32.2	2018	●	↑
Corporate Tax Haven Score (best 0–100 worst) *	0.0	2019	●	●

* Imputed data point

5. Country Profiles

▼ OVERALL PERFORMANCE

Index score

57.7

Regional average score

53.1

SDG Global rank **130** (OF 166)

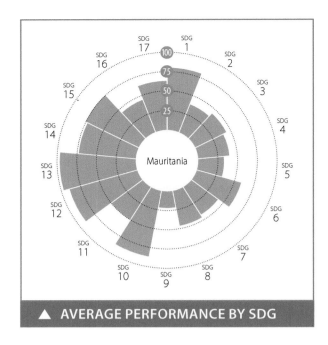

▲ AVERAGE PERFORMANCE BY SDG

▼ SPILLOVER INDEX

100 (best) to 0 (worst)

▼ CURRENT ASSESSMENT – SDG DASHBOARD

■ Major challenges ■ Significant challenges □ Challenges remain ■ SDG achieved ■ Information unavailable

▼ SDG TRENDS

1 NO POVERTY	2 ZERO HUNGER	3 GOOD HEALTH AND WELL-BEING	4 QUALITY EDUCATION	5 GENDER EQUALITY	6 CLEAN WATER AND SANITATION	7 AFFORDABLE AND CLEAN ENERGY	8 DECENT WORK AND ECONOMIC GROWTH	9 INDUSTRY, INNOVATION AND INFRASTRUCTURE
↑	↓	→	↗	→	↗	→	→	→

10 REDUCED INEQUALITIES	11 SUSTAINABLE CITIES AND COMMUNITIES	12 RESPONSIBLE CONSUMPTION AND PRODUCTION	13 CLIMATE ACTION	14 LIFE BELOW WATER	15 LIFE ON LAND	16 PEACE, JUSTICE AND STRONG INSTITUTIONS	17 PARTNERSHIPS FOR THE GOALS
•	→	•	↑	↗	↗	→	↓

↓ Decreasing → Stagnating ↗ Moderately improving ↑ On track or maintaining SDG achievement • Information unavailable

Notes: The full title of Goal 2 "Zero Hunger" is "End hunger, achieve food security and improved nutrition and promote sustainable agriculture".
The full title of each SDG is available here: https://sustainabledevelopment.un.org/topics/sustainabledevelopmentgoals

SDG1 – No Poverty

	Value	Year	Rating	Trend
Poverty headcount ratio at $1.90/day (%)	3.2	2020	○	↑
Poverty headcount ratio at $3.20/day (%)	16.9	2020	●	↑

SDG2 – Zero Hunger

	Value	Year	Rating	Trend
Prevalence of undernourishment (%)	10.4	2017	○	↓
Prevalence of stunting in children under 5 years of age (%)	27.9	2015	●	↓
Prevalence of wasting in children under 5 years of age (%)	14.8	2015	●	↓
Prevalence of obesity, BMI ≥ 30 (% of adult population)	12.7	2016	○	↓
Human Trophic Level (best 2–3 worst)	2.3	2017	●	→
Cereal yield (tonnes per hectare of harvested land)	1.4	2017	●	↓
Sustainable Nitrogen Management Index (best 0–1.41 worst)	0.9	2015	●	→

SDG3 – Good Health and Well-Being

	Value	Year	Rating	Trend
Maternal mortality rate (per 100,000 live births)	766	2017	●	→
Neonatal mortality rate (per 1,000 live births)	33.5	2018	●	→
Mortality rate, under-5 (per 1,000 live births)	75.7	2018	●	↗
Incidence of tuberculosis (per 100,000 population)	93.0	2018	●	↗
New HIV infections (per 1,000 uninfected population)	0.0	2018	●	↑
Age-standardized death rate due to cardiovascular disease, cancer, diabetes, or chronic respiratory disease in adults aged 30–70 years (%)	18.1	2016	○	↓
Age-standardized death rate attributable to household air pollution and ambient air pollution (per 100,000 population)	169	2016	●	●
Traffic deaths (per 100,000 population)	24.7	2016	●	↓
Life expectancy at birth (years)	63.9	2016	●	→
Adolescent fertility rate (births per 1,000 adolescent females aged 15 to 19)	71.0	2017	●	↗
Births attended by skilled health personnel (%)	69.3	2015	●	↗
Percentage of surviving infants who received 2 WHO-recommended vaccines (%)	78	2018	●	↑
Universal health coverage (UHC) index of service coverage (worst 0–100 best)	41.0	2017	●	→
Subjective well-being (average ladder score, worst 0–10 best)	4.2	2019	●	→

SDG4 – Quality Education

	Value	Year	Rating	Trend
Net primary enrollment rate (%)	79.6	2018	●	↗
Lower secondary completion rate (%)	41.9	2018	●	↗
Literacy rate (% of population aged 15 to 24)	63.9	2017	●	●

SDG5 – Gender Equality

	Value	Year	Rating	Trend
Demand for family planning satisfied by modern methods (% of females aged 15 to 49 who are married or in unions)	30.4	2015	●	→
Ratio of female-to-male mean years of education received (%)	67.3	2018	●	↗
Ratio of female-to-male labor force participation rate (%)	46.3	2019	●	→
Seats held by women in national parliament (%)	20.3	2020	●	↓

SDG6 – Clean Water and Sanitation

	Value	Year	Rating	Trend
Population using at least basic drinking water services (%)	70.7	2017	●	↗
Population using at least basic sanitation services (%)	48.4	2017	●	↗
Freshwater withdrawal (% of available freshwater resources)	13.2	2005	●	●
Anthropogenic wastewater that receives treatment (%)	0.0	2018	●	●
Scarce water consumption embodied in imports (m³/capita)	1.6	2013	●	↑

SDG7 – Affordable and Clean Energy

	Value	Year	Rating	Trend
Population with access to electricity (%)	42.9	2017	●	→
Population with access to clean fuels and technology for cooking (%)	46.6	2016	●	→
CO₂ emissions from fuel combustion for electricity and heating per total electricity output (MtCO₂/TWh)	NA	NA	●	●

SDG8 – Decent Work and Economic Growth

	Value	Year	Rating	Trend
Adjusted GDP growth (%)	-5.6	2018	●	●
Victims of modern slavery (per 1,000 population)	21.4	2018	●	●
Adults with an account at a bank or other financial institution or with a mobile-money-service provider (% of population aged 15 or over)	20.9	2017	●	↓
Unemployment rate (% of total labor force)	9.5	2019	●	→
Fatal work-related accidents embodied in imports (per 100,000 population)	0.1	2010	●	↑

SDG9 – Industry, Innovation and Infrastructure

	Value	Year	Rating	Trend
Population using the internet (%)	20.8	2017	●	↗
Mobile broadband subscriptions (per 100 population)	52.9	2018	●	↑
Logistics Performance Index: Quality of trade and transport-related infrastructure (worst 1–5 best)	2.3	2018	●	↓
The Times Higher Education Universities Ranking: Average score of top 3 universities (worst 0–100 best) *	0.0	2020	●	●
Scientific and technical journal articles (per 1,000 population)	0.0	2018	●	→
Expenditure on research and development (% of GDP)	NA	NA	●	●

SDG10 – Reduced Inequalities

	Value	Year	Rating	Trend
Gini coefficient adjusted for top income	32.6	2014	○	●

SDG11 – Sustainable Cities and Communities

	Value	Year	Rating	Trend
Annual mean concentration of particulate matter of less than 2.5 microns in diameter (PM2.5) (μg/m³)	47.4	2017	●	↓
Access to improved water source, piped (% of urban population)	65.5	2017	●	↗
Satisfaction with public transport (%)	42.5	2019	●	→

SDG12 – Responsible Consumption and Production

	Value	Year	Rating	Trend
Municipal solid waste (kg/capita/day)	0.5	2009	●	●
Electronic waste (kg/capita)	1.3	2016	●	●
Production-based SO₂ emissions (kg/capita)	33.0	2012	○	●
SO₂ emissions embodied in imports (kg/capita)	1.8	2012	●	●
Production-based nitrogen emissions (kg/capita)	36.9	2010	●	●
Nitrogen emissions embodied in imports (kg/capita)	0.7	2010	●	●

SDG13 – Climate Action

	Value	Year	Rating	Trend
Energy-related CO₂ emissions (tCO₂/capita)	0.7	2017	●	↑
CO₂ emissions embodied in imports (tCO₂/capita)	0.1	2015	●	↑
CO₂ emissions embodied in fossil fuel exports (kg/capita)	NA	NA	●	●

SDG14 – Life Below Water

	Value	Year	Rating	Trend
Mean area that is protected in marine sites important to biodiversity (%)	64.4	2018	●	↑
Ocean Health Index: Clean Waters score (worst 0–100 best)	60.8	2019	●	↓
Fish caught from overexploited or collapsed stocks (% of total catch)	15.6	2014	●	↑
Fish caught by trawling (%)	23.0	2014	○	↑
Marine biodiversity threats embodied in imports (per million population)	0.1	2018	●	●

SDG15 – Life on Land

	Value	Year	Rating	Trend
Mean area that is protected in terrestrial sites important to biodiversity (%)	14.6	2018	●	→
Mean area that is protected in freshwater sites important to biodiversity (%)	NA	NA	●	●
Red List Index of species survival (worst 0–1 best)	1.0	2019	●	↑
Permanent deforestation (% of forest area, 5-year average)	0.0	2018	●	●
Terrestrial and freshwater biodiversity threats embodied in imports (per million population)	0.1	2018	●	●

SDG16 – Peace, Justice and Strong Institutions

		Value	Year	Rating	Trend
Homicides (per 100,000 population)	*	9.9	2015	●	●
Unsentenced detainees (% of prison population)		41.0	2015	●	●
Percentage of population who feel safe walking alone at night in the city or area where they live (%)		50.6	2019	●	↗
Property Rights (worst 1–7 best)		2.2	2019	●	●
Birth registrations with civil authority (% of children under age 5)		65.6	2018	●	●
Corruption Perception Index (worst 0–100 best)		28	2019	●	↓
Children involved in child labor (% of population aged 5 to 14)		37.6	2016	●	●
Exports of major conventional weapons (TIV constant million USD per 100,000 population)	*	0.0	2019	●	●
Press Freedom Index (best 0–100 worst)		31.7	2019	○	↓

SDG17 – Partnerships for the Goals

		Value	Year	Rating	Trend
Government spending on health and education (% of GDP)		4.2	2016	●	↓
For high-income and all OECD DAC countries: International concessional public finance, including official development assistance (% of GNI)		NA	NA	●	●
Other countries: Government revenue excluding grants (% of GDP)		NA	NA	●	●
Corporate Tax Haven Score (best 0–100 worst)	*	0.0	2019	●	●

* Imputed data point

MAURITIUS

Sub-Saharan Africa

▼ OVERALL PERFORMANCE

Index score

63.8

Regional average score

53.1

SDG Global rank 108 (OF 166)

▼ SPILLOVER INDEX

100 (best) to 0 (worst)

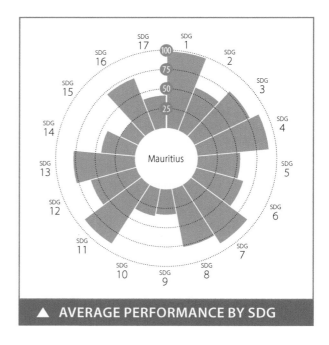

▲ AVERAGE PERFORMANCE BY SDG

▼ CURRENT ASSESSMENT – SDG DASHBOARD

■ Major challenges ■ Significant challenges ■ Challenges remain ■ SDG achieved ■ Information unavailable

▼ SDG TRENDS

↓ Decreasing → Stagnating ↗ Moderately improving ↑ On track or maintaining SDG achievement ● Information unavailable

Notes: The full title of Goal 2 "Zero Hunger" is "End hunger, achieve food security and improved nutrition and promote sustainable agriculture".
The full title of each SDG is available here: https://sustainabledevelopment.un.org/topics/sustainabledevelopmentgoals

SDG1 – No Poverty

	Value	Year	Rating	Trend
Poverty headcount ratio at $1.90/day (%)	0.2	2020	●	↑
Poverty headcount ratio at $3.20/day (%)	1.1	2020	●	↑

SDG2 – Zero Hunger

	Value	Year	Rating	Trend
Prevalence of undernourishment (%)	6.5	2017	●	↑
Prevalence of stunting in children under 5 years of age (%)	NA	NA	●	●
Prevalence of wasting in children under 5 years of age (%)	NA	NA	●	●
Prevalence of obesity, BMI ≥ 30 (% of adult population)	10.8	2016	●	↓
Human Trophic Level (best 2–3 worst)	2.2	2017	●	↑
Cereal yield (tonnes per hectare of harvested land)	5.2	2017	●	↑
Sustainable Nitrogen Management Index (best 0–1.41 worst)	1.1	2015	●	→

SDG3 – Good Health and Well-Being

	Value	Year	Rating	Trend
Maternal mortality rate (per 100,000 live births)	61	2017	●	↑
Neonatal mortality rate (per 1,000 live births)	9.2	2018	●	↑
Mortality rate, under-5 (per 1,000 live births)	15.5	2018	●	↑
Incidence of tuberculosis (per 100,000 population)	13.0	2018	●	→
New HIV infections (per 1,000 uninfected population)	0.7	2018	●	→
Age-standardized death rate due to cardiovascular disease, cancer, diabetes, or chronic respiratory disease in adults aged 30–70 years (%)	22.6	2016	●	↗
Age-standardized death rate attributable to household air pollution and ambient air pollution (per 100,000 population)	38	2016	●	●
Traffic deaths (per 100,000 population)	13.7	2016	●	↓
Life expectancy at birth (years)	74.8	2016	●	↗
Adolescent fertility rate (births per 1,000 adolescent females aged 15 to 19)	25.7	2017	●	↑
Births attended by skilled health personnel (%)	99.8	2016	●	↑
Percentage of surviving infants who received 2 WHO-recommended vaccines (%)	97	2018	●	↑
Universal health coverage (UHC) index of service coverage (worst 0–100 best)	63.0	2017	●	↗
Subjective well-being (average ladder score, worst 0–10 best)	6.2	2019	●	↑

SDG4 – Quality Education

	Value	Year	Rating	Trend
Net primary enrollment rate (%)	94.8	2018	●	→
Lower secondary completion rate (%)	86.8	2018	●	↑
Literacy rate (% of population aged 15 to 24)	99.0	2018	●	●

SDG5 – Gender Equality

	Value	Year	Rating	Trend
Demand for family planning satisfied by modern methods (% of females aged 15 to 49 who are married or in unions)	40.8	2014	●	↗
Ratio of female-to-male mean years of education received (%)	97.9	2018	●	↑
Ratio of female-to-male labor force participation rate (%)	62.9	2019	●	→
Seats held by women in national parliament (%)	20.0	2020	●	↗

SDG6 – Clean Water and Sanitation

	Value	Year	Rating	Trend
Population using at least basic drinking water services (%)	99.9	2017	●	↑
Population using at least basic sanitation services (%)	95.5	2017	●	↑
Freshwater withdrawal (% of available freshwater resources)	26.3	2005	●	●
Anthropogenic wastewater that receives treatment (%)	2.5	2018	●	●
Scarce water consumption embodied in imports (m³/capita)	72.4	2013	●	↓

SDG7 – Affordable and Clean Energy

	Value	Year	Rating	Trend
Population with access to electricity (%)	98.0	2017	●	↑
Population with access to clean fuels and technology for cooking (%)	93.3	2016	●	↑
CO_2 emissions from fuel combustion for electricity and heating per total electricity output (MtCO$_2$/TWh)	1.4	2017	●	→

SDG8 – Decent Work and Economic Growth

	Value	Year	Rating	Trend
Adjusted GDP growth (%)	0.7	2018	●	●
Victims of modern slavery (per 1,000 population)	1.0	2018	●	●
Adults with an account at a bank or other financial institution or with a mobile-money-service provider (% of population aged 15 or over)	89.8	2017	●	↑
Unemployment rate (% of total labor force)	6.7	2019	●	↑
Fatal work-related accidents embodied in imports (per 100,000 population)	3.3	2010	●	↓

SDG9 – Industry, Innovation and Infrastructure

	Value	Year	Rating	Trend
Population using the internet (%)	58.6	2018	●	↑
Mobile broadband subscriptions (per 100 population)	65.3	2018	●	↑
Logistics Performance Index: Quality of trade and transport-related infrastructure (worst 1–5 best)	2.8	2018	●	↑
The Times Higher Education Universities Ranking: Average score of top 3 universities (worst 0–100 best) *	0.0	2020	●	●
Scientific and technical journal articles (per 1,000 population)	0.1	2018	●	→
Expenditure on research and development (% of GDP)	0.4	2017	●	●

SDG10 – Reduced Inequalities

	Value	Year	Rating	Trend
Gini coefficient adjusted for top income	50.4	2012	●	●

SDG11 – Sustainable Cities and Communities

	Value	Year	Rating	Trend
Annual mean concentration of particulate matter of less than 2.5 microns in diameter (PM2.5) (μg/m³)	14.5	2017	●	↗
Access to improved water source, piped (% of urban population)	99.0	2017	●	↑
Satisfaction with public transport (%)	70.2	2019	●	↑

SDG12 – Responsible Consumption and Production

	Value	Year	Rating	Trend
Municipal solid waste (kg/capita/day)	2.3	2016	●	●
Electronic waste (kg/capita)	8.6	2016	●	●
Production-based SO_2 emissions (kg/capita)	225.4	2012	●	●
SO_2 emissions embodied in imports (kg/capita)	11.0	2012	●	●
Production-based nitrogen emissions (kg/capita)	26.8	2010	●	●
Nitrogen emissions embodied in imports (kg/capita)	19.2	2010	●	●

SDG13 – Climate Action

	Value	Year	Rating	Trend
Energy-related CO_2 emissions (tCO$_2$/capita)	3.6	2017	●	→
CO_2 emissions embodied in imports (tCO$_2$/capita)	1.7	2015	●	→
CO_2 emissions embodied in fossil fuel exports (kg/capita)	0.0	2016	●	→

SDG14 – Life Below Water

	Value	Year	Rating	Trend
Mean area that is protected in marine sites important to biodiversity (%)	11.8	2018	●	→
Ocean Health Index: Clean Waters score (worst 0–100 best)	65.0	2019	●	→
Fish caught from overexploited or collapsed stocks (% of total catch)	47.9	2014	●	↓
Fish caught by trawling (%)	6.5	2008	●	●
Marine biodiversity threats embodied in imports (per million population)	1.8	2018	●	●

SDG15 – Life on Land

	Value	Year	Rating	Trend
Mean area that is protected in terrestrial sites important to biodiversity (%)	9.3	2018	●	→
Mean area that is protected in freshwater sites important to biodiversity (%)	NA	NA	●	●
Red List Index of species survival (worst 0–1 best)	0.4	2019	●	↓
Permanent deforestation (% of forest area, 5-year average)	0.1	2018	●	●
Terrestrial and freshwater biodiversity threats embodied in imports (per million population)	22.1	2018	●	●

SDG16 – Peace, Justice and Strong Institutions

	Value	Year	Rating	Trend
Homicides (per 100,000 population)	1.8	2016	●	↓
Unsentenced detainees (% of prison population)	40.7	2018	●	↓
Percentage of population who feel safe walking alone at night in the city or area where they live	65.1	2019	●	↑
Property Rights (worst 1–7 best)	5.3	2019	●	●
Birth registrations with civil authority (% of children under age 5)	NA	NA	●	●
Corruption Perception Index (worst 0–100 best)	52	2019	●	↓
Children involved in child labor (% of population aged 5 to 14)	NA	NA	●	●
Exports of major conventional weapons (TIV constant million USD per 100,000 population) *	0.0	2019	●	●
Press Freedom Index (best 0–100 worst)	28.5	2019	●	↑

SDG17 – Partnerships for the Goals

	Value	Year	Rating	Trend
Government spending on health and education (% of GDP)	7.5	2016	●	↑
For high-income and all OECD DAC countries: International concessional public finance, including official development assistance (% of GNI)	NA	NA	●	●
Other countries: Government revenue excluding grants (% of GDP)	22.6	2018	●	↓
Corporate Tax Haven Score (best 0–100 worst)	79.8	2019	●	●

* Imputed data point

5. Country Profiles

MEXICO

▼ OVERALL PERFORMANCE

Index score

70.4

Regional average score

77.3

SDG Global rank 69 (OF 166)

▲ AVERAGE PERFORMANCE BY SDG

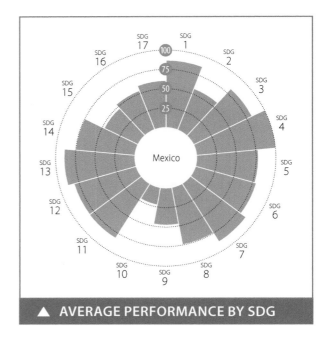

▼ SPILLOVER INDEX

100 (best) to 0 (worst)

▼ CURRENT ASSESSMENT – SDG DASHBOARD

■ Major challenges ■ Significant challenges ■ Challenges remain ■ SDG achieved ■ Information unavailable

▼ SDG TRENDS

1 NO POVERTY	2 ZERO HUNGER	3 GOOD HEALTH AND WELL-BEING	4 QUALITY EDUCATION	5 GENDER EQUALITY	6 CLEAN WATER AND SANITATION	7 AFFORDABLE AND CLEAN ENERGY	8 DECENT WORK AND ECONOMIC GROWTH	9 INDUSTRY, INNOVATION AND INFRASTRUCTURE
↗	↗	↗	↗	↗	↗	↗	→	→

10 REDUCED INEQUALITIES	11 SUSTAINABLE CITIES AND COMMUNITIES	12 RESPONSIBLE CONSUMPTION AND PRODUCTION	13 CLIMATE ACTION	14 LIFE BELOW WATER	15 LIFE ON LAND	16 PEACE, JUSTICE AND STRONG INSTITUTIONS	17 PARTNERSHIPS FOR THE GOALS
→	↑	●	↗	↗	→	→	→

↓ Decreasing → Stagnating ↗ Moderately improving ↑ On track or maintaining SDG achievement ● Information unavailable

Notes: The full title of Goal 2 "Zero Hunger" is "End hunger, achieve food security and improved nutrition and promote sustainable agriculture".
The full title of each SDG is available here: https://sustainabledevelopment.un.org/topics/sustainabledevelopmentgoals

MEXICO

SDG1 – No Poverty

	Value	Year	Rating	Trend
Poverty headcount ratio at $1.90/day (%)	1.7	2020	●	↑
Poverty headcount ratio at $3.20/day (%)	11.9	2020	●	↗
Poverty rate after taxes and transfers (%)	16.6	2016	●	→

SDG2 – Zero Hunger

	Value	Year	Rating	Trend
Prevalence of undernourishment (%)	3.6	2017	●	↑
Prevalence of stunting in children under 5 years of age (%)	12.4	2015	●	↑
Prevalence of wasting in children under 5 years of age (%)	1.0	2015	●	↑
Prevalence of obesity, BMI ≥ 30 (% of adult population)	28.9	2016	●	↓
Human Trophic Level (best 2–3 worst)	2.3	2017	●	→
Cereal yield (tonnes per hectare of harvested land)	3.8	2017	●	↑
Sustainable Nitrogen Management Index (best 0–1.41 worst)	0.8	2015	●	↓
Yield gap closure (% of potential yield)	NA	NA	●	●

SDG3 – Good Health and Well-Being

	Value	Year	Rating	Trend
Maternal mortality rate (per 100,000 live births)	33	2017	●	↑
Neonatal mortality rate (per 1,000 live births)	7.5	2018	●	↑
Mortality rate, under-5 (per 1,000 live births)	12.7	2018	●	↑
Incidence of tuberculosis (per 100,000 population)	23.0	2018	●	→
New HIV infections (per 1,000 uninfected population)	0.1	2018	●	↑
Age-standardized death rate due to cardiovascular disease, cancer, diabetes, or chronic respiratory disease in adults aged 30–70 years (%)	15.7	2016	●	↑
Age-standardized death rate attributable to household air pollution and ambient air pollution (per 100,000 population)	37	2016	●	●
Traffic deaths (per 100,000 population)	13.1	2016	●	↓
Life expectancy at birth (years)	76.6	2016	●	→
Adolescent fertility rate (births per 1,000 adolescent females aged 15 to 19)	60.4	2017	●	↓
Births attended by skilled health personnel (%)	97.7	2015	●	↓
Percentage of surviving infants who received 2 WHO-recommended vaccines (%)	88.0	2018	●	↑
Universal health coverage (UHC) index of service coverage (worst 0–100 best)	76.0	2017	●	↑
Subjective well-being (average ladder score, worst 0–10 best)	6.6	2018	●	↑
Gap in life expectancy at birth among regions (years)	3.7	2016	●	●
Gap in self-reported health status by income (percentage points)	NA	NA	●	●
Daily smokers (% of population aged 15 and over)	7.6	2017	●	↑

SDG4 – Quality Education

	Value	Year	Rating	Trend
Net primary enrollment rate (%)	* 100.0	2017	●	↑
Lower secondary completion rate (%)	* 100.0	2017	●	↑
Literacy rate (% of population aged 15 to 24)	99.3	2018	●	●
Participation rate in pre-primary organized learning (% of children aged 4 to 6)	99.0	2017	●	↑
Tertiary educational attainment (% of population aged 25 to 34)	23.4	2018	●	↗
PISA score (worst 0–600 best)	416.0	2018	●	→
Variation in science performance explained by socio-economic status (%)	12.1	2018	●	↓
Underachievers in science (% of 15-year-olds)	46.8	2018	●	→
Resilient students in science (% of 15-year-olds)	21.6	2018	●	↑

SDG5 – Gender Equality

	Value	Year	Rating	Trend
Demand for family planning satisfied by modern methods (% of females aged 15 to 49 who are married or in unions)	79.8	2015	●	↑
Ratio of female-to-male mean years of education received (%)	95.5	2018	●	→
Ratio of female-to-male labor force participation rate (%)	55.7	2019	●	→
Seats held by women in national parliament (%)	48.2	2020	●	↑
Gender wage gap (% of male median wage)	14.0	2018	●	↑
Gender gap in time spent doing unpaid work (minutes/day)	199.9	2014	●	●

SDG6 – Clean Water and Sanitation

	Value	Year	Rating	Trend
Population using at least basic drinking water services (%)	99.3	2017	●	●
Population using at least basic sanitation services (%)	91.2	2017	●	●
Freshwater withdrawal (% of available freshwater resources)	32.2	2015	●	●
Anthropogenic wastewater that receives treatment (%)	31.6	2018	●	●
Scarce water consumption embodied in imports (m3/capita)	4.3	2013	●	↑
Population using safely managed water services (%)	42.9	2017	●	→
Population using safely managed sanitation services (%)	50.4	2017	●	↗

SDG7 – Affordable and Clean Energy

	Value	Year	Rating	Trend
Population with access to electricity (%)	100.0	2017	●	↑
Population with access to clean fuels and technology for cooking (%)	85.4	2016	●	↑
CO2 emissions from fuel combustion for electricity and heating per total electricity output (MtCO2/TWh)	1.5	2017	●	↗
Share of renewable energy in total primary energy supply (%)	9.0	2018	●	→

SDG8 – Decent Work and Economic Growth

	Value	Year	Rating	Trend
Adjusted GDP growth (%)	-2.3	2018	●	●
Victims of modern slavery (per 1,000 population)	2.7	2018	●	●
Adults with an account at a bank or other financial institution or with a mobile-money-service provider (% of population aged 15 or over)	36.9	2017	●	↓
Fatal work-related accidents embodied in imports (per 100,000 population)	0.2	2010	●	↑
Employment-to-population ratio (%)	62.2	2019	●	↑
Youth not in employment, education or training (NEET) (% of population aged 15 to 29)	20.9	2018	●	→

SDG9 – Industry, Innovation and Infrastructure

	Value	Year	Rating	Trend
Population using the internet (%)	65.8	2018	●	↑
Mobile broadband subscriptions (per 100 population)	70.0	2018	●	↑
Logistics Performance Index: Quality of trade and transport-related infrastructure (worst 1–5 best)	2.8	2018	●	↓
The Times Higher Education Universities Ranking: Average score of top 3 universities (worst 0–100 best)	31.8	2020	●	●
Scientific and technical journal articles (per 1,000 population)	0.1	2018	●	→
Expenditure on research and development (% of GDP)	0.5	2016	●	↓
Researchers (per 1,000 employed population)	1.0	2016	●	→
Triadic patent families filed (per million population)	0.2	2017	●	↓
Gap in internet access by income (percentage points)	59.8	2012	●	●
Women in science and engineering (% of tertiary graduates in science and engineering)	29.2	2015	●	●

SDG10 – Reduced Inequalities

	Value	Year	Rating	Trend
Gini coefficient adjusted for top income	55.4	2016	●	→
Palma ratio	2.5	2016	●	→
Elderly poverty rate (% of population aged 66 or over)	24.7	2016	●	→

SDG11 – Sustainable Cities and Communities

	Value	Year	Rating	Trend
Annual mean concentration of particulate matter of less than 2.5 microns in diameter (PM2.5) (μg/m3)	20.9	2017	●	↗
Access to improved water source, piped (% of urban population)	98.1	2017	●	↑
Satisfaction with public transport (%)	60.7	2018	●	↑
Population with rent overburden (%)	6.7	2014	●	●

SDG12 – Responsible Consumption and Production

	Value	Year	Rating	Trend
Electronic waste (kg/capita)	8.2	2016	●	●
Production-based SO2 emissions (kg/capita)	18.1	2012	●	●
SO2 emissions embodied in imports (kg/capita)	2.1	2012	●	●
Production-based nitrogen emissions (kg/capita)	26.8	2010	●	●
Nitrogen emissions embodied in imports (kg/capita)	3.5	2010	●	●
Non-recycled municipal solid waste (kg/capita/day)	0.9	2012	●	●

SDG13 – Climate Action

	Value	Year	Rating	Trend
Energy-related CO2 emissions (tCO2/capita)	4.0	2017	●	→
CO2 emissions embodied in imports (tCO2/capita)	0.4	2015	●	↑
CO2 emissions embodied in fossil fuel exports (kg/capita)	651.8	2019	●	●
Effective carbon rate (EUR/tCO2)	0.3	2016	●	●

SDG14 – Life Below Water

	Value	Year	Rating	Trend
Mean area that is protected in marine sites important to biodiversity (%)	78.6	2018	●	↑
Ocean Health Index: Clean Waters score (worst 0–100 best)	64.4	2019	●	↗
Fish caught from overexploited or collapsed stocks (% of total catch)	35.5	2014	●	↓
Fish caught by trawling (%)	12.4	2014	●	↑
Marine biodiversity threats embodied in imports (per million population)	0.0	2018	●	●

SDG15 – Life on Land

	Value	Year	Rating	Trend
Mean area that is protected in terrestrial sites important to biodiversity (%)	31.7	2018	●	→
Mean area that is protected in freshwater sites important to biodiversity (%)	15.1	2018	●	→
Red List Index of species survival (worst 0–1 best)	0.7	2019	●	↓
Permanent deforestation (% of forest area, 5-year average)	0.3	2018	●	●
Terrestrial and freshwater biodiversity threats embodied in imports (per million population)	0.7	2018	●	●

SDG16 – Peace, Justice and Strong Institutions

	Value	Year	Rating	Trend
Homicides (per 100,000 population)	24.8	2017	●	↓
Unsentenced detainees (% of prison population)	34.3	2018	●	↑
Percentage of population who feel safe walking alone at night in the city or area where they live	42.0	2018	●	→
Property Rights (worst 1–7 best)	4.1	2019	●	●
Birth registrations with civil authority (% of children under age 5)	95.0	2018	●	●
Corruption Perception Index (worst 0–100 best)	29.0	2019	●	↓
Children involved in child labor (% of population aged 5 to 14)	12.4	2016	●	●
Exports of major conventional weapons (TIV constant million USD per 100,000 population)	0.0	2019	●	●
Press Freedom Index (best 0–100 worst)	46.8	2019	●	→
Persons held in prison (per 100,000 population)	140.9	2017	●	↑

SDG17 – Partnerships for the Goals

	Value	Year	Rating	Trend
Government spending on health and education (% of GDP)	7.8	2016	●	↓
For high-income and all OECD DAC countries: International concessional public finance, including official development assistance (% of GNI)	NA	NA	●	●
Other countries: Government revenue excluding grants (% of GDP)	18.9	2018	●	→
Corporate Tax Haven Score (best 0–100 worst)	* 0.0	2019	●	●
Financial Secrecy Score (best 0–100 worst)	52.8	2020	●	●
Shifted profits of multinationals (US$ billion)	11.1	2016	●	●

* Imputed data point

▼ OVERALL PERFORMANCE

Index score

na

Regional average score

49.6

SDG Global rank   **NA** (OF 166)

▼ SPILLOVER INDEX

100 (best) to 0 (worst)

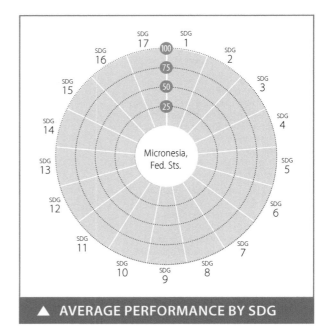

▲ AVERAGE PERFORMANCE BY SDG

▼ CURRENT ASSESSMENT – SDG DASHBOARD

■ Major challenges   ■ Significant challenges   ■ Challenges remain   ■ SDG achieved   ■ Information unavailable

▼ SDG TRENDS

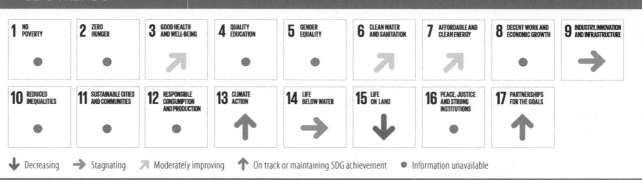

↓ Decreasing   → Stagnating   ↗ Moderately improving   ↑ On track or maintaining SDG achievement   ● Information unavailable

Notes: The full title of Goal 2 "Zero Hunger" is "End hunger, achieve food security and improved nutrition and promote sustainable agriculture".
The full title of each SDG is available here: https://sustainabledevelopment.un.org/topics/sustainabledevelopmentgoals

SDG1 – No Poverty

	Value	Year	Rating	Trend
Poverty headcount ratio at $1.90/day (%)	NA	NA	●	●
Poverty headcount ratio at $3.20/day (%)	NA	NA	●	●

SDG2 – Zero Hunger

	Value	Year	Rating	Trend
Prevalence of undernourishment (%)	NA	NA	●	●
Prevalence of stunting in children under 5 years of age (%)	NA	NA	●	●
Prevalence of wasting in children under 5 years of age (%)	NA	NA	●	●
Prevalence of obesity, BMI ≥ 30 (% of adult population)	45.8	2016	●	↓
Human Trophic Level (best 2–3 worst)	NA	NA	●	●
Cereal yield (tonnes per hectare of harvested land)	1.7	2017	●	→
Sustainable Nitrogen Management Index (best 0–1.41 worst)	1.1	2015	●	→

SDG3 – Good Health and Well-Being

	Value	Year	Rating	Trend
Maternal mortality rate (per 100,000 live births)	88	2017	◐	↑
Neonatal mortality rate (per 1,000 live births)	16.0	2018	●	↑
Mortality rate, under-5 (per 1,000 live births)	30.8	2018	◐	↑
Incidence of tuberculosis (per 100,000 population)	108.0	2018	●	↗
New HIV infections (per 1,000 uninfected population)	NA	NA	●	●
Age-standardized death rate due to cardiovascular disease, cancer, diabetes, or chronic respiratory disease in adults aged 30–70 years (%)	26.1	2016	●	→
Age-standardized death rate attributable to household air pollution and ambient air pollution (per 100,000 population)	152	2016	●	●
Traffic deaths (per 100,000 population)	1.9	2016	●	↑
Life expectancy at birth (years)	69.6	2016	●	→
Adolescent fertility rate (births per 1,000 adolescent females aged 15 to 19)	13.9	2017	●	↑
Births attended by skilled health personnel (%)	100.0	2009	●	●
Percentage of surviving infants who received 2 WHO-recommended vaccines (%)	73	2018	●	→
Universal health coverage (UHC) index of service coverage (worst 0–100 best)	47.0	2017	●	→
Subjective well-being (average ladder score, worst 0–10 best)	NA	NA	●	●

SDG4 – Quality Education

	Value	Year	Rating	Trend
Net primary enrollment rate (%)	85.5	2015	●	●
Lower secondary completion rate (%)	NA	NA	●	●
Literacy rate (% of population aged 15 to 24)	NA	NA	●	●

SDG5 – Gender Equality

	Value	Year	Rating	Trend
Demand for family planning satisfied by modern methods (% of females aged 15 to 49 who are married or in unions)	NA	NA	●	●
Ratio of female-to-male mean years of education received (%)	NA	NA	●	●
Ratio of female-to-male labor force participation rate (%)	NA	NA	●	●
Seats held by women in national parliament (%)	0.0	2020	●	→

SDG6 – Clean Water and Sanitation

	Value	Year	Rating	Trend
Population using at least basic drinking water services (%)	78.6	2017	●	↓
Population using at least basic sanitation services (%)	88.3	2017	◐	↑
Freshwater withdrawal (% of available freshwater resources)	NA	NA	●	●
Anthropogenic wastewater that receives treatment (%)	0.1	2018	●	●
Scarce water consumption embodied in imports (m³/capita)	NA	NA	●	●

SDG7 – Affordable and Clean Energy

	Value	Year	Rating	Trend
Population with access to electricity (%)	80.8	2017	◐	↑
Population with access to clean fuels and technology for cooking (%)	12.0	2016	●	→
CO$_2$ emissions from fuel combustion for electricity and heating per total electricity output (MtCO$_2$/TWh)	NA	NA	●	●

SDG8 – Decent Work and Economic Growth

	Value	Year	Rating	Trend
Adjusted GDP growth (%)	-5.7	2018	●	●
Victims of modern slavery (per 1,000 population)	NA	NA	●	●
Adults with an account at a bank or other financial institution or with a mobile-money-service provider (% of population aged 15 or over)	NA	NA	●	●
Unemployment rate (% of total labor force)	NA	NA	●	●
Fatal work-related accidents embodied in imports (per 100,000 population)	NA	NA	●	●

SDG9 – Industry, Innovation and Infrastructure

	Value	Year	Rating	Trend
Population using the internet (%)	35.3	2017	●	↗
Mobile broadband subscriptions (per 100 population)	0.0	2017	●	→
Logistics Performance Index: Quality of trade and transport-related infrastructure (worst 1–5 best)	NA	NA	●	●
The Times Higher Education Universities Ranking: Average score of top 3 universities (worst 0–100 best) *	0.0	2020	◐	●
Scientific and technical journal articles (per 1,000 population)	0.0	2018	●	↓
Expenditure on research and development (% of GDP)	NA	NA	●	●

SDG10 – Reduced Inequalities

	Value	Year	Rating	Trend
Gini coefficient adjusted for top income	45.7	2013	●	●

SDG11 – Sustainable Cities and Communities

	Value	Year	Rating	Trend
Annual mean concentration of particulate matter of less than 2.5 microns in diameter (PM2.5) (µg/m³)	11.3	2017	◐	↑
Access to improved water source, piped (% of urban population)	NA	NA	●	●
Satisfaction with public transport (%)	NA	NA	●	●

SDG12 – Responsible Consumption and Production

	Value	Year	Rating	Trend
Municipal solid waste (kg/capita/day)	0.2	2016	●	●
Electronic waste (kg/capita)	1.7	2016	●	●
Production-based SO$_2$ emissions (kg/capita)	NA	NA	●	●
SO$_2$ emissions embodied in imports (kg/capita)	NA	NA	●	●
Production-based nitrogen emissions (kg/capita)	NA	NA	●	●
Nitrogen emissions embodied in imports (kg/capita)	NA	NA	●	●

SDG13 – Climate Action

	Value	Year	Rating	Trend
Energy-related CO$_2$ emissions (tCO$_2$/capita)	0.3	2017	●	↑
CO$_2$ emissions embodied in imports (tCO$_2$/capita)	NA	NA	●	●
CO$_2$ emissions embodied in fossil fuel exports (kg/capita) *	0.0	2017	●	●

SDG14 – Life Below Water

	Value	Year	Rating	Trend
Mean area that is protected in marine sites important to biodiversity (%)	1.6	2018	●	→
Ocean Health Index: Clean Waters score (worst 0–100 best)	63.7	2019	●	↑
Fish caught from overexploited or collapsed stocks (% of total catch)	94.4	2014	●	↓
Fish caught by trawling (%)	NA	NA	●	●
Marine biodiversity threats embodied in imports (per million population)	NA	NA	●	●

SDG15 – Life on Land

	Value	Year	Rating	Trend
Mean area that is protected in terrestrial sites important to biodiversity (%)	0.0	2018	●	→
Mean area that is protected in freshwater sites important to biodiversity (%)	NA	NA	●	●
Red List Index of species survival (worst 0–1 best)	0.7	2019	●	↓
Permanent deforestation (% of forest area, 5-year average) *	0.0	2018	●	●
Terrestrial and freshwater biodiversity threats embodied in imports (per million population)	NA	NA	●	●

SDG16 – Peace, Justice and Strong Institutions

	Value	Year	Rating	Trend
Homicides (per 100,000 population) *	4.7	2015	●	●
Unsentenced detainees (% of prison population)	17.7	2015	●	●
Percentage of population who feel safe walking alone at night in the city or area where they live (%)	NA	NA	●	●
Property Rights (worst 1–7 best)	NA	NA	●	●
Birth registrations with civil authority (% of children under age 5)	NA	NA	●	●
Corruption Perception Index (worst 0–100 best)	NA	NA	●	●
Children involved in child labor (% of population aged 5 to 14)	NA	NA	●	●
Exports of major conventional weapons (TIV constant million USD per 100,000 population) *	0.0	2019	●	●
Press Freedom Index (best 0–100 worst)	NA	NA	●	●

SDG17 – Partnerships for the Goals

	Value	Year	Rating	Trend
Government spending on health and education (% of GDP)	15.7	2015	●	●
For high-income and all OECD DAC countries: International concessional public finance, including official development assistance (% of GNI)	NA	NA	●	●
Other countries: Government revenue excluding grants (% of GDP)	44.7	2018	●	↑
Corporate Tax Haven Score (best 0–100 worst) *	0.0	2019	●	●

* Imputed data point

5. Country Profiles

▼ OVERALL PERFORMANCE

Index score

74.4

Regional average score

70.9

SDG Global rank 42 (OF 166)

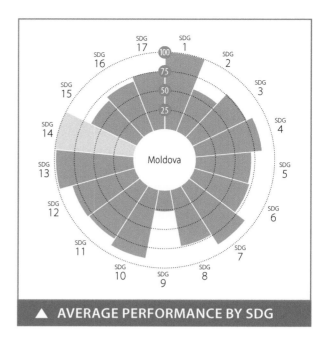

▲ AVERAGE PERFORMANCE BY SDG

▼ SPILLOVER INDEX

100 (best) to 0 (worst)

▼ CURRENT ASSESSMENT – SDG DASHBOARD

■ Major challenges   ■ Significant challenges   ■ Challenges remain   ■ SDG achieved   ■ Information unavailable

▼ SDG TRENDS

↓ Decreasing   → Stagnating   ↗ Moderately improving   ↑ On track or maintaining SDG achievement   ● Information unavailable

Notes: The full title of Goal 2 "Zero Hunger" is "End hunger, achieve food security and improved nutrition and promote sustainable agriculture".
The full title of each SDG is available here: https://sustainabledevelopment.un.org/topics/sustainabledevelopmentgoals

SDG1 – No Poverty

Indicator	Value	Year	Rating	Trend
Poverty headcount ratio at $1.90/day (%)	0.0	2020	●	↑
Poverty headcount ratio at $3.20/day (%)	0.3	2020	●	↑

SDG2 – Zero Hunger

Indicator	Value	Year	Rating	Trend
Prevalence of undernourishment (%)	NA	NA	●	●
Prevalence of stunting in children under 5 years of age (%)	6.4	2012	●	↑
Prevalence of wasting in children under 5 years of age (%)	1.9	2012	●	↑
Prevalence of obesity, BMI ≥ 30 (% of adult population)	18.9	2016	●	↓
Human Trophic Level (best 2–3 worst)	2.4	2017	●	→
Cereal yield (tonnes per hectare of harvested land)	3.6	2017	●	↑
Sustainable Nitrogen Management Index (best 0–1.41 worst)	0.6	2015	●	↓

SDG3 – Good Health and Well-Being

Indicator	Value	Year	Rating	Trend
Maternal mortality rate (per 100,000 live births)	19	2017	●	↑
Neonatal mortality rate (per 1,000 live births)	11.9	2018	●	↑
Mortality rate, under-5 (per 1,000 live births)	15.8	2018	●	↑
Incidence of tuberculosis (per 100,000 population)	86.0	2018	●	↗
New HIV infections (per 1,000 uninfected population)	0.3	2018	●	↑
Age-standardized death rate due to cardiovascular disease, cancer, diabetes, or chronic respiratory disease in adults aged 30–70 years (%)	24.9	2016	●	↑
Age-standardized death rate attributable to household air pollution and ambient air pollution (per 100,000 population)	78	2016	●	●
Traffic deaths (per 100,000 population)	9.7	2016	●	↑
Life expectancy at birth (years)	71.5	2016	●	→
Adolescent fertility rate (births per 1,000 adolescent females aged 15 to 19)	22.4	2017	●	↑
Births attended by skilled health personnel (%)	99.7	2014	●	●
Percentage of surviving infants who received 2 WHO-recommended vaccines (%)	93	2018	●	↑
Universal health coverage (UHC) index of service coverage (worst 0–100 best)	69.0	2017	●	↑
Subjective well-being (average ladder score, worst 0–10 best)	5.8	2019	●	↓

SDG4 – Quality Education

Indicator	Value	Year	Rating	Trend
Net primary enrollment rate (%)	86.3	2018	●	↓
Lower secondary completion rate (%)	85.1	2018	●	↗
Literacy rate (% of population aged 15 to 24)	99.8	2014	●	●

SDG5 – Gender Equality

Indicator	Value	Year	Rating	Trend
Demand for family planning satisfied by modern methods (% of females aged 15 to 49 who are married or in unions)	60.4	2012	●	↗
Ratio of female-to-male mean years of education received (%)	100.9	2018	●	↑
Ratio of female-to-male labor force participation rate (%)	84.6	2019	●	↑
Seats held by women in national parliament (%)	24.8	2020	●	→

SDG6 – Clean Water and Sanitation

Indicator	Value	Year	Rating	Trend
Population using at least basic drinking water services (%)	89.1	2017	●	↗
Population using at least basic sanitation services (%)	76.3	2017	●	→
Freshwater withdrawal (% of available freshwater resources)	15.8	2005	●	●
Anthropogenic wastewater that receives treatment (%)	9.0	2018	●	●
Scarce water consumption embodied in imports (m³/capita)	0.3	2013	●	↑

SDG7 – Affordable and Clean Energy

Indicator	Value	Year	Rating	Trend
Population with access to electricity (%)	100.0	2017	●	↑
Population with access to clean fuels and technology for cooking (%)	92.2	2016	●	↑
CO_2 emissions from fuel combustion for electricity and heating per total electricity output (MtCO$_2$/TWh)	1.6	2017	●	→

SDG8 – Decent Work and Economic Growth

Indicator	Value	Year	Rating	Trend
Adjusted GDP growth (%)	-0.6	2018	●	●
Victims of modern slavery (per 1,000 population)	5.5	2018	●	●
Adults with an account at a bank or other financial institution or with a mobile-money-service provider (% of population aged 15 or over)	43.8	2017	●	↑
Unemployment rate (% of total labor force)	5.5	2019	●	↓
Fatal work-related accidents embodied in imports (per 100,000 population)	0.0	2010	●	↑

SDG9 – Industry, Innovation and Infrastructure

Indicator	Value	Year	Rating	Trend
Population using the internet (%)	76.1	2017	●	↑
Mobile broadband subscriptions (per 100 population)	53.5	2018	●	↑
Logistics Performance Index: Quality of trade and transport-related infrastructure (worst 1–5 best)	2.0	2018	●	↓
The Times Higher Education Universities Ranking: Average score of top 3 universities (worst 0–100 best) *	0.0	2020	●	●
Scientific and technical journal articles (per 1,000 population)	0.1	2018	●	→
Expenditure on research and development (% of GDP)	0.3	2017	●	↓

SDG10 – Reduced Inequalities

Indicator	Value	Year	Rating	Trend
Gini coefficient adjusted for top income	31.4	2017	●	●

SDG11 – Sustainable Cities and Communities

Indicator	Value	Year	Rating	Trend
Annual mean concentration of particulate matter of less than 2.5 microns in diameter (PM2.5) (μg/m³)	16.3	2017	●	→
Access to improved water source, piped (% of urban population)	90.9	2017	●	↑
Satisfaction with public transport (%)	59.0	2019	●	↑

SDG12 – Responsible Consumption and Production

Indicator	Value	Year	Rating	Trend
Municipal solid waste (kg/capita/day)	6.3	2015	●	●
Electronic waste (kg/capita)	1.8	2016	●	●
Production-based SO_2 emissions (kg/capita)	9.7	2012	●	●
SO_2 emissions embodied in imports (kg/capita)	0.3	2012	●	●
Production-based nitrogen emissions (kg/capita)	2.2	2010	●	●
Nitrogen emissions embodied in imports (kg/capita)	0.1	2010	●	●

SDG13 – Climate Action

Indicator	Value	Year	Rating	Trend
Energy-related CO_2 emissions (tCO$_2$/capita)	1.3	2017	●	↑
CO_2 emissions embodied in imports (tCO$_2$/capita)	0.0	2015	●	↑
CO_2 emissions embodied in fossil fuel exports (kg/capita)	0.0	2018	●	●

SDG14 – Life Below Water

Indicator	Value	Year	Rating	Trend
Mean area that is protected in marine sites important to biodiversity (%)	NA	NA	●	●
Ocean Health Index: Clean Waters score (worst 0–100 best)	NA	NA	●	●
Fish caught from overexploited or collapsed stocks (% of total catch)	NA	NA	●	●
Fish caught by trawling (%)	NA	NA	●	●
Marine biodiversity threats embodied in imports (per million population)	0.0	2018	●	●

SDG15 – Life on Land

Indicator	Value	Year	Rating	Trend
Mean area that is protected in terrestrial sites important to biodiversity (%)	23.6	2018	●	→
Mean area that is protected in freshwater sites important to biodiversity (%)	10.8	2018	●	→
Red List Index of species survival (worst 0–1 best)	1.0	2019	●	↑
Permanent deforestation (% of forest area, 5-year average) *	0.0	2018	●	●
Terrestrial and freshwater biodiversity threats embodied in imports (per million population)	0.0	2018	●	●

SDG16 – Peace, Justice and Strong Institutions

Indicator	Value	Year	Rating	Trend
Homicides (per 100,000 population)	3.2	2014	●	●
Unsentenced detainees (% of prison population)	17.5	2018	●	↑
Percentage of population who feel safe walking alone at night in the city or area where they live (%)	66.1	2019	●	↑
Property Rights (worst 1–7 best)	3.9	2019	●	●
Birth registrations with civil authority (% of children under age 5)	99.6	2018	●	●
Corruption Perception Index (worst 0–100 best)	32	2019	●	↓
Children involved in child labor (% of population aged 5 to 14)	16.3	2016	●	●
Exports of major conventional weapons (TIV constant million USD per 100,000 population) *	0.0	2019	●	●
Press Freedom Index (best 0–100 worst)	31.2	2019	●	↓

SDG17 – Partnerships for the Goals

Indicator	Value	Year	Rating	Trend
Government spending on health and education (% of GDP)	10.0	2016	●	↓
For high-income and all OECD DAC countries: International concessional public finance, including official development assistance (% of GNI)	NA	NA	●	●
Other countries: Government revenue excluding grants (% of GDP)	27.7	2018	●	↑
Corporate Tax Haven Score (best 0–100 worst) *	0.0	2019	●	●

* Imputed data point

5. Country Profiles

▼ OVERALL PERFORMANCE

Index score

na

Regional average score

70.9

SDG Global rank   NA (OF 166)

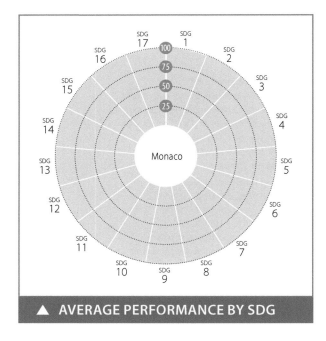

▼ SPILLOVER INDEX

100 (best) to 0 (worst)

▲ AVERAGE PERFORMANCE BY SDG

▼ CURRENT ASSESSMENT – SDG DASHBOARD

■ Major challenges   ■ Significant challenges   ■ Challenges remain   ■ SDG achieved   ■ Information unavailable

▼ SDG TRENDS

↓ Decreasing   → Stagnating   ↗ Moderately improving   ↑ On track or maintaining SDG achievement   ● Information unavailable

Notes: The full title of Goal 2 "Zero Hunger" is "End hunger, achieve food security and improved nutrition and promote sustainable agriculture".
The full title of each SDG is available here: https://sustainabledevelopment.un.org/topics/sustainabledevelopmentgoals

MONACO

SDG1 – No Poverty

	Value	Year	Rating	Trend
Poverty headcount ratio at $1.90/day (%)	NA	NA	●	●
Poverty headcount ratio at $3.20/day (%)	NA	NA	●	●

SDG2 – Zero Hunger

		Value	Year	Rating	Trend
Prevalence of undernourishment (%)	*	1.2	2017	●	●
Prevalence of stunting in children under 5 years of age (%)	*	2.6	2016	●	●
Prevalence of wasting in children under 5 years of age (%)	*	0.7	2016	●	●
Prevalence of obesity, BMI ≥ 30 (% of adult population)		NA	NA	●	●
Human Trophic Level (best 2–3 worst)		NA	NA	●	●
Cereal yield (tonnes per hectare of harvested land)		NA	NA	●	●
Sustainable Nitrogen Management Index (best 0–1.41 worst)		NA	NA	●	●

SDG3 – Good Health and Well-Being

	Value	Year	Rating	Trend
Maternal mortality rate (per 100,000 live births)	NA	NA	●	●
Neonatal mortality rate (per 1,000 live births)	1.7	2018	●	↑
Mortality rate, under-5 (per 1,000 live births)	3.2	2018	●	↑
Incidence of tuberculosis (per 100,000 population)	0.0	2018	●	↑
New HIV infections (per 1,000 uninfected population)	NA	NA	●	●
Age-standardized death rate due to cardiovascular disease, cancer, diabetes, or chronic respiratory disease in adults aged 30–70 years (%)	NA	NA	●	●
Age-standardized death rate attributable to household air pollution and ambient air pollution (per 100,000 population)	NA	NA	●	●
Traffic deaths (per 100,000 population)	0.0	2013	●	●
Life expectancy at birth (years)	NA	NA	●	●
Adolescent fertility rate (births per 1,000 adolescent females aged 15 to 19)	NA	NA	●	●
Births attended by skilled health personnel (%)	NA	NA	●	●
Percentage of surviving infants who received 2 WHO-recommended vaccines (%)	87	2018	●	→
Universal health coverage (UHC) index of service coverage (worst 0–100 best)	NA	NA	●	●
Subjective well-being (average ladder score, worst 0–10 best)	NA	NA	●	●

SDG4 – Quality Education

	Value	Year	Rating	Trend
Net primary enrollment rate (%)	NA	NA	●	●
Lower secondary completion rate (%)	NA	NA	●	●
Literacy rate (% of population aged 15 to 24)	NA	NA	●	●

SDG5 – Gender Equality

	Value	Year	Rating	Trend
Demand for family planning satisfied by modern methods (% of females aged 15 to 49 who are married or in unions)	NA	NA	●	●
Ratio of female-to-male mean years of education received (%)	NA	NA	●	●
Ratio of female-to-male labor force participation rate (%)	NA	NA	●	●
Seats held by women in national parliament (%)	33.3	2020	●	↑

SDG6 – Clean Water and Sanitation

	Value	Year	Rating	Trend
Population using at least basic drinking water services (%)	100.0	2017	●	↑
Population using at least basic sanitation services (%)	100.0	2017	●	↑
Freshwater withdrawal (% of available freshwater resources)	NA	NA	●	●
Anthropogenic wastewater that receives treatment (%)	100.0	2018	●	●
Scarce water consumption embodied in imports (m³/capita)	28.1	2013	●	↗

SDG7 – Affordable and Clean Energy

	Value	Year	Rating	Trend
Population with access to electricity (%)	100.0	2017	●	↑
Population with access to clean fuels and technology for cooking (%)	100.0	2016	●	↑
CO₂ emissions from fuel combustion for electricity and heating per total electricity output (MtCO₂/TWh)	NA	NA	●	●

SDG8 – Decent Work and Economic Growth

	Value	Year	Rating	Trend
Adjusted GDP growth (%)	NA	NA	●	●
Victims of modern slavery (per 1,000 population)	NA	NA	●	●
Adults with an account at a bank or other financial institution or with a mobile-money-service provider (% of population aged 15 or over)	NA	NA	●	●
Unemployment rate (% of total labor force)	NA	NA	●	●
Fatal work-related accidents embodied in imports (per 100,000 population)	2.0	2010	●	↑

SDG9 – Industry, Innovation and Infrastructure

		Value	Year	Rating	Trend
Population using the internet (%)		97.1	2017	●	↑
Mobile broadband subscriptions (per 100 population)		84.1	2018	●	↑
Logistics Performance Index: Quality of trade and transport-related infrastructure (worst 1–5 best)		NA	NA	●	●
The Times Higher Education Universities Ranking: Average score of top 3 universities (worst 0–100 best)	*	0.0	2020	●	●
Scientific and technical journal articles (per 1,000 population)		1.2	2018	●	↑
Expenditure on research and development (% of GDP)		0.0	2005	●	●

SDG10 – Reduced Inequalities

	Value	Year	Rating	Trend
Gini coefficient adjusted for top income	NA	NA	●	●

SDG11 – Sustainable Cities and Communities

	Value	Year	Rating	Trend
Annual mean concentration of particulate matter of less than 2.5 microns in diameter (PM2.5) (μg/m³)	NA	NA	●	●
Access to improved water source, piped (% of urban population)	99.0	2017	●	↑
Satisfaction with public transport (%)	NA	NA	●	●

SDG12 – Responsible Consumption and Production

	Value	Year	Rating	Trend
Municipal solid waste (kg/capita/day)	3.2	2012	●	●
Electronic waste (kg/capita)	NA	NA	●	●
Production-based SO₂ emissions (kg/capita)	109.5	2012	●	●
SO₂ emissions embodied in imports (kg/capita)	30.9	2012	●	●
Production-based nitrogen emissions (kg/capita)	48.0	2010	●	●
Nitrogen emissions embodied in imports (kg/capita)	13.8	2010	●	●

SDG13 – Climate Action

	Value	Year	Rating	Trend
Energy-related CO₂ emissions (tCO₂/capita)	1.8	2017	●	↑
CO₂ emissions embodied in imports (tCO₂/capita)	1.1	2015	●	↗
CO₂ emissions embodied in fossil fuel exports (kg/capita)	NA	NA	●	●

SDG14 – Life Below Water

	Value	Year	Rating	Trend
Mean area that is protected in marine sites important to biodiversity (%)	NA	NA	●	●
Ocean Health Index: Clean Waters score (worst 0–100 best)	19.6	2019	●	↓
Fish caught from overexploited or collapsed stocks (% of total catch)	NA	NA	●	●
Fish caught by trawling (%)	NA	NA	●	●
Marine biodiversity threats embodied in imports (per million population)	0.0	2018	●	●

SDG15 – Life on Land

	Value	Year	Rating	Trend
Mean area that is protected in terrestrial sites important to biodiversity (%)	NA	NA	●	●
Mean area that is protected in freshwater sites important to biodiversity (%)	NA	NA	●	●
Red List Index of species survival (worst 0–1 best)	0.8	2019	●	↓
Permanent deforestation (% of forest area, 5-year average)	NA	NA	●	●
Terrestrial and freshwater biodiversity threats embodied in imports (per million population)	0.4	2018	●	●

SDG16 – Peace, Justice and Strong Institutions

		Value	Year	Rating	Trend
Homicides (per 100,000 population)		2.9	2006	●	●
Unsentenced detainees (% of prison population)		35.5	2018	●	↑
Percentage of population who feel safe walking alone at night in the city or area where they live (%)		NA	NA	●	●
Property Rights (worst 1–7 best)		NA	NA	●	●
Birth registrations with civil authority (% of children under age 5)		100.0	2018	●	●
Corruption Perception Index (worst 0–100 best)		NA	NA	●	●
Children involved in child labor (% of population aged 5 to 14)		NA	NA	●	●
Exports of major conventional weapons (TIV constant million USD per 100,000 population)	*	0.0	2019	●	●
Press Freedom Index (best 0–100 worst)		NA	NA	●	●

SDG17 – Partnerships for the Goals

	Value	Year	Rating	Trend
Government spending on health and education (% of GDP)	2.8	2016	●	↓
For high-income and all OECD DAC countries: International concessional public finance, including official development assistance (% of GNI)	NA	NA	●	●
Other countries: Government revenue excluding grants (% of GDP)	NA	NA	●	●
Corporate Tax Haven Score (best 0–100 worst)	67.6	2019	●	●

* Imputed data point

5. Country Profiles

▼ OVERALL PERFORMANCE

Index score

64.0

Regional average score

67.2

SDG Global rank 107 (OF 166)

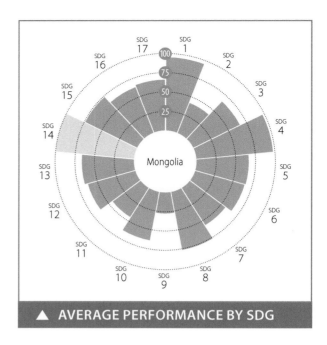

▲ AVERAGE PERFORMANCE BY SDG

▼ SPILLOVER INDEX

100 (best) to 0 (worst)

▼ CURRENT ASSESSMENT – SDG DASHBOARD

■ Major challenges   ■ Significant challenges   ■ Challenges remain   ■ SDG achieved   ■ Information unavailable

▼ SDG TRENDS

↓ Decreasing   → Stagnating   ↗ Moderately improving   ↑ On track or maintaining SDG achievement   ● Information unavailable

Notes: The full title of Goal 2 "Zero Hunger" is "End hunger, achieve food security and improved nutrition and promote sustainable agriculture".
The full title of each SDG is available here: https://sustainabledevelopment.un.org/topics/sustainabledevelopmentgoals

SDG1 – No Poverty

	Value	Year	Rating	Trend
Poverty headcount ratio at $1.90/day (%)	0.3	2020	●	↑
Poverty headcount ratio at $3.20/day (%)	4.3	2020	○	→

SDG2 – Zero Hunger

	Value	Year	Rating	Trend
Prevalence of undernourishment (%)	13.4	2017	●	↑
Prevalence of stunting in children under 5 years of age (%)	10.8	2013	○	↗
Prevalence of wasting in children under 5 years of age (%)	1.0	2013	●	↑
Prevalence of obesity, BMI ≥ 30 (% of adult population)	20.6	2016	●	↓
Human Trophic Level (best 2–3 worst)	2.5	2017	●	↓
Cereal yield (tonnes per hectare of harvested land)	0.6	2017	●	↓
Sustainable Nitrogen Management Index (best 0–1.41 worst)	1.1	2015	●	↓

SDG3 – Good Health and Well-Being

	Value	Year	Rating	Trend
Maternal mortality rate (per 100,000 live births)	45	2017	●	↑
Neonatal mortality rate (per 1,000 live births)	8.7	2018	●	↑
Mortality rate, under-5 (per 1,000 live births)	16.3	2018	●	↑
Incidence of tuberculosis (per 100,000 population)	428.0	2018	●	→
New HIV infections (per 1,000 uninfected population)	0.0	2018	●	↑
Age-standardized death rate due to cardiovascular disease, cancer, diabetes, or chronic respiratory disease in adults aged 30–70 years (%)	30.2	2016	●	→
Age-standardized death rate attributable to household air pollution and ambient air pollution (per 100,000 population)	156	2016	●	●
Traffic deaths (per 100,000 population)	16.5	2016	●	↑
Life expectancy at birth (years)	69.8	2016	●	→
Adolescent fertility rate (births per 1,000 adolescent females aged 15 to 19)	31.0	2017	○	→
Births attended by skilled health personnel (%)	98.9	2014	●	●
Percentage of surviving infants who received 2 WHO-recommended vaccines (%)	99	2018	●	↑
Universal health coverage (UHC) index of service coverage (worst 0–100 best)	62.0	2017	●	↗
Subjective well-being (average ladder score, worst 0–10 best)	5.6	2019	○	↑

SDG4 – Quality Education

	Value	Year	Rating	Trend
Net primary enrollment rate (%)	97.7	2018	●	↑
Lower secondary completion rate (%)	105.2	2018	●	●
Literacy rate (% of population aged 15 to 24)	98.6	2018	●	●

SDG5 – Gender Equality

	Value	Year	Rating	Trend
Demand for family planning satisfied by modern methods (% of females aged 15 to 49 who are married or in unions)	65.2	2013	●	↗
Ratio of female-to-male mean years of education received (%)	106.1	2018	●	↑
Ratio of female-to-male labor force participation rate (%)	79.8	2019	●	↑
Seats held by women in national parliament (%)	17.3	2020	●	→

SDG6 – Clean Water and Sanitation

	Value	Year	Rating	Trend
Population using at least basic drinking water services (%)	83.3	2017	○	↗
Population using at least basic sanitation services (%)	58.5	2017	●	→
Freshwater withdrawal (% of available freshwater resources)	3.4	2015	●	●
Anthropogenic wastewater that receives treatment (%)	3.3	2018	●	●
Scarce water consumption embodied in imports (m³/capita)	3.6	2013	●	↑

SDG7 – Affordable and Clean Energy

	Value	Year	Rating	Trend
Population with access to electricity (%)	85.9	2017	●	↑
Population with access to clean fuels and technology for cooking (%)	42.8	2016	●	↗
CO_2 emissions from fuel combustion for electricity and heating per total electricity output (MtCO$_2$/TWh)	3.4	2017	●	→

SDG8 – Decent Work and Economic Growth

	Value	Year	Rating	Trend
Adjusted GDP growth (%)	-1.2	2018	○	●
Victims of modern slavery (per 1,000 population)	12.3	2018	●	●
Adults with an account at a bank or other financial institution or with a mobile-money-service provider (% of population aged 15 or over)	93.0	2017	●	↑
Unemployment rate (% of total labor force)	6.0	2019	○	↓
Fatal work-related accidents embodied in imports (per 100,000 population)	0.2	2010	●	↑

SDG9 – Industry, Innovation and Infrastructure

	Value	Year	Rating	Trend
Population using the internet (%)	47.2	2018	●	↑
Mobile broadband subscriptions (per 100 population)	83.7	2018	●	↑
Logistics Performance Index: Quality of trade and transport-related infrastructure (worst 1–5 best)	2.1	2018	●	↓
The Times Higher Education Universities Ranking: Average score of top 3 universities (worst 0–100 best) *	0.0	2020	●	●
Scientific and technical journal articles (per 1,000 population)	0.0	2018	●	→
Expenditure on research and development (% of GDP)	0.1	2017	●	↓

SDG10 – Reduced Inequalities

	Value	Year	Rating	Trend
Gini coefficient adjusted for top income	40.5	2016	●	●

SDG11 – Sustainable Cities and Communities

	Value	Year	Rating	Trend
Annual mean concentration of particulate matter of less than 2.5 microns in diameter (PM2.5) (μg/m³)	40.1	2017	●	↓
Access to improved water source, piped (% of urban population)	34.5	2017	●	↓
Satisfaction with public transport (%)	47.7	2019	●	↗

SDG12 – Responsible Consumption and Production

	Value	Year	Rating	Trend
Municipal solid waste (kg/capita/day)	3.7	2016	●	●
Electronic waste (kg/capita)	4.7	2016	●	●
Production-based SO$_2$ emissions (kg/capita)	59.1	2012	○	●
SO$_2$ emissions embodied in imports (kg/capita)	4.2	2012	●	●
Production-based nitrogen emissions (kg/capita)	78.9	2010	●	●
Nitrogen emissions embodied in imports (kg/capita)	1.4	2010	●	●

SDG13 – Climate Action

	Value	Year	Rating	Trend
Energy-related CO_2 emissions (tCO$_2$/capita)	8.2	2017	●	↓
CO_2 emissions embodied in imports (tCO$_2$/capita)	0.6	2015	○	↑
CO_2 emissions embodied in fossil fuel exports (kg/capita)	20728.8	2018	●	↑

SDG14 – Life Below Water

	Value	Year	Rating	Trend
Mean area that is protected in marine sites important to biodiversity (%)	NA	NA	●	●
Ocean Health Index: Clean Waters score (worst 0–100 best)	NA	NA	●	●
Fish caught from overexploited or collapsed stocks (% of total catch)	NA	NA	●	●
Fish caught by trawling (%)	NA	NA	●	●
Marine biodiversity threats embodied in imports (per million population)	0.0	2018	●	●

SDG15 – Life on Land

	Value	Year	Rating	Trend
Mean area that is protected in terrestrial sites important to biodiversity (%)	43.7	2018	○	↑
Mean area that is protected in freshwater sites important to biodiversity (%)	42.1	2018	○	↑
Red List Index of species survival (worst 0–1 best)	0.9	2019	●	↑
Permanent deforestation (% of forest area, 5-year average)	0.0	2018	●	●
Terrestrial and freshwater biodiversity threats embodied in imports (per million population)	0.0	2018	●	●

SDG16 – Peace, Justice and Strong Institutions

	Value	Year	Rating	Trend
Homicides (per 100,000 population)	6.2	2017	●	↑
Unsentenced detainees (% of prison population)	23.1	2018	●	↑
Percentage of population who feel safe walking alone at night in the city or area where they live (%)	50.0	2019	●	↓
Property Rights (worst 1–7 best)	3.5	2019	●	●
Birth registrations with civil authority (% of children under age 5)	99.3	2018	●	●
Corruption Perception Index (worst 0–100 best)	35	2019	●	↓
Children involved in child labor (% of population aged 5 to 14)	17.3	2016	●	●
Exports of major conventional weapons (TIV constant million USD per 100,000 population) *	0.0	2019	●	●
Press Freedom Index (best 0–100 worst)	29.5	2019	●	↑

SDG17 – Partnerships for the Goals

	Value	Year	Rating	Trend
Government spending on health and education (% of GDP)	7.3	2016	●	↗
For high-income and all OECD DAC countries: International concessional public finance, including official development assistance (% of GNI)	NA	NA	●	●
Other countries: Government revenue excluding grants (% of GDP)	24.9	2017	○	↓
Corporate Tax Haven Score (best 0–100 worst) *	0.0	2019	●	●

* Imputed data point

5. Country Profiles

OVERALL PERFORMANCE

Index score
70.2

Regional average score
70.9

SDG Global rank 72 (OF 166)

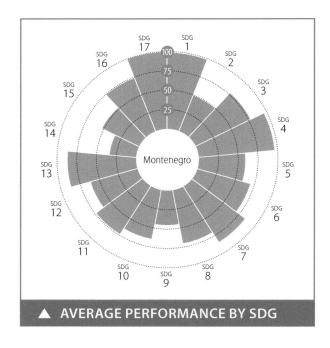

AVERAGE PERFORMANCE BY SDG

Montenegro

SPILLOVER INDEX

100 (best) to 0 (worst)

CURRENT ASSESSMENT – SDG DASHBOARD

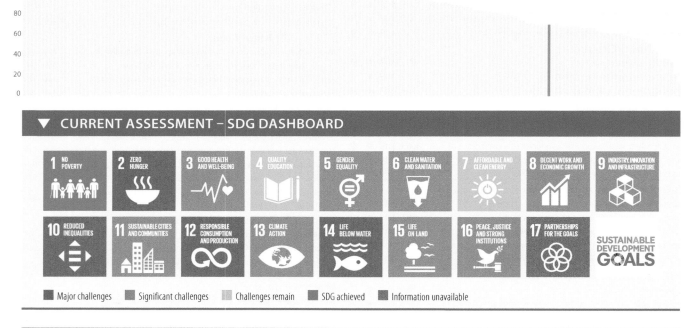

■ Major challenges   ■ Significant challenges   ■ Challenges remain   ■ SDG achieved   ■ Information unavailable

SDG TRENDS

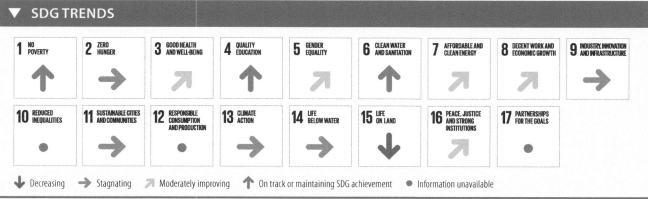

↓ Decreasing   → Stagnating   ↗ Moderately improving   ↑ On track or maintaining SDG achievement   ● Information unavailable

Notes: The full title of Goal 2 "Zero Hunger" is "End hunger, achieve food security and improved nutrition and promote sustainable agriculture".
The full title of each SDG is available here: https://sustainabledevelopment.un.org/topics/sustainabledevelopmentgoals

MONTENEGRO

SDG1 – No Poverty	Value	Year	Rating	Trend
Poverty headcount ratio at $1.90/day (%)	0.0	2020	●	↑
Poverty headcount ratio at $3.20/day (%)	0.1	2020	●	↑

SDG2 – Zero Hunger
	Value	Year	Rating	Trend
Prevalence of undernourishment (%)	2.5	2017	●	↑
Prevalence of stunting in children under 5 years of age (%)	9.4	2013	●	→
Prevalence of wasting in children under 5 years of age (%)	2.8	2013	●	↑
Prevalence of obesity, BMI ≥ 30 (% of adult population)	23.3	2016	●	↓
Human Trophic Level (best 2–3 worst)	2.5	2017	●	→
Cereal yield (tonnes per hectare of harvested land)	3.3	2017	●	↑
Sustainable Nitrogen Management Index (best 0–1.41 worst)	1.1	2015	●	↓

SDG3 – Good Health and Well-Being
	Value	Year	Rating	Trend
Maternal mortality rate (per 100,000 live births)	6	2017	●	↑
Neonatal mortality rate (per 1,000 live births)	1.7	2018	●	↑
Mortality rate, under-5 (per 1,000 live births)	2.5	2018	●	↑
Incidence of tuberculosis (per 100,000 population)	15.0	2018	●	→
New HIV infections (per 1,000 uninfected population)	0.1	2018	●	↑
Age-standardized death rate due to cardiovascular disease, cancer, diabetes, or chronic respiratory disease in adults aged 30–70 years (%)	20.6	2016	●	↗
Age-standardized death rate attributable to household air pollution and ambient air pollution (per 100,000 population)	79	2016	●	●
Traffic deaths (per 100,000 population)	10.7	2016	●	↑
Life expectancy at birth (years)	76.8	2016	●	↗
Adolescent fertility rate (births per 1,000 adolescent females aged 15 to 19)	9.3	2017	●	↑
Births attended by skilled health personnel (%)	99.0	2013	●	●
Percentage of surviving infants who received 2 WHO-recommended vaccines (%)	58	2018	●	↓
Universal health coverage (UHC) index of service coverage (worst 0–100 best)	68.0	2017	●	↗
Subjective well-being (average ladder score, worst 0–10 best)	5.4	2019	●	↑

SDG4 – Quality Education
	Value	Year	Rating	Trend
Net primary enrollment rate (%)	96.5	2018	●	↑
Lower secondary completion rate (%)	99.4	2017	●	↑
Literacy rate (% of population aged 15 to 24)	99.1	2018	●	●

SDG5 – Gender Equality
	Value	Year	Rating	Trend
Demand for family planning satisfied by modern methods (% of females aged 15 to 49 who are married or in unions)	42.8	2013	●	→
Ratio of female-to-male mean years of education received (%)	88.4	2018	●	↓
Ratio of female-to-male labor force participation rate (%)	75.2	2019	●	↑
Seats held by women in national parliament (%)	29.6	2020	●	↑

SDG6 – Clean Water and Sanitation
	Value	Year	Rating	Trend
Population using at least basic drinking water services (%)	97.0	2017	●	↑
Population using at least basic sanitation services (%)	97.8	2017	●	↑
Freshwater withdrawal (% of available freshwater resources)	NA	NA	●	●
Anthropogenic wastewater that receives treatment (%)	8.4	2018	●	●
Scarce water consumption embodied in imports (m3/capita)	21.6	2013	●	↑

SDG7 – Affordable and Clean Energy
	Value	Year	Rating	Trend
Population with access to electricity (%)	100.0	2017	●	↑
Population with access to clean fuels and technology for cooking (%)	69.4	2016	●	↗
CO_2 emissions from fuel combustion for electricity and heating per total electricity output (MtCO2/TWh)	0.9	2017	●	↑

SDG8 – Decent Work and Economic Growth
	Value	Year	Rating	Trend
Adjusted GDP growth (%)	2.9	2018	●	●
Victims of modern slavery (per 1,000 population)	5.9	2018	●	●
Adults with an account at a bank or other financial institution or with a mobile-money-service provider (% of population aged 15 or over)	68.4	2017	●	↑
Unemployment rate (% of total labor force)	14.9	2019	●	↗
Fatal work-related accidents embodied in imports (per 100,000 population)	1.5	2010	●	↓

SDG9 – Industry, Innovation and Infrastructure	Value	Year	Rating	Trend
Population using the internet (%)	71.5	2018	●	↑
Mobile broadband subscriptions (per 100 population)	73.2	2018	●	↑
Logistics Performance Index: Quality of trade and transport-related infrastructure (worst 1–5 best)	2.6	2018	●	↓
The Times Higher Education Universities Ranking: Average score of top 3 universities (worst 0–100 best)	16.4	2020	●	●
Scientific and technical journal articles (per 1,000 population)	0.4	2018	●	↗
Expenditure on research and development (% of GDP)	0.3	2016	●	↓

SDG10 – Reduced Inequalities
	Value	Year	Rating	Trend
Gini coefficient adjusted for top income	40.5	2014	●	●

SDG11 – Sustainable Cities and Communities
	Value	Year	Rating	Trend
Annual mean concentration of particulate matter of less than 2.5 microns in diameter (PM2.5) (µg/m3)	20.8	2017	●	↗
Access to improved water source, piped (% of urban population)	94.1	2017	●	→
Satisfaction with public transport (%)	46.1	2019	●	↓

SDG12 – Responsible Consumption and Production
	Value	Year	Rating	Trend
Municipal solid waste (kg/capita/day)	2.2	2015	●	●
Electronic waste (kg/capita)	10.0	2016	●	●
Production-based SO_2 emissions (kg/capita)	43.2	2012	●	●
SO_2 emissions embodied in imports (kg/capita)	23.0	2012	●	●
Production-based nitrogen emissions (kg/capita)	30.8	2010	●	●
Nitrogen emissions embodied in imports (kg/capita)	10.7	2010	●	●

SDG13 – Climate Action
	Value	Year	Rating	Trend
Energy-related CO_2 emissions (tCO2/capita)	4.1	2017	●	→
CO_2 emissions embodied in imports (tCO2/capita)	0.8	2015	●	↗
CO_2 emissions embodied in fossil fuel exports (kg/capita)	131.1	2018	●	●

SDG14 – Life Below Water
	Value	Year	Rating	Trend
Mean area that is protected in marine sites important to biodiversity (%)	0.0	2018	●	→
Ocean Health Index: Clean Waters score (worst 0–100 best)	61.3	2019	●	↗
Fish caught from overexploited or collapsed stocks (% of total catch)	NA	NA	●	●
Fish caught by trawling (%)	52.8	2014	●	↓
Marine biodiversity threats embodied in imports (per million population)	1.1	2018	●	●

SDG15 – Life on Land
	Value	Year	Rating	Trend
Mean area that is protected in terrestrial sites important to biodiversity (%)	12.5	2018	●	→
Mean area that is protected in freshwater sites important to biodiversity (%)	NA	NA	●	●
Red List Index of species survival (worst 0–1 best)	0.8	2019	●	↓
Permanent deforestation (% of forest area, 5-year average)	* 0.0	2018	●	●
Terrestrial and freshwater biodiversity threats embodied in imports (per million population)	5.3	2018	●	●

SDG16 – Peace, Justice and Strong Institutions
	Value	Year	Rating	Trend
Homicides (per 100,000 population)	2.4	2017	●	↑
Unsentenced detainees (% of prison population)	28.7	2018	●	↑
Percentage of population who feel safe walking alone at night in the city or area where they live (%)	79.2	2019	●	↑
Property Rights (worst 1–7 best)	4.3	2019	●	●
Birth registrations with civil authority (% of children under age 5)	99.4	2018	●	●
Corruption Perception Index (worst 0–100 best)	45	2019	●	→
Children involved in child labor (% of population aged 5 to 14)	12.5	2016	●	●
Exports of major conventional weapons (TIV constant million USD per 100,000 population)	0.0	2019	●	●
Press Freedom Index (best 0–100 worst)	32.7	2019	●	→

SDG17 – Partnerships for the Goals
	Value	Year	Rating	Trend
Government spending on health and education (% of GDP)	NA	NA	●	●
For high-income and all OECD DAC countries: International concessional public finance, including official development assistance (% of GNI)	NA	NA	●	●
Other countries: Government revenue excluding grants (% of GDP)	NA	NA	●	●
Corporate Tax Haven Score (best 0–100 worst)	* 0.0	2019	●	●

* Imputed data point

5. Country Profiles

▼ OVERALL PERFORMANCE

Index score

71.3

Regional average score

66.3

SDG Global rank 64 (OF 166)

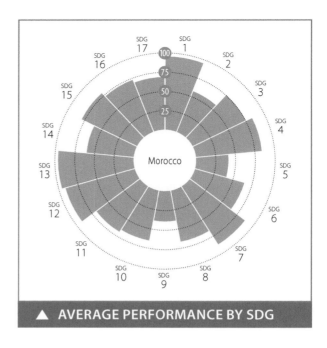

▲ AVERAGE PERFORMANCE BY SDG

▼ SPILLOVER INDEX

100 (best) to 0 (worst)

▼ CURRENT ASSESSMENT – SDG DASHBOARD

■ Major challenges ■ Significant challenges ■ Challenges remain ■ SDG achieved ■ Information unavailable

▼ SDG TRENDS

| 1 NO POVERTY | 2 ZERO HUNGER | 3 GOOD HEALTH AND WELL-BEING | 4 QUALITY EDUCATION | 5 GENDER EQUALITY | 6 CLEAN WATER AND SANITATION | 7 AFFORDABLE AND CLEAN ENERGY | 8 DECENT WORK AND ECONOMIC GROWTH | 9 INDUSTRY, INNOVATION AND INFRASTRUCTURE |

↓ Decreasing   → Stagnating   ↗ Moderately improving   ↑ On track or maintaining SDG achievement   ● Information unavailable

Notes: The full title of Goal 2 "Zero Hunger" is "End hunger, achieve food security and improved nutrition and promote sustainable agriculture".
The full title of each SDG is available here: https://sustainabledevelopment.un.org/topics/sustainabledevelopmentgoals

SDG1 – No Poverty

	Value	Year	Rating	Trend
Poverty headcount ratio at $1.90/day (%)	0.2	2020	●	↑
Poverty headcount ratio at $3.20/day (%)	4.5	2020	○	↑

SDG2 – Zero Hunger

	Value	Year	Rating	Trend
Prevalence of undernourishment (%)	3.4	2017	●	↑
Prevalence of stunting in children under 5 years of age (%)	14.9	2011	●	↗
Prevalence of wasting in children under 5 years of age (%)	2.3	2011	●	↑
Prevalence of obesity, BMI ≥ 30 (% of adult population)	26.1	2016	●	↓
Human Trophic Level (best 2–3 worst)	2.2	2017	●	↑
Cereal yield (tonnes per hectare of harvested land)	1.8	2017	●	↑
Sustainable Nitrogen Management Index (best 0–1.41 worst)	0.8	2015	●	→

SDG3 – Good Health and Well-Being

	Value	Year	Rating	Trend
Maternal mortality rate (per 100,000 live births)	70	2017	●	↑
Neonatal mortality rate (per 1,000 live births)	13.8	2018	○	↑
Mortality rate, under-5 (per 1,000 live births)	22.4	2018	●	↑
Incidence of tuberculosis (per 100,000 population)	99.0	2018	●	→
New HIV infections (per 1,000 uninfected population)	0.0	2018	●	↑
Age-standardized death rate due to cardiovascular disease, cancer, diabetes, or chronic respiratory disease in adults aged 30–70 years (%)	12.4	2016	●	↑
Age-standardized death rate attributable to household air pollution and ambient air pollution (per 100,000 population)	49	2016	●	●
Traffic deaths (per 100,000 population)	19.6	2016	●	↗
Life expectancy at birth (years)	76.0	2016	○	↗
Adolescent fertility rate (births per 1,000 adolescent females aged 15 to 19)	31.0	2017	●	↑
Births attended by skilled health personnel (%)	73.6	2011	●	●
Percentage of surviving infants who received 2 WHO-recommended vaccines (%)	99	2018	●	↑
Universal health coverage (UHC) index of service coverage (worst 0–100 best)	70.0	2017	○	↑
Subjective well-being (average ladder score, worst 0–10 best)	5.1	2019	●	↓

SDG4 – Quality Education

	Value	Year	Rating	Trend
Net primary enrollment rate (%)	99.1	2018	●	↑
Lower secondary completion rate (%)	64.9	2018	●	↓
Literacy rate (% of population aged 15 to 24)	97.7	2018	●	●

SDG5 – Gender Equality

	Value	Year	Rating	Trend
Demand for family planning satisfied by modern methods (% of females aged 15 to 49 who are married or in unions)	68.6	2018	●	↑
Ratio of female-to-male mean years of education received (%)	71.9	2018	●	↑
Ratio of female-to-male labor force participation rate (%)	30.4	2019	●	↓
Seats held by women in national parliament (%)	20.5	2020	●	→

SDG6 – Clean Water and Sanitation

	Value	Year	Rating	Trend
Population using at least basic drinking water services (%)	86.8	2017	○	↑
Population using at least basic sanitation services (%)	88.5	2017	○	↑
Freshwater withdrawal (% of available freshwater resources)	49.7	2010	○	●
Anthropogenic wastewater that receives treatment (%)	5.4	2018	●	●
Scarce water consumption embodied in imports (m³/capita)	2.0	2013	●	↑

SDG7 – Affordable and Clean Energy

	Value	Year	Rating	Trend
Population with access to electricity (%)	100.0	2017	●	↑
Population with access to clean fuels and technology for cooking (%)	96.8	2016	●	↑
CO₂ emissions from fuel combustion for electricity and heating per total electricity output (MtCO₂/TWh)	2.0	2017	●	→

SDG8 – Decent Work and Economic Growth

	Value	Year	Rating	Trend
Adjusted GDP growth (%)	-3.2	2018	●	●
Victims of modern slavery (per 1,000 population)	2.4	2018	●	●
Adults with an account at a bank or other financial institution or with a mobile-money-service provider (% of population aged 15 or over)	28.6	2017	●	●
Unemployment rate (% of total labor force)	9.0	2019	●	→
Fatal work-related accidents embodied in imports (per 100,000 population)	0.1	2010	●	↑

SDG9 – Industry, Innovation and Infrastructure

	Value	Year	Rating	Trend
Population using the internet (%)	64.8	2018	●	↑
Mobile broadband subscriptions (per 100 population)	59.1	2018	○	↑
Logistics Performance Index: Quality of trade and transport-related infrastructure (worst 1–5 best)	2.4	2018	●	●
The Times Higher Education Universities Ranking: Average score of top 3 universities (worst 0–100 best)	21.5	2020	○	●
Scientific and technical journal articles (per 1,000 population)	0.1	2018	●	→
Expenditure on research and development (% of GDP)	0.7	2010	●	●

SDG10 – Reduced Inequalities

	Value	Year	Rating	Trend
Gini coefficient adjusted for top income	39.8	2013	●	●

SDG11 – Sustainable Cities and Communities

	Value	Year	Rating	Trend
Annual mean concentration of particulate matter of less than 2.5 microns in diameter (PM2.5) (µg/m³)	32.6	2017	●	↓
Access to improved water source, piped (% of urban population)	94.1	2017	○	→
Satisfaction with public transport (%)	49.2	2019	●	↓

SDG12 – Responsible Consumption and Production

	Value	Year	Rating	Trend
Municipal solid waste (kg/capita/day)	0.8	2014	●	●
Electronic waste (kg/capita)	3.7	2016	●	●
Production-based SO₂ emissions (kg/capita)	12.8	2012	●	●
SO₂ emissions embodied in imports (kg/capita)	1.2	2012	●	●
Production-based nitrogen emissions (kg/capita)	10.3	2010	●	●
Nitrogen emissions embodied in imports (kg/capita)	0.7	2010	●	●

SDG13 – Climate Action

	Value	Year	Rating	Trend
Energy-related CO₂ emissions (tCO₂/capita)	1.6	2017	●	↑
CO₂ emissions embodied in imports (tCO₂/capita)	0.2	2015	●	↑
CO₂ emissions embodied in fossil fuel exports (kg/capita)	0.0	2018	●	●

SDG14 – Life Below Water

	Value	Year	Rating	Trend
Mean area that is protected in marine sites important to biodiversity (%)	38.7	2018	○	→
Ocean Health Index: Clean Waters score (worst 0–100 best)	55.3	2019	●	↓
Fish caught from overexploited or collapsed stocks (% of total catch)	6.2	2014	●	↑
Fish caught by trawling (%)	62.0	2014	●	→
Marine biodiversity threats embodied in imports (per million population)	0.0	2018	●	●

SDG15 – Life on Land

	Value	Year	Rating	Trend
Mean area that is protected in terrestrial sites important to biodiversity (%)	51.9	2018	●	↑
Mean area that is protected in freshwater sites important to biodiversity (%)	82.6	2018	●	↑
Red List Index of species survival (worst 0–1 best)	0.9	2019	○	→
Permanent deforestation (% of forest area, 5-year average)	0.2	2018	●	●
Terrestrial and freshwater biodiversity threats embodied in imports (per million population)	0.1	2018	●	●

SDG16 – Peace, Justice and Strong Institutions

	Value	Year	Rating	Trend
Homicides (per 100,000 population)	2.1	2017	○	↓
Unsentenced detainees (% of prison population)	23.4	2018	●	↑
Percentage of population who feel safe walking alone at night in the city or area where they live	57.4	2019	●	↓
Property Rights (worst 1–7 best)	5.3	2019	●	●
Birth registrations with civil authority (% of children under age 5)	96.1	2018	○	●
Corruption Perception Index (worst 0–100 best)	41	2019	●	↗
Children involved in child labor (% of population aged 5 to 14)	8.3	2016	●	●
Exports of major conventional weapons (TIV constant million USD per 100,000 population)	* 0.0	2019	●	●
Press Freedom Index (best 0–100 worst)	44.0	2019	●	↓

SDG17 – Partnerships for the Goals

	Value	Year	Rating	Trend
Government spending on health and education (% of GDP)	7.8	2009	○	●
For high-income and all OECD DAC countries: International concessional public finance, including official development assistance (% of GNI)	NA	NA	●	●
Other countries: Government revenue excluding grants (% of GDP)	25.8	2018	○	↓
Corporate Tax Haven Score (best 0–100 worst)	* 0.0	2019	●	●

* Imputed data point

5. Country Profiles

MOZAMBIQUE

▼ OVERALL PERFORMANCE

Index score

54.1

Regional average score

53.1

SDG Global rank 140 (OF 166)

▼ SPILLOVER INDEX

100 (best) to 0 (worst)

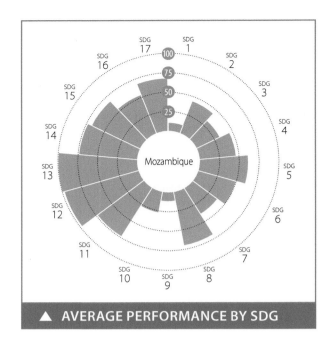

▲ AVERAGE PERFORMANCE BY SDG

▼ CURRENT ASSESSMENT – SDG DASHBOARD

■ Major challenges   ■ Significant challenges   ■ Challenges remain   ■ SDG achieved   ■ Information unavailable

▼ SDG TRENDS

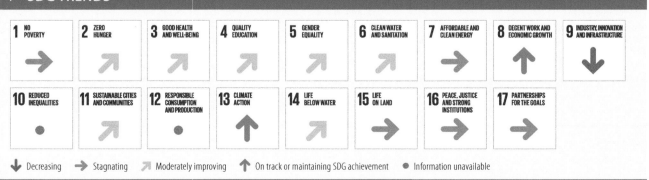

↓ Decreasing   → Stagnating   ↗ Moderately improving   ↑ On track or maintaining SDG achievement   ● Information unavailable

Notes: The full title of Goal 2 "Zero Hunger" is "End hunger, achieve food security and improved nutrition and promote sustainable agriculture".
The full title of each SDG is available here: https://sustainabledevelopment.un.org/topics/sustainabledevelopmentgoals

MOZAMBIQUE

SDG1 – No Poverty

Indicator	Value	Year	Rating	Trend
Poverty headcount ratio at $1.90/day (%)	55.5	2020	●	→
Poverty headcount ratio at $3.20/day (%)	77.5	2020	●	→

SDG2 – Zero Hunger

Indicator	Value	Year	Rating	Trend
Prevalence of undernourishment (%)	27.9	2017	●	↓
Prevalence of stunting in children under 5 years of age (%)	43.1	2011	●	→
Prevalence of wasting in children under 5 years of age (%)	6.1	2011	●	↑
Prevalence of obesity, BMI ≥ 30 (% of adult population)	7.2	2016	●	↑
Human Trophic Level (best 2–3 worst)	2.1	2017	●	↑
Cereal yield (tonnes per hectare of harvested land)	0.9	2017	●	↗
Sustainable Nitrogen Management Index (best 0–1.41 worst)	0.9	2015	●	→

SDG3 – Good Health and Well-Being

Indicator	Value	Year	Rating	Trend
Maternal mortality rate (per 100,000 live births)	289	2017	●	↗
Neonatal mortality rate (per 1,000 live births)	27.8	2018	●	↗
Mortality rate, under-5 (per 1,000 live births)	73.2	2018	●	↗
Incidence of tuberculosis (per 100,000 population)	551.0	2018	●	→
New HIV infections (per 1,000 uninfected population)	5.3	2018	●	↗
Age-standardized death rate due to cardiovascular disease, cancer, diabetes, or chronic respiratory disease in adults aged 30–70 years (%)	18.4	2016	●	↑
Age-standardized death rate attributable to household air pollution and ambient air pollution (per 100,000 population)	110	2016	●	●
Traffic deaths (per 100,000 population)	30.1	2016	●	→
Life expectancy at birth (years)	60.1	2016	●	↗
Adolescent fertility rate (births per 1,000 adolescent females aged 15 to 19)	148.6	2017	●	→
Births attended by skilled health personnel (%)	54.3	2011	●	●
Percentage of surviving infants who received 2 WHO-recommended vaccines (%)	80	2018	●	→
Universal health coverage (UHC) index of service coverage (worst 0–100 best)	46.0	2017	●	↗
Subjective well-being (average ladder score, worst 0–10 best)	4.9	2019	●	↗

SDG4 – Quality Education

Indicator	Value	Year	Rating	Trend
Net primary enrollment rate (%)	93.9	2018	●	↑
Lower secondary completion rate (%)	22.8	2017	●	↓
Literacy rate (% of population aged 15 to 24)	70.9	2017	●	●

SDG5 – Gender Equality

Indicator	Value	Year	Rating	Trend
Demand for family planning satisfied by modern methods (% of females aged 15 to 49 who are married or in unions)	55.5	2015	●	↗
Ratio of female-to-male mean years of education received (%)	54.3	2018	●	→
Ratio of female-to-male labor force participation rate (%)	97.2	2019	●	↑
Seats held by women in national parliament (%)	41.2	2020	●	↑

SDG6 – Clean Water and Sanitation

Indicator	Value	Year	Rating	Trend
Population using at least basic drinking water services (%)	55.7	2017	●	↗
Population using at least basic sanitation services (%)	29.4	2017	●	→
Freshwater withdrawal (% of available freshwater resources)	1.8	2015	●	●
Anthropogenic wastewater that receives treatment (%)	0.2	2018	●	●
Scarce water consumption embodied in imports (m³/capita)	0.2	2013	●	↑

SDG7 – Affordable and Clean Energy

Indicator	Value	Year	Rating	Trend
Population with access to electricity (%)	27.4	2017	●	→
Population with access to clean fuels and technology for cooking (%)	3.7	2016	●	→
CO$_2$ emissions from fuel combustion for electricity and heating per total electricity output (MtCO$_2$/TWh)	0.5	2017	●	↑

SDG8 – Decent Work and Economic Growth

Indicator	Value	Year	Rating	Trend
Adjusted GDP growth (%)	-6.5	2018	●	●
Victims of modern slavery (per 1,000 population)	5.4	2018	●	●
Adults with an account at a bank or other financial institution or with a mobile-money-service provider (% of population aged 15 or over)	41.7	2017	●	●
Unemployment rate (% of total labor force)	3.2	2019	●	↑
Fatal work-related accidents embodied in imports (per 100,000 population)	0.0	2010	●	↑

SDG9 – Industry, Innovation and Infrastructure

Indicator	Value	Year	Rating	Trend
Population using the internet (%)	10.0	2017	●	→
Mobile broadband subscriptions (per 100 population)	15.1	2018	●	↓
Logistics Performance Index: Quality of trade and transport-related infrastructure (worst 1–5 best)	2.2	2016	●	●
The Times Higher Education Universities Ranking: Average score of top 3 universities (worst 0–100 best) *	0.0	2020	●	●
Scientific and technical journal articles (per 1,000 population)	0.0	2018	●	→
Expenditure on research and development (% of GDP)	0.3	2015	●	●

SDG10 – Reduced Inequalities

Indicator	Value	Year	Rating	Trend
Gini coefficient adjusted for top income	53.9	2014	●	●

SDG11 – Sustainable Cities and Communities

Indicator	Value	Year	Rating	Trend
Annual mean concentration of particulate matter of less than 2.5 microns in diameter (PM2.5) (µg/m³)	21.3	2017	●	↗
Access to improved water source, piped (% of urban population)	74.6	2017	●	↗
Satisfaction with public transport (%)	58.3	2019	●	↑

SDG12 – Responsible Consumption and Production

Indicator	Value	Year	Rating	Trend
Municipal solid waste (kg/capita/day)	0.6	2014	●	●
Electronic waste (kg/capita)	0.6	2016	●	●
Production-based SO$_2$ emissions (kg/capita)	5.7	2012	●	●
SO$_2$ emissions embodied in imports (kg/capita)	0.4	2012	●	●
Production-based nitrogen emissions (kg/capita)	6.6	2010	●	●
Nitrogen emissions embodied in imports (kg/capita)	0.2	2010	●	●

SDG13 – Climate Action

Indicator	Value	Year	Rating	Trend
Energy-related CO$_2$ emissions (tCO$_2$/capita)	0.3	2017	●	↑
CO$_2$ emissions embodied in imports (tCO$_2$/capita)	0.0	2015	●	↑
CO$_2$ emissions embodied in fossil fuel exports (kg/capita)	733.2	2018	●	●

SDG14 – Life Below Water

Indicator	Value	Year	Rating	Trend
Mean area that is protected in marine sites important to biodiversity (%)	66.1	2018	●	↑
Ocean Health Index: Clean Waters score (worst 0–100 best)	54.1	2019	●	↓
Fish caught from overexploited or collapsed stocks (% of total catch)	19.9	2014	●	↑
Fish caught by trawling (%)	14.1	2014	●	↑
Marine biodiversity threats embodied in imports (per million population)	0.0	2018	●	●

SDG15 – Life on Land

Indicator	Value	Year	Rating	Trend
Mean area that is protected in terrestrial sites important to biodiversity (%)	26.1	2018	●	→
Mean area that is protected in freshwater sites important to biodiversity (%)	90.0	2018	●	↑
Red List Index of species survival (worst 0–1 best)	0.8	2019	●	↓
Permanent deforestation (% of forest area, 5-year average)	0.4	2018	●	●
Terrestrial and freshwater biodiversity threats embodied in imports (per million population)	0.0	2018	●	●

SDG16 – Peace, Justice and Strong Institutions

Indicator	Value	Year	Rating	Trend
Homicides (per 100,000 population)	3.4	2011	●	●
Unsentenced detainees (% of prison population)	34.8	2018	●	→
Percentage of population who feel safe walking alone at night in the city or area where they live (%)	53.2	2019	●	↗
Property Rights (worst 1–7 best)	3.4	2019	●	●
Birth registrations with civil authority (% of children under age 5)	55.0	2018	●	●
Corruption Perception Index (worst 0–100 best)	26	2019	●	↓
Children involved in child labor (% of population aged 5 to 14)	22.2	2016	●	●
Exports of major conventional weapons (TIV constant million USD per 100,000 population) *	0.0	2019	●	●
Press Freedom Index (best 0–100 worst)	32.7	2019	●	↓

SDG17 – Partnerships for the Goals

Indicator	Value	Year	Rating	Trend
Government spending on health and education (% of GDP)	9.1	2016	●	↑
For high-income and all OECD DAC countries: International concessional public finance, including official development assistance (% of GNI)	NA	NA	●	●
Other countries: Government revenue excluding grants (% of GDP) *	23.8	2018	●	↓
Corporate Tax Haven Score (best 0–100 worst) *	0.0	2019	●	●

* Imputed data point

▼ OVERALL PERFORMANCE

Index score

64.6

Regional average score

67.2

SDG Global rank 104 (OF 166)

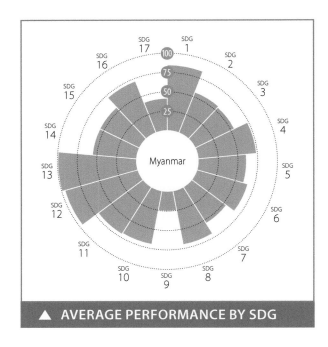

▲ AVERAGE PERFORMANCE BY SDG

▼ SPILLOVER INDEX

100 (best) to 0 (worst)

▼ CURRENT ASSESSMENT – SDG DASHBOARD

■ Major challenges ■ Significant challenges ▢ Challenges remain ■ SDG achieved ▨ Information unavailable

▼ SDG TRENDS

↓ Decreasing → Stagnating ↗ Moderately improving ↑ On track or maintaining SDG achievement ● Information unavailable

Notes: The full title of Goal 2 "Zero Hunger" is "End hunger, achieve food security and improved nutrition and promote sustainable agriculture".
The full title of each SDG is available here: https://sustainabledevelopment.un.org/topics/sustainabledevelopmentgoals

SDG1 – No Poverty

	Value	Year	Rating	Trend
Poverty headcount ratio at $1.90/day (%)	2.1	2020	○	↑
Poverty headcount ratio at $3.20/day (%)	13.8	2020	●	↑

SDG2 – Zero Hunger

	Value	Year	Rating	Trend
Prevalence of undernourishment (%)	10.6	2017	○	↑
Prevalence of stunting in children under 5 years of age (%)	29.2	2016	●	↗
Prevalence of wasting in children under 5 years of age (%)	7.0	2016	●	↑
Prevalence of obesity, BMI ≥ 30 (% of adult population)	5.8	2016	●	↑
Human Trophic Level (best 2–3 worst)	2.3	2017	●	→
Cereal yield (tonnes per hectare of harvested land)	3.6	2017	●	↑
Sustainable Nitrogen Management Index (best 0–1.41 worst)	0.6	2015	●	↓

SDG3 – Good Health and Well-Being

	Value	Year	Rating	Trend
Maternal mortality rate (per 100,000 live births)	250	2017	●	→
Neonatal mortality rate (per 1,000 live births)	23.1	2018	●	↗
Mortality rate, under-5 (per 1,000 live births)	46.2	2018	●	↑
Incidence of tuberculosis (per 100,000 population)	338.0	2018	●	↗
New HIV infections (per 1,000 uninfected population)	0.2	2018	●	↑
Age-standardized death rate due to cardiovascular disease, cancer, diabetes, or chronic respiratory disease in adults aged 30–70 years (%)	24.2	2016	●	→
Age-standardized death rate attributable to household air pollution and ambient air pollution (per 100,000 population)	156	2016	●	●
Traffic deaths (per 100,000 population)	19.9	2016	●	→
Life expectancy at birth (years)	66.8	2016	●	→
Adolescent fertility rate (births per 1,000 adolescent females aged 15 to 19)	28.5	2017	○	↗
Births attended by skilled health personnel (%)	60.2	2016	○	●
Percentage of surviving infants who received 2 WHO-recommended vaccines (%)	91	2018	●	↑
Universal health coverage (UHC) index of service coverage (worst 0–100 best)	61.0	2017	●	↑
Subjective well-being (average ladder score, worst 0–10 best)	4.4	2019	●	→

SDG4 – Quality Education

	Value	Year	Rating	Trend
Net primary enrollment rate (%)	97.9	2018	●	●
Lower secondary completion rate (%)	61.1	2017	●	↑
Literacy rate (% of population aged 15 to 24)	84.8	2016	●	●

SDG5 – Gender Equality

	Value	Year	Rating	Trend
Demand for family planning satisfied by modern methods (% of females aged 15 to 49 who are married or in unions)	74.9	2016	○	↑
Ratio of female-to-male mean years of education received (%)	102.0	2018	●	↑
Ratio of female-to-male labor force participation rate (%)	61.7	2019	●	↓
Seats held by women in national parliament (%)	11.1	2020	●	↓

SDG6 – Clean Water and Sanitation

	Value	Year	Rating	Trend
Population using at least basic drinking water services (%)	81.8	2017	●	↗
Population using at least basic sanitation services (%)	64.3	2017	●	↓
Freshwater withdrawal (% of available freshwater resources)	5.8	2000	●	●
Anthropogenic wastewater that receives treatment (%)	0.0	2018	●	●
Scarce water consumption embodied in imports (m³/capita)	0.0	2013	●	↑

SDG7 – Affordable and Clean Energy

	Value	Year	Rating	Trend
Population with access to electricity (%)	69.8	2017	●	↑
Population with access to clean fuels and technology for cooking (%)	18.4	2016	●	→
CO$_2$ emissions from fuel combustion for electricity and heating per total electricity output (MtCO$_2$/TWh)	1.4	2017	●	→

SDG8 – Decent Work and Economic Growth

	Value	Year	Rating	Trend
Adjusted GDP growth (%)	0.6	2018	●	●
Victims of modern slavery (per 1,000 population)	11.0	2018	●	●
Adults with an account at a bank or other financial institution or with a mobile-money-service provider (% of population aged 15 or over)	26.0	2017	●	→
Unemployment rate (% of total labor force)	1.6	2019	●	↑
Fatal work-related accidents embodied in imports (per 100,000 population)	0.0	2010	●	↑

SDG9 – Industry, Innovation and Infrastructure

	Value	Year	Rating	Trend
Population using the internet (%)	30.7	2017	●	↑
Mobile broadband subscriptions (per 100 population)	92.7	2018	●	↑
Logistics Performance Index: Quality of trade and transport-related infrastructure (worst 1–5 best)	2.0	2018	●	↓
The Times Higher Education Universities Ranking: Average score of top 3 universities (worst 0–100 best) *	0.0	2020	●	●
Scientific and technical journal articles (per 1,000 population)	0.0	2018	●	→
Expenditure on research and development (% of GDP)	0.0	2017	●	●

SDG10 – Reduced Inequalities

	Value	Year	Rating	Trend
Gini coefficient adjusted for top income	38.8	2015	●	●

SDG11 – Sustainable Cities and Communities

	Value	Year	Rating	Trend
Annual mean concentration of particulate matter of less than 2.5 microns in diameter (PM2.5) (μg/m³)	35.6	2017	●	↗
Access to improved water source, piped (% of urban population)	56.9	2017	●	↗
Satisfaction with public transport (%)	77.0	2019	●	↑

SDG12 – Responsible Consumption and Production

	Value	Year	Rating	Trend
Municipal solid waste (kg/capita/day)	0.8	2000	●	●
Electronic waste (kg/capita)	1.0	2016	●	●
Production-based SO$_2$ emissions (kg/capita)	3.2	2012	●	●
SO$_2$ emissions embodied in imports (kg/capita)	0.0	2012	●	●
Production-based nitrogen emissions (kg/capita)	9.3	2010	●	●
Nitrogen emissions embodied in imports (kg/capita)	0.0	2010	●	●

SDG13 – Climate Action

	Value	Year	Rating	Trend
Energy-related CO$_2$ emissions (tCO$_2$/capita)	0.5	2017	●	↑
CO$_2$ emissions embodied in imports (tCO$_2$/capita)	0.0	2015	●	↑
CO$_2$ emissions embodied in fossil fuel exports (kg/capita)	748.6	2018	○	●

SDG14 – Life Below Water

	Value	Year	Rating	Trend
Mean area that is protected in marine sites important to biodiversity (%)	21.4	2018	●	↑
Ocean Health Index: Clean Waters score (worst 0–100 best)	48.5	2019	●	↓
Fish caught from overexploited or collapsed stocks (% of total catch)	19.5	2014	●	↑
Fish caught by trawling (%)	46.9	2014	●	→
Marine biodiversity threats embodied in imports (per million population)	0.0	2018	●	●

SDG15 – Life on Land

	Value	Year	Rating	Trend
Mean area that is protected in terrestrial sites important to biodiversity (%)	27.5	2018	●	→
Mean area that is protected in freshwater sites important to biodiversity (%)	27.9	2018	●	→
Red List Index of species survival (worst 0–1 best)	0.8	2019	●	↓
Permanent deforestation (% of forest area, 5-year average)	0.4	2018	●	●
Terrestrial and freshwater biodiversity threats embodied in imports (per million population)	0.0	2018	●	●

SDG16 – Peace, Justice and Strong Institutions

	Value	Year	Rating	Trend
Homicides (per 100,000 population)	2.3	2016	○	↗
Unsentenced detainees (% of prison population)	11.1	2009	●	●
Percentage of population who feel safe walking alone at night in the city or area where they live (%)	67.3	2019	○	↓
Property Rights (worst 1–7 best)	NA	NA	●	●
Birth registrations with civil authority (% of children under age 5)	81.3	2018	●	●
Corruption Perception Index (worst 0–100 best)	29	2019	●	↗
Children involved in child labor (% of population aged 5 to 14)	9.3	2016	●	●
Exports of major conventional weapons (TIV constant million USD per 100,000 population) *	0.0	2019	●	●
Press Freedom Index (best 0–100 worst)	44.9	2019	●	→

SDG17 – Partnerships for the Goals

	Value	Year	Rating	Trend
Government spending on health and education (% of GDP)	1.0	2011	●	●
For high-income and all OECD DAC countries: International concessional public finance, including official development assistance (% of GNI)	NA	NA	●	●
Other countries: Government revenue excluding grants (% of GDP)	15.8	2017	●	↓
Corporate Tax Haven Score (best 0–100 worst) *	0.0	2019	●	↓

* Imputed data point

5. Country Profiles

NAMIBIA

▼ OVERALL PERFORMANCE

Index score

61.6

Regional average score

53.1

SDG Global rank 119 (OF 166)

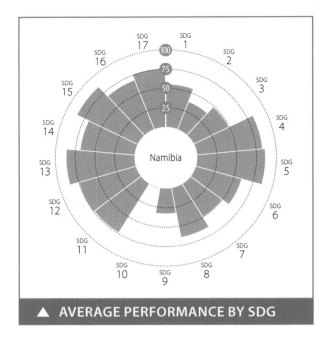

▲ AVERAGE PERFORMANCE BY SDG

▼ SPILLOVER INDEX

100 (best) to 0 (worst)

▼ CURRENT ASSESSMENT – SDG DASHBOARD

■ Major challenges   ■ Significant challenges   ■ Challenges remain   ■ SDG achieved   ■ Information unavailable

▼ SDG TRENDS

| 1 NO POVERTY → | 2 ZERO HUNGER → | 3 GOOD HEALTH AND WELL-BEING ↗ | 4 QUALITY EDUCATION ↑ | 5 GENDER EQUALITY ↑ | 6 CLEAN WATER AND SANITATION → | 7 AFFORDABLE AND CLEAN ENERGY → | 8 DECENT WORK AND ECONOMIC GROWTH ↗ | 9 INDUSTRY, INNOVATION AND INFRASTRUCTURE ↗ |

| 10 REDUCED INEQUALITIES ● | 11 SUSTAINABLE CITIES AND COMMUNITIES → | 12 RESPONSIBLE CONSUMPTION AND PRODUCTION ● | 13 CLIMATE ACTION ↗ | 14 LIFE BELOW WATER ↗ | 15 LIFE ON LAND ↑ | 16 PEACE, JUSTICE AND STRONG INSTITUTIONS → | 17 PARTNERSHIPS FOR THE GOALS ↑ |

↓ Decreasing   → Stagnating   ↗ Moderately improving   ↑ On track or maintaining SDG achievement   ● Information unavailable

Notes: The full title of Goal 2 "Zero Hunger" is "End hunger, achieve food security and improved nutrition and promote sustainable agriculture".
The full title of each SDG is available here: https://sustainabledevelopment.un.org/topics/sustainabledevelopmentgoals

SDG1 – No Poverty

	Value	Year	Rating	Trend
Poverty headcount ratio at $1.90/day (%)	19.6	2020	●	→
Poverty headcount ratio at $3.20/day (%)	31.2	2020	●	→

SDG2 – Zero Hunger

	Value	Year	Rating	Trend
Prevalence of undernourishment (%)	27.3	2017	●	↗
Prevalence of stunting in children under 5 years of age (%)	23.1	2013	●	↗
Prevalence of wasting in children under 5 years of age (%)	7.1	2013	◐	↗
Prevalence of obesity, BMI ≥ 30 (% of adult population)	17.2	2016	◐	↓
Human Trophic Level (best 2–3 worst)	2.2	2017	●	→
Cereal yield (tonnes per hectare of harvested land)	0.4	2017	●	→
Sustainable Nitrogen Management Index (best 0–1.41 worst)	1.2	2015	●	↓

SDG3 – Good Health and Well-Being

	Value	Year	Rating	Trend
Maternal mortality rate (per 100,000 live births)	195	2017	●	↗
Neonatal mortality rate (per 1,000 live births)	15.6	2018	●	↗
Mortality rate, under-5 (per 1,000 live births)	39.6	2018	●	↑
Incidence of tuberculosis (per 100,000 population)	524.0	2018	●	↗
New HIV infections (per 1,000 uninfected population)	2.8	2018	●	↑
Age-standardized death rate due to cardiovascular disease, cancer, diabetes, or chronic respiratory disease in adults aged 30–70 years (%)	21.3	2016	●	↗
Age-standardized death rate attributable to household air pollution and ambient air pollution (per 100,000 population)	145	2016	●	●
Traffic deaths (per 100,000 population)	30.4	2016	●	↓
Life expectancy at birth (years)	63.7	2016	●	→
Adolescent fertility rate (births per 1,000 adolescent females aged 15 to 19)	63.6	2017	●	↑
Births attended by skilled health personnel (%)	88.2	2013	●	●
Percentage of surviving infants who received 2 WHO-recommended vaccines (%)	82	2018	●	↓
Universal health coverage (UHC) index of service coverage (worst 0–100 best)	62.0	2017	●	→
Subjective well-being (average ladder score, worst 0–10 best)	4.4	2019	●	↓

SDG4 – Quality Education

	Value	Year	Rating	Trend
Net primary enrollment rate (%)	97.5	2018	●	↑
Lower secondary completion rate (%)	69.8	2017	●	●
Literacy rate (% of population aged 15 to 24)	95.2	2018	●	●

SDG5 – Gender Equality

	Value	Year	Rating	Trend
Demand for family planning satisfied by modern methods (% of females aged 15 to 49 who are married or in unions)	80.4	2013	●	↑
Ratio of female-to-male mean years of education received (%)	110.6	2018	●	↑
Ratio of female-to-male labor force participation rate (%)	85.7	2019	●	↑
Seats held by women in national parliament (%)	43.3	2020	●	↑

SDG6 – Clean Water and Sanitation

	Value	Year	Rating	Trend
Population using at least basic drinking water services (%)	82.5	2017	●	→
Population using at least basic sanitation services (%)	34.5	2017	●	→
Freshwater withdrawal (% of available freshwater resources)	0.9	2000	●	●
Anthropogenic wastewater that receives treatment (%)	6.3	2018	●	●
Scarce water consumption embodied in imports (m3/capita)	5.4	2013	●	↑

SDG7 – Affordable and Clean Energy

	Value	Year	Rating	Trend
Population with access to electricity (%)	52.5	2017	●	→
Population with access to clean fuels and technology for cooking (%)	42.2	2016	●	→
CO_2 emissions from fuel combustion for electricity and heating per total electricity output (MtCO2/TWh)	2.5	2017	●	→

SDG8 – Decent Work and Economic Growth

	Value	Year	Rating	Trend
Adjusted GDP growth (%)	-6.0	2018	●	●
Victims of modern slavery (per 1,000 population)	3.3	2018	●	●
Adults with an account at a bank or other financial institution or with a mobile-money-service provider (% of population aged 15 or over)	80.6	2017	●	↑
Unemployment rate (% of total labor force)	20.3	2019	●	→
Fatal work-related accidents embodied in imports (per 100,000 population)	0.6	2010	●	↑

SDG9 – Industry, Innovation and Infrastructure

	Value	Year	Rating	Trend
Population using the internet (%)	51.0	2017	●	↑
Mobile broadband subscriptions (per 100 population)	73.4	2018	◐	↑
Logistics Performance Index: Quality of trade and transport-related infrastructure (worst 1–5 best)	2.8	2016	◐	●
The Times Higher Education Universities Ranking: Average score of top 3 universities (worst 0–100 best) *	0.0	2020	●	●
Scientific and technical journal articles (per 1,000 population)	0.1	2018	●	→
Expenditure on research and development (% of GDP)	0.3	2014	●	●

SDG10 – Reduced Inequalities

	Value	Year	Rating	Trend
Gini coefficient adjusted for top income	64.2	2015	●	●

SDG11 – Sustainable Cities and Communities

	Value	Year	Rating	Trend
Annual mean concentration of particulate matter of less than 2.5 microns in diameter (PM2.5) (μg/m3)	25.4	2017	●	→
Access to improved water source, piped (% of urban population)	97.5	2017	◐	→
Satisfaction with public transport (%)	48.6	2019	●	↓

SDG12 – Responsible Consumption and Production

	Value	Year	Rating	Trend
Municipal solid waste (kg/capita/day)	NA	NA	●	●
Electronic waste (kg/capita)	6.0	2016	●	●
Production-based SO_2 emissions (kg/capita)	106.2	2012	●	●
SO_2 emissions embodied in imports (kg/capita)	10.2	2012	●	●
Production-based nitrogen emissions (kg/capita)	42.6	2010	●	●
Nitrogen emissions embodied in imports (kg/capita)	4.1	2010	●	●

SDG13 – Climate Action

	Value	Year	Rating	Trend
Energy-related CO_2 emissions (tCO2/capita)	1.6	2017	●	↑
CO_2 emissions embodied in imports (tCO2/capita)	1.2	2015	●	↗
CO_2 emissions embodied in fossil fuel exports (kg/capita)	0.0	2018	●	●

SDG14 – Life Below Water

	Value	Year	Rating	Trend
Mean area that is protected in marine sites important to biodiversity (%)	91.3	2018	●	↑
Ocean Health Index: Clean Waters score (worst 0–100 best)	83.2	2019	●	↑
Fish caught from overexploited or collapsed stocks (% of total catch)	12.3	2014	●	↑
Fish caught by trawling (%)	88.1	2014	●	→
Marine biodiversity threats embodied in imports (per million population)	0.3	2018	◐	●

SDG15 – Life on Land

	Value	Year	Rating	Trend
Mean area that is protected in terrestrial sites important to biodiversity (%)	83.5	2018	●	↑
Mean area that is protected in freshwater sites important to biodiversity (%)	85.4	2018	●	↑
Red List Index of species survival (worst 0–1 best)	1.0	2019	●	↑
Permanent deforestation (% of forest area, 5-year average)	0.3	2018	●	●
Terrestrial and freshwater biodiversity threats embodied in imports (per million population)	1.3	2018	◐	●

SDG16 – Peace, Justice and Strong Institutions

	Value	Year	Rating	Trend
Homicides (per 100,000 population)	17.1	2012	●	●
Unsentenced detainees (% of prison population)	3.2	2015	●	●
Percentage of population who feel safe walking alone at night in the city or area where they live (%)	39.5	2019	●	↓
Property Rights (worst 1–7 best)	5.0	2019	●	●
Birth registrations with civil authority (% of children under age 5)	77.4	2018	●	●
Corruption Perception Index (worst 0–100 best)	52	2019	◐	↓
Children involved in child labor (% of population aged 5 to 14)	NA	NA	●	●
Exports of major conventional weapons (TIV constant million USD per 100,000 population) *	0.0	2019	●	●
Press Freedom Index (best 0–100 worst)	19.0	2019	●	↑

SDG17 – Partnerships for the Goals

	Value	Year	Rating	Trend
Government spending on health and education (% of GDP)	8.4	2014	◐	●
For high-income and all OECD DAC countries: International concessional public finance, including official development assistance (% of GNI)	NA	NA	●	●
Other countries: Government revenue excluding grants (% of GDP)	31.6	2018	●	↑
Corporate Tax Haven Score (best 0–100 worst) *	0.0	2019	●	●

* Imputed data point

5. Country Profiles

▼ OVERALL PERFORMANCE

Index score

na

Regional average score

49.6

SDG Global rank NA (OF 166)

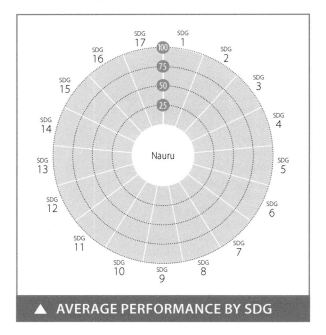

▲ AVERAGE PERFORMANCE BY SDG

▼ SPILLOVER INDEX

100 (best) to 0 (worst)

▼ CURRENT ASSESSMENT – SDG DASHBOARD

■ Major challenges ■ Significant challenges ▨ Challenges remain ■ SDG achieved ▨ Information unavailable

▼ SDG TRENDS

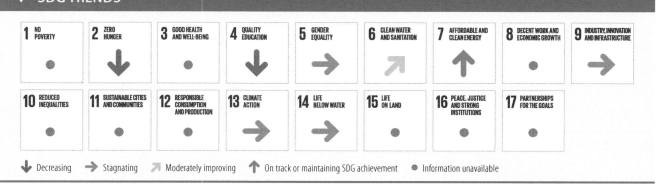

↓ Decreasing → Stagnating ↗ Moderately improving ↑ On track or maintaining SDG achievement ● Information unavailable

Notes: The full title of Goal 2 "Zero Hunger" is "End hunger, achieve food security and improved nutrition and promote sustainable agriculture".
The full title of each SDG is available here: https://sustainabledevelopment.un.org/topics/sustainabledevelopmentgoals

SDG1 – No Poverty	Value	Year	Rating	Trend
Poverty headcount ratio at $1.90/day (%)	NA	NA	●	●
Poverty headcount ratio at $3.20/day (%)	NA	NA	●	●

SDG2 – Zero Hunger	Value	Year	Rating	Trend
Prevalence of undernourishment (%)	NA	NA	●	●
Prevalence of stunting in children under 5 years of age (%)	24.0	2007	●	●
Prevalence of wasting in children under 5 years of age (%)	1.0	2007	●	●
Prevalence of obesity, BMI ≥ 30 (% of adult population)	61.0	2016	●	↓
Human Trophic Level (best 2–3 worst)	NA	NA	●	●
Cereal yield (tonnes per hectare of harvested land)	NA	NA	●	●
Sustainable Nitrogen Management Index (best 0–1.41 worst)	1.0	2015	●	→

SDG3 – Good Health and Well-Being	Value	Year	Rating	Trend
Maternal mortality rate (per 100,000 live births)	NA	NA	●	●
Neonatal mortality rate (per 1,000 live births)	19.9	2018	●	↑
Mortality rate, under-5 (per 1,000 live births)	31.8	2018	○	↑
Incidence of tuberculosis (per 100,000 population)	54.0	2018	●	↑
New HIV infections (per 1,000 uninfected population)	NA	NA	●	●
Age-standardized death rate due to cardiovascular disease, cancer, diabetes, or chronic respiratory disease in adults aged 30–70 years (%)	NA	NA	●	●
Age-standardized death rate attributable to household air pollution and ambient air pollution (per 100,000 population)	NA	NA	●	●
Traffic deaths (per 100,000 population)	NA	NA	●	●
Life expectancy at birth (years)	NA	NA	●	●
Adolescent fertility rate (births per 1,000 adolescent females aged 15 to 19)	NA	NA	●	●
Births attended by skilled health personnel (%)	97.4	2007	○	●
Percentage of surviving infants who received 2 WHO-recommended vaccines (%)	90	2018	●	↑
Universal health coverage (UHC) index of service coverage (worst 0–100 best)	NA	NA	●	●
Subjective well-being (average ladder score, worst 0–10 best)	NA	NA	●	●

SDG4 – Quality Education	Value	Year	Rating	Trend
Net primary enrollment rate (%)	93.7	2016	○	↓
Lower secondary completion rate (%)	73.3	2012	●	●
Literacy rate (% of population aged 15 to 24)	NA	NA	●	●

SDG5 – Gender Equality	Value	Year	Rating	Trend
Demand for family planning satisfied by modern methods (% of females aged 15 to 49 who are married or in unions)	42.5	2007	●	●
Ratio of female-to-male mean years of education received (%)	NA	NA	●	●
Ratio of female-to-male labor force participation rate (%)	NA	NA	●	●
Seats held by women in national parliament (%)	10.5	2020	●	→

SDG6 – Clean Water and Sanitation	Value	Year	Rating	Trend
Population using at least basic drinking water services (%)	99.5	2017	●	↑
Population using at least basic sanitation services (%)	65.6	2017	●	→
Freshwater withdrawal (% of available freshwater resources)	NA	NA	●	●
Anthropogenic wastewater that receives treatment (%)	0.9	2018	●	●
Scarce water consumption embodied in imports (m³/capita)	NA	NA	●	●

SDG7 – Affordable and Clean Energy	Value	Year	Rating	Trend
Population with access to electricity (%)	99.6	2017	●	↑
Population with access to clean fuels and technology for cooking (%)	91.3	2016	●	↑
CO₂ emissions from fuel combustion for electricity and heating per total electricity output (MtCO₂/TWh)	NA	NA	●	●

SDG8 – Decent Work and Economic Growth	Value	Year	Rating	Trend
Adjusted GDP growth (%)	2.4	2018	●	●
Victims of modern slavery (per 1,000 population)	NA	NA	●	●
Adults with an account at a bank or other financial institution or with a mobile-money-service provider (% of population aged 15 or over)	NA	NA	●	●
Unemployment rate (% of total labor force)	NA	NA	●	●
Fatal work-related accidents embodied in imports (per 100,000 population)	NA	NA	●	●

SDG9 – Industry, Innovation and Infrastructure	Value	Year	Rating	Trend
Population using the internet (%)	57.0	2017	●	●
Mobile broadband subscriptions (per 100 population)	37.8	2017	●	↑
Logistics Performance Index: Quality of trade and transport-related infrastructure (worst 1–5 best)	NA	NA	●	●
The Times Higher Education Universities Ranking: Average score of top 3 universities (worst 0–100 best) *	0.0	2020	○	●
Scientific and technical journal articles (per 1,000 population)	0.0	2018	●	↓
Expenditure on research and development (% of GDP)	NA	NA	●	●

SDG10 – Reduced Inequalities	Value	Year	Rating	Trend
Gini coefficient adjusted for top income	NA	NA	●	●

SDG11 – Sustainable Cities and Communities	Value	Year	Rating	Trend
Annual mean concentration of particulate matter of less than 2.5 microns in diameter (PM2.5) (μg/m³)	NA	NA	●	●
Access to improved water source, piped (% of urban population)	52.8	2017	●	→
Satisfaction with public transport (%)	NA	NA	●	●

SDG12 – Responsible Consumption and Production	Value	Year	Rating	Trend
Municipal solid waste (kg/capita/day)	1.5	2016	○	●
Electronic waste (kg/capita)	NA	NA	●	●
Production-based SO₂ emissions (kg/capita)	NA	NA	●	●
SO₂ emissions embodied in imports (kg/capita)	NA	NA	●	●
Production-based nitrogen emissions (kg/capita)	NA	NA	●	●
Nitrogen emissions embodied in imports (kg/capita)	NA	NA	●	●

SDG13 – Climate Action	Value	Year	Rating	Trend
Energy-related CO₂ emissions (tCO₂/capita)	5.5	2017	●	→
CO₂ emissions embodied in imports (tCO₂/capita)	NA	NA	●	●
CO₂ emissions embodied in fossil fuel exports (kg/capita) *	0.0	2018	●	●

SDG14 – Life Below Water	Value	Year	Rating	Trend
Mean area that is protected in marine sites important to biodiversity (%)	0.0	2018	●	→
Ocean Health Index: Clean Waters score (worst 0–100 best)	24.2	2019	●	↓
Fish caught from overexploited or collapsed stocks (% of total catch)	13.3	2014	●	↑
Fish caught by trawling (%)	NA	NA	●	●
Marine biodiversity threats embodied in imports (per million population)	NA	NA	●	●

SDG15 – Life on Land	Value	Year	Rating	Trend
Mean area that is protected in terrestrial sites important to biodiversity (%)	0.0	2018	●	→
Mean area that is protected in freshwater sites important to biodiversity (%)	NA	NA	●	●
Red List Index of species survival (worst 0–1 best)	0.8	2019	●	↓
Permanent deforestation (% of forest area, 5-year average)	NA	NA	●	●
Terrestrial and freshwater biodiversity threats embodied in imports (per million population)	NA	NA	●	●

SDG16 – Peace, Justice and Strong Institutions		Value	Year	Rating	Trend
Homicides (per 100,000 population)	*	NA	NA	●	●
Unsentenced detainees (% of prison population)		NA	NA	●	●
Percentage of population who feel safe walking alone at night in the city or area where they live (%)		NA	NA	●	●
Property Rights (worst 1–7 best)		NA	NA	●	●
Birth registrations with civil authority (% of children under age 5)		95.9	2018	○	●
Corruption Perception Index (worst 0–100 best)		NA	NA	●	●
Children involved in child labor (% of population aged 5 to 14)		NA	NA	●	●
Exports of major conventional weapons (TIV constant million USD per 100,000 population)	*	0.0	2019	●	●
Press Freedom Index (best 0–100 worst)		NA	NA	●	●

SDG17 – Partnerships for the Goals		Value	Year	Rating	Trend
Government spending on health and education (% of GDP)		NA	NA	●	●
For high-income and all OECD DAC countries: International concessional public finance, including official development assistance (% of GNI)		NA	NA	●	●
Other countries: Government revenue excluding grants (% of GDP)		96.8	2017	●	↑
Corporate Tax Haven Score (best 0–100 worst)	*	NA	NA	●	●

* Imputed data point

5. Country Profiles

▼ OVERALL PERFORMANCE

Index score	Regional average score
65.9	67.2

SDG Global rank 96 (OF 166)

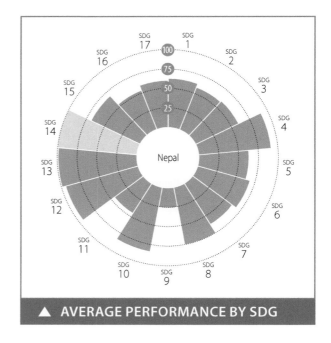

▲ AVERAGE PERFORMANCE BY SDG

▼ SPILLOVER INDEX

100 (best) to 0 (worst)

▼ CURRENT ASSESSMENT – SDG DASHBOARD

■ Major challenges   ■ Significant challenges   ■ Challenges remain   ■ SDG achieved   ■ Information unavailable

▼ SDG TRENDS

↓ Decreasing   → Stagnating   ↗ Moderately improving   ↑ On track or maintaining SDG achievement   ● Information unavailable

Notes: The full title of Goal 2 "Zero Hunger" is "End hunger, achieve food security and improved nutrition and promote sustainable agriculture".
The full title of each SDG is available here: https://sustainabledevelopment.un.org/topics/sustainabledevelopmentgoals

SDG1 – No Poverty

Indicator	Value	Year	Rating	Trend
Poverty headcount ratio at $1.90/day (%)	6.8	2020	●	↑
Poverty headcount ratio at $3.20/day (%)	33.0	2020	●	→

SDG2 – Zero Hunger

Indicator	Value	Year	Rating	Trend
Prevalence of undernourishment (%)	8.7	2017	●	↑
Prevalence of stunting in children under 5 years of age (%)	35.8	2016	●	→
Prevalence of wasting in children under 5 years of age (%)	9.7	2016	●	↗
Prevalence of obesity, BMI ≥ 30 (% of adult population)	4.1	2016	●	↑
Human Trophic Level (best 2–3 worst)	2.1	2017	●	↑
Cereal yield (tonnes per hectare of harvested land)	2.8	2017	●	↑
Sustainable Nitrogen Management Index (best 0–1.41 worst)	0.7	2015	●	↓

SDG3 – Good Health and Well-Being

Indicator	Value	Year	Rating	Trend
Maternal mortality rate (per 100,000 live births)	186	2017	●	↑
Neonatal mortality rate (per 1,000 live births)	19.9	2018	●	↑
Mortality rate, under-5 (per 1,000 live births)	32.2	2018	●	↑
Incidence of tuberculosis (per 100,000 population)	151.0	2018	●	→
New HIV infections (per 1,000 uninfected population)	0.0	2018	●	↑
Age-standardized death rate due to cardiovascular disease, cancer, diabetes, or chronic respiratory disease in adults aged 30–70 years (%)	21.8	2016	●	↗
Age-standardized death rate attributable to household air pollution and ambient air pollution (per 100,000 population)	194	2016	●	●
Traffic deaths (per 100,000 population)	15.9	2016	●	↗
Life expectancy at birth (years)	70.2	2016	●	↗
Adolescent fertility rate (births per 1,000 adolescent females aged 15 to 19)	65.1	2017	●	↗
Births attended by skilled health personnel (%)	58.0	2016	●	↑
Percentage of surviving infants who received 2 WHO-recommended vaccines (%)	91	2018	●	↑
Universal health coverage (UHC) index of service coverage (worst 0–100 best)	48.0	2017	●	→
Subjective well-being (average ladder score, worst 0–10 best)	5.4	2019	●	↑

SDG4 – Quality Education

Indicator	Value	Year	Rating	Trend
Net primary enrollment rate (%)	96.3	2019	●	↓
Lower secondary completion rate (%)	94.6	2017	●	↑
Literacy rate (% of population aged 15 to 24)	92.4	2018	●	●

SDG5 – Gender Equality

Indicator	Value	Year	Rating	Trend
Demand for family planning satisfied by modern methods (% of females aged 15 to 49 who are married or in unions)	56.0	2017	●	→
Ratio of female-to-male mean years of education received (%)	65.6	2018	●	↑
Ratio of female-to-male labor force participation rate (%)	96.9	2019	●	↑
Seats held by women in national parliament (%)	32.7	2020	●	↗

SDG6 – Clean Water and Sanitation

Indicator	Value	Year	Rating	Trend
Population using at least basic drinking water services (%)	88.8	2017	●	↗
Population using at least basic sanitation services (%)	62.1	2017	●	↑
Freshwater withdrawal (% of available freshwater resources)	8.3	2005	●	●
Anthropogenic wastewater that receives treatment (%)	0.0	2018	●	●
Scarce water consumption embodied in imports (m³/capita)	1.6	2013	●	↑

SDG7 – Affordable and Clean Energy

Indicator	Value	Year	Rating	Trend
Population with access to electricity (%)	95.5	2017	●	↑
Population with access to clean fuels and technology for cooking (%)	27.6	2016	●	→
CO$_2$ emissions from fuel combustion for electricity and heating per total electricity output (MtCO$_2$/TWh)	2.2	2017	●	→

SDG8 – Decent Work and Economic Growth

Indicator	Value	Year	Rating	Trend
Adjusted GDP growth (%)	-2.4	2018	●	●
Victims of modern slavery (per 1,000 population)	6.0	2018	●	●
Adults with an account at a bank or other financial institution or with a mobile-money-service provider (% of population aged 15 or over)	45.4	2017	●	↑
Unemployment rate (% of total labor force)	1.4	2019	●	↑
Fatal work-related accidents embodied in imports (per 100,000 population)	0.1	2010	●	↑

SDG9 – Industry, Innovation and Infrastructure

Indicator	Value	Year	Rating	Trend
Population using the internet (%)	34.0	2017	●	↑
Mobile broadband subscriptions (per 100 population)	47.5	2018	●	↑
Logistics Performance Index: Quality of trade and transport-related infrastructure (worst 1–5 best)	2.2	2018	●	↓
The Times Higher Education Universities Ranking: Average score of top 3 universities (worst 0–100 best)	16.4	2020	●	●
Scientific and technical journal articles (per 1,000 population)	0.0	2018	●	→
Expenditure on research and development (% of GDP)	0.3	2010	●	●

SDG10 – Reduced Inequalities

Indicator	Value	Year	Rating	Trend
Gini coefficient adjusted for top income	33.4	2010	●	●

SDG11 – Sustainable Cities and Communities

Indicator	Value	Year	Rating	Trend
Annual mean concentration of particulate matter of less than 2.5 microns in diameter (PM2.5) (µg/m³)	99.7	2017	●	↓
Access to improved water source, piped (% of urban population)	55.3	2017	●	↓
Satisfaction with public transport (%)	71.2	2019	●	↑

SDG12 – Responsible Consumption and Production

Indicator	Value	Year	Rating	Trend
Municipal solid waste (kg/capita/day)	0.8	2016	●	●
Electronic waste (kg/capita)	0.8	2016	●	●
Production-based SO$_2$ emissions (kg/capita)	5.4	2012	●	●
SO$_2$ emissions embodied in imports (kg/capita)	0.5	2012	●	●
Production-based nitrogen emissions (kg/capita)	10.0	2010	●	●
Nitrogen emissions embodied in imports (kg/capita)	0.4	2010	●	●

SDG13 – Climate Action

Indicator	Value	Year	Rating	Trend
Energy-related CO$_2$ emissions (tCO$_2$/capita)	0.3	2017	●	↑
CO$_2$ emissions embodied in imports (tCO$_2$/capita)	0.1	2015	●	↑
CO$_2$ emissions embodied in fossil fuel exports (kg/capita)	0.0	2017	●	●

SDG14 – Life Below Water

Indicator	Value	Year	Rating	Trend
Mean area that is protected in marine sites important to biodiversity (%)	NA	NA	●	●
Ocean Health Index: Clean Waters score (worst 0–100 best)	NA	NA	●	●
Fish caught from overexploited or collapsed stocks (% of total catch)	NA	NA	●	●
Fish caught by trawling (%)	NA	NA	●	●
Marine biodiversity threats embodied in imports (per million population)	0.0	2018	●	●

SDG15 – Life on Land

Indicator	Value	Year	Rating	Trend
Mean area that is protected in terrestrial sites important to biodiversity (%)	52.3	2018	●	↑
Mean area that is protected in freshwater sites important to biodiversity (%)	36.5	2018	●	→
Red List Index of species survival (worst 0–1 best)	0.8	2019	●	→
Permanent deforestation (% of forest area, 5-year average)	0.0	2018	●	●
Terrestrial and freshwater biodiversity threats embodied in imports (per million population)	0.0	2018	●	●

SDG16 – Peace, Justice and Strong Institutions

Indicator	Value	Year	Rating	Trend
Homicides (per 100,000 population)	2.2	2016	●	→
Unsentenced detainees (% of prison population)	NA	NA	●	●
Percentage of population who feel safe walking alone at night in the city or area where they live	57.5	2019	●	↓
Property Rights (worst 1–7 best)	4.0	2019	●	●
Birth registrations with civil authority (% of children under age 5)	56.2	2018	●	●
Corruption Perception Index (worst 0–100 best)	34	2019	●	↗
Children involved in child labor (% of population aged 5 to 14)	37.4	2016	●	●
Exports of major conventional weapons (TIV constant million USD per 100,000 population) *	0.0	2019	●	●
Press Freedom Index (best 0–100 worst)	33.4	2019	●	→

SDG17 – Partnerships for the Goals

Indicator	Value	Year	Rating	Trend
Government spending on health and education (% of GDP)	5.6	2016	●	↑
For high-income and all OECD DAC countries: International concessional public finance, including official development assistance (% of GNI)	NA	NA	●	●
Other countries: Government revenue excluding grants (% of GDP)	22.9	2017	●	↑
Corporate Tax Haven Score (best 0–100 worst) *	0.0	2019	●	●

* Imputed data point

▼ OVERALL PERFORMANCE

Index score

80.4

Regional average score

77.3

SDG Global rank   9   (OF 166)

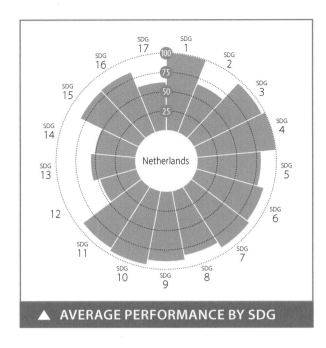

AVERAGE PERFORMANCE BY SDG

▼ SPILLOVER INDEX

100 (best) to 0 (worst)

▼ CURRENT ASSESSMENT – SDG DASHBOARD

| 1 NO POVERTY | 2 ZERO HUNGER | 3 GOOD HEALTH AND WELL-BEING | 4 QUALITY EDUCATION | 5 GENDER EQUALITY | 6 CLEAN WATER AND SANITATION | 7 AFFORDABLE AND CLEAN ENERGY | 8 DECENT WORK AND ECONOMIC GROWTH | 9 INDUSTRY, INNOVATION AND INFRASTRUCTURE |

| 10 REDUCED INEQUALITIES | 11 SUSTAINABLE CITIES AND COMMUNITIES | 12 RESPONSIBLE CONSUMPTION AND PRODUCTION | 13 CLIMATE ACTION | 14 LIFE BELOW WATER | 15 LIFE ON LAND | 16 PEACE, JUSTICE AND STRONG INSTITUTIONS | 17 PARTNERSHIPS FOR THE GOALS | SUSTAINABLE DEVELOPMENT GOALS |

■ Major challenges   ■ Significant challenges   Challenges remain   ■ SDG achieved   ■ Information unavailable

▼ SDG TRENDS

| 1 NO POVERTY ↑ | 2 ZERO HUNGER ↗ | 3 GOOD HEALTH AND WELL-BEING ↗ | 4 QUALITY EDUCATION ↗ | 5 GENDER EQUALITY ↗ | 6 CLEAN WATER AND SANITATION ↗ | 7 AFFORDABLE AND CLEAN ENERGY ↗ | 8 DECENT WORK AND ECONOMIC GROWTH ↑ | 9 INDUSTRY, INNOVATION AND INFRASTRUCTURE ↑ |

| 10 REDUCED INEQUALITIES ↑ | 11 SUSTAINABLE CITIES AND COMMUNITIES ↑ | 12 RESPONSIBLE CONSUMPTION AND PRODUCTION ● | 13 CLIMATE ACTION → | 14 LIFE BELOW WATER ↗ | 15 LIFE ON LAND ↑ | 16 PEACE, JUSTICE AND STRONG INSTITUTIONS ↑ | 17 PARTNERSHIPS FOR THE GOALS → |

↓ Decreasing   → Stagnating   ↗ Moderately improving   ↑ On track or maintaining SDG achievement   ● Information unavailable

Notes: The full title of Goal 2 "Zero Hunger" is "End hunger, achieve food security and improved nutrition and promote sustainable agriculture".
The full title of each SDG is available here: https://sustainabledevelopment.un.org/topics/sustainabledevelopmentgoals

SDG1 – No Poverty

Indicator	Value	Year	Rating	Trend
Poverty headcount ratio at $1.90/day (%)	0.2	2020	●	↑
Poverty headcount ratio at $3.20/day (%)	0.3	2020	●	↑
Poverty rate after taxes and transfers (%)	8.3	2016	●	↑

SDG2 – Zero Hunger

Indicator	Value	Year	Rating	Trend
Prevalence of undernourishment (%)	2.5	2017	●	↑
Prevalence of stunting in children under 5 years of age (%)	* 2.6	2016	●	↑
Prevalence of wasting in children under 5 years of age (%)	* 0.7	2016	●	↑
Prevalence of obesity, BMI ≥ 30 (% of adult population)	20.4	2016	●	↓
Human Trophic Level (best 2–3 worst)	2.5	2017	●	↓
Cereal yield (tonnes per hectare of harvested land)	8.8	2017	●	↑
Sustainable Nitrogen Management Index (best 0–1.41 worst)	0.8	2015	●	↓
Yield gap closure (% of potential yield)	76.2	2015	●	●

SDG3 – Good Health and Well-Being

Indicator	Value	Year	Rating	Trend
Maternal mortality rate (per 100,000 live births)	5	2017	●	↑
Neonatal mortality rate (per 1,000 live births)	2.1	2018	●	↑
Mortality rate, under-5 (per 1,000 live births)	3.9	2018	●	↑
Incidence of tuberculosis (per 100,000 population)	5.3	2018	●	↑
New HIV infections (per 1,000 uninfected population)	0.0	2017	●	↑
Age-standardized death rate due to cardiovascular disease, cancer, diabetes, or chronic respiratory disease in adults aged 30–70 years (%)	11.2	2016	●	↑
Age-standardized death rate attributable to household air pollution and ambient air pollution (per 100,000 population)	14	2016	●	●
Traffic deaths (per 100,000 population)	3.8	2016	●	↑
Life expectancy at birth (years)	81.6	2016	●	↑
Adolescent fertility rate (births per 1,000 adolescent females aged 15 to 19)	3.8	2017	●	↑
Births attended by skilled health personnel (%)	100.0	2003	●	●
Percentage of surviving infants who received 2 WHO-recommended vaccines (%)	93.0	2018	●	↑
Universal health coverage (UHC) index of service coverage (worst 0–100 best)	86.0	2017	●	↑
Subjective well-being (average ladder score, worst 0–10 best)	7.4	2019	●	●
Gap in life expectancy at birth among regions (years)	1.3	2016	●	●
Gap in self-reported health status by income (percentage points)	24.0	2017	●	↓
Daily smokers (% of population aged 15 and over)	16.8	2017	●	↑

SDG4 – Quality Education

Indicator	Value	Year	Rating	Trend
Net primary enrollment rate (%)	* 99.7	2017	●	↑
Lower secondary completion rate (%)	* 99.7	2017	●	↑
Literacy rate (% of population aged 15 to 24)	NA	NA	●	●
Participation rate in pre-primary organized learning (% of children aged 4 to 6)	99.7	2017	●	↑
Tertiary educational attainment (% of population aged 25 to 34)	47.6	2018	●	↑
PISA score (worst 0–600 best)	502.3	2018	●	↑
Variation in science performance explained by socio-economic status (%)	12.9	2018	●	↓
Underachievers in science (% of 15-year-olds)	20.0	2018	●	↓
Resilient students in science (% of 15-year-olds)	34.9	2018	●	↑

SDG5 – Gender Equality

Indicator	Value	Year	Rating	Trend
Demand for family planning satisfied by modern methods (% of females aged 15 to 49 who are married or in unions)	* 86.3	2017	●	↑
Ratio of female-to-male mean years of education received (%)	95.2	2018	●	↑
Ratio of female-to-male labor force participation rate (%)	84.4	2019	●	↑
Seats held by women in national parliament (%)	33.3	2020	●	↓
Gender wage gap (% of male median wage)	14.1	2014	●	●
Gender gap in time spent doing unpaid work (minutes/day)	79.5	2016	●	●

SDG6 – Clean Water and Sanitation

Indicator	Value	Year	Rating	Trend
Population using at least basic drinking water services (%)	100.0	2017	●	●
Population using at least basic sanitation services (%)	97.7	2017	●	●
Freshwater withdrawal (% of available freshwater resources)	16.9	2015	●	●
Anthropogenic wastewater that receives treatment (%)	100.0	2018	●	●
Scarce water consumption embodied in imports (m³/capita)	49.3	2013	●	↗
Population using safely managed water services (%)	100.0	2017	●	↑
Population using safely managed sanitation services (%)	97.5	2017	●	↑

SDG7 – Affordable and Clean Energy

Indicator	Value	Year	Rating	Trend
Population with access to electricity (%)	100.0	2017	●	↑
Population with access to clean fuels and technology for cooking (%)	100.0	2016	●	↑
CO$_2$ emissions from fuel combustion for electricity and heating per total electricity output (MtCO$_2$/TWh)	1.4	2017	●	↑
Share of renewable energy in total primary energy supply (%)	6.4	2018	●	→

SDG8 – Decent Work and Economic Growth

Indicator	Value	Year	Rating	Trend
Adjusted GDP growth (%)	0.3	2018	●	●
Victims of modern slavery (per 1,000 population)	1.8	2018	●	●
Adults with an account at a bank or other financial institution or with a mobile-money-service provider (% of population aged 15 or over)	99.6	2017	●	↑
Fatal work-related accidents embodied in imports (per 100,000 population)	2.2	2010	●	↑
Employment-to-population ratio (%)	78.2	2019	●	↑
Youth not in employment, education or training (NEET) (% of population aged 15 to 29)	7.0	2018	●	↑

SDG9 – Industry, Innovation and Infrastructure

Indicator	Value	Year	Rating	Trend
Population using the internet (%)	94.7	2018	●	↑
Mobile broadband subscriptions (per 100 population)	90.9	2017	●	↑
Logistics Performance Index: Quality of trade and transport-related infrastructure (worst 1–5 best)	4.2	2018	●	↑
The Times Higher Education Universities Ranking: Average score of top 3 universities (worst 0–100 best)	68.1	2020	●	●
Scientific and technical journal articles (per 1,000 population)	1.8	2018	●	↑
Expenditure on research and development (% of GDP)	2.0	2017	●	↑
Researchers (per 1,000 employed population)	10.3	2018	●	↑
Triadic patent families filed (per million population)	69.1	2017	●	↑
Gap in internet access by income (percentage points)	3.4	2019	●	↑
Women in science and engineering (% of tertiary graduates in science and engineering)	26.1	2015	●	●

SDG10 – Reduced Inequalities

Indicator	Value	Year	Rating	Trend
Gini coefficient adjusted for top income	28.8	2015	●	↑
Palma ratio	1.0	2016	●	↑
Elderly poverty rate (% of population aged 66 or over)	3.1	2016	●	↑

SDG11 – Sustainable Cities and Communities

Indicator	Value	Year	Rating	Trend
Annual mean concentration of particulate matter of less than 2.5 microns in diameter (PM2.5) (µg/m³)	12.0	2017	●	↑
Access to improved water source, piped (% of urban population)	99.0	2017	●	↑
Satisfaction with public transport (%)	73.9	2019	●	↑
Population with rent overburden (%)	7.0	2017	●	↑

SDG12 – Responsible Consumption and Production

Indicator	Value	Year	Rating	Trend
Electronic waste (kg/capita)	23.9	2016	●	●
Production-based SO$_2$ emissions (kg/capita)	50.8	2012	●	●
SO$_2$ emissions embodied in imports (kg/capita)	16.9	2012	●	●
Production-based nitrogen emissions (kg/capita)	62.6	2010	●	●
Nitrogen emissions embodied in imports (kg/capita)	20.4	2010	●	●
Non-recycled municipal solid waste (kg/capita/day)	0.6	2018	●	●

SDG13 – Climate Action

Indicator	Value	Year	Rating	Trend
Energy-related CO$_2$ emissions (tCO$_2$/capita)	10.1	2017	●	↓
CO$_2$ emissions embodied in imports (tCO$_2$/capita)	2.9	2015	●	→
CO$_2$ emissions embodied in fossil fuel exports (kg/capita)	37.8	2018	●	●
Effective carbon rate (EUR/tCO$_2$)	54.0	2016	●	●

SDG14 – Life Below Water

Indicator	Value	Year	Rating	Trend
Mean area that is protected in marine sites important to biodiversity (%)	81.5	2018	●	↑
Ocean Health Index: Clean Waters score (worst 0–100 best)	45.4	2019	●	→
Fish caught from overexploited or collapsed stocks (% of total catch)	31.7	2014	●	↑
Fish caught by trawling (%)	97.4	2014	●	→
Marine biodiversity threats embodied in imports (per million population)	0.3	2018	●	●

SDG15 – Life on Land

Indicator	Value	Year	Rating	Trend
Mean area that is protected in terrestrial sites important to biodiversity (%)	90.6	2018	●	↑
Mean area that is protected in freshwater sites important to biodiversity (%)	93.4	2018	●	↑
Red List Index of species survival (worst 0–1 best)	0.9	2019	●	↑
Permanent deforestation (% of forest area, 5-year average)	0.0	2018	●	●
Terrestrial and freshwater biodiversity threats embodied in imports (per million population)	6.0	2018	●	●

SDG16 – Peace, Justice and Strong Institutions

Indicator	Value	Year	Rating	Trend
Homicides (per 100,000 population)	0.8	2017	●	↑
Unsentenced detainees (% of prison population)	25.8	2018	●	↑
Percentage of population who feel safe walking alone at night in the city or area where they live	80.1	2019	●	↑
Property Rights (worst 1–7 best)	6.1	2019	●	●
Birth registrations with civil authority (% of children under age 5)	100.0	2018	●	●
Corruption Perception Index (worst 0–100 best)	82.0	2019	●	↑
Children involved in child labor (% of population aged 5 to 14)	* 0.0	2016	●	●
Exports of major conventional weapons (TIV constant million USD per 100,000 population)	3.2	2019	●	●
Press Freedom Index (best 0–100 worst)	8.6	2019	●	↑
Persons held in prison (per 100,000 population)	61.4	2017	●	↑

SDG17 – Partnerships for the Goals

Indicator	Value	Year	Rating	Trend
Government spending on health and education (% of GDP)	13.9	2016	●	↑
For high-income and all OECD DAC countries: International concessional public finance, including official development assistance (% of GNI)	0.6	2017	●	↓
Other countries: Government revenue excluding grants (% of GDP)	NA	NA	●	●
Corporate Tax Haven Score (best 0–100 worst)	78.0	2019	●	●
Financial Secrecy Score (best 0–100 worst)	71.8	2020	●	●
Shifted profits of multinationals (US$ billion)	-104.6	2016	●	●

* Imputed data point

OVERALL PERFORMANCE

Index score

79.2

Regional average score

77.3

SDG Global rank 16 (OF 166)

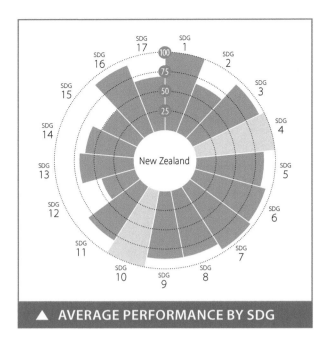

AVERAGE PERFORMANCE BY SDG

New Zealand

SPILLOVER INDEX

100 (best) to 0 (worst)

CURRENT ASSESSMENT – SDG DASHBOARD

| 1 NO POVERTY | 2 ZERO HUNGER | 3 GOOD HEALTH AND WELL-BEING | 4 QUALITY EDUCATION | 5 GENDER EQUALITY | 6 CLEAN WATER AND SANITATION | 7 AFFORDABLE AND CLEAN ENERGY | 8 DECENT WORK AND ECONOMIC GROWTH | 9 INDUSTRY, INNOVATION AND INFRASTRUCTURE |
| 10 REDUCED INEQUALITIES | 11 SUSTAINABLE CITIES AND COMMUNITIES | 12 RESPONSIBLE CONSUMPTION AND PRODUCTION | 13 CLIMATE ACTION | 14 LIFE BELOW WATER | 15 LIFE ON LAND | 16 PEACE, JUSTICE AND STRONG INSTITUTIONS | 17 PARTNERSHIPS FOR THE GOALS | SUSTAINABLE DEVELOPMENT GOALS |

■ Major challenges ■ Significant challenges ▨ Challenges remain ■ SDG achieved ■ Information unavailable

SDG TRENDS

| 1 NO POVERTY ↑ | 2 ZERO HUNGER ↗ | 3 GOOD HEALTH AND WELL-BEING ↗ | 4 QUALITY EDUCATION ↗ | 5 GENDER EQUALITY ↑ | 6 CLEAN WATER AND SANITATION ↑ | 7 AFFORDABLE AND CLEAN ENERGY ↑ | 8 DECENT WORK AND ECONOMIC GROWTH ↑ | 9 INDUSTRY, INNOVATION AND INFRASTRUCTURE ↗ |
| 10 REDUCED INEQUALITIES ● | 11 SUSTAINABLE CITIES AND COMMUNITIES ↗ | 12 RESPONSIBLE CONSUMPTION AND PRODUCTION ● | 13 CLIMATE ACTION → | 14 LIFE BELOW WATER ↗ | 15 LIFE ON LAND ↓ | 16 PEACE, JUSTICE AND STRONG INSTITUTIONS ↗ | 17 PARTNERSHIPS FOR THE GOALS → | |

↓ Decreasing → Stagnating ↗ Moderately improving ↑ On track or maintaining SDG achievement ● Information unavailable

Notes: The full title of Goal 2 "Zero Hunger" is "End hunger, achieve food security and improved nutrition and promote sustainable agriculture".
The full title of each SDG is available here: https://sustainabledevelopment.un.org/topics/sustainabledevelopmentgoals

SDG1 – No Poverty

	Value	Year	Rating	Trend
Poverty headcount ratio at $1.90/day (%)	0.0	2020	●	↑
Poverty headcount ratio at $3.20/day (%)	0.0	2020	●	↑
Poverty rate after taxes and transfers (%)	10.9	2014	◐	●

SDG2 – Zero Hunger

	Value	Year	Rating	Trend
Prevalence of undernourishment (%)	2.5	2017	●	↑
Prevalence of stunting in children under 5 years of age (%)	* 2.6	2016	●	↑
Prevalence of wasting in children under 5 years of age (%)	* 0.7	2016	●	↑
Prevalence of obesity, BMI ≥ 30 (% of adult population)	30.8	2016	●	↓
Human Trophic Level (best 2–3 worst)	2.4	2017	●	↓
Cereal yield (tonnes per hectare of harvested land)	8.5	2017	●	↑
Sustainable Nitrogen Management Index (best 0–1.41 worst)	0.6	2015	●	→
Yield gap closure (% of potential yield)	NA	NA	●	●

SDG3 – Good Health and Well-Being

	Value	Year	Rating	Trend
Maternal mortality rate (per 100,000 live births)	9	2017	●	↑
Neonatal mortality rate (per 1,000 live births)	3.5	2018	●	↑
Mortality rate, under-5 (per 1,000 live births)	5.7	2018	●	↑
Incidence of tuberculosis (per 100,000 population)	7.3	2018	●	↑
New HIV infections (per 1,000 uninfected population)	0.0	2018	●	↑
Age-standardized death rate due to cardiovascular disease, cancer, diabetes, or chronic respiratory disease in adults aged 30–70 years (%)	10.1	2016	●	↑
Age-standardized death rate attributable to household air pollution and ambient air pollution (per 100,000 population)	7	2016	●	●
Traffic deaths (per 100,000 population)	7.8	2016	●	↑
Life expectancy at birth (years)	82.2	2016	●	↑
Adolescent fertility rate (births per 1,000 adolescent females aged 15 to 19)	19.3	2017	●	↑
Births attended by skilled health personnel (%)	96.3	2015	◐	→
Percentage of surviving infants who received 2 WHO-recommended vaccines (%)	92.0	2018	●	↑
Universal health coverage (UHC) index of service coverage (worst 0–100 best)	87.0	2017	●	↑
Subjective well-being (average ladder score, worst 0–10 best)	7.2	2019	●	↑
Gap in life expectancy at birth among regions (years)	4.0	2013	●	●
Gap in self-reported health status by income (percentage points)	2.1	2018	●	↑
Daily smokers (% of population aged 15 and over)	13.1	2018	●	↑

SDG4 – Quality Education

	Value	Year	Rating	Trend
Net primary enrollment rate (%)	NA	NA	●	●
Lower secondary completion rate (%)	NA	NA	●	●
Literacy rate (% of population aged 15 to 24)	NA	NA	●	●
Participation rate in pre-primary organized learning (% of children aged 4 to 6)	91.8	2016	●	↑
Tertiary educational attainment (% of population aged 25 to 34)	45.8	2018	●	↑
PISA score (worst 0–600 best)	502.7	2018	●	↑
Variation in science performance explained by socio-economic status (%)	13.9	2018	●	↓
Underachievers in science (% of 15-year-olds)	18.0	2018	●	↓
Resilient students in science (% of 15-year-olds)	38.4	2018	●	↑

SDG5 – Gender Equality

	Value	Year	Rating	Trend
Demand for family planning satisfied by modern methods (% of females aged 15 to 49 who are married or in unions)	* 84.7	2017	●	↑
Ratio of female-to-male mean years of education received (%)	98.4	2018	●	↑
Ratio of female-to-male labor force participation rate (%)	85.4	2019	●	↑
Seats held by women in national parliament (%)	40.8	2020	●	↑
Gender wage gap (% of male median wage)	7.9	2018	●	↑
Gender gap in time spent doing unpaid work (minutes/day)	123.0	2010	◐	●

SDG6 – Clean Water and Sanitation

	Value	Year	Rating	Trend
Population using at least basic drinking water services (%)	100.0	2017	●	●
Population using at least basic sanitation services (%)	100.0	2017	●	●
Freshwater withdrawal (% of available freshwater resources)	4.2	2010	●	●
Anthropogenic wastewater that receives treatment (%)	79.9	2018	●	●
Scarce water consumption embodied in imports (m³/capita)	18.2	2013	●	↑
Population using safely managed water services (%)	100.0	2017	●	↑
Population using safely managed sanitation services (%)	88.7	2017	◐	↑

SDG7 – Affordable and Clean Energy

	Value	Year	Rating	Trend
Population with access to electricity (%)	100.0	2017	●	↑
Population with access to clean fuels and technology for cooking (%)	100.0	2016	●	↑
CO₂ emissions from fuel combustion for electricity and heating per total electricity output (MtCO₂/TWh)	0.8	2017	●	↑
Share of renewable energy in total primary energy supply (%)	41.8	2018	●	↑

SDG8 – Decent Work and Economic Growth

	Value	Year	Rating	Trend
Adjusted GDP growth (%)	-1.0	2018	◐	●
Victims of modern slavery (per 1,000 population)	0.6	2018	●	●
Adults with an account at a bank or other financial institution or with a mobile-money-service provider (% of population aged 15 or over)	99.2	2017	●	↑
Fatal work-related accidents embodied in imports (per 100,000 population)	1.0	2010	●	↑
Employment-to-population ratio (%)	77.4	2019	●	↑
Youth not in employment, education or training (NEET) (% of population aged 15 to 29)	10.2	2018	◐	↑

SDG9 – Industry, Innovation and Infrastructure

	Value	Year	Rating	Trend
Population using the internet (%)	90.8	2017	●	↑
Mobile broadband subscriptions (per 100 population)	114.5	2018	●	↑
Logistics Performance Index: Quality of trade and transport-related infrastructure (worst 1–5 best)	4.0	2018	●	↑
The Times Higher Education Universities Ranking: Average score of top 3 universities (worst 0–100 best)	51.9	2020	●	●
Scientific and technical journal articles (per 1,000 population)	1.7	2018	●	↑
Expenditure on research and development (% of GDP)	1.2	2015	●	●
Researchers (per 1,000 employed population)	10.1	2017	●	↑
Triadic patent families filed (per million population)	15.2	2017	●	↓
Gap in internet access by income (percentage points)	19.0	2012	●	●
Women in science and engineering (% of tertiary graduates in science and engineering)	26.7	2015	●	●

SDG10 – Reduced Inequalities

	Value	Year	Rating	Trend
Gini coefficient adjusted for top income	NA	NA	●	●
Palma ratio	1.4	2014	●	●
Elderly poverty rate (% of population aged 66 or over)	10.6	2014	◐	●

SDG11 – Sustainable Cities and Communities

	Value	Year	Rating	Trend
Annual mean concentration of particulate matter of less than 2.5 microns in diameter (PM2.5) (μg/m³)	6.0	2017	●	↑
Access to improved water source, piped (% of urban population)	99.0	2017	●	↑
Satisfaction with public transport (%)	49.9	2019	●	→
Population with rent overburden (%)	NA	NA	●	●

SDG12 – Responsible Consumption and Production

	Value	Year	Rating	Trend
Electronic waste (kg/capita)	20.1	2016	●	●
Production-based SO₂ emissions (kg/capita)	142.7	2012	●	●
SO₂ emissions embodied in imports (kg/capita)	15.6	2012	●	●
Production-based nitrogen emissions (kg/capita)	94.0	2010	●	●
Nitrogen emissions embodied in imports (kg/capita)	8.2	2010	◐	●
Non-recycled municipal solid waste (kg/capita/day)	NA	NA	●	●

SDG13 – Climate Action

	Value	Year	Rating	Trend
Energy-related CO₂ emissions (tCO₂/capita)	7.8	2017	●	↓
CO₂ emissions embodied in imports (tCO₂/capita)	1.9	2015	●	→
CO₂ emissions embodied in fossil fuel exports (kg/capita)	113.7	2019	◐	●
Effective carbon rate (EUR/tCO₂)	1.5	2016	●	●

SDG14 – Life Below Water

	Value	Year	Rating	Trend
Mean area that is protected in marine sites important to biodiversity (%)	44.6	2018	◐	→
Ocean Health Index: Clean Waters score (worst 0–100 best)	78.3	2019	●	↑
Fish caught from overexploited or collapsed stocks (% of total catch)	35.3	2014	◐	↑
Fish caught by trawling (%)	43.1	2014	●	↓
Marine biodiversity threats embodied in imports (per million population)	0.4	2018	●	●

SDG15 – Life on Land

	Value	Year	Rating	Trend
Mean area that is protected in terrestrial sites important to biodiversity (%)	43.0	2018	◐	→
Mean area that is protected in freshwater sites important to biodiversity (%)	29.3	2018	◐	→
Red List Index of species survival (worst 0–1 best)	0.6	2019	●	↓
Permanent deforestation (% of forest area, 5-year average)	0.0	2018	●	●
Terrestrial and freshwater biodiversity threats embodied in imports (per million population)	2.6	2018	●	●

SDG16 – Peace, Justice and Strong Institutions

	Value	Year	Rating	Trend
Homicides (per 100,000 population)	0.7	2017	●	↑
Unsentenced detainees (% of prison population)	18.4	2018	●	↑
Percentage of population who feel safe walking alone at night in the city or area where they live	68.0	2019	◐	↑
Property Rights (worst 1–7 best)	5.9	2019	●	●
Birth registrations with civil authority (% of children under age 5)	100.0	2018	●	●
Corruption Perception Index (worst 0–100 best)	87.0	2019	●	↑
Children involved in child labor (% of population aged 5 to 14)	* 0.0	2016	●	●
Exports of major conventional weapons (TIV constant million USD per 100,000 population)	0.1	2019	●	●
Press Freedom Index (best 0–100 worst)	10.8	2019	●	↑
Persons held in prison (per 100,000 population)	221.7	2017	◐	↓

SDG17 – Partnerships for the Goals

	Value	Year	Rating	Trend
Government spending on health and education (% of GDP)	13.7	2016	●	↑
For high-income and all OECD DAC countries: International concessional public finance, including official development assistance (% of GNI)	0.2	2017	●	↓
Other countries: Government revenue excluding grants (% of GDP)	NA	NA	●	●
Corporate Tax Haven Score (best 0–100 worst)	* 0.0	2019	●	●
Financial Secrecy Score (best 0–100 worst)	64.8	2020	●	●
Shifted profits of multinationals (US$ billion)	1.9	2016	●	●

* Imputed data point

5. Country Profiles

▼ OVERALL PERFORMANCE

Index score

68.7

Regional average score

70.4

SDG Global rank 85 (OF 166)

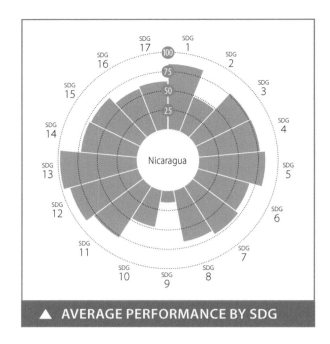

▲ AVERAGE PERFORMANCE BY SDG

▼ SPILLOVER INDEX

100 (best) to 0 (worst)

▼ CURRENT ASSESSMENT – SDG DASHBOARD

■ Major challenges   ■ Significant challenges   ■ Challenges remain   ■ SDG achieved   ■ Information unavailable

▼ SDG TRENDS

↓ Decreasing   → Stagnating   ↗ Moderately improving   ↑ On track or maintaining SDG achievement   ● Information unavailable

Notes: The full title of Goal 2 "Zero Hunger" is "End hunger, achieve food security and improved nutrition and promote sustainable agriculture".
The full title of each SDG is available here: https://sustainabledevelopment.un.org/topics/sustainabledevelopmentgoals

SDG1 – No Poverty

Indicator	Value	Year	Rating	Trend
Poverty headcount ratio at $1.90/day (%)	2.9	2020	○	→
Poverty headcount ratio at $3.20/day (%)	13.5	2020	●	↓

SDG2 – Zero Hunger

Indicator	Value	Year	Rating	Trend
Prevalence of undernourishment (%)	17.0	2017	●	→
Prevalence of stunting in children under 5 years of age (%)	17.3	2012	●	↗
Prevalence of wasting in children under 5 years of age (%)	2.2	2012	●	↑
Prevalence of obesity, BMI ≥ 30 (% of adult population)	23.7	2016	●	↓
Human Trophic Level (best 2–3 worst)	2.3	2017	●	↗
Cereal yield (tonnes per hectare of harvested land)	2.1	2017	●	↑
Sustainable Nitrogen Management Index (best 0–1.41 worst)	1.0	2015	●	↓

SDG3 – Good Health and Well-Being

Indicator	Value	Year	Rating	Trend
Maternal mortality rate (per 100,000 live births)	98	2017	○	↗
Neonatal mortality rate (per 1,000 live births)	9.4	2018	●	↑
Mortality rate, under-5 (per 1,000 live births)	18.3	2018	●	↑
Incidence of tuberculosis (per 100,000 population)	41.0	2018	●	↑
New HIV infections (per 1,000 uninfected population)	0.1	2018	●	↑
Age-standardized death rate due to cardiovascular disease, cancer, diabetes, or chronic respiratory disease in adults aged 30–70 years (%)	14.2	2016	●	↑
Age-standardized death rate attributable to household air pollution and ambient air pollution (per 100,000 population)	56	2016	●	●
Traffic deaths (per 100,000 population)	15.3	2013	●	●
Life expectancy at birth (years)	75.5	2016	●	↗
Adolescent fertility rate (births per 1,000 adolescent females aged 15 to 19)	85.0	2017	●	→
Births attended by skilled health personnel (%)	88.0	2012	●	↑
Percentage of surviving infants who received 2 WHO-recommended vaccines (%)	98	2018	●	↑
Universal health coverage (UHC) index of service coverage (worst 0–100 best)	73.0	2017	○	↑
Subjective well-being (average ladder score, worst 0–10 best)	5.8	2018	○	↓

SDG4 – Quality Education

Indicator	Value	Year	Rating	Trend
Net primary enrollment rate (%)	94.9	2010	○	●
Lower secondary completion rate (%)	66.4	2010	●	●
Literacy rate (% of population aged 15 to 24)	91.6	2015	○	●

SDG5 – Gender Equality

Indicator	Value	Year	Rating	Trend
Demand for family planning satisfied by modern methods (% of females aged 15 to 49 who are married or in unions)	92.6	2012	●	↑
Ratio of female-to-male mean years of education received (%)	109.2	2018	●	↑
Ratio of female-to-male labor force participation rate (%)	60.9	2019	○	↗
Seats held by women in national parliament (%)	47.3	2020	●	↑

SDG6 – Clean Water and Sanitation

Indicator	Value	Year	Rating	Trend
Population using at least basic drinking water services (%)	81.5	2017	●	→
Population using at least basic sanitation services (%)	74.4	2017	●	→
Freshwater withdrawal (% of available freshwater resources)	2.7	2010	●	●
Anthropogenic wastewater that receives treatment (%)	0.0	2018	●	●
Scarce water consumption embodied in imports (m³/capita)	0.8	2013	●	↑

SDG7 – Affordable and Clean Energy

Indicator	Value	Year	Rating	Trend
Population with access to electricity (%)	86.8	2017	●	↑
Population with access to clean fuels and technology for cooking (%)	52.3	2016	●	↗
CO₂ emissions from fuel combustion for electricity and heating per total electricity output (MtCO₂/TWh)	1.2	2017	○	→

SDG8 – Decent Work and Economic Growth

Indicator	Value	Year	Rating	Trend
Adjusted GDP growth (%)	-4.7	2018	●	●
Victims of modern slavery (per 1,000 population)	2.9	2018	●	●
Adults with an account at a bank or other financial institution or with a mobile-money-service provider (% of population aged 15 or over)	30.9	2017	●	↑
Unemployment rate (% of total labor force)	6.8	2019	○	↓
Fatal work-related accidents embodied in imports (per 100,000 population)	0.1	2010	●	↑

SDG9 – Industry, Innovation and Infrastructure

Indicator	Value	Year	Rating	Trend
Population using the internet (%)	27.9	2017	●	↗
Mobile broadband subscriptions (per 100 population)	18.7	2018	●	↗
Logistics Performance Index: Quality of trade and transport-related infrastructure (worst 1–5 best)	2.5	2016	●	●
The Times Higher Education Universities Ranking: Average score of top 3 universities (worst 0–100 best) *	0.0	2020	●	●
Scientific and technical journal articles (per 1,000 population)	0.0	2018	●	→
Expenditure on research and development (% of GDP)	0.1	2015	●	●

SDG10 – Reduced Inequalities

Indicator	Value	Year	Rating	Trend
Gini coefficient adjusted for top income	46.1	2014	●	●

SDG11 – Sustainable Cities and Communities

Indicator	Value	Year	Rating	Trend
Annual mean concentration of particulate matter of less than 2.5 microns in diameter (PM2.5) (µg/m³)	17.6	2017	●	↑
Access to improved water source, piped (% of urban population)	95.6	2017	○	↑
Satisfaction with public transport (%)	52.7	2018	●	↓

SDG12 – Responsible Consumption and Production

Indicator	Value	Year	Rating	Trend
Municipal solid waste (kg/capita/day)	1.1	2010	○	●
Electronic waste (kg/capita)	2.2	2016	●	●
Production-based SO₂ emissions (kg/capita)	28.3	2012	●	●
SO₂ emissions embodied in imports (kg/capita)	1.3	2012	●	●
Production-based nitrogen emissions (kg/capita)	16.4	2010	●	●
Nitrogen emissions embodied in imports (kg/capita)	0.8	2010	●	●

SDG13 – Climate Action

Indicator	Value	Year	Rating	Trend
Energy-related CO₂ emissions (tCO₂/capita)	0.9	2017	●	↑
CO₂ emissions embodied in imports (tCO₂/capita)	0.2	2015	●	↑
CO₂ emissions embodied in fossil fuel exports (kg/capita)	0.0	2017	●	●

SDG14 – Life Below Water

Indicator	Value	Year	Rating	Trend
Mean area that is protected in marine sites important to biodiversity (%)	52.9	2018	●	↑
Ocean Health Index: Clean Waters score (worst 0–100 best)	65.1	2019	○	↑
Fish caught from overexploited or collapsed stocks (% of total catch)	21.7	2014	○	↑
Fish caught by trawling (%)	21.7	2014	○	↑
Marine biodiversity threats embodied in imports (per million population)	0.0	2018	●	●

SDG15 – Life on Land

Indicator	Value	Year	Rating	Trend
Mean area that is protected in terrestrial sites important to biodiversity (%)	73.7	2018	●	↑
Mean area that is protected in freshwater sites important to biodiversity (%)	65.8	2018	●	↑
Red List Index of species survival (worst 0–1 best)	0.9	2019	○	→
Permanent deforestation (% of forest area, 5-year average)	0.7	2018	●	●
Terrestrial and freshwater biodiversity threats embodied in imports (per million population)	0.5	2018	●	●

SDG16 – Peace, Justice and Strong Institutions

Indicator	Value	Year	Rating	Trend
Homicides (per 100,000 population)	7.4	2016	●	↑
Unsentenced detainees (% of prison population)	21.4	2018	●	●
Percentage of population who feel safe walking alone at night in the city or area where they live (%)	46.2	2018	●	↓
Property Rights (worst 1–7 best)	3.6	2019	●	●
Birth registrations with civil authority (% of children under age 5)	84.7	2018	●	●
Corruption Perception Index (worst 0–100 best)	22	2019	●	↓
Children involved in child labor (% of population aged 5 to 14)	14.5	2016	●	●
Exports of major conventional weapons (TIV constant million USD per 100,000 population) *	0.0	2019	●	●
Press Freedom Index (best 0–100 worst)	35.5	2019	○	↓

SDG17 – Partnerships for the Goals

Indicator	Value	Year	Rating	Trend
Government spending on health and education (% of GDP)	9.4	2016	○	↑
For high-income and all OECD DAC countries: International concessional public finance, including official development assistance (% of GNI)	NA	NA	●	●
Other countries: Government revenue excluding grants (% of GDP)	16.8	2018	●	→
Corporate Tax Haven Score (best 0–100 worst) *	0.0	2019	●	●

* Imputed data point

5. Country Profiles

▼ OVERALL PERFORMANCE

Index score

50.1

Regional average score

53.1

SDG Global rank 157 (OF 166)

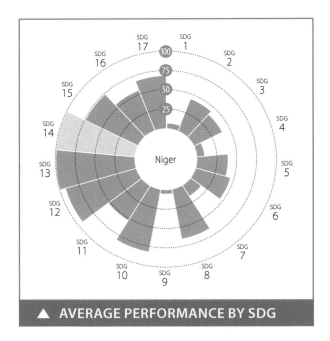

▲ AVERAGE PERFORMANCE BY SDG

▼ SPILLOVER INDEX

100 (best) to 0 (worst)

▼ CURRENT ASSESSMENT – SDG DASHBOARD

■ Major challenges   ■ Significant challenges   ■ Challenges remain   ■ SDG achieved   ■ Information unavailable

▼ SDG TRENDS

↓ Decreasing   → Stagnating   ↗ Moderately improving   ↑ On track or maintaining SDG achievement   ● Information unavailable

Notes: The full title of Goal 2 "Zero Hunger" is "End hunger, achieve food security and improved nutrition and promote sustainable agriculture".
The full title of each SDG is available here: https://sustainabledevelopment.un.org/topics/sustainabledevelopmentgoals

SDG1 – No Poverty

	Value	Year	Rating	Trend
Poverty headcount ratio at $1.90/day (%)	62.3	2020	●	→
Poverty headcount ratio at $3.20/day (%)	88.3	2020	●	→

SDG2 – Zero Hunger

	Value	Year	Rating	Trend
Prevalence of undernourishment (%)	16.5	2017	●	↓
Prevalence of stunting in children under 5 years of age (%)	42.2	2016	●	→
Prevalence of wasting in children under 5 years of age (%)	10.3	2016	●	→
Prevalence of obesity, BMI ≥ 30 (% of adult population)	5.5	2016	●	↑
Human Trophic Level (best 2–3 worst)	2.1	2017	●	↑
Cereal yield (tonnes per hectare of harvested land)	0.5	2017	●	→
Sustainable Nitrogen Management Index (best 0–1.41 worst)	0.9	2015	●	→

SDG3 – Good Health and Well-Being

	Value	Year	Rating	Trend
Maternal mortality rate (per 100,000 live births)	509	2017	●	↗
Neonatal mortality rate (per 1,000 live births)	25.2	2018	●	↗
Mortality rate, under-5 (per 1,000 live births)	83.7	2018	●	↗
Incidence of tuberculosis (per 100,000 population)	87.0	2018	●	→
New HIV infections (per 1,000 uninfected population)	0.1	2018	●	↑
Age-standardized death rate due to cardiovascular disease, cancer, diabetes, or chronic respiratory disease in adults aged 30–70 years (%)	20.0	2016	◐	→
Age-standardized death rate attributable to household air pollution and ambient air pollution (per 100,000 population)	252	2016	●	●
Traffic deaths (per 100,000 population)	26.2	2016	●	→
Life expectancy at birth (years)	59.8	2016	●	→
Adolescent fertility rate (births per 1,000 adolescent females aged 15 to 19)	186.5	2017	●	→
Births attended by skilled health personnel (%)	39.7	2015	●	↗
Percentage of surviving infants who received 2 WHO-recommended vaccines (%)	77	2018	●	↓
Universal health coverage (UHC) index of service coverage (worst 0–100 best)	37.0	2017	●	→
Subjective well-being (average ladder score, worst 0–10 best)	5.0	2019	●	↑

SDG4 – Quality Education

	Value	Year	Rating	Trend
Net primary enrollment rate (%)	65.1	2017	●	↗
Lower secondary completion rate (%)	19.0	2018	●	→
Literacy rate (% of population aged 15 to 24)	39.8	2012	●	●

SDG5 – Gender Equality

	Value	Year	Rating	Trend
Demand for family planning satisfied by modern methods (% of females aged 15 to 49 who are married or in unions)	45.5	2018	●	↗
Ratio of female-to-male mean years of education received (%)	51.9	2018	●	↓
Ratio of female-to-male labor force participation rate (%)	74.4	2019	●	↑
Seats held by women in national parliament (%)	17.0	2020	●	→

SDG6 – Clean Water and Sanitation

	Value	Year	Rating	Trend
Population using at least basic drinking water services (%)	50.3	2017	●	→
Population using at least basic sanitation services (%)	13.6	2017	●	→
Freshwater withdrawal (% of available freshwater resources)	7.5	2015	●	●
Anthropogenic wastewater that receives treatment (%)	0.0	2018	●	●
Scarce water consumption embodied in imports (m³/capita)	0.3	2013	●	↑

SDG7 – Affordable and Clean Energy

	Value	Year	Rating	Trend
Population with access to electricity (%)	20.0	2017	●	→
Population with access to clean fuels and technology for cooking (%)	1.9	2016	●	→
CO_2 emissions from fuel combustion for electricity and heating per total electricity output (MtCO₂/TWh)	3.9	2017	●	↑

SDG8 – Decent Work and Economic Growth

	Value	Year	Rating	Trend
Adjusted GDP growth (%)	-6.2	2018	●	●
Victims of modern slavery (per 1,000 population)	6.7	2018	◐	●
Adults with an account at a bank or other financial institution or with a mobile-money-service provider (% of population aged 15 or over)	15.5	2017	●	↗
Unemployment rate (% of total labor force)	0.5	2019	●	↑
Fatal work-related accidents embodied in imports (per 100,000 population)	0.0	2010	●	↑

SDG9 – Industry, Innovation and Infrastructure

	Value	Year	Rating	Trend
Population using the internet (%)	5.3	2018	●	→
Mobile broadband subscriptions (per 100 population)	3.9	2017	●	→
Logistics Performance Index: Quality of trade and transport-related infrastructure (worst 1–5 best)	2.0	2018	●	↓
The Times Higher Education Universities Ranking: Average score of top 3 universities (worst 0–100 best) *	0.0	2020	●	●
Scientific and technical journal articles (per 1,000 population)	0.0	2018	●	↓
Expenditure on research and development (% of GDP) *	0.0	2017	●	●

SDG10 – Reduced Inequalities

	Value	Year	Rating	Trend
Gini coefficient adjusted for top income	34.3	2014	◐	●

SDG11 – Sustainable Cities and Communities

	Value	Year	Rating	Trend
Annual mean concentration of particulate matter of less than 2.5 microns in diameter (PM2.5) (µg/m³)	94.1	2017	●	↓
Access to improved water source, piped (% of urban population)	82.9	2017	●	↓
Satisfaction with public transport (%)	66.7	2019	◐	↑

SDG12 – Responsible Consumption and Production

	Value	Year	Rating	Trend
Municipal solid waste (kg/capita/day)	NA	NA	●	●
Electronic waste (kg/capita)	0.4	2016	●	●
Production-based SO_2 emissions (kg/capita)	7.6	2012	●	●
SO_2 emissions embodied in imports (kg/capita)	0.3	2012	●	●
Production-based nitrogen emissions (kg/capita)	33.5	2010	◐	●
Nitrogen emissions embodied in imports (kg/capita)	0.3	2010	●	●

SDG13 – Climate Action

	Value	Year	Rating	Trend
Energy-related CO_2 emissions (tCO₂/capita)	0.1	2017	●	↑
CO_2 emissions embodied in imports (tCO₂/capita)	0.0	2015	●	↑
CO_2 emissions embodied in fossil fuel exports (kg/capita)	0.0	2015	●	●

SDG14 – Life Below Water

	Value	Year	Rating	Trend
Mean area that is protected in marine sites important to biodiversity (%)	NA	NA	●	●
Ocean Health Index: Clean Waters score (worst 0–100 best)	NA	NA	●	●
Fish caught from overexploited or collapsed stocks (% of total catch)	NA	NA	●	●
Fish caught by trawling (%)	NA	NA	●	●
Marine biodiversity threats embodied in imports (per million population)	0.0	2018	●	●

SDG15 – Life on Land

	Value	Year	Rating	Trend
Mean area that is protected in terrestrial sites important to biodiversity (%)	46.3	2018	◐	→
Mean area that is protected in freshwater sites important to biodiversity (%)	45.3	2018	◐	→
Red List Index of species survival (worst 0–1 best)	0.9	2019	●	↑
Permanent deforestation (% of forest area, 5-year average)	0.0	2018	●	●
Terrestrial and freshwater biodiversity threats embodied in imports (per million population)	0.0	2018	●	●

SDG16 – Peace, Justice and Strong Institutions

	Value	Year	Rating	Trend
Homicides (per 100,000 population)	4.4	2012	●	●
Unsentenced detainees (% of prison population)	53.9	2015	●	●
Percentage of population who feel safe walking alone at night in the city or area where they live (%)	60.3	2019	◐	↓
Property Rights (worst 1–7 best)	NA	NA	●	●
Birth registrations with civil authority (% of children under age 5)	63.9	2018	●	●
Corruption Perception Index (worst 0–100 best)	32	2019	●	↓
Children involved in child labor (% of population aged 5 to 14)	30.5	2016	●	●
Exports of major conventional weapons (TIV constant million USD per 100,000 population) *	0.0	2019	●	●
Press Freedom Index (best 0–100 worst)	29.3	2019	●	↑

SDG17 – Partnerships for the Goals

	Value	Year	Rating	Trend
Government spending on health and education (% of GDP)	5.6	2016	●	↓
For high-income and all OECD DAC countries: International concessional public finance, including official development assistance (% of GNI)	NA	NA	●	●
Other countries: Government revenue excluding grants (% of GDP)	NA	NA	●	●
Corporate Tax Haven Score (best 0–100 worst) *	0.0	2019	●	●

* Imputed data point

NIGERIA

▼ OVERALL PERFORMANCE

Index score

49.3

Regional average score

53.1

SDG Global rank 160 (OF 166)

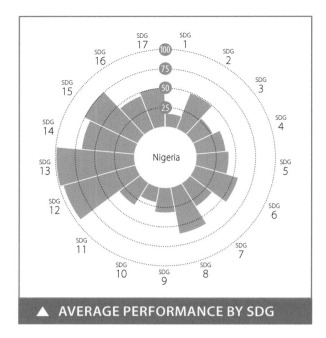

▲ AVERAGE PERFORMANCE BY SDG

▼ SPILLOVER INDEX

100 (best) to 0 (worst)

▼ CURRENT ASSESSMENT – SDG DASHBOARD

■ Major challenges ■ Significant challenges ■ Challenges remain ■ SDG achieved ■ Information unavailable

▼ SDG TRENDS

↓ Decreasing → Stagnating ↗ Moderately improving ↑ On track or maintaining SDG achievement ● Information unavailable

Notes: The full title of Goal 2 "Zero Hunger" is "End hunger, achieve food security and improved nutrition and promote sustainable agriculture".
The full title of each SDG is available here: https://sustainabledevelopment.un.org/topics/sustainabledevelopmentgoals

SDG1 – No Poverty

	Value	Year	Rating	Trend
Poverty headcount ratio at $1.90/day (%)	47.6	2020	●	↓
Poverty headcount ratio at $3.20/day (%)	76.9	2020	●	↓

SDG2 – Zero Hunger

	Value	Year	Rating	Trend
Prevalence of undernourishment (%)	13.4	2017	●	↓
Prevalence of stunting in children under 5 years of age (%)	43.6	2016	●	↑
Prevalence of wasting in children under 5 years of age (%)	10.8	2016	●	→
Prevalence of obesity, BMI ≥ 30 (% of adult population)	8.9	2016	●	↑
Human Trophic Level (best 2–3 worst)	2.0	2017	●	↑
Cereal yield (tonnes per hectare of harvested land)	1.5	2017	●	→
Sustainable Nitrogen Management Index (best 0–1.41 worst)	0.8	2015	●	↓

SDG3 – Good Health and Well-Being

	Value	Year	Rating	Trend
Maternal mortality rate (per 100,000 live births)	917	2017	●	→
Neonatal mortality rate (per 1,000 live births)	36.0	2018	●	→
Mortality rate, under-5 (per 1,000 live births)	119.9	2018	●	→
Incidence of tuberculosis (per 100,000 population)	219.0	2018	●	→
New HIV infections (per 1,000 uninfected population)	0.7	2018	●	→
Age-standardized death rate due to cardiovascular disease, cancer, diabetes, or chronic respiratory disease in adults aged 30–70 years (%)	22.5	2016	●	→
Age-standardized death rate attributable to household air pollution and ambient air pollution (per 100,000 population)	307	2016	●	●
Traffic deaths (per 100,000 population)	21.4	2016	●	↓
Life expectancy at birth (years)	55.2	2016	●	→
Adolescent fertility rate (births per 1,000 adolescent females aged 15 to 19)	107.3	2017	●	→
Births attended by skilled health personnel (%)	40.3	2017	●	→
Percentage of surviving infants who received 2 WHO-recommended vaccines (%)	57	2018	●	↑
Universal health coverage (UHC) index of service coverage (worst 0–100 best)	42.0	2017	●	→
Subjective well-being (average ladder score, worst 0–10 best)	5.3	2018	●	↑

SDG4 – Quality Education

	Value	Year	Rating	Trend
Net primary enrollment rate (%)	64.1	2010	●	●
Lower secondary completion rate (%)	47.1	2010	●	●
Literacy rate (% of population aged 15 to 24)	75.0	2018	●	●

SDG5 – Gender Equality

	Value	Year	Rating	Trend
Demand for family planning satisfied by modern methods (% of females aged 15 to 49 who are married or in unions)	42.8	2018	●	→
Ratio of female-to-male mean years of education received (%)	69.7	2018	●	→
Ratio of female-to-male labor force participation rate (%)	84.8	2019	●	↑
Seats held by women in national parliament (%)	3.6	2020	●	↓

SDG6 – Clean Water and Sanitation

	Value	Year	Rating	Trend
Population using at least basic drinking water services (%)	71.4	2017	●	↗
Population using at least basic sanitation services (%)	39.2	2017	●	→
Freshwater withdrawal (% of available freshwater resources)	9.7	2010	●	●
Anthropogenic wastewater that receives treatment (%)	0.2	2018	●	●
Scarce water consumption embodied in imports (m³/capita)	0.7	2013	●	↑

SDG7 – Affordable and Clean Energy

	Value	Year	Rating	Trend
Population with access to electricity (%)	54.4	2017	●	↓
Population with access to clean fuels and technology for cooking (%)	4.9	2016	●	→
CO₂ emissions from fuel combustion for electricity and heating per total electricity output (MtCO₂/TWh)	2.8	2017	●	→

SDG8 – Decent Work and Economic Growth

		Value	Year	Rating	Trend
Adjusted GDP growth (%)		-7.2	2018	●	●
Victims of modern slavery (per 1,000 population)	*	NA	NA	●	●
Adults with an account at a bank or other financial institution or with a mobile-money-service provider (% of population aged 15 or over)		39.7	2017	●	↓
Unemployment rate (% of total labor force)		8.1	2019	●	↓
Fatal work-related accidents embodied in imports (per 100,000 population)		0.0	2010	●	↑

SDG9 – Industry, Innovation and Infrastructure

	Value	Year	Rating	Trend
Population using the internet (%)	42.0	2017	●	↑
Mobile broadband subscriptions (per 100 population)	30.7	2018	●	↗
Logistics Performance Index: Quality of trade and transport-related infrastructure (worst 1–5 best)	2.6	2018	●	→
The Times Higher Education Universities Ranking: Average score of top 3 universities (worst 0–100 best)	34.3	2020	●	●
Scientific and technical journal articles (per 1,000 population)	0.0	2018	●	→
Expenditure on research and development (% of GDP)	0.2	2007	●	●

SDG10 – Reduced Inequalities

	Value	Year	Rating	Trend
Gini coefficient adjusted for top income	56.1	2003	●	●

SDG11 – Sustainable Cities and Communities

	Value	Year	Rating	Trend
Annual mean concentration of particulate matter of less than 2.5 microns in diameter (PM2.5) (μg/m³)	71.8	2017	●	↓
Access to improved water source, piped (% of urban population)	14.6	2017	●	↓
Satisfaction with public transport (%)	64.8	2018	●	↑

SDG12 – Responsible Consumption and Production

	Value	Year	Rating	Trend
Municipal solid waste (kg/capita/day)	0.8	2009	●	●
Electronic waste (kg/capita)	1.5	2016	●	●
Production-based SO₂ emissions (kg/capita)	2.2	2012	●	●
SO₂ emissions embodied in imports (kg/capita)	0.6	2012	●	●
Production-based nitrogen emissions (kg/capita)	10.7	2010	●	●
Nitrogen emissions embodied in imports (kg/capita)	0.3	2010	●	●

SDG13 – Climate Action

	Value	Year	Rating	Trend
Energy-related CO₂ emissions (tCO₂/capita)	0.6	2017	●	↑
CO₂ emissions embodied in imports (tCO₂/capita)	0.1	2015	●	↑
CO₂ emissions embodied in fossil fuel exports (kg/capita)	110.2	2018	●	●

SDG14 – Life Below Water

	Value	Year	Rating	Trend
Mean area that is protected in marine sites important to biodiversity (%)	NA	NA	●	●
Ocean Health Index: Clean Waters score (worst 0–100 best)	37.1	2019	●	↓
Fish caught from overexploited or collapsed stocks (% of total catch)	14.2	2014	●	↑
Fish caught by trawling (%)	28.5	2014	●	→
Marine biodiversity threats embodied in imports (per million population)	0.0	2018	●	●

SDG15 – Life on Land

	Value	Year	Rating	Trend
Mean area that is protected in terrestrial sites important to biodiversity (%)	79.6	2018	●	↑
Mean area that is protected in freshwater sites important to biodiversity (%)	59.1	2018	●	↑
Red List Index of species survival (worst 0–1 best)	0.9	2019	●	→
Permanent deforestation (% of forest area, 5-year average)	0.5	2018	●	●
Terrestrial and freshwater biodiversity threats embodied in imports (per million population)	0.0	2018	●	●

SDG16 – Peace, Justice and Strong Institutions

		Value	Year	Rating	Trend
Homicides (per 100,000 population)	*	9.8	2015	●	→
Unsentenced detainees (% of prison population)		67.8	2018	●	→
Percentage of population who feel safe walking alone at night in the city or area where they live (%)		54.3	2018	●	↓
Property Rights (worst 1–7 best)		3.6	2019	●	●
Birth registrations with civil authority (% of children under age 5)		42.6	2018	●	●
Corruption Perception Index (worst 0–100 best)		26	2019	●	→
Children involved in child labor (% of population aged 5 to 14)		24.7	2016	●	●
Exports of major conventional weapons (TIV constant million USD per 100,000 population)	*	0.0	2019	●	●
Press Freedom Index (best 0–100 worst)		36.5	2019	●	↓

SDG17 – Partnerships for the Goals

		Value	Year	Rating	Trend
Government spending on health and education (% of GDP)		NA	NA	●	●
For high-income and all OECD DAC countries: International concessional public finance, including official development assistance (% of GNI)		NA	NA	●	●
Other countries: Government revenue excluding grants (% of GDP)	*	5.0	2013	●	●
Corporate Tax Haven Score (best 0–100 worst)	*	0.0	2019	●	●

* Imputed data point

5. Country Profiles

▼ OVERALL PERFORMANCE

Index score
71.4

Regional average score
70.9

SDG Global rank 62 (OF 166)

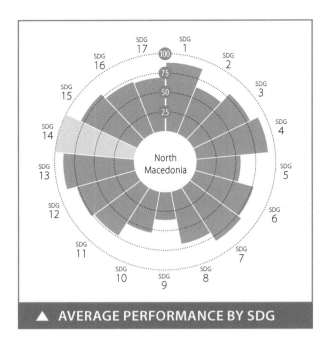

▲ AVERAGE PERFORMANCE BY SDG

▼ SPILLOVER INDEX

100 (best) to 0 (worst)

▼ CURRENT ASSESSMENT – SDG DASHBOARD

■ Major challenges ■ Significant challenges ■ Challenges remain ■ SDG achieved ■ Information unavailable

▼ SDG TRENDS

↓ Decreasing → Stagnating ↗ Moderately improving ↑ On track or maintaining SDG achievement ● Information unavailable

Notes: The full title of Goal 2 "Zero Hunger" is "End hunger, achieve food security and improved nutrition and promote sustainable agriculture".
The full title of each SDG is available here: https://sustainabledevelopment.un.org/topics/sustainabledevelopmentgoals

SDG1 – No Poverty

Indicator	Value	Year
Poverty headcount ratio at $1.90/day (%)	3.2	2020
Poverty headcount ratio at $3.20/day (%)	8.1	2020

SDG2 – Zero Hunger

Indicator	Value	Year
Prevalence of undernourishment (%)	3.2	2017
Prevalence of stunting in children under 5 years of age (%)	4.9	2011
Prevalence of wasting in children under 5 years of age (%)	1.8	2011
Prevalence of obesity, BMI ≥ 30 (% of adult population)	22.4	2016
Human Trophic Level (best 2–3 worst)	2.3	2017
Cereal yield (tonnes per hectare of harvested land)	3.9	2016
Sustainable Nitrogen Management Index (best 0–1.41 worst)	0.7	2015

SDG3 – Good Health and Well-Being

Indicator	Value	Year
Maternal mortality rate (per 100,000 live births)	7	2017
Neonatal mortality rate (per 1,000 live births)	7.4	2018
Mortality rate, under-5 (per 1,000 live births)	9.9	2018
Incidence of tuberculosis (per 100,000 population)	13.0	2018
New HIV infections (per 1,000 uninfected population)	0.0	2018
Age-standardized death rate due to cardiovascular disease, cancer, diabetes, or chronic respiratory disease in adults aged 30–70 years (%)	20.3	2016
Age-standardized death rate attributable to household air pollution and ambient air pollution (per 100,000 population)	82	2016
Traffic deaths (per 100,000 population)	6.4	2016
Life expectancy at birth (years)	75.9	2016
Adolescent fertility rate (births per 1,000 adolescent females aged 15 to 19)	15.7	2017
Births attended by skilled health personnel (%)	99.9	2016
Percentage of surviving infants who received 2 WHO-recommended vaccines (%)	83	2018
Universal health coverage (UHC) index of service coverage (worst 0–100 best)	72.0	2017
Subjective well-being (average ladder score, worst 0–10 best)	5.0	2019

SDG4 – Quality Education

Indicator	Value	Year
Net primary enrollment rate (%)	94.9	2017
Lower secondary completion rate (%)	88.1	2015
Literacy rate (% of population aged 15 to 24)	98.6	2014

SDG5 – Gender Equality

Indicator	Value	Year
Demand for family planning satisfied by modern methods (% of females aged 15 to 49 who are married or in unions)	22.3	2011
Ratio of female-to-male mean years of education received (%)	90.2	2018
Ratio of female-to-male labor force participation rate (%)	63.4	2019
Seats held by women in national parliament (%)	40.0	2020

SDG6 – Clean Water and Sanitation

Indicator	Value	Year
Population using at least basic drinking water services (%)	93.1	2017
Population using at least basic sanitation services (%)	99.1	2017
Freshwater withdrawal (% of available freshwater resources)	13.3	2005
Anthropogenic wastewater that receives treatment (%)	0.9	2018
Scarce water consumption embodied in imports (m³/capita)	6.5	2013

SDG7 – Affordable and Clean Energy

Indicator	Value	Year
Population with access to electricity (%)	100.0	2017
Population with access to clean fuels and technology for cooking (%)	65.6	2016
CO_2 emissions from fuel combustion for electricity and heating per total electricity output (MtCO2/TWh)	1.4	2017

SDG8 – Decent Work and Economic Growth

Indicator	Value	Year
Adjusted GDP growth (%)	0.2	2018
Victims of modern slavery (per 1,000 population)	8.7	2018
Adults with an account at a bank or other financial institution or with a mobile-money-service provider (% of population aged 15 or over)	76.6	2017
Unemployment rate (% of total labor force)	17.8	2019
Fatal work-related accidents embodied in imports (per 100,000 population)	0.2	2010

SDG9 – Industry, Innovation and Infrastructure

Indicator	Value	Year
Population using the internet (%)	79.2	2018
Mobile broadband subscriptions (per 100 population)	64.7	2018
Logistics Performance Index: Quality of trade and transport-related infrastructure (worst 1–5 best)	2.5	2018
The Times Higher Education Universities Ranking: Average score of top 3 universities (worst 0–100 best) *	0.0	2020
Scientific and technical journal articles (per 1,000 population)	0.2	2018
Expenditure on research and development (% of GDP)	0.4	2017

SDG10 – Reduced Inequalities

Indicator	Value	Year
Gini coefficient adjusted for top income	44.0	2015

SDG11 – Sustainable Cities and Communities

Indicator	Value	Year
Annual mean concentration of particulate matter of less than 2.5 microns in diameter (PM2.5) (μg/m³)	29.7	2017
Access to improved water source, piped (% of urban population)	98.3	2017
Satisfaction with public transport (%)	50.8	2019

SDG12 – Responsible Consumption and Production

Indicator	Value	Year
Municipal solid waste (kg/capita/day)	1.8	2016
Electronic waste (kg/capita)	7.2	2016
Production-based SO_2 emissions (kg/capita)	144.6	2012
SO_2 emissions embodied in imports (kg/capita)	3.9	2012
Production-based nitrogen emissions (kg/capita)	17.1	2010
Nitrogen emissions embodied in imports (kg/capita)	2.9	2010

SDG13 – Climate Action

Indicator	Value	Year
Energy-related CO_2 emissions (tCO2/capita)	3.5	2017
CO_2 emissions embodied in imports (tCO2/capita)	0.6	2015
CO_2 emissions embodied in fossil fuel exports (kg/capita)	2.3	2019

SDG14 – Life Below Water

Indicator	Value	Year
Mean area that is protected in marine sites important to biodiversity (%)	NA	NA
Ocean Health Index: Clean Waters score (worst 0–100 best)	NA	NA
Fish caught from overexploited or collapsed stocks (% of total catch)	NA	NA
Fish caught by trawling (%)	NA	NA
Marine biodiversity threats embodied in imports (per million population)	0.0	2018

SDG15 – Life on Land

Indicator	Value	Year
Mean area that is protected in terrestrial sites important to biodiversity (%)	23.6	2018
Mean area that is protected in freshwater sites important to biodiversity (%)	93.6	2018
Red List Index of species survival (worst 0–1 best)	1.0	2019
Permanent deforestation (% of forest area, 5-year average)	0.0	2018
Terrestrial and freshwater biodiversity threats embodied in imports (per million population)	0.7	2018

SDG16 – Peace, Justice and Strong Institutions

Indicator	Value	Year
Homicides (per 100,000 population)	1.5	2017
Unsentenced detainees (% of prison population)	10.0	2018
Percentage of population who feel safe walking alone at night in the city or area where they live (%)	68.3	2019
Property Rights (worst 1–7 best)	3.6	2019
Birth registrations with civil authority (% of children under age 5)	99.7	2018
Corruption Perception Index (worst 0–100 best)	35	2019
Children involved in child labor (% of population aged 5 to 14)	12.5	2016
Exports of major conventional weapons (TIV constant million USD per 100,000 population) *	0.0	2019
Press Freedom Index (best 0–100 worst)	31.7	2019

SDG17 – Partnerships for the Goals

Indicator	Value	Year
Government spending on health and education (% of GDP)	8.0	2002
For high-income and all OECD DAC countries: International concessional public finance, including official development assistance (% of GNI)	NA	NA
Other countries: Government revenue excluding grants (% of GDP)	26.8	2018
Corporate Tax Haven Score (best 0–100 worst) *	0.0	2019

* Imputed data point

5. Country Profiles

▼ OVERALL PERFORMANCE

Index score

80.8

Regional average score

77.3

SDG Global rank 6 (OF 166)

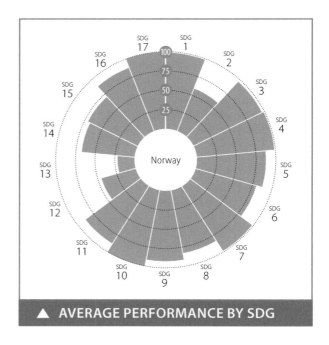

▲ AVERAGE PERFORMANCE BY SDG

▼ SPILLOVER INDEX

100 (best) to 0 (worst)

▼ CURRENT ASSESSMENT – SDG DASHBOARD

■ Major challenges   ■ Significant challenges   ■ Challenges remain   ■ SDG achieved   ■ Information unavailable

▼ SDG TRENDS

↓ Decreasing   → Stagnating   ↗ Moderately improving   ↑ On track or maintaining SDG achievement   ● Information unavailable

Notes: The full title of Goal 2 "Zero Hunger" is "End hunger, achieve food security and improved nutrition and promote sustainable agriculture".
The full title of each SDG is available here: https://sustainabledevelopment.un.org/topics/sustainabledevelopmentgoals

SDG1 – No Poverty

Indicator	Value	Year	Rating	Trend
Poverty headcount ratio at $1.90/day (%)	0.3	2020	●	↑
Poverty headcount ratio at $3.20/day (%)	0.3	2020	●	↑
Poverty rate after taxes and transfers (%)	8.4	2017	●	↑

SDG2 – Zero Hunger

Indicator	Value	Year	Rating	Trend
Prevalence of undernourishment (%)	2.5	2017	●	↑
Prevalence of stunting in children under 5 years of age (%)	* 2.6	2016	●	↑
Prevalence of wasting in children under 5 years of age (%)	* 0.7	2016	●	↑
Prevalence of obesity, BMI ≥ 30 (% of adult population)	23.1	2016	●	↓
Human Trophic Level (best 2–3 worst)	2.5	2017	●	→
Cereal yield (tonnes per hectare of harvested land)	4.5	2017	●	↑
Sustainable Nitrogen Management Index (best 0–1.41 worst)	0.8	2015	●	↓
Yield gap closure (% of potential yield)	56.9	2015	●	●

SDG3 – Good Health and Well-Being

Indicator	Value	Year	Rating	Trend
Maternal mortality rate (per 100,000 live births)	2	2017	●	↑
Neonatal mortality rate (per 1,000 live births)	1.5	2018	●	↑
Mortality rate, under-5 (per 1,000 live births)	2.5	2018	●	↑
Incidence of tuberculosis (per 100,000 population)	4.1	2018	●	↑
New HIV infections (per 1,000 uninfected population)	0.0	2018	●	↑
Age-standardized death rate due to cardiovascular disease, cancer, diabetes, or chronic respiratory disease in adults aged 30–70 years (%)	9.2	2016	●	↑
Age-standardized death rate attributable to household air pollution and ambient air pollution (per 100,000 population)	9	2016	●	●
Traffic deaths (per 100,000 population)	2.7	2016	●	↑
Life expectancy at birth (years)	82.5	2016	●	↑
Adolescent fertility rate (births per 1,000 adolescent females aged 15 to 19)	5.1	2017	●	↑
Births attended by skilled health personnel (%)	99.1	2016	●	↑
Percentage of surviving infants who received 2 WHO-recommended vaccines (%)	96.0	2018	●	↑
Universal health coverage (UHC) index of service coverage (worst 0–100 best)	87.0	2017	●	↑
Subjective well-being (average ladder score, worst 0–10 best)	7.4	2019	●	↑
Gap in life expectancy at birth among regions (years)	1.3	2016	●	↑
Gap in self-reported health status by income (percentage points)	16.6	2017	●	↑
Daily smokers (% of population aged 15 and over)	12.0	2018	●	↑

SDG4 – Quality Education

Indicator	Value	Year	Rating	Trend
Net primary enrollment rate (%)	* 99.4	2017	●	↑
Lower secondary completion rate (%)	* 99.4	2017	●	↑
Literacy rate (% of population aged 15 to 24)	NA	NA	●	●
Participation rate in pre-primary organized learning (% of children aged 4 to 6)	96.2	2017	●	↑
Tertiary educational attainment (% of population aged 25 to 34)	48.2	2018	●	↑
PISA score (worst 0–600 best)	496.7	2018	●	↑
Variation in science performance explained by socio-economic status (%)	8.9	2018	●	↑
Underachievers in science (% of 15-year-olds)	20.8	2018	●	↓
Resilient students in science (% of 15-year-olds)	25.7	2018	●	↓

SDG5 – Gender Equality

Indicator	Value	Year	Rating	Trend
Demand for family planning satisfied by modern methods (% of females aged 15 to 49 who are married or in unions)	* 84.3	2017	●	↑
Ratio of female-to-male mean years of education received (%)	100.8	2018	●	↑
Ratio of female-to-male labor force participation rate (%)	90.5	2019	●	↑
Seats held by women in national parliament (%)	41.4	2020	●	↑
Gender wage gap (% of male median wage)	7.1	2015	●	●
Gender gap in time spent doing unpaid work (minutes/day)	58.9	2011	●	●

SDG6 – Clean Water and Sanitation

Indicator	Value	Year	Rating	Trend
Population using at least basic drinking water services (%)	100.0	2017	●	●
Population using at least basic sanitation services (%)	98.1	2017	●	●
Freshwater withdrawal (% of available freshwater resources)	2.3	2005	●	●
Anthropogenic wastewater that receives treatment (%)	64.3	2018	●	●
Scarce water consumption embodied in imports (m³/capita)	60.1	2013	●	↓
Population using safely managed water services (%)	98.3	2017	●	↑
Population using safely managed sanitation services (%)	76.3	2017	●	→

SDG7 – Affordable and Clean Energy

Indicator	Value	Year	Rating	Trend
Population with access to electricity (%)	100.0	2017	●	●
Population with access to clean fuels and technology for cooking (%)	100.0	2016	●	↑
CO₂ emissions from fuel combustion for electricity and heating per total electricity output (MtCO₂/TWh)	0.2	2017	●	↑
Share of renewable energy in total primary energy supply (%)	47.1	2018	●	↑

SDG8 – Decent Work and Economic Growth

Indicator	Value	Year	Rating	Trend
Adjusted GDP growth (%)	-0.6	2018	●	●
Victims of modern slavery (per 1,000 population)	1.8	2018	●	●
Adults with an account at a bank or other financial institution or with a mobile-money-service provider (% of population aged 15 or over)	99.7	2017	●	↑
Fatal work-related accidents embodied in imports (per 100,000 population)	2.3	2010	●	↑
Employment-to-population ratio (%)	75.3	2019	●	↑
Youth not in employment, education or training (NEET) (% of population aged 15 to 29)	8.7	2018	●	↑

SDG9 – Industry, Innovation and Infrastructure

Indicator	Value	Year	Rating	Trend
Population using the internet (%)	96.5	2018	●	↑
Mobile broadband subscriptions (per 100 population)	99.2	2018	●	↑
Logistics Performance Index: Quality of trade and transport-related infrastructure (worst 1–5 best)	3.7	2018	●	↑
The Times Higher Education Universities Ranking: Average score of top 3 universities (worst 0–100 best)	50.4	2020	●	●
Scientific and technical journal articles (per 1,000 population)	2.2	2018	●	↑
Expenditure on research and development (% of GDP)	2.1	2017	●	↑
Researchers (per 1,000 employed population)	12.2	2018	●	↑
Triadic patent families filed (per million population)	18.8	2017	●	↓
Gap in internet access by income (percentage points)	3.6	2019	●	↑
Women in science and engineering (% of tertiary graduates in science and engineering)	26.6	2015	●	●

SDG10 – Reduced Inequalities

Indicator	Value	Year	Rating	Trend
Gini coefficient adjusted for top income	27.4	2015	●	↑
Palma ratio	0.9	2017	●	↑
Elderly poverty rate (% of population aged 66 or over)	4.3	2017	●	↑

SDG11 – Sustainable Cities and Communities

Indicator	Value	Year	Rating	Trend
Annual mean concentration of particulate matter of less than 2.5 microns in diameter (PM2.5) (µg/m³)	7.0	2017	●	↑
Access to improved water source, piped (% of urban population)	99.0	2017	●	↑
Satisfaction with public transport (%)	60.2	2019	●	↗
Population with rent overburden (%)	7.4	2017	●	↑

SDG12 – Responsible Consumption and Production

Indicator	Value	Year	Rating	Trend
Electronic waste (kg/capita)	28.5	2016	●	●
Production-based SO₂ emissions (kg/capita)	94.2	2012	●	●
SO₂ emissions embodied in imports (kg/capita)	27.8	2012	●	●
Production-based nitrogen emissions (kg/capita)	43.0	2010	●	●
Nitrogen emissions embodied in imports (kg/capita)	20.4	2010	●	●
Non-recycled municipal solid waste (kg/capita/day)	1.2	2018	●	●

SDG13 – Climate Action

Indicator	Value	Year	Rating	Trend
Energy-related CO₂ emissions (tCO₂/capita)	8.8	2017	●	→
CO₂ emissions embodied in imports (tCO₂/capita)	3.7	2015	●	→
CO₂ emissions embodied in fossil fuel exports (kg/capita)	45780.3	2018	●	●
Effective carbon rate (EUR/tCO₂)	51.0	2016	●	●

SDG14 – Life Below Water

Indicator	Value	Year	Rating	Trend
Mean area that is protected in marine sites important to biodiversity (%)	55.2	2018	●	↑
Ocean Health Index: Clean Waters score (worst 0–100 best)	77.0	2019	●	↑
Fish caught from overexploited or collapsed stocks (% of total catch)	21.2	2014	●	↑
Fish caught by trawling (%)	40.3	2014	●	↓
Marine biodiversity threats embodied in imports (per million population)	0.4	2018	●	●

SDG15 – Life on Land

Indicator	Value	Year	Rating	Trend
Mean area that is protected in terrestrial sites important to biodiversity (%)	51.3	2018	●	↑
Mean area that is protected in freshwater sites important to biodiversity (%)	55.9	2018	●	↑
Red List Index of species survival (worst 0–1 best)	0.9	2019	●	↑
Permanent deforestation (% of forest area, 5-year average)	0.0	2018	●	●
Terrestrial and freshwater biodiversity threats embodied in imports (per million population)	3.8	2018	●	●

SDG16 – Peace, Justice and Strong Institutions

Indicator	Value	Year	Rating	Trend
Homicides (per 100,000 population)	0.5	2017	●	↑
Unsentenced detainees (% of prison population)	25.2	2018	●	↑
Percentage of population who feel safe walking alone at night in the city or area where they live (%)	92.2	2019	●	↑
Property Rights (worst 1–7 best)	5.8	2019	●	●
Birth registrations with civil authority (% of children under age 5)	100.0	2018	●	●
Corruption Perception Index (worst 0–100 best)	84.0	2019	●	↑
Children involved in child labor (% of population aged 5 to 14)	* 0.0	2016	●	●
Exports of major conventional weapons (TIV constant million USD per 100,000 population)	2.1	2019	●	●
Press Freedom Index (best 0–100 worst)	7.8	2019	●	↑
Persons held in prison (per 100,000 population)	63.6	2017	●	↑

SDG17 – Partnerships for the Goals

Indicator	Value	Year	Rating	Trend
Government spending on health and education (% of GDP)	16.9	2016	●	↑
For high-income and all OECD DAC countries: International concessional public finance, including official development assistance (% of GNI)	1.0	2017	●	↑
Other countries: Government revenue excluding grants (% of GDP)	NA	NA	●	●
Corporate Tax Haven Score (best 0–100 worst)	* 0.0	2019	●	●
Financial Secrecy Score (best 0–100 worst)	44.3	2020	●	●
Shifted profits of multinationals (US$ billion)	6.2	2016	●	●

* Imputed data point

5. Country Profiles

▼ OVERALL PERFORMANCE

Index score

69.7

Regional average score

66.3

SDG Global rank 76 (OF 166)

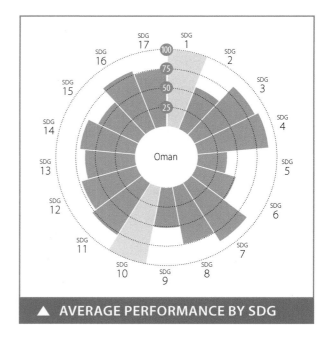

▲ AVERAGE PERFORMANCE BY SDG

▼ SPILLOVER INDEX

100 (best) to 0 (worst)

▼ CURRENT ASSESSMENT – SDG DASHBOARD

■ Major challenges ■ Significant challenges ■ Challenges remain ■ SDG achieved ■ Information unavailable

▼ SDG TRENDS

↓ Decreasing → Stagnating ↗ Moderately improving ↑ On track or maintaining SDG achievement ● Information unavailable

Notes: The full title of Goal 2 "Zero Hunger" is "End hunger, achieve food security and improved nutrition and promote sustainable agriculture".
The full title of each SDG is available here: https://sustainabledevelopment.un.org/topics/sustainabledevelopmentgoals

OMAN

SDG1 – No Poverty

		Value	Year	Rating	Trend
Poverty headcount ratio at $1.90/day (%)	*	NA	NA	●	●
Poverty headcount ratio at $3.20/day (%)	*	NA	NA	●	●

SDG2 – Zero Hunger

	Value	Year	Rating	Trend
Prevalence of undernourishment (%)	6.8	2017	●	↑
Prevalence of stunting in children under 5 years of age (%)	14.1	2014	●	↓
Prevalence of wasting in children under 5 years of age (%)	7.5	2014	●	→
Prevalence of obesity, BMI ≥ 30 (% of adult population)	27.0	2016	●	↓
Human Trophic Level (best 2–3 worst)	2.3	2017	●	↗
Cereal yield (tonnes per hectare of harvested land)	13.0	2017	●	↑
Sustainable Nitrogen Management Index (best 0–1.41 worst)	0.7	2015	●	↗

SDG3 – Good Health and Well-Being

	Value	Year	Rating	Trend
Maternal mortality rate (per 100,000 live births)	19	2017	●	↑
Neonatal mortality rate (per 1,000 live births)	5.1	2018	●	↑
Mortality rate, under-5 (per 1,000 live births)	11.4	2018	●	↑
Incidence of tuberculosis (per 100,000 population)	5.9	2018	●	↑
New HIV infections (per 1,000 uninfected population)	0.1	2018	●	↑
Age-standardized death rate due to cardiovascular disease, cancer, diabetes, or chronic respiratory disease in adults aged 30–70 years (%)	17.8	2016	●	↑
Age-standardized death rate attributable to household air pollution and ambient air pollution (per 100,000 population)	54	2016	●	●
Traffic deaths (per 100,000 population)	16.1	2016	●	↑
Life expectancy at birth (years)	77.0	2016	●	↗
Adolescent fertility rate (births per 1,000 adolescent females aged 15 to 19)	13.1	2017	●	↑
Births attended by skilled health personnel (%)	99.1	2014	●	●
Percentage of surviving infants who received 2 WHO-recommended vaccines (%)	99	2018	●	↑
Universal health coverage (UHC) index of service coverage (worst 0–100 best)	69.0	2017	●	→
Subjective well-being (average ladder score, worst 0–10 best)	6.9	2011	●	●

SDG4 – Quality Education

	Value	Year	Rating	Trend
Net primary enrollment rate (%)	86.3	2018	●	↓
Lower secondary completion rate (%)	103.5	2018	●	↑
Literacy rate (% of population aged 15 to 24)	98.6	2018	●	●

SDG5 – Gender Equality

	Value	Year	Rating	Trend
Demand for family planning satisfied by modern methods (% of females aged 15 to 49 who are married or in unions)	39.6	2014	●	→
Ratio of female-to-male mean years of education received (%)	112.8	2018	●	↑
Ratio of female-to-male labor force participation rate (%)	34.6	2019	●	→
Seats held by women in national parliament (%)	2.3	2020	●	→

SDG6 – Clean Water and Sanitation

	Value	Year	Rating	Trend
Population using at least basic drinking water services (%)	91.9	2017	●	↑
Population using at least basic sanitation services (%)	100.0	2017	●	↑
Freshwater withdrawal (% of available freshwater resources)	90.1	2005	●	●
Anthropogenic wastewater that receives treatment (%)	13.4	2018	●	●
Scarce water consumption embodied in imports (m³/capita)	55.5	2013	●	→

SDG7 – Affordable and Clean Energy

	Value	Year	Rating	Trend
Population with access to electricity (%)	100.0	2017	●	↑
Population with access to clean fuels and technology for cooking (%)	95.2	2016	●	↑
CO_2 emissions from fuel combustion for electricity and heating per total electricity output (MtCO2/TWh)	1.9	2017	●	↑

SDG8 – Decent Work and Economic Growth

		Value	Year	Rating	Trend
Adjusted GDP growth (%)		-3.9	2018	●	●
Victims of modern slavery (per 1,000 population)	*	NA	NA	●	●
Adults with an account at a bank or other financial institution or with a mobile-money-service provider (% of population aged 15 or over)		73.6	2011	●	●
Unemployment rate (% of total labor force)		2.7	2019	●	↑
Fatal work-related accidents embodied in imports (per 100,000 population)		1.3	2010	●	→

SDG9 – Industry, Innovation and Infrastructure

	Value	Year	Rating	Trend
Population using the internet (%)	80.2	2017	●	↑
Mobile broadband subscriptions (per 100 population)	85.2	2018	●	↑
Logistics Performance Index: Quality of trade and transport-related infrastructure (worst 1–5 best)	3.2	2018	●	↑
The Times Higher Education Universities Ranking: Average score of top 3 universities (worst 0–100 best)	25.2	2020	●	●
Scientific and technical journal articles (per 1,000 population)	0.2	2018	●	→
Expenditure on research and development (% of GDP)	0.2	2017	●	→

SDG10 – Reduced Inequalities

	Value	Year	Rating	Trend
Gini coefficient adjusted for top income	NA	NA	●	●

SDG11 – Sustainable Cities and Communities

	Value	Year	Rating	Trend
Annual mean concentration of particulate matter of less than 2.5 microns in diameter (PM2.5) (µg/m³)	41.1	2017	●	↓
Access to improved water source, piped (% of urban population)	93.2	2017	●	↑
Satisfaction with public transport (%)	72.8	2011	●	●

SDG12 – Responsible Consumption and Production

	Value	Year	Rating	Trend
Municipal solid waste (kg/capita/day)	1.2	2014	●	●
Electronic waste (kg/capita)	14.9	2016	●	●
Production-based SO_2 emissions (kg/capita)	49.4	2012	●	●
SO_2 emissions embodied in imports (kg/capita)	8.0	2012	●	●
Production-based nitrogen emissions (kg/capita)	23.0	2010	●	●
Nitrogen emissions embodied in imports (kg/capita)	7.7	2010	●	●

SDG13 – Climate Action

	Value	Year	Rating	Trend
Energy-related CO_2 emissions (tCO2/capita)	13.2	2017	●	↗
CO_2 emissions embodied in imports (tCO2/capita)	1.4	2015	●	↑
CO_2 emissions embodied in fossil fuel exports (kg/capita)	4773.1	2018	●	●

SDG14 – Life Below Water

	Value	Year	Rating	Trend
Mean area that is protected in marine sites important to biodiversity (%)	10.4	2018	●	→
Ocean Health Index: Clean Waters score (worst 0–100 best)	66.1	2019	●	↓
Fish caught from overexploited or collapsed stocks (% of total catch)	4.5	2014	●	↑
Fish caught by trawling (%)	0.4	2014	●	↑
Marine biodiversity threats embodied in imports (per million population)	0.1	2018	●	●

SDG15 – Life on Land

	Value	Year	Rating	Trend
Mean area that is protected in terrestrial sites important to biodiversity (%)	11.1	2018	●	→
Mean area that is protected in freshwater sites important to biodiversity (%)	NA	NA	●	●
Red List Index of species survival (worst 0–1 best)	0.9	2019	●	→
Permanent deforestation (% of forest area, 5-year average)	NA	NA	●	●
Terrestrial and freshwater biodiversity threats embodied in imports (per million population)	0.7	2018	●	●

SDG16 – Peace, Justice and Strong Institutions

		Value	Year	Rating	Trend
Homicides (per 100,000 population)	*	0.5	2017	●	↑
Unsentenced detainees (% of prison population)		NA	NA	●	●
Percentage of population who feel safe walking alone at night in the city or area where they live (%)		NA	NA	●	●
Property Rights (worst 1–7 best)		5.6	2019	●	●
Birth registrations with civil authority (% of children under age 5)		100.0	2018	●	●
Corruption Perception Index (worst 0–100 best)		52	2019	●	↑
Children involved in child labor (% of population aged 5 to 14)		NA	NA	●	●
Exports of major conventional weapons (TIV constant million USD per 100,000 population)		0.1	2019	●	●
Press Freedom Index (best 0–100 worst)		43.4	2019	●	↓

SDG17 – Partnerships for the Goals

		Value	Year	Rating	Trend
Government spending on health and education (% of GDP)		7.4	2013	●	●
For high-income and all OECD DAC countries: International concessional public finance, including official development assistance (% of GNI)		NA	NA	●	●
Other countries: Government revenue excluding grants (% of GDP)	*	NA	NA	●	●
Corporate Tax Haven Score (best 0–100 worst)	*	0.0	2019	●	●

* Imputed data point

5. Country Profiles

▼ OVERALL PERFORMANCE

Index score

56.2

Regional average score

67.2

SDG Global rank **134** (OF 166)

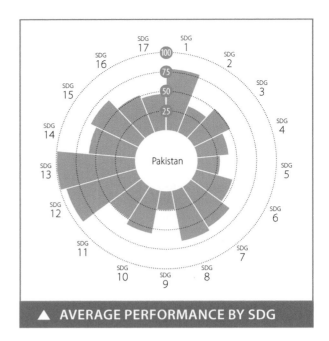

▲ AVERAGE PERFORMANCE BY SDG

▼ SPILLOVER INDEX

100 (best) to 0 (worst)

▼ CURRENT ASSESSMENT – SDG DASHBOARD

- ■ Major challenges
- ■ Significant challenges
- ■ Challenges remain
- ■ SDG achieved
- ■ Information unavailable

▼ SDG TRENDS

- ↓ Decreasing
- → Stagnating
- ↗ Moderately improving
- ↑ On track or maintaining SDG achievement
- ● Information unavailable

Notes: The full title of Goal 2 "Zero Hunger" is "End hunger, achieve food security and improved nutrition and promote sustainable agriculture".
The full title of each SDG is available here: https://sustainabledevelopment.un.org/topics/sustainabledevelopmentgoals

SDG1 – No Poverty

	Value	Year	Rating	Trend
Poverty headcount ratio at $1.90/day (%)	0.9	2020	●	↑
Poverty headcount ratio at $3.20/day (%)	20.7	2020	●	↑

SDG2 – Zero Hunger

	Value	Year	Rating	Trend
Prevalence of undernourishment (%)	20.3	2017	●	→
Prevalence of stunting in children under 5 years of age (%)	45.0	2012	●	→
Prevalence of wasting in children under 5 years of age (%)	10.5	2012	●	↗
Prevalence of obesity, BMI ≥ 30 (% of adult population)	8.6	2016	●	↑
Human Trophic Level (best 2–3 worst)	2.5	2017	●	↓
Cereal yield (tonnes per hectare of harvested land)	3.2	2017	●	↑
Sustainable Nitrogen Management Index (best 0–1.41 worst)	0.9	2015	●	→

SDG3 – Good Health and Well-Being

	Value	Year	Rating	Trend
Maternal mortality rate (per 100,000 live births)	140	2017	●	↑
Neonatal mortality rate (per 1,000 live births)	42.0	2018	●	→
Mortality rate, under-5 (per 1,000 live births)	69.3	2018	●	↗
Incidence of tuberculosis (per 100,000 population)	265.0	2018	●	→
New HIV infections (per 1,000 uninfected population)	0.1	2018	●	↑
Age-standardized death rate due to cardiovascular disease, cancer, diabetes, or chronic respiratory disease in adults aged 30–70 years (%)	24.7	2016	●	→
Age-standardized death rate attributable to household air pollution and ambient air pollution (per 100,000 population)	174	2016	●	●
Traffic deaths (per 100,000 population)	14.3	2016	●	↓
Life expectancy at birth (years)	66.5	2016	●	→
Adolescent fertility rate (births per 1,000 adolescent females aged 15 to 19)	38.8	2017	●	↗
Births attended by skilled health personnel (%)	69.3	2018	●	↑
Percentage of surviving infants who received 2 WHO-recommended vaccines (%)	75	2018	●	↗
Universal health coverage (UHC) index of service coverage (worst 0–100 best)	45.0	2017	●	↗
Subjective well-being (average ladder score, worst 0–10 best)	5.5	2018	●	↑

SDG4 – Quality Education

	Value	Year	Rating	Trend
Net primary enrollment rate (%)	67.6	2018	●	→
Lower secondary completion rate (%)	48.2	2018	●	→
Literacy rate (% of population aged 15 to 24)	74.5	2017	●	●

SDG5 – Gender Equality

	Value	Year	Rating	Trend
Demand for family planning satisfied by modern methods (% of females aged 15 to 49 who are married or in unions)	48.5	2018	●	↗
Ratio of female-to-male mean years of education received (%)	58.5	2018	●	→
Ratio of female-to-male labor force participation rate (%)	29.6	2019	●	→
Seats held by women in national parliament (%)	20.2	2020	●	↓

SDG6 – Clean Water and Sanitation

	Value	Year	Rating	Trend
Population using at least basic drinking water services (%)	91.5	2017	●	↗
Population using at least basic sanitation services (%)	59.9	2017	●	↗
Freshwater withdrawal (% of available freshwater resources)	112.5	2010	●	●
Anthropogenic wastewater that receives treatment (%)	0.1	2018	●	●
Scarce water consumption embodied in imports (m³/capita)	0.3	2013	●	↑

SDG7 – Affordable and Clean Energy

	Value	Year	Rating	Trend
Population with access to electricity (%)	70.8	2017	●	↓
Population with access to clean fuels and technology for cooking (%)	43.3	2016	●	→
CO₂ emissions from fuel combustion for electricity and heating per total electricity output (MtCO₂/TWh)	1.5	2017	●	→

SDG8 – Decent Work and Economic Growth

	Value	Year	Rating	Trend
Adjusted GDP growth (%)	-1.8	2018	●	●
Victims of modern slavery (per 1,000 population)	* NA	NA	●	●
Adults with an account at a bank or other financial institution or with a mobile-money-service provider (% of population aged 15 or over)	21.3	2017	●	↗
Unemployment rate (% of total labor force)	4.5	2019	●	↑
Fatal work-related accidents embodied in imports (per 100,000 population)	0.0	2010	●	↑

SDG9 – Industry, Innovation and Infrastructure

	Value	Year	Rating	Trend
Population using the internet (%)	15.5	2017	●	→
Mobile broadband subscriptions (per 100 population)	29.2	2018	●	↑
Logistics Performance Index: Quality of trade and transport-related infrastructure (worst 1–5 best)	2.2	2018	●	↓
The Times Higher Education Universities Ranking: Average score of top 3 universities (worst 0–100 best)	32.5	2020	●	●
Scientific and technical journal articles (per 1,000 population)	0.1	2018	●	→
Expenditure on research and development (% of GDP)	0.2	2017	●	↓

SDG10 – Reduced Inequalities

	Value	Year	Rating	Trend
Gini coefficient adjusted for top income	43.0	2015	●	●

SDG11 – Sustainable Cities and Communities

	Value	Year	Rating	Trend
Annual mean concentration of particulate matter of less than 2.5 microns in diameter (PM2.5) (µg/m³)	58.3	2017	●	→
Access to improved water source, piped (% of urban population)	51.3	2017	●	↓
Satisfaction with public transport (%)	60.2	2018	●	↗

SDG12 – Responsible Consumption and Production

	Value	Year	Rating	Trend
Municipal solid waste (kg/capita/day)	1.1	2017	●	●
Electronic waste (kg/capita)	1.6	2016	●	●
Production-based SO₂ emissions (kg/capita)	5.5	2012	●	●
SO₂ emissions embodied in imports (kg/capita)	0.2	2012	●	●
Production-based nitrogen emissions (kg/capita)	15.1	2010	●	●
Nitrogen emissions embodied in imports (kg/capita)	0.1	2010	●	●

SDG13 – Climate Action

	Value	Year	Rating	Trend
Energy-related CO₂ emissions (tCO₂/capita)	0.9	2017	●	↑
CO₂ emissions embodied in imports (tCO₂/capita)	0.0	2015	●	↑
CO₂ emissions embodied in fossil fuel exports (kg/capita)	0.0	2018	●	●

SDG14 – Life Below Water

	Value	Year	Rating	Trend
Mean area that is protected in marine sites important to biodiversity (%)	39.3	2018	●	→
Ocean Health Index: Clean Waters score (worst 0–100 best)	45.5	2019	●	→
Fish caught from overexploited or collapsed stocks (% of total catch)	40.3	2014	●	↓
Fish caught by trawling (%)	23.9	2014	●	→
Marine biodiversity threats embodied in imports (per million population)	0.0	2018	●	●

SDG15 – Life on Land

	Value	Year	Rating	Trend
Mean area that is protected in terrestrial sites important to biodiversity (%)	36.6	2018	●	→
Mean area that is protected in freshwater sites important to biodiversity (%)	37.0	2018	●	→
Red List Index of species survival (worst 0–1 best)	0.9	2019	●	↓
Permanent deforestation (% of forest area, 5-year average)	0.0	2018	●	●
Terrestrial and freshwater biodiversity threats embodied in imports (per million population)	0.0	2018	●	●

SDG16 – Peace, Justice and Strong Institutions

	Value	Year	Rating	Trend
Homicides (per 100,000 population)	4.2	2017	●	↑
Unsentenced detainees (% of prison population)	69.1	2015	●	●
Percentage of population who feel safe walking alone at night in the city or area where they live (%)	68.5	2018	●	↑
Property Rights (worst 1–7 best)	4.1	2019	●	●
Birth registrations with civil authority (% of children under age 5)	42.2	2018	●	●
Corruption Perception Index (worst 0–100 best)	32	2019	●	→
Children involved in child labor (% of population aged 5 to 14)	NA	NA	●	●
Exports of major conventional weapons (TIV constant million USD per 100,000 population)	0.0	2019	●	●
Press Freedom Index (best 0–100 worst)	45.8	2019	●	↗

SDG17 – Partnerships for the Goals

	Value	Year	Rating	Trend
Government spending on health and education (% of GDP)	3.8	2016	●	→
For high-income and all OECD DAC countries: International concessional public finance, including official development assistance (% of GNI)	NA	NA	●	●
Other countries: Government revenue excluding grants (% of GDP)	* 14.4	2015	●	●
Corporate Tax Haven Score (best 0–100 worst)	* 0.0	2019	●	●

* Imputed data point

PALAU

Oceania

▼ OVERALL PERFORMANCE

Index score

na

Regional average score

49.6

SDG Global rank NA (OF 166)

▼ SPILLOVER INDEX

100 (best) to 0 (worst)

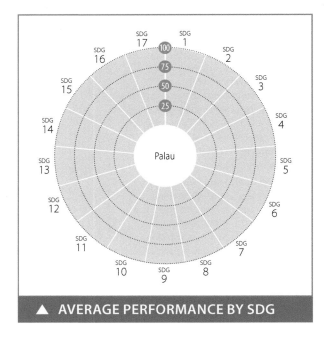

▲ AVERAGE PERFORMANCE BY SDG

▼ CURRENT ASSESSMENT – SDG DASHBOARD

■ Major challenges　■ Significant challenges　■ Challenges remain　■ SDG achieved　■ Information unavailable

▼ SDG TRENDS

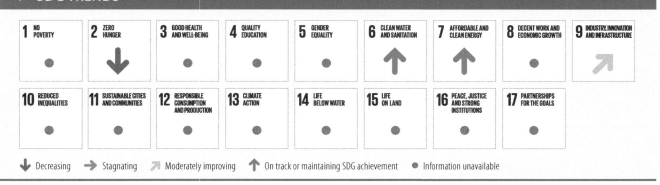

↓ Decreasing　→ Stagnating　↗ Moderately improving　↑ On track or maintaining SDG achievement　● Information unavailable

Notes: The full title of Goal 2 "Zero Hunger" is "End hunger, achieve food security and improved nutrition and promote sustainable agriculture".
The full title of each SDG is available here: https://sustainabledevelopment.un.org/topics/sustainabledevelopmentgoals

SDG1 – No Poverty

	Value	Year	Rating	Trend
Poverty headcount ratio at $1.90/day (%)	NA	NA	●	●
Poverty headcount ratio at $3.20/day (%)	NA	NA	●	●

SDG2 – Zero Hunger

		Value	Year	Rating	Trend
Prevalence of undernourishment (%)	*	1.2	2017	●	●
Prevalence of stunting in children under 5 years of age (%)	*	2.6	2016	●	●
Prevalence of wasting in children under 5 years of age (%)	*	0.7	2016	●	●
Prevalence of obesity, BMI ≥ 30 (% of adult population)		55.3	2016	●	↓
Human Trophic Level (best 2–3 worst)		NA	NA	●	●
Cereal yield (tonnes per hectare of harvested land)		NA	NA	●	●
Sustainable Nitrogen Management Index (best 0–1.41 worst)		NA	NA	●	●

SDG3 – Good Health and Well-Being

	Value	Year	Rating	Trend
Maternal mortality rate (per 100,000 live births)	NA	NA	●	●
Neonatal mortality rate (per 1,000 live births)	9.4	2018	●	↑
Mortality rate, under-5 (per 1,000 live births)	17.9	2018	●	↑
Incidence of tuberculosis (per 100,000 population)	109.0	2018	●	→
New HIV infections (per 1,000 uninfected population)	NA	NA	●	●
Age-standardized death rate due to cardiovascular disease, cancer, diabetes, or chronic respiratory disease in adults aged 30–70 years (%)	NA	NA	●	●
Age-standardized death rate attributable to household air pollution and ambient air pollution (per 100,000 population)	NA	NA	●	●
Traffic deaths (per 100,000 population)	4.8	2013	●	●
Life expectancy at birth (years)	NA	NA	●	●
Adolescent fertility rate (births per 1,000 adolescent females aged 15 to 19)	NA	NA	●	●
Births attended by skilled health personnel (%)	100.0	2016	●	↑
Percentage of surviving infants who received 2 WHO-recommended vaccines (%)	90	2018	●	↑
Universal health coverage (UHC) index of service coverage (worst 0–100 best)	NA	NA	●	●
Subjective well-being (average ladder score, worst 0–10 best)	NA	NA	●	●

SDG4 – Quality Education

	Value	Year	Rating	Trend
Net primary enrollment rate (%)	94.9	2014	●	●
Lower secondary completion rate (%)	108.5	2014	●	●
Literacy rate (% of population aged 15 to 24)	98.7	2015	●	●

SDG5 – Gender Equality

	Value	Year	Rating	Trend
Demand for family planning satisfied by modern methods (% of females aged 15 to 49 who are married or in unions)	NA	NA	●	●
Ratio of female-to-male mean years of education received (%)	NA	NA	●	●
Ratio of female-to-male labor force participation rate (%)	NA	NA	●	●
Seats held by women in national parliament (%)	12.5	2020	●	↗

SDG6 – Clean Water and Sanitation

	Value	Year	Rating	Trend
Population using at least basic drinking water services (%)	100.0	2017	●	↑
Population using at least basic sanitation services (%)	100.0	2017	●	↑
Freshwater withdrawal (% of available freshwater resources)	NA	NA	●	●
Anthropogenic wastewater that receives treatment (%)	40.0	2018	●	●
Scarce water consumption embodied in imports (m³/capita)	NA	NA	●	●

SDG7 – Affordable and Clean Energy

	Value	Year	Rating	Trend
Population with access to electricity (%)	100.0	2017	●	↑
Population with access to clean fuels and technology for cooking (%)	86.9	2016	●	↑
CO_2 emissions from fuel combustion for electricity and heating per total electricity output (MtCO₂/TWh)	NA	NA	●	●

SDG8 – Decent Work and Economic Growth

	Value	Year	Rating	Trend
Adjusted GDP growth (%)	-4.1	2018	●	●
Victims of modern slavery (per 1,000 population)	NA	NA	●	●
Adults with an account at a bank or other financial institution or with a mobile-money-service provider (% of population aged 15 or over)	NA	NA	●	●
Unemployment rate (% of total labor force)	NA	NA	●	●
Fatal work-related accidents embodied in imports (per 100,000 population)	NA	NA	●	●

SDG9 – Industry, Innovation and Infrastructure

		Value	Year	Rating	Trend
Population using the internet (%)		27.0	2004	●	●
Mobile broadband subscriptions (per 100 population)		NA	NA	●	●
Logistics Performance Index: Quality of trade and transport-related infrastructure (worst 1–5 best)		NA	NA	●	●
The Times Higher Education Universities Ranking: Average score of top 3 universities (worst 0–100 best)	*	0.0	2020	●	●
Scientific and technical journal articles (per 1,000 population)		0.4	2018	●	↗
Expenditure on research and development (% of GDP)		NA	NA	●	●

SDG10 – Reduced Inequalities

	Value	Year	Rating	Trend
Gini coefficient adjusted for top income	NA	NA	●	●

SDG11 – Sustainable Cities and Communities

	Value	Year	Rating	Trend
Annual mean concentration of particulate matter of less than 2.5 microns in diameter (PM2.5) (µg/m³)	NA	NA	●	●
Access to improved water source, piped (% of urban population)	99.0	2017	●	↑
Satisfaction with public transport (%)	NA	NA	●	●

SDG12 – Responsible Consumption and Production

	Value	Year	Rating	Trend
Municipal solid waste (kg/capita/day)	1.5	2016	●	●
Electronic waste (kg/capita)	9.3	2016	●	●
Production-based SO_2 emissions (kg/capita)	NA	NA	●	●
SO_2 emissions embodied in imports (kg/capita)	NA	NA	●	●
Production-based nitrogen emissions (kg/capita)	NA	NA	●	●
Nitrogen emissions embodied in imports (kg/capita)	NA	NA	●	●

SDG13 – Climate Action

	Value	Year	Rating	Trend
Energy-related CO_2 emissions (tCO₂/capita)	17.9	2017	●	↓
CO_2 emissions embodied in imports (tCO₂/capita)	NA	NA	●	●
CO_2 emissions embodied in fossil fuel exports (kg/capita)	NA	NA	●	●

SDG14 – Life Below Water

	Value	Year	Rating	Trend
Mean area that is protected in marine sites important to biodiversity (%)	NA	NA	●	●
Ocean Health Index: Clean Waters score (worst 0–100 best)	72.0	2019	●	↑
Fish caught from overexploited or collapsed stocks (% of total catch)	4.1	2014	●	↑
Fish caught by trawling (%)	NA	NA	●	●
Marine biodiversity threats embodied in imports (per million population)	NA	NA	●	●

SDG15 – Life on Land

	Value	Year	Rating	Trend
Mean area that is protected in terrestrial sites important to biodiversity (%)	NA	NA	●	●
Mean area that is protected in freshwater sites important to biodiversity (%)	NA	NA	●	●
Red List Index of species survival (worst 0–1 best)	0.7	2019	●	↓
Permanent deforestation (% of forest area, 5-year average)	0.0	2018	●	●
Terrestrial and freshwater biodiversity threats embodied in imports (per million population)	NA	NA	●	●

SDG16 – Peace, Justice and Strong Institutions

		Value	Year	Rating	Trend
Homicides (per 100,000 population)	*	3.1	2012	●	●
Unsentenced detainees (% of prison population)		4.1	2006	●	●
Percentage of population who feel safe walking alone at night in the city or area where they live (%)		NA	NA	●	●
Property Rights (worst 1–7 best)		NA	NA	●	●
Birth registrations with civil authority (% of children under age 5)		NA	NA	●	●
Corruption Perception Index (worst 0–100 best)		NA	NA	●	●
Children involved in child labor (% of population aged 5 to 14)		NA	NA	●	●
Exports of major conventional weapons (TIV constant million USD per 100,000 population)	*	0.0	2019	●	●
Press Freedom Index (best 0–100 worst)		NA	NA	●	●

SDG17 – Partnerships for the Goals

		Value	Year	Rating	Trend
Government spending on health and education (% of GDP)		11.2	2002	●	●
For high-income and all OECD DAC countries: International concessional public finance, including official development assistance (% of GNI)		NA	NA	●	●
Other countries: Government revenue excluding grants (% of GDP)		NA	NA	●	●
Corporate Tax Haven Score (best 0–100 worst)	*	0.0	2019	●	●

* Imputed data point

▼ OVERALL PERFORMANCE

Index score
69.2

Regional average score
70.4

SDG Global rank **81** (OF 166)

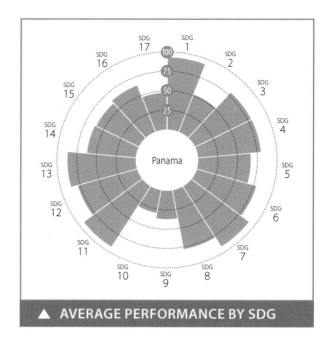

▲ AVERAGE PERFORMANCE BY SDG

▼ SPILLOVER INDEX

100 (best) to 0 (worst)

▼ CURRENT ASSESSMENT – SDG DASHBOARD

■ Major challenges ■ Significant challenges ■ Challenges remain ■ SDG achieved ■ Information unavailable

▼ SDG TRENDS

1 NO POVERTY ↑	2 ZERO HUNGER ↗	3 GOOD HEALTH AND WELL-BEING ↗	4 QUALITY EDUCATION ↓	5 GENDER EQUALITY ↗	6 CLEAN WATER AND SANITATION ↑	7 AFFORDABLE AND CLEAN ENERGY ↑	8 DECENT WORK AND ECONOMIC GROWTH ↗	9 INDUSTRY, INNOVATION AND INFRASTRUCTURE ↗
10 REDUCED INEQUALITIES ●	11 SUSTAINABLE CITIES AND COMMUNITIES ↑	12 RESPONSIBLE CONSUMPTION AND PRODUCTION ●	13 CLIMATE ACTION →	14 LIFE BELOW WATER ↗	15 LIFE ON LAND ↓	16 PEACE, JUSTICE AND STRONG INSTITUTIONS ↗	17 PARTNERSHIPS FOR THE GOALS ●	

↓ Decreasing → Stagnating ↗ Moderately improving ↑ On track or maintaining SDG achievement ● Information unavailable

Notes: The full title of Goal 2 "Zero Hunger" is "End hunger, achieve food security and improved nutrition and promote sustainable agriculture".
The full title of each SDG is available here: https://sustainabledevelopment.un.org/topics/sustainabledevelopmentgoals

SDG1 – No Poverty

	Value	Year	Rating	Trend
Poverty headcount ratio at $1.90/day (%)	1.6	2020	●	↑
Poverty headcount ratio at $3.20/day (%)	5.2	2020	○	↑

SDG2 – Zero Hunger

	Value	Year	Rating	Trend
Prevalence of undernourishment (%)	10.0	2017	○	→
Prevalence of stunting in children under 5 years of age (%)	19.1	2008	●	↑
Prevalence of wasting in children under 5 years of age (%)	1.2	2008	●	↑
Prevalence of obesity, BMI ≥ 30 (% of adult population)	22.7	2016	●	↓
Human Trophic Level (best 2–3 worst)	2.3	2017	●	↗
Cereal yield (tonnes per hectare of harvested land)	2.7	2017	●	↑
Sustainable Nitrogen Management Index (best 0–1.41 worst)	1.0	2015	●	↓

SDG3 – Good Health and Well-Being

	Value	Year	Rating	Trend
Maternal mortality rate (per 100,000 live births)	52	2017	●	↑
Neonatal mortality rate (per 1,000 live births)	8.5	2018	●	↑
Mortality rate, under-5 (per 1,000 live births)	15.3	2018	●	↑
Incidence of tuberculosis (per 100,000 population)	52.0	2018	●	→
New HIV infections (per 1,000 uninfected population)	0.3	2018	○	↑
Age-standardized death rate due to cardiovascular disease, cancer, diabetes, or chronic respiratory disease in adults aged 30–70 years (%)	13.0	2016	●	↑
Age-standardized death rate attributable to household air pollution and ambient air pollution (per 100,000 population)	26	2016	●	
Traffic deaths (per 100,000 population)	14.3	2016	●	↓
Life expectancy at birth (years)	78.0	2016	●	↗
Adolescent fertility rate (births per 1,000 adolescent females aged 15 to 19)	81.8	2017	●	→
Births attended by skilled health personnel (%)	94.6	2016	●	→
Percentage of surviving infants who received 2 WHO-recommended vaccines (%)	88	2018	●	↑
Universal health coverage (UHC) index of service coverage (worst 0–100 best)	79.0	2017	●	↑
Subjective well-being (average ladder score, worst 0–10 best)	6.1	2019	●	↑

SDG4 – Quality Education

	Value	Year	Rating	Trend
Net primary enrollment rate (%)	86.2	2017	●	↓
Lower secondary completion rate (%)	76.8	2017	●	●
Literacy rate (% of population aged 15 to 24)	99.1	2018	●	●

SDG5 – Gender Equality

	Value	Year	Rating	Trend
Demand for family planning satisfied by modern methods (% of females aged 15 to 49 who are married or in unions)	73.3	2013	●	↗
Ratio of female-to-male mean years of education received (%)	105.1	2018	●	↑
Ratio of female-to-male labor force participation rate (%)	65.3	2019	●	↗
Seats held by women in national parliament (%)	22.5	2020	●	↗

SDG6 – Clean Water and Sanitation

	Value	Year	Rating	Trend
Population using at least basic drinking water services (%)	96.4	2017	●	↑
Population using at least basic sanitation services (%)	83.3	2017	●	↑
Freshwater withdrawal (% of available freshwater resources)	0.8	2010	●	●
Anthropogenic wastewater that receives treatment (%)	23.1	2018	●	●
Scarce water consumption embodied in imports (m³/capita)	6.0	2013	●	↑

SDG7 – Affordable and Clean Energy

	Value	Year	Rating	Trend
Population with access to electricity (%)	100.0	2017	●	↑
Population with access to clean fuels and technology for cooking (%)	89.0	2016	●	↑
CO$_2$ emissions from fuel combustion for electricity and heating per total electricity output (MtCO$_2$/TWh)	0.9	2017	●	↑

SDG8 – Decent Work and Economic Growth

	Value	Year	Rating	Trend
Adjusted GDP growth (%)	-0.1	2018	○	●
Victims of modern slavery (per 1,000 population)	2.1	2018	●	●
Adults with an account at a bank or other financial institution or with a mobile-money-service provider (% of population aged 15 or over)	46.5	2017	●	→
Unemployment rate (% of total labor force)	3.9	2019	●	↑
Fatal work-related accidents embodied in imports (per 100,000 population)	0.5	2010	●	↑

SDG9 – Industry, Innovation and Infrastructure

	Value	Year	Rating	Trend
Population using the internet (%)	57.9	2017	●	↑
Mobile broadband subscriptions (per 100 population)	79.1	2018	●	↑
Logistics Performance Index: Quality of trade and transport-related infrastructure (worst 1–5 best)	3.1	2018	●	↑
The Times Higher Education Universities Ranking: Average score of top 3 universities (worst 0–100 best) *	3.4	2019	●	●
Scientific and technical journal articles (per 1,000 population)	0.0	2018	●	↓
Expenditure on research and development (% of GDP)	0.1	2013	●	●

SDG10 – Reduced Inequalities

	Value	Year	Rating	Trend
Gini coefficient adjusted for top income	52.6	2017	●	●

SDG11 – Sustainable Cities and Communities

	Value	Year	Rating	Trend
Annual mean concentration of particulate matter of less than 2.5 microns in diameter (PM2.5) (µg/m³)	11.4	2017	○	↑
Access to improved water source, piped (% of urban population)	98.3	2017	●	↑
Satisfaction with public transport (%)	73.0	2019	●	↑

SDG12 – Responsible Consumption and Production

	Value	Year	Rating	Trend
Municipal solid waste (kg/capita/day)	1.4	2015	○	●
Electronic waste (kg/capita)	8.0	2016	●	●
Production-based SO$_2$ emissions (kg/capita)	58.9	2012	●	●
SO$_2$ emissions embodied in imports (kg/capita)	6.4	2012	●	●
Production-based nitrogen emissions (kg/capita)	22.5	2010	●	●
Nitrogen emissions embodied in imports (kg/capita)	4.8	2010	●	●

SDG13 – Climate Action

	Value	Year	Rating	Trend
Energy-related CO$_2$ emissions (tCO$_2$/capita)	2.4	2017	○	↓
CO$_2$ emissions embodied in imports (tCO$_2$/capita)	1.0	2015	●	↗
CO$_2$ emissions embodied in fossil fuel exports (kg/capita)	0.0	2016	●	●

SDG14 – Life Below Water

	Value	Year	Rating	Trend
Mean area that is protected in marine sites important to biodiversity (%)	32.0	2018	●	→
Ocean Health Index: Clean Waters score (worst 0–100 best)	64.9	2019	●	↑
Fish caught from overexploited or collapsed stocks (% of total catch)	39.9	2014	●	↑
Fish caught by trawling (%)	9.3	2014	●	↑
Marine biodiversity threats embodied in imports (per million population)	0.4	2018	●	●

SDG15 – Life on Land

	Value	Year	Rating	Trend
Mean area that is protected in terrestrial sites important to biodiversity (%)	38.3	2018	○	→
Mean area that is protected in freshwater sites important to biodiversity (%)	NA	NA	●	●
Red List Index of species survival (worst 0–1 best)	0.7	2019	●	↓
Permanent deforestation (% of forest area, 5-year average)	0.2	2018	●	●
Terrestrial and freshwater biodiversity threats embodied in imports (per million population)	1.4	2018	○	●

SDG16 – Peace, Justice and Strong Institutions

	Value	Year	Rating	Trend
Homicides (per 100,000 population)	9.7	2017	●	↑
Unsentenced detainees (% of prison population)	52.8	2018	●	↑
Percentage of population who feel safe walking alone at night in the city or area where they live	49.6	2019	●	↓
Property Rights (worst 1–7 best)	4.5	2019	●	●
Birth registrations with civil authority (% of children under age 5)	95.6	2018	○	●
Corruption Perception Index (worst 0–100 best)	36	2019	●	↓
Children involved in child labor (% of population aged 5 to 14)	2.5	2016	●	●
Exports of major conventional weapons (TIV constant million USD per 100,000 population)	0.0	2019	●	●
Press Freedom Index (best 0–100 worst)	29.8	2019	●	↑

SDG17 – Partnerships for the Goals

	Value	Year	Rating	Trend
Government spending on health and education (% of GDP)	7.3	2011	●	●
For high-income and all OECD DAC countries: International concessional public finance, including official development assistance (% of GNI)	NA	NA	●	●
Other countries: Government revenue excluding grants (% of GDP) *	NA	NA	●	●
Corporate Tax Haven Score (best 0–100 worst)	71.8	2019	●	●

* Imputed data point

5. Country Profiles

PAPUA NEW GUINEA

Oceania

▼ OVERALL PERFORMANCE

Index score

51.7

Regional average score

49.6

SDG Global rank 155 (OF 166)

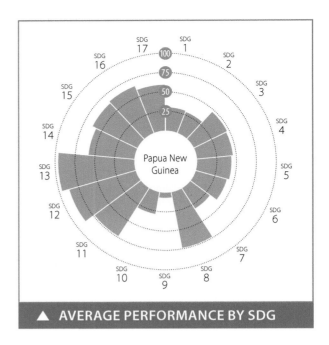

▲ AVERAGE PERFORMANCE BY SDG

▼ SPILLOVER INDEX

100 (best) to 0 (worst)

▼ CURRENT ASSESSMENT – SDG DASHBOARD

■ Major challenges ■ Significant challenges ■ Challenges remain ■ SDG achieved ■ Information unavailable

▼ SDG TRENDS

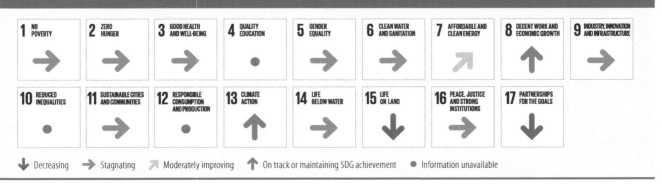

⬇ Decreasing ➡ Stagnating ⬈ Moderately improving ⬆ On track or maintaining SDG achievement ● Information unavailable

Notes: The full title of Goal 2 "Zero Hunger" is "End hunger, achieve food security and improved nutrition and promote sustainable agriculture".
The full title of each SDG is available here: https://sustainabledevelopment.un.org/topics/sustainabledevelopmentgoals

SDG1 – No Poverty

	Value	Year	Rating	Trend
Poverty headcount ratio at $1.90/day (%)	27.9	2020	●	→
Poverty headcount ratio at $3.20/day (%)	51.0	2020	●	→

SDG2 – Zero Hunger

	Value	Year	Rating	Trend
Prevalence of undernourishment (%)	NA	NA	●	●
Prevalence of stunting in children under 5 years of age (%)	49.5	2010	●	→
Prevalence of wasting in children under 5 years of age (%)	14.3	2010	●	↗
Prevalence of obesity, BMI ≥ 30 (% of adult population)	21.3	2016	●	↓
Human Trophic Level (best 2–3 worst)	NA	NA	●	●
Cereal yield (tonnes per hectare of harvested land)	4.8	2017	●	↑
Sustainable Nitrogen Management Index (best 0–1.41 worst)	0.9	2015	●	→

SDG3 – Good Health and Well-Being

	Value	Year	Rating	Trend
Maternal mortality rate (per 100,000 live births)	145	2017	●	↗
Neonatal mortality rate (per 1,000 live births)	22.1	2018	●	↗
Mortality rate, under-5 (per 1,000 live births)	47.8	2018	●	↗
Incidence of tuberculosis (per 100,000 population)	432.0	2018	●	→
New HIV infections (per 1,000 uninfected population)	0.3	2018	●	↑
Age-standardized death rate due to cardiovascular disease, cancer, diabetes, or chronic respiratory disease in adults aged 30–70 years (%)	30.0	2016	●	↓
Age-standardized death rate attributable to household air pollution and ambient air pollution (per 100,000 population)	152	2016	●	●
Traffic deaths (per 100,000 population)	14.2	2016	●	↑
Life expectancy at birth (years)	65.9	2016	●	→
Adolescent fertility rate (births per 1,000 adolescent females aged 15 to 19)	52.7	2017	●	→
Births attended by skilled health personnel (%)	53.0	2006	●	●
Percentage of surviving infants who received 2 WHO-recommended vaccines (%)	61	2018	●	↓
Universal health coverage (UHC) index of service coverage (worst 0–100 best)	40.0	2017	●	→
Subjective well-being (average ladder score, worst 0–10 best)	NA	NA	●	●

SDG4 – Quality Education

	Value	Year	Rating	Trend
Net primary enrollment rate (%)	73.7	2016	●	●
Lower secondary completion rate (%)	62.1	2016	●	●
Literacy rate (% of population aged 15 to 24)	67.9	2010	●	●

SDG5 – Gender Equality

	Value	Year	Rating	Trend
Demand for family planning satisfied by modern methods (% of females aged 15 to 49 who are married or in unions)	40.6	2007	●	→
Ratio of female-to-male mean years of education received (%)	72.2	2018	●	→
Ratio of female-to-male labor force participation rate (%)	96.3	2019	●	↑
Seats held by women in national parliament (%)	0.0	2020	●	↓

SDG6 – Clean Water and Sanitation

	Value	Year	Rating	Trend
Population using at least basic drinking water services (%)	41.3	2017	●	→
Population using at least basic sanitation services (%)	12.9	2017	●	↓
Freshwater withdrawal (% of available freshwater resources)	0.1	2005	●	●
Anthropogenic wastewater that receives treatment (%)	0.0	2018	●	●
Scarce water consumption embodied in imports (m³/capita)	0.9	2013	●	↑

SDG7 – Affordable and Clean Energy

	Value	Year	Rating	Trend
Population with access to electricity (%)	54.4	2017	●	↑
Population with access to clean fuels and technology for cooking (%)	13.4	2016	●	→
CO$_2$ emissions from fuel combustion for electricity and heating per total electricity output (MtCO$_2$/TWh)	NA	NA	●	●

SDG8 – Decent Work and Economic Growth

	Value	Year	Rating	Trend
Adjusted GDP growth (%)	-5.3	2018	●	●
Victims of modern slavery (per 1,000 population)	10.3	2018	●	●
Adults with an account at a bank or other financial institution or with a mobile-money-service provider (% of population aged 15 or over)	NA	NA	●	●
Unemployment rate (% of total labor force)	2.5	2019	●	↑
Fatal work-related accidents embodied in imports (per 100,000 population)	0.1	2010	●	↑

SDG9 – Industry, Innovation and Infrastructure

	Value	Year	Rating	Trend
Population using the internet (%)	11.2	2017	●	→
Mobile broadband subscriptions (per 100 population)	10.9	2017	●	↗
Logistics Performance Index: Quality of trade and transport-related infrastructure (worst 1–5 best)	2.0	2018	●	↓
The Times Higher Education Universities Ranking: Average score of top 3 universities (worst 0–100 best) *	0.0	2020	●	●
Scientific and technical journal articles (per 1,000 population)	0.0	2018	●	→
Expenditure on research and development (% of GDP)	0.0	2016	●	●

SDG10 – Reduced Inequalities

	Value	Year	Rating	Trend
Gini coefficient adjusted for top income	53.0	2009	●	●

SDG11 – Sustainable Cities and Communities

	Value	Year	Rating	Trend
Annual mean concentration of particulate matter of less than 2.5 microns in diameter (PM2.5) (µg/m³)	12.3	2017	◔	↑
Access to improved water source, piped (% of urban population)	55.4	2017	●	↓
Satisfaction with public transport (%)	NA	NA	●	●

SDG12 – Responsible Consumption and Production

	Value	Year	Rating	Trend
Municipal solid waste (kg/capita/day)	2.5	2014	●	●
Electronic waste (kg/capita)	0.9	2016	●	●
Production-based SO$_2$ emissions (kg/capita)	20.9	2012	●	●
SO$_2$ emissions embodied in imports (kg/capita)	2.0	2012	●	●
Production-based nitrogen emissions (kg/capita)	2.1	2010	●	●
Nitrogen emissions embodied in imports (kg/capita)	0.5	2010	●	●

SDG13 – Climate Action

	Value	Year	Rating	Trend
Energy-related CO$_2$ emissions (tCO$_2$/capita)	0.9	2017	●	↑
CO$_2$ emissions embodied in imports (tCO$_2$/capita)	0.2	2015	●	↑
CO$_2$ emissions embodied in fossil fuel exports (kg/capita)	NA	NA	●	●

SDG14 – Life Below Water

	Value	Year	Rating	Trend
Mean area that is protected in marine sites important to biodiversity (%)	1.9	2018	●	→
Ocean Health Index: Clean Waters score (worst 0–100 best)	64.9	2019	●	↗
Fish caught from overexploited or collapsed stocks (% of total catch)	56.9	2014	●	↓
Fish caught by trawling (%)	0.6	2014	●	↑
Marine biodiversity threats embodied in imports (per million population)	0.0	2018	●	●

SDG15 – Life on Land

	Value	Year	Rating	Trend
Mean area that is protected in terrestrial sites important to biodiversity (%)	7.5	2018	●	→
Mean area that is protected in freshwater sites important to biodiversity (%)	NA	NA	●	●
Red List Index of species survival (worst 0–1 best)	0.8	2019	●	↓
Permanent deforestation (% of forest area, 5-year average)	0.1	2018	◔	●
Terrestrial and freshwater biodiversity threats embodied in imports (per million population)	0.0	2018	●	●

SDG16 – Peace, Justice and Strong Institutions

	Value	Year	Rating	Trend
Homicides (per 100,000 population)	10.0	2010	●	●
Unsentenced detainees (% of prison population)	38.3	2018	◔	→
Percentage of population who feel safe walking alone at night in the city or area where they live (%)	NA	NA	●	●
Property Rights (worst 1–7 best)	NA	NA	●	●
Birth registrations with civil authority (% of children under age 5)	NA	NA	●	●
Corruption Perception Index (worst 0–100 best)	28	2019	●	→
Children involved in child labor (% of population aged 5 to 14)	NA	NA	●	●
Exports of major conventional weapons (TIV constant million USD per 100,000 population) *	0.0	2019	●	●
Press Freedom Index (best 0–100 worst)	24.7	2019	●	↑

SDG17 – Partnerships for the Goals

	Value	Year	Rating	Trend
Government spending on health and education (% of GDP)	NA	NA	●	●
For high-income and all OECD DAC countries: International concessional public finance, including official development assistance (% of GNI)	NA	NA	●	●
Other countries: Government revenue excluding grants (% of GDP)	15.9	2018	●	↓
Corporate Tax Haven Score (best 0–100 worst) *	0.0	2019	●	●

* Imputed data point

PARAGUAY

▼ OVERALL PERFORMANCE

Index score

67.7

Regional average score

70.4

SDG Global rank **90** (OF 166)

▼ SPILLOVER INDEX

100 (best) to 0 (worst)

▲ AVERAGE PERFORMANCE BY SDG

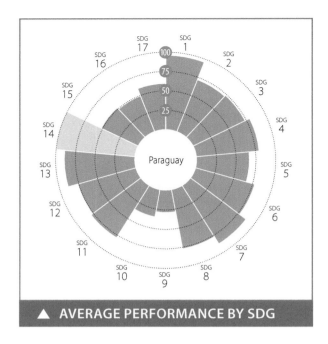

Paraguay

▼ CURRENT ASSESSMENT – SDG DASHBOARD

■ Major challenges ■ Significant challenges ■ Challenges remain ■ SDG achieved ■ Information unavailable

▼ SDG TRENDS

↓ Decreasing → Stagnating ↗ Moderately improving ↑ On track or maintaining SDG achievement ● Information unavailable

Notes: The full title of Goal 2 "Zero Hunger" is "End hunger, achieve food security and improved nutrition and promote sustainable agriculture".
The full title of each SDG is available here: https://sustainabledevelopment.un.org/topics/sustainabledevelopmentgoals

SDG1 – No Poverty

	Value	Year	Rating	Trend
Poverty headcount ratio at $1.90/day (%)	1.0	2020	○	↑
Poverty headcount ratio at $3.20/day (%)	4.5	2020	○	↑

SDG2 – Zero Hunger

	Value	Year	Rating	Trend
Prevalence of undernourishment (%)	10.7	2017	○	↑
Prevalence of stunting in children under 5 years of age (%)	5.6	2016	●	↑
Prevalence of wasting in children under 5 years of age (%)	1.0	2016	●	↑
Prevalence of obesity, BMI ≥ 30 (% of adult population)	20.3	2016	●	↓
Human Trophic Level (best 2–3 worst)	2.2	2017	●	↑
Cereal yield (tonnes per hectare of harvested land)	4.4	2017	●	↑
Sustainable Nitrogen Management Index (best 0–1.41 worst)	0.3	2015	●	↑

SDG3 – Good Health and Well-Being

	Value	Year	Rating	Trend
Maternal mortality rate (per 100,000 live births)	129	2017	●	→
Neonatal mortality rate (per 1,000 live births)	10.7	2018	●	↑
Mortality rate, under-5 (per 1,000 live births)	20.2	2018	●	↑
Incidence of tuberculosis (per 100,000 population)	43.0	2018	●	→
New HIV infections (per 1,000 uninfected population)	0.2	2018	●	↑
Age-standardized death rate due to cardiovascular disease, cancer, diabetes, or chronic respiratory disease in adults aged 30–70 years (%)	17.5	2016	○	↑
Age-standardized death rate attributable to household air pollution and ambient air pollution (per 100,000 population)	57	2016	●	●
Traffic deaths (per 100,000 population)	22.7	2016	●	↓
Life expectancy at birth (years)	74.2	2016	●	→
Adolescent fertility rate (births per 1,000 adolescent females aged 15 to 19)	70.5	2017	●	→
Births attended by skilled health personnel (%)	95.5	2016	●	→
Percentage of surviving infants who received 2 WHO-recommended vaccines (%)	88	2018	●	↑
Universal health coverage (UHC) index of service coverage (worst 0–100 best)	69.0	2017	●	↗
Subjective well-being (average ladder score, worst 0–10 best)	5.6	2018	○	↓

SDG4 – Quality Education

	Value	Year	Rating	Trend
Net primary enrollment rate (%)	87.2	2012	●	●
Lower secondary completion rate (%)	73.4	2012	●	●
Literacy rate (% of population aged 15 to 24)	98.3	2018	●	●

SDG5 – Gender Equality

	Value	Year	Rating	Trend
Demand for family planning satisfied by modern methods (% of females aged 15 to 49 who are married or in unions)	78.9	2016	●	↑
Ratio of female-to-male mean years of education received (%)	101.2	2018	●	↑
Ratio of female-to-male labor force participation rate (%)	68.1	2019	●	↗
Seats held by women in national parliament (%)	16.3	2020	●	→

SDG6 – Clean Water and Sanitation

	Value	Year	Rating	Trend
Population using at least basic drinking water services (%)	99.6	2017	●	↑
Population using at least basic sanitation services (%)	89.8	2017	○	↑
Freshwater withdrawal (% of available freshwater resources)	1.8	2010	●	●
Anthropogenic wastewater that receives treatment (%)	0.7	2018	●	●
Scarce water consumption embodied in imports (m³/capita)	2.7	2013	●	↑

SDG7 – Affordable and Clean Energy

	Value	Year	Rating	Trend
Population with access to electricity (%)	99.3	2017	●	↑
Population with access to clean fuels and technology for cooking (%)	66.2	2016	●	↗
CO₂ emissions from fuel combustion for electricity and heating per total electricity output (MtCO₂/TWh)	0.1	2017	●	↑

SDG8 – Decent Work and Economic Growth

	Value	Year	Rating	Trend
Adjusted GDP growth (%)	-0.9	2018	○	●
Victims of modern slavery (per 1,000 population)	1.6	2018	●	●
Adults with an account at a bank or other financial institution or with a mobile-money-service provider (% of population aged 15 or over)	48.6	2017	●	●
Unemployment rate (% of total labor force)	4.8	2019	●	↑
Fatal work-related accidents embodied in imports (per 100,000 population)	0.4	2010	●	↑

SDG9 – Industry, Innovation and Infrastructure

	Value	Year	Rating	Trend
Population using the internet (%)	65.0	2018	●	↑
Mobile broadband subscriptions (per 100 population)	57.7	2018	○	↑
Logistics Performance Index: Quality of trade and transport-related infrastructure (worst 1–5 best)	2.5	2018	○	↗
The Times Higher Education Universities Ranking: Average score of top 3 universities (worst 0–100 best) *	0.0	2020	●	●
Scientific and technical journal articles (per 1,000 population)	0.0	2018	●	→
Expenditure on research and development (% of GDP)	0.2	2016	●	→

SDG10 – Reduced Inequalities

	Value	Year	Rating	Trend
Gini coefficient adjusted for top income	50.5	2017	●	●

SDG11 – Sustainable Cities and Communities

	Value	Year	Rating	Trend
Annual mean concentration of particulate matter of less than 2.5 microns in diameter (PM2.5) (µg/m³)	11.9	2017	○	↑
Access to improved water source, piped (% of urban population)	97.3	2017	○	↑
Satisfaction with public transport (%)	48.6	2018	●	↗

SDG12 – Responsible Consumption and Production

	Value	Year	Rating	Trend
Municipal solid waste (kg/capita/day)	1.2	2015	○	●
Electronic waste (kg/capita)	6.4	2016	○	●
Production-based SO₂ emissions (kg/capita)	26.1	2012	●	●
SO₂ emissions embodied in imports (kg/capita)	3.6	2012	●	●
Production-based nitrogen emissions (kg/capita)	61.9	2010	●	●
Nitrogen emissions embodied in imports (kg/capita)	4.5	2010	●	●

SDG13 – Climate Action

	Value	Year	Rating	Trend
Energy-related CO₂ emissions (tCO₂/capita)	0.8	2017	●	↑
CO₂ emissions embodied in imports (tCO₂/capita)	0.6	2015	○	↑
CO₂ emissions embodied in fossil fuel exports (kg/capita)	NA	NA	●	●

SDG14 – Life Below Water

	Value	Year	Rating	Trend
Mean area that is protected in marine sites important to biodiversity (%)	NA	NA	●	●
Ocean Health Index: Clean Waters score (worst 0–100 best)	NA	NA	●	●
Fish caught from overexploited or collapsed stocks (% of total catch)	NA	NA	●	●
Fish caught by trawling (%)	NA	NA	●	●
Marine biodiversity threats embodied in imports (per million population)	0.0	2018	●	●

SDG15 – Life on Land

	Value	Year	Rating	Trend
Mean area that is protected in terrestrial sites important to biodiversity (%)	36.3	2018	○	→
Mean area that is protected in freshwater sites important to biodiversity (%)	38.8	2018	○	→
Red List Index of species survival (worst 0–1 best)	0.9	2019	●	↑
Permanent deforestation (% of forest area, 5-year average)	1.6	2018	●	●
Terrestrial and freshwater biodiversity threats embodied in imports (per million population)	0.4	2018	●	●

SDG16 – Peace, Justice and Strong Institutions

	Value	Year	Rating	Trend
Homicides (per 100,000 population)	8.9	2016	●	→
Unsentenced detainees (% of prison population)	76.1	2018	●	↓
Percentage of population who feel safe walking alone at night in the city or area where they live (%)	51.1	2018	●	↑
Property Rights (worst 1–7 best)	4.2	2019	●	●
Birth registrations with civil authority (% of children under age 5)	69.1	2018	●	●
Corruption Perception Index (worst 0–100 best)	28	2019	●	→
Children involved in child labor (% of population aged 5 to 14)	27.6	2016	●	●
Exports of major conventional weapons (TIV constant million USD per 100,000 population) *	0.0	2019	●	●
Press Freedom Index (best 0–100 worst)	32.4	2019	○	↑

SDG17 – Partnerships for the Goals

	Value	Year	Rating	Trend
Government spending on health and education (% of GDP)	7.6	2016	○	↓
For high-income and all OECD DAC countries: International concessional public finance, including official development assistance (% of GNI)	NA	NA	●	●
Other countries: Government revenue excluding grants (% of GDP)	17.4	2017	●	→
Corporate Tax Haven Score (best 0–100 worst) *	0.0	2019	●	●

* Imputed data point

5. Country Profiles

▼ OVERALL PERFORMANCE

Index score

71.8

Regional average score

70.4

SDG Global rank **61** (OF 166)

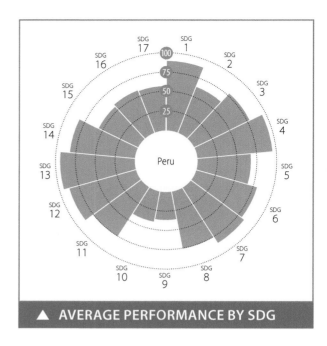

Peru

▲ AVERAGE PERFORMANCE BY SDG

▼ SPILLOVER INDEX

100 (best) to 0 (worst)

▼ CURRENT ASSESSMENT – SDG DASHBOARD

■ Major challenges   ■ Significant challenges   ■ Challenges remain   ■ SDG achieved   ■ Information unavailable

▼ SDG TRENDS

↓ Decreasing   → Stagnating   ↗ Moderately improving   ↑ On track or maintaining SDG achievement   ● Information unavailable

Notes: The full title of Goal 2 "Zero Hunger" is "End hunger, achieve food security and improved nutrition and promote sustainable agriculture".
The full title of each SDG is available here: https://sustainabledevelopment.un.org/topics/sustainabledevelopmentgoals

SDG1 – No Poverty

	Value	Year	Rating	Trend
Poverty headcount ratio at $1.90/day (%)	2.3	2020	●	↑
Poverty headcount ratio at $3.20/day (%)	8.5	2020	●	↗

SDG2 – Zero Hunger

	Value	Year	Rating	Trend
Prevalence of undernourishment (%)	9.7	2017	●	→
Prevalence of stunting in children under 5 years of age (%)	13.1	2016	●	↑
Prevalence of wasting in children under 5 years of age (%)	1.0	2016	●	↑
Prevalence of obesity, BMI ≥ 30 (% of adult population)	19.7	2016	●	↓
Human Trophic Level (best 2–3 worst)	2.2	2017	●	↓
Cereal yield (tonnes per hectare of harvested land)	4.2	2017	●	↑
Sustainable Nitrogen Management Index (best 0–1.41 worst)	0.8	2015	●	→

SDG3 – Good Health and Well-Being

	Value	Year	Rating	Trend
Maternal mortality rate (per 100,000 live births)	88	2017	●	↑
Neonatal mortality rate (per 1,000 live births)	7.3	2018	●	↑
Mortality rate, under-5 (per 1,000 live births)	14.3	2018	●	↑
Incidence of tuberculosis (per 100,000 population)	123.0	2018	●	→
New HIV infections (per 1,000 uninfected population)	0.1	2018	●	↑
Age-standardized death rate due to cardiovascular disease, cancer, diabetes, or chronic respiratory disease in adults aged 30–70 years (%)	12.6	2016	●	↑
Age-standardized death rate attributable to household air pollution and ambient air pollution (per 100,000 population)	64	2016	●	●
Traffic deaths (per 100,000 population)	13.5	2016	●	→
Life expectancy at birth (years)	75.9	2016	●	↗
Adolescent fertility rate (births per 1,000 adolescent females aged 15 to 19)	56.9	2017	●	→
Births attended by skilled health personnel (%)	92.4	2016	●	↑
Percentage of surviving infants who received 2 WHO-recommended vaccines (%)	84	2018	●	↓
Universal health coverage (UHC) index of service coverage (worst 0–100 best)	77.0	2017	●	↑
Subjective well-being (average ladder score, worst 0–10 best)	6.0	2019	●	↑

SDG4 – Quality Education

	Value	Year	Rating	Trend
Net primary enrollment rate (%)	95.7	2018	●	↑
Lower secondary completion rate (%)	98.0	2018	●	↑
Literacy rate (% of population aged 15 to 24)	99.0	2018	●	●

SDG5 – Gender Equality

	Value	Year	Rating	Trend
Demand for family planning satisfied by modern methods (% of females aged 15 to 49 who are married or in unions)	66.6	2017	●	↑
Ratio of female-to-male mean years of education received (%)	89.7	2018	●	↗
Ratio of female-to-male labor force participation rate (%)	82.8	2019	●	↑
Seats held by women in national parliament (%)	26.2	2020	●	↗

SDG6 – Clean Water and Sanitation

	Value	Year	Rating	Trend
Population using at least basic drinking water services (%)	91.1	2017	●	↑
Population using at least basic sanitation services (%)	74.3	2017	●	→
Freshwater withdrawal (% of available freshwater resources)	2.5	2010	●	●
Anthropogenic wastewater that receives treatment (%)	46.4	2018	●	●
Scarce water consumption embodied in imports (m3/capita)	1.6	2013	●	↑

SDG7 – Affordable and Clean Energy

	Value	Year	Rating	Trend
Population with access to electricity (%)	96.4	2017	●	↑
Population with access to clean fuels and technology for cooking (%)	75.1	2016	●	↑
CO_2 emissions from fuel combustion for electricity and heating per total electricity output (MtCO2/TWh)	1.0	2017	●	↑

SDG8 – Decent Work and Economic Growth

	Value	Year	Rating	Trend
Adjusted GDP growth (%)	-2.0	2018	●	●
Victims of modern slavery (per 1,000 population)	2.6	2018	●	●
Adults with an account at a bank or other financial institution or with a mobile-money-service provider (% of population aged 15 or over)	42.6	2017	●	↑
Unemployment rate (% of total labor force)	3.3	2019	●	↑
Fatal work-related accidents embodied in imports (per 100,000 population)	0.1	2010	●	↑

SDG9 – Industry, Innovation and Infrastructure

	Value	Year	Rating	Trend
Population using the internet (%)	52.5	2018	●	↑
Mobile broadband subscriptions (per 100 population)	65.7	2017	●	↑
Logistics Performance Index: Quality of trade and transport-related infrastructure (worst 1–5 best)	2.3	2018	●	↓
The Times Higher Education Universities Ranking: Average score of top 3 universities (worst 0–100 best)	31.1	2020	●	●
Scientific and technical journal articles (per 1,000 population)	0.1	2018	●	→
Expenditure on research and development (% of GDP)	0.1	2017	●	→

SDG10 – Reduced Inequalities

	Value	Year	Rating	Trend
Gini coefficient adjusted for top income	48.9	2017	●	●

SDG11 – Sustainable Cities and Communities

	Value	Year	Rating	Trend
Annual mean concentration of particulate matter of less than 2.5 microns in diameter (PM2.5) (μg/m3)	24.8	2017	●	↗
Access to improved water source, piped (% of urban population)	92.6	2017	●	↑
Satisfaction with public transport (%)	55.3	2019	●	→

SDG12 – Responsible Consumption and Production

	Value	Year	Rating	Trend
Municipal solid waste (kg/capita/day)	0.9	2014	●	●
Electronic waste (kg/capita)	5.8	2016	●	●
Production-based SO_2 emissions (kg/capita)	27.9	2012	●	●
SO_2 emissions embodied in imports (kg/capita)	2.0	2012	●	●
Production-based nitrogen emissions (kg/capita)	19.1	2010	●	●
Nitrogen emissions embodied in imports (kg/capita)	1.1	2010	●	●

SDG13 – Climate Action

	Value	Year	Rating	Trend
Energy-related CO_2 emissions (tCO2/capita)	2.0	2017	●	↓
CO_2 emissions embodied in imports (tCO2/capita)	0.3	2015	●	↑
CO_2 emissions embodied in fossil fuel exports (kg/capita)	365.4	2018	●	●

SDG14 – Life Below Water

	Value	Year	Rating	Trend
Mean area that is protected in marine sites important to biodiversity (%)	77.9	2018	●	↑
Ocean Health Index: Clean Waters score (worst 0–100 best)	57.0	2019	●	→
Fish caught from overexploited or collapsed stocks (% of total catch)	4.9	2014	●	↑
Fish caught by trawling (%)	2.2	2014	●	↑
Marine biodiversity threats embodied in imports (per million population)	0.0	2018	●	●

SDG15 – Life on Land

	Value	Year	Rating	Trend
Mean area that is protected in terrestrial sites important to biodiversity (%)	19.1	2018	●	↓
Mean area that is protected in freshwater sites important to biodiversity (%)	48.8	2018	●	→
Red List Index of species survival (worst 0–1 best)	0.7	2019	●	↓
Permanent deforestation (% of forest area, 5-year average)	0.2	2018	●	●
Terrestrial and freshwater biodiversity threats embodied in imports (per million population)	0.7	2018	●	●

SDG16 – Peace, Justice and Strong Institutions

	Value	Year	Rating	Trend
Homicides (per 100,000 population)	7.7	2017	●	→
Unsentenced detainees (% of prison population)	40.8	2018	●	↑
Percentage of population who feel safe walking alone at night in the city or area where they live (%)	44.9	2019	●	↗
Property Rights (worst 1–7 best)	3.5	2019	●	●
Birth registrations with civil authority (% of children under age 5)	97.7	2018	●	●
Corruption Perception Index (worst 0–100 best)	36	2019	●	→
Children involved in child labor (% of population aged 5 to 14)	21.8	2016	●	●
Exports of major conventional weapons (TIV constant million USD per 100,000 population)	* 0.0	2019	●	●
Press Freedom Index (best 0–100 worst)	30.2	2019	●	↓

SDG17 – Partnerships for the Goals

	Value	Year	Rating	Trend
Government spending on health and education (% of GDP)	7.1	2016	●	↑
For high-income and all OECD DAC countries: International concessional public finance, including official development assistance (% of GNI)	NA	NA	●	●
Other countries: Government revenue excluding grants (% of GDP)	17.0	2017	●	↓
Corporate Tax Haven Score (best 0–100 worst)	* 0.0	2019	●	●

5. Country Profiles

* Imputed data point

▼ OVERALL PERFORMANCE

Index score

65.5

Regional average score

67.2

SDG Global rank 99 (OF 166)

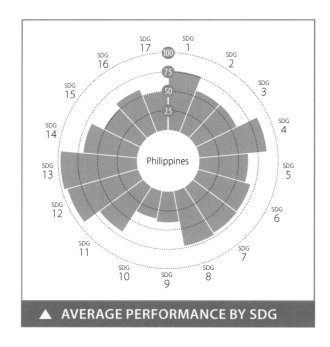

▲ AVERAGE PERFORMANCE BY SDG

▼ SPILLOVER INDEX

100 (best) to 0 (worst)

▼ CURRENT ASSESSMENT – SDG DASHBOARD

■ Major challenges ■ Significant challenges ■ Challenges remain ■ SDG achieved ■ Information unavailable

▼ SDG TRENDS

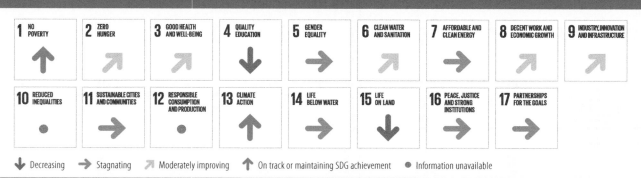

↓ Decreasing → Stagnating ↗ Moderately improving ↑ On track or maintaining SDG achievement ● Information unavailable

Notes: The full title of Goal 2 "Zero Hunger" is "End hunger, achieve food security and improved nutrition and promote sustainable agriculture".
The full title of each SDG is available here: https://sustainabledevelopment.un.org/topics/sustainabledevelopmentgoals

PHILIPPINES

SDG1 – No Poverty	Value	Year	Rating	Trend
Poverty headcount ratio at $1.90/day (%)	3.1	2020	○	↑
Poverty headcount ratio at $3.20/day (%)	22.1	2020	●	↑

SDG2 – Zero Hunger

	Value	Year	Rating	Trend
Prevalence of undernourishment (%)	13.3	2017	●	↗
Prevalence of stunting in children under 5 years of age (%)	33.4	2015	●	→
Prevalence of wasting in children under 5 years of age (%)	7.1	2015	○	→
Prevalence of obesity, BMI ≥ 30 (% of adult population)	6.4	2016	●	↑
Human Trophic Level (best 2–3 worst)	2.2	2017	●	↑
Cereal yield (tonnes per hectare of harvested land)	3.7	2017	●	↑
Sustainable Nitrogen Management Index (best 0–1.41 worst)	0.8	2015	●	↓

SDG3 – Good Health and Well-Being

	Value	Year	Rating	Trend
Maternal mortality rate (per 100,000 live births)	121	2017	●	↗
Neonatal mortality rate (per 1,000 live births)	13.5	2018	○	↑
Mortality rate, under-5 (per 1,000 live births)	28.4	2018	○	↑
Incidence of tuberculosis (per 100,000 population)	554.0	2018	●	↓
New HIV infections (per 1,000 uninfected population)	0.1	2018	●	↑
Age-standardized death rate due to cardiovascular disease, cancer, diabetes, or chronic respiratory disease in adults aged 30–70 years (%)	26.8	2016	●	→
Age-standardized death rate attributable to household air pollution and ambient air pollution (per 100,000 population)	185	2016	●	●
Traffic deaths (per 100,000 population)	12.3	2016	○	↓
Life expectancy at birth (years)	69.3	2016	●	→
Adolescent fertility rate (births per 1,000 adolescent females aged 15 to 19)	54.2	2017	●	→
Births attended by skilled health personnel (%)	84.4	2017	●	↑
Percentage of surviving infants who received 2 WHO-recommended vaccines (%)	65	2018	●	↗
Universal health coverage (UHC) index of service coverage (worst 0–100 best)	61.0	2017	●	↑
Subjective well-being (average ladder score, worst 0–10 best)	6.3	2019	●	↑

SDG4 – Quality Education

	Value	Year	Rating	Trend
Net primary enrollment rate (%)	93.8	2017	○	↓
Lower secondary completion rate (%)	78.2	2017	●	↓
Literacy rate (% of population aged 15 to 24)	99.1	2015	●	●

SDG5 – Gender Equality

	Value	Year	Rating	Trend
Demand for family planning satisfied by modern methods (% of females aged 15 to 49 who are married or in unions)	52.5	2017	●	→
Ratio of female-to-male mean years of education received (%)	104.3	2018	●	↑
Ratio of female-to-male labor force participation rate (%)	62.0	2019	●	↓
Seats held by women in national parliament (%)	28.0	2020	●	→

SDG6 – Clean Water and Sanitation

	Value	Year	Rating	Trend
Population using at least basic drinking water services (%)	93.6	2017	○	↑
Population using at least basic sanitation services (%)	76.5	2017	●	↗
Freshwater withdrawal (% of available freshwater resources)	26.0	2015	●	●
Anthropogenic wastewater that receives treatment (%)	0.7	2018	●	●
Scarce water consumption embodied in imports (m³/capita)	1.9	2013	●	↑

SDG7 – Affordable and Clean Energy

	Value	Year	Rating	Trend
Population with access to electricity (%)	93.0	2017	○	↑
Population with access to clean fuels and technology for cooking (%)	43.2	2016	●	→
CO₂ emissions from fuel combustion for electricity and heating per total electricity output (MtCO₂/TWh)	1.4	2017	●	→

SDG8 – Decent Work and Economic Growth

	Value	Year	Rating	Trend
Adjusted GDP growth (%)	0.5	2018	●	●
Victims of modern slavery (per 1,000 population)	7.7	2018	●	●
Adults with an account at a bank or other financial institution or with a mobile-money-service provider (% of population aged 15 or over)	34.5	2017	●	→
Unemployment rate (% of total labor force)	2.2	2019	●	↑
Fatal work-related accidents embodied in imports (per 100,000 population)	0.1	2010	●	↑

SDG9 – Industry, Innovation and Infrastructure

	Value	Year	Rating	Trend
Population using the internet (%)	60.1	2017	●	↑
Mobile broadband subscriptions (per 100 population)	68.4	2017	○	↑
Logistics Performance Index: Quality of trade and transport-related infrastructure (worst 1–5 best)	2.7	2018	●	↑
The Times Higher Education Universities Ranking: Average score of top 3 universities (worst 0–100 best)	28.5	2020	○	●
Scientific and technical journal articles (per 1,000 population)	0.0	2018	●	→
Expenditure on research and development (% of GDP)	0.1	2013	●	●

SDG10 – Reduced Inequalities

	Value	Year	Rating	Trend
Gini coefficient adjusted for top income	50.1	2015	●	●

SDG11 – Sustainable Cities and Communities

	Value	Year	Rating	Trend
Annual mean concentration of particulate matter of less than 2.5 microns in diameter (PM2.5) (μg/m³)	18.1	2017	●	↑
Access to improved water source, piped (% of urban population)	46.8	2017	●	↓
Satisfaction with public transport (%)	68.5	2019	○	↓

SDG12 – Responsible Consumption and Production

	Value	Year	Rating	Trend
Municipal solid waste (kg/capita/day)	0.8	2016	●	●
Electronic waste (kg/capita)	2.8	2016	●	●
Production-based SO₂ emissions (kg/capita)	9.2	2012	●	●
SO₂ emissions embodied in imports (kg/capita)	1.0	2012	●	●
Production-based nitrogen emissions (kg/capita)	8.0	2010	●	●
Nitrogen emissions embodied in imports (kg/capita)	0.9	2010	●	●

SDG13 – Climate Action

	Value	Year	Rating	Trend
Energy-related CO₂ emissions (tCO₂/capita)	1.2	2017	●	↑
CO₂ emissions embodied in imports (tCO₂/capita)	0.2	2015	●	↑
CO₂ emissions embodied in fossil fuel exports (kg/capita)	101.1	2018	○	●

SDG14 – Life Below Water

	Value	Year	Rating	Trend
Mean area that is protected in marine sites important to biodiversity (%)	44.2	2018	○	→
Ocean Health Index: Clean Waters score (worst 0–100 best)	54.0	2019	●	↗
Fish caught from overexploited or collapsed stocks (% of total catch)	30.9	2014	○	↓
Fish caught by trawling (%)	4.5	2014	●	↑
Marine biodiversity threats embodied in imports (per million population)	0.0	2018	●	●

SDG15 – Life on Land

	Value	Year	Rating	Trend
Mean area that is protected in terrestrial sites important to biodiversity (%)	40.9	2018	○	→
Mean area that is protected in freshwater sites important to biodiversity (%)	36.5	2018	○	→
Red List Index of species survival (worst 0–1 best)	0.6	2019	●	↓
Permanent deforestation (% of forest area, 5-year average)	0.4	2018	●	●
Terrestrial and freshwater biodiversity threats embodied in imports (per million population)	0.1	2018	●	●

SDG16 – Peace, Justice and Strong Institutions

	Value	Year	Rating	Trend
Homicides (per 100,000 population)	8.4	2017	●	↗
Unsentenced detainees (% of prison population)	74.7	2018	●	↓
Percentage of population who feel safe walking alone at night in the city or area where they live (%)	62.4	2019	○	→
Property Rights (worst 1–7 best)	4.5	2019	●	●
Birth registrations with civil authority (% of children under age 5)	91.8	2018	○	●
Corruption Perception Index (worst 0–100 best)	34	2019	●	↓
Children involved in child labor (% of population aged 5 to 14)	11.1	2016	●	●
Exports of major conventional weapons (TIV constant million USD per 100,000 population)	* 0.0	2019	●	●
Press Freedom Index (best 0–100 worst)	43.9	2019	○	→

SDG17 – Partnerships for the Goals

	Value	Year	Rating	Trend
Government spending on health and education (% of GDP)	4.0	2009	●	●
For high-income and all OECD DAC countries: International concessional public finance, including official development assistance (% of GNI)	NA	NA	●	●
Other countries: Government revenue excluding grants (% of GDP)	16.3	2018	●	→
Corporate Tax Haven Score (best 0–100 worst)	* 0.0	2019	●	●

* Imputed data point

▼ OVERALL PERFORMANCE

Index score

78.1

Regional average score

77.3

SDG Global rank 23 (OF 166)

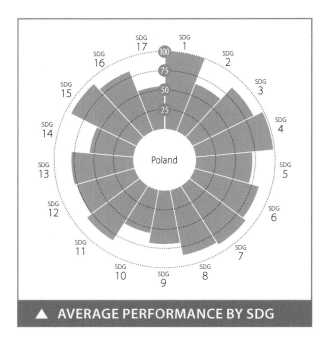

Poland

▲ AVERAGE PERFORMANCE BY SDG

▼ SPILLOVER INDEX

100 (best) to 0 (worst)

▼ CURRENT ASSESSMENT – SDG DASHBOARD

| 1 NO POVERTY | 2 ZERO HUNGER | 3 GOOD HEALTH AND WELL-BEING | 4 QUALITY EDUCATION | 5 GENDER EQUALITY | 6 CLEAN WATER AND SANITATION | 7 AFFORDABLE AND CLEAN ENERGY | 8 DECENT WORK AND ECONOMIC GROWTH | 9 INDUSTRY, INNOVATION AND INFRASTRUCTURE |
| 10 REDUCED INEQUALITIES | 11 SUSTAINABLE CITIES AND COMMUNITIES | 12 RESPONSIBLE CONSUMPTION AND PRODUCTION | 13 CLIMATE ACTION | 14 LIFE BELOW WATER | 15 LIFE ON LAND | 16 PEACE, JUSTICE AND STRONG INSTITUTIONS | 17 PARTNERSHIPS FOR THE GOALS | SUSTAINABLE DEVELOPMENT GOALS |

■ Major challenges   ■ Significant challenges   ■ Challenges remain   ■ SDG achieved   ■ Information unavailable

▼ SDG TRENDS

1 NO POVERTY	2 ZERO HUNGER	3 GOOD HEALTH AND WELL-BEING	4 QUALITY EDUCATION	5 GENDER EQUALITY	6 CLEAN WATER AND SANITATION	7 AFFORDABLE AND CLEAN ENERGY	8 DECENT WORK AND ECONOMIC GROWTH	9 INDUSTRY, INNOVATION AND INFRASTRUCTURE
↑	↗	↗	↑	↗	↑	→	↑	↗

10 REDUCED INEQUALITIES	11 SUSTAINABLE CITIES AND COMMUNITIES	12 RESPONSIBLE CONSUMPTION AND PRODUCTION	13 CLIMATE ACTION	14 LIFE BELOW WATER	15 LIFE ON LAND	16 PEACE, JUSTICE AND STRONG INSTITUTIONS	17 PARTNERSHIPS FOR THE GOALS
→	↗	●	↓	↗	↑	↗	→

↓ Decreasing   → Stagnating   ↗ Moderately improving   ↑ On track or maintaining SDG achievement   ● Information unavailable

Notes: The full title of Goal 2 "Zero Hunger" is "End hunger, achieve food security and improved nutrition and promote sustainable agriculture".
The full title of each SDG is available here: https://sustainabledevelopment.un.org/topics/sustainabledevelopmentgoals

SDG1 – No Poverty

	Value	Year	Rating	Trend
Poverty headcount ratio at $1.90/day (%)	0.0	2020	●	↑
Poverty headcount ratio at $3.20/day (%)	0.1	2020	●	↑
Poverty rate after taxes and transfers (%)	9.6	2017	●	↑

SDG2 – Zero Hunger

	Value	Year	Rating	Trend
Prevalence of undernourishment (%)	2.5	2017	●	↑
Prevalence of stunting in children under 5 years of age (%)	* 2.6	2016	●	↑
Prevalence of wasting in children under 5 years of age (%)	* 0.7	2016	●	↑
Prevalence of obesity, BMI ≥ 30 (% of adult population)	23.1	2016	●	↓
Human Trophic Level (best 2–3 worst)	2.4	2017	●	↓
Cereal yield (tonnes per hectare of harvested land)	4.2	2017	●	↑
Sustainable Nitrogen Management Index (best 0–1.41 worst)	0.6	2015	●	→
Yield gap closure (% of potential yield)	44.5	2015	●	●

SDG3 – Good Health and Well-Being

	Value	Year	Rating	Trend
Maternal mortality rate (per 100,000 live births)	2	2017	●	↑
Neonatal mortality rate (per 1,000 live births)	2.7	2018	●	↑
Mortality rate, under-5 (per 1,000 live births)	4.4	2018	●	↑
Incidence of tuberculosis (per 100,000 population)	16.0	2018	●	↑
New HIV infections (per 1,000 uninfected population)	0.0	2018	●	↑
Age-standardized death rate due to cardiovascular disease, cancer, diabetes, or chronic respiratory disease in adults aged 30–70 years (%)	18.7	2016	●	↑
Age-standardized death rate attributable to household air pollution and ambient air pollution (per 100,000 population)	38	2016	●	●
Traffic deaths (per 100,000 population)	9.7	2016	●	↑
Life expectancy at birth (years)	77.8	2016	●	↑
Adolescent fertility rate (births per 1,000 adolescent females aged 15 to 19)	10.5	2017	●	↑
Births attended by skilled health personnel (%)	99.8	2016	●	↑
Percentage of surviving infants who received 2 WHO-recommended vaccines (%)	93.0	2018	●	↑
Universal health coverage (UHC) index of service coverage (worst 0–100 best)	75.0	2017	●	↑
Subjective well-being (average ladder score, worst 0–10 best)	6.1	2018	●	↑
Gap in life expectancy at birth among regions (years)	2.8	2016	●	●
Gap in self-reported health status by income (percentage points)	24.2	2017	●	↓
Daily smokers (% of population aged 15 and over)	22.7	2014	●	●

SDG4 – Quality Education

	Value	Year	Rating	Trend
Net primary enrollment rate (%)	NA	NA	●	●
Lower secondary completion rate (%)	NA	NA	●	●
Literacy rate (% of population aged 15 to 24)	99.8	2008	●	●
Participation rate in pre-primary organized learning (% of children aged 4 to 6)	99.1	2017	●	●
Tertiary educational attainment (% of population aged 25 to 34)	43.5	2018	●	↑
PISA score (worst 0–600 best)	513.0	2018	●	↑
Variation in science performance explained by socio-economic status (%)	12.6	2018	●	↑
Underachievers in science (% of 15-year-olds)	13.8	2018	●	↑
Resilient students in science (% of 15-year-olds)	39.3	2018	●	↑

SDG5 – Gender Equality

	Value	Year	Rating	Trend
Demand for family planning satisfied by modern methods (% of females aged 15 to 49 who are married or in unions)	* 68.2	2017	●	↗
Ratio of female-to-male mean years of education received (%)	100.0	2018	●	●
Ratio of female-to-male labor force participation rate (%)	74.7	2019	●	↑
Seats held by women in national parliament (%)	28.7	2020	●	→
Gender wage gap (% of male median wage)	9.4	2016	●	↑
Gender gap in time spent doing unpaid work (minutes/day)	136.2	2013	●	●

SDG6 – Clean Water and Sanitation

	Value	Year	Rating	Trend
Population using at least basic drinking water services (%)	99.7	2017	●	●
Population using at least basic sanitation services (%)	98.8	2017	●	●
Freshwater withdrawal (% of available freshwater resources)	36.6	2015	●	●
Anthropogenic wastewater that receives treatment (%)	60.9	2018	●	●
Scarce water consumption embodied in imports (m³/capita)	9.0	2013	●	↑
Population using safely managed water services (%)	99.2	2017	●	↑
Population using safely managed sanitation services (%)	93.3	2017	●	↑

SDG7 – Affordable and Clean Energy

	Value	Year	Rating	Trend
Population with access to electricity (%)	100.0	2017	●	↑
Population with access to clean fuels and technology for cooking (%)	100.0	2016	●	↑
CO2 emissions from fuel combustion for electricity and heating per total electricity output (MtCO2/TWh)	1.9	2017	●	→
Share of renewable energy in total primary energy supply (%)	8.2	2018	●	↓

SDG8 – Decent Work and Economic Growth

	Value	Year	Rating	Trend
Adjusted GDP growth (%)	0.8	2018	●	●
Victims of modern slavery (per 1,000 population)	3.4	2018	●	●
Adults with an account at a bank or other financial institution or with a mobile-money-service provider (% of population aged 15 or over)	86.7	2017	●	↑
Fatal work-related accidents embodied in imports (per 100,000 population)	0.5	2010	●	↑
Employment-to-population ratio (%)	68.2	2019	●	↑
Youth not in employment, education or training (NEET) (% of population aged 15 to 29)	12.7	2018	●	↑

SDG9 – Industry, Innovation and Infrastructure

	Value	Year	Rating	Trend
Population using the internet (%)	77.5	2018	●	↑
Mobile broadband subscriptions (per 100 population)	171.7	2018	●	↑
Logistics Performance Index: Quality of trade and transport-related infrastructure (worst 1–5 best)	3.2	2018	●	↑
The Times Higher Education Universities Ranking: Average score of top 3 universities (worst 0–100 best)	29.6	2020	●	●
Scientific and technical journal articles (per 1,000 population)	0.9	2018	●	↑
Expenditure on research and development (% of GDP)	1.0	2017	●	↗
Researchers (per 1,000 employed population)	7.2	2018	●	↑
Triadic patent families filed (per million population)	2.0	2017	●	→
Gap in internet access by income (percentage points)	34.9	2019	●	↗
Women in science and engineering (% of tertiary graduates in science and engineering)	41.0	2015	●	●

SDG10 – Reduced Inequalities

	Value	Year	Rating	Trend
Gini coefficient adjusted for top income	42.9	2016	●	→
Palma ratio	1.0	2017	●	↑
Elderly poverty rate (% of population aged 66 or over)	11.2	2017	●	↓

SDG11 – Sustainable Cities and Communities

	Value	Year	Rating	Trend
Annual mean concentration of particulate matter of less than 2.5 microns in diameter (PM2.5) (µg/m³)	20.9	2017	●	↗
Access to improved water source, piped (% of urban population)	99.0	2017	●	↑
Satisfaction with public transport (%)	63.2	2018	●	↓
Population with rent overburden (%)	6.2	2017	●	↑

SDG12 – Responsible Consumption and Production

	Value	Year	Rating	Trend
Electronic waste (kg/capita)	11.9	2016	●	●
Production-based SO2 emissions (kg/capita)	30.7	2012	●	●
SO2 emissions embodied in imports (kg/capita)	5.2	2012	●	●
Production-based nitrogen emissions (kg/capita)	32.8	2010	●	●
Nitrogen emissions embodied in imports (kg/capita)	3.4	2010	●	●
Non-recycled municipal solid waste (kg/capita/day)	0.6	2018	●	●

SDG13 – Climate Action

	Value	Year	Rating	Trend
Energy-related CO2 emissions (tCO2/capita)	8.0	2017	●	↓
CO2 emissions embodied in imports (tCO2/capita)	1.0	2015	●	→
CO2 emissions embodied in fossil fuel exports (kg/capita)	387.1	2019	●	●
Effective carbon rate (EUR/tCO2)	11.9	2016	●	●

SDG14 – Life Below Water

	Value	Year	Rating	Trend
Mean area that is protected in marine sites important to biodiversity (%)	83.8	2018	●	↑
Ocean Health Index: Clean Waters score (worst 0–100 best)	44.3	2019	●	↗
Fish caught from overexploited or collapsed stocks (% of total catch)	59.9	2014	●	↑
Fish caught by trawling (%)	56.5	2014	●	↓
Marine biodiversity threats embodied in imports (per million population)	0.0	2018	●	●

SDG15 – Life on Land

	Value	Year	Rating	Trend
Mean area that is protected in terrestrial sites important to biodiversity (%)	87.6	2018	●	↑
Mean area that is protected in freshwater sites important to biodiversity (%)	91.8	2018	●	↑
Red List Index of species survival (worst 0–1 best)	1.0	2019	●	↑
Permanent deforestation (% of forest area, 5-year average)	0.0	2018	●	●
Terrestrial and freshwater biodiversity threats embodied in imports (per million population)	1.0	2018	●	●

SDG16 – Peace, Justice and Strong Institutions

	Value	Year	Rating	Trend
Homicides (per 100,000 population)	0.8	2017	●	↑
Unsentenced detainees (% of prison population)	9.1	2018	●	↑
Percentage of population who feel safe walking alone at night in the city or area where they live (%)	73.9	2018	●	↑
Property Rights (worst 1–7 best)	4.1	2019	●	●
Birth registrations with civil authority (% of children under age 5)	100.0	2018	●	●
Corruption Perception Index (worst 0–100 best)	58.0	2019	●	↓
Children involved in child labor (% of population aged 5 to 14)	* 0.0	2016	●	●
Exports of major conventional weapons (TIV constant million USD per 100,000 population)	0.0	2019	●	●
Press Freedom Index (best 0–100 worst)	28.9	2019	●	↑
Persons held in prison (per 100,000 population)	195.1	2017	●	↗

SDG17 – Partnerships for the Goals

	Value	Year	Rating	Trend
Government spending on health and education (% of GDP)	9.2	2016	●	↓
For high-income and all OECD DAC countries: International concessional public finance, including official development assistance (% of GNI)	0.1	2017	●	→
Other countries: Government revenue excluding grants (% of GDP)	NA	NA	●	●
Corporate Tax Haven Score (best 0–100 worst)	40.4	2019	●	●
Financial Secrecy Score (best 0–100 worst)	55.6	2020	●	●
Shifted profits of multinationals (US$ billion)	4.2	2016	●	●

* Imputed data point

5. Country Profiles

▼ OVERALL PERFORMANCE

Index score

77.6

Regional average score

77.3

SDG Global rank 25 (OF 166)

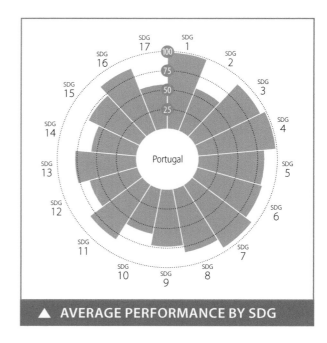

▲ AVERAGE PERFORMANCE BY SDG

▼ SPILLOVER INDEX

100 (best) to 0 (worst)

▼ CURRENT ASSESSMENT – SDG DASHBOARD

■ Major challenges   ■ Significant challenges   ■ Challenges remain   ■ SDG achieved   ■ Information unavailable

▼ SDG TRENDS

↓ Decreasing   → Stagnating   ↗ Moderately improving   ↑ On track or maintaining SDG achievement   ● Information unavailable

Notes: The full title of Goal 2 "Zero Hunger" is "End hunger, achieve food security and improved nutrition and promote sustainable agriculture".
The full title of each SDG is available here: https://sustainabledevelopment.un.org/topics/sustainabledevelopmentgoals

SDG1 – No Poverty

Indicator	Value	Year
Poverty headcount ratio at $1.90/day (%)	0.5	2020
Poverty headcount ratio at $3.20/day (%)	0.9	2020
Poverty rate after taxes and transfers (%)	10.7	2017

SDG2 – Zero Hunger

Indicator	Value	Year
Prevalence of undernourishment (%)	2.5	2017
Prevalence of stunting in children under 5 years of age (%)	* 2.6	2016
Prevalence of wasting in children under 5 years of age (%)	* 0.7	2016
Prevalence of obesity, BMI ≥ 30 (% of adult population)	20.8	2016
Human Trophic Level (best 2–3 worst)	2.4	2017
Cereal yield (tonnes per hectare of harvested land)	4.7	2017
Sustainable Nitrogen Management Index (best 0–1.41 worst)	1.1	2015
Yield gap closure (% of potential yield)	28.5	2015

SDG3 – Good Health and Well-Being

Indicator	Value	Year
Maternal mortality rate (per 100,000 live births)	8	2017
Neonatal mortality rate (per 1,000 live births)	2.1	2018
Mortality rate, under-5 (per 1,000 live births)	3.7	2018
Incidence of tuberculosis (per 100,000 population)	24.0	2018
New HIV infections (per 1,000 uninfected population)	0.1	2018
Age-standardized death rate due to cardiovascular disease, cancer, diabetes, or chronic respiratory disease in adults aged 30–70 years (%)	11.1	2016
Age-standardized death rate attributable to household air pollution and ambient air pollution (per 100,000 population)	10	2016
Traffic deaths (per 100,000 population)	7.4	2016
Life expectancy at birth (years)	81.5	2016
Adolescent fertility rate (births per 1,000 adolescent females aged 15 to 19)	8.4	2017
Births attended by skilled health personnel (%)	98.9	2015
Percentage of surviving infants who received 2 WHO-recommended vaccines (%)	99.0	2018
Universal health coverage (UHC) index of service coverage (worst 0–100 best)	82.0	2017
Subjective well-being (average ladder score, worst 0–10 best)	6.1	2019
Gap in life expectancy at birth among regions (years)	4.1	2016
Gap in self-reported health status by income (percentage points)	22.6	2017
Daily smokers (% of population aged 15 and over)	16.8	2014

SDG4 – Quality Education

Indicator	Value	Year
Net primary enrollment rate (%)	* 98.6	2017
Lower secondary completion rate (%)	* 98.6	2017
Literacy rate (% of population aged 15 to 24)	99.7	2018
Participation rate in pre-primary organized learning (% of children aged 4 to 6)	99.3	2017
Tertiary educational attainment (% of population aged 25 to 34)	35.1	2018
PISA score (worst 0–600 best)	492.0	2018
Variation in science performance explained by socio-economic status (%)	15.9	2018
Underachievers in science (% of 15-year-olds)	19.6	2018
Resilient students in science (% of 15-year-olds)	41.1	2018

SDG5 – Gender Equality

Indicator	Value	Year
Demand for family planning satisfied by modern methods (% of females aged 15 to 49 who are married or in unions)	* 79.1	2017
Ratio of female-to-male mean years of education received (%)	100.0	2018
Ratio of female-to-male labor force participation rate (%)	84.0	2019
Seats held by women in national parliament (%)	40.0	2020
Gender wage gap (% of male median wage)	14.8	2017
Gender gap in time spent doing unpaid work (minutes/day)	NA	NA

SDG6 – Clean Water and Sanitation

Indicator	Value	Year
Population using at least basic drinking water services (%)	99.9	2017
Population using at least basic sanitation services (%)	99.6	2017
Freshwater withdrawal (% of available freshwater resources)	1.2	2005
Anthropogenic wastewater that receives treatment (%)	55.0	2018
Scarce water consumption embodied in imports (m³/capita)	27.0	2013
Population using safely managed water services (%)	95.3	2017
Population using safely managed sanitation services (%)	84.7	2017

SDG7 – Affordable and Clean Energy

Indicator	Value	Year
Population with access to electricity (%)	100.0	2017
Population with access to clean fuels and technology for cooking (%)	100.0	2016
CO2 emissions from fuel combustion for electricity and heating per total electricity output (MtCO2/TWh)	0.9	2017
Share of renewable energy in total primary energy supply (%)	24.7	2018

SDG8 – Decent Work and Economic Growth

Indicator	Value	Year
Adjusted GDP growth (%)	-0.3	2018
Victims of modern slavery (per 1,000 population)	2.5	2018
Adults with an account at a bank or other financial institution or with a mobile-money-service provider (% of population aged 15 or over)	92.3	2017
Fatal work-related accidents embodied in imports (per 100,000 population)	1.1	2010
Employment-to-population ratio (%)	70.5	2019
Youth not in employment, education or training (NEET) (% of population aged 15 to 29)	11.6	2018

SDG9 – Industry, Innovation and Infrastructure

Indicator	Value	Year
Population using the internet (%)	74.7	2018
Mobile broadband subscriptions (per 100 population)	73.8	2018
Logistics Performance Index: Quality of trade and transport-related infrastructure (worst 1–5 best)	3.2	2018
The Times Higher Education Universities Ranking: Average score of top 3 universities (worst 0–100 best)	40.3	2020
Scientific and technical journal articles (per 1,000 population)	1.4	2018
Expenditure on research and development (% of GDP)	1.3	2017
Researchers (per 1,000 employed population)	9.5	2018
Triadic patent families filed (per million population)	3.4	2017
Gap in internet access by income (percentage points)	41.2	2019
Women in science and engineering (% of tertiary graduates in science and engineering)	38.1	2015

SDG10 – Reduced Inequalities

Indicator	Value	Year
Gini coefficient adjusted for top income	42.1	2015
Palma ratio	1.2	2017
Elderly poverty rate (% of population aged 66 or over)	10.1	2017

SDG11 – Sustainable Cities and Communities

Indicator	Value	Year
Annual mean concentration of particulate matter of less than 2.5 microns in diameter (PM2.5) (µg/m³)	8.2	2017
Access to improved water source, piped (% of urban population)	99.0	2017
Satisfaction with public transport (%)	52.2	2019
Population with rent overburden (%)	8.4	2017

SDG12 – Responsible Consumption and Production

Indicator	Value	Year
Electronic waste (kg/capita)	17.3	2016
Production-based SO2 emissions (kg/capita)	52.9	2012
SO2 emissions embodied in imports (kg/capita)	8.4	2012
Production-based nitrogen emissions (kg/capita)	35.5	2010
Nitrogen emissions embodied in imports (kg/capita)	12.9	2010
Non-recycled municipal solid waste (kg/capita/day)	1.0	2018

SDG13 – Climate Action

Indicator	Value	Year
Energy-related CO2 emissions (tCO2/capita)	4.8	2017
CO2 emissions embodied in imports (tCO2/capita)	1.6	2015
CO2 emissions embodied in fossil fuel exports (kg/capita)	0.0	2019
Effective carbon rate (EUR/tCO2)	9.0	2016

SDG14 – Life Below Water

Indicator	Value	Year
Mean area that is protected in marine sites important to biodiversity (%)	65.7	2018
Ocean Health Index: Clean Waters score (worst 0–100 best)	52.3	2019
Fish caught from overexploited or collapsed stocks (% of total catch)	67.2	2014
Fish caught by trawling (%)	11.3	2014
Marine biodiversity threats embodied in imports (per million population)	0.6	2018

SDG15 – Life on Land

Indicator	Value	Year
Mean area that is protected in terrestrial sites important to biodiversity (%)	74.1	2018
Mean area that is protected in freshwater sites important to biodiversity (%)	64.0	2018
Red List Index of species survival (worst 0–1 best)	0.9	2019
Permanent deforestation (% of forest area, 5-year average)	0.0	2018
Terrestrial and freshwater biodiversity threats embodied in imports (per million population)	4.0	2018

SDG16 – Peace, Justice and Strong Institutions

Indicator	Value	Year
Homicides (per 100,000 population)	0.7	2017
Unsentenced detainees (% of prison population)	15.9	2018
Percentage of population who feel safe walking alone at night in the city or area where they live (%)	83.3	2019
Property Rights (worst 1–7 best)	4.9	2019
Birth registrations with civil authority (% of children under age 5)	100.0	2018
Corruption Perception Index (worst 0–100 best)	62.0	2019
Children involved in child labor (% of population aged 5 to 14)	3.4	2016
Exports of major conventional weapons (TIV constant million USD per 100,000 population)	0.5	2019
Press Freedom Index (best 0–100 worst)	12.6	2019
Persons held in prison (per 100,000 population)	131.5	2017

SDG17 – Partnerships for the Goals

Indicator	Value	Year
Government spending on health and education (% of GDP)	10.8	2015
For high-income and all OECD DAC countries: International concessional public finance, including official development assistance (% of GNI)	0.2	2017
Other countries: Government revenue excluding grants (% of GDP)	NA	NA
Corporate Tax Haven Score (best 0–100 worst)	45.8	2019
Financial Secrecy Score (best 0–100 worst)	54.0	2020
Shifted profits of multinationals (US$ billion)	3.3	2016

* Imputed data point

5. Country Profiles

▼ OVERALL PERFORMANCE

Index score

64.7

Regional average score

66.3

SDG Global rank 103 (OF 166)

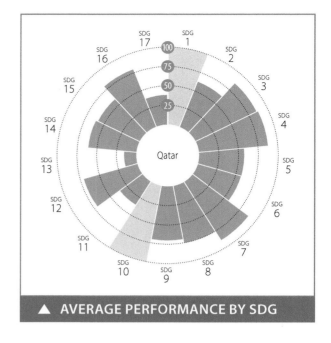

▲ AVERAGE PERFORMANCE BY SDG

▼ SPILLOVER INDEX

100 (best) to 0 (worst)

▼ CURRENT ASSESSMENT – SDG DASHBOARD

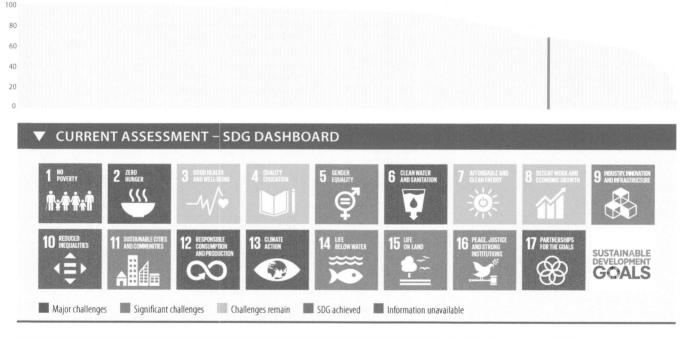

■ Major challenges   ■ Significant challenges   ■ Challenges remain   ■ SDG achieved   ■ Information unavailable

▼ SDG TRENDS

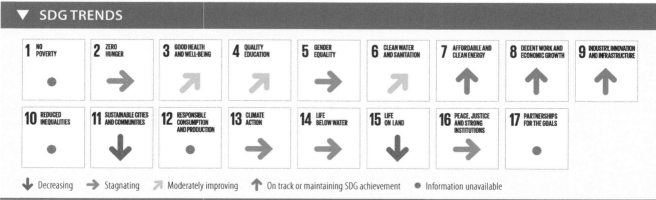

↓ Decreasing   → Stagnating   ↗ Moderately improving   ↑ On track or maintaining SDG achievement   ● Information unavailable

Notes: The full title of Goal 2 "Zero Hunger" is "End hunger, achieve food security and improved nutrition and promote sustainable agriculture".
The full title of each SDG is available here: https://sustainabledevelopment.un.org/topics/sustainabledevelopmentgoals

SDG1 – No Poverty

Indicator	Value	Year	Rating	Trend
Poverty headcount ratio at $1.90/day (%)	* NA	NA	●	●
Poverty headcount ratio at $3.20/day (%)	* NA	NA	●	●

SDG2 – Zero Hunger

Indicator	Value	Year	Rating	Trend
Prevalence of undernourishment (%)	* 1.2	2017	●	●
Prevalence of stunting in children under 5 years of age (%)	* 2.6	2016	●	↑
Prevalence of wasting in children under 5 years of age (%)	* 0.7	2016	●	↑
Prevalence of obesity, BMI ≥ 30 (% of adult population)	35.1	2016	●	↓
Human Trophic Level (best 2–3 worst)	NA	NA	●	●
Cereal yield (tonnes per hectare of harvested land)	5.1	2017	●	↑
Sustainable Nitrogen Management Index (best 0–1.41 worst)	1.0	2015	●	↓

SDG3 – Good Health and Well-Being

Indicator	Value	Year	Rating	Trend
Maternal mortality rate (per 100,000 live births)	9	2017	●	↑
Neonatal mortality rate (per 1,000 live births)	3.5	2018	●	↑
Mortality rate, under-5 (per 1,000 live births)	6.8	2018	●	↑
Incidence of tuberculosis (per 100,000 population)	31.0	2018	●	→
New HIV infections (per 1,000 uninfected population)	NA	NA	●	●
Age-standardized death rate due to cardiovascular disease, cancer, diabetes, or chronic respiratory disease in adults aged 30–70 years (%)	15.3	2016	●	↑
Age-standardized death rate attributable to household air pollution and ambient air pollution (per 100,000 population)	47	2016	●	●
Traffic deaths (per 100,000 population)	9.3	2016	●	↑
Life expectancy at birth (years)	78.1	2016	●	↗
Adolescent fertility rate (births per 1,000 adolescent females aged 15 to 19)	9.9	2017	●	↑
Births attended by skilled health personnel (%)	100.0	2015	●	↑
Percentage of surviving infants who received 2 WHO-recommended vaccines (%)	98	2018	●	↑
Universal health coverage (UHC) index of service coverage (worst 0–100 best)	68.0	2017	●	→
Subjective well-being (average ladder score, worst 0–10 best)	6.4	2014	●	●

SDG4 – Quality Education

Indicator	Value	Year	Rating	Trend
Net primary enrollment rate (%)	94.1	2018	●	↑
Lower secondary completion rate (%)	88.4	2018	●	→
Literacy rate (% of population aged 15 to 24)	94.6	2017	●	●

SDG5 – Gender Equality

Indicator	Value	Year	Rating	Trend
Demand for family planning satisfied by modern methods (% of females aged 15 to 49 who are married or in unions)	68.9	2012	●	→
Ratio of female-to-male mean years of education received (%)	119.4	2018	●	↑
Ratio of female-to-male labor force participation rate (%)	60.7	2019	●	↓
Seats held by women in national parliament (%)	9.8	2020	●	↗

SDG6 – Clean Water and Sanitation

Indicator	Value	Year	Rating	Trend
Population using at least basic drinking water services (%)	99.6	2017	●	↑
Population using at least basic sanitation services (%)	100.0	2017	●	↑
Freshwater withdrawal (% of available freshwater resources)	374.1	2005	●	●
Anthropogenic wastewater that receives treatment (%)	70.0	2018	●	●
Scarce water consumption embodied in imports (m³/capita)	83.6	2013	●	↗

SDG7 – Affordable and Clean Energy

Indicator	Value	Year	Rating	Trend
Population with access to electricity (%)	100.0	2017	●	↑
Population with access to clean fuels and technology for cooking (%)	98.5	2016	●	↑
CO_2 emissions from fuel combustion for electricity and heating per total electricity output (MtCO2/TWh)	1.9	2017	●	↑

SDG8 – Decent Work and Economic Growth

Indicator	Value	Year	Rating	Trend
Adjusted GDP growth (%)	-1.4	2018	●	●
Victims of modern slavery (per 1,000 population)	* NA	NA	●	●
Adults with an account at a bank or other financial institution or with a mobile-money-service provider (% of population aged 15 or over)	65.9	2011	●	●
Unemployment rate (% of total labor force)	0.1	2019	●	↑
Fatal work-related accidents embodied in imports (per 100,000 population)	1.7	2010	●	↑

SDG9 – Industry, Innovation and Infrastructure

Indicator	Value	Year	Rating	Trend
Population using the internet (%)	99.7	2018	●	↑
Mobile broadband subscriptions (per 100 population)	125.9	2018	●	↑
Logistics Performance Index: Quality of trade and transport-related infrastructure (worst 1–5 best)	3.4	2018	●	↑
The Times Higher Education Universities Ranking: Average score of top 3 universities (worst 0–100 best)	40.6	2020	●	●
Scientific and technical journal articles (per 1,000 population)	0.5	2018	●	↑
Expenditure on research and development (% of GDP)	0.5	2015	●	●

SDG10 – Reduced Inequalities

Indicator	Value	Year	Rating	Trend
Gini coefficient adjusted for top income	NA	NA	●	●

SDG11 – Sustainable Cities and Communities

Indicator	Value	Year	Rating	Trend
Annual mean concentration of particulate matter of less than 2.5 microns in diameter (PM2.5) (µg/m³)	91.2	2017	●	↓
Access to improved water source, piped (% of urban population)	NA	NA	●	●
Satisfaction with public transport (%)	64.7	2012	●	●

SDG12 – Responsible Consumption and Production

Indicator	Value	Year	Rating	Trend
Municipal solid waste (kg/capita/day)	1.0	2012	●	●
Electronic waste (kg/capita)	11.3	2016	●	●
Production-based SO_2 emissions (kg/capita)	66.7	2012	●	●
SO_2 emissions embodied in imports (kg/capita)	11.1	2012	●	●
Production-based nitrogen emissions (kg/capita)	33.2	2010	●	●
Nitrogen emissions embodied in imports (kg/capita)	10.7	2010	●	●

SDG13 – Climate Action

Indicator	Value	Year	Rating	Trend
Energy-related CO_2 emissions (tCO2/capita)	44.0	2017	●	↓
CO_2 emissions embodied in imports (tCO2/capita)	1.7	2015	●	↑
CO_2 emissions embodied in fossil fuel exports (kg/capita)	107901.6	2018	●	●

SDG14 – Life Below Water

Indicator	Value	Year	Rating	Trend
Mean area that is protected in marine sites important to biodiversity (%)	40.0	2018	●	→
Ocean Health Index: Clean Waters score (worst 0–100 best)	62.3	2019	●	↗
Fish caught from overexploited or collapsed stocks (% of total catch)	NA	NA	●	●
Fish caught by trawling (%)	NA	NA	●	●
Marine biodiversity threats embodied in imports (per million population)	0.1	2018	●	●

SDG15 – Life on Land

Indicator	Value	Year	Rating	Trend
Mean area that is protected in terrestrial sites important to biodiversity (%)	33.3	2018	●	→
Mean area that is protected in freshwater sites important to biodiversity (%)	NA	NA	●	●
Red List Index of species survival (worst 0–1 best)	0.8	2019	●	↓
Permanent deforestation (% of forest area, 5-year average)	NA	NA	●	●
Terrestrial and freshwater biodiversity threats embodied in imports (per million population)	1.0	2018	●	●

SDG16 – Peace, Justice and Strong Institutions

Indicator	Value	Year	Rating	Trend
Homicides (per 100,000 population)	0.4	2014	●	●
Unsentenced detainees (% of prison population)	43.5	2015	●	●
Percentage of population who feel safe walking alone at night in the city or area where they live (%)	92.1	2012	●	●
Property Rights (worst 1–7 best)	5.4	2019	●	●
Birth registrations with civil authority (% of children under age 5)	100.0	2018	●	●
Corruption Perception Index (worst 0–100 best)	62	2019	●	↑
Children involved in child labor (% of population aged 5 to 14)	NA	NA	●	●
Exports of major conventional weapons (TIV constant million USD per 100,000 population)	0.2	2019	●	●
Press Freedom Index (best 0–100 worst)	42.5	2019	●	↓

SDG17 – Partnerships for the Goals

Indicator	Value	Year	Rating	Trend
Government spending on health and education (% of GDP)	5.7	2014	●	●
For high-income and all OECD DAC countries: International concessional public finance, including official development assistance (% of GNI)	NA	NA	●	●
Other countries: Government revenue excluding grants (% of GDP)	NA	NA	●	●
Corporate Tax Haven Score (best 0–100 worst)	* NA	NA	●	●

* Imputed data point

5. Country Profiles

▼ OVERALL PERFORMANCE

Index score

74.8

Regional average score

70.9

SDG Global rank **38** (OF 166)

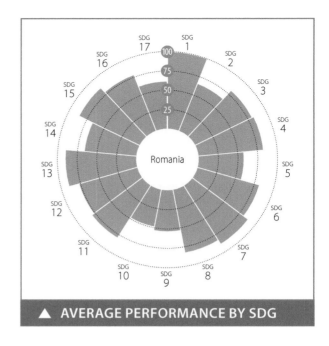

▲ AVERAGE PERFORMANCE BY SDG

▼ SPILLOVER INDEX

100 (best) to 0 (worst)

▼ CURRENT ASSESSMENT – SDG DASHBOARD

■ Major challenges ■ Significant challenges ■ Challenges remain ■ SDG achieved ■ Information unavailable

▼ SDG TRENDS

↓ Decreasing → Stagnating ↗ Moderately improving ↑ On track or maintaining SDG achievement ● Information unavailable

Notes: The full title of Goal 2 "Zero Hunger" is "End hunger, achieve food security and improved nutrition and promote sustainable agriculture".
The full title of each SDG is available here: https://sustainabledevelopment.un.org/topics/sustainabledevelopmentgoals

SDG1 – No Poverty

	Value	Year	Rating	Trend
Poverty headcount ratio at $1.90/day (%)	0.1	2020	●	↑
Poverty headcount ratio at $3.20/day (%)	0.9	2020	●	↑

SDG2 – Zero Hunger

	Value	Year	Rating	Trend
Prevalence of undernourishment (%)	2.5	2017	●	↑
Prevalence of stunting in children under 5 years of age (%)	12.8	2002	●	↗
Prevalence of wasting in children under 5 years of age (%)	3.5	2002	●	↑
Prevalence of obesity, BMI ≥ 30 (% of adult population)	22.5	2016	●	↓
Human Trophic Level (best 2–3 worst)	2.3	2017	●	→
Cereal yield (tonnes per hectare of harvested land)	5.2	2017	●	↑
Sustainable Nitrogen Management Index (best 0–1.41 worst)	0.5	2015	●	↑

SDG3 – Good Health and Well-Being

	Value	Year	Rating	Trend
Maternal mortality rate (per 100,000 live births)	19	2017	●	↑
Neonatal mortality rate (per 1,000 live births)	3.4	2018	●	↑
Mortality rate, under-5 (per 1,000 live births)	7.3	2018	●	↑
Incidence of tuberculosis (per 100,000 population)	68.0	2018	●	↗
New HIV infections (per 1,000 uninfected population)	0.0	2018	●	↑
Age-standardized death rate due to cardiovascular disease, cancer, diabetes, or chronic respiratory disease in adults aged 30–70 years (%)	21.4	2016	●	↗
Age-standardized death rate attributable to household air pollution and ambient air pollution (per 100,000 population)	59	2016	●	●
Traffic deaths (per 100,000 population)	10.3	2016	●	↓
Life expectancy at birth (years)	75.2	2016	●	→
Adolescent fertility rate (births per 1,000 adolescent females aged 15 to 19)	36.2	2017	●	→
Births attended by skilled health personnel (%)	95.2	2015	●	↓
Percentage of surviving infants who received 2 WHO-recommended vaccines (%)	86	2018	●	→
Universal health coverage (UHC) index of service coverage (worst 0–100 best)	74.0	2017	●	↑
Subjective well-being (average ladder score, worst 0–10 best)	6.1	2019	●	↑

SDG4 – Quality Education

	Value	Year	Rating	Trend
Net primary enrollment rate (%)	82.2	2017	●	↓
Lower secondary completion rate (%)	89.0	2016	●	●
Literacy rate (% of population aged 15 to 24)	99.4	2018	●	●

SDG5 – Gender Equality

	Value	Year	Rating	Trend
Demand for family planning satisfied by modern methods (% of females aged 15 to 49 who are married or in unions)	46.5	2004	●	↑
Ratio of female-to-male mean years of education received (%)	93.8	2018	●	↗
Ratio of female-to-male labor force participation rate (%)	70.8	2019	●	↑
Seats held by women in national parliament (%)	21.9	2020	●	↗

SDG6 – Clean Water and Sanitation

	Value	Year	Rating	Trend
Population using at least basic drinking water services (%)	100.0	2017	●	↑
Population using at least basic sanitation services (%)	84.3	2017	●	↗
Freshwater withdrawal (% of available freshwater resources)	6.0	2015	●	●
Anthropogenic wastewater that receives treatment (%)	30.4	2018	●	●
Scarce water consumption embodied in imports (m³/capita)	5.6	2013	●	↑

SDG7 – Affordable and Clean Energy

	Value	Year	Rating	Trend
Population with access to electricity (%)	100.0	2017	●	↑
Population with access to clean fuels and technology for cooking (%)	85.9	2016	●	↑
CO$_2$ emissions from fuel combustion for electricity and heating per total electricity output (MtCO$_2$/TWh)	1.2	2017	●	→

SDG8 – Decent Work and Economic Growth

	Value	Year	Rating	Trend
Adjusted GDP growth (%)	4.4	2018	●	●
Victims of modern slavery (per 1,000 population)	4.3	2018	●	●
Adults with an account at a bank or other financial institution or with a mobile-money-service provider (% of population aged 15 or over)	57.8	2017	●	↓
Unemployment rate (% of total labor force)	4.0	2019	●	↑
Fatal work-related accidents embodied in imports (per 100,000 population)	0.2	2010	●	↑

SDG9 – Industry, Innovation and Infrastructure

	Value	Year	Rating	Trend
Population using the internet (%)	70.7	2018	●	↑
Mobile broadband subscriptions (per 100 population)	88.0	2018	●	↑
Logistics Performance Index: Quality of trade and transport-related infrastructure (worst 1–5 best)	2.9	2018	●	↑
The Times Higher Education Universities Ranking: Average score of top 3 universities (worst 0–100 best)	22.3	2020	●	●
Scientific and technical journal articles (per 1,000 population)	0.5	2018	●	↓
Expenditure on research and development (% of GDP)	0.5	2017	●	↗

SDG10 – Reduced Inequalities

	Value	Year	Rating	Trend
Gini coefficient adjusted for top income	45.8	2016	●	●

SDG11 – Sustainable Cities and Communities

	Value	Year	Rating	Trend
Annual mean concentration of particulate matter of less than 2.5 microns in diameter (PM2.5) (μg/m³)	14.6	2017	●	→
Access to improved water source, piped (% of urban population)	89.8	2017	●	→
Satisfaction with public transport (%)	57.5	2019	●	↓

SDG12 – Responsible Consumption and Production

	Value	Year	Rating	Trend
Municipal solid waste (kg/capita/day)	1.3	2015	●	●
Electronic waste (kg/capita)	11.6	2016	●	●
Production-based SO$_2$ emissions (kg/capita)	29.4	2012	●	●
SO$_2$ emissions embodied in imports (kg/capita)	3.3	2012	●	●
Production-based nitrogen emissions (kg/capita)	41.3	2010	●	●
Nitrogen emissions embodied in imports (kg/capita)	2.2	2010	●	●

SDG13 – Climate Action

	Value	Year	Rating	Trend
Energy-related CO$_2$ emissions (tCO$_2$/capita)	3.5	2017	●	→
CO$_2$ emissions embodied in imports (tCO$_2$/capita)	0.6	2015	●	→
CO$_2$ emissions embodied in fossil fuel exports (kg/capita)	7.3	2019	●	●

SDG14 – Life Below Water

	Value	Year	Rating	Trend
Mean area that is protected in marine sites important to biodiversity (%)	99.3	2018	●	↑
Ocean Health Index: Clean Waters score (worst 0–100 best)	58.1	2019	●	→
Fish caught from overexploited or collapsed stocks (% of total catch)	NA	NA	●	●
Fish caught by trawling (%)	70.3	2014	●	↑
Marine biodiversity threats embodied in imports (per million population)	0.0	2018	●	●

SDG15 – Life on Land

	Value	Year	Rating	Trend
Mean area that is protected in terrestrial sites important to biodiversity (%)	77.3	2018	●	↑
Mean area that is protected in freshwater sites important to biodiversity (%)	65.9	2018	●	↑
Red List Index of species survival (worst 0–1 best)	0.9	2019	●	↑
Permanent deforestation (% of forest area, 5-year average)	0.0	2018	●	●
Terrestrial and freshwater biodiversity threats embodied in imports (per million population)	0.5	2018	●	●

SDG16 – Peace, Justice and Strong Institutions

	Value	Year	Rating	Trend
Homicides (per 100,000 population)	1.5	2017	●	↑
Unsentenced detainees (% of prison population)	6.1	2018	●	↑
Percentage of population who feel safe walking alone at night in the city or area where they live (%)	60.0	2019	●	↑
Property Rights (worst 1–7 best)	4.6	2019	●	●
Birth registrations with civil authority (% of children under age 5)	NA	NA	●	●
Corruption Perception Index (worst 0–100 best)	44	2019	●	↓
Children involved in child labor (% of population aged 5 to 14)	0.9	2016	●	●
Exports of major conventional weapons (TIV constant million USD per 100,000 population)	* 0.0	2019	●	●
Press Freedom Index (best 0–100 worst)	25.7	2019	●	↑

SDG17 – Partnerships for the Goals

	Value	Year	Rating	Trend
Government spending on health and education (% of GDP)	6.9	2016	●	↓
For high-income and all OECD DAC countries: International concessional public finance, including official development assistance (% of GNI)	NA	NA	●	●
Other countries: Government revenue excluding grants (% of GDP)	28.6	2017	●	↓
Corporate Tax Haven Score (best 0–100 worst)	55.6	2019	●	●

* Imputed data point

5. Country Profiles

▼ OVERALL PERFORMANCE

Index score

71.9

Regional average score

70.9

SDG Global rank **57** (OF 166)

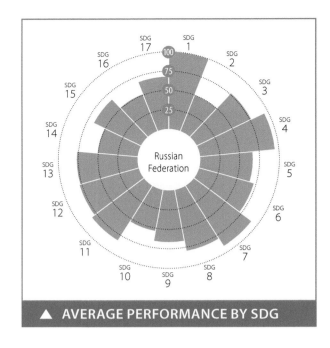

▲ AVERAGE PERFORMANCE BY SDG

▼ SPILLOVER INDEX

100 (best) to 0 (worst)

▼ CURRENT ASSESSMENT – SDG DASHBOARD

■ Major challenges ■ Significant challenges ■ Challenges remain ■ SDG achieved ■ Information unavailable

▼ SDG TRENDS

↓ Decreasing → Stagnating ↗ Moderately improving ↑ On track or maintaining SDG achievement ● Information unavailable

Notes: The full title of Goal 2 "Zero Hunger" is "End hunger, achieve food security and improved nutrition and promote sustainable agriculture".
The full title of each SDG is available here: https://sustainabledevelopment.un.org/topics/sustainabledevelopmentgoals

SDG1 – No Poverty

	Value	Year	Rating	Trend
Poverty headcount ratio at $1.90/day (%)	0.0	2020	●	↑
Poverty headcount ratio at $3.20/day (%)	0.0	2020	●	↑

SDG2 – Zero Hunger

	Value	Year	Rating	Trend
Prevalence of undernourishment (%)	2.5	2017	●	↑
Prevalence of stunting in children under 5 years of age (%)	NA	NA	●	●
Prevalence of wasting in children under 5 years of age (%)	NA	NA	●	●
Prevalence of obesity, BMI ≥ 30 (% of adult population)	23.1	2016	●	↓
Human Trophic Level (best 2–3 worst)	2.4	2017	●	→
Cereal yield (tonnes per hectare of harvested land)	3.0	2017	●	↑
Sustainable Nitrogen Management Index (best 0–1.41 worst)	0.6	2015	●	→

SDG3 – Good Health and Well-Being

	Value	Year	Rating	Trend
Maternal mortality rate (per 100,000 live births)	17	2017	●	↑
Neonatal mortality rate (per 1,000 live births)	3.2	2018	●	↑
Mortality rate, under-5 (per 1,000 live births)	7.2	2018	●	↑
Incidence of tuberculosis (per 100,000 population)	54.0	2018	●	↑
New HIV infections (per 1,000 uninfected population)	NA	NA	●	●
Age-standardized death rate due to cardiovascular disease, cancer, diabetes, or chronic respiratory disease in adults aged 30–70 years (%)	25.4	2016	●	↑
Age-standardized death rate attributable to household air pollution and ambient air pollution (per 100,000 population)	49	2016	◐	●
Traffic deaths (per 100,000 population)	18.0	2016	●	→
Life expectancy at birth (years)	71.9	2016	◐	↗
Adolescent fertility rate (births per 1,000 adolescent females aged 15 to 19)	20.7	2017	●	↑
Births attended by skilled health personnel (%)	99.7	2014	●	●
Percentage of surviving infants who received 2 WHO-recommended vaccines (%)	97	2018	●	↑
Universal health coverage (UHC) index of service coverage (worst 0–100 best)	74.0	2017	◐	↑
Subjective well-being (average ladder score, worst 0–10 best)	5.5	2018	◐	↓

SDG4 – Quality Education

	Value	Year	Rating	Trend
Net primary enrollment rate (%)	95.1	2017	◐	↑
Lower secondary completion rate (%)	95.9	2016	●	●
Literacy rate (% of population aged 15 to 24)	99.7	2018	●	●

SDG5 – Gender Equality

	Value	Year	Rating	Trend
Demand for family planning satisfied by modern methods (% of females aged 15 to 49 who are married or in unions)	72.4	2011	◐	↑
Ratio of female-to-male mean years of education received (%)	98.3	2018	●	↑
Ratio of female-to-male labor force participation rate (%)	77.8	2019	●	↑
Seats held by women in national parliament (%)	15.8	2020	●	→

SDG6 – Clean Water and Sanitation

	Value	Year	Rating	Trend
Population using at least basic drinking water services (%)	97.1	2017	◐	↑
Population using at least basic sanitation services (%)	90.5	2017	◐	↑
Freshwater withdrawal (% of available freshwater resources)	4.4	2015	●	●
Anthropogenic wastewater that receives treatment (%)	18.5	2018	●	●
Scarce water consumption embodied in imports (m³/capita)	43.1	2013	●	→

SDG7 – Affordable and Clean Energy

	Value	Year	Rating	Trend
Population with access to electricity (%)	100.0	2017	●	↑
Population with access to clean fuels and technology for cooking (%)	98.3	2016	●	↑
CO$_2$ emissions from fuel combustion for electricity and heating per total electricity output (MtCO$_2$/TWh)	1.5	2017	●	↗

SDG8 – Decent Work and Economic Growth

	Value	Year	Rating	Trend
Adjusted GDP growth (%)	-0.6	2018	◐	●
Victims of modern slavery (per 1,000 population)	5.5	2018	●	●
Adults with an account at a bank or other financial institution or with a mobile-money-service provider (% of population aged 15 or over)	75.8	2017	◐	↑
Unemployment rate (% of total labor force)	4.6	2019	●	↑
Fatal work-related accidents embodied in imports (per 100,000 population)	0.4	2010	●	↑

SDG9 – Industry, Innovation and Infrastructure

	Value	Year	Rating	Trend
Population using the internet (%)	80.9	2018	●	↑
Mobile broadband subscriptions (per 100 population)	87.3	2018	●	↑
Logistics Performance Index: Quality of trade and transport-related infrastructure (worst 1–5 best)	2.8	2018	◐	↑
The Times Higher Education Universities Ranking: Average score of top 3 universities (worst 0–100 best)	51.6	2020	●	●
Scientific and technical journal articles (per 1,000 population)	0.6	2018	◐	↑
Expenditure on research and development (% of GDP)	1.1	2017	●	→

SDG10 – Reduced Inequalities

	Value	Year	Rating	Trend
Gini coefficient adjusted for top income	44.0	2015	●	●

SDG11 – Sustainable Cities and Communities

	Value	Year	Rating	Trend
Annual mean concentration of particulate matter of less than 2.5 microns in diameter (PM2.5) (µg/m³)	16.2	2017	◐	→
Access to improved water source, piped (% of urban population)	96.3	2017	◐	↑
Satisfaction with public transport (%)	59.9	2018	◐	↗

SDG12 – Responsible Consumption and Production

	Value	Year	Rating	Trend
Municipal solid waste (kg/capita/day)	1.5	2012	●	●
Electronic waste (kg/capita)	9.7	2016	●	●
Production-based SO$_2$ emissions (kg/capita)	33.2	2012	◐	●
SO$_2$ emissions embodied in imports (kg/capita)	3.4	2012	●	●
Production-based nitrogen emissions (kg/capita)	27.2	2010	◐	●
Nitrogen emissions embodied in imports (kg/capita)	4.0	2010	●	●

SDG13 – Climate Action

	Value	Year	Rating	Trend
Energy-related CO$_2$ emissions (tCO$_2$/capita)	11.3	2017	●	→
CO$_2$ emissions embodied in imports (tCO$_2$/capita)	0.5	2015	●	↑
CO$_2$ emissions embodied in fossil fuel exports (kg/capita)	3625.6	2018	◐	●

SDG14 – Life Below Water

	Value	Year	Rating	Trend
Mean area that is protected in marine sites important to biodiversity (%)	24.8	2018	●	→
Ocean Health Index: Clean Waters score (worst 0–100 best)	67.9	2019	◐	↗
Fish caught from overexploited or collapsed stocks (% of total catch)	52.1	2014	●	↓
Fish caught by trawling (%)	60.0	2014	●	↗
Marine biodiversity threats embodied in imports (per million population)	0.1	2018	●	●

SDG15 – Life on Land

	Value	Year	Rating	Trend
Mean area that is protected in terrestrial sites important to biodiversity (%)	27.4	2018	●	→
Mean area that is protected in freshwater sites important to biodiversity (%)	27.3	2018	●	→
Red List Index of species survival (worst 0–1 best)	1.0	2019	●	↑
Permanent deforestation (% of forest area, 5-year average)	0.0	2018	●	●
Terrestrial and freshwater biodiversity threats embodied in imports (per million population)	0.9	2018	●	●

SDG16 – Peace, Justice and Strong Institutions

	Value	Year	Rating	Trend
Homicides (per 100,000 population)	9.2	2017	●	↑
Unsentenced detainees (% of prison population)	9.0	2018	●	↑
Percentage of population who feel safe walking alone at night in the city or area where they live (%)	57.5	2018	●	↑
Property Rights (worst 1–7 best)	3.7	2019	●	●
Birth registrations with civil authority (% of children under age 5)	100.0	2018	●	●
Corruption Perception Index (worst 0–100 best)	28	2019	●	↓
Children involved in child labor (% of population aged 5 to 14)	NA	NA	●	●
Exports of major conventional weapons (TIV constant million USD per 100,000 population)	4.1	2019	●	●
Press Freedom Index (best 0–100 worst)	50.3	2019	●	↓

SDG17 – Partnerships for the Goals

	Value	Year	Rating	Trend
Government spending on health and education (% of GDP)	6.7	2016	●	↓
For high-income and all OECD DAC countries: International concessional public finance, including official development assistance (% of GNI)	NA	NA	●	●
Other countries: Government revenue excluding grants (% of GDP)	27.5	2018	◐	↗
Corporate Tax Haven Score (best 0–100 worst) *	0.0	2019	●	●

* Imputed data point

5. Country Profiles

▼ OVERALL PERFORMANCE

Index score

56.6

Regional average score

53.1

SDG Global rank   132 (OF 166)

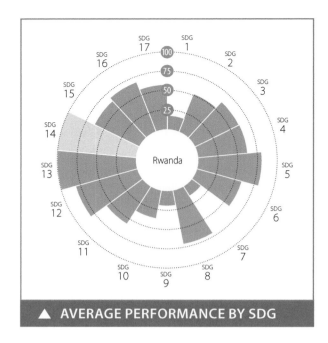

▲ AVERAGE PERFORMANCE BY SDG

▼ SPILLOVER INDEX

100 (best) to 0 (worst)

▼ CURRENT ASSESSMENT – SDG DASHBOARD

■ Major challenges   ■ Significant challenges   ■ Challenges remain   ■ SDG achieved   ■ Information unavailable

▼ SDG TRENDS

↓ Decreasing   → Stagnating   ↗ Moderately improving   ↑ On track or maintaining SDG achievement   ● Information unavailable

Notes: The full title of Goal 2 "Zero Hunger" is "End hunger, achieve food security and improved nutrition and promote sustainable agriculture".
The full title of each SDG is available here: https://sustainabledevelopment.un.org/topics/sustainabledevelopmentgoals

SDG1 – No Poverty

Indicator	Value	Year	Rating	Trend
Poverty headcount ratio at $1.90/day (%)	45.9	2020	●	→
Poverty headcount ratio at $3.20/day (%)	72.9	2020	●	→

SDG2 – Zero Hunger

Indicator	Value	Year	Rating	Trend
Prevalence of undernourishment (%)	36.8	2017	●	↓
Prevalence of stunting in children under 5 years of age (%)	37.9	2015	●	→
Prevalence of wasting in children under 5 years of age (%)	2.2	2015	●	↑
Prevalence of obesity, BMI ≥ 30 (% of adult population)	5.8	2016	●	↑
Human Trophic Level (best 2–3 worst)	2.1	2017	●	↑
Cereal yield (tonnes per hectare of harvested land)	1.3	2017	●	↓
Sustainable Nitrogen Management Index (best 0–1.41 worst)	0.8	2015	●	→

SDG3 – Good Health and Well-Being

Indicator	Value	Year	Rating	Trend
Maternal mortality rate (per 100,000 live births)	248	2017	●	↑
Neonatal mortality rate (per 1,000 live births)	15.9	2018	●	↑
Mortality rate, under-5 (per 1,000 live births)	35.3	2018	●	↑
Incidence of tuberculosis (per 100,000 population)	59.0	2018	●	→
New HIV infections (per 1,000 uninfected population)	0.3	2018	●	↑
Age-standardized death rate due to cardiovascular disease, cancer, diabetes, or chronic respiratory disease in adults aged 30–70 years (%)	18.2	2016	●	↗
Age-standardized death rate attributable to household air pollution and ambient air pollution (per 100,000 population)	121	2016	●	●
Traffic deaths (per 100,000 population)	29.7	2016	●	↗
Life expectancy at birth (years)	68.0	2016	●	↗
Adolescent fertility rate (births per 1,000 adolescent females aged 15 to 19)	39.1	2017	●	→
Births attended by skilled health personnel (%)	90.7	2015	●	●
Percentage of surviving infants who received 2 WHO-recommended vaccines (%)	97	2018	●	↑
Universal health coverage (UHC) index of service coverage (worst 0–100 best)	57.0	2017	●	↗
Subjective well-being (average ladder score, worst 0–10 best)	3.3	2019	●	↓

SDG4 – Quality Education

Indicator	Value	Year	Rating	Trend
Net primary enrollment rate (%)	94.8	2018	●	●
Lower secondary completion rate (%)	36.8	2018	●	→
Literacy rate (% of population aged 15 to 24)	86.5	2018	●	●

SDG5 – Gender Equality

Indicator	Value	Year	Rating	Trend
Demand for family planning satisfied by modern methods (% of females aged 15 to 49 who are married or in unions)	62.9	2015	●	↑
Ratio of female-to-male mean years of education received (%)	79.6	2018	●	↗
Ratio of female-to-male labor force participation rate (%)	100.8	2019	●	↑
Seats held by women in national parliament (%)	61.3	2020	●	↑

SDG6 – Clean Water and Sanitation

Indicator	Value	Year	Rating	Trend
Population using at least basic drinking water services (%)	57.7	2017	●	→
Population using at least basic sanitation services (%)	66.6	2017	●	↗
Freshwater withdrawal (% of available freshwater resources)	1.4	2000	●	●
Anthropogenic wastewater that receives treatment (%)	0.0	2018	●	●
Scarce water consumption embodied in imports (m³/capita)	0.6	2013	●	↑

SDG7 – Affordable and Clean Energy

Indicator	Value	Year	Rating	Trend
Population with access to electricity (%)	34.1	2017	●	↗
Population with access to clean fuels and technology for cooking (%)	0.6	2016	●	→
CO₂ emissions from fuel combustion for electricity and heating per total electricity output (MtCO₂/TWh)	NA	NA	●	●

SDG8 – Decent Work and Economic Growth

Indicator	Value	Year	Rating	Trend
Adjusted GDP growth (%)	-2.5	2018	●	●
Victims of modern slavery (per 1,000 population)	11.6	2018	●	●
Adults with an account at a bank or other financial institution or with a mobile-money-service provider (% of population aged 15 or over)	50.0	2017	●	↑
Unemployment rate (% of total labor force)	1.0	2019	●	↑
Fatal work-related accidents embodied in imports (per 100,000 population)	0.1	2010	●	↑

SDG9 – Industry, Innovation and Infrastructure

Indicator	Value	Year	Rating	Trend
Population using the internet (%)	21.8	2017	●	↗
Mobile broadband subscriptions (per 100 population)	39.0	2018	●	↑
Logistics Performance Index: Quality of trade and transport-related infrastructure (worst 1–5 best)	2.8	2018	●	↑
The Times Higher Education Universities Ranking: Average score of top 3 universities (worst 0–100 best) *	0.0	2020	●	●
Scientific and technical journal articles (per 1,000 population)	0.0	2018	●	→
Expenditure on research and development (% of GDP) *	0.0	2017	●	●

SDG10 – Reduced Inequalities

Indicator	Value	Year	Rating	Trend
Gini coefficient adjusted for top income	50.1	2016	●	●

SDG11 – Sustainable Cities and Communities

Indicator	Value	Year	Rating	Trend
Annual mean concentration of particulate matter of less than 2.5 microns in diameter (PM2.5) (µg/m³)	43.2	2017	●	↓
Access to improved water source, piped (% of urban population)	75.0	2017	●	→
Satisfaction with public transport (%)	47.2	2019	●	↓

SDG12 – Responsible Consumption and Production

Indicator	Value	Year	Rating	Trend
Municipal solid waste (kg/capita/day)	5.6	2016	●	●
Electronic waste (kg/capita)	0.5	2016	●	●
Production-based SO₂ emissions (kg/capita)	13.3	2012	●	●
SO₂ emissions embodied in imports (kg/capita)	0.7	2012	●	●
Production-based nitrogen emissions (kg/capita)	9.8	2010	●	●
Nitrogen emissions embodied in imports (kg/capita)	0.4	2010	●	●

SDG13 – Climate Action

Indicator	Value	Year	Rating	Trend
Energy-related CO₂ emissions (tCO₂/capita)	0.1	2017	●	↑
CO₂ emissions embodied in imports (tCO₂/capita)	0.0	2015	●	↑
CO₂ emissions embodied in fossil fuel exports (kg/capita)	0.0	2016	●	●

SDG14 – Life Below Water

Indicator	Value	Year	Rating	Trend
Mean area that is protected in marine sites important to biodiversity (%)	NA	NA	●	●
Ocean Health Index: Clean Waters score (worst 0–100 best)	NA	NA	●	●
Fish caught from overexploited or collapsed stocks (% of total catch)	NA	NA	●	●
Fish caught by trawling (%)	NA	NA	●	●
Marine biodiversity threats embodied in imports (per million population)	0.0	2018	●	●

SDG15 – Life on Land

Indicator	Value	Year	Rating	Trend
Mean area that is protected in terrestrial sites important to biodiversity (%)	46.5	2018	●	→
Mean area that is protected in freshwater sites important to biodiversity (%)	50.0	2018	●	→
Red List Index of species survival (worst 0–1 best)	0.8	2019	●	→
Permanent deforestation (% of forest area, 5-year average)	0.6	2018	●	●
Terrestrial and freshwater biodiversity threats embodied in imports (per million population)	0.3	2018	●	●

SDG16 – Peace, Justice and Strong Institutions

Indicator	Value	Year	Rating	Trend
Homicides (per 100,000 population)	2.5	2015	●	●
Unsentenced detainees (% of prison population)	6.8	2015	●	●
Percentage of population who feel safe walking alone at night in the city or area where they live (%)	80.3	2019	●	↑
Property Rights (worst 1–7 best)	5.0	2019	●	●
Birth registrations with civil authority (% of children under age 5)	56.0	2018	●	●
Corruption Perception Index (worst 0–100 best)	53	2019	●	↓
Children involved in child labor (% of population aged 5 to 14)	28.5	2016	●	●
Exports of major conventional weapons (TIV constant million USD per 100,000 population) *	0.0	2019	●	●
Press Freedom Index (best 0–100 worst)	52.4	2019	●	→

SDG17 – Partnerships for the Goals

Indicator	Value	Year	Rating	Trend
Government spending on health and education (% of GDP)	5.8	2016	●	↓
For high-income and all OECD DAC countries: International concessional public finance, including official development assistance (% of GNI)	NA	NA	●	●
Other countries: Government revenue excluding grants (% of GDP)	20.0	2017	●	↗
Corporate Tax Haven Score (best 0–100 worst) *	0.0	2019	●	●

* Imputed data point

5. Country Profiles

SAMOA

▼ OVERALL PERFORMANCE

Index score
na

Regional average score
49.6

SDG Global rank   NA (OF 166)

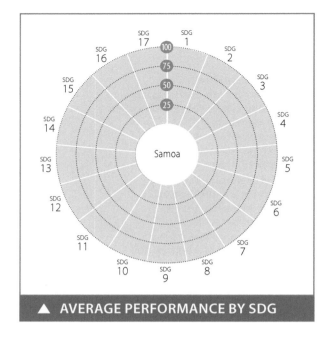

▲ AVERAGE PERFORMANCE BY SDG

▼ SPILLOVER INDEX

100 (best) to 0 (worst)

▼ CURRENT ASSESSMENT – SDG DASHBOARD

■ Major challenges   ■ Significant challenges   ■ Challenges remain   ■ SDG achieved   ■ Information unavailable

▼ SDG TRENDS

↓ Decreasing   → Stagnating   ↗ Moderately improving   ↑ On track or maintaining SDG achievement   ● Information unavailable

Notes: The full title of Goal 2 "Zero Hunger" is "End hunger, achieve food security and improved nutrition and promote sustainable agriculture".
The full title of each SDG is available here: https://sustainabledevelopment.un.org/topics/sustainabledevelopmentgoals

SDG1 – No Poverty

	Value	Year	Rating	Trend
Poverty headcount ratio at $1.90/day (%)	0.2	2020	●	↑
Poverty headcount ratio at $3.20/day (%)	4.1	2020	○	↑

SDG2 – Zero Hunger

	Value	Year	Rating	Trend
Prevalence of undernourishment (%)	2.7	2017	●	↑
Prevalence of stunting in children under 5 years of age (%)	4.7	2014	●	↑
Prevalence of wasting in children under 5 years of age (%)	3.7	2014	●	↑
Prevalence of obesity, BMI ≥ 30 (% of adult population)	47.3	2016	●	↓
Human Trophic Level (best 2–3 worst)	2.3	2017	○	→
Cereal yield (tonnes per hectare of harvested land)	NA	NA	●	●
Sustainable Nitrogen Management Index (best 0–1.41 worst)	1.0	2015	●	→

SDG3 – Good Health and Well-Being

	Value	Year	Rating	Trend
Maternal mortality rate (per 100,000 live births)	43	2017	●	↑
Neonatal mortality rate (per 1,000 live births)	8.3	2018	●	↑
Mortality rate, under-5 (per 1,000 live births)	15.8	2018	●	↑
Incidence of tuberculosis (per 100,000 population)	6.4	2018	●	↑
New HIV infections (per 1,000 uninfected population)	NA	NA	●	●
Age-standardized death rate due to cardiovascular disease, cancer, diabetes, or chronic respiratory disease in adults aged 30–70 years (%)	20.6	2016	●	↑
Age-standardized death rate attributable to household air pollution and ambient air pollution (per 100,000 population)	85	2016	●	●
Traffic deaths (per 100,000 population)	11.3	2016	○	↑
Life expectancy at birth (years)	75.1	2016	●	↗
Adolescent fertility rate (births per 1,000 adolescent females aged 15 to 19)	23.9	2017	●	↑
Births attended by skilled health personnel (%)	82.5	2014	●	●
Percentage of surviving infants who received 2 WHO-recommended vaccines (%)	31	2018	●	↓
Universal health coverage (UHC) index of service coverage (worst 0–100 best)	58.0	2017	●	↗
Subjective well-being (average ladder score, worst 0–10 best)	NA	NA	●	●

SDG4 – Quality Education

	Value	Year	Rating	Trend
Net primary enrollment rate (%)	94.4	2018	○	↓
Lower secondary completion rate (%)	105.5	2018	●	↑
Literacy rate (% of population aged 15 to 24)	99.1	2018	●	●

SDG5 – Gender Equality

	Value	Year	Rating	Trend
Demand for family planning satisfied by modern methods (% of females aged 15 to 49 who are married or in unions)	39.4	2014	●	→
Ratio of female-to-male mean years of education received (%)	NA	NA	●	●
Ratio of female-to-male labor force participation rate (%)	61.3	2019	○	→
Seats held by women in national parliament (%)	10.0	2020	●	→

SDG6 – Clean Water and Sanitation

	Value	Year	Rating	Trend
Population using at least basic drinking water services (%)	97.4	2017	○	↑
Population using at least basic sanitation services (%)	98.2	2017	●	↑
Freshwater withdrawal (% of available freshwater resources)	NA	NA	●	●
Anthropogenic wastewater that receives treatment (%)	0.3	2018	●	●
Scarce water consumption embodied in imports (m3/capita)	4.7	2013	●	↑

SDG7 – Affordable and Clean Energy

	Value	Year	Rating	Trend
Population with access to electricity (%)	96.8	2017	○	→
Population with access to clean fuels and technology for cooking (%)	32.3	2016	●	→
CO2 emissions from fuel combustion for electricity and heating per total electricity output (MtCO2/TWh)	NA	NA	●	●

SDG8 – Decent Work and Economic Growth

	Value	Year	Rating	Trend
Adjusted GDP growth (%)	-3.2	2018	●	●
Victims of modern slavery (per 1,000 population)	NA	NA	●	●
Adults with an account at a bank or other financial institution or with a mobile-money-service provider (% of population aged 15 or over)	NA	NA	●	●
Unemployment rate (% of total labor force)	8.4	2019	●	→
Fatal work-related accidents embodied in imports (per 100,000 population)	0.3	2010	●	↑

SDG9 – Industry, Innovation and Infrastructure

	Value	Year	Rating	Trend
Population using the internet (%)	33.6	2017	●	↑
Mobile broadband subscriptions (per 100 population)	26.2	2017	●	↑
Logistics Performance Index: Quality of trade and transport-related infrastructure (worst 1–5 best)	NA	NA	●	●
The Times Higher Education Universities Ranking: Average score of top 3 universities (worst 0–100 best) *	0.0	2020	●	●
Scientific and technical journal articles (per 1,000 population)	0.1	2018	○	↓
Expenditure on research and development (% of GDP)	NA	NA	●	●

SDG10 – Reduced Inequalities

	Value	Year	Rating	Trend
Gini coefficient adjusted for top income	43.3	2013	●	●

SDG11 – Sustainable Cities and Communities

	Value	Year	Rating	Trend
Annual mean concentration of particulate matter of less than 2.5 microns in diameter (PM2.5) (μg/m3)	11.5	2017	○	↑
Access to improved water source, piped (% of urban population)	90.1	2017	○	→
Satisfaction with public transport (%)	NA	NA	●	●

SDG12 – Responsible Consumption and Production

	Value	Year	Rating	Trend
Municipal solid waste (kg/capita/day)	2.1	2011	●	●
Electronic waste (kg/capita)	2.6	2016	●	●
Production-based SO2 emissions (kg/capita)	555.1	2012	●	●
SO2 emissions embodied in imports (kg/capita)	6.8	2012	○	●
Production-based nitrogen emissions (kg/capita)	15.8	2010	●	●
Nitrogen emissions embodied in imports (kg/capita)	2.5	2010	●	●

SDG13 – Climate Action

	Value	Year	Rating	Trend
Energy-related CO2 emissions (tCO2/capita)	1.4	2017	●	↑
CO2 emissions embodied in imports (tCO2/capita)	0.3	2015	●	↑
CO2 emissions embodied in fossil fuel exports (kg/capita)	0.0	2018	●	●

SDG14 – Life Below Water

	Value	Year	Rating	Trend
Mean area that is protected in marine sites important to biodiversity (%)	11.9	2018	●	→
Ocean Health Index: Clean Waters score (worst 0–100 best)	92.2	2019	●	↑
Fish caught from overexploited or collapsed stocks (% of total catch)	30.6	2014	○	↓
Fish caught by trawling (%)	NA	NA	●	●
Marine biodiversity threats embodied in imports (per million population)	0.0	2018	●	●

SDG15 – Life on Land

	Value	Year	Rating	Trend
Mean area that is protected in terrestrial sites important to biodiversity (%)	37.1	2018	○	↑
Mean area that is protected in freshwater sites important to biodiversity (%)	NA	NA	●	●
Red List Index of species survival (worst 0–1 best)	0.8	2019	●	↓
Permanent deforestation (% of forest area, 5-year average)	NA	NA	●	●
Terrestrial and freshwater biodiversity threats embodied in imports (per million population)	0.4	2018	●	●

SDG16 – Peace, Justice and Strong Institutions

	Value	Year	Rating	Trend
Homicides (per 100,000 population)	3.1	2013	●	●
Unsentenced detainees (% of prison population)	6.5	2018	●	●
Percentage of population who feel safe walking alone at night in the city or area where they live (%)	NA	NA	●	●
Property Rights (worst 1–7 best)	NA	NA	●	●
Birth registrations with civil authority (% of children under age 5)	58.6	2018	●	●
Corruption Perception Index (worst 0–100 best)	NA	NA	●	●
Children involved in child labor (% of population aged 5 to 14)	NA	NA	●	●
Exports of major conventional weapons (TIV constant million USD per 100,000 population) *	0.0	2019	●	●
Press Freedom Index (best 0–100 worst)	18.3	2019	●	↑

SDG17 – Partnerships for the Goals

	Value	Year	Rating	Trend
Government spending on health and education (% of GDP)	8.3	2016	○	●
For high-income and all OECD DAC countries: International concessional public finance, including official development assistance (% of GNI)	NA	NA	●	●
Other countries: Government revenue excluding grants (% of GDP)	33.1	2018	●	↑
Corporate Tax Haven Score (best 0–100 worst) *	0.0	2019	●	●

* Imputed data point

5. Country Profiles

▼ OVERALL PERFORMANCE

Index score
na

Regional average score
70.9

SDG Global rank NA (OF 166)

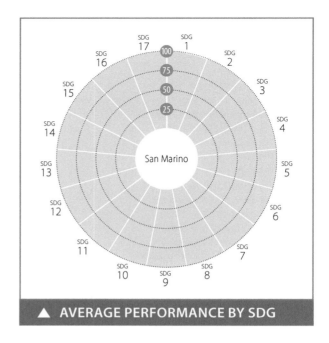

▲ AVERAGE PERFORMANCE BY SDG

▼ SPILLOVER INDEX

100 (best) to 0 (worst)

▼ CURRENT ASSESSMENT – SDG DASHBOARD

■ Major challenges ■ Significant challenges ■ Challenges remain ■ SDG achieved ■ Information unavailable

▼ SDG TRENDS

↓ Decreasing → Stagnating ↗ Moderately improving ↑ On track or maintaining SDG achievement ● Information unavailable

Notes: The full title of Goal 2 "Zero Hunger" is "End hunger, achieve food security and improved nutrition and promote sustainable agriculture".
The full title of each SDG is available here: https://sustainabledevelopment.un.org/topics/sustainabledevelopmentgoals

SDG1 – No Poverty

	Value	Year	Rating	Trend
Poverty headcount ratio at $1.90/day (%)	NA	NA	●	●
Poverty headcount ratio at $3.20/day (%)	NA	NA	●	●

SDG2 – Zero Hunger

		Value	Year	Rating	Trend
Prevalence of undernourishment (%)	*	1.2	2017	●	●
Prevalence of stunting in children under 5 years of age (%)	*	2.6	2016	●	●
Prevalence of wasting in children under 5 years of age (%)	*	0.7	2016	●	●
Prevalence of obesity, BMI ≥ 30 (% of adult population)		NA	NA	●	●
Human Trophic Level (best 2–3 worst)		NA	NA	●	●
Cereal yield (tonnes per hectare of harvested land)		NA	NA	●	●
Sustainable Nitrogen Management Index (best 0–1.41 worst)		NA	NA	●	●

SDG3 – Good Health and Well-Being

	Value	Year	Rating	Trend
Maternal mortality rate (per 100,000 live births)	NA	NA	●	●
Neonatal mortality rate (per 1,000 live births)	0.9	2018	●	↑
Mortality rate, under-5 (per 1,000 live births)	2.0	2018	●	↑
Incidence of tuberculosis (per 100,000 population)	0.0	2018	●	↑
New HIV infections (per 1,000 uninfected population)	NA	NA	●	●
Age-standardized death rate due to cardiovascular disease, cancer, diabetes, or chronic respiratory disease in adults aged 30–70 years (%)	NA	NA	●	●
Age-standardized death rate attributable to household air pollution and ambient air pollution (per 100,000 population)	NA	NA	●	●
Traffic deaths (per 100,000 population)	0.0	2016	●	↑
Life expectancy at birth (years)	NA	NA	●	●
Adolescent fertility rate (births per 1,000 adolescent females aged 15 to 19)	NA	NA	●	●
Births attended by skilled health personnel (%)	NA	NA	●	●
Percentage of surviving infants who received 2 WHO-recommended vaccines (%)	89	2018	◐	↑
Universal health coverage (UHC) index of service coverage (worst 0–100 best)	NA	NA	●	●
Subjective well-being (average ladder score, worst 0–10 best)	NA	NA	●	●

SDG4 – Quality Education

	Value	Year	Rating	Trend
Net primary enrollment rate (%)	93.9	2004	◐	●
Lower secondary completion rate (%)	103.2	2018	●	●
Literacy rate (% of population aged 15 to 24)	100.0	2018	●	●

SDG5 – Gender Equality

	Value	Year	Rating	Trend
Demand for family planning satisfied by modern methods (% of females aged 15 to 49 who are married or in unions)	NA	NA	●	●
Ratio of female-to-male mean years of education received (%)	NA	NA	●	●
Ratio of female-to-male labor force participation rate (%)	NA	NA	●	●
Seats held by women in national parliament (%)	31.7	2020	◐	↑

SDG6 – Clean Water and Sanitation

	Value	Year	Rating	Trend
Population using at least basic drinking water services (%)	100.0	2017	●	↑
Population using at least basic sanitation services (%)	100.0	2017	●	↑
Freshwater withdrawal (% of available freshwater resources)	NA	NA	●	●
Anthropogenic wastewater that receives treatment (%)	6.2	2018	●	●
Scarce water consumption embodied in imports (m³/capita)	177.3	2013	●	↓

SDG7 – Affordable and Clean Energy

	Value	Year	Rating	Trend
Population with access to electricity (%)	100.0	2017	●	↑
Population with access to clean fuels and technology for cooking (%)	100.0	2016	●	↑
CO₂ emissions from fuel combustion for electricity and heating per total electricity output (MtCO₂/TWh)	NA	NA	●	●

SDG8 – Decent Work and Economic Growth

	Value	Year	Rating	Trend
Adjusted GDP growth (%)	NA	NA	●	●
Victims of modern slavery (per 1,000 population)	NA	NA	●	●
Adults with an account at a bank or other financial institution or with a mobile-money-service provider (% of population aged 15 or over)	NA	NA	●	●
Unemployment rate (% of total labor force)	NA	NA	●	●
Fatal work-related accidents embodied in imports (per 100,000 population)	10.0	2010	●	↓

SDG9 – Industry, Innovation and Infrastructure

		Value	Year	Rating	Trend
Population using the internet (%)		60.2	2017	●	●
Mobile broadband subscriptions (per 100 population)		130.7	2017	●	↑
Logistics Performance Index: Quality of trade and transport-related infrastructure (worst 1–5 best)		NA	NA	●	●
The Times Higher Education Universities Ranking: Average score of top 3 universities (worst 0–100 best)	*	0.0	2020	●	●
Scientific and technical journal articles (per 1,000 population)		0.3	2018	●	↑
Expenditure on research and development (% of GDP)		NA	NA	●	●

SDG10 – Reduced Inequalities

	Value	Year	Rating	Trend
Gini coefficient adjusted for top income	NA	NA	●	●

SDG11 – Sustainable Cities and Communities

	Value	Year	Rating	Trend
Annual mean concentration of particulate matter of less than 2.5 microns in diameter (PM2.5) (μg/m³)	NA	NA	●	●
Access to improved water source, piped (% of urban population)	NA	NA	●	●
Satisfaction with public transport (%)	NA	NA	●	●

SDG12 – Responsible Consumption and Production

	Value	Year	Rating	Trend
Municipal solid waste (kg/capita/day)	1.4	2016	◐	●
Electronic waste (kg/capita)	NA	NA	●	●
Production-based SO₂ emissions (kg/capita)	251.2	2012	●	●
SO₂ emissions embodied in imports (kg/capita)	145.6	2012	●	●
Production-based nitrogen emissions (kg/capita)	148.1	2010	●	●
Nitrogen emissions embodied in imports (kg/capita)	74.6	2010	●	●

SDG13 – Climate Action

	Value	Year	Rating	Trend
Energy-related CO₂ emissions (tCO₂/capita)	5.2	2017	●	→
CO₂ emissions embodied in imports (tCO₂/capita)	21.3	2015	●	↗
CO₂ emissions embodied in fossil fuel exports (kg/capita)	NA	NA	●	●

SDG14 – Life Below Water

	Value	Year	Rating	Trend
Mean area that is protected in marine sites important to biodiversity (%)	NA	NA	●	●
Ocean Health Index: Clean Waters score (worst 0–100 best)	NA	NA	●	●
Fish caught from overexploited or collapsed stocks (% of total catch)	NA	NA	●	●
Fish caught by trawling (%)	NA	NA	●	●
Marine biodiversity threats embodied in imports (per million population)	6.5	2018	●	●

SDG15 – Life on Land

	Value	Year	Rating	Trend
Mean area that is protected in terrestrial sites important to biodiversity (%)	NA	NA	●	●
Mean area that is protected in freshwater sites important to biodiversity (%)	NA	NA	●	●
Red List Index of species survival (worst 0–1 best)	1.0	2019	●	↑
Permanent deforestation (% of forest area, 5-year average)	NA	NA	●	●
Terrestrial and freshwater biodiversity threats embodied in imports (per million population)	59.1	2018	●	●

SDG16 – Peace, Justice and Strong Institutions

		Value	Year	Rating	Trend
Homicides (per 100,000 population)		3.6	2002	●	●
Unsentenced detainees (% of prison population)		83.3	2018	●	↑
Percentage of population who feel safe walking alone at night in the city or area where they live (%)		NA	NA	●	●
Property Rights (worst 1–7 best)		NA	NA	●	●
Birth registrations with civil authority (% of children under age 5)		100.0	2018	●	●
Corruption Perception Index (worst 0–100 best)		NA	NA	●	●
Children involved in child labor (% of population aged 5 to 14)		NA	NA	●	●
Exports of major conventional weapons (TIV constant million USD per 100,000 population)	*	0.0	2019	●	●
Press Freedom Index (best 0–100 worst)		NA	NA	●	●

SDG17 – Partnerships for the Goals

	Value	Year	Rating	Trend
Government spending on health and education (% of GDP)	7.9	2011	◐	●
For high-income and all OECD DAC countries: International concessional public finance, including official development assistance (% of GNI)	NA	NA	●	●
Other countries: Government revenue excluding grants (% of GDP)	NA	NA	●	●
Corporate Tax Haven Score (best 0–100 worst)	61.5	2019	◐	●

* Imputed data point

5. Country Profiles

▼ OVERALL PERFORMANCE

Index score

62.6

Regional average score

53.1

SDG Global rank 115 (OF 166)

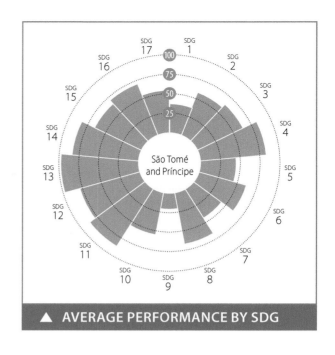

▲ AVERAGE PERFORMANCE BY SDG

São Tomé and Príncipe

▼ SPILLOVER INDEX

100 (best) to 0 (worst)

▼ CURRENT ASSESSMENT – SDG DASHBOARD

■ Major challenges ■ Significant challenges ■ Challenges remain ■ SDG achieved ■ Information unavailable

▼ SDG TRENDS

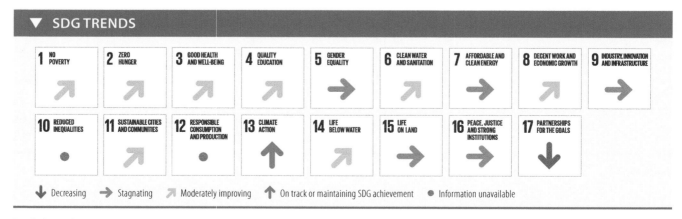

↓ Decreasing → Stagnating ↗ Moderately improving ↑ On track or maintaining SDG achievement ● Information unavailable

Notes: The full title of Goal 2 "Zero Hunger" is "End hunger, achieve food security and improved nutrition and promote sustainable agriculture".
The full title of each SDG is available here: https://sustainabledevelopment.un.org/topics/sustainabledevelopmentgoals

SDG1 – No Poverty

	Value	Year	Rating	Trend
Poverty headcount ratio at $1.90/day (%)	18.7	2020	●	↗
Poverty headcount ratio at $3.20/day (%)	50.2	2020	●	→

SDG2 – Zero Hunger

	Value	Year	Rating	Trend
Prevalence of undernourishment (%)	7.0	2017	●	↑
Prevalence of stunting in children under 5 years of age (%)	17.2	2014	●	↑
Prevalence of wasting in children under 5 years of age (%)	4.0	2014	●	↑
Prevalence of obesity, BMI ≥ 30 (% of adult population)	12.4	2016	◐	↓
Human Trophic Level (best 2–3 worst)	2.1	2017	●	↑
Cereal yield (tonnes per hectare of harvested land)	2.1	2017	◐	↓
Sustainable Nitrogen Management Index (best 0–1.41 worst)	1.1	2015	●	↓

SDG3 – Good Health and Well-Being

	Value	Year	Rating	Trend
Maternal mortality rate (per 100,000 live births)	130	2017	●	→
Neonatal mortality rate (per 1,000 live births)	14.0	2018	◐	↑
Mortality rate, under-5 (per 1,000 live births)	31.2	2018	◐	↑
Incidence of tuberculosis (per 100,000 population)	124.0	2018	●	↑
New HIV infections (per 1,000 uninfected population)	0.1	2018	●	↑
Age-standardized death rate due to cardiovascular disease, cancer, diabetes, or chronic respiratory disease in adults aged 30–70 years (%)	18.5	2016	◐	→
Age-standardized death rate attributable to household air pollution and ambient air pollution (per 100,000 population)	162	2016	●	●
Traffic deaths (per 100,000 population)	27.5	2016	●	↗
Life expectancy at birth (years)	68.7	2016	●	→
Adolescent fertility rate (births per 1,000 adolescent females aged 15 to 19)	94.6	2017	●	→
Births attended by skilled health personnel (%)	92.5	2014	●	●
Percentage of surviving infants who received 2 WHO-recommended vaccines (%)	95	2018	●	↑
Universal health coverage (UHC) index of service coverage (worst 0–100 best)	55.0	2017	●	→
Subjective well-being (average ladder score, worst 0–10 best)	NA	NA	●	●

SDG4 – Quality Education

	Value	Year	Rating	Trend
Net primary enrollment rate (%)	93.1	2017	◐	↑
Lower secondary completion rate (%)	73.5	2017	●	↗
Literacy rate (% of population aged 15 to 24)	97.8	2018	●	●

SDG5 – Gender Equality

	Value	Year	Rating	Trend
Demand for family planning satisfied by modern methods (% of females aged 15 to 49 who are married or in unions)	52.2	2014	●	↗
Ratio of female-to-male mean years of education received (%)	79.2	2018	●	↓
Ratio of female-to-male labor force participation rate (%)	56.8	2019	●	→
Seats held by women in national parliament (%)	14.6	2020	●	↓

SDG6 – Clean Water and Sanitation

	Value	Year	Rating	Trend
Population using at least basic drinking water services (%)	84.3	2017	●	↗
Population using at least basic sanitation services (%)	43.0	2017	●	→
Freshwater withdrawal (% of available freshwater resources)	1.9	2015	●	●
Anthropogenic wastewater that receives treatment (%)	0.2	2018	●	●
Scarce water consumption embodied in imports (m³/capita)	4.9	2013	●	↑

SDG7 – Affordable and Clean Energy

	Value	Year	Rating	Trend
Population with access to electricity (%)	72.5	2017	●	↗
Population with access to clean fuels and technology for cooking (%)	16.8	2016	●	↓
CO$_2$ emissions from fuel combustion for electricity and heating per total electricity output (MtCO$_2$/TWh)	NA	NA	●	●

SDG8 – Decent Work and Economic Growth

	Value	Year	Rating	Trend
Adjusted GDP growth (%)	-4.3	2018	●	●
Victims of modern slavery (per 1,000 population)	NA	NA	●	●
Adults with an account at a bank or other financial institution or with a mobile-money-service provider (% of population aged 15 or over)	NA	NA	●	●
Unemployment rate (% of total labor force)	13.4	2019	●	→
Fatal work-related accidents embodied in imports (per 100,000 population)	0.3	2010	●	↑

SDG9 – Industry, Innovation and Infrastructure

	Value	Year	Rating	Trend
Population using the internet (%)	29.9	2017	●	↗
Mobile broadband subscriptions (per 100 population)	33.5	2018	●	↑
Logistics Performance Index: Quality of trade and transport-related infrastructure (worst 1–5 best)	2.3	2018	●	↓
The Times Higher Education Universities Ranking: Average score of top 3 universities (worst 0–100 best) *	0.0	2020	●	●
Scientific and technical journal articles (per 1,000 population)	0.0	2018	●	↓
Expenditure on research and development (% of GDP)	NA	NA	●	●

SDG10 – Reduced Inequalities

	Value	Year	Rating	Trend
Gini coefficient adjusted for top income	44.1	2010	●	●

SDG11 – Sustainable Cities and Communities

	Value	Year	Rating	Trend
Annual mean concentration of particulate matter of less than 2.5 microns in diameter (PM2.5) (μg/m³)	28.5	2017	●	↓
Access to improved water source, piped (% of urban population)	98.5	2017	●	↑
Satisfaction with public transport (%)	NA	NA	●	●

SDG12 – Responsible Consumption and Production

	Value	Year	Rating	Trend
Municipal solid waste (kg/capita/day)	0.5	2014	●	●
Electronic waste (kg/capita)	1.2	2016	●	●
Production-based SO$_2$ emissions (kg/capita)	489.3	2012	●	●
SO$_2$ emissions embodied in imports (kg/capita)	5.1	2012	◐	●
Production-based nitrogen emissions (kg/capita)	9.5	2010	●	●
Nitrogen emissions embodied in imports (kg/capita)	2.3	2010	●	●

SDG13 – Climate Action

	Value	Year	Rating	Trend
Energy-related CO$_2$ emissions (tCO$_2$/capita)	0.7	2017	●	↑
CO$_2$ emissions embodied in imports (tCO$_2$/capita)	0.2	2015	●	↑
CO$_2$ emissions embodied in fossil fuel exports (kg/capita) *	0.0	2018	●	●

SDG14 – Life Below Water

	Value	Year	Rating	Trend
Mean area that is protected in marine sites important to biodiversity (%)	86.4	2018	●	↑
Ocean Health Index: Clean Waters score (worst 0–100 best)	57.8	2019	●	→
Fish caught from overexploited or collapsed stocks (% of total catch)	8.6	2014	●	↑
Fish caught by trawling (%)	2.1	2014	●	↑
Marine biodiversity threats embodied in imports (per million population)	0.0	2018	●	●

SDG15 – Life on Land

	Value	Year	Rating	Trend
Mean area that is protected in terrestrial sites important to biodiversity (%)	76.3	2018	●	↑
Mean area that is protected in freshwater sites important to biodiversity (%)	39.8	2018	◐	→
Red List Index of species survival (worst 0–1 best)	0.8	2019	●	↓
Permanent deforestation (% of forest area, 5-year average)	NA	NA	●	●
Terrestrial and freshwater biodiversity threats embodied in imports (per million population)	0.1	2018	●	●

SDG16 – Peace, Justice and Strong Institutions

	Value	Year	Rating	Trend
Homicides (per 100,000 population)	3.4	2011	●	●
Unsentenced detainees (% of prison population)	33.2	2018	◐	↓
Percentage of population who feel safe walking alone at night in the city or area where they live (%)	NA	NA	●	●
Property Rights (worst 1–7 best)	NA	NA	●	●
Birth registrations with civil authority (% of children under age 5)	95.2	2018	◐	●
Corruption Perception Index (worst 0–100 best)	46	2019	●	↗
Children involved in child labor (% of population aged 5 to 14)	26.0	2016	●	●
Exports of major conventional weapons (TIV constant million USD per 100,000 population) *	0.0	2019	●	●
Press Freedom Index (best 0–100 worst)	NA	NA	●	●

SDG17 – Partnerships for the Goals

	Value	Year	Rating	Trend
Government spending on health and education (% of GDP)	7.6	2016	◐	↓
For high-income and all OECD DAC countries: International concessional public finance, including official development assistance (% of GNI)	NA	NA	●	●
Other countries: Government revenue excluding grants (% of GDP) *	14.5	2018	●	↓
Corporate Tax Haven Score (best 0–100 worst) *	0.0	2019	●	●

* Imputed data point

5. Country Profiles

▼ OVERALL PERFORMANCE

Index score
65.8

Regional average score
66.3

SDG Global rank   97 (OF 166)

▼ SPILLOVER INDEX

100 (best) to 0 (worst)

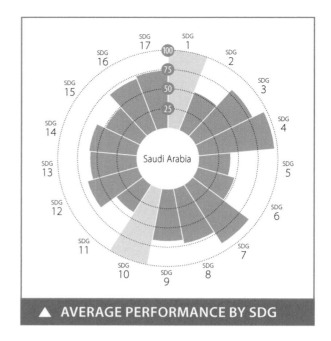

▲ AVERAGE PERFORMANCE BY SDG

▼ CURRENT ASSESSMENT – SDG DASHBOARD

| 1 NO POVERTY | 2 ZERO HUNGER | 3 GOOD HEALTH AND WELL-BEING | 4 QUALITY EDUCATION | 5 GENDER EQUALITY | 6 CLEAN WATER AND SANITATION | 7 AFFORDABLE AND CLEAN ENERGY | 8 DECENT WORK AND ECONOMIC GROWTH | 9 INDUSTRY, INNOVATION AND INFRASTRUCTURE |
| 10 REDUCED INEQUALITIES | 11 SUSTAINABLE CITIES AND COMMUNITIES | 12 RESPONSIBLE CONSUMPTION AND PRODUCTION | 13 CLIMATE ACTION | 14 LIFE BELOW WATER | 15 LIFE ON LAND | 16 PEACE, JUSTICE AND STRONG INSTITUTIONS | 17 PARTNERSHIPS FOR THE GOALS | SUSTAINABLE DEVELOPMENT GOALS |

■ Major challenges   ■ Significant challenges   ■ Challenges remain   ■ SDG achieved   ■ Information unavailable

▼ SDG TRENDS

| 1 NO POVERTY ● | 2 ZERO HUNGER ↗ | 3 GOOD HEALTH AND WELL-BEING ↗ | 4 QUALITY EDUCATION → | 5 GENDER EQUALITY → | 6 CLEAN WATER AND SANITATION ↗ | 7 AFFORDABLE AND CLEAN ENERGY ↗ | 8 DECENT WORK AND ECONOMIC GROWTH ↗ | 9 INDUSTRY, INNOVATION AND INFRASTRUCTURE ↗ |
| 10 REDUCED INEQUALITIES ● | 11 SUSTAINABLE CITIES AND COMMUNITIES ↗ | 12 RESPONSIBLE CONSUMPTION AND PRODUCTION ● | 13 CLIMATE ACTION ↗ | 14 LIFE BELOW WATER ↗ | 15 LIFE ON LAND → | 16 PEACE, JUSTICE AND STRONG INSTITUTIONS → | 17 PARTNERSHIPS FOR THE GOALS ● | |

↓ Decreasing   → Stagnating   ↗ Moderately improving   ↑ On track or maintaining SDG achievement   ● Information unavailable

Notes: The full title of Goal 2 "Zero Hunger" is "End hunger, achieve food security and improved nutrition and promote sustainable agriculture".
The full title of each SDG is available here: https://sustainabledevelopment.un.org/topics/sustainabledevelopmentgoals

SAUDI ARABIA

SDG1 – No Poverty		Value	Year	Rating	Trend
Poverty headcount ratio at $1.90/day (%)	*	NA	NA	●	●
Poverty headcount ratio at $3.20/day (%)	*	NA	NA	●	●

SDG2 – Zero Hunger
	Value	Year	Rating	Trend
Prevalence of undernourishment (%)	7.1	2017	●	↑
Prevalence of stunting in children under 5 years of age (%)	9.3	2005	●	↗
Prevalence of wasting in children under 5 years of age (%)	11.8	2005	●	↑
Prevalence of obesity, BMI ≥ 30 (% of adult population)	35.4	2016	●	↓
Human Trophic Level (best 2–3 worst)	2.3	2017	●	→
Cereal yield (tonnes per hectare of harvested land)	5.6	2017	●	↑
Sustainable Nitrogen Management Index (best 0–1.41 worst)	0.6	2015	●	↑

SDG3 – Good Health and Well-Being
	Value	Year	Rating	Trend
Maternal mortality rate (per 100,000 live births)	17	2017	●	↑
Neonatal mortality rate (per 1,000 live births)	3.7	2018	●	↑
Mortality rate, under-5 (per 1,000 live births)	7.1	2018	●	↑
Incidence of tuberculosis (per 100,000 population)	10.0	2018	●	↑
New HIV infections (per 1,000 uninfected population)	NA	NA	●	●
Age-standardized death rate due to cardiovascular disease, cancer, diabetes, or chronic respiratory disease in adults aged 30–70 years (%)	16.4	2016	●	↑
Age-standardized death rate attributable to household air pollution and ambient air pollution (per 100,000 population)	84	2016	●	●
Traffic deaths (per 100,000 population)	28.8	2016	●	↓
Life expectancy at birth (years)	74.8	2016	●	→
Adolescent fertility rate (births per 1,000 adolescent females aged 15 to 19)	7.3	2017	●	↑
Births attended by skilled health personnel (%)	98.0	2013	●	●
Percentage of surviving infants who received 2 WHO-recommended vaccines (%)	96	2018	●	↑
Universal health coverage (UHC) index of service coverage (worst 0–100 best)	74.0	2017	●	↑
Subjective well-being (average ladder score, worst 0–10 best)	6.6	2019	●	↑

SDG4 – Quality Education
	Value	Year	Rating	Trend
Net primary enrollment rate (%)	94.5	2018	●	↓
Lower secondary completion rate (%)	106.5	2017	●	↑
Literacy rate (% of population aged 15 to 24)	99.3	2017	●	●

SDG5 – Gender Equality
		Value	Year	Rating	Trend
Demand for family planning satisfied by modern methods (% of females aged 15 to 49 who are married or in unions)	*	41.5	2017	●	→
Ratio of female-to-male mean years of education received (%)		89.1	2018	●	→
Ratio of female-to-male labor force participation rate (%)		29.5	2019	●	→
Seats held by women in national parliament (%)		19.9	2020	●	↓

SDG6 – Clean Water and Sanitation
	Value	Year	Rating	Trend
Population using at least basic drinking water services (%)	100.0	2017	●	↑
Population using at least basic sanitation services (%)	100.0	2017	●	↑
Freshwater withdrawal (% of available freshwater resources)	907.1	2015	●	●
Anthropogenic wastewater that receives treatment (%)	11.8	2018	●	●
Scarce water consumption embodied in imports (m³/capita)	70.3	2013	●	↓

SDG7 – Affordable and Clean Energy
	Value	Year	Rating	Trend
Population with access to electricity (%)	100.0	2017	●	↑
Population with access to clean fuels and technology for cooking (%)	96.0	2016	●	↑
CO_2 emissions from fuel combustion for electricity and heating per total electricity output (MtCO₂/TWh)	1.6	2017	●	↗

SDG8 – Decent Work and Economic Growth
		Value	Year	Rating	Trend
Adjusted GDP growth (%)		-2.6	2018	●	●
Victims of modern slavery (per 1,000 population)	*	NA	NA	●	●
Adults with an account at a bank or other financial institution or with a mobile-money-service provider (% of population aged 15 or over)		71.7	2017	●	↑
Unemployment rate (% of total labor force)		5.9	2019	●	→
Fatal work-related accidents embodied in imports (per 100,000 population)		1.3	2010	●	↑

SDG9 – Industry, Innovation and Infrastructure	Value	Year	Rating	Trend
Population using the internet (%)	93.3	2018	●	↑
Mobile broadband subscriptions (per 100 population)	111.1	2018	●	↑
Logistics Performance Index: Quality of trade and transport-related infrastructure (worst 1–5 best)	3.1	2018	●	↑
The Times Higher Education Universities Ranking: Average score of top 3 universities (worst 0–100 best)	45.8	2020	●	●
Scientific and technical journal articles (per 1,000 population)	0.3	2018	●	→
Expenditure on research and development (% of GDP)	0.8	2013	●	●

SDG10 – Reduced Inequalities
	Value	Year	Rating	Trend
Gini coefficient adjusted for top income	NA	NA	●	●

SDG11 – Sustainable Cities and Communities
	Value	Year	Rating	Trend
Annual mean concentration of particulate matter of less than 2.5 microns in diameter (PM2.5) (μg/m³)	87.9	2017	●	↓
Access to improved water source, piped (% of urban population)	NA	NA	●	●
Satisfaction with public transport (%)	72.8	2019	●	↑

SDG12 – Responsible Consumption and Production
	Value	Year	Rating	Trend
Municipal solid waste (kg/capita/day)	1.6	2015	●	●
Electronic waste (kg/capita)	15.9	2016	●	●
Production-based SO_2 emissions (kg/capita)	72.3	2012	●	●
SO_2 emissions embodied in imports (kg/capita)	9.1	2012	●	●
Production-based nitrogen emissions (kg/capita)	32.9	2010	●	●
Nitrogen emissions embodied in imports (kg/capita)	9.3	2010	●	●

SDG13 – Climate Action
	Value	Year	Rating	Trend
Energy-related CO_2 emissions (tCO₂/capita)	17.9	2017	●	→
CO_2 emissions embodied in imports (tCO₂/capita)	1.5	2015	●	↗
CO_2 emissions embodied in fossil fuel exports (kg/capita)	214.2	2018	●	●

SDG14 – Life Below Water
	Value	Year	Rating	Trend
Mean area that is protected in marine sites important to biodiversity (%)	20.8	2018	●	→
Ocean Health Index: Clean Waters score (worst 0–100 best)	62.5	2019	●	↑
Fish caught from overexploited or collapsed stocks (% of total catch)	20.4	2014	●	↑
Fish caught by trawling (%)	17.9	2014	●	↑
Marine biodiversity threats embodied in imports (per million population)	0.5	2018	●	●

SDG15 – Life on Land
	Value	Year	Rating	Trend
Mean area that is protected in terrestrial sites important to biodiversity (%)	23.1	2018	●	→
Mean area that is protected in freshwater sites important to biodiversity (%)	17.7	2018	●	→
Red List Index of species survival (worst 0–1 best)	0.9	2019	●	↑
Permanent deforestation (% of forest area, 5-year average)	NA	NA	●	●
Terrestrial and freshwater biodiversity threats embodied in imports (per million population)	1.8	2018	●	●

SDG16 – Peace, Justice and Strong Institutions
		Value	Year	Rating	Trend
Homicides (per 100,000 population)		1.3	2017	●	↑
Unsentenced detainees (% of prison population)		48.3	2018	●	●
Percentage of population who feel safe walking alone at night in the city or area where they live (%)		87.9	2019	●	●
Property Rights (worst 1–7 best)		5.7	2019	●	●
Birth registrations with civil authority (% of children under age 5)		NA	NA	●	●
Corruption Perception Index (worst 0–100 best)		53	2019	●	→
Children involved in child labor (% of population aged 5 to 14)		NA	NA	●	●
Exports of major conventional weapons (TIV constant million USD per 100,000 population)		0.0	2019	●	●
Press Freedom Index (best 0–100 worst)		65.9	2019	●	↓

SDG17 – Partnerships for the Goals
		Value	Year	Rating	Trend
Government spending on health and education (% of GDP)		7.0	2008	●	●
For high-income and all OECD DAC countries: International concessional public finance, including official development assistance (% of GNI)		NA	NA	●	●
Other countries: Government revenue excluding grants (% of GDP)		NA	NA	●	●
Corporate Tax Haven Score (best 0–100 worst)	*	0.0	2019	●	●

* Imputed data point

5. Country Profiles

SENEGAL

▼ OVERALL PERFORMANCE

Index score

58.3

Regional average score

53.1

SDG Global rank   127 (OF 166)

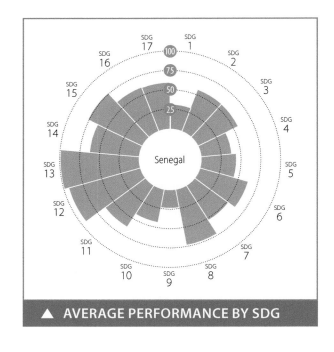

▲ AVERAGE PERFORMANCE BY SDG

▼ SPILLOVER INDEX

100 (best) to 0 (worst)

▼ CURRENT ASSESSMENT – SDG DASHBOARD

■ Major challenges   ■ Significant challenges   ■ Challenges remain   ■ SDG achieved   ■ Information unavailable

▼ SDG TRENDS

↓ Decreasing   → Stagnating   ↗ Moderately improving   ↑ On track or maintaining SDG achievement   ● Information unavailable

Notes: The full title of Goal 2 "Zero Hunger" is "End hunger, achieve food security and improved nutrition and promote sustainable agriculture".
The full title of each SDG is available here: https://sustainabledevelopment.un.org/topics/sustainabledevelopmentgoals

SDG1 – No Poverty

Indicator	Value	Year	Rating	Trend
Poverty headcount ratio at $1.90/day (%)	27.2	2020	●	↗
Poverty headcount ratio at $3.20/day (%)	52.9	2020	●	↗

SDG2 – Zero Hunger

Indicator	Value	Year	Rating	Trend
Prevalence of undernourishment (%)	11.3	2017	●	↑
Prevalence of stunting in children under 5 years of age (%)	17.0	2016	●	↗
Prevalence of wasting in children under 5 years of age (%)	7.2	2016	●	↑
Prevalence of obesity, BMI ≥ 30 (% of adult population)	8.8	2016	●	↑
Human Trophic Level (best 2–3 worst)	2.1	2017	●	↑
Cereal yield (tonnes per hectare of harvested land)	1.3	2017	●	↗
Sustainable Nitrogen Management Index (best 0–1.41 worst)	0.9	2015	●	↓

SDG3 – Good Health and Well-Being

Indicator	Value	Year	Rating	Trend
Maternal mortality rate (per 100,000 live births)	315	2017	●	↗
Neonatal mortality rate (per 1,000 live births)	20.6	2018	●	↗
Mortality rate, under-5 (per 1,000 live births)	43.6	2018	●	↑
Incidence of tuberculosis (per 100,000 population)	118.0	2018	●	→
New HIV infections (per 1,000 uninfected population)	0.1	2018	●	↑
Age-standardized death rate due to cardiovascular disease, cancer, diabetes, or chronic respiratory disease in adults aged 30–70 years (%)	18.1	2016	●	↑
Age-standardized death rate attributable to household air pollution and ambient air pollution (per 100,000 population)	161	2016	●	●
Traffic deaths (per 100,000 population)	23.4	2016	●	↑
Life expectancy at birth (years)	66.8	2016	●	↗
Adolescent fertility rate (births per 1,000 adolescent females aged 15 to 19)	72.7	2017	●	↗
Births attended by skilled health personnel (%)	68.4	2017	●	↑
Percentage of surviving infants who received 2 WHO-recommended vaccines (%)	81	2018	●	↗
Universal health coverage (UHC) index of service coverage (worst 0–100 best)	45.0	2017	●	→
Subjective well-being (average ladder score, worst 0–10 best)	5.5	2019	●	↑

SDG4 – Quality Education

Indicator	Value	Year	Rating	Trend
Net primary enrollment rate (%)	75.4	2017	●	→
Lower secondary completion rate (%)	37.4	2017	●	↓
Literacy rate (% of population aged 15 to 24)	69.5	2017	●	●

SDG5 – Gender Equality

Indicator	Value	Year	Rating	Trend
Demand for family planning satisfied by modern methods (% of females aged 15 to 49 who are married or in unions)	50.9	2017	●	↗
Ratio of female-to-male mean years of education received (%)	40.9	2018	●	↓
Ratio of female-to-male labor force participation rate (%)	60.3	2019	●	→
Seats held by women in national parliament (%)	43.0	2020	●	↑

SDG6 – Clean Water and Sanitation

Indicator	Value	Year	Rating	Trend
Population using at least basic drinking water services (%)	80.7	2017	●	↗
Population using at least basic sanitation services (%)	51.5	2017	●	→
Freshwater withdrawal (% of available freshwater resources)	11.8	2000	●	●
Anthropogenic wastewater that receives treatment (%)	0.5	2018	●	●
Scarce water consumption embodied in imports (m³/capita)	0.9	2013	●	↑

SDG7 – Affordable and Clean Energy

Indicator	Value	Year	Rating	Trend
Population with access to electricity (%)	61.7	2017	●	→
Population with access to clean fuels and technology for cooking (%)	31.7	2016	●	→
CO$_2$ emissions from fuel combustion for electricity and heating per total electricity output (MtCO$_2$/TWh)	1.9	2017	●	→

SDG8 – Decent Work and Economic Growth

Indicator	Value	Year	Rating	Trend
Adjusted GDP growth (%)	-2.0	2018	●	●
Victims of modern slavery (per 1,000 population)	2.9	2018	●	●
Adults with an account at a bank or other financial institution or with a mobile-money-service provider (% of population aged 15 or over)	42.3	2017	●	↑
Unemployment rate (% of total labor force)	6.6	2019	●	→
Fatal work-related accidents embodied in imports (per 100,000 population)	0.1	2010	●	↑

SDG9 – Industry, Innovation and Infrastructure

Indicator	Value	Year	Rating	Trend
Population using the internet (%)	46.0	2017	●	↑
Mobile broadband subscriptions (per 100 population)	42.1	2018	●	↑
Logistics Performance Index: Quality of trade and transport-related infrastructure (worst 1–5 best)	2.2	2018	●	↓
The Times Higher Education Universities Ranking: Average score of top 3 universities (worst 0–100 best) *	0.0	2020	●	●
Scientific and technical journal articles (per 1,000 population)	0.0	2018	●	↓
Expenditure on research and development (% of GDP)	0.8	2015	●	●

SDG10 – Reduced Inequalities

Indicator	Value	Year	Rating	Trend
Gini coefficient adjusted for top income	47.8	2011	●	●

SDG11 – Sustainable Cities and Communities

Indicator	Value	Year	Rating	Trend
Annual mean concentration of particulate matter of less than 2.5 microns in diameter (PM2.5) (µg/m³)	40.7	2017	●	↓
Access to improved water source, piped (% of urban population)	86.2	2017	●	→
Satisfaction with public transport (%)	48.8	2019	●	↑

SDG12 – Responsible Consumption and Production

Indicator	Value	Year	Rating	Trend
Municipal solid waste (kg/capita/day)	0.9	2016	●	●
Electronic waste (kg/capita)	1.0	2016	●	●
Production-based SO$_2$ emissions (kg/capita)	13.2	2012	●	●
SO$_2$ emissions embodied in imports (kg/capita)	0.5	2012	●	●
Production-based nitrogen emissions (kg/capita)	14.0	2010	●	●
Nitrogen emissions embodied in imports (kg/capita)	0.5	2010	●	●

SDG13 – Climate Action

Indicator	Value	Year	Rating	Trend
Energy-related CO$_2$ emissions (tCO$_2$/capita)	0.5	2017	●	↑
CO$_2$ emissions embodied in imports (tCO$_2$/capita)	0.1	2015	●	↑
CO$_2$ emissions embodied in fossil fuel exports (kg/capita)	0.0	2019	●	●

SDG14 – Life Below Water

Indicator	Value	Year	Rating	Trend
Mean area that is protected in marine sites important to biodiversity (%)	31.5	2018	●	↗
Ocean Health Index: Clean Waters score (worst 0–100 best)	46.6	2019	●	→
Fish caught from overexploited or collapsed stocks (% of total catch)	26.5	2014	●	↑
Fish caught by trawling (%)	15.2	2014	●	↑
Marine biodiversity threats embodied in imports (per million population)	0.0	2018	●	●

SDG15 – Life on Land

Indicator	Value	Year	Rating	Trend
Mean area that is protected in terrestrial sites important to biodiversity (%)	43.0	2018	●	↑
Mean area that is protected in freshwater sites important to biodiversity (%)	NA	NA	●	●
Red List Index of species survival (worst 0–1 best)	0.9	2019	●	↑
Permanent deforestation (% of forest area, 5-year average)	0.3	2018	●	●
Terrestrial and freshwater biodiversity threats embodied in imports (per million population)	0.1	2018	●	●

SDG16 – Peace, Justice and Strong Institutions

Indicator	Value	Year	Rating	Trend
Homicides (per 100,000 population) *	7.4	2015	●	●
Unsentenced detainees (% of prison population)	42.1	2018	●	●
Percentage of population who feel safe walking alone at night in the city or area where they live (%)	48.6	2019	●	↓
Property Rights (worst 1–7 best)	4.3	2019	●	●
Birth registrations with civil authority (% of children under age 5)	77.4	2018	●	●
Corruption Perception Index (worst 0–100 best)	45	2019	●	→
Children involved in child labor (% of population aged 5 to 14)	23.0	2016	●	●
Exports of major conventional weapons (TIV constant million USD per 100,000 population) *	0.0	2019	●	●
Press Freedom Index (best 0–100 worst)	25.8	2019	●	↑

SDG17 – Partnerships for the Goals

Indicator	Value	Year	Rating	Trend
Government spending on health and education (% of GDP)	7.0	2016	●	↓
For high-income and all OECD DAC countries: International concessional public finance, including official development assistance (% of GNI)	NA	NA	●	●
Other countries: Government revenue excluding grants (% of GDP)	19.2	2015	●	●
Corporate Tax Haven Score (best 0–100 worst) *	0.0	2019	●	●

* Imputed data point

▼ OVERALL PERFORMANCE

Index score

75.2

Regional average score

70.9

SDG Global rank 33 (OF 166)

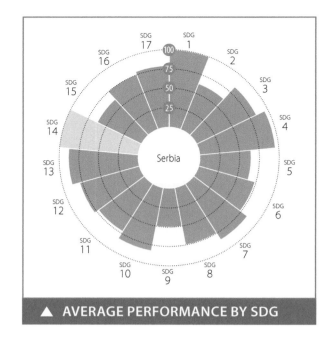

▲ AVERAGE PERFORMANCE BY SDG

▼ SPILLOVER INDEX

100 (best) to 0 (worst)

▼ CURRENT ASSESSMENT – SDG DASHBOARD

■ Major challenges ■ Significant challenges ■ Challenges remain ■ SDG achieved ■ Information unavailable

▼ SDG TRENDS

↓ Decreasing → Stagnating ↗ Moderately improving ↑ On track or maintaining SDG achievement ● Information unavailable

Notes: The full title of Goal 2 "Zero Hunger" is "End hunger, achieve food security and improved nutrition and promote sustainable agriculture".
The full title of each SDG is available here: https://sustainabledevelopment.un.org/topics/sustainabledevelopmentgoals

SDG1 – No Poverty

Indicator	Value	Year	Rating	Trend
Poverty headcount ratio at $1.90/day (%)	0.1	2020	●	↑
Poverty headcount ratio at $3.20/day (%)	0.4	2020	●	↑

SDG2 – Zero Hunger

Indicator	Value	Year	Rating	Trend
Prevalence of undernourishment (%)	5.7	2017	●	↑
Prevalence of stunting in children under 5 years of age (%)	6.0	2014	●	↑
Prevalence of wasting in children under 5 years of age (%)	3.9	2014	●	↑
Prevalence of obesity, BMI ≥ 30 (% of adult population)	21.5	2016	●	↓
Human Trophic Level (best 2–3 worst)	2.3	2017	●	→
Cereal yield (tonnes per hectare of harvested land)	4.0	2017	●	↑
Sustainable Nitrogen Management Index (best 0–1.41 worst)	0.5	2015	●	↑

SDG3 – Good Health and Well-Being

Indicator	Value	Year	Rating	Trend
Maternal mortality rate (per 100,000 live births)	12	2017	●	↑
Neonatal mortality rate (per 1,000 live births)	3.4	2018	●	↑
Mortality rate, under-5 (per 1,000 live births)	5.5	2018	●	↑
Incidence of tuberculosis (per 100,000 population)	17.0	2018	●	↑
New HIV infections (per 1,000 uninfected population)	0.0	2018	●	↑
Age-standardized death rate due to cardiovascular disease, cancer, diabetes, or chronic respiratory disease in adults aged 30–70 years (%)	19.1	2016	●	↑
Age-standardized death rate attributable to household air pollution and ambient air pollution (per 100,000 population)	62	2016	●	●
Traffic deaths (per 100,000 population)	7.4	2016	●	↑
Life expectancy at birth (years)	76.3	2016	●	↗
Adolescent fertility rate (births per 1,000 adolescent females aged 15 to 19)	14.7	2017	●	↑
Births attended by skilled health personnel (%)	98.4	2014	●	●
Percentage of surviving infants who received 2 WHO-recommended vaccines (%)	92	2018	●	↑
Universal health coverage (UHC) index of service coverage (worst 0–100 best)	65.0	2017	●	↑
Subjective well-being (average ladder score, worst 0–10 best)	5.9	2018	●	↑

SDG4 – Quality Education

Indicator	Value	Year	Rating	Trend
Net primary enrollment rate (%)	94.6	2018	●	↓
Lower secondary completion rate (%)	98.0	2018	●	↑
Literacy rate (% of population aged 15 to 24)	99.7	2016	●	●

SDG5 – Gender Equality

Indicator	Value	Year	Rating	Trend
Demand for family planning satisfied by modern methods (% of females aged 15 to 49 who are married or in unions)	38.7	2014	●	↗
Ratio of female-to-male mean years of education received (%)	92.2	2018	●	→
Ratio of female-to-male labor force participation rate (%)	75.3	2019	●	↑
Seats held by women in national parliament (%)	37.7	2020	●	↑

SDG6 – Clean Water and Sanitation

Indicator	Value	Year	Rating	Trend
Population using at least basic drinking water services (%)	85.5	2017	●	↓
Population using at least basic sanitation services (%)	97.6	2017	●	↑
Freshwater withdrawal (% of available freshwater resources)	5.2	2015	●	●
Anthropogenic wastewater that receives treatment (%)	1.7	2018	●	●
Scarce water consumption embodied in imports (m³/capita)	9.4	2013	●	↑

SDG7 – Affordable and Clean Energy

Indicator	Value	Year	Rating	Trend
Population with access to electricity (%)	100.0	2017	●	↑
Population with access to clean fuels and technology for cooking (%)	76.4	2016	●	↑
CO_2 emissions from fuel combustion for electricity and heating per total electricity output (MtCO2/TWh)	1.3	2017	●	→

SDG8 – Decent Work and Economic Growth

Indicator	Value	Year	Rating	Trend
Adjusted GDP growth (%)	-0.1	2018	●	●
Victims of modern slavery (per 1,000 population)	3.3	2018	●	●
Adults with an account at a bank or other financial institution or with a mobile-money-service provider (% of population aged 15 or over)	71.4	2017	●	↓
Unemployment rate (% of total labor force)	12.7	2019	●	↑
Fatal work-related accidents embodied in imports (per 100,000 population)	0.5	2010	●	↑

SDG9 – Industry, Innovation and Infrastructure

Indicator	Value	Year	Rating	Trend
Population using the internet (%)	73.4	2018	●	↑
Mobile broadband subscriptions (per 100 population)	66.0	2018	●	↑
Logistics Performance Index: Quality of trade and transport-related infrastructure (worst 1–5 best)	2.6	2018	●	↓
The Times Higher Education Universities Ranking: Average score of top 3 universities (worst 0–100 best)	22.5	2019	●	●
Scientific and technical journal articles (per 1,000 population)	0.5	2018	●	↓
Expenditure on research and development (% of GDP)	0.9	2017	●	↑

SDG10 – Reduced Inequalities

Indicator	Value	Year	Rating	Trend
Gini coefficient adjusted for top income	33.8	2015	●	●

SDG11 – Sustainable Cities and Communities

Indicator	Value	Year	Rating	Trend
Annual mean concentration of particulate matter of less than 2.5 microns in diameter (PM2.5) (µg/m³)	24.7	2017	●	↗
Access to improved water source, piped (% of urban population)	97.0	2017	●	→
Satisfaction with public transport (%)	46.4	2018	●	↗

SDG12 – Responsible Consumption and Production

Indicator	Value	Year	Rating	Trend
Municipal solid waste (kg/capita/day)	1.0	2015	●	●
Electronic waste (kg/capita)	7.1	2016	●	●
Production-based SO_2 emissions (kg/capita)	15.2	2012	●	●
SO_2 emissions embodied in imports (kg/capita)	13.9	2012	●	●
Production-based nitrogen emissions (kg/capita)	21.6	2010	●	●
Nitrogen emissions embodied in imports (kg/capita)	3.8	2010	●	●

SDG13 – Climate Action

Indicator	Value	Year	Rating	Trend
Energy-related CO_2 emissions (tCO2/capita)	5.7	2017	●	↓
CO_2 emissions embodied in imports (tCO2/capita)	0.4	2015	●	↑
CO_2 emissions embodied in fossil fuel exports (kg/capita)	10.5	2019	●	●

SDG14 – Life Below Water

Indicator	Value	Year	Rating	Trend
Mean area that is protected in marine sites important to biodiversity (%)	NA	NA	●	●
Ocean Health Index: Clean Waters score (worst 0–100 best)	NA	NA	●	●
Fish caught from overexploited or collapsed stocks (% of total catch)	NA	NA	●	●
Fish caught by trawling (%)	NA	NA	●	●
Marine biodiversity threats embodied in imports (per million population)	0.8	2018	●	●

SDG15 – Life on Land

Indicator	Value	Year	Rating	Trend
Mean area that is protected in terrestrial sites important to biodiversity (%)	29.5	2018	●	→
Mean area that is protected in freshwater sites important to biodiversity (%)	31.5	2018	●	→
Red List Index of species survival (worst 0–1 best)	1.0	2019	●	↑
Permanent deforestation (% of forest area, 5-year average)	0.0	2018	●	●
Terrestrial and freshwater biodiversity threats embodied in imports (per million population)	3.8	2018	●	●

SDG16 – Peace, Justice and Strong Institutions

Indicator	Value	Year	Rating	Trend
Homicides (per 100,000 population)	1.1	2017	●	↑
Unsentenced detainees (% of prison population)	15.6	2018	●	↑
Percentage of population who feel safe walking alone at night in the city or area where they live (%)	77.8	2018	●	↑
Property Rights (worst 1–7 best)	3.9	2019	●	●
Birth registrations with civil authority (% of children under age 5)	99.4	2018	●	●
Corruption Perception Index (worst 0–100 best)	39	2019	●	↓
Children involved in child labor (% of population aged 5 to 14)	9.5	2016	●	●
Exports of major conventional weapons (TIV constant million USD per 100,000 population)	0.2	2019	●	●
Press Freedom Index (best 0–100 worst)	31.2	2019	●	↓

SDG17 – Partnerships for the Goals

Indicator	Value	Year	Rating	Trend
Government spending on health and education (% of GDP)	8.9	2016	●	↓
For high-income and all OECD DAC countries: International concessional public finance, including official development assistance (% of GNI)	NA	NA	●	●
Other countries: Government revenue excluding grants (% of GDP)	32.8	2012	●	●
Corporate Tax Haven Score (best 0–100 worst) *	0.0	2019	●	●

* Imputed data point

OVERALL PERFORMANCE

Index score

na

Regional average score

53.1

SDG Global rank NA (OF 166)

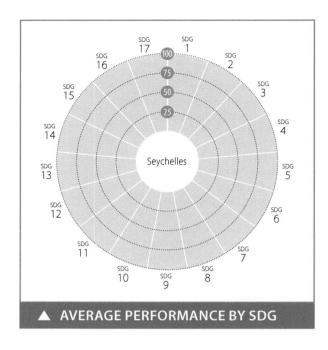

▲ AVERAGE PERFORMANCE BY SDG

SPILLOVER INDEX

100 (best) to 0 (worst)

CURRENT ASSESSMENT – SDG DASHBOARD

■ Major challenges ■ Significant challenges ■ Challenges remain ■ SDG achieved ■ Information unavailable

SDG TRENDS

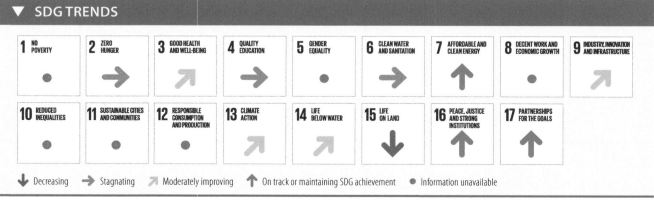

↓ Decreasing → Stagnating ↗ Moderately improving ↑ On track or maintaining SDG achievement ● Information unavailable

Notes: The full title of Goal 2 "Zero Hunger" is "End hunger, achieve food security and improved nutrition and promote sustainable agriculture".
The full title of each SDG is available here: https://sustainabledevelopment.un.org/topics/sustainabledevelopmentgoals

SDG1 – No Poverty

Indicator	Value	Year	Rating	Trend
Poverty headcount ratio at $1.90/day (%)	NA	NA	●	●
Poverty headcount ratio at $3.20/day (%)	NA	NA	●	●

SDG2 – Zero Hunger

Indicator	Value	Year	Rating	Trend
Prevalence of undernourishment (%)	* 1.2	2017	●	●
Prevalence of stunting in children under 5 years of age (%)	7.9	2012	●	→
Prevalence of wasting in children under 5 years of age (%)	4.3	2012	●	↑
Prevalence of obesity, BMI ≥ 30 (% of adult population)	14.0	2016	●	↓
Human Trophic Level (best 2–3 worst)	2.4	2007	●	●
Cereal yield (tonnes per hectare of harvested land)	NA	NA	●	●
Sustainable Nitrogen Management Index (best 0–1.41 worst)	1.2	2015	●	→

SDG3 – Good Health and Well-Being

Indicator	Value	Year	Rating	Trend
Maternal mortality rate (per 100,000 live births)	53	2017	●	↑
Neonatal mortality rate (per 1,000 live births)	8.8	2018	●	↑
Mortality rate, under-5 (per 1,000 live births)	14.5	2018	●	↑
Incidence of tuberculosis (per 100,000 population)	18.0	2018	●	↓
New HIV infections (per 1,000 uninfected population)	NA	NA	●	●
Age-standardized death rate due to cardiovascular disease, cancer, diabetes, or chronic respiratory disease in adults aged 30–70 years (%)	21.2	2016	●	↗
Age-standardized death rate attributable to household air pollution and ambient air pollution (per 100,000 population)	49	2016	●	●
Traffic deaths (per 100,000 population)	15.9	2016	●	↓
Life expectancy at birth (years)	73.3	2016	●	→
Adolescent fertility rate (births per 1,000 adolescent females aged 15 to 19)	62.1	2017	●	↓
Births attended by skilled health personnel (%)	99.0	2012	●	●
Percentage of surviving infants who received 2 WHO-recommended vaccines (%)	96	2018	●	↑
Universal health coverage (UHC) index of service coverage (worst 0–100 best)	71.0	2017	●	↑
Subjective well-being (average ladder score, worst 0–10 best)	NA	NA	●	●

SDG4 – Quality Education

Indicator	Value	Year	Rating	Trend
Net primary enrollment rate (%)	92.2	2018	●	↓
Lower secondary completion rate (%)	108.4	2018	●	↑
Literacy rate (% of population aged 15 to 24)	99.1	2018	●	●

SDG5 – Gender Equality

Indicator	Value	Year	Rating	Trend
Demand for family planning satisfied by modern methods (% of females aged 15 to 49 who are married or in unions)	NA	NA	●	●
Ratio of female-to-male mean years of education received (%)	NA	NA	●	●
Ratio of female-to-male labor force participation rate (%)	NA	NA	●	●
Seats held by women in national parliament (%)	21.2	2020	●	↓

SDG6 – Clean Water and Sanitation

Indicator	Value	Year	Rating	Trend
Population using at least basic drinking water services (%)	96.2	2017	●	→
Population using at least basic sanitation services (%)	100.0	2017	●	↑
Freshwater withdrawal (% of available freshwater resources)	NA	NA	●	●
Anthropogenic wastewater that receives treatment (%)	1.7	2018	●	●
Scarce water consumption embodied in imports (m³/capita)	34.6	2013	●	→

SDG7 – Affordable and Clean Energy

Indicator	Value	Year	Rating	Trend
Population with access to electricity (%)	100.0	2017	●	↑
Population with access to clean fuels and technology for cooking (%)	90.4	2016	●	↑
CO_2 emissions from fuel combustion for electricity and heating per total electricity output (MtCO2/TWh)	NA	NA	●	●

SDG8 – Decent Work and Economic Growth

Indicator	Value	Year	Rating	Trend
Adjusted GDP growth (%)	0.3	2018	●	●
Victims of modern slavery (per 1,000 population)	NA	NA	●	●
Adults with an account at a bank or other financial institution or with a mobile-money-service provider (% of population aged 15 or over)	NA	NA	●	●
Unemployment rate (% of total labor force)	NA	NA	●	●
Fatal work-related accidents embodied in imports (per 100,000 population)	1.8	2010	●	↑

SDG9 – Industry, Innovation and Infrastructure

Indicator	Value	Year	Rating	Trend
Population using the internet (%)	58.8	2017	●	↑
Mobile broadband subscriptions (per 100 population)	80.5	2018	●	↑
Logistics Performance Index: Quality of trade and transport-related infrastructure (worst 1–5 best)	NA	NA	●	●
The Times Higher Education Universities Ranking: Average score of top 3 universities (worst 0–100 best)	* 0.0	2020	●	●
Scientific and technical journal articles (per 1,000 population)	0.1	2018	●	↓
Expenditure on research and development (% of GDP)	0.2	2016	●	●

SDG10 – Reduced Inequalities

Indicator	Value	Year	Rating	Trend
Gini coefficient adjusted for top income	49.1	2013	●	●

SDG11 – Sustainable Cities and Communities

Indicator	Value	Year	Rating	Trend
Annual mean concentration of particulate matter of less than 2.5 microns in diameter (PM2.5) (µg/m³)	20.2	2017	●	→
Access to improved water source, piped (% of urban population)	NA	NA	●	●
Satisfaction with public transport (%)	NA	NA	●	●

SDG12 – Responsible Consumption and Production

Indicator	Value	Year	Rating	Trend
Municipal solid waste (kg/capita/day)	2.4	2012	●	●
Electronic waste (kg/capita)	11.5	2016	●	●
Production-based SO_2 emissions (kg/capita)	1155.8	2012	●	●
SO_2 emissions embodied in imports (kg/capita)	30.1	2012	●	●
Production-based nitrogen emissions (kg/capita)	35.8	2010	●	●
Nitrogen emissions embodied in imports (kg/capita)	11.5	2010	●	●

SDG13 – Climate Action

Indicator	Value	Year	Rating	Trend
Energy-related CO_2 emissions (tCO2/capita)	4.2	2017	●	↑
CO_2 emissions embodied in imports (tCO2/capita)	2.4	2015	●	→
CO_2 emissions embodied in fossil fuel exports (kg/capita)	0.0	2017	●	●

SDG14 – Life Below Water

Indicator	Value	Year	Rating	Trend
Mean area that is protected in marine sites important to biodiversity (%)	22.9	2018	●	→
Ocean Health Index: Clean Waters score (worst 0–100 best)	78.4	2019	●	↑
Fish caught from overexploited or collapsed stocks (% of total catch)	29.7	2014	●	↑
Fish caught by trawling (%)	NA	NA	●	●
Marine biodiversity threats embodied in imports (per million population)	0.0	2018	●	●

SDG15 – Life on Land

Indicator	Value	Year	Rating	Trend
Mean area that is protected in terrestrial sites important to biodiversity (%)	19.2	2018	●	→
Mean area that is protected in freshwater sites important to biodiversity (%)	NA	NA	●	●
Red List Index of species survival (worst 0–1 best)	0.7	2019	●	↓
Permanent deforestation (% of forest area, 5-year average)	NA	NA	●	●
Terrestrial and freshwater biodiversity threats embodied in imports (per million population)	0.5	2018	●	●

SDG16 – Peace, Justice and Strong Institutions

Indicator	Value	Year	Rating	Trend
Homicides (per 100,000 population)	12.7	2016	●	↑
Unsentenced detainees (% of prison population)	15.1	2018	●	↑
Percentage of population who feel safe walking alone at night in the city or area where they live (%)	NA	NA	●	●
Property Rights (worst 1–7 best)	4.7	2019	●	●
Birth registrations with civil authority (% of children under age 5)	NA	NA	●	●
Corruption Perception Index (worst 0–100 best)	66	2019	●	↑
Children involved in child labor (% of population aged 5 to 14)	NA	NA	●	●
Exports of major conventional weapons (TIV constant million USD per 100,000 population)	* 0.0	2019	●	●
Press Freedom Index (best 0–100 worst)	29.4	2019	●	↑

SDG17 – Partnerships for the Goals

Indicator	Value	Year	Rating	Trend
Government spending on health and education (% of GDP)	8.2	2016	●	↑
For high-income and all OECD DAC countries: International concessional public finance, including official development assistance (% of GNI)	NA	NA	●	●
Other countries: Government revenue excluding grants (% of GDP)	NA	NA	●	●
Corporate Tax Haven Score (best 0–100 worst)	68.1	2019	●	●

* Imputed data point

5. Country Profiles

▼ OVERALL PERFORMANCE

Index score
51.9

Regional average score
53.1

SDG Global rank 153 (OF 166)

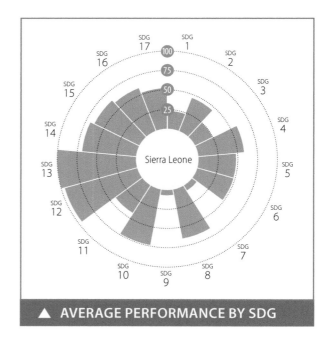

▲ AVERAGE PERFORMANCE BY SDG

▼ SPILLOVER INDEX

100 (best) to 0 (worst)

▼ CURRENT ASSESSMENT – SDG DASHBOARD

■ Major challenges ■ Significant challenges ■ Challenges remain ■ SDG achieved ■ Information unavailable

▼ SDG TRENDS

↓ Decreasing → Stagnating ↗ Moderately improving ↑ On track or maintaining SDG achievement ● Information unavailable

Notes: The full title of Goal 2 "Zero Hunger" is "End hunger, achieve food security and improved nutrition and promote sustainable agriculture".
The full title of each SDG is available here: https://sustainabledevelopment.un.org/topics/sustainabledevelopmentgoals

SDG1 – No Poverty

	Value	Year	Rating	Trend
Poverty headcount ratio at $1.90/day (%)	37.9	2020	●	↗
Poverty headcount ratio at $3.20/day (%)	70.3	2020	●	→

SDG2 – Zero Hunger

	Value	Year	Rating	Trend
Prevalence of undernourishment (%)	25.6	2017	●	↓
Prevalence of stunting in children under 5 years of age (%)	37.9	2013	●	→
Prevalence of wasting in children under 5 years of age (%)	9.4	2013	●	↗
Prevalence of obesity, BMI ≥ 30 (% of adult population)	8.7	2016	●	↑
Human Trophic Level (best 2–3 worst)	2.2	2017	●	↑
Cereal yield (tonnes per hectare of harvested land)	2.0	2017	●	↑
Sustainable Nitrogen Management Index (best 0–1.41 worst)	0.8	2015	●	→

SDG3 – Good Health and Well-Being

	Value	Year	Rating	Trend
Maternal mortality rate (per 100,000 live births)	1120	2017	●	→
Neonatal mortality rate (per 1,000 live births)	32.8	2018	●	↗
Mortality rate, under-5 (per 1,000 live births)	105.1	2018	●	↗
Incidence of tuberculosis (per 100,000 population)	298.0	2018	●	→
New HIV infections (per 1,000 uninfected population)	0.6	2018	○	↑
Age-standardized death rate due to cardiovascular disease, cancer, diabetes, or chronic respiratory disease in adults aged 30–70 years (%)	30.5	2016	●	→
Age-standardized death rate attributable to household air pollution and ambient air pollution (per 100,000 population)	324	2016	●	●
Traffic deaths (per 100,000 population)	27.3	2013	●	●
Life expectancy at birth (years)	53.1	2016	●	→
Adolescent fertility rate (births per 1,000 adolescent females aged 15 to 19)	112.8	2017	●	→
Births attended by skilled health personnel (%)	59.7	2013	●	●
Percentage of surviving infants who received 2 WHO-recommended vaccines (%)	80	2018	●	↗
Universal health coverage (UHC) index of service coverage (worst 0–100 best)	39.0	2017	●	↗
Subjective well-being (average ladder score, worst 0–10 best)	3.4	2019	●	↓

SDG4 – Quality Education

	Value	Year	Rating	Trend
Net primary enrollment rate (%)	98.1	2016	●	↑
Lower secondary completion rate (%)	51.0	2018	●	↗
Literacy rate (% of population aged 15 to 24)	66.6	2018	●	●

SDG5 – Gender Equality

	Value	Year	Rating	Trend
Demand for family planning satisfied by modern methods (% of females aged 15 to 49 who are married or in unions)	44.7	2017	●	→
Ratio of female-to-male mean years of education received (%)	63.6	2018	●	→
Ratio of female-to-male labor force participation rate (%)	98.7	2019	●	↑
Seats held by women in national parliament (%)	12.3	2020	●	↓

SDG6 – Clean Water and Sanitation

	Value	Year	Rating	Trend
Population using at least basic drinking water services (%)	60.8	2017	●	→
Population using at least basic sanitation services (%)	15.7	2017	●	→
Freshwater withdrawal (% of available freshwater resources)	0.5	2005	●	●
Anthropogenic wastewater that receives treatment (%)	0.0	2018	●	●
Scarce water consumption embodied in imports (m³/capita)	0.5	2013	●	↑

SDG7 – Affordable and Clean Energy

	Value	Year	Rating	Trend
Population with access to electricity (%)	23.4	2017	●	→
Population with access to clean fuels and technology for cooking (%)	1.0	2016	●	→
CO_2 emissions from fuel combustion for electricity and heating per total electricity output (MtCO$_2$/TWh)	NA	NA	●	●

SDG8 – Decent Work and Economic Growth

	Value	Year	Rating	Trend
Adjusted GDP growth (%)	-4.7	2018	●	●
Victims of modern slavery (per 1,000 population)	5.0	2018	○	●
Adults with an account at a bank or other financial institution or with a mobile-money-service provider (% of population aged 15 or over)	19.8	2017	●	→
Unemployment rate (% of total labor force)	4.4	2019	●	↑
Fatal work-related accidents embodied in imports (per 100,000 population)	0.0	2010	●	↑

SDG9 – Industry, Innovation and Infrastructure

	Value	Year	Rating	Trend
Population using the internet (%)	9.0	2017	●	→
Mobile broadband subscriptions (per 100 population)	25.8	2017	●	↑
Logistics Performance Index: Quality of trade and transport-related infrastructure (worst 1–5 best)	1.8	2018	●	●
The Times Higher Education Universities Ranking: Average score of top 3 universities (worst 0–100 best) *	0.0	2020	●	●
Scientific and technical journal articles (per 1,000 population)	0.0	2018	●	→
Expenditure on research and development (% of GDP) *	0.0	2017	●	●

SDG10 – Reduced Inequalities

	Value	Year	Rating	Trend
Gini coefficient adjusted for top income	36.9	2011	●	●

SDG11 – Sustainable Cities and Communities

	Value	Year	Rating	Trend
Annual mean concentration of particulate matter of less than 2.5 microns in diameter (PM2.5) (μg/m³)	21.6	2017	●	↓
Access to improved water source, piped (% of urban population)	37.8	2017	●	↓
Satisfaction with public transport (%)	28.4	2019	●	→

SDG12 – Responsible Consumption and Production

	Value	Year	Rating	Trend
Municipal solid waste (kg/capita/day)	0.5	2004	●	●
Electronic waste (kg/capita)	0.5	2016	●	●
Production-based SO$_2$ emissions (kg/capita)	20.8	2012	●	●
SO$_2$ emissions embodied in imports (kg/capita)	0.5	2012	●	●
Production-based nitrogen emissions (kg/capita)	12.0	2010	●	●
Nitrogen emissions embodied in imports (kg/capita)	0.2	2010	●	●

SDG13 – Climate Action

	Value	Year	Rating	Trend
Energy-related CO_2 emissions (tCO$_2$/capita)	0.1	2017	●	↑
CO_2 emissions embodied in imports (tCO$_2$/capita)	0.0	2015	●	↑
CO_2 emissions embodied in fossil fuel exports (kg/capita)	0.0	2017	●	●

SDG14 – Life Below Water

	Value	Year	Rating	Trend
Mean area that is protected in marine sites important to biodiversity (%)	57.6	2018	●	↑
Ocean Health Index: Clean Waters score (worst 0–100 best)	43.2	2019	●	→
Fish caught from overexploited or collapsed stocks (% of total catch)	2.5	2014	●	↑
Fish caught by trawling (%)	29.6	2014	○	↓
Marine biodiversity threats embodied in imports (per million population)	0.0	2018	●	●

SDG15 – Life on Land

	Value	Year	Rating	Trend
Mean area that is protected in terrestrial sites important to biodiversity (%)	68.8	2018	●	↑
Mean area that is protected in freshwater sites important to biodiversity (%)	72.5	2018	●	↑
Red List Index of species survival (worst 0–1 best)	0.9	2019	●	↑
Permanent deforestation (% of forest area, 5-year average)	2.0	2018	●	●
Terrestrial and freshwater biodiversity threats embodied in imports (per million population)	0.0	2018	●	●

SDG16 – Peace, Justice and Strong Institutions

	Value	Year	Rating	Trend
Homicides (per 100,000 population)	1.7	2015	○	●
Unsentenced detainees (% of prison population)	30.1	2018	○	↑
Percentage of population who feel safe walking alone at night in the city or area where they live (%)	49.3	2019	●	↓
Property Rights (worst 1–7 best)	NA	NA	●	●
Birth registrations with civil authority (% of children under age 5)	81.1	2018	●	●
Corruption Perception Index (worst 0–100 best)	33	2019	●	→
Children involved in child labor (% of population aged 5 to 14)	37.4	2016	●	●
Exports of major conventional weapons (TIV constant million USD per 100,000 population) *	0.0	2019	●	●
Press Freedom Index (best 0–100 worst)	30.4	2019	○	↓

SDG17 – Partnerships for the Goals

	Value	Year	Rating	Trend
Government spending on health and education (% of GDP)	4.9	2016	●	↑
For high-income and all OECD DAC countries: International concessional public finance, including official development assistance (% of GNI)	NA	NA	●	●
Other countries: Government revenue excluding grants (% of GDP) *	17.1	2018	●	↑
Corporate Tax Haven Score (best 0–100 worst) *	0.0	2019	●	●

* Imputed data point

5. Country Profiles

▼ OVERALL PERFORMANCE

Index score

67.0

Regional average score

67.2

SDG Global rank 93 (OF 166)

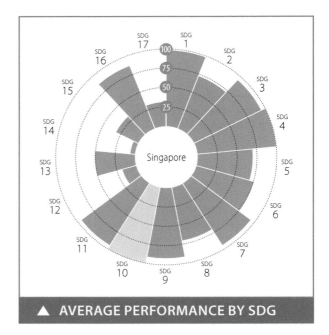

▲ AVERAGE PERFORMANCE BY SDG

▼ SPILLOVER INDEX

100 (best) to 0 (worst)

▼ CURRENT ASSESSMENT – SDG DASHBOARD

■ Major challenges   ■ Significant challenges   ■ Challenges remain   ■ SDG achieved   ■ Information unavailable

▼ SDG TRENDS

↓ Decreasing   → Stagnating   ↗ Moderately improving   ↑ On track or maintaining SDG achievement   ● Information unavailable

Notes: The full title of Goal 2 "Zero Hunger" is "End hunger, achieve food security and improved nutrition and promote sustainable agriculture".
The full title of each SDG is available here: https://sustainabledevelopment.un.org/topics/sustainabledevelopmentgoals

SDG1 – No Poverty

Indicator	Value	Year	Rating	Trend
Poverty headcount ratio at $1.90/day (%)	0.9	2020	●	↑
Poverty headcount ratio at $3.20/day (%)	1.1	2020	●	↑

SDG2 – Zero Hunger

Indicator	Value	Year	Rating	Trend
Prevalence of undernourishment (%)	* 1.2	2017	●	●
Prevalence of stunting in children under 5 years of age (%)	4.4	2000	●	↑
Prevalence of wasting in children under 5 years of age (%)	3.6	2000	●	↑
Prevalence of obesity, BMI ≥ 30 (% of adult population)	6.1	2016	●	↑
Human Trophic Level (best 2–3 worst)	NA	NA	●	●
Cereal yield (tonnes per hectare of harvested land)	NA	NA	●	●
Sustainable Nitrogen Management Index (best 0–1.41 worst)	1.1	2015	●	↓

SDG3 – Good Health and Well-Being

Indicator	Value	Year	Rating	Trend
Maternal mortality rate (per 100,000 live births)	8	2017	●	↑
Neonatal mortality rate (per 1,000 live births)	1.1	2018	●	↑
Mortality rate, under-5 (per 1,000 live births)	2.8	2018	●	↑
Incidence of tuberculosis (per 100,000 population)	47.0	2018	●	→
New HIV infections (per 1,000 uninfected population)	0.0	2018	●	↑
Age-standardized death rate due to cardiovascular disease, cancer, diabetes, or chronic respiratory disease in adults aged 30–70 years (%)	9.3	2016	●	↑
Age-standardized death rate attributable to household air pollution and ambient air pollution (per 100,000 population)	26	2016	●	●
Traffic deaths (per 100,000 population)	2.8	2016	●	↑
Life expectancy at birth (years)	82.9	2016	●	↑
Adolescent fertility rate (births per 1,000 adolescent females aged 15 to 19)	3.5	2017	●	↑
Births attended by skilled health personnel (%)	99.6	2016	●	↑
Percentage of surviving infants who received 2 WHO-recommended vaccines (%)	95	2018	●	↑
Universal health coverage (UHC) index of service coverage (worst 0–100 best)	86.0	2017	●	↑
Subjective well-being (average ladder score, worst 0–10 best)	6.4	2019	●	↑

SDG4 – Quality Education

Indicator	Value	Year	Rating	Trend
Net primary enrollment rate (%)	99.7	2017	●	●
Lower secondary completion rate (%)	104.6	2017	●	↑
Literacy rate (% of population aged 15 to 24)	99.9	2018	●	●

SDG5 – Gender Equality

Indicator	Value	Year	Rating	Trend
Demand for family planning satisfied by modern methods (% of females aged 15 to 49 who are married or in unions)	* 76.9	2017	●	↗
Ratio of female-to-male mean years of education received (%)	92.5	2018	●	↑
Ratio of female-to-male labor force participation rate (%)	79.3	2019	●	↑
Seats held by women in national parliament (%)	24.0	2020	●	→

SDG6 – Clean Water and Sanitation

Indicator	Value	Year	Rating	Trend
Population using at least basic drinking water services (%)	100.0	2017	●	↑
Population using at least basic sanitation services (%)	100.0	2017	●	↑
Freshwater withdrawal (% of available freshwater resources)	NA	NA	●	●
Anthropogenic wastewater that receives treatment (%)	100.0	2018	●	●
Scarce water consumption embodied in imports (m³/capita)	97.3	2013	●	→

SDG7 – Affordable and Clean Energy

Indicator	Value	Year	Rating	Trend
Population with access to electricity (%)	100.0	2017	●	↑
Population with access to clean fuels and technology for cooking (%)	100.0	2016	●	↑
CO_2 emissions from fuel combustion for electricity and heating per total electricity output (MtCO₂/TWh)	1.0	2017	●	↑

SDG8 – Decent Work and Economic Growth

Indicator	Value	Year	Rating	Trend
Adjusted GDP growth (%)	1.8	2018	●	●
Victims of modern slavery (per 1,000 population)	3.4	2018	●	●
Adults with an account at a bank or other financial institution or with a mobile-money-service provider (% of population aged 15 or over)	97.9	2017	●	↑
Unemployment rate (% of total labor force)	4.1	2019	●	↑
Fatal work-related accidents embodied in imports (per 100,000 population)	7.9	2010	●	↑

SDG9 – Industry, Innovation and Infrastructure

Indicator	Value	Year	Rating	Trend
Population using the internet (%)	88.2	2018	●	↑
Mobile broadband subscriptions (per 100 population)	148.8	2018	●	↑
Logistics Performance Index: Quality of trade and transport-related infrastructure (worst 1–5 best)	4.1	2018	●	↑
The Times Higher Education Universities Ranking: Average score of top 3 universities (worst 0–100 best)	77.4	2020	●	●
Scientific and technical journal articles (per 1,000 population)	2.0	2018	●	↑
Expenditure on research and development (% of GDP)	2.2	2016	●	↑

SDG10 – Reduced Inequalities

Indicator	Value	Year	Rating	Trend
Gini coefficient adjusted for top income	NA	NA	●	●

SDG11 – Sustainable Cities and Communities

Indicator	Value	Year	Rating	Trend
Annual mean concentration of particulate matter of less than 2.5 microns in diameter (PM2.5) (µg/m³)	19.1	2017	●	↓
Access to improved water source, piped (% of urban population)	99.0	2017	●	↑
Satisfaction with public transport (%)	94.5	2019	●	↑

SDG12 – Responsible Consumption and Production

Indicator	Value	Year	Rating	Trend
Municipal solid waste (kg/capita/day)	3.6	2017	●	●
Electronic waste (kg/capita)	17.9	2016	●	●
Production-based SO_2 emissions (kg/capita)	232.6	2012	●	●
SO_2 emissions embodied in imports (kg/capita)	58.1	2012	●	●
Production-based nitrogen emissions (kg/capita)	76.7	2010	●	●
Nitrogen emissions embodied in imports (kg/capita)	44.3	2010	●	●

SDG13 – Climate Action

Indicator	Value	Year	Rating	Trend
Energy-related CO_2 emissions (tCO₂/capita)	11.9	2017	●	↓
CO_2 emissions embodied in imports (tCO₂/capita)	9.3	2015	●	→
CO_2 emissions embodied in fossil fuel exports (kg/capita)	0.0	2018	●	●

SDG14 – Life Below Water

Indicator	Value	Year	Rating	Trend
Mean area that is protected in marine sites important to biodiversity (%)	3.3	2018	●	→
Ocean Health Index: Clean Waters score (worst 0–100 best)	38.7	2019	●	↓
Fish caught from overexploited or collapsed stocks (% of total catch)	NA	NA	●	●
Fish caught by trawling (%)	NA	NA	●	●
Marine biodiversity threats embodied in imports (per million population)	3.2	2018	●	●

SDG15 – Life on Land

Indicator	Value	Year	Rating	Trend
Mean area that is protected in terrestrial sites important to biodiversity (%)	21.1	2018	●	→
Mean area that is protected in freshwater sites important to biodiversity (%)	NA	NA	●	●
Red List Index of species survival (worst 0–1 best)	0.9	2019	●	↓
Permanent deforestation (% of forest area, 5-year average)	0.9	2018	●	●
Terrestrial and freshwater biodiversity threats embodied in imports (per million population)	12.6	2018	●	●

SDG16 – Peace, Justice and Strong Institutions

Indicator	Value	Year	Rating	Trend
Homicides (per 100,000 population)	0.2	2017	●	↑
Unsentenced detainees (% of prison population)	11.5	2018	●	↑
Percentage of population who feel safe walking alone at night in the city or area where they live	96.5	2019	●	↑
Property Rights (worst 1–7 best)	6.4	2019	●	●
Birth registrations with civil authority (% of children under age 5)	NA	NA	●	●
Corruption Perception Index (worst 0–100 best)	85	2019	●	↑
Children involved in child labor (% of population aged 5 to 14)	NA	NA	●	●
Exports of major conventional weapons (TIV constant million USD per 100,000 population)	0.8	2019	●	●
Press Freedom Index (best 0–100 worst)	51.4	2019	●	→

SDG17 – Partnerships for the Goals

Indicator	Value	Year	Rating	Trend
Government spending on health and education (% of GDP)	4.6	2013	●	●
For high-income and all OECD DAC countries: International concessional public finance, including official development assistance (% of GNI)	NA	NA	●	●
Other countries: Government revenue excluding grants (% of GDP)	NA	NA	●	●
Corporate Tax Haven Score (best 0–100 worst)	81.4	2019	●	●

* Imputed data point

5. Country Profiles

SLOVAK REPUBLIC

▼ OVERALL PERFORMANCE

Index score

77.5

Regional average score

77.3

SDG Global rank **27** (OF 166)

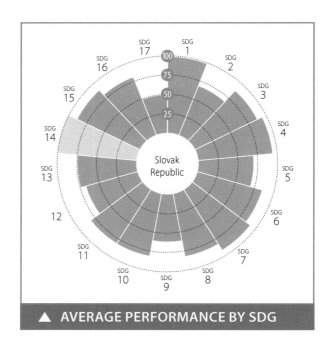

▲ AVERAGE PERFORMANCE BY SDG

▼ SPILLOVER INDEX

100 (best) to 0 (worst)

▼ CURRENT ASSESSMENT – SDG DASHBOARD

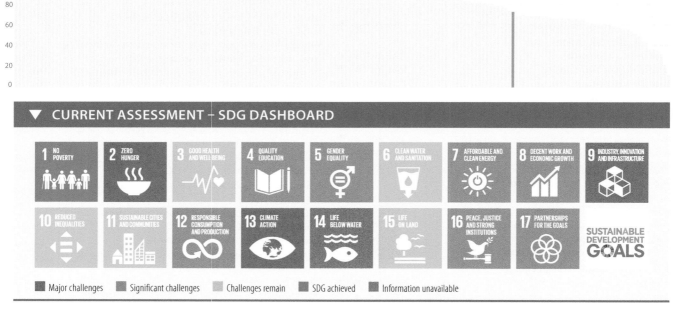

■ Major challenges　■ Significant challenges　■ Challenges remain　■ SDG achieved　■ Information unavailable

▼ SDG TRENDS

↓ Decreasing　→ Stagnating　↗ Moderately improving　↑ On track or maintaining SDG achievement　● Information unavailable

Notes: The full title of Goal 2 "Zero Hunger" is "End hunger, achieve food security and improved nutrition and promote sustainable agriculture".
The full title of each SDG is available here: https://sustainabledevelopment.un.org/topics/sustainabledevelopmentgoals

SDG1 – No Poverty

Indicator	Value	Year	Rating	Trend
Poverty headcount ratio at $1.90/day (%)	0.9	2020	●	↑
Poverty headcount ratio at $3.20/day (%)	1.2	2020	●	↑
Poverty rate after taxes and transfers (%)	8.5	2016	●	↑

SDG2 – Zero Hunger

Indicator	Value	Year	Rating	Trend
Prevalence of undernourishment (%)	3.4	2017	●	↑
Prevalence of stunting in children under 5 years of age (%)	* 2.6	2016	●	↑
Prevalence of wasting in children under 5 years of age (%)	* 0.7	2016	●	↑
Prevalence of obesity, BMI ≥ 30 (% of adult population)	20.5	2016	●	↓
Human Trophic Level (best 2–3 worst)	2.4	2017	●	↓
Cereal yield (tonnes per hectare of harvested land)	4.9	2017	●	↑
Sustainable Nitrogen Management Index (best 0–1.41 worst)	0.5	2015	●	↓
Yield gap closure (% of potential yield)	48.9	2015	●	●

SDG3 – Good Health and Well-Being

Indicator	Value	Year	Rating	Trend
Maternal mortality rate (per 100,000 live births)	5	2017	●	↑
Neonatal mortality rate (per 1,000 live births)	2.8	2018	●	↑
Mortality rate, under-5 (per 1,000 live births)	5.6	2018	●	↑
Incidence of tuberculosis (per 100,000 population)	5.8	2018	●	↑
New HIV infections (per 1,000 uninfected population)	0.0	2018	●	↑
Age-standardized death rate due to cardiovascular disease, cancer, diabetes, or chronic respiratory disease in adults aged 30–70 years (%)	17.2	2016	●	↑
Age-standardized death rate attributable to household air pollution and ambient air pollution (per 100,000 population)	34	2016	●	●
Traffic deaths (per 100,000 population)	6.1	2016	●	↑
Life expectancy at birth (years)	77.4	2016	●	↑
Adolescent fertility rate (births per 1,000 adolescent females aged 15 to 19)	25.7	2017	●	↓
Births attended by skilled health personnel (%)	98.5	2014	●	●
Percentage of surviving infants who received 2 WHO-recommended vaccines (%)	96.0	2018	●	↑
Universal health coverage (UHC) index of service coverage (worst 0–100 best)	77.0	2017	●	↑
Subjective well-being (average ladder score, worst 0–10 best)	6.2	2018	●	↑
Gap in life expectancy at birth among regions (years)	1.9	2016	●	●
Gap in self-reported health status by income (percentage points)	16.9	2017	●	↑
Daily smokers (% of population aged 15 and over)	22.9	2014	●	●

SDG4 – Quality Education

Indicator	Value	Year	Rating	Trend
Net primary enrollment rate (%)	* 94.8	2017	●	→
Lower secondary completion rate (%)	* 94.8	2017	●	↑
Literacy rate (% of population aged 15 to 24)	NA	NA	●	●
Participation rate in pre-primary organized learning (% of children aged 4 to 6)	82.3	2017	●	↓
Tertiary educational attainment (% of population aged 25 to 34)	37.2	2018	●	↑
PISA score (worst 0–600 best)	469.3	2018	●	↑
Variation in science performance explained by socio-economic status (%)	18.5	2018	●	↓
Underachievers in science (% of 15-year-olds)	29.3	2018	●	→
Resilient students in science (% of 15-year-olds)	19.3	2018	●	→

SDG5 – Gender Equality

Indicator	Value	Year	Rating	Trend
Demand for family planning satisfied by modern methods (% of females aged 15 to 49 who are married or in unions)	* 75.1	2017	●	↑
Ratio of female-to-male mean years of education received (%)	98.4	2018	●	↑
Ratio of female-to-male labor force participation rate (%)	78.3	2019	●	↑
Seats held by women in national parliament (%)	20.0	2020	●	→
Gender wage gap (% of male median wage)	15.7	2018	●	↓
Gender gap in time spent doing unpaid work (minutes/day)	NA	NA	●	●

SDG6 – Clean Water and Sanitation

Indicator	Value	Year	Rating	Trend
Population using at least basic drinking water services (%)	99.8	2017	●	●
Population using at least basic sanitation services (%)	97.9	2017	●	●
Freshwater withdrawal (% of available freshwater resources)	2.3	2015	●	●
Anthropogenic wastewater that receives treatment (%)	43.7	2018	●	●
Scarce water consumption embodied in imports (m³/capita)	16.4	2013	●	↑
Population using safely managed water services (%)	99.8	2017	●	↑
Population using safely managed sanitation services (%)	82.5	2017	●	↓

SDG7 – Affordable and Clean Energy

Indicator	Value	Year	Rating	Trend
Population with access to electricity (%)	100.0	2017	●	↑
Population with access to clean fuels and technology for cooking (%)	96.6	2016	●	↑
CO$_2$ emissions from fuel combustion for electricity and heating per total electricity output (MtCO$_2$/TWh)	1.2	2017	●	→
Share of renewable energy in total primary energy supply (%)	8.9	2018	●	↓

SDG8 – Decent Work and Economic Growth

Indicator	Value	Year	Rating	Trend
Adjusted GDP growth (%)	-0.3	2018	●	●
Victims of modern slavery (per 1,000 population)	2.9	2018	●	●
Adults with an account at a bank or other financial institution or with a mobile-money-service provider (% of population aged 15 or over)	84.2	2017	●	↑
Fatal work-related accidents embodied in imports (per 100,000 population)	0.7	2010	●	↑
Employment-to-population ratio (%)	68.4	2019	●	↑
Youth not in employment, education or training (NEET) (% of population aged 15 to 29)	15.1	2018	●	↑

SDG9 – Industry, Innovation and Infrastructure

Indicator	Value	Year	Rating	Trend
Population using the internet (%)	80.7	2018	●	↑
Mobile broadband subscriptions (per 100 population)	86.0	2018	●	↑
Logistics Performance Index: Quality of trade and transport-related infrastructure (worst 1–5 best)	3.0	2018	●	↑
The Times Higher Education Universities Ranking: Average score of top 3 universities (worst 0–100 best)	16.4	2020	●	●
Scientific and technical journal articles (per 1,000 population)	1.0	2018	●	↑
Expenditure on research and development (% of GDP)	0.9	2017	●	→
Researchers (per 1,000 employed population)	6.8	2018	●	→
Triadic patent families filed (per million population)	1.6	2017	●	→
Gap in internet access by income (percentage points)	28.5	2019	●	↑
Women in science and engineering (% of tertiary graduates in science and engineering)	33.9	2015	●	●

SDG10 – Reduced Inequalities

Indicator	Value	Year	Rating	Trend
Gini coefficient adjusted for top income	33.9	2015	●	↓
Palma ratio	0.8	2016	●	↑
Elderly poverty rate (% of population aged 66 or over)	4.4	2016	●	↑

SDG11 – Sustainable Cities and Communities

Indicator	Value	Year	Rating	Trend
Annual mean concentration of particulate matter of less than 2.5 microns in diameter (PM2.5) (μg/m³)	17.6	2017	●	→
Access to improved water source, piped (% of urban population)	97.2	2017	●	→
Satisfaction with public transport (%)	59.0	2018	●	↑
Population with rent overburden (%)	3.8	2015	●	●

SDG12 – Responsible Consumption and Production

Indicator	Value	Year	Rating	Trend
Electronic waste (kg/capita)	12.3	2016	●	●
Production-based SO$_2$ emissions (kg/capita)	80.1	2012	●	●
SO$_2$ emissions embodied in imports (kg/capita)	9.3	2012	●	●
Production-based nitrogen emissions (kg/capita)	39.1	2010	●	●
Nitrogen emissions embodied in imports (kg/capita)	7.4	2010	●	●
Non-recycled municipal solid waste (kg/capita/day)	0.7	2018	●	●

SDG13 – Climate Action

Indicator	Value	Year	Rating	Trend
Energy-related CO$_2$ emissions (tCO$_2$/capita)	5.9	2017	●	↓
CO$_2$ emissions embodied in imports (tCO$_2$/capita)	1.7	2015	●	→
CO$_2$ emissions embodied in fossil fuel exports (kg/capita)	64.0	2018	●	●
Effective carbon rate (EUR/tCO$_2$)	18.1	2016	●	●

SDG14 – Life Below Water

Indicator	Value	Year	Rating	Trend
Mean area that is protected in marine sites important to biodiversity (%)	NA	NA	●	●
Ocean Health Index: Clean Waters score (worst 0–100 best)	NA	NA	●	●
Fish caught from overexploited or collapsed stocks (% of total catch)	NA	NA	●	●
Fish caught by trawling (%)	NA	NA	●	●
Marine biodiversity threats embodied in imports (per million population)	0.1	2018	●	●

SDG15 – Life on Land

Indicator	Value	Year	Rating	Trend
Mean area that is protected in terrestrial sites important to biodiversity (%)	82.7	2018	●	↑
Mean area that is protected in freshwater sites important to biodiversity (%)	81.5	2018	●	↑
Red List Index of species survival (worst 0–1 best)	1.0	2019	●	↑
Permanent deforestation (% of forest area, 5-year average)	0.0	2018	●	●
Terrestrial and freshwater biodiversity threats embodied in imports (per million population)	1.4	2018	●	●

SDG16 – Peace, Justice and Strong Institutions

Indicator	Value	Year	Rating	Trend
Homicides (per 100,000 population)	1.5	2017	●	↑
Unsentenced detainees (% of prison population)	14.9	2018	●	↑
Percentage of population who feel safe walking alone at night in the city or area where they live (%)	67.5	2018	●	↑
Property Rights (worst 1–7 best)	4.4	2019	●	●
Birth registrations with civil authority (% of children under age 5)	100.0	2018	●	↓
Corruption Perception Index (worst 0–100 best)	50.0	2019	●	↓
Children involved in child labor (% of population aged 5 to 14)	* 0.0	2016	●	●
Exports of major conventional weapons (TIV constant million USD per 100,000 population)	0.3	2019	●	●
Press Freedom Index (best 0–100 worst)	23.6	2019	●	↑
Persons held in prison (per 100,000 population)	192.3	2017	●	↓

SDG17 – Partnerships for the Goals

Indicator	Value	Year	Rating	Trend
Government spending on health and education (% of GDP)	9.6	2016	●	→
For high-income and all OECD DAC countries: International concessional public finance, including official development assistance (% of GNI)	0.1	2017	●	→
Other countries: Government revenue excluding grants (% of GDP)	NA	NA	●	●
Corporate Tax Haven Score (best 0–100 worst)	53.0	2019	●	●
Financial Secrecy Score (best 0–100 worst)	50.9	2020	●	●
Shifted profits of multinationals (US$ billion)	0.9	2016	●	●

* Imputed data point

5. Country Profiles

▼ OVERALL PERFORMANCE

Index score

79.8

Regional average score

77.3

SDG Global rank **12** (OF 166)

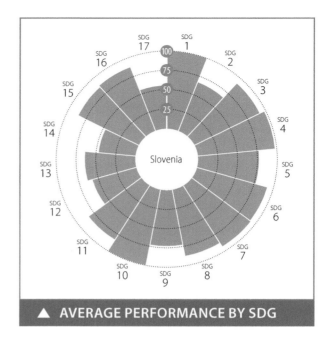

▲ AVERAGE PERFORMANCE BY SDG

▼ SPILLOVER INDEX

100 (best) to 0 (worst)

▼ CURRENT ASSESSMENT – SDG DASHBOARD

■ Major challenges ■ Significant challenges ■ Challenges remain ■ SDG achieved ■ Information unavailable

▼ SDG TRENDS

1 NO POVERTY	2 ZERO HUNGER	3 GOOD HEALTH AND WELL-BEING	4 QUALITY EDUCATION	5 GENDER EQUALITY	6 CLEAN WATER AND SANITATION	7 AFFORDABLE AND CLEAN ENERGY	8 DECENT WORK AND ECONOMIC GROWTH	9 INDUSTRY, INNOVATION AND INFRASTRUCTURE
↑	↗	↗	↗	↗	↗	↗	↑	↗

10 REDUCED INEQUALITIES	11 SUSTAINABLE CITIES AND COMMUNITIES	12 RESPONSIBLE CONSUMPTION AND PRODUCTION	13 CLIMATE ACTION	14 LIFE BELOW WATER	15 LIFE ON LAND	16 PEACE, JUSTICE AND STRONG INSTITUTIONS	17 PARTNERSHIPS FOR THE GOALS
↗	↗	●	↓	→	↑	↑	↗

↓ Decreasing → Stagnating ↗ Moderately improving ↑ On track or maintaining SDG achievement ● Information unavailable

Notes: The full title of Goal 2 "Zero Hunger" is "End hunger, achieve food security and improved nutrition and promote sustainable agriculture".
The full title of each SDG is available here: https://sustainabledevelopment.un.org/topics/sustainabledevelopmentgoals

SDG1 – No Poverty

Indicator	Value	Year	Rating	Trend
Poverty headcount ratio at $1.90/day (%)	0.2	2020	●	↑
Poverty headcount ratio at $3.20/day (%)	0.2	2020	●	↑
Poverty rate after taxes and transfers (%)	8.5	2017	●	↑

SDG2 – Zero Hunger

Indicator	Value	Year	Rating	Trend
Prevalence of undernourishment (%)	2.5	2017	●	↑
Prevalence of stunting in children under 5 years of age (%)	* 2.6	2016	●	↑
Prevalence of wasting in children under 5 years of age (%)	* 0.7	2016	●	↑
Prevalence of obesity, BMI ≥ 30 (% of adult population)	20.2	2016	●	↓
Human Trophic Level (best 2–3 worst)	2.4	2017	●	↑
Cereal yield (tonnes per hectare of harvested land)	5.5	2017	●	↑
Sustainable Nitrogen Management Index (best 0–1.41 worst)	0.7	2015	●	→
Yield gap closure (% of potential yield)	57.6	2015	●	●

SDG3 – Good Health and Well-Being

Indicator	Value	Year	Rating	Trend
Maternal mortality rate (per 100,000 live births)	7	2017	●	↑
Neonatal mortality rate (per 1,000 live births)	1.2	2018	●	↑
Mortality rate, under-5 (per 1,000 live births)	2.1	2018	●	↑
Incidence of tuberculosis (per 100,000 population)	5.3	2018	●	↑
New HIV infections (per 1,000 uninfected population)	NA	NA	●	●
Age-standardized death rate due to cardiovascular disease, cancer, diabetes, or chronic respiratory disease in adults aged 30–70 years (%)	12.7	2016	●	↑
Age-standardized death rate attributable to household air pollution and ambient air pollution (per 100,000 population)	23	2016	●	●
Traffic deaths (per 100,000 population)	6.4	2016	●	↑
Life expectancy at birth (years)	80.9	2016	●	↑
Adolescent fertility rate (births per 1,000 adolescent females aged 15 to 19)	3.8	2017	●	↑
Births attended by skilled health personnel (%)	99.8	2012	●	●
Percentage of surviving infants who received 2 WHO-recommended vaccines (%)	93.0	2018	●	↑
Universal health coverage (UHC) index of service coverage (worst 0–100 best)	79.0	2017	●	↑
Subjective well-being (average ladder score, worst 0–10 best)	6.7	2019	●	↑
Gap in life expectancy at birth among regions (years)	2.4	2016	●	●
Gap in self-reported health status by income (percentage points)	25.7	2017	●	↓
Daily smokers (% of population aged 15 and over)	18.9	2014	●	●

SDG4 – Quality Education

Indicator	Value	Year	Rating	Trend
Net primary enrollment rate (%)	* 98.0	2017	●	↑
Lower secondary completion rate (%)	* 98.0	2017	●	↑
Literacy rate (% of population aged 15 to 24)	99.8	2014	●	●
Participation rate in pre-primary organized learning (% of children aged 4 to 6)	94.1	2017	●	↑
Tertiary educational attainment (% of population aged 25 to 34)	40.7	2018	●	↑
PISA score (worst 0–600 best)	503.7	2018	●	↑
Variation in science performance explained by socio-economic status (%)	13.0	2018	●	↗
Underachievers in science (% of 15-year-olds)	14.6	2018	●	↑
Resilient students in science (% of 15-year-olds)	37.7	2018	●	↑

SDG5 – Gender Equality

Indicator	Value	Year	Rating	Trend
Demand for family planning satisfied by modern methods (% of females aged 15 to 49 who are married or in unions)	* 78.6	2017	●	↑
Ratio of female-to-male mean years of education received (%)	99.2	2018	●	↑
Ratio of female-to-male labor force participation rate (%)	85.3	2019	●	↑
Seats held by women in national parliament (%)	27.8	2020	●	↓
Gender wage gap (% of male median wage)	5.0	2014	●	●
Gender gap in time spent doing unpaid work (minutes/day)	119.7	2001	●	●

SDG6 – Clean Water and Sanitation

Indicator	Value	Year	Rating	Trend
Population using at least basic drinking water services (%)	99.5	2017	●	●
Population using at least basic sanitation services (%)	99.1	2017	●	●
Freshwater withdrawal (% of available freshwater resources)	0.6	2015	●	●
Anthropogenic wastewater that receives treatment (%)	89.1	2018	●	●
Scarce water consumption embodied in imports (m³/capita)	24.5	2013	●	↑
Population using safely managed water services (%)	98.1	2017	●	↑
Population using safely managed sanitation services (%)	83.0	2017	●	↗

SDG7 – Affordable and Clean Energy

Indicator	Value	Year	Rating	Trend
Population with access to electricity (%)	100.0	2017	●	↑
Population with access to clean fuels and technology for cooking (%)	96.2	2016	●	↑
CO2 emissions from fuel combustion for electricity and heating per total electricity output (MtCO2/TWh)	0.9	2017	●	↑
Share of renewable energy in total primary energy supply (%)	16.8	2018	●	↓

SDG8 – Decent Work and Economic Growth

Indicator	Value	Year	Rating	Trend
Adjusted GDP growth (%)	2.1	2018	●	●
Victims of modern slavery (per 1,000 population)	2.2	2018	●	●
Adults with an account at a bank or other financial institution or with a mobile-money-service provider (% of population aged 15 or over)	97.5	2017	●	↑
Fatal work-related accidents embodied in imports (per 100,000 population)	1.0	2010	●	↑
Employment-to-population ratio (%)	71.9	2019	●	↑
Youth not in employment, education or training (NEET) (% of population aged 15 to 29)	9.7	2018	●	↑

SDG9 – Industry, Innovation and Infrastructure

Indicator	Value	Year	Rating	Trend
Population using the internet (%)	79.8	2018	●	↑
Mobile broadband subscriptions (per 100 population)	77.7	2018	●	↑
Logistics Performance Index: Quality of trade and transport-related infrastructure (worst 1–5 best)	3.3	2018	●	↑
The Times Higher Education Universities Ranking: Average score of top 3 universities (worst 0–100 best)	28.5	2020	●	●
Scientific and technical journal articles (per 1,000 population)	1.5	2018	●	↑
Expenditure on research and development (% of GDP)	1.9	2017	●	↑
Researchers (per 1,000 employed population)	9.9	2018	●	↑
Triadic patent families filed (per million population)	3.8	2017	●	↓
Gap in internet access by income (percentage points)	29.3	2019	●	↑
Women in science and engineering (% of tertiary graduates in science and engineering)	31.1	2015	●	●

SDG10 – Reduced Inequalities

Indicator	Value	Year	Rating	Trend
Gini coefficient adjusted for top income	27.4	2015	●	↑
Palma ratio	0.8	2017	●	↑
Elderly poverty rate (% of population aged 66 or over)	13.2	2017	●	↓

SDG11 – Sustainable Cities and Communities

Indicator	Value	Year	Rating	Trend
Annual mean concentration of particulate matter of less than 2.5 microns in diameter (PM2.5) (µg/m³)	16.0	2017	●	→
Access to improved water source, piped (% of urban population)	99.0	2017	●	↑
Satisfaction with public transport (%)	59.7	2019	●	↓
Population with rent overburden (%)	5.2	2017	●	↑

SDG12 – Responsible Consumption and Production

Indicator	Value	Year	Rating	Trend
Electronic waste (kg/capita)	16.1	2016	●	●
Production-based SO2 emissions (kg/capita)	126.2	2012	●	●
SO2 emissions embodied in imports (kg/capita)	15.1	2012	●	●
Production-based nitrogen emissions (kg/capita)	29.2	2010	●	●
Nitrogen emissions embodied in imports (kg/capita)	11.9	2010	●	●
Non-recycled municipal solid waste (kg/capita/day)	0.3	2018	●	●

SDG13 – Climate Action

Indicator	Value	Year	Rating	Trend
Energy-related CO2 emissions (tCO2/capita)	6.4	2017	●	↓
CO2 emissions embodied in imports (tCO2/capita)	2.6	2015	●	→
CO2 emissions embodied in fossil fuel exports (kg/capita)	54.8	2018	●	●
Effective carbon rate (EUR/tCO2)	23.3	2016	●	●

SDG14 – Life Below Water

Indicator	Value	Year	Rating	Trend
Mean area that is protected in marine sites important to biodiversity (%)	88.6	2018	●	↑
Ocean Health Index: Clean Waters score (worst 0–100 best)	28.4	2019	●	↓
Fish caught from overexploited or collapsed stocks (% of total catch)	NA	NA	●	●
Fish caught by trawling (%)	89.7	2012	●	●
Marine biodiversity threats embodied in imports (per million population)	0.1	2018	●	●

SDG15 – Life on Land

Indicator	Value	Year	Rating	Trend
Mean area that is protected in terrestrial sites important to biodiversity (%)	85.1	2018	●	↑
Mean area that is protected in freshwater sites important to biodiversity (%)	77.5	2018	●	↑
Red List Index of species survival (worst 0–1 best)	0.9	2019	●	↑
Permanent deforestation (% of forest area, 5-year average)	* 0.0	2018	●	●
Terrestrial and freshwater biodiversity threats embodied in imports (per million population)	2.2	2018	●	●

SDG16 – Peace, Justice and Strong Institutions

Indicator	Value	Year	Rating	Trend
Homicides (per 100,000 population)	0.9	2017	●	↑
Unsentenced detainees (% of prison population)	18.3	2018	●	↑
Percentage of population who feel safe walking alone at night in the city or area where they live (%)	90.3	2019	●	↑
Property Rights (worst 1–7 best)	4.6	2019	●	●
Birth registrations with civil authority (% of children under age 5)	100.0	2018	●	●
Corruption Perception Index (worst 0–100 best)	60.0	2019	●	↑
Children involved in child labor (% of population aged 5 to 14)	* 0.0	2016	●	●
Exports of major conventional weapons (TIV constant million USD per 100,000 population)	0.0	2019	●	●
Press Freedom Index (best 0–100 worst)	22.3	2019	●	↑
Persons held in prison (per 100,000 population)	63.3	2017	●	↑

SDG17 – Partnerships for the Goals

Indicator	Value	Year	Rating	Trend
Government spending on health and education (% of GDP)	10.9	2016	●	↑
For high-income and all OECD DAC countries: International concessional public finance, including official development assistance (% of GNI)	0.2	2017	●	→
Other countries: Government revenue excluding grants (% of GDP)	NA	NA	●	●
Corporate Tax Haven Score (best 0–100 worst)	49.6	2019	●	●
Financial Secrecy Score (best 0–100 worst)	37.6	2020	●	●
Shifted profits of multinationals (US$ billion)	0.9	2016	●	●

* Imputed data point

SOLOMON ISLANDS

Oceania

▼ OVERALL PERFORMANCE

Index score

na

Regional average score

49.6

SDG Global rank   NA (OF 166)

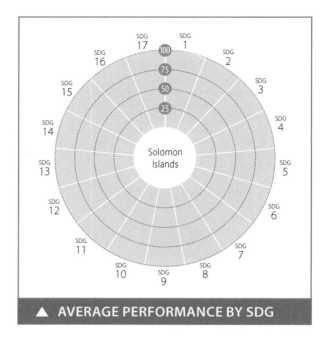

▲ AVERAGE PERFORMANCE BY SDG

▼ SPILLOVER INDEX

100 (best) to 0 (worst)

▼ CURRENT ASSESSMENT – SDG DASHBOARD

■ Major challenges   ■ Significant challenges   ■ Challenges remain   ■ SDG achieved   ■ Information unavailable

▼ SDG TRENDS

↓ Decreasing   → Stagnating   ↗ Moderately improving   ↑ On track or maintaining SDG achievement   ● Information unavailable

Notes: The full title of Goal 2 "Zero Hunger" is "End hunger, achieve food security and improved nutrition and promote sustainable agriculture".
The full title of each SDG is available here: https://sustainabledevelopment.un.org/topics/sustainabledevelopmentgoals

SOLOMON ISLANDS
Performance by Indicator

SDG1 – No Poverty	Value	Year	Rating	Trend
Poverty headcount ratio at $1.90/day (%)	23.0	2020	●	→
Poverty headcount ratio at $3.20/day (%)	52.9	2020	●	→

SDG2 – Zero Hunger	Value	Year	Rating	Trend
Prevalence of undernourishment (%)	8.9	2017	○	↑
Prevalence of stunting in children under 5 years of age (%)	31.6	2015	●	→
Prevalence of wasting in children under 5 years of age (%)	7.9	2015	●	↑
Prevalence of obesity, BMI ≥ 30 (% of adult population)	22.5	2016	●	↓
Human Trophic Level (best 2–3 worst)	2.1	2017	●	↑
Cereal yield (tonnes per hectare of harvested land)	1.6	2017	●	↓
Sustainable Nitrogen Management Index (best 0–1.41 worst)	1.2	2015	●	↓

SDG3 – Good Health and Well-Being	Value	Year	Rating	Trend
Maternal mortality rate (per 100,000 live births)	104	2017	○	↑
Neonatal mortality rate (per 1,000 live births)	8.2	2018	●	↑
Mortality rate, under-5 (per 1,000 live births)	20.0	2018	●	↑
Incidence of tuberculosis (per 100,000 population)	74.0	2018	●	↗
New HIV infections (per 1,000 uninfected population)	NA	NA	●	●
Age-standardized death rate due to cardiovascular disease, cancer, diabetes, or chronic respiratory disease in adults aged 30–70 years (%)	23.8	2016	●	↗
Age-standardized death rate attributable to household air pollution and ambient air pollution (per 100,000 population)	137	2016	●	●
Traffic deaths (per 100,000 population)	17.4	2016	●	↗
Life expectancy at birth (years)	71.1	2016	●	→
Adolescent fertility rate (births per 1,000 adolescent females aged 15 to 19)	78.0	2017	●	→
Births attended by skilled health personnel (%)	86.2	2015	●	●
Percentage of surviving infants who received 2 WHO-recommended vaccines (%)	85	2018	○	↑
Universal health coverage (UHC) index of service coverage (worst 0–100 best)	47.0	2017	●	→
Subjective well-being (average ladder score, worst 0–10 best)	NA	NA	●	●

SDG4 – Quality Education	Value	Year	Rating	Trend
Net primary enrollment rate (%)	67.5	2018	●	↓
Lower secondary completion rate (%)	71.4	2018	●	●
Literacy rate (% of population aged 15 to 24)	NA	NA	●	●

SDG5 – Gender Equality	Value	Year	Rating	Trend
Demand for family planning satisfied by modern methods (% of females aged 15 to 49 who are married or in unions)	38.0	2015	●	→
Ratio of female-to-male mean years of education received (%)	NA	NA	●	●
Ratio of female-to-male labor force participation rate (%)	77.7	2019	●	↑
Seats held by women in national parliament (%)	6.1	2020	●	→

SDG6 – Clean Water and Sanitation	Value	Year	Rating	Trend
Population using at least basic drinking water services (%)	67.8	2017	●	↓
Population using at least basic sanitation services (%)	33.5	2017	●	→
Freshwater withdrawal (% of available freshwater resources)	NA	NA	●	●
Anthropogenic wastewater that receives treatment (%)	0.0	2018	●	●
Scarce water consumption embodied in imports (m³/capita)	NA	NA	●	●

SDG7 – Affordable and Clean Energy	Value	Year	Rating	Trend
Population with access to electricity (%)	62.9	2017	●	↑
Population with access to clean fuels and technology for cooking (%)	8.5	2016	●	→
CO$_2$ emissions from fuel combustion for electricity and heating per total electricity output (MtCO$_2$/TWh)	NA	NA	●	●

SDG8 – Decent Work and Economic Growth	Value	Year	Rating	Trend
Adjusted GDP growth (%)	-5.5	2018	●	●
Victims of modern slavery (per 1,000 population)	NA	NA	●	●
Adults with an account at a bank or other financial institution or with a mobile-money-service provider (% of population aged 15 or over)	NA	NA	●	●
Unemployment rate (% of total labor force)	0.6	2019	●	↑
Fatal work-related accidents embodied in imports (per 100,000 population)	NA	NA	●	●

SDG9 – Industry, Innovation and Infrastructure	Value	Year	Rating	Trend
Population using the internet (%)	11.9	2017	●	→
Mobile broadband subscriptions (per 100 population)	17.5	2018	●	↗
Logistics Performance Index: Quality of trade and transport-related infrastructure (worst 1–5 best)	2.2	2018	●	↓
The Times Higher Education Universities Ranking: Average score of top 3 universities (worst 0–100 best) *	0.0	2020	●	●
Scientific and technical journal articles (per 1,000 population)	0.0	2018	●	↓
Expenditure on research and development (% of GDP)	NA	NA	●	●

SDG10 – Reduced Inequalities	Value	Year	Rating	Trend
Gini coefficient adjusted for top income	42.0	2013	●	●

SDG11 – Sustainable Cities and Communities	Value	Year	Rating	Trend
Annual mean concentration of particulate matter of less than 2.5 microns in diameter (PM2.5) (µg/m³)	11.9	2017	○	↗
Access to improved water source, piped (% of urban population)	70.5	2017	●	↓
Satisfaction with public transport (%)	NA	NA	●	●

SDG12 – Responsible Consumption and Production	Value	Year	Rating	Trend
Municipal solid waste (kg/capita/day)	3.3	2013	●	●
Electronic waste (kg/capita)	0.7	2016	●	●
Production-based SO$_2$ emissions (kg/capita)	NA	NA	●	●
SO$_2$ emissions embodied in imports (kg/capita)	NA	NA	●	●
Production-based nitrogen emissions (kg/capita)	NA	NA	●	●
Nitrogen emissions embodied in imports (kg/capita)	NA	NA	●	●

SDG13 – Climate Action	Value	Year	Rating	Trend
Energy-related CO$_2$ emissions (tCO$_2$/capita)	0.4	2017	●	↑
CO$_2$ emissions embodied in imports (tCO$_2$/capita)	NA	NA	●	●
CO$_2$ emissions embodied in fossil fuel exports (kg/capita)	0.0	2016	●	●

SDG14 – Life Below Water	Value	Year	Rating	Trend
Mean area that is protected in marine sites important to biodiversity (%)	9.4	2018	●	→
Ocean Health Index: Clean Waters score (worst 0–100 best)	72.6	2019	●	↑
Fish caught from overexploited or collapsed stocks (% of total catch)	28.7	2014	○	↓
Fish caught by trawling (%)	NA	NA	●	●
Marine biodiversity threats embodied in imports (per million population)	NA	NA	●	●

SDG15 – Life on Land	Value	Year	Rating	Trend
Mean area that is protected in terrestrial sites important to biodiversity (%)	9.0	2018	●	→
Mean area that is protected in freshwater sites important to biodiversity (%)	NA	NA	●	●
Red List Index of species survival (worst 0–1 best)	0.8	2018	●	↓
Permanent deforestation (% of forest area, 5-year average)	0.3	2018	●	●
Terrestrial and freshwater biodiversity threats embodied in imports (per million population)	NA	NA	●	●

SDG16 – Peace, Justice and Strong Institutions	Value	Year	Rating	Trend
Homicides (per 100,000 population)	3.8	2008	●	●
Unsentenced detainees (% of prison population)	48.2	2018	●	→
Percentage of population who feel safe walking alone at night in the city or area where they live (%)	NA	NA	●	●
Property Rights (worst 1–7 best)	NA	NA	●	●
Birth registrations with civil authority (% of children under age 5)	88.0	2018	○	●
Corruption Perception Index (worst 0–100 best)	42	2019	●	→
Children involved in child labor (% of population aged 5 to 14)	47.8	2016	●	●
Exports of major conventional weapons (TIV constant million USD per 100,000 population) *	0.0	2019	●	●
Press Freedom Index (best 0–100 worst)	NA	NA	●	●

SDG17 – Partnerships for the Goals	Value	Year	Rating	Trend
Government spending on health and education (% of GDP)	14.1	2010	●	●
For high-income and all OECD DAC countries: International concessional public finance, including official development assistance (% of GNI)	NA	NA	●	●
Other countries: Government revenue excluding grants (% of GDP)	33.8	2018	●	↑
Corporate Tax Haven Score (best 0–100 worst) *	0.0	2019	●	●

* Imputed data point

5. Country Profiles

Sustainable Development Report 2020　◐　The Sustainable Development Goals and Covid-19 | 413

SOMALIA

Sub-Saharan Africa

▼ OVERALL PERFORMANCE

Index score

46.2

Regional average score

53.1

SDG Global rank 163 (OF 166)

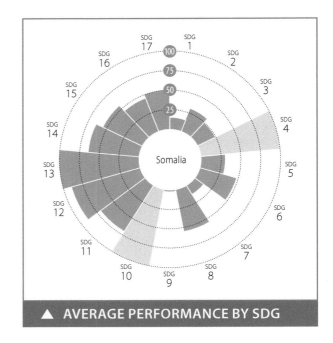

▲ AVERAGE PERFORMANCE BY SDG

▼ SPILLOVER INDEX

100 (best) to 0 (worst)

▼ CURRENT ASSESSMENT – SDG DASHBOARD

■ Major challenges   ■ Significant challenges   ■ Challenges remain   ■ SDG achieved   ■ Information unavailable

▼ SDG TRENDS

↓ Decreasing   → Stagnating   ↗ Moderately improving   ↑ On track or maintaining SDG achievement   ● Information unavailable

Notes: The full title of Goal 2 "Zero Hunger" is "End hunger, achieve food security and improved nutrition and promote sustainable agriculture".
The full title of each SDG is available here: https://sustainabledevelopment.un.org/topics/sustainabledevelopmentgoals

SDG1 – No Poverty

	Value	Year	Rating	Trend
Poverty headcount ratio at $1.90/day (%)	50.5	2020	●	→
Poverty headcount ratio at $3.20/day (%)	78.0	2020	●	→

SDG2 – Zero Hunger

	Value	Year	Rating	Trend
Prevalence of undernourishment (%)	NA	NA	●	●
Prevalence of stunting in children under 5 years of age (%)	25.3	2009	●	→
Prevalence of wasting in children under 5 years of age (%)	15.0	2009	●	→
Prevalence of obesity, BMI ≥ 30 (% of adult population)	8.3	2016	●	↑
Human Trophic Level (best 2–3 worst)	NA	NA	●	●
Cereal yield (tonnes per hectare of harvested land)	0.5	2017	●	↓
Sustainable Nitrogen Management Index (best 0–1.41 worst)	1.1	2015	●	→

SDG3 – Good Health and Well-Being

	Value	Year	Rating	Trend
Maternal mortality rate (per 100,000 live births)	829	2017	●	→
Neonatal mortality rate (per 1,000 live births)	37.5	2018	●	→
Mortality rate, under-5 (per 1,000 live births)	121.5	2018	●	↗
Incidence of tuberculosis (per 100,000 population)	262.0	2018	●	→
New HIV infections (per 1,000 uninfected population)	0.0	2018	●	↑
Age-standardized death rate due to cardiovascular disease, cancer, diabetes, or chronic respiratory disease in adults aged 30–70 years (%)	21.8	2016	●	↓
Age-standardized death rate attributable to household air pollution and ambient air pollution (per 100,000 population)	213	2016	●	●
Traffic deaths (per 100,000 population)	27.1	2016	●	↓
Life expectancy at birth (years)	55.4	2016	●	→
Adolescent fertility rate (births per 1,000 adolescent females aged 15 to 19)	100.1	2017	●	→
Births attended by skilled health personnel (%)	9.4	2006	●	●
Percentage of surviving infants who received 2 WHO-recommended vaccines (%)	42	2018	●	→
Universal health coverage (UHC) index of service coverage (worst 0–100 best)	25.0	2017	●	→
Subjective well-being (average ladder score, worst 0–10 best)	4.7	2016	●	●

SDG4 – Quality Education

	Value	Year	Rating	Trend
Net primary enrollment rate (%)	NA	NA	●	●
Lower secondary completion rate (%)	NA	NA	●	●
Literacy rate (% of population aged 15 to 24)	NA	NA	●	●

SDG5 – Gender Equality

	Value	Year	Rating	Trend
Demand for family planning satisfied by modern methods (% of females aged 15 to 49 who are married or in unions) *	48.3	2017	●	↗
Ratio of female-to-male mean years of education received (%)	NA	NA	●	●
Ratio of female-to-male labor force participation rate (%)	25.8	2019	●	→
Seats held by women in national parliament (%)	24.4	2020	●	↑

SDG6 – Clean Water and Sanitation

	Value	Year	Rating	Trend
Population using at least basic drinking water services (%)	52.4	2017	●	↗
Population using at least basic sanitation services (%)	38.3	2017	●	→
Freshwater withdrawal (% of available freshwater resources)	24.5	2005	●	●
Anthropogenic wastewater that receives treatment (%)	0.0	2018	●	●
Scarce water consumption embodied in imports (m³/capita)	0.0	2013	●	↑

SDG7 – Affordable and Clean Energy

	Value	Year	Rating	Trend
Population with access to electricity (%)	32.9	2017	●	→
Population with access to clean fuels and technology for cooking (%)	2.3	2016	●	→
CO₂ emissions from fuel combustion for electricity and heating per total electricity output (MtCO₂/TWh)	NA	NA	●	●

SDG8 – Decent Work and Economic Growth

	Value	Year	Rating	Trend
Adjusted GDP growth (%)	NA	NA	●	●
Victims of modern slavery (per 1,000 population)	15.5	2018	●	●
Adults with an account at a bank or other financial institution or with a mobile-money-service provider (% of population aged 15 or over)	38.7	2014	●	●
Unemployment rate (% of total labor force)	11.4	2019	●	→
Fatal work-related accidents embodied in imports (per 100,000 population)	0.0	2010	●	↑

SDG9 – Industry, Innovation and Infrastructure

	Value	Year	Rating	Trend
Population using the internet (%)	2.0	2017	●	→
Mobile broadband subscriptions (per 100 population)	2.5	2017	●	→
Logistics Performance Index: Quality of trade and transport-related infrastructure (worst 1–5 best)	1.8	2018	●	↗
The Times Higher Education Universities Ranking: Average score of top 3 universities (worst 0–100 best) *	0.0	2020	●	●
Scientific and technical journal articles (per 1,000 population)	0.0	2018	●	→
Expenditure on research and development (% of GDP) *	0.0	2017	●	●

SDG10 – Reduced Inequalities

	Value	Year	Rating	Trend
Gini coefficient adjusted for top income	NA	NA	●	●

SDG11 – Sustainable Cities and Communities

	Value	Year	Rating	Trend
Annual mean concentration of particulate matter of less than 2.5 microns in diameter (PM2.5) (µg/m³)	32.0	2017	●	↓
Access to improved water source, piped (% of urban population)	75.4	2017	●	↑
Satisfaction with public transport (%)	62.0	2016	◐	●

SDG12 – Responsible Consumption and Production

	Value	Year	Rating	Trend
Municipal solid waste (kg/capita/day)	0.9	2016	●	●
Electronic waste (kg/capita)	NA	NA	●	●
Production-based SO₂ emissions (kg/capita)	10.2	2012	●	●
SO₂ emissions embodied in imports (kg/capita)	0.0	2012	●	●
Production-based nitrogen emissions (kg/capita)	30.8	2010	◐	●
Nitrogen emissions embodied in imports (kg/capita)	0.0	2010	●	●

SDG13 – Climate Action

	Value	Year	Rating	Trend
Energy-related CO₂ emissions (tCO₂/capita)	0.0	2017	●	↑
CO₂ emissions embodied in imports (tCO₂/capita)	0.0	2015	●	↑
CO₂ emissions embodied in fossil fuel exports (kg/capita) *	0.0	2018	●	●

SDG14 – Life Below Water

	Value	Year	Rating	Trend
Mean area that is protected in marine sites important to biodiversity (%)	0.0	2018	●	→
Ocean Health Index: Clean Waters score (worst 0–100 best)	61.0	2019	●	→
Fish caught from overexploited or collapsed stocks (% of total catch)	15.4	2014	●	↑
Fish caught by trawling (%)	10.4	2014	◐	→
Marine biodiversity threats embodied in imports (per million population)	0.0	2018	●	●

SDG15 – Life on Land

	Value	Year	Rating	Trend
Mean area that is protected in terrestrial sites important to biodiversity (%)	0.0	2018	●	→
Mean area that is protected in freshwater sites important to biodiversity (%)	0.0	2018	●	→
Red List Index of species survival (worst 0–1 best)	0.9	2019	◐	↓
Permanent deforestation (% of forest area, 5-year average)	0.0	2018	●	●
Terrestrial and freshwater biodiversity threats embodied in imports (per million population)	0.0	2018	●	●

SDG16 – Peace, Justice and Strong Institutions

	Value	Year	Rating	Trend
Homicides (per 100,000 population) *	4.3	2015	●	●
Unsentenced detainees (% of prison population)	NA	NA	●	●
Percentage of population who feel safe walking alone at night in the city or area where they live (%)	85.4	2016	●	●
Property Rights (worst 1–7 best)	NA	NA	●	●
Birth registrations with civil authority (% of children under age 5)	3.0	2018	●	●
Corruption Perception Index (worst 0–100 best)	9	2019	●	→
Children involved in child labor (% of population aged 5 to 14)	49.0	2016	●	●
Exports of major conventional weapons (TIV constant million USD per 100,000 population) *	0.0	2019	●	●
Press Freedom Index (best 0–100 worst)	57.2	2019	●	↗

SDG17 – Partnerships for the Goals

	Value	Year	Rating	Trend
Government spending on health and education (% of GDP)	NA	NA	●	●
For high-income and all OECD DAC countries: International concessional public finance, including official development assistance (% of GNI)	NA	NA	●	●
Other countries: Government revenue excluding grants (% of GDP)	0.0	2018	●	●
Corporate Tax Haven Score (best 0–100 worst) *	0.0	2019	●	●

* Imputed data point

▼ OVERALL PERFORMANCE

Index score

63.4

Regional average score

53.1

SDG Global rank **110** (OF 166)

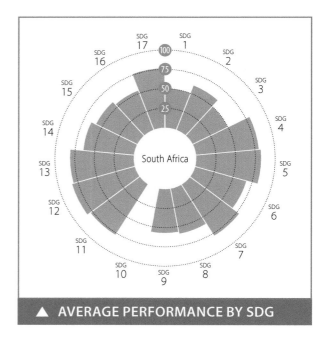

▲ AVERAGE PERFORMANCE BY SDG

▼ SPILLOVER INDEX

100 (best) to 0 (worst)

▼ CURRENT ASSESSMENT – SDG DASHBOARD

■ Major challenges ■ Significant challenges ■ Challenges remain ■ SDG achieved ■ Information unavailable

▼ SDG TRENDS

↓ Decreasing   → Stagnating   ↗ Moderately improving   ↑ On track or maintaining SDG achievement   ● Information unavailable

Notes: The full title of Goal 2 "Zero Hunger" is "End hunger, achieve food security and improved nutrition and promote sustainable agriculture".
The full title of each SDG is available here: https://sustainabledevelopment.un.org/topics/sustainabledevelopmentgoals

SDG1 – No Poverty

	Value	Year	Rating	Trend
Poverty headcount ratio at $1.90/day (%)	24.5	2020	●	→
Poverty headcount ratio at $3.20/day (%)	34.1	2020	●	→

SDG2 – Zero Hunger

	Value	Year	Rating	Trend
Prevalence of undernourishment (%)	6.2	2017	●	↑
Prevalence of stunting in children under 5 years of age (%)	27.4	2016	●	↗
Prevalence of wasting in children under 5 years of age (%)	2.5	2016	●	↑
Prevalence of obesity, BMI ≥ 30 (% of adult population)	28.3	2016	●	↓
Human Trophic Level (best 2–3 worst)	2.3	2017	○	→
Cereal yield (tonnes per hectare of harvested land)	5.6	2017	●	↑
Sustainable Nitrogen Management Index (best 0–1.41 worst)	0.5	2015	●	↗

SDG3 – Good Health and Well-Being

	Value	Year	Rating	Trend
Maternal mortality rate (per 100,000 live births)	119	2017	●	↗
Neonatal mortality rate (per 1,000 live births)	10.7	2018	●	↑
Mortality rate, under-5 (per 1,000 live births)	33.8	2018	○	↑
Incidence of tuberculosis (per 100,000 population)	520.0	2018	●	↑
New HIV infections (per 1,000 uninfected population)	4.9	2018	●	↑
Age-standardized death rate due to cardiovascular disease, cancer, diabetes, or chronic respiratory disease in adults aged 30–70 years (%)	26.2	2016	●	↗
Age-standardized death rate attributable to household air pollution and ambient air pollution (per 100,000 population)	87	2016	●	●
Traffic deaths (per 100,000 population)	25.9	2016	●	↓
Life expectancy at birth (years)	63.6	2016	●	↗
Adolescent fertility rate (births per 1,000 adolescent females aged 15 to 19)	67.9	2017	●	→
Births attended by skilled health personnel (%)	96.7	2016	●	●
Percentage of surviving infants who received 2 WHO-recommended vaccines (%)	70	2018	●	↓
Universal health coverage (UHC) index of service coverage (worst 0–100 best)	69.0	2017	●	↑
Subjective well-being (average ladder score, worst 0–10 best)	4.9	2018	●	↓

SDG4 – Quality Education

	Value	Year	Rating	Trend
Net primary enrollment rate (%)	87.0	2017	●	↑
Lower secondary completion rate (%)	80.8	2016	●	●
Literacy rate (% of population aged 15 to 24)	95.3	2017	●	●

SDG5 – Gender Equality

	Value	Year	Rating	Trend
Demand for family planning satisfied by modern methods (% of females aged 15 to 49 who are married or in unions)	77.9	2016	○	→
Ratio of female-to-male mean years of education received (%)	95.2	2018	○	↑
Ratio of female-to-male labor force participation rate (%)	77.9	2019	●	↑
Seats held by women in national parliament (%)	46.6	2020	●	↑

SDG6 – Clean Water and Sanitation

	Value	Year	Rating	Trend
Population using at least basic drinking water services (%)	92.7	2017	○	↑
Population using at least basic sanitation services (%)	75.7	2017	●	↗
Freshwater withdrawal (% of available freshwater resources)	44.4	2015	●	●
Anthropogenic wastewater that receives treatment (%)	21.7	2018	●	●
Scarce water consumption embodied in imports (m³/capita)	5.8	2013	●	↑

SDG7 – Affordable and Clean Energy

	Value	Year	Rating	Trend
Population with access to electricity (%)	84.4	2017	●	↓
Population with access to clean fuels and technology for cooking (%)	84.8	2016	○	↑
CO₂ emissions from fuel combustion for electricity and heating per total electricity output (MtCO₂/TWh)	1.8	2017	●	↗

SDG8 – Decent Work and Economic Growth

	Value	Year	Rating	Trend
Adjusted GDP growth (%)	-4.3	2018	●	●
Victims of modern slavery (per 1,000 population)	2.8	2018	●	●
Adults with an account at a bank or other financial institution or with a mobile-money-service provider (% of population aged 15 or over)	69.2	2017	○	↓
Unemployment rate (% of total labor force)	28.2	2019	●	↓
Fatal work-related accidents embodied in imports (per 100,000 population)	0.3	2010	●	↑

SDG9 – Industry, Innovation and Infrastructure

	Value	Year	Rating	Trend
Population using the internet (%)	56.2	2017	●	↑
Mobile broadband subscriptions (per 100 population)	77.5	2018	●	↑
Logistics Performance Index: Quality of trade and transport-related infrastructure (worst 1–5 best)	3.2	2018	●	↑
The Times Higher Education Universities Ranking: Average score of top 3 universities (worst 0–100 best)	53.6	2020	●	●
Scientific and technical journal articles (per 1,000 population)	0.2	2018	●	→
Expenditure on research and development (% of GDP)	0.8	2016	●	↗

SDG10 – Reduced Inequalities

	Value	Year	Rating	Trend
Gini coefficient adjusted for top income	67.3	2014	●	●

SDG11 – Sustainable Cities and Communities

	Value	Year	Rating	Trend
Annual mean concentration of particulate matter of less than 2.5 microns in diameter (PM2.5) (µg/m³)	25.1	2017	●	↗
Access to improved water source, piped (% of urban population)	98.3	2017	●	↑
Satisfaction with public transport (%)	57.1	2018	●	↓

SDG12 – Responsible Consumption and Production

	Value	Year	Rating	Trend
Municipal solid waste (kg/capita/day)	1.3	2011	○	●
Electronic waste (kg/capita)	5.7	2016	○	●
Production-based SO₂ emissions (kg/capita)	43.1	2012	●	●
SO₂ emissions embodied in imports (kg/capita)	2.9	2012	●	●
Production-based nitrogen emissions (kg/capita)	24.4	2010	●	●
Nitrogen emissions embodied in imports (kg/capita)	3.0	2010	●	●

SDG13 – Climate Action

	Value	Year	Rating	Trend
Energy-related CO₂ emissions (tCO₂/capita)	9.1	2017	●	↗
CO₂ emissions embodied in imports (tCO₂/capita)	0.5	2015	○	↑
CO₂ emissions embodied in fossil fuel exports (kg/capita)	1690.1	2018	◐	●

SDG14 – Life Below Water

	Value	Year	Rating	Trend
Mean area that is protected in marine sites important to biodiversity (%)	51.9	2018	●	↑
Ocean Health Index: Clean Waters score (worst 0–100 best)	55.6	2019	●	→
Fish caught from overexploited or collapsed stocks (% of total catch)	33.6	2014	○	↓
Fish caught by trawling (%)	26.6	2014	○	↓
Marine biodiversity threats embodied in imports (per million population)	0.1	2018	●	●

SDG15 – Life on Land

	Value	Year	Rating	Trend
Mean area that is protected in terrestrial sites important to biodiversity (%)	30.7	2018	○	→
Mean area that is protected in freshwater sites important to biodiversity (%)	35.8	2018	○	→
Red List Index of species survival (worst 0–1 best)	0.8	2019	●	↓
Permanent deforestation (% of forest area, 5-year average)	0.1	2018	●	●
Terrestrial and freshwater biodiversity threats embodied in imports (per million population)	0.8	2018	●	●

SDG16 – Peace, Justice and Strong Institutions

	Value	Year	Rating	Trend
Homicides (per 100,000 population)	35.9	2017	●	↓
Unsentenced detainees (% of prison population)	27.0	2018	●	↑
Percentage of population who feel safe walking alone at night in the city or area where they live (%)	31.5	2018	●	↓
Property Rights (worst 1–7 best)	4.1	2019	○	●
Birth registrations with civil authority (% of children under age 5)	88.6	2018	●	●
Corruption Perception Index (worst 0–100 best)	44	2019	●	→
Children involved in child labor (% of population aged 5 to 14)	NA	NA	●	●
Exports of major conventional weapons (TIV constant million USD per 100,000 population)	0.1	2019	●	●
Press Freedom Index (best 0–100 worst)	22.2	2019	●	↑

SDG17 – Partnerships for the Goals

	Value	Year	Rating	Trend
Government spending on health and education (% of GDP)	10.3	2016	●	↑
For high-income and all OECD DAC countries: International concessional public finance, including official development assistance (% of GNI)	NA	NA	●	●
Other countries: Government revenue excluding grants (% of GDP)	30.9	2017	●	↑
Corporate Tax Haven Score (best 0–100 worst)	47.1	2019	●	●

* Imputed data point

5. Country Profiles

SOUTH SUDAN

▼ OVERALL PERFORMANCE

Index score
43.7

Regional average score
53.1

SDG Global rank **165** (OF 166)

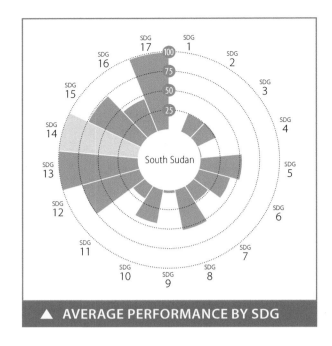

▲ AVERAGE PERFORMANCE BY SDG

▼ SPILLOVER INDEX

100 (best) to 0 (worst)

▼ CURRENT ASSESSMENT – SDG DASHBOARD

■ Major challenges　■ Significant challenges　■ Challenges remain　■ SDG achieved　■ Information unavailable

▼ SDG TRENDS

↓ Decreasing　→ Stagnating　↗ Moderately improving　↑ On track or maintaining SDG achievement　● Information unavailable

Notes: The full title of Goal 2 "Zero Hunger" is "End hunger, achieve food security and improved nutrition and promote sustainable agriculture".
The full title of each SDG is available here: https://sustainabledevelopment.un.org/topics/sustainabledevelopmentgoals

SDG1 – No Poverty

Indicator	Value	Year	Rating	Trend
Poverty headcount ratio at $1.90/day (%)	78.3	2020	●	↓
Poverty headcount ratio at $3.20/day (%)	94.0	2020	●	↓

SDG2 – Zero Hunger

Indicator	Value	Year	Rating	Trend
Prevalence of undernourishment (%)	NA	NA	●	●
Prevalence of stunting in children under 5 years of age (%)	31.1	2010	●	→
Prevalence of wasting in children under 5 years of age (%)	22.7	2010	●	↗
Prevalence of obesity, BMI ≥ 30 (% of adult population)	NA	NA	●	●
Human Trophic Level (best 2–3 worst)	2.3	2017	◐	↑
Cereal yield (tonnes per hectare of harvested land)	1.4	2017	●	↗
Sustainable Nitrogen Management Index (best 0–1.41 worst)	NA	NA	●	●

SDG3 – Good Health and Well-Being

Indicator	Value	Year	Rating	Trend
Maternal mortality rate (per 100,000 live births)	1150	2017	●	↓
Neonatal mortality rate (per 1,000 live births)	40.0	2018	●	→
Mortality rate, under-5 (per 1,000 live births)	98.6	2018	●	→
Incidence of tuberculosis (per 100,000 population)	146.0	2018	●	→
New HIV infections (per 1,000 uninfected population)	1.6	2018	●	→
Age-standardized death rate due to cardiovascular disease, cancer, diabetes, or chronic respiratory disease in adults aged 30–70 years (%)	19.8	2016	◐	→
Age-standardized death rate attributable to household air pollution and ambient air pollution (per 100,000 population)	165	2016	●	●
Traffic deaths (per 100,000 population)	29.9	2016	●	↓
Life expectancy at birth (years)	58.6	2016	●	→
Adolescent fertility rate (births per 1,000 adolescent females aged 15 to 19)	62.0	2017	●	↑
Births attended by skilled health personnel (%)	19.4	2010	●	●
Percentage of surviving infants who received 2 WHO-recommended vaccines (%)	49	2018	●	→
Universal health coverage (UHC) index of service coverage (worst 0–100 best)	31.0	2017	●	→
Subjective well-being (average ladder score, worst 0–10 best)	2.8	2017	●	●

SDG4 – Quality Education

Indicator	Value	Year	Rating	Trend
Net primary enrollment rate (%)	35.2	2015	●	●
Lower secondary completion rate (%)	18.0	2011	●	●
Literacy rate (% of population aged 15 to 24)	47.9	2018	●	●

SDG5 – Gender Equality

Indicator	Value	Year	Rating	Trend
Demand for family planning satisfied by modern methods (% of females aged 15 to 49 who are married or in unions)	5.6	2010	●	→
Ratio of female-to-male mean years of education received (%)	75.5	2018	●	→
Ratio of female-to-male labor force participation rate (%)	96.8	2019	●	↑
Seats held by women in national parliament (%)	28.5	2020	●	→

SDG6 – Clean Water and Sanitation

Indicator	Value	Year	Rating	Trend
Population using at least basic drinking water services (%)	40.7	2017	●	↓
Population using at least basic sanitation services (%)	11.3	2017	●	→
Freshwater withdrawal (% of available freshwater resources)	4.2	2010	●	●
Anthropogenic wastewater that receives treatment (%)	0.0	2018	●	●
Scarce water consumption embodied in imports (m³/capita)	0.1	2013	●	↑

SDG7 – Affordable and Clean Energy

Indicator	Value	Year	Rating	Trend
Population with access to electricity (%)	25.4	2017	●	↗
Population with access to clean fuels and technology for cooking (%)	0.6	2016	●	→
CO_2 emissions from fuel combustion for electricity and heating per total electricity output (MtCO$_2$/TWh)	3.0	2017	●	↗

SDG8 – Decent Work and Economic Growth

Indicator	Value	Year	Rating	Trend
Adjusted GDP growth (%)	NA	NA	●	●
Victims of modern slavery (per 1,000 population) *	NA	NA	●	●
Adults with an account at a bank or other financial institution or with a mobile-money-service provider (% of population aged 15 or over)	8.6	2017	●	●
Unemployment rate (% of total labor force)	12.2	2019	●	→
Fatal work-related accidents embodied in imports (per 100,000 population)	0.0	2010	●	↑

SDG9 – Industry, Innovation and Infrastructure

Indicator	Value	Year	Rating	Trend
Population using the internet (%)	8.0	2017	●	→
Mobile broadband subscriptions (per 100 population)	6.0	2018	●	→
Logistics Performance Index: Quality of trade and transport-related infrastructure (worst 1–5 best)	NA	NA	●	●
The Times Higher Education Universities Ranking: Average score of top 3 universities (worst 0–100 best) *	0.0	2020	●	●
Scientific and technical journal articles (per 1,000 population)	0.0	2018	●	→
Expenditure on research and development (% of GDP) *	0.0	2017	●	●

SDG10 – Reduced Inequalities

Indicator	Value	Year	Rating	Trend
Gini coefficient adjusted for top income	48.0	2009	●	●

SDG11 – Sustainable Cities and Communities

Indicator	Value	Year	Rating	Trend
Annual mean concentration of particulate matter of less than 2.5 microns in diameter (PM2.5) (µg/m³)	45.6	2017	●	↓
Access to improved water source, piped (% of urban population)	7.8	2017	●	↓
Satisfaction with public transport (%)	17.7	2017	●	●

SDG12 – Responsible Consumption and Production

Indicator	Value	Year	Rating	Trend
Municipal solid waste (kg/capita/day)	2.9	2013	●	●
Electronic waste (kg/capita)	NA	NA	●	●
Production-based SO$_2$ emissions (kg/capita)	0.2	2012	●	●
SO$_2$ emissions embodied in imports (kg/capita)	0.1	2012	●	●
Production-based nitrogen emissions (kg/capita)	50.0	2010	●	●
Nitrogen emissions embodied in imports (kg/capita)	0.0	2010	●	●

SDG13 – Climate Action

Indicator	Value	Year	Rating	Trend
Energy-related CO_2 emissions (tCO$_2$/capita)	0.2	2017	●	↑
CO_2 emissions embodied in imports (tCO$_2$/capita)	0.0	2015	●	↑
CO_2 emissions embodied in fossil fuel exports (kg/capita)	NA	NA	●	●

SDG14 – Life Below Water

Indicator	Value	Year	Rating	Trend
Mean area that is protected in marine sites important to biodiversity (%)	NA	NA	●	●
Ocean Health Index: Clean Waters score (worst 0–100 best)	NA	NA	●	●
Fish caught from overexploited or collapsed stocks (% of total catch)	NA	NA	●	●
Fish caught by trawling (%)	NA	NA	●	●
Marine biodiversity threats embodied in imports (per million population)	0.0	2018	●	●

SDG15 – Life on Land

Indicator	Value	Year	Rating	Trend
Mean area that is protected in terrestrial sites important to biodiversity (%)	33.6	2018	◐	→
Mean area that is protected in freshwater sites important to biodiversity (%)	58.6	2018	●	↑
Red List Index of species survival (worst 0–1 best)	0.9	2019	●	↑
Permanent deforestation (% of forest area, 5-year average)	0.0	2018	●	●
Terrestrial and freshwater biodiversity threats embodied in imports (per million population)	0.0	2018	●	●

SDG16 – Peace, Justice and Strong Institutions

Indicator	Value	Year	Rating	Trend
Homicides (per 100,000 population)	13.9	2012	●	●
Unsentenced detainees (% of prison population)	28.9	2015	●	●
Percentage of population who feel safe walking alone at night in the city or area where they live (%)	42.1	2017	●	●
Property Rights (worst 1–7 best)	NA	NA	●	●
Birth registrations with civil authority (% of children under age 5)	35.4	2018	●	↓
Corruption Perception Index (worst 0–100 best)	12	2019	●	↓
Children involved in child labor (% of population aged 5 to 14)	NA	NA	●	●
Exports of major conventional weapons (TIV constant million USD per 100,000 population) *	0.0	2019	●	●
Press Freedom Index (best 0–100 worst)	45.7	2019	◐	↓

SDG17 – Partnerships for the Goals

Indicator	Value	Year	Rating	Trend
Government spending on health and education (% of GDP)	NA	NA	●	●
For high-income and all OECD DAC countries: International concessional public finance, including official development assistance (% of GNI)	NA	NA	●	●
Other countries: Government revenue excluding grants (% of GDP)	NA	NA	●	●
Corporate Tax Haven Score (best 0–100 worst) *	0.0	2019	●	●

* Imputed data point

▼ OVERALL PERFORMANCE

Index score

78.1

Regional average score

77.3

SDG Global rank **22** (OF 166)

▼ SPILLOVER INDEX

100 (best) to 0 (worst)

▲ AVERAGE PERFORMANCE BY SDG

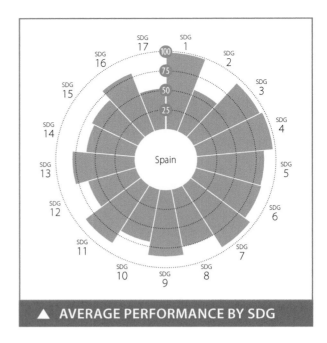

▼ CURRENT ASSESSMENT – SDG DASHBOARD

| 1 NO POVERTY | 2 ZERO HUNGER | 3 GOOD HEALTH AND WELL-BEING | 4 QUALITY EDUCATION | 5 GENDER EQUALITY | 6 CLEAN WATER AND SANITATION | 7 AFFORDABLE AND CLEAN ENERGY | 8 DECENT WORK AND ECONOMIC GROWTH | 9 INDUSTRY, INNOVATION AND INFRASTRUCTURE |
| 10 REDUCED INEQUALITIES | 11 SUSTAINABLE CITIES AND COMMUNITIES | 12 RESPONSIBLE CONSUMPTION AND PRODUCTION | 13 CLIMATE ACTION | 14 LIFE BELOW WATER | 15 LIFE ON LAND | 16 PEACE, JUSTICE AND STRONG INSTITUTIONS | 17 PARTNERSHIPS FOR THE GOALS | SUSTAINABLE DEVELOPMENT GOALS |

■ Major challenges ■ Significant challenges ■ Challenges remain ■ SDG achieved ■ Information unavailable

▼ SDG TRENDS

| 1 NO POVERTY ↗ | 2 ZERO HUNGER ↗ | 3 GOOD HEALTH AND WELL-BEING ↑ | 4 QUALITY EDUCATION ↗ | 5 GENDER EQUALITY ↗ | 6 CLEAN WATER AND SANITATION ↑ | 7 AFFORDABLE AND CLEAN ENERGY ↗ | 8 DECENT WORK AND ECONOMIC GROWTH ↑ | 9 INDUSTRY, INNOVATION AND INFRASTRUCTURE ↗ |
| 10 REDUCED INEQUALITIES → | 11 SUSTAINABLE CITIES AND COMMUNITIES ↗ | 12 RESPONSIBLE CONSUMPTION AND PRODUCTION ● | 13 CLIMATE ACTION ↓ | 14 LIFE BELOW WATER ↗ | 15 LIFE ON LAND → | 16 PEACE, JUSTICE AND STRONG INSTITUTIONS ↑ | 17 PARTNERSHIPS FOR THE GOALS ↗ | |

↓ Decreasing   → Stagnating   ↗ Moderately improving   ↑ On track or maintaining SDG achievement   ● Information unavailable

Notes: The full title of Goal 2 "Zero Hunger" is "End hunger, achieve food security and improved nutrition and promote sustainable agriculture".
The full title of each SDG is available here: https://sustainabledevelopment.un.org/topics/sustainabledevelopmentgoals

SDG1 – No Poverty

	Value	Year	Rating	Trend
Poverty headcount ratio at $1.90/day (%)	0.9	2020	●	↑
Poverty headcount ratio at $3.20/day (%)	1.3	2020	●	↑
Poverty rate after taxes and transfers (%)	14.8	2017	●	↗

SDG2 – Zero Hunger

		Value	Year	Rating	Trend
Prevalence of undernourishment (%)		2.5	2017	●	↑
Prevalence of stunting in children under 5 years of age (%)	*	2.6	2016	●	↑
Prevalence of wasting in children under 5 years of age (%)	*	0.7	2016	●	↑
Prevalence of obesity, BMI ≥ 30 (% of adult population)		23.8	2016	●	↓
Human Trophic Level (best 2–3 worst)		2.4	2017	●	↓
Cereal yield (tonnes per hectare of harvested land)		2.8	2017	●	↓
Sustainable Nitrogen Management Index (best 0–1.41 worst)		0.8	2015	●	↓
Yield gap closure (% of potential yield)		45.7	2015	●	●

SDG3 – Good Health and Well-Being

	Value	Year	Rating	Trend
Maternal mortality rate (per 100,000 live births)	4	2017	●	↑
Neonatal mortality rate (per 1,000 live births)	1.7	2018	●	↑
Mortality rate, under-5 (per 1,000 live births)	3.0	2018	●	↑
Incidence of tuberculosis (per 100,000 population)	9.4	2018	●	↑
New HIV infections (per 1,000 uninfected population)	0.1	2018	●	↑
Age-standardized death rate due to cardiovascular disease, cancer, diabetes, or chronic respiratory disease in adults aged 30–70 years (%)	9.9	2016	●	↑
Age-standardized death rate attributable to household air pollution and ambient air pollution (per 100,000 population)	10	2016	●	●
Traffic deaths (per 100,000 population)	4.1	2016	●	↑
Life expectancy at birth (years)	83.1	2016	●	↑
Adolescent fertility rate (births per 1,000 adolescent females aged 15 to 19)	7.7	2017	●	↑
Births attended by skilled health personnel (%)	NA	NA	●	●
Percentage of surviving infants who received 2 WHO-recommended vaccines (%)	93.0	2018	●	↑
Universal health coverage (UHC) index of service coverage (worst 0–100 best)	83.0	2017	●	↑
Subjective well-being (average ladder score, worst 0–10 best)	6.5	2019	●	↑
Gap in life expectancy at birth among regions (years)	3.0	2016	●	●
Gap in self-reported health status by income (percentage points)	12.3	2017	●	●
Daily smokers (% of population aged 15 and over)	22.1	2017	●	↗

SDG4 – Quality Education

		Value	Year	Rating	Trend
Net primary enrollment rate (%)	*	97.2	2017	●	↑
Lower secondary completion rate (%)	*	97.2	2017	●	↑
Literacy rate (% of population aged 15 to 24)		99.7	2018	●	●
Participation rate in pre-primary organized learning (% of children aged 4 to 6)		93.2	2017	●	↑
Tertiary educational attainment (% of population aged 25 to 34)		44.3	2018	●	↑
PISA score (worst 0–600 best)**		486.7	2018	●	↓
Variation in science performance explained by socio-economic status (%)		10.0	2018	●	↑
Underachievers in science (% of 15-year-olds)		21.3	2018	●	↓
Resilient students in science (% of 15-year-olds)		37.3	2018	●	↓

SDG5 – Gender Equality

		Value	Year	Rating	Trend
Demand for family planning satisfied by modern methods (% of females aged 15 to 49 who are married or in unions)	*	84.5	2017	●	↑
Ratio of female-to-male mean years of education received (%)		97.0	2018	●	→
Ratio of female-to-male labor force participation rate (%)		81.8	2019	●	↑
Seats held by women in national parliament (%)		44.0	2020	●	↑
Gender wage gap (% of male median wage)		11.5	2014	●	●
Gender gap in time spent doing unpaid work (minutes/day)		143.2	2010	●	●

SDG6 – Clean Water and Sanitation

	Value	Year	Rating	Trend
Population using at least basic drinking water services (%)	99.9	2017	●	●
Population using at least basic sanitation services (%)	99.9	2017	●	●
Freshwater withdrawal (% of available freshwater resources)	44.0	2015	●	●
Anthropogenic wastewater that receives treatment (%)	91.5	2018	●	●
Scarce water consumption embodied in imports (m³/capita)	24.0	2013	●	↑
Population using safely managed water services (%)	98.4	2017	●	↑
Population using safely managed sanitation services (%)	96.6	2017	●	↑

SDG7 – Affordable and Clean Energy

	Value	Year	Rating	Trend
Population with access to electricity (%)	100.0	2017	●	↑
Population with access to clean fuels and technology for cooking (%)	100.0	2016	●	↑
CO₂ emissions from fuel combustion for electricity and heating per total electricity output (MtCO₂/TWh)	1.0	2017	●	↑
Share of renewable energy in total primary energy supply (%)	14.6	2018	●	↓

SDG8 – Decent Work and Economic Growth

		Value	Year	Rating	Trend
Adjusted GDP growth (%)		0.3	2018	●	●
Victims of modern slavery (per 1,000 population)		2.3	2018	●	●
Adults with an account at a bank or other financial institution or with a mobile-money-service provider (% of population aged 15 or over)		93.8	2017	●	↑
Fatal work-related accidents embodied in imports (per 100,000 population)		1.8	2010	●	↑
Employment-to-population ratio (%)		63.3	2019	●	↑
Youth not in employment, education or training (NEET) (% of population aged 15 to 29)		19.1	2018	●	↑

SDG9 – Industry, Innovation and Infrastructure

	Value	Year	Rating	Trend
Population using the internet (%)	86.1	2018	●	↑
Mobile broadband subscriptions (per 100 population)	98.5	2018	●	↑
Logistics Performance Index: Quality of trade and transport-related infrastructure (worst 1–5 best)	3.8	2018	●	↑
The Times Higher Education Universities Ranking: Average score of top 3 universities (worst 0–100 best)	55.5	2020	●	●
Scientific and technical journal articles (per 1,000 population)	1.2	2018	●	↑
Expenditure on research and development (% of GDP)	1.2	2017	●	↓
Researchers (per 1,000 employed population)	7.0	2018	●	↗
Triadic patent families filed (per million population)	5.8	2017	●	→
Gap in internet access by income (percentage points)	21.2	2019	●	↑
Women in science and engineering (% of tertiary graduates in science and engineering)	27.1	2015	●	●

SDG10 – Reduced Inequalities

	Value	Year	Rating	Trend
Gini coefficient adjusted for top income	38.6	2015	●	↓
Palma ratio	1.3	2017	●	↗
Elderly poverty rate (% of population aged 66 or over)	10.2	2017	●	↓

SDG11 – Sustainable Cities and Communities

	Value	Year	Rating	Trend
Annual mean concentration of particulate matter of less than 2.5 microns in diameter (PM2.5) (µg/m³)	9.7	2017	●	↑
Access to improved water source, piped (% of urban population)	99.0	2017	●	↑
Satisfaction with public transport (%)	63.4	2019	●	↓
Population with rent overburden (%)	12.9	2017	●	↑

SDG12 – Responsible Consumption and Production

	Value	Year	Rating	Trend
Electronic waste (kg/capita)	20.1	2016	●	●
Production-based SO₂ emissions (kg/capita)	37.2	2012	●	●
SO₂ emissions embodied in imports (kg/capita)	8.2	2012	●	●
Production-based nitrogen emissions (kg/capita)	45.0	2010	●	●
Nitrogen emissions embodied in imports (kg/capita)	11.0	2010	●	●
Non-recycled municipal solid waste (kg/capita/day)	0.8	2018	●	●

SDG13 – Climate Action

	Value	Year	Rating	Trend
Energy-related CO₂ emissions (tCO₂/capita)	5.3	2017	●	↓
CO₂ emissions embodied in imports (tCO₂/capita)	1.3	2015	●	→
CO₂ emissions embodied in fossil fuel exports (kg/capita)	22.7	2018	●	●
Effective carbon rate (EUR/tCO₂)	12.5	2016	●	●

SDG14 – Life Below Water

	Value	Year	Rating	Trend
Mean area that is protected in marine sites important to biodiversity (%)	85.6	2018	●	↑
Ocean Health Index: Clean Waters score (worst 0–100 best)	48.6	2019	●	↓
Fish caught from overexploited or collapsed stocks (% of total catch)	35.5	2014	●	↑
Fish caught by trawling (%)	33.6	2014	●	↑
Marine biodiversity threats embodied in imports (per million population)	0.6	2018	●	●

SDG15 – Life on Land

	Value	Year	Rating	Trend
Mean area that is protected in terrestrial sites important to biodiversity (%)	56.6	2018	●	↑
Mean area that is protected in freshwater sites important to biodiversity (%)	46.1	2018	●	→
Red List Index of species survival (worst 0–1 best)	0.8	2019	●	↓
Permanent deforestation (% of forest area, 5-year average)	0.0	2018	●	●
Terrestrial and freshwater biodiversity threats embodied in imports (per million population)	3.6	2018	●	●

SDG16 – Peace, Justice and Strong Institutions

		Value	Year	Rating	Trend
Homicides (per 100,000 population)		0.7	2017	●	↑
Unsentenced detainees (% of prison population)		14.4	2018	●	↑
Percentage of population who feel safe walking alone at night in the city or area where they live (%)		77.5	2019	●	↑
Property Rights (worst 1–7 best)		4.8	2019	●	●
Birth registrations with civil authority (% of children under age 5)		100.0	2018	●	●
Corruption Perception Index (worst 0–100 best)		62.0	2019	●	↑
Children involved in child labor (% of population aged 5 to 14)	*	0.0	2016	●	●
Exports of major conventional weapons (TIV constant million USD per 100,000 population)		1.9	2019	●	●
Press Freedom Index (best 0–100 worst)		22.0	2019	●	↑
Persons held in prison (per 100,000 population)		126.9	2017	●	↑

SDG17 – Partnerships for the Goals

	Value	Year	Rating	Trend
Government spending on health and education (% of GDP)	10.6	2016	●	↑
For high-income and all OECD DAC countries: International concessional public finance, including official development assistance (% of GNI)	0.2	2017	●	↗
Other countries: Government revenue excluding grants (% of GDP)	NA	NA	●	●
Corporate Tax Haven Score (best 0–100 worst)	54.5	2019	●	●
Financial Secrecy Score (best 0–100 worst)	44.0	2020	●	●
Shifted profits of multinationals (US$ billion)	14.7	2016	●	●

* Imputed data point   **For Spain, the reading score for 2015 was carried forward to 2018.

5. Country Profiles

▼ OVERALL PERFORMANCE

Index score

66.9

Regional average score

67.2

SDG Global rank 94 (OF 166)

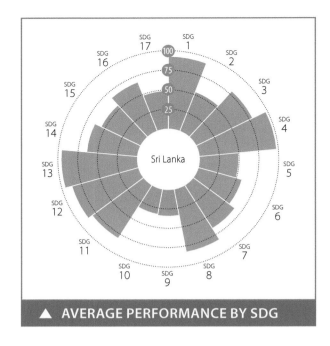

▲ AVERAGE PERFORMANCE BY SDG

▼ SPILLOVER INDEX

100 (best) to 0 (worst)

▼ CURRENT ASSESSMENT – SDG DASHBOARD

■ Major challenges   ■ Significant challenges   ■ Challenges remain   ■ SDG achieved   ■ Information unavailable

▼ SDG TRENDS

↓ Decreasing   → Stagnating   ↗ Moderately improving   ↑ On track or maintaining SDG achievement   ● Information unavailable

Notes: The full title of Goal 2 "Zero Hunger" is "End hunger, achieve food security and improved nutrition and promote sustainable agriculture".
The full title of each SDG is available here: https://sustainabledevelopment.un.org/topics/sustainabledevelopmentgoals

SDG1 – No Poverty

Indicator	Value	Year
Poverty headcount ratio at $1.90/day (%)	0.3	2020
Poverty headcount ratio at $3.20/day (%)	8.0	2020

SDG2 – Zero Hunger

Indicator	Value	Year
Prevalence of undernourishment (%)	9.0	2017
Prevalence of stunting in children under 5 years of age (%)	17.3	2016
Prevalence of wasting in children under 5 years of age (%)	15.1	2016
Prevalence of obesity, BMI ≥ 30 (% of adult population)	5.2	2016
Human Trophic Level (best 2–3 worst)	2.2	2017
Cereal yield (tonnes per hectare of harvested land)	2.1	2017
Sustainable Nitrogen Management Index (best 0–1.41 worst)	0.9	2015

SDG3 – Good Health and Well-Being

Indicator	Value	Year
Maternal mortality rate (per 100,000 live births)	36	2017
Neonatal mortality rate (per 1,000 live births)	4.5	2018
Mortality rate, under-5 (per 1,000 live births)	7.4	2018
Incidence of tuberculosis (per 100,000 population)	64.0	2018
New HIV infections (per 1,000 uninfected population)	0.0	2018
Age-standardized death rate due to cardiovascular disease, cancer, diabetes, or chronic respiratory disease in adults aged 30–70 years (%)	17.4	2016
Age-standardized death rate attributable to household air pollution and ambient air pollution (per 100,000 population)	80	2016
Traffic deaths (per 100,000 population)	14.9	2016
Life expectancy at birth (years)	75.3	2016
Adolescent fertility rate (births per 1,000 adolescent females aged 15 to 19)	20.9	2017
Births attended by skilled health personnel (%)	100.0	2014
Percentage of surviving infants who received 2 WHO-recommended vaccines (%)	99	2018
Universal health coverage (UHC) index of service coverage (worst 0–100 best)	66.0	2017
Subjective well-being (average ladder score, worst 0–10 best)	4.4	2018

SDG4 – Quality Education

Indicator	Value	Year
Net primary enrollment rate (%)	99.1	2018
Lower secondary completion rate (%)	96.4	2017
Literacy rate (% of population aged 15 to 24)	98.8	2018

SDG5 – Gender Equality

Indicator	Value	Year
Demand for family planning satisfied by modern methods (% of females aged 15 to 49 who are married or in unions)	74.3	2016
Ratio of female-to-male mean years of education received (%)	90.5	2018
Ratio of female-to-male labor force participation rate (%)	48.4	2019
Seats held by women in national parliament (%)	5.3	2020

SDG6 – Clean Water and Sanitation

Indicator	Value	Year
Population using at least basic drinking water services (%)	89.4	2017
Population using at least basic sanitation services (%)	95.8	2017
Freshwater withdrawal (% of available freshwater resources)	90.8	2005
Anthropogenic wastewater that receives treatment (%)	0.0	2018
Scarce water consumption embodied in imports (m³/capita)	5.1	2013

SDG7 – Affordable and Clean Energy

Indicator	Value	Year
Population with access to electricity (%)	97.5	2017
Population with access to clean fuels and technology for cooking (%)	26.3	2016
CO_2 emissions from fuel combustion for electricity and heating per total electricity output (MtCO₂/TWh)	1.5	2017

SDG8 – Decent Work and Economic Growth

Indicator	Value	Year
Adjusted GDP growth (%)	-1.3	2018
Victims of modern slavery (per 1,000 population)	2.1	2018
Adults with an account at a bank or other financial institution or with a mobile-money-service provider (% of population aged 15 or over)	73.6	2017
Unemployment rate (% of total labor force)	4.2	2019
Fatal work-related accidents embodied in imports (per 100,000 population)	0.2	2010

SDG9 – Industry, Innovation and Infrastructure

Indicator	Value	Year
Population using the internet (%)	34.1	2017
Mobile broadband subscriptions (per 100 population)	65.0	2018
Logistics Performance Index: Quality of trade and transport-related infrastructure (worst 1–5 best)	2.5	2018
The Times Higher Education Universities Ranking: Average score of top 3 universities (worst 0–100 best)	28.5	2020
Scientific and technical journal articles (per 1,000 population)	0.1	2018
Expenditure on research and development (% of GDP)	0.1	2015

SDG10 – Reduced Inequalities

Indicator	Value	Year
Gini coefficient adjusted for top income	51.4	2016

SDG11 – Sustainable Cities and Communities

Indicator	Value	Year
Annual mean concentration of particulate matter of less than 2.5 microns in diameter (PM2.5) (μg/m³)	11.1	2017
Access to improved water source, piped (% of urban population)	73.8	2017
Satisfaction with public transport (%)	67.3	2018

SDG12 – Responsible Consumption and Production

Indicator	Value	Year
Municipal solid waste (kg/capita/day)	1.9	2016
Electronic waste (kg/capita)	4.5	2016
Production-based SO_2 emissions (kg/capita)	11.5	2012
SO_2 emissions embodied in imports (kg/capita)	1.8	2012
Production-based nitrogen emissions (kg/capita)	4.3	2010
Nitrogen emissions embodied in imports (kg/capita)	1.0	2010

SDG13 – Climate Action

Indicator	Value	Year
Energy-related CO_2 emissions (tCO₂/capita)	1.3	2017
CO_2 emissions embodied in imports (tCO₂/capita)	0.3	2015
CO_2 emissions embodied in fossil fuel exports (kg/capita)	0.0	2017

SDG14 – Life Below Water

Indicator	Value	Year
Mean area that is protected in marine sites important to biodiversity (%)	43.4	2018
Ocean Health Index: Clean Waters score (worst 0–100 best)	58.1	2019
Fish caught from overexploited or collapsed stocks (% of total catch)	20.9	2014
Fish caught by trawling (%)	35.8	2014
Marine biodiversity threats embodied in imports (per million population)	0.1	2018

SDG15 – Life on Land

Indicator	Value	Year
Mean area that is protected in terrestrial sites important to biodiversity (%)	43.7	2018
Mean area that is protected in freshwater sites important to biodiversity (%)	40.6	2018
Red List Index of species survival (worst 0–1 best)	0.6	2019
Permanent deforestation (% of forest area, 5-year average)	0.1	2018
Terrestrial and freshwater biodiversity threats embodied in imports (per million population)	0.1	2018

SDG16 – Peace, Justice and Strong Institutions

Indicator	Value	Year
Homicides (per 100,000 population)	2.3	2017
Unsentenced detainees (% of prison population)	53.4	2018
Percentage of population who feel safe walking alone at night in the city or area where they live (%)	63.8	2018
Property Rights (worst 1–7 best)	3.9	2019
Birth registrations with civil authority (% of children under age 5)	97.2	2018
Corruption Perception Index (worst 0–100 best)	38	2019
Children involved in child labor (% of population aged 5 to 14)	1.0	2016
Exports of major conventional weapons (TIV constant million USD per 100,000 population) *	0.0	2019
Press Freedom Index (best 0–100 worst)	39.6	2019

SDG17 – Partnerships for the Goals

Indicator	Value	Year
Government spending on health and education (% of GDP)	5.1	2016
For high-income and all OECD DAC countries: International concessional public finance, including official development assistance (% of GNI)	NA	NA
Other countries: Government revenue excluding grants (% of GDP)	13.3	2018
Corporate Tax Haven Score (best 0–100 worst) *	0.0	2019

* Imputed data point

5. Country Profiles

▼ OVERALL PERFORMANCE

Index score
na

Regional average score
70.4

SDG Global rank   NA (OF 166)

▼ SPILLOVER INDEX
100 (best) to 0 (worst)

100
80
60
40
20
0

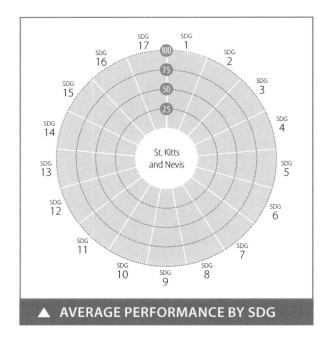

▲ AVERAGE PERFORMANCE BY SDG

▼ CURRENT ASSESSMENT – SDG DASHBOARD

■ Major challenges   ■ Significant challenges   ■ Challenges remain   ■ SDG achieved   ■ Information unavailable

▼ SDG TRENDS

↓ Decreasing   → Stagnating   ↗ Moderately improving   ↑ On track or maintaining SDG achievement   ● Information unavailable

Notes: The full title of Goal 2 "Zero Hunger" is "End hunger, achieve food security and improved nutrition and promote sustainable agriculture".
The full title of each SDG is available here: https://sustainabledevelopment.un.org/topics/sustainabledevelopmentgoals

SDG1 – No Poverty

		Value	Year	Rating	Trend
Poverty headcount ratio at $1.90/day (%)		NA	NA	●	●
Poverty headcount ratio at $3.20/day (%)		NA	NA	●	●

SDG2 – Zero Hunger

		Value	Year	Rating	Trend
Prevalence of undernourishment (%)	*	1.2	2017	●	●
Prevalence of stunting in children under 5 years of age (%)	*	2.6	2016	●	●
Prevalence of wasting in children under 5 years of age (%)	*	0.7	2016	●	●
Prevalence of obesity, BMI ≥ 30 (% of adult population)		22.9	2016	●	↓
Human Trophic Level (best 2–3 worst)		2.4	2017	●	↗
Cereal yield (tonnes per hectare of harvested land)		NA	NA	●	●
Sustainable Nitrogen Management Index (best 0–1.41 worst)		1.2	2015	●	→

SDG3 – Good Health and Well-Being

	Value	Year	Rating	Trend
Maternal mortality rate (per 100,000 live births)	NA	NA	●	●
Neonatal mortality rate (per 1,000 live births)	7.9	2018	●	↑
Mortality rate, under-5 (per 1,000 live births)	12.0	2018	●	↑
Incidence of tuberculosis (per 100,000 population)	0.0	2018	●	↑
New HIV infections (per 1,000 uninfected population)	0.3	2018	●	→
Age-standardized death rate due to cardiovascular disease, cancer, diabetes, or chronic respiratory disease in adults aged 30–70 years (%)	NA	NA	●	●
Age-standardized death rate attributable to household air pollution and ambient air pollution (per 100,000 population)	NA	NA	●	●
Traffic deaths (per 100,000 population)	NA	NA	●	●
Life expectancy at birth (years)	NA	NA	●	●
Adolescent fertility rate (births per 1,000 adolescent females aged 15 to 19)	NA	NA	●	●
Births attended by skilled health personnel (%)	100.0	2014	●	●
Percentage of surviving infants who received 2 WHO-recommended vaccines (%)	96	2018	●	↑
Universal health coverage (UHC) index of service coverage (worst 0–100 best)	NA	NA	●	●
Subjective well-being (average ladder score, worst 0–10 best)	NA	NA	●	●

SDG4 – Quality Education

	Value	Year	Rating	Trend
Net primary enrollment rate (%)	93.8	2016	●	↓
Lower secondary completion rate (%)	111.2	2016	●	●
Literacy rate (% of population aged 15 to 24)	NA	NA	●	●

SDG5 – Gender Equality

	Value	Year	Rating	Trend
Demand for family planning satisfied by modern methods (% of females aged 15 to 49 who are married or in unions)	NA	NA	●	●
Ratio of female-to-male mean years of education received (%)	NA	NA	●	●
Ratio of female-to-male labor force participation rate (%)	NA	NA	●	●
Seats held by women in national parliament (%)	20.0	2020	●	↗

SDG6 – Clean Water and Sanitation

	Value	Year	Rating	Trend
Population using at least basic drinking water services (%)	99.0	2013	●	●
Population using at least basic sanitation services (%)	91.6	2013	●	●
Freshwater withdrawal (% of available freshwater resources)	51.3	2010	●	●
Anthropogenic wastewater that receives treatment (%)	0.6	2018	●	●
Scarce water consumption embodied in imports (m³/capita)	NA	NA	●	●

SDG7 – Affordable and Clean Energy

	Value	Year	Rating	Trend
Population with access to electricity (%)	100.0	2017	●	↑
Population with access to clean fuels and technology for cooking (%)	100.0	2016	●	↑
CO_2 emissions from fuel combustion for electricity and heating per total electricity output (MtCO₂/TWh)	NA	NA	●	●

SDG8 – Decent Work and Economic Growth

		Value	Year	Rating	Trend
Adjusted GDP growth (%)		-2.2	2018	●	●
Victims of modern slavery (per 1,000 population)		NA	NA	●	●
Adults with an account at a bank or other financial institution or with a mobile-money-service provider (% of population aged 15 or over)		NA	NA	●	●
Unemployment rate (% of total labor force)		NA	NA	●	●
Fatal work-related accidents embodied in imports (per 100,000 population)		NA	NA	●	●

SDG9 – Industry, Innovation and Infrastructure

		Value	Year	Rating	Trend
Population using the internet (%)		80.7	2017	●	↑
Mobile broadband subscriptions (per 100 population)		69.9	2017	●	↓
Logistics Performance Index: Quality of trade and transport-related infrastructure (worst 1–5 best)		NA	NA	●	●
The Times Higher Education Universities Ranking: Average score of top 3 universities (worst 0–100 best)	*	0.0	2020	●	●
Scientific and technical journal articles (per 1,000 population)		0.5	2018	●	↑
Expenditure on research and development (% of GDP)		NA	NA	●	●

SDG10 – Reduced Inequalities

	Value	Year	Rating	Trend
Gini coefficient adjusted for top income	NA	NA	●	●

SDG11 – Sustainable Cities and Communities

	Value	Year	Rating	Trend
Annual mean concentration of particulate matter of less than 2.5 microns in diameter (PM2.5) (µg/m³)	NA	NA	●	●
Access to improved water source, piped (% of urban population)	NA	NA	●	●
Satisfaction with public transport (%)	NA	NA	●	●

SDG12 – Responsible Consumption and Production

	Value	Year	Rating	Trend
Municipal solid waste (kg/capita/day)	5.2	2015	●	●
Electronic waste (kg/capita)	12.1	2016	●	●
Production-based SO_2 emissions (kg/capita)	NA	NA	●	●
SO_2 emissions embodied in imports (kg/capita)	NA	NA	●	●
Production-based nitrogen emissions (kg/capita)	NA	NA	●	●
Nitrogen emissions embodied in imports (kg/capita)	NA	NA	●	●

SDG13 – Climate Action

		Value	Year	Rating	Trend
Energy-related CO_2 emissions (tCO₂/capita)		4.6	2017	●	→
CO_2 emissions embodied in imports (tCO₂/capita)		NA	NA	●	●
CO_2 emissions embodied in fossil fuel exports (kg/capita)	*	0.0	2018	●	●

SDG14 – Life Below Water

	Value	Year	Rating	Trend
Mean area that is protected in marine sites important to biodiversity (%)	19.5	2018	●	→
Ocean Health Index: Clean Waters score (worst 0–100 best)	56.6	2019	●	→
Fish caught from overexploited or collapsed stocks (% of total catch)	NA	NA	●	●
Fish caught by trawling (%)	NA	NA	●	●
Marine biodiversity threats embodied in imports (per million population)	NA	NA	●	●

SDG15 – Life on Land

	Value	Year	Rating	Trend
Mean area that is protected in terrestrial sites important to biodiversity (%)	29.2	2018	●	→
Mean area that is protected in freshwater sites important to biodiversity (%)	NA	NA	●	●
Red List Index of species survival (worst 0–1 best)	0.7	2019	●	↓
Permanent deforestation (% of forest area, 5-year average)	0.0	2018	●	●
Terrestrial and freshwater biodiversity threats embodied in imports (per million population)	NA	NA	●	●

SDG16 – Peace, Justice and Strong Institutions

		Value	Year	Rating	Trend
Homicides (per 100,000 population)		34.2	2012	●	●
Unsentenced detainees (% of prison population)		30.5	2018	●	↓
Percentage of population who feel safe walking alone at night in the city or area where they live (%)		NA	NA	●	●
Property Rights (worst 1–7 best)		NA	NA	●	●
Birth registrations with civil authority (% of children under age 5)		NA	NA	●	●
Corruption Perception Index (worst 0–100 best)		NA	NA	●	●
Children involved in child labor (% of population aged 5 to 14)		NA	NA	●	●
Exports of major conventional weapons (TIV constant million USD per 100,000 population)	*	0.0	2019	●	●
Press Freedom Index (best 0–100 worst)		NA	NA	●	●

SDG17 – Partnerships for the Goals

		Value	Year	Rating	Trend
Government spending on health and education (% of GDP)		4.7	2015	●	●
For high-income and all OECD DAC countries: International concessional public finance, including official development assistance (% of GNI)		NA	NA	●	●
Other countries: Government revenue excluding grants (% of GDP)		NA	NA	●	●
Corporate Tax Haven Score (best 0–100 worst)	*	0.0	2019	●	●

* Imputed data point

ST. LUCIA

▼ OVERALL PERFORMANCE

Index score
na

Regional average score
70.4

SDG Global rank NA (OF 166)

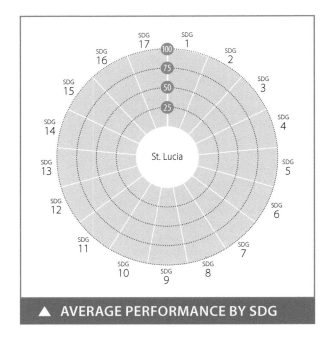

▲ AVERAGE PERFORMANCE BY SDG

▼ SPILLOVER INDEX

100 (best) to 0 (worst)

▼ CURRENT ASSESSMENT – SDG DASHBOARD

■ Major challenges ■ Significant challenges ■ Challenges remain ■ SDG achieved ■ Information unavailable

▼ SDG TRENDS

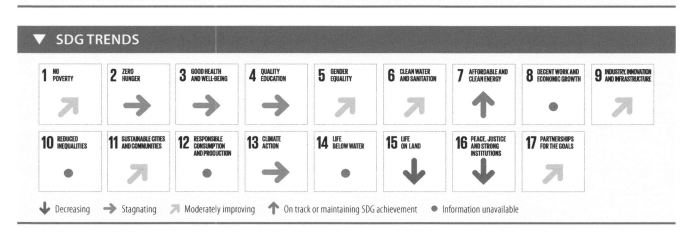

↓ Decreasing → Stagnating ↗ Moderately improving ↑ On track or maintaining SDG achievement ● Information unavailable

Notes: The full title of Goal 2 "Zero Hunger" is "End hunger, achieve food security and improved nutrition and promote sustainable agriculture".
The full title of each SDG is available here: https://sustainabledevelopment.un.org/topics/sustainabledevelopmentgoals

SDG1 – No Poverty

Indicator	Value	Year	Rating	Trend
Poverty headcount ratio at $1.90/day (%)	4.8	2020	◐	↑
Poverty headcount ratio at $3.20/day (%)	10.4	2020	◐	↗

SDG2 – Zero Hunger

Indicator	Value	Year	Rating	Trend
Prevalence of undernourishment (%)	NA	NA	●	●
Prevalence of stunting in children under 5 years of age (%)	2.5	2012	●	↑
Prevalence of wasting in children under 5 years of age (%)	3.7	2012	●	↑
Prevalence of obesity, BMI ≥ 30 (% of adult population)	19.7	2016	●	↓
Human Trophic Level (best 2–3 worst)	2.4	2017	●	↗
Cereal yield (tonnes per hectare of harvested land)	NA	NA	●	●
Sustainable Nitrogen Management Index (best 0–1.41 worst)	1.3	2015	●	↓

SDG3 – Good Health and Well-Being

Indicator	Value	Year	Rating	Trend
Maternal mortality rate (per 100,000 live births)	117	2017	●	→
Neonatal mortality rate (per 1,000 live births)	12.4	2018	●	↑
Mortality rate, under-5 (per 1,000 live births)	16.6	2018	●	↑
Incidence of tuberculosis (per 100,000 population)	3.2	2018	●	↑
New HIV infections (per 1,000 uninfected population)	0.3	2018	◐	→
Age-standardized death rate due to cardiovascular disease, cancer, diabetes, or chronic respiratory disease in adults aged 30–70 years (%)	18.8	2016	◐	→
Age-standardized death rate attributable to household air pollution and ambient air pollution (per 100,000 population)	30	2016	●	●
Traffic deaths (per 100,000 population)	35.4	2016	●	↓
Life expectancy at birth (years)	75.6	2016	◐	↗
Adolescent fertility rate (births per 1,000 adolescent females aged 15 to 19)	40.5	2017	◐	↗
Births attended by skilled health personnel (%)	98.7	2012	●	●
Percentage of surviving infants who received 2 WHO-recommended vaccines (%)	86	2018	◐	↓
Universal health coverage (UHC) index of service coverage (worst 0–100 best)	68.0	2017	●	↑
Subjective well-being (average ladder score, worst 0–10 best)	NA	NA	●	●

SDG4 – Quality Education

Indicator	Value	Year	Rating	Trend
Net primary enrollment rate (%)	95.4	2018	◐	↑
Lower secondary completion rate (%)	86.2	2018	◐	↓
Literacy rate (% of population aged 15 to 24)	NA	NA	●	●

SDG5 – Gender Equality

Indicator	Value	Year	Rating	Trend
Demand for family planning satisfied by modern methods (% of females aged 15 to 49 who are married or in unions)	72.4	2012	◐	↗
Ratio of female-to-male mean years of education received (%)	107.3	2018	●	↑
Ratio of female-to-male labor force participation rate (%)	80.2	2019	●	↑
Seats held by women in national parliament (%)	16.7	2020	●	↓

SDG6 – Clean Water and Sanitation

Indicator	Value	Year	Rating	Trend
Population using at least basic drinking water services (%)	98.2	2017	●	↑
Population using at least basic sanitation services (%)	88.4	2017	◐	→
Freshwater withdrawal (% of available freshwater resources)	14.3	2005	●	●
Anthropogenic wastewater that receives treatment (%)	0.9	2018	●	●
Scarce water consumption embodied in imports (m³/capita)	NA	NA	●	●

SDG7 – Affordable and Clean Energy

Indicator	Value	Year	Rating	Trend
Population with access to electricity (%)	98.8	2017	●	↑
Population with access to clean fuels and technology for cooking (%)	97.2	2016	●	↑
CO_2 emissions from fuel combustion for electricity and heating per total electricity output (MtCO$_2$/TWh)	NA	NA	●	●

SDG8 – Decent Work and Economic Growth

Indicator	Value	Year	Rating	Trend
Adjusted GDP growth (%)	-2.2	2018	●	●
Victims of modern slavery (per 1,000 population)	NA	NA	●	●
Adults with an account at a bank or other financial institution or with a mobile-money-service provider (% of population aged 15 or over)	NA	NA	●	●
Unemployment rate (% of total labor force)	20.7	2019	●	↗
Fatal work-related accidents embodied in imports (per 100,000 population)	NA	NA	●	●

SDG9 – Industry, Innovation and Infrastructure

Indicator	Value	Year	Rating	Trend
Population using the internet (%)	50.8	2017	●	↑
Mobile broadband subscriptions (per 100 population)	42.5	2018	●	↗
Logistics Performance Index: Quality of trade and transport-related infrastructure (worst 1–5 best)	NA	NA	●	●
The Times Higher Education Universities Ranking: Average score of top 3 universities (worst 0–100 best) *	0.0	2020	●	●
Scientific and technical journal articles (per 1,000 population)	0.0	2018	●	→
Expenditure on research and development (% of GDP)	NA	NA	●	●

SDG10 – Reduced Inequalities

Indicator	Value	Year	Rating	Trend
Gini coefficient adjusted for top income	51.3	2016	●	●

SDG11 – Sustainable Cities and Communities

Indicator	Value	Year	Rating	Trend
Annual mean concentration of particulate matter of less than 2.5 microns in diameter (PM2.5) (µg/m³)	22.4	2017	●	↗
Access to improved water source, piped (% of urban population)	99.0	2017	●	↑
Satisfaction with public transport (%)	NA	NA	●	●

SDG12 – Responsible Consumption and Production

Indicator	Value	Year	Rating	Trend
Municipal solid waste (kg/capita/day)	6.3	2015	●	●
Electronic waste (kg/capita)	9.3	2016	●	●
Production-based SO$_2$ emissions (kg/capita)	NA	NA	●	●
SO$_2$ emissions embodied in imports (kg/capita)	NA	NA	●	●
Production-based nitrogen emissions (kg/capita)	NA	NA	●	●
Nitrogen emissions embodied in imports (kg/capita)	NA	NA	●	●

SDG13 – Climate Action

Indicator	Value	Year	Rating	Trend
Energy-related CO_2 emissions (tCO$_2$/capita)	2.4	2017	●	→
CO_2 emissions embodied in imports (tCO$_2$/capita)	NA	NA	●	●
CO_2 emissions embodied in fossil fuel exports (kg/capita)	0.0	2016	●	●

SDG14 – Life Below Water

Indicator	Value	Year	Rating	Trend
Mean area that is protected in marine sites important to biodiversity (%)	15.5	2018	●	→
Ocean Health Index: Clean Waters score (worst 0–100 best)	52.8	2019	●	↓
Fish caught from overexploited or collapsed stocks (% of total catch)	NA	NA	●	●
Fish caught by trawling (%)	NA	NA	●	●
Marine biodiversity threats embodied in imports (per million population)	NA	NA	●	●

SDG15 – Life on Land

Indicator	Value	Year	Rating	Trend
Mean area that is protected in terrestrial sites important to biodiversity (%)	46.0	2018	◐	→
Mean area that is protected in freshwater sites important to biodiversity (%)	NA	NA	●	●
Red List Index of species survival (worst 0–1 best)	0.8	2019	●	↓
Permanent deforestation (% of forest area, 5-year average)	0.1	2018	●	●
Terrestrial and freshwater biodiversity threats embodied in imports (per million population)	NA	NA	●	●

SDG16 – Peace, Justice and Strong Institutions

Indicator	Value	Year	Rating	Trend
Homicides (per 100,000 population)	29.6	2017	●	↓
Unsentenced detainees (% of prison population)	51.8	2018	●	●
Percentage of population who feel safe walking alone at night in the city or area where they live (%)	NA	NA	●	●
Property Rights (worst 1–7 best)	NA	NA	●	●
Birth registrations with civil authority (% of children under age 5)	92.0	2018	●	●
Corruption Perception Index (worst 0–100 best)	55	2019	◐	↓
Children involved in child labor (% of population aged 5 to 14)	3.9	2016	●	●
Exports of major conventional weapons (TIV constant million USD per 100,000 population) *	0.0	2019	●	●
Press Freedom Index (best 0–100 worst)	NA	NA	●	●

SDG17 – Partnerships for the Goals

Indicator	Value	Year	Rating	Trend
Government spending on health and education (% of GDP)	8.0	2016	◐	↑
For high-income and all OECD DAC countries: International concessional public finance, including official development assistance (% of GNI)	NA	NA	●	●
Other countries: Government revenue excluding grants (% of GDP)	21.4	2017	◐	↓
Corporate Tax Haven Score (best 0–100 worst) *	0.0	2019	●	●

* Imputed data point

5. Country Profiles

▼ OVERALL PERFORMANCE

Index score

na

Regional average score

70.4

SDG Global rank   NA (OF 166)

▼ SPILLOVER INDEX

100 (best) to 0 (worst)

100
80
60
40
20
0

▲ AVERAGE PERFORMANCE BY SDG

St. Vincent and the Grenadines

SDG 1, SDG 2, SDG 3, SDG 4, SDG 5, SDG 6, SDG 7, SDG 8, SDG 9, SDG 10, SDG 11, SDG 12, SDG 13, SDG 14, SDG 15, SDG 16, SDG 17

▼ CURRENT ASSESSMENT – SDG DASHBOARD

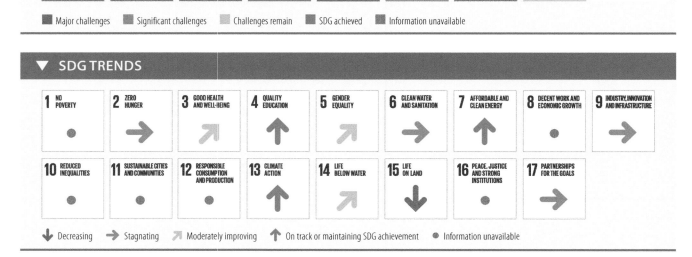

| 1 NO POVERTY | 2 ZERO HUNGER | 3 GOOD HEALTH AND WELL-BEING | 4 QUALITY EDUCATION | 5 GENDER EQUALITY | 6 CLEAN WATER AND SANITATION | 7 AFFORDABLE AND CLEAN ENERGY | 8 DECENT WORK AND ECONOMIC GROWTH | 9 INDUSTRY, INNOVATION AND INFRASTRUCTURE |

| 10 REDUCED INEQUALITIES | 11 SUSTAINABLE CITIES AND COMMUNITIES | 12 RESPONSIBLE CONSUMPTION AND PRODUCTION | 13 CLIMATE ACTION | 14 LIFE BELOW WATER | 15 LIFE ON LAND | 16 PEACE, JUSTICE AND STRONG INSTITUTIONS | 17 PARTNERSHIPS FOR THE GOALS | SUSTAINABLE DEVELOPMENT GOALS |

■ Major challenges   ■ Significant challenges   ■ Challenges remain   ■ SDG achieved   ■ Information unavailable

▼ SDG TRENDS

| 1 NO POVERTY ● | 2 ZERO HUNGER → | 3 GOOD HEALTH AND WELL-BEING ↗ | 4 QUALITY EDUCATION ↑ | 5 GENDER EQUALITY ↗ | 6 CLEAN WATER AND SANITATION → | 7 AFFORDABLE AND CLEAN ENERGY ↑ | 8 DECENT WORK AND ECONOMIC GROWTH ● | 9 INDUSTRY, INNOVATION AND INFRASTRUCTURE → |

| 10 REDUCED INEQUALITIES ● | 11 SUSTAINABLE CITIES AND COMMUNITIES ● | 12 RESPONSIBLE CONSUMPTION AND PRODUCTION ● | 13 CLIMATE ACTION ↑ | 14 LIFE BELOW WATER ↗ | 15 LIFE ON LAND ↓ | 16 PEACE, JUSTICE AND STRONG INSTITUTIONS ● | 17 PARTNERSHIPS FOR THE GOALS → | |

↓ Decreasing   → Stagnating   ↗ Moderately improving   ↑ On track or maintaining SDG achievement   ● Information unavailable

Notes: The full title of Goal 2 "Zero Hunger" is "End hunger, achieve food security and improved nutrition and promote sustainable agriculture".
The full title of each SDG is available here: https://sustainabledevelopment.un.org/topics/sustainabledevelopmentgoals

SDG1 – No Poverty

		Value	Year	Rating	Trend
Poverty headcount ratio at $1.90/day (%)	*	NA	NA	●	●
Poverty headcount ratio at $3.20/day (%)	*	NA	NA	●	●

SDG2 – Zero Hunger

	Value	Year	Rating	Trend
Prevalence of undernourishment (%)	5.7	2017	●	↑
Prevalence of stunting in children under 5 years of age (%)	NA	NA	●	●
Prevalence of wasting in children under 5 years of age (%)	NA	NA	●	●
Prevalence of obesity, BMI ≥ 30 (% of adult population)	23.7	2016	●	↓
Human Trophic Level (best 2–3 worst)	2.3	2017	○	→
Cereal yield (tonnes per hectare of harvested land)	26.1	2017	●	↑
Sustainable Nitrogen Management Index (best 0–1.41 worst)	0.9	2015	●	→

SDG3 – Good Health and Well-Being

	Value	Year	Rating	Trend
Maternal mortality rate (per 100,000 live births)	68	2017	●	↑
Neonatal mortality rate (per 1,000 live births)	9.7	2018	●	↑
Mortality rate, under-5 (per 1,000 live births)	16.4	2018	●	↑
Incidence of tuberculosis (per 100,000 population)	6.3	2018	●	↑
New HIV infections (per 1,000 uninfected population)	0.9	2018	●	→
Age-standardized death rate due to cardiovascular disease, cancer, diabetes, or chronic respiratory disease in adults aged 30–70 years (%)	23.2	2016	●	↓
Age-standardized death rate attributable to household air pollution and ambient air pollution (per 100,000 population)	48	2016	○	●
Traffic deaths (per 100,000 population)	8.2	2013	●	●
Life expectancy at birth (years)	72.0	2016	●	→
Adolescent fertility rate (births per 1,000 adolescent females aged 15 to 19)	49.0	2017	●	↗
Births attended by skilled health personnel (%)	99.0	2014	●	●
Percentage of surviving infants who received 2 WHO-recommended vaccines (%)	97	2018	●	↑
Universal health coverage (UHC) index of service coverage (worst 0–100 best)	71.0	2017	○	↑
Subjective well-being (average ladder score, worst 0–10 best)	NA	NA	●	●

SDG4 – Quality Education

	Value	Year	Rating	Trend
Net primary enrollment rate (%)	93.6	2017	○	↑
Lower secondary completion rate (%)	92.0	2018	●	↑
Literacy rate (% of population aged 15 to 24)	NA	NA	●	●

SDG5 – Gender Equality

		Value	Year	Rating	Trend
Demand for family planning satisfied by modern methods (% of females aged 15 to 49 who are married or in unions)	*	81.0	2017	●	↑
Ratio of female-to-male mean years of education received (%)		NA	NA	●	●
Ratio of female-to-male labor force participation rate (%)		72.6	2019	●	↑
Seats held by women in national parliament (%)		13.0	2020	●	→

SDG6 – Clean Water and Sanitation

	Value	Year	Rating	Trend
Population using at least basic drinking water services (%)	95.1	2017	○	→
Population using at least basic sanitation services (%)	87.2	2017	●	→
Freshwater withdrawal (% of available freshwater resources)	11.2	2015	●	●
Anthropogenic wastewater that receives treatment (%)	0.7	2018	●	●
Scarce water consumption embodied in imports (m3/capita)	NA	NA	●	●

SDG7 – Affordable and Clean Energy

	Value	Year	Rating	Trend
Population with access to electricity (%)	100.0	2017	●	↑
Population with access to clean fuels and technology for cooking (%)	96.0	2016	●	↑
CO2 emissions from fuel combustion for electricity and heating per total electricity output (MtCO2/TWh)	NA	NA	●	●

SDG8 – Decent Work and Economic Growth

	Value	Year	Rating	Trend
Adjusted GDP growth (%)	-2.6	2018	●	●
Victims of modern slavery (per 1,000 population)	NA	NA	●	●
Adults with an account at a bank or other financial institution or with a mobile-money-service provider (% of population aged 15 or over)	NA	NA	●	●
Unemployment rate (% of total labor force)	18.9	2019	●	→
Fatal work-related accidents embodied in imports (per 100,000 population)	NA	NA	●	●

SDG9 – Industry, Innovation and Infrastructure

		Value	Year	Rating	Trend
Population using the internet (%)		22.4	2018	●	↓
Mobile broadband subscriptions (per 100 population)		53.9	2018	●	↑
Logistics Performance Index: Quality of trade and transport-related infrastructure (worst 1–5 best)		NA	NA	●	●
The Times Higher Education Universities Ranking: Average score of top 3 universities (worst 0–100 best)	*	0.0	2020	●	●
Scientific and technical journal articles (per 1,000 population)		0.0	2018	●	→
Expenditure on research and development (% of GDP)		0.1	2002	●	●

SDG10 – Reduced Inequalities

	Value	Year	Rating	Trend
Gini coefficient adjusted for top income	NA	NA	●	●

SDG11 – Sustainable Cities and Communities

	Value	Year	Rating	Trend
Annual mean concentration of particulate matter of less than 2.5 microns in diameter (PM2.5) (μg/m3)	22.2	2017	●	→
Access to improved water source, piped (% of urban population)	NA	NA	●	●
Satisfaction with public transport (%)	NA	NA	●	●

SDG12 – Responsible Consumption and Production

	Value	Year	Rating	Trend
Municipal solid waste (kg/capita/day)	1.5	2015	●	●
Electronic waste (kg/capita)	8.3	2016	●	●
Production-based SO2 emissions (kg/capita)	NA	NA	●	●
SO2 emissions embodied in imports (kg/capita)	NA	NA	●	●
Production-based nitrogen emissions (kg/capita)	NA	NA	●	●
Nitrogen emissions embodied in imports (kg/capita)	NA	NA	●	●

SDG13 – Climate Action

	Value	Year	Rating	Trend
Energy-related CO2 emissions (tCO2/capita)	2.0	2017	●	↑
CO2 emissions embodied in imports (tCO2/capita)	NA	NA	●	●
CO2 emissions embodied in fossil fuel exports (kg/capita)	0.0	2017	●	●

SDG14 – Life Below Water

	Value	Year	Rating	Trend
Mean area that is protected in marine sites important to biodiversity (%)	26.3	2018	●	→
Ocean Health Index: Clean Waters score (worst 0–100 best)	59.3	2019	●	↑
Fish caught from overexploited or collapsed stocks (% of total catch)	NA	NA	●	●
Fish caught by trawling (%)	80.2	2012	●	●
Marine biodiversity threats embodied in imports (per million population)	NA	NA	●	●

SDG15 – Life on Land

	Value	Year	Rating	Trend
Mean area that is protected in terrestrial sites important to biodiversity (%)	42.8	2018	○	→
Mean area that is protected in freshwater sites important to biodiversity (%)	NA	NA	●	●
Red List Index of species survival (worst 0–1 best)	0.8	2019	●	↓
Permanent deforestation (% of forest area, 5-year average)	0.0	2018	●	●
Terrestrial and freshwater biodiversity threats embodied in imports (per million population)	NA	NA	●	●

SDG16 – Peace, Justice and Strong Institutions

		Value	Year	Rating	Trend
Homicides (per 100,000 population)		36.5	2016	●	●
Unsentenced detainees (% of prison population)		24.3	2018	●	↑
Percentage of population who feel safe walking alone at night in the city or area where they live (%)		NA	NA	●	●
Property Rights (worst 1–7 best)		NA	NA	●	●
Birth registrations with civil authority (% of children under age 5)		NA	NA	●	●
Corruption Perception Index (worst 0–100 best)		59	2019	○	↓
Children involved in child labor (% of population aged 5 to 14)		NA	NA	●	●
Exports of major conventional weapons (TIV constant million USD per 100,000 population)	*	0.0	2019	●	●
Press Freedom Index (best 0–100 worst)		NA	NA	●	●

SDG17 – Partnerships for the Goals

		Value	Year	Rating	Trend
Government spending on health and education (% of GDP)		8.5	2016	○	●
For high-income and all OECD DAC countries: International concessional public finance, including official development assistance (% of GNI)		NA	NA	●	●
Other countries: Government revenue excluding grants (% of GDP)		27.2	2017	○	→
Corporate Tax Haven Score (best 0–100 worst)	*	0.0	2019	●	●

* Imputed data point

5. Country Profiles

SUDAN

▼ OVERALL PERFORMANCE

Index score

49.6

Regional average score

53.1

SDG Global rank **159** (OF 166)

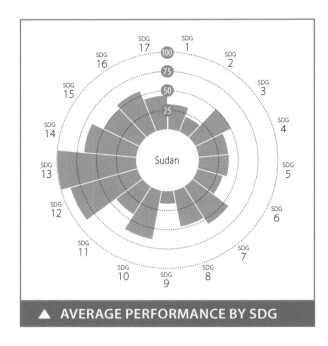

▲ AVERAGE PERFORMANCE BY SDG

▼ SPILLOVER INDEX

100 (best) to 0 (worst)

▼ CURRENT ASSESSMENT – SDG DASHBOARD

■ Major challenges ■ Significant challenges ■ Challenges remain ■ SDG achieved ■ Information unavailable

▼ SDG TRENDS

↓ Decreasing   → Stagnating   ↗ Moderately improving   ↑ On track or maintaining SDG achievement   ● Information unavailable

Notes: The full title of Goal 2 "Zero Hunger" is "End hunger, achieve food security and improved nutrition and promote sustainable agriculture".
The full title of each SDG is available here: https://sustainabledevelopment.un.org/topics/sustainabledevelopmentgoals

SDG1 – No Poverty

	Value	Year	Rating	Trend
Poverty headcount ratio at $1.90/day (%)	24.6	2020	●	↓
Poverty headcount ratio at $3.20/day (%)	53.1	2020	●	↓

SDG2 – Zero Hunger

	Value	Year	Rating	Trend
Prevalence of undernourishment (%)	20.1	2017	●	→
Prevalence of stunting in children under 5 years of age (%)	38.2	2014	●	→
Prevalence of wasting in children under 5 years of age (%)	16.3	2014	●	↗
Prevalence of obesity, BMI ≥ 30 (% of adult population)	NA	NA	●	●
Human Trophic Level (best 2–3 worst)	2.4	2011	●	●
Cereal yield (tonnes per hectare of harvested land)	0.7	2017	●	↓
Sustainable Nitrogen Management Index (best 0–1.41 worst)	NA	NA	●	●

SDG3 – Good Health and Well-Being

	Value	Year	Rating	Trend
Maternal mortality rate (per 100,000 live births)	295	2017	●	↗
Neonatal mortality rate (per 1,000 live births)	28.6	2018	●	→
Mortality rate, under-5 (per 1,000 live births)	60.5	2018	●	↗
Incidence of tuberculosis (per 100,000 population)	71.0	2018	●	↑
New HIV infections (per 1,000 uninfected population)	0.1	2018	●	↑
Age-standardized death rate due to cardiovascular disease, cancer, diabetes, or chronic respiratory disease in adults aged 30–70 years (%)	26.0	2016	●	→
Age-standardized death rate attributable to household air pollution and ambient air pollution (per 100,000 population)	185	2016	●	●
Traffic deaths (per 100,000 population)	25.7	2016	●	↓
Life expectancy at birth (years)	65.1	2016	●	→
Adolescent fertility rate (births per 1,000 adolescent females aged 15 to 19)	64.0	2017	●	↑
Births attended by skilled health personnel (%)	77.5	2014	●	●
Percentage of surviving infants who received 2 WHO-recommended vaccines (%)	88	2018	○	↑
Universal health coverage (UHC) index of service coverage (worst 0–100 best)	44.0	2017	●	↗
Subjective well-being (average ladder score, worst 0–10 best)	4.1	2014	●	●

SDG4 – Quality Education

	Value	Year	Rating	Trend
Net primary enrollment rate (%)	60.0	2017	●	→
Lower secondary completion rate (%)	57.5	2017	●	↑
Literacy rate (% of population aged 15 to 24)	73.0	2018	●	●

SDG5 – Gender Equality

	Value	Year	Rating	Trend
Demand for family planning satisfied by modern methods (% of females aged 15 to 49 who are married or in unions)	30.1	2014	●	→
Ratio of female-to-male mean years of education received (%)	76.2	2018	●	↗
Ratio of female-to-male labor force participation rate (%)	34.8	2019	●	→
Seats held by women in national parliament (%)	30.5	2018	○	→

SDG6 – Clean Water and Sanitation

	Value	Year	Rating	Trend
Population using at least basic drinking water services (%)	60.3	2017	●	→
Population using at least basic sanitation services (%)	36.6	2017	●	→
Freshwater withdrawal (% of available freshwater resources)	118.7	2010	●	●
Anthropogenic wastewater that receives treatment (%)	0.0	2018	●	●
Scarce water consumption embodied in imports (m³/capita)	0.0	2013	●	↑

SDG7 – Affordable and Clean Energy

	Value	Year	Rating	Trend
Population with access to electricity (%)	56.5	2017	●	↑
Population with access to clean fuels and technology for cooking (%)	41.3	2016	●	↗
CO_2 emissions from fuel combustion for electricity and heating per total electricity output (MtCO₂/TWh)	1.2	2017	○	→

SDG8 – Decent Work and Economic Growth

	Value	Year	Rating	Trend
Adjusted GDP growth (%)	-5.7	2018	●	●
Victims of modern slavery (per 1,000 population)	12.0	2018	●	●
Adults with an account at a bank or other financial institution or with a mobile-money-service provider (% of population aged 15 or over)	15.3	2014	●	●
Unemployment rate (% of total labor force)	16.5	2019	●	→
Fatal work-related accidents embodied in imports (per 100,000 population)	0.0	2010	●	↑

SDG9 – Industry, Innovation and Infrastructure

	Value	Year	Rating	Trend
Population using the internet (%)	30.9	2017	●	↗
Mobile broadband subscriptions (per 100 population)	32.4	2018	●	→
Logistics Performance Index: Quality of trade and transport-related infrastructure (worst 1–5 best)	2.2	2018	●	↑
The Times Higher Education Universities Ranking: Average score of top 3 universities (worst 0–100 best) *	0.0	2020	●	●
Scientific and technical journal articles (per 1,000 population)	0.0	2018	●	→
Expenditure on research and development (% of GDP)	0.3	2005	●	●

SDG10 – Reduced Inequalities

	Value	Year	Rating	Trend
Gini coefficient adjusted for top income	40.3	2009	●	●

SDG11 – Sustainable Cities and Communities

	Value	Year	Rating	Trend
Annual mean concentration of particulate matter of less than 2.5 microns in diameter (PM2.5) (μg/m³)	55.4	2017	●	↓
Access to improved water source, piped (% of urban population)	68.6	2017	●	→
Satisfaction with public transport (%)	33.3	2014	●	●

SDG12 – Responsible Consumption and Production

	Value	Year	Rating	Trend
Municipal solid waste (kg/capita/day)	0.5	2015	●	●
Electronic waste (kg/capita)	1.3	2016	●	●
Production-based SO_2 emissions (kg/capita)	0.0	2012	●	●
SO_2 emissions embodied in imports (kg/capita)	0.0	2012	●	●
Production-based nitrogen emissions (kg/capita)	57.0	2010	●	●
Nitrogen emissions embodied in imports (kg/capita)	0.0	2010	●	●

SDG13 – Climate Action

	Value	Year	Rating	Trend
Energy-related CO_2 emissions (tCO₂/capita)	0.4	2017	●	↑
CO_2 emissions embodied in imports (tCO₂/capita)	0.0	2015	●	↑
CO_2 emissions embodied in fossil fuel exports (kg/capita)	0.0	2017	●	↑

SDG14 – Life Below Water

	Value	Year	Rating	Trend
Mean area that is protected in marine sites important to biodiversity (%)	87.5	2018	●	↑
Ocean Health Index: Clean Waters score (worst 0–100 best)	45.0	2019	●	↓
Fish caught from overexploited or collapsed stocks (% of total catch)	39.2	2014	●	↗
Fish caught by trawling (%)	2.0	2014	●	↑
Marine biodiversity threats embodied in imports (per million population)	NA	NA	●	●

SDG15 – Life on Land

	Value	Year	Rating	Trend
Mean area that is protected in terrestrial sites important to biodiversity (%)	25.0	2018	●	↑
Mean area that is protected in freshwater sites important to biodiversity (%)	0.0	2018	●	→
Red List Index of species survival (worst 0–1 best)	0.9	2019	●	↑
Permanent deforestation (% of forest area, 5-year average)	0.0	2018	●	●
Terrestrial and freshwater biodiversity threats embodied in imports (per million population)	NA	NA	●	●

SDG16 – Peace, Justice and Strong Institutions

	Value	Year	Rating	Trend
Homicides (per 100,000 population)	5.2	2008	●	●
Unsentenced detainees (% of prison population)	20.4	2015	●	●
Percentage of population who feel safe walking alone at night in the city or area where they live (%)	71.3	2014	●	●
Property Rights (worst 1–7 best)	NA	NA	●	●
Birth registrations with civil authority (% of children under age 5)	67.3	2018	●	●
Corruption Perception Index (worst 0–100 best)	16	2019	●	→
Children involved in child labor (% of population aged 5 to 14)	24.9	2016	●	●
Exports of major conventional weapons (TIV constant million USD per 100,000 population) *	0.0	2019	●	●
Press Freedom Index (best 0–100 worst)	72.5	2019	●	→

SDG17 – Partnerships for the Goals

	Value	Year	Rating	Trend
Government spending on health and education (% of GDP)	4.8	2009	●	●
For high-income and all OECD DAC countries: International concessional public finance, including official development assistance (% of GNI)	NA	NA	●	●
Other countries: Government revenue excluding grants (% of GDP)	9.5	2016	●	↓
Corporate Tax Haven Score (best 0–100 worst) *	0.0	2019	●	●

* Imputed data point

5. Country Profiles

SURINAME

▼ OVERALL PERFORMANCE

Index score

68.4

Regional average score

70.4

SDG Global rank   86 (OF 166)

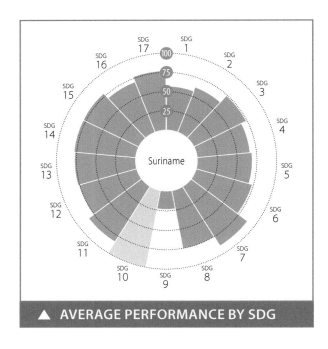

AVERAGE PERFORMANCE BY SDG ▲

▼ SPILLOVER INDEX

100 (best) to 0 (worst)

▼ CURRENT ASSESSMENT – SDG DASHBOARD

■ Major challenges   ■ Significant challenges   ■ Challenges remain   ■ SDG achieved   ■ Information unavailable

▼ SDG TRENDS

⬇ Decreasing   ➡ Stagnating   ↗ Moderately improving   ⬆ On track or maintaining SDG achievement   ● Information unavailable

Notes: The full title of Goal 2 "Zero Hunger" is "End hunger, achieve food security and improved nutrition and promote sustainable agriculture".
The full title of each SDG is available here: https://sustainabledevelopment.un.org/topics/sustainabledevelopmentgoals

SDG1 – No Poverty

Indicator	Value	Year	Rating	Trend
Poverty headcount ratio at $1.90/day (%)	20.4	2020	●	↓
Poverty headcount ratio at $3.20/day (%)	30.3	2020	●	↓

SDG2 – Zero Hunger

Indicator	Value	Year	Rating	Trend
Prevalence of undernourishment (%)	8.5	2017	●	→
Prevalence of stunting in children under 5 years of age (%)	8.8	2010	●	↑
Prevalence of wasting in children under 5 years of age (%)	5.0	2010	●	↑
Prevalence of obesity, BMI ≥ 30 (% of adult population)	26.4	2016	●	↓
Human Trophic Level (best 2–3 worst)	2.2	2017	●	↑
Cereal yield (tonnes per hectare of harvested land)	4.5	2017	●	↑
Sustainable Nitrogen Management Index (best 0–1.41 worst)	0.7	2015	●	→

SDG3 – Good Health and Well-Being

Indicator	Value	Year	Rating	Trend
Maternal mortality rate (per 100,000 live births)	120	2017	●	→
Neonatal mortality rate (per 1,000 live births)	10.0	2018	●	↑
Mortality rate, under-5 (per 1,000 live births)	18.9	2018	●	↑
Incidence of tuberculosis (per 100,000 population)	38.0	2018	●	→
New HIV infections (per 1,000 uninfected population)	0.5	2018	●	↑
Age-standardized death rate due to cardiovascular disease, cancer, diabetes, or chronic respiratory disease in adults aged 30–70 years (%)	21.7	2016	●	↗
Age-standardized death rate attributable to household air pollution and ambient air pollution (per 100,000 population)	57	2016	●	●
Traffic deaths (per 100,000 population)	14.5	2016	●	↑
Life expectancy at birth (years)	71.8	2016	●	→
Adolescent fertility rate (births per 1,000 adolescent females aged 15 to 19)	61.7	2017	●	→
Births attended by skilled health personnel (%)	80.0	2015	●	●
Percentage of surviving infants who received 2 WHO-recommended vaccines (%)	95	2018	●	↑
Universal health coverage (UHC) index of service coverage (worst 0–100 best)	71.0	2017	●	↑
Subjective well-being (average ladder score, worst 0–10 best)	6.3	2012	●	●

SDG4 – Quality Education

Indicator	Value	Year	Rating	Trend
Net primary enrollment rate (%)	86.0	2018	●	↓
Lower secondary completion rate (%)	45.2	2018	●	↓
Literacy rate (% of population aged 15 to 24)	98.6	2018	●	●

SDG5 – Gender Equality

Indicator	Value	Year	Rating	Trend
Demand for family planning satisfied by modern methods (% of females aged 15 to 49 who are married or in unions)	73.2	2010	●	↗
Ratio of female-to-male mean years of education received (%)	97.8	2018	●	↗
Ratio of female-to-male labor force participation rate (%)	61.5	2019	●	↓
Seats held by women in national parliament (%)	31.4	2020	●	↑

SDG6 – Clean Water and Sanitation

Indicator	Value	Year	Rating	Trend
Population using at least basic drinking water services (%)	95.4	2017	●	↑
Population using at least basic sanitation services (%)	84.5	2017	●	→
Freshwater withdrawal (% of available freshwater resources)	4.0	2005	●	●
Anthropogenic wastewater that receives treatment (%)	0.0	2018	●	●
Scarce water consumption embodied in imports (m³/capita)	8.2	2013	●	↑

SDG7 – Affordable and Clean Energy

Indicator	Value	Year	Rating	Trend
Population with access to electricity (%)	96.8	2017	●	↑
Population with access to clean fuels and technology for cooking (%)	89.6	2016	●	↑
CO_2 emissions from fuel combustion for electricity and heating per total electricity output (MtCO₂/TWh)	1.1	2017	●	→

SDG8 – Decent Work and Economic Growth

Indicator	Value	Year	Rating	Trend
Adjusted GDP growth (%)	-5.3	2018	●	●
Victims of modern slavery (per 1,000 population)	2.3	2018	●	●
Adults with an account at a bank or other financial institution or with a mobile-money-service provider (% of population aged 15 or over)	NA	NA	●	●
Unemployment rate (% of total labor force)	7.3	2019	●	→
Fatal work-related accidents embodied in imports (per 100,000 population)	0.5	2010	●	↑

SDG9 – Industry, Innovation and Infrastructure

Indicator	Value	Year	Rating	Trend
Population using the internet (%)	48.9	2017	●	↑
Mobile broadband subscriptions (per 100 population)	42.1	2018	●	↓
Logistics Performance Index: Quality of trade and transport-related infrastructure (worst 1–5 best)	NA	NA	●	●
The Times Higher Education Universities Ranking: Average score of top 3 universities (worst 0–100 best) *	0.0	2020	●	●
Scientific and technical journal articles (per 1,000 population)	0.0	2018	●	→
Expenditure on research and development (% of GDP)	NA	NA	●	●

SDG10 – Reduced Inequalities

Indicator	Value	Year	Rating	Trend
Gini coefficient adjusted for top income	NA	NA	●	●

SDG11 – Sustainable Cities and Communities

Indicator	Value	Year	Rating	Trend
Annual mean concentration of particulate matter of less than 2.5 microns in diameter (PM2.5) (µg/m³)	24.8	2017	●	→
Access to improved water source, piped (% of urban population)	87.8	2017	●	→
Satisfaction with public transport (%)	73.3	2012	●	●

SDG12 – Responsible Consumption and Production

Indicator	Value	Year	Rating	Trend
Municipal solid waste (kg/capita/day)	0.6	2010	●	●
Electronic waste (kg/capita)	9.6	2016	●	●
Production-based SO_2 emissions (kg/capita)	206.8	2012	●	●
SO_2 emissions embodied in imports (kg/capita)	8.2	2012	●	●
Production-based nitrogen emissions (kg/capita)	22.7	2010	●	●
Nitrogen emissions embodied in imports (kg/capita)	3.6	2010	●	●

SDG13 – Climate Action

Indicator	Value	Year	Rating	Trend
Energy-related CO_2 emissions (tCO₂/capita)	4.2	2017	●	→
CO_2 emissions embodied in imports (tCO₂/capita)	1.0	2015	●	→
CO_2 emissions embodied in fossil fuel exports (kg/capita)	NA	NA	●	●

SDG14 – Life Below Water

Indicator	Value	Year	Rating	Trend
Mean area that is protected in marine sites important to biodiversity (%)	74.2	2018	●	↑
Ocean Health Index: Clean Waters score (worst 0–100 best)	78.8	2019	●	↑
Fish caught from overexploited or collapsed stocks (% of total catch)	30.0	2014	●	↓
Fish caught by trawling (%)	22.5	2014	●	↑
Marine biodiversity threats embodied in imports (per million population)	0.0	2018	●	●

SDG15 – Life on Land

Indicator	Value	Year	Rating	Trend
Mean area that is protected in terrestrial sites important to biodiversity (%)	51.2	2018	●	↑
Mean area that is protected in freshwater sites important to biodiversity (%)	49.4	2018	●	→
Red List Index of species survival (worst 0–1 best)	1.0	2019	●	↑
Permanent deforestation (% of forest area, 5-year average)	0.1	2018	●	●
Terrestrial and freshwater biodiversity threats embodied in imports (per million population)	0.3	2018	●	●

SDG16 – Peace, Justice and Strong Institutions

Indicator	Value	Year	Rating	Trend
Homicides (per 100,000 population)	5.5	2017	●	→
Unsentenced detainees (% of prison population)	221.0	2015	●	●
Percentage of population who feel safe walking alone at night in the city or area where they live (%)	60.2	2012	●	●
Property Rights (worst 1–7 best)	NA	NA	●	●
Birth registrations with civil authority (% of children under age 5)	98.3	2018	●	●
Corruption Perception Index (worst 0–100 best)	44	2019	●	↑
Children involved in child labor (% of population aged 5 to 14)	4.1	2016	●	●
Exports of major conventional weapons (TIV constant million USD per 100,000 population) *	0.0	2019	●	●
Press Freedom Index (best 0–100 worst)	16.4	2019	●	↑

SDG17 – Partnerships for the Goals

Indicator	Value	Year	Rating	Trend
Government spending on health and education (% of GDP)	NA	NA	●	●
For high-income and all OECD DAC countries: International concessional public finance, including official development assistance (% of GNI)	NA	NA	●	●
Other countries: Government revenue excluding grants (% of GDP) *	25.7	2012	●	●
Corporate Tax Haven Score (best 0–100 worst) *	0.0	2019	●	●

* Imputed data point

5. Country Profiles

SWEDEN

▼ OVERALL PERFORMANCE

Index score	Regional average score
84.7	77.3

SDG Global rank **1** (OF 166)

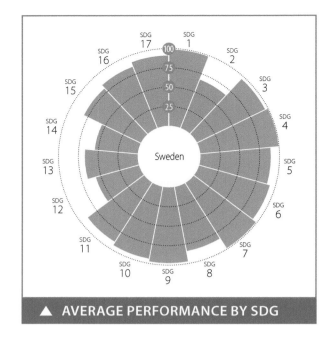

▲ AVERAGE PERFORMANCE BY SDG

▼ SPILLOVER INDEX

100 (best) to 0 (worst)

▼ CURRENT ASSESSMENT – SDG DASHBOARD

■ Major challenges ■ Significant challenges ■ Challenges remain ■ SDG achieved ■ Information unavailable

▼ SDG TRENDS

↓ Decreasing → Stagnating ↗ Moderately improving ↑ On track or maintaining SDG achievement • Information unavailable

Notes: The full title of Goal 2 "Zero Hunger" is "End hunger, achieve food security and improved nutrition and promote sustainable agriculture".
The full title of each SDG is available here: https://sustainabledevelopment.un.org/topics/sustainabledevelopmentgoals

SWEDEN

SDG1 – No Poverty

	Value	Year	Rating	Trend
Poverty headcount ratio at $1.90/day (%)	0.5	2020	●	↑
Poverty headcount ratio at $3.20/day (%)	0.6	2020	●	↑
Poverty rate after taxes and transfers (%)	9.3	2017	●	↑

SDG2 – Zero Hunger

		Value	Year	Rating	Trend
Prevalence of undernourishment (%)		2.5	2017	●	↑
Prevalence of stunting in children under 5 years of age (%)	*	2.6	2016	●	↑
Prevalence of wasting in children under 5 years of age (%)	*	0.7	2016	●	↑
Prevalence of obesity, BMI ≥ 30 (% of adult population)		20.6	2016	●	↓
Human Trophic Level (best 2–3 worst)		2.5	2017	●	→
Cereal yield (tonnes per hectare of harvested land)		6.0	2017	●	↑
Sustainable Nitrogen Management Index (best 0–1.41 worst)		0.5	2015	◐	↓
Yield gap closure (% of potential yield)		68.6	2015	◐	●

SDG3 – Good Health and Well-Being

	Value	Year	Rating	Trend
Maternal mortality rate (per 100,000 live births)	4	2017	●	↑
Neonatal mortality rate (per 1,000 live births)	1.5	2018	●	↑
Mortality rate, under-5 (per 1,000 live births)	2.7	2018	●	↑
Incidence of tuberculosis (per 100,000 population)	5.5	2018	●	↑
New HIV infections (per 1,000 uninfected population)	NA	NA	●	●
Age-standardized death rate due to cardiovascular disease, cancer, diabetes, or chronic respiratory disease in adults aged 30–70 years (%)	9.1	2016	●	↑
Age-standardized death rate attributable to household air pollution and ambient air pollution (per 100,000 population)	7	2016	●	●
Traffic deaths (per 100,000 population)	2.8	2016	●	↑
Life expectancy at birth (years)	82.4	2016	●	↑
Adolescent fertility rate (births per 1,000 adolescent females aged 15 to 19)	5.1	2017	●	↑
Births attended by skilled health personnel (%)	NA	NA	●	●
Percentage of surviving infants who received 2 WHO-recommended vaccines (%)	97.0	2018	●	↑
Universal health coverage (UHC) index of service coverage (worst 0–100 best)	86.0	2017	●	↑
Subjective well-being (average ladder score, worst 0–10 best)	7.4	2019	●	↑
Gap in life expectancy at birth among regions (years)	1.2	2016	●	↑
Gap in self-reported health status by income (percentage points)	19.9	2017	●	↑
Daily smokers (% of population aged 15 and over)	10.4	2017	●	↑

SDG4 – Quality Education

		Value	Year	Rating	Trend
Net primary enrollment rate (%)	*	100.0	2017	●	↑
Lower secondary completion rate (%)	*	100.0	2017	●	↑
Literacy rate (% of population aged 15 to 24)		NA	NA	●	●
Participation rate in pre-primary organized learning (% of children aged 4 to 6)		99.9	2017	●	↑
Tertiary educational attainment (% of population aged 25 to 34)		47.5	2018	●	↑
PISA score (worst 0–600 best)		502.3	2018	●	↑
Variation in science performance explained by socio-economic status (%)		12.7	2018	◐	↓
Underachievers in science (% of 15-year-olds)		19.0	2018	●	↑
Resilient students in science (% of 15-year-olds)		30.4	2018	◐	↑

SDG5 – Gender Equality

		Value	Year	Rating	Trend
Demand for family planning satisfied by modern methods (% of females aged 15 to 49 who are married or in unions)	*	80.0	2017	●	↑
Ratio of female-to-male mean years of education received (%)		101.6	2018	●	↑
Ratio of female-to-male labor force participation rate (%)		90.5	2019	●	↑
Seats held by women in national parliament (%)		47.0	2020	●	↑
Gender wage gap (% of male median wage)		7.1	2018	●	↑
Gender gap in time spent doing unpaid work (minutes/day)		49.2	2010	●	●

SDG6 – Clean Water and Sanitation

	Value	Year	Rating	Trend
Population using at least basic drinking water services (%)	100.0	2017	●	●
Population using at least basic sanitation services (%)	99.3	2017	●	●
Freshwater withdrawal (% of available freshwater resources)	3.9	2010	●	●
Anthropogenic wastewater that receives treatment (%)	100.0	2018	●	●
Scarce water consumption embodied in imports (m³/capita)	32.3	2013	◐	→
Population using safely managed water services (%)	99.9	2017	●	↑
Population using safely managed sanitation services (%)	93.4	2017	●	↑

SDG7 – Affordable and Clean Energy

	Value	Year	Rating	Trend
Population with access to electricity (%)	100.0	2017	●	↑
Population with access to clean fuels and technology for cooking (%)	100.0	2016	●	↑
CO₂ emissions from fuel combustion for electricity and heating per total electricity output (MtCO₂/TWh)	0.2	2017	●	↑
Share of renewable energy in total primary energy supply (%)	37.8	2018	●	↑

SDG8 – Decent Work and Economic Growth

	Value	Year	Rating	Trend
Adjusted GDP growth (%)	-0.8	2018	◐	●
Victims of modern slavery (per 1,000 population)	1.6	2018	●	●
Adults with an account at a bank or other financial institution or with a mobile-money-service provider (% of population aged 15 or over)	99.7	2017	●	↑
Fatal work-related accidents embodied in imports (per 100,000 population)	1.3	2010	◐	↑
Employment-to-population ratio (%)	77.1	2019	●	↑
Youth not in employment, education or training (NEET) (% of population aged 15 to 29)	8.9	2018	●	↑

SDG9 – Industry, Innovation and Infrastructure

		Value	Year	Rating	Trend
Population using the internet (%)		92.1	2018	●	↑
Mobile broadband subscriptions (per 100 population)		127.0	2018	●	↑
Logistics Performance Index: Quality of trade and transport-related infrastructure (worst 1–5 best)		4.2	2018	●	↑
The Times Higher Education Universities Ranking: Average score of top 3 universities (worst 0–100 best)		66.3	2020	●	●
Scientific and technical journal articles (per 1,000 population)		2.0	2018	●	↑
Expenditure on research and development (% of GDP)		3.3	2017	●	↑
Researchers (per 1,000 employed population)		14.8	2018	●	↑
Triadic patent families filed (per million population)		74.0	2017	●	↑
Gap in internet access by income (percentage points)		6.3	2019	●	↑
Women in science and engineering (% of tertiary graduates in science and engineering)		30.0	2015	◐	●

SDG10 – Reduced Inequalities

	Value	Year	Rating	Trend
Gini coefficient adjusted for top income	29.8	2015	●	↑
Palma ratio	1.0	2017	◐	↓
Elderly poverty rate (% of population aged 66 or over)	11.3	2017	◐	↓

SDG11 – Sustainable Cities and Communities

	Value	Year	Rating	Trend
Annual mean concentration of particulate matter of less than 2.5 microns in diameter (PM2.5) (μg/m³)	6.2	2017	●	↑
Access to improved water source, piped (% of urban population)	99.0	2017	●	↑
Satisfaction with public transport (%)	62.6	2019	◐	→
Population with rent overburden (%)	9.9	2017	◐	↓

SDG12 – Responsible Consumption and Production

	Value	Year	Rating	Trend
Electronic waste (kg/capita)	21.5	2016	●	●
Production-based SO₂ emissions (kg/capita)	63.3	2012	◐	●
SO₂ emissions embodied in imports (kg/capita)	18.4	2012	●	●
Production-based nitrogen emissions (kg/capita)	36.1	2010	◐	●
Nitrogen emissions embodied in imports (kg/capita)	13.3	2010	●	●
Non-recycled municipal solid waste (kg/capita/day)	0.7	2018	●	●

SDG13 – Climate Action

	Value	Year	Rating	Trend
Energy-related CO₂ emissions (tCO₂/capita)	4.3	2017	●	→
CO₂ emissions embodied in imports (tCO₂/capita)	2.7	2015	●	→
CO₂ emissions embodied in fossil fuel exports (kg/capita)	0.0	2019	●	●
Effective carbon rate (EUR/tCO₂)	43.8	2016	●	●

SDG14 – Life Below Water

	Value	Year	Rating	Trend
Mean area that is protected in marine sites important to biodiversity (%)	59.1	2018	●	↑
Ocean Health Index: Clean Waters score (worst 0–100 best)	63.4	2019	●	↓
Fish caught from overexploited or collapsed stocks (% of total catch)	41.3	2014	●	↓
Fish caught by trawling (%)	79.3	2014	●	→
Marine biodiversity threats embodied in imports (per million population)	0.1	2018	●	●

SDG15 – Life on Land

	Value	Year	Rating	Trend
Mean area that is protected in terrestrial sites important to biodiversity (%)	58.4	2018	●	↑
Mean area that is protected in freshwater sites important to biodiversity (%)	61.9	2018	●	↑
Red List Index of species survival (worst 0–1 best)	1.0	2019	●	↑
Permanent deforestation (% of forest area, 5-year average)	0.0	2018	●	●
Terrestrial and freshwater biodiversity threats embodied in imports (per million population)	1.6	2018	◐	●

SDG16 – Peace, Justice and Strong Institutions

		Value	Year	Rating	Trend
Homicides (per 100,000 population)		1.1	2017	●	↑
Unsentenced detainees (% of prison population)		26.9	2018	●	↑
Percentage of population who feel safe walking alone at night in the city or area where they live		76.7	2019	●	↑
Property Rights (worst 1–7 best)		5.5	2019	●	●
Birth registrations with civil authority (% of children under age 5)		100.0	2018	●	●
Corruption Perception Index (worst 0–100 best)		85.0	2019	●	↑
Children involved in child labor (% of population aged 5 to 14)	*	0.0	2016	●	●
Exports of major conventional weapons (TIV constant million USD per 100,000 population)		1.8	2019	●	●
Press Freedom Index (best 0–100 worst)		8.3	2019	●	↑
Persons held in prison (per 100,000 population)		57.6	2017	●	↑

SDG17 – Partnerships for the Goals

	Value	Year	Rating	Trend
Government spending on health and education (% of GDP)	16.8	2016	●	↑
For high-income and all OECD DAC countries: International concessional public finance, including official development assistance (% of GNI)	1.0	2017	●	↑
Other countries: Government revenue excluding grants (% of GDP)	NA	NA	●	●
Corporate Tax Haven Score (best 0–100 worst)	56.0	2019	●	●
Financial Secrecy Score (best 0–100 worst)	45.7	2020	●	●
Shifted profits of multinationals (US$ billion)	10.3	2016	●	●

* Imputed data point

5. Country Profiles

▼ OVERALL PERFORMANCE

Index score

79.4

Regional average score

77.3

SDG Global rank 15 (OF 166)

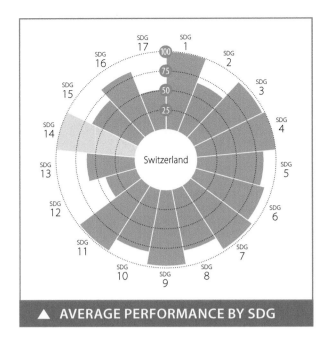

▲ AVERAGE PERFORMANCE BY SDG

▼ SPILLOVER INDEX

100 (best) to 0 (worst)

▼ CURRENT ASSESSMENT – SDG DASHBOARD

■ Major challenges ■ Significant challenges ■ Challenges remain ■ SDG achieved ■ Information unavailable

▼ SDG TRENDS

↓ Decreasing → Stagnating ↗ Moderately improving ↑ On track or maintaining SDG achievement ● Information unavailable

Notes: The full title of Goal 2 "Zero Hunger" is "End hunger, achieve food security and improved nutrition and promote sustainable agriculture".
The full title of each SDG is available here: https://sustainabledevelopment.un.org/topics/sustainabledevelopmentgoals

SWITZERLAND

SDG1 – No Poverty

	Value	Year	Rating	Trend
Poverty headcount ratio at $1.90/day (%)	0.1	2020	●	↑
Poverty headcount ratio at $3.20/day (%)	0.1	2020	●	↑
Poverty rate after taxes and transfers (%)	9.1	2015	●	↑

SDG2 – Zero Hunger

	Value	Year	Rating	Trend
Prevalence of undernourishment (%)	2.5	2017	●	↑
Prevalence of stunting in children under 5 years of age (%)	* 2.6	2016	●	↑
Prevalence of wasting in children under 5 years of age (%)	* 0.7	2016	●	↑
Prevalence of obesity, BMI ≥ 30 (% of adult population)	19.5	2016	●	↓
Human Trophic Level (best 2–3 worst)	2.5	2017	●	→
Cereal yield (tonnes per hectare of harvested land)	6.8	2017	●	↑
Sustainable Nitrogen Management Index (best 0–1.41 worst)	0.7	2015	●	↓
Yield gap closure (% of potential yield)	64.2	2015	○	●

SDG3 – Good Health and Well-Being

	Value	Year	Rating	Trend
Maternal mortality rate (per 100,000 live births)	5	2017	●	↑
Neonatal mortality rate (per 1,000 live births)	2.9	2018	●	↑
Mortality rate, under-5 (per 1,000 live births)	4.1	2018	●	↑
Incidence of tuberculosis (per 100,000 population)	6.4	2018	●	↑
New HIV infections (per 1,000 uninfected population)	NA	NA	●	●
Age-standardized death rate due to cardiovascular disease, cancer, diabetes, or chronic respiratory disease in adults aged 30–70 years (%)	8.6	2016	●	↑
Age-standardized death rate attributable to household air pollution and ambient air pollution (per 100,000 population)	10	2016	●	●
Traffic deaths (per 100,000 population)	2.7	2016	●	↑
Life expectancy at birth (years)	83.3	2016	●	↑
Adolescent fertility rate (births per 1,000 adolescent females aged 15 to 19)	2.8	2017	●	↑
Births attended by skilled health personnel (%)	100.0	2006	●	●
Percentage of surviving infants who received 2 WHO-recommended vaccines (%)	96.0	2018	●	↑
Universal health coverage (UHC) index of service coverage (worst 0–100 best)	83.0	2017	●	↑
Subjective well-being (average ladder score, worst 0–10 best)	7.7	2019	●	↑
Gap in life expectancy at birth among regions (years)	1.9	2016	●	●
Gap in self-reported health status by income (percentage points)	21.4	2017	○	↑
Daily smokers (% of population aged 15 and over)	19.1	2017	○	●

SDG4 – Quality Education

	Value	Year	Rating	Trend
Net primary enrollment rate (%)	* 99.9	2017	●	●
Lower secondary completion rate (%)	* 99.9	2017	●	↑
Literacy rate (% of population aged 15 to 24)	NA	NA	●	●
Participation rate in pre-primary organized learning (% of children aged 4 to 6)	99.4	2017	●	↑
Tertiary educational attainment (% of population aged 25 to 34)	51.2	2018	●	↑
PISA score (worst 0–600 best)	498.0	2018	●	↑
Variation in science performance explained by socio-economic status (%)	16.3	2018	●	↓
Underachievers in science (% of 15-year-olds)	20.2	2018	●	↓
Resilient students in science (% of 15-year-olds)	31.2	2018	○	↑

SDG5 – Gender Equality

	Value	Year	Rating	Trend
Demand for family planning satisfied by modern methods (% of females aged 15 to 49 who are married or in unions)	* 86.4	2017	●	↑
Ratio of female-to-male mean years of education received (%)	93.4	2018	○	→
Ratio of female-to-male labor force participation rate (%)	84.8	2019	●	↑
Seats held by women in national parliament (%)	41.5	2020	●	↑
Gender wage gap (% of male median wage)	14.8	2016	●	↑
Gender gap in time spent doing unpaid work (minutes/day)	NA	NA	●	●

SDG6 – Clean Water and Sanitation

	Value	Year	Rating	Trend
Population using at least basic drinking water services (%)	100.0	2017	●	●
Population using at least basic sanitation services (%)	99.9	2017	●	●
Freshwater withdrawal (% of available freshwater resources)	7.6	2010	●	●
Anthropogenic wastewater that receives treatment (%)	96.7	2018	●	●
Scarce water consumption embodied in imports (m³/capita)	47.6	2013	●	→
Population using safely managed water services (%)	95.5	2017	●	↑
Population using safely managed sanitation services (%)	99.5	2017	●	↑

SDG7 – Affordable and Clean Energy

	Value	Year	Rating	Trend
Population with access to electricity (%)	100.0	2017	●	●
Population with access to clean fuels and technology for cooking (%)	100.0	2016	●	↑
CO₂ emissions from fuel combustion for electricity and heating per total electricity output (MtCO₂/TWh)	0.6	2017	●	↑
Share of renewable energy in total primary energy supply (%)	21.5	2018	●	↑

SDG8 – Decent Work and Economic Growth

	Value	Year	Rating	Trend
Adjusted GDP growth (%)	-1.1	2018	○	●
Victims of modern slavery (per 1,000 population)	1.7	2018	●	●
Adults with an account at a bank or other financial institution or with a mobile-money-service provider (% of population aged 15 or over)	98.4	2017	●	↑
Fatal work-related accidents embodied in imports (per 100,000 population)	2.8	2010	●	↑
Employment-to-population ratio (%)	80.5	2019	●	↑
Youth not in employment, education or training (NEET) (% of population aged 15 to 29)	8.1	2018	●	●

SDG9 – Industry, Innovation and Infrastructure

	Value	Year	Rating	Trend
Population using the internet (%)	89.7	2017	●	↑
Mobile broadband subscriptions (per 100 population)	99.4	2018	●	↑
Logistics Performance Index: Quality of trade and transport-related infrastructure (worst 1–5 best)	4.0	2018	●	↑
The Times Higher Education Universities Ranking: Average score of top 3 universities (worst 0–100 best)	75.5	2020	●	●
Scientific and technical journal articles (per 1,000 population)	2.5	2018	●	↑
Expenditure on research and development (% of GDP)	3.4	2015	●	●
Researchers (per 1,000 employed population)	9.2	2017	●	↑
Triadic patent families filed (per million population)	151.9	2017	●	↑
Gap in internet access by income (percentage points)	26.7	2014	●	●
Women in science and engineering (% of tertiary graduates in science and engineering)	21.6	2015	●	●

SDG10 – Reduced Inequalities

	Value	Year	Rating	Trend
Gini coefficient adjusted for top income	34.3	2015	○	↓
Palma ratio	1.1	2015	○	→
Elderly poverty rate (% of population aged 66 or over)	19.5	2015	●	→

SDG11 – Sustainable Cities and Communities

	Value	Year	Rating	Trend
Annual mean concentration of particulate matter of less than 2.5 microns in diameter (PM2.5) (µg/m³)	10.3	2017	○	↑
Access to improved water source, piped (% of urban population)	99.0	2017	●	↑
Satisfaction with public transport (%)	83.3	2019	●	↑
Population with rent overburden (%)	6.7	2016	●	↑

SDG12 – Responsible Consumption and Production

	Value	Year	Rating	Trend
Electronic waste (kg/capita)	22.2	2016	●	●
Production-based SO₂ emissions (kg/capita)	58.3	2012	○	●
SO₂ emissions embodied in imports (kg/capita)	27.5	2012	●	●
Production-based nitrogen emissions (kg/capita)	43.3	2010	●	●
Nitrogen emissions embodied in imports (kg/capita)	21.8	2010	●	●
Non-recycled municipal solid waste (kg/capita/day)	0.9	2018	●	●

SDG13 – Climate Action

	Value	Year	Rating	Trend
Energy-related CO₂ emissions (tCO₂/capita)	3.9	2017	●	→
CO₂ emissions embodied in imports (tCO₂/capita)	4.8	2015	●	→
CO₂ emissions embodied in fossil fuel exports (kg/capita)	0.0	2019	●	●
Effective carbon rate (EUR/tCO₂)	28.6	2016	●	●

SDG14 – Life Below Water

	Value	Year	Rating	Trend
Mean area that is protected in marine sites important to biodiversity (%)	NA	NA	●	●
Ocean Health Index: Clean Waters score (worst 0–100 best)	NA	NA	●	●
Fish caught from overexploited or collapsed stocks (% of total catch)	NA	NA	●	●
Fish caught by trawling (%)	NA	NA	●	●
Marine biodiversity threats embodied in imports (per million population)	0.5	2018	○	●

SDG15 – Life on Land

	Value	Year	Rating	Trend
Mean area that is protected in terrestrial sites important to biodiversity (%)	35.2	2018	○	→
Mean area that is protected in freshwater sites important to biodiversity (%)	60.1	2018	●	↑
Red List Index of species survival (worst 0–1 best)	1.0	2019	●	↑
Permanent deforestation (% of forest area, 5-year average)	0.0	2018	●	●
Terrestrial and freshwater biodiversity threats embodied in imports (per million population)	5.8	2018	●	●

SDG16 – Peace, Justice and Strong Institutions

	Value	Year	Rating	Trend
Homicides (per 100,000 population)	0.5	2017	●	↑
Unsentenced detainees (% of prison population)	43.2	2018	●	↓
Percentage of population who feel safe walking alone at night in the city or area where they live (%)	87.6	2019	●	↑
Property Rights (worst 1–7 best)	6.4	2019	●	●
Birth registrations with civil authority (% of children under age 5)	100.0	2018	●	●
Corruption Perception Index (worst 0–100 best)	85.0	2019	●	↑
Children involved in child labor (% of population aged 5 to 14)	* 0.0	2016	●	●
Exports of major conventional weapons (TIV constant million USD per 100,000 population)	3.1	2019	●	●
Press Freedom Index (best 0–100 worst)	10.5	2019	●	↑
Persons held in prison (per 100,000 population)	77.4	2017	●	↑

SDG17 – Partnerships for the Goals

	Value	Year	Rating	Trend
Government spending on health and education (% of GDP)	12.8	2016	●	↑
For high-income and all OECD DAC countries: International concessional public finance, including official development assistance (% of GNI)	0.5	2017	●	↓
Other countries: Government revenue excluding grants (% of GDP)	NA	NA	●	●
Corporate Tax Haven Score (best 0–100 worst)	83.3	2019	●	●
Financial Secrecy Score (best 0–100 worst)	74.1	2020	●	●
Shifted profits of multinationals (US$ billion)	-73.2	2016	●	●

* Imputed data point

5. Country Profiles

▼ OVERALL PERFORMANCE

Index score
59.3

Regional average score
66.3

SDG Global rank 126 (OF 166)

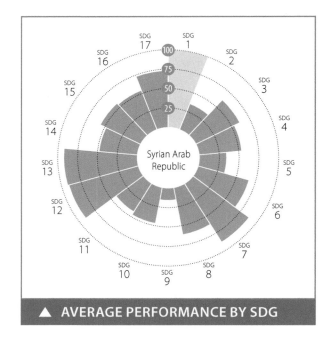

▲ AVERAGE PERFORMANCE BY SDG

▼ SPILLOVER INDEX

100 (best) to 0 (worst)

▼ CURRENT ASSESSMENT – SDG DASHBOARD

■ Major challenges   ■ Significant challenges   ▨ Challenges remain   ■ SDG achieved   ■ Information unavailable

▼ SDG TRENDS

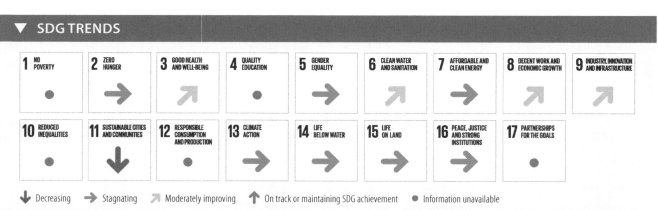

↓ Decreasing   → Stagnating   ↗ Moderately improving   ↑ On track or maintaining SDG achievement   ● Information unavailable

Notes: The full title of Goal 2 "Zero Hunger" is "End hunger, achieve food security and improved nutrition and promote sustainable agriculture".
The full title of each SDG is available here: https://sustainabledevelopment.un.org/topics/sustainabledevelopmentgoals

SYRIAN ARAB REPUBLIC

SDG1 – No Poverty

	Value	Year	Rating	Trend
Poverty headcount ratio at $1.90/day (%)	NA	NA	●	●
Poverty headcount ratio at $3.20/day (%)	NA	NA	●	●

SDG2 – Zero Hunger

	Value	Year	Rating	Trend
Prevalence of undernourishment (%)	NA	NA	●	●
Prevalence of stunting in children under 5 years of age (%)	27.5	2009	●	→
Prevalence of wasting in children under 5 years of age (%)	11.5	2009	●	↓
Prevalence of obesity, BMI ≥ 30 (% of adult population)	27.8	2016	●	↓
Human Trophic Level (best 2–3 worst)	2.2	2007	●	●
Cereal yield (tonnes per hectare of harvested land)	1.6	2017	●	↑
Sustainable Nitrogen Management Index (best 0–1.41 worst)	0.7	2015	●	→

SDG3 – Good Health and Well-Being

	Value	Year	Rating	Trend
Maternal mortality rate (per 100,000 live births)	31	2017	●	↑
Neonatal mortality rate (per 1,000 live births)	8.8	2018	●	↑
Mortality rate, under-5 (per 1,000 live births)	16.7	2018	●	↑
Incidence of tuberculosis (per 100,000 population)	19.0	2018	●	→
New HIV infections (per 1,000 uninfected population)	0.0	2018	●	↑
Age-standardized death rate due to cardiovascular disease, cancer, diabetes, or chronic respiratory disease in adults aged 30–70 years (%)	21.8	2016	●	→
Age-standardized death rate attributable to household air pollution and ambient air pollution (per 100,000 population)	75	2016	●	●
Traffic deaths (per 100,000 population)	26.5	2016	●	↓
Life expectancy at birth (years)	63.8	2016	●	↗
Adolescent fertility rate (births per 1,000 adolescent females aged 15 to 19)	38.6	2017	●	↗
Births attended by skilled health personnel (%)	96.2	2009	●	●
Percentage of surviving infants who received 2 WHO-recommended vaccines (%)	47	2018	●	↗
Universal health coverage (UHC) index of service coverage (worst 0–100 best)	60.0	2017	●	→
Subjective well-being (average ladder score, worst 0–10 best)	3.5	2015	●	●

SDG4 – Quality Education

	Value	Year	Rating	Trend
Net primary enrollment rate (%)	68.0	2013	●	●
Lower secondary completion rate (%)	53.8	2013	●	●
Literacy rate (% of population aged 15 to 24)	92.5	2004	●	●

SDG5 – Gender Equality

	Value	Year	Rating	Trend
Demand for family planning satisfied by modern methods (% of females aged 15 to 49 who are married or in unions)	53.3	2009	●	→
Ratio of female-to-male mean years of education received (%)	82.1	2018	●	→
Ratio of female-to-male labor force participation rate (%)	16.8	2019	●	↓
Seats held by women in national parliament (%)	12.4	2020	●	→

SDG6 – Clean Water and Sanitation

	Value	Year	Rating	Trend
Population using at least basic drinking water services (%)	97.2	2017	●	↑
Population using at least basic sanitation services (%)	91.2	2017	●	→
Freshwater withdrawal (% of available freshwater resources)	126.0	2005	●	●
Anthropogenic wastewater that receives treatment (%)	48.0	2018	●	●
Scarce water consumption embodied in imports (m³/capita)	1.9	2013	●	↑

SDG7 – Affordable and Clean Energy

	Value	Year	Rating	Trend
Population with access to electricity (%)	89.6	2017	●	→
Population with access to clean fuels and technology for cooking (%)	99.0	2016	●	↑
CO₂ emissions from fuel combustion for electricity and heating per total electricity output (MtCO₂/TWh)	1.3	2017	●	→

SDG8 – Decent Work and Economic Growth

		Value	Year	Rating	Trend
Adjusted GDP growth (%)		NA	NA	●	●
Victims of modern slavery (per 1,000 population)	*	NA	NA	●	●
Adults with an account at a bank or other financial institution or with a mobile-money-service provider (% of population aged 15 or over)		23.3	2011	●	●
Unemployment rate (% of total labor force)		8.4	2019	●	→
Fatal work-related accidents embodied in imports (per 100,000 population)		0.1	2010	●	↑

SDG9 – Industry, Innovation and Infrastructure

		Value	Year	Rating	Trend
Population using the internet (%)		34.3	2017	●	↗
Mobile broadband subscriptions (per 100 population)		16.5	2018	●	→
Logistics Performance Index: Quality of trade and transport-related infrastructure (worst 1–5 best)		2.5	2018	●	↑
The Times Higher Education Universities Ranking: Average score of top 3 universities (worst 0–100 best)	*	0.0	2020	●	●
Scientific and technical journal articles (per 1,000 population)		0.0	2018	●	→
Expenditure on research and development (% of GDP)		0.0	2015	●	●

SDG10 – Reduced Inequalities

	Value	Year	Rating	Trend
Gini coefficient adjusted for top income	46.5	2004	●	●

SDG11 – Sustainable Cities and Communities

	Value	Year	Rating	Trend
Annual mean concentration of particulate matter of less than 2.5 microns in diameter (PM2.5) (µg/m³)	43.8	2017	●	↓
Access to improved water source, piped (% of urban population)	74.7	2017	●	↓
Satisfaction with public transport (%)	15.3	2015	●	●

SDG12 – Responsible Consumption and Production

	Value	Year	Rating	Trend
Municipal solid waste (kg/capita/day)	1.2	2009	●	●
Electronic waste (kg/capita)	NA	NA	●	●
Production-based SO₂ emissions (kg/capita)	24.9	2012	●	●
SO₂ emissions embodied in imports (kg/capita)	1.0	2012	●	●
Production-based nitrogen emissions (kg/capita)	10.4	2010	●	●
Nitrogen emissions embodied in imports (kg/capita)	0.5	2010	●	●

SDG13 – Climate Action

	Value	Year	Rating	Trend
Energy-related CO₂ emissions (tCO₂/capita)	2.6	2017	●	↓
CO₂ emissions embodied in imports (tCO₂/capita)	0.2	2015	●	↑
CO₂ emissions embodied in fossil fuel exports (kg/capita)	NA	NA	●	●

SDG14 – Life Below Water

	Value	Year	Rating	Trend
Mean area that is protected in marine sites important to biodiversity (%)	0.0	2018	●	→
Ocean Health Index: Clean Waters score (worst 0–100 best)	37.6	2019	●	→
Fish caught from overexploited or collapsed stocks (% of total catch)	NA	NA	●	●
Fish caught by trawling (%)	22.0	2014	●	↑
Marine biodiversity threats embodied in imports (per million population)	0.0	2018	●	●

SDG15 – Life on Land

	Value	Year	Rating	Trend
Mean area that is protected in terrestrial sites important to biodiversity (%)	0.9	2018	●	→
Mean area that is protected in freshwater sites important to biodiversity (%)	3.2	2018	●	→
Red List Index of species survival (worst 0–1 best)	0.9	2019	●	↑
Permanent deforestation (% of forest area, 5-year average)	0.2	2018	●	●
Terrestrial and freshwater biodiversity threats embodied in imports (per million population)	0.1	2018	●	●

SDG16 – Peace, Justice and Strong Institutions

		Value	Year	Rating	Trend
Homicides (per 100,000 population)		2.2	2010	●	●
Unsentenced detainees (% of prison population)		50.5	2006	●	●
Percentage of population who feel safe walking alone at night in the city or area where they live (%)		32.2	2015	●	●
Property Rights (worst 1–7 best)		NA	NA	●	●
Birth registrations with civil authority (% of children under age 5)		96.0	2018	●	●
Corruption Perception Index (worst 0–100 best)		13	2019	●	↓
Children involved in child labor (% of population aged 5 to 14)		4.0	2016	●	●
Exports of major conventional weapons (TIV constant million USD per 100,000 population)	*	0.0	2019	●	●
Press Freedom Index (best 0–100 worst)		71.8	2019	●	↗

SDG17 – Partnerships for the Goals

		Value	Year	Rating	Trend
Government spending on health and education (% of GDP)		6.7	2009	●	●
For high-income and all OECD DAC countries: International concessional public finance, including official development assistance (% of GNI)		NA	NA	●	●
Other countries: Government revenue excluding grants (% of GDP)		NA	NA	●	●
Corporate Tax Haven Score (best 0–100 worst)	*	0.0	2019	●	●

* Imputed data point

5. Country Profiles

▼ OVERALL PERFORMANCE

Index score

69.4

Regional average score

70.9

SDG Global rank 78 (OF 166)

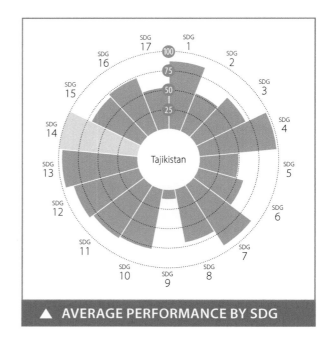

▲ AVERAGE PERFORMANCE BY SDG

▼ SPILLOVER INDEX

100 (best) to 0 (worst)

▼ CURRENT ASSESSMENT – SDG DASHBOARD

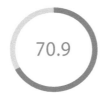

■ Major challenges ■ Significant challenges ■ Challenges remain ■ SDG achieved ■ Information unavailable

▼ SDG TRENDS

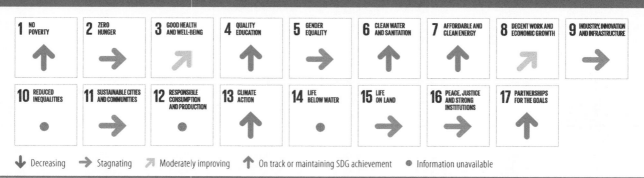

↓ Decreasing   → Stagnating   ↗ Moderately improving   ↑ On track or maintaining SDG achievement   ● Information unavailable

Notes: The full title of Goal 2 "Zero Hunger" is "End hunger, achieve food security and improved nutrition and promote sustainable agriculture".
The full title of each SDG is available here: https://sustainabledevelopment.un.org/topics/sustainabledevelopmentgoals

SDG1 – No Poverty

	Value	Year	Rating	Trend
Poverty headcount ratio at $1.90/day (%)	1.5	2020	●	↑
Poverty headcount ratio at $3.20/day (%)	11.6	2020	●	↑

SDG2 – Zero Hunger

	Value	Year	Rating	Trend
Prevalence of undernourishment (%)	NA	NA	●	●
Prevalence of stunting in children under 5 years of age (%)	26.8	2012	●	→
Prevalence of wasting in children under 5 years of age (%)	9.9	2012	●	→
Prevalence of obesity, BMI ≥ 30 (% of adult population)	14.2	2016	●	↓
Human Trophic Level (best 2–3 worst)	2.1	2017	●	↑
Cereal yield (tonnes per hectare of harvested land)	3.5	2017	●	↑
Sustainable Nitrogen Management Index (best 0–1.41 worst)	0.7	2015	●	→

SDG3 – Good Health and Well-Being

	Value	Year	Rating	Trend
Maternal mortality rate (per 100,000 live births)	17	2017	●	↑
Neonatal mortality rate (per 1,000 live births)	15.0	2018	●	↑
Mortality rate, under-5 (per 1,000 live births)	34.8	2018	●	↑
Incidence of tuberculosis (per 100,000 population)	84.0	2018	●	→
New HIV infections (per 1,000 uninfected population)	0.1	2018	●	↑
Age-standardized death rate due to cardiovascular disease, cancer, diabetes, or chronic respiratory disease in adults aged 30–70 years (%)	25.3	2016	●	→
Age-standardized death rate attributable to household air pollution and ambient air pollution (per 100,000 population)	129	2016	●	●
Traffic deaths (per 100,000 population)	18.1	2016	●	→
Life expectancy at birth (years)	70.8	2016	●	→
Adolescent fertility rate (births per 1,000 adolescent females aged 15 to 19)	57.1	2017	●	↓
Births attended by skilled health personnel (%)	94.8	2017	●	↑
Percentage of surviving infants who received 2 WHO-recommended vaccines (%)	96	2018	●	↑
Universal health coverage (UHC) index of service coverage (worst 0–100 best)	68.0	2017	●	↑
Subjective well-being (average ladder score, worst 0–10 best)	5.5	2018	●	↑

SDG4 – Quality Education

	Value	Year	Rating	Trend
Net primary enrollment rate (%)	98.3	2017	●	↑
Lower secondary completion rate (%)	96.2	2017	●	↑
Literacy rate (% of population aged 15 to 24)	99.9	2014	●	●

SDG5 – Gender Equality

	Value	Year	Rating	Trend
Demand for family planning satisfied by modern methods (% of females aged 15 to 49 who are married or in unions)	44.8	2017	●	→
Ratio of female-to-male mean years of education received (%)	90.2	2018	●	↑
Ratio of female-to-male labor force participation rate (%)	46.2	2019	●	↓
Seats held by women in national parliament (%)	23.8	2020	●	↗

SDG6 – Clean Water and Sanitation

	Value	Year	Rating	Trend
Population using at least basic drinking water services (%)	81.2	2017	●	↑
Population using at least basic sanitation services (%)	97.0	2017	●	↑
Freshwater withdrawal (% of available freshwater resources)	73.9	2005	●	●
Anthropogenic wastewater that receives treatment (%)	2.3	2018	●	●
Scarce water consumption embodied in imports (m3/capita)	5.1	2013	●	↑

SDG7 – Affordable and Clean Energy

	Value	Year	Rating	Trend
Population with access to electricity (%)	99.3	2017	●	↑
Population with access to clean fuels and technology for cooking (%)	80.4	2016	●	↑
CO_2 emissions from fuel combustion for electricity and heating per total electricity output (MtCO2/TWh)	0.3	2017	●	↑

SDG8 – Decent Work and Economic Growth

	Value	Year	Rating	Trend
Adjusted GDP growth (%)	-1.3	2018	●	●
Victims of modern slavery (per 1,000 population)	4.5	2018	●	●
Adults with an account at a bank or other financial institution or with a mobile-money-service provider (% of population aged 15 or over)	47.0	2017	●	↑
Unemployment rate (% of total labor force)	11.0	2019	●	→
Fatal work-related accidents embodied in imports (per 100,000 population)	0.1	2010	●	↑

SDG9 – Industry, Innovation and Infrastructure

	Value	Year	Rating	Trend
Population using the internet (%)	22.0	2017	●	→
Mobile broadband subscriptions (per 100 population)	22.8	2017	●	↑
Logistics Performance Index: Quality of trade and transport-related infrastructure (worst 1–5 best)	2.2	2018	●	↓
The Times Higher Education Universities Ranking: Average score of top 3 universities (worst 0–100 best) *	0.0	2020	●	●
Scientific and technical journal articles (per 1,000 population)	0.0	2018	●	→
Expenditure on research and development (% of GDP)	0.1	2017	●	→

SDG10 – Reduced Inequalities

	Value	Year	Rating	Trend
Gini coefficient adjusted for top income	35.3	2015	●	●

SDG11 – Sustainable Cities and Communities

	Value	Year	Rating	Trend
Annual mean concentration of particulate matter of less than 2.5 microns in diameter (PM2.5) (μg/m3)	46.2	2017	●	→
Access to improved water source, piped (% of urban population)	90.8	2017	●	→
Satisfaction with public transport (%)	84.7	2018	●	↑

SDG12 – Responsible Consumption and Production

	Value	Year	Rating	Trend
Municipal solid waste (kg/capita/day)	2.0	2013	●	●
Electronic waste (kg/capita)	NA	NA	●	●
Production-based SO_2 emissions (kg/capita)	17.2	2012	●	●
SO_2 emissions embodied in imports (kg/capita)	2.1	2012	●	●
Production-based nitrogen emissions (kg/capita)	9.3	2010	●	●
Nitrogen emissions embodied in imports (kg/capita)	0.5	2010	●	●

SDG13 – Climate Action

	Value	Year	Rating	Trend
Energy-related CO_2 emissions (tCO2/capita)	0.4	2017	●	↑
CO_2 emissions embodied in imports (tCO2/capita)	0.2	2015	●	↑
CO_2 emissions embodied in fossil fuel exports (kg/capita)	NA	NA	●	●

SDG14 – Life Below Water

	Value	Year	Rating	Trend
Mean area that is protected in marine sites important to biodiversity (%)	NA	NA	●	●
Ocean Health Index: Clean Waters score (worst 0–100 best)	NA	NA	●	●
Fish caught from overexploited or collapsed stocks (% of total catch)	NA	NA	●	●
Fish caught by trawling (%)	NA	NA	●	●
Marine biodiversity threats embodied in imports (per million population)	0.0	2018	●	●

SDG15 – Life on Land

	Value	Year	Rating	Trend
Mean area that is protected in terrestrial sites important to biodiversity (%)	20.8	2018	●	→
Mean area that is protected in freshwater sites important to biodiversity (%)	35.2	2018	●	→
Red List Index of species survival (worst 0–1 best)	1.0	2019	●	↑
Permanent deforestation (% of forest area, 5-year average) *	0.0	2018	●	●
Terrestrial and freshwater biodiversity threats embodied in imports (per million population)	0.0	2018	●	●

SDG16 – Peace, Justice and Strong Institutions

	Value	Year	Rating	Trend
Homicides (per 100,000 population)	1.6	2011	●	●
Unsentenced detainees (% of prison population)	15.0	2009	●	●
Percentage of population who feel safe walking alone at night in the city or area where they live	88.1	2018	●	↑
Property Rights (worst 1–7 best)	4.6	2019	●	●
Birth registrations with civil authority (% of children under age 5)	95.8	2018	●	●
Corruption Perception Index (worst 0–100 best)	25	2019	●	↓
Children involved in child labor (% of population aged 5 to 14)	10.0	2016	●	●
Exports of major conventional weapons (TIV constant million USD per 100,000 population) *	0.0	2019	●	●
Press Freedom Index (best 0–100 worst)	54.0	2019	●	↓

SDG17 – Partnerships for the Goals

	Value	Year	Rating	Trend
Government spending on health and education (% of GDP)	7.2	2015	●	↑
For high-income and all OECD DAC countries: International concessional public finance, including official development assistance (% of GNI)	NA	NA	●	●
Other countries: Government revenue excluding grants (% of GDP)	13.5	2004	●	●
Corporate Tax Haven Score (best 0–100 worst) *	0.0	2019	●	●

* Imputed data point

5. Country Profiles

TANZANIA

▼ OVERALL PERFORMANCE

Index score

56.6

Regional average score

53.1

SDG Global rank **131** (OF 166)

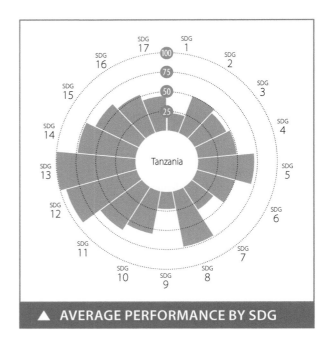

▲ AVERAGE PERFORMANCE BY SDG

▼ SPILLOVER INDEX

100 (best) to 0 (worst)

▼ CURRENT ASSESSMENT – SDG DASHBOARD

■ Major challenges   ■ Significant challenges   ■ Challenges remain   ■ SDG achieved   ■ Information unavailable

▼ SDG TRENDS

↓ Decreasing   → Stagnating   ↗ Moderately improving   ↑ On track or maintaining SDG achievement   ● Information unavailable

Notes: The full title of Goal 2 "Zero Hunger" is "End hunger, achieve food security and improved nutrition and promote sustainable agriculture".
The full title of each SDG is available here: https://sustainabledevelopment.un.org/topics/sustainabledevelopmentgoals

SDG1 – No Poverty

	Value	Year	Rating	Trend
Poverty headcount ratio at $1.90/day (%)	38.6	2020	●	→
Poverty headcount ratio at $3.20/day (%)	70.6	2020	●	→

SDG2 – Zero Hunger

	Value	Year	Rating	Trend
Prevalence of undernourishment (%)	30.7	2017	●	→
Prevalence of stunting in children under 5 years of age (%)	34.4	2015	●	↗
Prevalence of wasting in children under 5 years of age (%)	4.5	2015	●	↑
Prevalence of obesity, BMI ≥ 30 (% of adult population)	8.4	2016	●	↑
Human Trophic Level (best 2–3 worst)	2.1	2017	●	↑
Cereal yield (tonnes per hectare of harvested land)	1.5	2017	●	↓
Sustainable Nitrogen Management Index (best 0–1.41 worst)	0.8	2015	●	→

SDG3 – Good Health and Well-Being

	Value	Year	Rating	Trend
Maternal mortality rate (per 100,000 live births)	524	2017	●	↗
Neonatal mortality rate (per 1,000 live births)	21.3	2018	●	↗
Mortality rate, under-5 (per 1,000 live births)	53.0	2018	●	↗
Incidence of tuberculosis (per 100,000 population)	253.0	2018	●	↗
New HIV infections (per 1,000 uninfected population)	1.4	2018	●	↑
Age-standardized death rate due to cardiovascular disease, cancer, diabetes, or chronic respiratory disease in adults aged 30–70 years (%)	17.9	2016	○	→
Age-standardized death rate attributable to household air pollution and ambient air pollution (per 100,000 population)	139	2016	●	●
Traffic deaths (per 100,000 population)	29.2	2016	●	↗
Life expectancy at birth (years)	63.9	2016	●	↗
Adolescent fertility rate (births per 1,000 adolescent females aged 15 to 19)	118.4	2017	●	→
Births attended by skilled health personnel (%)	63.7	2016	●	→
Percentage of surviving infants who received 2 WHO-recommended vaccines (%)	98	2018	●	↑
Universal health coverage (UHC) index of service coverage (worst 0–100 best)	43.0	2017	●	→
Subjective well-being (average ladder score, worst 0–10 best)	3.6	2019	●	↓

SDG4 – Quality Education

	Value	Year	Rating	Trend
Net primary enrollment rate (%)	81.3	2018	●	↓
Lower secondary completion rate (%)	29.6	2018	●	↓
Literacy rate (% of population aged 15 to 24)	85.8	2015	●	●

SDG5 – Gender Equality

	Value	Year	Rating	Trend
Demand for family planning satisfied by modern methods (% of females aged 15 to 49 who are married or in unions)	54.0	2016	●	↗
Ratio of female-to-male mean years of education received (%)	87.5	2018	○	↗
Ratio of female-to-male labor force participation rate (%)	90.9	2019	●	↑
Seats held by women in national parliament (%)	36.9	2020	○	↗

SDG6 – Clean Water and Sanitation

	Value	Year	Rating	Trend
Population using at least basic drinking water services (%)	56.7	2017	●	↗
Population using at least basic sanitation services (%)	29.9	2017	●	→
Freshwater withdrawal (% of available freshwater resources)	13.0	2000	●	●
Anthropogenic wastewater that receives treatment (%)	1.4	2018	●	●
Scarce water consumption embodied in imports (m³/capita)	0.6	2013	●	↑

SDG7 – Affordable and Clean Energy

	Value	Year	Rating	Trend
Population with access to electricity (%)	32.8	2017	●	↗
Population with access to clean fuels and technology for cooking (%)	2.2	2016	●	→
CO$_2$ emissions from fuel combustion for electricity and heating per total electricity output (MtCO$_2$/TWh)	1.3	2017	●	↑

SDG8 – Decent Work and Economic Growth

	Value	Year	Rating	Trend
Adjusted GDP growth (%)	-3.0	2018	●	●
Victims of modern slavery (per 1,000 population)	6.2	2018	○	●
Adults with an account at a bank or other financial institution or with a mobile-money-service provider (% of population aged 15 or over)	46.8	2017	●	↗
Unemployment rate (% of total labor force)	2.0	2019	●	↑
Fatal work-related accidents embodied in imports (per 100,000 population)	0.1	2010	●	↑

SDG9 – Industry, Innovation and Infrastructure

	Value	Year	Rating	Trend
Population using the internet (%)	25.0	2017	●	↑
Mobile broadband subscriptions (per 100 population)	9.1	2018	●	↓
Logistics Performance Index: Quality of trade and transport-related infrastructure (worst 1–5 best)	2.8	2016	○	●
The Times Higher Education Universities Ranking: Average score of top 3 universities (worst 0–100 best)	16.4	2020	○	●
Scientific and technical journal articles (per 1,000 population)	0.0	2018	●	→
Expenditure on research and development (% of GDP)	0.5	2013	●	●

SDG10 – Reduced Inequalities

	Value	Year	Rating	Trend
Gini coefficient adjusted for top income	43.0	2011	●	●

SDG11 – Sustainable Cities and Communities

	Value	Year	Rating	Trend
Annual mean concentration of particulate matter of less than 2.5 microns in diameter (PM2.5) (μg/m³)	29.1	2017	●	↓
Access to improved water source, piped (% of urban population)	58.8	2017	●	↓
Satisfaction with public transport (%)	62.9	2019	○	↑

SDG12 – Responsible Consumption and Production

	Value	Year	Rating	Trend
Municipal solid waste (kg/capita/day)	1.3	2012	○	●
Electronic waste (kg/capita)	0.8	2016	●	●
Production-based SO$_2$ emissions (kg/capita)	2.8	2012	●	●
SO$_2$ emissions embodied in imports (kg/capita)	0.3	2012	●	●
Production-based nitrogen emissions (kg/capita)	10.6	2010	●	●
Nitrogen emissions embodied in imports (kg/capita)	0.4	2010	●	●

SDG13 – Climate Action

	Value	Year	Rating	Trend
Energy-related CO$_2$ emissions (tCO$_2$/capita)	0.2	2017	●	↑
CO$_2$ emissions embodied in imports (tCO$_2$/capita)	0.0	2015	●	↑
CO$_2$ emissions embodied in fossil fuel exports (kg/capita)	1.9	2018	●	↑

SDG14 – Life Below Water

	Value	Year	Rating	Trend
Mean area that is protected in marine sites important to biodiversity (%)	55.7	2018	●	↑
Ocean Health Index: Clean Waters score (worst 0–100 best)	50.5	2019	●	→
Fish caught from overexploited or collapsed stocks (% of total catch)	17.0	2014	●	↑
Fish caught by trawling (%)	2.8	2014	●	↑
Marine biodiversity threats embodied in imports (per million population)	0.0	2018	●	●

SDG15 – Life on Land

	Value	Year	Rating	Trend
Mean area that is protected in terrestrial sites important to biodiversity (%)	64.0	2018	●	↑
Mean area that is protected in freshwater sites important to biodiversity (%)	43.1	2018	○	→
Red List Index of species survival (worst 0–1 best)	0.7	2019	●	↓
Permanent deforestation (% of forest area, 5-year average)	0.3	2018	●	●
Terrestrial and freshwater biodiversity threats embodied in imports (per million population)	0.0	2018	●	●

SDG16 – Peace, Justice and Strong Institutions

	Value	Year	Rating	Trend
Homicides (per 100,000 population)	6.2	2016	●	↑
Unsentenced detainees (% of prison population)	48.6	2015	●	●
Percentage of population who feel safe walking alone at night in the city or area where they live (%)	70.7	2019	○	↑
Property Rights (worst 1–7 best)	4.2	2019	●	●
Birth registrations with civil authority (% of children under age 5)	26.4	2018	●	●
Corruption Perception Index (worst 0–100 best)	37	2019	●	↗
Children involved in child labor (% of population aged 5 to 14)	28.8	2016	●	●
Exports of major conventional weapons (TIV constant million USD per 100,000 population) *	0.0	2019	●	●
Press Freedom Index (best 0–100 worst)	36.3	2019	○	↓

SDG17 – Partnerships for the Goals

	Value	Year	Rating	Trend
Government spending on health and education (% of GDP)	4.6	2014	●	●
For high-income and all OECD DAC countries: International concessional public finance, including official development assistance (% of GNI)	NA	NA	●	●
Other countries: Government revenue excluding grants (% of GDP)	13.7	2018	●	→
Corporate Tax Haven Score (best 0–100 worst)	46.1	2019	●	●

* Imputed data point

5. Country Profiles

▼ OVERALL PERFORMANCE

Index score

74.5

Regional average score

67.2

SDG Global rank **41** (OF 166)

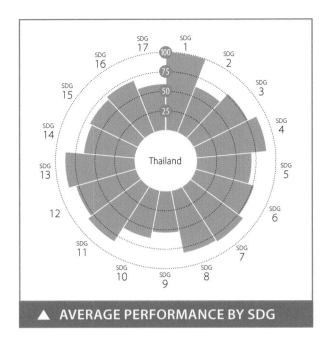

▲ AVERAGE PERFORMANCE BY SDG

▼ SPILLOVER INDEX

100 (best) to 0 (worst)

▼ CURRENT ASSESSMENT – SDG DASHBOARD

■ Major challenges   ■ Significant challenges   ■ Challenges remain   ■ SDG achieved   ■ Information unavailable

▼ SDG TRENDS

↓ Decreasing   → Stagnating   ↗ Moderately improving   ↑ On track or maintaining SDG achievement   ● Information unavailable

Notes: The full title of Goal 2 "Zero Hunger" is "End hunger, achieve food security and improved nutrition and promote sustainable agriculture".
The full title of each SDG is available here: https://sustainabledevelopment.un.org/topics/sustainabledevelopmentgoals

SDG1 – No Poverty

Indicator	Value	Year	Rating	Trend
Poverty headcount ratio at $1.90/day (%)	0.0	2020	●	↑
Poverty headcount ratio at $3.20/day (%)	0.0	2020	●	↑

SDG2 – Zero Hunger

Indicator	Value	Year	Rating	Trend
Prevalence of undernourishment (%)	7.8	2017	○	↑
Prevalence of stunting in children under 5 years of age (%)	10.5	2016	○	→
Prevalence of wasting in children under 5 years of age (%)	5.4	2016	●	→
Prevalence of obesity, BMI ≥ 30 (% of adult population)	10.0	2016	●	↑
Human Trophic Level (best 2–3 worst)	2.2	2017	●	↑
Cereal yield (tonnes per hectare of harvested land)	3.2	2017	●	↑
Sustainable Nitrogen Management Index (best 0–1.41 worst)	0.9	2015	●	↓

SDG3 – Good Health and Well-Being

Indicator	Value	Year	Rating	Trend
Maternal mortality rate (per 100,000 live births)	37	2017	●	↑
Neonatal mortality rate (per 1,000 live births)	5.0	2018	●	↑
Mortality rate, under-5 (per 1,000 live births)	9.1	2018	●	↑
Incidence of tuberculosis (per 100,000 population)	153.0	2018	●	→
New HIV infections (per 1,000 uninfected population)	0.1	2018	●	↑
Age-standardized death rate due to cardiovascular disease, cancer, diabetes, or chronic respiratory disease in adults aged 30–70 years (%)	14.5	2016	●	↑
Age-standardized death rate attributable to household air pollution and ambient air pollution (per 100,000 population)	61	2016	○	●
Traffic deaths (per 100,000 population)	32.7	2016	●	↗
Life expectancy at birth (years)	75.5	2016	○	↗
Adolescent fertility rate (births per 1,000 adolescent females aged 15 to 19)	44.9	2017	●	↗
Births attended by skilled health personnel (%)	99.1	2016	●	↑
Percentage of surviving infants who received 2 WHO-recommended vaccines (%)	96	2018	●	↑
Universal health coverage (UHC) index of service coverage (worst 0–100 best)	80.0	2017	●	↑
Subjective well-being (average ladder score, worst 0–10 best)	6.0	2019	●	↑

SDG4 – Quality Education

Indicator	Value	Year	Rating	Trend
Net primary enrollment rate (%)	98.1	2009	●	●
Lower secondary completion rate (%)	78.4	2017	●	↓
Literacy rate (% of population aged 15 to 24)	98.1	2018	●	●

SDG5 – Gender Equality

Indicator	Value	Year	Rating	Trend
Demand for family planning satisfied by modern methods (% of females aged 15 to 49 who are married or in unions)	89.2	2016	●	↑
Ratio of female-to-male mean years of education received (%)	93.8	2018	○	→
Ratio of female-to-male labor force participation rate (%)	78.0	2019	●	↑
Seats held by women in national parliament (%)	15.8	2020	●	↗

SDG6 – Clean Water and Sanitation

Indicator	Value	Year	Rating	Trend
Population using at least basic drinking water services (%)	99.9	2017	●	↑
Population using at least basic sanitation services (%)	98.8	2017	●	↑
Freshwater withdrawal (% of available freshwater resources)	23.0	2005	●	●
Anthropogenic wastewater that receives treatment (%)	2.0	2018	●	●
Scarce water consumption embodied in imports (m³/capita)	3.9	2013	●	↑

SDG7 – Affordable and Clean Energy

Indicator	Value	Year	Rating	Trend
Population with access to electricity (%)	100.0	2017	●	↑
Population with access to clean fuels and technology for cooking (%)	74.4	2016	○	→
CO₂ emissions from fuel combustion for electricity and heating per total electricity output (MtCO₂/TWh)	1.4	2017	●	↑

SDG8 – Decent Work and Economic Growth

Indicator	Value	Year	Rating	Trend
Adjusted GDP growth (%)	0.1	2018	●	●
Victims of modern slavery (per 1,000 population)	8.9	2018	●	●
Adults with an account at a bank or other financial institution or with a mobile-money-service provider (% of population aged 15 or over)	81.6	2017	●	↑
Unemployment rate (% of total labor force)	0.8	2019	●	↑
Fatal work-related accidents embodied in imports (per 100,000 population)	0.3	2010	●	↑

SDG9 – Industry, Innovation and Infrastructure

Indicator	Value	Year	Rating	Trend
Population using the internet (%)	56.8	2018	●	↑
Mobile broadband subscriptions (per 100 population)	104.7	2018	●	↑
Logistics Performance Index: Quality of trade and transport-related infrastructure (worst 1–5 best)	3.1	2018	●	↑
The Times Higher Education Universities Ranking: Average score of top 3 universities (worst 0–100 best)	29.6	2020	○	●
Scientific and technical journal articles (per 1,000 population)	0.2	2018	●	→
Expenditure on research and development (% of GDP)	0.8	2016	●	↑

SDG10 – Reduced Inequalities

Indicator	Value	Year	Rating	Trend
Gini coefficient adjusted for top income	40.9	2017	●	●

SDG11 – Sustainable Cities and Communities

Indicator	Value	Year	Rating	Trend
Annual mean concentration of particulate matter of less than 2.5 microns in diameter (PM2.5) (µg/m³)	26.3	2017	●	↗
Access to improved water source, piped (% of urban population)	86.8	2017	○	↑
Satisfaction with public transport (%)	75.7	2019	●	↑

SDG12 – Responsible Consumption and Production

Indicator	Value	Year	Rating	Trend
Municipal solid waste (kg/capita/day)	2.1	2015	●	●
Electronic waste (kg/capita)	7.4	2016	○	●
Production-based SO₂ emissions (kg/capita)	28.4	2012	●	●
SO₂ emissions embodied in imports (kg/capita)	3.3	2012	●	●
Production-based nitrogen emissions (kg/capita)	23.8	2010	○	●
Nitrogen emissions embodied in imports (kg/capita)	1.8	2010	●	●

SDG13 – Climate Action

Indicator	Value	Year	Rating	Trend
Energy-related CO₂ emissions (tCO₂/capita)	4.6	2017	●	→
CO₂ emissions embodied in imports (tCO₂/capita)	0.6	2015	○	↑
CO₂ emissions embodied in fossil fuel exports (kg/capita)	1.7	2018	●	●

SDG14 – Life Below Water

Indicator	Value	Year	Rating	Trend
Mean area that is protected in marine sites important to biodiversity (%)	60.4	2018	●	↑
Ocean Health Index: Clean Waters score (worst 0–100 best)	60.2	2019	●	↑
Fish caught from overexploited or collapsed stocks (% of total catch)	55.6	2014	●	↓
Fish caught by trawling (%)	17.7	2014	○	↓
Marine biodiversity threats embodied in imports (per million population)	0.1	2018	●	●

SDG15 – Life on Land

Indicator	Value	Year	Rating	Trend
Mean area that is protected in terrestrial sites important to biodiversity (%)	71.3	2018	●	↑
Mean area that is protected in freshwater sites important to biodiversity (%)	43.6	2018	○	→
Red List Index of species survival (worst 0–1 best)	0.8	2019	●	↓
Permanent deforestation (% of forest area, 5-year average)	0.2	2018	●	●
Terrestrial and freshwater biodiversity threats embodied in imports (per million population)	1.0	2018	○	●

SDG16 – Peace, Justice and Strong Institutions

Indicator	Value	Year	Rating	Trend
Homicides (per 100,000 population)	3.2	2016	●	↑
Unsentenced detainees (% of prison population)	17.2	2018	●	↑
Percentage of population who feel safe walking alone at night in the city or area where they live (%)	63.9	2019	○	↓
Property Rights (worst 1–7 best)	4.3	2019	●	●
Birth registrations with civil authority (% of children under age 5)	99.5	2018	●	●
Corruption Perception Index (worst 0–100 best)	36	2019	●	↓
Children involved in child labor (% of population aged 5 to 14)	8.3	2016	●	●
Exports of major conventional weapons (TIV constant million USD per 100,000 population)	0.0	2019	●	●
Press Freedom Index (best 0–100 worst)	44.1	2019	●	→

SDG17 – Partnerships for the Goals

Indicator	Value	Year	Rating	Trend
Government spending on health and education (% of GDP)	6.8	2013	●	●
For high-income and all OECD DAC countries: International concessional public finance, including official development assistance (% of GNI)	NA	NA	●	●
Other countries: Government revenue excluding grants (% of GDP)	19.5	2018	●	↓
Corporate Tax Haven Score (best 0–100 worst)	* 0.0	2019	●	●

* Imputed data point

5. Country Profiles

▼ OVERALL PERFORMANCE

Index score

na

Regional average score

67.2

SDG Global rank NA (OF 166)

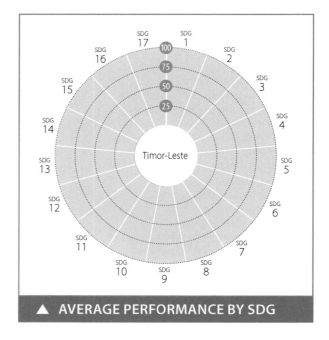

▲ AVERAGE PERFORMANCE BY SDG

▼ SPILLOVER INDEX

100 (best) to 0 (worst)

▼ CURRENT ASSESSMENT – SDG DASHBOARD

■ Major challenges ■ Significant challenges ■ Challenges remain ■ SDG achieved ■ Information unavailable

▼ SDG TRENDS

1 NO POVERTY	2 ZERO HUNGER	3 GOOD HEALTH AND WELL-BEING	4 QUALITY EDUCATION	5 GENDER EQUALITY	6 CLEAN WATER AND SANITATION	7 AFFORDABLE AND CLEAN ENERGY	8 DECENT WORK AND ECONOMIC GROWTH	9 INDUSTRY, INNOVATION AND INFRASTRUCTURE
→	↗	↗	↑	→	↗	↗	↑	→

10 REDUCED INEQUALITIES	11 SUSTAINABLE CITIES AND COMMUNITIES	12 RESPONSIBLE CONSUMPTION AND PRODUCTION	13 CLIMATE ACTION	14 LIFE BELOW WATER	15 LIFE ON LAND	16 PEACE, JUSTICE AND STRONG INSTITUTIONS	17 PARTNERSHIPS FOR THE GOALS
●	↗	●	●	→	↓	↑	↑

↓ Decreasing → Stagnating ↗ Moderately improving ↑ On track or maintaining SDG achievement ● Information unavailable

Notes: The full title of Goal 2 "Zero Hunger" is "End hunger, achieve food security and improved nutrition and promote sustainable agriculture".
The full title of each SDG is available here: https://sustainabledevelopment.un.org/topics/sustainabledevelopmentgoals

SDG1 – No Poverty

	Value	Year	Rating	Trend
Poverty headcount ratio at $1.90/day (%)	28.1	2020	●	↗
Poverty headcount ratio at $3.20/day (%)	69.2	2020	●	→

SDG2 – Zero Hunger

	Value	Year	Rating	Trend
Prevalence of undernourishment (%)	24.9	2017	●	→
Prevalence of stunting in children under 5 years of age (%)	50.2	2013	●	→
Prevalence of wasting in children under 5 years of age (%)	11.0	2013	●	↗
Prevalence of obesity, BMI ≥ 30 (% of adult population)	3.8	2016	●	↑
Human Trophic Level (best 2–3 worst)	2.1	2017	●	↑
Cereal yield (tonnes per hectare of harvested land)	2.5	2017	●	↑
Sustainable Nitrogen Management Index (best 0–1.41 worst)	0.9	2015	●	→

SDG3 – Good Health and Well-Being

	Value	Year	Rating	Trend
Maternal mortality rate (per 100,000 live births)	142	2017	●	↑
Neonatal mortality rate (per 1,000 live births)	20.4	2018	●	↗
Mortality rate, under-5 (per 1,000 live births)	45.8	2018	●	↗
Incidence of tuberculosis (per 100,000 population)	498.0	2018	●	→
New HIV infections (per 1,000 uninfected population)	NA	NA	●	●
Age-standardized death rate due to cardiovascular disease, cancer, diabetes, or chronic respiratory disease in adults aged 30–70 years (%)	19.9	2016	●	↑
Age-standardized death rate attributable to household air pollution and ambient air pollution (per 100,000 population)	140	2016	●	●
Traffic deaths (per 100,000 population)	12.7	2016	●	↑
Life expectancy at birth (years)	68.6	2016	●	→
Adolescent fertility rate (births per 1,000 adolescent females aged 15 to 19)	33.8	2017	●	↑
Births attended by skilled health personnel (%)	56.7	2016	●	●
Percentage of surviving infants who received 2 WHO-recommended vaccines (%)	77	2018	●	↑
Universal health coverage (UHC) index of service coverage (worst 0–100 best)	52.0	2017	●	↗
Subjective well-being (average ladder score, worst 0–10 best)	NA	NA	●	●

SDG4 – Quality Education

	Value	Year	Rating	Trend
Net primary enrollment rate (%)	92.3	2018	●	↗
Lower secondary completion rate (%)	90.9	2018	●	↑
Literacy rate (% of population aged 15 to 24)	83.5	2018	●	●

SDG5 – Gender Equality

	Value	Year	Rating	Trend
Demand for family planning satisfied by modern methods (% of females aged 15 to 49 who are married or in unions)	37.4	2016	●	→
Ratio of female-to-male mean years of education received (%)	67.9	2018	●	→
Ratio of female-to-male labor force participation rate (%)	47.4	2019	●	↓
Seats held by women in national parliament (%)	38.5	2020	●	→

SDG6 – Clean Water and Sanitation

	Value	Year	Rating	Trend
Population using at least basic drinking water services (%)	78.3	2017	●	↑
Population using at least basic sanitation services (%)	53.5	2017	●	→
Freshwater withdrawal (% of available freshwater resources)	28.3	2005	●	●
Anthropogenic wastewater that receives treatment (%)	0.3	2018	●	●
Scarce water consumption embodied in imports (m3/capita)	NA	NA	●	●

SDG7 – Affordable and Clean Energy

	Value	Year	Rating	Trend
Population with access to electricity (%)	80.4	2017	●	↑
Population with access to clean fuels and technology for cooking (%)	6.9	2016	●	→
CO2 emissions from fuel combustion for electricity and heating per total electricity output (MtCO2/TWh)	NA	NA	●	●

SDG8 – Decent Work and Economic Growth

	Value	Year	Rating	Trend
Adjusted GDP growth (%)	-8.5	2018	●	●
Victims of modern slavery (per 1,000 population)	7.7	2018	●	●
Adults with an account at a bank or other financial institution or with a mobile-money-service provider (% of population aged 15 or over)	NA	NA	●	●
Unemployment rate (% of total labor force)	4.5	2019	●	↑
Fatal work-related accidents embodied in imports (per 100,000 population)	NA	NA	●	●

SDG9 – Industry, Innovation and Infrastructure

	Value	Year	Rating	Trend
Population using the internet (%)	27.5	2017	●	↗
Mobile broadband subscriptions (per 100 population)	31.6	2018	●	↓
Logistics Performance Index: Quality of trade and transport-related infrastructure (worst 1–5 best)	NA	NA	●	●
The Times Higher Education Universities Ranking: Average score of top 3 universities (worst 0–100 best) *	0.0	2020	●	●
Scientific and technical journal articles (per 1,000 population)	0.0	2018	●	→
Expenditure on research and development (% of GDP)	NA	NA	●	●

SDG10 – Reduced Inequalities

	Value	Year	Rating	Trend
Gini coefficient adjusted for top income	30.9	2014	●	●

SDG11 – Sustainable Cities and Communities

	Value	Year	Rating	Trend
Annual mean concentration of particulate matter of less than 2.5 microns in diameter (PM2.5) (μg/m3)	19.3	2017	●	↗
Access to improved water source, piped (% of urban population)	82.7	2017	●	↑
Satisfaction with public transport (%)	NA	NA	●	●

SDG12 – Responsible Consumption and Production

	Value	Year	Rating	Trend
Municipal solid waste (kg/capita/day)	0.4	2016	●	●
Electronic waste (kg/capita)	3.0	2016	●	●
Production-based SO2 emissions (kg/capita)	NA	NA	●	●
SO2 emissions embodied in imports (kg/capita)	NA	NA	●	●
Production-based nitrogen emissions (kg/capita)	NA	NA	●	●
Nitrogen emissions embodied in imports (kg/capita)	NA	NA	●	●

SDG13 – Climate Action

	Value	Year	Rating	Trend
Energy-related CO2 emissions (tCO2/capita)	0.4	2017	●	↑
CO2 emissions embodied in imports (tCO2/capita)	NA	NA	●	●
CO2 emissions embodied in fossil fuel exports (kg/capita)	NA	NA	●	●

SDG14 – Life Below Water

	Value	Year	Rating	Trend
Mean area that is protected in marine sites important to biodiversity (%)	18.8	2018	●	→
Ocean Health Index: Clean Waters score (worst 0–100 best)	53.3	2019	●	→
Fish caught from overexploited or collapsed stocks (% of total catch)	10.0	2014	●	↑
Fish caught by trawling (%)	NA	NA	●	●
Marine biodiversity threats embodied in imports (per million population)	NA	NA	●	●

SDG15 – Life on Land

	Value	Year	Rating	Trend
Mean area that is protected in terrestrial sites important to biodiversity (%)	33.6	2018	●	→
Mean area that is protected in freshwater sites important to biodiversity (%)	NA	NA	●	●
Red List Index of species survival (worst 0–1 best)	0.9	2019	●	↓
Permanent deforestation (% of forest area, 5-year average)	0.1	2018	●	●
Terrestrial and freshwater biodiversity threats embodied in imports (per million population)	NA	NA	●	●

SDG16 – Peace, Justice and Strong Institutions

	Value	Year	Rating	Trend
Homicides (per 100,000 population)	3.9	2015	●	●
Unsentenced detainees (% of prison population)	23.8	2018	●	↑
Percentage of population who feel safe walking alone at night in the city or area where they live (%)	NA	NA	●	●
Property Rights (worst 1–7 best)	NA	NA	●	●
Birth registrations with civil authority (% of children under age 5)	60.4	2018	●	●
Corruption Perception Index (worst 0–100 best)	38	2019	●	↑
Children involved in child labor (% of population aged 5 to 14)	4.2	2016	●	●
Exports of major conventional weapons (TIV constant million USD per 100,000 population) *	0.0	2019	●	●
Press Freedom Index (best 0–100 worst)	29.9	2019	●	↑

SDG17 – Partnerships for the Goals

	Value	Year	Rating	Trend
Government spending on health and education (% of GDP)	7.6	2016	●	↑
For high-income and all OECD DAC countries: International concessional public finance, including official development assistance (% of GNI)	NA	NA	●	●
Other countries: Government revenue excluding grants (% of GDP)	38.4	2017	●	↑
Corporate Tax Haven Score (best 0–100 worst) *	0.0	2019	●	●

* Imputed data point

5. Country Profiles

TOGO

▼ OVERALL PERFORMANCE

Index score

52.7

Regional average score

53.1

SDG Global rank 147 (OF 166)

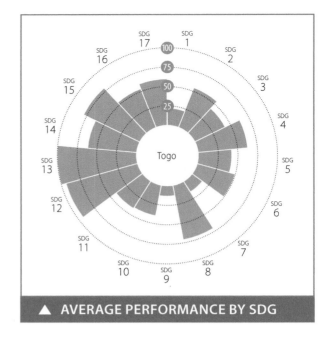

▲ AVERAGE PERFORMANCE BY SDG

▼ SPILLOVER INDEX

100 (best) to 0 (worst)

▼ CURRENT ASSESSMENT – SDG DASHBOARD

■ Major challenges   ■ Significant challenges   ■ Challenges remain   ■ SDG achieved   ▓ Information unavailable

▼ SDG TRENDS

↓ Decreasing   → Stagnating   ↗ Moderately improving   ↑ On track or maintaining SDG achievement   ● Information unavailable

Notes: The full title of Goal 2 "Zero Hunger" is "End hunger, achieve food security and improved nutrition and promote sustainable agriculture".
The full title of each SDG is available here: https://sustainabledevelopment.un.org/topics/sustainabledevelopmentgoals

SDG1 – No Poverty

Indicator	Value	Year	Rating	Trend
Poverty headcount ratio at $1.90/day (%)	41.0	2020	●	→
Poverty headcount ratio at $3.20/day (%)	65.5	2020	●	→

SDG2 – Zero Hunger

Indicator	Value	Year	Rating	Trend
Prevalence of undernourishment (%)	16.1	2017	●	↗
Prevalence of stunting in children under 5 years of age (%)	27.5	2014	●	↗
Prevalence of wasting in children under 5 years of age (%)	6.7	2014	◐	↓
Prevalence of obesity, BMI ≥ 30 (% of adult population)	8.4	2016	●	↑
Human Trophic Level (best 2–3 worst)	2.1	2017	●	↑
Cereal yield (tonnes per hectare of harvested land)	1.1	2017	●	↓
Sustainable Nitrogen Management Index (best 0–1.41 worst)	0.9	2015	●	→

SDG3 – Good Health and Well-Being

Indicator	Value	Year	Rating	Trend
Maternal mortality rate (per 100,000 live births)	396	2017	●	→
Neonatal mortality rate (per 1,000 live births)	24.9	2018	●	→
Mortality rate, under-5 (per 1,000 live births)	69.8	2018	●	↗
Incidence of tuberculosis (per 100,000 population)	36.0	2018	◐	↑
New HIV infections (per 1,000 uninfected population)	0.7	2018	◐	↑
Age-standardized death rate due to cardiovascular disease, cancer, diabetes, or chronic respiratory disease in adults aged 30–70 years (%)	23.6	2016	●	→
Age-standardized death rate attributable to household air pollution and ambient air pollution (per 100,000 population)	250	2016	●	●
Traffic deaths (per 100,000 population)	29.2	2016	●	→
Life expectancy at birth (years)	60.6	2016	●	→
Adolescent fertility rate (births per 1,000 adolescent females aged 15 to 19)	89.1	2017	●	→
Births attended by skilled health personnel (%)	44.6	2014	●	●
Percentage of surviving infants who received 2 WHO-recommended vaccines (%)	85	2018	◐	→
Universal health coverage (UHC) index of service coverage (worst 0–100 best)	43.0	2017	●	↗
Subjective well-being (average ladder score, worst 0–10 best)	4.2	2019	●	↗

SDG4 – Quality Education

Indicator	Value	Year	Rating	Trend
Net primary enrollment rate (%)	90.7	2018	◐	→
Lower secondary completion rate (%)	47.9	2018	●	↗
Literacy rate (% of population aged 15 to 24)	84.3	2015	●	●

SDG5 – Gender Equality

Indicator	Value	Year	Rating	Trend
Demand for family planning satisfied by modern methods (% of females aged 15 to 49 who are married or in unions)	37.4	2014	●	→
Ratio of female-to-male mean years of education received (%)	50.0	2018	●	↓
Ratio of female-to-male labor force participation rate (%)	95.6	2019	●	↑
Seats held by women in national parliament (%)	18.7	2020	●	→

SDG6 – Clean Water and Sanitation

Indicator	Value	Year	Rating	Trend
Population using at least basic drinking water services (%)	65.1	2017	●	→
Population using at least basic sanitation services (%)	16.1	2017	●	→
Freshwater withdrawal (% of available freshwater resources)	2.6	2000	●	●
Anthropogenic wastewater that receives treatment (%)	0.0	2018	●	●
Scarce water consumption embodied in imports (m3/capita)	0.4	2013	●	↑

SDG7 – Affordable and Clean Energy

Indicator	Value	Year	Rating	Trend
Population with access to electricity (%)	48.0	2017	●	→
Population with access to clean fuels and technology for cooking (%)	6.7	2016	●	→
CO_2 emissions from fuel combustion for electricity and heating per total electricity output (MtCO2/TWh)	8.9	2017	●	↑

SDG8 – Decent Work and Economic Growth

Indicator	Value	Year	Rating	Trend
Adjusted GDP growth (%)	-4.6	2018	●	●
Victims of modern slavery (per 1,000 population)	6.8	2018	◐	●
Adults with an account at a bank or other financial institution or with a mobile-money-service provider (% of population aged 15 or over)	45.3	2017	●	↑
Unemployment rate (% of total labor force)	2.0	2019	●	↑
Fatal work-related accidents embodied in imports (per 100,000 population)	0.0	2010	●	↑

SDG9 – Industry, Innovation and Infrastructure

Indicator	Value	Year	Rating	Trend
Population using the internet (%)	12.4	2017	●	→
Mobile broadband subscriptions (per 100 population)	32.0	2018	●	↑
Logistics Performance Index: Quality of trade and transport-related infrastructure (worst 1–5 best)	2.2	2018	●	↗
The Times Higher Education Universities Ranking: Average score of top 3 universities (worst 0–100 best) *	0.0	2020	●	●
Scientific and technical journal articles (per 1,000 population)	0.0	2018	●	→
Expenditure on research and development (% of GDP)	0.3	2014	●	●

SDG10 – Reduced Inequalities

Indicator	Value	Year	Rating	Trend
Gini coefficient adjusted for top income	48.9	2015	●	●

SDG11 – Sustainable Cities and Communities

Indicator	Value	Year	Rating	Trend
Annual mean concentration of particulate matter of less than 2.5 microns in diameter (PM2.5) ($\mu g/m^3$)	35.7	2017	●	↓
Access to improved water source, piped (% of urban population)	44.7	2017	●	↓
Satisfaction with public transport (%)	32.4	2019	●	→

SDG12 – Responsible Consumption and Production

Indicator	Value	Year	Rating	Trend
Municipal solid waste (kg/capita/day)	0.9	2014	●	●
Electronic waste (kg/capita)	0.9	2016	●	●
Production-based SO_2 emissions (kg/capita)	19.0	2012	●	●
SO_2 emissions embodied in imports (kg/capita)	0.6	2012	●	●
Production-based nitrogen emissions (kg/capita)	9.9	2010	●	●
Nitrogen emissions embodied in imports (kg/capita)	0.6	2010	●	●

SDG13 – Climate Action

Indicator	Value	Year	Rating	Trend
Energy-related CO_2 emissions (tCO2/capita)	0.3	2017	●	↑
CO_2 emissions embodied in imports (tCO2/capita)	0.0	2015	●	↑
CO_2 emissions embodied in fossil fuel exports (kg/capita)	0.0	2017	●	●

SDG14 – Life Below Water

Indicator	Value	Year	Rating	Trend
Mean area that is protected in marine sites important to biodiversity (%)	NA	NA	●	●
Ocean Health Index: Clean Waters score (worst 0–100 best)	21.4	2019	●	→
Fish caught from overexploited or collapsed stocks (% of total catch)	NA	NA	●	●
Fish caught by trawling (%)	15.4	2014	◐	↓
Marine biodiversity threats embodied in imports (per million population)	0.0	2018	●	●

SDG15 – Life on Land

Indicator	Value	Year	Rating	Trend
Mean area that is protected in terrestrial sites important to biodiversity (%)	97.0	2018	●	↑
Mean area that is protected in freshwater sites important to biodiversity (%)	NA	NA	●	●
Red List Index of species survival (worst 0–1 best)	0.9	2019	◐	→
Permanent deforestation (% of forest area, 5-year average)	0.7	2018	●	●
Terrestrial and freshwater biodiversity threats embodied in imports (per million population)	0.0	2018	●	●

SDG16 – Peace, Justice and Strong Institutions

Indicator	Value	Year	Rating	Trend
Homicides (per 100,000 population) *	9.0	2015	●	●
Unsentenced detainees (% of prison population)	64.6	2018	●	↓
Percentage of population who feel safe walking alone at night in the city or area where they live (%)	50.6	2019	●	↓
Property Rights (worst 1–7 best)	NA	NA	●	●
Birth registrations with civil authority (% of children under age 5)	78.1	2018	●	●
Corruption Perception Index (worst 0–100 best)	29	2019	●	↓
Children involved in child labor (% of population aged 5 to 14)	27.9	2016	●	●
Exports of major conventional weapons (TIV constant million USD per 100,000 population) *	0.0	2019	●	●
Press Freedom Index (best 0–100 worst)	29.7	2019	●	↑

SDG17 – Partnerships for the Goals

Indicator	Value	Year	Rating	Trend
Government spending on health and education (% of GDP)	6.4	2016	●	↗
For high-income and all OECD DAC countries: International concessional public finance, including official development assistance (% of GNI)	NA	NA	●	●
Other countries: Government revenue excluding grants (% of GDP)	20.3	2018	●	→
Corporate Tax Haven Score (best 0–100 worst) *	0.0	2019	●	●

* Imputed data point

5. Country Profiles

TONGA

▼ OVERALL PERFORMANCE

Index score

na

Regional average score

49.6

SDG Global rank NA (OF 166)

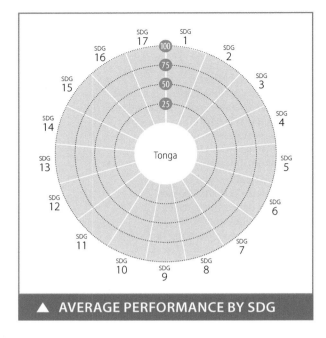

▲ AVERAGE PERFORMANCE BY SDG

▼ SPILLOVER INDEX

100 (best) to 0 (worst)

▼ CURRENT ASSESSMENT – SDG DASHBOARD

■ Major challenges   ■ Significant challenges   ■ Challenges remain   ■ SDG achieved   ■ Information unavailable

▼ SDG TRENDS

↓ Decreasing   → Stagnating   ↗ Moderately improving   ↑ On track or maintaining SDG achievement   • Information unavailable

Notes: The full title of Goal 2 "Zero Hunger" is "End hunger, achieve food security and improved nutrition and promote sustainable agriculture".
The full title of each SDG is available here: https://sustainabledevelopment.un.org/topics/sustainabledevelopmentgoals

TONGA

SDG1 – No Poverty	Value	Year	Rating	Trend
Poverty headcount ratio at $1.90/day (%)	0.1	2020	●	↑
Poverty headcount ratio at $3.20/day (%)	4.2	2020	◐	↑

SDG2 – Zero Hunger	Value	Year	Rating	Trend
Prevalence of undernourishment (%)	NA	NA	●	●
Prevalence of stunting in children under 5 years of age (%)	8.1	2012	◐	↗
Prevalence of wasting in children under 5 years of age (%)	5.2	2012	●	↑
Prevalence of obesity, BMI ≥ 30 (% of adult population)	48.2	2016	●	↓
Human Trophic Level (best 2–3 worst)	NA	NA	●	●
Cereal yield (tonnes per hectare of harvested land)	NA	NA	●	●
Sustainable Nitrogen Management Index (best 0–1.41 worst)	1.0	2015	●	↓

SDG3 – Good Health and Well-Being	Value	Year	Rating	Trend
Maternal mortality rate (per 100,000 live births)	52	2017	●	↑
Neonatal mortality rate (per 1,000 live births)	6.5	2018	●	↑
Mortality rate, under-5 (per 1,000 live births)	15.6	2018	●	↑
Incidence of tuberculosis (per 100,000 population)	10.0	2018	●	↑
New HIV infections (per 1,000 uninfected population)	NA	NA	●	●
Age-standardized death rate due to cardiovascular disease, cancer, diabetes, or chronic respiratory disease in adults aged 30–70 years (%)	23.3	2016	●	→
Age-standardized death rate attributable to household air pollution and ambient air pollution (per 100,000 population)	73	2016	◐	●
Traffic deaths (per 100,000 population)	16.8	2016	●	↓
Life expectancy at birth (years)	73.4	2016	●	→
Adolescent fertility rate (births per 1,000 adolescent females aged 15 to 19)	14.7	2017	●	↑
Births attended by skilled health personnel (%)	95.5	2012	◐	●
Percentage of surviving infants who received 2 WHO-recommended vaccines (%)	81	2018	●	↑
Universal health coverage (UHC) index of service coverage (worst 0–100 best)	58.0	2017	●	→
Subjective well-being (average ladder score, worst 0–10 best)	NA	NA	●	●

SDG4 – Quality Education	Value	Year	Rating	Trend
Net primary enrollment rate (%)	85.9	2015	●	●
Lower secondary completion rate (%)	78.7	2004	●	●
Literacy rate (% of population aged 15 to 24)	99.4	2018	●	●

SDG5 – Gender Equality	Value	Year	Rating	Trend
Demand for family planning satisfied by modern methods (% of females aged 15 to 49 who are married or in unions)	47.9	2012	●	→
Ratio of female-to-male mean years of education received (%)	100.9	2018	●	↑
Ratio of female-to-male labor force participation rate (%)	61.0	2019	◐	→
Seats held by women in national parliament (%)	7.4	2020	●	↗

SDG6 – Clean Water and Sanitation	Value	Year	Rating	Trend
Population using at least basic drinking water services (%)	99.9	2017	●	↑
Population using at least basic sanitation services (%)	93.4	2017	◐	→
Freshwater withdrawal (% of available freshwater resources)	NA	NA	●	●
Anthropogenic wastewater that receives treatment (%)	0.3	2018	●	●
Scarce water consumption embodied in imports (m3/capita)	NA	NA	●	●

SDG7 – Affordable and Clean Energy	Value	Year	Rating	Trend
Population with access to electricity (%)	98.0	2017	◐	↑
Population with access to clean fuels and technology for cooking (%)	59.2	2016	●	→
CO2 emissions from fuel combustion for electricity and heating per total electricity output (MtCO2/TWh)	NA	NA	●	●

SDG8 – Decent Work and Economic Growth	Value	Year	Rating	Trend
Adjusted GDP growth (%)	-3.7	2018	●	●
Victims of modern slavery (per 1,000 population)	NA	NA	●	●
Adults with an account at a bank or other financial institution or with a mobile-money-service provider (% of population aged 15 or over)	NA	NA	●	●
Unemployment rate (% of total labor force)	1.1	2019	●	↑
Fatal work-related accidents embodied in imports (per 100,000 population)	NA	NA	●	●

SDG9 – Industry, Innovation and Infrastructure	Value	Year	Rating	Trend
Population using the internet (%)	41.2	2017	●	↗
Mobile broadband subscriptions (per 100 population)	65.1	2018	◐	↑
Logistics Performance Index: Quality of trade and transport-related infrastructure (worst 1–5 best)	NA	NA	●	●
The Times Higher Education Universities Ranking: Average score of top 3 universities (worst 0–100 best) *	0.0	2020	●	●
Scientific and technical journal articles (per 1,000 population)	0.0	2018	●	→
Expenditure on research and development (% of GDP)	NA	NA	●	●

SDG10 – Reduced Inequalities	Value	Year	Rating	Trend
Gini coefficient adjusted for top income	40.1	2015	●	●

SDG11 – Sustainable Cities and Communities	Value	Year	Rating	Trend
Annual mean concentration of particulate matter of less than 2.5 microns in diameter (PM2.5) (μg/m3)	10.8	2017	◐	↑
Access to improved water source, piped (% of urban population)	99.0	2017	●	↑
Satisfaction with public transport (%)	NA	NA	●	●

SDG12 – Responsible Consumption and Production	Value	Year	Rating	Trend
Municipal solid waste (kg/capita/day)	1.9	2012	●	●
Electronic waste (kg/capita)	2.4	2016	●	●
Production-based SO2 emissions (kg/capita)	NA	NA	●	●
SO2 emissions embodied in imports (kg/capita)	NA	NA	●	●
Production-based nitrogen emissions (kg/capita)	NA	NA	●	●
Nitrogen emissions embodied in imports (kg/capita)	NA	NA	●	●

SDG13 – Climate Action	Value	Year	Rating	Trend
Energy-related CO2 emissions (tCO2/capita)	1.5	2017	●	↑
CO2 emissions embodied in imports (tCO2/capita)	NA	NA	●	●
CO2 emissions embodied in fossil fuel exports (kg/capita) *	0.0	2018	●	●

SDG14 – Life Below Water	Value	Year	Rating	Trend
Mean area that is protected in marine sites important to biodiversity (%)	5.9	2018	●	→
Ocean Health Index: Clean Waters score (worst 0–100 best)	66.9	2019	◐	↑
Fish caught from overexploited or collapsed stocks (% of total catch)	39.8	2014	●	↓
Fish caught by trawling (%)	NA	NA	●	●
Marine biodiversity threats embodied in imports (per million population)	NA	NA	●	●

SDG15 – Life on Land	Value	Year	Rating	Trend
Mean area that is protected in terrestrial sites important to biodiversity (%)	9.3	2018	●	→
Mean area that is protected in freshwater sites important to biodiversity (%)	NA	NA	●	●
Red List Index of species survival (worst 0–1 best)	0.7	2019	●	↓
Permanent deforestation (% of forest area, 5-year average)	NA	NA	●	●
Terrestrial and freshwater biodiversity threats embodied in imports (per million population)	NA	NA	●	●

SDG16 – Peace, Justice and Strong Institutions	Value	Year	Rating	Trend
Homicides (per 100,000 population)	1.0	2012	●	●
Unsentenced detainees (% of prison population)	7.4	2015	●	●
Percentage of population who feel safe walking alone at night in the city or area where they live (%)	NA	NA	●	●
Property Rights (worst 1–7 best)	NA	NA	●	●
Birth registrations with civil authority (% of children under age 5)	93.4	2018	◐	●
Corruption Perception Index (worst 0–100 best)	NA	NA	●	●
Children involved in child labor (% of population aged 5 to 14)	NA	NA	●	●
Exports of major conventional weapons (TIV constant million USD per 100,000 population) *	0.0	2019	●	●
Press Freedom Index (best 0–100 worst)	25.4	2019	●	↑

SDG17 – Partnerships for the Goals	Value	Year	Rating	Trend
Government spending on health and education (% of GDP)	6.3	2004	●	●
For high-income and all OECD DAC countries: International concessional public finance, including official development assistance (% of GNI)	NA	NA	●	●
Other countries: Government revenue excluding grants (% of GDP)	25.6	2017	◐	↑
Corporate Tax Haven Score (best 0–100 worst) *	0.0	2019	●	●

* Imputed data point

5. Country Profiles

TRINIDAD AND TOBAGO Latin America and the Caribbean

OVERALL PERFORMANCE

Index score
65.8

Regional average score
70.4

SDG Global rank 98 (OF 166)

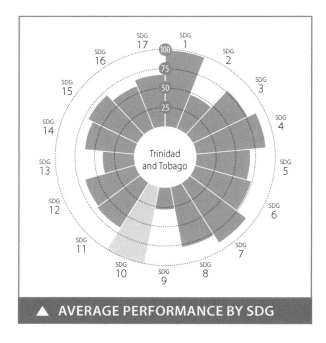

▲ AVERAGE PERFORMANCE BY SDG

SPILLOVER INDEX
100 (best) to 0 (worst)

CURRENT ASSESSMENT – SDG DASHBOARD

■ Major challenges ■ Significant challenges ■ Challenges remain ■ SDG achieved ■ Information unavailable

SDG TRENDS

↓ Decreasing → Stagnating ↗ Moderately improving ↑ On track or maintaining SDG achievement ● Information unavailable

Notes: The full title of Goal 2 "Zero Hunger" is "End hunger, achieve food security and improved nutrition and promote sustainable agriculture".
The full title of each SDG is available here: https://sustainabledevelopment.un.org/topics/sustainabledevelopmentgoals

SDG1 – No Poverty

	Value	Year	Rating	Trend
Poverty headcount ratio at $1.90/day (%)	0.3	2020	●	↑
Poverty headcount ratio at $3.20/day (%)	1.3	2020	●	↑

SDG2 – Zero Hunger

	Value	Year	Rating	Trend
Prevalence of undernourishment (%)	5.5	2017	●	↑
Prevalence of stunting in children under 5 years of age (%)	11.0	2011	●	↑
Prevalence of wasting in children under 5 years of age (%)	6.3	2011	●	↑
Prevalence of obesity, BMI ≥ 30 (% of adult population)	18.6	2016	●	↓
Human Trophic Level (best 2–3 worst)	2.3	2017	●	→
Cereal yield (tonnes per hectare of harvested land)	1.4	2017	●	→
Sustainable Nitrogen Management Index (best 0–1.41 worst)	1.3	2015	●	↓

SDG3 – Good Health and Well-Being

	Value	Year	Rating	Trend
Maternal mortality rate (per 100,000 live births)	67	2017	●	↑
Neonatal mortality rate (per 1,000 live births)	11.7	2018	●	↑
Mortality rate, under-5 (per 1,000 live births)	18.3	2018	●	↑
Incidence of tuberculosis (per 100,000 population)	21.0	2018	●	→
New HIV infections (per 1,000 uninfected population)	NA	NA	●	●
Age-standardized death rate due to cardiovascular disease, cancer, diabetes, or chronic respiratory disease in adults aged 30–70 years (%)	21.3	2016	●	↗
Age-standardized death rate attributable to household air pollution and ambient air pollution (per 100,000 population)	39	2016	●	●
Traffic deaths (per 100,000 population)	12.1	2016	●	↑
Life expectancy at birth (years)	71.8	2016	●	→
Adolescent fertility rate (births per 1,000 adolescent females aged 15 to 19)	30.1	2017	●	↑
Births attended by skilled health personnel (%)	100.0	2015	●	↑
Percentage of surviving infants who received 2 WHO-recommended vaccines (%)	90	2018	●	↑
Universal health coverage (UHC) index of service coverage (worst 0–100 best)	74.0	2017	●	↑
Subjective well-being (average ladder score, worst 0–10 best)	6.2	2017	●	●

SDG4 – Quality Education

	Value	Year	Rating	Trend
Net primary enrollment rate (%)	95.3	2010	●	●
Lower secondary completion rate (%)	80.9	2010	●	●
Literacy rate (% of population aged 15 to 24)	99.6	2010	●	●

SDG5 – Gender Equality

	Value	Year	Rating	Trend
Demand for family planning satisfied by modern methods (% of females aged 15 to 49 who are married or in unions)	58.2	2011	●	→
Ratio of female-to-male mean years of education received (%)	101.8	2018	●	↑
Ratio of female-to-male labor force participation rate (%)	70.9	2019	●	↑
Seats held by women in national parliament (%)	31.0	2020	●	↓

SDG6 – Clean Water and Sanitation

	Value	Year	Rating	Trend
Population using at least basic drinking water services (%)	98.2	2017	●	↑
Population using at least basic sanitation services (%)	93.4	2017	●	→
Freshwater withdrawal (% of available freshwater resources)	20.3	2010	●	●
Anthropogenic wastewater that receives treatment (%)	3.2	2018	●	●
Scarce water consumption embodied in imports (m³/capita)	13.7	2013	●	↑

SDG7 – Affordable and Clean Energy

	Value	Year	Rating	Trend
Population with access to electricity (%)	100.0	2017	●	↑
Population with access to clean fuels and technology for cooking (%)	99.3	2016	●	↑
CO_2 emissions from fuel combustion for electricity and heating per total electricity output (MtCO2/TWh)	1.7	2017	●	↑

SDG8 – Decent Work and Economic Growth

	Value	Year	Rating	Trend
Adjusted GDP growth (%)	-5.9	2018	●	●
Victims of modern slavery (per 1,000 population)	3.0	2018	●	●
Adults with an account at a bank or other financial institution or with a mobile-money-service provider (% of population aged 15 or over)	80.8	2017	●	●
Unemployment rate (% of total labor force)	2.7	2019	●	↑
Fatal work-related accidents embodied in imports (per 100,000 population)	0.6	2010	●	↑

SDG9 – Industry, Innovation and Infrastructure

	Value	Year	Rating	Trend
Population using the internet (%)	77.3	2017	●	↑
Mobile broadband subscriptions (per 100 population)	40.7	2018	●	↗
Logistics Performance Index: Quality of trade and transport-related infrastructure (worst 1–5 best)	2.4	2018	●	●
The Times Higher Education Universities Ranking: Average score of top 3 universities (worst 0–100 best) *	0.0	2020	●	●
Scientific and technical journal articles (per 1,000 population)	0.2	2018	●	→
Expenditure on research and development (% of GDP)	0.1	2016	●	→

SDG10 – Reduced Inequalities

	Value	Year	Rating	Trend
Gini coefficient adjusted for top income	NA	NA	●	●

SDG11 – Sustainable Cities and Communities

	Value	Year	Rating	Trend
Annual mean concentration of particulate matter of less than 2.5 microns in diameter (PM2.5) (µg/m³)	24.1	2017	●	→
Access to improved water source, piped (% of urban population)	NA	NA	●	●
Satisfaction with public transport (%)	56.2	2017	●	●

SDG12 – Responsible Consumption and Production

	Value	Year	Rating	Trend
Municipal solid waste (kg/capita/day)	2.7	2010	●	●
Electronic waste (kg/capita)	15.8	2016	●	●
Production-based SO_2 emissions (kg/capita)	64.7	2012	●	●
SO_2 emissions embodied in imports (kg/capita)	8.1	2012	●	●
Production-based nitrogen emissions (kg/capita)	14.0	2010	●	●
Nitrogen emissions embodied in imports (kg/capita)	6.7	2010	●	●

SDG13 – Climate Action

	Value	Year	Rating	Trend
Energy-related CO_2 emissions (tCO2/capita)	30.4	2017	●	↗
CO_2 emissions embodied in imports (tCO2/capita)	1.3	2015	●	→
CO_2 emissions embodied in fossil fuel exports (kg/capita)	17806.5	2015	●	●

SDG14 – Life Below Water

	Value	Year	Rating	Trend
Mean area that is protected in marine sites important to biodiversity (%)	23.7	2018	●	→
Ocean Health Index: Clean Waters score (worst 0–100 best)	62.3	2019	●	↓
Fish caught from overexploited or collapsed stocks (% of total catch)	26.8	2014	●	↓
Fish caught by trawling (%)	23.0	2014	●	↓
Marine biodiversity threats embodied in imports (per million population)	0.1	2018	●	●

SDG15 – Life on Land

	Value	Year	Rating	Trend
Mean area that is protected in terrestrial sites important to biodiversity (%)	40.7	2018	●	→
Mean area that is protected in freshwater sites important to biodiversity (%)	NA	NA	●	●
Red List Index of species survival (worst 0–1 best)	0.8	2019	●	↓
Permanent deforestation (% of forest area, 5-year average)	0.1	2018	●	●
Terrestrial and freshwater biodiversity threats embodied in imports (per million population)	0.6	2018	●	●

SDG16 – Peace, Justice and Strong Institutions

	Value	Year	Rating	Trend
Homicides (per 100,000 population)	30.9	2015	●	●
Unsentenced detainees (% of prison population)	59.7	2018	●	↓
Percentage of population who feel safe walking alone at night in the city or area where they live (%)	51.7	2017	●	●
Property Rights (worst 1–7 best)	4.3	2019	●	●
Birth registrations with civil authority (% of children under age 5)	96.5	2018	●	●
Corruption Perception Index (worst 0–100 best)	40	2019	●	→
Children involved in child labor (% of population aged 5 to 14)	0.7	2016	●	●
Exports of major conventional weapons (TIV constant million USD per 100,000 population) *	0.0	2019	●	●
Press Freedom Index (best 0–100 worst)	24.7	2019	●	↑

SDG17 – Partnerships for the Goals

	Value	Year	Rating	Trend
Government spending on health and education (% of GDP)	5.1	2003	●	●
For high-income and all OECD DAC countries: International concessional public finance, including official development assistance (% of GNI)	NA	NA	●	●
Other countries: Government revenue excluding grants (% of GDP)	NA	NA	●	●
Corporate Tax Haven Score (best 0–100 worst) *	0.0	2019	●	●

* Imputed data point

5. Country Profiles

▼ OVERALL PERFORMANCE

Index score

71.4

Regional average score

66.3

SDG Global rank 63 (OF 166)

Tunisia

▲ AVERAGE PERFORMANCE BY SDG

▼ SPILLOVER INDEX

100 (best) to 0 (worst)

▼ CURRENT ASSESSMENT – SDG DASHBOARD

■ Major challenges   ■ Significant challenges   ■ Challenges remain   ■ SDG achieved   ■ Information unavailable

▼ SDG TRENDS

1 NO POVERTY	2 ZERO HUNGER	3 GOOD HEALTH AND WELL-BEING	4 QUALITY EDUCATION	5 GENDER EQUALITY	6 CLEAN WATER AND SANITATION	7 AFFORDABLE AND CLEAN ENERGY	8 DECENT WORK AND ECONOMIC GROWTH	9 INDUSTRY, INNOVATION AND INFRASTRUCTURE
↑	→	↗	↑	→	↑	↗	↗	→

10 REDUCED INEQUALITIES	11 SUSTAINABLE CITIES AND COMMUNITIES	12 RESPONSIBLE CONSUMPTION AND PRODUCTION	13 CLIMATE ACTION	14 LIFE BELOW WATER	15 LIFE ON LAND	16 PEACE, JUSTICE AND STRONG INSTITUTIONS	17 PARTNERSHIPS FOR THE GOALS
●	→	●	↑	→	→	→	↑

↓ Decreasing   → Stagnating   ↗ Moderately improving   ↑ On track or maintaining SDG achievement   ● Information unavailable

Notes: The full title of Goal 2 "Zero Hunger" is "End hunger, achieve food security and improved nutrition and promote sustainable agriculture".
The full title of each SDG is available here: https://sustainabledevelopment.un.org/topics/sustainabledevelopmentgoals

SDG1 – No Poverty

	Value	Year	Rating	Trend
Poverty headcount ratio at $1.90/day (%)	0.2	2020	●	↑
Poverty headcount ratio at $3.20/day (%)	2.2	2020	○	↑

SDG2 – Zero Hunger

	Value	Year	Rating	Trend
Prevalence of undernourishment (%)	4.3	2017	●	↑
Prevalence of stunting in children under 5 years of age (%)	10.1	2012	●	↗
Prevalence of wasting in children under 5 years of age (%)	2.8	2012	●	↑
Prevalence of obesity, BMI ≥ 30 (% of adult population)	26.9	2016	●	↓
Human Trophic Level (best 2–3 worst)	2.2	2017	○	→
Cereal yield (tonnes per hectare of harvested land)	1.5	2017	●	↓
Sustainable Nitrogen Management Index (best 0–1.41 worst)	1.0	2015	●	↓

SDG3 – Good Health and Well-Being

	Value	Year	Rating	Trend
Maternal mortality rate (per 100,000 live births)	43	2017	●	↑
Neonatal mortality rate (per 1,000 live births)	11.5	2018	●	↑
Mortality rate, under-5 (per 1,000 live births)	17.0	2018	●	↑
Incidence of tuberculosis (per 100,000 population)	35.0	2018	●	↑
New HIV infections (per 1,000 uninfected population)	0.0	2018	●	↑
Age-standardized death rate due to cardiovascular disease, cancer, diabetes, or chronic respiratory disease in adults aged 30–70 years (%)	16.1	2016	○	↑
Age-standardized death rate attributable to household air pollution and ambient air pollution (per 100,000 population)	56	2016	○	●
Traffic deaths (per 100,000 population)	22.8	2016	●	↗
Life expectancy at birth (years)	76.0	2016	○	↗
Adolescent fertility rate (births per 1,000 adolescent females aged 15 to 19)	7.8	2017	●	↑
Births attended by skilled health personnel (%)	73.6	2012	●	●
Percentage of surviving infants who received 2 WHO-recommended vaccines (%)	96	2018	●	↑
Universal health coverage (UHC) index of service coverage (worst 0–100 best)	70.0	2017	○	↗
Subjective well-being (average ladder score, worst 0–10 best)	4.3	2019	●	↓

SDG4 – Quality Education

	Value	Year	Rating	Trend
Net primary enrollment rate (%)	97.8	2013	●	●
Lower secondary completion rate (%)	77.4	2018	●	↑
Literacy rate (% of population aged 15 to 24)	96.2	2014	●	●

SDG5 – Gender Equality

	Value	Year	Rating	Trend
Demand for family planning satisfied by modern methods (% of females aged 15 to 49 who are married or in unions)	73.2	2012	○	↑
Ratio of female-to-male mean years of education received (%)	81.0	2018	●	→
Ratio of female-to-male labor force participation rate (%)	34.3	2019	●	↓
Seats held by women in national parliament (%)	24.9	2020	●	↓

SDG6 – Clean Water and Sanitation

	Value	Year	Rating	Trend
Population using at least basic drinking water services (%)	96.3	2017	○	↑
Population using at least basic sanitation services (%)	90.9	2017	○	↑
Freshwater withdrawal (% of available freshwater resources)	121.1	2015	●	●
Anthropogenic wastewater that receives treatment (%)	43.0	2018	●	●
Scarce water consumption embodied in imports (m³/capita)	10.1	2013	●	↑

SDG7 – Affordable and Clean Energy

	Value	Year	Rating	Trend
Population with access to electricity (%)	100.0	2017	●	↑
Population with access to clean fuels and technology for cooking (%)	99.1	2016	●	↑
CO₂ emissions from fuel combustion for electricity and heating per total electricity output (MtCO₂/TWh)	1.4	2017	●	→

SDG8 – Decent Work and Economic Growth

	Value	Year	Rating	Trend
Adjusted GDP growth (%)	-3.2	2018	●	●
Victims of modern slavery (per 1,000 population)	2.2	2018	●	●
Adults with an account at a bank or other financial institution or with a mobile-money-service provider (% of population aged 15 or over)	36.9	2017	●	↗
Unemployment rate (% of total labor force)	16.0	2019	●	↓
Fatal work-related accidents embodied in imports (per 100,000 population)	0.3	2010	●	↑

SDG9 – Industry, Innovation and Infrastructure

	Value	Year	Rating	Trend
Population using the internet (%)	64.2	2018	●	↑
Mobile broadband subscriptions (per 100 population)	76.1	2018	●	↑
Logistics Performance Index: Quality of trade and transport-related infrastructure (worst 1–5 best)	2.1	2018	●	↓
The Times Higher Education Universities Ranking: Average score of top 3 universities (worst 0–100 best)	16.4	2020	○	●
Scientific and technical journal articles (per 1,000 population)	0.5	2018	○	↗
Expenditure on research and development (% of GDP)	0.6	2016	●	↓

SDG10 – Reduced Inequalities

	Value	Year	Rating	Trend
Gini coefficient adjusted for top income	40.0	2015	●	●

SDG11 – Sustainable Cities and Communities

	Value	Year	Rating	Trend
Annual mean concentration of particulate matter of less than 2.5 microns in diameter (PM2.5) (µg/m³)	37.7	2017	●	↓
Access to improved water source, piped (% of urban population)	99.0	2017	●	↑
Satisfaction with public transport (%)	42.6	2019	●	→

SDG12 – Responsible Consumption and Production

	Value	Year	Rating	Trend
Municipal solid waste (kg/capita/day)	0.9	2014	●	●
Electronic waste (kg/capita)	5.6	2016	○	●
Production-based SO₂ emissions (kg/capita)	21.1	2012	●	●
SO₂ emissions embodied in imports (kg/capita)	2.5	2012	●	●
Production-based nitrogen emissions (kg/capita)	13.7	2010	●	●
Nitrogen emissions embodied in imports (kg/capita)	2.3	2010	●	●

SDG13 – Climate Action

	Value	Year	Rating	Trend
Energy-related CO₂ emissions (tCO₂/capita)	1.8	2017	●	↑
CO₂ emissions embodied in imports (tCO₂/capita)	0.5	2015	●	↑
CO₂ emissions embodied in fossil fuel exports (kg/capita)	0.0	2017	●	●

SDG14 – Life Below Water

	Value	Year	Rating	Trend
Mean area that is protected in marine sites important to biodiversity (%)	31.1	2018	○	→
Ocean Health Index: Clean Waters score (worst 0–100 best)	49.1	2019	●	→
Fish caught from overexploited or collapsed stocks (% of total catch)	5.1	2014	●	↑
Fish caught by trawling (%)	28.1	2014	●	↓
Marine biodiversity threats embodied in imports (per million population)	0.1	2018	●	●

SDG15 – Life on Land

	Value	Year	Rating	Trend
Mean area that is protected in terrestrial sites important to biodiversity (%)	40.2	2018	○	→
Mean area that is protected in freshwater sites important to biodiversity (%)	43.4	2018	○	→
Red List Index of species survival (worst 0–1 best)	1.0	2019	●	↑
Permanent deforestation (% of forest area, 5-year average)	0.5	2018	●	●
Terrestrial and freshwater biodiversity threats embodied in imports (per million population)	0.3	2018	●	●

SDG16 – Peace, Justice and Strong Institutions

	Value	Year	Rating	Trend
Homicides (per 100,000 population)	3.0	2012	●	●
Unsentenced detainees (% of prison population)	50.9	2018	●	→
Percentage of population who feel safe walking alone at night in the city or area where they live (%)	57.9	2019	●	↓
Property Rights (worst 1–7 best)	4.3	2019	○	●
Birth registrations with civil authority (% of children under age 5)	99.9	2018	●	●
Corruption Perception Index (worst 0–100 best)	43	2019	●	↗
Children involved in child labor (% of population aged 5 to 14)	2.1	2016	●	●
Exports of major conventional weapons (TIV constant million USD per 100,000 population) *	0.0	2019	●	●
Press Freedom Index (best 0–100 worst)	29.6	2019	●	↑

SDG17 – Partnerships for the Goals

	Value	Year	Rating	Trend
Government spending on health and education (% of GDP)	10.6	2015	●	↑
For high-income and all OECD DAC countries: International concessional public finance, including official development assistance (% of GNI)	NA	NA	●	●
Other countries: Government revenue excluding grants (% of GDP)	31.4	2012	●	●
Corporate Tax Haven Score (best 0–100 worst) *	0.0	2019	●	●

* Imputed data point

5. Country Profiles

▼ OVERALL PERFORMANCE

Index score

70.3

Regional average score

77.3

SDG Global rank 70 (OF 166)

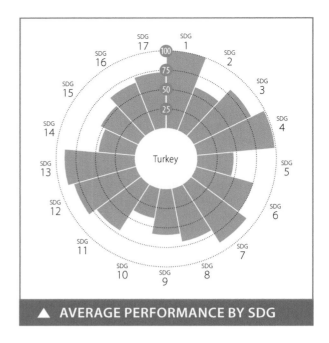

Turkey

▲ AVERAGE PERFORMANCE BY SDG

▼ SPILLOVER INDEX

100 (best) to 0 (worst)

▼ CURRENT ASSESSMENT – SDG DASHBOARD

■ Major challenges   ■ Significant challenges   ■ Challenges remain   ■ SDG achieved   ■ Information unavailable

▼ SDG TRENDS

↓ Decreasing   → Stagnating   ↗ Moderately improving   ↑ On track or maintaining SDG achievement   ● Information unavailable

Notes: The full title of Goal 2 "Zero Hunger" is "End hunger, achieve food security and improved nutrition and promote sustainable agriculture".
The full title of each SDG is available here: https://sustainabledevelopment.un.org/topics/sustainabledevelopmentgoals

SDG1 – No Poverty	Value	Year	Rating	Trend
Poverty headcount ratio at $1.90/day (%)	0.0	2020	●	↑
Poverty headcount ratio at $3.20/day (%)	0.3	2020	●	↑
Poverty rate after taxes and transfers (%)	17.2	2015	●	↓

SDG2 – Zero Hunger				
Prevalence of undernourishment (%)	2.5	2017	●	↑
Prevalence of stunting in children under 5 years of age (%)	9.5	2013	●	↑
Prevalence of wasting in children under 5 years of age (%)	1.7	2013	●	↑
Prevalence of obesity, BMI ≥ 30 (% of adult population)	32.1	2016	●	↓
Human Trophic Level (best 2–3 worst)	2.3	2017	●	↗
Cereal yield (tonnes per hectare of harvested land)	3.3	2017	●	↑
Sustainable Nitrogen Management Index (best 0–1.41 worst)	0.6	2015	●	→
Yield gap closure (% of potential yield)	NA	NA	●	●

SDG3 – Good Health and Well-Being				
Maternal mortality rate (per 100,000 live births)	17	2017	●	↑
Neonatal mortality rate (per 1,000 live births)	5.5	2018	●	↑
Mortality rate, under-5 (per 1,000 live births)	10.6	2018	●	↑
Incidence of tuberculosis (per 100,000 population)	16.0	2018	●	↑
New HIV infections (per 1,000 uninfected population)	NA	NA	●	●
Age-standardized death rate due to cardiovascular disease, cancer, diabetes, or chronic respiratory disease in adults aged 30–70 years (%)	16.1	2016	●	↑
Age-standardized death rate attributable to household air pollution and ambient air pollution (per 100,000 population)	47	2016	●	
Traffic deaths (per 100,000 population)	12.3	2016	●	↓
Life expectancy at birth (years)	76.4	2016	●	↑
Adolescent fertility rate (births per 1,000 adolescent females aged 15 to 19)	26.6	2017	●	↑
Births attended by skilled health personnel (%)	97.4	2014	●	●
Percentage of surviving infants who received 2 WHO-recommended vaccines (%)	96.0	2018	●	↑
Universal health coverage (UHC) index of service coverage (worst 0–100 best)	74.0	2017	●	↑
Subjective well-being (average ladder score, worst 0–10 best)	5.2	2018	●	↓
Gap in life expectancy at birth among regions (years)	2.9	2016	●	●
Gap in self-reported health status by income (percentage points)	13.1	2017	●	↑
Daily smokers (% of population aged 15 and over)	26.5	2016	●	↗

SDG4 – Quality Education				
Net primary enrollment rate (%)	* 99.0	2017	●	↑
Lower secondary completion rate (%)	* 99.0	2017	●	↑
Literacy rate (% of population aged 15 to 24)	99.8	2017	●	●
Participation rate in pre-primary organized learning (% of children aged 4 to 6)	67.6	2017	●	↓
Tertiary educational attainment (% of population aged 25 to 34)	33.3	2018	●	↑
PISA score (worst 0–600 best)	462.7	2018	●	↑
Variation in science performance explained by socio-economic status (%)	11.0	2018	●	↓
Underachievers in science (% of 15-year-olds)	25.2	2018	●	↑
Resilient students in science (% of 15-year-olds)	48.2	2018	●	↑

SDG5 – Gender Equality				
Demand for family planning satisfied by modern methods (% of females aged 15 to 49 who are married or in unions)	59.7	2013	●	→
Ratio of female-to-male mean years of education received (%)	82.1	2018	●	→
Ratio of female-to-male labor force participation rate (%)	46.2	2019	●	→
Seats held by women in national parliament (%)	17.3	2020	●	→
Gender wage gap (% of male median wage)	6.9	2014	●	●
Gender gap in time spent doing unpaid work (minutes/day)	237.5	2015	●	●

SDG6 – Clean Water and Sanitation				
Population using at least basic drinking water services (%)	98.9	2017	●	●
Population using at least basic sanitation services (%)	97.3	2017	●	●
Freshwater withdrawal (% of available freshwater resources)	42.9	2015	●	●
Anthropogenic wastewater that receives treatment (%)	30.4	2018	●	●
Scarce water consumption embodied in imports (m³/capita)	13.2	2013	●	↑
Population using safely managed water services (%)	NA	NA	●	●
Population using safely managed sanitation services (%)	65.2	2017	●	→

SDG7 – Affordable and Clean Energy				
Population with access to electricity (%)	100.0	2017	●	↑
Population with access to clean fuels and technology for cooking (%)	NA	NA	●	●
CO₂ emissions from fuel combustion for electricity and heating per total electricity output (MtCO₂/TWh)	1.3	2017	●	→
Share of renewable energy in total primary energy supply (%)	13.1	2018	●	↑

SDG8 – Decent Work and Economic Growth				
Adjusted GDP growth (%)	-1.5	2018	●	●
Victims of modern slavery (per 1,000 population)	6.5	2018	●	●
Adults with an account at a bank or other financial institution or with a mobile-money-service provider (% of population aged 15 or over)	68.6	2017	●	↑
Fatal work-related accidents embodied in imports (per 100,000 population)	0.2	2010	●	↑
Employment-to-population ratio (%)	50.3	2019	●	→
Youth not in employment, education or training (NEET) (% of population aged 15 to 29)	26.5	2018	●	↗

SDG9 – Industry, Innovation and Infrastructure	Value	Year	Rating	Trend
Population using the internet (%)	71.0	2018	●	↑
Mobile broadband subscriptions (per 100 population)	74.2	2018	●	↑
Logistics Performance Index: Quality of trade and transport-related infrastructure (worst 1–5 best)	3.2	2018	●	↑
The Times Higher Education Universities Ranking: Average score of top 3 universities (worst 0–100 best)	39.4	2020	●	●
Scientific and technical journal articles (per 1,000 population)	0.4	2018	●	↓
Expenditure on research and development (% of GDP)	1.0	2017	●	↗
Researchers (per 1,000 employed population)	4.0	2017	●	↗
Triadic patent families filed (per million population)	0.7	2017	●	→
Gap in internet access by income (percentage points)	NA	NA	●	●
Women in science and engineering (% of tertiary graduates in science and engineering)	30.7	2015	●	●

SDG10 – Reduced Inequalities				
Gini coefficient adjusted for top income	49.0	2016	●	↓
Palma ratio	1.9	2015	●	↓
Elderly poverty rate (% of population aged 66 or over)	17.0	2015	●	↑

SDG11 – Sustainable Cities and Communities				
Annual mean concentration of particulate matter of less than 2.5 microns in diameter (PM2.5) (µg/m³)	44.3	2017	●	↓
Access to improved water source, piped (% of urban population)	98.6	2017	●	↑
Satisfaction with public transport (%)	57.8	2018	●	↓
Population with rent overburden (%)	NA	NA	●	●

SDG12 – Responsible Consumption and Production				
Electronic waste (kg/capita)	7.9	2016	●	●
Production-based SO₂ emissions (kg/capita)	28.7	2012	●	●
SO₂ emissions embodied in imports (kg/capita)	2.7	2012	●	●
Production-based nitrogen emissions (kg/capita)	25.5	2010	●	●
Nitrogen emissions embodied in imports (kg/capita)	1.7	2010	●	●
Non-recycled municipal solid waste (kg/capita/day)	1.0	2018	●	●

SDG13 – Climate Action				
Energy-related CO₂ emissions (tCO₂/capita)	4.4	2017	●	↓
CO₂ emissions embodied in imports (tCO₂/capita)	0.5	2015	●	↑
CO₂ emissions embodied in fossil fuel exports (kg/capita)	3.0	2018	●	●
Effective carbon rate (EUR/tCO₂)	8.1	2016	●	●

SDG14 – Life Below Water				
Mean area that is protected in marine sites important to biodiversity (%)	4.1	2018	●	→
Ocean Health Index: Clean Waters score (worst 0–100 best)	50.5	2019	●	↓
Fish caught from overexploited or collapsed stocks (% of total catch)	61.6	2014	●	↓
Fish caught by trawling (%)	33.8	2014	●	↗
Marine biodiversity threats embodied in imports (per million population)	0.0	2018	●	●

SDG15 – Life on Land				
Mean area that is protected in terrestrial sites important to biodiversity (%)	2.5	2018	●	→
Mean area that is protected in freshwater sites important to biodiversity (%)	4.4	2018	●	→
Red List Index of species survival (worst 0–1 best)	0.9	2019	●	→
Permanent deforestation (% of forest area, 5-year average)	0.0	2018	●	●
Terrestrial and freshwater biodiversity threats embodied in imports (per million population)	0.7	2018	●	●

SDG16 – Peace, Justice and Strong Institutions				
Homicides (per 100,000 population)	4.3	2012	●	●
Unsentenced detainees (% of prison population)	30.6	2018	●	↓
Percentage of population who feel safe walking alone at night in the city or area where they live (%)	56.8	2018	●	↓
Property Rights (worst 1–7 best)	4.3	2019	●	●
Birth registrations with civil authority (% of children under age 5)	98.8	2018	●	●
Corruption Perception Index (worst 0–100 best)	39.0	2019	●	↓
Children involved in child labor (% of population aged 5 to 14)	5.9	2016	●	●
Exports of major conventional weapons (TIV constant million USD per 100,000 population)	0.3	2019	●	●
Press Freedom Index (best 0–100 worst)	52.8	2019	●	↓
Persons held in prison (per 100,000 population)	322.0	2017	●	↓

SDG17 – Partnerships for the Goals				
Government spending on health and education (% of GDP)	* 7.0	2015	●	↓
For high-income and all OECD DAC countries: International concessional public finance, including official development assistance (% of GNI)	NA	NA	●	●
Other countries: Government revenue excluding grants (% of GDP)	30.7	2018	●	↑
Corporate Tax Haven Score (best 0–100 worst)	* 0.0	2019	●	●
Financial Secrecy Score (best 0–100 worst)	59.5	2020	●	●
Shifted profits of multinationals (US$ billion)	3.9	2016	●	●

* Imputed data point

5. Country Profiles

▼ OVERALL PERFORMANCE

Index score

63.0

Regional average score

70.9

SDG Global rank **114** (OF 166)

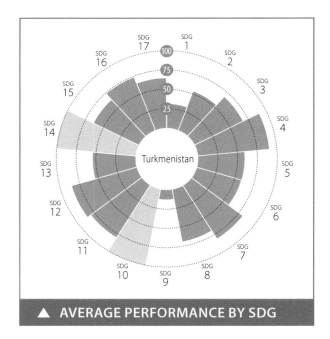

▲ AVERAGE PERFORMANCE BY SDG

▼ SPILLOVER INDEX

100 (best) to 0 (worst)

▼ CURRENT ASSESSMENT – SDG DASHBOARD

■ Major challenges ■ Significant challenges ■ Challenges remain ■ SDG achieved ■ Information unavailable

▼ SDG TRENDS

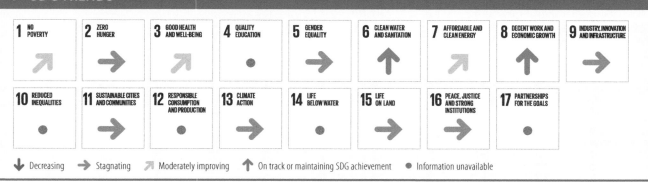

↓ Decreasing   → Stagnating   ↗ Moderately improving   ↑ On track or maintaining SDG achievement   ● Information unavailable

Notes: The full title of Goal 2 "Zero Hunger" is "End hunger, achieve food security and improved nutrition and promote sustainable agriculture".
The full title of each SDG is available here: https://sustainabledevelopment.un.org/topics/sustainabledevelopmentgoals

SDG1 – No Poverty

	Value	Year	Rating	Trend
Poverty headcount ratio at $1.90/day (%)	26.6	2020	●	↑
Poverty headcount ratio at $3.20/day (%)	54.1	2020	●	↗

SDG2 – Zero Hunger

	Value	Year	Rating	Trend
Prevalence of undernourishment (%)	5.4	2017	●	↑
Prevalence of stunting in children under 5 years of age (%)	11.5	2015	●	↑
Prevalence of wasting in children under 5 years of age (%)	4.2	2015	●	↑
Prevalence of obesity, BMI ≥ 30 (% of adult population)	18.6	2016	●	↓
Human Trophic Level (best 2–3 worst)	2.3	2017	●	→
Cereal yield (tonnes per hectare of harvested land)	1.1	2017	●	→
Sustainable Nitrogen Management Index (best 0–1.41 worst)	0.7	2015	●	↓

SDG3 – Good Health and Well-Being

	Value	Year	Rating	Trend
Maternal mortality rate (per 100,000 live births)	7	2017	●	↑
Neonatal mortality rate (per 1,000 live births)	21.0	2018	●	↗
Mortality rate, under-5 (per 1,000 live births)	45.8	2018	●	↗
Incidence of tuberculosis (per 100,000 population)	46.0	2018	●	→
New HIV infections (per 1,000 uninfected population)	NA	NA	●	●
Age-standardized death rate due to cardiovascular disease, cancer, diabetes, or chronic respiratory disease in adults aged 30–70 years (%)	29.5	2016	●	→
Age-standardized death rate attributable to household air pollution and ambient air pollution (per 100,000 population)	79	2016	◐	●
Traffic deaths (per 100,000 population)	14.5	2016	●	↑
Life expectancy at birth (years)	68.2	2016	●	→
Adolescent fertility rate (births per 1,000 adolescent females aged 15 to 19)	24.4	2017	●	↑
Births attended by skilled health personnel (%)	100.0	2016	●	●
Percentage of surviving infants who received 2 WHO-recommended vaccines (%)	99	2018	●	↑
Universal health coverage (UHC) index of service coverage (worst 0–100 best)	70.0	2017	◐	↑
Subjective well-being (average ladder score, worst 0–10 best)	5.5	2019	●	↓

SDG4 – Quality Education

	Value	Year	Rating	Trend
Net primary enrollment rate (%)	NA	NA	●	●
Lower secondary completion rate (%)	NA	NA	●	●
Literacy rate (% of population aged 15 to 24)	99.8	2014	●	●

SDG5 – Gender Equality

	Value	Year	Rating	Trend
Demand for family planning satisfied by modern methods (% of females aged 15 to 49 who are married or in unions)	75.6	2016	◐	↗
Ratio of female-to-male mean years of education received (%)	NA	NA	●	●
Ratio of female-to-male labor force participation rate (%)	67.4	2019	◐	→
Seats held by women in national parliament (%)	25.0	2020	●	↓

SDG6 – Clean Water and Sanitation

	Value	Year	Rating	Trend
Population using at least basic drinking water services (%)	98.8	2017	●	↑
Population using at least basic sanitation services (%)	98.7	2017	●	↑
Freshwater withdrawal (% of available freshwater resources)	143.6	2005	●	●
Anthropogenic wastewater that receives treatment (%)	9.8	2018	●	●
Scarce water consumption embodied in imports (m3/capita)	13.2	2013	●	↑

SDG7 – Affordable and Clean Energy

	Value	Year	Rating	Trend
Population with access to electricity (%)	100.0	2017	●	↑
Population with access to clean fuels and technology for cooking (%)	99.3	2016	●	↑
CO_2 emissions from fuel combustion for electricity and heating per total electricity output (MtCO2/TWh)	3.3	2017	●	↗

SDG8 – Decent Work and Economic Growth

	Value	Year	Rating	Trend
Adjusted GDP growth (%)	1.1	2018	●	●
Victims of modern slavery (per 1,000 population)	11.2	2018	●	●
Adults with an account at a bank or other financial institution or with a mobile-money-service provider (% of population aged 15 or over)	40.6	2017	●	●
Unemployment rate (% of total labor force)	3.9	2019	●	↑
Fatal work-related accidents embodied in imports (per 100,000 population)	0.4	2010	●	↑

SDG9 – Industry, Innovation and Infrastructure

	Value	Year	Rating	Trend
Population using the internet (%)	21.3	2017	●	↗
Mobile broadband subscriptions (per 100 population)	15.3	2017	●	↗
Logistics Performance Index: Quality of trade and transport-related infrastructure (worst 1–5 best)	2.2	2018	●	↗
The Times Higher Education Universities Ranking: Average score of top 3 universities (worst 0–100 best) *	0.0	2020	●	●
Scientific and technical journal articles (per 1,000 population)	0.0	2018	●	→
Expenditure on research and development (% of GDP)	NA	NA	●	●

SDG10 – Reduced Inequalities

	Value	Year	Rating	Trend
Gini coefficient adjusted for top income	NA	NA	●	●

SDG11 – Sustainable Cities and Communities

	Value	Year	Rating	Trend
Annual mean concentration of particulate matter of less than 2.5 microns in diameter (PM2.5) ($\mu g/m^3$)	21.8	2017	●	→
Access to improved water source, piped (% of urban population)	77.8	2017	●	↓
Satisfaction with public transport (%)	71.0	2019	◐	↓

SDG12 – Responsible Consumption and Production

	Value	Year	Rating	Trend
Municipal solid waste (kg/capita/day)	0.5	2013	●	●
Electronic waste (kg/capita)	NA	NA	●	●
Production-based SO_2 emissions (kg/capita)	29.6	2012	●	●
SO_2 emissions embodied in imports (kg/capita)	8.2	2012	●	●
Production-based nitrogen emissions (kg/capita)	30.1	2010	◐	●
Nitrogen emissions embodied in imports (kg/capita)	2.4	2010	●	●

SDG13 – Climate Action

	Value	Year	Rating	Trend
Energy-related CO_2 emissions (tCO2/capita)	14.6	2017	●	↓
CO_2 emissions embodied in imports (tCO2/capita)	1.0	2015	●	↑
CO_2 emissions embodied in fossil fuel exports (kg/capita)	NA	NA	●	●

SDG14 – Life Below Water

	Value	Year	Rating	Trend
Mean area that is protected in marine sites important to biodiversity (%)	NA	NA	●	●
Ocean Health Index: Clean Waters score (worst 0–100 best)	NA	NA	●	●
Fish caught from overexploited or collapsed stocks (% of total catch)	NA	NA	●	●
Fish caught by trawling (%)	NA	NA	●	●
Marine biodiversity threats embodied in imports (per million population)	0.0	2018	●	●

SDG15 – Life on Land

	Value	Year	Rating	Trend
Mean area that is protected in terrestrial sites important to biodiversity (%)	14.4	2018	●	→
Mean area that is protected in freshwater sites important to biodiversity (%)	13.1	2018	●	→
Red List Index of species survival (worst 0–1 best)	1.0	2019	●	↑
Permanent deforestation (% of forest area, 5-year average)	0.0	2018	●	●
Terrestrial and freshwater biodiversity threats embodied in imports (per million population)	0.2	2018	●	●

SDG16 – Peace, Justice and Strong Institutions

	Value	Year	Rating	Trend
Homicides (per 100,000 population)	4.2	2006	●	●
Unsentenced detainees (% of prison population)	14.0	2012	●	●
Percentage of population who feel safe walking alone at night in the city or area where they live (%)	92.5	2019	●	↑
Property Rights (worst 1–7 best)	NA	NA	●	●
Birth registrations with civil authority (% of children under age 5)	99.6	2018	●	●
Corruption Perception Index (worst 0–100 best)	19	2019	●	→
Children involved in child labor (% of population aged 5 to 14)	0.3	2016	●	●
Exports of major conventional weapons (TIV constant million USD per 100,000 population) *	0.0	2019	●	●
Press Freedom Index (best 0–100 worst)	85.4	2019	●	↓

SDG17 – Partnerships for the Goals

	Value	Year	Rating	Trend
Government spending on health and education (% of GDP)	4.3	2012	●	●
For high-income and all OECD DAC countries: International concessional public finance, including official development assistance (% of GNI)	NA	NA	●	●
Other countries: Government revenue excluding grants (% of GDP)	NA	NA	●	●
Corporate Tax Haven Score (best 0–100 worst) *	0.0	2019	●	●

* Imputed data point

5. Country Profiles

TUVALU

▼ OVERALL PERFORMANCE

Index score
na

Regional average score
49.6

SDG Global rank   NA (OF 166)

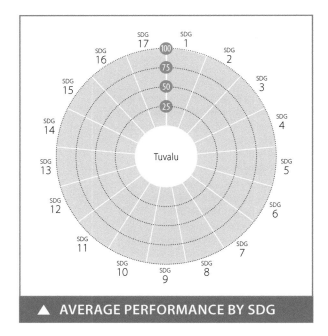

▲ AVERAGE PERFORMANCE BY SDG

▼ SPILLOVER INDEX

100 (best) to 0 (worst)

▼ CURRENT ASSESSMENT – SDG DASHBOARD

■ Major challenges   ■ Significant challenges   ■ Challenges remain   ■ SDG achieved   ■ Information unavailable

▼ SDG TRENDS

↓ Decreasing   → Stagnating   ↗ Moderately improving   ↑ On track or maintaining SDG achievement   ● Information unavailable

Notes: The full title of Goal 2 "Zero Hunger" is "End hunger, achieve food security and improved nutrition and promote sustainable agriculture".
The full title of each SDG is available here: https://sustainabledevelopment.un.org/topics/sustainabledevelopmentgoals

SDG1 – No Poverty

	Value	Year	Rating	Trend
Poverty headcount ratio at $1.90/day (%)	NA	NA	●	●
Poverty headcount ratio at $3.20/day (%)	NA	NA	●	●

SDG2 – Zero Hunger

	Value	Year	Rating	Trend
Prevalence of undernourishment (%)	NA	NA	●	●
Prevalence of stunting in children under 5 years of age (%)	10.0	2007	○	●
Prevalence of wasting in children under 5 years of age (%)	3.3	2007	●	●
Prevalence of obesity, BMI ≥ 30 (% of adult population)	51.6	2016	●	↓
Human Trophic Level (best 2–3 worst)	NA	NA	●	●
Cereal yield (tonnes per hectare of harvested land)	NA	NA	●	●
Sustainable Nitrogen Management Index (best 0–1.41 worst)	1.3	2015	●	↓

SDG3 – Good Health and Well-Being

	Value	Year	Rating	Trend
Maternal mortality rate (per 100,000 live births)	NA	NA	●	●
Neonatal mortality rate (per 1,000 live births)	15.7	2018	●	↑
Mortality rate, under-5 (per 1,000 live births)	24.4	2018	●	↑
Incidence of tuberculosis (per 100,000 population)	270.0	2018	●	↓
New HIV infections (per 1,000 uninfected population)	NA	NA	●	●
Age-standardized death rate due to cardiovascular disease, cancer, diabetes, or chronic respiratory disease in adults aged 30–70 years (%)	NA	NA	●	●
Age-standardized death rate attributable to household air pollution and ambient air pollution (per 100,000 population)	NA	NA	●	●
Traffic deaths (per 100,000 population)	NA	NA	●	●
Life expectancy at birth (years)	NA	NA	●	●
Adolescent fertility rate (births per 1,000 adolescent females aged 15 to 19)	NA	NA	●	●
Births attended by skilled health personnel (%)	93.1	2007	○	●
Percentage of surviving infants who received 2 WHO-recommended vaccines (%)	88	2018	○	↓
Universal health coverage (UHC) index of service coverage (worst 0–100 best)	NA	NA	●	●
Subjective well-being (average ladder score, worst 0–10 best)	NA	NA	●	●

SDG4 – Quality Education

	Value	Year	Rating	Trend
Net primary enrollment rate (%)	76.2	2016	●	↓
Lower secondary completion rate (%)	61.1	2016	●	↓
Literacy rate (% of population aged 15 to 24)	NA	NA	●	●

SDG5 – Gender Equality

	Value	Year	Rating	Trend
Demand for family planning satisfied by modern methods (% of females aged 15 to 49 who are married or in unions)	41.0	2007	●	●
Ratio of female-to-male mean years of education received (%)	NA	NA	●	●
Ratio of female-to-male labor force participation rate (%)	NA	NA	●	●
Seats held by women in national parliament (%)	6.3	2020	●	↓

SDG6 – Clean Water and Sanitation

	Value	Year	Rating	Trend
Population using at least basic drinking water services (%)	99.3	2017	●	↑
Population using at least basic sanitation services (%)	84.1	2017	●	↓
Freshwater withdrawal (% of available freshwater resources)	NA	NA	●	●
Anthropogenic wastewater that receives treatment (%)	0.1	2018	●	●
Scarce water consumption embodied in imports (m³/capita)	NA	NA	●	●

SDG7 – Affordable and Clean Energy

	Value	Year	Rating	Trend
Population with access to electricity (%)	100.0	2017	●	↑
Population with access to clean fuels and technology for cooking (%)	50.4	2016	●	↗
CO$_2$ emissions from fuel combustion for electricity and heating per total electricity output (MtCO$_2$/TWh)	NA	NA	●	●

SDG8 – Decent Work and Economic Growth

	Value	Year	Rating	Trend
Adjusted GDP growth (%)	-3.7	2018	●	●
Victims of modern slavery (per 1,000 population)	NA	NA	●	●
Adults with an account at a bank or other financial institution or with a mobile-money-service provider (% of population aged 15 or over)	NA	NA	●	●
Unemployment rate (% of total labor force)	NA	NA	●	●
Fatal work-related accidents embodied in imports (per 100,000 population)	NA	NA	●	●

SDG9 – Industry, Innovation and Infrastructure

	Value	Year	Rating	Trend
Population using the internet (%)	49.3	2017	●	↑
Mobile broadband subscriptions (per 100 population)	0.0	2017	●	→
Logistics Performance Index: Quality of trade and transport-related infrastructure (worst 1–5 best)	NA	NA	●	●
The Times Higher Education Universities Ranking: Average score of top 3 universities (worst 0–100 best) *	0.0	2020	●	●
Scientific and technical journal articles (per 1,000 population)	0.1	2018	●	→
Expenditure on research and development (% of GDP)	NA	NA	●	●

SDG10 – Reduced Inequalities

	Value	Year	Rating	Trend
Gini coefficient adjusted for top income	39.4	2010	●	●

SDG11 – Sustainable Cities and Communities

	Value	Year	Rating	Trend
Annual mean concentration of particulate matter of less than 2.5 microns in diameter (PM2.5) (µg/m³)	NA	NA	●	●
Access to improved water source, piped (% of urban population)	99.0	2017	●	↑
Satisfaction with public transport (%)	NA	NA	●	●

SDG12 – Responsible Consumption and Production

	Value	Year	Rating	Trend
Municipal solid waste (kg/capita/day)	1.6	2016	●	●
Electronic waste (kg/capita)	1.2	2016	●	●
Production-based SO$_2$ emissions (kg/capita)	NA	NA	●	●
SO$_2$ emissions embodied in imports (kg/capita)	NA	NA	●	●
Production-based nitrogen emissions (kg/capita)	NA	NA	●	●
Nitrogen emissions embodied in imports (kg/capita)	NA	NA	●	●

SDG13 – Climate Action

	Value	Year	Rating	Trend
Energy-related CO$_2$ emissions (tCO$_2$/capita)	1.2	2017	●	↑
CO$_2$ emissions embodied in imports (tCO$_2$/capita)	NA	NA	●	●
CO$_2$ emissions embodied in fossil fuel exports (kg/capita) *	0.0	2017	●	●

SDG14 – Life Below Water

	Value	Year	Rating	Trend
Mean area that is protected in marine sites important to biodiversity (%)	NA	NA	●	●
Ocean Health Index: Clean Waters score (worst 0–100 best)	52.4	2019	●	→
Fish caught from overexploited or collapsed stocks (% of total catch)	3.8	2014	●	↑
Fish caught by trawling (%)	NA	NA	●	●
Marine biodiversity threats embodied in imports (per million population)	NA	NA	●	●

SDG15 – Life on Land

	Value	Year	Rating	Trend
Mean area that is protected in terrestrial sites important to biodiversity (%)	NA	NA	●	●
Mean area that is protected in freshwater sites important to biodiversity (%)	NA	NA	●	●
Red List Index of species survival (worst 0–1 best)	0.8	2019	●	↓
Permanent deforestation (% of forest area, 5-year average)	NA	NA	●	●
Terrestrial and freshwater biodiversity threats embodied in imports (per million population)	NA	NA	●	●

SDG16 – Peace, Justice and Strong Institutions

	Value	Year	Rating	Trend
Homicides (per 100,000 population)	18.6	2012	●	●
Unsentenced detainees (% of prison population)	0.0	2015	●	●
Percentage of population who feel safe walking alone at night in the city or area where they live (%)	NA	NA	●	●
Property Rights (worst 1–7 best)	NA	NA	●	●
Birth registrations with civil authority (% of children under age 5)	49.9	2018	●	●
Corruption Perception Index (worst 0–100 best)	NA	NA	●	●
Children involved in child labor (% of population aged 5 to 14)	NA	NA	●	●
Exports of major conventional weapons (TIV constant million USD per 100,000 population) *	0.0	2019	●	●
Press Freedom Index (best 0–100 worst)	NA	NA	●	●

SDG17 – Partnerships for the Goals

	Value	Year	Rating	Trend
Government spending on health and education (% of GDP)	NA	NA	●	●
For high-income and all OECD DAC countries: International concessional public finance, including official development assistance (% of GNI)	NA	NA	●	●
Other countries: Government revenue excluding grants (% of GDP)	NA	NA	●	●
Corporate Tax Haven Score (best 0–100 worst) *	0.0	2019	●	●

* Imputed data point

5. Country Profiles

UGANDA

▼ OVERALL PERFORMANCE

Index score

53.5

Regional average score

53.1

SDG Global rank 142 (OF 166)

▼ AVERAGE PERFORMANCE BY SDG

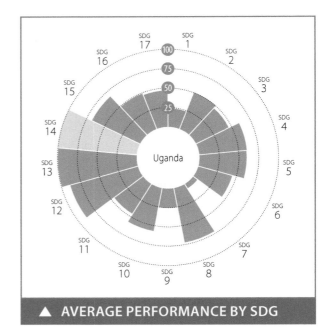

▼ SPILLOVER INDEX

100 (best) to 0 (worst)

```
100
 80
 60
 40
 20
  0
```

▼ CURRENT ASSESSMENT – SDG DASHBOARD

■ Major challenges ■ Significant challenges ■ Challenges remain ■ SDG achieved ■ Information unavailable

▼ SDG TRENDS

↓ Decreasing → Stagnating ↗ Moderately improving ↑ On track or maintaining SDG achievement ● Information unavailable

Notes: The full title of Goal 2 "Zero Hunger" is "End hunger, achieve food security and improved nutrition and promote sustainable agriculture".
The full title of each SDG is available here: https://sustainabledevelopment.un.org/topics/sustainabledevelopmentgoals

SDG1 – No Poverty

Indicator	Value	Year	Rating	Trend
Poverty headcount ratio at $1.90/day (%)	37.0	2020	●	→
Poverty headcount ratio at $3.20/day (%)	64.3	2020	●	→

SDG2 – Zero Hunger

Indicator	Value	Year	Rating	Trend
Prevalence of undernourishment (%)	41.0	2017	●	↓
Prevalence of stunting in children under 5 years of age (%)	28.9	2016	●	→
Prevalence of wasting in children under 5 years of age (%)	3.6	2016	●	↑
Prevalence of obesity, BMI ≥ 30 (% of adult population)	5.3	2016	●	↑
Human Trophic Level (best 2–3 worst)	2.1	2017	●	↑
Cereal yield (tonnes per hectare of harvested land)	2.1	2017	◐	→
Sustainable Nitrogen Management Index (best 0–1.41 worst)	0.8	2015	●	→

SDG3 – Good Health and Well-Being

Indicator	Value	Year	Rating	Trend
Maternal mortality rate (per 100,000 live births)	375	2017	●	→
Neonatal mortality rate (per 1,000 live births)	19.9	2018	●	↗
Mortality rate, under-5 (per 1,000 live births)	46.4	2018	●	↑
Incidence of tuberculosis (per 100,000 population)	200.0	2018	●	→
New HIV infections (per 1,000 uninfected population)	1.4	2018	●	↑
Age-standardized death rate due to cardiovascular disease, cancer, diabetes, or chronic respiratory disease in adults aged 30–70 years (%)	21.9	2016	●	→
Age-standardized death rate attributable to household air pollution and ambient air pollution (per 100,000 population)	156	2016	●	●
Traffic deaths (per 100,000 population)	29.0	2016	●	↓
Life expectancy at birth (years)	62.5	2016	●	↗
Adolescent fertility rate (births per 1,000 adolescent females aged 15 to 19)	118.8	2017	●	→
Births attended by skilled health personnel (%)	74.2	2016	●	↑
Percentage of surviving infants who received 2 WHO-recommended vaccines (%)	86	2018	◐	↑
Universal health coverage (UHC) index of service coverage (worst 0–100 best)	45.0	2017	●	→
Subjective well-being (average ladder score, worst 0–10 best)	4.3	2018	●	→

SDG4 – Quality Education

Indicator	Value	Year	Rating	Trend
Net primary enrollment rate (%)	95.5	2013	◐	●
Lower secondary completion rate (%)	26.4	2017	●	↓
Literacy rate (% of population aged 15 to 24)	89.4	2018	●	●

SDG5 – Gender Equality

Indicator	Value	Year	Rating	Trend
Demand for family planning satisfied by modern methods (% of females aged 15 to 49 who are married or in unions)	53.5	2018	●	↑
Ratio of female-to-male mean years of education received (%)	64.9	2018	●	↓
Ratio of female-to-male labor force participation rate (%)	89.7	2019	●	↑
Seats held by women in national parliament (%)	34.9	2020	◐	↓

SDG6 – Clean Water and Sanitation

Indicator	Value	Year	Rating	Trend
Population using at least basic drinking water services (%)	49.1	2017	●	→
Population using at least basic sanitation services (%)	18.5	2017	●	→
Freshwater withdrawal (% of available freshwater resources)	5.8	2010	●	●
Anthropogenic wastewater that receives treatment (%)	0.4	2018	●	●
Scarce water consumption embodied in imports (m3/capita)	0.6	2013	●	↑

SDG7 – Affordable and Clean Energy

Indicator	Value	Year	Rating	Trend
Population with access to electricity (%)	22.0	2017	●	→
Population with access to clean fuels and technology for cooking (%)	0.8	2016	●	↓
CO_2 emissions from fuel combustion for electricity and heating per total electricity output (MtCO2/TWh)	NA	NA	●	●

SDG8 – Decent Work and Economic Growth

Indicator	Value	Year	Rating	Trend
Adjusted GDP growth (%)	-5.6	2018	●	●
Victims of modern slavery (per 1,000 population)	7.6	2018	●	●
Adults with an account at a bank or other financial institution or with a mobile-money-service provider (% of population aged 15 or over)	59.2	2017	●	↑
Unemployment rate (% of total labor force)	1.8	2019	●	↑
Fatal work-related accidents embodied in imports (per 100,000 population)	0.1	2010	●	↑

SDG9 – Industry, Innovation and Infrastructure

Indicator	Value	Year	Rating	Trend
Population using the internet (%)	23.7	2017	●	↗
Mobile broadband subscriptions (per 100 population)	33.6	2018	●	↑
Logistics Performance Index: Quality of trade and transport-related infrastructure (worst 1–5 best)	2.2	2018	●	●
The Times Higher Education Universities Ranking: Average score of top 3 universities (worst 0–100 best)	31.8	2020	●	●
Scientific and technical journal articles (per 1,000 population)	0.0	2018	●	→
Expenditure on research and development (% of GDP)	0.2	2014	●	●

SDG10 – Reduced Inequalities

Indicator	Value	Year	Rating	Trend
Gini coefficient adjusted for top income	42.7	2016	●	●

SDG11 – Sustainable Cities and Communities

Indicator	Value	Year	Rating	Trend
Annual mean concentration of particulate matter of less than 2.5 microns in diameter (PM2.5) (μg/m3)	50.5	2017	●	↓
Access to improved water source, piped (% of urban population)	53.3	2017	●	↓
Satisfaction with public transport (%)	46.2	2018	●	↓

SDG12 – Responsible Consumption and Production

Indicator	Value	Year	Rating	Trend
Municipal solid waste (kg/capita/day)	1.8	2011	●	●
Electronic waste (kg/capita)	0.6	2016	●	●
Production-based SO_2 emissions (kg/capita)	5.6	2012	●	●
SO_2 emissions embodied in imports (kg/capita)	0.5	2012	●	●
Production-based nitrogen emissions (kg/capita)	16.4	2010	●	●
Nitrogen emissions embodied in imports (kg/capita)	0.3	2010	●	●

SDG13 – Climate Action

Indicator	Value	Year	Rating	Trend
Energy-related CO_2 emissions (tCO2/capita)	0.1	2017	●	↑
CO_2 emissions embodied in imports (tCO2/capita)	0.1	2015	●	↑
CO_2 emissions embodied in fossil fuel exports (kg/capita)	0.0	2018	●	●

SDG14 – Life Below Water

Indicator	Value	Year	Rating	Trend
Mean area that is protected in marine sites important to biodiversity (%)	NA	NA	●	●
Ocean Health Index: Clean Waters score (worst 0–100 best)	NA	NA	●	●
Fish caught from overexploited or collapsed stocks (% of total catch)	NA	NA	●	●
Fish caught by trawling (%)	NA	NA	●	●
Marine biodiversity threats embodied in imports (per million population)	0.0	2018	●	●

SDG15 – Life on Land

Indicator	Value	Year	Rating	Trend
Mean area that is protected in terrestrial sites important to biodiversity (%)	75.7	2018	●	↑
Mean area that is protected in freshwater sites important to biodiversity (%)	65.7	2018	●	↑
Red List Index of species survival (worst 0–1 best)	0.7	2019	●	↓
Permanent deforestation (% of forest area, 5-year average)	0.6	2018	●	●
Terrestrial and freshwater biodiversity threats embodied in imports (per million population)	0.2	2018	●	●

SDG16 – Peace, Justice and Strong Institutions

Indicator	Value	Year	Rating	Trend
Homicides (per 100,000 population)	11.0	2017	●	→
Unsentenced detainees (% of prison population)	51.2	2018	●	↗
Percentage of population who feel safe walking alone at night in the city or area where they live (%)	52.3	2018	●	↓
Property Rights (worst 1–7 best)	4.1	2019	◐	●
Birth registrations with civil authority (% of children under age 5)	32.2	2018	●	●
Corruption Perception Index (worst 0–100 best)	28	2019	●	→
Children involved in child labor (% of population aged 5 to 14)	16.3	2016	●	●
Exports of major conventional weapons (TIV constant million USD per 100,000 population)	0.0	2019	●	●
Press Freedom Index (best 0–100 worst)	39.4	2019	◐	↓

SDG17 – Partnerships for the Goals

Indicator	Value	Year	Rating	Trend
Government spending on health and education (% of GDP)	3.6	2016	●	→
For high-income and all OECD DAC countries: International concessional public finance, including official development assistance (% of GNI)	NA	NA	●	●
Other countries: Government revenue excluding grants (% of GDP)	15.0	2018	●	→
Corporate Tax Haven Score (best 0–100 worst) *	0.0	2019	●	●

* Imputed data point

5. Country Profiles

▼ OVERALL PERFORMANCE

Index score

74.2

Regional average score

70.9

SDG Global rank **47** (OF 166)

▼ AVERAGE PERFORMANCE BY SDG

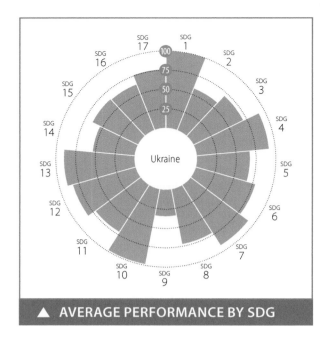

▼ SPILLOVER INDEX

100 (best) to 0 (worst)

▼ CURRENT ASSESSMENT – SDG DASHBOARD

■ Major challenges ■ Significant challenges ■ Challenges remain ■ SDG achieved ■ Information unavailable

▼ SDG TRENDS

↓ Decreasing   → Stagnating   ↗ Moderately improving   ↑ On track or maintaining SDG achievement   ● Information unavailable

Notes: The full title of Goal 2 "Zero Hunger" is "End hunger, achieve food security and improved nutrition and promote sustainable agriculture".
The full title of each SDG is available here: https://sustainabledevelopment.un.org/topics/sustainabledevelopmentgoals

SDG1 – No Poverty

	Value	Year	Rating	Trend
Poverty headcount ratio at $1.90/day (%)	0.1	2020	●	↑
Poverty headcount ratio at $3.20/day (%)	0.2	2020	●	↑

SDG2 – Zero Hunger

	Value	Year	Rating	Trend
Prevalence of undernourishment (%)	3.5	2017	●	↑
Prevalence of stunting in children under 5 years of age (%)	22.9	2000	●	→
Prevalence of wasting in children under 5 years of age (%)	8.2	2000	●	↑
Prevalence of obesity, BMI ≥ 30 (% of adult population)	24.1	2016	●	↓
Human Trophic Level (best 2–3 worst)	2.3	2017	●	→
Cereal yield (tonnes per hectare of harvested land)	4.3	2017	●	↑
Sustainable Nitrogen Management Index (best 0–1.41 worst)	0.4	2015	●	↑

SDG3 – Good Health and Well-Being

	Value	Year	Rating	Trend
Maternal mortality rate (per 100,000 live births)	19	2017	●	↑
Neonatal mortality rate (per 1,000 live births)	5.2	2018	●	↑
Mortality rate, under-5 (per 1,000 live births)	8.7	2018	●	↑
Incidence of tuberculosis (per 100,000 population)	80.0	2018	●	↗
New HIV infections (per 1,000 uninfected population)	0.3	2018	●	↗
Age-standardized death rate due to cardiovascular disease, cancer, diabetes, or chronic respiratory disease in adults aged 30–70 years (%)	24.7	2016	●	↑
Age-standardized death rate attributable to household air pollution and ambient air pollution (per 100,000 population)	71	2016	●	●
Traffic deaths (per 100,000 population)	13.7	2016	●	↓
Life expectancy at birth (years)	72.5	2016	●	↗
Adolescent fertility rate (births per 1,000 adolescent females aged 15 to 19)	23.7	2017	●	↑
Births attended by skilled health personnel (%)	99.9	2014	●	●
Percentage of surviving infants who received 2 WHO-recommended vaccines (%)	50	2018	●	↑
Universal health coverage (UHC) index of service coverage (worst 0–100 best)	68.0	2017	●	↑
Subjective well-being (average ladder score, worst 0–10 best)	4.7	2019	●	↑

SDG4 – Quality Education

	Value	Year	Rating	Trend
Net primary enrollment rate (%)	91.7	2014	●	●
Lower secondary completion rate (%)	94.4	2014	●	●
Literacy rate (% of population aged 15 to 24)	100.0	2012	●	●

SDG5 – Gender Equality

	Value	Year	Rating	Trend
Demand for family planning satisfied by modern methods (% of females aged 15 to 49 who are married or in unions)	68.0	2012	●	↗
Ratio of female-to-male mean years of education received (%)	100.0	2018	●	↑
Ratio of female-to-male labor force participation rate (%)	74.2	2019	●	↑
Seats held by women in national parliament (%)	20.8	2020	●	↗

SDG6 – Clean Water and Sanitation

	Value	Year	Rating	Trend
Population using at least basic drinking water services (%)	93.8	2017	●	→
Population using at least basic sanitation services (%)	96.2	2017	●	↑
Freshwater withdrawal (% of available freshwater resources)	12.8	2015	●	●
Anthropogenic wastewater that receives treatment (%)	14.1	2018	●	●
Scarce water consumption embodied in imports (m³/capita)	6.2	2013	●	↑

SDG7 – Affordable and Clean Energy

	Value	Year	Rating	Trend
Population with access to electricity (%)	100.0	2017	●	↑
Population with access to clean fuels and technology for cooking (%)	95.7	2016	●	↑
CO₂ emissions from fuel combustion for electricity and heating per total electricity output (MtCO₂/TWh)	1.2	2017	●	↑

SDG8 – Decent Work and Economic Growth

	Value	Year	Rating	Trend
Adjusted GDP growth (%)	-1.3	2018	●	●
Victims of modern slavery (per 1,000 population)	6.4	2018	●	●
Adults with an account at a bank or other financial institution or with a mobile-money-service provider (% of population aged 15 or over)	62.9	2017	●	↑
Unemployment rate (% of total labor force)	8.9	2019	●	→
Fatal work-related accidents embodied in imports (per 100,000 population)	0.2	2010	●	↑

SDG9 – Industry, Innovation and Infrastructure

	Value	Year	Rating	Trend
Population using the internet (%)	62.6	2018	●	↑
Mobile broadband subscriptions (per 100 population)	47.2	2018	●	↑
Logistics Performance Index: Quality of trade and transport-related infrastructure (worst 1–5 best)	2.2	2018	●	↓
The Times Higher Education Universities Ranking: Average score of top 3 universities (worst 0–100 best)	19.3	2020	●	●
Scientific and technical journal articles (per 1,000 population)	0.2	2018	●	↗
Expenditure on research and development (% of GDP)	0.4	2017	●	↓

SDG10 – Reduced Inequalities

	Value	Year	Rating	Trend
Gini coefficient adjusted for top income	28.0	2016	●	●

SDG11 – Sustainable Cities and Communities

	Value	Year	Rating	Trend
Annual mean concentration of particulate matter of less than 2.5 microns in diameter (PM2.5) (μg/m³)	20.3	2017	●	→
Access to improved water source, piped (% of urban population)	81.5	2017	●	↓
Satisfaction with public transport (%)	53.1	2019	●	↓

SDG12 – Responsible Consumption and Production

	Value	Year	Rating	Trend
Municipal solid waste (kg/capita/day)	1.4	2016	●	●
Electronic waste (kg/capita)	6.5	2016	●	●
Production-based SO₂ emissions (kg/capita)	32.3	2012	●	●
SO₂ emissions embodied in imports (kg/capita)	2.9	2012	●	●
Production-based nitrogen emissions (kg/capita)	23.5	2010	●	●
Nitrogen emissions embodied in imports (kg/capita)	1.6	2010	●	●

SDG13 – Climate Action

	Value	Year	Rating	Trend
Energy-related CO₂ emissions (tCO₂/capita)	3.9	2017	●	↑
CO₂ emissions embodied in imports (tCO₂/capita)	0.5	2015	●	↑
CO₂ emissions embodied in fossil fuel exports (kg/capita)	24.7	2018	●	●

SDG14 – Life Below Water

	Value	Year	Rating	Trend
Mean area that is protected in marine sites important to biodiversity (%)	47.9	2018	●	→
Ocean Health Index: Clean Waters score (worst 0–100 best)	58.9	2019	●	↓
Fish caught from overexploited or collapsed stocks (% of total catch)	21.5	2014	●	↑
Fish caught by trawling (%)	90.0	2014	●	↓
Marine biodiversity threats embodied in imports (per million population)	0.0	2018	●	●

SDG15 – Life on Land

	Value	Year	Rating	Trend
Mean area that is protected in terrestrial sites important to biodiversity (%)	23.8	2018	●	→
Mean area that is protected in freshwater sites important to biodiversity (%)	17.5	2018	●	→
Red List Index of species survival (worst 0–1 best)	0.9	2019	●	↑
Permanent deforestation (% of forest area, 5-year average)	0.0	2018	●	●
Terrestrial and freshwater biodiversity threats embodied in imports (per million population)	0.3	2018	●	●

SDG16 – Peace, Justice and Strong Institutions

	Value	Year	Rating	Trend
Homicides (per 100,000 population)	6.2	2017	●	→
Unsentenced detainees (% of prison population)	33.8	2018	●	●
Percentage of population who feel safe walking alone at night in the city or area where they live (%)	52.6	2019	●	↑
Property Rights (worst 1–7 best)	3.3	2019	●	●
Birth registrations with civil authority (% of children under age 5)	99.8	2018	●	●
Corruption Perception Index (worst 0–100 best)	30	2019	●	→
Children involved in child labor (% of population aged 5 to 14)	2.4	2016	●	●
Exports of major conventional weapons (TIV constant million USD per 100,000 population)	0.6	2019	●	●
Press Freedom Index (best 0–100 worst)	32.5	2019	●	↗

SDG17 – Partnerships for the Goals

	Value	Year	Rating	Trend
Government spending on health and education (% of GDP)	7.9	2016	●	↓
For high-income and all OECD DAC countries: International concessional public finance, including official development assistance (% of GNI)	NA	NA	●	●
Other countries: Government revenue excluding grants (% of GDP)	32.1	2018	●	↑
Corporate Tax Haven Score (best 0–100 worst) *	0.0	2019	●	●

* Imputed data point

5. Country Profiles

UNITED ARAB EMIRATES

▼ OVERALL PERFORMANCE

Index score

70.3

Regional average score

66.3

SDG Global rank **71** (OF 166)

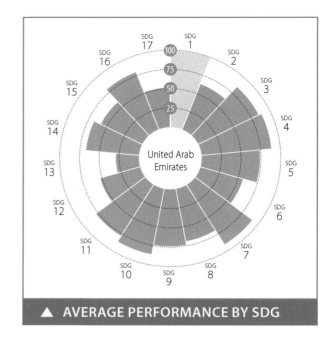

▲ AVERAGE PERFORMANCE BY SDG

▼ SPILLOVER INDEX

100 (best) to 0 (worst)

▼ CURRENT ASSESSMENT – SDG DASHBOARD

1 NO POVERTY	2 ZERO HUNGER	3 GOOD HEALTH AND WELL-BEING
4 QUALITY EDUCATION	5 GENDER EQUALITY	6 CLEAN WATER AND SANITATION
7 AFFORDABLE AND CLEAN ENERGY	8 DECENT WORK AND ECONOMIC GROWTH	9 INDUSTRY, INNOVATION AND INFRASTRUCTURE
10 REDUCED INEQUALITIES	11 SUSTAINABLE CITIES AND COMMUNITIES	12 RESPONSIBLE CONSUMPTION AND PRODUCTION
13 CLIMATE ACTION	14 LIFE BELOW WATER	15 LIFE ON LAND
16 PEACE, JUSTICE AND STRONG INSTITUTIONS	17 PARTNERSHIPS FOR THE GOALS	SUSTAINABLE DEVELOPMENT GOALS

■ Major challenges ■ Significant challenges Challenges remain ■ SDG achieved ■ Information unavailable

▼ SDG TRENDS

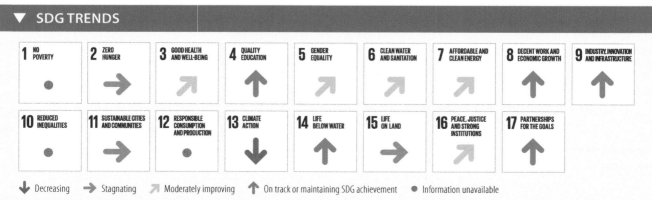

↓ Decreasing → Stagnating ↗ Moderately improving ↑ On track or maintaining SDG achievement ● Information unavailable

Notes: The full title of Goal 2 "Zero Hunger" is "End hunger, achieve food security and improved nutrition and promote sustainable agriculture".
The full title of each SDG is available here: https://sustainabledevelopment.un.org/topics/sustainabledevelopmentgoals

SDG1 – No Poverty

Indicator	Value	Year	Rating	Trend
Poverty headcount ratio at $1.90/day (%)	* NA	NA	●	●
Poverty headcount ratio at $3.20/day (%)	* NA	NA	●	●

SDG2 – Zero Hunger

Indicator	Value	Year	Rating	Trend
Prevalence of undernourishment (%)	2.6	2017	●	↑
Prevalence of stunting in children under 5 years of age (%)	* 2.6	2016	●	↑
Prevalence of wasting in children under 5 years of age (%)	* 0.7	2016	●	↑
Prevalence of obesity, BMI ≥ 30 (% of adult population)	31.7	2016	●	↓
Human Trophic Level (best 2–3 worst)	2.3	2017	◐	↑
Cereal yield (tonnes per hectare of harvested land)	23.6	2017	●	↑
Sustainable Nitrogen Management Index (best 0–1.41 worst)	1.2	2015	●	→

SDG3 – Good Health and Well-Being

Indicator	Value	Year	Rating	Trend
Maternal mortality rate (per 100,000 live births)	3	2017	●	↑
Neonatal mortality rate (per 1,000 live births)	4.0	2018	●	↑
Mortality rate, under-5 (per 1,000 live births)	7.6	2018	●	↑
Incidence of tuberculosis (per 100,000 population)	1.0	2018	●	↑
New HIV infections (per 1,000 uninfected population)	NA	NA	●	●
Age-standardized death rate due to cardiovascular disease, cancer, diabetes, or chronic respiratory disease in adults aged 30–70 years (%)	16.8	2016	◐	↑
Age-standardized death rate attributable to household air pollution and ambient air pollution (per 100,000 population)	55	2016	◐	●
Traffic deaths (per 100,000 population)	18.1	2016	●	↓
Life expectancy at birth (years)	77.2	2016	◐	↗
Adolescent fertility rate (births per 1,000 adolescent females aged 15 to 19)	6.5	2017	●	↑
Births attended by skilled health personnel (%)	99.9	2015	●	↑
Percentage of surviving infants who received 2 WHO-recommended vaccines (%)	99	2018	●	↑
Universal health coverage (UHC) index of service coverage (worst 0–100 best)	76.0	2017	◐	↑
Subjective well-being (average ladder score, worst 0–10 best)	6.7	2019	●	↑

SDG4 – Quality Education

Indicator	Value	Year	Rating	Trend
Net primary enrollment rate (%)	95.0	2017	◐	↑
Lower secondary completion rate (%)	81.7	2014	●	●
Literacy rate (% of population aged 15 to 24)	99.4	2015	●	●

SDG5 – Gender Equality

Indicator	Value	Year	Rating	Trend
Demand for family planning satisfied by modern methods (% of females aged 15 to 49 who are married or in unions)	* 60.9	2017	●	→
Ratio of female-to-male mean years of education received (%)	122.4	2018	●	↑
Ratio of female-to-male labor force participation rate (%)	54.7	2019	◐	↗
Seats held by women in national parliament (%)	50.0	2020	●	↑

SDG6 – Clean Water and Sanitation

Indicator	Value	Year	Rating	Trend
Population using at least basic drinking water services (%)	98.0	2017	●	↑
Population using at least basic sanitation services (%)	98.6	2017	●	↑
Freshwater withdrawal (% of available freshwater resources)	1866.7	2005	●	●
Anthropogenic wastewater that receives treatment (%)	76.8	2018	●	●
Scarce water consumption embodied in imports (m³/capita)	91.4	2013	●	→

SDG7 – Affordable and Clean Energy

Indicator	Value	Year	Rating	Trend
Population with access to electricity (%)	100.0	2017	●	↑
Population with access to clean fuels and technology for cooking (%)	98.5	2016	●	↑
CO$_2$ emissions from fuel combustion for electricity and heating per total electricity output (MtCO$_2$/TWh)	1.6	2017	●	→

SDG8 – Decent Work and Economic Growth

Indicator	Value	Year	Rating	Trend
Adjusted GDP growth (%)	-0.8	2018	◐	●
Victims of modern slavery (per 1,000 population)	* NA	NA	●	●
Adults with an account at a bank or other financial institution or with a mobile-money-service provider (% of population aged 15 or over)	88.2	2017	●	↑
Unemployment rate (% of total labor force)	2.3	2019	●	↑
Fatal work-related accidents embodied in imports (per 100,000 population)	4.5	2010	●	↑

SDG9 – Industry, Innovation and Infrastructure

Indicator	Value	Year	Rating	Trend
Population using the internet (%)	98.5	2018	●	↑
Mobile broadband subscriptions (per 100 population)	250.0	2018	●	↑
Logistics Performance Index: Quality of trade and transport-related infrastructure (worst 1–5 best)	4.0	2018	●	↑
The Times Higher Education Universities Ranking: Average score of top 3 universities (worst 0–100 best)	40.3	2020	●	●
Scientific and technical journal articles (per 1,000 population)	0.3	2018	◐	↗
Expenditure on research and development (% of GDP)	1.3	2018	◐	↑

SDG10 – Reduced Inequalities

Indicator	Value	Year	Rating	Trend
Gini coefficient adjusted for top income	* 32.5	2017	◐	●

SDG11 – Sustainable Cities and Communities

Indicator	Value	Year	Rating	Trend
Annual mean concentration of particulate matter of less than 2.5 microns in diameter (PM2.5) (μg/m³)	40.9	2017	●	↓
Access to improved water source, piped (% of urban population)	NA	NA	●	●
Satisfaction with public transport (%)	81.3	2019	●	↑

SDG12 – Responsible Consumption and Production

Indicator	Value	Year	Rating	Trend
Municipal solid waste (kg/capita/day)	1.8	2016	●	●
Electronic waste (kg/capita)	13.6	2016	●	●
Production-based SO$_2$ emissions (kg/capita)	43.4	2012	◐	●
SO$_2$ emissions embodied in imports (kg/capita)	25.2	2012	●	●
Production-based nitrogen emissions (kg/capita)	41.4	2010	●	●
Nitrogen emissions embodied in imports (kg/capita)	22.5	2010	●	●

SDG13 – Climate Action

Indicator	Value	Year	Rating	Trend
Energy-related CO$_2$ emissions (tCO$_2$/capita)	23.5	2017	●	↓
CO$_2$ emissions embodied in imports (tCO$_2$/capita)	4.3	2015	●	→
CO$_2$ emissions embodied in fossil fuel exports (kg/capita)	6281.1	2018	●	●

SDG14 – Life Below Water

Indicator	Value	Year	Rating	Trend
Mean area that is protected in marine sites important to biodiversity (%)	49.7	2018	◐	↑
Ocean Health Index: Clean Waters score (worst 0–100 best)	68.3	2019	◐	↑
Fish caught from overexploited or collapsed stocks (% of total catch)	17.7	2014	●	↑
Fish caught by trawling (%)	* 0.0	2014	●	↑
Marine biodiversity threats embodied in imports (per million population)	1.0	2018	●	●

SDG15 – Life on Land

Indicator	Value	Year	Rating	Trend
Mean area that is protected in terrestrial sites important to biodiversity (%)	57.9	2018	●	↑
Mean area that is protected in freshwater sites important to biodiversity (%)	NA	NA	●	●
Red List Index of species survival (worst 0–1 best)	0.9	2019	◐	↓
Permanent deforestation (% of forest area, 5-year average)	NA	NA	●	●
Terrestrial and freshwater biodiversity threats embodied in imports (per million population)	4.6	2018	●	●

SDG16 – Peace, Justice and Strong Institutions

Indicator	Value	Year	Rating	Trend
Homicides (per 100,000 population)	0.5	2017	●	↑
Unsentenced detainees (% of prison population)	35.8	2015	◐	●
Percentage of population who feel safe walking alone at night in the city or area where they live (%)	92.0	2019	●	●
Property Rights (worst 1–7 best)	5.7	2019	●	●
Birth registrations with civil authority (% of children under age 5)	100.0	2018	●	●
Corruption Perception Index (worst 0–100 best)	71	2019	●	↑
Children involved in child labor (% of population aged 5 to 14)	NA	NA	●	●
Exports of major conventional weapons (TIV constant million USD per 100,000 population)	1.1	2019	◐	●
Press Freedom Index (best 0–100 worst)	43.6	2019	●	↓

SDG17 – Partnerships for the Goals

Indicator	Value	Year	Rating	Trend
Government spending on health and education (% of GDP)	NA	NA	●	●
For high-income and all OECD DAC countries: International concessional public finance, including official development assistance (% of GNI)	1.0	2017	●	↑
Other countries: Government revenue excluding grants (% of GDP)	NA	NA	●	●
Corporate Tax Haven Score (best 0–100 worst)	98.3	2019	●	●

* Imputed data point

5. Country Profiles

▼ OVERALL PERFORMANCE

Index score

79.8

Regional average score

77.3

SDG Global rank **13** (OF 166)

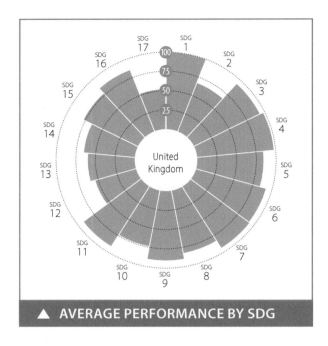

▲ AVERAGE PERFORMANCE BY SDG

▼ SPILLOVER INDEX

100 (best) to 0 (worst)

▼ CURRENT ASSESSMENT – SDG DASHBOARD

■ Major challenges   ■ Significant challenges   Challenges remain   ■ SDG achieved   ■ Information unavailable

▼ SDG TRENDS

1 NO POVERTY	2 ZERO HUNGER	3 GOOD HEALTH AND WELL-BEING	4 QUALITY EDUCATION	5 GENDER EQUALITY	6 CLEAN WATER AND SANITATION	7 AFFORDABLE AND CLEAN ENERGY	8 DECENT WORK AND ECONOMIC GROWTH	9 INDUSTRY, INNOVATION AND INFRASTRUCTURE
↗	→	↗	↗	↗	↗	↑	↑	↑

10 REDUCED INEQUALITIES	11 SUSTAINABLE CITIES AND COMMUNITIES	12 RESPONSIBLE CONSUMPTION AND PRODUCTION	13 CLIMATE ACTION	14 LIFE BELOW WATER	15 LIFE ON LAND	16 PEACE, JUSTICE AND STRONG INSTITUTIONS	17 PARTNERSHIPS FOR THE GOALS
↓	↗	●	↗	↗	↗	↗	↑

↓ Decreasing   → Stagnating   ↗ Moderately improving   ↑ On track or maintaining SDG achievement   ● Information unavailable

Notes: The full title of Goal 2 "Zero Hunger" is "End hunger, achieve food security and improved nutrition and promote sustainable agriculture".
The full title of each SDG is available here: https://sustainabledevelopment.un.org/topics/sustainabledevelopmentgoals

SDG1 – No Poverty	Value	Year	Rating	Trend
Poverty headcount ratio at $1.90/day (%)	0.2	2020	●	↑
Poverty headcount ratio at $3.20/day (%)	0.2	2020	●	↑
Poverty rate after taxes and transfers (%)	11.9	2017	○	↓

SDG2 – Zero Hunger	Value	Year	Rating	Trend
Prevalence of undernourishment (%)	2.5	2017	●	↑
Prevalence of stunting in children under 5 years of age (%)	* 2.6	2016	●	↑
Prevalence of wasting in children under 5 years of age (%)	* 0.7	2016	●	↑
Prevalence of obesity, BMI ≥ 30 (% of adult population)	27.8	2016	●	↓
Human Trophic Level (best 2–3 worst)	2.4	2017	●	→
Cereal yield (tonnes per hectare of harvested land)	7.2	2017	●	↑
Sustainable Nitrogen Management Index (best 0–1.41 worst)	0.6	2015	●	↓
Yield gap closure (% of potential yield)	67.8	2015	○	●

SDG3 – Good Health and Well-Being	Value	Year	Rating	Trend
Maternal mortality rate (per 100,000 live births)	7	2017	●	↑
Neonatal mortality rate (per 1,000 live births)	2.6	2018	●	↑
Mortality rate, under-5 (per 1,000 live births)	4.3	2018	●	↑
Incidence of tuberculosis (per 100,000 population)	8.0	2018	●	↑
New HIV infections (per 1,000 uninfected population)	NA	NA	●	●
Age-standardized death rate due to cardiovascular disease, cancer, diabetes, or chronic respiratory disease in adults aged 30–70 years (%)	10.9	2016	●	↑
Age-standardized death rate attributable to household air pollution and ambient air pollution (per 100,000 population)	14	2016	●	●
Traffic deaths (per 100,000 population)	3.1	2016	●	↑
Life expectancy at birth (years)	81.4	2016	●	↑
Adolescent fertility rate (births per 1,000 adolescent females aged 15 to 19)	13.4	2017	●	↑
Births attended by skilled health personnel (%)	NA	NA	●	●
Percentage of surviving infants who received 2 WHO-recommended vaccines (%)	92.0	2018	●	↑
Universal health coverage (UHC) index of service coverage (worst 0–100 best)	87.0	2017	●	↑
Subjective well-being (average ladder score, worst 0–10 best)	7.2	2019	●	↑
Gap in life expectancy at birth among regions (years)	3.5	2016	●	●
Gap in self-reported health status by income (percentage points)	22.0	2017	○	→
Daily smokers (% of population aged 15 and over)	17.2	2017	●	↑

SDG4 – Quality Education	Value	Year	Rating	Trend
Net primary enrollment rate (%)	* 98.4	2017	●	↑
Lower secondary completion rate (%)	* 98.4	2017	●	↑
Literacy rate (% of population aged 15 to 24)	NA	NA	●	●
Participation rate in pre-primary organized learning (% of children aged 4 to 6)	99.9	2017	●	↑
Tertiary educational attainment (% of population aged 25 to 34)	50.8	2018	●	↑
PISA score (worst 0–600 best)	503.7	2018	●	↑
Variation in science performance explained by socio-economic status (%)	10.7	2018	○	↓
Underachievers in science (% of 15-year-olds)	17.4	2018	●	→
Resilient students in science (% of 15-year-olds)	37.0	2018	○	↑

SDG5 – Gender Equality	Value	Year	Rating	Trend
Demand for family planning satisfied by modern methods (% of females aged 15 to 49 who are married or in unions)	* 93.0	2017	●	↑
Ratio of female-to-male mean years of education received (%)	99.2	2018	●	↑
Ratio of female-to-male labor force participation rate (%)	84.4	2019	●	↑
Seats held by women in national parliament (%)	33.9	2020	●	↑
Gender wage gap (% of male median wage)	16.4	2018	●	→
Gender gap in time spent doing unpaid work (minutes/day)	108.6	2015	○	●

SDG6 – Clean Water and Sanitation	Value	Year	Rating	Trend
Population using at least basic drinking water services (%)	100.0	2017	●	●
Population using at least basic sanitation services (%)	99.1	2017	●	●
Freshwater withdrawal (% of available freshwater resources)	13.7	2010	●	●
Anthropogenic wastewater that receives treatment (%)	98.5	2018	●	●
Scarce water consumption embodied in imports (m³/capita)	33.9	2013	○	↗
Population using safely managed water services (%)	100.0	2017	●	↑
Population using safely managed sanitation services (%)	97.8	2017	●	↑

SDG7 – Affordable and Clean Energy	Value	Year	Rating	Trend
Population with access to electricity (%)	100.0	2017	●	↑
Population with access to clean fuels and technology for cooking (%)	100.0	2016	●	↑
CO₂ emissions from fuel combustion for electricity and heating per total electricity output (MtCO₂/TWh)	1.1	2017	○	↑
Share of renewable energy in total primary energy supply (%)	11.5	2018	●	↑

SDG8 – Decent Work and Economic Growth	Value	Year	Rating	Trend
Adjusted GDP growth (%)	-1.2	2018	○	●
Victims of modern slavery (per 1,000 population)	2.1	2018	●	●
Adults with an account at a bank or other financial institution or with a mobile-money-service provider (% of population aged 15 or over)	96.4	2017	●	↑
Fatal work-related accidents embodied in imports (per 100,000 population)	1.8	2010	●	↑
Employment-to-population ratio (%)	75.2	2019	●	↑
Youth not in employment, education or training (NEET) (% of population aged 15 to 29)	12.6	2018	●	↑

SDG9 – Industry, Innovation and Infrastructure	Value	Year	Rating	Trend
Population using the internet (%)	94.9	2018	●	↑
Mobile broadband subscriptions (per 100 population)	98.5	2018	●	↑
Logistics Performance Index: Quality of trade and transport-related infrastructure (worst 1–5 best)	4.0	2018	●	↑
The Times Higher Education Universities Ranking: Average score of top 3 universities (worst 0–100 best)	93.2	2020	●	●
Scientific and technical journal articles (per 1,000 population)	1.5	2018	●	↑
Expenditure on research and development (% of GDP)	1.7	2017	●	↑
Researchers (per 1,000 employed population)	9.5	2018	●	↑
Triadic patent families filed (per million population)	23.5	2017	●	↑
Gap in internet access by income (percentage points)	36.5	2008	●	●
Women in science and engineering (% of tertiary graduates in science and engineering)	35.3	2015	●	●

SDG10 – Reduced Inequalities	Value	Year	Rating	Trend
Gini coefficient adjusted for top income	37.0	2015	●	↓
Palma ratio	1.5	2017	●	→
Elderly poverty rate (% of population aged 66 or over)	15.3	2017	●	↓

SDG11 – Sustainable Cities and Communities	Value	Year	Rating	Trend
Annual mean concentration of particulate matter of less than 2.5 microns in diameter (PM2.5) (µg/m³)	10.5	2017	○	↑
Access to improved water source, piped (% of urban population)	99.0	2017	●	↑
Satisfaction with public transport (%)	69.8	2019	○	↓
Population with rent overburden (%)	10.4	2017	○	↑

SDG12 – Responsible Consumption and Production	Value	Year	Rating	Trend
Electronic waste (kg/capita)	24.9	2016	●	●
Production-based SO₂ emissions (kg/capita)	53.9	2012	●	●
SO₂ emissions embodied in imports (kg/capita)	17.0	2012	●	●
Production-based nitrogen emissions (kg/capita)	38.0	2010	●	●
Nitrogen emissions embodied in imports (kg/capita)	16.2	2010	●	●
Non-recycled municipal solid waste (kg/capita/day)	0.7	2018	●	●

SDG13 – Climate Action	Value	Year	Rating	Trend
Energy-related CO₂ emissions (tCO₂/capita)	5.5	2017	●	↑
CO₂ emissions embodied in imports (tCO₂/capita)	3.2	2015	●	→
CO₂ emissions embodied in fossil fuel exports (kg/capita)	331.4	2019	○	●
Effective carbon rate (EUR/tCO₂)	14.6	2016	●	●

SDG14 – Life Below Water	Value	Year	Rating	Trend
Mean area that is protected in marine sites important to biodiversity (%)	84.0	2018	●	↑
Ocean Health Index: Clean Waters score (worst 0–100 best)	64.2	2019	●	→
Fish caught from overexploited or collapsed stocks (% of total catch)	18.6	2014	●	↑
Fish caught by trawling (%)	71.2	2014	●	↓
Marine biodiversity threats embodied in imports (per million population)	0.2	2018	○	●

SDG15 – Life on Land	Value	Year	Rating	Trend
Mean area that is protected in terrestrial sites important to biodiversity (%)	84.3	2018	●	↑
Mean area that is protected in freshwater sites important to biodiversity (%)	88.1	2018	●	↑
Red List Index of species survival (worst 0–1 best)	0.8	2019	●	↓
Permanent deforestation (% of forest area, 5-year average)	0.0	2018	●	●
Terrestrial and freshwater biodiversity threats embodied in imports (per million population)	3.2	2018	●	●

SDG16 – Peace, Justice and Strong Institutions	Value	Year	Rating	Trend
Homicides (per 100,000 population)	1.2	2017	●	↑
Unsentenced detainees (% of prison population)	8.8	2018	●	↑
Percentage of population who feel safe walking alone at night in the city or area where they live (%)	74.5	2019	●	↑
Property Rights (worst 1–7 best)	5.5	2019	●	●
Birth registrations with civil authority (% of children under age 5)	100.0	2018	●	●
Corruption Perception Index (worst 0–100 best)	77.0	2019	●	↑
Children involved in child labor (% of population aged 5 to 14)	* 0.0	2016	●	●
Exports of major conventional weapons (TIV constant million USD per 100,000 population)	1.6	2019	○	●
Press Freedom Index (best 0–100 worst)	22.2	2019	●	↑
Persons held in prison (per 100,000 population)	141.3	2017	○	→

SDG17 – Partnerships for the Goals	Value	Year	Rating	Trend
Government spending on health and education (% of GDP)	13.3	2016	●	↑
For high-income and all OECD DAC countries: International concessional public finance, including official development assistance (% of GNI)	0.7	2017	●	↑
Other countries: Government revenue excluding grants (% of GDP)	NA	NA	●	●
Corporate Tax Haven Score (best 0–100 worst)	100.0	2019	●	●
Financial Secrecy Score (best 0–100 worst)	70.8	2020	●	●
Shifted profits of multinationals (US$ billion)	12.8	2016	●	●

* Imputed data point

5. Country Profiles

UNITED STATES

▼ OVERALL PERFORMANCE

Index score

76.4

Regional average score

77.3

SDG Global rank **31** (OF 166)

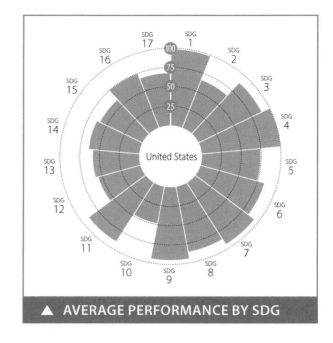

▲ AVERAGE PERFORMANCE BY SDG

▼ SPILLOVER INDEX

100 (best) to 0 (worst)

▼ CURRENT ASSESSMENT – SDG DASHBOARD

- ■ Major challenges
- ■ Significant challenges
- ■ Challenges remain
- ■ SDG achieved
- ■ Information unavailable

▼ SDG TRENDS

1 NO POVERTY	2 ZERO HUNGER	3 GOOD HEALTH AND WELL-BEING	4 QUALITY EDUCATION	5 GENDER EQUALITY	6 CLEAN WATER AND SANITATION	7 AFFORDABLE AND CLEAN ENERGY	8 DECENT WORK AND ECONOMIC GROWTH	9 INDUSTRY, INNOVATION AND INFRASTRUCTURE
↗	→	↗	↗	↗	↑	↗	↑	↑

10 REDUCED INEQUALITIES	11 SUSTAINABLE CITIES AND COMMUNITIES	12 RESPONSIBLE CONSUMPTION AND PRODUCTION	13 CLIMATE ACTION	14 LIFE BELOW WATER	15 LIFE ON LAND	16 PEACE, JUSTICE AND STRONG INSTITUTIONS	17 PARTNERSHIPS FOR THE GOALS
→	↑	●	→	→	↓	↗	→

↓ Decreasing   → Stagnating   ↗ Moderately improving   ↑ On track or maintaining SDG achievement   ● Information unavailable

Notes: The full title of Goal 2 "Zero Hunger" is "End hunger, achieve food security and improved nutrition and promote sustainable agriculture".
The full title of each SDG is available here: https://sustainabledevelopment.un.org/topics/sustainabledevelopmentgoals

SDG1 – No Poverty

Indicator	Value	Year	Rating	Trend
Poverty headcount ratio at $1.90/day (%)	0.5	2020	●	↑
Poverty headcount ratio at $3.20/day (%)	0.7	2020	●	↑
Poverty rate after taxes and transfers (%)	17.8	2017	●	↓

SDG2 – Zero Hunger

Indicator	Value	Year	Rating	Trend
Prevalence of undernourishment (%)	2.5	2017	●	↑
Prevalence of stunting in children under 5 years of age (%)	2.1	2012	●	↑
Prevalence of wasting in children under 5 years of age (%)	0.5	2012	●	↑
Prevalence of obesity, BMI ≥ 30 (% of adult population)	36.2	2016	●	↓
Human Trophic Level (best 2–3 worst)	2.5	2017	●	↓
Cereal yield (tonnes per hectare of harvested land)	8.3	2017	●	↑
Sustainable Nitrogen Management Index (best 0–1.41 worst)	0.3	2015	◐	→
Yield gap closure (% of potential yield)	77.6	2015	●	●

SDG3 – Good Health and Well-Being

Indicator	Value	Year	Rating	Trend
Maternal mortality rate (per 100,000 live births)	19	2017	●	↑
Neonatal mortality rate (per 1,000 live births)	3.5	2018	●	↑
Mortality rate, under-5 (per 1,000 live births)	6.5	2018	●	↑
Incidence of tuberculosis (per 100,000 population)	3.0	2018	●	↑
New HIV infections (per 1,000 uninfected population)	0.1	2016	●	
Age-standardized death rate due to cardiovascular disease, cancer, diabetes, or chronic respiratory disease in adults aged 30–70 years (%)	14.6	2016	●	↑
Age-standardized death rate attributable to household air pollution and ambient air pollution (per 100,000 population)	13	2016	●	●
Traffic deaths (per 100,000 population)	12.4	2016	◐	↓
Life expectancy at birth (years)	78.5	2016	◐	→
Adolescent fertility rate (births per 1,000 adolescent females aged 15 to 19)	19.9	2017	●	↑
Births attended by skilled health personnel (%)	99.1	2015	●	↑
Percentage of surviving infants who received 2 WHO-recommended vaccines (%)	92.0	2018	●	↑
Universal health coverage (UHC) index of service coverage (worst 0–100 best)	84.0	2017	●	↑
Subjective well-being (average ladder score, worst 0–10 best)	6.9	2019	●	↑
Gap in life expectancy at birth among regions (years)	6.3	2010	●	●
Gap in self-reported health status by income (percentage points)	21.7	2017	◐	→
Daily smokers (% of population aged 15 and over)	10.5	2017	●	↑

SDG4 – Quality Education

Indicator	Value	Year	Rating	Trend
Net primary enrollment rate (%)	* 100.0	2017	●	↑
Lower secondary completion rate (%)	* 100.0	2017	●	↑
Literacy rate (% of population aged 15 to 24)	NA	NA	●	●
Participation rate in pre-primary organized learning (% of children aged 4 to 6)	* 91.2	2016	●	●
Tertiary educational attainment (% of population aged 25 to 34)	49.4	2018	●	↑
PISA score (worst 0–600 best)	495.0	2018	●	↑
Variation in science performance explained by socio-economic status (%)	12.3	2018	◐	↓
Underachievers in science (% of 15-year-olds)	18.6	2018	●	↑
Resilient students in science (% of 15-year-olds)	38.6	2018	●	↑

SDG5 – Gender Equality

Indicator	Value	Year	Rating	Trend
Demand for family planning satisfied by modern methods (% of females aged 15 to 49 who are married or in unions)	77.2	2015	◐	↑
Ratio of female-to-male mean years of education received (%)	100.7	2018	●	↑
Ratio of female-to-male labor force participation rate (%)	82.1	2019	●	↑
Seats held by women in national parliament (%)	23.8	2020	●	↗
Gender wage gap (% of male median wage)	18.9	2018	●	↓
Gender gap in time spent doing unpaid work (minutes/day)	96.0	2018	●	●

SDG6 – Clean Water and Sanitation

Indicator	Value	Year	Rating	Trend
Population using at least basic drinking water services (%)	99.3	2017	●	●
Population using at least basic sanitation services (%)	100.0	2017	●	●
Freshwater withdrawal (% of available freshwater resources)	30.6	2010	◐	●
Anthropogenic wastewater that receives treatment (%)	58.9	2018	●	●
Scarce water consumption embodied in imports (m³/capita)	18.3	2013	●	↑
Population using safely managed water services (%)	99.0	2017	◐	↑
Population using safely managed sanitation services (%)	90.0	2017	◐	↑

SDG7 – Affordable and Clean Energy

Indicator	Value	Year	Rating	Trend
Population with access to electricity (%)	100.0	2017	●	↑
Population with access to clean fuels and technology for cooking (%)	100.0	2016	●	↑
CO₂ emissions from fuel combustion for electricity and heating per total electricity output (MtCO₂/TWh)	1.2	2017	◐	↑
Share of renewable energy in total primary energy supply (%)	7.8	2018	●	→

SDG8 – Decent Work and Economic Growth

Indicator	Value	Year	Rating	Trend
Adjusted GDP growth (%)	0.0	2018	●	●
Victims of modern slavery (per 1,000 population)	1.3	2018	●	●
Adults with an account at a bank or other financial institution or with a mobile-money-service provider (% of population aged 15 or over)	93.1	2017	●	↑
Fatal work-related accidents embodied in imports (per 100,000 population)	1.4	2010	◐	↑
Employment-to-population ratio (%)	71.4	2019	●	↑
Youth not in employment, education or training (NEET) (% of population aged 15 to 29)	12.7	2018	●	↑

SDG9 – Industry, Innovation and Infrastructure

Indicator	Value	Year	Rating	Trend
Population using the internet (%)	87.3	2017	●	↑
Mobile broadband subscriptions (per 100 population)	144.8	2018	●	↑
Logistics Performance Index: Quality of trade and transport-related infrastructure (worst 1–5 best)	4.0	2018	●	↑
The Times Higher Education Universities Ranking: Average score of top 3 universities (worst 0–100 best)	94.1	2020	●	●
Scientific and technical journal articles (per 1,000 population)	1.3	2018	●	↑
Expenditure on research and development (% of GDP)	2.8	2017	●	↑
Researchers (per 1,000 employed population)	9.2	2017	●	↑
Triadic patent families filed (per million population)	38.3	2017	●	↑
Gap in internet access by income (percentage points)	29.1	2017	●	↑
Women in science and engineering (% of tertiary graduates in science and engineering)	28.6	2015	●	●

SDG10 – Reduced Inequalities

Indicator	Value	Year	Rating	Trend
Gini coefficient adjusted for top income	46.1	2013	●	●
Palma ratio	1.8	2017	●	→
Elderly poverty rate (% of population aged 66 or over)	23.1	2017	●	↓

SDG11 – Sustainable Cities and Communities

Indicator	Value	Year	Rating	Trend
Annual mean concentration of particulate matter of less than 2.5 microns in diameter (PM2.5) (μg/m³)	7.4	2017	●	↑
Access to improved water source, piped (% of urban population)	99.0	2017	●	↑
Satisfaction with public transport (%)	64.0	2019	◐	↑
Population with rent overburden (%)	11.9	2016	◐	↑

SDG12 – Responsible Consumption and Production

Indicator	Value	Year	Rating	Trend
Electronic waste (kg/capita)	19.4	2016	●	●
Production-based SO₂ emissions (kg/capita)	51.0	2012	●	●
SO₂ emissions embodied in imports (kg/capita)	11.3	2012	●	●
Production-based nitrogen emissions (kg/capita)	54.0	2010	●	●
Nitrogen emissions embodied in imports (kg/capita)	8.4	2010	●	●
Non-recycled municipal solid waste (kg/capita/day)	1.3	2017	●	●

SDG13 – Climate Action

Indicator	Value	Year	Rating	Trend
Energy-related CO₂ emissions (tCO₂/capita)	15.3	2017	●	→
CO₂ emissions embodied in imports (tCO₂/capita)	1.9	2015	●	→
CO₂ emissions embodied in fossil fuel exports (kg/capita)	869.0	2019	◐	●
Effective carbon rate (EUR/tCO₂)	0.8	2016	●	●

SDG14 – Life Below Water

Indicator	Value	Year	Rating	Trend
Mean area that is protected in marine sites important to biodiversity (%)	61.4	2018	●	↑
Ocean Health Index: Clean Waters score (worst 0–100 best)	72.6	2019	●	↑
Fish caught from overexploited or collapsed stocks (% of total catch)	29.8	2014	◐	↓
Fish caught by trawling (%)	44.4	2014	●	↓
Marine biodiversity threats embodied in imports (per million population)	0.5	2018	●	●

SDG15 – Life on Land

Indicator	Value	Year	Rating	Trend
Mean area that is protected in terrestrial sites important to biodiversity (%)	48.3	2018	◐	→
Mean area that is protected in freshwater sites important to biodiversity (%)	33.3	2018	◐	→
Red List Index of species survival (worst 0–1 best)	0.8	2019	●	↓
Permanent deforestation (% of forest area, 5-year average)	0.0	2018	●	●
Terrestrial and freshwater biodiversity threats embodied in imports (per million population)	3.7	2018	●	●

SDG16 – Peace, Justice and Strong Institutions

Indicator	Value	Year	Rating	Trend
Homicides (per 100,000 population)	5.3	2017	●	↓
Unsentenced detainees (% of prison population)	23.4	2018	●	↑
Percentage of population who feel safe walking alone at night in the city or area where they live (%)	74.5	2019	●	↑
Property Rights (worst 1–7 best)	5.6	2019	●	●
Birth registrations with civil authority (% of children under age 5)	100.0	2018	●	●
Corruption Perception Index (worst 0–100 best)	69.0	2019	●	↑
Children involved in child labor (% of population aged 5 to 14)	* 0.0	2016	●	●
Exports of major conventional weapons (TIV constant million USD per 100,000 population)	3.2	2019	●	●
Press Freedom Index (best 0–100 worst)	25.7	2019	●	↑
Persons held in prison (per 100,000 population)	671.1	2016	●	→

SDG17 – Partnerships for the Goals

Indicator	Value	Year	Rating	Trend
Government spending on health and education (% of GDP)	* 15.3	2018	●	↑
For high-income and all OECD DAC countries: International concessional public finance, including official development assistance (% of GNI)	0.2	2017	●	↓
Other countries: Government revenue excluding grants (% of GDP)	NA	NA	●	●
Corporate Tax Haven Score (best 0–100 worst)	43.2	2019	●	●
Financial Secrecy Score (best 0–100 worst)	70.0	2020	●	●
Shifted profits of multinationals (US$ billion)	113.7	2016	●	●

* Imputed data point

5. Country Profiles

▼ OVERALL PERFORMANCE

Index score

74.3

Regional average score

70.4

SDG Global rank 45 (OF 166)

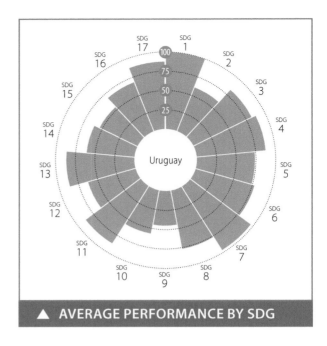

▲ AVERAGE PERFORMANCE BY SDG

▼ SPILLOVER INDEX

100 (best) to 0 (worst)

▼ CURRENT ASSESSMENT – SDG DASHBOARD

■ Major challenges ■ Significant challenges ■ Challenges remain ■ SDG achieved ■ Information unavailable

▼ SDG TRENDS

↓ Decreasing → Stagnating ↗ Moderately improving ↑ On track or maintaining SDG achievement ● Information unavailable

Notes: The full title of Goal 2 "Zero Hunger" is "End hunger, achieve food security and improved nutrition and promote sustainable agriculture".
The full title of each SDG is available here: https://sustainabledevelopment.un.org/topics/sustainabledevelopmentgoals

SDG1 – No Poverty

	Value	Year	Rating	Trend
Poverty headcount ratio at $1.90/day (%)	0.0	2020	●	↑
Poverty headcount ratio at $3.20/day (%)	0.1	2020	●	↑

SDG2 – Zero Hunger

	Value	Year	Rating	Trend
Prevalence of undernourishment (%)	2.5	2017	●	↑
Prevalence of stunting in children under 5 years of age (%)	10.7	2011	○	↗
Prevalence of wasting in children under 5 years of age (%)	1.3	2011	●	↑
Prevalence of obesity, BMI ≥ 30 (% of adult population)	27.9	2016	●	↓
Human Trophic Level (best 2–3 worst)	2.4	2017	●	↗
Cereal yield (tonnes per hectare of harvested land)	4.3	2017	●	↑
Sustainable Nitrogen Management Index (best 0–1.41 worst)	0.5	2015	○	↓

SDG3 – Good Health and Well-Being

	Value	Year	Rating	Trend
Maternal mortality rate (per 100,000 live births)	17	2017	●	↑
Neonatal mortality rate (per 1,000 live births)	4.5	2018	●	↑
Mortality rate, under-5 (per 1,000 live births)	7.6	2018	●	↑
Incidence of tuberculosis (per 100,000 population)	33.0	2018	○	→
New HIV infections (per 1,000 uninfected population)	0.3	2018	●	→
Age-standardized death rate due to cardiovascular disease, cancer, diabetes, or chronic respiratory disease in adults aged 30–70 years (%)	16.7	2016	●	↑
Age-standardized death rate attributable to household air pollution and ambient air pollution (per 100,000 population)	18	2016	●	●
Traffic deaths (per 100,000 population)	13.4	2016	●	↑
Life expectancy at birth (years)	77.1	2016	●	↗
Adolescent fertility rate (births per 1,000 adolescent females aged 15 to 19)	58.7	2017	●	→
Births attended by skilled health personnel (%)	99.9	2014	●	●
Percentage of surviving infants who received 2 WHO-recommended vaccines (%)	91	2018	●	↑
Universal health coverage (UHC) index of service coverage (worst 0–100 best)	80.0	2017	●	↑
Subjective well-being (average ladder score, worst 0–10 best)	6.4	2018	●	↑

SDG4 – Quality Education

	Value	Year	Rating	Trend
Net primary enrollment rate (%)	99.4	2017	●	●
Lower secondary completion rate (%)	74.3	2010	●	●
Literacy rate (% of population aged 15 to 24)	98.9	2018	●	●

SDG5 – Gender Equality

	Value	Year	Rating	Trend
Demand for family planning satisfied by modern methods (% of females aged 15 to 49 who are married or in unions) *	89.5	2017	●	↑
Ratio of female-to-male mean years of education received (%)	107.1	2018	●	↑
Ratio of female-to-male labor force participation rate (%)	75.8	2019	●	↑
Seats held by women in national parliament (%)	21.2	2020	●	↗

SDG6 – Clean Water and Sanitation

	Value	Year	Rating	Trend
Population using at least basic drinking water services (%)	99.4	2017	●	↑
Population using at least basic sanitation services (%)	96.6	2017	●	↑
Freshwater withdrawal (% of available freshwater resources)	9.8	2000	●	●
Anthropogenic wastewater that receives treatment (%)	2.2	2018	●	●
Scarce water consumption embodied in imports (m³/capita)	5.8	2013	●	↑

SDG7 – Affordable and Clean Energy

	Value	Year	Rating	Trend
Population with access to electricity (%)	100.0	2017	●	↑
Population with access to clean fuels and technology for cooking (%)	98.0	2016	●	↑
CO_2 emissions from fuel combustion for electricity and heating per total electricity output (MtCO₂/TWh)	0.4	2017	●	↑

SDG8 – Decent Work and Economic Growth

	Value	Year	Rating	Trend
Adjusted GDP growth (%)	-1.4	2018	○	●
Victims of modern slavery (per 1,000 population)	1.0	2018	●	●
Adults with an account at a bank or other financial institution or with a mobile-money-service provider (% of population aged 15 or over)	63.9	2017	●	↑
Unemployment rate (% of total labor force)	8.7	2019	●	↓
Fatal work-related accidents embodied in imports (per 100,000 population)	0.5	2010	●	↑

SDG9 – Industry, Innovation and Infrastructure

	Value	Year	Rating	Trend
Population using the internet (%)	74.8	2018	○	↑
Mobile broadband subscriptions (per 100 population)	123.9	2018	●	↑
Logistics Performance Index: Quality of trade and transport-related infrastructure (worst 1–5 best)	2.4	2018	●	↓
The Times Higher Education Universities Ranking: Average score of top 3 universities (worst 0–100 best) *	12.0	2019	●	●
Scientific and technical journal articles (per 1,000 population)	0.2	2018	●	→
Expenditure on research and development (% of GDP)	0.4	2016	●	→

SDG10 – Reduced Inequalities

	Value	Year	Rating	Trend
Gini coefficient adjusted for top income	42.9	2017	●	●

SDG11 – Sustainable Cities and Communities

	Value	Year	Rating	Trend
Annual mean concentration of particulate matter of less than 2.5 microns in diameter (PM2.5) (μg/m³)	9.3	2017	●	↑
Access to improved water source, piped (% of urban population)	99.0	2017	●	↑
Satisfaction with public transport (%)	60.7	2018	○	↑

SDG12 – Responsible Consumption and Production

	Value	Year	Rating	Trend
Municipal solid waste (kg/capita/day)	1.0	2015	○	●
Electronic waste (kg/capita)	10.8	2016	●	●
Production-based SO_2 emissions (kg/capita)	124.5	2012	●	●
SO_2 emissions embodied in imports (kg/capita)	5.9	2012	○	●
Production-based nitrogen emissions (kg/capita)	101.2	2010	●	●
Nitrogen emissions embodied in imports (kg/capita)	6.6	2010	○	●

SDG13 – Climate Action

	Value	Year	Rating	Trend
Energy-related CO_2 emissions (tCO₂/capita)	2.5	2017	○	↓
CO_2 emissions embodied in imports (tCO₂/capita)	1.1	2015	●	↗
CO_2 emissions embodied in fossil fuel exports (kg/capita)	0.0	2018	●	●

SDG14 – Life Below Water

	Value	Year	Rating	Trend
Mean area that is protected in marine sites important to biodiversity (%)	52.5	2018	●	↑
Ocean Health Index: Clean Waters score (worst 0–100 best)	58.3	2019	●	→
Fish caught from overexploited or collapsed stocks (% of total catch)	36.3	2014	○	↑
Fish caught by trawling (%)	46.8	2014	●	↗
Marine biodiversity threats embodied in imports (per million population)	0.0	2018	●	●

SDG15 – Life on Land

	Value	Year	Rating	Trend
Mean area that is protected in terrestrial sites important to biodiversity (%)	20.8	2018	●	→
Mean area that is protected in freshwater sites important to biodiversity (%)	2.3	2018	●	→
Red List Index of species survival (worst 0–1 best)	0.8	2019	●	↓
Permanent deforestation (% of forest area, 5-year average)	0.1	2018	●	●
Terrestrial and freshwater biodiversity threats embodied in imports (per million population)	0.7	2018	●	●

SDG16 – Peace, Justice and Strong Institutions

	Value	Year	Rating	Trend
Homicides (per 100,000 population)	8.2	2017	●	→
Unsentenced detainees (% of prison population)	69.7	2018	●	↓
Percentage of population who feel safe walking alone at night in the city or area where they live	39.5	2018	●	↓
Property Rights (worst 1–7 best)	5.1	2019	●	●
Birth registrations with civil authority (% of children under age 5)	99.8	2018	●	●
Corruption Perception Index (worst 0–100 best)	71	2019	●	↑
Children involved in child labor (% of population aged 5 to 14)	7.9	2016	●	●
Exports of major conventional weapons (TIV constant million USD per 100,000 population) *	0.0	2019	●	●
Press Freedom Index (best 0–100 worst)	16.1	2019	●	↑

SDG17 – Partnerships for the Goals

	Value	Year	Rating	Trend
Government spending on health and education (% of GDP)	11.3	2016	●	●
For high-income and all OECD DAC countries: International concessional public finance, including official development assistance (% of GNI)	NA	NA	●	●
Other countries: Government revenue excluding grants (% of GDP)	NA	NA	●	●
Corporate Tax Haven Score (best 0–100 worst) *	0.0	2019	●	●

* Imputed data point

5. Country Profiles

UZBEKISTAN

▼ OVERALL PERFORMANCE

Index score

71.0

Regional average score

70.9

SDG Global rank **66** (OF 166)

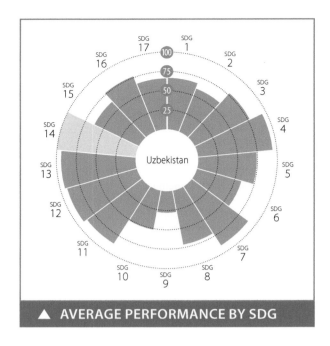

▲ AVERAGE PERFORMANCE BY SDG

▼ SPILLOVER INDEX

100 (best) to 0 (worst)

▼ CURRENT ASSESSMENT – SDG DASHBOARD

■ Major challenges   ■ Significant challenges   ■ Challenges remain   ■ SDG achieved   ■ Information unavailable

▼ SDG TRENDS

↓ Decreasing   → Stagnating   ↗ Moderately improving   ↑ On track or maintaining SDG achievement   ● Information unavailable

Notes: The full title of Goal 2 "Zero Hunger" is "End hunger, achieve food security and improved nutrition and promote sustainable agriculture".
The full title of each SDG is available here: https://sustainabledevelopment.un.org/topics/sustainabledevelopmentgoals

SDG1 – No Poverty

Indicator	Value	Year	Rating	Trend
Poverty headcount ratio at $1.90/day (%)	6.8	2020	●	↑
Poverty headcount ratio at $3.20/day (%)	28.7	2020	●	↗

SDG2 – Zero Hunger

Indicator	Value	Year	Rating	Trend
Prevalence of undernourishment (%)	6.3	2017	●	↑
Prevalence of stunting in children under 5 years of age (%)	19.6	2006	●	↗
Prevalence of wasting in children under 5 years of age (%)	4.5	2006	●	↑
Prevalence of obesity, BMI ≥ 30 (% of adult population)	16.6	2016	●	↓
Human Trophic Level (best 2–3 worst)	2.3	2017	●	→
Cereal yield (tonnes per hectare of harvested land)	4.3	2017	●	↑
Sustainable Nitrogen Management Index (best 0–1.41 worst)	0.7	2015	●	↓

SDG3 – Good Health and Well-Being

Indicator	Value	Year	Rating	Trend
Maternal mortality rate (per 100,000 live births)	29	2017	●	↑
Neonatal mortality rate (per 1,000 live births)	11.6	2018	●	↑
Mortality rate, under-5 (per 1,000 live births)	21.4	2018	●	↑
Incidence of tuberculosis (per 100,000 population)	70.0	2018	●	↗
New HIV infections (per 1,000 uninfected population)	0.2	2018	●	↑
Age-standardized death rate due to cardiovascular disease, cancer, diabetes, or chronic respiratory disease in adults aged 30–70 years (%)	24.5	2016	●	↗
Age-standardized death rate attributable to household air pollution and ambient air pollution (per 100,000 population)	81	2016	●	●
Traffic deaths (per 100,000 population)	11.5	2016	●	→
Life expectancy at birth (years)	72.3	2016	●	→
Adolescent fertility rate (births per 1,000 adolescent females aged 15 to 19)	23.8	2017	●	↑
Births attended by skilled health personnel (%)	100.0	2015	●	↑
Percentage of surviving infants who received 2 WHO-recommended vaccines (%)	96	2018	●	↑
Universal health coverage (UHC) index of service coverage (worst 0–100 best)	73.0	2017	●	↑
Subjective well-being (average ladder score, worst 0–10 best)	6.2	2019	●	↑

SDG4 – Quality Education

Indicator	Value	Year	Rating	Trend
Net primary enrollment rate (%)	94.6	2018	●	↗
Lower secondary completion rate (%)	95.9	2018	●	↑
Literacy rate (% of population aged 15 to 24)	100.0	2018	●	●

SDG5 – Gender Equality

Indicator	Value	Year	Rating	Trend
Demand for family planning satisfied by modern methods (% of females aged 15 to 49 who are married or in unions) *	83.5	2017	●	↑
Ratio of female-to-male mean years of education received (%)	95.8	2018	●	→
Ratio of female-to-male labor force participation rate (%)	68.4	2019	●	→
Seats held by women in national parliament (%)	32.0	2020	●	↑

SDG6 – Clean Water and Sanitation

Indicator	Value	Year	Rating	Trend
Population using at least basic drinking water services (%)	97.8	2017	●	↑
Population using at least basic sanitation services (%)	100.0	2017	●	↑
Freshwater withdrawal (% of available freshwater resources)	136.9	2015	●	●
Anthropogenic wastewater that receives treatment (%)	0.0	2018	●	●
Scarce water consumption embodied in imports (m³/capita)	4.6	2013	●	↑

SDG7 – Affordable and Clean Energy

Indicator	Value	Year	Rating	Trend
Population with access to electricity (%)	100.0	2017	●	↑
Population with access to clean fuels and technology for cooking (%)	92.1	2016	●	↑
CO₂ emissions from fuel combustion for electricity and heating per total electricity output (MtCO₂/TWh)	1.4	2017	●	↑

SDG8 – Decent Work and Economic Growth

Indicator	Value	Year	Rating	Trend
Adjusted GDP growth (%)	-1.2	2018	●	●
Victims of modern slavery (per 1,000 population)	5.2	2018	●	●
Adults with an account at a bank or other financial institution or with a mobile-money-service provider (% of population aged 15 or over)	37.1	2017	●	↓
Unemployment rate (% of total labor force)	5.9	2019	●	↓
Fatal work-related accidents embodied in imports (per 100,000 population)	0.1	2010	●	↑

SDG9 – Industry, Innovation and Infrastructure

Indicator	Value	Year	Rating	Trend
Population using the internet (%)	55.2	2018	●	↑
Mobile broadband subscriptions (per 100 population)	62.4	2018	●	↑
Logistics Performance Index: Quality of trade and transport-related infrastructure (worst 1–5 best)	2.6	2018	●	↑
The Times Higher Education Universities Ranking: Average score of top 3 universities (worst 0–100 best) *	0.0	2020	●	●
Scientific and technical journal articles (per 1,000 population)	0.0	2018	●	→
Expenditure on research and development (% of GDP)	0.2	2017	●	↓

SDG10 – Reduced Inequalities

Indicator	Value	Year	Rating	Trend
Gini coefficient adjusted for top income	44.8	2003	●	●

SDG11 – Sustainable Cities and Communities

Indicator	Value	Year	Rating	Trend
Annual mean concentration of particulate matter of less than 2.5 microns in diameter (PM2.5) (µg/m³)	28.5	2017	●	→
Access to improved water source, piped (% of urban population)	88.1	2017	●	↓
Satisfaction with public transport (%)	85.2	2019	●	↑

SDG12 – Responsible Consumption and Production

Indicator	Value	Year	Rating	Trend
Municipal solid waste (kg/capita/day)	0.7	2012	●	●
Electronic waste (kg/capita)	NA	NA	●	●
Production-based SO₂ emissions (kg/capita)	23.6	2012	●	●
SO₂ emissions embodied in imports (kg/capita)	0.9	2012	●	●
Production-based nitrogen emissions (kg/capita)	20.3	2010	●	●
Nitrogen emissions embodied in imports (kg/capita)	0.3	2010	●	●

SDG13 – Climate Action

Indicator	Value	Year	Rating	Trend
Energy-related CO₂ emissions (tCO₂/capita)	3.3	2017	●	↗
CO₂ emissions embodied in imports (tCO₂/capita)	0.1	2015	●	↑
CO₂ emissions embodied in fossil fuel exports (kg/capita)	468.2	2018	●	●

SDG14 – Life Below Water

Indicator	Value	Year	Rating	Trend
Mean area that is protected in marine sites important to biodiversity (%)	NA	NA	●	●
Ocean Health Index: Clean Waters score (worst 0–100 best)	NA	NA	●	●
Fish caught from overexploited or collapsed stocks (% of total catch)	NA	NA	●	●
Fish caught by trawling (%)	NA	NA	●	●
Marine biodiversity threats embodied in imports (per million population)	0.0	2018	●	●

SDG15 – Life on Land

Indicator	Value	Year	Rating	Trend
Mean area that is protected in terrestrial sites important to biodiversity (%)	15.5	2018	●	→
Mean area that is protected in freshwater sites important to biodiversity (%)	10.4	2018	●	→
Red List Index of species survival (worst 0–1 best)	1.0	2019	●	↑
Permanent deforestation (% of forest area, 5-year average) *	0.0	2018	●	●
Terrestrial and freshwater biodiversity threats embodied in imports (per million population)	0.0	2018	●	●

SDG16 – Peace, Justice and Strong Institutions

Indicator	Value	Year	Rating	Trend
Homicides (per 100,000 population)	1.1	2017	●	↑
Unsentenced detainees (% of prison population)	10.0	2009	●	●
Percentage of population who feel safe walking alone at night in the city or area where they live (%)	87.1	2019	●	↑
Property Rights (worst 1–7 best)	NA	NA	●	●
Birth registrations with civil authority (% of children under age 5)	99.9	2018	●	●
Corruption Perception Index (worst 0–100 best)	25	2019	●	↗
Children involved in child labor (% of population aged 5 to 14)	NA	NA	●	●
Exports of major conventional weapons (TIV constant million USD per 100,000 population)	0.2	2019	●	●
Press Freedom Index (best 0–100 worst)	53.5	2019	●	↗

SDG17 – Partnerships for the Goals

Indicator	Value	Year	Rating	Trend
Government spending on health and education (% of GDP)	8.6	2016	●	↓
For high-income and all OECD DAC countries: International concessional public finance, including official development assistance (% of GNI)	NA	NA	●	●
Other countries: Government revenue excluding grants (% of GDP)	22.3	2018	●	→
Corporate Tax Haven Score (best 0–100 worst) *	0.0	2019	●	●

* Imputed data point

▼ OVERALL PERFORMANCE

Index score

60.9

Regional average score

49.6

SDG Global rank 122 (OF 166)

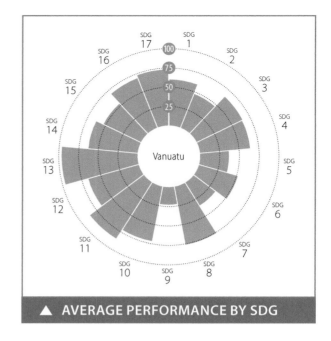

▲ AVERAGE PERFORMANCE BY SDG

▼ SPILLOVER INDEX

100 (best) to 0 (worst)

▼ CURRENT ASSESSMENT – SDG DASHBOARD

■ Major challenges   ■ Significant challenges   ■ Challenges remain   ■ SDG achieved   ■ Information unavailable

▼ SDG TRENDS

↓ Decreasing   → Stagnating   ↗ Moderately improving   ↑ On track or maintaining SDG achievement   ● Information unavailable

Notes: The full title of Goal 2 "Zero Hunger" is "End hunger, achieve food security and improved nutrition and promote sustainable agriculture".
The full title of each SDG is available here: https://sustainabledevelopment.un.org/topics/sustainabledevelopmentgoals

SDG1 – No Poverty

Indicator	Value	Year
Poverty headcount ratio at $1.90/day (%)	10.6	2020
Poverty headcount ratio at $3.20/day (%)	33.6	2020

SDG2 – Zero Hunger

Indicator	Value	Year
Prevalence of undernourishment (%)	7.2	2017
Prevalence of stunting in children under 5 years of age (%)	28.5	2013
Prevalence of wasting in children under 5 years of age (%)	4.4	2013
Prevalence of obesity, BMI ≥ 30 (% of adult population)	25.2	2016
Human Trophic Level (best 2–3 worst)	2.2	2017
Cereal yield (tonnes per hectare of harvested land)	0.6	2017
Sustainable Nitrogen Management Index (best 0–1.41 worst)	0.9	2015

SDG3 – Good Health and Well-Being

Indicator	Value	Year
Maternal mortality rate (per 100,000 live births)	72	2017
Neonatal mortality rate (per 1,000 live births)	11.5	2018
Mortality rate, under-5 (per 1,000 live births)	26.4	2018
Incidence of tuberculosis (per 100,000 population)	46.0	2018
New HIV infections (per 1,000 uninfected population)	NA	NA
Age-standardized death rate due to cardiovascular disease, cancer, diabetes, or chronic respiratory disease in adults aged 30–70 years (%)	23.3	2016
Age-standardized death rate attributable to household air pollution and ambient air pollution (per 100,000 population)	136	2016
Traffic deaths (per 100,000 population)	15.9	2016
Life expectancy at birth (years)	72.0	2016
Adolescent fertility rate (births per 1,000 adolescent females aged 15 to 19)	49.4	2017
Births attended by skilled health personnel (%)	89.4	2013
Percentage of surviving infants who received 2 WHO-recommended vaccines (%)	75	2018
Universal health coverage (UHC) index of service coverage (worst 0–100 best)	48.0	2017
Subjective well-being (average ladder score, worst 0–10 best)	NA	NA

SDG4 – Quality Education

Indicator	Value	Year
Net primary enrollment rate (%)	79.8	2015
Lower secondary completion rate (%)	53.3	2013
Literacy rate (% of population aged 15 to 24)	96.3	2018

SDG5 – Gender Equality

Indicator	Value	Year
Demand for family planning satisfied by modern methods (% of females aged 15 to 49 who are married or in unions)	50.7	2013
Ratio of female-to-male mean years of education received (%)	NA	NA
Ratio of female-to-male labor force participation rate (%)	77.2	2019
Seats held by women in national parliament (%)	0.0	2020

SDG6 – Clean Water and Sanitation

Indicator	Value	Year
Population using at least basic drinking water services (%)	91.3	2017
Population using at least basic sanitation services (%)	34.1	2017
Freshwater withdrawal (% of available freshwater resources)	NA	NA
Anthropogenic wastewater that receives treatment (%)	0.0	2018
Scarce water consumption embodied in imports (m³/capita)	5.1	2013

SDG7 – Affordable and Clean Energy

Indicator	Value	Year
Population with access to electricity (%)	62.8	2017
Population with access to clean fuels and technology for cooking (%)	12.6	2016
CO_2 emissions from fuel combustion for electricity and heating per total electricity output (MtCO$_2$/TWh)	NA	NA

SDG8 – Decent Work and Economic Growth

Indicator	Value	Year
Adjusted GDP growth (%)	-4.9	2018
Victims of modern slavery (per 1,000 population)	NA	NA
Adults with an account at a bank or other financial institution or with a mobile-money-service provider (% of population aged 15 or over)	NA	NA
Unemployment rate (% of total labor force)	4.4	2019
Fatal work-related accidents embodied in imports (per 100,000 population)	0.4	2010

SDG9 – Industry, Innovation and Infrastructure

Indicator	Value	Year
Population using the internet (%)	25.7	2017
Mobile broadband subscriptions (per 100 population)	65.1	2018
Logistics Performance Index: Quality of trade and transport-related infrastructure (worst 1–5 best)	NA	NA
The Times Higher Education Universities Ranking: Average score of top 3 universities (worst 0–100 best) *	0.0	2020
Scientific and technical journal articles (per 1,000 population)	0.0	2018
Expenditure on research and development (% of GDP)	NA	NA

SDG10 – Reduced Inequalities

Indicator	Value	Year
Gini coefficient adjusted for top income	37.6	2010

SDG11 – Sustainable Cities and Communities

Indicator	Value	Year
Annual mean concentration of particulate matter of less than 2.5 microns in diameter (PM2.5) (µg/m³)	11.7	2017
Access to improved water source, piped (% of urban population)	78.5	2017
Satisfaction with public transport (%)	NA	NA

SDG12 – Responsible Consumption and Production

Indicator	Value	Year
Municipal solid waste (kg/capita/day)	2.7	2016
Electronic waste (kg/capita)	1.0	2016
Production-based SO_2 emissions (kg/capita)	407.7	2012
SO_2 emissions embodied in imports (kg/capita)	6.5	2012
Production-based nitrogen emissions (kg/capita)	23.9	2010
Nitrogen emissions embodied in imports (kg/capita)	2.6	2010

SDG13 – Climate Action

Indicator	Value	Year
Energy-related CO_2 emissions (tCO$_2$/capita)	0.7	2017
CO_2 emissions embodied in imports (tCO$_2$/capita)	0.3	2015
CO_2 emissions embodied in fossil fuel exports (kg/capita) *	0.0	2018

SDG14 – Life Below Water

Indicator	Value	Year
Mean area that is protected in marine sites important to biodiversity (%)	4.7	2018
Ocean Health Index: Clean Waters score (worst 0–100 best)	61.9	2019
Fish caught from overexploited or collapsed stocks (% of total catch)	34.4	2014
Fish caught by trawling (%)	1.0	2014
Marine biodiversity threats embodied in imports (per million population)	0.0	2018

SDG15 – Life on Land

Indicator	Value	Year
Mean area that is protected in terrestrial sites important to biodiversity (%)	6.4	2018
Mean area that is protected in freshwater sites important to biodiversity (%)	NA	NA
Red List Index of species survival (worst 0–1 best)	0.7	2019
Permanent deforestation (% of forest area, 5-year average)	0.0	2018
Terrestrial and freshwater biodiversity threats embodied in imports (per million population)	0.3	2018

SDG16 – Peace, Justice and Strong Institutions

Indicator	Value	Year
Homicides (per 100,000 population) *	2.1	2015
Unsentenced detainees (% of prison population)	22.4	2018
Percentage of population who feel safe walking alone at night in the city or area where they live (%)	NA	NA
Property Rights (worst 1–7 best)	NA	NA
Birth registrations with civil authority (% of children under age 5)	43.4	2018
Corruption Perception Index (worst 0–100 best)	46	2019
Children involved in child labor (% of population aged 5 to 14)	15.2	2016
Exports of major conventional weapons (TIV constant million USD per 100,000 population) *	0.0	2019
Press Freedom Index (best 0–100 worst)	NA	NA

SDG17 – Partnerships for the Goals

Indicator	Value	Year
Government spending on health and education (% of GDP)	7.6	2015
For high-income and all OECD DAC countries: International concessional public finance, including official development assistance (% of GNI)	NA	NA
Other countries: Government revenue excluding grants (% of GDP)	30.3	2018
Corporate Tax Haven Score (best 0–100 worst) *	0.0	2019

* Imputed data point

5. Country Profiles

VENEZUELA, RB

▼ OVERALL PERFORMANCE

Index score

61.7

Regional average score

70.4

SDG Global rank 118 (OF 166)

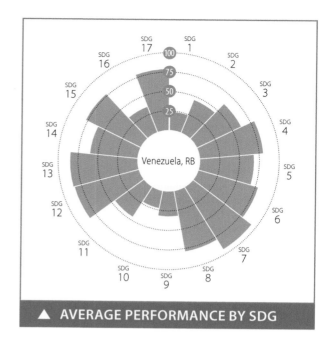

▲ AVERAGE PERFORMANCE BY SDG

▼ SPILLOVER INDEX

100 (best) to 0 (worst)

▼ CURRENT ASSESSMENT – SDG DASHBOARD

■ Major challenges ■ Significant challenges ▦ Challenges remain ■ SDG achieved ■ Information unavailable

▼ SDG TRENDS

↓ Decreasing → Stagnating ↗ Moderately improving ↑ On track or maintaining SDG achievement ● Information unavailable

Notes: The full title of Goal 2 "Zero Hunger" is "End hunger, achieve food security and improved nutrition and promote sustainable agriculture".
The full title of each SDG is available here: https://sustainabledevelopment.un.org/topics/sustainabledevelopmentgoals

VENEZUELA, RB

SDG1 – No Poverty	Value	Year	Rating	Trend
Poverty headcount ratio at $1.90/day (%)	36.6	2020	●	↓
Poverty headcount ratio at $3.20/day (%)	59.7	2020	●	↓

SDG2 – Zero Hunger	Value	Year	Rating	Trend
Prevalence of undernourishment (%)	21.2	2017	●	↓
Prevalence of stunting in children under 5 years of age (%)	13.4	2009	●	→
Prevalence of wasting in children under 5 years of age (%)	4.1	2009	●	↑
Prevalence of obesity, BMI ≥ 30 (% of adult population)	25.6	2016	●	↓
Human Trophic Level (best 2–3 worst)	2.3	2017	●	↑
Cereal yield (tonnes per hectare of harvested land)	3.1	2017	●	↑
Sustainable Nitrogen Management Index (best 0–1.41 worst)	1.0	2015	●	↓

SDG3 – Good Health and Well-Being	Value	Year	Rating	Trend
Maternal mortality rate (per 100,000 live births)	125	2017	●	→
Neonatal mortality rate (per 1,000 live births)	15.1	2018	●	→
Mortality rate, under-5 (per 1,000 live births)	24.5	2018	●	↑
Incidence of tuberculosis (per 100,000 population)	48.0	2018	●	→
New HIV infections (per 1,000 uninfected population)	NA	NA	●	●
Age-standardized death rate due to cardiovascular disease, cancer, diabetes, or chronic respiratory disease in adults aged 30–70 years (%)	18.1	2016	◐	→
Age-standardized death rate attributable to household air pollution and ambient air pollution (per 100,000 population)	35	2016	◐	●
Traffic deaths (per 100,000 population)	33.7	2016	●	↑
Life expectancy at birth (years)	74.1	2016	●	→
Adolescent fertility rate (births per 1,000 adolescent females aged 15 to 19)	85.3	2017	●	→
Births attended by skilled health personnel (%)	96.2	2016	◐	→
Percentage of surviving infants who received 2 WHO-recommended vaccines (%)	60	2018	●	↓
Universal health coverage (UHC) index of service coverage (worst 0–100 best)	74.0	2017	◐	↑
Subjective well-being (average ladder score, worst 0–10 best)	5.1	2019	●	↓

SDG4 – Quality Education	Value	Year	Rating	Trend
Net primary enrollment rate (%)	87.4	2017	●	↓
Lower secondary completion rate (%)	75.2	2017	●	↓
Literacy rate (% of population aged 15 to 24)	98.8	2016	●	●

SDG5 – Gender Equality	Value	Year	Rating	Trend
Demand for family planning satisfied by modern methods (% of females aged 15 to 49 who are married or in unions) *	81.4	2017	●	↑
Ratio of female-to-male mean years of education received (%)	107.0	2018	●	↑
Ratio of female-to-male labor force participation rate (%)	62.1	2019	◐	↓
Seats held by women in national parliament (%)	22.2	2020	●	↗

SDG6 – Clean Water and Sanitation	Value	Year	Rating	Trend
Population using at least basic drinking water services (%)	95.7	2017	◐	→
Population using at least basic sanitation services (%)	93.9	2017	◐	→
Freshwater withdrawal (% of available freshwater resources)	7.5	2005	●	●
Anthropogenic wastewater that receives treatment (%)	6.4	2018	●	●
Scarce water consumption embodied in imports (m3/capita)	1.9	2013	●	↑

SDG7 – Affordable and Clean Energy	Value	Year	Rating	Trend
Population with access to electricity (%)	100.0	2017	●	↑
Population with access to clean fuels and technology for cooking (%)	96.2	2016	●	↑
CO2 emissions from fuel combustion for electricity and heating per total electricity output (MtCO2/TWh)	1.1	2017	◐	↑

SDG8 – Decent Work and Economic Growth	Value	Year	Rating	Trend
Adjusted GDP growth (%)	NA	NA	●	●
Victims of modern slavery (per 1,000 population)	5.6	2018	◐	●
Adults with an account at a bank or other financial institution or with a mobile-money-service provider (% of population aged 15 or over)	73.5	2017	◐	↑
Unemployment rate (% of total labor force)	8.8	2019	●	↓
Fatal work-related accidents embodied in imports (per 100,000 population)	0.1	2010	●	↑

SDG9 – Industry, Innovation and Infrastructure	Value	Year	Rating	Trend
Population using the internet (%)	72.0	2017	◐	↑
Mobile broadband subscriptions (per 100 population)	54.5	2018	●	↑
Logistics Performance Index: Quality of trade and transport-related infrastructure (worst 1–5 best)	2.1	2018	●	↓
The Times Higher Education Universities Ranking: Average score of top 3 universities (worst 0–100 best)	16.4	2020	◐	●
Scientific and technical journal articles (per 1,000 population)	0.0	2018	●	↓
Expenditure on research and development (% of GDP)	0.1	2016	●	↓

SDG10 – Reduced Inequalities	Value	Year	Rating	Trend
Gini coefficient adjusted for top income	55.3	2006	●	●

SDG11 – Sustainable Cities and Communities	Value	Year	Rating	Trend
Annual mean concentration of particulate matter of less than 2.5 microns in diameter (PM2.5) (μg/m3)	17.0	2017	◐	↑
Access to improved water source, piped (% of urban population)	NA	NA	●	●
Satisfaction with public transport (%)	22.6	2019	●	↓

SDG12 – Responsible Consumption and Production	Value	Year	Rating	Trend
Municipal solid waste (kg/capita/day)	0.9	2012	●	●
Electronic waste (kg/capita)	8.2	2016	◐	●
Production-based SO2 emissions (kg/capita)	32.8	2012	◐	●
SO2 emissions embodied in imports (kg/capita)	1.8	2012	●	●
Production-based nitrogen emissions (kg/capita)	27.6	2010	◐	●
Nitrogen emissions embodied in imports (kg/capita)	1.7	2010	●	●

SDG13 – Climate Action	Value	Year	Rating	Trend
Energy-related CO2 emissions (tCO2/capita)	5.3	2017	●	↗
CO2 emissions embodied in imports (tCO2/capita)	0.3	2015	●	↑
CO2 emissions embodied in fossil fuel exports (kg/capita)	NA	NA	●	●

SDG14 – Life Below Water	Value	Year	Rating	Trend
Mean area that is protected in marine sites important to biodiversity (%)	48.7	2018	◐	→
Ocean Health Index: Clean Waters score (worst 0–100 best)	62.0	2019	●	→
Fish caught from overexploited or collapsed stocks (% of total catch)	80.1	2014	●	↓
Fish caught by trawling (%)	5.1	2014	●	↑
Marine biodiversity threats embodied in imports (per million population)	0.0	2018	●	●

SDG15 – Life on Land	Value	Year	Rating	Trend
Mean area that is protected in terrestrial sites important to biodiversity (%)	66.5	2018	●	↑
Mean area that is protected in freshwater sites important to biodiversity (%)	85.8	2018	●	↑
Red List Index of species survival (worst 0–1 best)	0.8	2019	●	↓
Permanent deforestation (% of forest area, 5-year average)	0.1	2018	●	●
Terrestrial and freshwater biodiversity threats embodied in imports (per million population)	0.8	2018	●	●

SDG16 – Peace, Justice and Strong Institutions	Value	Year	Rating	Trend
Homicides (per 100,000 population)	56.3	2016	●	↗
Unsentenced detainees (% of prison population)	63.0	2018	●	→
Percentage of population who feel safe walking alone at night in the city or area where they live (%)	29.4	2019	●	↑
Property Rights (worst 1–7 best)	1.6	2019	●	●
Birth registrations with civil authority (% of children under age 5)	81.3	2018	●	●
Corruption Perception Index (worst 0–100 best)	16	2019	●	↓
Children involved in child labor (% of population aged 5 to 14)	7.7	2016	●	●
Exports of major conventional weapons (TIV constant million USD per 100,000 population) *	0.0	2019	●	●
Press Freedom Index (best 0–100 worst)	49.1	2019	◐	↓

SDG17 – Partnerships for the Goals	Value	Year	Rating	Trend
Government spending on health and education (% of GDP)	8.9	2009	●	●
For high-income and all OECD DAC countries: International concessional public finance, including official development assistance (% of GNI)	NA	NA	●	●
Other countries: Government revenue excluding grants (% of GDP)	NA	NA	●	●
Corporate Tax Haven Score (best 0–100 worst) *	0.0	2019	●	●

* Imputed data point

VIETNAM

▼ OVERALL PERFORMANCE

Index score

73.8

Regional average score

67.2

SDG Global rank 49 (OF 166)

▲ AVERAGE PERFORMANCE BY SDG

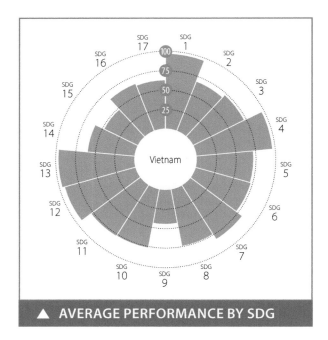

▼ SPILLOVER INDEX

100 (best) to 0 (worst)

▼ CURRENT ASSESSMENT – SDG DASHBOARD

■ Major challenges   ■ Significant challenges   ■ Challenges remain   ■ SDG achieved   ■ Information unavailable

▼ SDG TRENDS

↓ Decreasing   → Stagnating   ↗ Moderately improving   ↑ On track or maintaining SDG achievement   ● Information unavailable

Notes: The full title of Goal 2 "Zero Hunger" is "End hunger, achieve food security and improved nutrition and promote sustainable agriculture".
The full title of each SDG is available here: https://sustainabledevelopment.un.org/topics/sustainabledevelopmentgoals

SDG1 – No Poverty

Indicator	Value	Year
Poverty headcount ratio at $1.90/day (%)	0.6	2020
Poverty headcount ratio at $3.20/day (%)	3.5	2020

SDG2 – Zero Hunger

Indicator	Value	Year
Prevalence of undernourishment (%)	9.3	2017
Prevalence of stunting in children under 5 years of age (%)	24.6	2015
Prevalence of wasting in children under 5 years of age (%)	6.4	2015
Prevalence of obesity, BMI ≥ 30 (% of adult population)	2.1	2016
Human Trophic Level (best 2–3 worst)	2.2	2017
Cereal yield (tonnes per hectare of harvested land)	5.4	2017
Sustainable Nitrogen Management Index (best 0–1.41 worst)	0.6	2015

SDG3 – Good Health and Well-Being

Indicator	Value	Year
Maternal mortality rate (per 100,000 live births)	43	2017
Neonatal mortality rate (per 1,000 live births)	10.6	2018
Mortality rate, under-5 (per 1,000 live births)	20.7	2018
Incidence of tuberculosis (per 100,000 population)	182.0	2018
New HIV infections (per 1,000 uninfected population)	0.1	2018
Age-standardized death rate due to cardiovascular disease, cancer, diabetes, or chronic respiratory disease in adults aged 30–70 years (%)	17.1	2016
Age-standardized death rate attributable to household air pollution and ambient air pollution (per 100,000 population)	64	2016
Traffic deaths (per 100,000 population)	26.4	2016
Life expectancy at birth (years)	76.3	2016
Adolescent fertility rate (births per 1,000 adolescent females aged 15 to 19)	30.9	2017
Births attended by skilled health personnel (%)	93.8	2014
Percentage of surviving infants who received 2 WHO-recommended vaccines (%)	75	2018
Universal health coverage (UHC) index of service coverage (worst 0–100 best)	75.0	2017
Subjective well-being (average ladder score, worst 0–10 best)	5.5	2019

SDG4 – Quality Education

Indicator	Value	Year
Net primary enrollment rate (%)	98.0	2013
Lower secondary completion rate (%)	97.7	2018
Literacy rate (% of population aged 15 to 24)	98.4	2018

SDG5 – Gender Equality

Indicator	Value	Year
Demand for family planning satisfied by modern methods (% of females aged 15 to 49 who are married or in unions)	69.6	2014
Ratio of female-to-male mean years of education received (%)	92.9	2018
Ratio of female-to-male labor force participation rate (%)	88.1	2019
Seats held by women in national parliament (%)	26.7	2020

SDG6 – Clean Water and Sanitation

Indicator	Value	Year
Population using at least basic drinking water services (%)	94.7	2017
Population using at least basic sanitation services (%)	83.5	2017
Freshwater withdrawal (% of available freshwater resources)	18.1	2005
Anthropogenic wastewater that receives treatment (%)	0.3	2018
Scarce water consumption embodied in imports (m³/capita)	1.2	2013

SDG7 – Affordable and Clean Energy

Indicator	Value	Year
Population with access to electricity (%)	100.0	2017
Population with access to clean fuels and technology for cooking (%)	66.9	2016
CO$_2$ emissions from fuel combustion for electricity and heating per total electricity output (MtCO$_2$/TWh)	1.1	2017

SDG8 – Decent Work and Economic Growth

Indicator	Value	Year
Adjusted GDP growth (%)	0.8	2018
Victims of modern slavery (per 1,000 population)	4.5	2018
Adults with an account at a bank or other financial institution or with a mobile-money-service provider (% of population aged 15 or over)	30.8	2017
Unemployment rate (% of total labor force)	2.0	2019
Fatal work-related accidents embodied in imports (per 100,000 population)	0.1	2010

SDG9 – Industry, Innovation and Infrastructure

Indicator	Value	Year
Population using the internet (%)	70.4	2018
Mobile broadband subscriptions (per 100 population)	71.9	2018
Logistics Performance Index: Quality of trade and transport-related infrastructure (worst 1–5 best)	3.0	2018
The Times Higher Education Universities Ranking: Average score of top 3 universities (worst 0–100 best)	22.3	2020
Scientific and technical journal articles (per 1,000 population)	0.0	2018
Expenditure on research and development (% of GDP)	0.5	2017

SDG10 – Reduced Inequalities

Indicator	Value	Year
Gini coefficient adjusted for top income	35.6	2016

SDG11 – Sustainable Cities and Communities

Indicator	Value	Year
Annual mean concentration of particulate matter of less than 2.5 microns in diameter (PM2.5) (µg/m³)	29.6	2017
Access to improved water source, piped (% of urban population)	81.0	2017
Satisfaction with public transport (%)	71.7	2019

SDG12 – Responsible Consumption and Production

Indicator	Value	Year
Municipal solid waste (kg/capita/day)	0.8	2010
Electronic waste (kg/capita)	1.5	2016
Production-based SO$_2$ emissions (kg/capita)	11.7	2012
SO$_2$ emissions embodied in imports (kg/capita)	1.1	2012
Production-based nitrogen emissions (kg/capita)	14.2	2010
Nitrogen emissions embodied in imports (kg/capita)	0.6	2010

SDG13 – Climate Action

Indicator	Value	Year
Energy-related CO$_2$ emissions (tCO$_2$/capita)	1.8	2017
CO$_2$ emissions embodied in imports (tCO$_2$/capita)	0.2	2015
CO$_2$ emissions embodied in fossil fuel exports (kg/capita)	45.7	2018

SDG14 – Life Below Water

Indicator	Value	Year
Mean area that is protected in marine sites important to biodiversity (%)	44.2	2018
Ocean Health Index: Clean Waters score (worst 0–100 best)	45.2	2019
Fish caught from overexploited or collapsed stocks (% of total catch)	1.6	2014
Fish caught by trawling (%)	64.0	2014
Marine biodiversity threats embodied in imports (per million population)	0.0	2018

SDG15 – Life on Land

Indicator	Value	Year
Mean area that is protected in terrestrial sites important to biodiversity (%)	41.1	2018
Mean area that is protected in freshwater sites important to biodiversity (%)	37.7	2018
Red List Index of species survival (worst 0–1 best)	0.7	2019
Permanent deforestation (% of forest area, 5-year average)	1.1	2018
Terrestrial and freshwater biodiversity threats embodied in imports (per million population)	0.1	2018

SDG16 – Peace, Justice and Strong Institutions

Indicator	Value	Year
Homicides (per 100,000 population)	1.5	2011
Unsentenced detainees (% of prison population)	12.5	2018
Percentage of population who feel safe walking alone at night in the city or area where they live (%)	66.1	2019
Property Rights (worst 1–7 best)	4.0	2019
Birth registrations with civil authority (% of children under age 5)	96.1	2018
Corruption Perception Index (worst 0–100 best)	37	2019
Children involved in child labor (% of population aged 5 to 14)	16.4	2016
Exports of major conventional weapons (TIV constant million USD per 100,000 population)	* 0.0	2019
Press Freedom Index (best 0–100 worst)	74.9	2019

SDG17 – Partnerships for the Goals

Indicator	Value	Year
Government spending on health and education (% of GDP)	7.0	2016
For high-income and all OECD DAC countries: International concessional public finance, including official development assistance (% of GNI)	NA	NA
Other countries: Government revenue excluding grants (% of GDP)	* 21.5	2013
Corporate Tax Haven Score (best 0–100 worst)	* 0.0	2019

* Imputed data point

5. Country Profiles

YEMEN, REPUBLIC OF

▼ OVERALL PERFORMANCE

Index score
52.3

Regional average score
66.3

SDG Global rank **151** (OF 166)

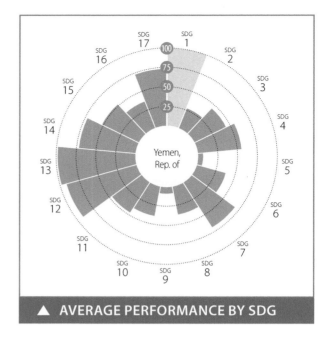

▲ AVERAGE PERFORMANCE BY SDG

▼ SPILLOVER INDEX

100 (best) to 0 (worst)

▼ CURRENT ASSESSMENT – SDG DASHBOARD

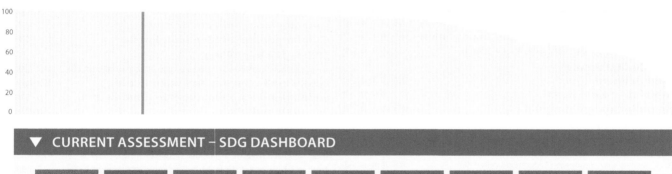

■ Major challenges   ■ Significant challenges   ■ Challenges remain   ■ SDG achieved   ■ Information unavailable

▼ SDG TRENDS

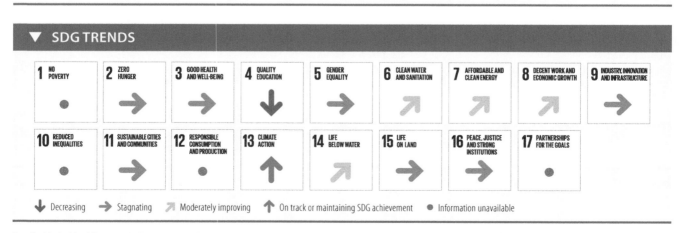

↓ Decreasing   → Stagnating   ↗ Moderately improving   ↑ On track or maintaining SDG achievement   ● Information unavailable

Notes: The full title of Goal 2 "Zero Hunger" is "End hunger, achieve food security and improved nutrition and promote sustainable agriculture".
The full title of each SDG is available here: https://sustainabledevelopment.un.org/topics/sustainabledevelopmentgoals

SDG1 – No Poverty

Indicator	Value	Year	Rating	Trend
Poverty headcount ratio at $1.90/day (%)	* NA	NA	●	●
Poverty headcount ratio at $3.20/day (%)	* NA	NA	●	●

SDG2 – Zero Hunger

Indicator	Value	Year	Rating	Trend
Prevalence of undernourishment (%)	38.9	2017	●	↓
Prevalence of stunting in children under 5 years of age (%)	46.5	2013	●	↗
Prevalence of wasting in children under 5 years of age (%)	16.3	2013	●	↓
Prevalence of obesity, BMI ≥ 30 (% of adult population)	17.1	2016	●	↓
Human Trophic Level (best 2–3 worst)	2.1	2017	●	↑
Cereal yield (tonnes per hectare of harvested land)	0.7	2017	●	↓
Sustainable Nitrogen Management Index (best 0–1.41 worst)	0.8	2015	●	↓

SDG3 – Good Health and Well-Being

Indicator	Value	Year	Rating	Trend
Maternal mortality rate (per 100,000 live births)	164	2017	●	↗
Neonatal mortality rate (per 1,000 live births)	27.0	2018	●	→
Mortality rate, under-5 (per 1,000 live births)	55.0	2018	●	→
Incidence of tuberculosis (per 100,000 population)	48.0	2018	●	→
New HIV infections (per 1,000 uninfected population)	0.0	2018	●	↑
Age-standardized death rate due to cardiovascular disease, cancer, diabetes, or chronic respiratory disease in adults aged 30–70 years (%)	30.6	2016	●	→
Age-standardized death rate attributable to household air pollution and ambient air pollution (per 100,000 population)	194	2016	●	●
Traffic deaths (per 100,000 population)	21.5	2013	●	●
Life expectancy at birth (years)	65.3	2016	●	→
Adolescent fertility rate (births per 1,000 adolescent females aged 15 to 19)	60.4	2017	●	↗
Births attended by skilled health personnel (%)	44.7	2013	●	●
Percentage of surviving infants who received 2 WHO-recommended vaccines (%)	64	2018	●	↓
Universal health coverage (UHC) index of service coverage (worst 0–100 best)	42.0	2017	●	→
Subjective well-being (average ladder score, worst 0–10 best)	3.1	2018	●	→

SDG4 – Quality Education

Indicator	Value	Year	Rating	Trend
Net primary enrollment rate (%)	84.2	2016	●	↓
Lower secondary completion rate (%)	53.1	2016	●	●
Literacy rate (% of population aged 15 to 24)	77.0	2004	●	●

SDG5 – Gender Equality

Indicator	Value	Year	Rating	Trend
Demand for family planning satisfied by modern methods (% of females aged 15 to 49 who are married or in unions)	37.7	2013	●	↗
Ratio of female-to-male mean years of education received (%)	43.2	2018	●	→
Ratio of female-to-male labor force participation rate (%)	8.2	2019	●	↓
Seats held by women in national parliament (%)	0.3	2020	●	→

SDG6 – Clean Water and Sanitation

Indicator	Value	Year	Rating	Trend
Population using at least basic drinking water services (%)	63.5	2017	●	→
Population using at least basic sanitation services (%)	59.1	2017	●	→
Freshwater withdrawal (% of available freshwater resources)	168.3	2005	●	●
Anthropogenic wastewater that receives treatment (%)	0.0	2018	●	●
Scarce water consumption embodied in imports (m³/capita)	1.6	2013	●	↑

SDG7 – Affordable and Clean Energy

Indicator	Value	Year	Rating	Trend
Population with access to electricity (%)	79.2	2017	●	↑
Population with access to clean fuels and technology for cooking (%)	64.9	2016	●	→
CO_2 emissions from fuel combustion for electricity and heating per total electricity output (MtCO₂/TWh)	2.0	2017	●	↑

SDG8 – Decent Work and Economic Growth

Indicator	Value	Year	Rating	Trend
Adjusted GDP growth (%)	-15.8	2018	●	●
Victims of modern slavery (per 1,000 population)	* NA	NA	●	●
Adults with an account at a bank or other financial institution or with a mobile-money-service provider (% of population aged 15 or over)	6.4	2014	●	●
Unemployment rate (% of total labor force)	12.9	2019	●	→
Fatal work-related accidents embodied in imports (per 100,000 population)	0.1	2010	●	↑

SDG9 – Industry, Innovation and Infrastructure

Indicator	Value	Year	Rating	Trend
Population using the internet (%)	26.7	2017	●	→
Mobile broadband subscriptions (per 100 population)	6.0	2017	●	→
Logistics Performance Index: Quality of trade and transport-related infrastructure (worst 1–5 best)	2.1	2018	●	↗
The Times Higher Education Universities Ranking: Average score of top 3 universities (worst 0–100 best)	* 0.0	2020	●	●
Scientific and technical journal articles (per 1,000 population)	0.0	2018	●	→
Expenditure on research and development (% of GDP)	* 0.0	2017	●	●

SDG10 – Reduced Inequalities

Indicator	Value	Year	Rating	Trend
Gini coefficient adjusted for top income	49.0	2014	●	●

SDG11 – Sustainable Cities and Communities

Indicator	Value	Year	Rating	Trend
Annual mean concentration of particulate matter of less than 2.5 microns in diameter (PM2.5) (µg/m³)	50.5	2017	●	↓
Access to improved water source, piped (% of urban population)	77.0	2017	●	→
Satisfaction with public transport (%)	32.9	2018	●	↗

SDG12 – Responsible Consumption and Production

Indicator	Value	Year	Rating	Trend
Municipal solid waste (kg/capita/day)	1.3	2016	●	●
Electronic waste (kg/capita)	1.5	2016	●	●
Production-based SO_2 emissions (kg/capita)	11.0	2012	●	●
SO_2 emissions embodied in imports (kg/capita)	0.7	2012	●	●
Production-based nitrogen emissions (kg/capita)	9.8	2010	●	●
Nitrogen emissions embodied in imports (kg/capita)	0.4	2010	●	●

SDG13 – Climate Action

Indicator	Value	Year	Rating	Trend
Energy-related CO_2 emissions (tCO₂/capita)	0.8	2017	●	↑
CO_2 emissions embodied in imports (tCO₂/capita)	0.1	2015	●	↑
CO_2 emissions embodied in fossil fuel exports (kg/capita)	0.0	2015	●	●

SDG14 – Life Below Water

Indicator	Value	Year	Rating	Trend
Mean area that is protected in marine sites important to biodiversity (%)	30.8	2018	●	→
Ocean Health Index: Clean Waters score (worst 0–100 best)	53.6	2019	●	↓
Fish caught from overexploited or collapsed stocks (% of total catch)	0.1	2014	●	↑
Fish caught by trawling (%)	8.2	2014	●	↑
Marine biodiversity threats embodied in imports (per million population)	0.0	2018	●	●

SDG15 – Life on Land

Indicator	Value	Year	Rating	Trend
Mean area that is protected in terrestrial sites important to biodiversity (%)	31.1	2018	●	→
Mean area that is protected in freshwater sites important to biodiversity (%)	7.7	2018	●	→
Red List Index of species survival (worst 0–1 best)	0.9	2019	●	→
Permanent deforestation (% of forest area, 5-year average)	NA	NA	●	●
Terrestrial and freshwater biodiversity threats embodied in imports (per million population)	0.0	2018	●	●

SDG16 – Peace, Justice and Strong Institutions

Indicator	Value	Year	Rating	Trend
Homicides (per 100,000 population)	6.7	2013	●	●
Unsentenced detainees (% of prison population)	70.9	2015	●	●
Percentage of population who feel safe walking alone at night in the city or area where they live (%)	53.0	2018	●	↓
Property Rights (worst 1–7 best)	2.9	2019	●	●
Birth registrations with civil authority (% of children under age 5)	30.7	2018	●	●
Corruption Perception Index (worst 0–100 best)	15	2019	●	↓
Children involved in child labor (% of population aged 5 to 14)	22.7	2016	●	●
Exports of major conventional weapons (TIV constant million USD per 100,000 population)	* 0.0	2019	●	●
Press Freedom Index (best 0–100 worst)	61.7	2019	●	↗

SDG17 – Partnerships for the Goals

Indicator	Value	Year	Rating	Trend
Government spending on health and education (% of GDP)	6.8	2008	●	●
For high-income and all OECD DAC countries: International concessional public finance, including official development assistance (% of GNI)	NA	NA	●	●
Other countries: Government revenue excluding grants (% of GDP)	NA	NA	●	●
Corporate Tax Haven Score (best 0–100 worst)	* 0.0	2019	●	●

* Imputed data point

5. Country Profiles

▼ OVERALL PERFORMANCE

Index score

52.7

Regional average score

53.1

SDG Global rank 148 (OF 166)

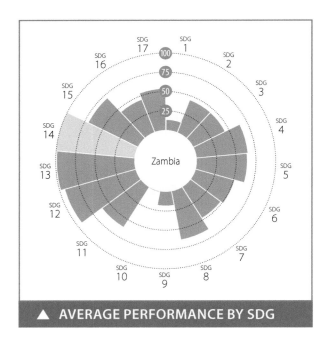

▲ AVERAGE PERFORMANCE BY SDG

▼ SPILLOVER INDEX

100 (best) to 0 (worst)

▼ CURRENT ASSESSMENT – SDG DASHBOARD

■ Major challenges   ■ Significant challenges   ■ Challenges remain   ■ SDG achieved   ■ Information unavailable

▼ SDG TRENDS

↓ Decreasing   → Stagnating   ↗ Moderately improving   ↑ On track or maintaining SDG achievement   ● Information unavailable

Notes: The full title of Goal 2 "Zero Hunger" is "End hunger, achieve food security and improved nutrition and promote sustainable agriculture".
The full title of each SDG is available here: https://sustainabledevelopment.un.org/topics/sustainabledevelopmentgoals

SDG1 – No Poverty

Indicator	Value	Year	Rating	Trend
Poverty headcount ratio at $1.90/day (%)	53.6	2020	●	→
Poverty headcount ratio at $3.20/day (%)	72.1	2020	●	→

SDG2 – Zero Hunger

Indicator	Value	Year	Rating	Trend
Prevalence of undernourishment (%)	46.7	2017	●	↓
Prevalence of stunting in children under 5 years of age (%)	40.0	2013	●	→
Prevalence of wasting in children under 5 years of age (%)	6.3	2013	●	→
Prevalence of obesity, BMI ≥ 30 (% of adult population)	8.1	2016	●	↑
Human Trophic Level (best 2–3 worst)	2.1	2017	●	↑
Cereal yield (tonnes per hectare of harvested land)	2.5	2017	●	↓
Sustainable Nitrogen Management Index (best 0–1.41 worst)	0.8	2015	●	→

SDG3 – Good Health and Well-Being

Indicator	Value	Year	Rating	Trend
Maternal mortality rate (per 100,000 live births)	213	2017	●	↗
Neonatal mortality rate (per 1,000 live births)	23.5	2018	●	→
Mortality rate, under-5 (per 1,000 live births)	57.8	2018	●	↗
Incidence of tuberculosis (per 100,000 population)	346.0	2018	●	↗
New HIV infections (per 1,000 uninfected population)	3.0	2018	●	↗
Age-standardized death rate due to cardiovascular disease, cancer, diabetes, or chronic respiratory disease in adults aged 30–70 years (%)	17.9	2016	●	↑
Age-standardized death rate attributable to household air pollution and ambient air pollution (per 100,000 population)	127	2016	●	●
Traffic deaths (per 100,000 population)	24.7	2013	●	●
Life expectancy at birth (years)	62.3	2016	●	↗
Adolescent fertility rate (births per 1,000 adolescent females aged 15 to 19)	120.1	2017	●	↗
Births attended by skilled health personnel (%)	63.3	2014	●	●
Percentage of surviving infants who received 2 WHO-recommended vaccines (%)	90	2018	●	↑
Universal health coverage (UHC) index of service coverage (worst 0–100 best)	53.0	2017	●	→
Subjective well-being (average ladder score, worst 0–10 best)	3.3	2019	●	↓

SDG4 – Quality Education

Indicator	Value	Year	Rating	Trend
Net primary enrollment rate (%)	83.2	2017	●	↓
Lower secondary completion rate (%)	54.8	2013	●	●
Literacy rate (% of population aged 15 to 24)	92.1	2018	●	●

SDG5 – Gender Equality

Indicator	Value	Year	Rating	Trend
Demand for family planning satisfied by modern methods (% of females aged 15 to 49 who are married or in unions)	62.4	2014	●	↑
Ratio of female-to-male mean years of education received (%)	89.3	2018	●	↑
Ratio of female-to-male labor force participation rate (%)	88.8	2019	●	↑
Seats held by women in national parliament (%)	16.8	2020	●	→

SDG6 – Clean Water and Sanitation

Indicator	Value	Year	Rating	Trend
Population using at least basic drinking water services (%)	60.0	2017	●	→
Population using at least basic sanitation services (%)	26.4	2017	●	→
Freshwater withdrawal (% of available freshwater resources)	2.8	2000	●	●
Anthropogenic wastewater that receives treatment (%)	4.2	2018	●	●
Scarce water consumption embodied in imports (m³/capita)	0.8	2013	●	↑

SDG7 – Affordable and Clean Energy

Indicator	Value	Year	Rating	Trend
Population with access to electricity (%)	40.3	2017	●	↗
Population with access to clean fuels and technology for cooking (%)	16.4	2016	●	→
CO_2 emissions from fuel combustion for electricity and heating per total electricity output (MtCO$_2$/TWh)	0.4	2017	●	↑

SDG8 – Decent Work and Economic Growth

Indicator	Value	Year	Rating	Trend
Adjusted GDP growth (%)	-5.0	2018	●	●
Victims of modern slavery (per 1,000 population)	5.7	2018	●	●
Adults with an account at a bank or other financial institution or with a mobile-money-service provider (% of population aged 15 or over)	45.9	2017	●	↑
Unemployment rate (% of total labor force)	11.4	2019	●	↓
Fatal work-related accidents embodied in imports (per 100,000 population)	0.1	2010	●	↑

SDG9 – Industry, Innovation and Infrastructure

Indicator	Value	Year	Rating	Trend
Population using the internet (%)	14.3	2018	●	↓
Mobile broadband subscriptions (per 100 population)	56.6	2018	●	↑
Logistics Performance Index: Quality of trade and transport-related infrastructure (worst 1–5 best)	2.3	2018	●	↓
The Times Higher Education Universities Ranking: Average score of top 3 universities (worst 0–100 best) *	0.0	2020	●	●
Scientific and technical journal articles (per 1,000 population)	0.0	2018	●	→
Expenditure on research and development (% of GDP)	0.3	2008	●	●

SDG10 – Reduced Inequalities

Indicator	Value	Year	Rating	Trend
Gini coefficient adjusted for top income	62.7	2015	●	●

SDG11 – Sustainable Cities and Communities

Indicator	Value	Year	Rating	Trend
Annual mean concentration of particulate matter of less than 2.5 microns in diameter (PM2.5) (µg/m³)	27.4	2017	●	→
Access to improved water source, piped (% of urban population)	68.2	2017	●	↓
Satisfaction with public transport (%)	48.0	2019	●	↑

SDG12 – Responsible Consumption and Production

Indicator	Value	Year	Rating	Trend
Municipal solid waste (kg/capita/day)	0.9	2011	●	●
Electronic waste (kg/capita)	0.9	2016	●	●
Production-based SO_2 emissions (kg/capita)	11.6	2012	●	●
SO_2 emissions embodied in imports (kg/capita)	1.1	2012	●	●
Production-based nitrogen emissions (kg/capita)	8.7	2010	●	●
Nitrogen emissions embodied in imports (kg/capita)	0.6	2010	●	●

SDG13 – Climate Action

Indicator	Value	Year	Rating	Trend
Energy-related CO_2 emissions (tCO$_2$/capita)	0.2	2017	●	↑
CO_2 emissions embodied in imports (tCO$_2$/capita)	0.1	2015	●	↑
CO_2 emissions embodied in fossil fuel exports (kg/capita)	0.5	2019	●	●

SDG14 – Life Below Water

Indicator	Value	Year	Rating	Trend
Mean area that is protected in marine sites important to biodiversity (%)	NA	NA	●	●
Ocean Health Index: Clean Waters score (worst 0–100 best)	NA	NA	●	●
Fish caught from overexploited or collapsed stocks (% of total catch)	NA	NA	●	●
Fish caught by trawling (%)	NA	NA	●	●
Marine biodiversity threats embodied in imports (per million population)	0.0	2018	●	●

SDG15 – Life on Land

Indicator	Value	Year	Rating	Trend
Mean area that is protected in terrestrial sites important to biodiversity (%)	48.4	2018	●	→
Mean area that is protected in freshwater sites important to biodiversity (%)	57.4	2018	●	↑
Red List Index of species survival (worst 0–1 best)	0.9	2019	●	→
Permanent deforestation (% of forest area, 5-year average)	0.3	2018	●	●
Terrestrial and freshwater biodiversity threats embodied in imports (per million population)	0.5	2018	●	●

SDG16 – Peace, Justice and Strong Institutions

Indicator	Value	Year	Rating	Trend
Homicides (per 100,000 population)	5.3	2015	●	●
Unsentenced detainees (% of prison population)	32.4	2018	●	↓
Percentage of population who feel safe walking alone at night in the city or area where they live (%)	44.1	2019	●	↓
Property Rights (worst 1–7 best)	4.1	2019	●	●
Birth registrations with civil authority (% of children under age 5)	11.3	2018	●	●
Corruption Perception Index (worst 0–100 best)	34	2019	●	↓
Children involved in child labor (% of population aged 5 to 14)	40.6	2016	●	●
Exports of major conventional weapons (TIV constant million USD per 100,000 population) *	0.0	2019	●	●
Press Freedom Index (best 0–100 worst)	36.4	2019	●	↓

SDG17 – Partnerships for the Goals

Indicator	Value	Year	Rating	Trend
Government spending on health and education (% of GDP)	5.5	2016	●	●
For high-income and all OECD DAC countries: International concessional public finance, including official development assistance (% of GNI)	NA	NA	●	●
Other countries: Government revenue excluding grants (% of GDP)	16.9	2017	●	↓
Corporate Tax Haven Score (best 0–100 worst) *	0.0	2019	●	●

* Imputed data point

5. Country Profiles

ZIMBABWE

Sub-Saharan Africa

▼ OVERALL PERFORMANCE

Index score
59.5

Regional average score
53.1

SDG Global rank 125 (OF 166)

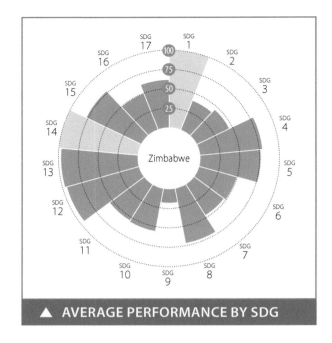

▲ AVERAGE PERFORMANCE BY SDG

▼ SPILLOVER INDEX

100 (best) to 0 (worst)

▼ CURRENT ASSESSMENT – SDG DASHBOARD

■ Major challenges ■ Significant challenges ■ Challenges remain ■ SDG achieved ■ Information unavailable

▼ SDG TRENDS

↓ Decreasing → Stagnating ↗ Moderately improving ↑ On track or maintaining SDG achievement ● Information unavailable

Notes: The full title of Goal 2 "Zero Hunger" is "End hunger, achieve food security and improved nutrition and promote sustainable agriculture".
The full title of each SDG is available here: https://sustainabledevelopment.un.org/topics/sustainabledevelopmentgoals

486 | Sustainable Development Report 2020 ○ The Sustainable Development Goals and Covid-19

SDG1 – No Poverty

		Value	Year	Rating	Trend
Poverty headcount ratio at $1.90/day (%)	*	NA	NA	●	●
Poverty headcount ratio at $3.20/day (%)	*	NA	NA	●	●

SDG2 – Zero Hunger

	Value	Year	Rating	Trend
Prevalence of undernourishment (%)	51.3	2017	●	↓
Prevalence of stunting in children under 5 years of age (%)	26.8	2015	●	↗
Prevalence of wasting in children under 5 years of age (%)	3.2	2015	●	↑
Prevalence of obesity, BMI ≥ 30 (% of adult population)	15.5	2016	●	↓
Human Trophic Level (best 2–3 worst)	2.2	2017	●	↑
Cereal yield (tonnes per hectare of harvested land)	0.6	2017	●	↓
Sustainable Nitrogen Management Index (best 0–1.41 worst)	1.0	2015	●	→

SDG3 – Good Health and Well-Being

	Value	Year	Rating	Trend
Maternal mortality rate (per 100,000 live births)	458	2017	●	→
Neonatal mortality rate (per 1,000 live births)	20.9	2018	●	↗
Mortality rate, under-5 (per 1,000 live births)	46.2	2018	●	↑
Incidence of tuberculosis (per 100,000 population)	210.0	2018	●	↗
New HIV infections (per 1,000 uninfected population)	2.8	2018	●	↑
Age-standardized death rate due to cardiovascular disease, cancer, diabetes, or chronic respiratory disease in adults aged 30–70 years (%)	19.3	2016	●	↗
Age-standardized death rate attributable to household air pollution and ambient air pollution (per 100,000 population)	133	2016	●	●
Traffic deaths (per 100,000 population)	34.7	2016	●	↓
Life expectancy at birth (years)	61.4	2016	●	↗
Adolescent fertility rate (births per 1,000 adolescent females aged 15 to 19)	86.1	2017	●	↗
Births attended by skilled health personnel (%)	78.1	2015	●	↑
Percentage of surviving infants who received 2 WHO-recommended vaccines (%)	88	2018	●	↑
Universal health coverage (UHC) index of service coverage (worst 0–100 best)	54.0	2017	●	↗
Subjective well-being (average ladder score, worst 0–10 best)	2.7	2019	●	↓

SDG4 – Quality Education

	Value	Year	Rating	Trend
Net primary enrollment rate (%)	94.1	2013	●	●
Lower secondary completion rate (%)	71.1	2013	●	●
Literacy rate (% of population aged 15 to 24)	90.4	2014	●	●

SDG5 – Gender Equality

	Value	Year	Rating	Trend
Demand for family planning satisfied by modern methods (% of females aged 15 to 49 who are married or in unions)	84.8	2015	●	↑
Ratio of female-to-male mean years of education received (%)	84.4	2018	●	→
Ratio of female-to-male labor force participation rate (%)	88.4	2019	●	↑
Seats held by women in national parliament (%)	31.9	2020	●	→

SDG6 – Clean Water and Sanitation

	Value	Year	Rating	Trend
Population using at least basic drinking water services (%)	64.1	2017	●	↓
Population using at least basic sanitation services (%)	36.2	2017	●	↓
Freshwater withdrawal (% of available freshwater resources)	33.5	2005	●	●
Anthropogenic wastewater that receives treatment (%)	0.0	2018	●	●
Scarce water consumption embodied in imports (m³/capita)	0.9	2013	●	↑

SDG7 – Affordable and Clean Energy

	Value	Year	Rating	Trend
Population with access to electricity (%)	40.4	2017	●	↗
Population with access to clean fuels and technology for cooking (%)	29.1	2016	●	↓
CO$_2$ emissions from fuel combustion for electricity and heating per total electricity output (MtCO$_2$/TWh)	1.3	2017	●	→

SDG8 – Decent Work and Economic Growth

		Value	Year	Rating	Trend
Adjusted GDP growth (%)		-3.8	2018	●	●
Victims of modern slavery (per 1,000 population)		6.7	2018	●	●
Adults with an account at a bank or other financial institution or with a mobile-money-service provider (% of population aged 15 or over)		55.3	2017	●	↑
Unemployment rate (% of total labor force)		5.0	2019	●	↑
Fatal work-related accidents embodied in imports (per 100,000 population)		0.0	2010	●	↑

SDG9 – Industry, Innovation and Infrastructure

		Value	Year	Rating	Trend
Population using the internet (%)		27.1	2017	●	↗
Mobile broadband subscriptions (per 100 population)		51.7	2018	●	↑
Logistics Performance Index: Quality of trade and transport-related infrastructure (worst 1–5 best)		1.8	2018	●	↓
The Times Higher Education Universities Ranking: Average score of top 3 universities (worst 0–100 best)	*	0.0	2020	●	●
Scientific and technical journal articles (per 1,000 population)		0.0	2018	●	→
Expenditure on research and development (% of GDP)		NA	NA	●	●

SDG10 – Reduced Inequalities

	Value	Year	Rating	Trend
Gini coefficient adjusted for top income	43.1	2011	●	●

SDG11 – Sustainable Cities and Communities

	Value	Year	Rating	Trend
Annual mean concentration of particulate matter of less than 2.5 microns in diameter (PM2.5) (µg/m³)	22.3	2017	●	→
Access to improved water source, piped (% of urban population)	74.4	2017	●	↓
Satisfaction with public transport (%)	27.6	2019	●	↓

SDG12 – Responsible Consumption and Production

	Value	Year	Rating	Trend
Municipal solid waste (kg/capita/day)	0.7	2002	●	●
Electronic waste (kg/capita)	0.9	2016	●	●
Production-based SO$_2$ emissions (kg/capita)	3.9	2012	●	●
SO$_2$ emissions embodied in imports (kg/capita)	1.5	2012	●	●
Production-based nitrogen emissions (kg/capita)	5.7	2010	●	●
Nitrogen emissions embodied in imports (kg/capita)	0.3	2010	●	●

SDG13 – Climate Action

	Value	Year	Rating	Trend
Energy-related CO$_2$ emissions (tCO$_2$/capita)	0.9	2017	●	↑
CO$_2$ emissions embodied in imports (tCO$_2$/capita)	0.2	2015	●	↑
CO$_2$ emissions embodied in fossil fuel exports (kg/capita)	13.1	2019	●	●

SDG14 – Life Below Water

	Value	Year	Rating	Trend
Mean area that is protected in marine sites important to biodiversity (%)	NA	NA	●	●
Ocean Health Index: Clean Waters score (worst 0–100 best)	NA	NA	●	●
Fish caught from overexploited or collapsed stocks (% of total catch)	NA	NA	●	●
Fish caught by trawling (%)	NA	NA	●	●
Marine biodiversity threats embodied in imports (per million population)	0.0	2018	●	●

SDG15 – Life on Land

	Value	Year	Rating	Trend
Mean area that is protected in terrestrial sites important to biodiversity (%)	85.9	2018	●	↑
Mean area that is protected in freshwater sites important to biodiversity (%)	79.0	2018	●	↑
Red List Index of species survival (worst 0–1 best)	0.8	2019	●	↓
Permanent deforestation (% of forest area, 5-year average)	0.3	2018	●	●
Terrestrial and freshwater biodiversity threats embodied in imports (per million population)	0.3	2018	●	●

SDG16 – Peace, Justice and Strong Institutions

		Value	Year	Rating	Trend
Homicides (per 100,000 population)		6.7	2012	●	●
Unsentenced detainees (% of prison population)		17.1	2015	●	●
Percentage of population who feel safe walking alone at night in the city or area where they live (%)		45.1	2019	●	↓
Property Rights (worst 1–7 best)		2.8	2019	●	●
Birth registrations with civil authority (% of children under age 5)		38.2	2018	●	●
Corruption Perception Index (worst 0–100 best)		24	2019	●	→
Children involved in child labor (% of population aged 5 to 14)		NA	NA	●	●
Exports of major conventional weapons (TIV constant million USD per 100,000 population)	*	0.0	2019	●	●
Press Freedom Index (best 0–100 worst)		42.2	2019	●	↓

SDG17 – Partnerships for the Goals

		Value	Year	Rating	Trend
Government spending on health and education (% of GDP)		9.2	2014	●	●
For high-income and all OECD DAC countries: International concessional public finance, including official development assistance (% of GNI)		NA	NA	●	●
Other countries: Government revenue excluding grants (% of GDP)		16.9	2017	●	↓
Corporate Tax Haven Score (best 0–100 worst)	*	0.0	2019	●	●

* Imputed data point

5. Country Profiles

EAST AND SOUTH ASIA

▼ OVERALL PERFORMANCE

Regional average score

67.2

SDG Global rank **NA** (OF 166)

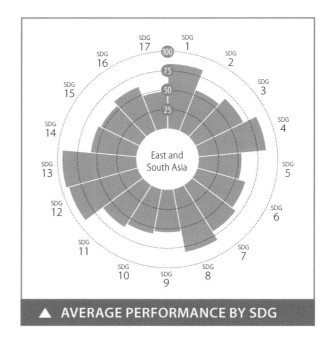

▲ AVERAGE PERFORMANCE BY SDG

▼ SPILLOVER INDEX

100 (best) to 0 (worst)

▼ CURRENT ASSESSMENT – SDG DASHBOARD

■ Major challenges ■ Significant challenges ■ Challenges remain ■ SDG achieved ■ Information unavailable

▼ SDG TRENDS

⬇ Decreasing ➡ Stagnating ➚ Moderately improving ⬆ On track or maintaining SDG achievement ● Information unavailable

Notes: The full title of Goal 2 "Zero Hunger" is "End hunger, achieve food security and improved nutrition and promote sustainable agriculture".
The full title of each SDG is available here: https://sustainabledevelopment.un.org/topics/sustainabledevelopmentgoals

SDG1 – No Poverty

	Value	Year	Rating	Trend
Poverty headcount ratio at $1.90/day (%)	1.6	2020	●	↑
Poverty headcount ratio at $3.20/day (%)	14.7	2020	●	↑

SDG2 – Zero Hunger

	Value	Year	Rating	Trend
Prevalence of undernourishment (%)	12.0	2017	●	↑
Prevalence of stunting in children under 5 years of age (%)	26.0	2016	●	→
Prevalence of wasting in children under 5 years of age (%)	11.0	2016	●	→
Prevalence of obesity, BMI ≥ 30 (% of adult population)	5.5	2016	●	↑
Human Trophic Level (best 2–3 worst)	2.2	2017	●	→
Cereal yield (tonnes per hectare of harvested land)	4.5	2017	●	↑
Sustainable Nitrogen Management Index (best 0–1.41 worst)	0.8	2015	●	→

SDG3 – Good Health and Well-Being

	Value	Year	Rating	Trend
Maternal mortality rate (per 100,000 live births)	100	2017	●	↑
Neonatal mortality rate (per 1,000 live births)	14.9	2018	●	↑
Mortality rate, under-5 (per 1,000 live births)	25.6	2018	●	↑
Incidence of tuberculosis (per 100,000 population)	172.5	2018	●	→
New HIV infections (per 1,000 uninfected population)	0.1	2018	●	↑
Age-standardized death rate due to cardiovascular disease, cancer, diabetes, or chronic respiratory disease in adults aged 30–70 years (%)	20.9	2016	●	→
Age-standardized death rate attributable to household air pollution and ambient air pollution (per 100,000 population)	144	2016	●	●
Traffic deaths (per 100,000 population)	19.3	2016	●	↓
Life expectancy at birth (years)	72.1	2016	●	→
Adolescent fertility rate (births per 1,000 adolescent females aged 15 to 19)	20.8	2017	●	↑
Births attended by skilled health personnel (%)	87.5	2016	●	●
Percentage of surviving infants who received 2 WHO-recommended vaccines (%)	91	2018	●	↑
Universal health coverage (UHC) index of service coverage (worst 0–100 best)	64.5	2017	●	↑
Subjective well-being (average ladder score, worst 0–10 best)	4.8	2019	●	↓

SDG4 – Quality Education

	Value	Year	Rating	Trend
Net primary enrollment rate (%)	90.9	2018	●	→
Lower secondary completion rate (%)	88.4	2018	●	↑
Literacy rate (% of population aged 15 to 24)	94.8	2018	●	●

SDG5 – Gender Equality

	Value	Year	Rating	Trend
Demand for family planning satisfied by modern methods (% of females aged 15 to 49 who are married or in unions)	77.9	2017	●	↑
Ratio of female-to-male mean years of education received (%)	76.9	2018	●	↑
Ratio of female-to-male labor force participation rate (%)	56.5	2019	●	↓
Seats held by women in national parliament (%)	20.1	2020	●	→

SDG6 – Clean Water and Sanitation

	Value	Year	Rating	Trend
Population using at least basic drinking water services (%)	92.6	2017	●	↑
Population using at least basic sanitation services (%)	71.8	2017	●	↑
Freshwater withdrawal (% of available freshwater resources)	50.0	2015	●	●
Anthropogenic wastewater that receives treatment (%)	4.5	2018	●	●
Scarce water consumption embodied in imports (m³/capita)	2.6	2013	●	↑

SDG7 – Affordable and Clean Energy

	Value	Year	Rating	Trend
Population with access to electricity (%)	94.1	2017	●	↑
Population with access to clean fuels and technology for cooking (%)	49.0	2016	●	→
CO_2 emissions from fuel combustion for electricity and heating per total electricity output (MtCO₂/TWh)	2.0	2017	●	↗

SDG8 – Decent Work and Economic Growth

	Value	Year	Rating	Trend
Adjusted GDP growth (%)	1.4	2018	●	●
Victims of modern slavery (per 1,000 population)	5.5	2018	●	●
Adults with an account at a bank or other financial institution or with a mobile-money-service provider (% of population aged 15 or over)	69.5	2017	●	↑
Unemployment rate (% of total labor force)	4.4	2019	●	↑
Fatal work-related accidents embodied in imports (per 100,000 population)	0.1	2010	●	↑

SDG9 – Industry, Innovation and Infrastructure

	Value	Year	Rating	Trend
Population using the internet (%)	42.4	2018	●	↑
Mobile broadband subscriptions (per 100 population)	65.8	2018	●	↑
Logistics Performance Index: Quality of trade and transport-related infrastructure (worst 1–5 best)	3.1	2018	●	↑
The Times Higher Education Universities Ranking: Average score of top 3 universities (worst 0–100 best)	50.0	2020	●	●
Scientific and technical journal articles (per 1,000 population)	0.2	2018	●	→
Expenditure on research and development (% of GDP)	1.1	2017	●	●

SDG10 – Reduced Inequalities

	Value	Year	Rating	Trend
Gini coefficient adjusted for top income	42.6	2017	●	●

SDG11 – Sustainable Cities and Communities

	Value	Year	Rating	Trend
Annual mean concentration of particulate matter of less than 2.5 microns in diameter (PM2.5) (µg/m³)	61.4	2017	●	→
Access to improved water source, piped (% of urban population)	71.7	2017	●	↓
Satisfaction with public transport (%)	74.5	2019	●	↑

SDG12 – Responsible Consumption and Production

	Value	Year	Rating	Trend
Municipal solid waste (kg/capita/day)	0.9	2016	●	●
Electronic waste (kg/capita)	3.3	2016	●	●
Production-based SO_2 emissions (kg/capita)	16.7	2012	●	●
SO_2 emissions embodied in imports (kg/capita)	0.8	2012	●	●
Production-based nitrogen emissions (kg/capita)	16.9	2010	●	●
Nitrogen emissions embodied in imports (kg/capita)	0.7	2010	●	●

SDG13 – Climate Action

	Value	Year	Rating	Trend
Energy-related CO_2 emissions (tCO₂/capita)	3.4	2017	●	→
CO_2 emissions embodied in imports (tCO₂/capita)	0.1	2015	●	↑
CO_2 emissions embodied in fossil fuel exports (kg/capita)	270.0	2019	●	●

SDG14 – Life Below Water

	Value	Year	Rating	Trend
Mean area that is protected in marine sites important to biodiversity (%)	30.8	2018	●	→
Ocean Health Index: Clean Waters score (worst 0–100 best)	37.2	2019	●	→
Fish caught from overexploited or collapsed stocks (% of total catch)	14.1	2014	●	↑
Fish caught by trawling (%)	34.0	2014	●	↓
Marine biodiversity threats embodied in imports (per million population)	0.0	2018	●	●

SDG15 – Life on Land

	Value	Year	Rating	Trend
Mean area that is protected in terrestrial sites important to biodiversity (%)	33.6	2018	●	→
Mean area that is protected in freshwater sites important to biodiversity (%)	27.6	2018	●	→
Red List Index of species survival (worst 0–1 best)	0.7	2019	●	↓
Permanent deforestation (% of forest area, 5-year average)	0.2	2018	●	●
Terrestrial and freshwater biodiversity threats embodied in imports (per million population)	0.3	2018	●	●

SDG16 – Peace, Justice and Strong Institutions

	Value	Year	Rating	Trend
Homicides (per 100,000 population)	2.1	2017	●	↑
Unsentenced detainees (% of prison population)	59.0	2018	●	↓
Percentage of population who feel safe walking alone at night in the city or area where they live (%)	75.6	2019	●	↑
Property Rights (worst 1–7 best)	4.4	2019	●	●
Birth registrations with civil authority (% of children under age 5)	75.8	2018	●	●
Corruption Perception Index (worst 0–100 best)	39	2019	●	↗
Children involved in child labor (% of population aged 5 to 14)	10.9	2016	●	●
Exports of major conventional weapons (TIV constant million USD per 100,000 population)	0.0	2019	●	●
Press Freedom Index (best 0–100 worst)	58.1	2019	●	→

SDG17 – Partnerships for the Goals

	Value	Year	Rating	Trend
Government spending on health and education (% of GDP)	4.5	2016	●	→
For high-income and all OECD DAC countries: International concessional public finance, including official development assistance (% of GNI)	NA	NA	●	●
Other countries: Government revenue excluding grants (% of GDP)	14.5	2018	●	→
Corporate Tax Haven Score (best 0–100 worst)	21.3	2019	●	●

* Imputed data point

5. Country Profiles

EASTERN EUROPE AND CENTRAL ASIA

Regional average score

70.9

SDG Global rank **NA** (OF 166)

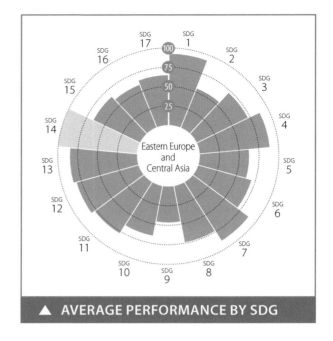

▲ AVERAGE PERFORMANCE BY SDG

▼ SPILLOVER INDEX

100 (best) to 0 (worst)

▼ CURRENT ASSESSMENT – SDG DASHBOARD

■ Major challenges   ■ Significant challenges   ■ Challenges remain   ■ SDG achieved   ■ Information unavailable

▼ SDG TRENDS

↓ Decreasing   → Stagnating   ↗ Moderately improving   ↑ On track or maintaining SDG achievement   ● Information unavailable

Notes: The full title of Goal 2 "Zero Hunger" is "End hunger, achieve food security and improved nutrition and promote sustainable agriculture".
The full title of each SDG is available here: https://sustainabledevelopment.un.org/topics/sustainabledevelopmentgoals

SDG1 – No Poverty

	Value	Year	Rating	Trend
Poverty headcount ratio at $1.90/day (%)	1.3	2020	●	↑
Poverty headcount ratio at $3.20/day (%)	4.8	2020	◐	↑

SDG2 – Zero Hunger

	Value	Year	Rating	Trend
Prevalence of undernourishment (%)	6.2	2017	●	↑
Prevalence of stunting in children under 5 years of age (%)	19.5	2016	●	→
Prevalence of wasting in children under 5 years of age (%)	5.6	2016	◐	↑
Prevalence of obesity, BMI ≥ 30 (% of adult population)	20.1	2016	●	↓
Human Trophic Level (best 2–3 worst)	2.3	2017	●	→
Cereal yield (tonnes per hectare of harvested land)	3.3	2017	●	↑
Sustainable Nitrogen Management Index (best 0–1.41 worst)	0.6	2015	●	→

SDG3 – Good Health and Well-Being

	Value	Year	Rating	Trend
Maternal mortality rate (per 100,000 live births)	81	2017	◐	↑
Neonatal mortality rate (per 1,000 live births)	8.8	2018	◐	↑
Mortality rate, under-5 (per 1,000 live births)	16.2	2018	●	↑
Incidence of tuberculosis (per 100,000 population)	72.3	2018	●	↗
New HIV infections (per 1,000 uninfected population)	0.1	2018	●	↑
Age-standardized death rate due to cardiovascular disease, cancer, diabetes, or chronic respiratory disease in adults aged 30–70 years (%)	25.0	2016	●	↗
Age-standardized death rate attributable to household air pollution and ambient air pollution (per 100,000 population)	78	2016	◐	●
Traffic deaths (per 100,000 population)	14.9	2016	●	→
Life expectancy at birth (years)	71.6	2016	●	↗
Adolescent fertility rate (births per 1,000 adolescent females aged 15 to 19)	29.6	2017	◐	↑
Births attended by skilled health personnel (%)	94.3	2016	◐	●
Percentage of surviving infants who received 2 WHO-recommended vaccines (%)	87	2018	◐	↑
Universal health coverage (UHC) index of service coverage (worst 0–100 best)	68.3	2017	●	↑
Subjective well-being (average ladder score, worst 0–10 best)	5.3	2019	●	↓

SDG4 – Quality Education

	Value	Year	Rating	Trend
Net primary enrollment rate (%)	92.9	2018	◐	→
Lower secondary completion rate (%)	90.6	2018	●	●
Literacy rate (% of population aged 15 to 24)	96.2	2018	●	●

SDG5 – Gender Equality

	Value	Year	Rating	Trend
Demand for family planning satisfied by modern methods (% of females aged 15 to 49 who are married or in unions)	63.9	2017	◐	↗
Ratio of female-to-male mean years of education received (%)	90.7	2018	◐	→
Ratio of female-to-male labor force participation rate (%)	73.7	2019	●	↑
Seats held by women in national parliament (%)	22.0	2020	●	↗

SDG6 – Clean Water and Sanitation

	Value	Year	Rating	Trend
Population using at least basic drinking water services (%)	92.8	2017	◐	↗
Population using at least basic sanitation services (%)	88.1	2017	◐	↗
Freshwater withdrawal (% of available freshwater resources)	30.9	2015	◐	●
Anthropogenic wastewater that receives treatment (%)	13.9	2018	●	●
Scarce water consumption embodied in imports (m³/capita)	20.0	2013	●	↑

SDG7 – Affordable and Clean Energy

	Value	Year	Rating	Trend
Population with access to electricity (%)	99.7	2017	●	↑
Population with access to clean fuels and technology for cooking (%)	87.5	2016	●	↑
CO_2 emissions from fuel combustion for electricity and heating per total electricity output (MtCO₂/TWh)	1.4	2017	●	↗

SDG8 – Decent Work and Economic Growth

	Value	Year	Rating	Trend
Adjusted GDP growth (%)	-1.3	2018	◐	●
Victims of modern slavery (per 1,000 population)	7.2	2018	●	●
Adults with an account at a bank or other financial institution or with a mobile-money-service provider (% of population aged 15 or over)	58.9	2017	●	↑
Unemployment rate (% of total labor force)	6.7	2019	◐	↑
Fatal work-related accidents embodied in imports (per 100,000 population)	0.3	2010	●	↑

SDG9 – Industry, Innovation and Infrastructure

	Value	Year	Rating	Trend
Population using the internet (%)	64.8	2018	●	↑
Mobile broadband subscriptions (per 100 population)	68.3	2018	◐	↑
Logistics Performance Index: Quality of trade and transport-related infrastructure (worst 1–5 best)	2.5	2018	◐	→
The Times Higher Education Universities Ranking: Average score of top 3 universities (worst 0–100 best)	25.8	2020	◐	●
Scientific and technical journal articles (per 1,000 population)	0.3	2018	●	↗
Expenditure on research and development (% of GDP)	0.6	2017	●	↓

SDG10 – Reduced Inequalities

	Value	Year	Rating	Trend
Gini coefficient adjusted for top income	40.4	2017	●	●

SDG11 – Sustainable Cities and Communities

	Value	Year	Rating	Trend
Annual mean concentration of particulate matter of less than 2.5 microns in diameter (PM2.5) (µg/m³)	23.4	2017	●	→
Access to improved water source, piped (% of urban population)	88.0	2017	◐	→
Satisfaction with public transport (%)	59.8	2019	◐	↓

SDG12 – Responsible Consumption and Production

	Value	Year	Rating	Trend
Municipal solid waste (kg/capita/day)	1.5	2016	●	●
Electronic waste (kg/capita)	7.7	2016	●	●
Production-based SO_2 emissions (kg/capita)	34.2	2012	●	●
SO_2 emissions embodied in imports (kg/capita)	3.2	2012	●	●
Production-based nitrogen emissions (kg/capita)	23.5	2010	●	●
Nitrogen emissions embodied in imports (kg/capita)	2.4	2010	●	●

SDG13 – Climate Action

	Value	Year	Rating	Trend
Energy-related CO_2 emissions (tCO₂/capita)	6.9	2017	●	→
CO_2 emissions embodied in imports (tCO₂/capita)	0.4	2015	●	↑
CO_2 emissions embodied in fossil fuel exports (kg/capita)	1795.8	2019	◐	●

SDG14 – Life Below Water

	Value	Year	Rating	Trend
Mean area that is protected in marine sites important to biodiversity (%)	NA	NA	●	●
Ocean Health Index: Clean Waters score (worst 0–100 best)	NA	NA	●	●
Fish caught from overexploited or collapsed stocks (% of total catch)	NA	NA	●	●
Fish caught by trawling (%)	NA	NA	●	●
Marine biodiversity threats embodied in imports (per million population)	0.0	2018	●	●

SDG15 – Life on Land

	Value	Year	Rating	Trend
Mean area that is protected in terrestrial sites important to biodiversity (%)	28.5	2018	●	↓
Mean area that is protected in freshwater sites important to biodiversity (%)	27.2	2018	●	↓
Red List Index of species survival (worst 0–1 best)	0.9	2019	●	↑
Permanent deforestation (% of forest area, 5-year average)	0.0	2018	●	●
Terrestrial and freshwater biodiversity threats embodied in imports (per million population)	0.6	2018	●	●

SDG16 – Peace, Justice and Strong Institutions

	Value	Year	Rating	Trend
Homicides (per 100,000 population)	5.8	2017	●	↗
Unsentenced detainees (% of prison population)	15.8	2018	●	↑
Percentage of population who feel safe walking alone at night in the city or area where they live	59.4	2019	●	↗
Property Rights (worst 1–7 best)	3.9	2019	●	●
Birth registrations with civil authority (% of children under age 5)	93.4	2018	●	●
Corruption Perception Index (worst 0–100 best)	30	2019	●	→
Children involved in child labor (% of population aged 5 to 14)	10.0	2016	●	●
Exports of major conventional weapons (TIV constant million USD per 100,000 population)	1.7	2019	◐	●
Press Freedom Index (best 0–100 worst)	44.5	2019	●	↓

SDG17 – Partnerships for the Goals

	Value	Year	Rating	Trend
Government spending on health and education (% of GDP)	6.9	2016	●	↓
For high-income and all OECD DAC countries: International concessional public finance, including official development assistance (% of GNI)	NA	NA	●	●
Other countries: Government revenue excluding grants (% of GDP)	25.6	2018	◐	↓
Corporate Tax Haven Score (best 0–100 worst)	4.7	2019	●	●

* Imputed data point

5. Country Profiles

LATIN AMERICA AND THE CARIBBEAN

Regional average score

70.4

SDG Global rank NA (OF 166)

Latin America and the Caribbean

▲ AVERAGE PERFORMANCE BY SDG

▼ SPILLOVER INDEX

100 (best) to 0 (worst)

▼ CURRENT ASSESSMENT – SDG DASHBOARD

■ Major challenges   ■ Significant challenges   ■ Challenges remain   ■ SDG achieved   ■ Information unavailable

▼ SDG TRENDS

↓ Decreasing   → Stagnating   ↗ Moderately improving   ↑ On track or maintaining SDG achievement   ● Information unavailable

Notes: The full title of Goal 2 "Zero Hunger" is "End hunger, achieve food security and improved nutrition and promote sustainable agriculture".
The full title of each SDG is available here: https://sustainabledevelopment.un.org/topics/sustainabledevelopmentgoals

SDG1 – No Poverty

	Value	Year	Rating	Trend
Poverty headcount ratio at $1.90/day (%)	6.0	2020	○	→
Poverty headcount ratio at $3.20/day (%)	14.1	2020	●	↓

SDG2 – Zero Hunger

	Value	Year	Rating	Trend
Prevalence of undernourishment (%)	7.4	2017	●	↑
Prevalence of stunting in children under 5 years of age (%)	11.7	2016	●	↗
Prevalence of wasting in children under 5 years of age (%)	1.7	2016	●	↑
Prevalence of obesity, BMI ≥ 30 (% of adult population)	22.9	2016	●	↓
Human Trophic Level (best 2–3 worst)	2.3	2017	●	→
Cereal yield (tonnes per hectare of harvested land)	4.3	2017	●	↑
Sustainable Nitrogen Management Index (best 0–1.41 worst)	0.7	2015	●	↓

SDG3 – Good Health and Well-Being

	Value	Year	Rating	Trend
Maternal mortality rate (per 100,000 live births)	80	2017	○	↑
Neonatal mortality rate (per 1,000 live births)	9.1	2018	●	↑
Mortality rate, under-5 (per 1,000 live births)	16.6	2018	●	↑
Incidence of tuberculosis (per 100,000 population)	49.7	2018	●	→
New HIV infections (per 1,000 uninfected population)	0.2	2018	○	→
Age-standardized death rate due to cardiovascular disease, cancer, diabetes, or chronic respiratory disease in adults aged 30–70 years (%)	16.2	2016	●	↑
Age-standardized death rate attributable to household air pollution and ambient air pollution (per 100,000 population)	41	2016	●	●
Traffic deaths (per 100,000 population)	19.0	2016	●	↗
Life expectancy at birth (years)	75.0	2016	●	↗
Adolescent fertility rate (births per 1,000 adolescent females aged 15 to 19)	64.1	2017	●	→
Births attended by skilled health personnel (%)	95.1	2016	●	↑
Percentage of surviving infants who received 2 WHO-recommended vaccines (%)	84	2018	●	↓
Universal health coverage (UHC) index of service coverage (worst 0–100 best)	75.4	2017	●	↑
Subjective well-being (average ladder score, worst 0–10 best)	6.1	2019	●	↑

SDG4 – Quality Education

	Value	Year	Rating	Trend
Net primary enrollment rate (%)	94.1	2018	○	↑
Lower secondary completion rate (%)	76.9	2018	●	↓
Literacy rate (% of population aged 15 to 24)	98.4	2018	●	●

SDG5 – Gender Equality

	Value	Year	Rating	Trend
Demand for family planning satisfied by modern methods (% of females aged 15 to 49 who are married or in unions)	82.0	2017	●	↑
Ratio of female-to-male mean years of education received (%)	102.2	2018	●	↑
Ratio of female-to-male labor force participation rate (%)	70.1	2019	●	↑
Seats held by women in national parliament (%)	22.7	2020	●	→

SDG6 – Clean Water and Sanitation

	Value	Year	Rating	Trend
Population using at least basic drinking water services (%)	96.0	2017	○	↑
Population using at least basic sanitation services (%)	85.5	2017	●	↗
Freshwater withdrawal (% of available freshwater resources)	5.9	2015	●	●
Anthropogenic wastewater that receives treatment (%)	28.4	2018	●	●
Scarce water consumption embodied in imports (m³/capita)	2.5	2013	●	↑

SDG7 – Affordable and Clean Energy

	Value	Year	Rating	Trend
Population with access to electricity (%)	97.5	2017	○	↑
Population with access to clean fuels and technology for cooking (%)	87.0	2016	●	↑
CO$_2$ emissions from fuel combustion for electricity and heating per total electricity output (MtCO$_2$/TWh)	1.0	2017	○	↑

SDG8 – Decent Work and Economic Growth

	Value	Year	Rating	Trend
Adjusted GDP growth (%)	-3.9	2018	●	●
Victims of modern slavery (per 1,000 population)	2.4	2018	●	●
Adults with an account at a bank or other financial institution or with a mobile-money-service provider (% of population aged 15 or over)	58.6	2017	●	↑
Unemployment rate (% of total labor force)	9.1	2019	●	↓
Fatal work-related accidents embodied in imports (per 100,000 population)	0.2	2010	●	↑

SDG9 – Industry, Innovation and Infrastructure

	Value	Year	Rating	Trend
Population using the internet (%)	64.6	2018	●	↑
Mobile broadband subscriptions (per 100 population)	69.7	2018	●	↑
Logistics Performance Index: Quality of trade and transport-related infrastructure (worst 1–5 best)	2.6	2018	○	↓
The Times Higher Education Universities Ranking: Average score of top 3 universities (worst 0–100 best)	25.5	2020	○	●
Scientific and technical journal articles (per 1,000 population)	0.2	2018	●	→
Expenditure on research and development (% of GDP)	0.7	2017	●	●

SDG10 – Reduced Inequalities

	Value	Year	Rating	Trend
Gini coefficient adjusted for top income	52.0	2017	●	●

SDG11 – Sustainable Cities and Communities

	Value	Year	Rating	Trend
Annual mean concentration of particulate matter of less than 2.5 microns in diameter (PM2.5) (μg/m³)	15.6	2017	○	↑
Access to improved water source, piped (% of urban population)	94.6	2017	○	→
Satisfaction with public transport (%)	54.1	2019	●	↓

SDG12 – Responsible Consumption and Production

	Value	Year	Rating	Trend
Municipal solid waste (kg/capita/day)	1.1	2016	●	●
Electronic waste (kg/capita)	6.8	2016	●	●
Production-based SO$_2$ emissions (kg/capita)	22.0	2012	●	●
SO$_2$ emissions embodied in imports (kg/capita)	2.3	2012	●	●
Production-based nitrogen emissions (kg/capita)	38.7	2010	●	●
Nitrogen emissions embodied in imports (kg/capita)	2.0	2010	●	●

SDG13 – Climate Action

	Value	Year	Rating	Trend
Energy-related CO$_2$ emissions (tCO$_2$/capita)	2.4	2017	○	↑
CO$_2$ emissions embodied in imports (tCO$_2$/capita)	0.4	2015	●	↑
CO$_2$ emissions embodied in fossil fuel exports (kg/capita)	635.5	2019	○	●

SDG14 – Life Below Water

	Value	Year	Rating	Trend
Mean area that is protected in marine sites important to biodiversity (%)	58.7	2018	●	↑
Ocean Health Index: Clean Waters score (worst 0–100 best)	60.9	2019	●	→
Fish caught from overexploited or collapsed stocks (% of total catch)	34.0	2014	●	↓
Fish caught by trawling (%)	18.4	2014	●	→
Marine biodiversity threats embodied in imports (per million population)	0.1	2018	●	●

SDG15 – Life on Land

	Value	Year	Rating	Trend
Mean area that is protected in terrestrial sites important to biodiversity (%)	40.9	2018	○	→
Mean area that is protected in freshwater sites important to biodiversity (%)	31.8	2018	○	→
Red List Index of species survival (worst 0–1 best)	0.8	2019	●	↓
Permanent deforestation (% of forest area, 5-year average)	0.4	2018	●	●
Terrestrial and freshwater biodiversity threats embodied in imports (per million population)	0.6	2018	●	●

SDG16 – Peace, Justice and Strong Institutions

	Value	Year	Rating	Trend
Homicides (per 100,000 population)	24.1	2017	●	→
Unsentenced detainees (% of prison population)	42.7	2018	●	↗
Percentage of population who feel safe walking alone at night in the city or area where they live (%)	43.4	2019	●	↓
Property Rights (worst 1–7 best)	3.7	2019	●	●
Birth registrations with civil authority (% of children under age 5)	94.5	2018	○	●
Corruption Perception Index (worst 0–100 best)	35	2019	●	↓
Children involved in child labor (% of population aged 5 to 14)	9.8	2016	●	●
Exports of major conventional weapons (TIV constant million USD per 100,000 population)	0.0	2019	●	●
Press Freedom Index (best 0–100 worst)	34.6	2019	○	→

SDG17 – Partnerships for the Goals

	Value	Year	Rating	Trend
Government spending on health and education (% of GDP)	9.4	2016	○	↑
For high-income and all OECD DAC countries: International concessional public finance, including official development assistance (% of GNI)	NA	NA	●	●
Other countries: Government revenue excluding grants (% of GDP)	23.5	2018	○	●
Corporate Tax Haven Score (best 0–100 worst)	0.7	2019	●	●

* Imputed data point

5. Country Profiles

▼ OVERALL PERFORMANCE

Regional average score

66.3

SDG Global rank NA (OF 166)

▼ SPILLOVER INDEX

100 (best) to 0 (worst)

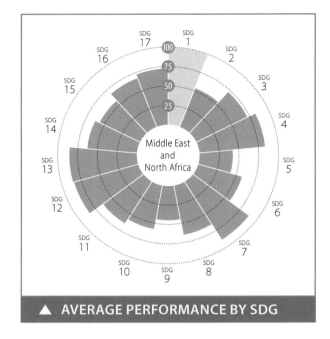

▲ AVERAGE PERFORMANCE BY SDG

▼ CURRENT ASSESSMENT – SDG DASHBOARD

■ Major challenges ■ Significant challenges ■ Challenges remain ■ SDG achieved ■ Information unavailable

▼ SDG TRENDS

↓ Decreasing → Stagnating ↗ Moderately improving ↑ On track or maintaining SDG achievement ● Information unavailable

Notes: The full title of Goal 2 "Zero Hunger" is "End hunger, achieve food security and improved nutrition and promote sustainable agriculture".

The full title of each SDG is available here: https://sustainabledevelopment.un.org/topics/sustainabledevelopmentgoals

SDG1 – No Poverty

Indicator	Value	Year	Rating	Trend
Poverty headcount ratio at $1.90/day (%)	NA	NA	●	●
Poverty headcount ratio at $3.20/day (%)	NA	NA	●	●

SDG2 – Zero Hunger

Indicator	Value	Year	Rating	Trend
Prevalence of undernourishment (%)	9.6	2017	●	→
Prevalence of stunting in children under 5 years of age (%)	16.9	2016	●	↗
Prevalence of wasting in children under 5 years of age (%)	7.1	2016	○	↑
Prevalence of obesity, BMI ≥ 30 (% of adult population)	28.8	2016	●	↓
Human Trophic Level (best 2–3 worst)	2.2	2017	●	↑
Cereal yield (tonnes per hectare of harvested land)	4.0	2017	●	↑
Sustainable Nitrogen Management Index (best 0–1.41 worst)	0.8	2015	●	↗

SDG3 – Good Health and Well-Being

Indicator	Value	Year	Rating	Trend
Maternal mortality rate (per 100,000 live births)	53	2017	●	↑
Neonatal mortality rate (per 1,000 live births)	11.5	2018	●	↑
Mortality rate, under-5 (per 1,000 live births)	20.5	2018	○	↑
Incidence of tuberculosis (per 100,000 population)	31.1	2018	○	→
New HIV infections (per 1,000 uninfected population)	0.0	2018	●	↑
Age-standardized death rate due to cardiovascular disease, cancer, diabetes, or chronic respiratory disease in adults aged 30–70 years (%)	19.9	2016	○	↗
Age-standardized death rate attributable to household air pollution and ambient air pollution (per 100,000 population)	80	2016	○	●
Traffic deaths (per 100,000 population)	19.2	2016	●	↑
Life expectancy at birth (years)	72.9	2016	●	→
Adolescent fertility rate (births per 1,000 adolescent females aged 15 to 19)	37.5	2017	○	→
Births attended by skilled health personnel (%)	88.0	2016	●	●
Percentage of surviving infants who received 2 WHO-recommended vaccines (%)	89	2018	○	↑
Universal health coverage (UHC) index of service coverage (worst 0–100 best)	68.2	2017	●	↑
Subjective well-being (average ladder score, worst 0–10 best)	4.8	2019	●	↓

SDG4 – Quality Education

Indicator	Value	Year	Rating	Trend
Net primary enrollment rate (%)	94.3	2018	○	→
Lower secondary completion rate (%)	78.1	2018	●	→
Literacy rate (% of population aged 15 to 24)	93.9	2018	○	●

SDG5 – Gender Equality

Indicator	Value	Year	Rating	Trend
Demand for family planning satisfied by modern methods (% of females aged 15 to 49 who are married or in unions)	64.6	2017	●	↗
Ratio of female-to-male mean years of education received (%)	85.3	2018	●	↗
Ratio of female-to-male labor force participation rate (%)	26.4	2019	●	→
Seats held by women in national parliament (%)	16.2	2020	●	→

SDG6 – Clean Water and Sanitation

Indicator	Value	Year	Rating	Trend
Population using at least basic drinking water services (%)	94.0	2017	○	↗
Population using at least basic sanitation services (%)	90.4	2017	○	↗
Freshwater withdrawal (% of available freshwater resources)	233.9	2015	●	●
Anthropogenic wastewater that receives treatment (%)	23.8	2018	●	●
Scarce water consumption embodied in imports (m^3/capita)	15.6	2013	●	↑

SDG7 – Affordable and Clean Energy

Indicator	Value	Year	Rating	Trend
Population with access to electricity (%)	97.8	2017	○	↑
Population with access to clean fuels and technology for cooking (%)	95.0	2016	○	↑
CO_2 emissions from fuel combustion for electricity and heating per total electricity output (MtCO$_2$/TWh)	1.6	2017	●	↑

SDG8 – Decent Work and Economic Growth

Indicator	Value	Year	Rating	Trend
Adjusted GDP growth (%)	-2.8	2018	●	●
Victims of modern slavery (per 1,000 population)	NA	NA	●	●
Adults with an account at a bank or other financial institution or with a mobile-money-service provider (% of population aged 15 or over)	48.4	2017	●	↗
Unemployment rate (% of total labor force)	10.5	2019	●	→
Fatal work-related accidents embodied in imports (per 100,000 population)	0.4	2010	●	↑

SDG9 – Industry, Innovation and Infrastructure

Indicator	Value	Year	Rating	Trend
Population using the internet (%)	60.7	2018	●	↑
Mobile broadband subscriptions (per 100 population)	65.3	2018	○	↑
Logistics Performance Index: Quality of trade and transport-related infrastructure (worst 1–5 best)	2.6	2018	○	↓
The Times Higher Education Universities Ranking: Average score of top 3 universities (worst 0–100 best)	29.4	2020	○	●
Scientific and technical journal articles (per 1,000 population)	0.2	2018	●	↗
Expenditure on research and development (% of GDP)	0.4	2017	●	●

SDG10 – Reduced Inequalities

Indicator	Value	Year	Rating	Trend
Gini coefficient adjusted for top income	42.8	2017	●	●

SDG11 – Sustainable Cities and Communities

Indicator	Value	Year	Rating	Trend
Annual mean concentration of particulate matter of less than 2.5 microns in diameter (PM2.5) (μg/m^3)	56.8	2017	●	↓
Access to improved water source, piped (% of urban population)	91.0	2017	○	→
Satisfaction with public transport (%)	59.6	2019	○	↑

SDG12 – Responsible Consumption and Production

Indicator	Value	Year	Rating	Trend
Municipal solid waste (kg/capita/day)	1.2	2016	○	●
Electronic waste (kg/capita)	7.1	2016	○	●
Production-based SO_2 emissions (kg/capita)	25.4	2012	●	●
SO_2 emissions embodied in imports (kg/capita)	3.1	2012	●	●
Production-based nitrogen emissions (kg/capita)	17.0	2010	●	●
Nitrogen emissions embodied in imports (kg/capita)	2.9	2010	●	●

SDG13 – Climate Action

Indicator	Value	Year	Rating	Trend
Energy-related CO_2 emissions (tCO$_2$/capita)	5.9	2017	●	→
CO_2 emissions embodied in imports (tCO$_2$/capita)	0.5	2015	○	↑
CO_2 emissions embodied in fossil fuel exports (kg/capita)	1128.1	2019	●	●

SDG14 – Life Below Water

Indicator	Value	Year	Rating	Trend
Mean area that is protected in marine sites important to biodiversity (%)	39.9	2018	○	→
Ocean Health Index: Clean Waters score (worst 0–100 best)	53.5	2019	●	↓
Fish caught from overexploited or collapsed stocks (% of total catch)	25.9	2014	○	↓
Fish caught by trawling (%)	24.7	2014	○	↑
Marine biodiversity threats embodied in imports (per million population)	0.1	2018	●	●

SDG15 – Life on Land

Indicator	Value	Year	Rating	Trend
Mean area that is protected in terrestrial sites important to biodiversity (%)	33.8	2018	○	→
Mean area that is protected in freshwater sites important to biodiversity (%)	31.5	2018	○	↓
Red List Index of species survival (worst 0–1 best)	0.9	2019	○	→
Permanent deforestation (% of forest area, 5-year average)	NA	NA	●	●
Terrestrial and freshwater biodiversity threats embodied in imports (per million population)	0.4	2018	●	●

SDG16 – Peace, Justice and Strong Institutions

Indicator	Value	Year	Rating	Trend
Homicides (per 100,000 population)	3.1	2017	●	●
Unsentenced detainees (% of prison population)	28.7	2018	●	●
Percentage of population who feel safe walking alone at night in the city or area where they live	71.0	2019	●	↑
Property Rights (worst 1–7 best)	4.5	2019	●	●
Birth registrations with civil authority (% of children under age 5)	93.6	2018	●	●
Corruption Perception Index (worst 0–100 best)	33	2019	●	↓
Children involved in child labor (% of population aged 5 to 14)	8.3	2016	●	●
Exports of major conventional weapons (TIV constant million USD per 100,000 population)	0.0	2019	●	●
Press Freedom Index (best 0–100 worst)	55.1	2019	●	↓

SDG17 – Partnerships for the Goals

Indicator	Value	Year	Rating	Trend
Government spending on health and education (% of GDP)	6.9	2016	●	●
For high-income and all OECD DAC countries: International concessional public finance, including official development assistance (% of GNI)	NA	NA	●	●
Other countries: Government revenue excluding grants (% of GDP)	NA	NA	●	●
Corporate Tax Haven Score (best 0–100 worst)	3.3	2019	●	●

* Imputed data point

5. Country Profiles

OCEANIA

▼ OVERALL PERFORMANCE

Regional average score

49.6

SDG Global rank   NA (OF 166)

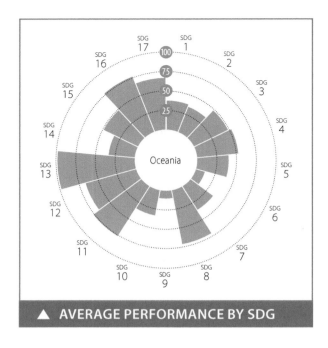

▲ AVERAGE PERFORMANCE BY SDG

▼ SPILLOVER INDEX

100 (best) to 0 (worst)

▼ CURRENT ASSESSMENT – SDG DASHBOARD

■ Major challenges   ■ Significant challenges   □ Challenges remain   ■ SDG achieved   ■ Information unavailable

▼ SDG TRENDS

↓ Decreasing   → Stagnating   ↗ Moderately improving   ↑ On track or maintaining SDG achievement   ● Information unavailable

Notes: The full title of Goal 2 "Zero Hunger" is "End hunger, achieve food security and improved nutrition and promote sustainable agriculture".
The full title of each SDG is available here: https://sustainabledevelopment.un.org/topics/sustainabledevelopmentgoals

SDG1 – No Poverty

Indicator	Value	Year	Rating	Trend
Poverty headcount ratio at $1.90/day (%)	24.1	2020	●	→
Poverty headcount ratio at $3.20/day (%)	45.8	2020	●	→

SDG2 – Zero Hunger

Indicator	Value	Year	Rating	Trend
Prevalence of undernourishment (%)	5.6	2017	●	●
Prevalence of stunting in children under 5 years of age (%)	43.1	2016	●	→
Prevalence of wasting in children under 5 years of age (%)	12.7	2016	●	↗
Prevalence of obesity, BMI ≥ 30 (% of adult population)	23.7	2016	●	↓
Human Trophic Level (best 2–3 worst)	NA	NA	●	●
Cereal yield (tonnes per hectare of harvested land)	NA	NA	●	●
Sustainable Nitrogen Management Index (best 0–1.41 worst)	1.0	2015	●	→

SDG3 – Good Health and Well-Being

Indicator	Value	Year	Rating	Trend
Maternal mortality rate (per 100,000 live births)	128	2017	●	↗
Neonatal mortality rate (per 1,000 live births)	19.6	2018	●	↗
Mortality rate, under-5 (per 1,000 live births)	42.7	2018	●	↗
Incidence of tuberculosis (per 100,000 population)	354.3	2018	●	→
New HIV infections (per 1,000 uninfected population)	NA	NA	●	●
Age-standardized death rate due to cardiovascular disease, cancer, diabetes, or chronic respiratory disease in adults aged 30–70 years (%)	29.2	2016	●	↓
Age-standardized death rate attributable to household air pollution and ambient air pollution (per 100,000 population)	144	2016	●	●
Traffic deaths (per 100,000 population)	13.8	2016	●	↑
Life expectancy at birth (years)	67.0	2016	●	→
Adolescent fertility rate (births per 1,000 adolescent females aged 15 to 19)	52.2	2017	●	→
Births attended by skilled health personnel (%)	61.8	2016	●	●
Percentage of surviving infants who received 2 WHO-recommended vaccines (%)	66	2018	●	↓
Universal health coverage (UHC) index of service coverage (worst 0–100 best)	43.1	2017	●	→
Subjective well-being (average ladder score, worst 0–10 best)	NA	NA	●	●

SDG4 – Quality Education

Indicator	Value	Year	Rating	Trend
Net primary enrollment rate (%)	76.1	2018	●	↓
Lower secondary completion rate (%)	67.2	2018	●	●
Literacy rate (% of population aged 15 to 24)	72.6	2018	●	●

SDG5 – Gender Equality

Indicator	Value	Year	Rating	Trend
Demand for family planning satisfied by modern methods (% of females aged 15 to 49 who are married or in unions)	42.9	2017	●	→
Ratio of female-to-male mean years of education received (%)	NA	NA	●	●
Ratio of female-to-male labor force participation rate (%)	89.9	2019	●	↑
Seats held by women in national parliament (%)	2.3	2020	●	↓

SDG6 – Clean Water and Sanitation

Indicator	Value	Year	Rating	Trend
Population using at least basic drinking water services (%)	51.0	2017	●	→
Population using at least basic sanitation services (%)	25.1	2017	●	↓
Freshwater withdrawal (% of available freshwater resources)	NA	NA	●	●
Anthropogenic wastewater that receives treatment (%)	0.4	2018	●	●
Scarce water consumption embodied in imports (m³/capita)	NA	NA	●	●

SDG7 – Affordable and Clean Energy

Indicator	Value	Year	Rating	Trend
Population with access to electricity (%)	60.6	2017	●	↑
Population with access to clean fuels and technology for cooking (%)	16.3	2016	●	→
CO_2 emissions from fuel combustion for electricity and heating per total electricity output (MtCO₂/TWh)	NA	NA	●	●

SDG8 – Decent Work and Economic Growth

Indicator	Value	Year	Rating	Trend
Adjusted GDP growth (%)	-4.9	2018	●	●
Victims of modern slavery (per 1,000 population)	NA	NA	●	●
Adults with an account at a bank or other financial institution or with a mobile-money-service provider (% of population aged 15 or over)	NA	NA	●	●
Unemployment rate (% of total labor force)	2.6	2019	●	↑
Fatal work-related accidents embodied in imports (per 100,000 population)	NA	NA	●	●

SDG9 – Industry, Innovation and Infrastructure

Indicator	Value	Year	Rating	Trend
Population using the internet (%)	15.9	2018	●	→
Mobile broadband subscriptions (per 100 population)	23.9	2018	●	↑
Logistics Performance Index: Quality of trade and transport-related infrastructure (worst 1–5 best)	NA	NA	●	●
The Times Higher Education Universities Ranking: Average score of top 3 universities (worst 0–100 best)	0.0	2020	●	●
Scientific and technical journal articles (per 1,000 population)	0.0	2018	●	→
Expenditure on research and development (% of GDP)	NA	NA	●	●

SDG10 – Reduced Inequalities

Indicator	Value	Year	Rating	Trend
Gini coefficient adjusted for top income	51.3	2017	●	●

SDG11 – Sustainable Cities and Communities

Indicator	Value	Year	Rating	Trend
Annual mean concentration of particulate matter of less than 2.5 microns in diameter (PM2.5) (µg/m³)	12.1	2017	●	↑
Access to improved water source, piped (% of urban population)	61.2	2017	●	↓
Satisfaction with public transport (%)	NA	NA	●	●

SDG12 – Responsible Consumption and Production

Indicator	Value	Year	Rating	Trend
Municipal solid waste (kg/capita/day)	2.4	2016	●	●
Electronic waste (kg/capita)	1.3	2016	●	●
Production-based SO_2 emissions (kg/capita)	NA	NA	●	●
SO_2 emissions embodied in imports (kg/capita)	NA	NA	●	●
Production-based nitrogen emissions (kg/capita)	NA	NA	●	●
Nitrogen emissions embodied in imports (kg/capita)	NA	NA	●	●

SDG13 – Climate Action

Indicator	Value	Year	Rating	Trend
Energy-related CO_2 emissions (tCO₂/capita)	1.0	2017	●	↑
CO_2 emissions embodied in imports (tCO₂/capita)	NA	NA	●	●
CO_2 emissions embodied in fossil fuel exports (kg/capita)	0.0	2019	●	●

SDG14 – Life Below Water

Indicator	Value	Year	Rating	Trend
Mean area that is protected in marine sites important to biodiversity (%)	4.2	2018	●	↓
Ocean Health Index: Clean Waters score (worst 0–100 best)	65.8	2019	●	↑
Fish caught from overexploited or collapsed stocks (% of total catch)	50.8	2014	●	↓
Fish caught by trawling (%)	NA	NA	●	●
Marine biodiversity threats embodied in imports (per million population)	NA	NA	●	●

SDG15 – Life on Land

Indicator	Value	Year	Rating	Trend
Mean area that is protected in terrestrial sites important to biodiversity (%)	8.5	2018	●	→
Mean area that is protected in freshwater sites important to biodiversity (%)	NA	NA	●	●
Red List Index of species survival (worst 0–1 best)	0.8	2019	●	↓
Permanent deforestation (% of forest area, 5-year average)	0.1	2018	●	●
Terrestrial and freshwater biodiversity threats embodied in imports (per million population)	NA	NA	●	●

SDG16 – Peace, Justice and Strong Institutions

Indicator	Value	Year	Rating	Trend
Homicides (per 100,000 population)	8.5	2017	●	●
Unsentenced detainees (% of prison population)	35.9	2018	●	→
Percentage of population who feel safe walking alone at night in the city or area where they live (%)	NA	NA	●	●
Property Rights (worst 1–7 best)	NA	NA	●	●
Birth registrations with civil authority (% of children under age 5)	75.4	2018	●	●
Corruption Perception Index (worst 0–100 best)	NA	NA	●	●
Children involved in child labor (% of population aged 5 to 14)	NA	NA	●	●
Exports of major conventional weapons (TIV constant million USD per 100,000 population)	0.0	2019	●	●
Press Freedom Index (best 0–100 worst)	NA	NA	●	●

SDG17 – Partnerships for the Goals

Indicator	Value	Year	Rating	Trend
Government spending on health and education (% of GDP)	10.3	2016	●	●
For high-income and all OECD DAC countries: International concessional public finance, including official development assistance (% of GNI)	NA	NA	●	●
Other countries: Government revenue excluding grants (% of GDP)	19.9	2018	●	↓
Corporate Tax Haven Score (best 0–100 worst)	0.0	2019	●	●

* Imputed data point

5. Country Profiles

OECD MEMBERS

▼ OVERALL PERFORMANCE

Regional average score

77.3

SDG Global rank **NA** (OF 166)

▼ SPILLOVER INDEX

100 (best) to 0 (worst)

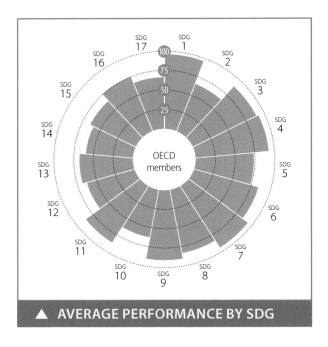

▲ AVERAGE PERFORMANCE BY SDG

▼ CURRENT ASSESSMENT – SDG DASHBOARD

■ Major challenges   ■ Significant challenges   ▨ Challenges remain   ■ SDG achieved   ■ Information unavailable

▼ SDG TRENDS

↓ Decreasing   → Stagnating   ↗ Moderately improving   ↑ On track or maintaining SDG achievement   ● Information unavailable

Notes: The full title of Goal 2 "Zero Hunger" is "End hunger, achieve food security and improved nutrition and promote sustainable agriculture".
The full title of each SDG is available here: https://sustainabledevelopment.un.org/topics/sustainabledevelopmentgoals

SDG1 – No Poverty

	Value	Year	Rating	Trend
Poverty headcount ratio at $1.90/day (%)	0.6	2020	●	↑
Poverty headcount ratio at $3.20/day (%)	1.7	2020	●	↑

SDG2 – Zero Hunger

	Value	Year	Rating	Trend
Prevalence of undernourishment (%)	2.6	2017	●	↑
Prevalence of stunting in children under 5 years of age (%)	4.2	2016	●	↑
Prevalence of wasting in children under 5 years of age (%)	0.9	2016	●	↑
Prevalence of obesity, BMI ≥ 30 (% of adult population)	25.3	2016	●	↓
Human Trophic Level (best 2–3 worst)	2.4	2017	●	↓
Cereal yield (tonnes per hectare of harvested land)	6.1	2017	●	↑
Sustainable Nitrogen Management Index (best 0–1.41 worst)	0.5	2015	●	↓

SDG3 – Good Health and Well-Being

	Value	Year	Rating	Trend
Maternal mortality rate (per 100,000 live births)	13	2017	●	↑
Neonatal mortality rate (per 1,000 live births)	3.2	2018	●	↑
Mortality rate, under-5 (per 1,000 live births)	5.7	2018	●	↑
Incidence of tuberculosis (per 100,000 population)	11.9	2018	◐	↑
New HIV infections (per 1,000 uninfected population)	0.1	2018	●	↑
Age-standardized death rate due to cardiovascular disease, cancer, diabetes, or chronic respiratory disease in adults aged 30–70 years (%)	12.6	2016	●	↑
Age-standardized death rate attributable to household air pollution and ambient air pollution (per 100,000 population)	19	2016	◐	●
Traffic deaths (per 100,000 population)	8.4	2016	◐	↑
Life expectancy at birth (years)	80.2	2016	●	↑
Adolescent fertility rate (births per 1,000 adolescent females aged 15 to 19)	17.4	2017	●	↑
Births attended by skilled health personnel (%)	98.9	2016	●	↑
Percentage of surviving infants who received 2 WHO-recommended vaccines (%)	93	2018	●	↑
Universal health coverage (UHC) index of service coverage (worst 0–100 best)	81.6	2017	●	↑
Subjective well-being (average ladder score, worst 0–10 best)	6.6	2019	●	↑

SDG4 – Quality Education

	Value	Year	Rating	Trend
Net primary enrollment rate (%)	99.2	2018	●	↑
Lower secondary completion rate (%)	99.2	2018	●	↑
Literacy rate (% of population aged 15 to 24)	NA	NA	●	●

SDG5 – Gender Equality

	Value	Year	Rating	Trend
Demand for family planning satisfied by modern methods (% of females aged 15 to 49 who are married or in unions)	77.6	2017	◐	↑
Ratio of female-to-male mean years of education received (%)	97.4	2018	◐	↑
Ratio of female-to-male labor force participation rate (%)	75.5	2019	●	↑
Seats held by women in national parliament (%)	28.7	2020	●	↗

SDG6 – Clean Water and Sanitation

	Value	Year	Rating	Trend
Population using at least basic drinking water services (%)	99.5	2017	●	●
Population using at least basic sanitation services (%)	98.5	2017	●	●
Freshwater withdrawal (% of available freshwater resources)	31.6	2015	◐	●
Anthropogenic wastewater that receives treatment (%)	67.2	2018	●	●
Scarce water consumption embodied in imports (m³/capita)	22.9	2013	●	↑

SDG7 – Affordable and Clean Energy

	Value	Year	Rating	Trend
Population with access to electricity (%)	100.0	2017	●	↑
Population with access to clean fuels and technology for cooking (%)	98.1	2016	●	↑
CO₂ emissions from fuel combustion for electricity and heating per total electricity output (MtCO₂/TWh)	1.2	2017	◐	↗

SDG8 – Decent Work and Economic Growth

	Value	Year	Rating	Trend
Adjusted GDP growth (%)	-0.6	2018	◐	●
Victims of modern slavery (per 1,000 population)	2.1	2018	●	●
Adults with an account at a bank or other financial institution or with a mobile-money-service provider (% of population aged 15 or over)	87.1	2017	●	↑
Unemployment rate (% of total labor force)	5.4	2019	◐	●
Fatal work-related accidents embodied in imports (per 100,000 population)	1.2	2010	◐	↑

SDG9 – Industry, Innovation and Infrastructure

	Value	Year	Rating	Trend
Population using the internet (%)	84.1	2018	●	↑
Mobile broadband subscriptions (per 100 population)	115.6	2018	●	↑
Logistics Performance Index: Quality of trade and transport-related infrastructure (worst 1–5 best)	3.8	2018	●	↑
The Times Higher Education Universities Ranking: Average score of top 3 universities (worst 0–100 best)	66.3	2020	●	●
Scientific and technical journal articles (per 1,000 population)	1.1	2018	●	↑
Expenditure on research and development (% of GDP)	2.2	2017	●	↑

SDG10 – Reduced Inequalities

	Value	Year	Rating	Trend
Gini coefficient adjusted for top income	41.3	2017	●	●

SDG11 – Sustainable Cities and Communities

	Value	Year	Rating	Trend
Annual mean concentration of particulate matter of less than 2.5 microns in diameter (PM2.5) (μg/m³)	14.5	2017	◐	↗
Access to improved water source, piped (% of urban population)	98.6	2017	●	↑
Satisfaction with public transport (%)	62.0	2019	◐	→

SDG12 – Responsible Consumption and Production

	Value	Year	Rating	Trend
Municipal solid waste (kg/capita/day)	1.8	2016	●	●
Electronic waste (kg/capita)	17.4	2016	●	●
Production-based SO₂ emissions (kg/capita)	46.4	2012	●	●
SO₂ emissions embodied in imports (kg/capita)	10.1	2012	●	●
Production-based nitrogen emissions (kg/capita)	41.9	2010	●	●
Nitrogen emissions embodied in imports (kg/capita)	9.7	2010	◐	●

SDG13 – Climate Action

	Value	Year	Rating	Trend
Energy-related CO₂ emissions (tCO₂/capita)	9.1	2017	●	→
CO₂ emissions embodied in imports (tCO₂/capita)	1.8	2015	●	→
CO₂ emissions embodied in fossil fuel exports (kg/capita)	1503.8	2019	◐	●

SDG14 – Life Below Water

	Value	Year	Rating	Trend
Mean area that is protected in marine sites important to biodiversity (%)	64.7	2018	●	↑
Ocean Health Index: Clean Waters score (worst 0–100 best)	62.0	2019	●	→
Fish caught from overexploited or collapsed stocks (% of total catch)	40.9	2014	●	↓
Fish caught by trawling (%)	41.9	2014	●	↓
Marine biodiversity threats embodied in imports (per million population)	0.4	2018	◐	●

SDG15 – Life on Land

	Value	Year	Rating	Trend
Mean area that is protected in terrestrial sites important to biodiversity (%)	55.0	2018	●	↑
Mean area that is protected in freshwater sites important to biodiversity (%)	50.1	2018	●	↑
Red List Index of species survival (worst 0–1 best)	0.8	2019	●	↓
Permanent deforestation (% of forest area, 5-year average)	0.0	2018	●	●
Terrestrial and freshwater biodiversity threats embodied in imports (per million population)	3.4	2018	●	●

SDG16 – Peace, Justice and Strong Institutions

	Value	Year	Rating	Trend
Homicides (per 100,000 population)	4.6	2017	●	→
Unsentenced detainees (% of prison population)	23.6	2018	●	↑
Percentage of population who feel safe walking alone at night in the city or area where they live (%)	69.4	2019	◐	↑
Property Rights (worst 1–7 best)	5.2	2019	●	●
Birth registrations with civil authority (% of children under age 5)	99.4	2018	●	●
Corruption Perception Index (worst 0–100 best)	63	2019	●	↑
Children involved in child labor (% of population aged 5 to 14)	1.7	2016	●	●
Exports of major conventional weapons (TIV constant million USD per 100,000 population)	1.6	2019	●	●
Press Freedom Index (best 0–100 worst)	27.2	2019	●	↑

SDG17 – Partnerships for the Goals

	Value	Year	Rating	Trend
Government spending on health and education (% of GDP)	12.1	2016	●	↑
For high-income and all OECD DAC countries: International concessional public finance, including official development assistance (% of GNI)	0.3	2017	●	→
Other countries: Government revenue excluding grants (% of GDP)	NA	NA	●	●
Corporate Tax Haven Score (best 0–100 worst)	33.6	2019	●	●

* Imputed data point

5. Country Profiles

SUB-SAHARAN AFRICA

▼ OVERALL PERFORMANCE

Regional average score

53.1

SDG Global rank NA (OF 166)

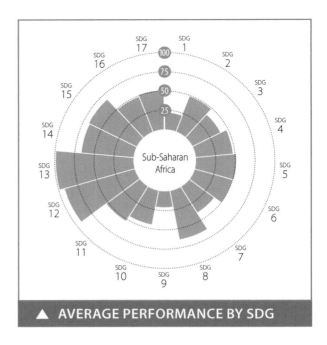

▲ AVERAGE PERFORMANCE BY SDG

▼ SPILLOVER INDEX

100 (best) to 0 (worst)

▼ CURRENT ASSESSMENT – SDG DASHBOARD

■ Major challenges   ■ Significant challenges   ■ Challenges remain   ■ SDG achieved   ■ Information unavailable

▼ SDG TRENDS

↓ Decreasing   → Stagnating   ↗ Moderately improving   ↑ On track or maintaining SDG achievement   ● Information unavailable

Notes: The full title of Goal 2 "Zero Hunger" is "End hunger, achieve food security and improved nutrition and promote sustainable agriculture".
The full title of each SDG is available here: https://sustainabledevelopment.un.org/topics/sustainabledevelopmentgoals

SDG1 – No Poverty

Indicator	Value	Year	Rating	Trend
Poverty headcount ratio at $1.90/day (%)	40.2	2020	●	→
Poverty headcount ratio at $3.20/day (%)	65.1	2020	●	→

SDG2 – Zero Hunger

Indicator	Value	Year	Rating	Trend
Prevalence of undernourishment (%)	21.4	2017	●	↓
Prevalence of stunting in children under 5 years of age (%)	35.9	2016	●	↗
Prevalence of wasting in children under 5 years of age (%)	8.2	2016	●	↗
Prevalence of obesity, BMI ≥ 30 (% of adult population)	8.9	2016	●	↑
Human Trophic Level (best 2–3 worst)	2.1	2017	●	↑
Cereal yield (tonnes per hectare of harvested land)	1.7	2017	●	→
Sustainable Nitrogen Management Index (best 0–1.41 worst)	0.8	2015	●	→

SDG3 – Good Health and Well-Being

Indicator	Value	Year	Rating	Trend
Maternal mortality rate (per 100,000 live births)	514	2017	●	→
Neonatal mortality rate (per 1,000 live births)	27.1	2018	●	→
Mortality rate, under-5 (per 1,000 live births)	74.7	2018	●	↗
Incidence of tuberculosis (per 100,000 population)	230.7	2018	●	↗
New HIV infections (per 1,000 uninfected population)	1.1	2018	●	↑
Age-standardized death rate due to cardiovascular disease, cancer, diabetes, or chronic respiratory disease in adults aged 30–70 years (%)	20.8	2016	●	→
Age-standardized death rate attributable to household air pollution and ambient air pollution (per 100,000 population)	187	2016	●	●
Traffic deaths (per 100,000 population)	26.9	2016	●	↓
Life expectancy at birth (years)	61.1	2016	●	→
Adolescent fertility rate (births per 1,000 adolescent females aged 15 to 19)	102.8	2017	●	→
Births attended by skilled health personnel (%)	58.1	2016	●	●
Percentage of surviving infants who received 2 WHO-recommended vaccines (%)	72	2018	●	↗
Universal health coverage (UHC) index of service coverage (worst 0–100 best)	43.8	2017	●	→
Subjective well-being (average ladder score, worst 0–10 best)	4.5	2019	●	→

SDG4 – Quality Education

Indicator	Value	Year	Rating	Trend
Net primary enrollment rate (%)	78.8	2018	●	→
Lower secondary completion rate (%)	44.5	2018	●	→
Literacy rate (% of population aged 15 to 24)	76.5	2018	●	●

SDG5 – Gender Equality

Indicator	Value	Year	Rating	Trend
Demand for family planning satisfied by modern methods (% of females aged 15 to 49 who are married or in unions)	48.2	2017	●	↗
Ratio of female-to-male mean years of education received (%)	68.3	2018	●	→
Ratio of female-to-male labor force participation rate (%)	83.9	2019	●	↑
Seats held by women in national parliament (%)	23.0	2020	●	→

SDG6 – Clean Water and Sanitation

Indicator	Value	Year	Rating	Trend
Population using at least basic drinking water services (%)	60.7	2017	●	→
Population using at least basic sanitation services (%)	30.7	2017	●	→
Freshwater withdrawal (% of available freshwater resources)	17.4	2015	●	●
Anthropogenic wastewater that receives treatment (%)	1.4	2018	●	●
Scarce water consumption embodied in imports (m³/capita)	1.0	2013	●	↑

SDG7 – Affordable and Clean Energy

Indicator	Value	Year	Rating	Trend
Population with access to electricity (%)	44.4	2017	●	↗
Population with access to clean fuels and technology for cooking (%)	14.1	2016	●	→
CO₂ emissions from fuel combustion for electricity and heating per total electricity output (MtCO2/TWh)	1.9	2017	●	↗

SDG8 – Decent Work and Economic Growth

Indicator	Value	Year	Rating	Trend
Adjusted GDP growth (%)	-5.0	2018	●	●
Victims of modern slavery (per 1,000 population)	8.3	2018	●	●
Adults with an account at a bank or other financial institution or with a mobile-money-service provider (% of population aged 15 or over)	40.0	2017	●	↗
Unemployment rate (% of total labor force)	6.6	2019	●	→
Fatal work-related accidents embodied in imports (per 100,000 population)	0.1	2010	●	↑

SDG9 – Industry, Innovation and Infrastructure

Indicator	Value	Year	Rating	Trend
Population using the internet (%)	25.1	2018	●	↗
Mobile broadband subscriptions (per 100 population)	29.4	2018	●	↗
Logistics Performance Index: Quality of trade and transport-related infrastructure (worst 1–5 best)	2.4	2018	●	→
The Times Higher Education Universities Ranking: Average score of top 3 universities (worst 0–100 best)	13.0	2020	●	●
Scientific and technical journal articles (per 1,000 population)	0.0	2018	●	→
Expenditure on research and development (% of GDP)	0.4	2017	●	●

SDG10 – Reduced Inequalities

Indicator	Value	Year	Rating	Trend
Gini coefficient adjusted for top income	47.2	2017	●	●

SDG11 – Sustainable Cities and Communities

Indicator	Value	Year	Rating	Trend
Annual mean concentration of particulate matter of less than 2.5 microns in diameter (PM2.5) (µg/m³)	44.7	2017	●	↓
Access to improved water source, piped (% of urban population)	59.2	2017	●	↓
Satisfaction with public transport (%)	50.3	2019	●	↗

SDG12 – Responsible Consumption and Production

Indicator	Value	Year	Rating	Trend
Municipal solid waste (kg/capita/day)	1.0	2016	●	●
Electronic waste (kg/capita)	1.3	2016	●	●
Production-based SO₂ emissions (kg/capita)	9.7	2012	●	●
SO₂ emissions embodied in imports (kg/capita)	0.7	2012	●	●
Production-based nitrogen emissions (kg/capita)	15.9	2010	●	●
Nitrogen emissions embodied in imports (kg/capita)	0.6	2010	●	●

SDG13 – Climate Action

Indicator	Value	Year	Rating	Trend
Energy-related CO₂ emissions (tCO2/capita)	0.8	2017	●	↑
CO₂ emissions embodied in imports (tCO2/capita)	0.1	2015	●	↑
CO₂ emissions embodied in fossil fuel exports (kg/capita)	147.7	2019	●	●

SDG14 – Life Below Water

Indicator	Value	Year	Rating	Trend
Mean area that is protected in marine sites important to biodiversity (%)	50.7	2018	●	↑
Ocean Health Index: Clean Waters score (worst 0–100 best)	44.3	2019	●	↓
Fish caught from overexploited or collapsed stocks (% of total catch)	22.6	2014	●	↑
Fish caught by trawling (%)	17.2	2014	●	●
Marine biodiversity threats embodied in imports (per million population)	0.0	2018	●	●

SDG15 – Life on Land

Indicator	Value	Year	Rating	Trend
Mean area that is protected in terrestrial sites important to biodiversity (%)	52.1	2018	●	↑
Mean area that is protected in freshwater sites important to biodiversity (%)	48.6	2018	●	↑
Red List Index of species survival (worst 0–1 best)	0.9	2019	●	→
Permanent deforestation (% of forest area, 5-year average)	0.4	2018	●	●
Terrestrial and freshwater biodiversity threats embodied in imports (per million population)	0.2	2018	●	●

SDG16 – Peace, Justice and Strong Institutions

Indicator	Value	Year	Rating	Trend
Homicides (per 100,000 population)	9.1	2017	●	●
Unsentenced detainees (% of prison population)	45.1	2018	●	→
Percentage of population who feel safe walking alone at night in the city or area where they live (%)	53.2	2019	●	↓
Property Rights (worst 1–7 best)	3.7	2019	●	●
Birth registrations with civil authority (% of children under age 5)	45.9	2018	●	●
Corruption Perception Index (worst 0–100 best)	29	2019	●	→
Children involved in child labor (% of population aged 5 to 14)	29.3	2016	●	●
Exports of major conventional weapons (TIV constant million USD per 100,000 population)	0.0	2019	●	●
Press Freedom Index (best 0–100 worst)	37.4	2019	●	→

SDG17 – Partnerships for the Goals

Indicator	Value	Year	Rating	Trend
Government spending on health and education (% of GDP)	5.7	2016	●	→
For high-income and all OECD DAC countries: International concessional public finance, including official development assistance (% of GNI)	NA	NA	●	●
Other countries: Government revenue excluding grants (% of GDP)	14.2	2018	●	↓
Corporate Tax Haven Score (best 0–100 worst)	9.2	2019	●	●

* Imputed data point

5. Country Profiles

LOW-INCOME COUNTRIES

Regional average score

52.5

SDG Global rank NA (OF 166)

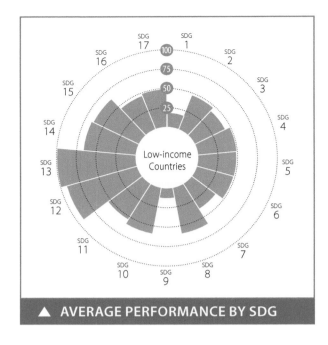

▲ AVERAGE PERFORMANCE BY SDG

▼ SPILLOVER INDEX

100 (best) to 0 (worst)

▼ CURRENT ASSESSMENT – SDG DASHBOARD

■ Major challenges ■ Significant challenges ■ Challenges remain ■ SDG achieved ■ Information unavailable

▼ SDG TRENDS

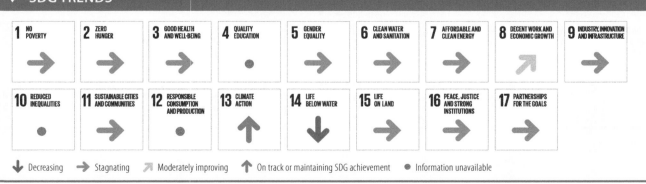

↓ Decreasing → Stagnating ↗ Moderately improving ↑ On track or maintaining SDG achievement ● Information unavailable

Notes: The full title of Goal 2 "Zero Hunger" is "End hunger, achieve food security and improved nutrition and promote sustainable agriculture".
The full title of each SDG is available here: https://sustainabledevelopment.un.org/topics/sustainabledevelopmentgoals

SDG1 – No Poverty

Indicator	Value	Year	Rating	Trend
Poverty headcount ratio at $1.90/day (%)	44.6	2020	●	→
Poverty headcount ratio at $3.20/day (%)	70.7	2020	●	→

SDG2 – Zero Hunger

Indicator	Value	Year	Rating	Trend
Prevalence of undernourishment (%)	27.7	2017	●	↓
Prevalence of stunting in children under 5 years of age (%)	37.1	2016	●	→
Prevalence of wasting in children under 5 years of age (%)	8.7	2016	●	→
Prevalence of obesity, BMI ≥ 30 (% of adult population)	7.6	2016	●	↑
Human Trophic Level (best 2–3 worst)	2.1	2017	●	↑
Cereal yield (tonnes per hectare of harvested land)	1.7	2017	●	→
Sustainable Nitrogen Management Index (best 0–1.41 worst)	0.8	2015	●	→

SDG3 – Good Health and Well-Being

Indicator	Value	Year	Rating	Trend
Maternal mortality rate (per 100,000 live births)	440	2017	●	↗
Neonatal mortality rate (per 1,000 live births)	25.7	2018	●	↗
Mortality rate, under-5 (per 1,000 live births)	64.7	2018	●	↗
Incidence of tuberculosis (per 100,000 population)	205.3	2018	●	→
New HIV infections (per 1,000 uninfected population)	0.7	2018	●	↗
Age-standardized death rate due to cardiovascular disease, cancer, diabetes, or chronic respiratory disease in adults aged 30–70 years (%)	21.5	2016	●	→
Age-standardized death rate attributable to household air pollution and ambient air pollution (per 100,000 population)	173	2016	●	●
Traffic deaths (per 100,000 population)	26.9	2016	●	↓
Life expectancy at birth (years)	63.0	2016	●	→
Adolescent fertility rate (births per 1,000 adolescent females aged 15 to 19)	97.2	2017	●	→
Births attended by skilled health personnel (%)	57.5	2016	●	●
Percentage of surviving infants who received 2 WHO-recommended vaccines (%)	74	2018	●	→
Universal health coverage (UHC) index of service coverage (worst 0–100 best)	42.1	2017	●	→
Subjective well-being (average ladder score, worst 0–10 best)	4.2	2019	●	→

SDG4 – Quality Education

Indicator	Value	Year	Rating	Trend
Net primary enrollment rate (%)	84.0	2018	●	●
Lower secondary completion rate (%)	39.2	2018	●	●
Literacy rate (% of population aged 15 to 24)	75.3	2018	●	●

SDG5 – Gender Equality

Indicator	Value	Year	Rating	Trend
Demand for family planning satisfied by modern methods (% of females aged 15 to 49 who are married or in unions)	47.3	2017	●	→
Ratio of female-to-male mean years of education received (%)	60.4	2018	●	→
Ratio of female-to-male labor force participation rate (%)	80.9	2019	●	↑
Seats held by women in national parliament (%)	24.8	2020	●	→

SDG6 – Clean Water and Sanitation

Indicator	Value	Year	Rating	Trend
Population using at least basic drinking water services (%)	57.2	2017	●	→
Population using at least basic sanitation services (%)	30.0	2017	●	→
Freshwater withdrawal (% of available freshwater resources)	24.1	2015	●	●
Anthropogenic wastewater that receives treatment (%)	1.3	2018	●	●
Scarce water consumption embodied in imports (m³/capita)	0.7	2013	●	↑

SDG7 – Affordable and Clean Energy

Indicator	Value	Year	Rating	Trend
Population with access to electricity (%)	40.7	2017	●	↗
Population with access to clean fuels and technology for cooking (%)	11.5	2016	●	→
CO_2 emissions from fuel combustion for electricity and heating per total electricity output (MtCO$_2$/TWh)	1.9	2017	●	●

SDG8 – Decent Work and Economic Growth

Indicator	Value	Year	Rating	Trend
Adjusted GDP growth (%)	-5.2	2018	●	●
Victims of modern slavery (per 1,000 population)	13.4	2018	●	●
Adults with an account at a bank or other financial institution or with a mobile-money-service provider (% of population aged 15 or over)	32.3	2017	●	↗
Unemployment rate (% of total labor force)	4.4	2019	●	↑
Fatal work-related accidents embodied in imports (per 100,000 population)	0.0	2010	●	↑

SDG9 – Industry, Innovation and Infrastructure

Indicator	Value	Year	Rating	Trend
Population using the internet (%)	16.0	2018	●	↗
Mobile broadband subscriptions (per 100 population)	18.1	2018	●	↗
Logistics Performance Index: Quality of trade and transport-related infrastructure (worst 1–5 best)	2.2	2018	●	→
The Times Higher Education Universities Ranking: Average score of top 3 universities (worst 0–100 best)	3.9	2020	●	●
Scientific and technical journal articles (per 1,000 population)	0.0	2018	●	→
Expenditure on research and development (% of GDP)	0.3	2017	●	●

SDG10 – Reduced Inequalities

Indicator	Value	Year	Rating	Trend
Gini coefficient adjusted for top income	41.9	2017	●	●

SDG11 – Sustainable Cities and Communities

Indicator	Value	Year	Rating	Trend
Annual mean concentration of particulate matter of less than 2.5 microns in diameter (PM2.5) (µg/m³)	43.2	2017	●	↓
Access to improved water source, piped (% of urban population)	67.0	2017	●	→
Satisfaction with public transport (%)	46.3	2019	●	↗

SDG12 – Responsible Consumption and Production

Indicator	Value	Year	Rating	Trend
Municipal solid waste (kg/capita/day)	1.3	2016	◐	●
Electronic waste (kg/capita)	0.7	2016	●	●
Production-based SO_2 emissions (kg/capita)	8.5	2012	●	●
SO_2 emissions embodied in imports (kg/capita)	0.4	2012	●	●
Production-based nitrogen emissions (kg/capita)	13.3	2010	●	●
Nitrogen emissions embodied in imports (kg/capita)	0.2	2010	●	●

SDG13 – Climate Action

Indicator	Value	Year	Rating	Trend
Energy-related CO_2 emissions (tCO$_2$/capita)	0.3	2017	●	↑
CO_2 emissions embodied in imports (tCO$_2$/capita)	0.0	2015	●	↑
CO_2 emissions embodied in fossil fuel exports (kg/capita)	41.7	2019	●	●

SDG14 – Life Below Water

Indicator	Value	Year	Rating	Trend
Mean area that is protected in marine sites important to biodiversity (%)	33.9	2018	◐	●
Ocean Health Index: Clean Waters score (worst 0–100 best)	46.8	2019	●	↓
Fish caught from overexploited or collapsed stocks (% of total catch)	14.2	2014	●	●
Fish caught by trawling (%)	12.4	2014	●	●
Marine biodiversity threats embodied in imports (per million population)	0.0	2018	●	●

SDG15 – Life on Land

Indicator	Value	Year	Rating	Trend
Mean area that is protected in terrestrial sites important to biodiversity (%)	41.4	2018	◐	→
Mean area that is protected in freshwater sites important to biodiversity (%)	40.1	2018	◐	↗
Red List Index of species survival (worst 0–1 best)	0.9	2019	●	→
Permanent deforestation (% of forest area, 5-year average)	0.3	2018	●	●
Terrestrial and freshwater biodiversity threats embodied in imports (per million population)	0.1	2018	●	●

SDG16 – Peace, Justice and Strong Institutions

Indicator	Value	Year	Rating	Trend
Homicides (per 100,000 population)	7.2	2017	●	●
Unsentenced detainees (% of prison population)	44.9	2018	●	●
Percentage of population who feel safe walking alone at night in the city or area where they live (%)	52.2	2019	●	↓
Property Rights (worst 1–7 best)	3.6	2019	●	●
Birth registrations with civil authority (% of children under age 5)	42.0	2018	●	●
Corruption Perception Index (worst 0–100 best)	27	2019	●	→
Children involved in child labor (% of population aged 5 to 14)	30.5	2016	●	●
Exports of major conventional weapons (TIV constant million USD per 100,000 population)	0.0	2019	●	●
Press Freedom Index (best 0–100 worst)	41.5	2019	●	→

SDG17 – Partnerships for the Goals

Indicator	Value	Year	Rating	Trend
Government spending on health and education (% of GDP)	5.1	2016	●	→
For high-income and all OECD DAC countries: International concessional public finance, including official development assistance (% of GNI)	NA	NA	●	●
Other countries: Government revenue excluding grants (% of GDP)	14.0	2018	●	●
Corporate Tax Haven Score (best 0–100 worst)	4.2	2019	●	●

* Imputed data point

LOWER-MIDDLE-INCOME COUNTRIES

▼ OVERALL PERFORMANCE

Regional average score

61.6

SDG Global rank NA (OF 166)

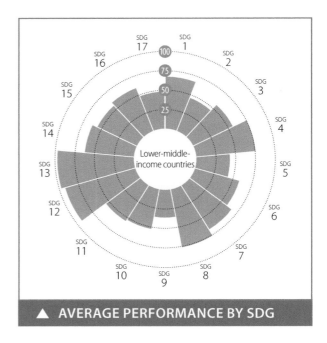

▲ AVERAGE PERFORMANCE BY SDG

SDG 17 · SDG 1 · SDG 2 · SDG 3 · SDG 4 · SDG 5 · SDG 6 · SDG 7 · SDG 8 · SDG 9 · SDG 10 · SDG 11 · SDG 12 · SDG 13 · SDG 14 · SDG 15 · SDG 16

Lower-middle-income countries

100 · 75 · 50 · 25

▼ SPILLOVER INDEX

100 (best) to 0 (worst)

100
80
60
40
20
0

▼ CURRENT ASSESSMENT – SDG DASHBOARD

■ Major challenges ■ Significant challenges ■ Challenges remain ■ SDG achieved ■ Information unavailable

▼ SDG TRENDS

↓ Decreasing → Stagnating ↗ Moderately improving ↑ On track or maintaining SDG achievement ● Information unavailable

Notes: The full title of Goal 2 "Zero Hunger" is "End hunger, achieve food security and improved nutrition and promote sustainable agriculture".
The full title of each SDG is available here: https://sustainabledevelopment.un.org/topics/sustainabledevelopmentgoals

SDG1 – No Poverty

	Value	Year	Rating	Trend
Poverty headcount ratio at $1.90/day (%)	7.2	2020	●	↑
Poverty headcount ratio at $3.20/day (%)	27.5	2020	●	↗

SDG2 – Zero Hunger

	Value	Year	Rating	Trend
Prevalence of undernourishment (%)	14.0	2017	●	↗
Prevalence of stunting in children under 5 years of age (%)	35.6	2016	●	↗
Prevalence of wasting in children under 5 years of age (%)	14.6	2016	●	→
Prevalence of obesity, BMI ≥ 30 (% of adult population)	7.4	2016	●	↑
Human Trophic Level (best 2–3 worst)	2.2	2017	●	→
Cereal yield (tonnes per hectare of harvested land)	3.4	2017	●	↑
Sustainable Nitrogen Management Index (best 0–1.41 worst)	0.8	2015	●	→

SDG3 – Good Health and Well-Being

	Value	Year	Rating	Trend
Maternal mortality rate (per 100,000 live births)	209	2017	●	↗
Neonatal mortality rate (per 1,000 live births)	22.2	2018	●	↗
Mortality rate, under-5 (per 1,000 live births)	42.9	2018	●	↑
Incidence of tuberculosis (per 100,000 population)	220.7	2018	●	→
New HIV infections (per 1,000 uninfected population)	0.3	2018	●	↑
Age-standardized death rate due to cardiovascular disease, cancer, diabetes, or chronic respiratory disease in adults aged 30–70 years (%)	23.1	2016	●	→
Age-standardized death rate attributable to household air pollution and ambient air pollution (per 100,000 population)	167	2016	●	●
Traffic deaths (per 100,000 population)	19.8	2016	●	↓
Life expectancy at birth (years)	68.0	2016	●	→
Adolescent fertility rate (births per 1,000 adolescent females aged 15 to 19)	40.4	2017	●	↑
Births attended by skilled health personnel (%)	76.7	2016	●	↑
Percentage of surviving infants who received 2 WHO-recommended vaccines (%)	83	2018	●	↑
Universal health coverage (UHC) index of service coverage (worst 0–100 best)	54.8	2017	●	↗
Subjective well-being (average ladder score, worst 0–10 best)	4.5	2019	●	↓

SDG4 – Quality Education

	Value	Year	Rating	Trend
Net primary enrollment rate (%)	88.1	2018	●	→
Lower secondary completion rate (%)	77.2	2018	●	→
Literacy rate (% of population aged 15 to 24)	89.7	2018	●	●

SDG5 – Gender Equality

	Value	Year	Rating	Trend
Demand for family planning satisfied by modern methods (% of females aged 15 to 49 who are married or in unions)	64.2	2017	●	↗
Ratio of female-to-male mean years of education received (%)	70.3	2018	●	↓
Ratio of female-to-male labor force participation rate (%)	47.5	2019	●	→
Seats held by women in national parliament (%)	17.4	2020	●	→

SDG6 – Clean Water and Sanitation

	Value	Year	Rating	Trend
Population using at least basic drinking water services (%)	88.5	2017	●	↗
Population using at least basic sanitation services (%)	60.8	2017	●	↗
Freshwater withdrawal (% of available freshwater resources)	52.1	2015	●	●
Anthropogenic wastewater that receives treatment (%)	3.0	2018	●	●
Scarce water consumption embodied in imports (m³/capita)	2.1	2013	●	↑

SDG7 – Affordable and Clean Energy

	Value	Year	Rating	Trend
Population with access to electricity (%)	85.9	2017	●	↑
Population with access to clean fuels and technology for cooking (%)	42.6	2016	●	→
CO₂ emissions from fuel combustion for electricity and heating per total electricity output (MtCO₂/TWh)	1.6	2017	●	↗

SDG8 – Decent Work and Economic Growth

	Value	Year	Rating	Trend
Adjusted GDP growth (%)	-0.5	2018	●	●
Victims of modern slavery (per 1,000 population)	6.0	2018	●	●
Adults with an account at a bank or other financial institution or with a mobile-money-service provider (% of population aged 15 or over)	57.4	2017	●	↑
Unemployment rate (% of total labor force)	5.5	2019	●	→
Fatal work-related accidents embodied in imports (per 100,000 population)	0.1	2010	●	↑

SDG9 – Industry, Innovation and Infrastructure

	Value	Year	Rating	Trend
Population using the internet (%)	35.9	2018	●	↑
Mobile broadband subscriptions (per 100 population)	46.5	2018	●	↑
Logistics Performance Index: Quality of trade and transport-related infrastructure (worst 1–5 best)	2.7	2018	●	↓
The Times Higher Education Universities Ranking: Average score of top 3 universities (worst 0–100 best)	31.6	2020	●	●
Scientific and technical journal articles (per 1,000 population)	0.1	2018	●	→
Expenditure on research and development (% of GDP)	0.5	2017	●	●

SDG10 – Reduced Inequalities

	Value	Year	Rating	Trend
Gini coefficient adjusted for top income	44.7	2017	●	●

SDG11 – Sustainable Cities and Communities

	Value	Year	Rating	Trend
Annual mean concentration of particulate matter of less than 2.5 microns in diameter (PM2.5) (μg/m³)	64.3	2017	●	↓
Access to improved water source, piped (% of urban population)	58.9	2017	●	↓
Satisfaction with public transport (%)	68.7	2019	●	↑

SDG12 – Responsible Consumption and Production

	Value	Year	Rating	Trend
Municipal solid waste (kg/capita/day)	1.0	2016	●	●
Electronic waste (kg/capita)	2.1	2016	●	●
Production-based SO₂ emissions (kg/capita)	8.3	2012	●	●
SO₂ emissions embodied in imports (kg/capita)	0.6	2012	●	●
Production-based nitrogen emissions (kg/capita)	13.7	2010	●	●
Nitrogen emissions embodied in imports (kg/capita)	0.6	2010	●	●

SDG13 – Climate Action

	Value	Year	Rating	Trend
Energy-related CO₂ emissions (tCO₂/capita)	1.4	2017	●	↑
CO₂ emissions embodied in imports (tCO₂/capita)	0.1	2015	●	↑
CO₂ emissions embodied in fossil fuel exports (kg/capita)	332.0	2019	●	●

SDG14 – Life Below Water

	Value	Year	Rating	Trend
Mean area that is protected in marine sites important to biodiversity (%)	38.6	2018	●	→
Ocean Health Index: Clean Waters score (worst 0–100 best)	39.1	2019	●	→
Fish caught from overexploited or collapsed stocks (% of total catch)	17.6	2014	●	↑
Fish caught by trawling (%)	20.4	2014	●	↓
Marine biodiversity threats embodied in imports (per million population)	0.0	2018	●	●

SDG15 – Life on Land

	Value	Year	Rating	Trend
Mean area that is protected in terrestrial sites important to biodiversity (%)	35.1	2018	●	→
Mean area that is protected in freshwater sites important to biodiversity (%)	27.5	2018	●	→
Red List Index of species survival (worst 0–1 best)	0.8	2019	●	↓
Permanent deforestation (% of forest area, 5-year average)	0.3	2018	●	●
Terrestrial and freshwater biodiversity threats embodied in imports (per million population)	0.1	2018	●	●

SDG16 – Peace, Justice and Strong Institutions

	Value	Year	Rating	Trend
Homicides (per 100,000 population)	4.0	2017	●	●
Unsentenced detainees (% of prison population)	55.3	2018	●	↓
Percentage of population who feel safe walking alone at night in the city or area where they live (%)	67.5	2019	●	→
Property Rights (worst 1–7 best)	4.3	2019	●	●
Birth registrations with civil authority (% of children under age 5)	73.3	2018	●	●
Corruption Perception Index (worst 0–100 best)	36	2019	●	→
Children involved in child labor (% of population aged 5 to 14)	13.2	2016	●	●
Exports of major conventional weapons (TIV constant million USD per 100,000 population)	0.0	2019	●	●
Press Freedom Index (best 0–100 worst)	44.8	2019	●	↓

SDG17 – Partnerships for the Goals

	Value	Year	Rating	Trend
Government spending on health and education (% of GDP)	4.8	2016	●	↓
For high-income and all OECD DAC countries: International concessional public finance, including official development assistance (% of GNI)	NA	NA	●	●
Other countries: Government revenue excluding grants (% of GDP)	14.3	2018	●	→
Corporate Tax Haven Score (best 0–100 worst)	1.4	2019	●	●

* Imputed data point

UPPER-MIDDLE-INCOME COUNTRIES

▼ OVERALL PERFORMANCE

Regional average score

73.2

SDG Global rank NA (OF 166)

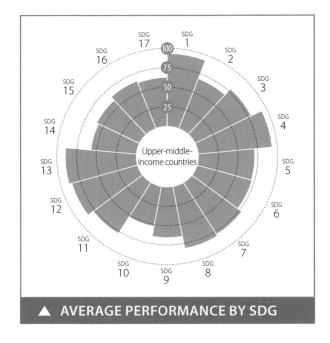

Upper-middle-income countries

▲ AVERAGE PERFORMANCE BY SDG

▼ SPILLOVER INDEX

100 (best) to 0 (worst)

▼ CURRENT ASSESSMENT – SDG DASHBOARD

■ Major challenges ■ Significant challenges ■ Challenges remain ■ SDG achieved ■ Information unavailable

▼ SDG TRENDS

↓ Decreasing → Stagnating ↗ Moderately improving ↑ On track or maintaining SDG achievement ● Information unavailable

Notes: The full title of Goal 2 "Zero Hunger" is "End hunger, achieve food security and improved nutrition and promote sustainable agriculture".
The full title of each SDG is available here: https://sustainabledevelopment.un.org/topics/sustainabledevelopmentgoals

SDG1 – No Poverty

	Value	Year	Rating	Trend
Poverty headcount ratio at $1.90/day (%)	1.8	2020	●	↑
Poverty headcount ratio at $3.20/day (%)	5.2	2020	◐	↑

SDG2 – Zero Hunger

	Value	Year	Rating	Trend
Prevalence of undernourishment (%)	7.2	2017	●	↑
Prevalence of stunting in children under 5 years of age (%)	10.0	2016	◐	↗
Prevalence of wasting in children under 5 years of age (%)	2.4	2016	●	↑
Prevalence of obesity, BMI ≥ 30 (% of adult population)	14.5	2016	◐	↓
Human Trophic Level (best 2–3 worst)	2.2	2017	●	→
Cereal yield (tonnes per hectare of harvested land)	4.9	2017	●	↑
Sustainable Nitrogen Management Index (best 0–1.41 worst)	0.7	2015	●	→

SDG3 – Good Health and Well-Being

	Value	Year	Rating	Trend
Maternal mortality rate (per 100,000 live births)	39	2017	●	↑
Neonatal mortality rate (per 1,000 live births)	5.9	2018	●	↑
Mortality rate, under-5 (per 1,000 live births)	11.4	2018	●	↑
Incidence of tuberculosis (per 100,000 population)	66.2	2018	◐	↗
New HIV infections (per 1,000 uninfected population)	0.5	2018	●	↑
Age-standardized death rate due to cardiovascular disease, cancer, diabetes, or chronic respiratory disease in adults aged 30–70 years (%)	17.5	2016	◐	↑
Age-standardized death rate attributable to household air pollution and ambient air pollution (per 100,000 population)	83	2016	◐	●
Traffic deaths (per 100,000 population)	18.6	2016	●	↗
Life expectancy at birth (years)	75.4	2016	◐	↗
Adolescent fertility rate (births per 1,000 adolescent females aged 15 to 19)	26.1	2017	◐	↑
Births attended by skilled health personnel (%)	98.5	2016	●	●
Percentage of surviving infants who received 2 WHO-recommended vaccines (%)	94	2018	●	↑
Universal health coverage (UHC) index of service coverage (worst 0–100 best)	76.7	2017	◐	↑
Subjective well-being (average ladder score, worst 0–10 best)	5.4	2019	●	↓

SDG4 – Quality Education

	Value	Year	Rating	Trend
Net primary enrollment rate (%)	95.4	2018	◐	↗
Lower secondary completion rate (%)	92.7	2018	●	↑
Literacy rate (% of population aged 15 to 24)	99.2	2018	●	●

SDG5 – Gender Equality

	Value	Year	Rating	Trend
Demand for family planning satisfied by modern methods (% of females aged 15 to 49 who are married or in unions)	86.2	2017	●	↑
Ratio of female-to-male mean years of education received (%)	93.5	2018	◐	↗
Ratio of female-to-male labor force participation rate (%)	71.6	2019	●	↑
Seats held by women in national parliament (%)	24.3	2020	●	→

SDG6 – Clean Water and Sanitation

	Value	Year	Rating	Trend
Population using at least basic drinking water services (%)	94.7	2017	◐	↑
Population using at least basic sanitation services (%)	87.3	2017	◐	↑
Freshwater withdrawal (% of available freshwater resources)	38.3	2015	◐	●
Anthropogenic wastewater that receives treatment (%)	15.9	2018	●	●
Scarce water consumption embodied in imports (m³/capita)	5.8	2013	●	↑

SDG7 – Affordable and Clean Energy

	Value	Year	Rating	Trend
Population with access to electricity (%)	99.4	2017	●	↑
Population with access to clean fuels and technology for cooking (%)	72.8	2016	◐	↗
CO$_2$ emissions from fuel combustion for electricity and heating per total electricity output (MtCO$_2$/TWh)	2.2	2017	●	↑

SDG8 – Decent Work and Economic Growth

	Value	Year	Rating	Trend
Adjusted GDP growth (%)	0.4	2018	●	●
Victims of modern slavery (per 1,000 population)	3.7	2018	●	●
Adults with an account at a bank or other financial institution or with a mobile-money-service provider (% of population aged 15 or over)	72.1	2017	◐	↑
Unemployment rate (% of total labor force)	6.5	2019	◐	→
Fatal work-related accidents embodied in imports (per 100,000 population)	0.2	2010	●	↑

SDG9 – Industry, Innovation and Infrastructure

	Value	Year	Rating	Trend
Population using the internet (%)	60.5	2018	●	↑
Mobile broadband subscriptions (per 100 population)	85.1	2018	●	↑
Logistics Performance Index: Quality of trade and transport-related infrastructure (worst 1–5 best)	3.3	2018	●	↑
The Times Higher Education Universities Ranking: Average score of top 3 universities (worst 0–100 best)	55.7	2020	●	●
Scientific and technical journal articles (per 1,000 population)	0.3	2018	●	↗
Expenditure on research and development (% of GDP)	1.5	2017	◐	●

SDG10 – Reduced Inequalities

	Value	Year	Rating	Trend
Gini coefficient adjusted for top income	44.7	2017	●	●

SDG11 – Sustainable Cities and Communities

	Value	Year	Rating	Trend
Annual mean concentration of particulate matter of less than 2.5 microns in diameter (PM2.5) (µg/m³)	38.9	2017	●	↗
Access to improved water source, piped (% of urban population)	93.4	2017	◐	↗
Satisfaction with public transport (%)	69.0	2019	◐	↑

SDG12 – Responsible Consumption and Production

	Value	Year	Rating	Trend
Municipal solid waste (kg/capita/day)	1.0	2016	●	●
Electronic waste (kg/capita)	6.3	2016	●	●
Production-based SO$_2$ emissions (kg/capita)	28.5	2012	●	●
SO$_2$ emissions embodied in imports (kg/capita)	1.6	2012	●	●
Production-based nitrogen emissions (kg/capita)	26.2	2010	●	●
Nitrogen emissions embodied in imports (kg/capita)	1.5	2010	●	●

SDG13 – Climate Action

	Value	Year	Rating	Trend
Energy-related CO$_2$ emissions (tCO$_2$/capita)	5.9	2017	●	→
CO$_2$ emissions embodied in imports (tCO$_2$/capita)	0.3	2015	●	↑
CO$_2$ emissions embodied in fossil fuel exports (kg/capita)	460.5	2019	◐	●

SDG14 – Life Below Water

	Value	Year	Rating	Trend
Mean area that is protected in marine sites important to biodiversity (%)	34.4	2018	◐	→
Ocean Health Index: Clean Waters score (worst 0–100 best)	46.4	2019	●	→
Fish caught from overexploited or collapsed stocks (% of total catch)	22.5	2014	●	↑
Fish caught by trawling (%)	44.8	2014	●	↓
Marine biodiversity threats embodied in imports (per million population)	0.1	2018	●	●

SDG15 – Life on Land

	Value	Year	Rating	Trend
Mean area that is protected in terrestrial sites important to biodiversity (%)	36.9	2018	◐	→
Mean area that is protected in freshwater sites important to biodiversity (%)	32.6	2018	◐	→
Red List Index of species survival (worst 0–1 best)	0.8	2019	●	↓
Permanent deforestation (% of forest area, 5-year average)	0.1	2018	●	●
Terrestrial and freshwater biodiversity threats embodied in imports (per million population)	0.6	2018	●	●

SDG16 – Peace, Justice and Strong Institutions

	Value	Year	Rating	Trend
Homicides (per 100,000 population)	7.4	2017	●	→
Unsentenced detainees (% of prison population)	29.6	2018	●	↑
Percentage of population who feel safe walking alone at night in the city or area where they live	70.4	2019	●	↑
Property Rights (worst 1–7 best)	4.3	2019	●	●
Birth registrations with civil authority (% of children under age 5)	96.5	2018	◐	●
Corruption Perception Index (worst 0–100 best)	38	2019	●	→
Children involved in child labor (% of population aged 5 to 14)	8.3	2016	●	●
Exports of major conventional weapons (TIV constant million USD per 100,000 population)	0.3	2019	●	●
Press Freedom Index (best 0–100 worst)	61.8	2019	●	→

SDG17 – Partnerships for the Goals

	Value	Year	Rating	Trend
Government spending on health and education (% of GDP)	8.1	2016	◐	●
For high-income and all OECD DAC countries: International concessional public finance, including official development assistance (% of GNI)	NA	NA	●	●
Other countries: Government revenue excluding grants (% of GDP)	19.9	2018	●	↓
Corporate Tax Haven Score (best 0–100 worst)	32.7	2019	●	●

* Imputed data point

5. Country Profiles

▼ OVERALL PERFORMANCE

Regional average score

77.7

SDG Global rank   NA (OF 166)

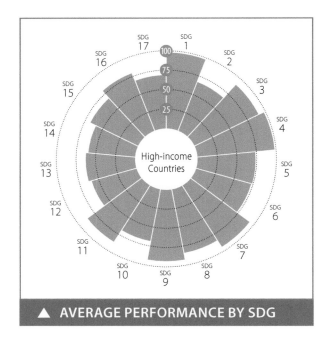

High-income Countries

▲ AVERAGE PERFORMANCE BY SDG

▼ SPILLOVER INDEX

100 (best) to 0 (worst)

▼ CURRENT ASSESSMENT – SDG DASHBOARD

■ Major challenges ■ Significant challenges ■ Challenges remain ■ SDG achieved ■ Information unavailable

▼ SDG TRENDS

⬇ Decreasing   ➡ Stagnating   ↗ Moderately improving   ⬆ On track or maintaining SDG achievement   ● Information unavailable

Notes: The full title of Goal 2 "Zero Hunger" is "End hunger, achieve food security and improved nutrition and promote sustainable agriculture".
The full title of each SDG is available here: https://sustainabledevelopment.un.org/topics/sustainabledevelopmentgoals

SDG1 – No Poverty

Indicator	Value	Year	Rating	Trend
Poverty headcount ratio at $1.90/day (%)	0.5	2020	●	↑
Poverty headcount ratio at $3.20/day (%)	0.7	2020	●	↑

SDG2 – Zero Hunger

Indicator	Value	Year	Rating	Trend
Prevalence of undernourishment (%)	2.7	2017	●	↑
Prevalence of stunting in children under 5 years of age (%)	3.2	2016	●	↑
Prevalence of wasting in children under 5 years of age (%)	1.3	2016	●	↑
Prevalence of obesity, BMI ≥ 30 (% of adult population)	24.8	2016	●	↓
Human Trophic Level (best 2–3 worst)	2.4	2017	●	↓
Cereal yield (tonnes per hectare of harvested land)	6.7	2017	●	↑
Sustainable Nitrogen Management Index (best 0–1.41 worst)	0.5	2015	●	→

SDG3 – Good Health and Well-Being

Indicator	Value	Year	Rating	Trend
Maternal mortality rate (per 100,000 live births)	10	2017	●	↑
Neonatal mortality rate (per 1,000 live births)	2.6	2018	●	↑
Mortality rate, under-5 (per 1,000 live births)	4.7	2018	●	↑
Incidence of tuberculosis (per 100,000 population)	10.7	2018	●	↑
New HIV infections (per 1,000 uninfected population)	0.1	2018	●	↑
Age-standardized death rate due to cardiovascular disease, cancer, diabetes, or chronic respiratory disease in adults aged 30–70 years (%)	12.2	2016	●	↑
Age-standardized death rate attributable to household air pollution and ambient air pollution (per 100,000 population)	18	2016	●	●
Traffic deaths (per 100,000 population)	8.4	2016	●	↑
Life expectancy at birth (years)	80.7	2016	●	↑
Adolescent fertility rate (births per 1,000 adolescent females aged 15 to 19)	11.8	2017	●	↑
Births attended by skilled health personnel (%)	99.1	2016	●	↑
Percentage of surviving infants who received 2 WHO-recommended vaccines (%)	94	2018	●	↑
Universal health coverage (UHC) index of service coverage (worst 0–100 best)	82.3	2017	●	↑
Subjective well-being (average ladder score, worst 0–10 best)	6.7	2019	●	↑

SDG4 – Quality Education

Indicator	Value	Year	Rating	Trend
Net primary enrollment rate (%)	98.7	2018	●	↑
Lower secondary completion rate (%)	99.0	2018	●	↑
Literacy rate (% of population aged 15 to 24)	99.5	2018	●	●

SDG5 – Gender Equality

Indicator	Value	Year	Rating	Trend
Demand for family planning satisfied by modern methods (% of females aged 15 to 49 who are married or in unions)	77.1	2017	●	↗
Ratio of female-to-male mean years of education received (%)	98.9	2018	●	↑
Ratio of female-to-male labor force participation rate (%)	78.0	2019	●	↑
Seats held by women in national parliament (%)	26.9	2020	●	↗

SDG6 – Clean Water and Sanitation

Indicator	Value	Year	Rating	Trend
Population using at least basic drinking water services (%)	99.5	2017	●	●
Population using at least basic sanitation services (%)	99.4	2017	●	●
Freshwater withdrawal (% of available freshwater resources)	80.5	2015	●	●
Anthropogenic wastewater that receives treatment (%)	71.5	2018	●	●
Scarce water consumption embodied in imports (m³/capita)	29.1	2013	●	↗

SDG7 – Affordable and Clean Energy

Indicator	Value	Year	Rating	Trend
Population with access to electricity (%)	100.0	2017	●	↑
Population with access to clean fuels and technology for cooking (%)	99.4	2016	●	↑
CO_2 emissions from fuel combustion for electricity and heating per total electricity output (MtCO$_2$/TWh)	1.2	2017	●	↗

SDG8 – Decent Work and Economic Growth

Indicator	Value	Year	Rating	Trend
Adjusted GDP growth (%)	-0.4	2018	●	●
Victims of modern slavery (per 1,000 population)	1.7	2018	●	●
Adults with an account at a bank or other financial institution or with a mobile-money-service provider (% of population aged 15 or over)	93.2	2017	●	↑
Unemployment rate (% of total labor force)	4.9	2019	●	●
Fatal work-related accidents embodied in imports (per 100,000 population)	1.5	2010	●	↑

SDG9 – Industry, Innovation and Infrastructure

Indicator	Value	Year	Rating	Trend
Population using the internet (%)	87.4	2018	●	↑
Mobile broadband subscriptions (per 100 population)	124.2	2018	●	↑
Logistics Performance Index: Quality of trade and transport-related infrastructure (worst 1–5 best)	3.9	2018	●	↑
The Times Higher Education Universities Ranking: Average score of top 3 universities (worst 0–100 best)	70.0	2020	●	●
Scientific and technical journal articles (per 1,000 population)	1.2	2018	●	↑
Expenditure on research and development (% of GDP)	2.3	2017	●	↑

SDG10 – Reduced Inequalities

Indicator	Value	Year	Rating	Trend
Gini coefficient adjusted for top income	39.0	2017	●	●

SDG11 – Sustainable Cities and Communities

Indicator	Value	Year	Rating	Trend
Annual mean concentration of particulate matter of less than 2.5 microns in diameter (PM2.5) (µg/m³)	14.6	2017	●	→
Access to improved water source, piped (% of urban population)	98.7	2017	●	↑
Satisfaction with public transport (%)	63.1	2019	●	→

SDG12 – Responsible Consumption and Production

Indicator	Value	Year	Rating	Trend
Municipal solid waste (kg/capita/day)	1.9	2016	●	●
Electronic waste (kg/capita)	18.9	2016	●	●
Production-based SO$_2$ emissions (kg/capita)	54.6	2012	●	●
SO$_2$ emissions embodied in imports (kg/capita)	12.0	2012	●	●
Production-based nitrogen emissions (kg/capita)	44.4	2010	●	●
Nitrogen emissions embodied in imports (kg/capita)	11.4	2010	●	●

SDG13 – Climate Action

Indicator	Value	Year	Rating	Trend
Energy-related CO_2 emissions (tCO$_2$/capita)	10.5	2017	●	→
CO_2 emissions embodied in imports (tCO$_2$/capita)	2.0	2015	●	→
CO_2 emissions embodied in fossil fuel exports (kg/capita)	1980.3	2019	●	●

SDG14 – Life Below Water

Indicator	Value	Year	Rating	Trend
Mean area that is protected in marine sites important to biodiversity (%)	65.1	2018	●	↑
Ocean Health Index: Clean Waters score (worst 0–100 best)	62.5	2019	●	↓
Fish caught from overexploited or collapsed stocks (% of total catch)	38.8	2014	●	→
Fish caught by trawling (%)	44.3	2014	●	↓
Marine biodiversity threats embodied in imports (per million population)	0.5	2018	●	●

SDG15 – Life on Land

Indicator	Value	Year	Rating	Trend
Mean area that is protected in terrestrial sites important to biodiversity (%)	59.8	2018	●	↑
Mean area that is protected in freshwater sites important to biodiversity (%)	56.5	2018	●	↑
Red List Index of species survival (worst 0–1 best)	0.9	2019	●	→
Permanent deforestation (% of forest area, 5-year average)	0.0	2018	●	●
Terrestrial and freshwater biodiversity threats embodied in imports (per million population)	3.8	2018	●	●

SDG16 – Peace, Justice and Strong Institutions

Indicator	Value	Year	Rating	Trend
Homicides (per 100,000 population)	2.3	2017	●	→
Unsentenced detainees (% of prison population)	23.0	2018	●	↑
Percentage of population who feel safe walking alone at night in the city or area where they live (%)	74.1	2019	●	↑
Property Rights (worst 1–7 best)	5.4	2019	●	●
Birth registrations with civil authority (% of children under age 5)	100.0	2018	●	●
Corruption Perception Index (worst 0–100 best)	68	2019	●	↑
Children involved in child labor (% of population aged 5 to 14)	0.2	2016	●	●
Exports of major conventional weapons (TIV constant million USD per 100,000 population)	1.8	2019	●	●
Press Freedom Index (best 0–100 worst)	24.8	2019	●	↑

SDG17 – Partnerships for the Goals

Indicator	Value	Year	Rating	Trend
Government spending on health and education (% of GDP)	12.6	2016	●	↑
For high-income and all OECD DAC countries: International concessional public finance, including official development assistance (% of GNI)	0.3	2017	●	→
Other countries: Government revenue excluding grants (% of GDP)	NA	NA	●	●
Corporate Tax Haven Score (best 0–100 worst)	39.3	2019	●	●

* Imputed data point

5. Country Profiles